The English translation of the psalm responses, gospel
verses, and Lenten gospel acclamations from the
Lectionary for Mass © 1969, 1981, 1997, International
Committee on English in the Liturgy, Inc. (ICEL);
excerpts from the English translation of Rite of Holy
Week © 1970, ICEL; excerpts from the English translation of The Roman Missal © 1973, ICEL; excerpts from
the English translation of Liturgy of the Hours © 1974,
ICEL; excerpts from the English translation of the Order
of Christian Funerals © 1985, ICEL. All rights reserved.

The text of the scripture readings © 1970, 1997, 1998
Confraternity of Christian Doctrine, Inc., Washington,
DC. All rights reserved.

Book design is based upon Worship—Third Edition by
Michael Tapia. Cover design by Jill Smith.

Published with the approval of the Committee on the
Liturgy, National Conference of Catholic Bishops

ISBN 1-57999-037-1

5 6 7 8 9 10 11 12 13 14 15 16 17 18

GATHER
COMPREHENSIVE

GIA PUBLICATIONS, INC.

CHICAGO

PREFACE

The year 1994 marks the publication of two related, yet different GIA hymnals, *Gather—Second Edition* and *Gather Comprehensive*. The former, as the name implies, is the second generation of a hymnal published in 1988. It is indeed an entirely new hymnal, almost double the size of the original *Gather*.

When GIA's acclaimed classical hymnal, *Worship—Third Edition,* was published in 1986, followed in 1988 by the original *Gather*, it was stated that the two were carefully designed to be used in combination—one complementing the other. The classical hymnody of *Worship* and the contemporary "folk" hymnody of *Gather* were isolated into two volumes, however, precisely for the reason which now becomes apparent with the publication of *Gather—Second Edition*. Music of the genre generally included in *Gather* (almost exclusively the work of living composers) tends to be generated at a quicker rate than the classical hymnody of *Worship* (which includes an extensive offering of hymnody from past centuries along with that of contemporary writers); therefore, *Gather* calls for revision more frequently than does the more classical hymnal.

The increased size of *Gather—Second Edition* is due to three main factors. First, the well-known composers whose work was found in the original edition have continued to write and have in this volume been joined by others. Second, this edition paves new territory, untouched in the 1988 collection. The second edition includes a representative offering of music from the Hispanic and African-American churches, as well as songs from the repertoire of the world church. Third, the psalm section has been significantly expanded to cover the entire church year.

This book, *Gather Comprehensive*, is an extension of *Gather—Second Edition*. It combines *Gather—Second Edition* with approximately 250 of the most standard classical hymns, psalms, and service music pieces. It has been published especially for parishes whose music programs tend to utilize a greater amount of contemporary "folk" art music than classical organ-based music. The mix is approximately 70/30. Other GIA hymnals slated for future publication will offer more of a 50/50 distribution between styles, pointing to this publisher's commitment to producing a diverse offering of bound hymnals intended to meet the differing needs of American parishes.

It should be kept in mind that both *Gather — Second Edition* and *Gather Comprehensive* are hymnals, inherently books intended for the assembly. Many of the selections contained herein have been edited from the familiar recorded octavo versions into versions which can essentially be sung by an assembly with basic keyboard accompaniment. Those wishing fuller arrangements of selections need only revert to the choral editions where they exist. When the choir and instruments are using a more complex version, however, the assembly can still sing their part by simply using the hymnal.

Acknowledgment is given to Diana Kodner, project director and editor; to staff engraver Marc Southard, assisted by Arne Eigenfeldt, Clarence Reiels and Jeffry Mickus; to Robert M. Sacha, book layout; to Alec Harris, technical coordinator; to Neil Borgstrom, Kelly Dobbs Mickus, and Edwina Schaufler, proofreaders; to Deborah L. Schmitz, permissions editor; and to David Blaszak, production.

Further acknowledgment is given to Mary Beth Kunde-Anderson, Rory Cooney, David Haas, and Marty Haugen for their invaluable study of and detailed comments on the draft version of *Gather—Second Edition*, the basis for this collection.

Finally, a distinguishing quality of this and all GIA hymnals published in the past twenty years is the extensive scriptural, liturgical, and topical indexes carefully prepared by Robert H. Oldershaw.

That God may be glorified.

Edward Harris
    Publisher
Robert J. Batastini
Michael A. Cymbala
    General Editors

Contents

Lectionary

Indexes

Morning Praise

The Church's sense for how to pray in the morning comes from our Jewish heritage. Whatever the day, whatever the difficulties, the tradition has been to begin the day with praise for the creator. The sign of the cross, first traced on the Christian at baptism, is again made to begin the new day and its prayer. In the hymn and the psalms, in the scripture and intercessions, each one who prays and the community together finds what it is to stand at the beginning of a new day as a Christian. The morning's prayer gives the day its meaning when, through the years, these prayers become one's own.

OPENING DIALOG   1

Stand

Ho-ly God! Fill us this day with new breath! And we shall be liv-ing words of praise!

Text: J. Tasch Jordan, adapt.
Music: David Haas
© 1986, GIA Publications, Inc.

2 MORNING HYMN

1. Sing your joy, pro - claim God's glo - ry!
2. All the earth is filled with re - joic - ing,
3. May we learn to be - come your King - dom.
4. Light our way, O God of the liv - ing,

Rise and sing, the morn - ing has come!
Light and life the won - der of God!
May we be your kind - ness and truth!
May we learn to see with new eyes!

Bless our God and praise all cre - a - tion;
Christ has tri - umphed! Ris - en for ev - er!
Love is our call - ing, gift of your pres - ence;
Je - sus the Lord, our pow - er and prom - ise;

Song of the earth, and light from heav - en:
Joy of our hearts, and hope of our dream - ing:
Chil - dren of God, and spir - it of Je - sus:
Light for the blind, and food for the hun - gry:

God is a - live! Al - le - lu - ia!
God is a - live! Al - le - lu - ia!
God is a - live! Al - le - lu - ia!
God is a - live! Al - le - lu - ia!

Text: David Haas, b.1957
Tune: SUMMIT HILL, Irregular; David Haas, b.1957
© 1987, GIA Publications, Inc.

PSALMODY

The singing of one or more psalms is a central part of Morning Praise. Psalm 63, given below, is one of the premier morning psalms. Psalm 51 is commonly substituted for Psalm 63 on Wednesday and Friday, as well as during Lent. Other appropriate psalms for morning are Psalms 5, 8, 33, 42, 47, 66, 72, 80, 85, 93, 95, 98, 100, 118, 148, 149, and 150.

PSALM 63

3

Sit

Refrain

As morn-ing breaks I look to you; I look to

you, O Lord, to be my strength this day, as morn-ing

breaks, as morn - ing breaks.

Verses

1. O God, you are my God, for you I long; for you my soul is thirsting.
   My body pines for you like a dry, weary land without water.
   So I gaze on you in your holy place to see your strength and your glory.

2. For your love is better than life, my lips will speak your praise.
   So I will bless you all my life, in your name I will lift up my hands.
   My soul shall be filled as with a banquet, my mouth shall praise you with joy.

3. On my bed I remember you. On you I muse through the night
   for you have been my help; in the shadow of your wings I rejoice.
   My soul clings to you; your right hand holds me fast.

Text: Psalm 63:2-3, 4-6, 7-9; © 1963, 1986, The Grail, GIA Publications, Inc. agent: refrain trans. © 1974, ICEL
Music: Michael Joncas, © 1985, New Dawn Music

PSALM PRAYER

Stand
All respond: Amen.

WORD OF GOD

4

Sit
Reader concludes: The word of the Lord.
       Assembly: Thanks be to God.

5 GOSPEL CANTICLE

Stand. All make the sign of the cross as the canticle begins.

1. Now bless the God of Is - ra - el, Who comes in love and pow'r, Who rais - es from the roy - al house De - liv - 'rance in this hour. Through ho - ly proph - ets God has sworn To free us from a - larm, To save us from the heav - y hand Of all who wish us harm.

2. Re - mem - ber - ing the cov - e - nant, God res - cues us from fear, That we might serve in hol - i - ness And peace from year to year. And you, my child, shall go be - fore To preach, to proph - e - sy, That all may know the ten - der love, The grace of God most high.

3. In ten - der mer - cy, God will send The day - spring from on high, Our ris - ing sun, the light of life For those who sit and sigh. God comes to guide our way to peace, That death shall reign no more. Ho - ly One! O wor - ship and a - dore!

Text: *Benedictus*, Luke 1:68-79; Ruth Duck, b.1947, © 1992, GIA Publications, Inc.
Tune: MELBOURNE, 8 6 8 6 D; Marty Haugen, b.1950, © 1994, GIA Publications, Inc.

MORNING PRAYERS

6

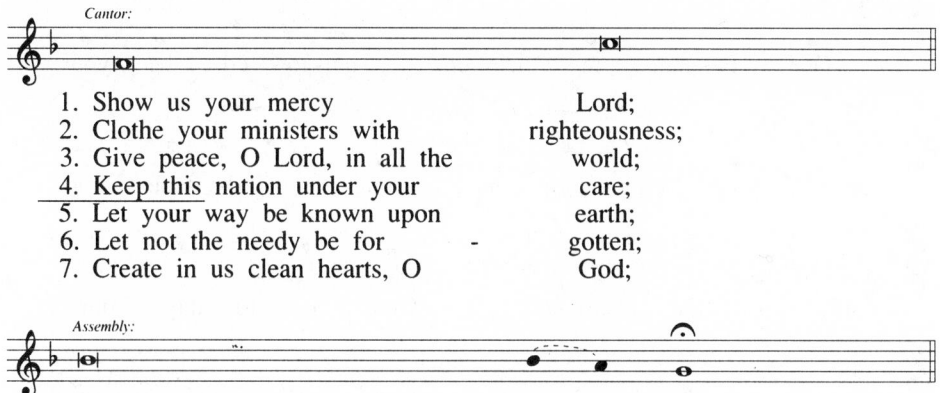

Cantor:

1. Show us your mercy   Lord;
2. Clothe your ministers with   righteousness;
3. Give peace, O Lord, in all the   world;
4. Keep this nation under your   care;
5. Let your way be known upon   earth;
6. Let not the needy be for   -   gotten;
7. Create in us clean hearts, O   God;

Assembly:

And grant us your sal   -   va - tion.
Let your people   sing   for   joy.
In you we can live in   safe - ty.
Guide us in justice   and   in   truth.
Your saving health among all   na - tions.
Nor the hope of all to   be   de - nied.
And sustain us in your holy   Spir - it.

Text: *The Book of Common Prayer*
Music: David Haas, © 1986, GIA Publications, Inc.

CONCLUDING PRAYER
All respond: Amen.

7 LORD'S PRAYER

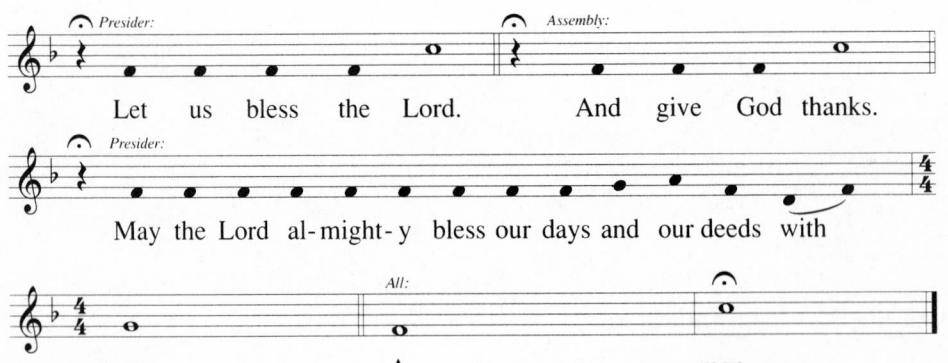

Our Fa-ther in heav-en, hal-low-ed be your name, your king-dom come, your will be done on earth as in heav-en. Give us to-day our dai-ly bread. For-give us our sins as we for-give those who sin a-gainst us. Save us from the time of trial and de-liv-er us from e-vil, for the king-dom, the pow'r and the glo-ry are yours, now and for ev-er.

Music: David Haas, © 1986, GIA Publications, Inc.

8 FINAL BLESSING

Presider: Let us bless the Lord. *Assembly:* And give God thanks.

Presider: May the Lord al-might-y bless our days and our deeds with peace.

All: A - men.

Text: David Haas
Music: David Haas
© 1986, GIA Publications, Inc.

Evensong

The Church gathers in the evening to give thanks for the day that is ending. In the earliest tradition, this began with the lighting of the lamps as darkness fell and the hymn of praise of Christ who is "radiant Light . . . of God the Father's deathless face." The evening psalms and the Magnificat bring the day just past to focus for the Christian: "God has cast down the mighty from their thrones, and has lifted up the lowly"; "God has remembered the promise of mercy, the promise made to our ancestors." Prayers of intercession are almost always part of the church's liturgy, but those which conclude evening prayer are especially important. As day ends, the church again and again lifts up to God the needs and sorrows and failures of all the world. Such intercession is the daily task and joy of the baptized.

LIGHT PROCLAMATION   9
Stand

Light and peace in Je-sus Christ our Lord. Thanks be to God.

Music: Michael Joncas, © 1979, GIA Publications, Inc.

10 EVENING HYMN

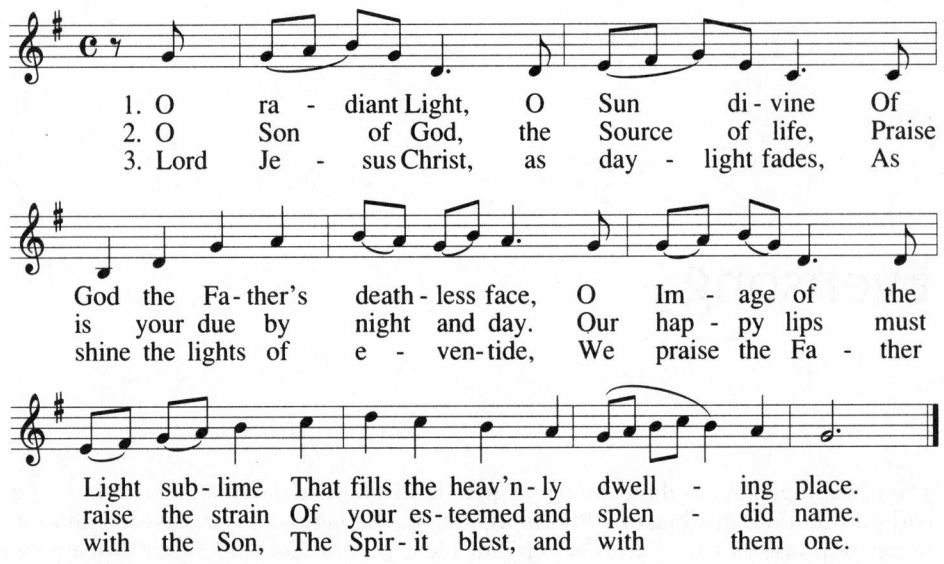

1. O   ra - diant Light,   O   Sun   di - vine   Of
2. O   Son   of God,   the   Source   of life,   Praise
3. Lord   Je - sus Christ,   as   day - light fades,   As

God   the   Fa - ther's   death - less face,   O   Im - age of   the
is   your due   by   night   and day.   Our   hap - py lips   must
shine the lights of   e - ven - tide,   We   praise   the Fa - ther

Light   sub - lime   That fills the heav'n - ly   dwell - ing   place.
raise   the strain   Of   your es - teemed and   splen - did   name.
with   the Son,   The Spir - it   blest, and   with   them one.

Text: *Phos Hilaron;* tr. by William G. Storey, ©
Tune: RADIANT LIGHT, LM: Michael Joncas, b. 1951, © 1979, GIA Publications, Inc.

11 EVENING THANKSGIVING

Assistant or Presider:

Let us give thanks to God our Fa - ther, al - ways and for ev - 'ry thing.

Assembly:

In   the   name   of   our   Lord   Je - sus   Christ.

The assistant sings the Thanksgiving to which all respond:

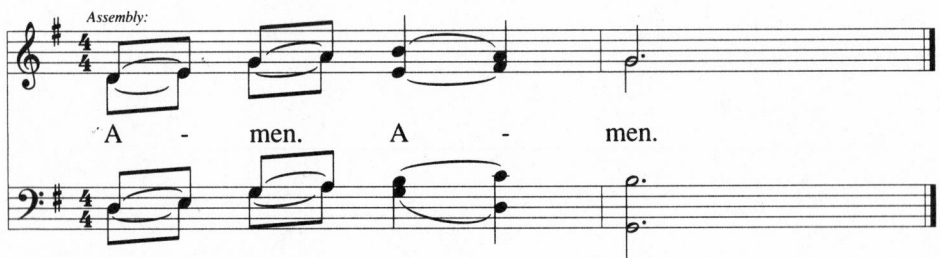

Assembly:

A - men.   A - men.

Music: Michael Joncas, © 1979, GIA Publications, Inc.

PSALMODY

The singing of one or more psalms is a central part of Evensong. Psalm 141, given below, is one of the premier evening psalms. It is customary to use incense as it is sung. Other appropriate psalms for evening are Psalms 4, 19, 23, 27, 84, 91, 104, 110, 111, 112, 114, 115, 117, 118, 121, 122, 130, 136, 139, and 145.

PSALM 141/INCENSE PSALM   12

Refrain

Like   burn-ing   in-cense, O   Lord, let my   prayer rise up to   you.

Verses

1. I have called to you, Lord; hasten to help me! Hear my voice when I cry to you.
   Let my prayer arise before you like incense,
   the raising of my hands like an evening oblation.

2. Set, O Lord, a guard over my mouth; Keep watch, O Lord, at the door of my lips!
   Do not turn my heart to things that are wrong,
   to evil deeds with those who are sinners.

3. Never allow me to share in their feasting.
   If the upright strike or reprove me it is kindness;
   but let the oil of the wicked not anoint my head.
   Let my prayer be ever against their malice.

4. To you, Lord God, my eyes are turned: in you I take refuge, spare my soul!
   From the trap they have laid for me keep me safe:
   Keep me from the snares of those who do evil.

5. Glory to the Father, and to the Son, and to the Holy Spirit:
   as it was in the beginning, is now, and will be for ever. Amen.

Text: Psalm 141; © 1963,The Grail, GIA Publications, Inc., agent
Music: Michael Joncas, © 1988, GIA Publications, Inc.

PSALM PRAYER
All respond: Amen.

13 WORD OF GOD

Sit
Reader concludes: The Word of the Lord.
        Assembly: Thanks be to God.

14 GOSPEL CANTICLE

Stand. All make the sign of the cross as the canticle begins.

1. My soul gives glo - ry to the Lord, In
2. His mer - cy goes to all who fear, From
3. He raised his ser - vant Is - ra - el, Re-

God my Sav - ior I re - joice. My low - li -
age to age and to all parts. His arm of
mem - b'ring his e - ter - nal grace, As from of

ness he did re - gard, Ex - alt - ing me by
strength to all is near; He scat - ters those who
old he did fore - tell To A - bra - ham and

his own choice. From this day all shall call me
have proud hearts. He casts the might - y from their
all his race. O Fa - ther, Son and Spir - it

blest, For he has done great things for me, Of
throne And rais - es those of low de - gree; He
blest, In three - fold Name are you a - dored, To

all great names his is the best, For
feeds the hun - gry as his own, The
you be ev - 'ry prayer ad - dressed, From

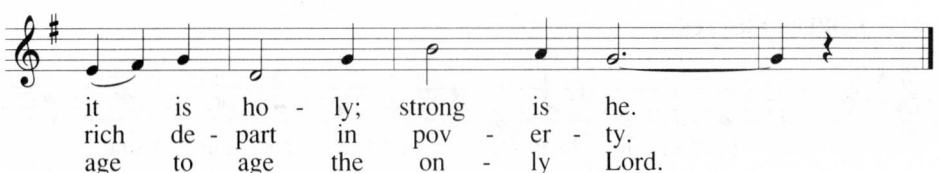

it   is   ho - ly;   strong   is   he.
rich   de - part   in   pov - er - ty.
age   to   age   the   on - ly   Lord.

Text: Luke 1:46-55; J.T. Mueller, 1885-1967, alt.
Tune: MAGNIFICAT, LMD; Michael Joncas, b.1951. © 1979, 1988, GIA Publications, Inc.

PETITIONS   15
Invitation

Assistant:
Let   us com - plete our eve - ning   prayer   to   the   Lord.

Refrain

Assembly:
Lord,   have mer - cy.   Lord,   have mer - cy.

Assistant: **D.S.**
let   us   pray   to   the   Lord:

Text: Michael Joncas
Music: Michael Joncas
© 1988, GIA Publications, Inc.

CONCLUDING PRAYER
All respond: Amen.

16 LORD'S PRAYER

Our Fa-ther in heav-en, hal-lowed be your name, your

king - dom come, your will be done on earth as in heav-en.

Give us to - day our dai - ly bread; give us to -

day our dai - ly bread. For-give us our sins as we for-give

those who sin a - gainst us. Save us from the time of trial

and de - liv - er us from e - vil. For the king-dom, the

pow-er, and the glo-ry are yours, now and for ev - er.

Music: Michael Joncas, © 1988, GIA Publications, Inc.

FINAL BLESSING

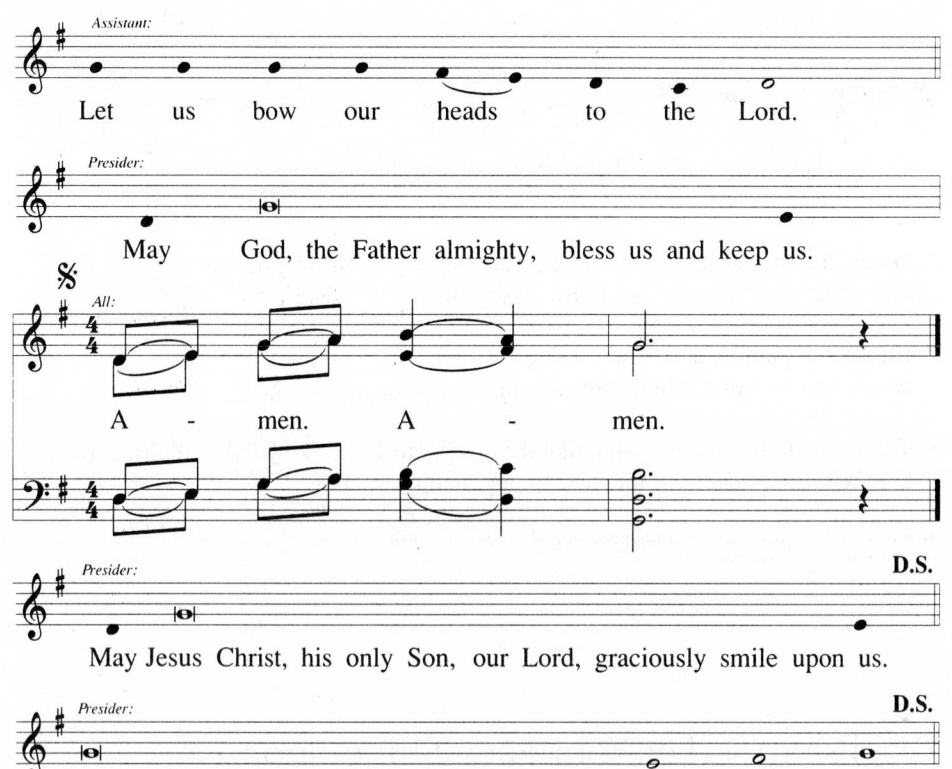

Assistant:
Let us bow our heads to the Lord.

Presider:
May God, the Father almighty, bless us and keep us.

All:
A - men. A - men.

Presider: **D.S.**
May Jesus Christ, his only Son, our Lord, graciously smile upon us.

Presider: **D.S.**
May the Holy Spirit, the Lord and giver of life, grant us peace.

Music: Michael Joncas, © 1988, GIA Publications, Inc.

18 Psalm 1: Happy Are They

Refrain

Hap - py are they who hope in God.

Verses

1. Happy are they who do not seek to walk the way of those who sin,
   but delight in the law of the Lord. Happy, happy are they.

2. Like a tree planted near water, there it blooms, like our God,
   whose leaves will not fade, but remain. Happy, happy are they.

3. The wicked, the lawless, who, like the chaff, our God, like wind, will drive away.
   God will keep watch for the just. Happy, happy are they.

Text: Psalm 1:1-2, 3-4, 6; David Haas. © 1989, GIA Publications, Inc.; refrain trans. © 1969, ICEL
Music: David Haas. © 1989, GIA Publications, Inc.

19 Psalm 4: Let Your Face Shine upon Us

Refrain

Lord, let your face shine up - on us, shine up -

on us, shine up - on us.

Verses

1. Listen to my song, hear me when I call, Oh Lord, my God, be gracious,
   hear my prayer.

2. You have called my name, set your seal upon my heart,
   you hear me when I call.

3. Fill me with your joy, grant to me your peaceful rest,
   to dwell in safety with my Lord.

Text: Psalm 4:2, 4, 9; Marty Haugen
Music: Marty Haugen
© 1980, GIA Publications, Inc.

Psalm 8: How Glorious Is Your Name   20

Refrain

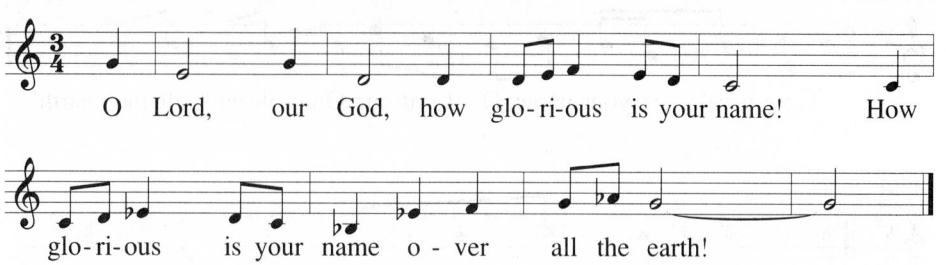

O Lord, our God, how glo-ri-ous is your name! How glo-ri-ous is your name o - ver all the earth!

Verses

1. When I see the heavens, the work of your hands,
   the moon and the stars which you arranged,
   What are we that you keep us in mind? Your children that you remember them at all?

2. Yet you have made us little less than gods, with glory and honor you crowned us,
   Gave us pow'r over the work of your hands, dominion over all that you have made.

3. All sheep and oxen, birds of the air, all things that swim in the sea.
   Beasts without number, life without names, you have placed under our feet.

Text: Psalm 8:4-5, 6-7, 8-9; Rory Cooney
Music: Rory Cooney
© 1990, GIA Publications, Inc.

21   Psalm 8: How Great Is Your Name

Antiphon I

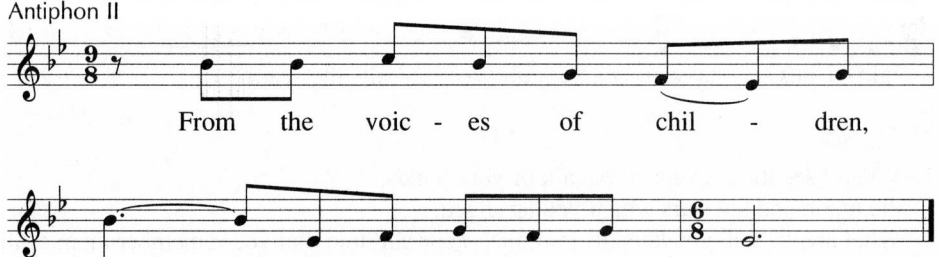

How great   is your name, O   Lord our God,   through all the   earth!

Antiphon II

From   the   voic - es   of   chil - dren,

Lord,   comes the   sound   of   your   praise.

Text: The Grail
Music: A. Gregory Murray, OSB
© 1963, The Grail, GIA Publications, Inc., agent

Psalm Tone

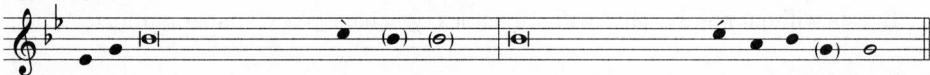

Music: Chant tone 5; acc. by Robert J. Batastini, © 1975, GIA Publications, Inc.

Gelineau Tone

Omit for 2-line stanzas

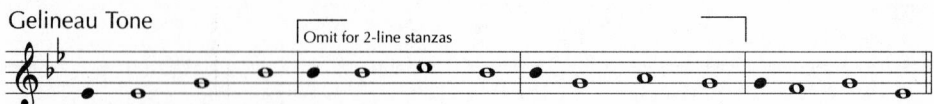

Domine, Dominus noster

*²How **great** is your **name**, O Lòrd our **God**,
thróugh all the **earth**!

Your **maj**esty is **praised** above the **hèav**ens:
³ on the **lips** of **chíl**dren and of **babes**
you have found **praise** to **foil** your **ène**my,
to **silence** the **fóe** and the **reb**el.

⁴ When I see the **heav**ens, the **work** of yòur **hands**,
the **moon** and the **stárs** which you ar**ranged**,
⁵ what are **we** that you should **keep** us in **mìnd**,
mere **mor**tals thát you **care** for **us**?

Omitted when Antiphon I is used.

⁶ Yet you have **made** us little **less** than **gòds**;
   and **crowned** us with **glóry** and **hon**or,
⁷ you gave us **pow**er over the **work** of yòur **hands**,
   put **all** things **ún**der our **feet**.

⁸ **All** of them. **sheep** and **càt**tle,
   yes, **e**ven thé **sav**age **beasts**,
⁹ **birds** of the **air**, and **fish**
   that **make** their **way** throúgh the **wa**ters.

^{*10} How **great** is your **name**, O Lòrd our **God**,
   Throúgh all the **earth**!

Give **glo**ry to the **Fa**ther Al**mìght**y,
to his **Son**, Jèsus **Christ**, the **Lord**,
to the **Spir**it who **dwells** in òur **hearts**,
both **now** and for **é**ver. **Amen**.

Text: Psalm 8; The Grail
Music: Joseph Gelineau
© 1963, 1993. The Grail, GIA Publications, Inc., agent

22 Psalm 15: They Who Do Justice

Refrain

They who do jus-tice will live in the pres-ence of God!

They who do jus-tice will live in the pres-ence of God!

Verses

1. Those who walk blamelessly and live their lives doing justice,
   who keep the truth in their heart, and slander not with their tongue!

2. Who harm not another, nor take up reproach to their neighbor,
   who hate the sight of the wicked, but honor the people of God!

3. Who show no condition in sharing the gifts of their treasure,
   who live not off the poor: They will stand firm forever!

Text: Psalm 15: 2-5: David Haas, © 1989. GIA Publications, Inc.; refrain trans. © 1969. ICEL
Music: David Haas. ©1989. GIA Publications. Inc.

23 Psalm 16: Keep Me Safe, O God

Refrain

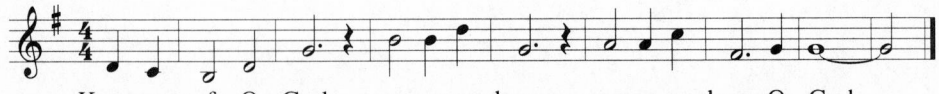

Keep me safe, O God: you are my hope; you are my hope, O God.

Verses

1. I say to God, "you are my only God, I have no good except in you."

2. I find in God always my cup of joy; and God will keep my life secure.

3. I bless my God: God who has counseled me. At night my heart gives counsel too.

4. I keep my God always before my eyes; with God beside me I'm secure.

5. And so my heart always is glad in God; my body too shall dwell secure.

6. For you will not ever abandon me, or let your servant lose the path.

7. The path of life you have revealed to me, and in your presence is my joy.

Text: Psalm 16: John Foley, SJ. © 1993, GIA Publications, Inc.; refrain trans., © 1969, ICEL
Music: John Foley, SJ. © 1993, GIA Publications, Inc.

Psalm 16: You Will Show Me the Path of Life 24

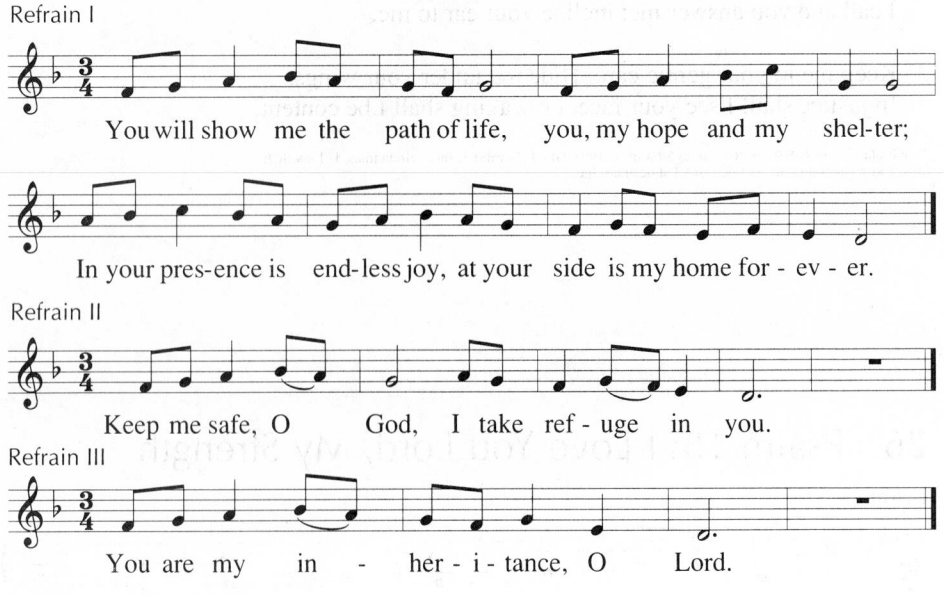

Refrain I

You will show me the path of life, you, my hope and my shel-ter;

In your pres-ence is end-less joy, at your side is my home for - ev - er.

Refrain II

Keep me safe, O God, I take ref - uge in you.

Refrain III

You are my in - her - i - tance, O Lord.

Verses

1. Faithful God, I look to you, you alone my life and fortune,
   never shall I look to other gods, you shall be my one hope.

2. From of old you are my heritage, you my wisdom and my safety,
   through the night you speak within my heart, silently you teach me.

3. So my heart shall sing for joy, in your arms I rest securely,
   you will not abandon me to death, you shall not desert me.

Text: Psalm 16:1-2, 6-8, 9-10; Marty Haugen. © 1988, GIA Publications, Inc.; refrain III trans., © 1969, ICEL
Music: Marty Haugen; refrain II and III adapt. by Diana Kodner. © 1988, 1994, GIA Publications, Inc.

25 Psalm 17: Lord, When Your Glory Appears

Refrain

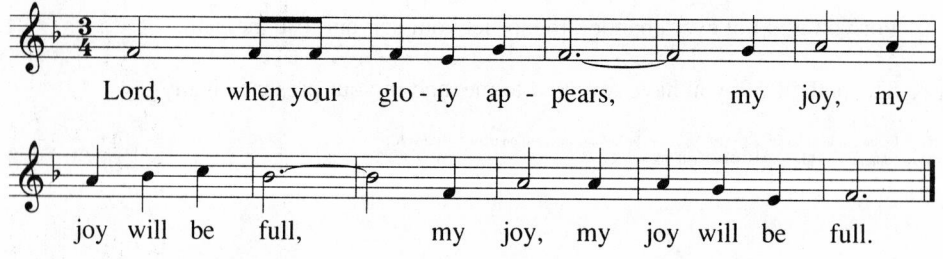

Lord, when your glo - ry ap - pears, my joy, my joy will be full, my joy, my joy will be full.

Verses

1. Hear, O Lord, a just suit, attend to my outcry. Hear the pray'r of my lips;
   lips without deceit.

2. My steps are fast in your path, my feet have faltered not.
   I call and you answer me; incline your ear to me.

3. Keep me in your gentle care. Hide me under your wings.
   In justice shall I see your face, on waking shall I be content.

Text: Psalm 17:1, 5-6, 8-9, 15; Roy James Stewart, © 1993, GIA Publications, Inc.: refrain trans. © 1969, ICEL
Music: Roy James Stewart, © 1993, GIA Publications. Inc.

26 Psalm 18: I Love You Lord, My Strength

Refrain

I love you, Lord, my strength, my strength.

Verses

1. I love you, Lord, my strength, my rock, my fortress, my savior.
   God, you are the rock where I take refuge;
   my shield, my mighty help, my stronghold.
   Lord, you are worthy of all praise, when I call I am saved from my foes.

2. Long life to you, Lord, my rock! Praise to you, God, who saves me,
   You have given great victories to your king and shown your love for your anointed.

Text: Psalm 18:2-3, 3-4, 47, 51: © 1963, 1993. The Grail, GIA Publications, Inc., agent: refrain trans. © 1969, ICEL
Music: Michel Guimont, © 1994, GIA Publications. Inc.

Psalm 19: Lord, You Have the Words   27

Refrain

Lord, you have the words of ev-er-last-ing life.

Verses

1. The law of the Lord is perfect, refreshing the soul;
   the Lord's rule is to be trusted, the simple find wisdom.

2. The fear of the Lord is holy, abiding for ever;
   the decrees of the Lord are true, all of them just.

3. The precepts of the Lord are right, they gladden the heart,
   the command of the Lord is clear, giving light to the eye.

4. They are worth more than gold, than the finest gold,
   sweeter than honey, than honey from the comb.

Psalm 22: I Will Praise You, Lord   28

Refrain

I will praise you, Lord, in the as-sem-bly of your peo - ple.

Verses

1. My vows I will pay before those who fear God.
   The poor shall eat and shall have their fill.
   Those who seek the Lord shall praise the Lord.
   May their hearts live for ever and ever!

2. All the earth shall remember and return to the Lord,
   all families of the nations shall bow down in awe.
   They shall bow down in awe, all the mighty of the earth,
   all who must die and go down to the dust.

3. My soul shall live for God and my children too shall serve.
   They shall tell of the Lord to generations yet to come;
   declare to those unborn, the faithfulness of God. These things the Lord has done.

29   Psalm 22: My God, My God

Refrain

My God, my God, O why have you a-ban-doned me?

Verses

1. All who see me laugh at me, they mock me and they shake their heads:
   "He relied on the Lord, let the Lord be his refuge."

2. As dogs around me, they circle me about.
   Wounded me and pierced me, I can number all my bones.

3. My clothing they divided, for my garments casting lots,
   O Lord, do not desert me, but hasten to my aid.

4. I will praise you to my people, and proclaim you in their midst,
   O fear the Lord, my people, give glory to God's name.

Text: Psalm 22:8-9, 17-18; 19-20; 23-24; Marty Haugen. © 1983. GIA Publications, Inc.; refrain trans. © 1969, ICEL
Music: Marty Haugen. © 1983. GIA Publications, Inc.

30   Psalm 23: My Shepherd Is the Lord

Antiphon I

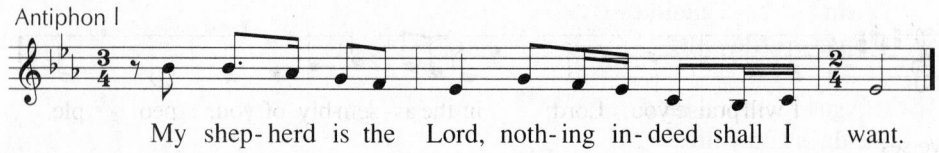

My shep-herd is the Lord, noth-ing in-deed shall I want.

Text: Psalm 23; The Grail
Music: Joseph Gelineau
© 1963, The Grail, GIA Publications, Inc., agent

Antiphon II

The Lord is my shep-herd, noth-ing shall I want: he

leads me by safe paths, noth-ing shall I fear.

Text: Psalm 23; The Grail
Music: A. Gregory Murray, OSB
© 1963, The Grail, GIA Publications, Inc., agent

Psalm Tone

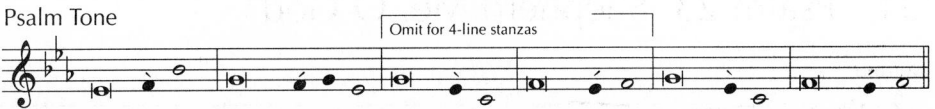

Omit for 4-line stanzas

Music: Richard Proulx, © 1975, GIA Publications, Inc.

Gelineau Tone

Omit for 4-line stanzas

Dominus regit me

¹ **Lord, you** are mỳ **shep**herd;
there is **noth**ing Í shall **want**.
² **Fresh** and **green** are thè **pas**tures
where you **give** me ré**pose.**
Near **restful wa**ters yòu **lead** me,
³ to re**vive** my droopíng **spirit.**

You **guide** me alòng the rìght **path**;
You are **true** tó your **name.**
⁴ If I should **walk** in the **val**ley òf **dark**ness
no evil would Í **fear.**
You are **there** with your **crook** and yòur **staff**;
with **these** you give mé **comfort.**

⁵ You have pre**pared** a **ban**quet fòr **me**
in the **sight** óf my **foes.**
My **head** you have a**noin**ted wìth **oil**;
my **cup** is ovér**flowing.**

⁶ Surely **good**ness and **kind**ness shàll **fol**low me
all the **days** óf my **life.**
In the **Lord's** own **house** shall Ì **dwell**
for **ev**er ánd **ever.**

To the **Fa**ther and **Son** gìve **glo**ry,
give **glo**ry tó the **Spir**it.
To God who **is**, who **was**, and whò **will** be
for **ev**er ánd **ever.**

Text: Psalm 23; The Grail
Music: Joseph Gelineau
© 1963, 1993, The Grail, GIA Publications, Inc., agent

31 Psalm 23: Shepherd Me, O God

Refrain

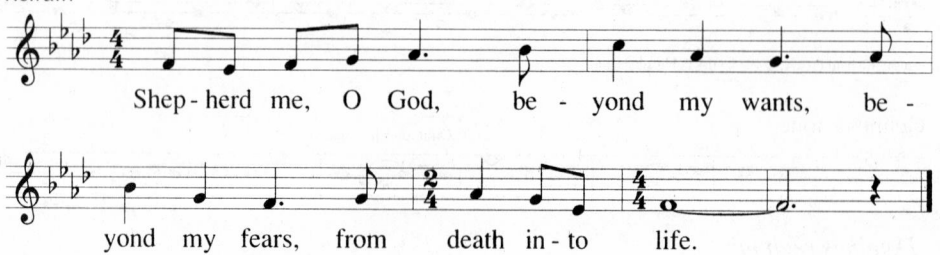

Shep - herd me, O God, be - yond my wants, be -
yond my fears, from death in - to life.

Verses

1. God is my shepherd, so nothing shall I want,
   I rest in the meadows of faithfulness and love,
   I walk by the quiet waters of peace.

2. Gently you raise me and heal my weary soul,
   you lead me by pathways of righteousness and truth,
   my spirit shall sing the music of your name.

3. Though I should wander the valley of death,
   I fear no evil, for you are at my side, your rod and your staff,
   my comfort and my hope.

4. You have set me a banquet of love in the face of hatred,
   crowning me with love beyond my pow'r to hold.

5. Surely your kindness and mercy follow me all the days of my life;
   I will dwell in the house of my God for evermore.

Text: Psalm 23; Marty Haugen
Music: Marty Haugen
© 1986. GIA Publications, Inc.

Psalm 23: The Lord Is My Shepherd   32

Refrain

The Lord is my shep-herd, I shall not want. The

Lord is my shep - herd, I shall not want.

Verses

1. The pastures are fresh where you give me rest; Calm waters lift up my soul.
   You lead me on paths that are righteous and good; Your name is hallowed by all.

2. Though I am brought down to the valley deep, No evil great will I fear;
   The strength of your rod and the pow'r of your staff Will give me comfort and cheer.

3. A feast you have held in the sight of foes; Oil has anointed my head;
   My cup overflows with your mercy and love: With blessings great am I fed.

4. Today and for all of my days to come Goodness and love follow me,
   And now I will dwell in the house of the Lord As long as life there shall be.

Text: Psalm 23; Randall Sensmeier
Music: Randall Sensmeier
© 1994, GIA Publications, Inc.

33   Psalm 23: Nada Me Falta

Refrain

El Se - ñor es mi pas - tor, na - da me fal - ta. El Se -
ñor es mi pas - tor, na - da me fal - ta - rá.

Verses

1. El Señor es mi pastor, nada me falta: En verdes praderas me hace recostar;
   Me conduce hacia fuentes tranquilas y repara mis fuerzas.

2. Me guía por el sendero justo en gracia de su nombre.
   Aunque camine por cañadas oscuras, nada temo porque tú vas conmigo:
   tu vara y tu cayado me sosiegan.

3. Preparas una mesa ante mí, enfrente de mis enemigos;
   me unges la cabeza con perfume, y mi copa rebosa.

4. Tu bondad y tu engencia me acompañan. Todos los días de mi vida,
   y habitaré en la casa del Señor por siempre.

Text: Psalm 23, Spanish Lectionary; Donna Peña
Music: Donna Peña; acc. by Diana Kodner
© 1988, 1993 GIA Publications, Inc.

34   Psalm 24: We Long to See Your Face

Refrain I

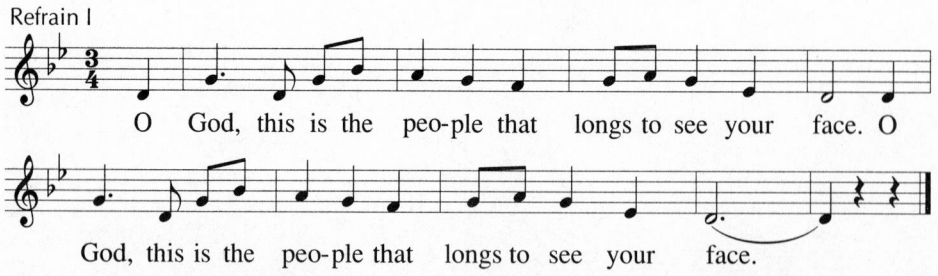

O God, this is the peo-ple that longs to see your face. O
God, this is the peo-ple that longs to see your face.

Refrain II

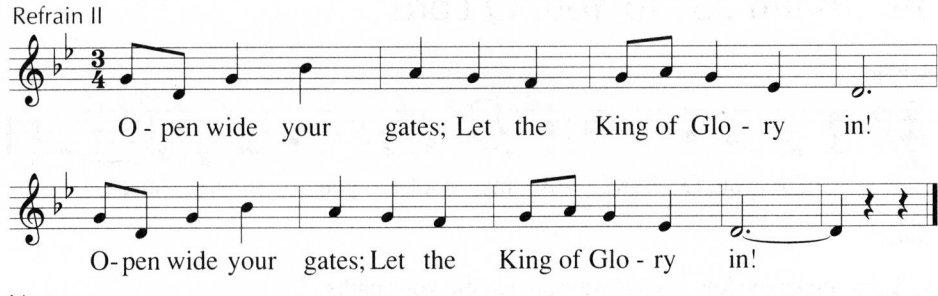

O - pen wide your gates; Let the King of Glo - ry in!

O - pen wide your gates; Let the King of Glo - ry in!

Verses

1. All the earth is yours, O God, the world and those who dwell on it.
   You have founded it upon the seas and established it upon the rivers.

2. Who can ascend your mountain, God? Or who may stand in this holy place?
   Those whose hands are sinless, hearts are clean, and desire not the vanity of earth.

3. They shall receive your blessing, God, their Savior shall reward them.
   Such is the face that seeks for you, that seeks your face, O God of Jacob.

Text: Psalm 24: Kevin Keil. © 1993, GIA Publications. Inc.: refrain I trans. © 1969, ICEL
Music: Kevin Keil. © 1993 GIA Publications. Inc.

Psalm 25: Remember Your Mercies   35

Refrain I

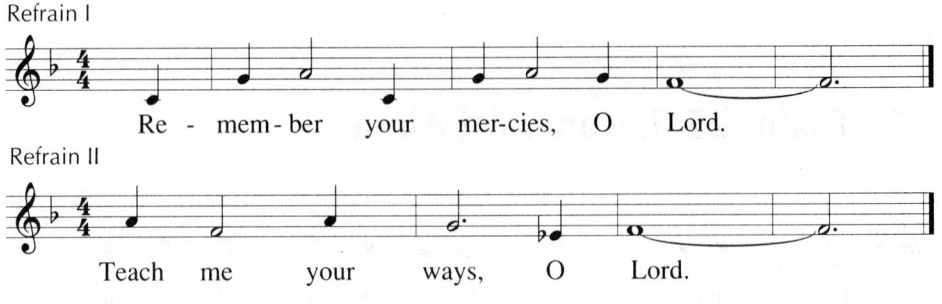

Re - mem - ber your mer-cies, O Lord.

Refrain II

Teach me your ways, O Lord.

Verses

1. Your ways, O Lord, make known to me, teach me your paths.
   Guide me, teach me, for you are my Savior.

2. Remember your compassion, Lord, and your kindness of old.
   Remember this, and not my sins, in your goodness, O Lord.

3. Good and just is the Lord, the sinners know the way.
   God guides the meek to justice, and teaches the humble.

Text: Psalm 25:4-5. 6-7. 8-9: David Haas. © 1985. GIA Publications. Inc.: refrain trans. © 1969. ICEL
Music: David Haas. © 1985. GIA Publications. Inc.

36 Psalm 25: To You, O Lord

Refrain

To you, O Lord, I lift my soul, to you, I lift my soul.

Verses

1. Lord, make me know your ways, teach me your paths
   and keep me in the way of your truth, for you are God, my Savior.

2. For the Lord is good and righteous, revealing the way to those who wander,
   gently leading the poor and the humble.

3. To the ones who seek the Lord, who look to God's word, who live God's love,
   God will always be near, and will show them mercy.

Text: Psalm 25:4-5, 8-9, 12-14; Marty Haugen, © 1982. GIA Publications, Inc.; refrain trans. © 1969, ICEL
Music: Marty Haugen, © 1982, GIA Publications, Inc.

37 Psalm 25: Levanto Mi Alma

Refrain

Oh Dios mí-o, le-van-to mi al - ma,
le-van-to a ti Se-ñor, mi sal-va-ción.

Verses

1. Sólo en ti confio, estaré sin vergüenza. Y no triunfaran mis enemigos.
   No hay dudas.

2. Muestrame tus caminos. Enseñame tus sendas.
   Guíame Señor en tu verdad y a mi salvación.

3. Todo el día espero en ti, espero por tu bondad.
   No recuerdes Señor los pecados de mi juventud, sino, dame tu amor.

4. Mis ojos estan en Yahveh. Mirame y ten compasión,
   porque estoy solo y estoy desdichado.

Text: Psalm 25: Donna Peña
Music: Donna Peña: acc. by Diana Kodner
© 1988, 1993. GIA Publications, Inc.

Psalm 27: In the Land of the Living   38

Refrain

I be - lieve I shall see the good things of the

Lord in the land of the liv - ing.

Verses

1. The Lord is my light, the Lord is my help, of whom should I be afraid?
   The Lord is the stronghold of my life, before whom should I shrink?

2. When I cry out, O Lord, hear my voice! Have mercy on me and answer.
   My heart has told me, "seek his face!" It is your face, Lord, I seek.

3. There is only one thing I ask of the Lord: to live in God's house forever,
   to savor the sweetness of the Lord, to behold his temple.

Text: Psalm 27: *The Jerusalem Bible*. © 1966. Darton. Longman and Todd. Ltd. and Doubleday. a division of Bantam Doubleday Dell
    Publishing Group. Inc.
Music: Carl Johengen. © 1993. GIA Publications. Inc.

39   Psalm 27: The Lord Is My Light

Refrain

The Lord is my light and my sal - va - tion, of whom should I be a - fraid, of whom should I be a - fraid?

Verses

1. The Lord is my light and my help; whom should I fear?
   The Lord is the stronghold of my life; before whom should I shrink?

2. There is one thing I ask of the Lord; for this I long:
   to live in the house of the Lord all the days of my life.

3. I believe I shall see the goodness of the Lord in the land of the living;
   hope in God, and take heart. Hope in the Lord!

Text: Psalm 27:1-2, 4, 13-14; David Haas
Music: David Haas
© 1983, GIA Publications, Inc.

40   Psalm 29: The Lord Will Bless His People

Refrain

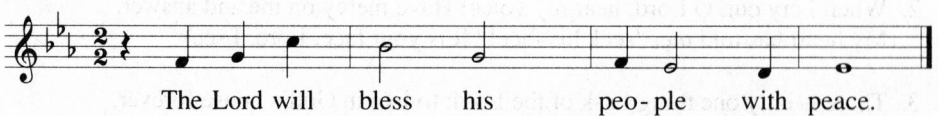

The Lord will bless his peo - ple with peace.

Verses

1. O give the Lord, you children of God, give the Lord glory and power;
   give the Lord the glory of his name. Adore the Lord, resplendent and holy.

2. The Lord's voice resounding on the waters; the Lord on the immensity of waters;
   the voice of the Lord, full of power, the voice of the Lord, full of splendor.

3. The God of glory thunders. In his temple they all cry:
   "Glory!" the Lord sat enthroned over the flood; the Lord sits as king for ever.

Text: Psalm 29:1-2, 3-4, 3, 9-10; © 1963, 1993, The Grail, GIA Publications, Inc., agent; refrain trans. © 1969, ICEL
Music: Michel Guimont, © 1994, GIA Publications, Inc.

Psalm 30: I Will Praise You, Lord   41

Refrain

I will praise you, Lord, you have res-cued me, I will praise you, Lord, for your mer-cy. I will praise you, Lord, you have res-cued me: I will praise you, Lord.

Verses

1. I will praise you, Lord, you have rescued me
   and have not let my enemies rejoice over me.
   O Lord, you have raised my soul from the dead,
   restored me to life from those who sink into the grave.

2. Sing psalms to the Lord, you who love him, give thanks to his holy name.
   His anger lasts but a moment; his favor through life.
   At night there are tears, but joy comes with dawn.

3. The Lord listened and had pity. The Lord came to my help.
   For me you have changed my mourning into dancing;
   O Lord my God, I will thank you for ever.

Text: Psalm 30:2, 4, 5-6, 11-13; © 1963, The Grail, GIA Publications, Inc., agent; refrain, Paul Inwood, © 1985
Music: Paul Inwood, © 1985
Published by OCP Publications

42 Psalm 31: I Put My Life in Your Hands / Pongo Mi Vida

Refrain

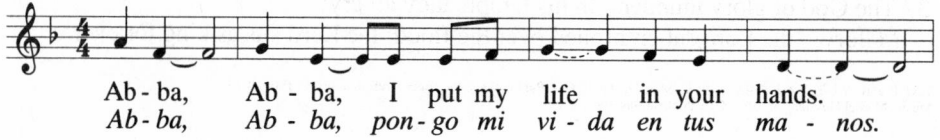

Ab-ba,   Ab-ba,   I   put   my   life   in   your   hands.
Ab-ba,   Ab-ba,   pon-go   mi   vi-da   en   tus   ma - nos.

Ab-ba,   Ab-ba,   I   put   my   life   in   your   hands.
Ab-ba,   Ab-ba,   pon-go   mi   vi-da   en   tus   ma - nos.

Verses

1. In you, O Lord I take refuge; let me never be put to shame.
   In your justice rescue me, in your hands I commend my spirit.

2. For all my foes reproach me; all my friends are now put to flight.
   I am forgotten, like the dead, like a dish that now is broken.

3. I place my trust in you; in your hands is my destiny.
   Let your face shine upon your servant, in your hands I will place my life.

1. *En ti busco protección. No me defraudes nunca jamás.*
   Ponme a salvo pues tú eres justo. En tus manos encomiendo mi espíritu.

2. *En ti pongo toda mi fe hablaré de tu bondad,*
   por favor está siempre conmigo. Tú haces la luz del caos.

3. *Tú eres mi esperanza; sólo tú mi salvación.*
   Con tu misericordia, ven. Escucha mi oración.

Text: Psalm 31; David Haas; Spanish trans. by Jeffrey Judge
Music: David Haas
© 1993, GIA Publications, Inc.

Psalm 31: I Put My Life in Your Hands 43

Refrain I

Fa - ther, I put my life in your hands.

Refrain II

O Lord, be my rock of safe - ty.

Verses

1. In you, O Lord I take refuge; let me never be put to shame.
   In your justice rescue me, oh my faithful Lord, in your hands I commend my spirit.

2. For all my foes reproach me; all my friends are now put to flight.
   I am forgotten, like the unremembered dead, like a dish that now is broken.

3. I place my trust in you, Lord; in your hands is my destiny.
   Let your face shine upon your servant, Lord, in your hands I will place my life.

Text: Psalm 31: 2, 6, 12-13, 15-16, 17; Marty Haugen. © 1983, GIA Publications, Inc., refrains trans. © 1969, ICEL
Music: Marty Haugen; refrain II adapt. by Diana Kodner. © 1983, 1994 GIA Publications, Inc.

44 Psalm 32: I Turn to You

Refrain

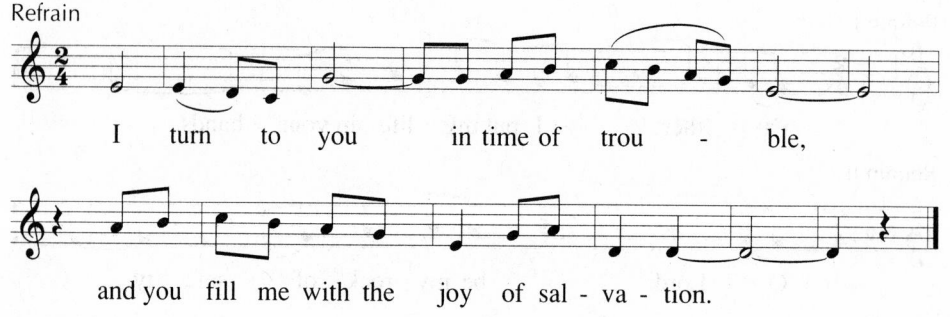

I turn to you in time of trou - ble,

and you fill me with the joy of sal - va - tion.

Verses

1. Happy is he whose sin is forgiven, whose fault is taken away.
   Happy is she whom God shall find of an innocent heart,
   in whose soul there is no guile.

2. I kept my sin held deep in my soul, and my frame was wasted away.
   Night and day was your hand a weight upon my heart:
   I was weak, wracked with fever and alone.

3. Then I acknowledged the pain of my sin, and my guilt I covered not.
   I said I confess my fault unto you, and you took away the guilt of my sin.

4. O be glad in our God; exult, you just; rejoice, all you upright of heart.

Text: Psalm 32:1-2, 3-4, 5, 11; Rory Cooney. © 1991, GIA Publications, Inc.: refrain trans. © 1969, ICEL
Music: Rory Cooney. © 1991, GIA Publications, Inc.

Psalm 33: Let Your Mercy Be on Us   45

Refrain I

Let your mer - cy be on us, O God, as we place our trust in you.

Refrain II

The earth is full of the good - ness of God, the good - ness of our God.

Refrain III

Hap - py are the peo - ple the Lord has cho - sen, cho - sen to be his own.

Verses

1. Your words, O God, are truth indeed, and all your works are ever faithful;
   you love justice and right, your compassion fills all creation.

2. See how the eye of God is watching, ever guarding all who wait in hope,
   to deliver them from death and sustain them in time of famine.

3. Exult, you just, in the Lord, for praise is the song of the righteous!
   How happy the people of God, the ones whom God has chosen!

4. Our soul is waiting for God, for God is our help and our shield.
   May your kindness, O God, be upon us who place our hope in you.

Text: Psalm 33:1, 4-5, 12, 18-19, 20, 22: Marty Haugen; refrain I trans. © 1969, ICEL; refrains II, III, and verses © 1987, 1994 GIA Publications, Inc.
Music: Marty Haugen; refrain III adapt. by Diana Kodner. © 1987, 1994, GIA Publications, Inc.

46 Psalm 34: I Will Bless the Lord

Refrain

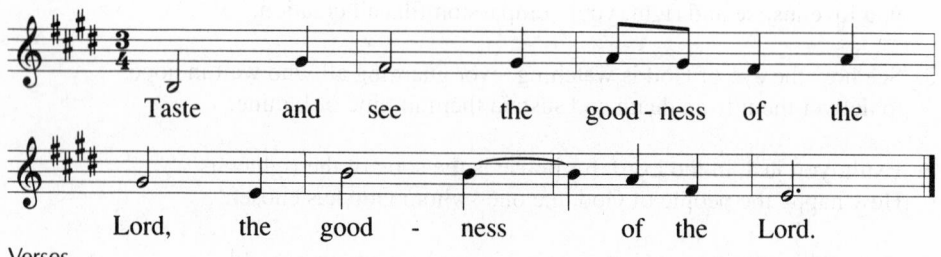

I will bless the Lord; God's praise shall be ev-er on my lips.

Verses

1. Let my soul glory in the Lord. Let the lowly hear me and be glad.
   Glorify the Lord with me! Let us all praise God's holy name.

2. I looked to God and my prayer was answered; God delivered me from all my fear.
   Look to God that you may be radiant with joy;
   that your faces may not blush with shame.

3. Taste and see the goodness of God; happy those who take shelter in the Lord.
   Fear the Lord, all you holy ones, for nothing is lacking to those who fear the Lord.

Text: Psalm 34: Normand Gouin
Music: Normand Gouin
© 1993, GIA Publications, Inc.

47 Psalm 34: Taste and See

Refrain

Taste and see the good-ness of the

Lord, the good - ness of the Lord.

Verses

1. I will bless the Lord at all times, God's praise ever in my mouth.
   Glory in the Lord for ever, and the lowly will hear and be glad.

2. Glory in the Lord with me, let us together extol God's name.
   I sought the Lord, who answered me and delivered me from all my fears.

3. Look to God that you might be radiant with joy,
   and your faces free from all shame.
   The Lord hears the suffering souls, and saves them from all distress.

Text: Psalm 34:2-3, 4-5, 6-7: Marty Haugen, ' 1980, GIA Publications, Inc.: refrain trans. ' 1969, ICEL
Music: Marty Haugen, ' 1980, GIA Publications, Inc.

Psalm 34: The Cry of the Poor   48

Refrain

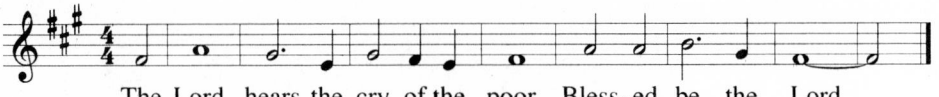

The Lord hears the cry of the poor. Bless-ed be the Lord.

Verses

1. I will bless the Lord at all times, with praise ever in my mouth.
   Let my soul glory in the Lord, who will hear the cry of the poor.

2. Let the lowly hear and be glad: the Lord listens to their pleas;
   and to hearts broken God is near, who will hear the cry of the poor.

3. Ev'ry spirit crushed God will save; will be ransom for their lives;
   will be safe shelter for their fears, and will hear the cry of the poor.

4. We proclaim your greatness, O God, your praise ever in our mouth;
   ev'ry face brightened in your light, for you hear the cry of the poor.

Text: Psalm 34:2-3, 6-7, 18-19, 23: John Foley, SJ
Music: John Foley, SJ
' 1978, 1990, John B. Foley, SJ, and New Dawn Music

49   Psalm 40: Here I Am

Refrain

Here I am, Lord, here I am. I come to do your will.

Verses

1. Long was I waiting for God, and then he heard my cry.
   It was he who taught this song to me, a song of praise to God.

2. You asked me not for sacrifice, for slaughtered goats or lambs.
   No, my heart, you gave me ears to hear you, then I said, "Here I am."

3. You wrote it in the scrolls of law what you would have me do.
   Doing that is what has made me happy, your law is in my heart.

4. I spoke before your holy people, the good news that you save.
   Now you know that I will not be silent. I'll always sing your praise.

Text: Psalm 40; Rory Cooney
Music: Rory Cooney
© 1971, 1991, NALR

50   Psalm 41: Lord, Heal My Soul

Refrain

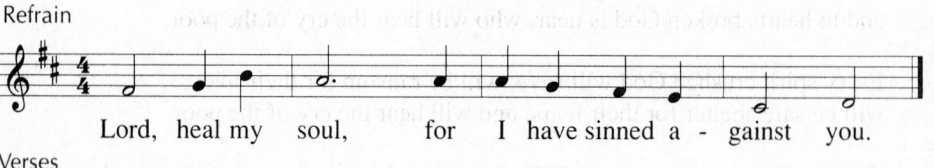

Lord, heal my soul, for I have sinned a - gainst you.

Verses

1. Happy those who consider the poor and the weak.
   The Lord will save them in the evil day,
   will guard them, give them life, make them happy in the land
   and will not give them up to the will of their foes.

2. The Lord will give them strength in their pain,
   will bring them back from sickness to health.
   As for me, I said: Lord, have mercy on me,
   heal my soul for I have sinned against you.

3. If you uphold me I shall be unharmed and set in your presence for evermore.
   Blessed be the Lord, the God of Israel from age to age. Amen. Amen.

Text: Psalm 41:2-3, 4-5, 13-14; © 1963, 1993, The Grail, GIA Publications, Inc., agent; refrain trans. © 1969, ICEL
Music: Michel Guimont, © 1994, GIA Publications, Inc.

Psalm 41-42: Song of Longing   51

Refrain

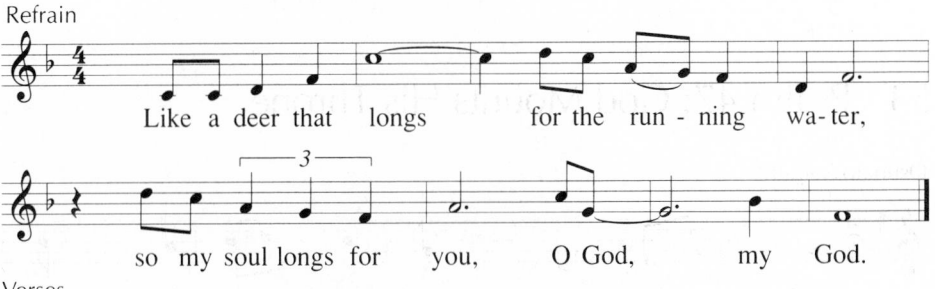

Like a deer that longs for the run - ning wa - ter,

so my soul longs for you, O God, my God.

Verses

1. My soul is longing for God, When shall I look on the face of God?
   The God who gives me my life. When shall I look on the face of God?
   Like a land rainless and barren, So do I long for my God.
   Like a man far from his homeland, So do I long for my God.
   O your love is better than living, and my lips shall sing your praise.
   In your name I lift my hands, I will bless you all my days.

2. My God is gladness and joy, When shall I look on the face of God?
   My rock and shelter is God, When shall I look on the face of God?
   As the sky gladdens the sparrow, So do I long for my God.
   As the dawn gladdens the watchman, So do I long for my God.
   To my eyes your light is a vision, to my heart your truth you give.
   These, O God, shall lead me on to the mountain where you live.

3. Why are you so downcast, my soul? Why do you sigh within me?
   Hope in God! O I will praise him still.

Text: Psalm 41, 42: Rory Cooney
Music: Rory Cooney
© 1974, 1991, NALR

52   Psalm 45: The Queen Stands at Your Right Hand

Refrain

The queen stands at your right hand, ar-rayed in gold.

Verses

1. Listen, O Daughter, give ear to my words:
   Forget your people and your father's house.
   So will the king desire your beauty; He is your lord, pay homage to him.

2. They are escorted with gladness and joy; they pass within the palace of the king,
   He is our God, pay homage to him.

Text: Psalm 45:10, 11, 12, 16; verses trans. © 1970, Confraternity of Christian Doctrine, Washington, D.C., alt.; refrain trans. © 1969, 1981, ICEL
Music: Diana Kodner, © 1994, GIA Publications, Inc.

53   Psalm 47: God Mounts His Throne

Ostinato Refrain*

God mounts his throne to shouts of joy, O

sing your prais-es to the Lord!

Verses

1. All you peoples, clap your hands, shout to God in gladness,
   the Lord we must fear, king of all the earth.

2. God goes up to shouts of joy, sound the trumpet blast.
   Sing praise to our God, praise unto our king!

3. God is king of all the earth, sing with all your skill
   to the king of all nations, God enthroned on high!

May be sung in canon.

Text: Psalm 47:2-3, 6-7, 8-9; Marty Haugen. © 1983, GIA Publications, Inc.; refrain trans. © 1969, ICEL
Music: Marty Haugen. © 1983, GIA Publications, Inc.

Psalm 50: To the Upright   54

Refrain

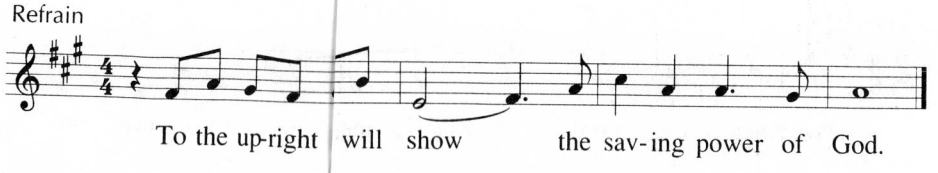

To the up-right will show   the sav-ing power of God.

Verses

1. The God of gods, the Lord has spoken and summoned the earth,
   from the rising of the sun to its setting,
   "I find no fault with your sacrifices, your offerings are always before me.

2. Were I hungry, I would not tell you, for I own the world and all it holds.
   Do you think I eat the flesh of bulls, or drink the blood of goats?

3. Offer to God your sacrifice; to the Most High pay your vows.
   Call on me in the day of distress. I will free you and you shall honor me."

Text: Psalm 50:1, 8, 12-13, 14-15: © 1963, 1993, The Grail, GIA Publications, Inc., agent: refrain trans. © 1969, ICEL.
Music: Michel Guimont, © 1994, GIA Publications, Inc.

55 Psalm 51: Have Mercy, Lord

Antiphon

Have mer - cy, Lord, cleanse me from all my sins.

Text: Psalm 51; The Grail
Music: Joseph Gelineau
© 1963, The Grail, GIA Publications, Inc., agent

Psalm Tone

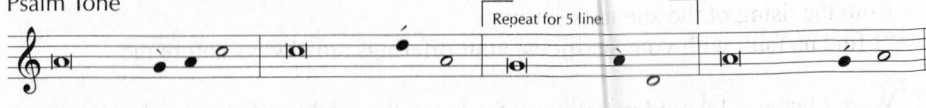

Music: Chrysogonus Waddell, OCSO, © Gethsemani Abbey

Gelineau Tone

Miserere mei, Deus

[3] Have **mercy** on me, **God** in your **kind**ness.
In your com**pas**sion blot **out** my óffense.
[4] O **wash** me more and **more** from mỳ **guilt**
and **cleanse** me **from** mý **sin**.

[5] My **offens**es trulỳ I **know** them;
my **sin** is **always** béfore me.
[6] Against **you**, you a**lone**, have Ì **sinned**;
what is **evil** in your **sight** I háve **done**.

That you may be **justi**fied **when** yòu give **sen**tence
and be with**out** re**proach** when yóu **judge**,
[7] O **see**, in **guilt** I wàs **born**,
a **sinner** was **I** cónceived.

[8] **Indeed** you love **truth** ìn the **heart**;
then in the **secret** of my **heart** teach mé **wis**dom.
[9] O **purify** me, **then** I shall bè **clean**;
O **wash** me, I shall be **whit**er thán **snow**.

[10] Make me **hear** rejoicìng and **glad**ness,
that the **bones** you have **crushed** máy re**vive**.
[11] **From my sins** turn away yòur **face**
and **blot** out **all** mý **guilt**.

¹² A **pure** heart cre**ate** for mè, O **God**,
   put a **stead**fast **spir**it wíth**in** me.
¹³ Do not **cast** me a**way** from yòur **pres**ence,
   nor de**prive** me of your holý **spir**it.

¹⁴ Give me a**gain** the **joy** òf your **help**;
   with a **spir**it of **fer**vor sús**tain** me,
¹⁵ that I may **teach** trans**gress**ors yòur **ways**,
   and **sin**ners may re**turn** tó **you**.

¹⁶ O **res**cue me, **Gòd**, my **help**er,
   and my **tongue** shall **ring** out yóur **good**ness.
¹⁷ O **Lord**, open mỳ **lips**
   and my **mouth** shall de**clare** yóur **praise**.

¹⁸ For in **sac**rifice you **take** nò de**light**,
   burnt **offer**ing from **me** you would ré**fuse**;
¹⁹ my **sac**rifice, a con**trìte spir**it,
   a **hum**bled, contrite **heart** you will nót **spurn**.

²⁰ In your **good**ness, show fa**vòr** to **Zion**;
   re**build** the **walls** of Jé**ru**salem.
²¹ **Then** you will be **pleased** with lawfùl **sacrifice**,
   (burnt **offer**ings **whol**ly còn**sumed**),
   then you will be **offer**ed young **bulls** on yóur **al**tar.

Give **glor**y to the **Fathèr** Al**might**y,
to his **Son**, Jesus **Christ**, thé **Lord**,
to the **Spir**it who **dwells** in oùr **hearts**,
both **now** and for **ever**, Ámen.

Text: Psalm 51; The Grail
Music: Joseph Gelineau
© 1963, 1993, The Grail, GIA Publications, Inc., agent

56 Psalm 51: Be Merciful, O Lord

Refrain

Be mer-ci-ful, O Lord, for we have sinned; be

mer-ci-ful, O Lord, for we have sinned.

Verses

1. Have mercy on me, God, in your kindness, in your compassion,
   blot out my offense.
   O wash me more and more from my guilt and my sorrow,
   and cleanse me from all of my sin.

2. My offenses, truly I know them, and my sins are always before me;
   against you alone have I sinned, O Lord, what is evil in your sight I have done.

3. Create in me a clean heart, O God, put your steadfast spirit in my soul.
   Cast me not away from your presence, O Lord, and take not your spirit from me.

4. Give back to me the joy of your salvation, let your willing spirit bear me up
   and I shall teach your way to the ones who have wandered,
   and bring them all home to your side.

Text: Psalm 51:3-4, 5-6, 12-13, 14-15; Marty Haugen. © 1983. GIA Publications, Inc.; refrain trans. © 1969. ICEL
Music: Marty Haugen. © 1983. GIA Publications, Inc.

Psalm 51: Create in Me   57

Refrains

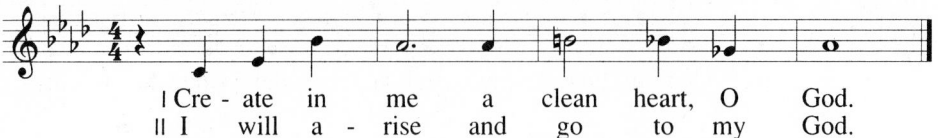

I Cre - ate in me a clean heart, O God.
II I will a - rise and go to my God.

Verses

1. Have mercy on me, O God. In the greatness of your love,
   cleanse me from my sin. Wash me.

2. Stay close to me, O God. In your presence keep me safe.
   Fill me with your spirit. Renew me.

3. Your salvation is joy to me. In your wisdom show the way. Lead me back to you.
   Teach me.

Text: Psalm 51:3-4, 12-13, 14-15: David Haas
Music: David Haas
© 1987. GIA Publications. Inc.

Psalm 54: The Lord Upholds My Life   58

Refrain

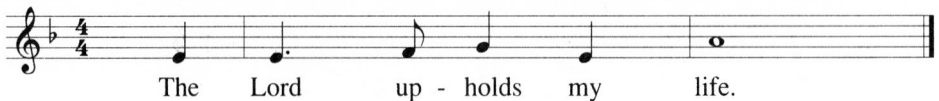

The Lord up - holds my life.

Verses

1. O God, save me by your name; by your power, uphold my cause.
   O God, hear my prayer; listen to the words of my mouth.

2. For the proud have risen against me, ruthless foes seek my life.
   They have no regard for God. (They have no regard for God).

3. But I have God for my help. The Lord upholds my life.
   I will sacrifice to you with willing heart and praise your name,
   O Lord, for it is good.

Text: Psalm 54:3-4, 6-8. © 1963. 1986. The Grail, GIA Publications, Inc., agent; refrain trans. © 1969. ICEL
Music: Michel Guimont. © 1994. GIA Publications. Inc.

59 Psalm 62: In God Alone

Refrain

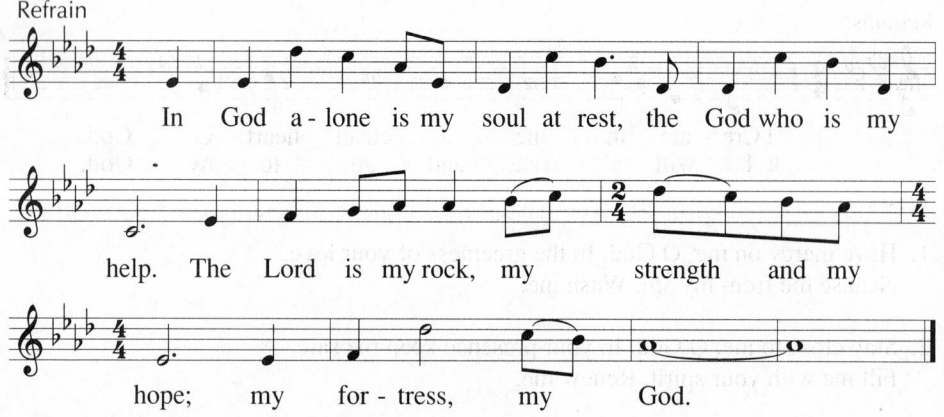

In God a-lone is my soul at rest, the God who is my
help. The Lord is my rock, my strength and my
hope; my for-tress, my God.

Verses

1. Only in God is my soul at rest, from my God comes my salvation.
   God is my rock, the salvation of my life.
   I shall not be shaken, for the Lord is my strength!

2. Only in God is my soul at rest, from my God comes my hope.
   God is my rock, my salvation and my hope.
   I will rest in the Lord. I will not be afraid!

3. Glory and safety, God is my joy, God is my rock and my strength.
   God is my refuge, I trust with all my strength.
   Pour out your hearts, before the Lord!

Text: Psalm 62: 2-3, 6-7, 8-9; David Haas
Music: David Haas
© 1989, GIA Publications, Inc.

Psalm 63: My Soul Is Thirsting 60

Antiphon I

My soul is thirst-ing for you, O Lord, thirst-ing for you my God.

Text: *Lectionary for Mass*, © 1969, 1981, ICEL
Music: Richard Proulx. © 1975, GIA Publications, Inc.

Antiphon II

In the morn-ing I will sing, will sing glad songs of praise to you.

Text: *Praise God in Song*
Music: David Clark Isele
© 1979, GIA Publications, Inc.

Psalm Tone

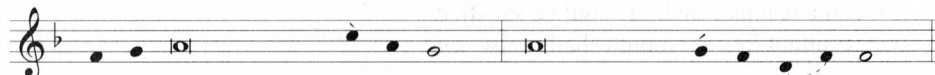

Music : Richard Proulx, © 1986, GIA Publications, Inc.

Gelineau Tone

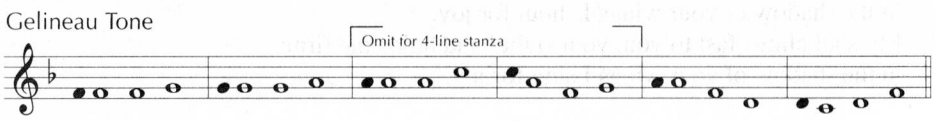

Deus, Deus meus

² O **God**, you are my **God**, for yòu I **long**;
for **yóu** my **soul** is **thirst**ing.
My **bod**y **pìnes** for **you**
like a **dry**, weary **lánd** without **wa**ter.
³ So I **gaze** on **you** in the **sànc**tuary
to **see** your **stréngth** and **your glory**.

⁴ For your **love** is **bèt**ter than **life**,
my **líps** will **speak** your **praise**.
⁵ So I will **bless** you **àll** my **life**,
in your **name** I will **líft** up **my hands**.
⁶ My **soul** shall be **filled** as with a **ban**quet,

my **mouth** shall **práise** you **with joy**.

⁷ On my **bed** I re**mèm**ber **you**.
On **you** I **múse** through **the night**
⁸ for **you** have **bèen** my **help**;
in the **shad**ow of your **wíngs** I **re**joice.
⁹ My **soul clìngs** to **you**;
your **ríght** hand **holds** me **fast**.

Give **praise** to the **Fàther Almigh**ty,
to his **Son**, Jésus **Christ** the **Lord**,
to the **Spir**it who **dwèlls** in our **hearts**,
both **now** and for **éver**. **Amen**.

Text: Psalm 63:2-9; The Grail
Music: Joseph Gelineau
© 1963, The Grail, GIA Publications, Inc., agent

61 Psalm 63: My Soul Is Thirsting

Refrain

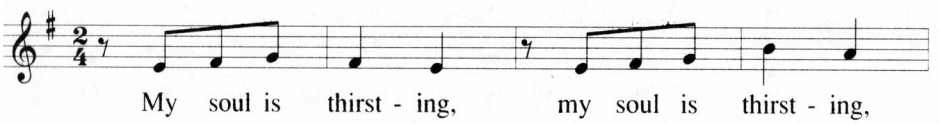

My soul is thirst - ing, my soul is thirst - ing,

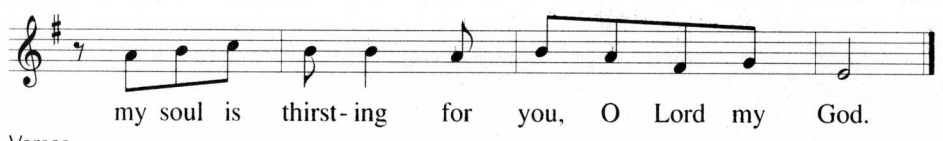

my soul is thirst-ing for you, O Lord my God.

Verses

1. O God, you are my God whom I seek;
   O God, you are my God whom I seek;
   for you my flesh pines, my soul thirsts like the earth, parched, lifeless,
   without water.

2. Thus have I gazed toward you in your holy place to see your power
   and your glory.
   Your kindness is a greater good than life itself; my lips will glorify you.

3. Thus will I bless you while I live;
   Lifting up my hands I will call upon your name.
   As with a banquet shall my soul be satisfied;
   with exultant lips my mouth shall praise you.

4. For you have been my help, you have been my help;
   in the shadow of your wings I shout for joy.
   My soul clings fast to you; your right hand holds me firm;
   in the shadow of your wings I sing for joy.

Text: Psalm 63:2, 3-4, 5-6, 8-9; verses trans. © 1970, Confraternity of Christian Doctrine, Washington, D.C.; refrain by Michael Joncas, © 1987, GIA Publications, Inc.
Music: Michael Joncas, © 1987, GIA Publications, Inc.

Psalm 63: Your Love Is Finer Than Life   62

Refrain

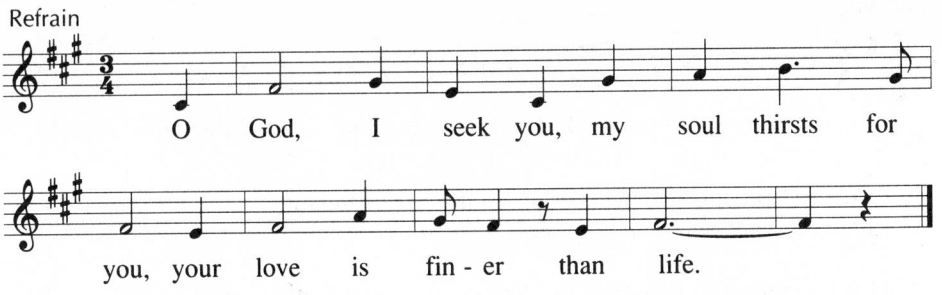

O God, I seek you, my soul thirsts for you, your love is fin-er than life.

Verses

1. As a dry and weary desert land, so my soul is thirsting for my God,
   and my flesh is faint for the God I seek, for your love is more to me than life.

2. I think of you when at night I rest, I reflect upon your steadfast love,
   I will cling to you, O Lord my God, in the shadow of your wings I sing.

3. I will bless your name all the days I live, I will raise my hands and call on you,
   my joyful lips shall sing your praise, you alone have filled my hungry soul.

Text: Psalm 63: Marty Haugen
Music: Marty Haugen
© 1982. GIA Publications. Inc.

63   Psalm 63: I Long for You

Refrain

I long for you, O Lord. With all my soul I thirst for you.

Verses

1. God, my God, it is you I seek; for you my soul is thirsting.
   Like a dry and weary land my spirit longs for you.

2. I have sought your presence, Lord; to see your pow'r and glory.
   Lord, your love means more than life; I shall sing your praise.

3. Thus will I bless you while I live, and I will call your name, Lord.
   As with the riches of a feast, my soul is filled by you.

4. Through the night I remember you for you have been my savior.
   In the shadow of your wings I will shout for joy.

Text: Psalm 63:2, 3-4, 5-6, 7-9; Mike Balhoff, Gary Daigle, Darryl Ducote
Music: Mike Balhoff, Gary Daigle, Darryl Ducote
© 1981, 1993, Damean Music. Distributed by GIA Publications, Inc.

Psalm 65: The Seed That Falls on Good Ground   64

Refrain

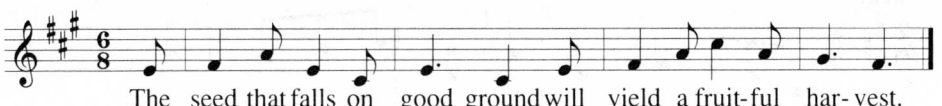

The seed that falls on good ground will yield a fruit-ful har-vest.

Verses

1. You care for the earth, give it water; you fill it with riches.
   Your river in heaven brims over to provide its grain.

2. And thus you provide for the earth; you drench its furrows;
   you level it, soften it with showers; you bless its growth.

3. You crown the year with your goodness. Abundance flows in your steps;
   in the pastures of the wilderness it flows.

4. The hills are girded with joy, the meadows covered with flocks,
   the valleys are decked with wheat. They shout for joy, yes they sing.

Text: Psalm 65:10-11, 12-13, 14: © 1963, 1993, The Grail, GIA Publications, Inc., agent; refrain trans. © 1969, ICEL
Music: Michel Guimont, © 1994, GIA Publications, Inc.

65 Psalm 66: Let All the Earth

Refrain

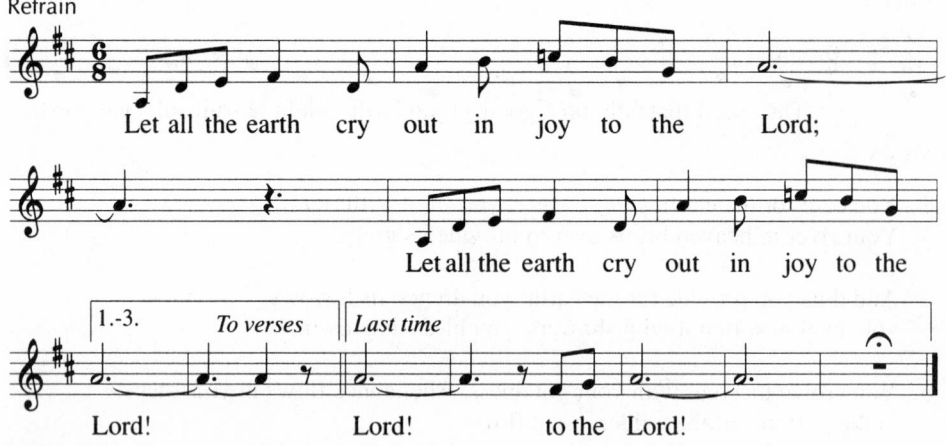

Let all the earth cry out in joy to the Lord;

Let all the earth cry out in joy to the

1.-3. *To verses* **Last time**

Lord! Lord! to the Lord!

Verses

1. Cry out in joy to the Lord, all peoples on earth,
   sing to the praise of God's name, proclaiming for ever,
   "tremendous your deeds for us."

2. Leading your people safe through fire and water,
   bringing their souls to life, we sing of your glory, your love is eternal.

3. Hearken to me as I sing my love of the Lord,
   who answers the prayer of my heart. God leads me in safety, from death unto life.

Text: Psalm 66:1-3, 12, 16; Marty Haugen
Music: Marty Haugen
© 1982, GIA Publications, Inc.

Psalm 67: May God Bless Us in His Mercy   66

Refrain I

May God bless us in his mer - cy,

may God bless us in his mer - cy.

Refrain II

O God, O God, let all the na-tions praise you.

Verses

1. O God, be gracious and bless us and let your face shed its light upon us.
   So will your ways be known upon earth and all nations learn your saving help.

2. Let the nations be glad and exult for you rule the world with justice.
   With fairness you rule the peoples, you guide the nations on earth.

3. Let the peoples praise you, O God; let all the peoples praise you.
   May God still give us blessing till the ends of the earth stand in awe.

67 Psalm 68: You Have Made a Home for the Poor

Refrain

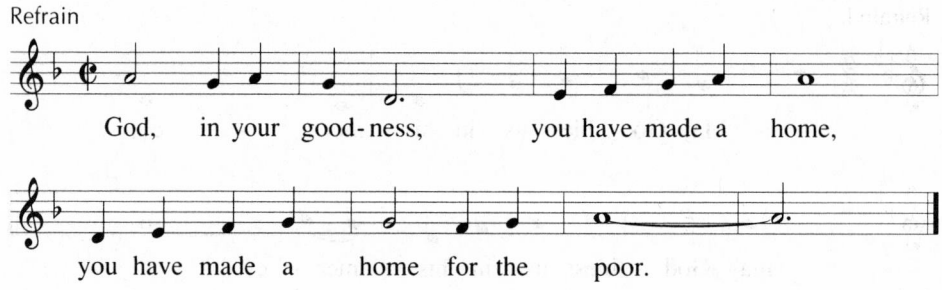

God, in your good-ness, you have made a home,

you have made a home for the poor.

Verses

1. Your presence all around them, the just proclaim your glory;
   Laughing, dancing, singing, they revel in your story.
   O let us sing our praises! God's name inspire our song,
   For God is ever near us, let our praise be loud and long.

2. A parent to the orphan, the widow's strong defender,
   This is how our God is, both terrible and tender.
   With mercy for the lowly, God builds for them a home,
   To lead them into freedom in a land to call their own.

3. Upon a thirsty nation, you rained refreshing rain,
   And when your own were starving, you gave them life again.
   So where there once was nothing, a nation formed and grew;
   A home at last, a country vast the poor received from you.

Text: Psalm 68:4-5, 6-7, 10-11: Rory Cooney, © 1991. GIA Publications, Inc.; refrain trans. © 1969. ICEL
Music: Rory Cooney. © 1991. GIA Publications. Inc.

Psalm 69: Lord, in Your Great Love   68

Refrain

Lord, in your great love, an - swer me.

Verses

1. It is for you that I suffer taunts, that shame covers my face,
   that I have become a stranger to my family, an alien to my brothers and sisters.
   I burn with zeal for your house and taunts against you fall on me.

2. This is my prayer to you, my prayer for your favor.
   In your great love, answer me, O God, with your help that never fails;
   Lord, answer, for your love is kind; in your compassion, turn towards me.

3. The poor when they see it will be glad and God-seeking hearts will revive;
   for the Lord listens to the needy and does not spurn captives in their chains.
   Let the heavens and the earth give God praise, the sea and all its living creatures.

69 Psalm 69: Turn to the Lord in Your Need

Refrain

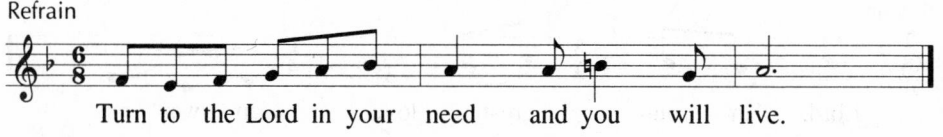

Turn to the Lord in your need and you will live.

Verses

1. This is my prayer to you, my prayer for your favor.
   In your great love, answer me, O God, with your help that never fails;
   Lord, answer, for your love is kind; in your compassion turn towards me.

2. As for me in my poverty and pain, let your help, O God, lift me up.
   I will praise God's name with a song; I will glorify God with thanksgiving.

3. The poor when they see it will be glad and God-seeking hearts will revive;
   for the Lord listens to the needy and does not spurn captives in their chains.

4. For God will bring help to Zion and rebuild the cities of Judah.
   The children of God's servants shall inherit it; those who love God's name shall
   dwell there.

Text: Psalm 69:14, 17, 30-31, 33-34, 36, 37; © 1963, 1993, The Grail, GIA Publications, Inc., agent; refrain trans. © 1969, ICEL
Music: Michel Guimont, © 1994, GIA Publications, Inc.

Psalm 69: Turn to the Lord in Your Need   70

Antiphon

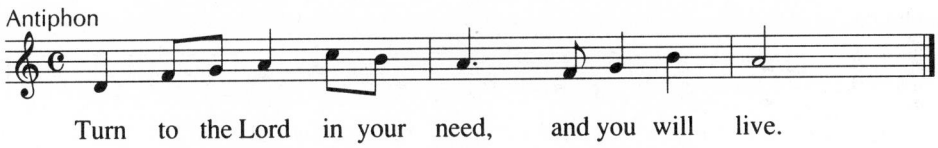

Turn to the Lord in your need, and you will live.

Text: Lectionary for Mass, © 1969, 1981, ICEL
Music: J. Robert Carroll: acc. by Robert J. Batastini, © 1975, GIA Publications, Inc.

Psalm Tone

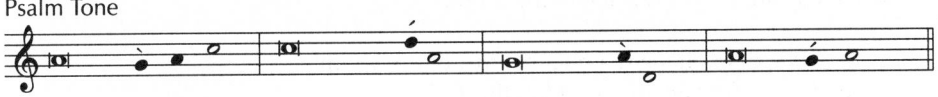

Music: Chrysogonus Waddell. © Gethsemani Abbey

Gelineau Tone

Repeat for 6-line stanza

Domine, ne in furore

¹⁴ **This** is my **pràyer** to **you,**
my **prayer for** yóur **favor.**
In your great **love, an**swer me, Ò **God,**
with your **help** that nevér **fails;**
¹⁷ Lord, **an**swer, for your **love** ìs **kind;**
in your compas**sion,** túrn **to**wards me.

³⁰ As for **me** in my **pove**rtỳ and **pain,**
let your **help,** O **God,** lift mé **up.**
³¹ I will **praise** God's **name** with à **song;**
I will **glo**rify **God** with thánks**giv**ing.

³³ The **poor** when they **see** it wìll be **glad**
and **God-**seeking **hearts** will ré**vive;**
³⁴ for the **Lord lis**tens to thè **needy**
and does not **spurn cap**tives in théir **chains.**

³⁶ For **God** will bring **hèlp** to **Zion**
and re**build** the **cit**ies óf **Ju**dah.
³⁷ The **chil**dren of God's **ser**vants shall ìn**her**it it;
those who **love** God's **name** sháll **dwell** there.

Text: Psalm 69: 14, 17, 30-31, 33-34, 36, 37: The Grail
Music: Joseph Gelineau
© 1963, 1993, The Grail, GIA Publications, Inc., agent

71 Psalm 71: I Will Sing

Refrain

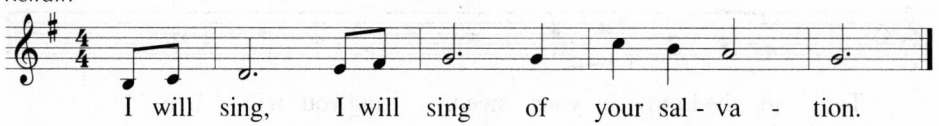

I will sing, I will sing of your sal - va - tion.

Verses

1. In you, O God, I place my fears, protect me from all shame.
   Save me from my guilt, listen to me, Lord.

2. In you, O God, my hope returns, the trust of my youth.
   To you I pray, for you are my strength.

3. My mouth shall proclaim your name, your praises day by day.
   O God, you are my song; forever I will sing.

Text: Psalm 71:1, 5, 15; David Haas. © 1989. GIA Publications, Inc.; refrain trans. © 1969. ICEL
Music: David Haas. © 1989. GIA Publications, Inc.

Psalm 72: Every Nation on Earth   72

Refrain I

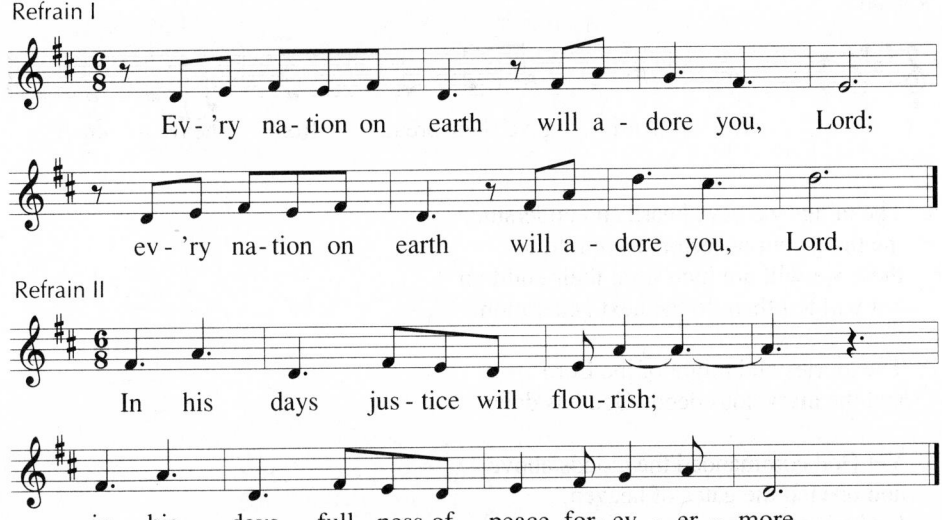

Ev - 'ry na - tion on earth will a - dore you, Lord;
ev - 'ry na - tion on earth will a - dore you, Lord.

Refrain II

In his days jus - tice will flou - rish;
in his days full - ness of peace for - ev - er - more.

Verses

1. O God, with your judgment endow the king;
   with your justice endow the king's son.
   With justice he will govern your people,
   your afflicted ones with right judgment.

2. Justice shall flow'r in his days,
   lasting peace 'til the moon be no more.
   May he rule from sea to sea,
   from the river to the ends of the earth.

3. The kings of Tarsish and the Isles offer gifts,
   those from Seba and Arabia bring tribute.
   All kings shall pay him their homage,
   all nations shall serve him.

4. He rescues the poor when they cry out,
   the afflicted with no one to help.
   The lowly and poor he shall pity,
   the lives of the poor he will save.

Text: Psalm 72:1-2, 7-8, 10-11, 12-13; Michael Joncas
Music: Michael Joncas
© 1987, 1994, GIA Publications, Inc.

73 Psalm 78: The Lord Gave Them Bread

Refrain

The Lord gave them bread from heav - en.

Verses

1. The things we have heard and understood,
   the things our ancestors have told us,
   these we will not hide from their children
   but will tell them to the next generation:

2. The glories and might of the Lord
   and the marvelous deeds God has done.

3. Yet God commanded the clouds above
   and opened the gates of heaven;
   God rained down manna for their food,
   and gave them bread from heaven.

4. Mere mortals ate the bread of angels.
   The Lord sent them meat in abundance.
   So God brought them to that holy land,
   to the mountain that was won by his hand.

Psalm 80: The Vineyard of the Lord   74

Refrain

The vine-yard of the Lord is the house of Is-ra-el.

Verses

1. You brought a vine out of Egypt; to plant it you drove out the nations.
   It stretched out its branches to the sea,
   to the Great River it stretched out its shoots.

2. Then why have you broken down its walls?
   It is plucked by all who pass by.
   It is ravaged by the boar of the forest, devoured by the beasts of the field.

3. God of hosts, turn again, we implore look down from heaven and see.
   Visit the vine and protect it, the vine your right hand has planted.

4. And we shall never forsake you again;
   give us life that we may call upon your name.
   God of hosts, bring us back;
   let your face shine on us and we shall be saved.

Text: Psalm 80:9, 12-14, 15-16, 19-20; © 1963, 1993, The Grail, GIA Publications, Inc., agent; refrain trans. © 1969, ICEL
Music: Michel Guimont, © 1994, GIA Publications, Inc.

75 Psalm 80/85/Luke 1: Lord, Make Us Turn to You

Refrain

Lord, make us turn to you, show us your face, and

we shall be saved.

Verses

1. Shepherd of Israel, hearken from your throne and shine forth,
   O rouse your power, and come to save us.

2. We are your chosen vine, only by your care do we live,
   reach out your hand, O Lord, unto your people.

3. If you will dwell with us, we shall live anew in your love,
   O shine upon us, great Lord of life.

4. Lord, we are present here, show us your kindness and love,
   O speak your word of peace unto your people.

5. Lord, let salvation rain, shower down your justice and peace,
   the earth shall bring forth truth, the skies your love.

6. See, Lord, we look to you, you alone can bring us to life,
   O walk before us to light our pathways.

7. You have done wondrous things, holy is your name for all time,
   your mercy and your love are with your people.

8. You are my joy and song, I would have my life speak your praise,
   on me your love has shown, your blessings given.

9. You fill all hungry hearts, sending the rich empty forth,
   and holding up in love the meek and lowly.

Text: Psalm 80:2-3, 15-16, 18-20; Psalm 85:9-14; Luke 1:46-55; Marty Haugen
Music: Marty Haugen
© 1982, GIA Publications, Inc.

Psalm 81: Sing with Joy to God   76

Refrain

Sing with joy to God!   Sing to God our help!

Verses

1. Raise a song and sound the timbrel, the sweet-sounding harp and the lute;
   blow the trumpet at the new moon, when the moon is full, on our feast.

2. For this is Israel's law, a command of the God of Jacob.
   Imposed as a law on Joseph's people,
   when they went out against the land of Egypt.

3. A voice I did not know said to me:
   "I freed your shoulder from the burden;
   your hands were freed from the load.
   You called in distress and I saved you.

4. Let there be no foreign god among you, no worship of an alien god.
   I am the Lord your God, who brought you from the land of Egypt."

77 Psalm 84: Happy Are They

Refrain

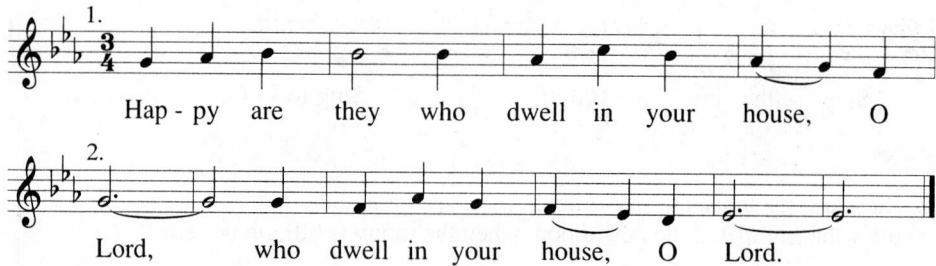

Hap - py are they who dwell in your house, O Lord, who dwell in your house, O Lord.

Verses

1. My soul yearns and pines for the courts of the Lord.
   My heart and my flesh cry to the living God.

2. The sparrow finds a home and the swallow a nest;
   Your altars, O Lord, my King and my God.

3. Happy are they who abide in your house.
   You are their strength, your praises they will sing.

Text: Psalm 84:2, 3, 4, 5-6; Thomas J. Porter
Music: Thomas J. Porter
© 1987. GIA Publications, Inc.

Psalm 84: How Lovely Is Your Dwelling Place 78

Antiphon

How love-ly is your dwell-ing place, O Lord of hosts.

Text: Psalm 84:2, The Grail
Music: A. Gregory Murray, OSB
© 1963, The Grail, GIA Publications, Inc., agent

Psalm Tone

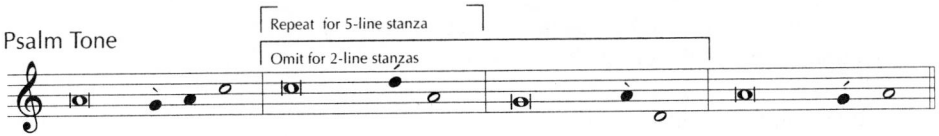

Music: Chrysogonus Waddell, © Gethsemani Abbey

Gelineau Tone

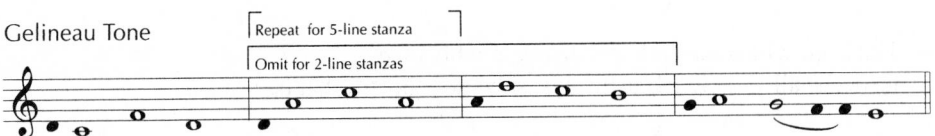

Quam dilecta

² How **lovely is** your **dwè**lling place,
Lord, God óf **hosts.**

³ My **soul is long**ìng and **yearn**ing,
is **yearn**ing for the **courts** of thé **Lord.**
My **heart** and my **soul** ring out thèir **joy**
to **God,** the **liv**íng **God.**

⁴ The **spar**row her**self** finds a **home**
and the **swal**low a **nest** for hér **brood;**
she **lays** her **young** by yòur **altars,**
Lord of **hosts,** my **king** and mý **God.**

⁵ They are **hap**py, who **dwell** ìn your **house,**
for **ever sing**ing yóur **praise.**
⁶ They are **hap**py, whose **strength** is ìn **you,**
in whose **hearts** are the **roads** tó **Zion.**

⁷ As they **go** through the **Bìt**ter **Valley**
they **make** it a **place** óf **springs,**
[the **autumn** rain **cov**ers it wíth **blessings**].
⁸ They **walk** with **ever** growìng **strength,**
they will **see** the God of **gods** ín **Zion.**

⁹ O **Lord** God of **hosts,** hèar my **prayer,**
give **ear,** O **God** óf **Jacob.**
¹⁰Turn your **eyes,** O **God,** òur **shield,**
look on the **face** of your **á**nointed.

¹¹ **One** day withìn your **courts**
is **bet**ter than a **thous**ánd **else**where.
The **thresh**old of the **house** òf **God**
I **pre**fer to the **dwell**ings of thé **wick**ed.

¹²For the Lord **God** is a **ram**pàrt, a **shield.**
The Lord will **give** us **fa**vor ánd **glory.**
The **Lord** will not **re**fuse anỳ **good**
to **those** who **walk** withóut **blame.**

¹³**Lord, Gòd** of **hosts,**
happy are **those** who **trust** ín **you!**

Give **praise** to the **Fathèr Al**mighty,
to his **Son,** Jesus **Christ** thé **Lord,**
to the **Spir**it who **dwells** in òur **hearts,**
both **now** and for **ever. Á**men.

Text: Psalm 84:2-10: The Grail
Music: Joseph Gelineau
© 1963, 1993, The Grail, GIA Publications, Inc., agent

79 Psalm 85: Lord, Let Us See Your Kindness

Refrain

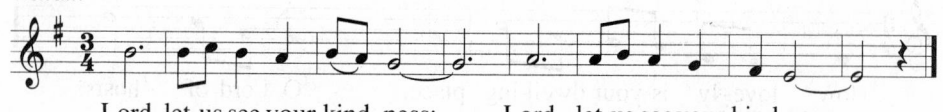

Lord, let us see your kind-ness;   Lord, let us see your kind-ness.

Verses

1. Let us hear what our God proclaims: Peace to the people of God,
   salvation is near to the ones who fear God.

2. Kindness and truth, justice and peace;
   truth shall spring up as the water from the earth,
   justice shall rain from the heavens.

3. The Lord will come and you shall know his love,
   justice shall walk in his pathways, salvation the gift that he brings.

Text: Psalm 85:9-10, 11-12, 13-14; Marty Haugen, © 1983, GIA Publications, Inc.; refrain trans. © 1969, ICEL
Music: Marty Haugen, © 1983, GIA Publications, Inc.

Psalm 85: Come, O Lord, and Set Us Free   80

Refrain I

Come, O Lord, and set us free. Come, and set us free.

Refrain II

Lord, let us see your kind - ness; Lord, grant us your sal-va - tion.

Verses

1. Now I will hear what God proclaims, the Lord who speaks of peace.
   Near to us now, God's saving love for those who believe.

2. Mercy and faithfulness shall meet, in justice and peace, embrace.
   Truth shall blossom from the earth as the heavens rejoice.

3. Our God shall grant abundant gifts, the earth shall yield its fruit.
   Justice shall march before our God and guide us to peace.

Text: Psalm 85: refrains I and II, © 1969, ICEL; verses by Mike Balhoff, Gary Daigle, Darryl Ducote, © 1978, 1993, Damean Music.
Distributed by GIA Publications, Inc.
Music: Mike Balhoff, Gary Daigle, Darryl Ducote, © 1978, 1993, Damean Music. Distributed by GIA Publications, Inc.

81　Psalm 86: Lord, You Are Good and Forgiving

Refrain

Lord, you are good and for - giv - ing.

Verses

1. O Lord, you are good and forgiving, full of love to all who call.
   Give heed, O Lord, to my prayer and attend to the sound of my voice.

2. All the nations shall come to adore you and glorify your name, O Lord,
   for you are great and do marvelous deeds, you who alone are God.

3. But you, God of mercy and compassion,
   slow to anger, O Lord, abounding in love and truth,
   turn and take pity on me. O give your strength to your servant.

Text: Psalm 86:5-6, 9-10, 15-17; © 1963, 1993, The Grail, GIA Publications, Inc., agent; refrain trans. © 1969, ICEL
Music: Michel Guimont, © 1994, GIA Publications, Inc.

82　Psalm 89: For Ever I Will Sing

Refrain

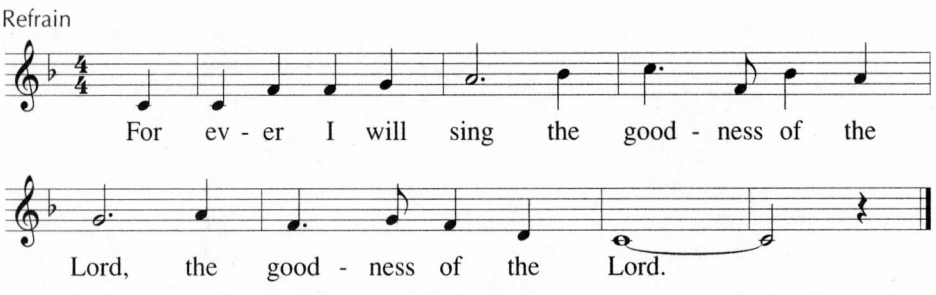

For ev - er I will sing the good - ness of the
Lord, the good - ness of the Lord.

Verses

1. "With my chosen one I have made a covenant; I have sworn to David my servant:
   I will establish your dynasty forever and set up your throne through all ages."

2. Happy the people who acclaim such a God,
   who walk, O Lord, in the light of your face,
   who find their joy ev'ry day in your name,
   who make your justice the source of their bliss.

3. He will say to me: "You are my father, my God, the rock who saves me!"
   I will keep my love for him always; with him my covenant shall last.

Alternate Verses

1. I have found David my servant,
   with my holy oil I have anointed him,
   that my hand may ever be with him
   and my arm make him strong.

2. My faithfulness and love shall be with you,
   in my Name your name will be exalted.

3. He shall cry to me, "My God, my rock of salvation, my salvation."

Text: Psalm 89: 4-5. 16-17. 27-29. © 1963, 1993, The Grail, GIA Publications, Inc., agent; alt. verses 21-22. 25. 27. Marty Haugen. © 1988, 1994.
    GIA Publications, Inc.; refrain trans. © 1969. ICEL
Music: Marty Haugen. © 1988, 1994. GIA Publications, Inc.

Psalm 90: In Ev'ry Age   83

Refrain

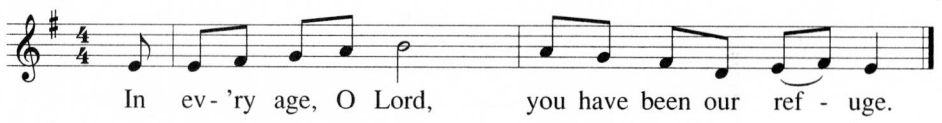

In ev-'ry age, O Lord,   you have been our   ref - uge.

Verses

1. You turn us back into dust and say: "Go back, children of the earth."
   To your eyes a thousand years are like yesterday, come and gone,
   no more than a watch in the night.

2. You sweep us away like a dream,
   like grass which springs up in the morning.
   In the morning it springs up and flowers; by evening it withers and fades.

3. Make us know the shortness of our life that we may gain wisdom of heart.
   Lord, relent! Is your anger for ever? Show pity to your servants.

4. In the morning, fill us with love; we shall exult and rejoice all our days.
   Let the favor of the Lord be upon us: give success to the work of our hands.

Text: Psalm 90:3-4, 5-6, 12-13, 14, 17: © 1963, 1993, The Grail, GIA Publications, Inc., agent; refrain trans. © 1969. ICEL
Music: Michel Guimont. © 1994. GIA Publications, Inc.

84   Psalm 90: Fill Us with Your Love, O Lord

Refrain

Fill us with your love, O Lord, and we will sing for joy!

Verses

1. Teach us to number our days, that we may gain wisdom of heart.
   Return, O Lord our God, have pity on your servants.

2. Fill us at dawn with your kindness,
   that we may shout for joy and gladness.
   Make us glad for the days when you afflicted us,
   for the years when we saw evil.

3. Let your work be seen by your servants, and your glory by their children.
   May your gracious care be ours. Prosper the work of our hands.

85   Psalm 91: Be with Me

Refrain

Be with me, Lord, when I am in trou-ble, be with me, Lord, I pray.

Verses

1. You who dwell in the shelter of the Lord, Most High,
   who abide in the shadow of our God,
   say to the Lord: "My refuge and fortress, the God in whom I trust."

2. No evil shall befall you, no pain come near,
   for the angels stand close by your side,
   guarding you always and bearing you gently, watching over your life.

3. Those who cling to the Lord live secure in God's love,
   lifted high, those who trust in God's name,
   call on the Lord, who will never forsake you.
   God will bring you salvation and joy.

Text: Psalm 91: 1-2, 10-11, 14-15: Marty Haugen
Music: Marty Haugen
© 1980, GIA Publications, Inc.

Psalm 92: Lord, It Is Good   86

Refrain

Lord, it is good to give thanks to you.

Verses

1. It is good to give thanks to the Lord,
   to make music to your name, O Most High,
   to proclaim your love in the morning
   and your truth in the watches of the night.

2. The just will flourish like the palm tree and grow like a Lebanon cedar.
   Planted in the house of the Lord they will flourish in the courts of our God.

3. Still bearing fruit when they are old, still full of sap, still green,
   to proclaim that the Lord is just. My rock, in whom there is no wrong.

Text: Psalm 92:2-3, 13-14, 15-16: © 1963, 1993, The Grail, GIA Publications, Inc., agent: refrain trans. © 1969, ICEL
Music: Michel Guimont, © 1994, GIA Publications, Inc.

87 Psalm 93: The Lord Is King

Refrain

The Lord is king; he is robed in maj-es-ty.

Verses

1. The Lord is king, with majesty enrobed;
   the Lord is robed with might, and girded round with power.

2. The world you made firm, not to be moved;
   your throne has stood firm from of old. From all eternity, O Lord, you are.

3. Truly your decrees are to be trusted.
   Holiness is fitting to your house, O Lord, until the end of time.

Text: Psalm 93:1, 1-2, 5; © 1963, 1993, The Grail; refrain trans. © 1969, ICEL
Music: Michel Guimont, © 1994, GIA Publications, Inc.

Psalm 93: The Lord Is King for Evermore   88

Antiphon I

The Lord is King for ev - er - more.

Antiphon II

Al - le - lu - ia, al - le - lu - ia, al - le - lu - ia.

Text: Psalm 93; The Grail
Music: A. Gregory Murray, OSB
© 1963, The Grail, GIA Publications, Inc., agent

Psalm Tone

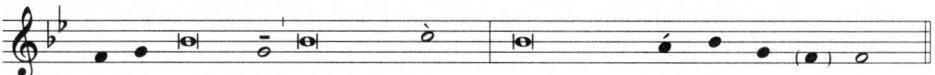

Music: Psalm tone 8-g; acc. by Richard Proulx, © 1975, GIA Publications, Inc.

Gelineau Tone

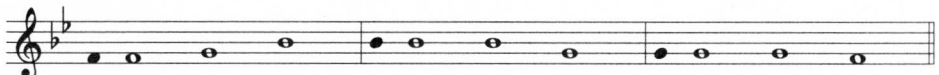

Dominus regnavit

¹The Lord is **king**, with **maj**esty en**rōbed**;
the **Lord** is **robed** with **mìght**,
and **gird**ed **róund** with **pow**er.

The **world** you made **firm**, not to be **mōved**;
²your **throne** has stood **firm** from of **òld**.
From all e**ter**nitý, O **Lord**, you **are**.

³The **wa**ters have **lift**ed up, O **Lōrd**,
the **wa**ters have **lift**ed up their **vòice**,
the **wa**ters have **lift**ed **úp** their **thun**der.

⁴**Great**er than the **roar** of mighty **watērs**,
more **glo**rious than the **surg**ings of the **sèa**,
the **Lord** is **gló**rious on **high**.

⁵**Tru**ly, your de**crees** are to be **trust**ēd.
Holiness is **fit**ting to your **hòuse**,
O **Lord**, until the **end** of **time**.

Give **glo**ry to the **Father Almight**ȳ,
to his **Son**, Jesus **Christ**, the **Lòrd**,
to the **Spir**it who **dwélls** in our **hearts**.

Text: Psalm 93; The Grail
Music: Joseph Gelineau
© 1963, 1993, The Grail, GIA Publications, Inc., agent

89 Psalm 95: If Today You Hear God's Voice

Refrain

If to-day you hear God's voice, hard-en not your hearts.

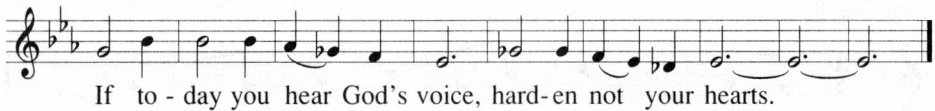

If to-day you hear God's voice, hard-en not your hearts.

Verses

1. Come, ring out our joy to the Lord, hail the rock who saves us,
   let us come now before our God, with songs let us hail the Lord.

2. Come, let us bow and bend low, let us kneel before God who made us,
   for here is our God; we the people, the flock that is led by God's hand.

3. O that today you would hear God's voice, "Harden not your hearts,
   as on that day in the desert, when your parents put me to the test."

Text: Psalm 95:1-2, 6-7, 8-9: David Haas
Music: David Haas
© 1983, 1994, GIA Publications, Inc.

90 Psalm 96: Today Is Born Our Savior

Refrain

To - day is born our Sav-ior, Christ the Lord. To -

day is born our Sav-ior, Christ the Lord.

Verses

1. Sing to the Lord a new song;
   sing to the Lord, all you lands.
   Sing to the Lord; bless his name.

2. Announce his salvation, day after day.
Tell his glory among the nations;
Among all peoples, his wondrous deeds.

3. Let the heavens be glad and the earth rejoice;
let the sea and what fills it resound;
let the plains be joyful and all that is in them!
Then shall all the trees of the forest exult.

4. They shall exult before the Lord, for he comes;
for he comes to rule the earth.
He shall rule the world with justice
and the peoples with his constancy.

Music: Psalm 96; verses tr. © 1970, Confraternity of Christian Doctrine, Washington, D.C.; refrain tr. © 1969, ICEL
Music: Howard Hughes, SM, © 1976, GIA Publications, Inc.

Psalm 96: Today Is Born Our Savior   91

Refrain

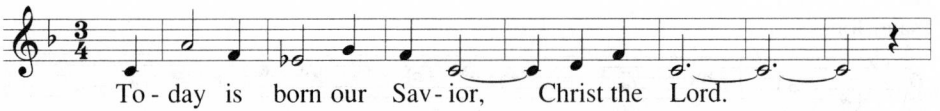

To-day is born our Sav-ior, Christ the Lord.

To-day is born our Sav-ior, Christ the Lord.

Verses

1. Sing out to God a new song, Sing out to God all you lands;
Sing out in joy, sing out in love to our God!

2. Announce God's salvation forever, and glory proclaim to the earth;
tell all the peoples the wondrous deeds of our God.

3. Let us rejoice in our Savior, who has come now to rule the earth;
rule it in justice, rule it in mercy forever!

4. Let the heavens be glad and the earth rejoice,
let the seas now resound in your praise!
Let the plains be joyful, and the forests exult!

Text: Psalm 96:1-2, 2-3, 11-12, 13; Marty Haugen. © 1988, GIA Publications, Inc.; refrain trans. © 1969, ICEL
Music: Marty Haugen. © 1988, GIA Publications, Inc.

92　Psalm 96: Great Is the Lord

Antiphon I

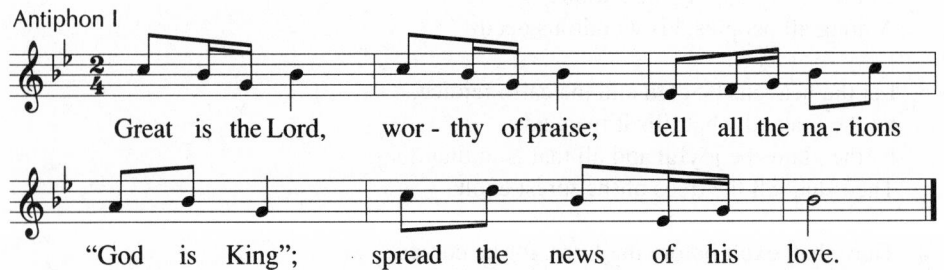

Great is the Lord, wor-thy of praise; tell all the na-tions

"God is King"; spread the news of his love.

Text: Psalm 96:3-4; The Grail
Music: Joseph Gelineau
© 1963, The Grail, GIA Publications, Inc., agent

Antiphon II

Bring an of-fer-ing and en-ter God's courts:

in the tem - ple wor-ship the Lord.

Text: Psalm 96:6; The Grail
Music: Clifford Howell, SJ
© 1963, 1993, The Grail, GIA Publications, Inc., agent

Psalm Tone

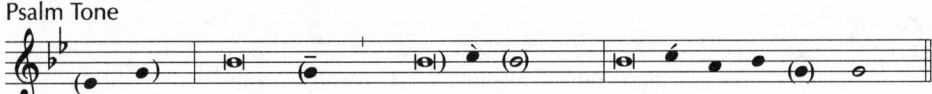

Music: Chant tone 5; acc. by Robert J. Batastini, © 1975, GIA Publications, Inc.

Gelineau Tone

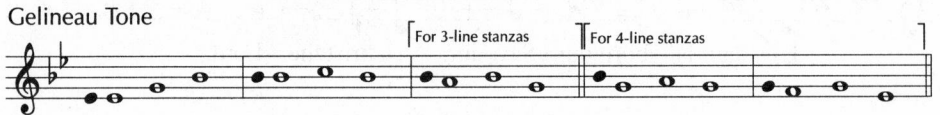

For 3-line stanzas　　For 4-line stanzas

Cantate Domino

¹O **sing** a new **song** to the **Lōrd**,
　sing to the **Lord** all the **eàrth**.
²O **sing** to the **Lórd**, bless his **name**.

　Pro**claim** God's **help** day by dăy,
³**tell** among the **na**tions his **glòry**
　and his **won**ders a**móng** all the **peo**ples.

⁴The Lord is **great** and **wor**thy of **prāise**,
to be **feared above** all **gòds**;
⁵the **gods** of the **héath**ens are **naught**.

It was the **Lord** who **made** the **heavēns**,
⁶ his are **maj**esty and **hon**or and **pòw**er
and **splen**dor in thé **holy place**.

⁷ Give the **Lord**, you **fam**ilies of **peoplēs**,
give the **Lord glory** and **pòw**er;
⁸ give the **Lord** the **glóry** of his **name**.

Bring an **off**ering and **en**ter God's **cōurts**,
⁹ **wor**ship the **Lord** in the **tèm**ple,
O **earth**, stand in **féar** of the **Lord**.

¹⁰ Pro**claim** to the **na**tions: "God is **kīng**."
The **world** was made **firm** in its **plàce**;
God will **judge** the **péo**ples in **fair**ness.

¹¹ Let the **heav**ens re**joice** and earth be **glàd**,
let the **sea** and all with**ín** it thunder **praise**,
¹² let the **land** and all it **bears** re**jòice**,
all the **trees** of the **wóod** shout for **joy**

¹³ at the **pres**ence of the **Lord** who **còmes**,
who **cómes** to **rule** the **earth**.
Comes with **justice** to **rule** the **wòrld**,
and to **judge** the **péo**ples with **truth**.

Give **praise** to the **Father** Al**mìgh**ty,
to his **Son**, Jésus **Christ**, the **Lord**,
to the **Spir**it who **dwells** in òur **hearts**,
both **now** and for **év**er. **Amen**.

Text: Psalm 96; The Grail
Music: Joseph Gelineau
© 1963, 1993, The Grail, GIA Publications, Inc., agent

93 Psalm 96: Proclaim to All the Nations

Refrain I

Pro - claim to all the na - tions the mar - vel-ous deeds of the Lord! Pro - claim to all the na - tions the mar - vel-ous deeds of the Lord!

Refrain II

Give the Lord glo - ry and hon - or.

Give the Lord glo - ry and hon - or.

Verses

1. Sing to the Lord a new song. Sing to the Lord all you lands!
   Sing to the Lord with all your heart, and bless God's name!

2. Announce salvation day by day, God's glory throughout the earth!
   Among all the people in ev'ry land, God's wondrous deeds!

3. Give to the Lord, you nations, praise to the Lord of all!
   Sing glory and praise and sing to the name, above all names!

4. Worship the Lord, and tremble, proclaim the one who reigns!
   Say to the nations: "The Lord is King;" who rules with justice!

Text: Psalm 96:1-2, 3, 7-8, 9; David Haas, © 1989, GIA Publications, Inc.; refrains trans. © 1969, ICEL
Music: Marty Haugen: refrain I; David Haas: refrain II adapt. by Diana Kodner; © 1989, 1994, GIA Publications, Inc.

Psalm 97: The Lord Is King   94

Refrain

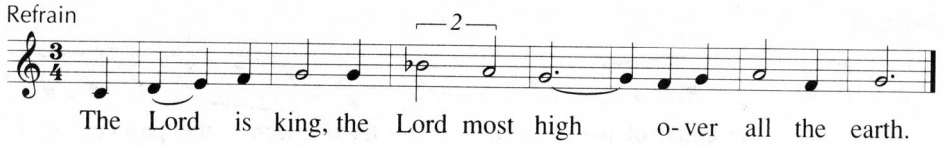

The Lord is king, the Lord most high   o-ver all the earth.

Verses

1. The Lord is king, let earth rejoice, let all the coastlands be glad.
   Justice and right, God's throne.

2. The skies proclaim God's justice; all peoples see God's glory.
   All you spirits worship the Lord.

3. For you indeed are the Lord most high above all the earth,
   exalted far above all spirits.

Text: Psalm 97:1-2, 6-7, 9; © 1963, 1993, The Grail, GIA Publications, Inc., agent; refrain trans. © 1969, ICEL
Music: Michel Guimont, © 1994, GIA Publications, Inc.

95   Psalm 98: All the Ends of the Earth

Refrain I

All the ends of the earth have seen the pow-er of God; all the ends of the earth have seen the pow - er of God.

Refrain II

Sing to the Lord a new song, for God has done won-der-ful deeds. Sing to the Lord a new song, for God has done won - der - ful deeds.

Refrain III

The Lord comes to the earth to rule the earth with jus - tice. The Lord comes to the earth to rule the earth with jus - tice.

Verses

1. Sing to the Lord a new song, for God has done wondrous deeds;
   whose right hand has won the vict'ry for us, God's holy arm.

2. The Lord has made salvation known, and justice revealed to all,
   remembering kindness and faithfulness to Israel.

3. All of the ends of earth have seen salvation by our God.
   Joyfully sing out all you lands, break forth in song.

4. Sing to the Lord with harp and song, with trumpet and with horn.
   Sing in your joy before the king, the king, our Lord.

Text: Psalm 98:1, 2-3, 3-4, 5-6; David Haas, Marty Haugen
Music: David Haas, Marty Haugen; refrain II, III adapt. by Diana Kodner
© 1983, 1994, GIA Publications, Inc.

96 Psalm 100: Arise, Come to Your God

Antiphon I

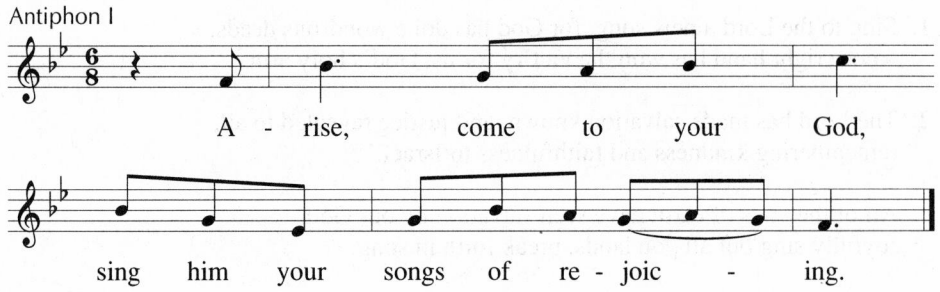

A - rise, come to your God,

sing him your songs of re - joic - ing.

Text: The Grail
Music: Joseph Gelineau
© 1963, The Grail, GIA Publications, Inc., agent

Antiphon II

Al - le - lu - ia, al - le - lu - ia, al - le - lu - ia.

Music: A. Gregory Murray, OSB
© 1963, The Grail, GIA Publications, Inc., agent

Psalm Tone

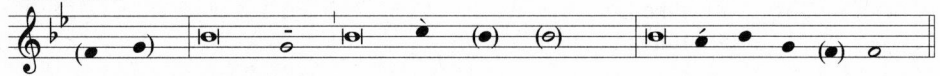

Music: Chant tone 8-g; acc. by Richard Proulx, © 1975, GIA Publications, Inc.

Gelineau Tone

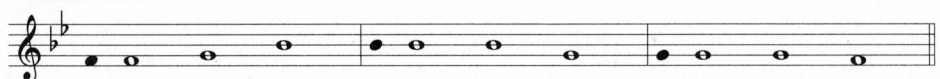

Jubilate Deo

¹Cry out with **joy** to the **Lord,** all the **earth**.
²**Serve** the **Lord** with **glàd**ness.
Come be**fore** God, **sí**nging for **joy**.

³**Know** that the **Lord** is **Gōd,**
our **Mak**er, to **whom** we be**lòng**.
We are God's **people, shéep** of the **flock**.

⁴**En**ter the **gates** with thanks**givīng**.
God's **courts** with **sòngs** of **praise**.
Give **thanks** to **Gód** and **bless** his **name**.

⁵**Indeed**, how **good** is the **Lōrd,**
whose **mer**ciful **love** is et**èr**nal;
whose **faith**fulness **lásts** for **ev**er.

Give **glo**ry to the **Fa**ther Al**mightȳ,**
to his **Son,** Jesus **Chrìst,** the **Lord,**
to the **Spir**it who **dwélls** in our **hearts**.

Text: Psalm 100; The Grail
Music: Joseph Gelineau, SJ
© 1963, 1993, The Grail, GIA Publications, Inc., agent

Psalm 100: We Are God's People   97

Ostinato Refrain

We are God's peo - ple, the flock of the Lord.

Verses

1. Cry out with joy to the Lord, all you lands, all you lands.
   Serve the Lord now with gladness, come before God singing for joy!

2. Know that the Lord is God! Know that the Lord is God,
   who made us, to God we belong, God's people, the sheep of the flock!

3. Go, now within the gates giving thanks, giving thanks.
   Enter the courts singing praise, give thanks and bless God's name!

4. Indeed, how good is the Lord, whose mercy endures for ever,
   for the Lord is faithful, is faithful from age to age!

Text: Psalm 100:1-2, 3, 4, 5: David Haas
Music: David Haas
© 1983, GIA Publications, Inc.

98 Psalm 103: My Soul, Give Thanks to the Lord

Antiphon

My soul, give thanks to the Lord, and bless God's Ho - ly Name.

Text: Psalm 103:1; The Grail © 1963, 1993, GIA Publications, Inc., agent
Music: Richard Proulx, © 1986, GIA Publications, Inc.

Psalm Tone

Music: Richard Proulx, © 1986, GIA Publications, Inc.

Gelineau Tone

Omit for 5 lines

Omit for 4-line stanzas

Benedic, anima mea

¹ My **soul**, give **thanks** tò the **Lord**,
   all my **being**, **bléss** God's holy **name**.
² My **soul**, give **thanks** tò the **Lord**
   and **never forget** áll God's **blessings**.

³ It is **God** who for**gives** àll your **guilt**,
   who **heals** every óne of your **ills**,
⁴ who re**deems** your **life** fròm the **grave**,
   who **crowns** you with **love** ánd com**passion**,
⁵ who **fills** your **life** wìth good **things**,
   re**new**ing your **youth** líke an **eagle**'s.

⁶ The **Lord** does **deeds** of **jùs**tice,
   gives **judge**ment for **áll** who are op**pressed**.
⁷ The Lord's **ways** were made **known** to **Mòs**es;
   the Lord's **deeds** to **Ís**rael's **sons**.

⁸ The **Lord** is com**pass**ion ànd **love**,
   slow to **anger** and **rích** in **mer**cy.
⁹ The **Lord** will not **alwàys** **chide**,
   will **not** be **án**gry for **ever**.
¹⁰ God does not **treat** us ac**cord**ing tò our **sins**
   nor re**pay** us ac**cór**ding to our **faults**.

[11] For as the **heav**ens are **high** abòve the **earth**
so **strong** is God's **love** fór the **God**-fearing;
[12] As **far** as the **east** is fròm the **west**
so **far** does hé re**move** our **sins**.

[13] As **par**ents have com**pass**ion on their **chìl**dren,
the Lord has **pity** on **those** who áre **God**-fearing;
[14] for he **knows** of **what** wè are **made**,
he re**mem**bers thát **we** are **dust**.

[15] As for **us**, our **days** are like **gràss**;
we **flow**er like the **flów**er of the **field**;
[16] the wind **blows** and **wè** are **gone**
and our **place** never **sées** us a**gain**.

[17] But the **love** of the **Lord** is everlàsting
upon **thóse** who **fear** the **Lord**.
God's **jus**tice reaches **out** to children's **chil**dren
[18] when they **keep** his **cov**enant ìn **truth**,
when they **keep** his **wíll** in their **mind**.

[19] The **Lord** has set his **throne** in **hèa**ven
and his **king**dom **rúles** over **all**.
[20] Give **thanks** to the **Lord**, all you **an**gels,
mighty in **pow**er, ful**fill**ing Gòd's **word**,
who **heed** the **vóice** of that **word**.

[21] Give **thanks** to the **Lord**, àll you **hosts**,
you **serv**ants whó **do** God's **will**.
[22] Give **thanks** to the **Lord**, all his **works**,
in **ev**ery **place** whère God **rules**.
My **soul**, give **thánks** to the **Lord**!

Give **praise** to the **Fa**ther Almìghty,
to his **Son**, Jésus **Christ**, the **Lord**,
to the **Spir**it who **dwells** in òur **hearts**,
both **now** and for **é**ver. **Amen.**

Text: Psalm 103: The Grail
Music: Joseph Gelineau
© 1963. 1993. The Grail. GIA Publications. Inc.. agent

99 Psalm 103: The Lord Is Kind and Merciful

Refrain

The Lord is kind and mer-ci-ful; the Lord is kind and mer-ci-ful. Slow to an-ger, rich in kind-ness, the Lord is kind and mer-ci-ful.

Verses

1. Bless the Lord, O my soul; all my being bless God's name.
   Bless the Lord, O my soul; forget not all God's blessings.

2. The Lord is gracious and merciful, slow to anger, full of kindness.
   God is good to all creation, full of compassion.

3. The goodness of God is from age to age,
   blessing those who choose to love.
   And justice toward God's children; on all who keep the covenant.

Text: Psalm 103: Jeanne Cotter
Music: Jeanne Cotter
© 1993. GIA Publications. Inc.

100 Psalm 103: The Lord Is Kind and Merciful

Refrain

The Lord is kind and mer-ci-ful, the Lord is kind and mer-ci-ful.

Verses

1. Bless the Lord, O my soul, and all my being bless God's name;
   bless the Lord, and forget not God's benefits.

2. God pardons all your iniquities, and comforts your sorrows,
   redeems your life from destruction and crowns you with kindness.

3. Merciful, merciful, and gracious is our God;
   slow to anger, abounding in kindness.

Text: Psalm 103:1-2, 3-4, 8; para. by Marty Haugen. © 1983. GIA Publications, Inc.; refrain trans. © 1969. ICEL
Music: Marty Haugen. © 1983, GIA Publications, Inc.

Psalm 104: Lord, Send Out Your Spirit   101

Refrain

Lord, send out your Spir-it, and re - new the face of the earth!

Verses

1. Bless the Lord, O my soul; O Lord, my God, you are great indeed!
   How manifold are your works, O Lord! The earth is full of your creatures!

2. If you take away their breath, they die and they return to their dust.
   When you send forth your Spirit of life, they are created in your sight!

3. May his glory last for all time; may the Lord be glad in his works.
   Pleasing to him will be my theme; I will be glad in the Lord!

Text: Psalm 104:1, 24, 29-30, 31, 34; Paul Lisicky. © 1985. GIA Publications, Inc.; refrain trans. © 1969. ICEL
Music: Paul Lisicky, © 1985. GIA Publications, Inc.

102 Psalm 107: Give Thanks to the Lord

Refrain

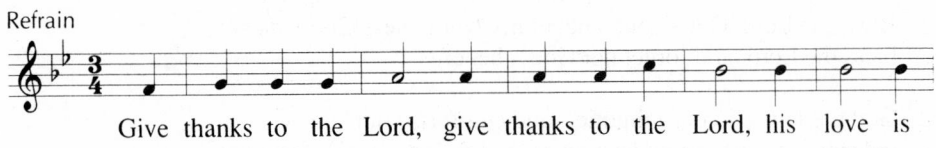

Give thanks to the Lord, give thanks to the Lord, his love is

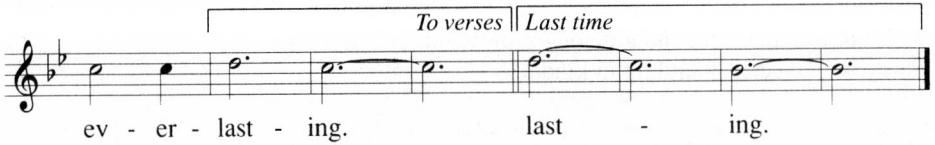

To verses | *Last time*

ev - er - last - ing.   last - ing.

Verses

1. Those who sailed the sea in ships trading on the deep waters;
   they saw the works of the Lord and his wonders in the abyss.

2. God's command raised up a storm wind which tossed its waves on high.
   They sank down to the depths; their hearts melted away.

3. They cried to the Lord in distress. From their straits he rescued them.
   God hushed the storm to a breeze and the waves of the sea were stilled.

Psalm 107: 23-24, 25-26, 28-29; Roy James Stewart. © 1993. GIA Publications. Inc.; refrain trans. © 1969. ICEL
Music: Roy James Stewart. © 1993. GIA Publications. Inc.

103 Psalm 110: You Are a Priest for Ever

Refrain

You are a priest for ev - er   in the line of Mel - chi - ze - dek.

Verses

1. The Lord's revelation to my Master: "Sit on my right;
   your foes I will put beneath your feet."

2. The Lord will wield from Zion your scepter of power;
   rule in the midst of all your foes.

3. A prince from the day of your birth on the holy mountains;
   from the womb before the dawn I begot you.

4. The Lord has sworn an oath and will not change.
   "You are a priest for ever, a priest like Melchizedek of old."

Text: Psalm 110:1, 2, 3, 4; © 1963, 1993, The Grail, GIA Publications, Inc., agent: refrain trans. © 1969, ICEL
Music: Michel Guimont. © 1994, GIA Publications, Inc.

Psalm 112: A Light Rises in the Darkness   104

Refrain

A   light   ris-es   in   the   dark-ness;   a   light   for the   up - right.

Verses

1. They are lights in the darkness for the upright;
   they are generous, merciful and just.
   Good people take pity and lend, they conduct their affairs with honor.

2. The just will never waver, they will be remembered for ever.
   They have no fear of evil news; with firm hearts they trust in the Lord.

3. With steadfast hearts they will not fear. Openhanded, they give to the poor;
   their justice stands firm for ever. Their heads will be raised in glory.

Text: Psalm 112:4-5, 6-7, 8-9; © 1963, 1993, The Grail, GIA Publications, Inc., agent: refrain trans. © 1969, ICEL
Music: Michel Guimont. © 1994, GIA Publications, Inc.

105 Psalm 113: Praise God's Name

Refrain

Al - le - lu - ia! Al - le - lu - ia! Al - le - lu - ia!

Verses

1. You servants of the Lord, bless the Lord: Blessed be the name for ever!
   From east to west, praised be the name of the Lord our God!

2. High above the nations the Lord is God;
   high above the heavens God's glory!
   Who is like God, enthroned on the stars above earth and sky?

3. Raising up the lowly and the poor from the dust,
   God gives them a home among rulers:
   blessing the barren, giving them children singing for joy!

4. Glory to the Father and glory to the Son; glory to the Holy Spirit:
   glory and honor, wisdom and power for evermore!

Text: Psalm 113: Michael Joncas
Music: Michael Joncas
© 1979, New Dawn Music

Psalm 113: Praise the Lord 106

Refrain

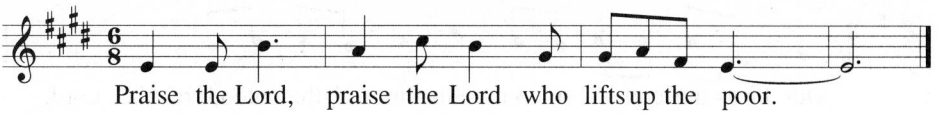

Praise the Lord, praise the Lord who lifts up the poor.

Verses

1. Praise, O servants of the Lord; praise the name of the Lord!
   May the name of the Lord be blessed both now and for evermore!

2. High above all nations is the Lord, above the heavens God's glory.
   Who is like the Lord, our God, the one enthroned on high,
   who stoops from the heights to look down,
   to look down upon heaven and earth?

3. From the dust God lifts up the lowly,
   from the dungheap God raises the poor
   to set them in the company of rulers, yes, with the rulers of the people.

Text: Psalm 113:1-2, 4-6, 7-8; © 1963, 1993, The Grail, GIA Publications, Inc., agent; refrain trans. © 1969, ICEL
Music: Michel Guimont, © 1994, GIA Publications, Inc.

107   Psalm 116: Our Blessing-Cup

Refrain

Our bless-ing-cup is a com-mun-ion with the blood of the Lord.

Verses

1. How can I make a return to the Lord for all God has done for me?
   The cup of salvation I will take up, I will call on the name of the Lord.

2. Precious, indeed, in the sight of the Lord is the death of his faithful ones;
   and I am your servant, your chosen one, for you have set me free.

3. Unto your name I will offer my thanks for the debt that I owe to you.
   In the presence of all who have called on your name,
   in the courts of the house of the Lord.

Text: Psalm 116:12-13, 15-16, 17-19; Marty Haugen
Music: Marty Haugen
© 1983, GIA Publications, Inc.

Psalm 116: I Will Walk in the Presence 108

Antiphon

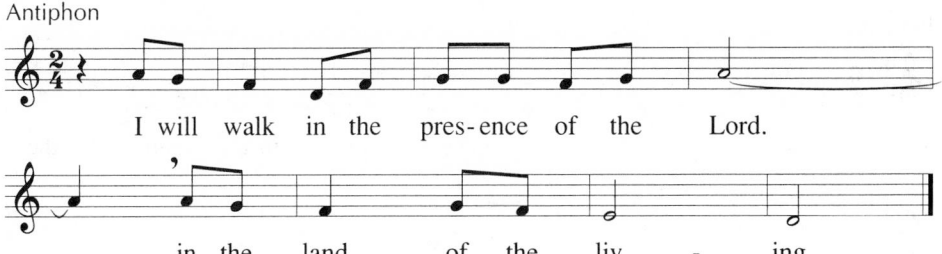

I will walk in the pres-ence of the Lord. in the land of the liv - ing.

Text: Psalm 116:9; The Grail, © 1963, GIA Publications, Inc., agent
Music: Richard Proulx, © 1975, GIA Publications, Inc.

Psalm Tone

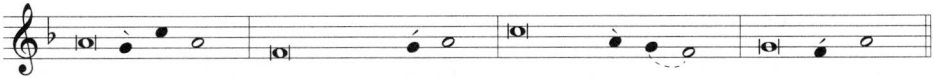

Music: Richard Proulx, © 1986, GIA Publications, Inc.

Gelineau Tone

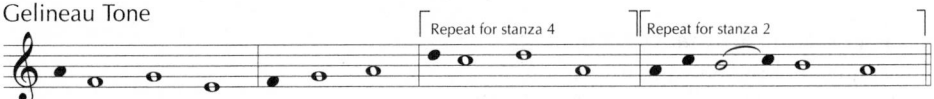

Repeat for stanza 4   Repeat for stanza 2

Dilexi, quoniam

I love the **Lord**, for the **Lòrd** has **heard**
the **cry** of my áp**peal**.
[2]The **Lord** was at**ten**tive tò **me**
in the **day** when **Í called**.

[3]They sur**round**ed me, the **snàres** of **death**,
with the **an**guish of thé **tomb**;
they **caught** me, **sor**row and dì**stress**.
[4]I **called** on the **Lord's name**.
O **Lord**, my **God**, dé**liv**er me!

[5]How **gra**cious is the **Lòrd**, and **just**;
our **God** has cóm**pas**sion.
[6]The **Lord** pro**tects** the simplè **hearts**;
I was **help**less so **Gód saved me**.

[7]Turn **back**, my **soul**, tò your **rest**
for the **Lord** has beén **good**,
[8]and has **kept** my **soul** from **death**,
(my **eyes** fròm **tears**,)
my **feet** fróm **stumbling**.

[9]I will **walk** in the **pres**ence òf the **Lord**
in the **land** of thé **living**.
Praise the **Father**, the **Son** and Holỳ **Spir**it,
for **ev**er ánd **ever**.

Text: Psalm 116:1-9; The Grail
Music: Joseph Gelineau
© 1963, 1993, The Grail, GIA Publications, Inc., agent

109 Psalm 116: I Will Walk in the Presence of God

Refrain

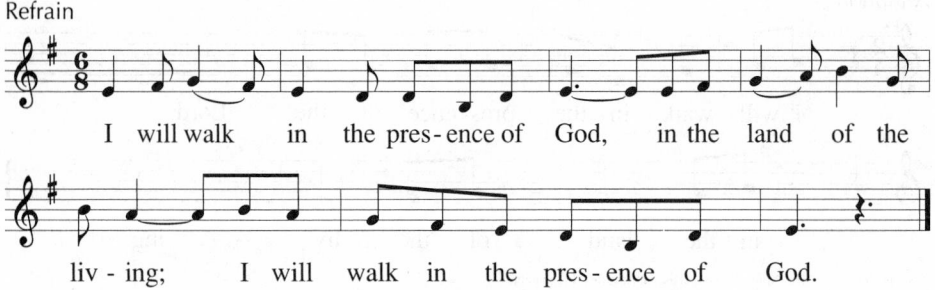

I will walk in the pres-ence of God, in the land of the liv-ing; I will walk in the pres-ence of God.

Verses

1. In my hour of despair, bereft and betrayed,
   I prayed, "Save me! Be my breath!"
   The death of a servant cuts close to your heart,
   For God of the living you are.

2. Your servant am I like my mother before me.
   You restore me, loosing my bonds.
   My hands in thanksgiving to God I will raise.
   O join me in glorious praise!

3. My vows I will make, and may ev'ryone hear me!
   Draw near me, O servants of God.
   I stand here in the midst of them:
   Your house, your heart, Jerusalem.

Text: Psalm 116 adapt. by Rory Cooney, © 1990, GIA Publications, Inc.; refrain trans. © 1969, ICEL.
Music: Gary Daigle and Rory Cooney, © 1990, GIA Publications, Inc.

110 Psalm 116: The Name of God

Refrain I

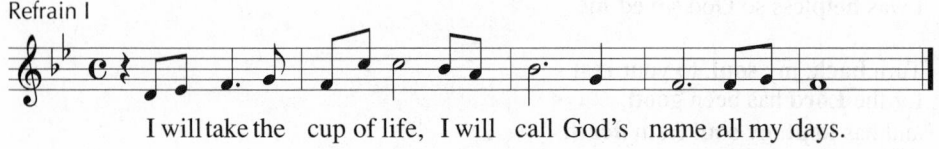

I will take the cup of life, I will call God's name all my days.

Refrain II

Our bless-ing cup is a com-mun-ion with the blood of Christ.

Refrain III

In the land of the liv-ing, I will walk with God all my days.

Verses

1. How can I make a return for the goodness of God?
   This saving cup I will bless and sing, and call the name of God!

2. The dying of those who keep faith is precious to our God.
   I am your servant called from your hands, you have set me free!

3. To you I will offer my thanks and call upon your name.
   You are my promise for all to see. I love your name, O God!

Text: Psalm 116; David Haas, © 1987, GIA Publications, Inc.; refrain II trans. © 1969, ICEL
Music: David Haas, © 1987, GIA Publications, Inc.

Psalm 117: Holy Is God, Holy and Strong   111

Refrain

Ho - ly is God! Ho - ly and strong!

Ho-ly is God! Ho-ly and strong! Ho-ly and liv-ing for ev - er!

Verses

1. O praise the Lord, all you nations, acclaim God, all you peoples!
   Strong is God's love for us, the Lord is faithful for ever!

2. Give glory to the Father Almighty, to his Son Jesus Christ the Lord,
   to the Spirit who dwells in our hearts, both now and for ever. Amen!

Text: Psalm 117; The Grail, © 1963, 1993, GIA Publications, Inc., agent; refrain trans. © 1969, ICEL
Music: Michael Joncas, © 1979, GIA Publications, Inc.

112 Psalm 117: Go Out to All the World

Refrain

Go out to all the world, and tell the good news!

Go out to all the world, and sing: "Al - le - lu - ia!"

Verses

1. Praise the Lord, all you nations! Glorify God, all you peoples!

2. Steadfast is God's love to all people!
   And the promise of God endures for ever!

Text: Psalm 117; David Haas, © 1991, GIA Publications, Inc.; refrain trans. © 1969, ICEL
Music: David Haas; © 1991, GIA Publications, Inc.

113 Psalm 118: Alleluia, Alleluia

Refrain

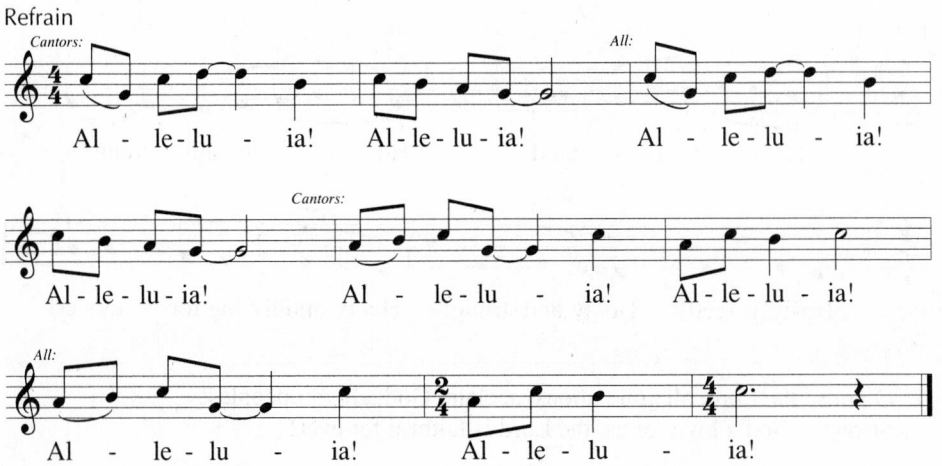

Cantors: Al - le - lu - ia! Al - le - lu - ia! *All:* Al - le - lu - ia!

Al - le - lu - ia! *Cantors:* Al - le - lu - ia! Al - le - lu - ia!

All: Al - le - lu - ia! Al - le - lu - ia!

Verses

1. This is the day the Lord has made, let us rejoice, be glad, and sing!
   Thanks and praise be to our God, for his mercy endures for evermore!

2. The right hand of God has come with power,
   the Lord, our God, is lifted high!
   I shall not die, but I shall live and rejoice in the works of the Lord!

3. The stone which the builders once denied now has become the cornerstone.
   By the Lord has this been done; it has brought wonder to our eyes!

Text: Psalm 118:24, 1, 16-17, 22-23; David Haas
Music: David Haas
© 1986, GIA Publications, Inc.

Psalm 118: Let Us Rejoice   114

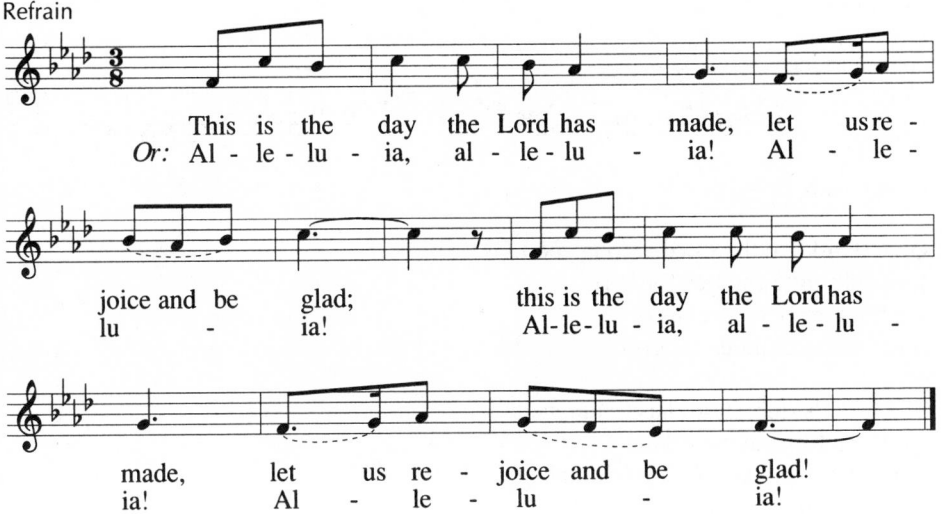

Refrain

This is the day the Lord has made, let us re-
Or: Al - le - lu - ia, al - le - lu - ia! Al - le -

joice and be glad; this is the day the Lord has
lu - ia! Al - le - lu - ia, al - le - lu -

made, let us re - joice and be glad!
ia! Al - le - lu - ia!

Verses

1. Give thanks to the Lord, for God is good; God's mercy endures for ever;
   Let the house of Israel say: "God's mercy endures for ever."

2. The hand of the Lord has struck with power, God's right hand is exalted,
   I shall not die, but live anew, declaring the works of the Lord.

3. The stone which the builders rejected has become the cornerstone,
   the Lord of love and mercy has brought wonder to our eyes!

Text: Psalm 118:1-2, 16-17, 22-23; Marty Haugen, © 1983, GIA Publications, Inc.; refrain trans. © 1969, ICEL
Music: Marty Haugen, © 1983, GIA Publications, Inc.

115   Psalm 118: This Is the Day

Antiphon

This is   the day the   Lord has made;

let us   re-joice,   let us   re-joice,   let us   re-joice and be   glad.

May be sung as a canon.

Psalm Tone

Gelineau Tone

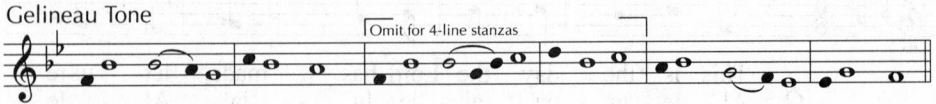

Confitemini Domino

¹Give **thanks** to the **Lord** who is **gòod**,
for God's **love** endures for **éver**.
²Let the **fam**ily of Israel **sày**:
"God's **love** endúres for **ever**."

The **Lord's** right **hand** has **trìumphed**;
¹⁶God's **right** hand **raised mé**.
The **Lord's** right **hand** has **trìumphed**;
¹⁷I **shall** not **die**,
I shall **live** and recóunt God's **dèeds**,
and recóunt God's **deeds**.

²²The **stone** which the **build**ers re**jèct**ed
has be**come** the **cornér**stone.
²³**This** is the **work** of the **Lòrd**,
a **mar**vel in our **éyes**.

Psalm 119: Happy Are Those Who Follow   116

Refrain

Hap-py are those who fol-low in the law of the Lord.

Hap-py are those who fol-low in the law of the Lord.

Verses

1. Happy are they whose way is blameless, who walk in the law of the Lord.
   Happy are they who observe God's decrees, who seek God with all their heart.
   Happy are they who walk in the law of the Lord.

2. You have commanded that all your precepts be kept with diligence.
   Oh, that I might be strong in the ways of keeping to your law.
   Happy are they who walk in the law of the Lord.

3. Be good to your servant that I may live, may live to keep your word.
   Open my heart that I may consider the wonders of your law.
   Happy are they who walk in the law of the Lord.

4. Instruct me, O God, in the way of your statutes,
   that I may exactly observe them.
   Give me discernment, that I may observe your law.
   Give me discernment to keep it with all my heart.
   Happy are they who walk in the law of the Lord.

Text: Psalm 119:1-2, 5-6, 17-18, 33-34; Rory Cooney
Music: Rory Cooney
© 1991, GIA Publications, Inc.

117   Psalm 119: Lord, I Love Your Commands

Refrain

Lord,   I   love   your   com - mands.

Verses

1. My part, I have resolved, O Lord, is to obey your word.
   The law from your mouth means more to me than silver and gold.

2. Let your love be ready to console me by your promise to your servant.
   Let your love come and I shall live for your law is my delight.

3. That is why I love your commands more than finest gold,
   why I rule my life by your precepts, and hate false ways.

4. Your will is wonderful indeed; therefore I obey it.
   The unfolding of your word gives light and teaches the simple.

Text: Psalm 119:57, 72, 76-77, 127-128, 129-130; © 1963, 1993, The Grail, GIA Publications, Inc., agent; refrain trans. © 1969, ICEL
Music: Michel Guimont, © 1994, GIA Publications, Inc.

Psalm 121: I Lift Up My Eyes   118

Verses

1. I lift up my eyes to the mountains; from where shall come my help?
   My help shall come from the Lord who made the heavens and the earth.

2. The Lord is your guard and your shade, for ever by your side.
   By day the sun shall not smite you nor the moon in the night.

3. The Lord ever watches over you, the guardian of your soul.
   The Lord will guard your coming and your going now and for ever.

Text: Psalm 121:1-2, 5-6, 7-8; Michel Guimont
Music: Michel Guimont

119   Psalm 121: Our Help Comes from the Lord

Refrain

[Musical notation]

Our help comes from the Lord, the
mak - er of heav - en and earth.

Verses

1. I lift up my eyes to the mountains: from where shall come my help?
   My help shall come from the Lord who made heaven and earth.

2. May God never allow you to stumble! Let God sleep not, your guard.
   Neither sleeping nor slumbering, God, Israel's guard.

3. The Lord is your guard and your shade: and at your right side stands,
   By day the sun shall not smite you nor the moon in the night.

4. The Lord will guard you from evil: God will guard your soul.
   The Lord will guard your going and coming both now and for ever.

5. Glory to the Father, and to the Son, and to the Holy Spirit:
   as it was in the beginning, is now, and will be for ever. Amen.

Text: Psalm 121; © 1963, 1993, The Grail, GIA Publications, Inc., agent; refrain by Michael Joncas, © 1979, GIA Publications, Inc.
Music: Michael Joncas, © 1979, GIA Publications, Inc.

Psalm 122: Let Us Go Rejoicing   120

Refrain

Let us go re-joic-ing to the house of the Lord;

Let us go, re-joic-ing to the house of the Lord.

Verses

1. I rejoiced when I heard them say: "Let us go to the house of the Lord,"
   and now our feet are standing within your gates, O Jerusalem.

2. Jerusalem is a city built with unity and strength.
   It is there, it is there that the tribes go up, the tribes of the Lord.

3. For Israel's law is to praise God's name and there to give God thanks.
   There are set the judgment thrones for all of David's house.

4. Pray for the peace of Jerusalem! "May those who love you prosper;
   May peace ever reign within your walls, and wealth within your buildings!"

5. For love of my fam'ly and love of my friends, I pray that peace be yours.
   For love of the house of the Lord our God I pray for your good.

Text: Psalm 122; Michael Joncas, © 1987, GIA Publications, Inc.; refrain trans.© 1969, ICEL
Music: Michael Joncas, © 1987, GIA Publications, Inc.

121   Psalm 122: I Was Glad

Refrain

I was glad when they said to me,
"Come with us to the house of the Lord!"

Verses

1. I was glad when they said to me: "Come with us to the house of the Lord."
   Now our feet are standing firm, within your gates, O Jerusalem!

2. Jerusalem— strongly built, walled around with unity.
   It is there that the tribes of God are lifted high, to the mountain of God!

3. Israel, this is your law to praise the name of the Lord.
   Here are placed the judgment seats, for the just, here the house of David!

4. For the love of my fam'ly and friends, "may the peace of God be with you!"
   For the love of the house of God I will pray, I will pray for your good!"

Text: Psalm 122; David Haas
Music: David Haas
© 1994, GIA Publications, Inc.

Psalm 123: Our Eyes Are Fixed on the Lord   122

Refrain

Our eyes are fixed on the Lord, plead-ing for his mer - cy.

Verses

1. To you I have lifted up my eyes, you who dwell in the heavens;
   my eyes, like the eyes of slaves on the hand of their lords.

2. Like the eyes of a servant on the hand of her mistress,
   so our eyes are on the Lord our God till we are shown mercy.

3. Have mercy on us Lord, have mercy. We are filled with contempt.
   Indeed all too full is our soul with the scorn of the rich,
   (the disdain of the proud).

Text: Psalm 123:1-2, 3-4; © 1963, 1993, The Grail, GIA Publications, Inc., agent; refrain trans. © 1969, ICEL
Music: Michel Guimont, © 1994, GIA Publications, Inc.

123   Psalm 126: The Lord Has Done Great Things

Antiphon

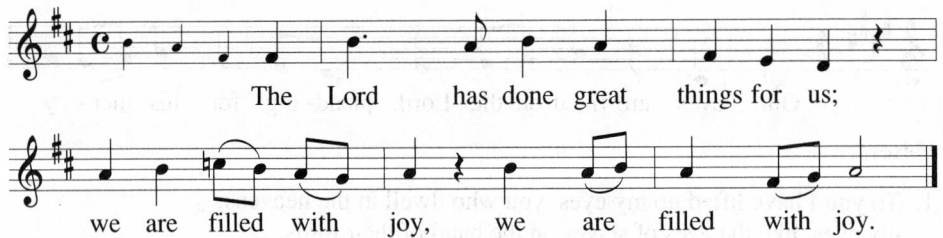

The Lord has done great things for us;
we are filled with joy, we are filled with joy.

Text: *Lectionary for Mass*, © 1969, 1981, ICEL
Music: Richard Proulx, © 1975, GIA Publications, Inc.

Psalm Tone

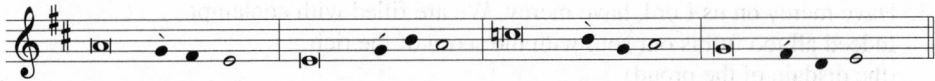

Music: Joseph B. Smith, © 1986, GIA Publications, Inc.

Gelineau Tone

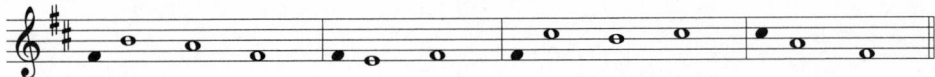

In convertendo

¹When the **Lord** delivered **Zìon** from **bond**age,
  it **seemed** líke a **dream.**
²**Then** was our **mouth** filled with **laugh**ter,
  on our **lips** thére were **songs.**

The **heath**ens them**selves** sàid: "What **mar**vels
  the **Lord** wórked for **them!**"
³What **mar**vels the **Lord** wòrked for **us!**
  In**deed**, wé were **glad.**

⁴**Deliver** us, O **Lord**, fròm our **bond**age
  as **streams** ín dry **land.**
⁵**Those** who are sowìng in **tears**
  will **sing** whén they **reap.**

⁶They go **out**, they go **out**, fùll of **tears**,
  carrying **seed** fór the **sow**ing;
  they come **back**, they come **back**, fùll of **song**,
  carryíng their **sheaves.**

Praise the **Father**, the **Son** and Hòly **Spir**it,
both **now** ánd for **ever**,
the God who **is**, who **was** ànd who **will** be,
world wíthout **end**.

Psalm 126: God Has Done Great Things for Us   124

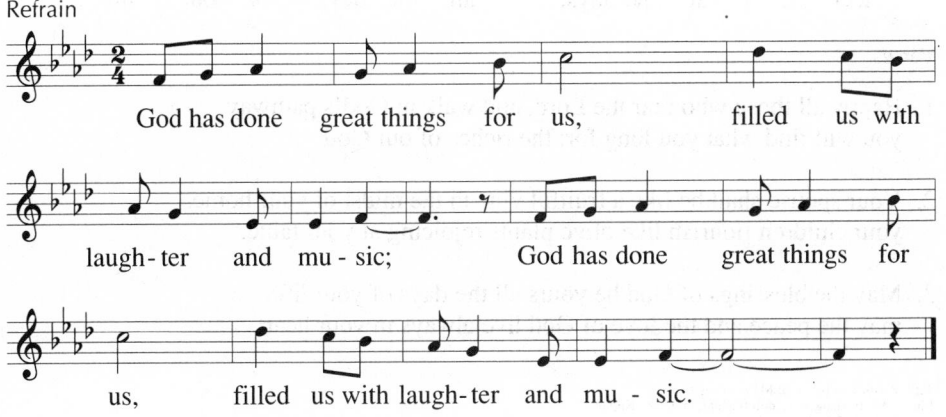

Refrain

God has done   great things   for   us,   filled   us with
laugh-ter   and   mu - sic;   God has done   great things   for
us,   filled   us with laugh-ter   and   mu - sic.

Verses

1. When our God led us back to freedom,
   like dreamers we beheld the promised land again;
   our mouths were filled with laughter and rejoicing.

2. We proclaimed to the nations what you had done for us;
   your mighty deeds of love, restoring us to life,
   you lead your people home to you rejoicing.

3. Come restore our fortune, renew us in your love,
   as rivers through the sand, as springs within the desert;
   those who sow in tears shall reap rejoicing.

125 Psalm 128: Blest Are Those Who Love You

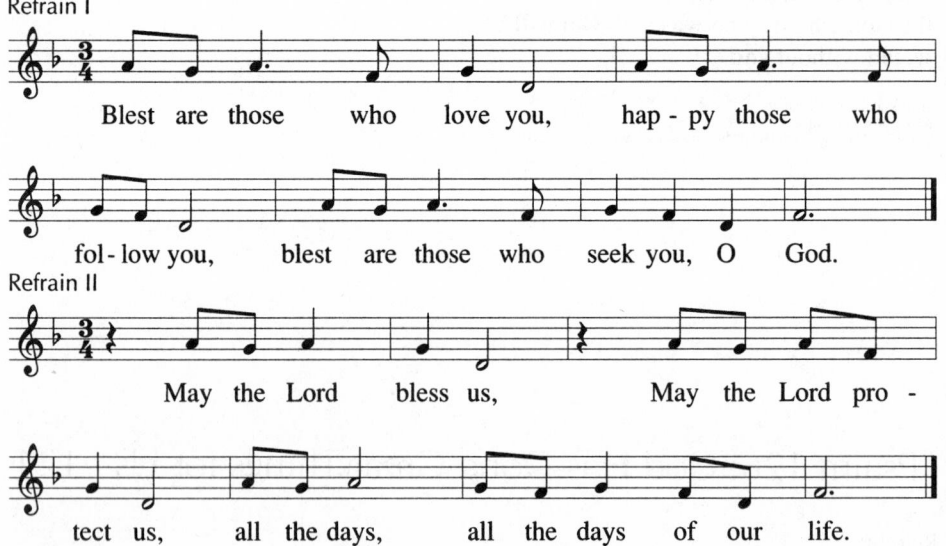

Refrain I

Blest are those who love you, hap-py those who fol-low you, blest are those who seek you, O God.

Refrain II

May the Lord bless us, May the Lord pro-tect us, all the days, all the days of our life.

Verses

1. Happy all those who fear the Lord, and walk in God's pathway;
   you will find what you long for: the riches of our God.

2. Your spouse shall be like a fruitful vine in the midst of your home,
   your children flourish like olive plants rejoicing at your table.

3. May the blessings of God be yours all the days of your life,
   may the peace and the love of God live always in your heart.

Text: Psalm 128:1-2, 3, 5; Marty Haugen
Music: Marty Haugen; refrain II adapt. by Diana Kodner
© 1987, 1993, GIA Publications, Inc.

126 Psalm 130: If You, O God, Laid Bare Our Guilt

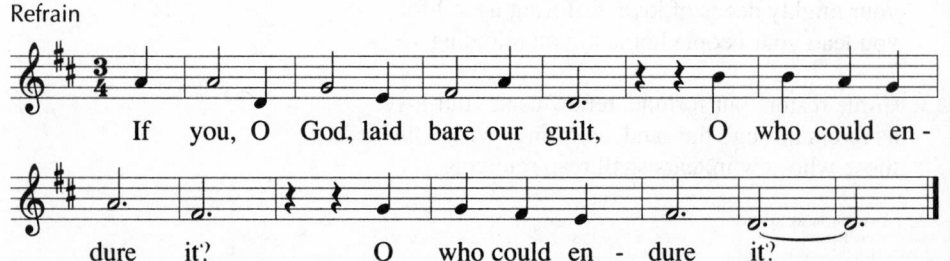

Refrain

If you, O God, laid bare our guilt, O who could en-dure it? O who could en-dure it?

verses

1. Out of the depths I cry to you. Lord, hear my plea.
   Let your ear be attentive to the sound of my call.

2. If you, O God, lay bare our sin, Lord, who can stand?
   But with you is forgiveness, so your name is revered.

3. Waiting for you, our souls await, hoping in God.
   Like the sent'nel for daybreak, so our souls wait for you.

4. For with the Lord is steadfast love: pow'r to redeem.
   God will save us from sorrows, bring us back from our sin.

Text: Psalm 130; John Foley, SJ
Music: John Foley, SJ
© 1994, GIA Publications, Inc.

Psalm 130: With the Lord There Is Mercy 127

Refrain

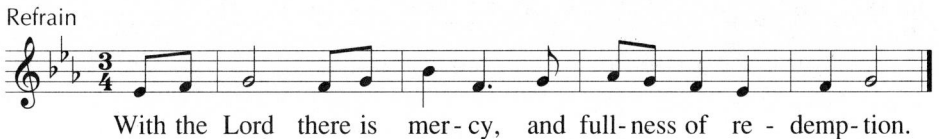

With the Lord there is mer-cy, and full-ness of re-demp-tion.

Verses

1. From out of the depths, I cry unto you,
   Lord, hear my voice, come hear my prayer;
   O let your ear be open to my pleading.

2. If you, O Lord, should mark our guilt,
   then who could stand within your sight?
   But in you is found forgiveness for our failings.

3. Just as those who wait for the morning light,
   even more I long for the Lord, my God,
   whose word to me shall ever be my comfort.

Text: Psalm 130:1-2, 3-4, 5-6; Marty Haugen, © 1983, GIA Publications, Inc.; refrain trans. © 1969, ICEL
Music: Marty Haugen, © 1983, GIA Publications, Inc.

128   Psalm 130: I Place All My Trust In You

Antiphon I

I place all my trust in you, my God; all my hope is in your sav - ing word.

Text: Joseph Gelineau
Music: Joseph Gelineau
© 1963, The Grail, GIA Publications, Inc., agent

Antiphon II

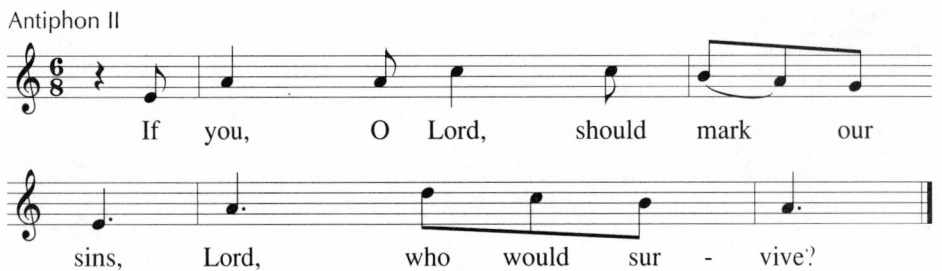

If you, O Lord, should mark our sins, Lord, who would sur - vive?

Text: Psalm 130:3; The Grail
Music: Clifford W. Howell
© 1963, The Grail, GIA Publications, Inc., agent

Psalm Tone

Repeat for 6-line stanza

Music: A. Gregory Murray , OSB, © L. J. Carey and Co. Ltd. (Ascherberg, Hopwood & Crow, Ltd.)

Gelineau Tone

Repeat for 6-line stanza

De profundis

¹ Out of the **depths I cry** to yòu, O **Lord**,
² **Lord**, héar my **voice**!
O **let** your **ears** bè at**ten**tive
to the **voice** óf my **pleading**.

³ If you, O Lord, should **màrk** our **guilt**,
Lord, who wóuld sur**vive**?
⁴ But with **you** is **fòund** for**give**ness:
for **this** wé re**vere you**.

⁵ My **soul** is **wait**ing fòr the **Lord**.
    I **count** ón God's **word**.
⁶ My **soul** is **long**ing fòr the **Lord**
    more than **those** who wátch for **daybreak**.
    (Let the **watch**ers còunt on **day**break
⁷ and **Is**rael ón the **Lord**.)

    Be**cause** with the **Lord** thère is **mer**cy
    and **full**ness óf re**demp**tion,
⁸ **Is**rael in**deed** God wìll re**deem**
    from **all** íts in**iqui**ty.

    To the **Fa**ther Al**might**ỳ give **glo**ry,
    give **glo**ry tó his **Son**,
    to the **Spir**it most **Hol**ỳ give **praise**,
    whose **reign** ís for **ever**.

Text: Psalm 130; The Grail
Music: Joseph Gelineau, SJ
© 1963, 1993, The Grail, GIA Publications, Inc., agent

129 Psalm 131: My Soul Is Still

Refrain

In you, O Lord, I have found my peace, I have found my peace.

Verses

1. My heart is not proud, my eyes not above you;
   You fill my soul. I am not filled with great things,
   nor with thoughts beyond me.

2. My soul is still, my soul stays quiet,
   longing for you like a weaned child
   in its mother's arms; so is my soul a child with you.

Text: Psalm 131; verses, David Haas, © 1985, GIA Publications, Inc.; refrain trans. © 1969, ICEL
Music: David Haas, © 1985, GIA Publications, Inc.

Psalm 134: In the Silent Hours of Night 130

Antiphon

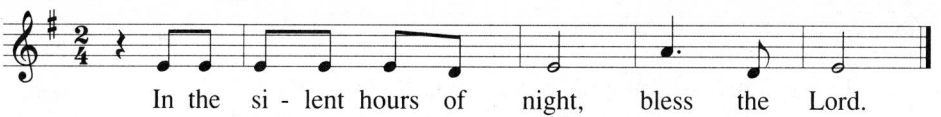

In the si - lent hours of night, bless the Lord.

Verses

1. O come, bless the Lord,
   all you who serve the Lord,
   who stand in the house of the Lord,
   in the courts of the house of our God.

2. Lift up your hands to the holy place
   and bless the Lord through the night.

3. May the Lord bless you from Zion,
   he who made both heaven and earth.

4. Gory to the Father, and the Son,
   and to the Holy Spirit:
   as it was in the beginning, is now,
   and will be for ever. Amen.

Text: Psalm 134; The Grail, © 1963, 1993, GIA Publications, Inc., agent
Music: Howard Hughes, SM, © 1979, GIA Publications, Inc.

131 Psalm 136: Love Is Never Ending

Cantor:

1. We give thanks un - to you, O God of might:
2. In your wis - dom and love you shaped the skies:
3. You have filled all the skies with glo - ry and light:
4. From of old you have led your peo - ple in faith:
5. You de - liv - ered the ones who called un - to you:
6. You have o - pened the sea and brought your peo-ple through:
7. You re - mem - ber your prom - ise age to age:
8. You give food and life to all liv - ing things:

All:

for your love is nev - er end - ing,

Cantor:

We give thanks un - to you, the God of gods:
You spread out the earth up - on the sea:
The sun for the day and moon for night:
You have shown your com-pas-sion, strength and love:
From bond - age to free-dom, you brought them forth:
Brought them in - to a land that flows with life:
You show mer - cy on those of low de - gree:
We give thanks un - to you, the God of all:

All:

for your love is nev - er end - ing.

Text: Psalm 136; Marty Haugen
Music: Marty Haugen
© 1987, GIA Publications, Inc.

Psalm 137: Let My Tongue Be Silent   132

Refrain

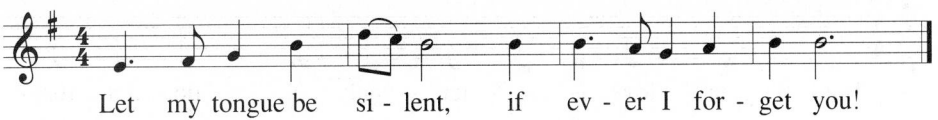

Let my tongue be si - lent, if ev - er I for - get you!

Verses

1. By Babylonian rivers, we sat and wept, rememb'ring Zion.
   There on the poplars we retired our harps.

2. For there our captors demanded songs of joy:
   "Sing to us one of the songs of Zion!"

3. How can we sing the songs of the Lord while in a foreign land?
   How can we sing the songs of the Lord while in a foreign land?

4. If I should fail to remember you, O Zion, Let my tongue be silenced,
   let my right hand be forgotten,
   If I do not consider Jerusalem to be my highest joy.

Text: Psalm 137:1-6; Carl Johengen, © 1992, GIA Publications, Inc.; refrain trans. © 1969, ICEL
Music: Carl Johengen, © 1992, GIA Publications, Inc.

133   Psalm 138: Lord, Your Love Is Eternal

Refrain

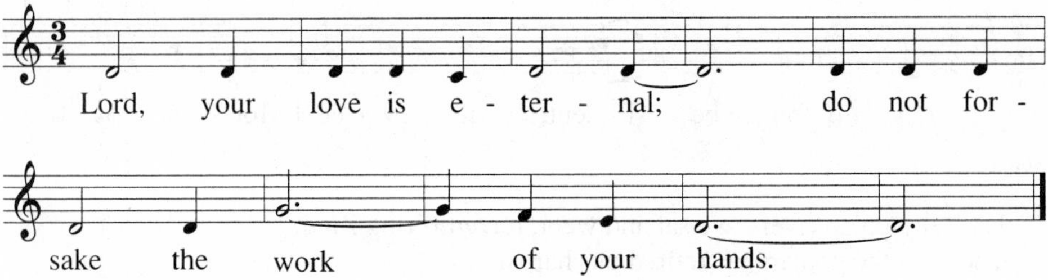

Lord, your love is e-ter-nal; do not for-sake the work of your hands.

Verses

1. I give thanks to you, O Lord, with all my heart, with all my soul.
   I will sing your praise with the angels. I will worship in your temple.

2. I give thanks to your holy name, for all your kindness and your truth.
   When I called, you answered me, and you built up strength within me.

3. The Lord God is exalted, yet he sees you, he sees me.
   And his kindness endures for ever, O forsake not the work of your hands.

Text: Psalm 138:1-2, 3, 7; Roy James Stewart, © 1993, GIA Publications, Inc.; refrain trans. © 1969, ICEL
Music: Roy James Stewart, © 1993, GIA Publications, Inc.

Psalm 138: The Fragrance of Christ   134

Refrains I-III

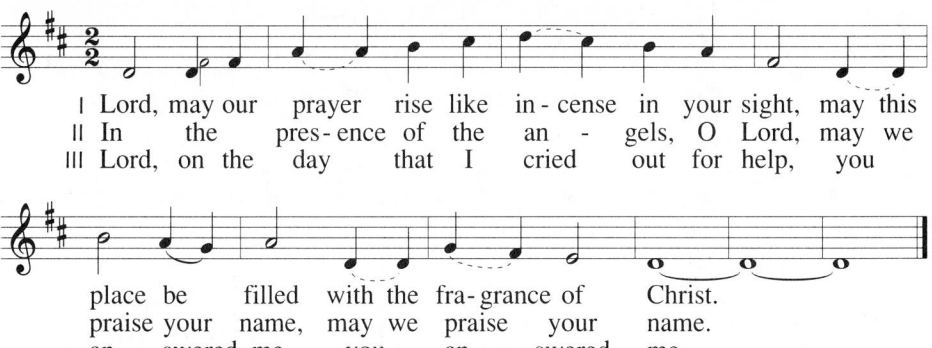

I   Lord, may our   prayer   rise like   in - cense   in   your sight, may this
II   In   the   pres - ence of   the   an -   gels,   O   Lord,   may we
III   Lord, on the   day   that   I   cried   out   for help,   you

place be   filled   with the   fra - grance of   Christ.
praise your   name,   may we   praise   your   name.
an - swered me,   you   an - swered   me.

Verses

1. I will thank you, Lord, with all of my heart,
   you have heard the words of my mouth.
   In the presence of the angels I will bless you,
   I will adore before your holy temple.

2. I will thank you, Lord, for your faithfulness and love,
   beyond all my hopes and dreams.
   On the day that I called you answered;
   you gave life to the strength of my soul.

3. All who live on earth shall give you thanks when they hear
   the words of your voice.
   And all shall sing of your ways: "How great is the glory of God!"

Text: Psalm 138:1-5; David Haas
Music: David Haas

135 Psalm 139: Filling Me with Joy

Refrain

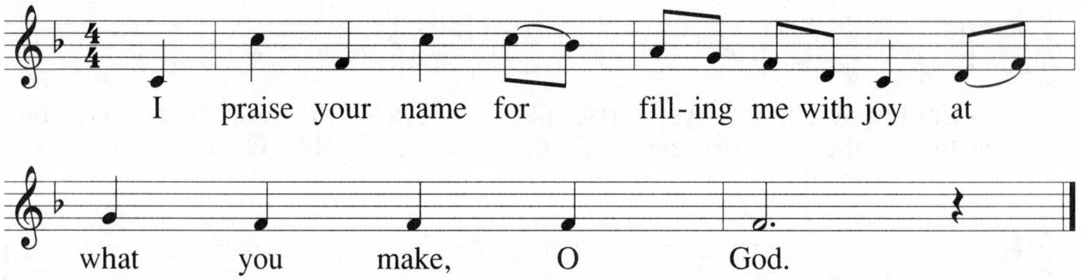

I praise your name for fill-ing me with joy at what you make, O God.

Verses

1. O God, you search me and you know me.
   You know when I sit and when I stand.
   You understand my thoughts from afar.
   With all my ways you are familiar.

2. God, you have formed my inmost being.
   You knit me in my mother's womb.
   I give you thanks for you have made me.
   How wondrous, wondrous are your works.

3. You knew my soul completely.
   Nor was my frame unknown to you
   when I was formed in the depths,
   when I was fashioned in secret.

Text: Psalm 139; Paul Lisicky
Music: Paul Lisicky
© 1992, GIA Publications, Inc.

Psalm 141: Evening Offering   136

Refrain

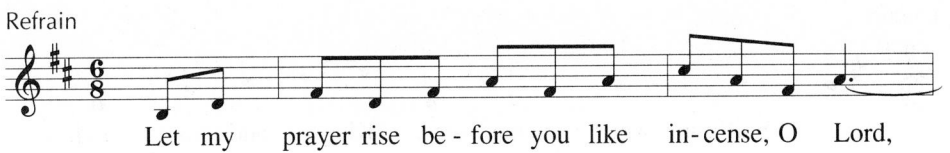

Let my   prayer rise be - fore you like   in-cense, O   Lord,

and my   hands like   an   eve - ning   of - f'ring.

Verses

1. To you, O Lord, I call out for help.
   O hear my voice when I cry out to you.
   Let my prayer rise up before you like incense,
   my hands lifted up at the end of the day.

2. May my words, O Lord, speak only your truth;
   my heart be filled with a longing for you.
   Keep my hands, O Lord, from all wicked deeds;
   let me not rejoice with those set against you.

3. Let your holy ones confront me in kindness;
   their words I hear as your wisdom for me.
   But the wicked ones shall never mislead me;
   I will pray for strength to conquer their evil.

4. I look to you, O Lord, for my hope.
   For you, my God, are the strength of my soul.
   Keep me safe from those who tempt me to sin,
   and free my heart to rest in your peace.

Text: Psalm 141; Darryl Ducote
Music: Darryl Ducote; arr. by Gary Daigle
© 1985, 1993, Damean Music. Distributed by GIA Publications, Inc.

137　Psalm 145: I Will Praise Your Name

Refrain

I will praise your name, my King and my God.

I will praise your name, my King and my God.

Verses

1. I will give you glory, my God above, and I will bless your name for ever.
   Ev'ry day I will bless and praise your name for ever.

2. The Lord is full of grace and mercy, who is kind and slow to anger.
   God is good in ev'ry way, and full of compassion.

3. Let all your works give you thanks, O Lord,
   and let all the faithful bless you.
   Let them speak of your might, O Lord, the glory of your kingdom.

4. The Lord is faithful in word and deed,
   and always near, his name is holy.
   Lifting up all those who fall, God raises up the lowly.

Text: Psalm 145:1-2, 8-9, 10-11, 13b-14; David Haas
Music: David Haas
© 1983, GIA Publications, Inc.

Psalm 145: Our God Is Compassion   138

Refrain

Our God is com-pas-sion to all cre-a-tion. Our
God is com-pas-sion to all cre-a-tion.

Verses

1. The Lord is grace and mercy, slow to anger, full of love.
   God is good to all creation; full of compassion.

2. Let all your works give thanks, O God. Let the faithful bless you.
   The eyes of all are filled with hope; you give them all they need.

3. The Lord is just in ev'ry way, full of love for all.
   God is near to those in need; who call out from their hearts.

Text: Psalm 145; Jeanne Cotter
Music: Jeanne Cotter
© 1993, GIA Publications, Inc.

Psalm 146: Happy the Poor in Spirit   139

Refrain

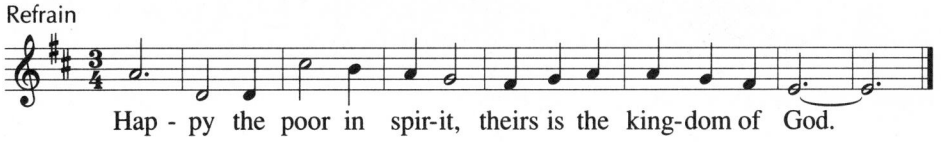

Hap-py the poor in spir-it, theirs is the king-dom of God.

Verses

1. Lord, you keep faith for ever, secure justice for the oppressed.
   You give food to all who are hungry. O Lord, you set captives free.

2. Lord, you open up blind eyes, and you raise up all those bowed down.
   The alien people are welcomed. The just, secure in your love.

3. Orphans, widows find comfort, but the wicked you take to their ruin.
   Your reign lasts for all generations, both now and for evermore.

Text: Psalm 146:7, 8-9, 8c-10; Thomas J. Porter
Music: Thomas J. Porter
© 1990, GIA Publications, Inc.

140 Psalm 146: Lord, Come and Save Us

Refrain

Lord, come and save us. Lord, come and save us. Lord, come and save us.

Verses

1. For all my life I will sing to you, O ever faithful God.
   You fill the heavens with wondrous lights, the earth sings out your glory.

2. Put not your trust in those who rule, the mighty of this earth.
   Their breath shall fail, their power die, their plans shall fade and vanish.

3. You give your sight to all the blind, you raise up those bent low.
   Your heart is near to the broken ones, you welcome in the stranger.

4. Happy those who keep faith with you, securing justice for the oppressed,
   who give your food to each hungry heart, your freedom to each captive.

5. The weak and poor you sustain in love,
   the wicked ones you bring to destruction;
   for ever more shall your reign endure, to ev'ry generation.

Text: Psalm 146:3-4, 8-9, 6b-7, 8c-10; Marty Haugen, © 1987, GIA Publications, Inc.; refrain trans. © 1969, ICEL
Music: Marty Haugen, © 1987, GIA Publications, Inc.

Psalm 147: Bless the Lord, My Soul   141

Refrain

Bless the Lord, my soul, who heals the bro - ken - heart - ed.

Verses

1. Praise the Lord, O Jerusalem, chant praises to your God.
   The strength of God is your fortress sure, and blessed are your children.

2. All praise to you, O gracious God, your goodness fills the earth.
   You raise anew Jerusalem, and gather all your lost ones.

3. You heal the hurt and broken heart, you bind up ev'ry wound,
   you number all the stars of night and call each one by name.

4. The peace of God shall be your hope, God's finest wheat, your food,
   the word of God fills all the earth, as rapid as the whirlwind.

Text: Psalm 147:12-13, 1-2, 3-4, 14-15; Marty Haugen
Music: Marty Haugen
© 1987, GIA Publications, Inc.

142 Psalm 150: Praise God in His Holy Dwelling

Al-le - lu - ia, al - le - lu - ia, al-le - lu - ia.

1. Praise God in his ho - ly dwell-ing; Praise him on his
2. Praise him with the blast of trum - pet; Praise him now with
3. Praise him with re - sound-ing cym-bals; With cym - bals that
4. Praise God the al - might-y Fa - ther; Praise Christ his be -

might - y throne; Praise him for his won - der-ful
lyre and harps; Praise him with the tim - brel and
crash, give praise; O let ev - 'ry-thing that has
lov - ed Son; Give praise to the Spir - it of

deeds; Praise him for his sov - 'reign maj - es - ty.
dance; Praise him with the sound of string and reed.
breath, Let all liv-ing crea - tures praise the Lord.
love; For ev - er the Tri - une God be praised.

Al - le - lu - ia, al - le - lu - ia,

1.-3.
al - le - lu - ia.

4.
lu - ia.

Text: Psalm 150:1-2, 3-4, 5-6; adapt. by Omer Westendorf
Music: Jan M. Vermulst
© 1964, World Library Publications, Inc.

Song at the Sea / Exodus 15   143

Refrain

Let us sing   to the Lord   who is cov-ered in   won-drous glo-ry.

Verses

1. I will sing to the Lord, in glory triumphant;
   horse and rider are thrown to the sea.
   God of strength, of song, of salvation, God of mine, hear these praises.

2. My God is a warrior whose name is "The Lord."
   Pharoah's army is thrown to the sea.
   Your right hand is magnificent in pow'r,
   your right hand has crushed the enemy.

3. In your mercy you led the people you redeemed.
   You brought them to your sacred home.
   There you will plant them on the mountain that is yours.
   The Lord shall reign for ever!

Text: Exodus 15; Niamh O'Kelly-Fischer
Music: Niamh O'Kelly-Fischer
© 1992, GIA Publications, Inc.

144   Canticle of Simeon / Luke 2:29-32

Antiphon

Guard us, O Lord, while we sleep, and keep us in peace.

Text: The Grail
Music: Guy Weitz and A. Gregory Murray, OSB
© 1963, The Grail, GIA Publications, Inc., agent

Psalm Tone

Music: Psalm tone 3-b; acc. by Richard Proulx, © 1975, GIA Publications, Inc.

Gelineau Tone

Omit for 3-line stanza

Nunc dimittis

1. At **last** all-**pow**erful **Mas**ter,
   you give **leave** to your **sèr**vant to go
   in **peace**, according to yóur **prom**ise.

2. For my **eyes** have **sèen** your sal**va**tion
   which **you** have pre**pared** for áll **na**tions,
   the **light** to en**lìgh**ten the **Gen**tiles
   and give **glo**ry to **Is**rael, yóur **peo**ple.

3. Give **praise** to the **Fà**ther Al**might**y,
   to his **Son**, Jesus **Chríst**, the **Lord**,
   to the **Spir**it who **dwèlls** in our **hearts**,
   both **now** and for evér. **Amen**.

Text: Luke 2:29-32; The Grail
Music: Joseph Gelineau
© 1963, The Grail, GIA Publications, Inc., agent

Canticle of Mary / Luke 1:46-55   145

Antiphon

My soul re - joic - es,   my soul re - joic - es in my God.

Text: Luke 1:46; Robert J. Batastini
Music: Robert J. Batastini
© 1972, GIA Publications, Inc.

Psalm Tone

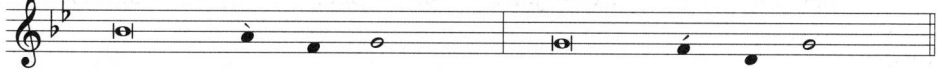

Music: *Lutheran Worship*, © 1982, Concordia Publishing House

Gelineau Tone

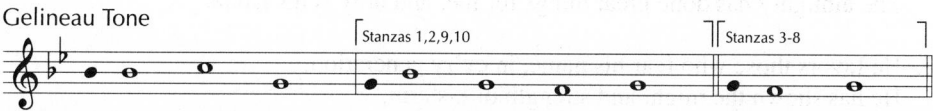

Stanzas 1,2,9,10   Stanzas 3-8

Magnificat anima mea

1. My **soul glori**fies the **Lord,**
   my **spir**it re**joic**es in **Gód,** my **Sav**ior.

2. He **looks** on his **ser**vant
      ìn her **noth**ingness;
   hence**forth** all **ag**es will
      cáll me **blessed.**

3. The Al**mighty** works **mar**vèls for **me.**
   Holỳ **his name!**

4. His **mer**cy is from **àge** to **age,**
   on **thóse** who **fear** him.

5. He **puts** forth his **àrm** in **strength**
   and **scat**ters thé proud**heart**ed.

6. He **casts** the **might**y fròm their **thrones**
   and **rais**és the **low**ly.

7. He **fills** the **star**ving wìth good **things,**
   sends the **rich** áway **empty.**

8. He pro**tects** Isra**è**l his **ser**vant,
   re**mem**beríng his **mer**cy,

9. the **mer**cy **prom**ised tò our **fa**thers,
   for **Abra**ham and his **sóns** for **ever.**

10. Praise the **Father,** the **Son**
      and Hòly **Spir**it,
    both **now** and for **ag**es un**end**íng. **Amen.**

Text: Luke 1:46-55; The Grail
Music: Joseph Gelineau
© 1963 The Grail, GIA Publications, Inc., agent

146 Magnificat / Luke 1:46-55

Refrain

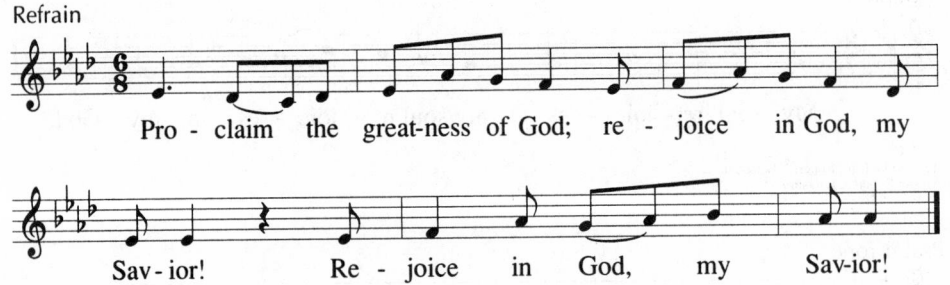

Pro - claim the great-ness of God; re - joice in God, my

Sav - ior! Re - joice in God, my Sav-ior!

Verses

1. For he has favored his lowly one, and all shall call me blessed.
   The almighty has done great things for me, and holy is his name.

2. He favors those who fear his name, in ev'ry generation.
   He has shown the might and strength of his arm,
   and scattered the proud of heart.

3. He has cast the mighty from their thrones, and lifted up the lowly.
   He has filled the hungry with all good gifts, and sent the rich away.

4. He has helped his servant Israel, remembering his mercy.
   He promised his mercy to Abraham and his children for evermore.

Text: Luke 1:46-55; James J. Chepponis
Music: James J. Chepponis
© 1980, GIA Publications, Inc.

Holy Is Your Name / Luke 1:46-55 147

Refrain

And ho - ly is your name through all gen - er -
a - tions! Ev - er - last - ing is your mer-cy to the
peo - ple you have cho-sen, and ho - ly is your name.

Verses

1. My soul is filled with joy as I sing to God my savior:
   you have looked upon your servant, you have visited your people.

2. I am lowly as a child, but I know from this day forward
   that my name will be remembered, for all will call me blessed.

3. I proclaim the pow'r of God, you do marvels for your servants;
   though you scatter the proud hearted, and destroy the might of princes.

4. To the hungry you give food, send the rich away empty.
   In your mercy you are mindful of the people you have chosen.

5. In your love you now fulfill what you promised to your people.
   I will praise you Lord, my savior, everlasting is your mercy.

Text: Luke 1:46-55, David Haas
Music: WILD MOUNTAIN THYME, Irregular; Irish traditional; arr. by David Haas
© 1989, GIA Publications, Inc.

148 Isaiah 12:2-3, 4, 6

Refrain I

With joy you shall draw wa - ter from the springs of end-less life; With joy you shall draw wa - ter from the liv-ing well of God.

Refrain II

Cry out with joy and glad - ness, for the Lord is in your midst, the ho - ly one of Is-ra - el, cry out, cry out with joy.

Verses

1. God indeed is my Savior, I will never be afraid,
   my strength and courage is the Lord, my Savior and my song.

2. Give thanks and praise the name of God, sing out to all the earth
   the wondrous deeds that God has done, our Savior and our song.

3. Shout with joy, O Zion, for dwelling in your midst
   is the Holy One of Israel, your Savior and your song.

Text: Isaiah 12:2-3, 4, 6; Marty Haugen
Music: Marty Haugen; refrain II adapt. by Diana Kodner
© 1988, 1994, GIA Publications, Inc.

Revelation 19:1-7   149

Antiphon

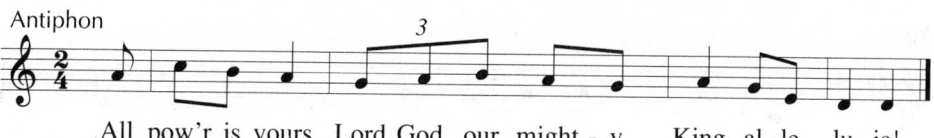

All pow'r is yours, Lord God, our might - y   King, al - le - lu - ia!

Refrain I

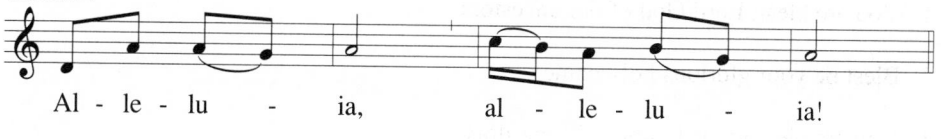

Al - le - lu - ia,   al - le - lu - ia!

Verse   **Refrain II**
Cantor:

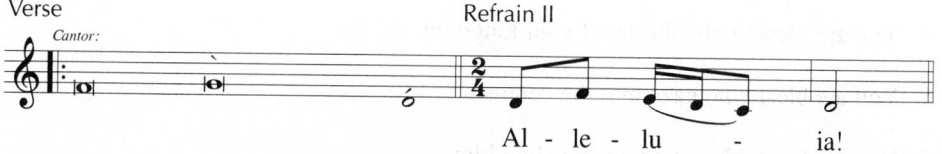

Al - le - lu - ia!

Verse   **Refrain I**
Cantor:

Al - le - lu - ia,   al - le - lu - ia!

Salus, et gloria

1. Salvation, glory and pòwer to our Gód: (Alleluia!)
   his judgements are hònest and trúe. (Alleluia, alleluia!)

2. Sing praise to our God, àll you his sérvants, (Alleluia!)
   all who worship him reverently, greàt and smáll. (Alleluia, alleluia!)

3. The Lord our all-powerful Gòd is Kíng; (Alleluia!)
   let us rejoice, sing pràise, and give him glóry. (Alleluia, alleluia!)

4. The wedding feast of the Làmb has begún, (Alleluia!)
   and his bride is prepàred to wélcome him. (Alleluia, alleluia!)

5. Glory to the Father, and to the Sòn, and to the Holy Spírit, (Alleluia!)
   as it was in the beginning, is now, and will be for èver. Amén. (Alleluia,
   alleluia!)

Text: Revelation 19:1-7; Howard Hughes, SM
Music: Howard Hughes, SM
© 1979, GIA Publications, Inc.

150　Song of the Three Children / Daniel 3:52-56

Refrain

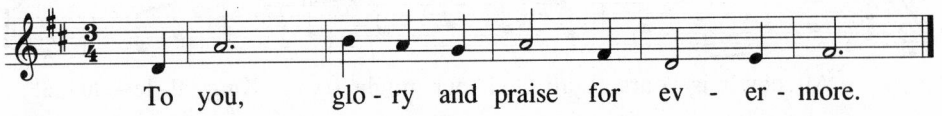

To you,　glo - ry and praise for ev - er - more.

Verses

1. You are blest, Lord God of our ancestors.

2. Blest be your glorious holy name.

3. You are blest in the temple of your glory.

4. You are blest on the throne of your kingdom.

5. You are blest who gaze into the depths.

6. You are blest who sit above the cherubim.

7. You are blest in the firmament of heaven.

Text: Daniel 3:52, 53, 54, 55, 56; © 1963, The Grail, GIA Publications, Inc., agent
Music: Michel Guimont, © 1994, GIA Publications, Inc.

Song of the Three Children / Daniel 3:52-57 151

Cantor:

1.	You	are	blest,	Lord	
2.	Blest		be	your	
3.	You	are	blest	in	the
4.	You	are	blest	on	the
5.	You	are	blest	who	
6.	You	are	blest	who	
7.	You	are	blest	in	the
8.	You	are	blest,	Lord	

God		of	our	fa -	thers.
glo -		ri -	ous	ho - ly	name.
tem -	ple	of	your	glo -	ry
throne		of	your	king -	dom
gaze		in -	to	the	depths.
sit	a -	bove	the	che - ru -	bim.
firm -	a -	ment	of	heav -	en.
God,		in		all	your	works.

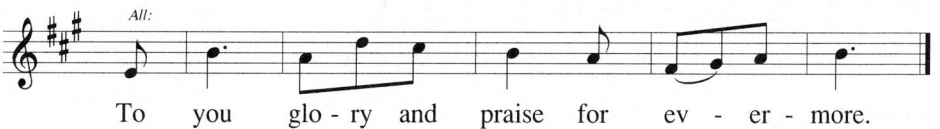

All:

To   you   glo - ry   and   praise   for   ev - er - more.

Text: Daniel 2:52-57; The Grail
Music: Joseph Gelineau

152 Song of the Three Children / Daniel 3:57-88

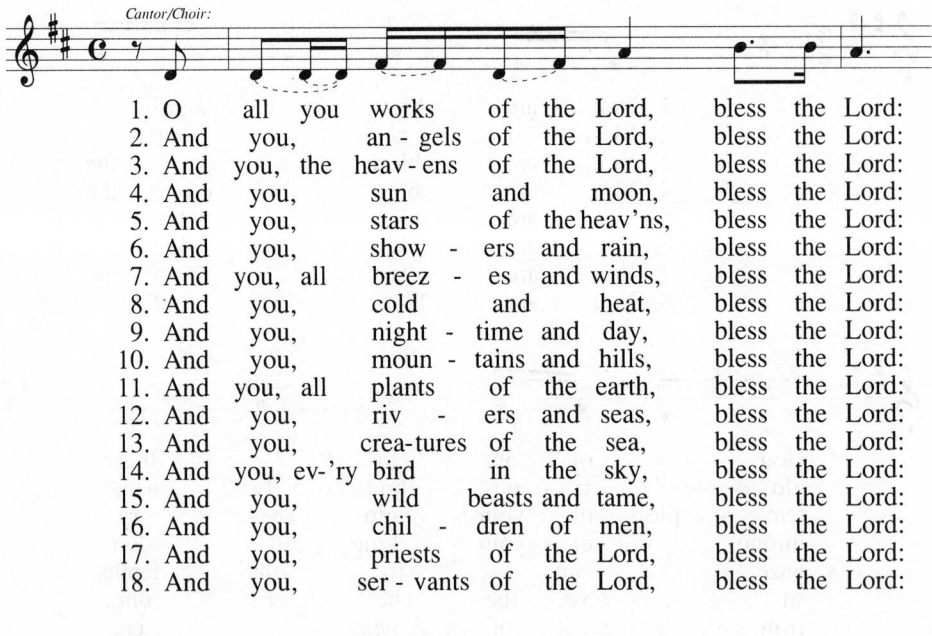

Cantor/Choir:

1. O all you works of the Lord, bless the Lord:
2. And you, an - gels of the Lord, bless the Lord:
3. And you, the heav - ens of the Lord, bless the Lord:
4. And you, sun and moon, bless the Lord:
5. And you, stars of the heav'ns, bless the Lord:
6. And you, show - ers and rain, bless the Lord:
7. And you, all breez - es and winds, bless the Lord:
8. And you, cold and heat, bless the Lord:
9. And you, night - time and day, bless the Lord:
10. And you, moun - tains and hills, bless the Lord:
11. And you, all plants of the earth, bless the Lord:
12. And you, riv - ers and seas, bless the Lord:
13. And you, crea-tures of the sea, bless the Lord:
14. And you, ev-'ry bird in the sky, bless the Lord:
15. And you, wild beasts and tame, bless the Lord:
16. And you, chil - dren of men, bless the Lord:
17. And you, priests of the Lord, bless the Lord:
18. And you, ser - vants of the Lord, bless the Lord:

All:

To him be high-est glo - ry and praise for ev - er.

Text: Daniel 3:57-88; The Grail
Music: A. Gregory Murray, OSB
© 1963, The Grail, GIA Publications, Inc., agent

The Order of Mass

153

Each church gathers on the Lord's Day to listen to the Scriptures, to offer prayers, to give thanks and praise to God while recalling God's gifts in creation and saving deeds in Jesus, and to share in holy communion.

In these rites of word and eucharist, the Church keeps Sunday as the Lord's Day, the day of creation and resurrection, the "eighth day" when the fullness of God's kingdom is anticipated. The Mass or eucharistic celebration of the Christian community has rites of gathering, of word, of eucharist, of dismissal. All those who gather constitute the assembly. One member of this assembly who has been ordained to the presbyterate or episcopate, the priesthood, leads the opening and closing prayers and the eucharistic prayer, and presides over the whole assembly. A member ordained to the diaconate may assist, read the gospel, and preach. Other members of the assembly are chosen and trained for various ministries: These are the readers, servers, ushers, musicians, communion ministers. All of these assist the assembly. It is the assembly itself, all those present, that does the liturgy.

The Order of Mass which follows is familiar to all who regularly join in this assembly. It is learned through repetition. This Order of Mass leaves many decisions to the local community and others are determined by the various seasons of the liturgical year.

INTRODUCTORY RITES

The rites which precede the liturgy of the word assist the assembly to gather as a community. They prepare that community to listen to the Scriptures and to celebrate the eucharist together. The procession and entrance song are ways of expressing the unity and spirit of the assembly.

GREETING
All make the sign of the cross.
> *Priest:* In the name of the Father, and of the Son, and of the Holy Spirit.

> *Assembly:* **Amen.**

After the sign of the cross one of the greetings is given.

| A | *Priest:* | The grace of our Lord Jesus Christ and the love of God and the fellowship of the Holy Spirit be with you all. |
| | *Assembly:* | **And also with you.** |

| B | *Priest:* | The grace and peace of God our Father and the Lord Jesus Christ be with you. |
| | *Assembly:* | **Blessed be God, the Father of our Lord Jesus Christ.** *or:* **And also with you.** |

| C | *Priest:* | The Lord be with you. (*Bishop:* Peace be with you.) |
| | *Assembly:* | **And also with you.** |

154 BLESSING AND SPRINKLING OF HOLY WATER

On Sundays, especially during the season of Easter, instead of the penitential rite below, the blessing and sprinkling of holy water may be done. The following or another appropriate song is sung as the water is sprinkled.

Refrain

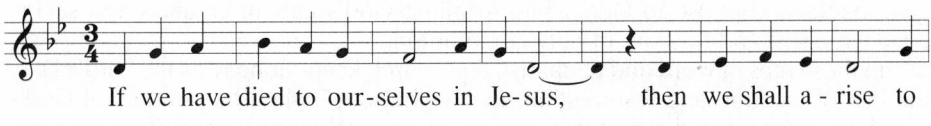

If we have died to our-selves in Je-sus, then we shall a - rise to

new life in him. Al - le - lu - ia, al - le - lu - ia!

Verses

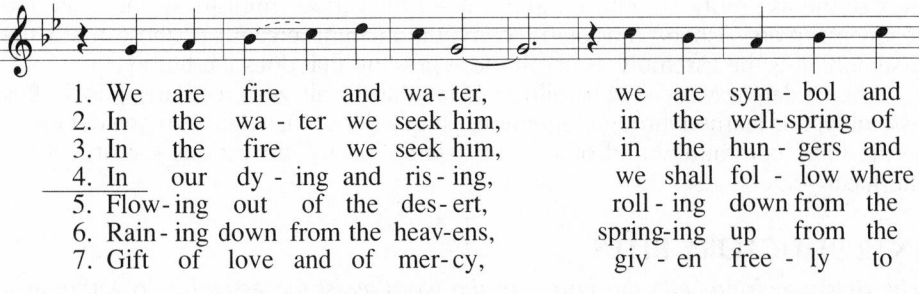

1.	We	are	fire	and	wa - ter,		we	are	sym - bol	and
2.	In	the	wa - ter	we	seek him,		in	the	well-spring	of
3.	In	the	fire	we	seek him,		in	the	hun - gers	and
4.	In	our	dy - ing	and	ris - ing,		we	shall	fol - low	where
5.	Flow-ing	out	of	the	des - ert,		roll - ing	down	from	the
6.	Rain - ing	down	from	the	heav-ens,		spring-ing	up	from	the
7.	Gift	of	love	and	of	mer-cy,	giv - en	free - ly	to

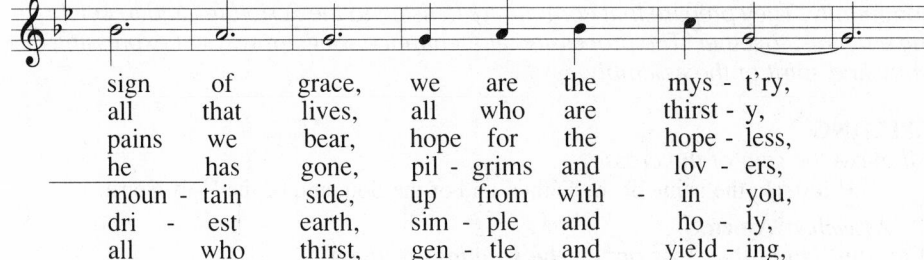

sign	of	grace,	we	are	the	mys - t'ry,
all	that	lives,	all	who	are	thirst - y,
pains	we	bear,	hope	for	the	hope - less,
he	has	gone,	pil - grims	and	lov - ers,
moun - tain	side,	up	from	with - in	you,
dri - est	earth,	sim - ple	and	ho - ly,
all	who	thirst,	gen - tle	and	yield - ing,

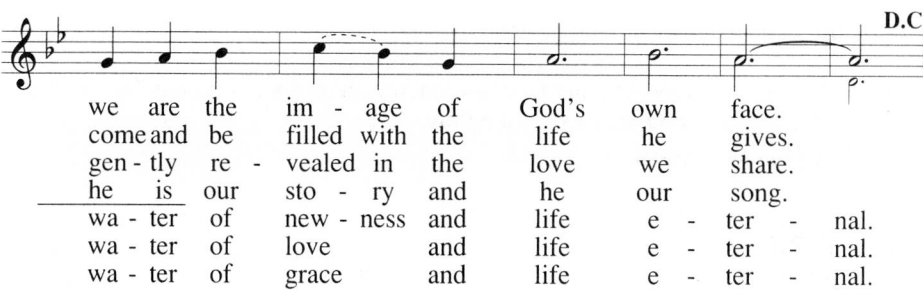

we	are	the	im - age	of	God's	own	face.
come and	be		filled with	the	life	he	gives.
gen - tly	re -		vealed in	the	love	we	share.
he	is	our	sto - ry	and	he	our	song.
wa - ter	of		new - ness	and	life	e - ter -	nal.
wa - ter	of		love	and	life	e - ter -	nal.
wa - ter	of		grace	and	life	e - ter -	nal.

Text: *Mass of Creation*, Marty Haugen
Music: *Mass of Creation*, Marty Haugen
© 1984, GIA Publications, Inc.

PENITENTIAL RITE 155

The priest invites all to be mindful of their sins and of the great mercy of God. After a time of silence, one of the following forms is used.

| A | *Assembly:* | **I confess to almighty God,**
and to you, my brothers and sisters,
that I have sinned through my own fault
in my thoughts and in my words,
in what I have done,
and in what I have failed to do;
and I ask blessed Mary, ever virgin,
all the angels and saints,
and you, my brothers and sisters,
to pray for me to the Lord our God. |

B	*Priest:*	Lord, we have sinned against you: Lord, have mercy.
	Assembly:	**Lord, have mercy.**
	Priest:	Lord, show us your mercy and love.
	Assembly:	**And grant us your salvation.**

| C | *The priest or another minister makes a series of invocations according to the following pattern.* |

	Priest:	(Invocation) Lord, have mercy.
	Assembly:	**Lord, have mercy.**
	Priest:	(Invocation) Christ, have mercy.
	Assembly:	**Christ, have mercy.**
	Priest:	(Invocation) Lord, have mercy.
	Assembly:	**Lord, have mercy.**

The penitential rite always concludes:

> *Priest:* May almighty God have mercy on us, forgive us our sins, and
> bring us to everlasting life.
>
> *Assembly:* **Amen.**

156 KYRIE
Unless form C of the penitential rite has been used, the Kyrie follows.

Refrain

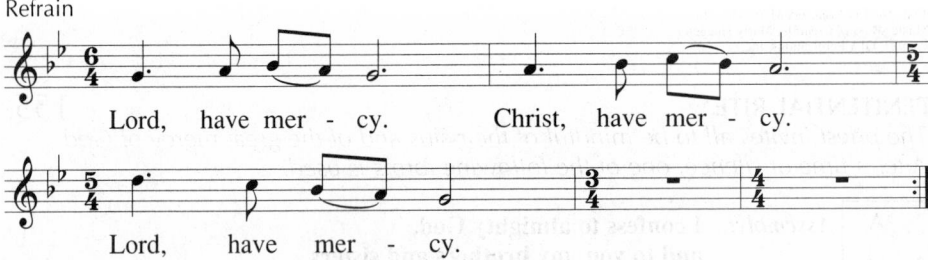

Music: *Mass of Creation,* Marty Haugen, © 1984, GIA Publications, Inc.

157 GLORIA
The Gloria is omitted during Advent, Lent, and most weekdays.

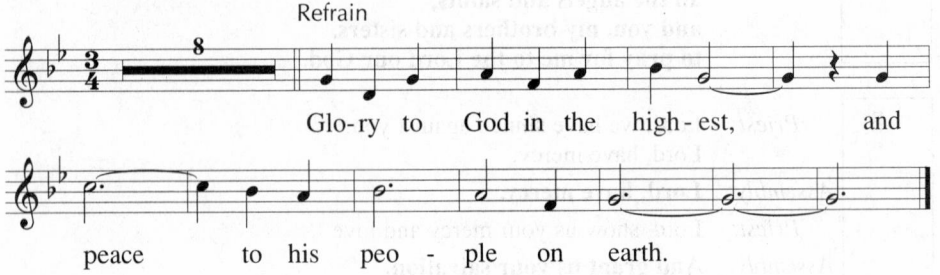

Verses

1. Lord God, heavenly King, almighty God and Father,
   we worship you, we give you thanks,
   we praise you for your glory.

2. Lord Jesus Christ, only Son of the Father,
   Lord God, Lamb of God,
   you take away the sin of the world: have mercy on us;
   you are seated at the right hand of the Father:
   receive our prayer.

3. For you alone are the Holy One,
   you alone are the Lord,
   you alone are the Most High, Jesus Christ,
   with the Holy Spirit,
   in the glory of God, the Father. Amen! Amen!

Music: *Mass of Creation*, Marty Haugen, © 1984, GIA Publications, Inc.

OPENING PRAYER   158
After the invitation from the priest, all pray for a while. The introductory rites con-
clude with the proper opening prayer and the Amen of the assembly.

LITURGY OF THE WORD   159
When the Church assembles, the book containing the Scriptures (Lectionary) is
opened and all listen as the readers and deacon (or priest) read from the places
assigned. The first reading is normally from the Hebrew Scriptures (Old Testament),
the second from the letters of the New Testament, and the third from the Book of
Gospels. Over a three-year cycle, the Church reads through the letters and gospels
and a portion of the Hebrew Scriptures. During the Sundays of Ordinary Time, the
letters and gospels are read in order, each Sunday continuing near the place where
the previous Sunday's readings ended. During Advent/Christmas and Lent/Easter,
the readings are those which are traditional and appropriate to these seasons.

The Church listens to and—through the weeks and years—is shaped by the
Scriptures. Those who have gathered for the Sunday liturgy are to give their full
attention to the words of the reader. A time of silence and reflection follows each of
the two readings. After the first reading, this reflection continues in the singing of
the psalm. A homily, bringing together the Scriptures and the life of the community, follows the gospel. The liturgy of the word concludes with the creed, the dismissal of the catechumens and the prayers of intercession. In the latter, the assembly continues its constant work of recalling and praying for the universal Church
and all those in need.

This reading and hearing of the word—simple things that they are—are the
foundation of the liturgical celebration. The public reading of the Scriptures and the
rituals which surround this—silence and psalm and acclamation, posture and gesture, preaching and litany of intercession—gather the Church generation after generation. They gather and sustain and gradually make of us the image of Christ.

READING I
In conclusion:

> *Reader:*   The word of the Lord.
> *Assembly:* **Thanks be to God.**

After a period of silence, the responsorial psalm is sung.

READING II

In conclusion:

> *Reader:*   The word of the Lord.
>
> *Assembly:*   **Thanks be to God.**

A time of silence follows the reading.

160 GOSPEL

Before the gospel, an acclamation is sung.

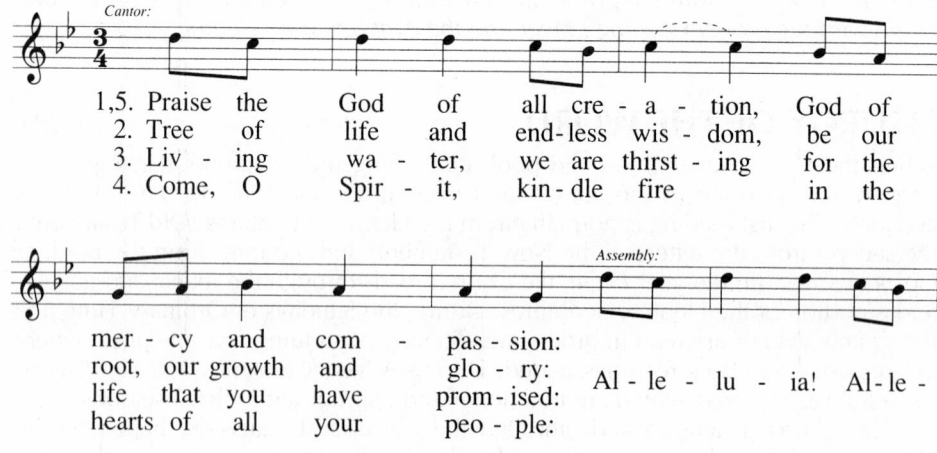

1,5. Praise the God of all cre - a - tion, God of
2. Tree of life and end-less wis - dom, be our
3. Liv - ing wa - ter, we are thirst - ing for the
4. Come, O Spir - it, kin-dle fire in the

mer - cy and com - pas - sion:
root, our growth and glo - ry:
life that you have prom-ised:
hearts of all your peo - ple:

Al - le - lu - ia! Al-le -

lu - ia! Praise the Word of truth and life!

Text: *Mass of Creation,* Marty Haugen
Music: *Mass of Creation,* Marty Haugen
© 1984, GIA Publications, Inc.

During Lent one of the following acclamations replaces the alleluia.

A

Praise to you, Lord   Je - sus Christ,   king of end - less   glo-ry!

Music: *Mass of Creation.* Marty Haugen, © 1984, GIA Publications, Inc.

Or:

B	**Praise and honor to you, Lord Jesus Christ!**
C	**Glory and praise to you, Lord Jesus Christ!**
D	**Glory to you, Word of God, Lord Jesus Christ!**

Deacon (or priest): The Lord be with you.

Assembly: **And also with you.**

Deacon: A reading from the holy gospel according to N.

Assembly: **Glory to you, Lord.**

After the reading:

Deacon: The gospel of the Lord.

Assembly: **Praise to you, Lord Jesus Christ.**

HOMILY

PROFESSION OF FAITH 161

We believe in one God,
the Father, the Almighty,
maker of heaven and earth,
of all that is seen and unseen.

We believe in one Lord, Jesus Christ,
the only Son of God,
eternally begotten of the Father,
God from God, Light from Light,
true God from true God,
begotten, not made, one in Being with the Father.
Through him all things were made.
For us men and for our salvation he came down from heaven:

All bow at the following words up to: and became man.

by the power of the Holy Spirit
he was born of the Virgin Mary, and became man.
For our sake he was crucified under Pontius Pilate;
he suffered, died, and was buried.
On the third day he rose again
in fulfillment of the Scriptures;
he ascended into heaven
and is seated at the right hand of the Father.
He will come again in glory to judge the living and the dead,
and his kingdom will have no end.

We believe in the Holy Spirit, the Lord, the giver of life,
who proceeds from the Father and the Son.
With the Father and the Son he is worshiped and glorified.
He has spoken through the Prophets.
We believe in one holy catholic and apostolic Church.
We acknowledge one baptism for the forgiveness of sins.
We look for the resurrection of the dead,
and the life of the world to come. Amen.

162 *At Masses with children, the Apostles' Creed may be used:*

We believe in God, the Father almighty,
    creator of heaven and earth.

We believe in Jesus Christ, his only Son, our Lord.
    He was conceived by the power of the Holy Spirit
        and born of the Virgin Mary.
    He suffered under Pontius Pilate,
        was crucified, died, and was buried.
    He descended to the dead.
    On the third day he arose again.
    He ascended into heaven,
        and is seated at the right hand of the Father.
    He will come again to judge the living and the dead.

We believe in the Holy Spirit,
    the holy catholic Church,
    the communion of saints,
    the forgiveness of sins,
    the resurrection of the body,
    and the life everlasting. Amen.

163 GENERAL INTERCESSIONS
The people respond to each petition as follows, or according to local practice.

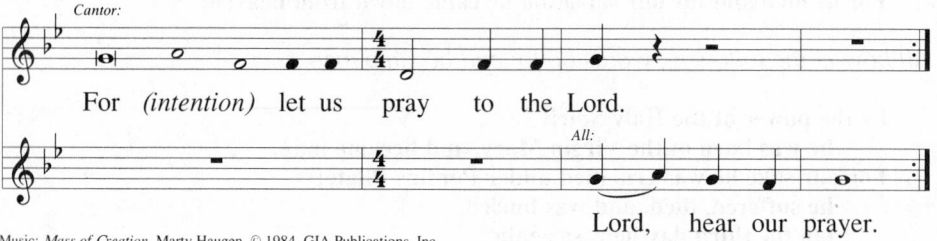

Cantor: For *(intention)* let us pray to the Lord.
All: Lord, hear our prayer.

Music: *Mass of Creation*, Marty Haugen, © 1984, GIA Publications, Inc.

LITURGY OF THE EUCHARIST 164

To celebrate the eucharist means to give God thanks and praise. When the table has been prepared with the bread and wine, the assembly joins the priest in remembering the gracious gifts of God in creation and God's saving deeds. The center of this is the paschal mystery, the death of our Lord Jesus Christ which destroyed the power of death and his rising which brings us life. That mystery into which we were baptized we proclaim each Sunday at the eucharist. It is the very shape of Christian life. We find this in the simple bread and wine which stir our remembering and draw forth our prayer of thanksgiving. "Fruit of the earth and work of human hands," the bread and wine become our holy communion in the body and blood of the Lord. We eat and drink and so proclaim that we belong to one another and to the Lord.

The members of the assembly quietly prepare themselves even as the table is prepared. The priest then invites all to lift up their hearts and join in the eucharistic prayer. All do this by giving their full attention and by singing the acclamations from the "Holy, holy" to the great "Amen." Then the assembly joins in the Lord's Prayer, the sign of peace and the "Lamb of God" litany which accompanies the breaking of bread. Ministers of communion assist the assembly to share the bread and wine. A time of silence and prayer concludes the liturgy of the eucharist.

PREPARATION OF THE ALTAR AND THE GIFTS
Bread and wine are brought to the table and the deacon or priest prepares these gifts. If there is no music, the prayers may be said aloud, and all may respond: "Blessed be God for ever." The priest then invites all to pray.

> *Assembly:* **May the Lord accept the sacrifice at your hands**
> **for the praise and glory of his name,**
> **for our good, and the good of all his Church.**

The priest says the prayer over the gifts and all respond: Amen.

EUCHARISTIC PRAYER 165
The central prayer of the Mass begins with this greeting and invitation between priest and assembly.

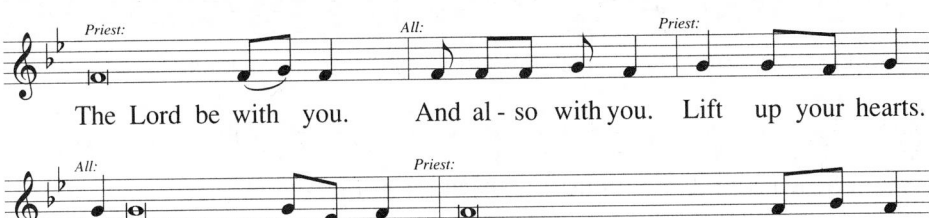

Music: *Mass of Creation*, Marty Haugen, © 1984, GIA Publications, Inc.

166 *The Sanctus acclamation is sung to conclude the introduction to the eucharistic prayer.*

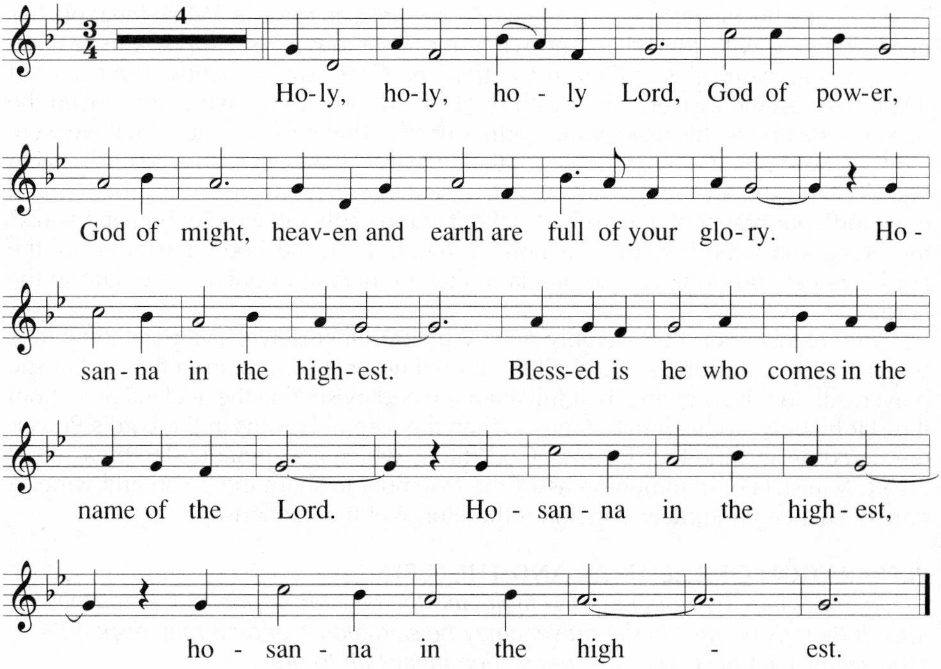

Ho-ly, ho-ly, ho - ly Lord, God of pow-er,

God of might, heav-en and earth are full of your glo-ry. Ho -

san - na in the high- est. Bless-ed is he who comes in the

name of the Lord. Ho - san - na in the high - est,

ho - san - na in the high - est.

Music: *Mass of Creation,* Marty Haugen, © 1984, GIA Publications, Inc.

167 *One of the following acclamations follows the priest's invitation: "Let us proclaim the mystery of faith."*

A

Priest:

Let us pro-claim the mys - ter - y of faith:

All:

Christ has died, Christ is ris-en, Christ will come a - gain.

Christ has died, Christ is ris-en, Christ will come a - gain!

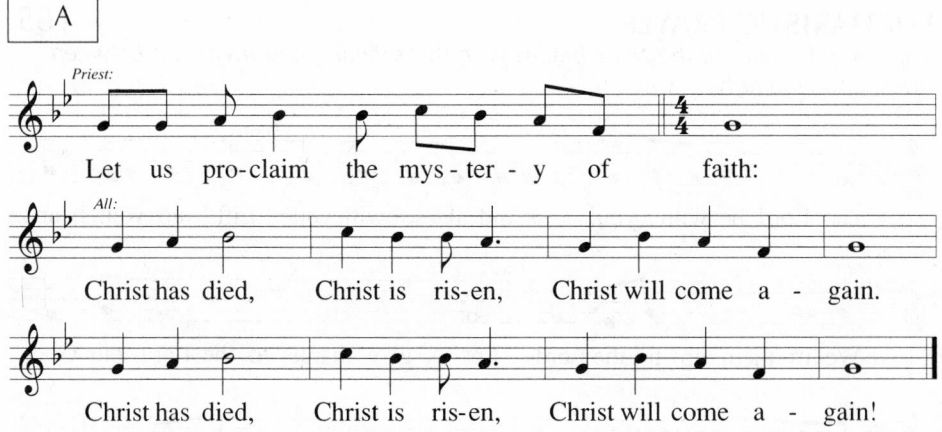

Music: *Mass of Creation,* Marty Haugen, © 1984, GIA Publications, Inc.

Priest:

Let us pro-claim the mys-ter-y of faith:

Cantor:

Dy-ing you de-

Cantor:

stroyed our death, ris-ing you re-

All:

Dy-ing you de-stroyed our death,

stored our life. Lord Je-sus, come in

ris-ing you re-stored our life. Lord

glo-ry.

Je-sus, come in glo-ry.

Music: *Mass of Creation*, Marty Haugen, ©1990, GIA Publications, Inc.

C

Priest:
Let us pro-claim the mys-ter-y of faith:

All:
When we eat this bread, when we drink this cup, we pro-claim your death, Lord Je-sus, un-til you come in glo-ry.

Music: *Mass of Creation,* Marty Haugen, © 1993, GIA Publications, Inc.

D

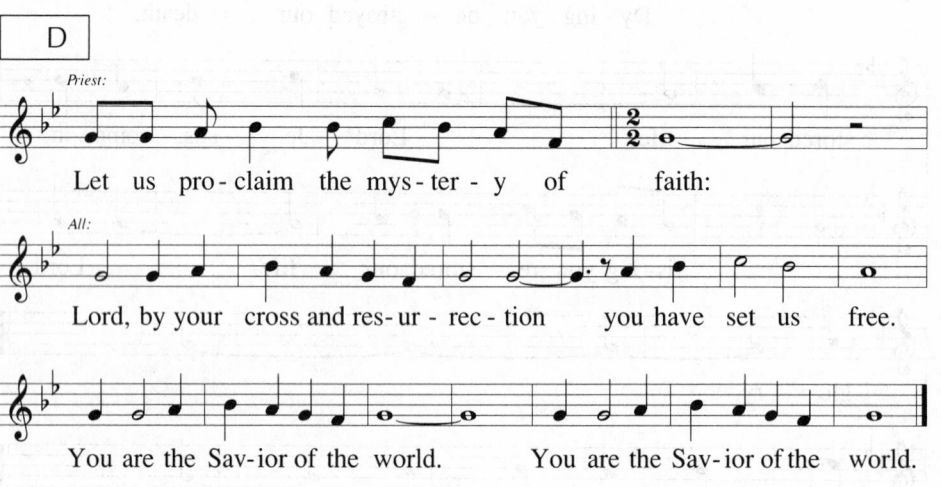

Priest:
Let us pro-claim the mys-ter-y of faith:

All:
Lord, by your cross and res-ur-rec-tion you have set us free.

You are the Sav-ior of the world. You are the Sav-ior of the world.

Music: *Mass of Creation,* Marty Haugen, © 1993, GIA Publications, Inc.

The eucharistic prayer concludes: 168

Priest: Through him, with him, in him, in the unity of the Holy Spirit,
          all glory and honor is yours, almighty Father, for ever and
          ever.

A - men,   a - men,   a -   men!

A - men,   a - men,   a -   men!

Music: *Mass of Creation*, Marty Haugen. © 1984, GIA Publications, Inc.

169 COMMUNION RITE

The priest invites all to join in the Lord's Prayer.

Our Fa - ther, who art in heav-en,

hal - low-ed be thy name; thy king-dom come; thy

will be done on earth as it is in heav - en.

Give us this day our dai-ly bread; and for - give us our tres-pass-es

as we for-give those who tres - pass a - gainst us; and

lead us not in - to temp - ta - tion, but de -

liv - er us from e - vil.

Priest: Deliver us, Lord...
for the coming our Savior, Jesus Christ.

All:
For the king-dom, the pow - er, and the glo - ry are yours,

now and for ev - er - more. A - men.

Following the prayer "Lord, Jesus Christ," the priest invites all to exchange **170**
the sign of peace.

> *Priest:* The peace of the Lord be with you always.
> *Assembly:* **And also with you.**

All exchange a sign of peace. **171**

Then the bread is solemnly broken and the bread and wine are prepared for holy communion. The litany "Lamb of God" is sung during the breaking of the bread.

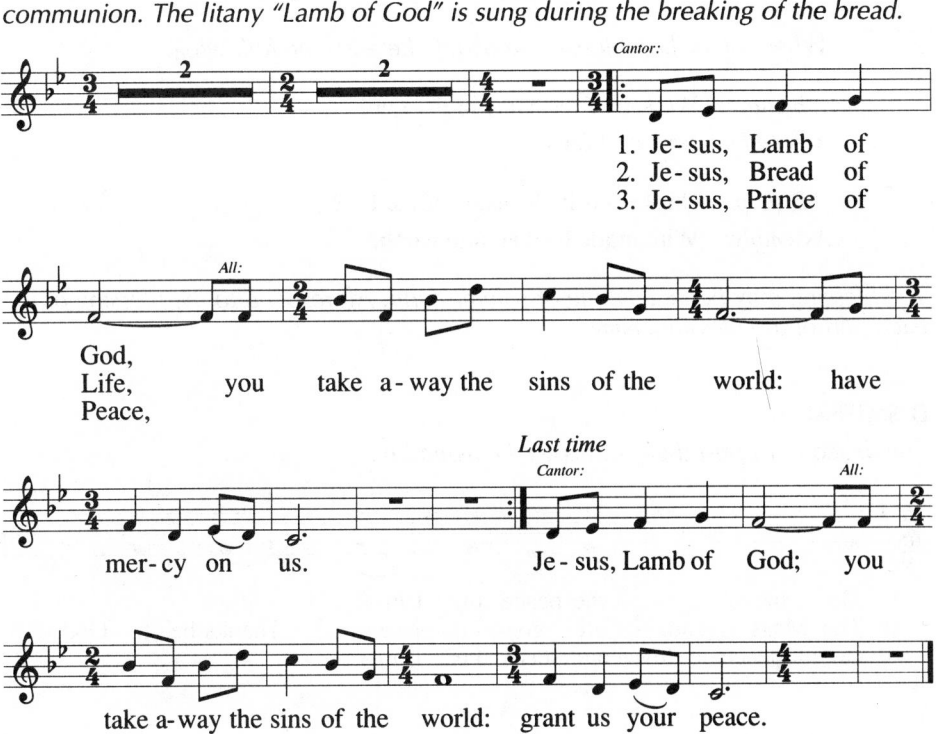

1. Je-sus, Lamb of
2. Je-sus, Bread of
3. Je-sus, Prince of

God,
Life, you take a-way the sins of the world: have
Peace,

mer-cy on us. Je-sus, Lamb of God; you

take a-way the sins of the world: grant us your peace.

Music: *Mass of Creation*, Marty Haugen, © 1984, GIA Publications, Inc.

The priest then invites all to share in holy communion. **172**

> *Priest:* This is the Lamb of God...his supper.
> *Assembly:* **Lord, I am not worthy to receive you, but only say the word and I shall be healed.**
> *Minister of communion:* The body (blood) of Christ.
> *Communicant:* **Amen.**

A song or psalm is ordinarily sung during communion. After communion, a time of silence is observed or a song of thanksgiving is sung. The rite concludes with the prayer after communion to which all respond: **Amen.**

173 CONCLUDING RITE

The liturgy of word and eucharist ends very simply. There may be announcements of events and concerns for the community, then the priest gives a blessing and the assembly is dismissed.

GREETING AND BLESSING

> *Priest:* The Lord be with you.
>
> *Assembly:* **And also with you.**

Optional

When the bishop blesses the people he adds the following:

> *Bishop:* Blessed be the name of the Lord.
>
> *Assembly:* **Now and for ever.**
>
> *Bishop:* Our help is in the name of the Lord.
>
> *Assembly:* **Who made heaven and earth.**

The blessing may be in a simple or solemn form. All respond to the blessing or to each part of the blessing: **Amen.**

DISMISSAL

The deacon or priest then dismisses the assembly:

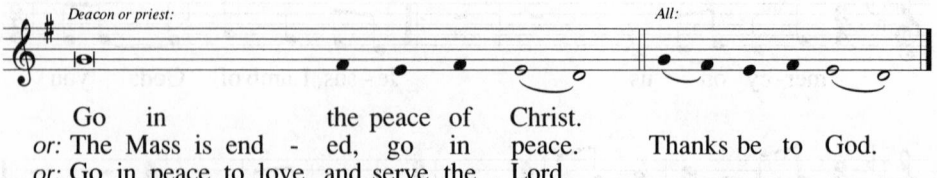

Go in the peace of Christ.
or: The Mass is end - ed, go in peace. Thanks be to God.
or: Go in peace to love and serve the Lord.

EASTER DISMISSAL

The deacon or priest then dismisses the assembly:

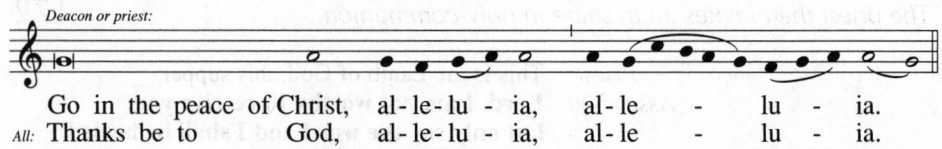

Go in the peace of Christ, al-le-lu - ia, al-le - lu - ia.
All: Thanks be to God, al-le-lu - ia, al-le - lu - ia.

Composite Setting

Cleanse us, O Lord, from all our sins; wash us, and we shall be clean, clean as new snow. snow. I will pour clean wa - ter o - ver you and wash a - way all your sins. snow. A new heart will I give you, says the Lord.

Music: Joseph Roff, © 1985, GIA Publications, Inc.

175   KYRIE ELEISON

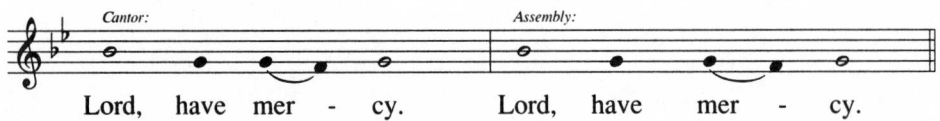

Lord, have mer - cy.   Lord, have mer - cy.

Christ, have mer - cy.   Christ, have mer - cy.

Lord, have mer - cy.   Lord, have mer - cy.

Music: Traditional chant; acc. by Richard Proulx, © 1971, GIA Publications, Inc.

Or:

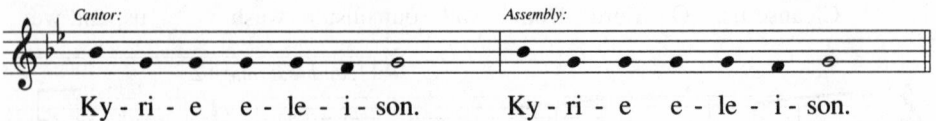

Ky - ri - e e - le - i - son.   Ky - ri - e e - le - i - son.

Chri - ste e - le - i - son.   Chri - ste e - le - i - son.

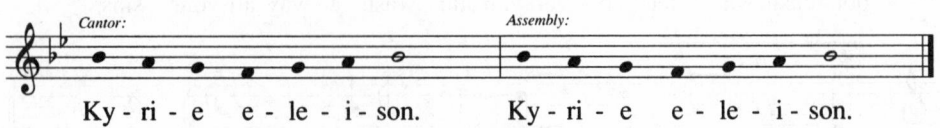

Ky - ri - e e - le - i - son.   Ky - ri - e e - le - i - son.

Music: Traditional chant; acc. by Richard Proulx, © 1971, GIA Publications, Inc.

GLORIA

Glo - ry to God in the high - est, and peace to his peo - ple on earth. Lord God, heav - en - ly King, al - might - y God and Fa - ther, we wor - ship you, we give you thanks, we praise you for your glo - ry.

Choir (Congr. ad lib):

Lord Je - sus Christ, on - ly Son of the Fa - ther, Lord God, Lamb of God, you take a - way the sin of the world: have mer - cy on us; you are seat - ed at the right hand of the Fa - ther: re - ceive our prayer.

For you a - lone are the Ho - ly One, you a - lone are the
Lord, you a - lone are the Most High,
Je - sus Christ, with the Ho - ly Spir - it, in the glo - ry of
God the Fa - ther. A - men.

Music: *A New Mass for Congregations,* Carroll T. Andrews, © 1970, GIA Publications, Inc.

177 GOSPEL ACCLAMATION

Cantor, then all:

Al - le - lu - ia, al - le - lu - ia, al - le - lu - ia.

Music: Chant Mode VI; acc. by Richard Proulx, © 1985, GIA Publications, Inc.

Lenten Acclamation

Cantor, then all:

Praise to you, Lord Je - sus Christ, king of end - less glo - ry!

Music: Frank Schoen, © 1971, GIA Publications, Inc.

GENERAL INTERCESSIONS

178

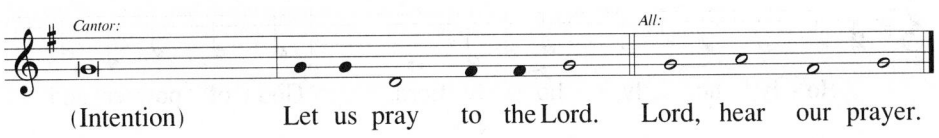

(Intention)   Let us pray   to the Lord.   Lord, hear   our prayer.

Music: Byzantine chant

PREFACE DIALOG

179

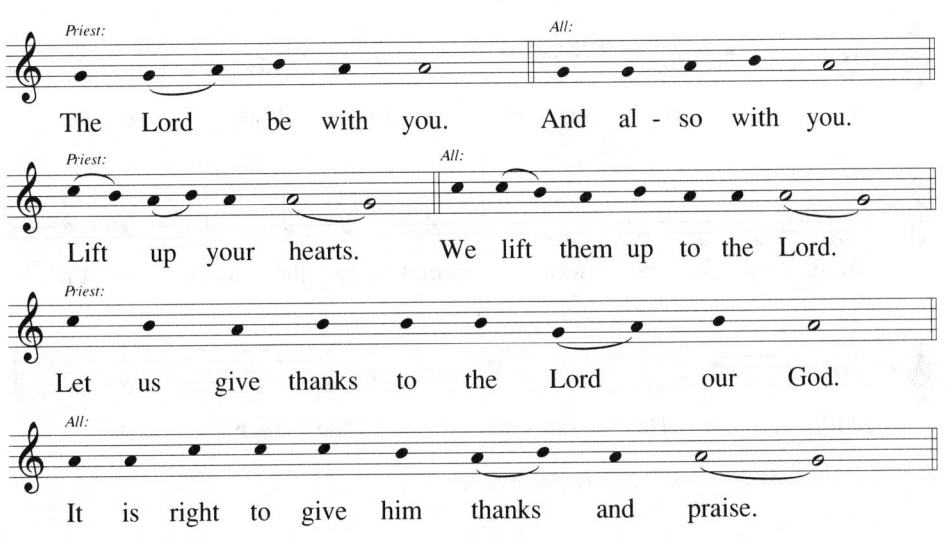

The   Lord   be   with   you.   And   al - so   with   you.

Lift   up   your   hearts.   We   lift   them   up   to   the   Lord.

Let   us   give   thanks   to   the   Lord   our   God.

It   is   right   to   give   him   thanks   and   praise.

Music: Sacramentary, 1974

180 SANCTUS

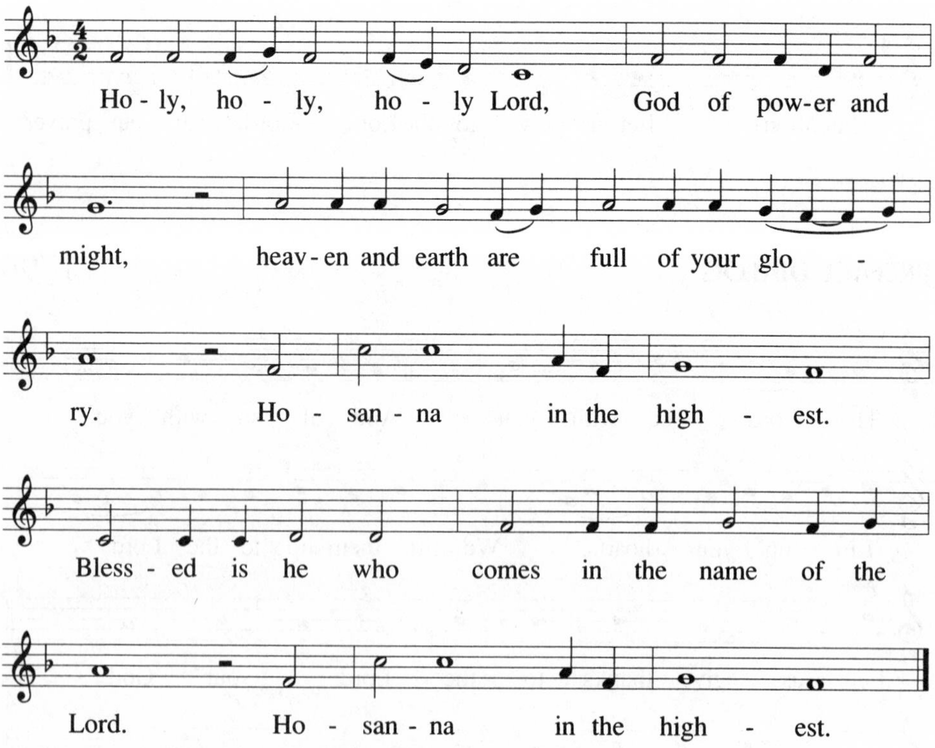

Ho - ly, ho - ly, ho - ly Lord, God of pow-er and might, heav - en and earth are full of your glo - ry. Ho - san - na in the high - est. Bless - ed is he who comes in the name of the Lord. Ho - san - na in the high - est.

Music: *People's Mass*, Jan Martin Vermulst; © 1970, World Library Publications, Inc.

181 MEMORIAL ACCLAMATION

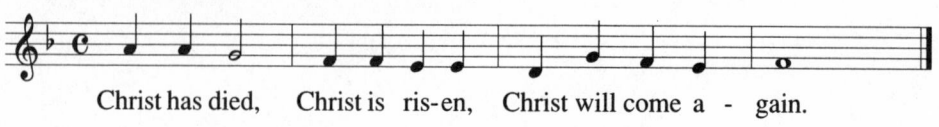

Christ has died, Christ is ris-en, Christ will come a - gain.

Music: *Danish Amen Mass*, Charles George Frischmann and David Kraehenbuehl; © 1970, J. S. Paluch Company, Inc.

182 AMEN

A - men, a - men, a - men.

Music: Danish Amen

COMMUNION RITE 183

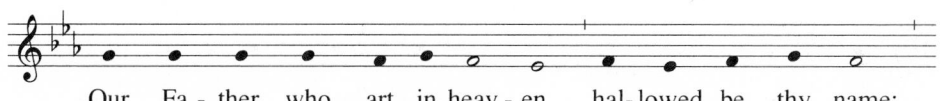

Our Fa - ther, who art in heav - en, hal - lowed be thy name;

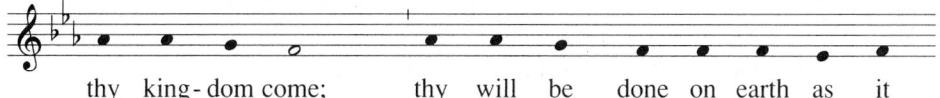

thy king - dom come; thy will be done on earth as it

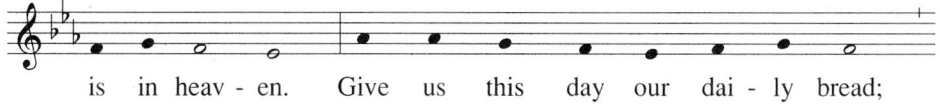

is in heav - en. Give us this day our dai - ly bread;

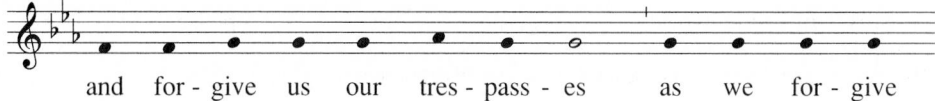

and for - give us our tres - pass - es as we for - give

those who tres - pass a - gainst us; and lead us not

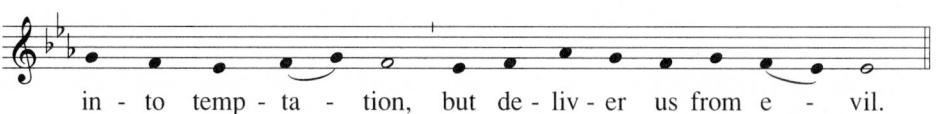

in - to temp - ta - tion, but de - liv - er us from e - vil.

Presider: Deliver us, Lord...
for the coming of our Savior, Jesus Christ.

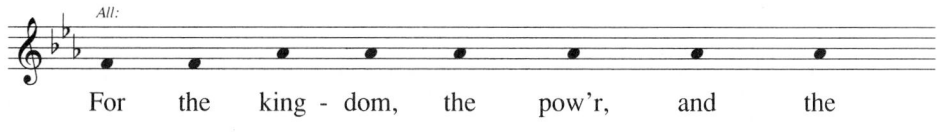

For the king - dom, the pow'r, and the

glo - ry are yours, now and for ev - er.

Music: Traditional chant, adapt. by Robert Snow, 1964; acc. by Robert J. Batastini. © 1975, 1993, GIA Publications, Inc.

184 AGNUS DEI

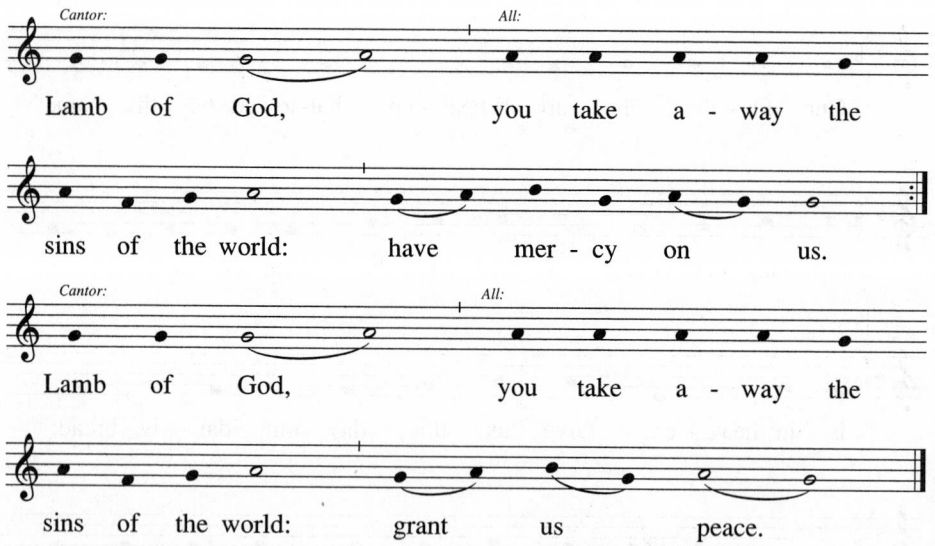

Lamb of God, you take a - way the sins of the world: have mer - cy on us.

Lamb of God, you take a - way the sins of the world: grant us peace.

Music: Agnus Dei XVIII, Vatican Edition; acc. by Robert J. Batastini, © 1993, GIA Publications, Inc.

Setting One

KYRIE ELEISON 185

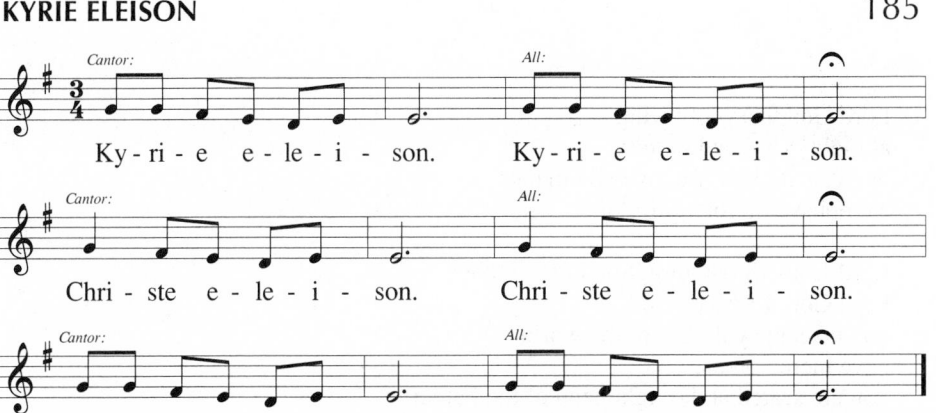

Ky - ri - e e - le - i - son. Ky - ri - e e - le - i - son.

Chri - ste e - le - i - son. Chri - ste e - le - i - son.

Ky - ri - e e - le - i - son. Ky - ri - e e - le - i - son.

186 GLORIA

Refrain

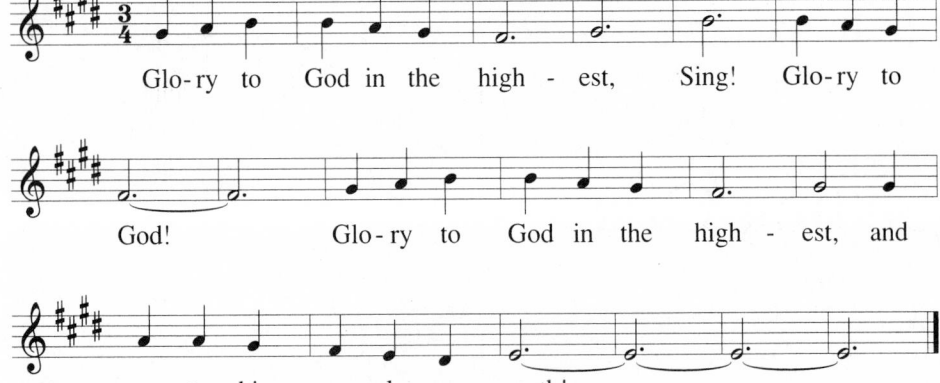

Glo-ry to God in the high - est, Sing! Glo-ry to

God! Glo-ry to God in the high - est, and

peace to his peo-ple on earth!

Verses

1. Lord God, heavenly King,
   almighty God and Father,
   we worship you, we give you thanks,
   we praise you for your glory!

2. Lord Jesus Christ, only Son of the Father,
   Lord God, Lamb of God,
   you take away the sin of the world:
   have mercy on us;
   you are seated at the right hand of the Father:
   receive our prayer!

3. For you alone are the Holy One,
   you alone are the Lord,
   the Most High, Jesus Christ,
   with the Holy Spirit,
   in the glory of God the Father!

Music: *Mass of Light*, David Haas, © 1988, GIA Publications, Inc.

187 ALLELUIA

Cantor or choir, then all:

Al-le-lu-ia! Al-le-lu-ia! Al - le-lu - ia!

Music: *Mass of Light*, David Haas, © 1988, GIA Publications, Inc.

GOSPEL ACCLAMATION 188

Cantor or choir, then all:

Glo-ry to you, O Word of God, Lord Je - sus Christ!

Music: *Mass of Light*, David Haas. © 1988, GIA Publications, Inc.

PREFACE DIALOG 189

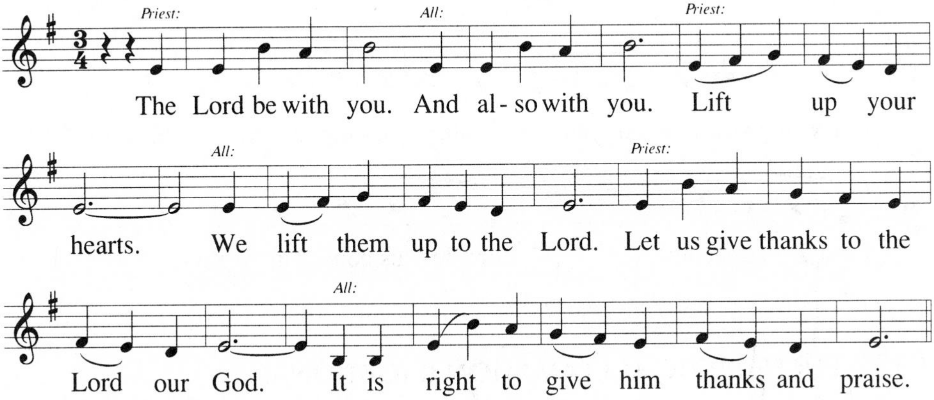

Priest: The Lord be with you. *All:* And al-so with you. *Priest:* Lift up your

hearts. *All:* We lift them up to the Lord. *Priest:* Let us give thanks to the

Lord our God. *All:* It is right to give him thanks and praise.

Music: *Mass of Light*, David Haas. © 1988, GIA Publications, Inc.

SANCTUS 190

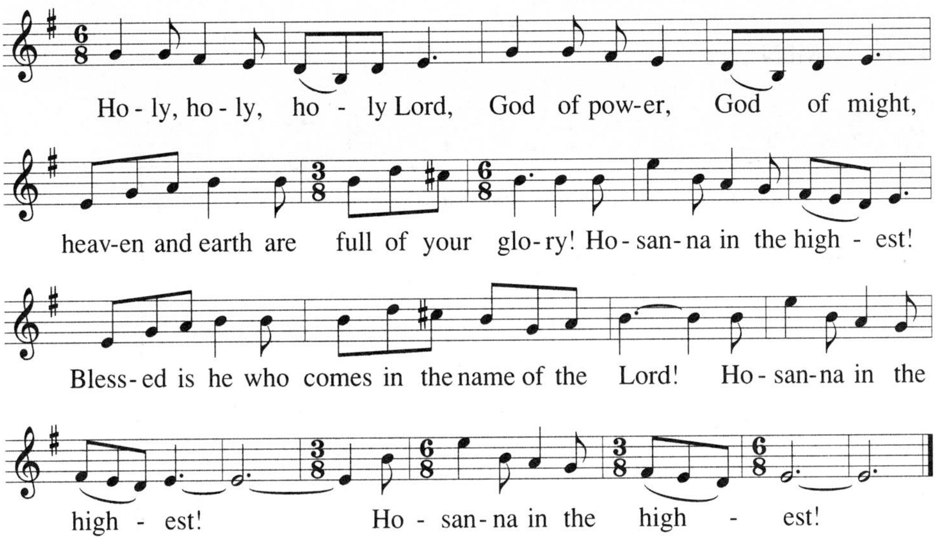

Ho - ly, ho - ly, ho - ly Lord, God of pow-er, God of might,

heav-en and earth are full of your glo-ry! Ho - san - na in the high - est!

Bless-ed is he who comes in the name of the Lord! Ho - san - na in the

high - est! Ho - san - na in the high - est!

Music: *Mass of Light*, David Haas. © 1988, GIA Publications, Inc.

191 EUCHARISTIC ACCLAMATION I (OPTIONAL)*

Ho - san - na in the high - est!

Music: *Mass of Light*, David Haas, © 1988, GIA Publications, Inc.

As in the Eucharistic Prayers for Masses with Children.

192 MEMORIAL ACCLAMATION

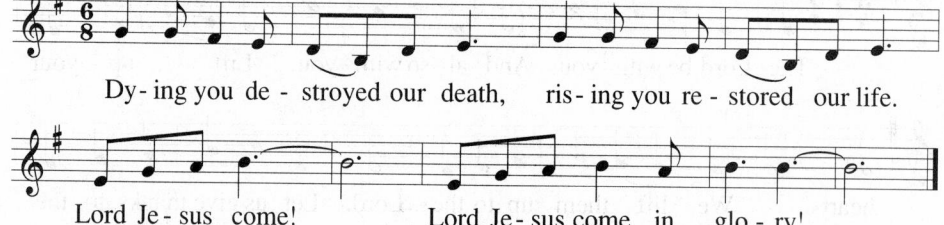

Dy-ing you de - stroyed our death, ris-ing you re - stored our life.

Lord Je - sus come! Lord Je - sus come in glo - ry!

Music: *Mass of Light*, David Haas, © 1988, GIA Publications, Inc.

193 EUCHARISTIC ACCLAMATION II (OPTIONAL)

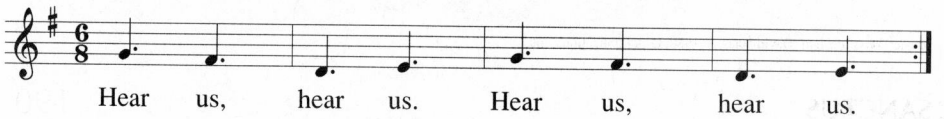

Hear us, hear us. Hear us, hear us.

Music: *Mass of Light*, David Haas, © 1988, GIA Publications, Inc.

194 AMEN

A - men, a - men! A - men, a - men!

Music: *Mass of Light*, David Haas, © 1988, GIA Publications, Inc.

AGNUS DEI

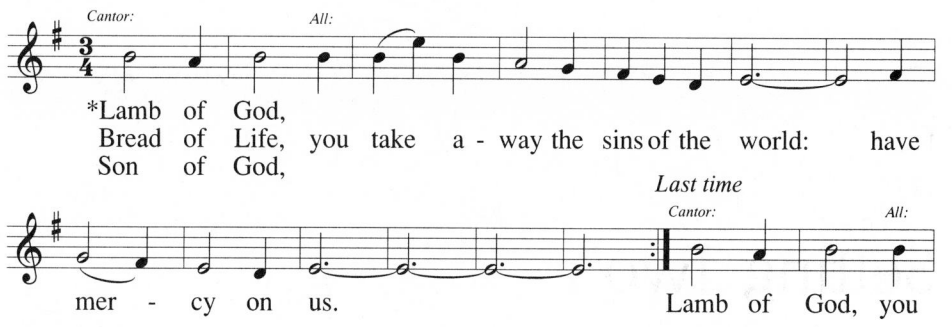

*Lamb of God,
Bread of Life, you take a - way the sins of the world: have
Son of God,

mer - cy on us. Lamb of God, you

take a - way the sins of the world grant us your peace.

*"Lamb of God" is sung the first and last times. Alternate intervening invocations include: "Saving Cup," "Hope for all," "Prince of Peace," "Wine of Peace," etc.

Music: *Mass of Light*, David Haas, © 1988, GIA Publications, Inc.

Setting Two

196 KYRIE

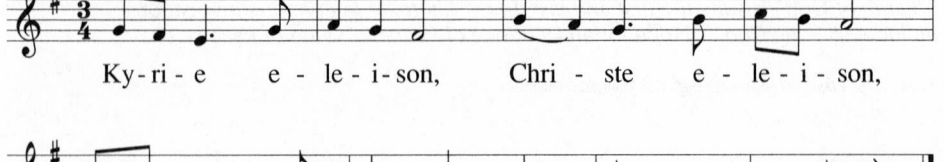

Ky-ri-e e-le-i-son, Chri-ste e-le-i-son,

Ky-ri-e e-le - i - son.

Music: *Mass of Remembrance*, Marty Haugen, © 1987, GIA Publications, Inc.

197 GLORIA

Refrain

Priest or cantor:

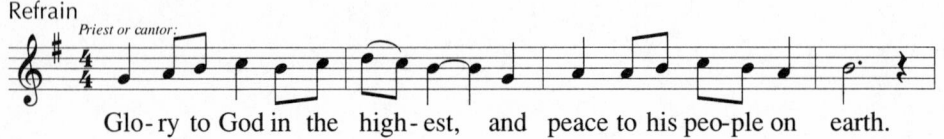

Glo-ry to God in the high-est, and peace to his peo-ple on earth.

All:

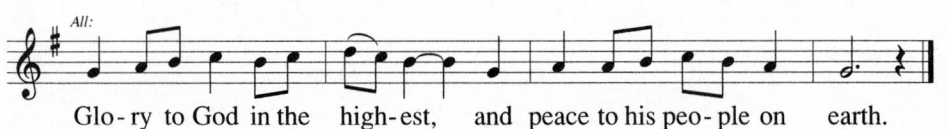

Glo-ry to God in the high-est, and peace to his peo-ple on earth.

Verses

Choir: Lord God, heavenly King, almighty God and Father,
       we worship you, we give you thanks,
       we praise you for your glory.
                    All sing entire refrain

Lord Jesus Christ, only Son of the Father,
Lord God, Lamb of God, you take away the sin of the world:
have mercy on us;
you are seated at the right hand of the Father:
receive our prayer.
All sing entire refrain

For you alone are the Holy One, you alone are the Lord,
you alone are the Most High, Jesus Christ,
with the Holy Spirit, in the glory of God the Father. Amen.
All sing entire refrain

Music: *Mass of Remembrance*, Marty Haugen, © 1987, GIA Publications, Inc.

ALLELUIA 198

Music: *Mass of Remembrance*, Marty Haugen, © 1987, GIA Publications, Inc.

PREFACE DIALOG 199

Music: *Mass of Remembrance*, Marty Haugen, © 1987, GIA Publications, Inc.

200 EUCHARISTIC ACCLAMATION IA (OPTIONAL)*

As in the Eucharistic Prayers for Masses with Children.

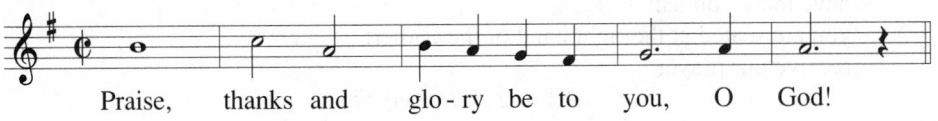

Praise, thanks and glo - ry be to you, O God!

Music: *Mass of Remembrance*, Marty Haugen, © 1987, GIA Publications, Inc.

201 SANCTUS

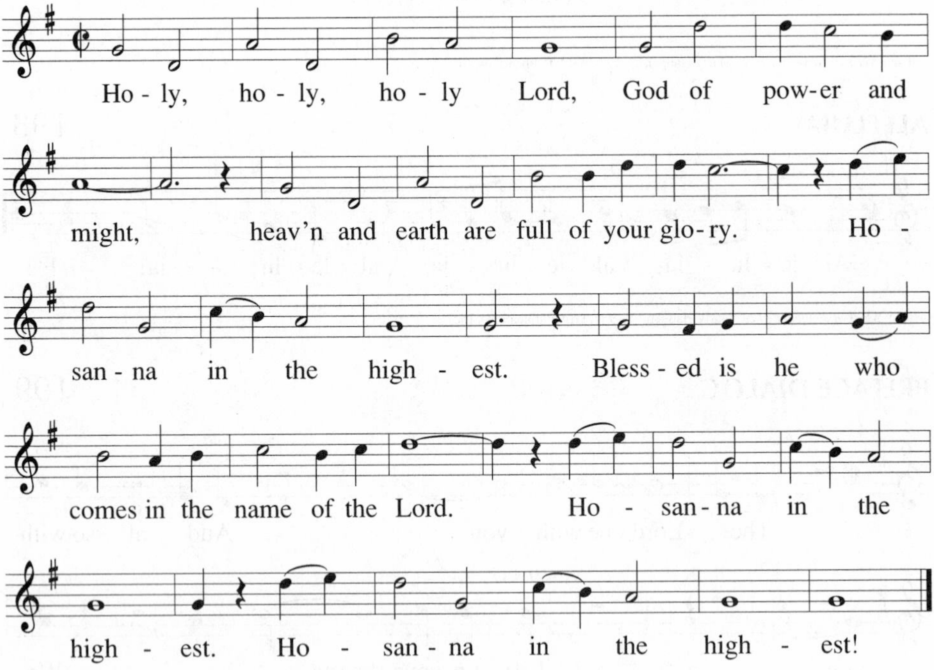

Ho - ly, ho - ly, ho - ly Lord, God of pow-er and

might, heav'n and earth are full of your glo-ry. Ho -

san - na in the high - est. Bless - ed is he who

comes in the name of the Lord. Ho - san-na in the

high - est. Ho - san - na in the high - est!

Music: *Mass of Remembrance*, Marty Haugen, © 1987, GIA Publications, Inc.

202 EUCHARISTIC ACCLAMATION IB (OPTIONAL)

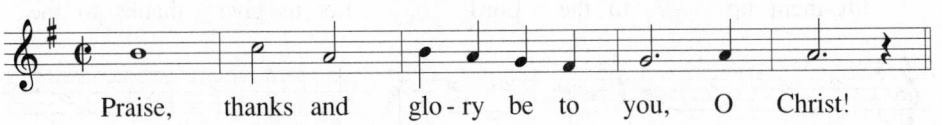

Praise, thanks and glo - ry be to you, O Christ!

Music: *Mass of Remembrance*, Marty Haugen, © 1987, GIA Publications, Inc.

MEMORIAL ACCLAMATION 203

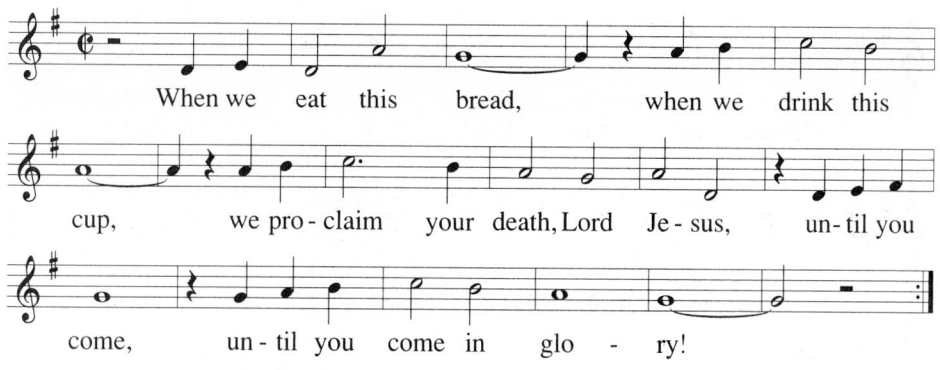

When we eat this bread, when we drink this cup, we pro-claim your death, Lord Je-sus, un-til you come, un-til you come in glo - ry!

Music: *Mass of Remembrance*, Marty Haugen, © 1987, GIA Publications, Inc.

EUCHARISTIC ACCLAMATION II (OPTIONAL) 204

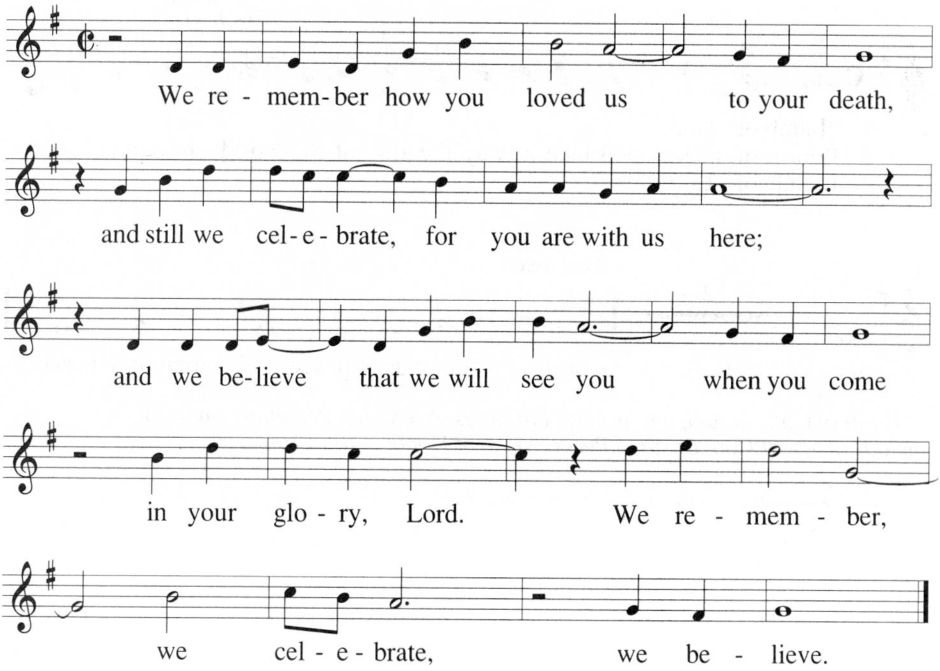

We re - mem-ber how you loved us to your death, and still we cel-e-brate, for you are with us here; and we be-lieve that we will see you when you come in your glo - ry, Lord. We re - mem - ber, we cel-e-brate, we be - lieve.

Music: *Mass of Remembrance*, Marty Haugen, © 1987, GIA Publications, Inc.

EUCHARISTIC ACCLAMATION III (OPTIONAL) 205

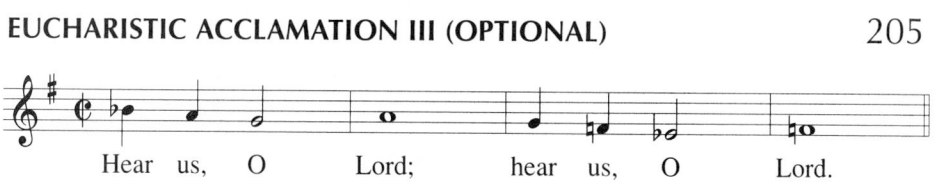

Hear us, O Lord; hear us, O Lord.

Music: *Mass of Remembrance*, Marty Haugen, © 1987, GIA Publications, Inc.

206 AMEN

Al - le - lu - ia,   a - men!
*Praise to   you, Lord,   a - men!

Al - le - lu - ia,   a - men!
Praise to   you, Lord,   a - men!

* During Lent

Music: *Mass of Remembrance*, Marty Haugen. © 1987. GIA Publications, Inc.

207 AGNUS DEI

1. *Lamb of God,
2. Prince of Peace, you take a-way the sins of the world: have mer-cy on
3. Bread of Life,

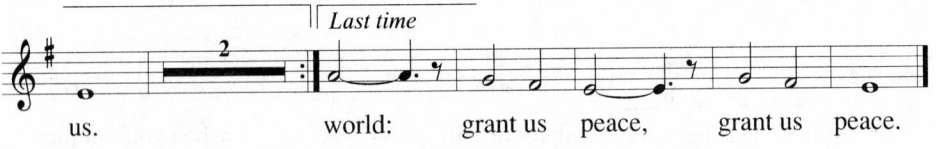

us.   world: grant us peace,   grant us peace.

** "Lamb of God" is sung the first and last times. Alternate intervening invocations
include: Ancient Cup, Bread of Peace, Wine of Hope, Lord of Lords.*

Music: *Mass of Remembrance*, Marty Haugen. © 1987. GIA Publications, Inc.

Setting Three

Lord, have mer-cy. Lord, have mer-cy.

Christ, have mer-cy. Christ, have mer-cy.

Lord, have mer-cy. Lord, have mer-cy.

Music: *The Psallite Mass*, Michael Joncas, © 1988, GIA Publications, Inc.

209 GLORIA

Refrain I

Glo-ri-a in ex - cel - sis De-o, glo-ri-a in ex - cel - sis De-o,

glo-ri-a in ex - cel - sis De-o, et in ter-ra pax.

Verses

Choir: Glory to God in the highest, and peace to his people on earth.
Glory to God in the highest, and peace to his people on earth.
Refrain I

Lord, God, heavenly King, almighty God and Father,
we worship you, we give you thanks, we praise you for your glory.
Refrain I

Lord Jesus Christ, only Son of the Father,
Lord Jesus Christ, Lord God, Lamb of God,
Refrain II

Refrain II

Do-mi-ne Je - su Chri- ste, Do-mi-ne Je - su Chri- ste,

mi - se - re - re no - bis, mi - se - re - re.

Verses

You take away the sin of the world: have mercy on us;
you are seated at the right hand of the Father: receive our prayer.
Refrain II

For you alone are the Holy One, you alone are the Lord,
you alone are the Most High, Jesus Christ, *(begin Refrain I)*
with the Holy Spirit, with the Holy Spirit
in the glory of God the Father. Amen.

Music: *The Psallite Mass*, Michael Joncas. © 1988, GIA Publications, Inc.

SANCTUS

210

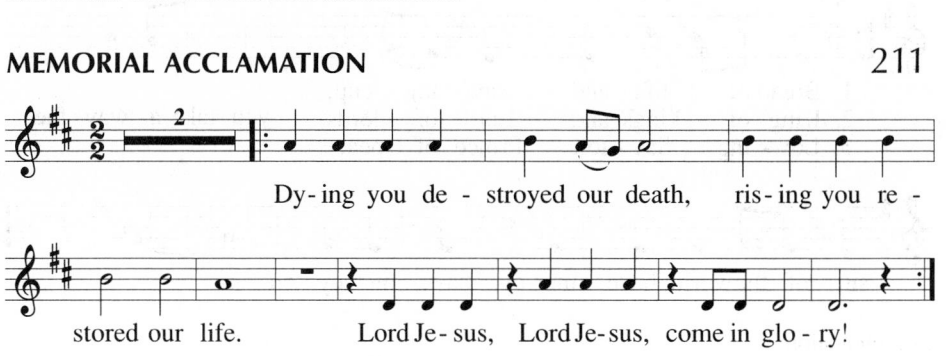

Ho - ly, ho - ly, ho - ly.

Ho - ly, ho - ly, ho - ly. Ho - san - na,

ho - san - na in the high - est! Ho - ly, ho - ly,

ho - ly. Ho - ly, ho - ly, ho - ly.

Ho - san - na, ho - san - na in the high - est!

Music: *The Psallite Mass*, Michael Joncas, © 1988, GIA Publications, Inc.

MEMORIAL ACCLAMATION

211

Dy- ing you de - stroyed our death, ris - ing you re -

stored our life. Lord Je - sus, Lord Je - sus, come in glo - ry!

Music: *The Psallite Mass*, Michael Joncas, © 1988, GIA Publications, Inc.

212 AMEN

A - men, a - men, a - men.

Al-le-lu - ia, al-le-lu - ia, al-le-lu - ia!

Music: *The Psallite Mass,* Michael Joncas, © 1988, GIA Publications, Inc.

213 AGNUS DEI

First Invocation

Cantor: *Assembly:*

Je - sus, Lamb of God, you take a-way the sins of the world:

have mer - cy, have mer-cy on us.

Invocations

Cantor: *All:*

1. Bread of life and sav - ing cup,
2. King of kings and Lord of lords, you take a - way the
3. Lov - ing Sav - ior, Prince of peace,

sins of the world: have mer - cy, have mer-cy on us.

Last Invocation

Cantor: *Assembly:*

Je - sus, Lamb of God, you take a-way the sins of the world:

have mer - cy, and grant us your peace.

Music: *The Psallite Mass,* Michael Joncas, © 1988, GIA Publications, Inc.

Setting Four

O Lord, have mer - cy,
Se - ñor, ten pie - dad,

O Christ, have mer - cy, O
Cri - sto, ten pie - dad, Se -

Lord, have mer - cy 3 on us, O
ñor, ten pie - dad de no - so - tros, Se -

Lord, have mer 3 cy on us.
ñor, ten pie - dad de no - so - tros.

Music: *Mass for the Life of the World,* Joe Camacho, David Haas; acc. by Rob Glover, © 1993, GIA Publications, Inc.

215   GLORIA / GLORIA A DIOS

Refrain

Glo - ry to God in the high-est! Glo - ry to God in the
¡Glo-ria a Dios en el cie - lo! ¡Glo-ria a Dios en el

high - est! Peace to all peo - ple on the earth!
cie - lo! ¡Y en la tie - rra paz a los hom - bres!

Peace to all peo - ple on the earth!
¡Y en la tie - rra paz a los hom - bres!

Last time

Peace to all peo - ple on the earth!
¡Y en la tie - rra paz a los hom - bres!

Verses

1. Lord God, heavenly King,
   almighty God and Father,
   we worship you, we give you thanks,
   we praise you for your glory!

2. Lord Jesus Christ, only Son of the Father,
   Lord God, Lamb of God,
   you take away the sin of the world:
   have mercy on us;
   you are seated at the right hand of the Father:
   receive our prayer.

3. For you alone are the Holy One,
   you alone are the Lord, you alone are the Most High, Jesus Christ,
   with the Holy Spirit, in the glory of God,
   in the glory of God the Father!

Music: *Mass for the Life of the World,* David Haas; acc. by Rob Glover, © 1993, GIA Publications, Inc.

ALLELUIA / ALELUYA 216

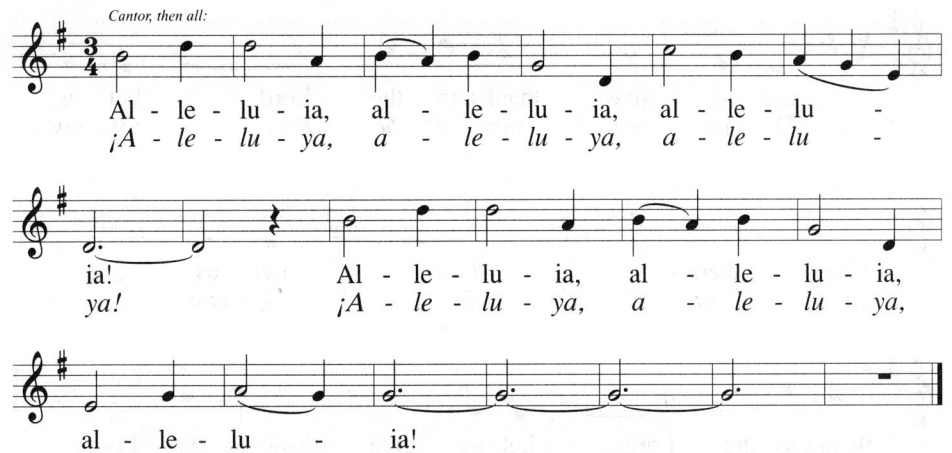

Al - le - lu - ia, al - le - lu - ia, al - le - lu - ia!
¡A - le - lu - ya, a - le - lu - ya, a - le - lu - ya!

Al - le - lu - ia, al - le - lu - ia,
¡A - le - lu - ya, a - le - lu - ya,

al - le - lu - ia!
a - le - lu - ya!

Music: *Mass for the Life of the World,* David Haas, arr. by Rob Glover, © 1993, GIA Publications, Inc.

O LORD, HEAR OUR PRAYER / SEÑOR, OYENOS 217

O Lord, hear our prayer; O
Se - ñor, ó - ye - nos; Se -

Lord, hear our prayer; O Lord, hear our prayer;
ñor, ó - ye - nos; Se - ñor, ó - ye - nos;

To repeat *To end*

O Lord, hear our prayer; O
Se - ñor, ó - ye - nos; Se -

Music: *Mass for the Life of the World,* David Haas, arr. by Rob Glover, © 1993, GIA Publications, Inc.

218 OSTINATO 1 (OPTIONAL)

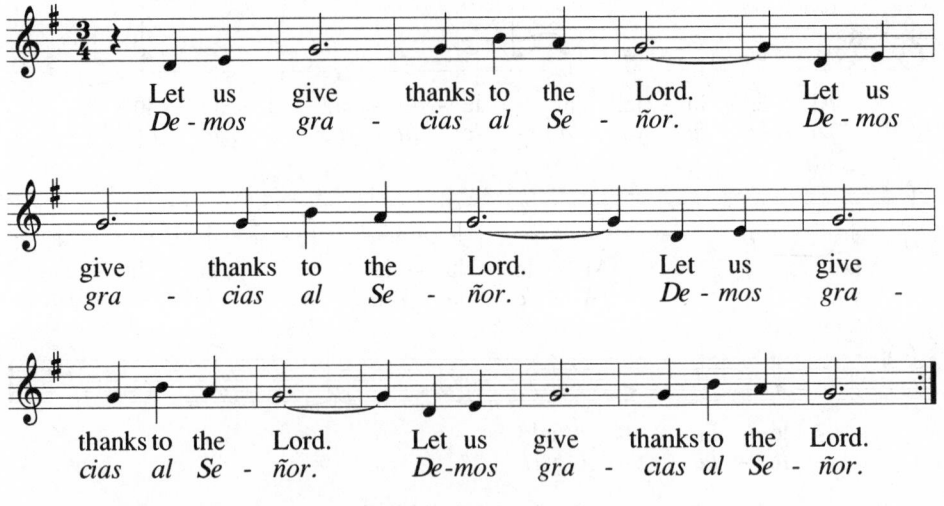

Let us give thanks to the Lord. Let us
De - mos gra - cias al Se - ñor. De - mos

give thanks to the Lord. Let us give
gra - cias al Se - ñor. De - mos gra -

thanks to the Lord. Let us give thanks to the Lord.
cias al Se - ñor. De - mos gra - cias al Se - ñor.

Music: *Mass for the Life of the World*, David Haas; arr. by Rob Glover, © 1993, GIA Publications, Inc.

219 ACCLAMATION 1: SANCTUS

Ho - ly, ho - ly, ho - ly Lord, God of pow'r, God of
San - to, San - to es el Se - ñor, e - res Dios del U - ni -

might, heav - en and earth are full of your glo - ry,
ver - so. Lle - nos es - tán el cie - lo y la tie - rra de tu glo - ria.

Ho - san - na in the high - est! Blest is he who
¡Ho - san - na en el cie - lo! Ben - di - to él que

comes in the name of the Lord. Ho - san -
vie - ne en nom - bre del Se - ñor. ¡Ho - san -

na! Ho - san - na in the high - est!
na! ¡Ho - san - na en el cie - lo!

Music: *Mass for the Life of the World*, David Haas, arr. by Rob Glover, © 1993, GIA Publications, Inc.

OSTINATO 2 / ACCLAMATION 2 (OPTIONAL)

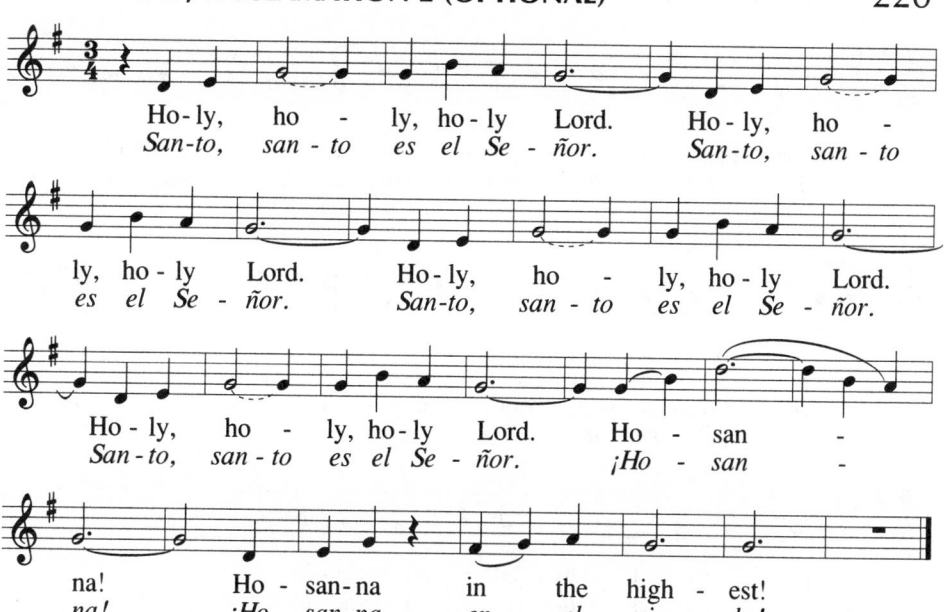

Ho-ly, ho - ly, ho-ly Lord. Ho-ly, ho -
San-to, san - to es el Se - ñor. San-to, san - to

ly, ho-ly Lord. Ho-ly, ho - ly, ho-ly Lord.
es el Se - ñor. San-to, san - to es el Se - ñor.

Ho - ly, ho - ly, ho-ly Lord. Ho - san -
San-to, san - to es el Se - ñor. ¡Ho - san -

na! Ho - san-na in the high - est!
na! ¡Ho - san-na en el cie - lo!

Music: *Mass for the Life of the World,* David Haas, arr. by Rob Glover, © 1993, GIA Publications, Inc.

OSTINATO 3 (OPTIONAL)

(Hum)

Music: *Mass for the Life of the World,* David Haas, arr. by Rob Glover, © 1993, GIA Publications, Inc.

222 ACCLAMATION 3: CHRIST HAS DIED

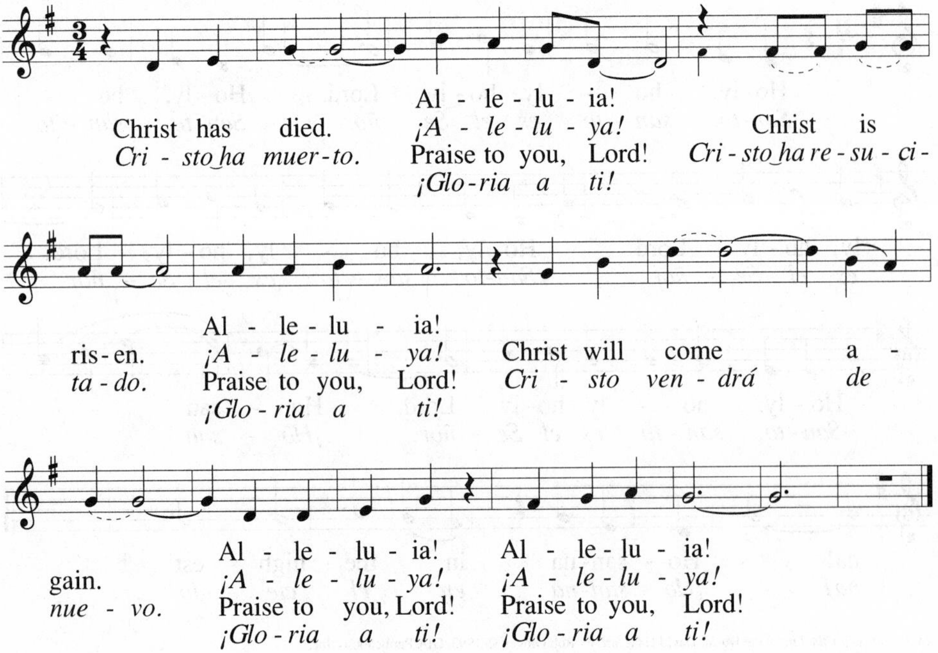

Christ has died.
Cri - sto ha muer - to.

Al - le - lu - ia!
¡A - le - lu - ya!
¡Glo - ria a ti!

Christ is

ris - en.
ta - do.

Al - le - lu - ia!
¡A - le - lu - ya!
¡Glo - ria a ti!

Christ will come a -
Cri - sto ven - drá de

gain.
nue - vo.

Al - le - lu - ia!
¡A - le - lu - ya!
¡Glo - ria a ti!

Al - le - lu - ia!
¡A - le - lu - ya!
¡Glo - ria a ti!

Music: *Mass for the Life of the World,* David Haas, arr. by Rob Glover, © 1993, GIA Publications, Inc.

223 OSTINATO 4 (OPTIONAL)

O Lord, hear our prayer; O
Se - ñor, ó - ye - nos; Se -

Lord, hear our prayer; O Lord, hear our
ñor, ó - ye - nos; Se - ñor, ó - ye -

prayer; O Lord, hear our prayer;
nos; Se - ñor, ó - ye - nos;

Music: *Mass for the Life of the World,* David Haas, arr. by Rob Glover, © 1993, GIA Publications, Inc.

ACCLAMATION 4

224

All:

Al - le - lu - ia!
A - men! ¡A - le - lu - ya! A -
¡A - mén! Praise to you, Lord! ¡A -
¡Glo - ria a ti!

Al - le - lu - ia!
men! ¡A - le - lu - ya! A -
mén! Praise to you, Lord! ¡A -
¡Glo - ria a ti!

men! A - men! Al - le -
mén! ¡A - mén! ¡A - le -
Praise to
¡Glo - ria

lu - ia! Al - le - lu - ia!
lu - ya! ¡A - le - lu - ya! We will
you, Lord! Praise to you, Lord! ¡Es ver -
a ti! ¡Glo - ria a ti!

rise to our cre - a - tor! We will rise with
dad, le - van - tar - e - mos con Je - sús, el

Je - sus, the Son! We will rise through the Spir - it!
hi - jo de Dios! ¡Es ver - dad! ¡A - mén!

Al - le - lu - ia! A - men!
¡A - le - lu - ya! ¡A - mén!
Praise to you, Lord.
¡Glo - ria a ti!

225 AGNUS DEI

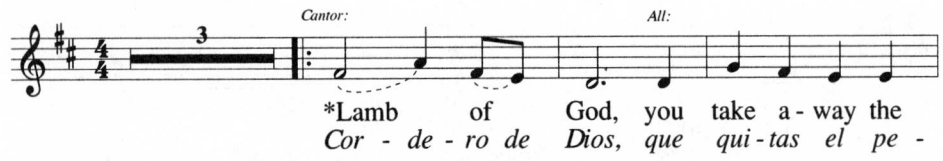

*Lamb of God, you take a-way the
Cor - de - ro de Dios, que qui-tas el pe -

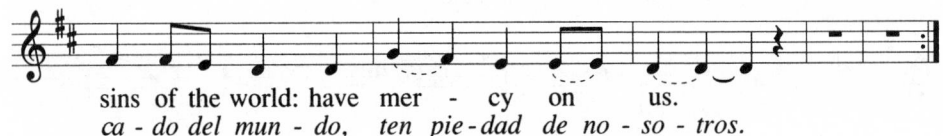

sins of the world: have mer - cy on us.
ca - do del mun - do, ten pie-dad de no - so - tros.

Last time:

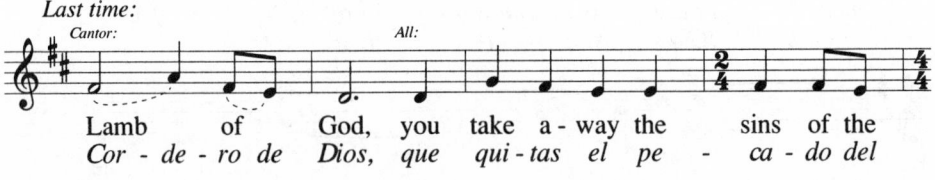

Lamb of God, you take a-way the sins of the
Cor - de - ro de Dios, que qui-tas el pe - ca - do del

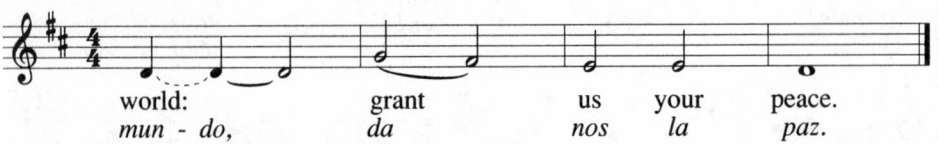

world: grant us your peace.
mun - do, da nos la paz.

*Other invocations may be used: King of kings, Prince of Peace, Bread of Life, Ancient Cup,
Pan de Vida (Bread of Life), Copa de Promesa (Cup of Promise), Sangre de la Cruz,
(Blood of the Cross), Mi Redentor (My Redeemer), etc.

Music: *Mass for the Life of the World*, David Haas, © 1987, 1993, GIA Publications, Inc.

Setting Five

Cantor: Lord, have mer - cy. *Assembly:* Lord, have mer - cy.

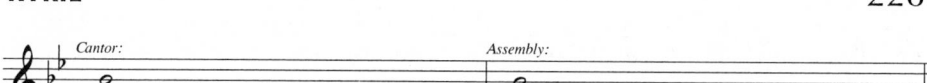

Cantor: Christ, have mer - cy. *Assembly:* Christ, have mer - cy.

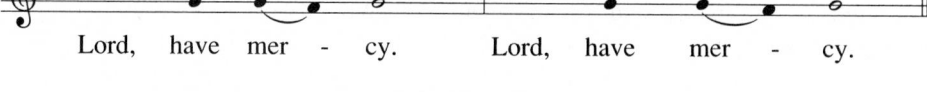

Cantor: Lord, have mer - cy. *Assembly:* Lord, have mer - cy.

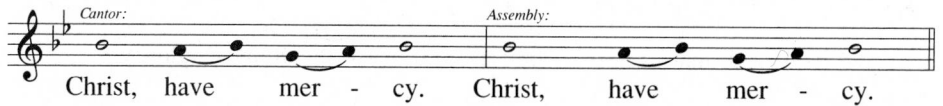

Music: *A Community Mass,* Richard Proulx, © 1971, 1977, GIA Publications, Inc.

227 GLORIA

Glo - ry to God in the high - est, and peace to his peo - ple on earth. Lord God, heav-en - ly King, al - might - y God and Fa - ther, We wor - ship you, we give you thanks, we praise you for your glo-ry. Lord Je - sus Christ, on - ly Son of the Fa - ther, Lord, God, Lamb of God, you take a - way the sin of the world: have mer - cy on us;

Music: *A Community Mass*, Richard Proulx, © 1971, 1977, GIA Publications, Inc.

228 **SANCTUS**

Ho- ly, ho- ly, ho - ly Lord, God of pow- er and

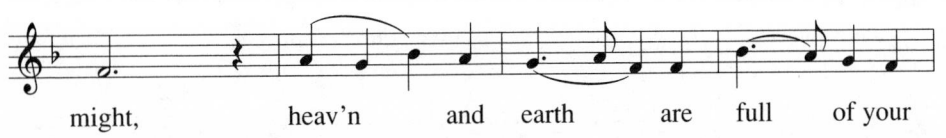

might, heav'n and earth are full of your

glo - ry. Ho - san - na in the high - est, ho -

san - na in the high- est. Blest is he who comes in the

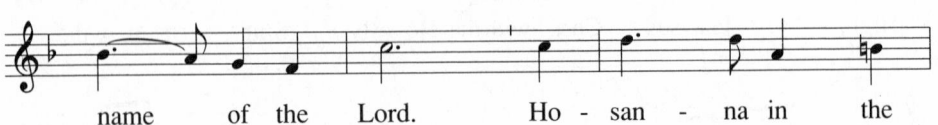

name of the Lord. Ho - san - na in the

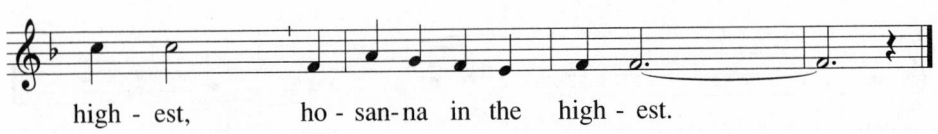

high - est, ho - san- na in the high - est.

Music: *A Community Mass*, by Richard Proulx, © 1971, 1977, GIA Publications, Inc.

MEMORIAL ACCLAMATION 229

Christ has died; Christ is ris- en;

Christ will come a - gain.

Music: *A Community Mass,* Richard Proulx, © 1971, 1977, GIA Publications, Inc.

MEMORIAL ACCLAMATION 230

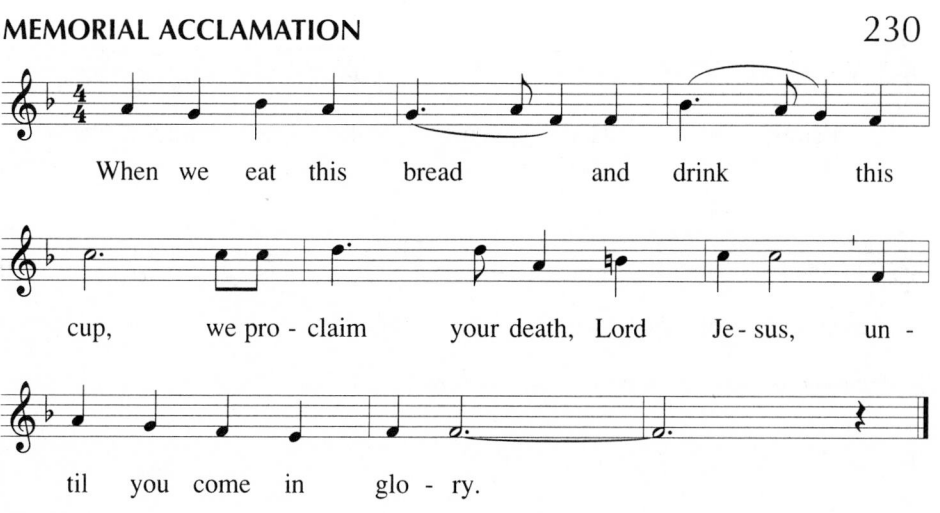

When we eat this bread and drink this

cup, we pro - claim your death, Lord Je - sus, un -

til you come in glo - ry.

Music: *A Community Mass,* Richard Proulx, © 1988, GIA Publications, Inc.

AMEN 231

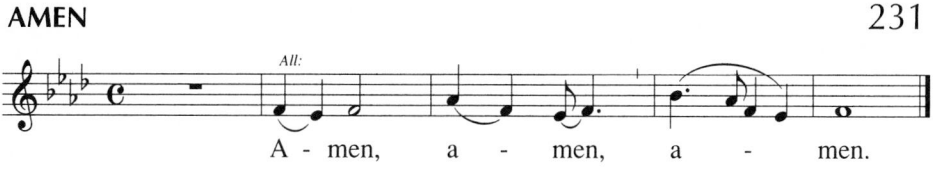

A - men, a - men, a - men.

Music: *A Community Mass,* Richard Proulx, © 1971, 1977, GIA Publications, Inc.

232 AGNUS DEI

Lamb of God, you take a - way the

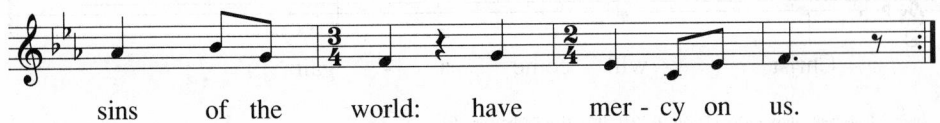

sins of the world: have mer - cy on us.

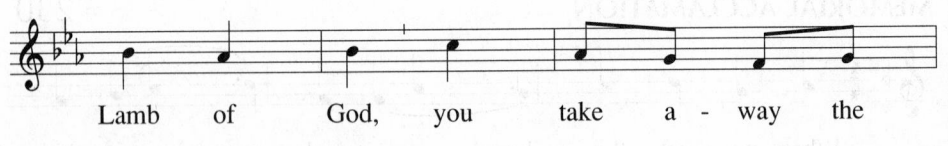

Lamb of God, you take a - way the

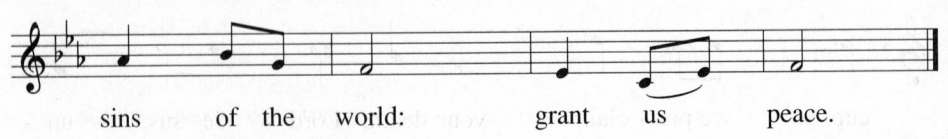

sins of the world: grant us peace.

Music: *A Community Mass,* Richard Proulx, © 1971, 1977, GIA Publications, Inc.

Setting Six

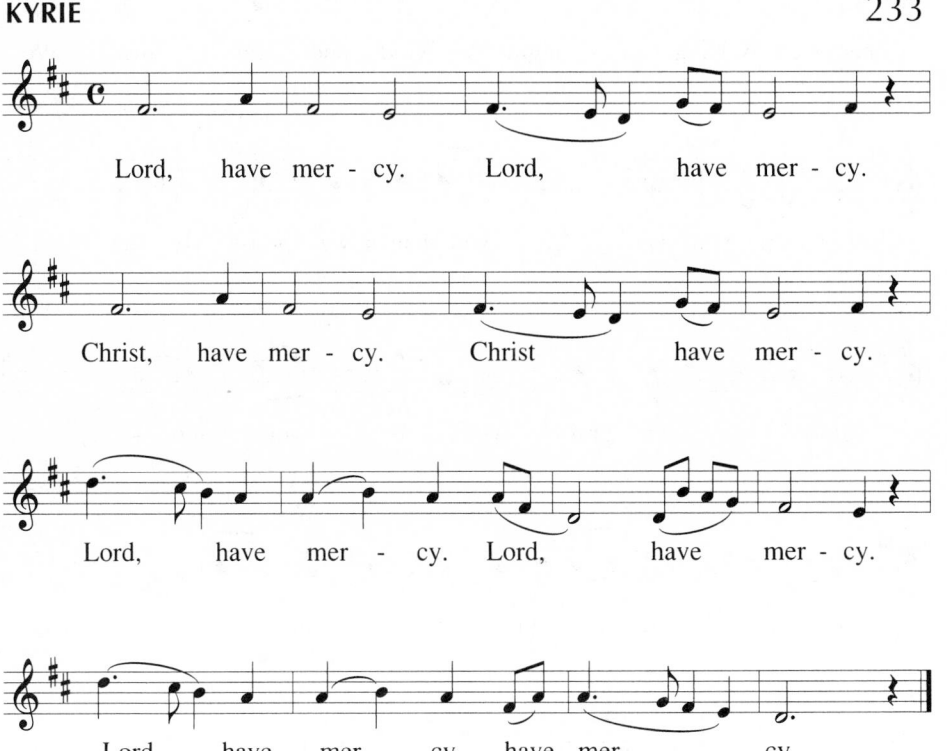

Lord, have mer - cy. Lord, have mer - cy.

Christ, have mer - cy. Christ have mer - cy.

Lord, have mer - cy. Lord, have mer - cy.

Lord, have mer - cy, have mer - cy.

Music: *Deutsche Messe,* Franz Schubert, 1797-1828, adapt. by Richard Proulx, © 1985, 1989, GIA Publications, Inc.

234 GLORIA

Glo - ry, glo - ry to God in the high - est,

and peace to his peo - ple on earth. Lord God,

heav - en - ly King, al - might - y God and Fa - ther. We

wor - ship you, we give you thanks, we praise you for your

glo - ry, we praise you for your glo - ry,

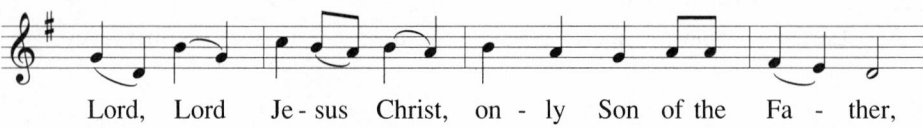

Lord, Lord Je - sus Christ, on - ly Son of the Fa - ther,

Lord God, Lamb of God, you take a - way the sin of the world, have

mer - cy on us, You are seat - ed at the right hand of the

Fa - ther, re - ceive our pray'r, re - ceive our pray'r.

For you a - lone are the Ho - ly One, you a - lone

are the Lord. You a - lone are the Most High,

Je - sus Christ, with the Ho - ly Spir - it in the

glo - ry of God the Fa - ther. A - men. A - men.

Music: *Deutsche Messe;* Franz Schubert, 1797-1828; adapt. by Richard Proulx, © 1985, 1989, GIA Publications, Inc.

235 SANCTUS

Ho - ly, ho - ly, ho - ly Lord, God of pow'r and
might. Ho - ly, ho - ly, ho - ly Lord,
God of pow'r and might. Heav - en and earth are
full, full of your glo - ry. Ho -
san - na in the high - est, ho - san - na in the
high - est. Bless - ed is he who comes
in the name of the Lord. Ho - san - na in the
high - est, ho - san - na in the high - est.

Music: *Deutsche Messe,* Franz Schubert, 1797-1828; adapt. by Richard Proulx, © 1985, 1989, GIA Publications, Inc.

MEMORIAL ACCLAMATION

Dy - ing you de-stroyed our death, Ris - ing you re - stored our life. Lord Je - sus come in glo - ry, Lord Je - sus come in glo - ry.

repeat ad lib.

Music: *Deutsche Messe*, Franz Schubert, 1797-1828; adapt. by Richard Proulx, © 1985, 1989, GIA Publications, Inc.

237 MEMORIAL ACCLAMATION

Lord, by your cross and res - ur - rec - tion,

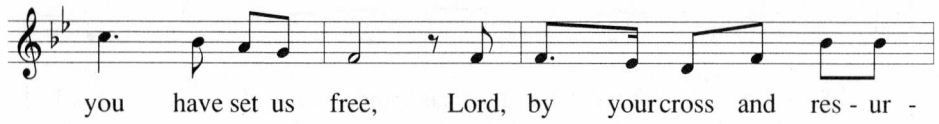

you have set us free, Lord, by your cross and res - ur -

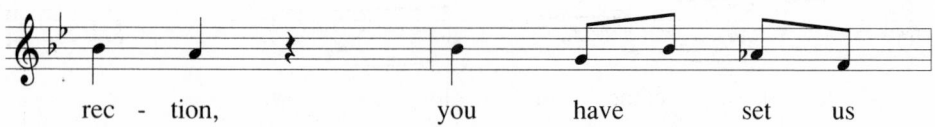

rec - tion, you have set us

repeat ad lib.

free, you are the Sav - ior of the world.

Music: *Deutsche Messe,* Franz Schubert, 1797-1828, adapt. by Richard Proulx, © 1985, 1989, GIA Publications, Inc.

238 AMEN

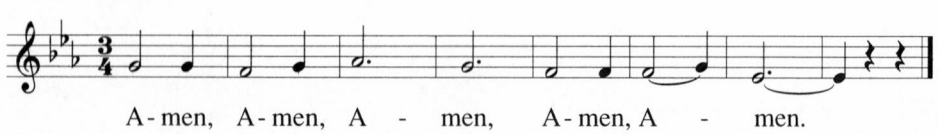

A - men, A - men, A - men, A - men, A - men.

Music: *Deutsche Messe,* Franz Schubert, 1797-1828, adapt. by Richard Proulx, © 1985, 1989, GIA Publications, Inc.

LORD'S PRAYER 239

Our Fa - ther, who art in heav - en, hal - lowed be thy

name; thy King - dom come, thy will be done on

earth, as it is in heav - en. Give us this day our

dai - ly bread; and for - give us our tres - pas-ses, as

we for - give those who tres - pass a - gainst us, and lead us not

in - to temp - ta - tion, but de - liv - er us from e - vil.

Priest: Deliver us Lord…
for the coming of our Savior, Jesus Christ.

For the king - dom, the pow'r and the glo - ry are yours,

now and for ev - er.

Music: *Deutsche Messe*, Franz Schubert, 1797-1828, adapt. by Richard Proulx, © 1985, 1989, GIA Publications, Inc.

240 AGNUS DEI

Je - sus, Lamb of God, have mer - cy on

us. Je - sus, Bear - er of our sins, have

mer - cy on us. Je - sus, Re - deem - er, Re -

deem - er of the world, give us your peace,

give us your peace.

Music: *Deutsche Messe,* Franz Schubert, 1797-1828, adapt. by Richard Proulx, © 1985, 1989, GIA Publications, Inc.

Service Music

RITE OF SPRINKLING 241

Cleanse us, Lord, from all our sins; wash us and we shall be clean as new snow. Cleanse us, Lord, from all our sins; wash us and we shall be clean as new snow.

Text: Psalm 51:9; Michael Joncas
Music: Michael Joncas
© 1988, GIA Publications, Inc.

RITE OF SPRINKLING 242

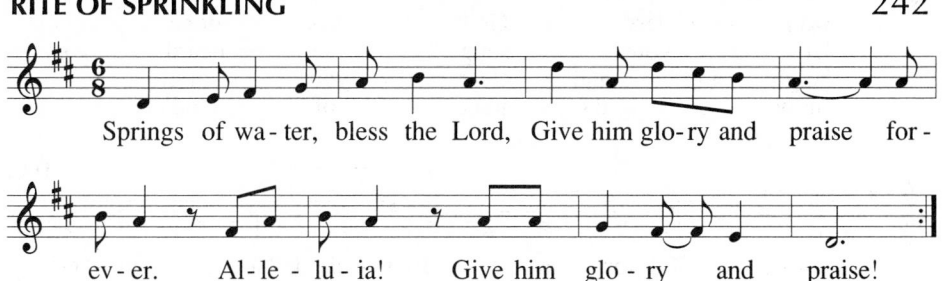

Springs of wa-ter, bless the Lord, Give him glo-ry and praise for-ev-er. Al-le-lu-ia! Give him glo-ry and praise!

Text: Refrain trans. © 1973, ICEL; additional text by Marty Haugen, © 1994, GIA Publications, Inc.
Music: Marty Haugen, © 1994, GIA Publications, Inc.

243 RITE OF SPRINKLING

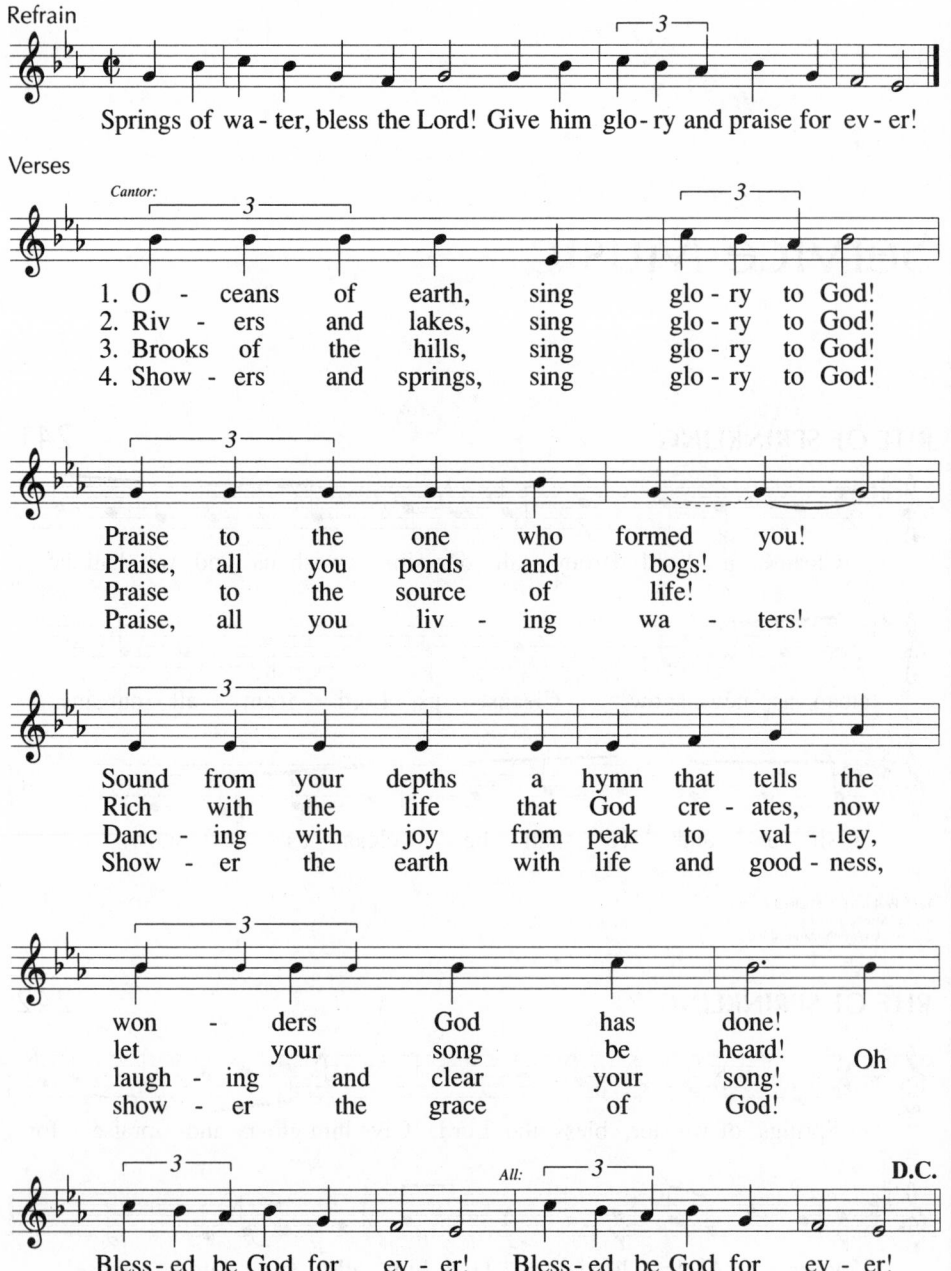

Refrain

Springs of wa-ter, bless the Lord! Give him glo-ry and praise for ev-er!

Verses

Cantor:

1. O - ceans of earth, sing glo - ry to God!
2. Riv - ers and lakes, sing glo - ry to God!
3. Brooks of the hills, sing glo - ry to God!
4. Show - ers and springs, sing glo - ry to God!

Praise to the one who formed you!
Praise, all you ponds and bogs!
Praise to the source of life!
Praise, all you liv - ing wa - ters!

Sound from your depths a hymn that tells the
Rich with the life that God cre - ates, now
Danc - ing with joy from peak to val - ley,
Show - er the earth with life and good - ness,

won - ders God has done!
let your song be heard! Oh
laugh - ing and clear your song!
show - er the grace of God!

All: D.C.

Bless-ed be God for ev - er! Bless-ed be God for ev - er!

Text: Refrain trans. © 1973, ICEL; additional text by Marty Haugen, © 1994, GIA Publications, Inc.
Music: Marty Haugen, © 1994, GIA Publications, Inc.

RITE OF SPRINKLING
244

All:

Lord Je - sus, from   your wound - ed

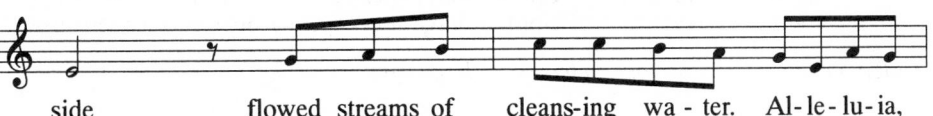

side   flowed streams of   cleans-ing wa - ter. Al - le - lu - ia,

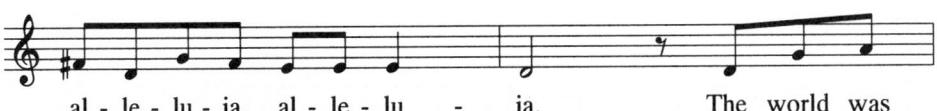

al - le - lu - ia, al - le - lu - ia.   The world was

washed of all   its sin, all life made   new a - gain. Al - le - lu - ia, al -

le - lu - ia, al - le - lu - ia.

Music: *Festival Liturgy,* Richard Hillert, © 1983, GIA Publications, Inc.

YOU HAVE PUT ON CHRIST
245

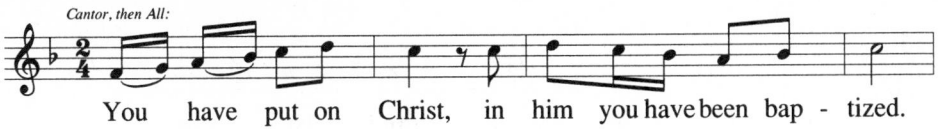

Cantor, then All:

You   have   put on   Christ, in   him you have been bap - tized.

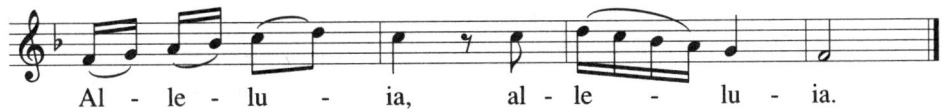

Al - le - lu - ia,   al - le - lu - ia.

Music: Howard Hughes, SM, © 1977, ICEL

246 KYRIE

Cantor, then all
*Lord have mer- cy, Lord have mer - cy.
(Invocation) Christ have mer- cy, Christ have mer - cy.
Lord have mer- cy, Lord have mer - cy.

*Alternate text, "Show us your mercy, be with us now!"

Music: Gary Daigle, © 1993, GIA Publications, Inc.

247 KYRIE

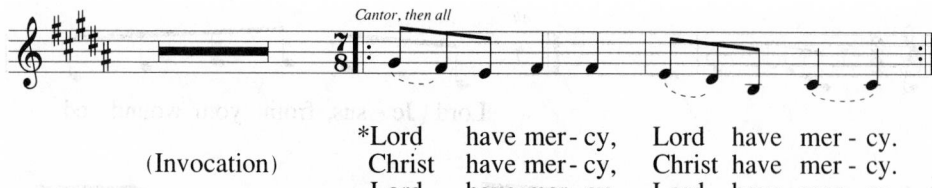

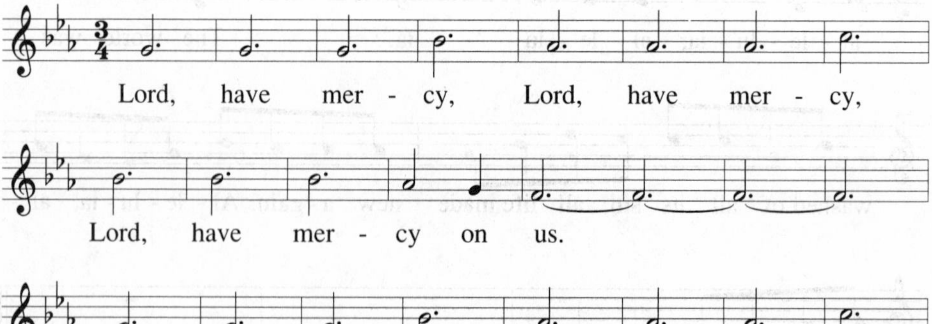

Lord, have mer - cy, Lord, have mer - cy,
Lord, have mer - cy on us.
Christ, have mer - cy, Christ, have mer - cy,
Christ, have mer - cy on us.
Lord, have mer - cy, Lord, have mer - cy,
Lord, have mer - cy, have mer - cy on us.

Music: *Mass of St. Augustine*, Leon C. Roberts, © 1981, GIA Publications, Inc.

KYRIE

248

Cantor or choir, then all:

Ky-ri-e e-le-i-son,

Ky-ri-e e-le-i-son, Ky-ri-e e-le-i-son.

Chris - te e-le-i-son,

Chris - te e-le-i-son,

Chris - te e-le-i-son,

e-le-i-son.

Ky-ri-e e-le-i-son, Ky-ri-e e-le-i-son,

Ky-ri-e e-le-i-son, e-

le-i-son.

Music: *Music for Celebration,* David Hurd, © 1979, GIA Publications, Inc.

249 GLORIA

Refrain

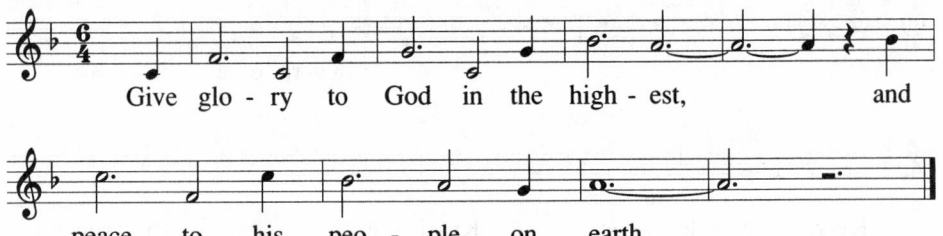

Give glo - ry to God in the high - est, and peace to his peo - ple on earth.

Verses

1. Lord God, heavenly King,
   almighty God and Father,
   we worship you,
   we give you thanks,
   we praise you for your glory.

2. Lord Jesus Christ,
   only Son of the Father,
   Lord God, Lamb of God,
   you take away the sin of the world:
   have mercy upon us;
   you are seated at the right hand of the Father:
   receive our prayer.

3. You alone are the Holy One,
   you alone are the Lord,
   you alone are the Most High, Jesus Christ,
   with the Holy Spirit, in the glory of God the Father.

Music: John B. Foley, S.J., © 1978, and New Dawn Music

250 GLORIA

Canon—*4 voices*

Glo - ri - a, glo - ri - a, in ex - cel - sis De - o!
Glo - ri - a, glo - ri - a, al - le - lu - ia, al - le - lu - ia!

Tune: Jacques Berthier. © 1979, 1988, Les Presses de Taizé, GIA Publications, Inc., agent

GLORIA

Refrain

Glo - ry to God in the high - est, give glo - ry to our God! Glo - ry to God in the high - est, and peace to all peo - ple on earth.

Verses

1. Lord God, heavenly King,
   almighty God and Father,
   we worship you, we give you thanks,
   we praise you for your glory.

2. Lord Jesus Christ, Son of the Father,
   Lord God, Lamb of God,
   you take away the sin of the world:
   have mercy on us;
   you are seated at the right hand of the Father:
   receive the prayer of your people.

3. You alone are the Most Holy,
   you alone are the Lord Most High, Jesus Christ,
   with the Holy Spirit,
   in the glory of God the Father!

Music: Michel Guimont, © 1992, GIA Publications, Inc.

252 GLORIA

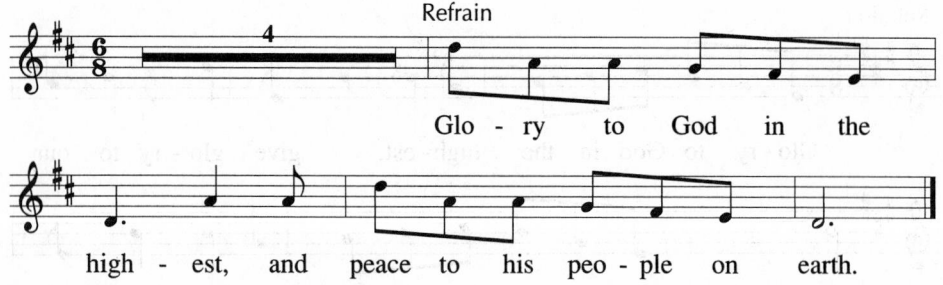

Refrain

Glo - ry to God in the high - est, and peace to his peo - ple on earth.

Verses

1. Lord God, heavenly King,
   almighty God and Father,
   we worship you, we give you thanks,
   we praise you for your glory.

2. Lord Jesus Christ, only Son of the Father,
   Lord God, Lamb of God,
   you take away sin of the world,
   have mercy on us;
   you are seated at the right hand of the Father,
   receive our prayer.

3. You alone are the holy one,
   you alone are the Lord,
   you alone are the Most High, Jesus Christ,
   with the Holy Spirit, in the glory of God the Father.

Music: *Assembly Mass,* Thomas Porter, © 1987, GIA Publications, Inc.

GLORIA

All:
Glo-ry to God in the high-est, and peace to his peo-ple on earth. Glo-ry to God in the high-est, and peace to his peo-ple on earth.

Cantor or T. B.:
Lord God, heav-en-ly King, al-might-y God and Fa - ther.

All:
Glo-ry to God in the high-est, and peace to his peo-ple on earth.

Cantor or S. A.:
We wor-ship you, we give you thanks, we praise you for your glo - ry.

All:
Glo-ry to God in the high-est, and peace to his peo-ple on earth.

Cantor or T. B.:
Lord Je - sus Christ, on - ly Son of the Fa - ther.

Music: *Mass of the Bells;* Alexander Peloquin, © 1972, 1973, GIA Publications, Inc.

254 GLORIA

I (Cantor/choir)
Glo-ry to God in the high - est, and peace to his peo-ple on earth.

II (Assembly)
Lord God, heav'n-ly King, al-might-y God and Fa - ther.

I
We wor-ship you, we give you thanks, we praise you for your glo - ry.

II
Lord Je-sus Christ, on - ly Son of the Fa - ther,

I
Lord God, Lamb of God, you take a-way the sin of the world:

II
have mer-cy on us; you are seat-ed at the right hand of the

Fa - ther: re - ceive our prayer.

I
For you a - lone are the Ho - ly One,

you a - lone are the Lord, you a -

lone are the Most High, Je - sus Christ, with the Ho - ly Spir - it,

in the glo - ry of God the Fa - ther. A - men.

Music: *Congregational Mass;* John Lee, © 1970, GIA Publications, Inc.

255 GLORIA

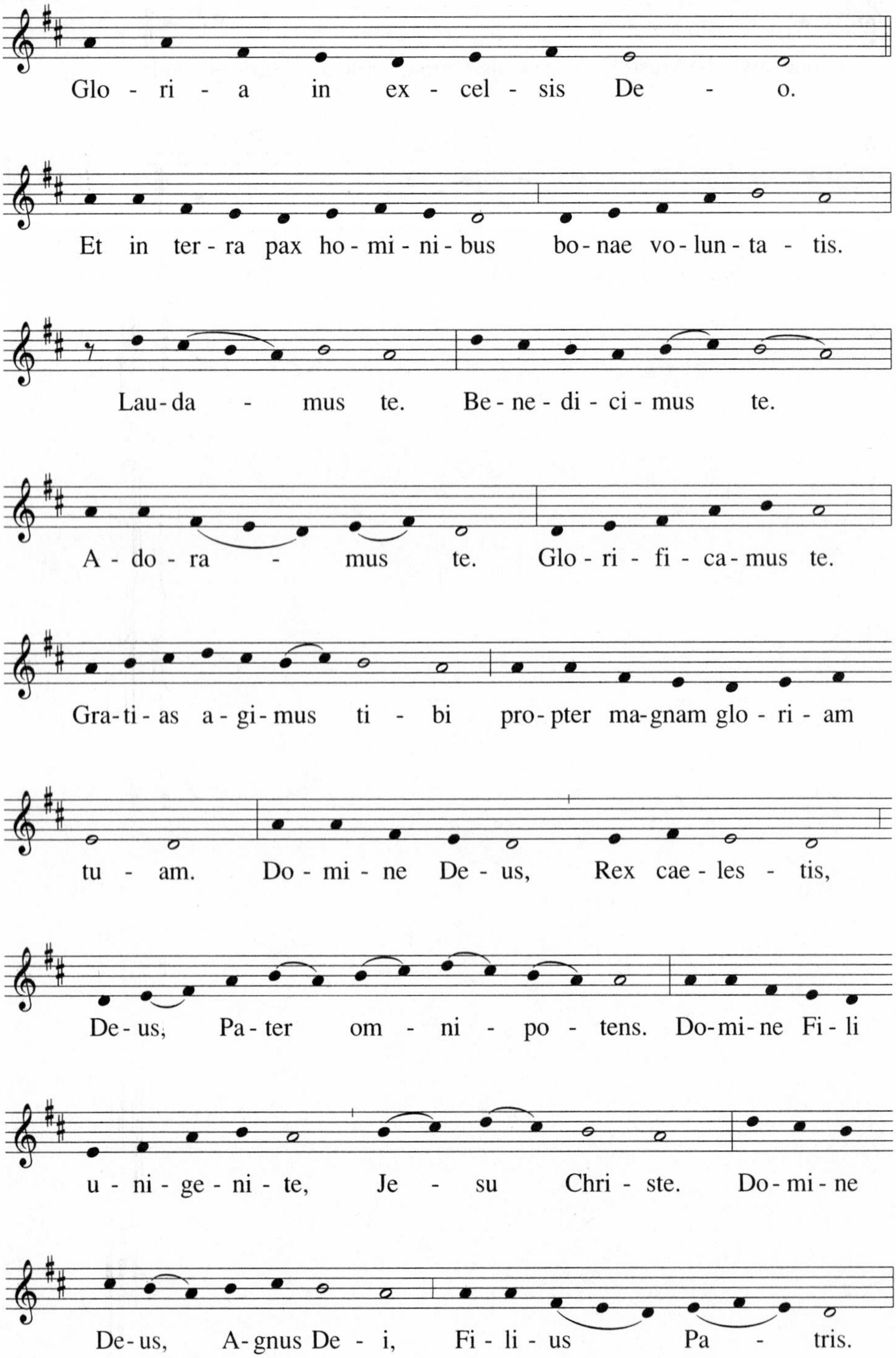

Glo - ri - a in ex - cel - sis De - o.

Et in ter - ra pax ho - mi - ni - bus bo - nae vo - lun - ta - tis.

Lau - da - mus te. Be - ne - di - ci - mus te.

A - do - ra - mus te. Glo - ri - fi - ca - mus te.

Gra - ti - as a - gi - mus ti - bi pro - pter ma - gnam glo - ri - am

tu - am. Do - mi - ne De - us, Rex cae - les - tis,

De - us, Pa - ter om - ni - po - tens. Do - mi - ne Fi - li

u - ni - ge - ni - te, Je - su Chri - ste. Do - mi - ne

De - us, A - gnus De - i, Fi - li - us Pa - tris.

Music: Gloria VIII, Vatican Edition; acc. by Gerard Farrell, OSB. © 1986, GIA Publications, Inc.

256 ALLELUIA

Al - le - lu - ia, al - le - lu - ia,

al - le - lu - ia, al - le - lu - ia, al - le - lu - ia.

Music: Joe Wise; acc. by Kelly Dobbs Mickus, © 1966, 1973, 1986, GIA Publications, Inc.

257 ALLELUIA

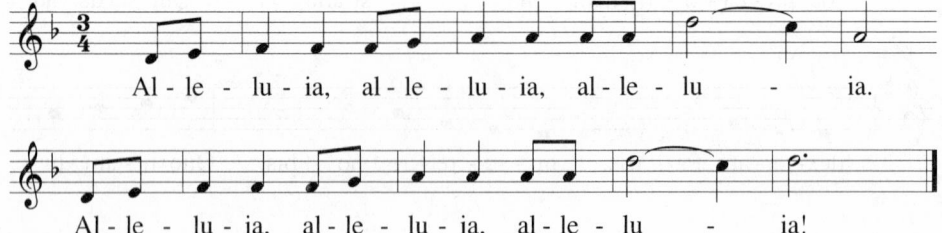

Al - le - lu - ia, al - le - lu - ia, al - le - lu - ia.

Al - le - lu - ia, al - le - lu - ia, al - le - lu - ia!

Music: Alleluia 7; Jacques Berthier, © 1984, Les Presses de Taizé, GIA Publications, Inc., agent

258 CELTIC ALLELUIA

Al - le - lu - ia, al - le - lu - ia!

Al - le - lu - ia, al - le - lu - ia!

Text: Fintan O'Carroll and Christopher Walker
Music: Fintan O'Carroll and Christopher Walker
© 1985, Fintan O'Carroll and Christopher Walker, published by OCP Publications

HALLE, HALLE, HALLE 259

Hal-le, hal-le, hal - le - lu - jah! Halle, hal-le, hal-
le - lu - ia! Hal - le, hal - le, hal - le -
lu - jah! Hal-le-lu-jah! Hal - le - lu - jah!

Music: Traditional Carribean, arr. by John L. Bell, © 1990, Iona Community, GIA Publications, Inc., agent; verses and acc. by Marty Haugen, © 1993, GIA Publications, Inc.

ALLELUIA 260

Al - le - lu - ia! Al - le - lu - ia!
Al - le - lu - ia! Al - le - lu - ia!

Text: Normand Gouin and Jennifer Kerr
Music: Normand Gouin and Jennifer Kerr
© 1992, GIA Publications, Inc.

ALLELUIA 261

Al - le - lu - ia, al - le - lu - ia, al - le - lu - ia.

Music: A. Gregory Murray, OSB, © 1958, The Grail, GIA Publications, Inc., agent

262 ALLELUIA

Cantor:

Al - le - lu - ia, al - le - lu - ia!

Assembly: *Cantor:*

Al - le - lu - ia, al - le - lu - ia! Al - le - lu - ia, al - le - lu - ia!

Assembly: *Cantor:*

Al - le - lu - ia, al - le - lu - ia! Al - le - lu - ia, al - le - lu - ia!

Assembly: *Cantor:*

Al - le - lu - ia, al - le - lu - ia! Al - le - lu - ia, al - le - lu - ia!

Assembly:

Al - le - lu - ia, al - le - lu - ia!

Music: *Joyful Alleluia;* Howard Hughes, SM, © 1973, 1979, GIA Publications, Inc.

263 ALLELUIA

Cantor: ***f*** *Assembly:*   *Cantor:*

Al - le - lu - ia. Al - le - lu - ia. Al - le - lu - ia.

f *Assembly:*   *Cantor:*   ***f*** *Assembly:*

Al - le - lu - ia. Al - le - lu - ia. Al - le - lu - ia.

Music: *Alleluia in C,* Howard Hughes, SM, © 1973, 1982, GIA Publications, Inc.

ALLELUIA

264

Al - le - lu - ia, al - le -
lu - ia, al - le - lu - ia, al - le - lu - ia,
al - le - lu - ia.

Music: Richard Proulx, © 1980 ICEL

ALLELUIA

265

Al - le - lu - ia, al - le - lu - ia, al - le - lu - ia,
al - le - lu - ia, al - le - lu - ia, al - le - lu - ia,

To repeat *Last time*

al - le - lu - ia, al - le - lu - ia. lu - ia.

Music: Jerry Sinclair, © 1972, Manna Music, Inc.; arr. by Betty C. Pulkingham, © 1971, 1975, Celebration

266 LENTEN ACCLAMATION

Praise to you, Lord Je-sus, king of end - less glo- ry,

Sav- ior of the world, Sav- ior of the world.

Text: Marty Haugen
Music: Marty Haugen
© 1983, GIA Publications, Inc.

267 LENTEN ACCLAMATION

Melody:

Glo - ry to you, O

Word of God, Lord Je - sus Christ!

Music: Richard Proulx, © 1975, GIA Publications, Inc.

268 GENERAL INTERCESSIONS

O Lord, hear our prayer.

Text: Ray East
Music: Ray East
© 1987, GIA Publications, Inc.

269 GENERAL INTERCESSIONS

O God, hear us; hear our prayer.

Text: Bob Hurd, © 1984
Music: Bob Hurd, © 1984; acc. by Craig S. Kingsbury, © 1984, OCP Publications
Published by OCP Publications

GENERAL INTERCESSIONS 270

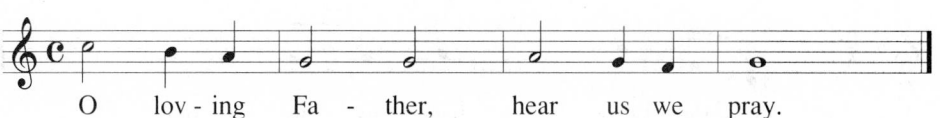

O lov - ing Fa - ther, hear us we pray.

Music: James Moore. © 1983, GIA Publications, Inc.

GENERAL INTERCESSIONS 271

Ky - ri - e, Ky - ri - e, e - le - i - son.

Music: Jacques Berthier, © 1980, Les Presses de Taizé, GIA Publications, Inc., agent

GENERAL INTERCESSIONS 272

Ky - ri - e e - lei - son. Ky - ri - e e - lei - son.
Chri - ste e - lei - son. Chri - ste e - lei - son.

Ky - ri - e e - lei - son.
Chri - ste e - lei - son.

Music: Russian Orthodox; arr. by John L. Bell, © 1990, Iona Community, GIA Publications, Inc., agent

GENERAL INTERCESSIONS 273

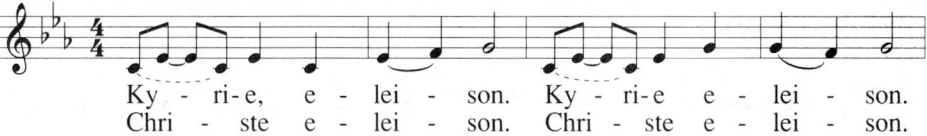

Ky - ri - e, e - lei - son. Ky - ri - e e - lei - son.
Chri - ste e - lei - son. Chri - ste e - lei - son.

Ky - ri - e e - lei - son. Ky - ri - e e - lei - son.
Chri - ste e - lei - son. Chri - ste e - lei - son.

Music: Dinah Reindorf, © 1987; arr. by John L. Bell, © 1990, Iona Community, GIA Publications, Inc., agent

274 GENERAL INTERCESSIONS

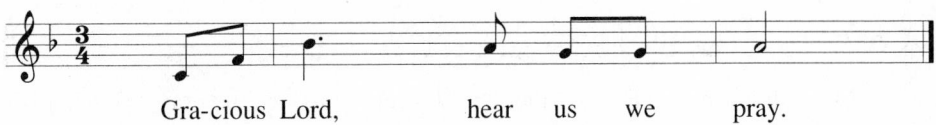

Gra-cious Lord, hear us we pray.

Music: Ronald F. Krisman, © 1977, GIA Publications, Inc.

275 PREFACE DIALOG

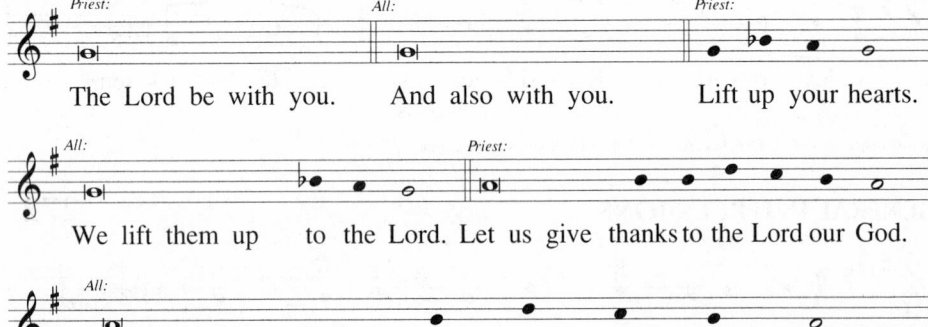

Priest: The Lord be with you. *All:* And also with you. *Priest:* Lift up your hearts.

All: We lift them up to the Lord. *Priest:* Let us give thanks to the Lord our God.

All: It is right to give him thanks and praise.

Music: *Agapé,* Marty Haugen, © 1993, GIA Publications, Inc.

276 EUCHARISTIC ACCLAMATION I (OPTIONAL)

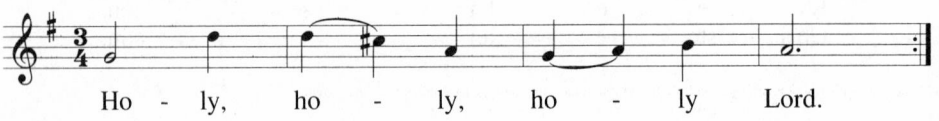

Ho - ly, ho - ly, ho - ly Lord.

Music: *Agapé,* Marty Haugen, © 1993, GIA Publications, Inc.

277 SANCTUS

Ho - ly, ho - ly, ho - ly, Lord,

God of pow - er and might, heav-en and earth are

full of your glo-ry! Ho - san - na in the high - est!

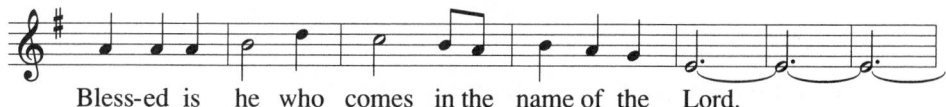

Bless-ed is he who comes in the name of the Lord.

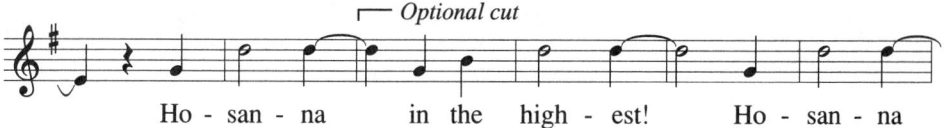

Optional cut

Ho - san - na in the high - est! Ho - san - na

End cut

in the high - est! Ho - san - na in the

high - est!

Music: *Agapé*, Marty Haugen, © 1993, GIA Publications, Inc.

EUCHARISTIC ACCLAMATION II (OPTIONAL)   278

We re - mem - ber, O God, we re - mem - ber, O God.

Music: *Agapé*, Marty Haugen, © 1993, GIA Publications, Inc.

MEMORIAL ACCLAMATION   279

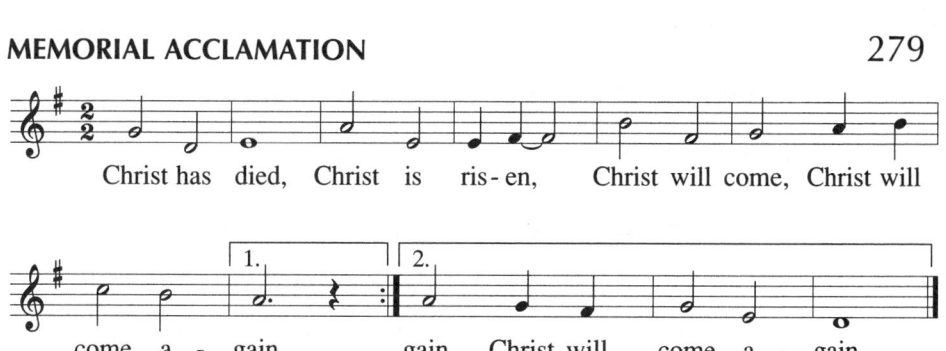

Christ has died, Christ is ris - en, Christ will come, Christ will

come a - gain. gain, Christ will come a - gain.

Music: *Agapé*, Marty Haugen, © 1993, GIA Publications, Inc.

280   EUCHARISTIC ACCLAMATION III (OPTIONAL)

Re - mem - ber, O   God,   re - mem - ber, O   God.

Music: *Agapé,* Marty Haugen, © 1993, GIA Publications, Inc.

281   DOXOLOGY AND GREAT AMEN

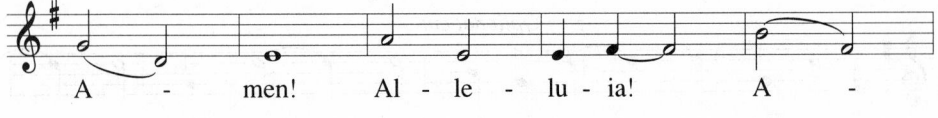

A - men!   Al - le - lu - ia!   A -

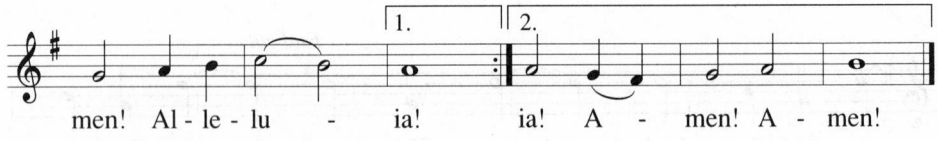

men! Al - le - lu - ia!   ia! A - men! A - men!

Music: *Agapé,* Marty Haugen, © 1993, GIA Publications, Inc.

282   EUCHARISTIC PRAYER FOR CHILDREN

The Lord be with you.   And al - so with you.   Lift   up your hearts.

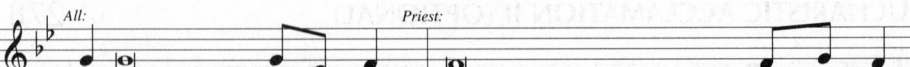

We lift them up to the Lord.   Let us give thanks to the Lord, our God.

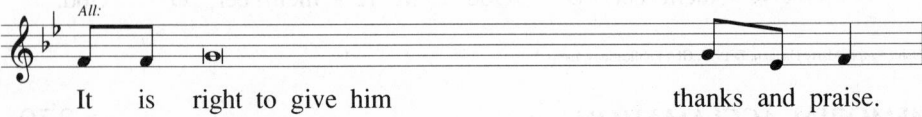

It   is   right to give him   thanks and praise.

Music: *Mass of Creation,* Marty Haugen, © 1984, GIA Publications, Inc.

283   ACCLAMATION 1

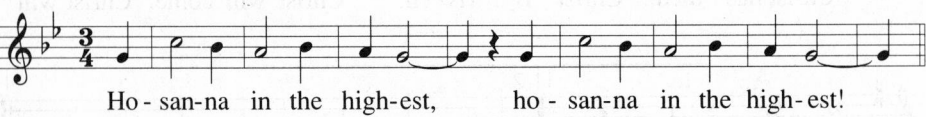

Ho - san-na in the high-est,   ho - san-na in the high-est!

Music: Eucharistic Prayer for Children, *Mass of Creation,* Marty Haugen, adapt. by Rob Glover, © 1989, GIA Publications, Inc.

SANCTUS 284

Ho-ly, ho-ly, ho-ly Lord, God of pow-er, God of might, heav-en and earth are full of your glo-ry. Ho-san-na in the high-est. Bless-ed is he who comes in the name of the Lord. Ho-san-na in the high-est, ho-san-na in the high - est.

Music: *Mass of Creation,* Marty Haugen, © 1984, GIA Publications, Inc.

ACCLAMATION 2 285

Bless-ed is he who comes in the name of the Lord. Ho-san-na in the high-est, ho-san-na in the high - est!

Music: Eucharistic Prayer for Children, *Mass of Creation,* Marty Haugen, adapt. by Rob Glover, © 1989, GIA Publications, Inc.

286 ACCLAMATION 3

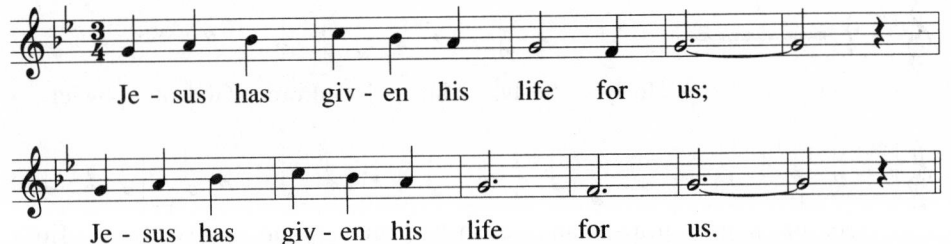

Je - sus has giv - en his life for us;

Je - sus has giv - en his life for us.

Music: Eucharistic Prayer for Children, *Mass of Creation*, Marty Haugen, adapt. by Rob Glover, © 1989, GIA Publications, Inc.

287 ACCLAMATION 4

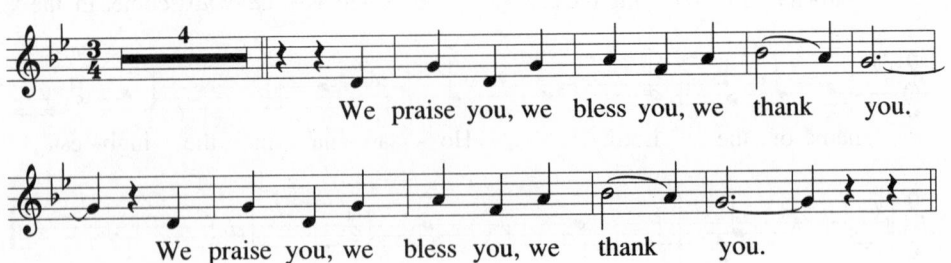

We praise you, we bless you, we thank you.

We praise you, we bless you, we thank you.

Music: Eucharistic Prayer for Children, *Mass of Creation*, Marty Haugen, adapt. by Rob Glover, © 1989, GIA Publications, Inc.

288 DOXOLOGY AND GREAT AMEN

A - men, a - men, a - men!

A - men, a - men, a - men!

Music: *Mass of Creation*, Marty Haugen, © 1984, GIA Publications, Inc.

EUCHARISTIC PRAYER II: PREFACE DIALOG 289

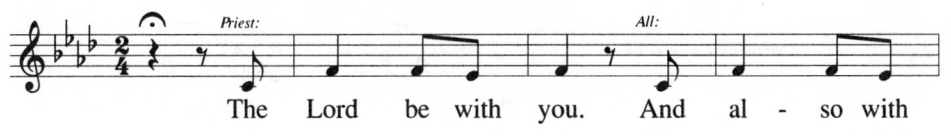

Priest: The Lord be with you. *All:* And al - so with

you. *Priest:* Lift up your hearts. *All:* We lift them up to the Lord.

Priest: Let us give thanks to the Lord our God. *All:* It is

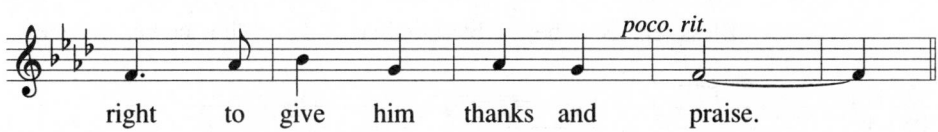

right to give him thanks and praise.

Music: *Eucharistic Prayer II,* Marty Haugen, © 1990, GIA Publications, Inc.

ADDITIONAL ACCLAMATION 1 (OPTIONAL) 290

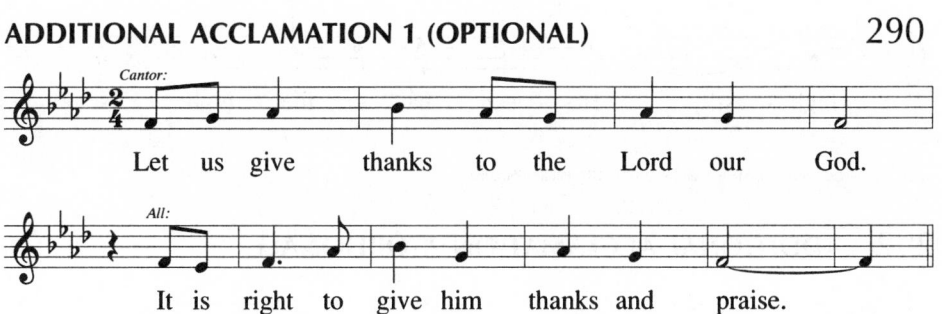

Cantor: Let us give thanks to the Lord our God.

All: It is right to give him thanks and praise.

Music: *Eucharistic Prayer II,* Marty Haugen, © 1990, GIA Publications, Inc.

291 SANCTUS

Ho - ly, ho - ly, ho - ly Lord, God of pow-er and might; heav-en and earth are full of your glo - ry: Ho - san - na in the high - est! Bless-ed is he, bless-ed is he who comes in the name of the Lord. Ho - san - na in the high - est! Ho - san - na in the high - est!

Music: *Eucharistic Prayer II*, Marty Haugen, © 1990, GIA Publications, Inc.

292 ADDITIONAL ACCLAMATION 2 (OPTIONAL)

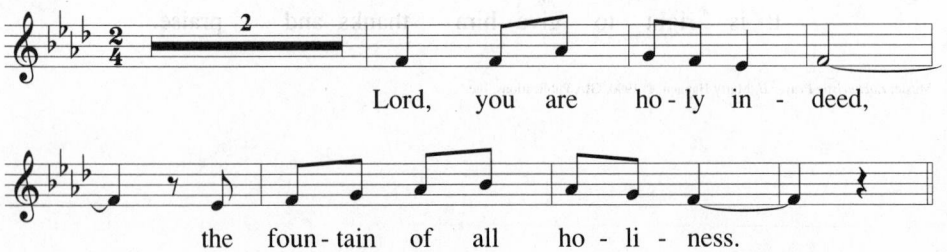

Lord, you are ho - ly in - deed, the foun - tain of all ho - li - ness.

Music: *Eucharistic Prayer II*, Marty Haugen, © 1990, GIA Publications, Inc.

ADDITIONAL ACCLAMATION 3 (OPTIONAL) 293

Cantor, then all:

Glo-ry and praise to you, O Christ! Sav-ior of the world!

MEMORIAL ACCLAMATION 294

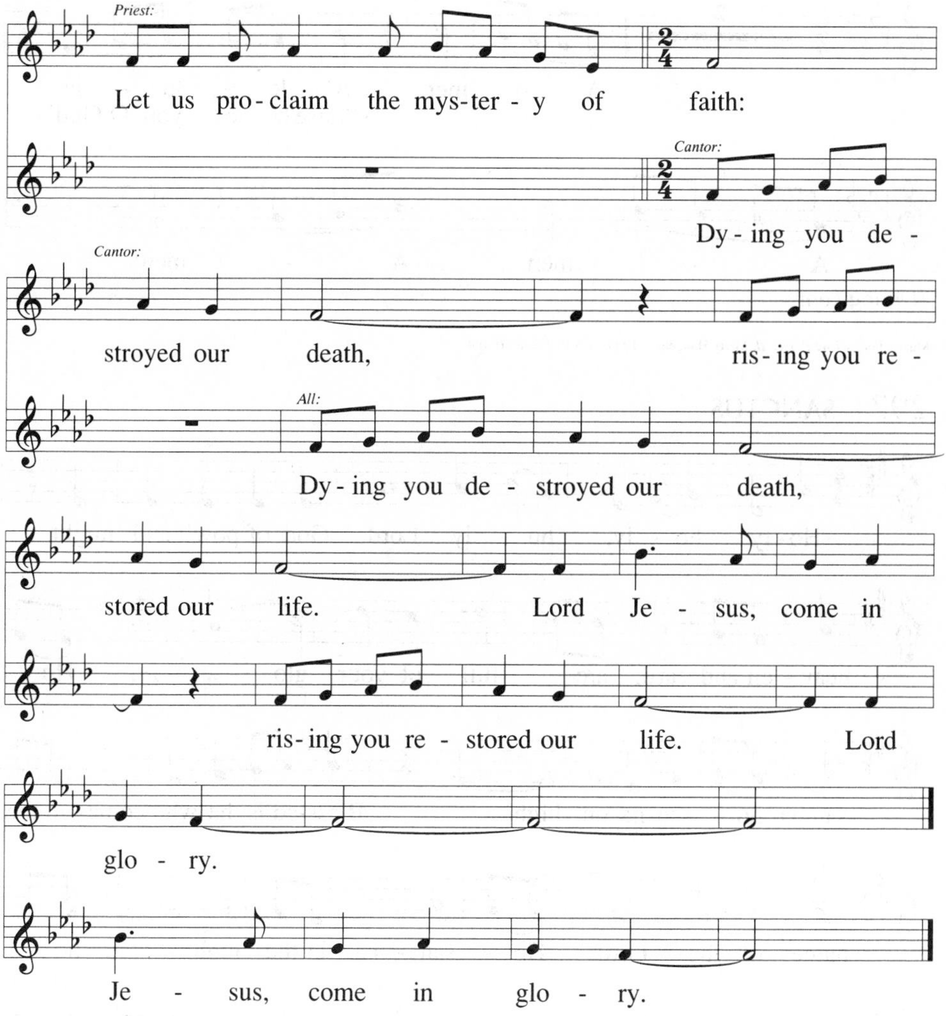

Priest:

Let us pro-claim the mys-ter-y of faith:

Cantor:

Dy-ing you de-

Cantor:

stroyed our death, ris-ing you re-

All:

Dy-ing you de-stroyed our death,

stored our life. Lord Je-sus, come in

ris-ing you re-stored our life. Lord

glo-ry.

Je-sus, come in glo-ry.

295 ADDITIONAL ACCLAMATION 4 (OPTIONAL)

Cantor, then all:

Good and gra - cious God, hear and re - mem-ber us.

Music: *Eucharistic Prayer II,* Marty Haugen, © 1990, GIA Publications, Inc.

296 DOXOLOGY AND GREAT AMEN

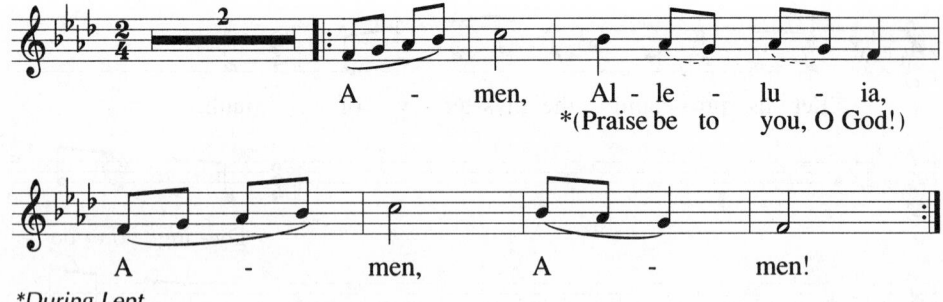

A - men, Al - le - lu - ia,
*(Praise be to you, O God!)

A - men, A - men!

*During Lent

Music: *Eucharistic Prayer II,* Marty Haugen, © 1990, GIA Publications, Inc.

297 SANCTUS

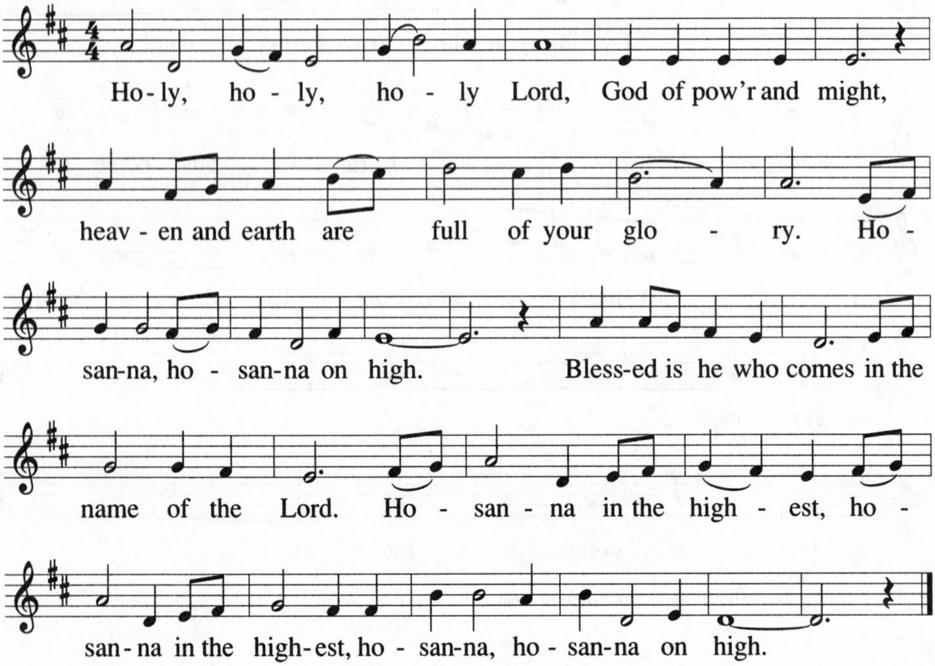

Ho - ly, ho - ly, ho - ly Lord, God of pow'r and might,

heav - en and earth are full of your glo - ry. Ho -

san - na, ho - san - na on high. Bless-ed is he who comes in the

name of the Lord. Ho - san - na in the high - est, ho -

san - na in the high-est, ho - san-na, ho - san-na on high.

Music: *St. Louis Jesuits Mass;* Robert J. Dufford, SJ, and Daniel L. Schutte, © 1973, administered by New Dawn Music; acc. by Diana Kodner, © 1993, GIA Publications, Inc.

WHEN WE EAT THIS BREAD 298

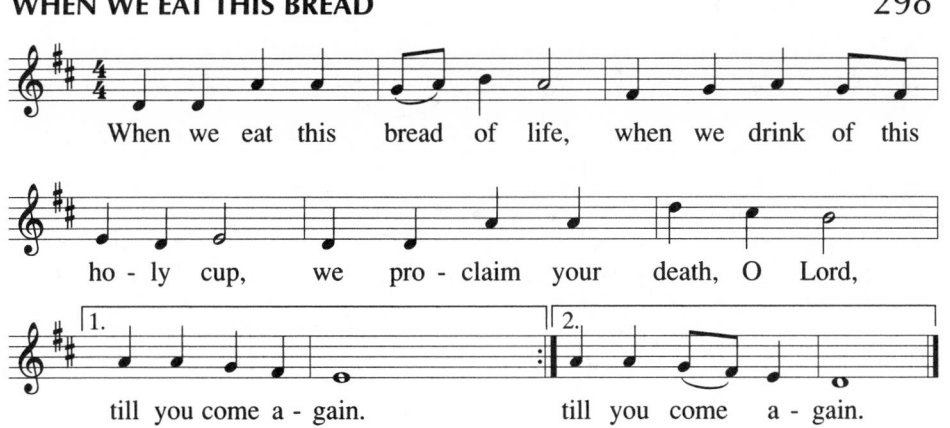

When we eat this bread of life, when we drink of this

ho - ly cup, we pro - claim your death, O Lord,

1. till you come a - gain.

2. till you come a - gain.

Music: *St. Louis Jesuits Mass;* Robert J. Dufford, SJ, and Daniel L. Schutte, © 1977, 1979, administered by New Dawn Music

AMEN 299

A - men, al - le - lu - ia, for

ev - er and ev - er, for ev - er, al - le - lu - ia, for

ev - er and ev - er. A - men.

Music: *St. Louis Jesuits Mass,* Robert J. Dufford, SJ, and Daniel L. Schutte, © 1973, administered by New Dawn Music; acc. by Diana Kodner, © 1993, GIA Publications, Inc.

300 SANCTUS

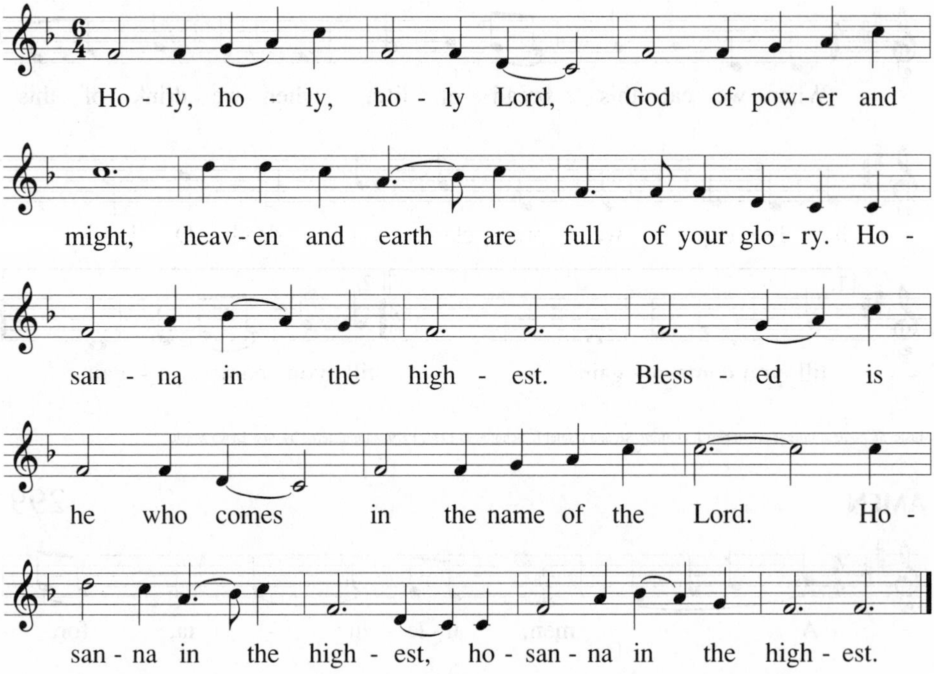

Ho - ly, ho - ly, ho - ly Lord, God of pow-er and might, heav - en and earth are full of your glo - ry. Ho - san - na in the high - est. Bless - ed is he who comes in the name of the Lord. Ho - san - na in the high - est, ho - san - na in the high - est.

Music: *Land of Rest;* adapt. by Marcia Pruner, © 1980, Church Pension Fund; acc. by Richard Proulx, © 1986, GIA Publications, Inc.

301 MEMORIAL ACCLAMATION

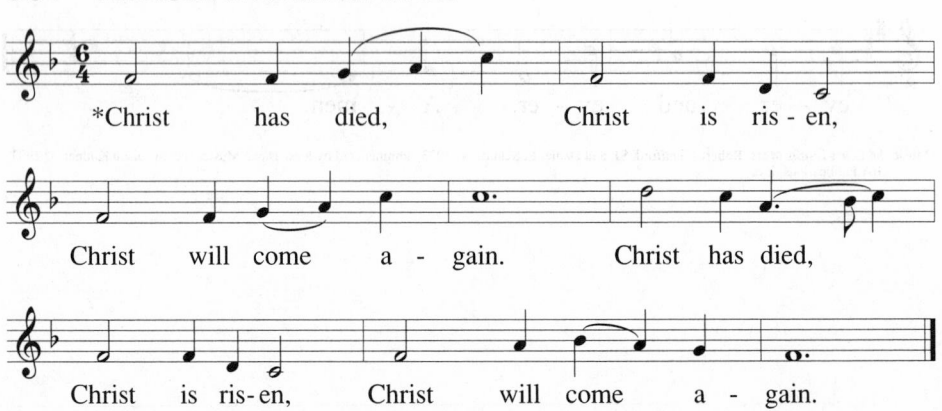

*Christ has died, Christ is ris - en, Christ will come a - gain. Christ has died, Christ is ris- en, Christ will come a - gain.

For a shorter version of this acclamation, sing the first two measures and the last two measures.

Music: *Land of Rest,* adapt. by Richard Proulx, © 1986, GIA Publications, Inc.

AMEN 302

A - men, a - men, a - men.

Music: *Land of Rest,* adapt. by Richard Proulx, GIA Publications, Inc.

SANCTUS 303

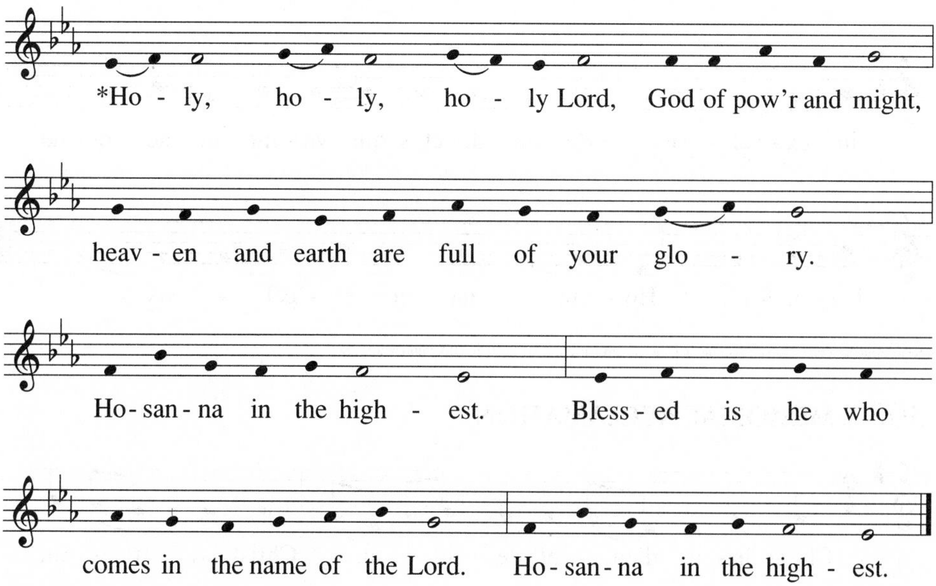

*Ho - ly, ho - ly, ho - ly Lord, God of pow'r and might,

heav - en and earth are full of your glo - ry.

Ho - san - na in the high - est. Bless - ed is he who

comes in the name of the Lord. Ho - san - na in the high - est.

May be sung unaccompanied.

Music: *Sacramentary,* 1974; adapt. by Robert J. Batastini, © 1975, GIA Publications, Inc.

MEMORIAL ACCLAMATION AND AMEN 304

Christ has died, Christ is ris - en, Christ will come a - gain.
A - men, a - men, a - men.

Music: *Sacramentary,* 1974; adapt. by Robert J. Batastini, © 1980, GIA Publications, Inc.

305 SANCTUS

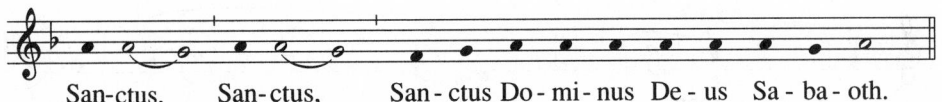

San-ctus,   San-ctus,   San-ctus Do-mi-nus De-us Sa-ba-oth.

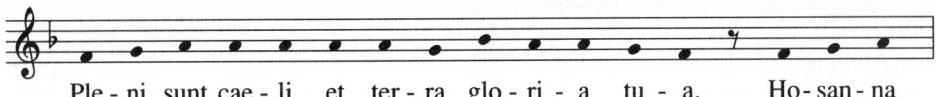

Ple-ni sunt cae-li et ter-ra glo-ri-a tu-a.   Ho-san-na

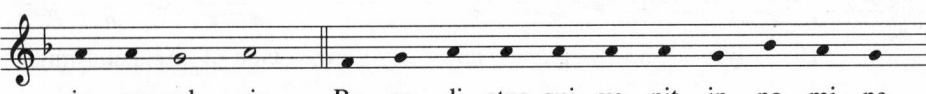

in ex-cel-sis.   Be-ne-di-ctus qui ve-nit in no-mi-ne

Do-mi-ni.   Ho-san-na in ex-cel-sis.

Music: *Sanctus XVIII, Vatican Edition;* acc. by Gerard Farrell, OSB © 1986, GIA Publications, Inc.

306 MEMORIAL ACCLAMATION

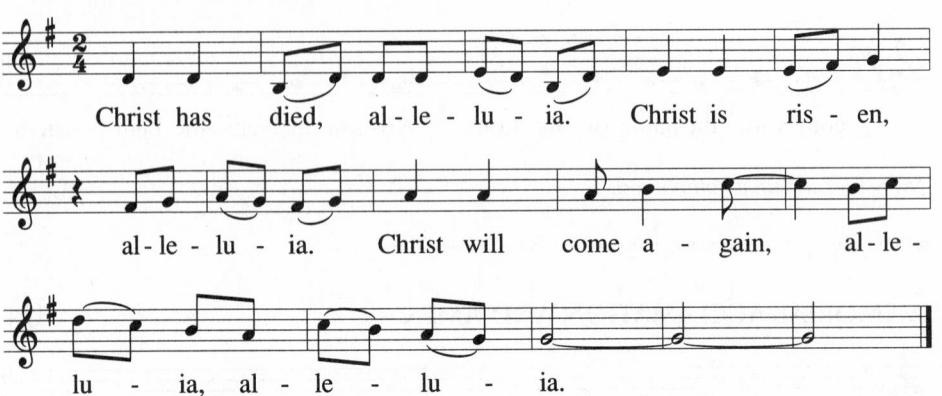

Christ has   died, al-le-lu-ia. Christ is   ris-en,

al-le-lu-ia. Christ will   come a-gain,   al-le-

lu-ia, al-le-lu-ia.

Music: Joe Wise; acc. by T.F. and R.P., © 1971, 1972, GIA Publications, Inc.

LORD'S PRAYER

Our Fa - ther, who art in heav - en,

hal-lowed be thy name; thy king - dom come; thy

will be done on earth as it is in heav - en.

Give us this day our dai - ly bread; and for - give us our

tres - pass - es as we for - give those who

tres - pass a - gainst us; and lead us not in - to temp -

ta - tion, but de - liv - er us from e - vil.

After the prayer "Deliver Us":

For the King-dom, the pow - er, and the

glo - ry are yours, now and for ev - er.

Music: *A Festival Eucharist,* Richard Proulx, © 1975, GIA Publications, Inc.

308 LAMB OF GOD

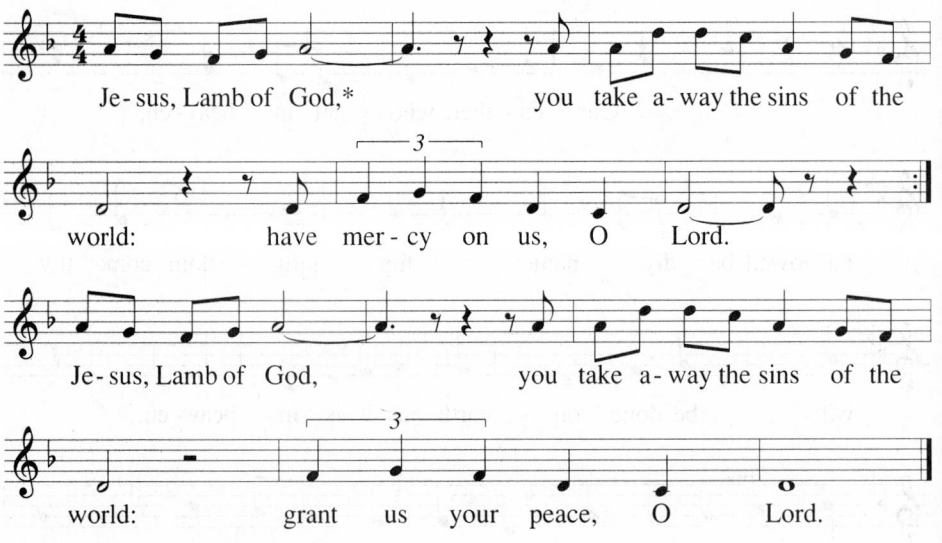

Je- sus, Lamb of God,*   you take a- way the sins   of the

world: have mer - cy   on   us,   O   Lord.

Je- sus, Lamb of God,   you take a- way the sins   of the

world: grant   us   your   peace,   O   Lord.

Alternate invocations:

Jesus, Word of God...
Jesus, Bread of Life...
Jesus, Cup of Life...
Jesus, Light of Peace...
Jesus, Hope of all...

Music: *Agapé*, Marty Haugen, © 1993, GIA Publications, Inc.

309 LAMB OF GOD

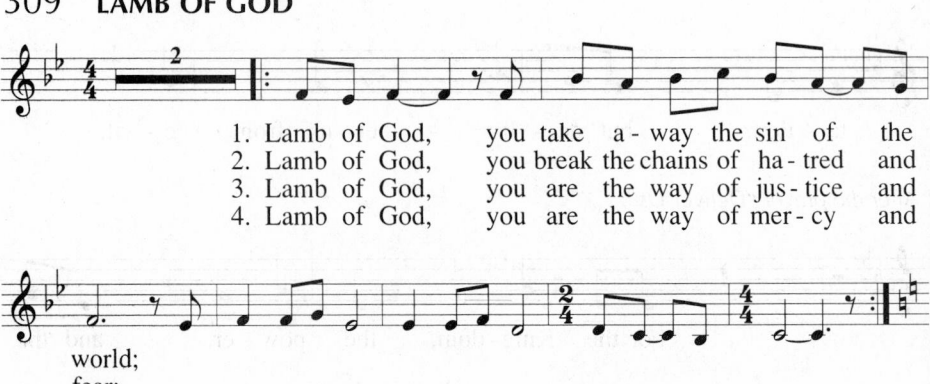

1. Lamb of God,   you take a - way the sin of   the
2. Lamb of God,   you break the chains of ha - tred   and
3. Lamb of God,   you are   the way of jus - tice   and
4. Lamb of God,   you are   the way of mer - cy   and

world;
fear;   have mer-cy on us, mer-cy on us,   mer-cy   on   us.
peace:
love:

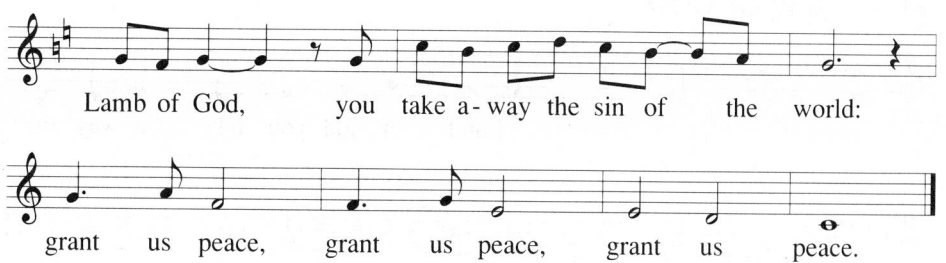

Lamb of God, you take a-way the sin of the world: grant us peace, grant us peace, grant us peace.

Text: ICET; additional text by Marty Haugen, © 1990, GIA Publications, Inc.
Music: *Now the Feast and Celebration*, Marty Haugen, © 1990, GIA Publications, Inc.

LAMB OF GOD
310

Cantor: *All:*

1. Je - sus, Lamb of God you
2. Je - sus, Pas - chal vic - tim you

take a - way the sins of the world, have mer - cy on us.

Last time
Cantor: *All:*

Je - sus, Lamb of God you take a - way the

sins of the world, grant us peace, grant us peace.

Additional invocations:

3. Jesus, Food of Pilgrims...
4. Jesus, True Bread from Heaven...
5. Jesus, Wine of Peace...
6. Jesus, Good Shepherd...

Music: Tony Way, © 1993

311 LAMB OF GOD

Lamb of God, you take a-way the sins of the world: have mer - cy on us.

Lamb of God, you take a-way the sins of the world: grant us peace, grant us peace.

Music: Richard Proulx, © 1975, GIA Publications, Inc.

312 LAMB OF GOD

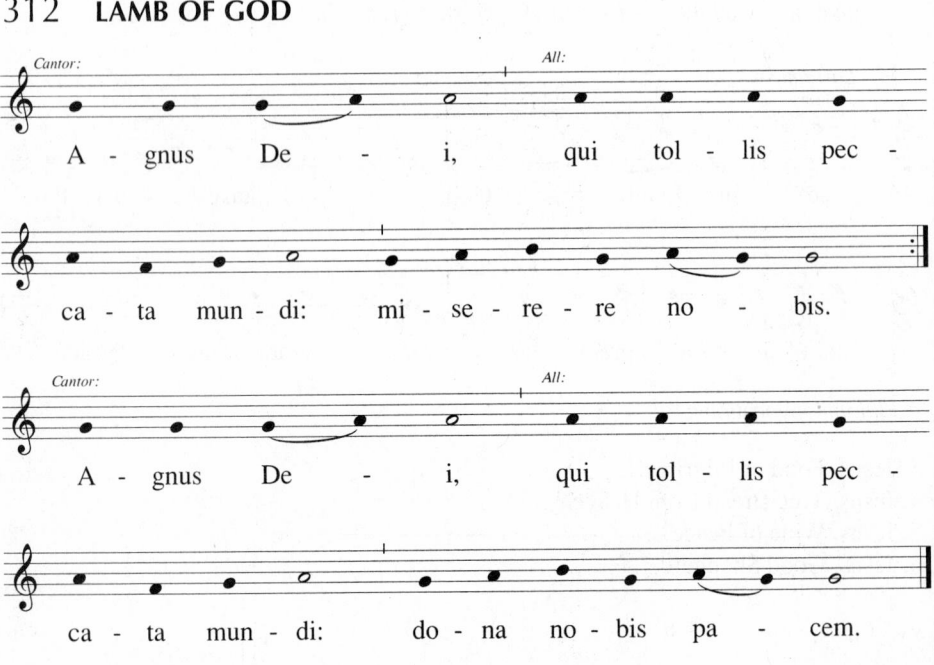

Cantor:
A - gnus De - i, qui tol - lis pec -

All:
ca - ta mun - di: mi - se - re - re no - bis.

Cantor:
A - gnus De - i, qui tol - lis pec -

All:
ca - ta mun - di: do - na no - bis pa - cem.

Music: Agnus Dei XVIII, Vatican Edition; acc. by Robert J. Batastini, © 1993, GIA Publications, Inc.

LAMB OF GOD

313

Choir or cantor:

*Lamb of God,

All:

you take a-way the sins of the world, have

mer - cy on us. world, grant

us peace.

*Alternates: 1. Bread of life, 2. Prince of peace, 3. King of kings.

Music: *Festival Liturgy*, Richard Hillert, © 1983, GIA Publications, Inc.

LAMB OF GOD

314

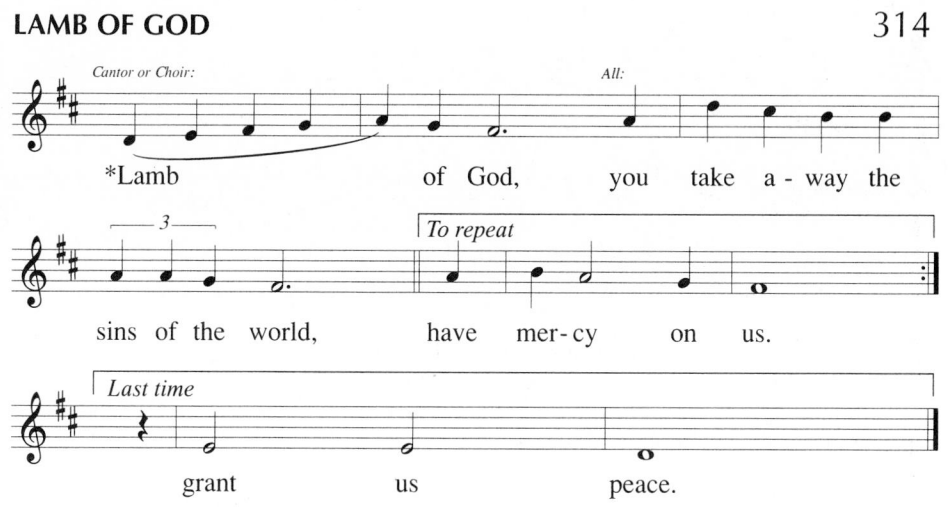

Cantor or Choir:

All:

*Lamb of God, you take a - way the

sins of the world, have mer-cy on us.

grant us peace.

*Alternates: 1. Emmanuel, 2. Prince of peace, 3. Son of God, 4. Word made flesh,
5. Paschal Lamb, 6. Bread of Life, 7. Lord Jesus Christ, 8. Lord of Love,
9. Christ the Lord, 10. King of kings.

Music: *Holy Cross Mass*; David Clark Isele. © 1979, GIA Publications, Inc.

315   LAMB OF GOD: MAY WE BE ONE

Cantor(s):

1. Lamb of God, you take a - way the sins of the world:
2. Lamb of God, un - blem - ished of - f'ring made for our sin:
3. Lamb of God, de - stroyed that all who eat might be healed:
4. Lamb of God, whose blood will save your peo - ple from death:
5. Lamb of God, our com - mon mem - 'ry, cov - e - nant feast:
6. Lamb of God, our free - dom won, re - mem - bered for ev - er:

All:

have mer - cy on us, have mer - cy on us.

Last time

Cantor(s):

Lamb of God, you take a - way the sins of the world,

All:

grant us peace, grant us peace.

Additional invocations:

Lamb of God, the shepherd of all who hunger and thirst...
Lamb of God, joy of the martyrs, song of the saints...
Lamb of God, all peoples will sing your victory song...
Lamb of God, unconquered light of the city of God...
Lamb of God, how blessed are those who are called to your feast...

Text: *Agnus Dei;* additional text by Rory Cooney
Music: Gary Daigle
© 1993, GIA Publications, Inc.

MAY WE BE ONE (COMMUNION HYMN)

Refrain

When we eat this bread and drink this cup,

we pro-claim your death, Lord Je - sus. So as we

share this feast may we be - come, heal-ing and

To verses ‖ *Last time*

light and peace. May we be one. one.

Verses

A - men, a - men.

A - men, a - men. A - men, a -

men. A - men, a - men.

Text: Rory Cooney, b.1952
Tune: Gary Daigle, b.1957
© 1993, GIA Publications, Inc.

317 O Come, O Come, Emmanuel

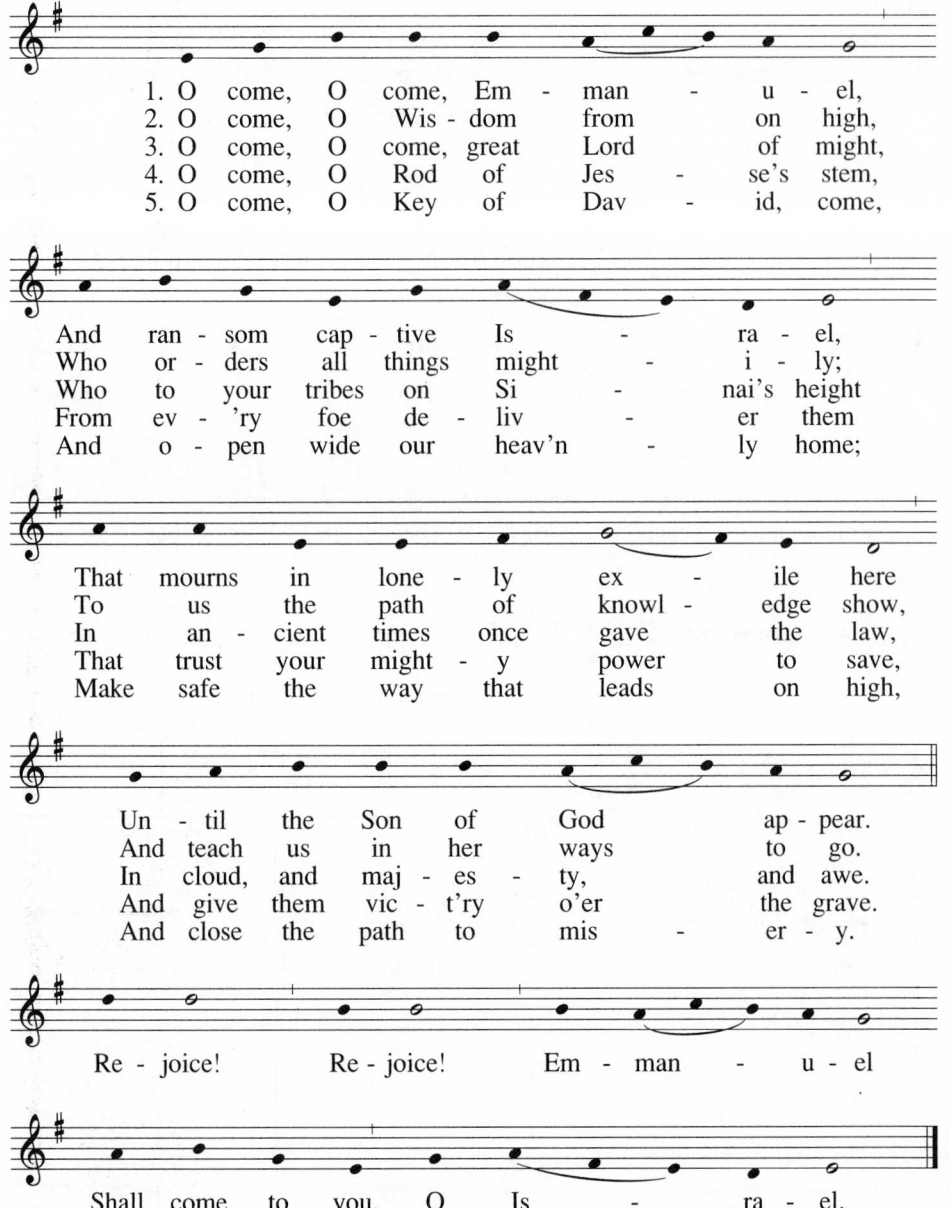

1. O come, O come, Em - man - u - el,
2. O come, O Wis - dom from on high,
3. O come, O come, great Lord of might,
4. O come, O Rod of Jes - se's stem,
5. O come, O Key of Dav - id, come,

And ran - som cap - tive Is - ra - el,
Who or - ders all things might - i - ly;
Who to your tribes on Si - nai's height
From ev - 'ry foe de - liv - er them
And o - pen wide our heav'n - ly home;

That mourns in lone - ly ex - ile here
To us the path of knowl - edge show,
In an - cient times once gave the law,
That trust your might - y power to save,
Make safe the way that leads on high,

Un - til the Son of God ap - pear.
And teach us in her ways to go.
In cloud, and maj - es - ty, and awe.
And give them vic - t'ry o'er the grave.
And close the path to mis - er - y.

Re - joice! Re - joice! Em - man - u - el

Shall come to you, O Is - ra - el.

6. O come, O Dayspring from on high
   And cheer us by your drawing nigh;
   Disperse the gloomy clouds of night,
   And death's dark shadow put to flight.

7. O come, Desire of nations, bind
   In one the hearts of humankind;
   O bid our sad divisions cease,
   And be for us our King of Peace.

Text: *Veni, veni Emmanuel;* Latin 9th C.; tr. by John M. Neale, 1818-1866, alt.
Tune: VENI VENI EMMANUEL, LM with refrain; Mode I; adapt. by Thomas Helmore, 1811-1890; acc. by Richard Proulx, b. 1937, © 1975,
GIA Publications, Inc.

People, Look East   318

1. Peo - ple, look East. The time is near
2. Fur - rows, be glad. Though earth is bare.
3. Birds, though you long have ceased to build,
4. Stars, keep the watch. When night is dim
5. An - gels an - nounce with shouts of mirth

Of the crown - ing of the year.
One more seed is plant - ed there:
Guard the nest that must be filled.
One more light the bowl shall brim,
Him who brings new life to earth.

Make your house fair as you are a - ble,
Give up your strength the seed to nour - ish,
E - ven the hour when wings are fro - zen
Shin - ing be - yond the frost - y weath - er,
Set ev - 'ry peak and val - ley hum - ming

Trim the hearth and set the ta - ble.
That in course the flow'r may flour - ish.
He for fledg - ing time has cho - sen.
Bright as sun and moon to - geth - er.
With the word, the Lord is com - ing.

Peo - ple look East and sing to - day:

Love the Guest is on the way.
Love the Rose is on the way.
Love the Bird is on the way.
Love the Star is on the way.
Love the Lord is on the way.

Text: Eleanor Farjeon, 1881-1965. © David Higham Assoc. Ltd.
Tune: BESANCON. 87 98 87: French Traditional; harm. by Martin Shaw, 1875-1958. © Oxford University Press

319 Walk in the Reign

Refrain

Close as to-mor-row the sun shall ap-pear.

Free-dom is com-ing and heal-ing is near. And I shall be

with you in laugh-ter and pain to stand in the wind and

walk in the reign, to walk in the reign.

Verses

1. In days to come the des-ert shall bloom.
2. Com-fort each oth-er, for pain soon must end. A
3. A cur-tain of fear is be-ing torn down.
4. The streets of So-we-to, the docks at G-dansk, Ti-

Riv-ers will run there, soon, ver-y soon. So
day comes when li-on and lamb shall be friends. The
Pris-ons are o-pened; the lost have been found. So
en-an-men Square, the slums of The Bronx, When

what shall we fear, though death do its
sight-less shall see then, the speech-less sing
go tell the seek-er what we've seen and
we stand to-geth-er to stand a-gainst

worst? The word of our God is the
songs. The name of our God is the
heard: The name of our God is the
hell, The name of this peo-ple is

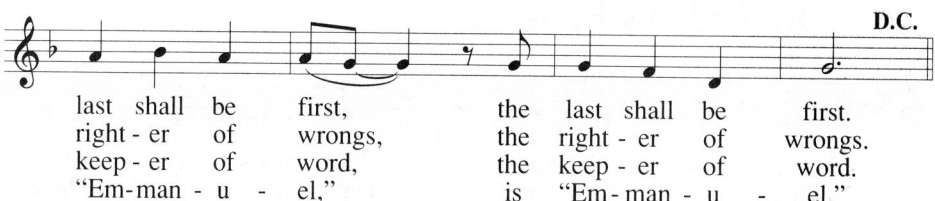

last shall be first, the last shall be first.
right - er of wrongs, the right - er of wrongs.
keep - er of word, the keep - er of word.
"Em-man - u - el," is "Em-man - u - el."

Text: Rory Cooney, b.1952
Tune: Rory Cooney, b.1952
© 1990, GIA Publications, Inc.

The King Shall Come When Morning Dawns 320

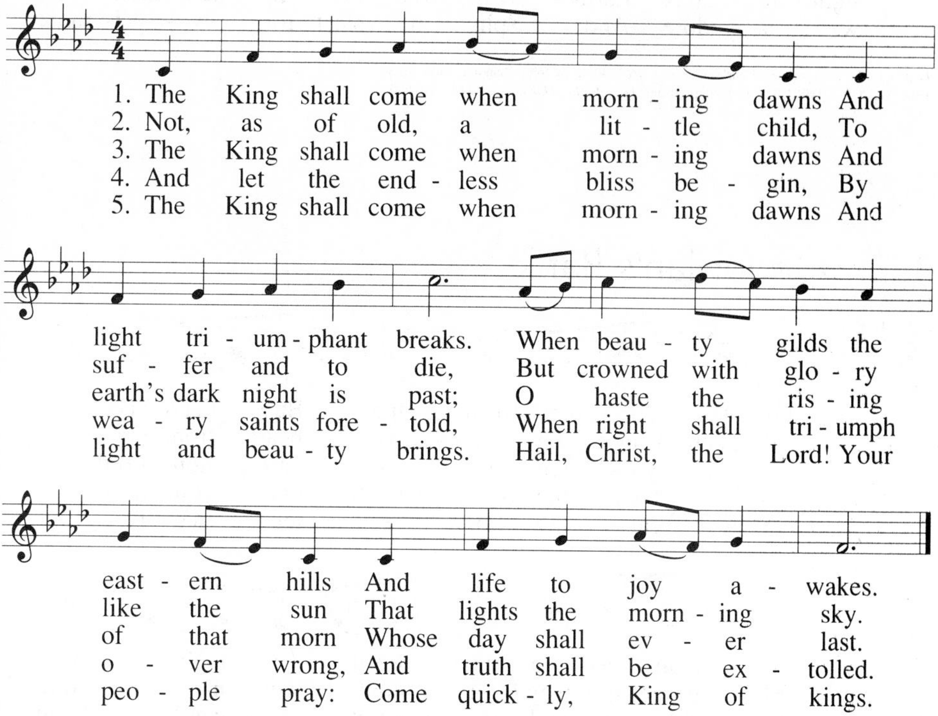

1. The King shall come when morn - ing dawns And
2. Not, as of old, a lit - tle child, To
3. The King shall come when morn - ing dawns And
4. And let the end - less bliss be - gin, By
5. The King shall come when morn - ing dawns And

light tri - um - phant breaks. When beau - ty gilds the
suf - fer and to die, But crowned with glo - ry
earth's dark night is past; O haste the ris - ing
wea - ry saints fore - told, When right shall tri - umph
light and beau - ty brings. Hail, Christ, the Lord! Your

east - ern hills And life to joy a - wakes.
like the sun That lights the morn - ing sky.
of that morn Whose day shall ev - er last.
o - ver wrong, And truth shall be ex - tolled.
peo - ple pray: Come quick - ly, King of kings.

Text: John Brownlie, 1857-1925
Tune: MORNING SONG. CM; John Wyeth, 1770-1858; arr. by Robert J. Batastini, b.1942, © 1994, GIA Publications, Inc.

321 On Jordan's Bank

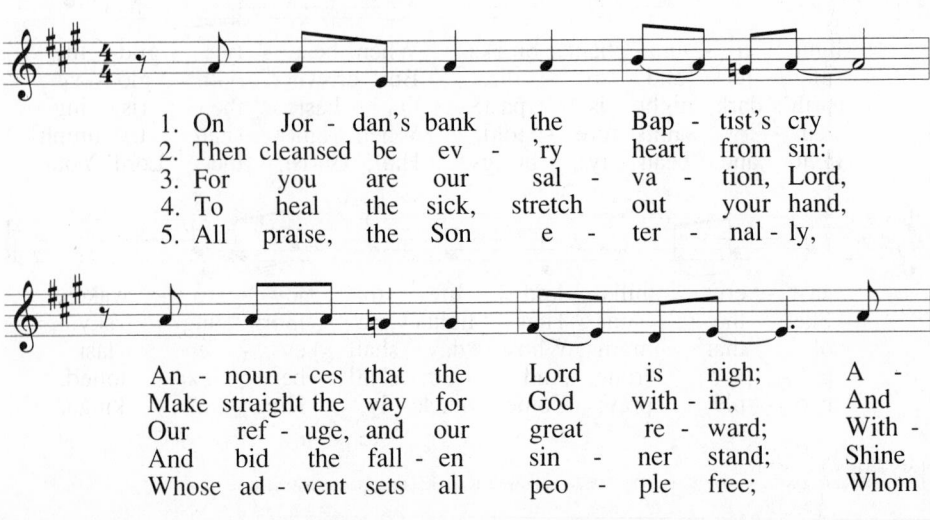

1. On Jor - dan's bank the Bap - tist's cry An -
2. Then cleansed be ev - ery heart from sin; Make
3. For you are our sal - va - tion, Lord, Our
4. To heal the sick stretch out your hand, And
5. All praise the Son e - ter - nal - ly, Whose

noun - ces that the Lord is nigh; A - wake and heark - en,
straight the way of God with - in, And let each heart pre -
ref - uge, and our great re - ward; With - out your grace we
bid the fall - en sin - ner stand; Shine forth, and let your
ad - vent sets his peo - ple free; Whom with the Fa - ther

for he brings Glad tid - ings of the King of kings.
pare a home Where such a might - y guest may come.
waste a - way Like flow'rs that with - er and de - cay.
light re - store Earth's own true love - li - ness once more.
we a - dore And Spir - it blest for ev - er - more.

Text: *Jordanis oras praevia;* Charles Coffin, 1676-1749; tr. by John Chandler, 1806-1876
Tune: WINCHESTER NEW, LM; adapt. from *Musikalisches Handbuch,* Hamburg, 1690

322 On Jordan's Bank

1. On Jor - dan's bank the Bap - tist's cry
2. Then cleansed be ev - 'ry heart from sin:
3. For you are our sal - va - tion, Lord,
4. To heal the sick, stretch out your hand,
5. All praise, the Son e - ter - nal - ly,

An - noun - ces that the Lord is nigh; A -
Make straight the way for God with - in, And
Our ref - uge, and our great re - ward; With -
And bid the fall - en sin - ner stand; Shine
Whose ad - vent sets all peo - ple free; Whom

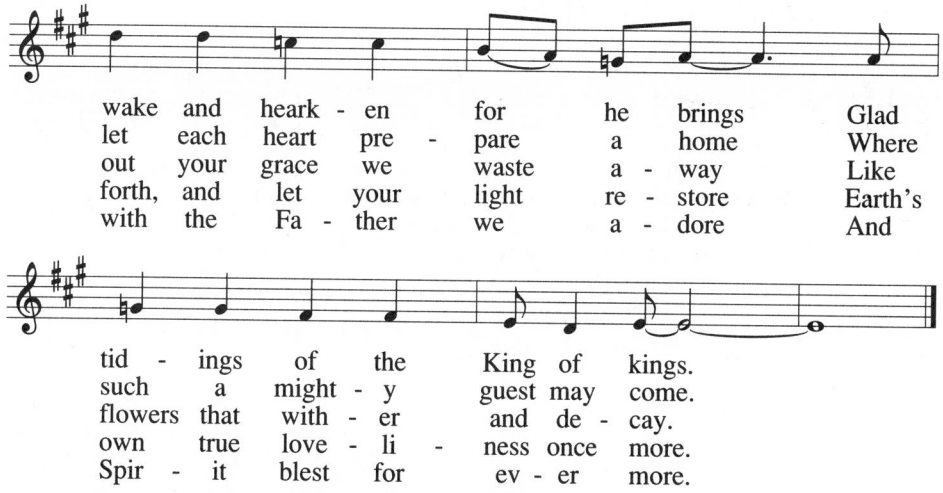

wake and heark - en for he brings Glad
let each heart pre - pare a home Where
out your grace we waste a - way Like
forth, and let your light re - store Earth's
with the Fa - ther we a - dore And

tid - ings of the King of kings.
such a might - y guest may come.
flowers that with - er and de - cay.
own true love - li - ness once more.
Spir - it blest for ev - er more.

Text: *Jordanis oras praevia;* Charles Coffin, 1676-1749; tr. by John Chandler, 1806-1876
Tune: ST. JOHN THE BAPTIST, LM; Gary Miles, © 1974, 1975, Celebration

Come, O Long Expected Jesus   323

1. Come, O long ex - pect - ed Je - sus,
2. Is - rael's strength and con - so - la - tion,
3. Born your peo - ple to de - liv - er;
4. By your own e - ter - nal Spir - it

Born to set your peo - ple free; From our fears and
You, the hope of all the earth, Dear de - sire of
Born a child and yet a king! Born to reign in
Rule in all our hearts a - lone; By your all suf -

sins re - lease us; Free us from cap - tiv - i - ty.
ev - 'ry na - tion, Come, and save us by your birth.
us for ev - er, Now your grac - ious king - dom bring.
fi - cient mer - it Raise us to your glo - rious throne.

Text: Haggai 2:7; Charles Wesley, 1707-1788, alt.
Tune: STUTTGART, 8 7 8 7; Christian F. Witt, 1660-1716; adapt. by Henry J. Gauntlett, 1805-1876

324 Advent Gathering

Verses

1. Here in this world where dark-ness sur-rounds us,
2. Where is the peace you prom-ised the wid-ow? Show us your
3. Where is the road you prom-ise the ex-ile?
4. Where is the heart whose "yes" is sal-va-tion?

face, O prom-ise of dawn.
We seek a sign that
Where is the home you
Where is the good news
Where is the child whose

you are a-mong us.
prom-ised the or-phan? Show us your face, O Lord Je-sus come.
preached to the low-ly?
life is our fu-ture?

Refrain

Come, O hope of your peo-ple. Come a-mong us and

Come, O hope of your peo-ple.

stay. Lead us in mer-cy up from the

Come a-mong us and stay.

shad-ows, Shine in our dark-ness, be here to-day.

Text: Rory Cooney, b.1952
Tune: Gary Daigle, b.1957
© 1993, GIA Publications, Inc.

Like a Shepherd 325

Refrain

Like a shep-herd he feeds his flock and gath-ers the
lambs in his arms, hold-ing them care-ful-ly
close to his heart, lead-ing them home.

Verses 1, 2

1. Say to the cit-ies of Ju - dah: Pre - pare the
2. I my-self will shep-herd them, for oth-ers have

way of the Lord. Go to the moun-tain top,
led them a - stray. The lost I will res - cue and

D.C.

lift your voice; Je - ru - sa - lem, here is your God.
heal their wounds and pas-ture them, giv-ing them rest.

Verse 3

3. Come un - to me if you are

heav - i-ly bur - dened, and take my yoke up-

D.C.

on your shoul-ders, I will give you rest.

Text: Isaiah 40:9ff, Ezekiel 34:11, Matthew 11:28ff; Bob Dufford, SJ, b.1943
Tune: Bob Dufford, SJ, b.1943; acc. by Sr. Theophane Hytrek, OSF, 1915-1992, alt.
© 1976, Robert J. Dufford, SJ, and New Dawn Music

326 Comfort, Comfort, O My People

1. Com - fort, com - fort, O my peo - ple, Speak of peace, now
2. Hark, the voice of one who's cry - ing In the des - ert
3. O make straight what long was crook-ed, Make the rough - er

says our God; Com - fort those who sit in dark - ness,
far and near, Bid - ding all to full re - pent - ance
plac - es plain; Let your hearts be true and hum - ble,

Mourn - ing 'neath their sor - row's load. Speak un - to Je -
Since the king - dom now is here. O that warn-ing
As be - fits his ho - ly reign. For the glo - ry

ru - sa - lem Of the peace that waits for them;
cry o - bey! Now pre - pare for God a way;
of the Lord Now o'er earth is shed a - broad;

Tell of all the sins I cov - er, And that war-fare now is o - ver.
Let the val - leys rise to meet him And the hills bow down to greet him.
And all flesh shall see the to - ken That his word is nev - er bro-ken.

Text: Isaiah 40:1-8; *Tröstet, tröstet, meine Lieben;* Johann Olearius, 1611-1684; tr. by Catherine Winkworth, 1827-1878, alt.
Tune: GENEVA 42, 8 7 8 7 77 88; *Genevan Psalter,* 1551; harm. adapt. from Claude Goudimel, 1505-1572

When the King Shall Come Again 327

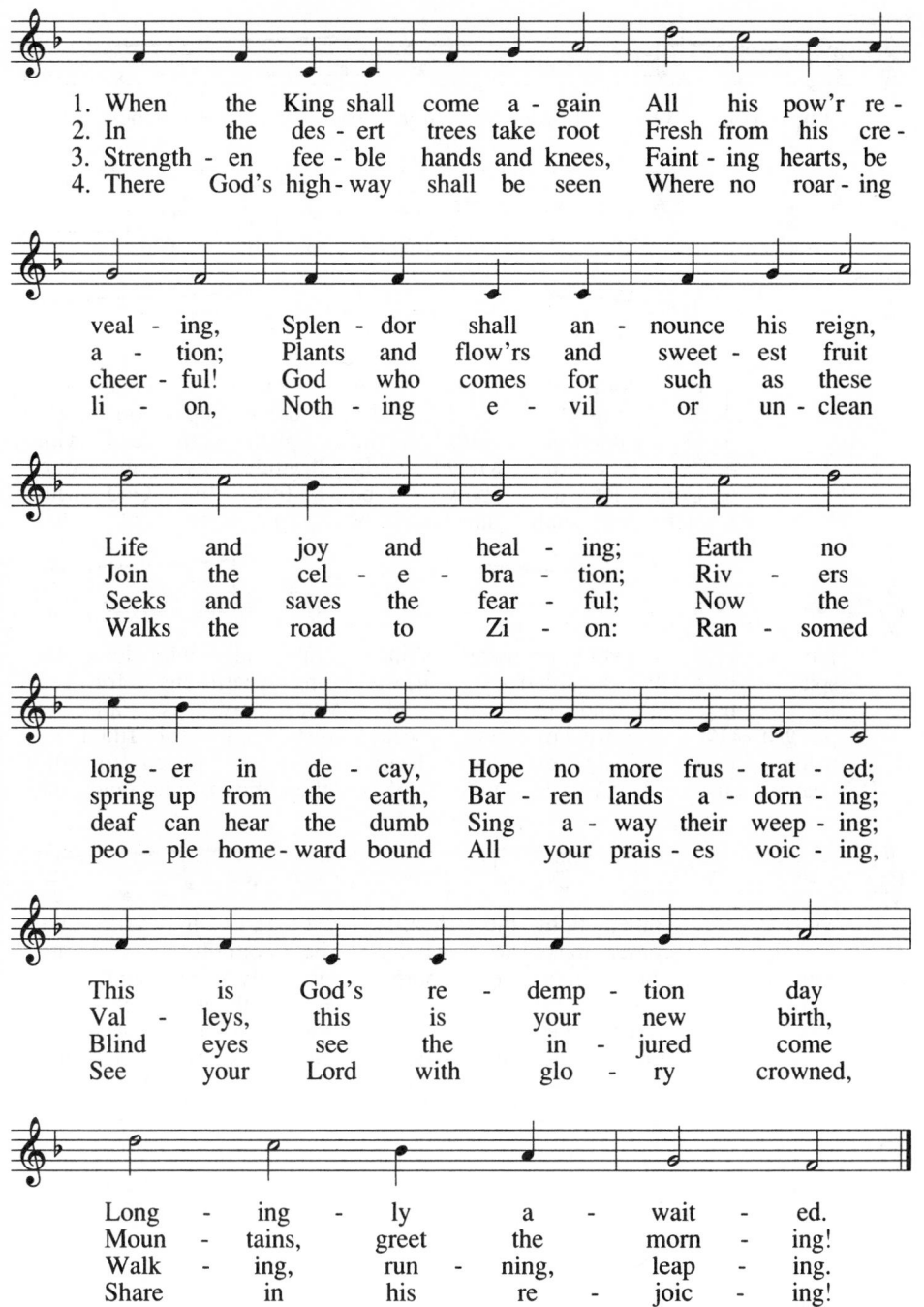

1. When the King shall come a - gain All his pow'r re -
2. In the des - ert trees take root Fresh from his cre -
3. Strength - en fee - ble hands and knees, Faint - ing hearts, be
4. There God's high - way shall be seen Where no roar - ing

veal - ing, Splen - dor shall an - nounce his reign,
a - tion; Plants and flow'rs and sweet - est fruit
cheer - ful! God who comes for such as these
li - on, Noth - ing e - vil or un - clean

Life and joy and heal - ing; Earth no
Join the cel - e - bra - tion; Riv - ers
Seeks and saves the fear - ful; Now the
Walks the road to Zi - on: Ran - somed

long - er in de - cay, Hope no more frus - trat - ed;
spring up from the earth, Bar - ren lands a - dorn - ing;
deaf can hear the dumb Sing a - way their weep - ing;
peo - ple home - ward bound All your prais - es voic - ing,

This is God's re - demp - tion day
Val - leys, this is your new birth,
Blind eyes see the in - jured come
See your Lord with glo - ry crowned,

Long - ing - ly a - wait - ed.
Moun - tains, greet the morn - ing!
Walk - ing, run - ning, leap - ing.
Share in his re - joic - ing!

Text: Isaiah 35; Christopher Idle, b.1938, © 1982, Hope Publishing Co.
Tune: GAUDEAMUS PARITER, 7 6 7 6 D; Johann Horn, c. 1495-1547

328 My Soul in Stillness Waits

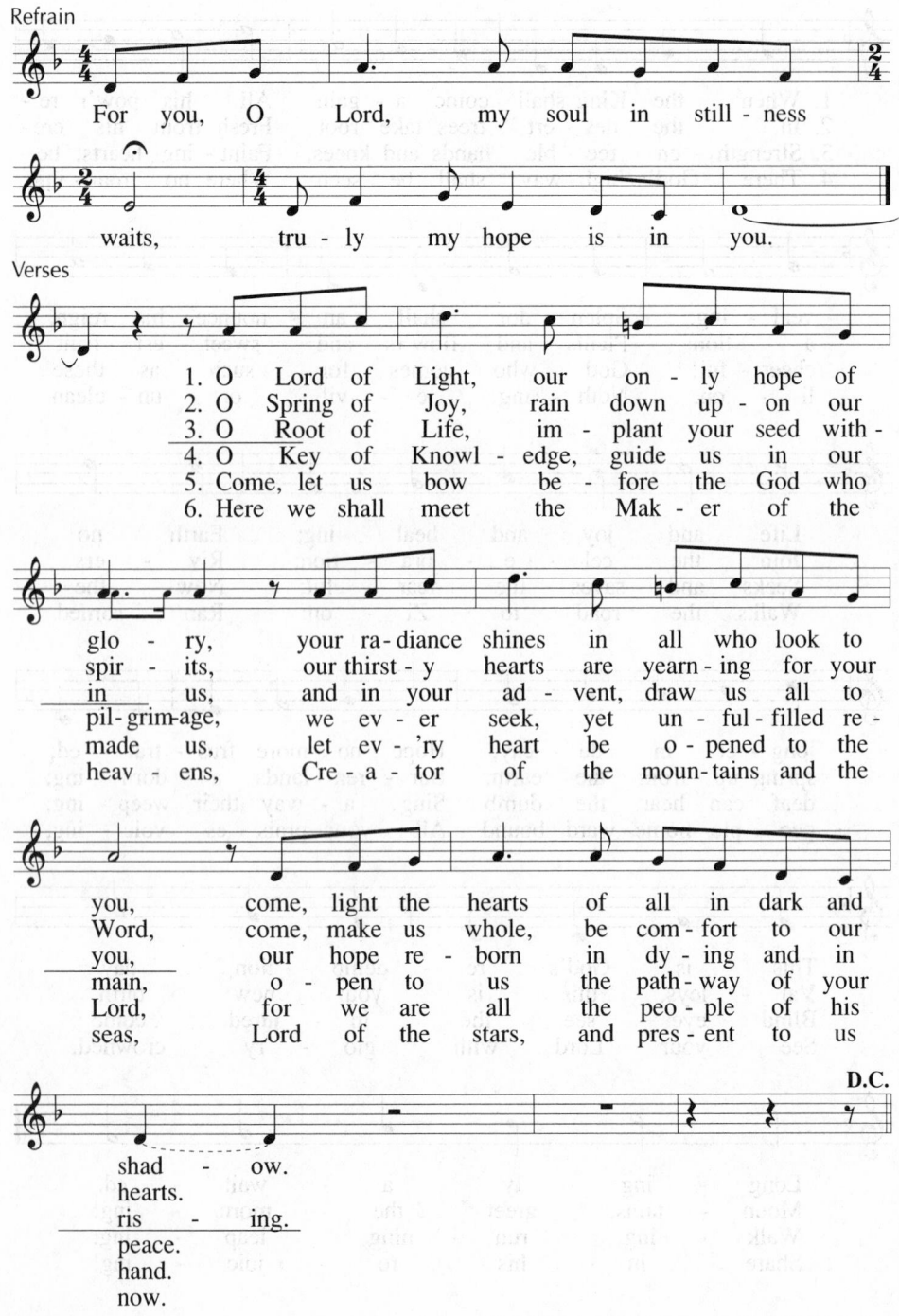

Refrain

For you, O Lord, my soul in still - ness waits, tru - ly my hope is in you.

Verses

1. O Lord of Light, our on - ly hope of
2. O Spring of Joy, rain down up - on our
3. O Root of Life, im - plant your seed with -
4. O Key of Knowl - edge, guide us in our
5. Come, let us bow be - fore the God who
6. Here we shall meet the Mak - er of the

glo - ry, your ra - diance shines in all who look to
spir - its, our thirst - y hearts are yearn - ing for your
in us, and in your ad - vent, draw us all to
pil - grim-age, we ev - er seek, yet un - ful - filled re -
made us, let ev - 'ry heart be o - pened to the
heav - ens, Cre - a - tor of the moun - tains and the

you, come, light the hearts of all in dark and
Word, come, make us whole, be com - fort to our
you, our hope re - born in dy - ing and in
main, o - pen to us the path - way of your
Lord, for we are all the peo - ple of his
seas, Lord of the stars, and pres - ent to us

D.C.

shad - ow.
hearts.
ris - ing.
peace.
hand.
now.

Text: Psalm 95 and "O" Antiphons; Marty Haugen, b.1950
Tune: Marty Haugen, b.1950
© 1982, GIA Publications, Inc.

Within Our Hearts Be Born 329

1. O an - cient love, pro - cess - ing through the
2. O home - less love, that dwells a - mong the
3. O gen - tle love, car - ess - ing those in
4. O suf - f'ring love, that bears our hu - man

a - ges: O hid - den love, re - vealed in hu - man
stran - ger: O low - ly love, that knows the might - y's
sor - row: O ten - der love, that com - forts those for -
weak - ness: O bound - less love, that ris - es with the

form: O prom - ised love, the dream of seers and
scorn: O hun - gry love, that lay with - in a
lorn: O hope - ful love, that prom - is - es to -
morn: O might - y love, con - cealed in in - fant

sa - ges:
man - ger: O liv - ing Love, with - in our hearts be
mor - row:
meek - ness:

born, O liv - ing Love, with - in our hearts be borne.

Text: Michael Joncas, b.1951
Tune: BEDFORD ABBEY, 11 10 11 10 10; Michael Joncas, b.1951
© 1994, GIA Publications, Inc.

330 Your Mercy Like Rain

Refrain

Let me taste   your   mer - cy   like   rain   on my

face;   here   in my   life,   show   me   your

peace.   Let us   see   with our   own   eyes   your   day   break - ing

bright.   Come, O   Morn - ing;   come, O   Light!

Verses

1. What God has spoken I will declare:
   Peace to the people of God ev'rywhere.
   God's saving presence is close at hand:
   glory as near as our land!

2. Here faithful love and truth will embrace;
   here peace and justice will come face to face.
   God's truth shall water the earth like a spring,
   while justice will bend down and sing.

3. God will keep the promise indeed;
   our land will yield the food that we need.
   Justice shall walk before you that day,
   clearing a path, preparing your way.

Text: Psalm 85; Rory Cooney, b.1952
Tune: Rory Cooney, b.1952
© 1993, GIA Publications, Inc.

God of All People 331

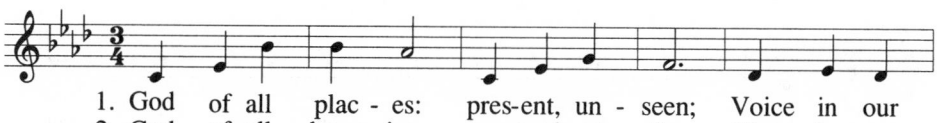

1. God of all plac - es: pres-ent, un - seen; Voice in our
2. God of all dream-ing, near and yet far. Vi - sion un -
3. God of all peo - ple, dust and the clay. Breath of a

si - lence, song in our midst. We are your peo-ple, know-ing, unheard of, wake us to rest. We are your pres-ence, sent forth a -
new wind, fire in our hearts. Light born of heav-en, peace on the

sure.   Come, Lord Je - sus, come!
fraid.   Come, Lord Je - sus, come!
earth.   Come, Lord Je - sus, come!

Text: David Haas, b.1957
Tune: KINGDOM, 9 9 9 6; David Haas, b.1957
© 1988, GIA Publications, Inc.

Wait for the Lord 332

Wait for the Lord, whose day is near.

Wait for the Lord: be strong, take heart!

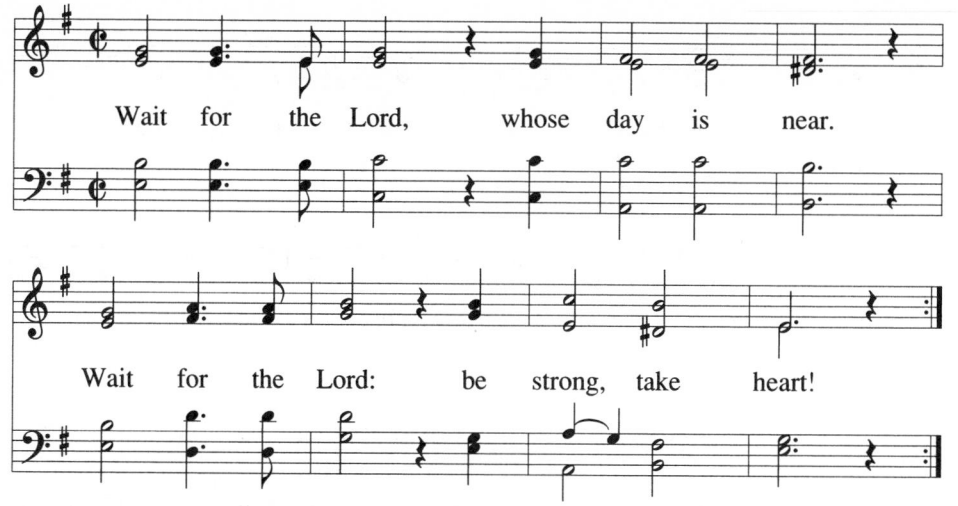

Text: Isaiah 40, Philippians 4, Matthew 6-7; Taizé Community, 1984
Tune: Jacques Berthier, 1923-1994
© 1984, Les Presses de Taizé, GIA Publications, Inc., agent

333 O Come, Divine Messiah

1. O come, Di-vine Mes - si - ah, The
2. O come De-sired of na - tions, Whom
3. O come in peace and meek - ness, For

world in si - lence waits the day When
priest and proph - et long fore - told, Will
low - ly will your cra - dle be: Though

hope shall sing its tri - umph, And
break the cap - tive fet - ters, Re -
clothed in hu - man weak - ness We

sad - ness flee a - way.
deem the long - lost fold.
shall your God - head see.

Dear Sav - ior, haste! Come, come to earth. Dis - pel the

night and show your face, And bid us hail the dawn of

grace. O come, Di - vine Mes - si - ah, The

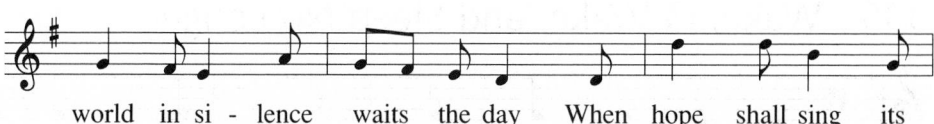

world in si - lence waits the day When hope shall sing its

tri - umph, And sad - ness flee a - way.

Text: *Venez, divin Messie;* Abbé Simon-Joseph Pellegrin, 1663-1745; tr. by S. Mary of St. Philip, 1877
Tune: VENEZ, DIVIN MESSIE, 7 8 7 6 with refrain; French Noël, 16th C.; harm. by Healey Willan, 1880-1968, © 1958,
Ralph Jusko Publications, Inc.

Savior of the Nations, Come   334

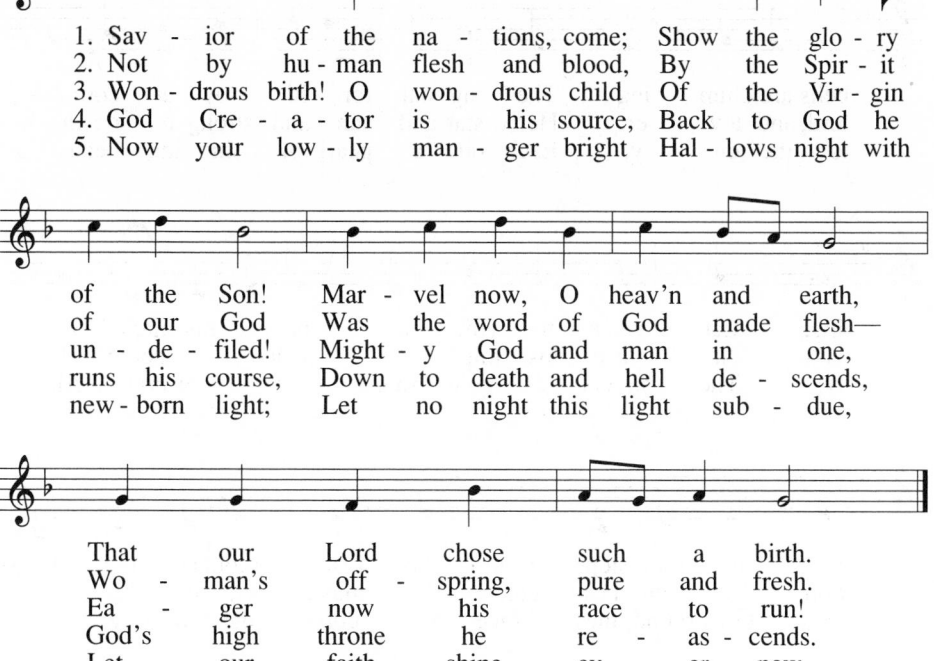

1. Sav - ior   of   the   na - tions, come;   Show   the   glo - ry
2. Not   by   hu - man   flesh   and blood,   By   the   Spir - it
3. Won - drous birth! O   won - drous child   Of   the   Vir - gin
4. God   Cre - a - tor   is   his source,   Back   to   God   he
5. Now   your   low - ly   man - ger bright   Hal - lows   night with

of   the   Son!   Mar - vel   now,   O   heav'n   and   earth,
of   our   God   Was   the   word   of   God   made   flesh—
un - de - filed!   Might - y   God   and   man   in   one,
runs   his   course,   Down   to   death and   hell   de - scends,
new - born   light;   Let   no   night this   light   sub - due,

That   our   Lord   chose   such   a   birth.
Wo - man's   off - spring,   pure   and   fresh.
Ea - ger   now   his   race   to   run!
God's   high   throne   he   re - as - cends.
Let   our   faith   shine   ev - er   new.

Text: *Veni, Redemptor gentium;* ascr. to St. Ambrose, 340-397; tr. sts. 1-3a, William Reynolds, 1812-1876; sts. 3b-5, Martin L. Seltz, 1909-1967, alt.
Tune: NUN KOMM DER HEIDEN HEILAND, 77 77; *Geystliche gesangk Buchleyn,* Wittenberg, 1524; harm. by Melchior Vulpius, c. 1560-1615

335 Wake, O Wake, and Sleep No Longer

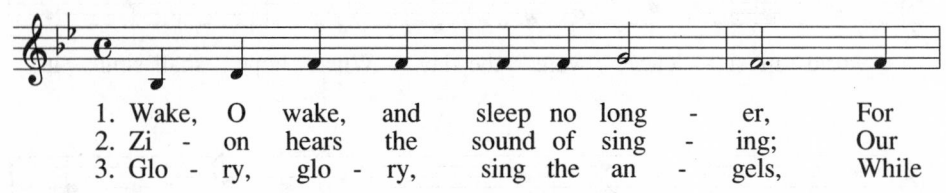

1. Wake, O wake, and sleep no long - er, For
2. Zi - on hears the sound of sing - ing; Our
3. Glo - ry, glo - ry, sing the an - gels, While

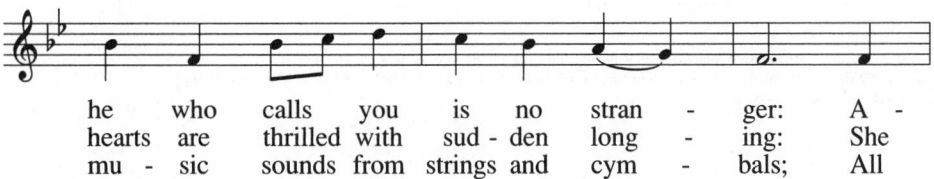

he who calls you is no stran - ger: A -
hearts are thrilled with sud - den long - ing: She
mu - sic sounds from strings and cym - bals; All

wake, God's own Je - ru - sa - lem! Hear, the mid - night
stirs, and wakes, and stands pre-pared. Christ, her friend, and
hu - man - kind, with songs a - rise! Twelve the gates in -

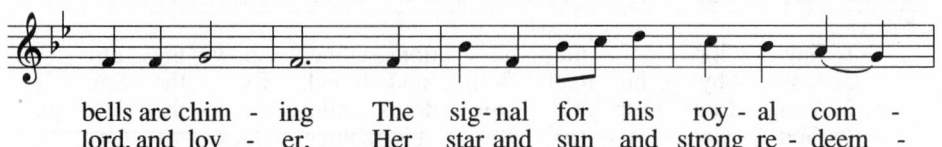

bells are chim - ing The sig - nal for his roy - al com -
lord, and lov - er, Her star and sun and strong re - deem -
to the cit - y, Each one a pearl of shin - ing beau -

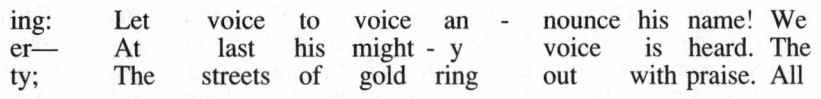

ing: Let voice to voice an - nounce his name! We
er— At last his might - y voice is heard. The
ty; The streets of gold ring out with praise. All

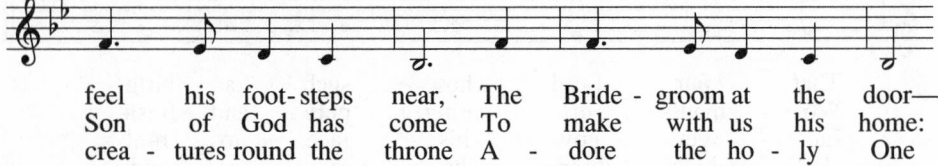

feel his foot-steps near, The Bride - groom at the door—
Son of God has come To make with us his home:
crea - tures round the throne A - dore the ho - ly One

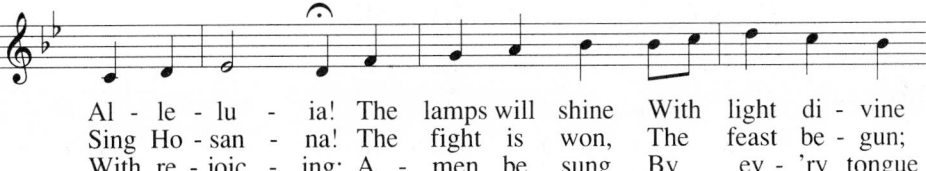

Al - le - lu - ia! The lamps will shine With light di - vine
Sing Ho - san - na! The fight is won, The feast be - gun;
With re - joic - ing: A - men be sung By ev - 'ry tongue

As Christ the sav - ior comes to reign.
We fix our eyes on Christ a - lone.
To crown their wel - come to the King.

Text: Matthew 25:1-13; *Wachet auf, ruft uns die Stimme*, Philipp Nicolai, 1556-1608; tr. and adapt. by Christopher Idle, b. 1938. © 1982, Hope
  Publishing Co.
Tune: WACHET AUF, 89 8 89 8 66 4 44 8; Philipp Nicolai, 1556-1608; harm. by J.S. Bach, 1685-1750

Prepare the Way of the Lord 336

Pre - pare the way of the Lord. Pre - pare the way of the Lord, and

all peo - ple will see the sal - va - tion of our God. Pre-

Text: Luke 3:4,6; Taizé Community, 1984
Tune: Jacques Berthier, 1923-1994
© 1984, Les Presses de Taizé, GIA Publications, Inc., agent

337 Creator of the Stars of Night

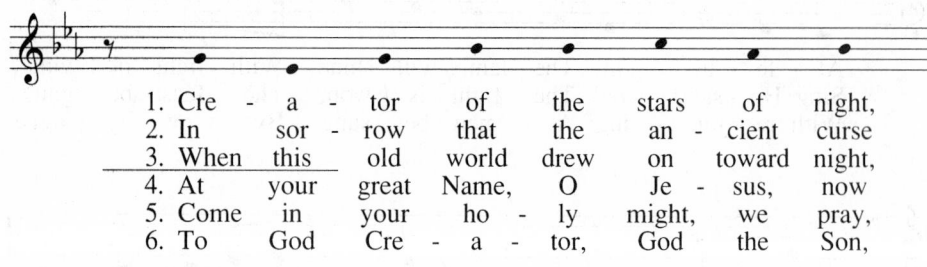

1. Cre - a - tor of the stars of night,
2. In sor - row that the an - cient curse
3. When this old world drew on toward night,
4. At your great Name, O Je - sus, now
5. Come in your ho - ly might, we pray,
6. To God Cre - a - tor, God the Son,

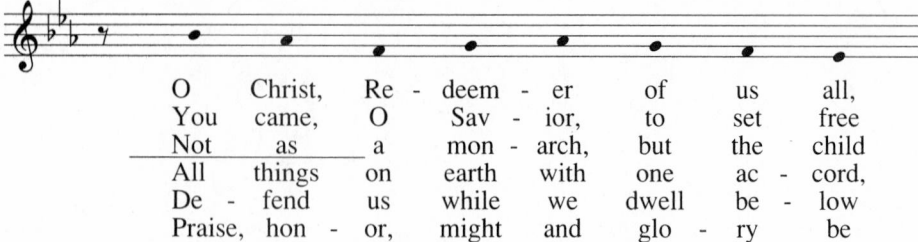

Your peo - ple's ev - er - last - ing light,
Should doom to death a u - ni - verse,
You came; but not in splen - dor bright,
All knees must bend, all hearts must bow:
Re - deem us for e - ter - nal day;
And God the Spir - it, Three in One,

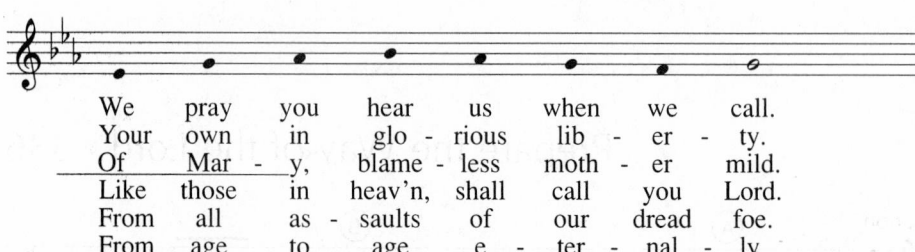

O Christ, Re - deem - er of us all,
You came, O Sav - ior, to set free
Not as a mon - arch, but the child
All things on earth with one ac - cord,
De - fend us while we dwell be - low
Praise, hon - or, might and glo - ry be

We pray you hear us when we call.
Your own in glo - rious lib - er - ty.
Of Mar - y, blame - less moth - er mild.
Like those in heav'n, shall call you Lord.
From all as - saults of our dread foe.
From age to age e - ter - nal - ly.

Text; *Conditor alme siderum*, Latin 9th. C.; tr. *The Hymnal 1982*, © 1985, The Church Pension Fund
Tune: CONDITOR ALME SIDERUM, LM; Mode IV; acc. by Gerard Farrell, OSB, b. 1919, © 1986, GIA Publications, Inc.

Come to Set Us Free 338

Refrain

Come to set us free, come to make us your own.

Come to show the way to your peo-ple, your cho - sen.

O - pen our lives to the light of your prom - ise.

Come to our hearts with heal-ing, come to our minds with pow-er,

come to us and bring us your life.

Verses

1. You are light which shines in dark - ness, Morn - ing
2. You are hope which brings us cour - age, you are
3. You are prom - ise of sal - va - tion, you are

Star which nev - er sets. O - pen our eyes which on - ly dim - ly
strength which nev - er fails. O - pen our minds to ways we do not
God in hu - man form. Bring to our world of emp - ti - ness and

D.C.

see the truth which sets us free.
know, but where your Spir - it grows.
fear the Word we long to hear.

Text: Bernadette Farrell, b.1957
Tune: Bernadette Farrell, b.1957
© 1982, Bernadette Farrell, published by OCP Publications

339 Each Winter As the Year Grows Older

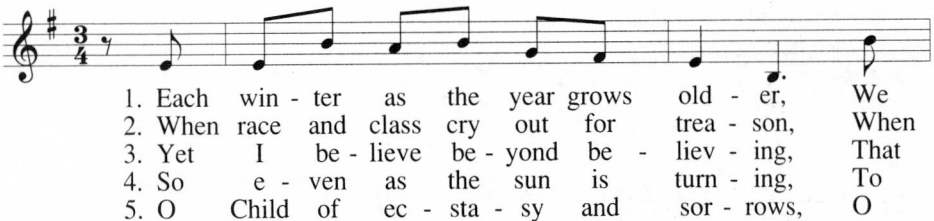

1. Each win - ter as the year grows old - er, We
2. When race and class cry out for trea - son, When
3. Yet I be - lieve be - yond be - liev - ing, That
4. So e - ven as the sun is turn - ing, To
5. O Child of ec - sta - sy and sor - rows, O

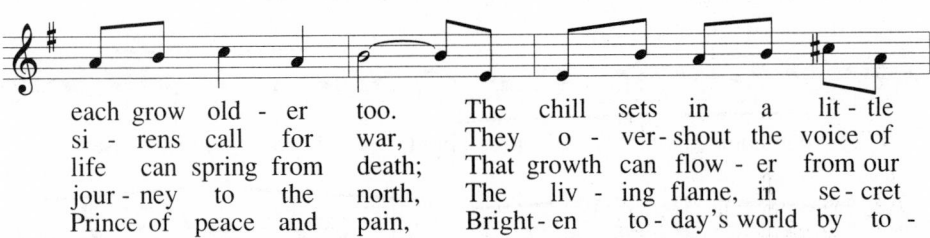

each grow old - er too. The chill sets in a lit - tle
si - rens call for war, They o - ver - shout the voice of
life can spring from death; That growth can flow - er from our
jour - ney to the north, The liv - ing flame, in se - cret
Prince of peace and pain, Bright - en to - day's world by to -

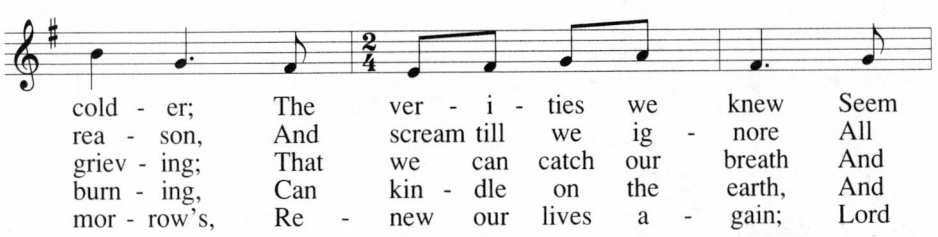

cold - er; The ver - i - ties we knew Seem
rea - son, And scream till we ig - nore All
griev - ing; That we can catch our breath And
burn - ing, Can kin - dle on the earth, And
mor - row's, Re - new our lives a - gain; Lord

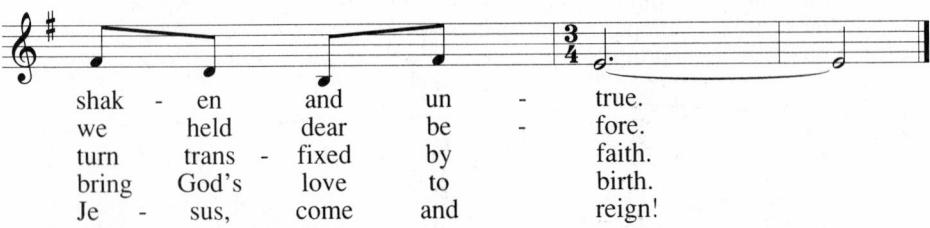

shak - en and un - true.
we held dear be - fore.
turn trans - fixed by faith.
bring God's love to birth.
Je - sus, come and reign!

Text: William Gay, fl. 1969, © 1971, United Church Press
Tune: CAROL OF HOPE, 9 6 9 66; Annabeth Gay, b.1925, © 1971, United Church Press; acc. by Marty Haugen, b.1950, alt.,
    © 1987, GIA Publications, Inc.

People of the Night 340

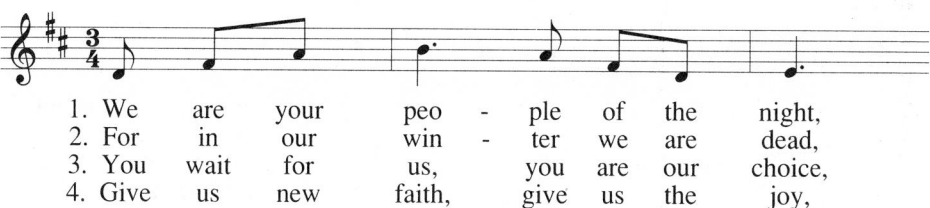

```
1. We    are   your   peo  -  ple   of   the   night,
2. For    in    our    win  -  ter   we   are   dead,
3. You   wait  for    us,        you  are  our   choice,
4. Give   us   new    faith,     give  us   the   joy,
```

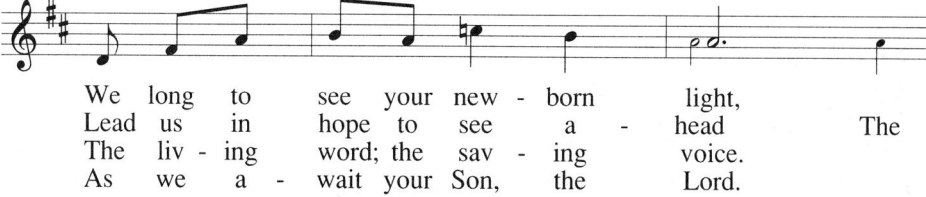

```
We  long   to    see   your  new - born      light,
Lead us    in    hope   to    see    a  -    head        The
The  liv - ing   word; the   sav  -  ing     voice.
As   we   a  -   wait  your  Son,   the       Lord.
```

```
Dis - tant  glim - mer;  ris  -  ing  from  a  -  far.
spring-time  and   the   gift  that   is   to   come.
Break  the   si  -  lence,  lis  -  ten  to  our  call.
In    our   pres - ence,  child born  of  your  breath,
```

```
We   a - wait  you,   ho  -  ly  morn-ing   star.
Come and  save   us,    be  God's  on - ly   Son.
Be   our  an - swer,   new  life  for  us   all.
Sav - ior broth - er;  life  that  shat-ters  death.
```

Text: David Haas, b.1957
Tune: SHEPHERD'S SONG, 88 99; David Haas, b.1957
© 1983, GIA Publications, Inc.

341　O Come, All Ye Faithful / Adeste Fideles

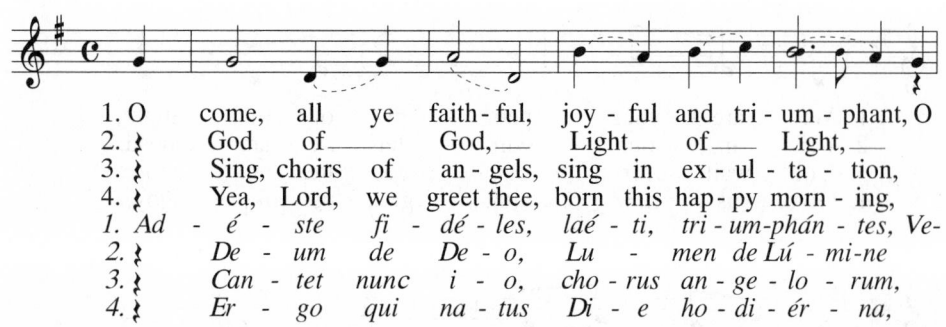

1. O come, all ye faith-ful, joy - ful and tri - um - phant, O
2. ⸱ God of___ God,___ Light__ of___ Light,___
3. ⸱ Sing, choirs of an - gels, sing in ex - ul - ta - tion,
4. ⸱ Yea, Lord, we greet thee, born this hap- py morn - ing,
1. *Ad - é - ste fi - dé - les, laé - ti, tri - um-phán - tes, Ve-*
2. *⸱ De - um de De - o, Lu - men de Lú - mi-ne*
3. *⸱ Can - tet nunc i - o, cho - rus an - ge - lo - rum,*
4. *⸱ Er - go qui na - tus Di - e ho - di - ér - na,*

come ye, O come ye to Beth - le - hem;
Lo! He comes forth from the Vir - gin's womb.
Sing, all ye cit - i - zens of heav'n a - bove!
Je - sus, to thee be all glo - ry giv'n;
ní - te, ve - ní - te in Béth - le - hem.
Ge - stant pu - él - lae ví - sce - ra.
Can - tet nunc au - la cae - lés - ti - um.
Je - su___ ti - bi sit gló - ri - a.

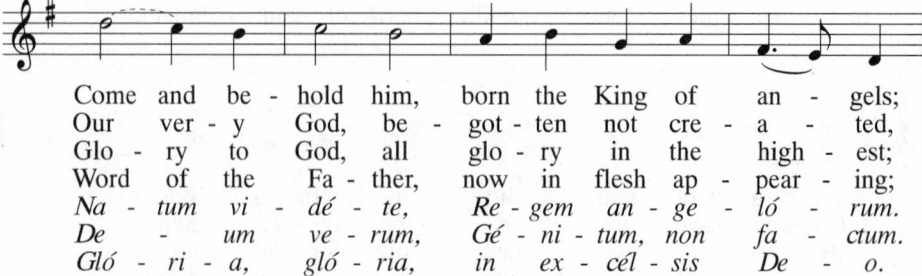

Come and be - hold him, born the King of an - gels;
Our ver - y God, be - got - ten not cre - a - ted,
Glo - ry to God, all glo - ry in the high - est;
Word of the Fa - ther, now in flesh ap - pear - ing;
Na - tum vi - dé - te, Re - gem an - ge - ló - rum.
De - um ve - rum, Gé - ni - tum, non fa - ctum.
Gló - ri - a, gló - ria, in ex - cél - sis De - o.
Pa - tris ae - ter - nae ver - bum ca - ro fa - ctum.

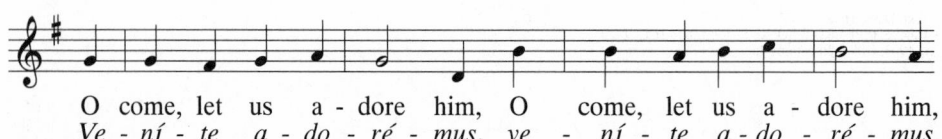

O come, let us a - dore him, O come, let us a - dore him,
Ve - ní - te a - do - ré - mus, ve - ní - te a - do - ré - mus,

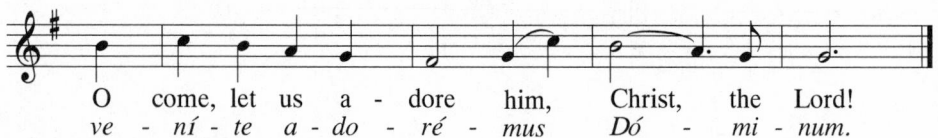

O come, let us a - dore him, Christ, the Lord!
ve - ní - te a - do - ré - mus Dó - mi - num.

Text: *Adeste fideles;* John F. Wade, c.1711-1786; tr. by Frederick Oakeley, 1802-1880, alt.
Tune: ADESTE FIDELES, Irr. with refrain; John F. Wade c.1711-1786

Night of Silence 342

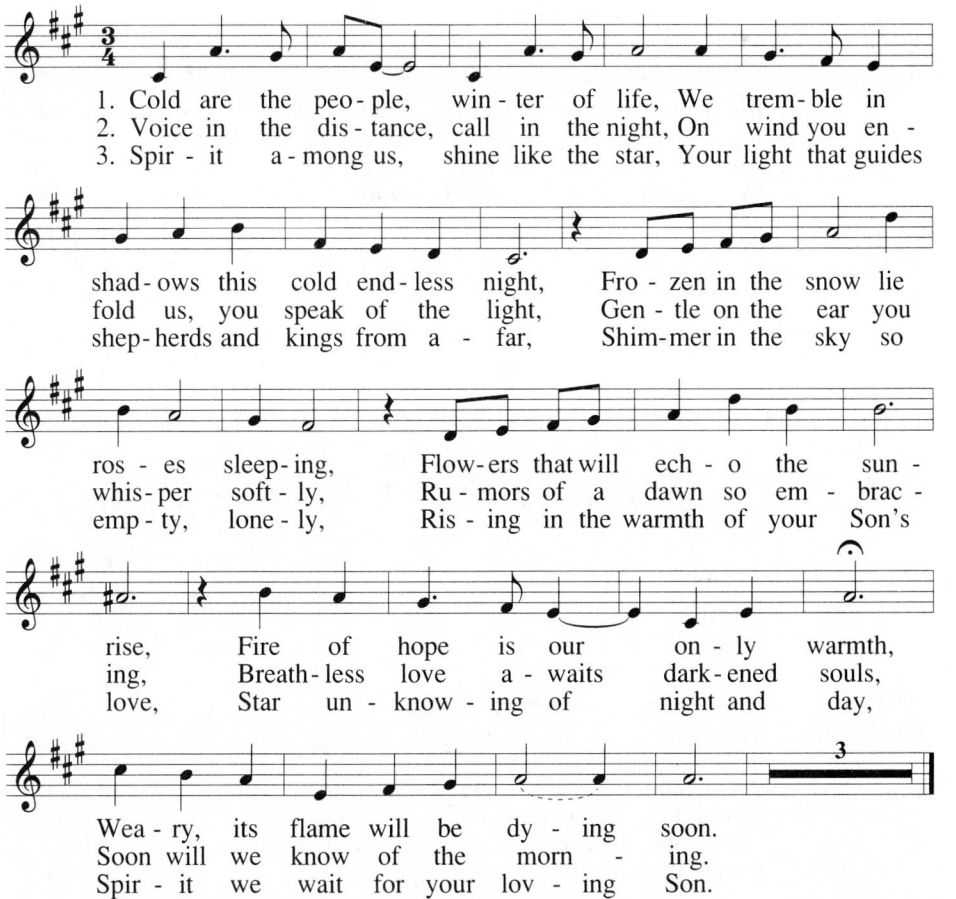

1. Cold are the peo-ple, win-ter of life, We trem-ble in
2. Voice in the dis-tance, call in the night, On wind you en -
3. Spir - it a-mong us, shine like the star, Your light that guides

shad-ows this cold end-less night, Fro - zen in the snow lie
fold us, you speak of the light, Gen - tle on the ear you
shep-herds and kings from a - far, Shim-mer in the sky so

ros - es sleep-ing, Flow-ers that will ech - o the sun -
whis-per soft - ly, Ru - mors of a dawn so em - brac -
emp - ty, lone - ly, Ris - ing in the warmth of your Son's

rise, Fire of hope is our on - ly warmth,
ing, Breath-less love a - waits dark-ened souls,
love, Star un - know-ing of night and day,

Wea - ry, its flame will be dy - ing soon.
Soon will we know of the morn - ing.
Spir - it we wait for your lov - ing Son.

Text: Daniel Kantor, b.1960
Tune: Daniel Kantor, b.1960

343 Joy to the World

1. Joy to the world! the Lord is come:
2. Joy to the world! the Sav - ior reigns:
3. No more let sin and sor - rows grow,
4. He rules the world with truth and grace,

Let earth re - ceive her King;
Let us, our songs em - ploy;
Nor thorns in - fest the ground;
And makes the na - tions prove

Let ev - 'ry heart pre - pare him room,
While fields and floods, rocks, hills and plains
He comes to make his bless - ings flow
The glo - ries of his right - eous - ness,

And heav'n and na - ture sing, And
Re - peat the sound - ing joy, Re -
Far as the curse is found, Far
And won - ders of his love, And

heav'n and na - ture sing, And
peat the sound - ing joy, Re -
as the curse is found, Far
won - ders of his love, And

heav'n, and heav'n and na - ture sing.
peat, re - peat the sound - ing joy.
as, far as the curse is found.
won - ders, won - ders of his love.

Text: Psalm 98; Isaac Watts, 1674-1748
Tune: ANTIOCH. CM; arr. from George F. Handel, 1685-1759, in T. Hawkes' *Collection of Tunes*, 1833

Gloria 344

¡Glo - ria, glo - ria, glo - ria   en   las al - tur - as a Dios!
Glo - ry, glo - ry, glo - ry,   glo - ry be to God on high!

Y_en la tie - rra paz   pa - ra_a - que - llos   que_a - ma el Se - ñor.
And on earth   peace   to the   peo - ple in whom God is well   pleased.

Text: Luke 2:14
Tune: Pablo Sosa, © 1990

345　The Virgin Mary Had a Baby Boy

Verses

1. The vir - gin Mar - y had a ba - by boy, the
2. The an - gels sang when the ba - by born, the
3. The wise men saw where the ba - by born, the

vir - gin Mar - y had a ba - by boy, the
an - gels sang when the ba - by born, the
wise men saw where the ba - by born, the

vir - gin Mar - y had a ba - by boy, and they
an - gels sang when the ba - by born, and they
wise men went where the ba - by born, and they

say that his name was Je - sus.
say that his name was Je - sus.
say that his name was Je - sus.

Refrain

He come from the glo - ry, he come from the

glo - rious king-dom. Oh, yes! be-liev - er! Oh,

yes! be - liev - er! He come from the glo - ry,

he come from the glo - rious king-dom.

Text: West Indian carol, © 1945, Boosey and Co., Ltd.
Tune: West Indian carol, © 1945, Boosey and Co., Ltd.; acc. by Diana Kodner, b. 1957, © 1993, GIA Publications, Inc.

Awake! Awake, and Greet the New Morn 346

1. A - wake! a - wake, and greet the new morn, For
2. To us, to all in sor - row and fear, Em -
3. In dark - est night his com - ing shall be, When
4. Re - joice, re - joice, take heart in the night, Though

an - gels her - ald its dawn - ing, Sing out your joy, for
man - u-el comes a - sing - ing, His hum - ble song is
all the world is de - spair - ing, As morn - ing light so
dark the win-ter and cheer-less, The ris - ing sun shall

now he is born, Be - hold! the Child of our long - ing.
qui - et and near, Yet fills the earth with its ring - ing;
qui - et and free, So warm and gen - tle and car - ing.
crown you with light, Be strong and lov - ing and fear - less;

Come as a ba - by weak and poor, To bring all hearts to -
Mu - sic to heal the bro - ken soul And hymns of lov - ing
Then shall the mute break forth in song, The lame shall leap in
Love be our song and love our prayer, And love, our end - less

geth - er, He o - pens wide the heav'n - ly door And
kind - ness, The thun - der of his an - thems roll To
won - der, The weak be raised a - bove the strong, And
sto - ry, May God fill ev - 'ry day we share, And

lives now in - side us for ev - er.
shat - ter all ha - tred and blind - ness.
weap - ons be bro - ken a - sun - der.
bring us at last in - to glo - ry.

Text: Marty Haugen, b.1950
Tune: REJOICE, REJOICE, 9 8 9 8 8 7 8 9; Marty Haugen, b.1950
© 1983, GIA Publications, Inc.

347 Angels We Have Heard on High

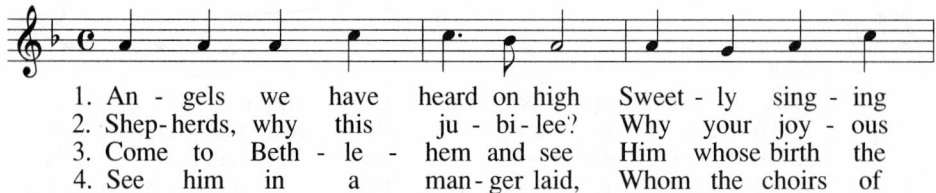

1. An - gels we have heard on high Sweet - ly sing - ing
2. Shep-herds, why this ju - bi - lee? Why your joy - ous
3. Come to Beth - le - hem and see Him whose birth the
4. See him in a man-ger laid, Whom the choirs of

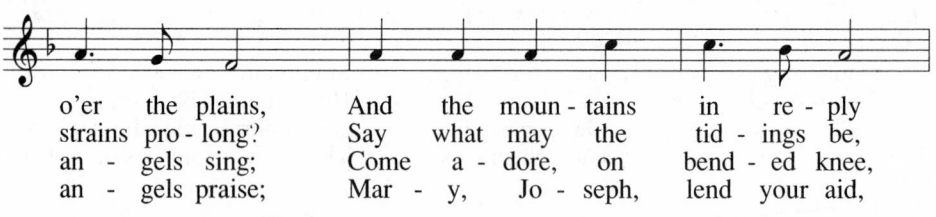

o'er the plains, And the moun - tains in re - ply
strains pro - long? Say what may the tid - ings be,
an - gels sing; Come a - dore, on bend - ed knee,
an - gels praise; Mar - y, Jo - seph, lend your aid,

Ech - o back their joy - ous strains.
Which in - spire your heav'n - ly song.
Christ, the Lord, the new - born King.
While our hearts in love we raise.

Glo - - - ri - a

in ex - cel - sis De - o, Glo - -

- - ri - a in ex - cel - sis De - o.

Text: *Les anges dans nos campagnes;* French, c. 18th C.; tr. from *Crown of Jesus Music,* London, 1862
Tune: GLORIA, 7 7 7 7 with refrain; French traditional

Hark! The Herald Angels Sing   348

1. Hark! the her - ald an - gels sing, "Glo - ry to the
2. Christ, by high - est heaven a - dored, Christ the ev - er-
3. Hail the heav'n - born Prince of Peace! Hail the Sun of

new - born King; Peace on earth, and mer - cy mild
last - ing Lord: Late in time be - hold him come,
Right-eous-ness! Light and life to all he brings,

God and sin - ners rec - on - ciled!" Joy - ful, all you
Off - spring of the Vir - gin's womb. Veiled in flesh the
Ris'n with heal - ing in his wings. Mild he lays his

na - tions, rise, Join the tri - umph of the skies;
God-head see: Hail the in - car - nate De - i - ty,
glo - ry by, Born that we no more may die,

With the an-gel - ic host pro-claim, "Christ is born in Beth - le-hem!"
Pleased as man with us to dwell, Je - sus, our Em - man - u - el.
Born to raise us from the earth, Born to give us sec - ond birth.

Hark! the her-ald an - gels sing, "Glo-ry to the new-born King!"

Text: Charles Wesley, 1707-1788, alt.
Tune: MENDELSSOHN, 77 77 D with refrain; Felix Mendelssohn, 1809-1847

349   The Age of Expectation

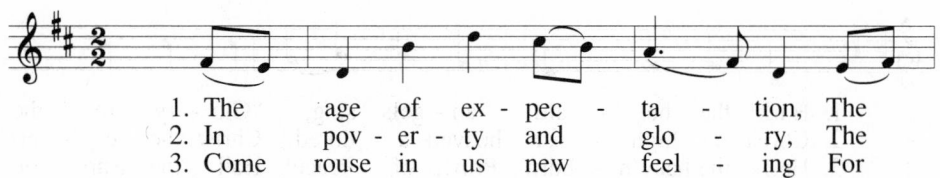

1. The age of ex - pec - ta - tion, The
2. In pov - er - ty and glo - ry, The
3. Come rouse in us new feel - ing For

heav - y years have passed. The light of God's sal -
sta - ble and the stars Be - gin to sing your
what we have seen and known. Come give all peo - ple

va - tion Now dawns for us at last.
sto - ry And how you come to ours.
heal - ing And make us as your own.

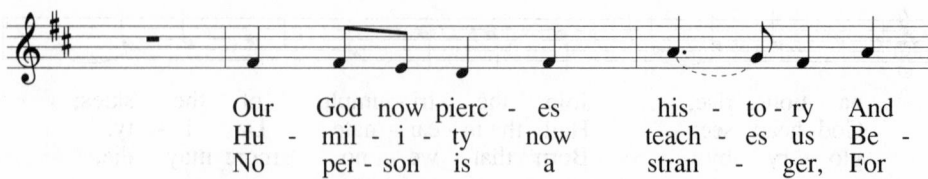

Our God now pierc - es his - to - ry And
Hu - mil - i - ty now teach - es us Be -
No per - son is a stran - ger, For

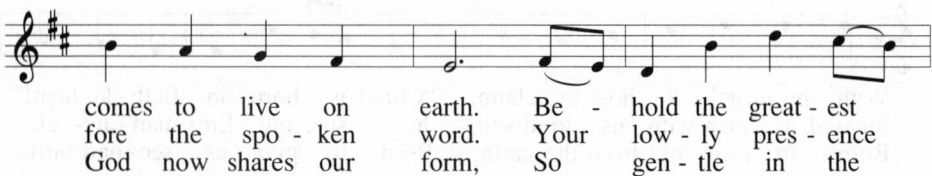

comes to live on earth. Be - hold the great - est
fore the spo - ken word. Your low - ly pres - ence
God now shares our form, So gen - tle in the

mys - ter - y, A God of hu - man birth.
reach - es us. No heart is left un - stirred.
man - ger, So meek and hu - man born.

Text: Todd Flowerday
Tune: ASHWOOD, 7 6 7 6 D; Bobby Fisher, b.1952
© 1992, GIA Publications, Inc.

God's Surprise 350

1. Who would think that what was need-ed To trans-
2. Shep - herds watch and wise men won-der, Mon - archs
3. Cen - tu - ries of skill and sci-ence Span the

form and save the earth Might not be a
scorn and an - gels sing; Such a place as
past from which we move, Yet ex - pe - rience

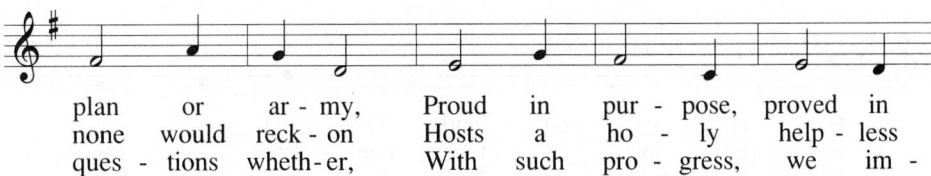

plan or ar - my, Proud in pur - pose, proved in
none would reck - on Hosts a ho - ly help - less
ques - tions wheth-er, With such pro - gress, we im -

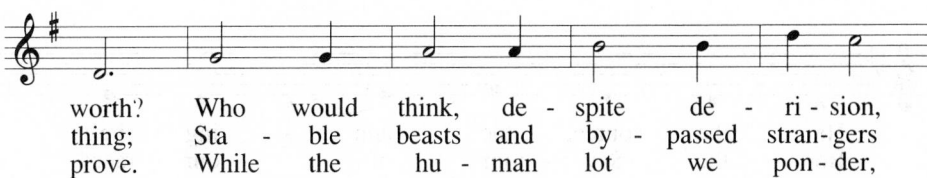

worth? Who would think, de - spite de - ri - sion,
thing; Sta - ble beasts and by - passed stran-gers
prove. While the hu - man lot we pon - der,

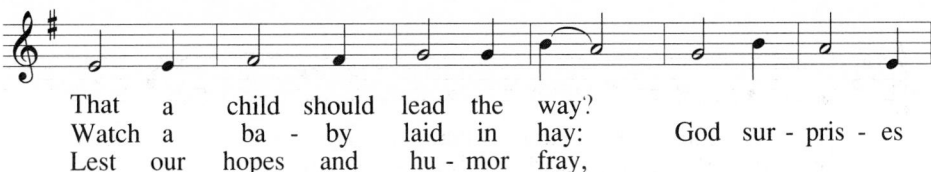

That a child should lead the way?
Watch a ba - by laid in hay: God sur - pris - es
Lest our hopes and hu - mor fray,

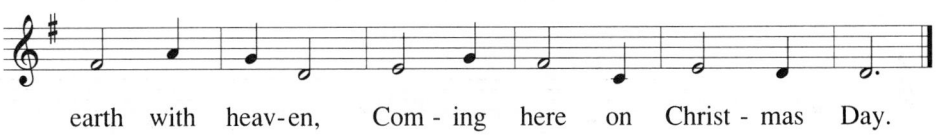

earth with heav-en, Com - ing here on Christ - mas Day.

Text: John L. Bell, b.1949
Tune: SCARLET RIBBONS, 8 7 8 7 D; English traditional; arr. by John L. Bell, b.1949
© 1987, Iona Community, GIA Publications, Inc., agent

351 Of the Father's Love Begotten

1. Of the Fa - ther's love be - got - ten,
2. O that birth for ev - er bless - ed,
3. Let the heights of heav'n a - dore him;
4. Christ, to you with God the Fa - ther,

Ere the worlds be - gan to be,
When the Vir - gin, full of grace,
An - gel hosts, his prais - es sing;
Spir - it blest e - ter - nal - ly,

He is Al - pha and O - me - ga,
By the Spir - it blest con - ceiv - ing,
Pow'rs, do - min - ions, bow be - fore him,
Hymn and chant and high thanks - giv - ing,

He the source, the end - ing he,
Bore the Sav - ior of our race;
And ex - tol our God and King;
And un - end - ing prais - es be:

Of the things that are, that have been,
And the Babe, the world's Re - deem - er,
Let no tongue on earth be si - lent,
Hon - or, glo - ry, and do - min - ion,

And that fu - ture years shall see,
First re - vealed his sa - cred face,
Ev - 'ry voice in con - cert ring,
And e - ter - nal vic - to - ry,

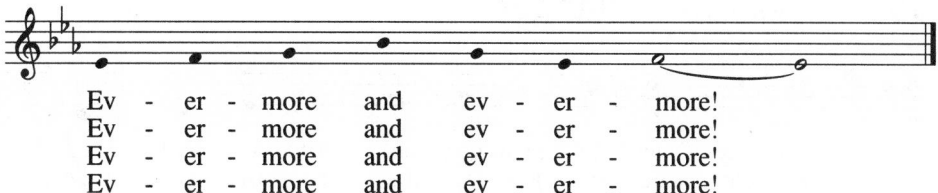

Ev - er - more and ev - er - more!
Ev - er - more and ev - er - more!
Ev - er - more and ev - er - more!
Ev - er - more and ev - er - more!

Text: *Corde natus ex Parentis;* Aurelius Prudentius, 348-413; tr. by John M. Neale, 1818-1866 and Henry W. Baker, 1821-1877
Tune: DIVINUM MYSTERIUM, 8 7 8 7 8 7 7; 12th C.; Mode V; acc. by Richard Proulx, b. 1937, © 1985, GIA Publications, Inc.

Silent Night, Holy Night 352

1. Si - lent night, ho - ly night, All is calm,
2. Si - lent night, ho - ly night, Shep - herds quake
3. Si - lent night, ho - ly night, Son of God,

all is bright Round yon Vir - gin Moth - er and Child,
at the sight; Glo - ries stream from heav - en a - far,
love's pure light Ra - diant beams from thy ho - ly face,

Ho - ly In - fant so ten - der and mild, Sleep in heav - en - ly
Heav'n-ly hosts sing al - le - lu - ia; Christ, the Sav - ior, is
With the dawn of re - deem - ing grace, Je - sus, Lord, at thy

peace, Sleep in heav - en - ly peace.
born! Christ, the Sav - ior, is born!
birth, Je - sus, Lord, at thy birth.

Text: *Stille Nacht, helige Nacht;* Joseph Mohr, 1792-1849; tr. John F. Young, 1820-1885
Tune: STILLE NACHT, 66 89 66; Franz X. Gruber, 1787-1863

353 Away in a Manger

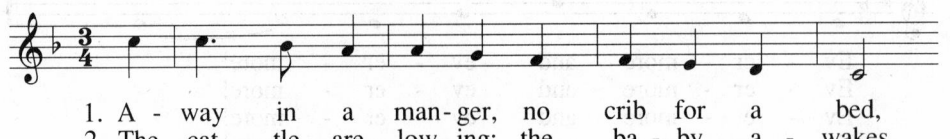

1. A - way in a man- ger, no crib for a bed,
2. The cat - tle are low - ing; the ba - by a - wakes,
3. Be near me, Lord Je - sus; I ask you to stay

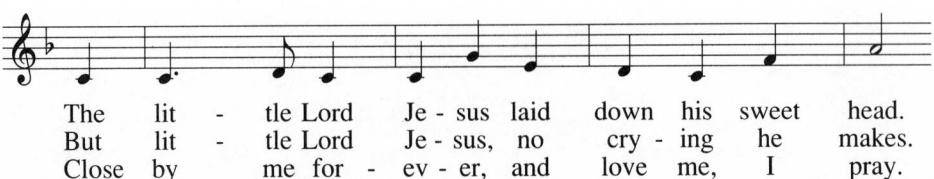

The lit - tle Lord Je - sus laid down his sweet head.
But lit - tle Lord Je - sus, no cry - ing he makes.
Close by me for - ev - er, and love me, I pray.

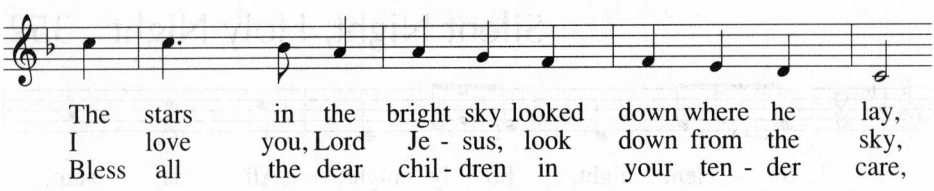

The stars in the bright sky looked down where he lay,
I love you, Lord Je - sus, look down from the sky,
Bless all the dear chil - dren in your ten - der care,

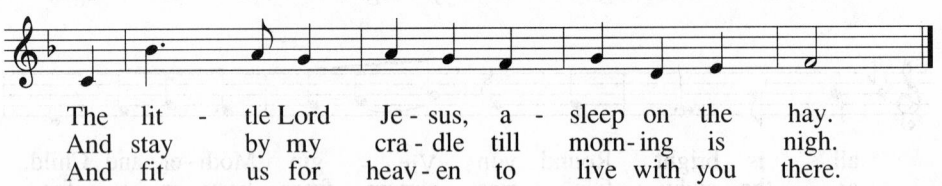

The lit - tle Lord Je - sus, a - sleep on the hay.
And stay by my cra - dle till morn - ing is nigh.
And fit us for heav - en to live with you there.

Text: St. 1-2, anonymous, st. 3, John T. McFarland, 1851-1913
Tune: MUELLER, 11 11 11 11; James R. Murray, 1841-1905; harm. by Robert J. Batastini, b. 1942, © 1994, GIA Publications, Inc.

Infant Holy, Infant Lowly   354

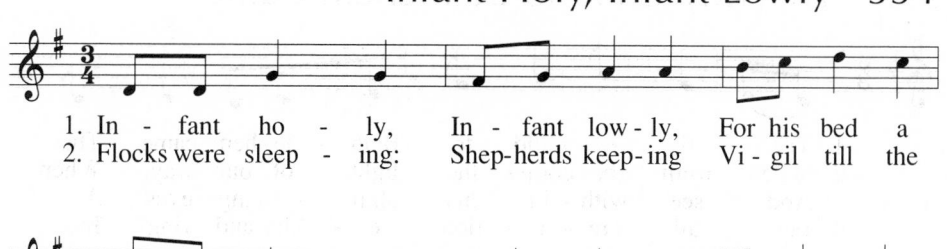

1. In - fant ho - ly, In - fant low - ly, For his bed a
2. Flocks were sleep - ing: Shep-herds keep-ing Vi - gil till the

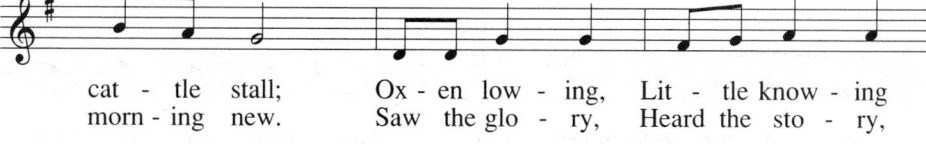

cat - tle stall; Ox - en low - ing, Lit - tle know - ing
morn - ing new. Saw the glo - ry, Heard the sto - ry,

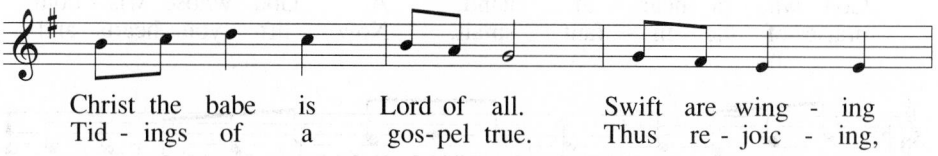

Christ the babe is Lord of all. Swift are wing - ing
Tid - ings of a gos-pel true. Thus re - joic - ing,

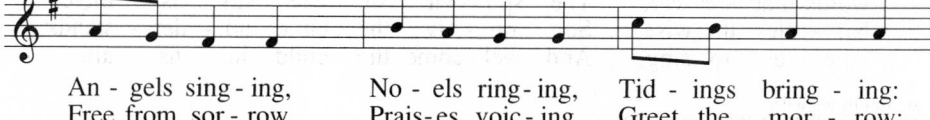

An - gels sing - ing, No - els ring-ing, Tid - ings bring - ing:
Free from sor - row, Prais-es voic - ing Greet the mor - row:

Christ the babe is Lord of all.
Christ the babe was born for you.

Text: Polish carol; para. by Edith M.G. Reed, 1885-1933
Tune: W ZLOBIE LEZY, 44 7 44 7 4444 7; Polish carol; harm. by A.E. Rusbridge, 1917-1969, © Rosalind Rusbridge.

355 The Tiny Child to Bethlehem Came

1. The ti - ny child to Beth - le - hem came That
2. When truth be - comes the light of our way, When
3. And see with - in his shin - ing eyes A
4. Let all cre - a - tion e - cho and ring In

all of the world might turn And care for ev - 'ry
peace is the gift we share, When love is more than
God who is near at hand, A God whose wis - dom
praise of the In - fant small, Now lift your hearts and

crea - ture the same, The way of com - pas - sion to learn.
words that we say, The spir - it of Je - sus is there.
baf - fles the wise, So on - ly the child un - der - stands.
voic - es to sing, And wel - come the child in us all.

Text: Marty Haugen, b.1950
Tune: TINY CHILD, 9 7 9 8; Marty Haugen, b.1950
© 1992, GIA Publications, Inc.

A Stable Lamp Is Lighted   356

1. A   sta - ble lamp is   light-ed   Whose glow shall wake the
2. This child through Da-vid's cit - y   Shall   ride   in   tri - umph
3. Yet   he   shall be   for - sak - en, And   yield-ed up   to
4. But   now, as   at   the   end-ing, The   low   is   lift - ed

sky;   The   stars shall bend   their voic - es,   And
by;   The   palm   shall strew its   branch - es, And
die;   The   sky   shall groan and   dark - en,   And
high;   The   stars shall bend   their voic - es,   And

ev - 'ry stone shall cry.   And ev - 'ry stone shall cry, And
ev - 'ry stone shall cry.   And ev - 'ry stone shall cry, Though
ev - 'ry stone shall cry.   And ev - 'ry stone shall cry, For
ev - 'ry stone shall cry.   And ev - 'ry stone shall cry, In

straw like gold shall shine; A   barn shall har - bor
heav - y,   dull, and   dumb, And lie   with - in the
hearts made hard by   sin: God's blood up - on   the
prais - es of   the   child By   whose de - scent a -

heav - en,   A   stall be - come a   shrine.
road - way   To   pave the king - dom come.
spear-head, God's love re - fused a - gain.
mong us   The worlds are rec - on - ciled.

Text: Richard Wilbur, © 1961
Tune: ANNIKA, 7 6 7 66 6 7 6; Marty Haugen, b.1950, © 1992, GIA Publications, Inc.

357 Child of Mercy

Refrain

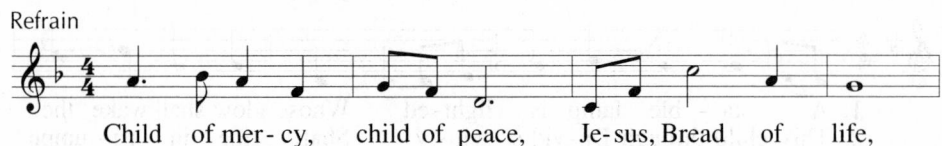

Child of mer-cy, child of peace, Je-sus, Bread of life,

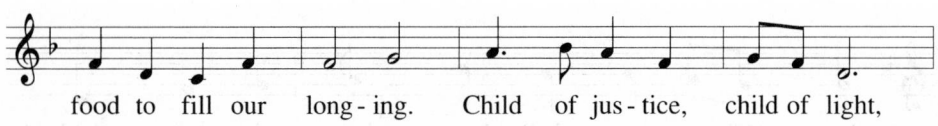

food to fill our long-ing. Child of jus-tice, child of light,

Je-sus, sav-ing cup, Em-man-u-el, God with us.

Verses

1. All who walk in dark-ness have seen a great light, to
2. ᵧ A child is born to us, a son is giv-en us, up-
3. ᵧ We name him: "Won-der, coun-s'lor, he-ro, might-y God," The
4. We pro-claim good news to you, great ti-dings of joy: To

D.C.

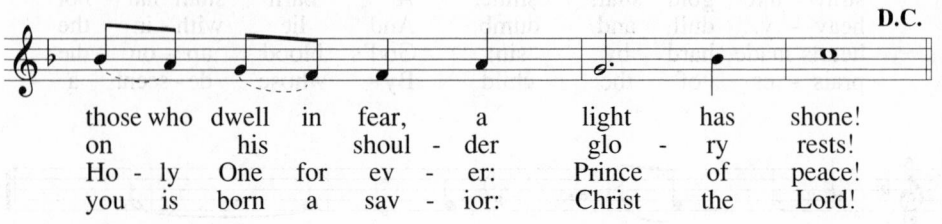

those who dwell in fear, a light has shone!
on his shoul-der glo-ry rests!
Ho-ly One for ev-er: Prince of peace!
you is born a sav-ior: Christ the Lord!

Text: Isaiah 9:1, 5; David Haas, b.1957
Tune: David Haas, b.1957
© 1991, GIA Publications, Inc.

Angels, from the Realms of Glory 358

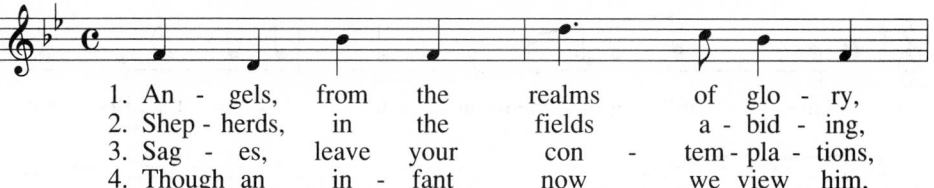

1. An - gels, from the realms of glo - ry,
2. Shep - herds, in the fields a - bid - ing,
3. Sag - es, leave your con - tem - pla - tions,
4. Though an in - fant now we view him,

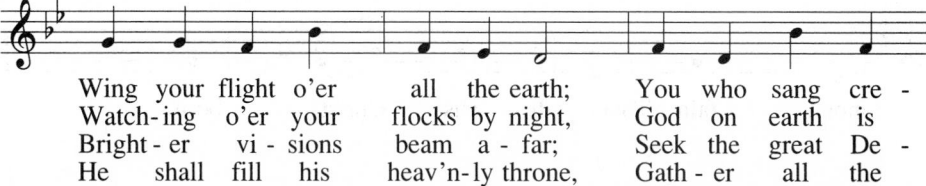

Wing your flight o'er all the earth; You who sang cre -
Watch-ing o'er your flocks by night, God on earth is
Bright - er vi - sions beam a - far; Seek the great De -
He shall fill his heav'n-ly throne, Gath - er all the

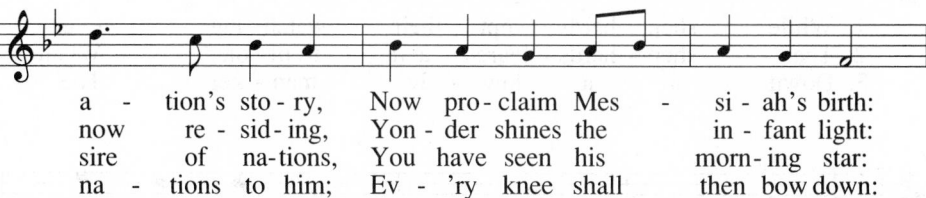

a - tion's sto - ry, Now pro - claim Mes - si - ah's birth:
now re - sid - ing, Yon - der shines the in - fant light:
sire of na - tions, You have seen his morn - ing star:
na - tions to him; Ev - 'ry knee shall then bow down:

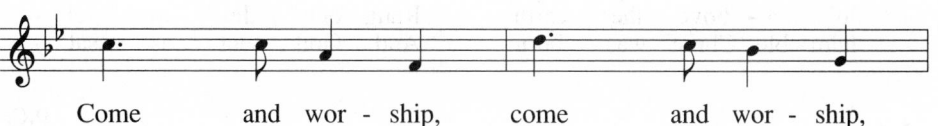

Come and wor - ship, come and wor - ship,

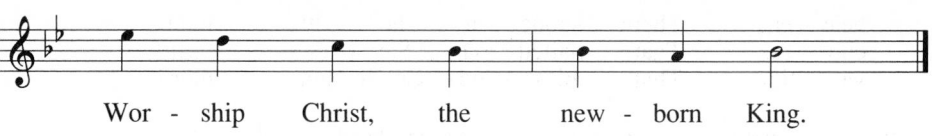

Wor - ship Christ, the new - born King.

Text: Sts. 1-3, James Montgomery, 1771-1854; st. 4, *Christmas Box*, 1825
Tune: REGENT SQUARE, 8 7 8 7 8 7; Henry Smart, 1813-1879

359   Go Tell It on the Mountain

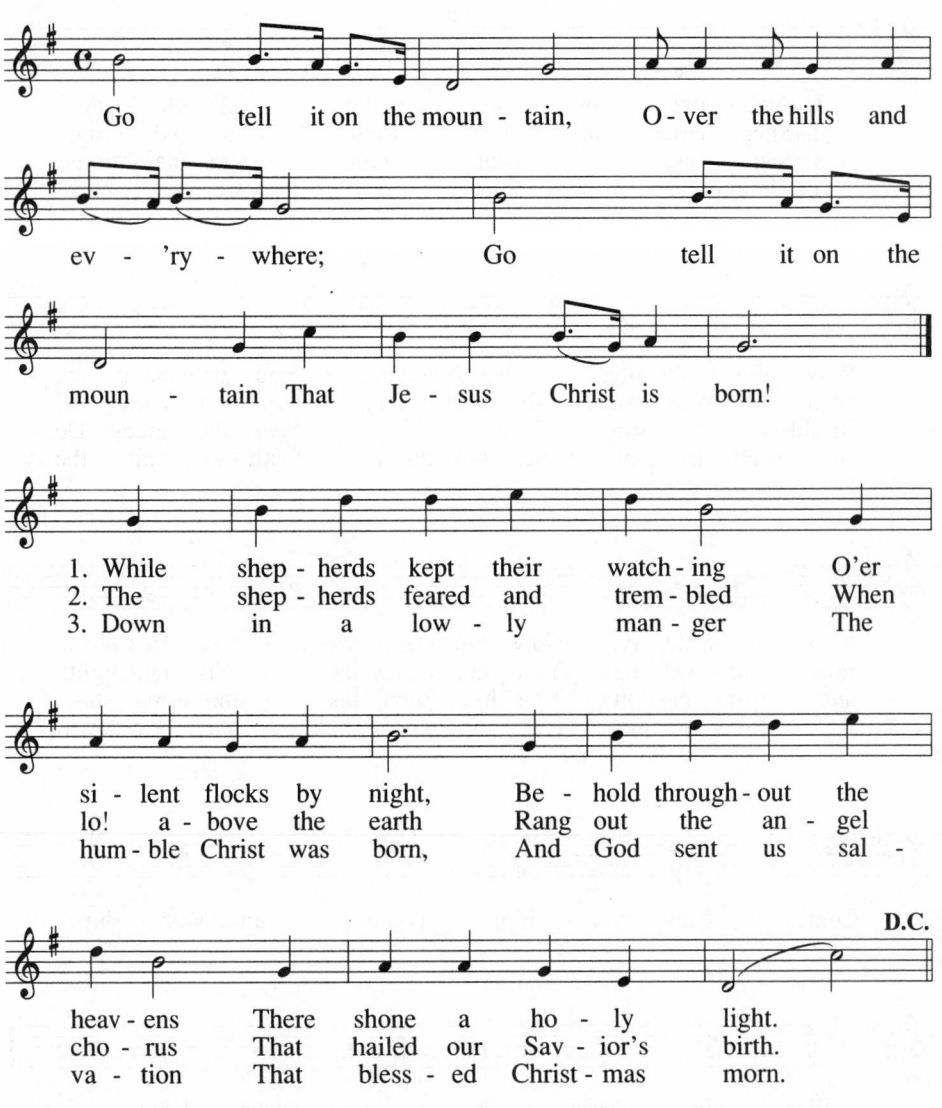

Go tell it on the moun - tain, O - ver the hills and ev - 'ry - where; Go tell it on the moun - tain That Je - sus Christ is born!

1. While shep - herds kept their watch - ing O'er
2. The shep - herds feared and trem - bled When
3. Down in a low - ly man - ger The

si - lent flocks by night, Be - hold through - out the
lo! a - bove the earth Rang out the an - gel
hum - ble Christ was born, And God sent us sal -

D.C.

heav - ens There shone a ho - ly light.
cho - rus That hailed our Sav - ior's birth.
va - tion That bless - ed Christ - mas morn.

Text: African-American spiritual; adapt. by John W. Work, Jr. 1871-1925, © Mrs. John W. Work III
Tune: GO TELL IT ON THE MOUNTAIN, 7 6 7 6 with refrain; African-American spiritual; harm. by Paul Sjolund, b. 1935, © Walton Music Corp.

Rise Up, Shepherd, and Follow   360

Verses

1. There's a star in the East on Christ-mas morn,
2. If you take good heed to the an - gel's words,

Rise up, shep-herd, and fol-low, It will lead to the place where the
Rise up, shep-herd, and fol-low, You'll for- get your flocks, you'll for-

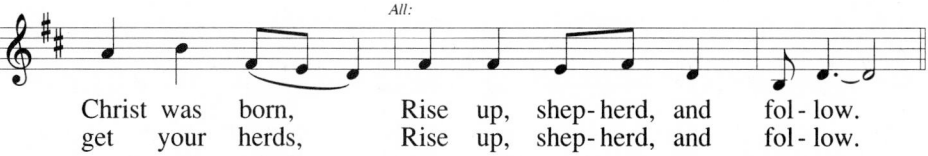

Christ was born, Rise up, shep- herd, and fol - low.
get your herds, Rise up, shep- herd, and fol - low.

Refrain

Fol - low, fol - low, Rise up, shep-herd, and fol-low,

Fol- low the Star of Beth- le - hem, Rise up, shep-herd, and fol- low.

Text: Traditional
Tune: African-American spiritual

361   'Twas in the Moon of Wintertime

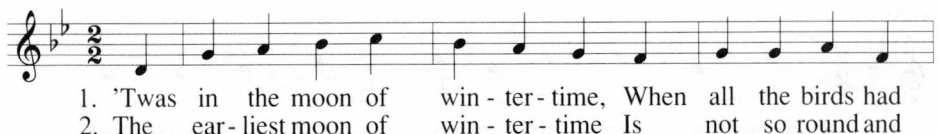

1. 'Twas in the moon of win - ter - time, When all the birds had
2. The ear - liest moon of win - ter - time Is not so round and
3. Oh, chil-dren of the for - est free, The an - gel song is

fled,   That God the Lord of all the earth Sent
fair   As was the ring of glo - ry 'round The
true;   The ho - ly child of earth and sky Is

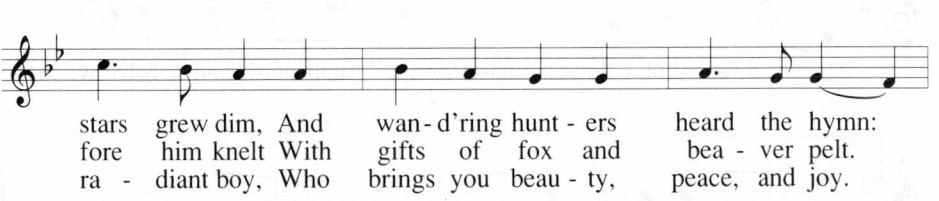

an - gel choirs in - stead;   Be - fore their light the
help - less in - fant there.   The chiefs from far be -
born this day for you;   Come kneel be - fore the

stars grew dim, And wan - d'ring hunt - ers heard the hymn:
fore him knelt With gifts of fox and bea - ver pelt.
ra - diant boy, Who brings you beau - ty, peace, and joy.

Je - sus your   king is born; Je - sus is born, in ex -

cel - sis glo - ri - a.

Text: Jean de Brebeuf, 1593-1649; trans. by Jesse E. Middleton, 1872-1960, © 1927, Frederick Harris Music Co. Ltd.
Tune: UNE JEUNE PUCELLE, 8 6 8 6 88 with refrain; French melody; arr. by Marty Haugen, b.1950, © 1992, GIA Publications, Inc.

Good Christian Friends, Rejoice   362

1. Good Chris-tian friends, re - joice With heart and
2. Good Chris-tian friends, re - joice With heart and
3. Good Chris-tian friends, re - joice With heart and

soul and voice; O give heed to what we say:
soul and voice; Now you hear of end - less bliss:
soul and voice; Now you need not fear the grave:

Je - sus Christ is born to - day! Ox and ass be -
Je - sus Christ was born for this! He has o - pened
Je - sus Christ was born to save! Calls you one and

fore him bow, And he is in the man - ger now.
heav - en's door, And we are blest for ev - er - more.
calls you all To gain his ev - er - last - ing hall.

Christ is born to - day! Christ is born to - day!
Christ was born for this! Christ was born for this!
Christ was born to save! Christ was born to save!

Text: *In dulci jubilo;* Latin and German, 14th C.: tr. by John M. Neal, 1818-1866
Tune: IN DULCI JUBILO, 66 77 77 55 ; Klug's *Geistliche Lieder,* Wittenberg, 1535; harm. by Robert L. Pearsall, 1795-1856

363 O Little Town of Bethlehem

1. O lit - tle town of Beth - le - hem, How
2. For Christ is born of Mar - y, And
3. How si - lent - ly, how si - lent - ly, The
4. O ho - ly Child of Beth - le - hem! De -

still we see thee lie! A - bove thy deep and
gath - ered all a - bove, While mor - tals sleep, the
won - drous gift is giv'n! So God im - parts to
scend to us we pray; Cast out our sin and

dream - less sleep The si - lent stars go by;
an - gels keep Their watch of won - d'ring love.
hu - man hearts The bless - ings of his heav'n.
en - ter in, Be born in us to - day.

Yet in the dark streets shin - eth The ev - er - last - ing
O morn - ing stars, to - geth - er Pro - claim the ho - ly
No ear may hear his com - ing, But in this world of
We hear the Christ - mas an - gels The great glad tid - ings

Light; The hopes and fears of
birth! And prais - es sing to
sin, Where meek souls will re -
tell; O come to us, a -

all the years Are met in thee to - night.
God the King, And peace to all on earth.
ceive him, still The dear Christ en - ters in.
bide with us, Our Lord Em - man - u - el!

Text: Phillips Brooks, 1835-1893
Tune: ST. LOUIS, 8 6 8 6 7 6 8 6; Lewis H. Redner, 1831-1908

Song of the Stable 364

1. Chill of the night-fall, Lamps in the win-dows,
2. Si - lence of mid-night, Voic - es of an - gels,
3. Splen - dor of star-light High on the hill - side,
4. Glo - ry of day-break! Sor - rows and shad-ows,

Let - ting their light fall Clear on the snow;
Sing - ing to bid night Yield to the dawn;
Faint is the far light Burn - ing be - low;
Sud - den - ly they break Forth in - to morn;

Bit - ter De - cem - ber Bids us re - mem - ber
Dark - ness is end - ed, Sin - ners be - friend - ed,
Kneel - ing be - fore him Shep - herds a - dore him,
Sing out and tell now All shall be well now;

Christ in the sta - ble Long, long a - go.
Where in the sta - ble Je - sus is born.
Christ in the sta - ble Long, long a - go.
For in the sta - ble Je - sus is born!

Text: *Chill of the Nightfall,* Timothy Dudley-Smith, b.1926, © 1980, Hope Publishing Co.
Tune: PRIOR LAKE, 5 5 5 4; David Haas, b.1957, © 1985, GIA Publications, Inc.

365 Nativity Carol

Verses

1. Si - lent, in the chill of mid - night,
2. "Fear not," said an - gel - ic voic - es;
3. Je - sus, Lord of all cre - a - tion,

star - light shines up - on a low - ly man - ger.
"ti - dings of a won - drous love we bring you.
sleep now close be - side your moth - er, Mar - y.

Won - der, won - der of the a - ges;
Go now, find him in a man - ger;
Bring us light a - mid the dark - ness,

heav - en breaks forth on the earth.
vis - it God's home on the earth."
prom - ise of life with - out end.

Refrain

For a child is born, the world re - joic - es! Shep-herds and

an - gels pro - claim his birth. This is Je - sus the Lord, our

Sav - ior and broth - er, bear - ing God's peace to the earth.

Text: Francis Patrick O'Brien, b.1958
Tune: Francis Patrick O'Brien, b.1958
© 1992, GIA Publications, Inc.

God Rest You Merry, Gentlemen   366

1. God   rest   you   mer - ry,   gen-tle-men,   Let   noth-ing   you   dis - may,
2. In   Beth - le - hem   in   Ju - dah   This   bless-ed   babe   was   born,
3. From God   our   great   Cre - a - tor   A   bless-ed   an - gel   came,
4. The   shep-herds   at   those   tid - ings   Re - joic - ed   much   in   mind,
5. Now   to   the   Lord   sing   prais - es,   All   you   with - in   this   place,

For   Je - sus   Christ   our   Sav - ior   Was   born   up - on   this   day,
And   laid   with - in   a   man - ger   Up - on   this   bless - ed   morn:
And   un - to   cer - tain   shep - herds   Brought   tid - ings   of   the   same,
And   left   their flocks   a - feed - ing   In   tem - pest,   storm,   and   wind,
And   with   true   love   and char - i - ty   Each   oth - er   now   em - brace;

To   save   us   all   from   Sa - tan's   power   When   we   were   gone   a - stray.
For   which   his moth - er   Mar - y   Did   noth-ing   take   in   scorn.
How   that   in   Beth - le - hem   was   born   The   Son   of   God   by   name.
And   went   to   Beth - le - hem straight-way,   The   bless - ed   babe   to   find.
This   ho - ly   tide   of   Christ - mas   All   oth - ers   shall   re - place.

O   tid - ings   of   com - fort   and   joy,   com - fort   and

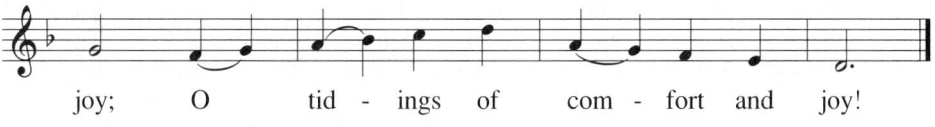

joy;   O   tid - ings   of   com - fort   and   joy!

Text: English carol, 18th C.
Tune: GOD REST YOU MERRY, 8 6 8 6 8 6 with refrain; English 18th C.; harm by John Stainer, 1840-1901

367 It Came upon the Midnight Clear

1. It came up - on the mid - night clear, That
2. Still through the clo - ven skies they come, With
3. Yet with the woes of sin and strife, The
4. For, lo, the days are has - tening on, By

glo - rious song of old, From
peace - ful wings un - furled, And
world has suf - fered long; Be -
proph - ets seen of old, When

an - gels bend - ing near the earth To
still their heav'n - ly mu - sic floats O'er
neath the heav'n - ly hymn have rolled Two
with the ev - er - cir - cling years Shall

touch their harps of gold: "Peace
all the wea - ry world: A -
thou - sand years of wrong; And
come the time fore - told, When

on the earth, good will to all From
bove its sad and low - ly plains They
war - ring hu - man - kind hears not The
peace shall o - ver all the earth Its

heaven's all gra - cious King"; The
bend on hov - 'ring wing, And
tid - ings which they bring; O
an - cient splen - dors fling, And

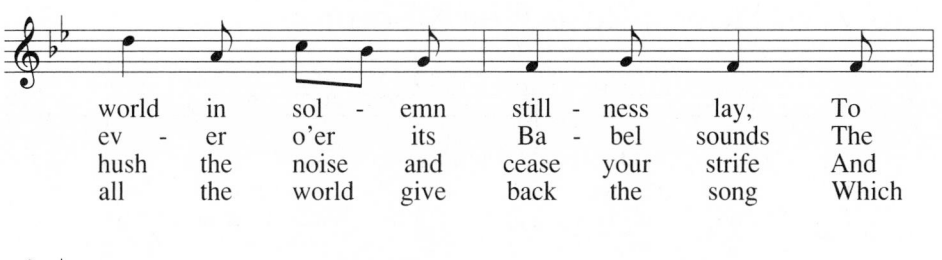

world	in	sol - emn	still - ness	lay,	To
ev - er	o'er	its	Ba - bel	sounds	The
hush	the	noise and	cease	your	strife	And
all	the	world give	back	the	song	Which

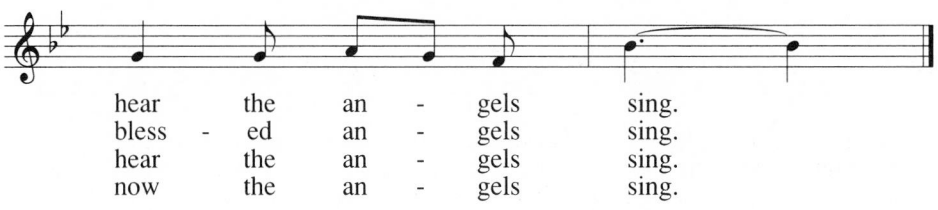

hear	the	an - gels	sing.
bless - ed	an - gels	sing.
hear	the	an - gels	sing.
now	the	an - gels	sing.

Text: Edmund H. Sears, 1810-1876, alt.
Tune: CAROL, CMD; Richard S. Willis, 1819-1900

368 Lo, How a Rose E'er Blooming

1. Lo, how a Rose e'er bloom-ing From ten-der stem hath
2. I - sa - iah 'twas for - told it, The Rose I have in
3. O Flower, whose fra - grance ten - der With sweet-ness fills the

sprung! Of Jes-se's lin-eage com-ing As seers of old have
mind, With Mar - y we be - hold it, The Vir - gin Moth - er
air, Dis - pel in glo-rious splen-dor The dark-ness ev - 'ry -

sung. It came, a blos-som bright, A - mid the cold of
kind. To show God's love a - right, She bore to us a
where; True man, yet ver - y God, From sin and death now

win - ter, When half spent was the night.
Sav - ior, When half spent was the night.
save us, And share our ev - 'ry load.

Text: Isaiah 11:1; *Es ist ein' Ros' entsprungen; Speier Gesangbuch,* 1599; tr. sts. 1-2 by Theodore Baker, 1851-1934; st. 3, The Hymnal, 1940
Tune: ES IST EIN' ROS' ENSTSPRUNGEN, 7 6 7 6 6 7 6; *Geistliche Kirchengesang,* Cologne, 1599; harm. by Michael Praetorius, 1571-1621

Carol at the Manger 369

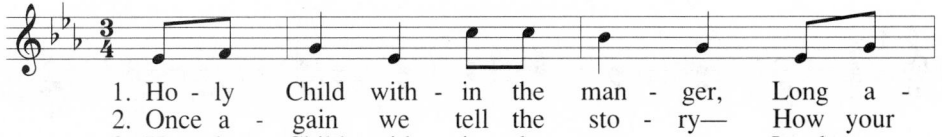

1. Ho - ly Child with - in the man - ger, Long a -
2. Once a - gain we tell the sto - ry— How your
3. Ho - ly Child with - in the man - ger, Lead us

go yet ev - er near; Come as friend to ev - 'ry
love for us was shown, When the Im - age of your
ev - er in your way, So we see in ev - 'ry

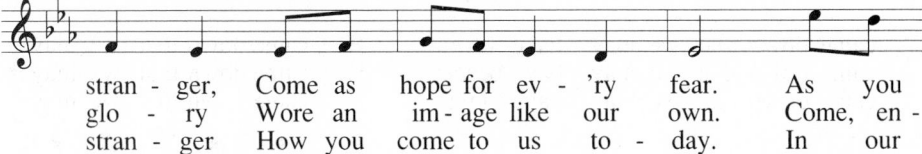

stran - ger, Come as hope for ev - 'ry fear. As you
glo - ry Wore an im - age like our own. Come, en -
stran - ger How you come to us to - day. In our

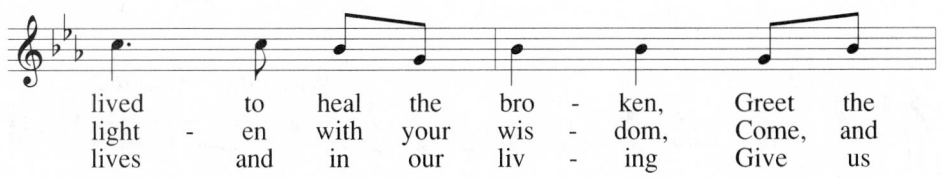

lived to heal the bro - ken, Greet the
light - en with your wis - dom, Come, and
lives and in our liv - ing Give us

out - cast, free the bound, As you taught us love un -
fill us with your grace, May the fire of your com -
strength to live as you, That our hearts might be for -

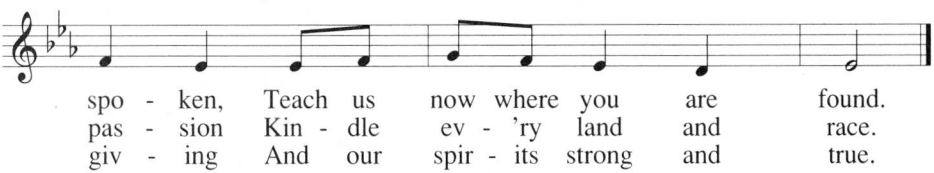

spo - ken, Teach us now where you are found.
pas - sion Kin - dle ev - 'ry land and race.
giv - ing And our spir - its strong and true.

Text: Marty Haugen, b.1950
Tune: JOYOUS LIGHT, 8 7 8 7 D; Marty Haugen, b.1950
© 1987, GIA Publications, Inc.

370 He Came Down

1. He came down that we may have love;
2. He came down that we may have peace;
3. He came down that we may have joy;

He came down that we may have love;
He came down that we may have peace;
He came down that we may have joy;

He came down that we may
He came down that we may
He came down that we may

Cantor: Why did he come?

have love, Hal-le - lu - jah for ev - er - more.
have peace, Hal-le - lu - jah for ev - er - more.
have joy; Hal-le - lu - jah for ev - er - more.

Text: Cameroon traditional
Tune: Cameroon traditional; transcribed and arr. by John L. Bell, b. 1949, © 1990, Iona Community, GIA Publications, Inc., agent

The Aye Carol   371

1. Who   is   the   ba - by   an   hour   or   two   old
2. Who   is   the   wom - an   with   child   at   her   breast,
3. Who   is   the   man   who   looks   on   at   the   door,
4. Who   are   the   peo - ple   come   in   from   the   street,
5. Will   you   come   with   me,   ev'n   though   I   feel   shy,

Looked   for   by   shep - herds   far   strayed   from   their   fold,
Giv - ing   her   milk   to   earth's   heav - en - ly   guest,
Wel - com - ing   stran - gers,   some   rich   but   most   poor,
Some   to   bring   pres - ents   and   some   just   to   meet,
Come   to   his   cra - dle   and   come   to   his   cry,

Lost   in   the   world   though   more   pre - cious   than   gold?
Tell - ing   her   mind   to   be   calm   and   at   rest?
Scan - ning   the   world   as   if   some - how   un - sure?
Join - ing   their   song   to   what   an - gels   re - peat?
Give   him   your   nod   or   your   "yes"   or   your   "aye,"

This   is   God   with   us   in   Je - sus.
Mar - y,   the   moth - er   of   Je - sus.
Jo - seph,   the   fa - ther   of   Je - sus.
These   are   the   new   friends   of   Je - sus.
Give   what   you   can   give   to   Je - sus?

Text: John L. Bell, b.1949
Tune: AYE CAROL; 10 10 10 8; John L. Bell, b.1949
© 1987, Iona Community, GIA Publications, Inc., agent

372 Once in Royal David's City

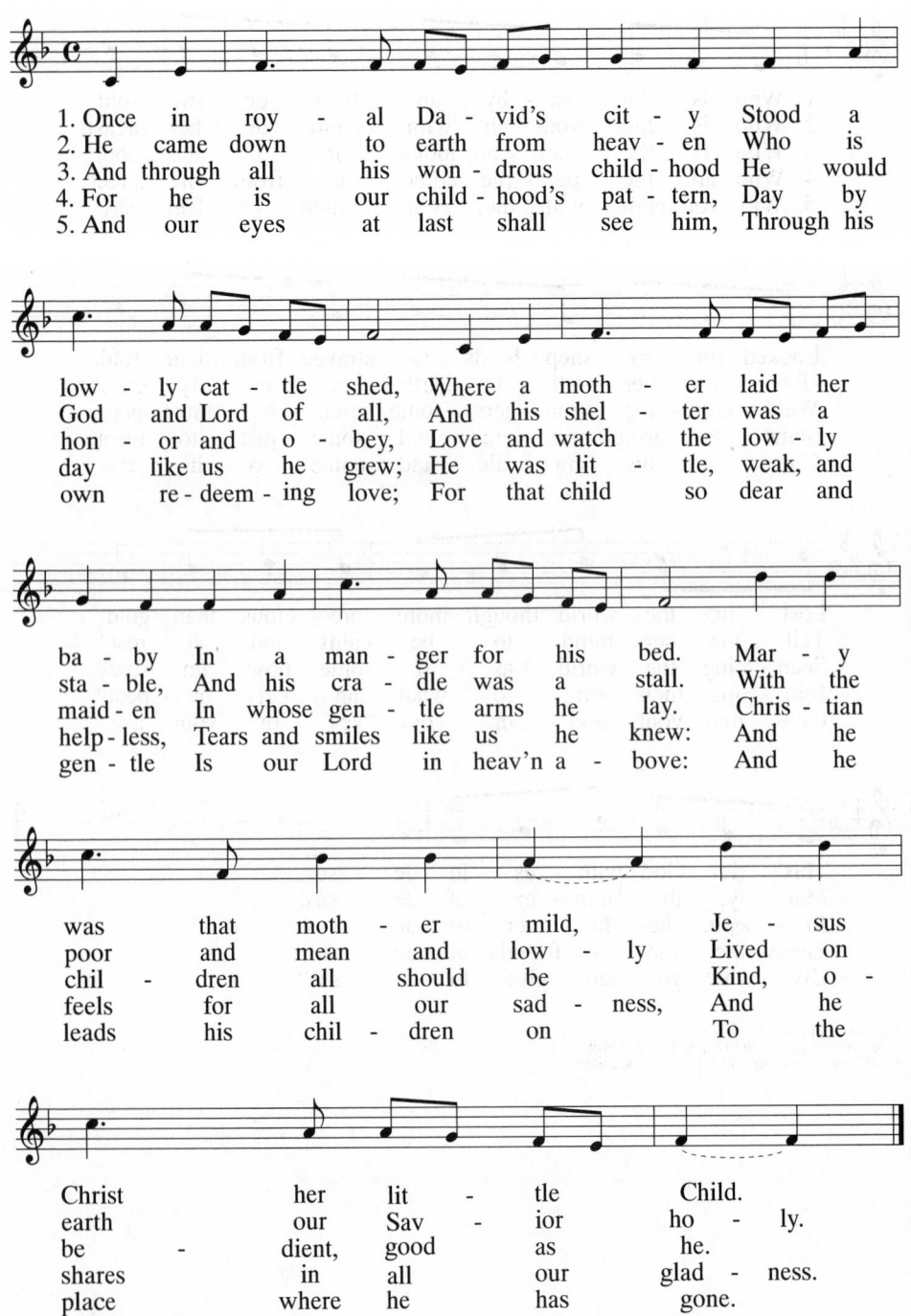

1. Once in roy - al Da - vid's cit - y Stood a
2. He came down to earth from heav - en Who is
3. And through all his won - drous child - hood He would
4. For he is our child - hood's pat - tern, Day by
5. And our eyes at last shall see him, Through his

low - ly cat - tle shed, Where a moth - er laid her
God and Lord of all, And his shel - ter was a
hon - or and o - bey, Love and watch the low - ly
day like us he grew; He was lit - tle, weak, and
own re - deem - ing love; For that child so dear and

ba - by In a man - ger for his bed. Mar - y
sta - ble, And his cra - dle was a stall. With the
maid - en In whose gen - tle arms he lay. Chris - tian
help - less, Tears and smiles like us he knew: And he
gen - tle Is our Lord in heav'n a - bove: And he

was that moth - er mild, Je - sus
poor and mean and low - ly Lived on
chil - dren all should be Kind, o -
feels for all our sad - ness, And he
leads his chil - dren on To the

Christ her lit - tle Child.
earth our Sav - ior ho - ly.
be - dient, good as he.
shares in all our glad - ness.
place where he has gone.

Text: Cecil Frances Alexander, 1818-1895
Tune: IRBY, 8 7 8 7 77; Henry J. Gauntlett, 1805-1876; harm. by Arthur H. Mann, 1850-1929. © 1957, Novello and Co. Ltd.

We Three Kings of Orient Are   373

1. We three kings of O - ri - ent are,
2. Born a babe on Beth - le - hem's plain,
3. Frank - in - cense to of - fer have I;
4. Myrrh is mine: its bit - ter per - fume
5. Glo - rious now be - hold him rise,

Bear - ing gifts we trav - erse a - far
Gold we bring to crown him a - gain;
In - cense owns a De - i - ty nigh,
Breathes a life of gath - 'ring gloom;
King and God and sac - ri - fice:

Field and foun - tain, Moor and
King for - ev - er, Ceas - ing
Prayer and prais - ing Glad - ly
Sor - rowing, sigh - ing, Bleed - ing
Heav'n sings, "Hal - le - lu - jah!"

moun - tain, Fol - low - ing yon - der star.
nev - er, O - ver us all to reign.
rais - ing, Wor - ship - ing God on high.
dy - ing, Sealed in the stone cold tomb.
"Hal - le - lu - jah!" earth re - plies.

O star of won - der, star of night, Star with roy-al beau-ty

bright, West-ward lead-ing, still pro-ceed-ing, Guide us to the per-fect Light.

Text: Matthew 2:1-11; John H. Hopkins, Jr., 1820-1891
Tune: KINGS OF ORIENT, 88 44 6 with refrain; John H. Hopkins, Jr., 1820-1891

374 As with Gladness Men of Old

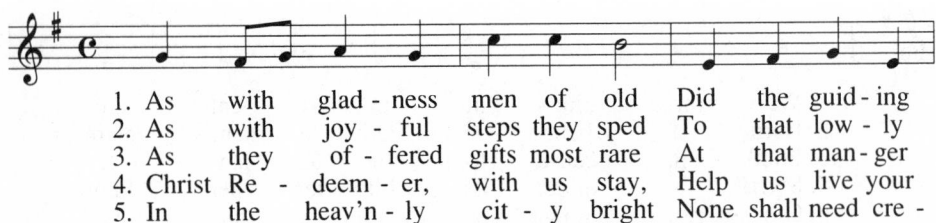

1. As with glad - ness men of old Did the guid - ing
2. As with joy - ful steps they sped To that low - ly
3. As they of - fered gifts most rare At that man - ger
4. Christ Re - deem - er, with us stay, Help us live your
5. In the heav'n - ly cit - y bright None shall need cre -

star be - hold; As with joy they hailed its light,
man - ger - bed, There to bend the knee be - fore
crude and bare; So may we this ho - ly day,
ho - ly way; And when earth - ly things are past,
a - ted light; You, its light, its joy, its crown,

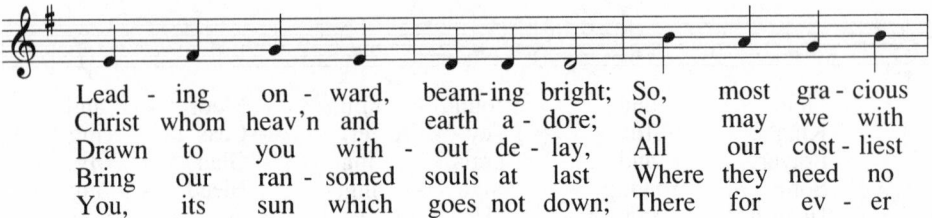

Lead - ing on - ward, beam-ing bright; So, most gra - cious
Christ whom heav'n and earth a - dore; So may we with
Drawn to you with - out de - lay, All our cost - liest
Bring our ran - somed souls at last Where they need no
You, its sun which goes not down; There for ev - er

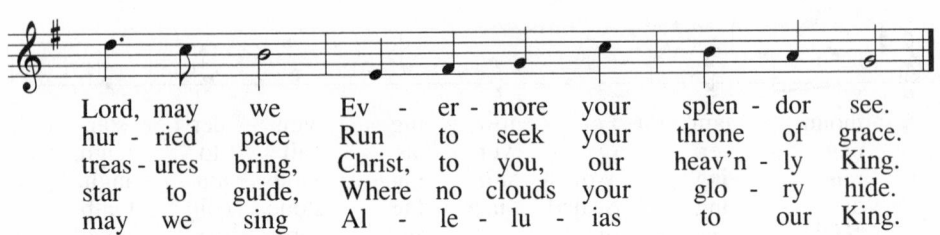

Lord, may we Ev - er - more your splen - dor see.
hur - ried pace Run to seek your throne of grace.
treas - ures bring, Christ, to you, our heav'n - ly King.
star to guide, Where no clouds your glo - ry hide.
may we sing Al - le - lu - ias to our King.

Text: William C. Dix, 1837-1898
Tune: DIX, 77 77 77; arr. from Conrad Kocher, 1786-1872, by William H. Monk, 1823-1889

Lord, Today 375

Refrain

Lord, to-day we have seen your glo-ry, dawn fol-lows the night. We, your peo-ple who walked in dark-ness now have seen a great light.

Verses

1. A child is born, a Son giv-en us, on him do-min-ion shall rest. The His name shall be Won-der-ful God, Coun-sel-or, Prince of Peace.

2. The Lord is king, the na-tions re-joice, let all God's peo-ple be glad. The heav-ens pro-claim jus-tice for all. Glo-ry has filled the land.

3. O Beth-le-hem, you are from of old, too small a-mong Ju-dah's clans. From you shall come a rul-er this day, shep-herd to guide the land.

4. The days will come, the Lord prom-ised us, when God would raise up a shoot to rule the land, reign as a king, whose name is Lord the Just.

5. New light has dawned up-on all the just, glad-ness for up-right of heart. Re-joice in the Lord, you faith-ful ones. Give thanks to God's great name.

D.C.

Text: Mike Balhoff, b.1946
Tune: Darryl Ducote, b.1945, Gary Daigle, b.1957
© 1978, Damean Music. Distributed by GIA Publications, Inc.

376 Songs of Thankfulness and Praise

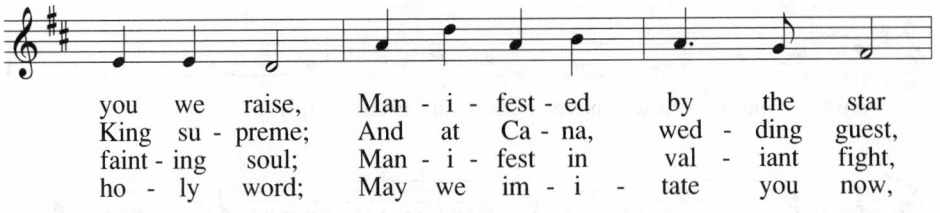

1. Songs of thank-ful - ness and praise, Je - sus, Lord, to
2. Man - i - fest at Jor - dan's stream, Proph- et, Priest, and
3. Man - i - fest in mak - ing whole Pal - sied limbs and
4. Grant us grace to see you, Lord, Mir - rored in your

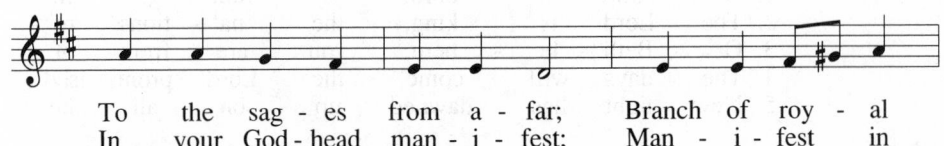

you we raise, Man - i - fest - ed by the star
King su - preme; And at Ca - na, wed - ding guest,
faint - ing soul; Man - i - fest in val - iant fight,
ho - ly word; May we im - i - tate you now,

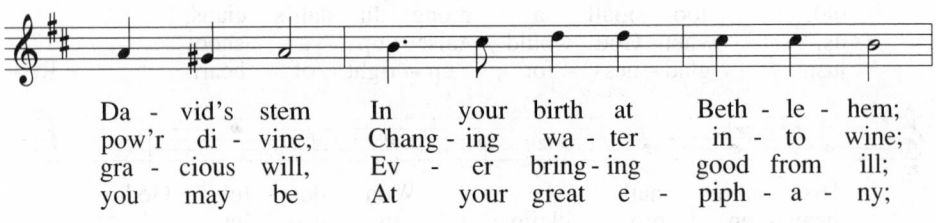

To the sag - es from a - far; Branch of roy - al
In your God- head man - i - fest; Man - i - fest in
Quell - ing all the dev - il's might; Man - i - fest in
And on us your grace en - dow; That we like to

David's stem In your birth at Beth - le - hem;
pow'r di - vine, Chang - ing wa - ter in - to wine;
gra - cious will, Ev - er bring- ing good from ill;
you may be At your great e - piph - a - ny;

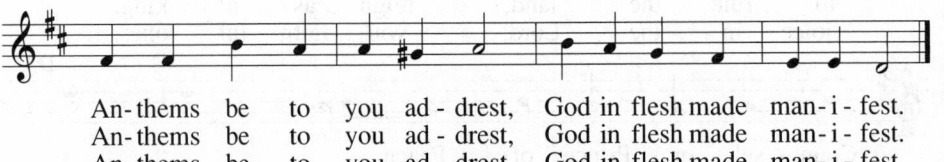

An- thems be to you ad - drest, God in flesh made man- i - fest.
An- thems be to you ad - drest, God in flesh made man- i - fest.
An- thems be to you ad - drest, God in flesh made man- i - fest.
And may praise you ev - er blest, God in flesh made man- i - fest.

Text: Christopher Wordsworth, 1807-1885
Tune: SALZBURG, 77 77 D; Jakob Hintze, 1622-1702, alt; harm. by J.S. Bach, 1685-1750

The First Nowell   377

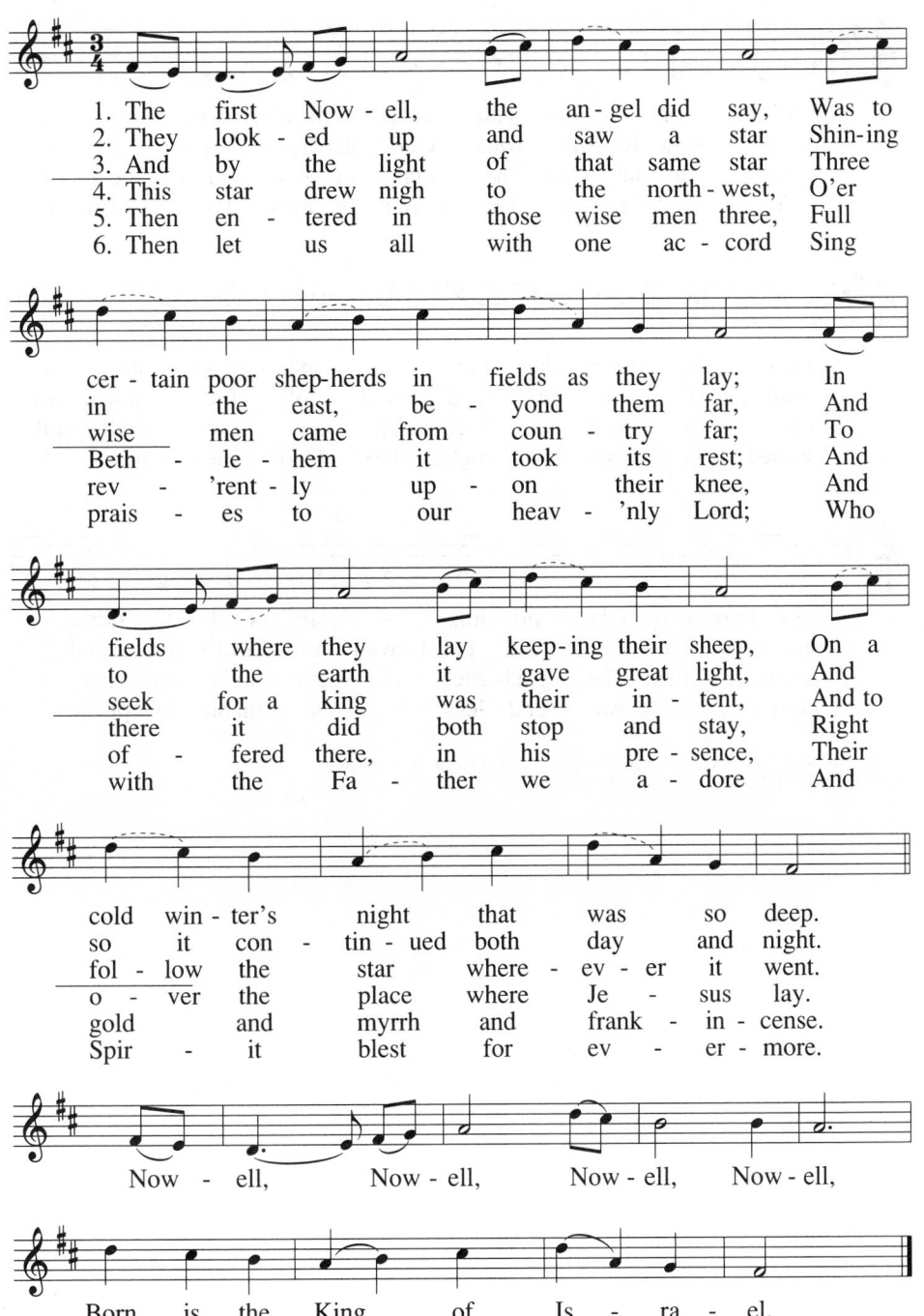

1. The first Now-ell, the an-gel did say, Was to
2. They look-ed up and saw a star Shin-ing
3. And by the light of that same star Three
4. This star drew nigh to the north-west, O'er
5. Then en-tered in those wise men three, Full
6. Then let us all with one ac-cord Sing

cer-tain poor shep-herds in fields as they lay; In
in the east, be-yond them far, And
wise men came from coun-try far; To
Beth-le-hem it took its rest; And
rev-'rent-ly up-on their knee, And
prais-es to our heav-'nly Lord; Who

fields where they lay keep-ing their sheep, On a
to the earth it gave great light, And
seek for a king was their in-tent, And to
there it did both stop and stay, Right
of-fered there, in his pre-sence, Their
with the Fa-ther we a-dore And

cold win-ter's night that was so deep.
so it con-tin-ued both day and night.
fol-low the star where-ev-er it went.
o-ver the place where Je-sus lay.
gold and myrrh and frank-in-cense.
Spir-it blest for ev-er-more.

Now-ell, Now-ell, Now-ell, Now-ell,

Born is the King of Is-ra-el.

Text: English Carol, 17th C.
Tune: THE FIRST NOWELL, Irregular; English Melody; harm. by David Willcocks, b. 1919, © 1961, Oxford University Press

378 What Star Is This

1. What star is this with beams so bright, More love-ly
2. 'Tis now ful-filled what God de-creed, "From Ja - cob
3. O Je - sus, while the star of grace Im - pels us
4. To God Cre - a - tor, heav'n - ly light, To Christ, re -

than the noon - day light? 'Tis sent to an - nounce a
shall a star pro - ceed"; And lo! the east - ern
on to seek your face, Let not our sloth - ful
vealed in earth - ly night, To God the Spir - it

new - born king, Glad tid - ings of our God to bring.
sag - es stand, To read in heaven the Lord's com-mand.
hearts re - fuse The guid-ance of your light to use.
blest we raise An end - less song of thank - ful praise!

Text: *Quem stella sole pulchrior,* Charles Coffin, 1676-1749; tr. by John Chandler, 1806-1876, alt.
Tune: PUER NOBIS, LM; adapt. by Michael Praetorius, 1571-1621

Brightest and Best 379

1. Bright - est and best of the stars of the morn - ing,
2. Cold on his cra - dle the dew - drops are shin - ing,
3. Shall we then yield him, in cost - ly de - vo - tion,
4. Vain - ly we of - fer each am - ple o - bla - tion,
5. Bright - est and best of the stars of the morn - ing,

Dawn on our dark - ness, and lend us thine aid;
Low lies his head with the beasts of the stall;
O - dors of E - dom, and of - f'rings di - vine,
Vain - ly with gifts would his fa - vor se - cure,
Dawn on our dark - ness, and lend us thine aid;

Star of the east, the hor - i - zon a - dorn - ing,
An - gels a - dore him in slum - ber re - clin - ing,
Gems of the moun - tain, and pearls of the o - cean,
Rich - er by far is the heart's ad - o - ra - tion,
Star of the east, the ho - ri - zon a - dorn - ing,

Guide where our in - fant Re - deem - er is laid.
Mak - er and Mon - arch and Sav - ior of all.
Myrrh from the for - est, and gold from the mine?
Dear - er to God are the pray'rs of the poor.
Guide where our in - fant Re - deem - er is laid.

Bright - est and best of the stars of the morn - ing,

Dawn on our dark - ness, and lend us thine aid;

Star of the east, the ho - ri - zon a - dorn - ing,

Guide where our in - fant Re - deem - er is laid.

Text: Reginald Heber, 1783-1826, alt.
Tune: STAR IN THE EAST, 11 10 11 10 with refrain; *Southern Harmony*, 1835; harm. by Marty Haugen, b.1950, © 1987, GIA Publications, Inc.

380 What Child Is This

1. What child is this, who, laid to rest, On
2. Why lies he in such mean es - tate Where
3. So bring him in - cense, gold and myrrh, Come

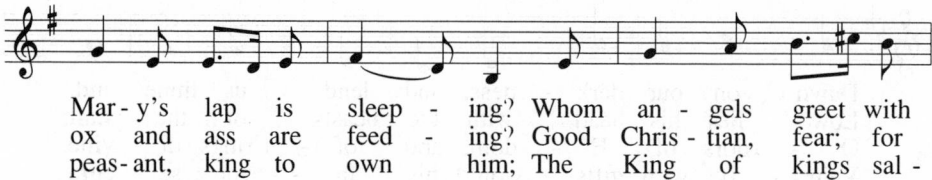

Mar - y's lap is sleep - ing? Whom an - gels greet with
ox and ass are feed - ing? Good Chris - tian, fear; for
peas-ant, king to own him; The King of kings sal -

an - thems sweet, While shep-herds watch are keep - ing?
sin - ners here The si - lent Word is plead - ing.
va - tion brings, Let lov - ing hearts en - throne him.

This, this is Christ the King, Whom shep-herds guard and an - gels sing;

Haste, haste to bring him laud, The babe, the son of Mar-y.

Text: William C. Dix, 1827-1898
Tune: GREENSLEEVES, 8 7 8 7 with refrain; English melody, 16th C.; harm. by John Stainer, 1840-1901

Dust and Ashes 381

Verses

1. Dust and ash - es touch our face,   mark our fail - ure and our
2. Dust and ash - es soil our hands—   greed of mar - ket, pride of
3. Dust and ash - es choke our tongue   in   the waste - land of de -

fall - ing.   Ho - ly Spir - it, come,   walk with   us   to - mor - row,
na - tion.   Ho - ly Spir - it, come,   walk with   us   to - mor - row,
pres - sion. Ho - ly Spir - it, come,   walk with   us   to - mor - row,

take   us   as   dis - ci - ples, washed and wak - ened by your call - ing.
as   we   pray and strug - gle through the mesh - es   of   op - pres - sion.
through all gloom and griev - ing   to   the paths of   res - ur - rec - tion.

Refrain

Take us by the hand and lead   us, lead us through the des - ert   sands,

bring us liv - ing   wa - ter, Ho - ly Spir - it, come.

Text: Brian Wren, b.1936, © 1989, Hope Publishing Co.
Tune: David Haas, b.1957, © 1991, GIA Publications, Inc.

382 Again We Keep This Solemn Fast

1. A - gain we keep this sol - emn fast
2. The law and proph - ets from of old
3. More spar - ing, there - fore, let us make
4. Let us a - void each harm - ful way
5. We pray, O bless - ed Three in One,

A gift of faith from a - ges past,
In fig - ured ways this Lent fore - told,
The words we speak, the food we take,
That lures the care - less mind a - stray;
Our God while end - less a - ges run,

This Lent which binds us lov - ing - ly
Which Christ, all a - ges' Lord and Guide,
Our sleep, our laugh - ter, ev - 'ry sense;
By watch - ful prayer our spir - its free
That this, our Lent of for - ty days,

To faith and hope and char - i - ty.
In these last days has sanc - ti - fied.
Learn peace through ho - ly pen - i - tence.
From schem - ing of the En - e - my.
May bring us growth and give you praise.

Text: *Ex more docti mystico*; ascr. to Gregory the Great, c. 540-604, tr. by Peter J. Scagnelli, b. 1949, ©
Tune: OLD HUNDREDTH, LM; Louis Bourgeois, c.1510-1561

383 Parce Domine

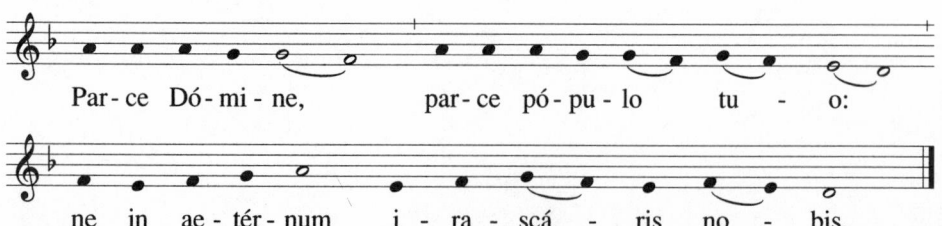

Par - ce Dó - mi - ne, par - ce pó - pu - lo tu - o:

ne in ae - tér - num i - ra - scá - ris no - bis.

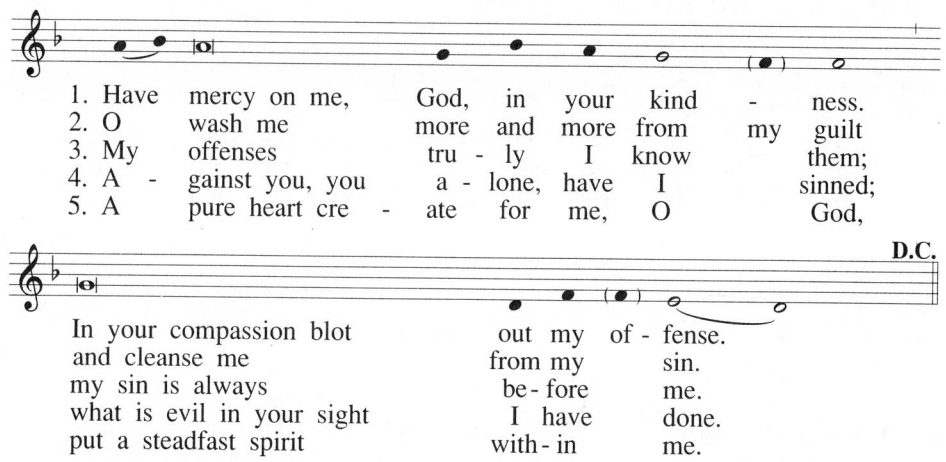

1. Have mercy on me, God, in your kind - ness.
2. O wash me more and more from my guilt
3. My offenses tru - ly I know them;
4. A - gainst you, you a - lone, have I sinned;
5. A pure heart cre - ate for me, O God,

D.C.

In your compassion blot out my of - fense.
and cleanse me from my sin.
my sin is always be - fore me.
what is evil in your sight I have done.
put a steadfast spirit with - in me.

Text: Joel 2:17, Psalm 51:3-6, 12; tr. The Grail, © 1963, GIA Publications, Inc., agent
Tune: PARCE DOMINE, Irregular; Mode I with Tonus Peregrinus; acc. by Robert LeBlanc, OSB, b.1948, © 1986, GIA Publications, Inc.

Forty Days and Forty Nights 384

1. For - ty days and for - ty nights You were fast - ing
2. Shall not we your sor - row share And from world - ly
3. Then if Sa - tan on us press, Flesh or spir - it
4. So shall we have peace di - vine: Ho - lier glad - ness
5. Keep, O keep us, Sav - ior dear, Ev - er con - stant

in the wild; For - ty days and for - ty nights
joys ab - stain, Fast - ing with un - ceas - ing prayer,
to as - sail, Vic - tor in the wil - der - ness,
ours shall be; Round us, too, shall an - gels shine,
by your side; That with you we may ap - pear

Tempt - ed and yet un - de - filed.
Strong with you to suf - fer pain?
Grant we may not faint nor fail!
Such as served you faith - ful - ly.
At the e - ter - nal East - er - tide.

Text: George H. Smyttan, 1822-1870, alt.
Tune: HEINLEIN, 7 7 7 7; attr. to Martin Herbst, 1654-1681, *Nürnbergisches Gesangbuch*, 1676

385 Eternal Lord of Love

1. E - ter - nal Lord of love, be - hold your Church,
2. So dai - ly dy - ing to the way of self,
3. If dead in you, so in you we a - rise,

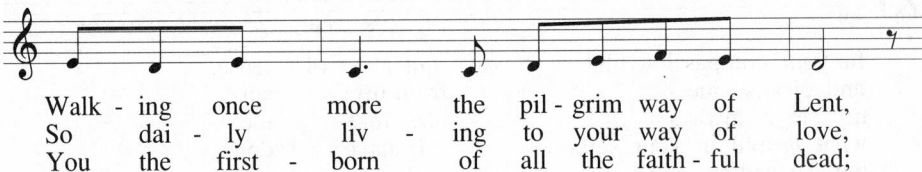

Walk - ing once more the pil - grim way of Lent,
So dai - ly liv - ing to your way of love,
You the first - born of all the faith - ful dead;

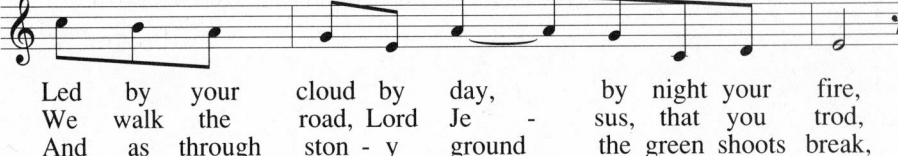

Led by your cloud by day, by night your fire,
We walk the road, Lord Je - sus, that you trod,
And as through ston - y ground the green shoots break,

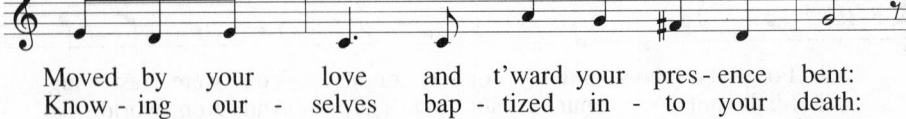

Moved by your love and t'ward your pres - ence bent:
Know - ing our - selves bap - tized in - to your death:
Glo - rious in spring - time dress of leaf and flower,

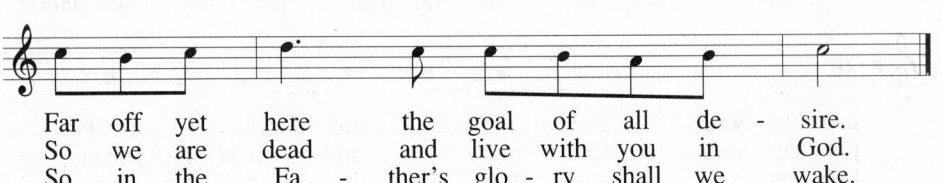

Far off yet here the goal of all de - sire.
So we are dead and live with you in God.
So in the Fa - ther's glo - ry shall we wake.

Text: Thomas H. Cain, b.1931, © 1982
Tune: FENN HOUSE, 10 10 10 10 10 10; Michael Joncas, b.1951, © 1988; GIA Publications, Inc.

Hosea 386

Verses

1. Come back to me with all your heart.
   Trees do bend, 'though straight and tall;
2. The wil - der - ness will lead you
   In - teg - ri - ty and jus - tice,
3. You shall sleep se - cure with peace;

Don't let fear keep us a - part.
so must we to oth - ers' call.
to your heart where I will speak.
With ten - der - ness, you shall know.
faith - ful - ness will be your joy. *(To refrain)*

Refrain

Long have I wait-ed for your com - ing home to me and

D.C.

liv - ing deep - ly our new life.

Text: Based on Hosea 6:1, 3:3, 2:16,21; Joel 2:12; Gregory Norbet, b.1940
Tune: Gregory Norbet, b.1940; arr. by Mary David Callahan, b.1923
© 1972, 1980, The Benedictine Foundation of the State of Vermont, Inc.

387 Hear Us, Almighty Lord / Attende Domine

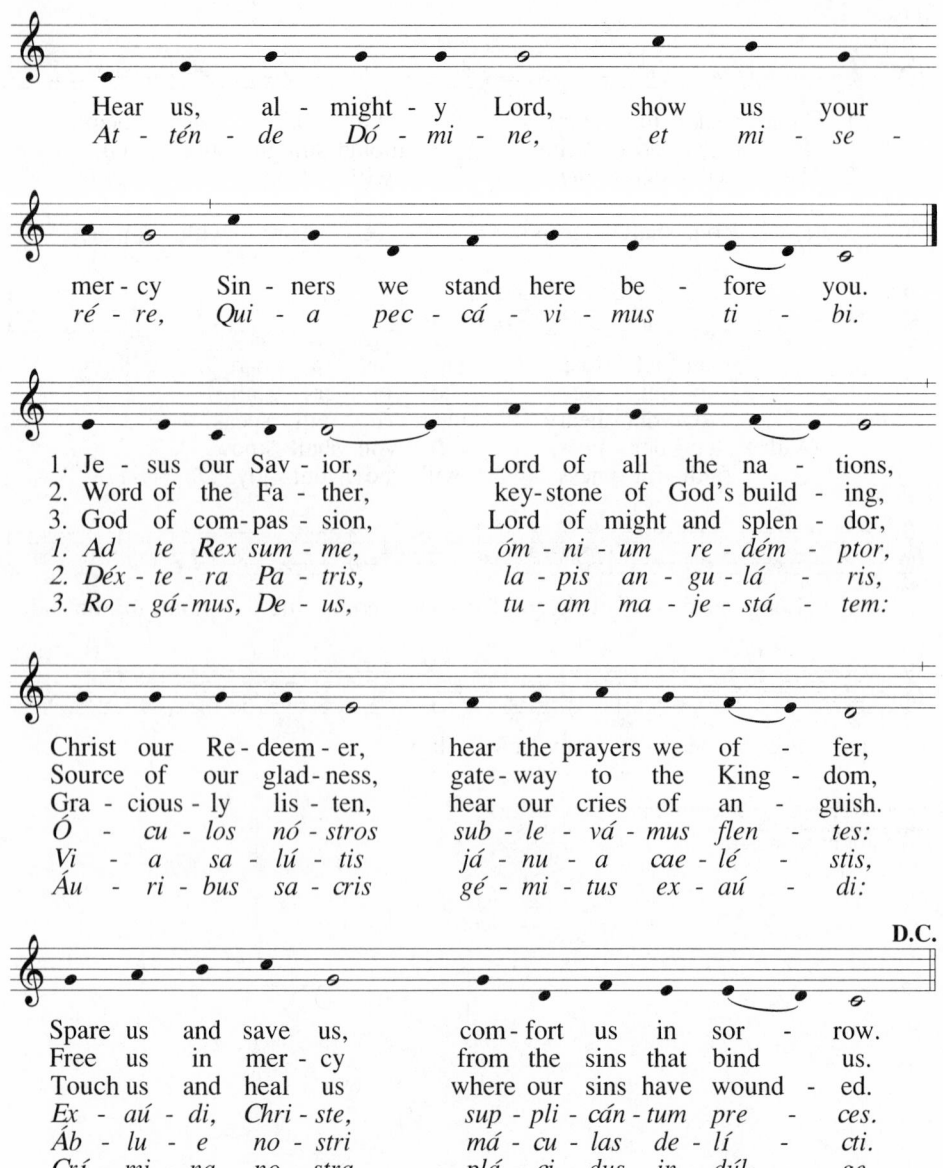

Hear us, al - might - y Lord, show us your
At - tén - de Dó - mi - ne, et mi - se -

mer - cy Sin - ners we stand here be - fore you.
ré - re, Qui - a pec - cá - vi - mus ti - bi.

1. Je - sus our Sav - ior, Lord of all the na - tions,
2. Word of the Fa - ther, key - stone of God's build - ing,
3. God of com - pas - sion, Lord of might and splen - dor,
1. Ad te Rex sum - me, óm - ni - um re - dém - ptor,
2. Déx - te - ra Pa - tris, la - pis an - gu - lá - ris,
3. Ro - gá - mus, De - us, tu - am ma - je - stá - tem:

Christ our Re - deem - er, hear the prayers we of - fer,
Source of our glad - ness, gate - way to the King - dom,
Gra - cious - ly lis - ten, hear our cries of an - guish.
Ó - cu - los nó - stros sub - le - vá - mus flen - tes:
Vi - a sa - lú - tis já - nu - a cae - lé - stis,
Áu - ri - bus sa - cris gé - mi - tus ex - aú - di:

D.C.

Spare us and save us, com - fort us in sor - row.
Free us in mer - cy from the sins that bind us.
Touch us and heal us where our sins have wound - ed.
Ex - aú - di, Chri - ste, sup - pli - cán - tum pre - ces.
Áb - lu - e no - stri má - cu - las de - lí - cti.
Crí - mi - na no - stra plá - ci - dus in - dúl - ge.

4. Humbly confessing that we have offended,
   Stripped of illusions, naked in our sorrow,
   Pardon, Lord Jesus, those your blood has ransomed.

5. Innocent captive, you were led to slaughter,
   Sentenced by sinners when they brought false witness,
   Keep from damnation those your death has rescued.

4. *Tibi fatémur, crímina admíssa:*
   Contríto corde pándimus occúlta:
   Túa redémptor, píetas ignóscat.

5. *Innocens captus, nec repúgnans ductus,*
   Téstibus falsis, pro ímpiis damnátus:
   Quos redemísti, tu consérva, Christe.

Text: Latin, 10th C.; tr. by Ralph Wright, OSB, b.1938, © 1980, ICEL
Tune: ATTENDE DOMINE, 11 11 11 with refrain; Mode V; acc. by Richard Proulx, b.1937, © 1975, GIA Publications, Inc.

The Glory of These Forty Days   388

1. The glo - ry of these for - ty days
2. A - lone and fast - ing Mo - ses saw
3. So Dan - iel trained his mys - tic sight,
4. Then grant that we like them be true,

We cel - e - brate with songs of praise;
The lov - ing God who gave the law;
De - liv - ered from the li - on's might;
Con - sumed in fast and prayer with you;

For Christ, by whom all things were made,
And to E - li - jah, fast - ing, came
And John, the Bride - groom's friend, be - came
Our spir - its strength - en with your grace,

Him - self has fast - ed and has prayed.
The steeds and char - i - ots of flame.
The her - ald of Mes - si - ah's name.
And give us joy to see your face.

Text: *Clarum decus jejunii*; Gregory the Great, c. 540-604; tr. by Maurice F. Bell, 1862-1947, © Oxford University Press
Tune: OLD HUNDREDTH, LM; Louis Bourgeois, c.1510-1561

389 Return to God

Refrain

Re - turn to God with all your heart, the source of grace and mer - cy; come seek the ten - der faith - ful - ness of God.

Verses

1. Now the time of grace has come,
   the day of salvation;
   come and learn now the way of our God.

2. I will take your heart of stone
   and place a heart within you,
   a heart of compassion and love.

3. If you break the chains of oppression,
   if you set the pris'ner free;
   if you share your bread with the hungry,
   give protection to the lost;
   give a shelter to the homeless,
   clothe the naked in your midst,
   then your light shall break forth like the dawn.

Text: Marty Haugen, b.1950
Tune: Marty Haugen, b.1950
© 1990, 1991, GIA Publications, Inc.

Jerusalem, My Destiny 390

Refrain

I have fixed my eyes on your hills, Je-ru-sa-lem, my des-ti-ny! Though I can-not see the end for me, I can-not turn a-way. We have set our hearts for the way; this jour-ney is our des-ti-ny. Let no-one walk a-lone. The jour-ney makes us one.

Verses

1. Oth - er spir - its, less - er gods, have court-ed
2. See, I leave the past be - hind; a new land
3. In my thirst, you let me drink the wa - ters
4. All the worlds I have not seen you o - pen
5. To the tombs I went to mourn the hope I

me with lies. Here a - mong you
calls to me. Here a - mong you
of your life. Here a - mong you
to my view. Here a - mong you
thought was gone. Here a - mong you

D.C.

I have found a truth which bids me rise.
now I find a glimpse of what might be.
I have met the sa - viour, Je - sus Christ.
I have found a vi - sion, bright and new.
I a - woke to un - ex - pect - ed dawn.

Text: Rory Cooney, b.1952
Tune: Rory Cooney, b.1952
© 1990, GIA Publications, Inc.

391 God of Abraham

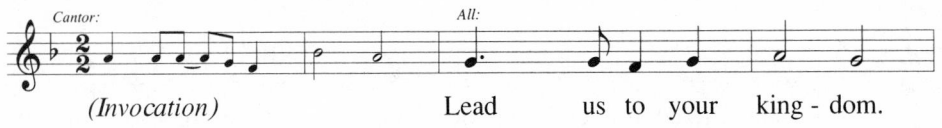

(Invocation) — Lead us to your king-dom.

(Invocation) — Lead us to-geth-er, lead us to free-dom.

Last time

lead us to free-dom. Lead us to free-dom now.

Text: Bernadette Farrell, b.1957
Tune: Bernadette Farrell, b.1957
© 1990, Bernadette Farrell, published by OCP Publications

392 Lord, Who throughout These Forty Days

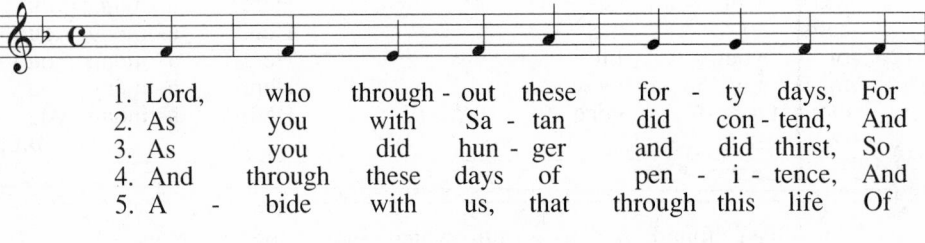

1. Lord, who through-out these for - ty days, For
2. As you with Sa - tan did con - tend, And
3. As you did hun - ger and did thirst, So
4. And through these days of pen - i - tence, And
5. A - bide with us, that through this life Of

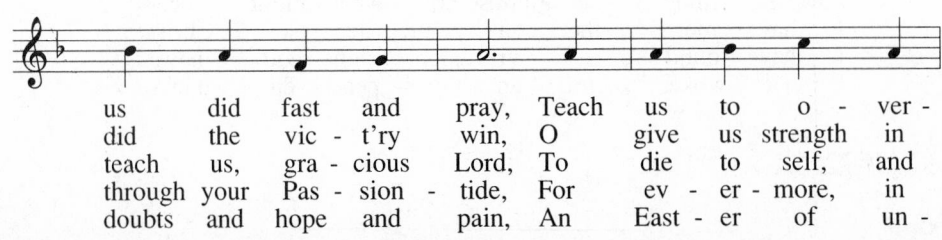

us did fast and pray, Teach us to o - ver-
did the vic - t'ry win, O give us strength in
teach us, gra - cious Lord, To die to self, and
through your Pas - sion - tide, For ev - er - more, in
doubts and hope and pain, An East - er of un -

come	our	sins,	And	close	by	you	to	stay.
you	to	fight,	In	you	to	con - quer		sin.
so	to	live	By	your	most	ho - ly		word.
life	and	death,	O	Lord!	with	us	a -	bide.
end -	ing	joy	We	may	at	last	at -	tain!

Text: Claudia F. Hernaman, 1838-1898, alt.
Tune: ST. FLAVIAN, CM; *John's Day Psalter*, 1562; harm. based on the original *faux-bourdon* setting

Jesus Walked This Lonesome Valley   393

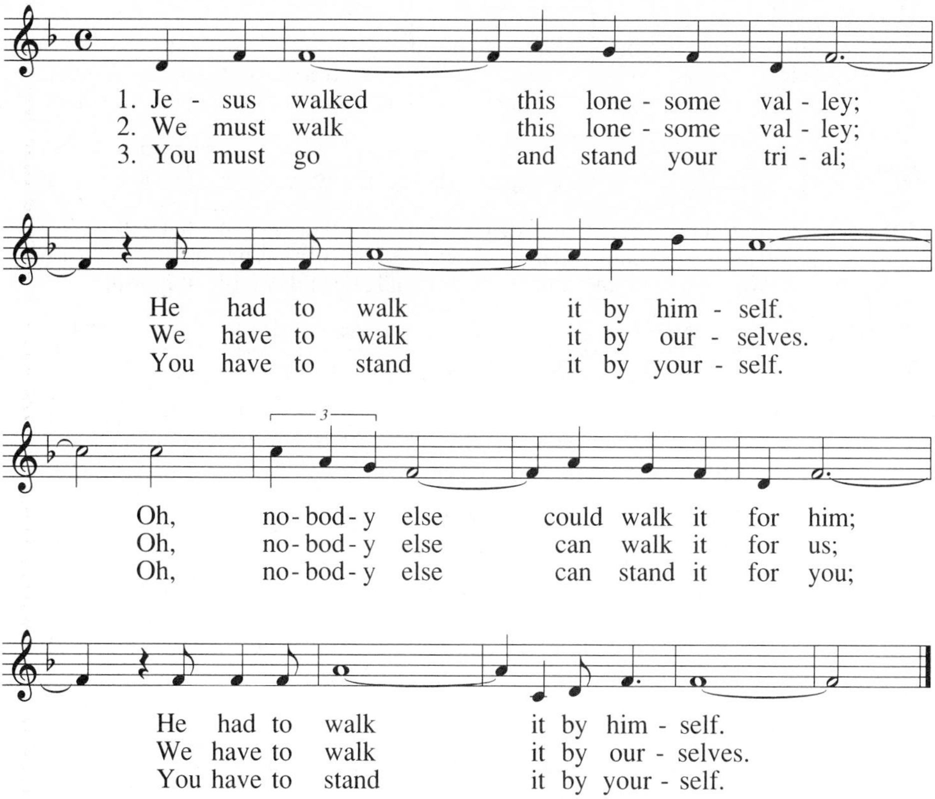

1. Je - sus walked   this lone - some val - ley;
2. We must walk   this lone - some val - ley;
3. You must go   and stand your tri - al;

He had to walk   it by him - self.
We have to walk   it by our - selves.
You have to stand   it by your - self.

Oh, no-bod-y else   could walk it for him;
Oh, no-bod-y else   can walk it for us;
Oh, no-bod-y else   can stand it for you;

He had to walk   it by him - self.
We have to walk   it by our - selves.
You have to stand   it by your - self.

Text: American Folk Hymn
Tune: LONESOME VALLEY, 8 8 10 8; American folk hymn; harm. by Richard Proulx, b.1937, © 1975, GIA Publications, Inc.

394 Change Our Hearts

Refrain

Change our hearts this time, Your word says it can
be. Change our minds, this time, Your life could make us
free. We are the peo - ple Your call set a - part,
Lord, this time change our hearts.

Verses

1. Brought by your hand to the edge of our dreams.
2. Now as we watch you stretch out your hands,
3. Show us the way that leads to your side,

One foot in par - a - dise, one in the waste.
of - 'fring a - bun - dan - ces, full - ness of joy.
o - ver the moun - tains and sands of the soul.

Drawn by your prom - is - es, still we are
Your milk and hon - ey seem dis - tant, un -
Be for us man - na, wa - ter from

D.C.

lured by the shad - ows and the chains we leave be - hind. But
real, when we have bread and wa - ter in our hands. But
stone, ʼ light which says we nev - er walk a - lone. And

Text: Rory Cooney, b.1952
Tune: Rory Cooney, b.1952
© 1984, North American Liturgy Resources

Somebody's Knockin' at Your Door   395

Some-bod - y's knock-in' at your door; Some-bod - y's
knock-in' at your door; O sin - ner, why don't you
an-swer? Some-bod - y's knock-in' at your door.

Solo: / *All:*

1. Knocks like Je - sus,
2. Can't you hear him?
3. Je - sus calls you,
4. Can't you trust him?

Some-bod - y's knock-in' at your door.

Solo: / *All:*

Knocks like Je - sus,
Can't you hear him?
Je - sus calls you,
Can't you trust him?

Some-bod - y's knock - in' at your door.

O sin - ner, why don't you an - swer?

Some-bod - y's knock- in' at your door.

Text: African-American spiritual
Tune: SOMEBODY'S KNOCKIN', Irregular; African-American spiritual; harm. by Richard Proulx, b.1937, © 1986, GIA Publications, Inc.

396 Adoramus Te Christe

Canon Refrain

1.
A - do - ra - mus te Chri - ste, a - do - ra - mus te Chri - ste,

3.
a - do - ra - mus te Chri - ste, a - do - ra - mus Chri - ste.

Verses

1. A - do - ra - mus te Chri - ste, et be - ne -

di - ci - mus ti - bi, 2. Qui - a per san - ctam

Cru - cem tu - am re - de - mi - sti mun - dum.

Text: Antiphon from Good Friday Liturgy; *We adore you, O Christ, and we bless you, because by your holy cross you have redeemed the world.*
Tune: Marty Haugen, b.1950, © 1984, GIA Publications, Inc.

397 Tree of Life

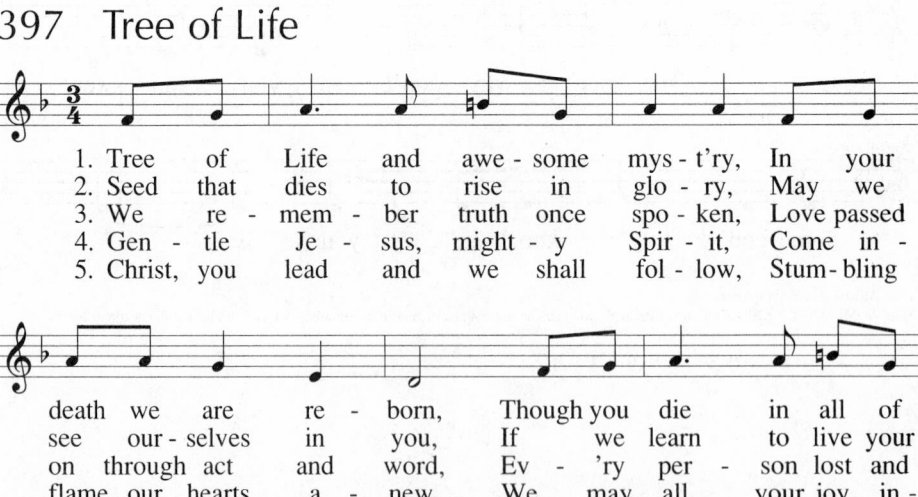

1. Tree of Life and awe - some mys - t'ry, In your
2. Seed that dies to rise in glo - ry, May we
3. We re - mem - ber truth once spo - ken, Love passed
4. Gen - tle Je - sus, might - y Spir - it, Come in -
5. Christ, you lead and we shall fol - low, Stum- bling

death we are re - born, Though you die in all of
see our - selves in you, If we learn to live your
on through act and word, Ev - 'ry per - son lost and
flame our hearts a - new, We may all your joy in -
though our steps may be, One with you in joy and

his - t'ry, Still you rise with ev - 'ry morn, Still you
sto - ry We may die to rise a - new, We may
bro - ken Wears the bod - y of our Lord, Wears the
her - it If we bear the cross with you, If we
sor - row, We the riv - er, you the sea, We the

rise with ev - 'ry morn.
die to rise a - new.
bod - y of our Lord.
bear the cross with you.
riv - er, you the sea.

Lenten Verses:

General: Light of life beyond conceiving, Mighty Spirit of our Lord;
Give new strength to our believing, Give us faith to live your word.

1st Sunday: From the dawning of creation, You have loved us as your own;
Stay with us through all temptation, Make us turn to you alone.

2nd Sunday: In our call to be a blessing, May we be a blessing true;
May we live and die confessing Christ as Lord of all we do.

3rd Sunday: Living Water of salvation, Be the fountain of each soul;
Springing up in new creation, Flow in us and make us whole.

4th Sunday: Give us eyes to see you clearly, Make us children of your light;
Give us hearts to live more nearly As your gospel shining bright.

5th Sunday: God of all our fear and sorrow, God who lives beyond our death;
Hold us close through each tomorrow, Love as near as every breath.

Text: Marty Haugen, b.1950
Tune: THOMAS, 8 7 8 77; Marty Haugen, b.1950
© 1984, GIA Publications, Inc.

398 Hold Us in Your Mercy: Penitential Litany

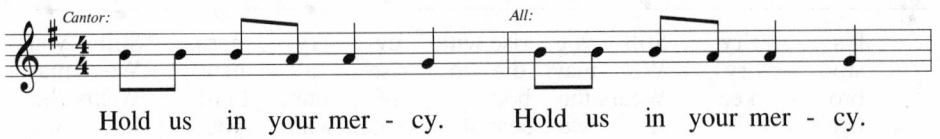

Hold us in your mer - cy. Hold us in your mer - cy.

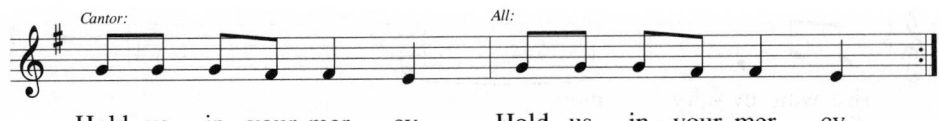

Hold us in your mer - cy. Hold us in your mer - cy.

(Invocation) Hold us in your mer - cy.

(Invocation) Hold us in your mer - cy.

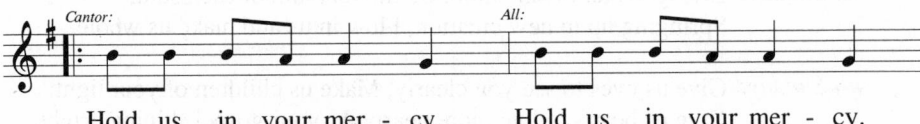

Hold us in your mer - cy. Hold us in your mer - cy.

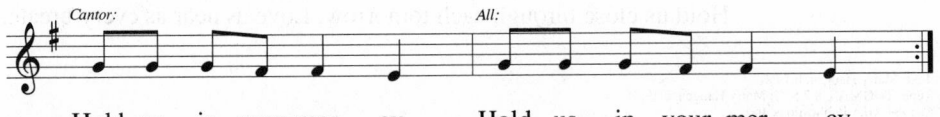

Hold us in your mer - cy. Hold us in your mer - cy.

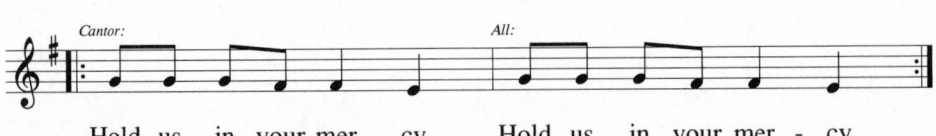

Hold us in your mer - cy Hold us in your mer - cy.

Text: Rory Cooney, b.1952
Tune: Gary Daigle, b.1957
© 1993, GIA Publications, Inc.

Deep Within   399

Refrain

Deep with - in I will plant my law, not on stone, but in your heart. Fol - low me, I will bring you back, you will be my own, and I will be your God.

Verses

1. I will give you a new heart, a new spir - it with-
2. ⁊ Seek my face, and see your
3. Re - turn to me, with all your

D.C.

in you, for I will be your strength.
God, ⁊ for I will be your hope.
heart, ⁊ and I will bring you back.

Text: Jeremiah 31:33, Ezekiel 36:26, Joel 2:12; David Haas, b.1957
Tune: David Haas, b.1957; acc. by Jeanne Cotter, b.1964
© 1987, GIA Publications, Inc.

400 Wash Me, Cleanse Me

Verses

1. Wash me, cleanse me and I shall be
2. Ash to ash, dust to dust, ev - 'ry - thing re -
3. Fear - ful, faith - ful, I a - wait new
4. Hear me, spare me, do not face me

bright - er than the snow. For my soul is
turn - ing to your heart. You are al - ways
heav - en and new earth. Yet a day to
sud - den - ly with death. Give me grace to

long - ing for your pres - ence, Lord, and my
mer - ci - ful and gra - cious, Lord, slow to
you is as a thou - sand years, and a
heal my sin and ig - no - rance, and the

bro - ken heart you know.
an - ger, just and kind.
thou - sand years a day.
time to change my heart.

Refrain

O Lord, please wash me, cleanse me
and I shall be bright-er than the snow. Wash me, cleanse

me and I shall be bright - er than the snow.

Text: Jeremy Young, b.1948
Tune: Jeremy Young, b.1948
© 1990, GIA Publications, Inc.

At the Cross Her Station Keeping 401

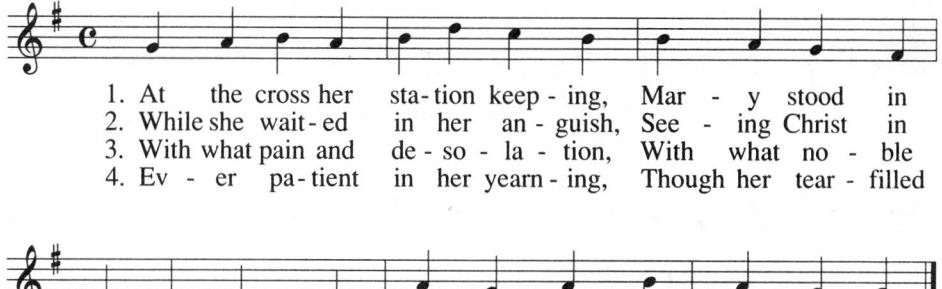

1. At the cross her sta-tion keep-ing, Mar - y stood in
2. While she wait-ed in her an - guish, See - ing Christ in
3. With what pain and de - so - la - tion, With what no - ble
4. Ev - er pa-tient in her yearn-ing, Though her tear - filled

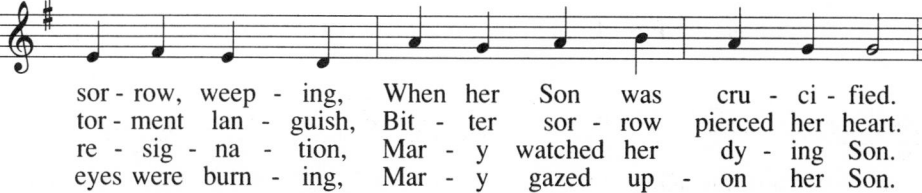

sor - row, weep - ing, When her Son was cru - ci - fied.
tor - ment lan - guish, Bit - ter sor - row pierced her heart.
re - sig - na - tion, Mar - y watched her dy - ing Son.
eyes were burn - ing, Mar - y gazed up - on her Son.

5. Who, that sorrow contemplating,
   On that passion meditating,
   Would not share the Virgin's grief?

6. Christ she saw, for our salvation,
   Scourged with cruel acclamation,
   Bruised and beaten by the rod.

7. Christ she saw with life-blood failing,
   All her anguish unavailing,
   Saw him breathe his very last.

8. Mary, fount of love's devotion,
   Let me share with true emotion
   All the sorrow you endured.

9. Virgin, ever interceding,
   Hear me in my fervent pleading:
   Fire me with your love of Christ.

10. Mother, may this prayer be granted:
    That Christ's love may be implanted
    In the depths of my poor soul.

11. At the cross, your sorrow sharing,
    All your grief and torment bearing,
    Let me stand and mourn with you.

12. Fairest maid of all creation,
    Queen of hope and consolation,
    Let me feel your grief sublime.

13. Virgin, in your love befriend me,
    At the Judgment Day defend me.
    Help me by your constant prayer.

14. Savior, when my life shall leave me,
    Through your mother's prayers receive me
    With the fruits of victory.

15. Let me to your love be taken,
    Let my soul in death awaken
    To the joys of Paradise.

Text: *Stabat mater dolorosa;* Jacopone da Todi, 1230-1306; trans. by Anthony G. Petti, 1932-1985. © 1971, Faber Music, Ltd.
Tune: STABAT MATER, 88 7; *Mainz Gesangbuch,* 1661; harm. by Richard Proulx, b.1937. © 1986, GIA Publications, Inc.

402 All Glory, Laud, and Honor

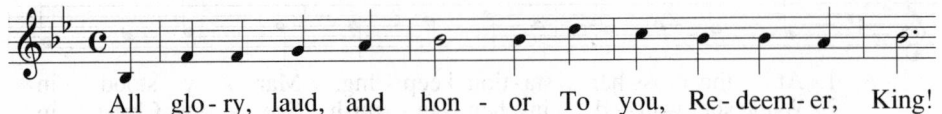

All glo - ry, laud, and hon - or To you, Re - deem - er, King!

To whom the lips of chil - dren Made sweet ho - san - nas ring.

1. You are the King of Is - ra - el, And Da - vid's roy - al Son,
2. The com - pa - ny of an - gels Are prais - ing you on high;
3. The peo - ple of the He - brews With palms be - fore you went:
4. To you be - fore your pas - sion They sang their hymns of praise:
5. Their prais - es you ac - cept - ed, Ac - cept the prayers we bring,

D.C.

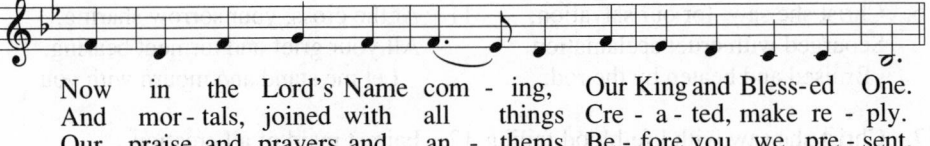

Now in the Lord's Name com - ing, Our King and Bless - ed One.
And mor - tals, joined with all things Cre - a - ted, make re - ply.
Our praise and prayers and an - thems Be - fore you we pre - sent.
To you, now high ex - alt - ed, Our mel - o - dy we raise.
Great source of love and good - ness, Our Sav - ior and our King.

Text: *Gloria, laus et honor*; Theodulph of Orleans, c.760-821; tr. by John M. Neale, 1818-1866, alt.
Tune: ST. THEODULPH, 7 6 7 6 D; Melchior Teschner, 1584-1635

Hosanna 403

Refrain

Ho - san - na, ho - san - na, ho - san -

na! Ho - san - na, ho - san -

na, ho - san - na!

Verses

1. Blessed is he,
   blessed is he who comes in the name of the Lord!
   Blessed is he,
   blessed is he who comes in the name of the Lord!

2. Blessed is the reign of our father, David.
   Blessed is the reign of our father, David, to come!

Text: Mark 11:9-10; David Haas, b.1957
Tune: David Haas, b.1957
© 1988, GIA Publications, Inc.

404 Jesus, Remember Me

Ostinato Refrain

Je-sus, re-mem-ber me when you come in-to your King-dom.

Je-sus, re-mem-ber me when you come in-to your King-dom.

Text: Luke 23:42; Taizé Community, 1981
Tune: Jacques Berthier, 1923-1994
© 1981, Les Presses de Taizé, GIA Publications, Inc., agent

Ride On, Jesus, Ride   405

Ride   on,   Je - sus,   ride.   Ride   on,   Je - sus,   ride.

Ride   on, Je - sus,   con - quering   King,   Ride   on,   Je - sus   ride.

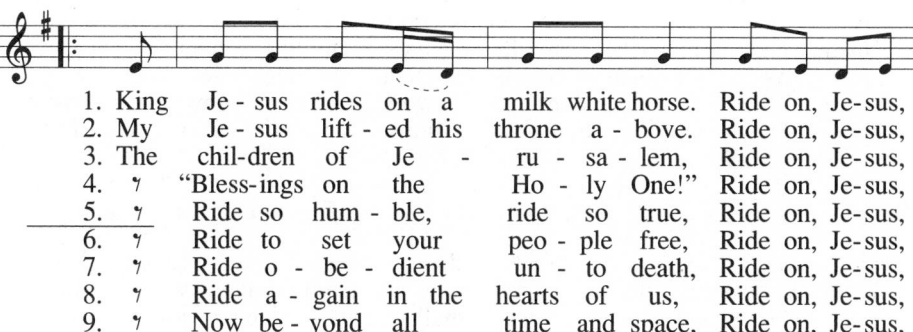

1. King   Je - sus rides on   a   milk white horse. Ride on, Je - sus,
2. My   Je - sus lift - ed his   throne a - bove. Ride on, Je - sus,
3. The   chil-dren of   Je   -   ru - sa - lem,   Ride on, Je - sus,
4. ⁊   "Bless-ings on   the   Ho - ly One!"   Ride on, Je - sus,
5. ⁊   Ride so   hum - ble,   ride   so   true,   Ride on, Je - sus,
6. ⁊   Ride to   set   your   peo - ple free,   Ride on, Je - sus,
7. ⁊   Ride o - be - dient   un - to   death,   Ride on, Je - sus,
8. ⁊   Ride a - gain in the   hearts of   us,   Ride on, Je - sus,
9. ⁊   Now be - yond all   time and space,   Ride on, Je - sus,

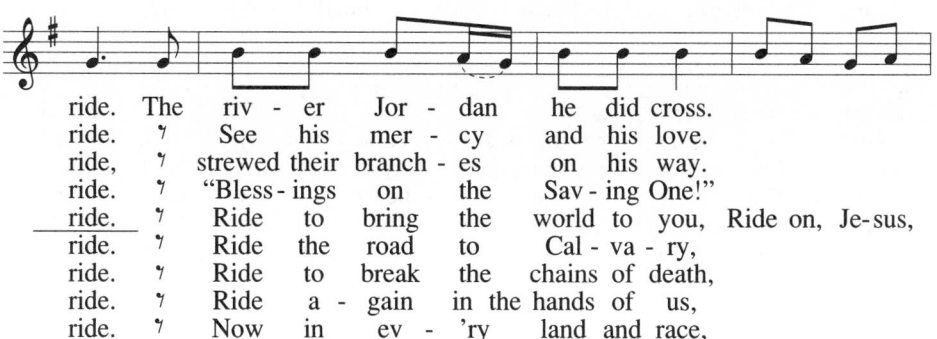

ride. The   riv - er   Jor - dan   he   did cross.
ride. ⁊   See   his   mer - cy   and his love.
ride, ⁊   strewed their branch - es   on   his way.
ride. ⁊   "Bless - ings on   the   Sav - ing One!"
ride. ⁊   Ride to   bring the   world to you, Ride on, Je - sus,
ride. ⁊   Ride the   road to   Cal - va - ry,
ride. ⁊   Ride to   break the   chains of death,
ride. ⁊   Ride a - gain in the hands of   us,
ride. ⁊   Now in   ev - 'ry   land and race,

ride. Ride on, Je - sus, con - quering King. Ride on, Je - sus ride.

Text: African-American spiritual; verses 3-9, Marty Haugen, b.1950, © 1991, GIA Publications, Inc.
Tune: African-American spiritual; harm. by Barbara Jackson Martin, © 1987, GIA Publications, Inc.

406 Triduum Hymn: Wondrous Love

Holy Thursday Verses

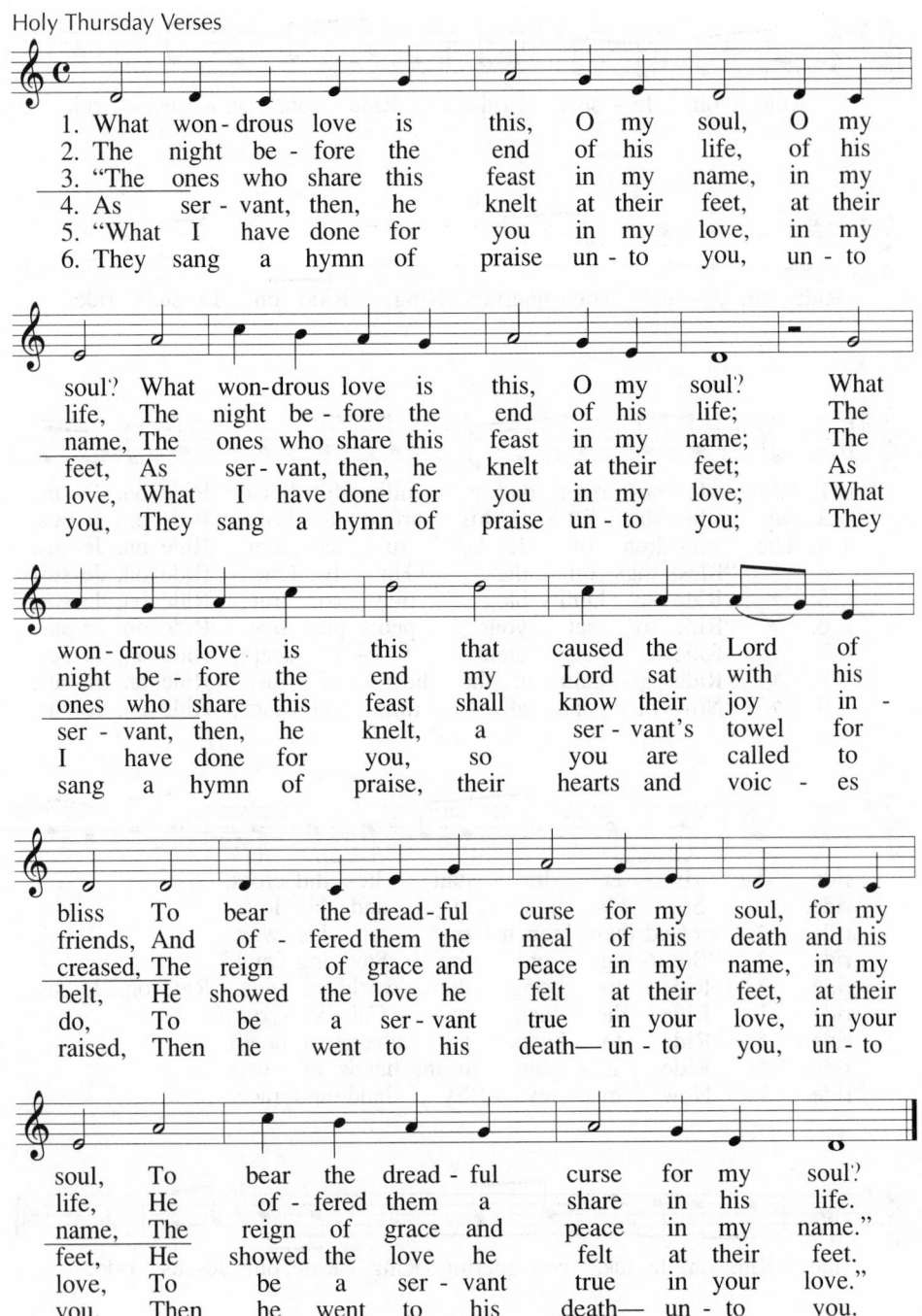

1. What won-drous love is this, O my soul, O my
2. The night be - fore the end of his life, of his
3. "The ones who share this feast in my name, in my
4. As ser - vant, then, he knelt at their feet, at their
5. "What I have done for you in my love, in my
6. They sang a hymn of praise un - to you, un - to

soul? What won-drous love is this, O my soul? What
life, The night be - fore the end of his life; The
name, The ones who share this feast in my name; The
feet, As ser - vant, then, he knelt at their feet; As
love, What I have done for you in my love; What
you, They sang a hymn of praise un - to you; They

won - drous love is this that caused the Lord of
night be - fore the end my Lord sat with his
ones who share this feast shall know their joy in -
ser - vant, then, he knelt, a ser - vant's towel for
I have done for you, so you are called to
sang a hymn of praise, their hearts and voic - es

bliss To bear the dread-ful curse for my soul, for my
friends, And of - fered them the meal of his death and his
creased, The reign of grace and peace in my name, in my
belt, He showed the love he felt at their feet, at their
do, To be a ser - vant true in your love, in your
raised, Then he went to his death— un - to you, un - to

soul, To bear the dread - ful curse for my soul?
life, He of - fered them a share in his life.
name, The reign of grace and peace in my name."
feet, He showed the love he felt at their feet.
love, To be a ser - vant true in your love."
you, Then he went to his death— un - to you.

Text: St. 1, Alexander Means, 1801-1853; remainder, Marty Haugen, b.1950, © 1987, GIA Publications, Inc.
Tune: WONDROUS LOVE, 12 9 12 12 9; *Southern Harmony*, 1835; acc. by Marty Haugen, b.1950, © 1987, GIA Publications, Inc.

Good Friday Verses

What wondrous love is this, O my
    soul, O my soul?
What wondrous love is this, O my soul?
What wondrous love is this that
    caused the Lord of bliss
To bear the dreadful curse for my soul,
    for my soul,
To bear the dreadful curse for my soul?

As you have shown the way, let us
    love, let us love,
As you have shown the way, let us love;
As you have shown the way, so teach
    us ev'ry day
To simply be the way of your love, of
    your love,
To simply be the way of your love.

Wherever you are found, may we be,
    may we be,
Wherever you are found, may we be;
Wherever you are found in souls and
    bodies bound,
Where suffering is found, may we be,
    may we be,
Where suffering is found, may we be.

As instruments of peace, may we
    grow, may we grow,
As instruments of peace, may we grow;
As instruments of peace to bring the
    bound release,
And make oppression cease, help us
    grow, help us grow,
To make oppression cease,
    help us grow.

O let us hear your call to be love,
    to be love,
O let us hear your call to be love;
O let us hear your call, great servant
    of us all,
To be the least of all, as your love, as
    your love,
To be the least of all, as your love.

Easter Vigil Verses

No more within the grave does he lie,
    does he lie,
No more within the grave does he lie;
No more within the grave, but risen
    now to save,
No more within the earth does he lie,
    does he lie
No more within the earth does he lie.

The God who raised my Lord will raise
    me, will raise me,
The God who raised my Lord will
    raise me;
The God who raised my Lord, who
    spoke the living word
Will shout into my tomb and raise me,
    and raise me,
Will shout into my tomb and raise me.

Up from the holy flood, I will rise, I
    will rise,
Up from the holy flood, I will rise;
Up from the holy flood, the water and
    the blood,
To praise the living God, I will rise, I
    will rise,
To praise the living God, I will rise.

To God and to the lamb I will sing, I
    will sing,
To God and to the lamb I will sing;
To God and to the lamb, who is the
    great "I am,"
While millions join the theme, I will
    sing, I will sing,
While millions join the theme, I will sing.

And when from death I'm free, I'll
    sing on, I'll sing on,
And when from death I'm free, I'll sing on;
And when from death I'm free, I'll sing
    and joyful be,
And through eternity I'll sing on,
    I'll sing on,
And through eternity I'll sing on.

Text: St. 1, Alexander Means, 1801-1853; remainder, Marty Haugen, b.1950, © 1987, GIA Publications, Inc.
Tune: WONDROUS LOVE, 12 9 12 12 9; *Southern Harmony*, 1835; acc. by Marty Haugen, b.1950, © 1987, GIA Publications, Inc.

407 Hail Our Savior's Glorious Body / Pange Lingua

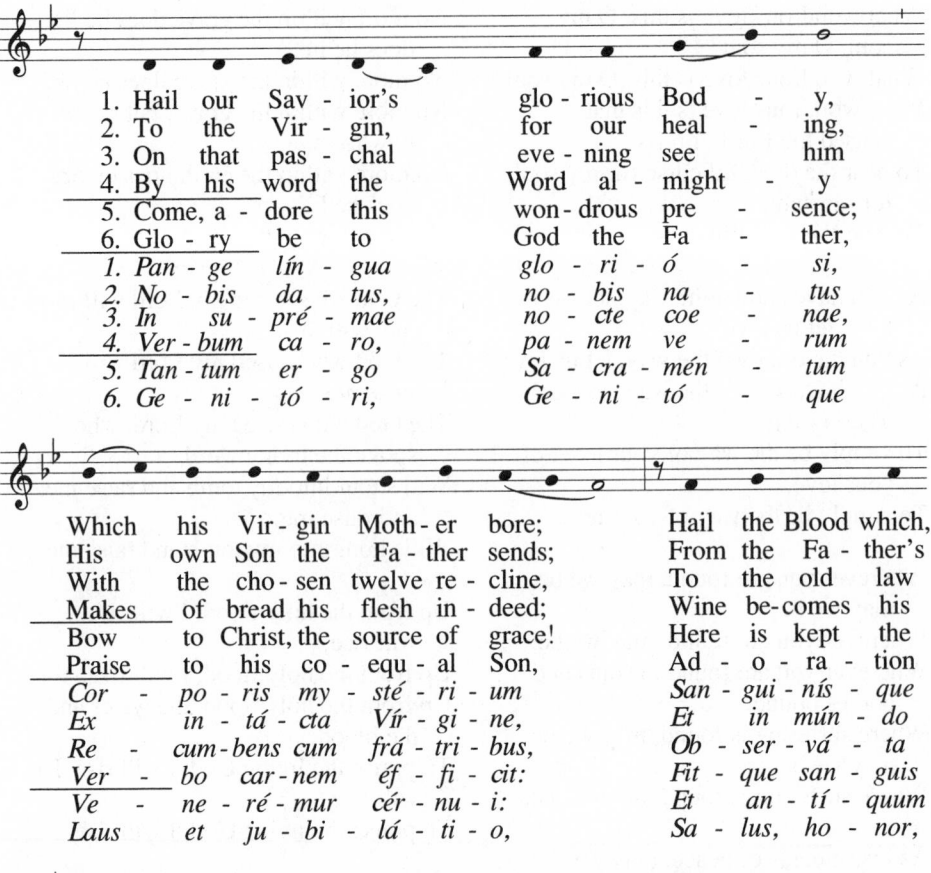

1. Hail our Sav - ior's glo - rious Bod - y,
2. To the Vir - gin, for our heal - ing,
3. On that pas - chal eve - ning see him
4. By his word the Word al - might - y
5. Come, a - dore this won - drous pre - sence;
6. Glo - ry be to God the Fa - ther,

1. Pan - ge lín - gua glo - ri - ó - si,
2. No - bis da - tus, no - bis na - tus
3. In su - pré - mae no - cte coe - nae,
4. Ver - bum ca - ro, pa - nem ve - rum
5. Tan - tum er - go Sa - cra - mén - tum
6. Ge - ni - tó - ri, Ge - ni - tó - que

Which his Vir - gin Moth - er bore; Hail the Blood which,
His own Son the Fa - ther sends; From the Fa - ther's
With the cho - sen twelve re - cline, To the old law
Makes of bread his flesh in - deed; Wine be - comes his
Bow to Christ, the source of grace! Here is kept the
Praise to his co - equ - al Son, Ad - o - ra - tion

Cor - po - ris my - sté - ri - um, San - gui - nís - que
Ex in - tá - cta Vír - gi - ne, Et in mún - do
Re - cum - bens cum frá - tri - bus, Ob - ser - vá - ta
Ver - bo car - nem éf - fi - cit: Fit - que san - guis
Ve - ne - ré - mur cér - nu - i: Et an - tí - quum
Laus et ju - bi - lá - ti - o, Sa - lus, ho - nor,

shed for sin - ners, Did a bro - ken world re - store;
love pro - ceed - ing Sow - er, seed and word de - scends;
still o - be - dient In its feast of love di - vine;
ver - y life - blood; Faith God's liv - ing Word must heed!
an - cient prom - ise Of God's earth - ly dwell - ing place!
to the Spir - it, Bond of love, in God - head one!

pre - ti - ó - si, Quem in mún - di pré - ti - um
con - ver - sá - tus, Spar - so vér - bi sé - mi - ne,
le - ge ple - ne Ci - bis in le - gá - li - bus,
Chri - sti me - rum, Et si sen - sus dé - fi - cit,
do - cu - mén - tum No - vo ce - dat rí - tu - i;
vir - tus quo - que Sit et be - ne - dí - cti - o:

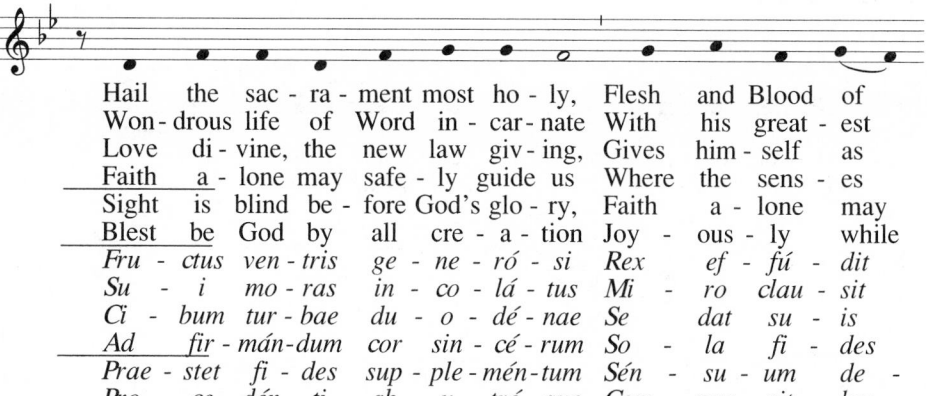

Hail	the	sac - ra - ment most ho - ly,	Flesh	and	Blood	of
Won - drous	life	of Word in - car - nate	With	his	great - est
Love	di - vine, the	new law giv - ing,	Gives	him - self	as
Faith	a - lone may	safe - ly guide us	Where	the	sens - es
Sight	is	blind be - fore God's glo - ry,	Faith	a - lone	may
Blest	be	God by all cre - a - tion	Joy - ous - ly	while
Fru - ctus	*ven - tris*	*ge - ne - ró - si*	*Rex*	*ef - fú - dit*
Su - i	*mo - ras*	*in - co - lá - tus*	*Mi - ro*	*clau - sit*
Ci - bum	*tur - bae*	*du - o - dé - nae*	*Se*	*dat*	*su - is*
Ad	*fir - mán - dum*	*cor sin - cé - rum*	*So - la*	*fi - des*
Prae - stet	*fi - des*	*sup - ple - mén - tum*	*Sén - su - um*	*de -*
Pro - ce - dén - ti	*ab u - tró - que*	*Com - par sit*	*lau -*

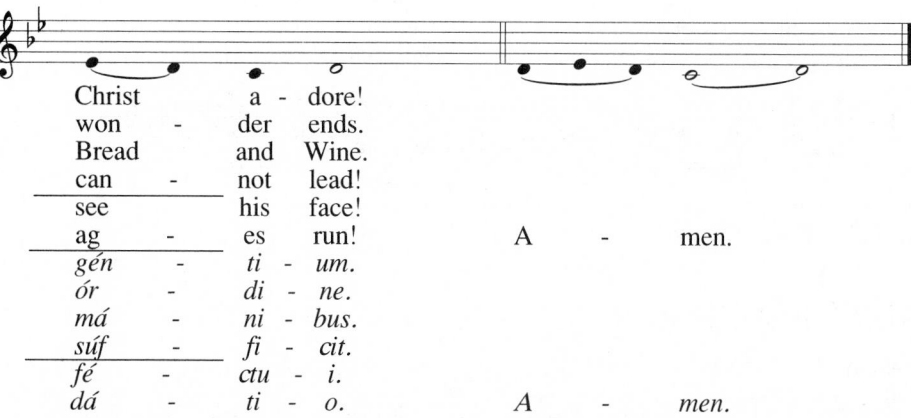

Christ	a - dore!		
won - der	ends.		
Bread	and Wine.		
can - not	lead!		
see	his face!		
ag - es	run!	A - men.
gén - ti - um.		
ór - di - ne.		
má - ni - bus.		
súf - fi - cit.		
fé - ctu - i.		
dá - ti - o.	A - men.

Text: *Pange lingua*, Thomas Aquinas, 1227-1274; tr. by James Quinn, SJ, b.1919, © 1969; Used by permission of Selah Publishing, Inc., Kingston, N.Y.
Tune: Mode III; acc. by Eugene Lapierre, © 1964, GIA Publications, Inc.

408 Ubi Caritas

Refrain

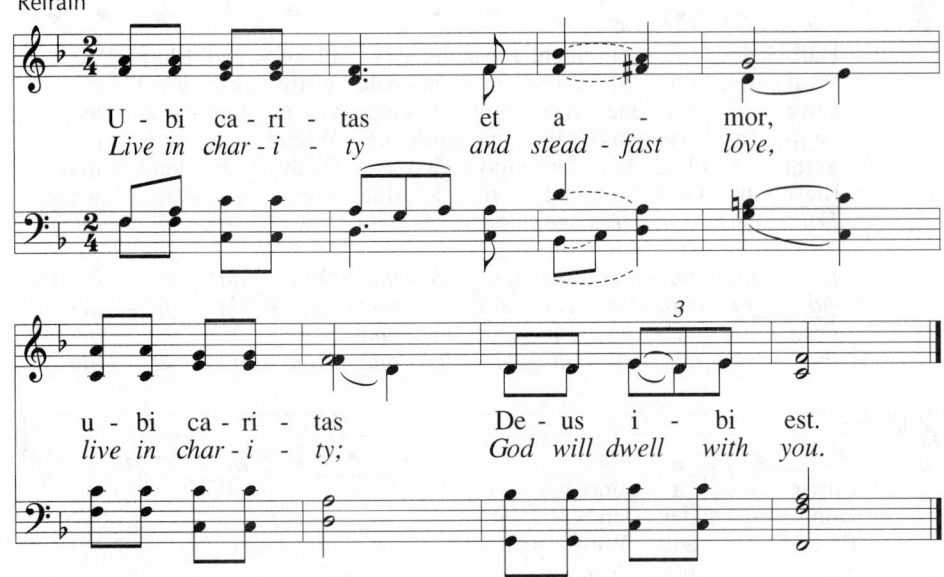

U - bi ca - ri - tas et a - mor,
Live in char - i - ty and stead - fast love,

u - bi ca - ri - tas De - us i - bi est.
live in char - i - ty; God will dwell with you.

Text: I Corinthians 13:2-8; *Where charity and love are found, God is there;* Taizé Community, 1978
Tune: Jacques Berthier, 1923-1994
© 1979, Les Presses de Taizé, GIA Publications, Inc., agent

409 Jesu, Jesu

Refrain

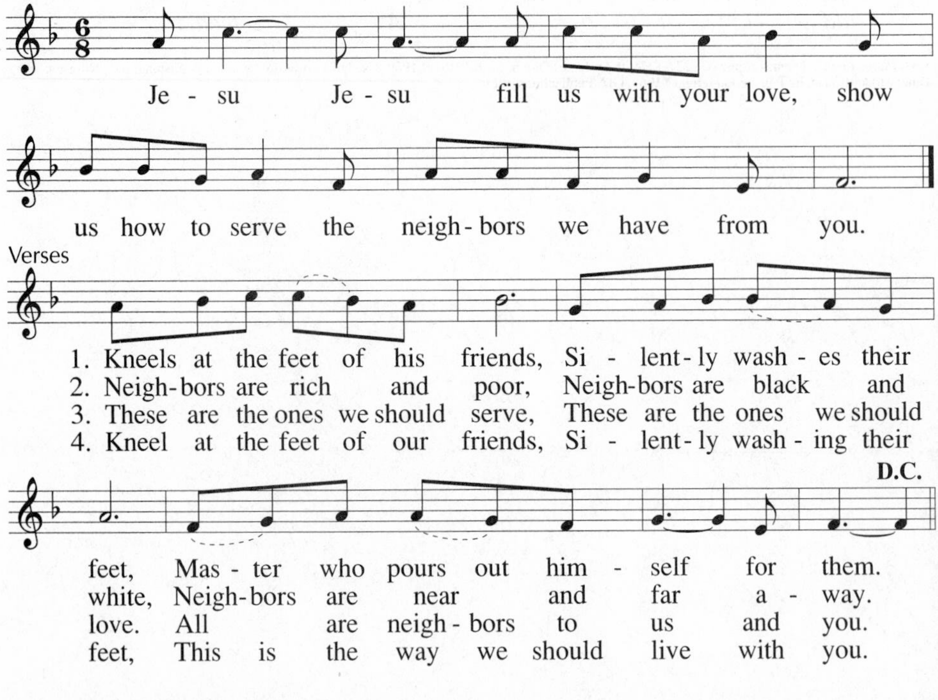

Je - su Je - su fill us with your love, show

us how to serve the neigh - bors we have from you.

Verses

1. Kneels at the feet of his friends, Si - lent - ly wash - es their
2. Neigh - bors are rich and poor, Neigh - bors are black and
3. These are the ones we should serve, These are the ones we should
4. Kneel at the feet of our friends, Si - lent - ly wash - ing their

D.C.

feet, Mas - ter who pours out him - self for them.
white, Neigh - bors are near and far a - way.
love. All are neigh - bors to us and you.
feet, This is the way we should live with you.

Text: John 13:3-5; Ghana folk song; tr. by Tom Colvin, b.1925
Tune: CHEREPONI, Irregular; Ghana folk song; Tom Colvin, b.1925; acc. by Jane M. Marshall, b.1924, © 1982, Hope Publishing Co.

Serving You 410

Refrain

In a spir - it of thank-ful - ness we wash each oth-er's feet,
up-hold each oth-er's lives. In a spir - it of joy and praise
we serve each oth-er now at the ta-ble of the Lord.

Verses

1. A new com - mand I give to you: love one an -
2. Hap-py are you, the faith - ful ser - vants who stand a -
3. I am the vine, you are the branch - es, those who a -
4. No great-er love than this, my friend, to give your
5. My peace I leave with all who live in the true
6. Al-ways re - mem-ber, a - mong your - selves, the great-est

oth - er as I've loved you. This love you share
wake at the Lord's com - ing. Hap - py are you,
bide in me will bear great fruit. Re - main in me,
life for an - oth - er. These words I share
spir - it of my word. My peace I give
one must be the ser - vant. Just as the Lord,

D.C.

will be a sign, a sign that you are my friends.
for at the ban - quet sure - ly the Lord will wait on you.
re - main in me and God will grant you what you need.
with all who hear so that your joy may be com-plete.
to all who choose to serve each oth - er in my name.
a - mong his own, has made him - self ser-vant of all.

411 Stay Here and Keep Watch

Ostinato Refrain

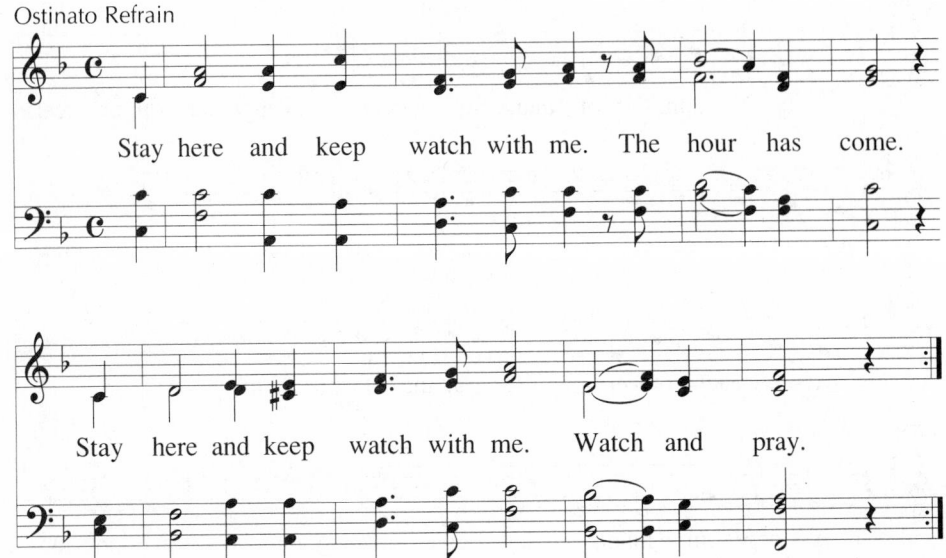

Stay here and keep watch with me. The hour has come.

Stay here and keep watch with me. Watch and pray.

Text: from Matthew 26; Taizé Community
Tune: Jacques Berthier, 1923-1994
© 1984, Les Presses de Taizé, GIA Publications, Inc., agent

412 Song of the Lord's Supper

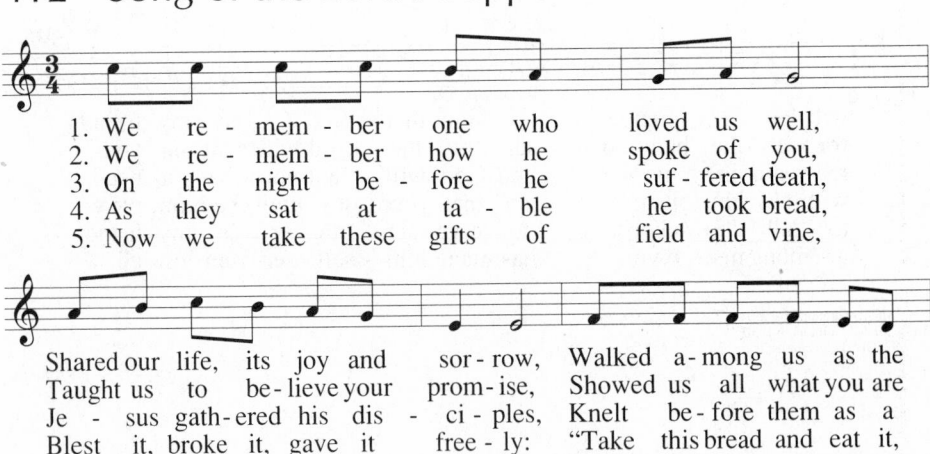

1. We re - mem - ber one who loved us well,
2. We re - mem - ber how he spoke of you,
3. On the night be - fore he suf - fered death,
4. As they sat at ta - ble he took bread,
5. Now we take these gifts of field and vine,

Shared our life, its joy and sor - row, Walked a - mong us as the
Taught us to be - lieve your prom - ise, Showed us all what you are
Je - sus gath - ered his dis - ci - ples, Knelt be - fore them as a
Blest it, broke it, gave it free - ly: "Take this bread and eat it,
Bless and share them in his mem - 'ry: Bread of life and cup of

least of all,   Gave him - self   in - to   our   keep - ing.
real - ly like—   Faith - ful,   ten - der,   God   of   peo - ple:
ser - vant might,   Washed their   feet   and   bid   them   wel - come:
all   of   you;   Take   and   eat,   this   is   my   bod - y."
cov - e - nant,   King - dom - feast   in   pledge   and   prom - ise.

He   is   light   that   dawns   for   blind - ed   eyes,
Not   a   God   to   break   the   wound - ed   heart,
"Do   you   know   what   I   have   done   for   you,
Then   he   took   the   cup   and   passed   it   round:
When   we   eat   this   bread   and   drink   this   cup

He   is   hope   for   the   de - spair - ing;   All   on   earth   can   find   a
Not   the   thun - der   of   the   might - y,   But   a   God   that   wel - comes
I   who   am   your Lord   and   Mas - ter?   If   I   bend   to   you   and
"Take   and drink,   this   is   my   life - blood,   Shed   for   you   and   for   all
We   pro - claim   the   death   of   Je - sus,   Taste   his   pres - ence,   liv - ing

place with   him,   Saint   and   sin - ner   at   his   ta - ble.
sin - ners   home,   Meets   the   low - ly   with   com - pas - sion.
wash   your   feet,   So   must   you   for   one   an - oth - er."
hu - man - kind,   Shed   that   sins   may   be   for - giv - en"
in   our   midst,   Look   for   him   to   come   in   glo - ry.

Text: Michael Joncas, b.1951
Tune: Michael Joncas, b.1951
© 1988, GIA Publications, Inc.

413 Faithful Family

Refrain

Be like our God, who chose to live and learn our ways, and die in deep, un-bound-ed love. For-give each oth - er ten-der - ly. The faith-ful fam-'ly of our God.

Verses

1. Where ev - er there is char - i - ty, self - less, giv - ing care, sure - ly our God is there.
2. And let us love the Liv - ing God, mer - ci - ful, and kind, bod - y and heart and mind.
3. { When we are to - geth - er, let us act as one, ways of greed and con - flict done.
4. { One day in the com - pan - y of the saints in light, may we see your face shine bright;

The love of Christ has gath - ered us to one from is - land ways: let us sing for joy all our days.
{ Let us love each oth - er well, hold the stran - ger dear, reach-ing out to all with - out fear.
{ Let there be no bit - ter-ness, quar - rel - ing, nor strife. In our midst is Christ, our life.
{ Bright up - on your fam - i - ly, faith - ful, hu - man, flawed. Shine in glo - ry, Christ, our God.

D.C.

Text: Verses based on *Ubi Caritas;* Rory Cooney, b.1952
Tune: Rory Cooney, b.1952
© 1986, North American Liturgy Resources

Jesus Took a Towel   414

Refrain

Je - sus took a tow - el and he gird - ed him - self, Then he

washed my feet, yes, he washed my feet, Je - sus took a ba - sin and he

knelt him - self down, And he washed, yes, he washed my feet.

Verse 1

1. The heav-ens are the Lord's, and the earth is his, The clouds are his

char-iot, glo-ry his cloak; He made the moun-tains, set the

D.C.

lim-its of the sea; And he stooped and washed my feet.

Verse 2

2. The hour had come, the Pasch was near; Je - sus loved his

own, loved them to the end. O Lord, let me see, let me

D.C.

un - der-stand Why you stooped and washed my feet.

Verse 3

3. Je - sus came to Pe-ter; Pe - ter said to him, "Do you

wash my feet? Lord, do you wash my feet?" Je - sus knelt down, but

D.C.

Pe - ter cried out, "Lord, you'll nev - er wash my feet!"

Verse 4

4. Je - sus said to Pe - ter, "Don't you un - der-stand? If you

want to be mine, I must wash your feet." "Then not just my

D.C.

feet, but my head and my hands! O Lord, I want to be yours."

Verse 5

5. He is King of kings and Lord of lords, Who dwells in light in-ac-

ces - si - ble; No one has seen him where he

D.C.

sits on high, Yet he stooped to wash my feet.

Verse 6

6. "Do you know, lit - tle chil - dren, what I've done for you? You

call me Mas-ter, and you call me Lord. If I am your Mas-ter, and if

D.C.

I am your Lord, Then, what I've done, you must do.

Verses 7-8

7. Now friends, let's be glad, let our joy be full. For
8. Who is like you, Lord, now en - throned on high, Where you

God is love, and he a - bides in us. He
look up - on the heav - ens and the earth be - low? Be -

washed our feet, he wash - es them still When we
fore your face the earth trem - bles and quakes, Yet you

D.C.

do what he once did.
stoop to wash my feet!

Verse 9

9. O the path is rug - ged, and the go - ing is rough, The

jour-ney is long to our heav'n - ly home, Our feet are wea-ry and

D.C.

cov - ered with mud, So the Lord still wash-es our feet.

Text: John 13; Chrysogonus Waddell, OSCO, b.1930
Tune: JESUS TOOK A TOWEL, Irregular; Chrysogonus Waddell, OCSO, b.1930
© 1986, GIA Publications, Inc.

415   O Sacred Head Surrounded

1. O Sa-cred Head sur-round-ed By crown of pierc-ing
2. I see your strength and vig-or All fad-ing in the
3. In this, your bit-ter pas-sion, Good Shep-herd, think of

thorn! O bleed-ing Head, so wound-ed, Re-
strife, And death with cru-el rig-or, Be-
me With your most sweet com-pas-sion, Un-

viled and put to scorn! The pow'r of death comes
reav-ing you of life; O ag-o-ny and
worth-y though I be: Be-neath your cross a-

o'er you, The glow of life de-cays, Yet
dy-ing! O love to sin-ners free! Je-
bid-ing For ev-er would I rest, In

an-gel hosts a-dore you, And trem-ble as they gaze.
sus, all grace sup-ply-ing, O turn your face on me.
your dear love con-fid-ing, And with your pres-ence blest.

Text: *Salve caput cruentatum;* ascr. to Bernard of Clairvaux, 1091-1153; tr. by Henry Baker, 1821-1877
Tune: PASSION CHORALE, 7 6 7 6 D; Hans Leo Hassler, 1564-1612; harm. by J. S. Bach, 1685-1750

Were You There 416

1. Were you there when they cru - ci - fied my Lord?
2. Were you there when they nailed him to the tree?
3. Were you there when they pierced him in the side?
4. Were you there when the sun re - fused to shine?
5. Were you there when they laid him in the tomb?
6. Were you there when they rolled the stone a - way?

Were you there when they cru - ci - fied my Lord?
Were you there when they nailed him to the tree?
Were you there when they pierced him in the side?
Were you there when the sun re - fused to shine?
Were you there when they laid him in the tomb?
Were you there when they rolled the stone a - way?

Oh! Some - times it caus - es me to

trem- ble, trem- ble, trem - ble, Were you

there when they cru - ci - fied my Lord?
there when they nailed him to the tree?
there when they pierced him in the side?
there when the sun re - fused to shine?
there when they laid him in the tomb?
there when they rolled the stone a - way?

Text: African-American spiritual
Tune: WERE YOU THERE, 10 10 with refrain; African-American spiritual; harm. by Robert J. Batastini, b.1942, © 1987, GIA Publications, Inc.

417 Crucem Tuam / O Lord, Your Cross

Cru - cem tu - am a - do - ra - mus Do - mi -
O Lord, your cross, we a - dore and glo - ri -

ne, re - sur - re - cti - o - nem tu - am lau - da - mus Do - mi -
fy, for your ho - ly re - sur - rec - tion, we praise you Lord of

ne. Lau - da - mus et glo - ri - fi - ca - mus.
life. We praise you and we glo - ri - fy you.

Re - sur - re - cti - o - nem tu - am lau - da - mus Do - mi - ne.
For your ho - ly re - sur - rec - tion, we praise you Lord of life.

Text: Taizé Community, 1991
Tune: Jacques Berthier, 1923-1994
© 1991, Les Presses de Taizé, GIA Publications, Inc., agent

Jesus, the Lord 418

Refrain

Je - sus. Je - sus. Let all cre - a-tion bend the knee to the Lord.

Verse 1

1. In him we live, we move and have our be - ing; in him the Christ, in him the King. Je - sus, the Lord.

Verses 2, 3

2. Though Son, he did not cling to god - li - ness; but
3. He lived o - be-dient-ly his Fa-ther's will ac -

emp - tied him - self, be - came a
cept - ing his death, death on a

slave!
tree! Je - sus, the Lord.

Text: *Jesus Prayer,* Philippians 2:5-11; Acts 17:28; Roc O'Connor, SJ, b.1949
Tune: Roc O'Connor, SJ, b.1949; arr. by John Foley, SJ, b.1939, alt.
© 1981, Robert F. O'Connor, SJ, and New Dawn Music

419 Calvary

Refrain

Cal - va - ry,   Cal - va - ry,   Cal - va -

ry,   Cal - va - ry,   Cal - va - ry,

Cal - va - ry,   Sure - ly he died on   Cal - va - ry.

Verses

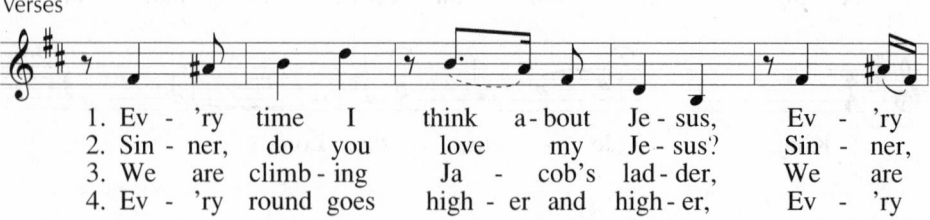

1. Ev - 'ry time I think a - bout Je - sus,   Ev - 'ry
2. Sin - ner, do you love my Je - sus?   Sin - ner,
3. We are climb - ing Ja - cob's lad - der,   We are
4. Ev - 'ry round goes high - er and high - er,   Ev - 'ry

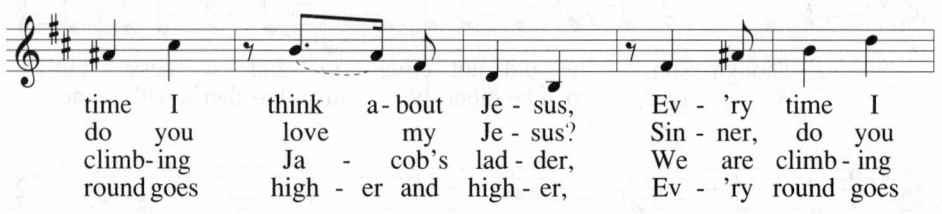

time I think a - bout Je - sus,   Ev - 'ry time I
do you love my Je - sus?   Sin - ner, do you
climb-ing Ja - cob's lad - der,   We are climb-ing
round goes high - er and high - er,   Ev - 'ry round goes

D.C.

think a - bout Je - sus,
love my Je - sus?
Ja - cob's lad - der,   Sure-ly he died on   Cal - va - ry.
high - er and high - er,

Text: African-American spiritual
Tune: African-American spiritual

Behold the Wood   420

Refrain

Be - hold, be - hold the wood of the
cross, on which is hung our sal - va - tion.
O come, let us a - dore.

Verses

1. Un -	less	a	grain	of	wheat	shall	fall	up -
2. And	when	my	hour	of	glo - ry	comes	as
3. For	there	can	be	no	great - er	love
4. My	Fa - ther,	if	it	be	your	plan,	this
5. For	sure - ly	he	has	borne	our	tears,	is
6. My	bod - y	now	is	torn	with	pain,	my

on the ground and die, it shall re - main but a
all was meant to be, you shall see me
shown up - on this land than in the one who
cup might pass me by, yet let it hap - pen
wound - ed by our sin, and yet he o - pens
friends have left and gone. O lov - ing Fa - ther,

D.C.

sin - gle grain and not give life.
lift - ed up up - on a tree.
came to die that we might live.
as you will if I must die.
not his mouth that we might live.
take my life in - to your hands.

Text: John 12; Dan Schutte, b.1947
Tune: Dan Schutte, b.1947
© 1976, Daniel L. Schutte and New Dawn Music

421 All You Who Pass This Way

Text: From the Passion Gospels; Taizé Community, 1984
Tune: Jacques Berthier, 1923-1994
© 1984, Les Presses de Taizé, GIA Publications, Inc., agent

Jesus Christ Is Risen Today 422

1. Je - sus Christ is ris'n to - day, Al - le - lu - ia!
2. Hymns of praise then let us sing, Al - le - lu - ia!
3. But the pains which he en - dured, Al - le - lu - ia!
4. Sing we to our God a - bove, Al - le - lu - ia!

Our tri - um - phant ho - ly day, Al - le - lu - ia!
Un - to Christ, our heav'n - ly King, Al - le - lu - ia!
Our sal - va - tion have pro - cured; Al - le - lu - ia!
Praise e - ter - nal as his love; Al - le - lu - ia!

Who did once up - on the cross, Al - le - lu - ia!
Who en - dured the cross and grave, Al - le - lu - ia!
Now a - bove the sky he's King, Al - le - lu - ia!
Praise him, now his might con - fess, Al - le - lu - ia!

Suf - fer to re - deem our loss. Al - le - lu - ia!
Sin - ners to re - deem and save. Al - le - lu - ia!
Where the an - gels ev - er sing. Al - le - lu - ia!
Fa - ther, Son, and Spir - it blest. Al - le - lu - ia!

Text: St. 1, *Surrexit Christus hodie*, Latin, 14th C.; para. in *Lyra Davidica*, 1708, alt.; st. 2, 3, *The Compleat Psalmodist*, c.1750, alt.; st. 4, Charles Wesley, 1707-1788
Tune: EASTER HYMN, 77 77 with alleluias, *Lyra Davidica*, 1708

423 O Sons and Daughters

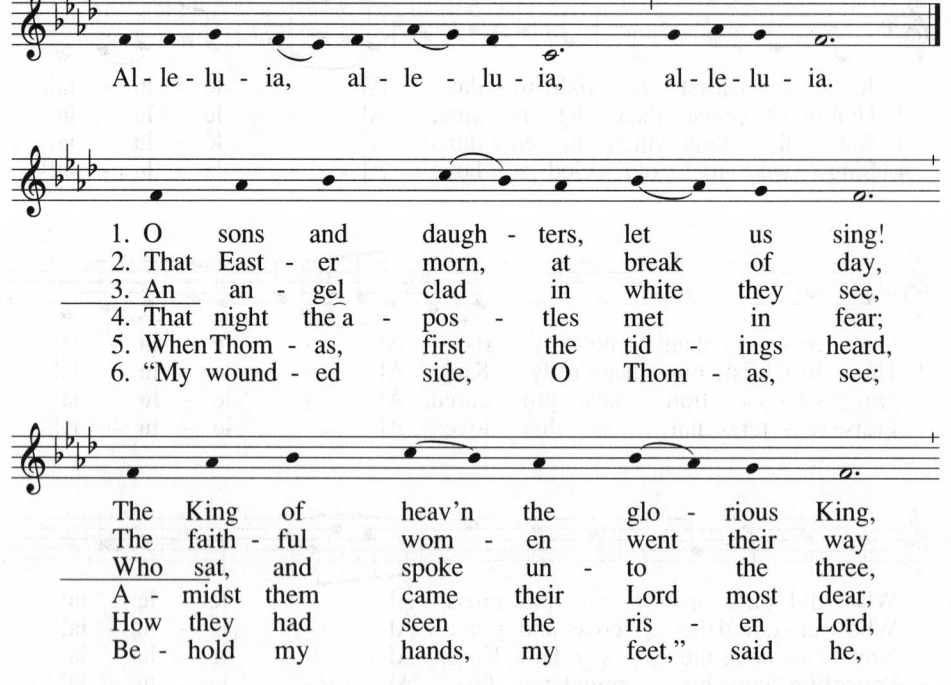

Al - le - lu - ia,   al - le - lu - ia,   al - le - lu - ia.

1. O	sons	and	daugh -	ters,	let	us	sing!
2. That	East -	er	morn,	at	break	of	day,
3. An	an -	gel	clad	in	white	they	see,
4. That	night	the a -	pos -	tles	met	in	fear;
5. When Thom -	as,		first	the	tid -	ings	heard,
6. "My wound -	ed		side,	O	Thom -	as,	see;

The	King	of	heav'n	the	glo -	rious	King,
The	faith -	ful	wom -	en	went	their	way
Who	sat,	and	spoke	un -	to	the	three,
A -	midst	them	came	their	Lord	most	dear,
How	they	had	seen	the	ris -	en	Lord,
Be -	hold	my	hands,	my	feet,"	said	he,

D.C.

O'er	death	to -	day	rose	tri -	umph - ing.	Al- le - lu- ia!
To	seek	the	tomb	where	Je -	sus lay.	Al- le - lu- ia!
"Your	Lord	has	gone	to	Gal -	i - lee."	Al- le - lu- ia!
And	said,	"My	peace	be	on	all here."	Al- le - lu- ia!
He	doubt -	ed	the	dis -	ci -	ples' word.	Al- le - lu- ia!
"Not	faith-	less,	but	be -	liev -	ing be."	Al- le - lu- ia!

7. No longer Thomas then denied,
   He saw the feet, the hands, the side;
   "You are my Lord and God," he cried. Alleluia!

8. How blest are they who have not seen,
   And yet whose faith has constant been,
   For they eternal life shall win. Alleluia!

9. On this most holy day of days,
   To God your hearts and voices raise,
   In laud, and jubilee and praise. Alleluia!

Text: *O filii et filiae;* Jean Tisserand, d.1494; tr. by John M. Neale, 1818-1866, alt.
Tune: O FILII ET FILIAE, 888 with alleluias; Mode II; acc. by Richard Proulx, b.1937, © 1975, GIA Publications, Inc.

Easter Alleluia 424

Refrain

Al-le-lu-ia, al - le - lu-ia, al-le-lu - ia!

Verses

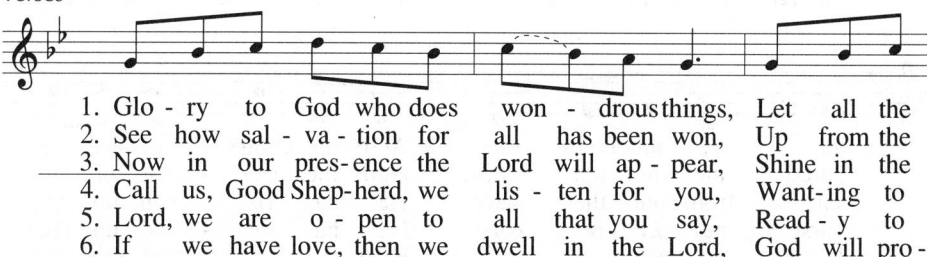

1. Glo - ry to God who does won - drous things, Let all the
2. See how sal - va - tion for all has been won, Up from the
3. Now in our pres-ence the Lord will ap - pear, Shine in the
4. Call us, Good Shep-herd, we lis - ten for you, Want-ing to
5. Lord, we are o - pen to all that you say, Read - y to
6. If we have love, then we dwell in the Lord, God will pro -

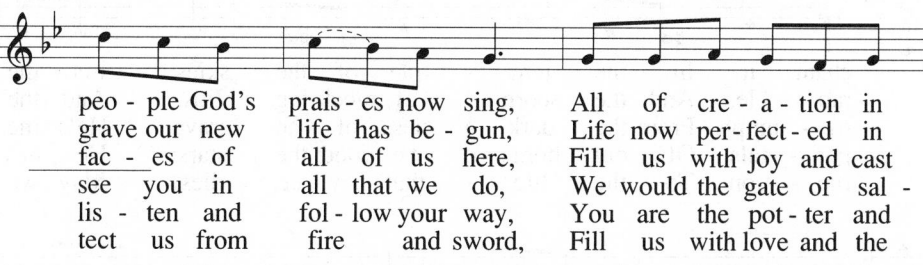

peo - ple God's prais-es now sing, All of cre - a - tion in
grave our new life has be - gun, Life now per-fect-ed in
fac - es of all of us here, Fill us with joy and cast
see you in all that we do, We would the gate of sal -
lis - ten and fol - low your way, You are the pot - ter and
tect us from fire and sword, Fill us with love and the

D.C.

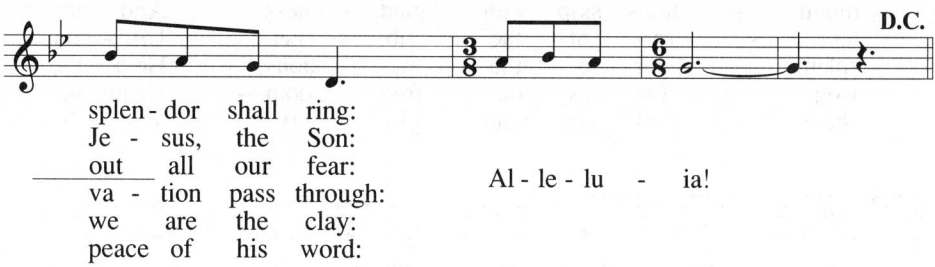

splen - dor shall ring:
Je - sus, the Son:
out all our fear: Al - le - lu - ia!
va - tion pass through:
we are the clay:
peace of his word:

Text: Marty Haugen, b.1950
Tune: O FILII ET FILIAE; 10 10 10 with alleluias; adapt. by Marty Haugen, b.1950
© 1986, GIA Publications, Inc.

425 Alleluia! Alleluia! Let the Holy Anthem Rise

1. Al - le - lu - ia! Al - le - lu - ia! Let the
2. Al - le - lu - ia! Al - le - lu - ia! He en -
3. Al - le - lu - ia! Al - le - lu - ia! Like the
4. Al - le - lu - ia! Al - le - lu - ia! He has
5. Al - le - lu - ia! Al - le - lu - ia! Bless-ed

ho - ly an - them rise, And the choirs of heav-en
dured the knot-ted whips, And the jeer - ing of the
sun from out the wave He has ris - en up in
burst our pris-on bars; He has lift - ed up the
Je - sus, make us rise From the life of this cor -

chant it In the tem - ple of the skies; Let the
rab - ble, And the scorn of mock-ing lips, And the
tri - umph From the dark - ness of the grave. He's the
por - tals Of our home be-yond the stars; He has
rup - tion To the life that nev - er dies. May we

moun - tains skip with glad - ness And the
ter - rors of the gib - bet Up - on
splen - dor of the na - tions; He's the
won for us our free - dom— 'Neath his
share with you your glo - ry When the

joy - ful val - leys ring With ho - san - nas in the
which he would be slain, But his death was on - ly
lamp of end-less day; He's the ver - y Lord of
feet our foes are trod; He has pur - chased back our
days of time are past, And the dead shall be a -

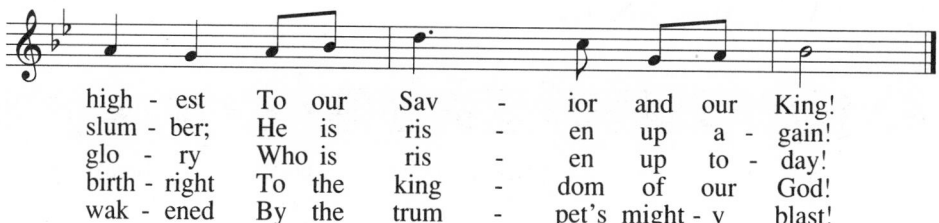

high - est To our Sav - ior and our King!
slum - ber; He is ris - en up a - gain!
glo - ry Who is ris - en up to - day!
birth - right To the king - dom of our God!
wak - ened By the trum - pet's might - y blast!

Text: Edward Caswall, 1814-1878
Tune: HOLY ANTHEM, 8 7 8 7 D; traditional melody; harm. Jerry R. Brubaker, © 1975, Romda Ltd.

Be Joyful, Mary 426

1. Be joy - ful, Mar - y, heav'n - ly Queen, be
2. The Son you bore by heav - en's grace, be
3. The Lord has ris - en from the dead, be
4. Then pray to God, O Vir - gin fair, be

joy - ful, Mar - y! Your grief is changed to
joy - ful, Mar - y! Did by his death our
joy - ful, Mar - y! He rose in glo - ry
joy - ful, Mar - y! That he our souls to

joy se - rene, Al - le - lu -
guilt e - rase, Al - le - lu -
as he said, Al - le - lu -
heav - en bear, Al - le - lu -

ia! Re - joice, re - joice, O Mar - y!
ia! Re - joice, re - joice, O Mar - y!
ia! Re - joice, re - joice, O Mar - y!
ia! Re - joice, re - joice, O Mar - y!

Text: *Regina caeli, jubila;* Latin, 17th C.; tr. anon. in *Psallite,* 1901
Tune: REGINA CAELI, 8 5 8 4 7; Leisentritt's *Gesangbuch,* 1584, alt.

427 All Things New

Refrain

Sing a new song! Re-joice! The dawn is break-ing,

the earth is wak-ing, its dreams come true. And do you

hear the voice, dark-ness sur-pris - ing, sing in its

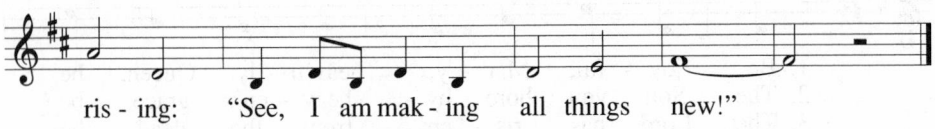

ris - ing: "See, I am mak - ing all things new!"

Verses

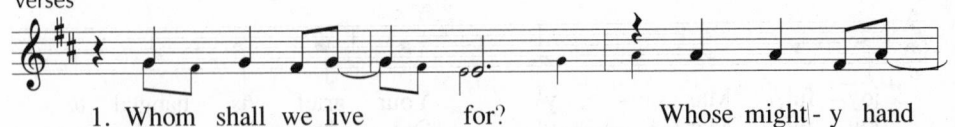

1. Whom shall we live for? Whose might - y hand
2. Who found us wan - der-ers, and made us in - to one?
3. Who is known to ev - 'ry heart and called by man - y names?

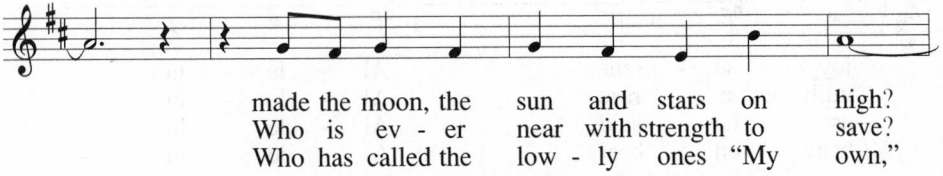

made the moon, the sun and stars on high?
Who is ev - er near with strength to save?
Who has called the low - ly ones "My own,"

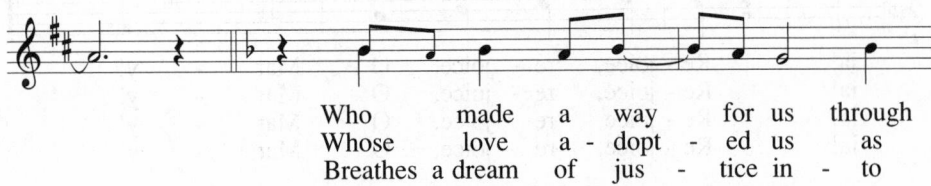

Who made a way for us through
Whose love a - dopt - ed us as
Breathes a dream of jus - tice in - to

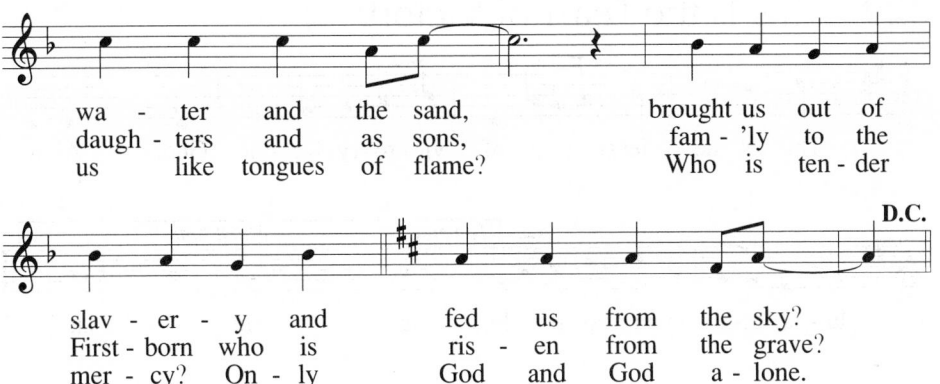

wa - ter and the sand, brought us out of
daugh - ters and as sons, fam - 'ly to the
us like tongues of flame? Who is ten - der

D.C.

slav - er - y and fed us from the sky?
First - born who is ris - en from the grave?
mer - cy? On - ly God and God a - lone.

Text: Rory Cooney, b. 1952
Tune: Rory Cooney, b. 1952
© 1993, GIA Publications, Inc.

Surrexit Dominus Vere II   428

Canon—*4 voices*

1. Sur - re - xit Do - mi - nus ve - re.

2. Al - le - lu - ia, al - le - lu - ia.

3. Sur - re - xit Chri - stus ho - di - e,

4. Al - le - lu - ia, al - le - lu - ia.

Text: *The Lord is truly risen! Christ is risen today!* Taizé Community, 1978
Tune: Jacques Berthier, 1923-1994
© 1978, Les Presses de Taizé, GIA Publications, Inc., agent

429 This Is the Feast of Victory

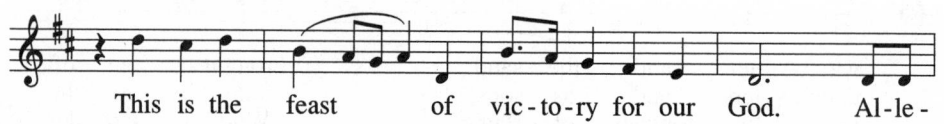

This is the   feast   of vic-to-ry for our   God.   Al-le-

To verses   *Last time*

lu - ia, al-le - lu-ia, al-le - lu - ia.   lu - ia.

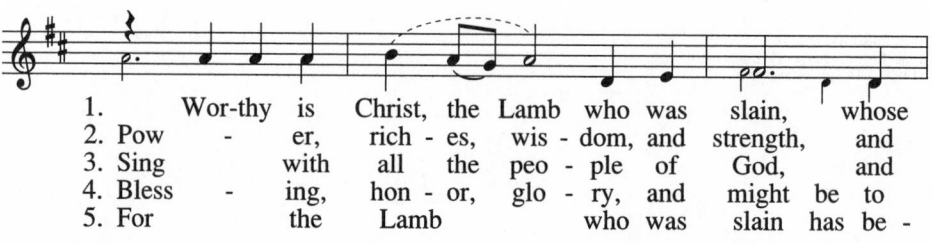

1. Wor-thy is   Christ, the Lamb who was   slain, whose
2. Pow - er,   rich - es, wis - dom, and strength,   and
3. Sing   with   all   the peo - ple of   God,   and
4. Bless - ing, hon - or, glo - ry, and   might be to
5. For   the   Lamb   who was   slain has be -

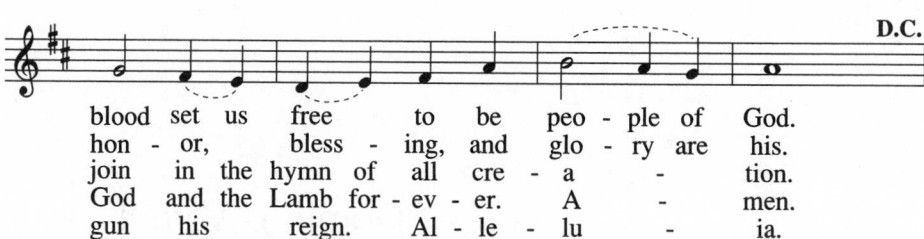

D.C.

blood set us   free   to be peo - ple of God.
hon - or,   bless - ing, and   glo - ry are   his.
join in the hymn of   all cre - a -   tion.
God and the Lamb for - ev - er.   A -   men.
gun his   reign. Al - le - lu -   ia.

Text: Based on Revelation 5, © 1978, *Lutheran Book of Worship*
Tune: FESTIVAL CANTICLE, Irregular; Richard Hillert, b.1923, © 1975, 1988, Richard Hillert

I Know That My Redeemer Lives   430

1. I know that my Re - deem - er lives;
2. He lives, to bless me with his love;
3. He lives, and grants me dai - ly breath;
4. He lives, all glo - ry to his name;

What joy the blest as - sur - ance gives!
He lives, to plead for me a - bove;
He lives, and I shall con - quer death;
He lives, my Sav - ior still the same;

He lives, he lives, who once was dead;
He lives, my hun - gry soul to feed;
He lives, my man - sion to pre - pare;
What joy the blest as - sur - ance gives;

He lives, my ev - er - last - ing Head!
He lives, to help in time of need.
He lives, to bring me safe - ly there.
I know that my Re - deem - er lives!

Text: Samuel Medley, 1738-1799
Tune: DUKE STREET, LM; John Hatton, c.1710-1793

431 Christ Is Risen! Shout Hosanna!

1. Christ is ris - en! Shout Ho - san - na! Cel - e - brate this
2. Christ is ris - en! Raise your spir - its From the cav - erns
3. Christ is ris - en! Earth and heav - en Nev - er - more shall

day of days! Christ is ris - en! Hush in won - der:
of des - pair. Walk with glad - ness in the morn - ing.
be the same. Break the bread of new cre - a - tion

All cre - a - tion is a - mazed. In the des - ert
See what love can do and dare. Drink the wine of
Where the world is still in pain. Tell its grim, de -

all sur - round - ing, See, a spread - ing tree has grown.
res - ur - rec - tion, Not a ser - vant, but a friend.
mon - ic cho - rus: "Christ is ris - en! Get you gone!"

Heal - ing leaves of grace a - bound - ing
Je - sus is our strong com - pan - ion.
God the First and Last is with us.

Bring a taste of love un - known.
Joy and peace shall nev - er end.
Sing Ho - san - na ev - 'ry one!

Text: Brian Wren, b.1936, © 1986, Hope Publishing Co.
Tune: HOSANNA, 8 7 8 7 D; David Haas, b.1957, © 1991, GIA Publications, Inc.

Resucitó   432

Refrain

Re - su - ci - tó,   re - su - ci - tó,   re - su - ci -
A - le - lu - ya,   a - le - lu - ya,   a - le - lu -

Final ending

tó,   a - le - lu - ya.   A - le - lu - ya.
ya,   re - su - ci - tó.

Verses

1.   La   muer - te   ¿dón - de es - tá la
2.   Gra - cias se - an   da - das al
3.   A - le - grí - a,   a - le - grí - a her -
4. Si con Él mo - ri - mos   y con Él vi -
1.   *And*   *death now,*   *van - ished is the*
2.   *The*   *king - dom,*   *praise to God, the*
3.   *Our*   *glad - ness,*   *bliss - ful in our*
4.   *With*   *him then,*   *die and live with*

muer - te?   ¿Dón - de es - tá mi
Pa - dre   que nos pa - só a su
ma - nos,   que si hoy nos que -
vi - mos,   y con Él can -
fear now,   *ban - ished are my*
king - dom!   *Raised up to the*
glad - ness,   *this will be our*
him then,   *rise and sing our*

D.C.

muer - te?   ¿Dón - de su vic - to - ria?
rei - no.   ¿Dón - de se vi - ve de a - mor?
re - mos.   Es que re - su - ci - tó.
ta - mos.   y A - le - lu - ya.
tears now,   *death has passed a - way.*
king - dom,   *we shall live in love.*
glad - ness,   *that he is a - live.*
hymn then,   *sing al - le - lu - ia.*

Text: Kiko Argüello, © 1972, Ediciones Musical PAX, U.S. agent: OCP Publications; trans. by Robert C. Trupia, © 1988, OCP Publications
Tune: Kiko Argüello, © 1972, Ediciones Musical PAX, U.S. agent: OCP Publications; acc. by Diana Kodner, © 1993, GIA Publications, Inc.

433 At the Lamb's High Feast We Sing

1. At the Lamb's high feast we sing Praise to our vic-
2. Where the Pas-chal blood is poured, Death's dark an-gel
3. Might-y vic-tim from the sky, Hell's fierce powers be-
4. East-er tri-umph, East-er joy, This a-lone can

to-rious King. Who has washed us in the tide
sheathes his sword; Is-rael's hosts tri-umph-ant go
neath you lie; You have con-quered in the fight,
sin de-stroy; From sin's power, Lord, set us free

Flow-ing from his pierc-ed side; Praise we him, whose
Through the wave that drowns the foe. Praise we Christ, whose
You have brought us life and light: Now no more can
New-born souls in you to be. Fa-ther, who the

love di-vine Gives his sa-cred Blood for wine,
blood was shed, Pas-chal vic-tim, Pas-chal bread;
death ap-pall, Now no more the grave en-thrall;
crown shall give, Sav-ior, by whose death we live,

Gives his Bod-y for the feast,
With sin-cer-i-ty and love
You have o-pened par-a-dise,
Spir-it, guide through all our days,

Christ the vic-tim, Christ the priest.
Eat we man-na from a-bove.
And in you your saints shall rise.
Three in One, your name we praise.

Text: *Ad regias agni dapes;* Latin, 4th C.; tr. by Robert Campbell, 1814-1868
Tune: SALZBURG, 77 77 D; Jakob Hintze, 1622-1702; harm. by J.S. Bach, 1685-1750

This Joyful Eastertide 434

1. This joy-ful East-er-tide
2. My flesh in hope shall rest
3. Death's flood has lost its chill

A-way with sin and
And for a sea-son
Since Je - sus crossed the

sor - row! My love, the Cru - ci - fied,
slum - ber Till trump from east to west
riv - er; Lov - er of souls, from ill

Has sprung to life this mor - row:
Shall wake the dead in num - ber:
My pass - ing soul de - liv - er:

Had Christ, who once was slain, Not burst his three-day pris - on,

Our faith had been in vain: But now has Christ a - ris - en,

a - ris - en, a - ris - en; But now has Christ a - ris - en!

Text: George R. Woodward, 1848-1934
Tune: VRUECHTEN, 6 7 6 7 D; Melody in Oudaen's *David's Psalmen*, 1685; harm. by Paul G. Bunjes, b.1914. © 1969 Concordia Publishing House

435 Sing to the Mountains

Refrain

Sing to the moun-tains, sing to the sea. Raise your
voic - es, lift your hearts. This is the day the
Lord has made. Let all the earth re - joice.

Verse 1

1. I will give thanks to you, my Lord. You have
an - swered my plea. You have saved my
soul from death. You are my strength and my song.

Verse 2

2. Ho - ly, ho - ly, ho - ly Lord,
heav - en and earth are full of your glo - ry.

Verse 3

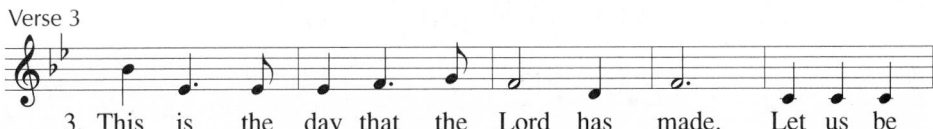

3. This is the day that the Lord has made. Let us be

glad and re - joice. He has turned all

D.C.

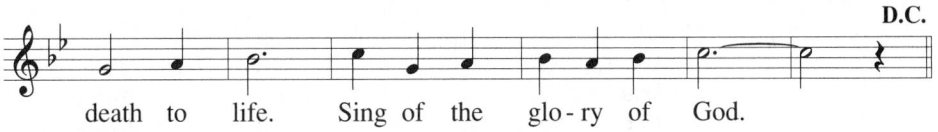

death to life. Sing of the glo - ry of God.

Text: Psalm 118; Bob Dufford, SJ, b.1943
Tune: Bob Dufford, SJ, b.1943; acc. by Sr. Theophane Hytrek, OSF, 1915-1992, alt.
© 1975, Robert J. Dufford, SJ, and New Dawn Music

Surrexit Christus 436

Ostinato Refrain

(hum) Sur - re - xit Chri - stus, al - le - lu - ia!

(hum) Can - ta - te Do - mi - no, al - le - lu - ia!

Text: *Christ is risen, sing to the Lord;* Daniel 3; Taizé Community, 1984
Tune: Jacques Berthier, 1923-1994
© 1984, Les Presses de Taizé, GIA Publications, Inc., agent

437 Christ the Lord Is Risen Today

1. Christ the Lord is ris'n to-day, Al - le -
2. Lives a - gain our glo - rious King; Al - le -
3. Love's re - deem - ing work is done, Al - le -
4. Soar we now where Christ has led, Al - le -

lu - ia! All on earth with an - gels say,
lu - ia! Where, O death, is now your sting?
lu - ia! Fought the fight, the bat - tle won.
lu - ia! Fol - l'wing our ex - alt - ed head;

Al - le - lu - ia! Raise your joys and
Al - le - lu - ia! Once he died our
Al - le - lu - ia! Death in vain for -
Al - le - lu - ia! Made like him, like

tri - umphs high, Al - le - lu - ia!
souls to save, Al - le - lu - ia!
bids him rise; Al - le - lu - ia!
him we rise, Al - le - lu - ia!

Sing, O heav'ns, and earth re - ply,
Where your vic - to - ry, O grave?
Christ has o - pened par - a - dise.
Ours the cross, the grave, the skies.

Al - le - lu - ia!

Text: Charles Wesley, 1707-1788
Tune: LLANFAIR, 77 77 with alleluias; Robert Williams, 1781-1821

Sequence for Easter   438

1. Chris - tians, praise the pas-chal vic-tim! Of - fer thank-ful sac - ri-fice!
1. *Ví - cti - mae Pa-schá - li lau-des im - mó - lent Chri - sti - á - ni.*

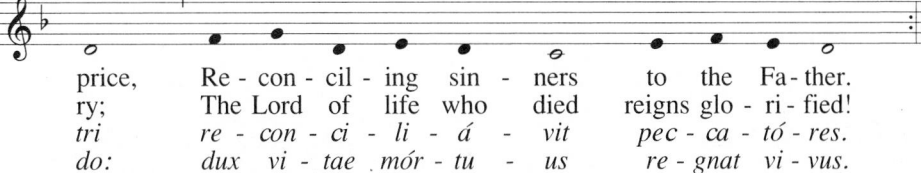

2. Christ the Lamb has saved the sheep, Christ the just one paid the
3. Death and life fought bit - ter - ly   For this won-drous vic - to -
2. *A - gnus ré - de - mit ó - ves: Chri - stus ín - no - cens Pá -*
3. *Mors et   vi - ta   du - él - lo   con - fli - xé - re   mi - rán -*

price,   Re - con - cil - ing sin - ners   to   the Fa - ther.
ry;   The Lord of   life who   died reigns glo - ri - fied!
tri   *re - con - ci - li - á - vit   pec - ca - tó - res.*
do: *dux vi - tae mór - tu - us   re - gnat vi - vus.*

4. O   Mar - y, come and   say   what you saw   at break of day.
6. Bright an - gels tes - ti - fied, Shroud and grave clothes side by side!
4. *Dic   no - bis Ma - rí - a,   quid vi - dí - sti   in vi - a?*
6. *An - gé - li - cos   te - stes,   su - dá - ri - um,   et ve-stes.*

5. "The emp - ty tomb of my liv - ing Lord! I   saw Christ Je - sus ri -
7. "Yes, Christ my hope rose glo - ri - ous - ly. He goes   be - fore you in -
5. *Se - púl - crum Chri - sti vi - vén - tis, et gló - ri - am vi - di*
7. *Sur - ré - xit Chri-stus spes me - a: prae-cé - det su - os in*

sen and a - dored! 8. Share the good news, sing joy - ful - ly:
to Ga - li - lee." 8. *Scí - mus Chrí - stum sur - re - xís - se*
re - sur - gén - tis.
Ga - li - láe - am.

His death is vic - to - ry! Lord Je - sus, Vic - tor King, Show us mer - cy.
a   mór-tu - is ve - re: tu no - bis vi - ctor Rex, mi - se - ré - re.

Text: Sequence for Easter, ascr. to Wipo of Burgundy, d.1048; tr. by Peter J. Scagnelli, b.1949, © 1983
Tune: Mode I; acc. by Richard Proulx, b.1937. © 1975, GIA Publications, Inc.

439 Christ the Lord Is Risen!

1. Christ the Lord is ris'n! Christ the Lord is ris'n!
2. He has con - quered death. He has con - quered death.
3. Sin has done its worst. Sin has done its worst.
4. He is King of kings. He is King of kings.
5. He is Lord of lords. He is Lord of lords.
6. All the world is his. All the world is his.
7. Come and wor - ship him. Come and wor - ship him.
8. Christ our Lord is ris'n! Christ our Lord is ris'n!
9. Hal - le - lu - jah! Hal - le - lu - jah!

Je - su. Christ the Lord is ris'n!
Je - su. He has con - quered death.
Je - su. Sin has done its worst.
Je - su. He is King of kings.
Je - su. He is Lord of lords.
Je - su. All the world is his.
Je - su. Come and wor - ship him.
Je - su. Christ our Lord is ris'n!
Je - su. Hal - le - lu - jah!

Christ the Lord is ris'n! Je - su.
He has con - quered death. Je - su.
Sin has done its worst. Je - su.
He is King of kings. Je - su.
He is Lord of lords. Je - su.
All the world is his. Je - su.
Come and wor - ship him. Je - su.
Christ our Lord is ris'n! Je - su.
Hal - le - lu - jah! Je - su.

Text: Tom Colvin, b.1925
Tune: Garu, Ghanian folk song, arr. by Kevin R. Hackett
© 1969, Hope Publishing Company

Come Away to the Skies   440

1. Come a - way to the skies, My be -
2. Now with sing - ing and praise, Let us
3. For the glo - ry we were First cre -
4. We with thanks do ap - prove The de -
5. Hal - le - lu - jah we sing, To our

lov - ed, a - rise And re - joice in the
spend all the days, By our heav - en - ly
at - ed to share, Both the na - ture and
sign of that love Which has joined us to
Fa - ther and King, And his rap - tu - rous

day you were born; On this
Fa - ther be - stowed, While his
king - dom di - vine! Now cre -
Je - sus' name; So u -
prais - es, re - peat: To the

fes - ti - val day, Come ex - ult - ing a -
grace we re - ceive From his boun - ty, and
at - ed a - gain That our lives may re -
nit - ed in heart, Let us nev - er - more
Lamb that was slain, Hal - le - lu - jah a -

way, And with sing - ing to Zi - on re - turn.
live, To the hon - or and glo - ry of God.
main, Through-out time and e - ter - ni - ty, thine.
part, Till we meet at the feast of the Lamb.
gain, Sing, all heav - en, and fall at his feet.

Text: Anonymous, *Southern Harmony*, 1835, alt.
Tune: MIDDLEBURY, 66 9 66 9; *Southern Harmony*, 1835; harm. by Jack W. Burnam, b.1946, © 1984

441 Come, Ye Faithful, Raise the Strain

1. Come, ye faith-ful raise the strain Of tri-um-phant glad-ness;
2. 'Tis the spring of souls to-day; Christ has burst the pris-on,
3. Now the queen of sea-sons, bright With the day of splen-dor,
4. Nei-ther could the gates of death, Nor the tomb's dark por-tal,
5. "Al-le-lu-ia!" now we cry To our King im-mor-tal,

God has brought his Is-ra-el In-to joy from
And from three days' sleep in death As a sun has
With the roy-al feast of feasts, Comes its joy to
Nor the watch-ers, nor the seal Hold him as a
Who, tri-um-phant, burst the bars Of the tomb's dark

sad-ness; Loosed from Phar-aoh's bit-ter yoke
ris-en; All the win-ter of our sins,
ren-der; Comes to glad-den faith-ful hearts
mor-tal; For to-day a-mong the Twelve
por-tal; "Al-le-lu-ia!" with the Son,

Ja-cob's sons and daugh-ters; Led them with un -
Long and dark is fly-ing From his light, to
Who with true af-fec-tion Wel-come in un -
Christ ap-peared be-stow-ing Last-ing peace which
God the Fa-ther prais-ing; "Al-le-lu-ia!"

moist-ened foot Through the Red Sea wa-ters.
whom we give Laud and praise un-dy-ing.
wea-ried strains Je-sus' res-ur-rec-tion.
ev-er-more Pass-es hu-man know-ing.
yet a-gain To the Spir-it rais-ing.

Text: Exodus 15; Ασωμεν παντες λαοι; John of Damascus, c.675-c.749; tr. by John M. Neale, 1818-1886, alt.
Tune: GAUDEAMUS PARITER, 7 6 7 6 D; Johann Horn, c. 1495-1547

Sing with All the Saints in Glory 442

1. Sing with all the saints in glo - ry, Sing the res - ur -
2. O what glo - ry, far ex - ceed - ing All that eye has
3. Life e - ter - nal! heav'n re - joic - es: Je - sus lives who
4. Life e - ter - nal! O what won - ders Crowd on faith; what

rec - tion song! Death and sor - row, earth's dark sto - ry,
yet per - ceived! Ho - liest hearts for a - ges plead - ing,
once was dead; Shout with joy, O death - less voic - es!
joy un - known, When, a - midst earth's clos - ing thun - ders,

To the for - mer days be - long. All a - round the
Nev - er that full joy con - ceived. God has prom - ised,
Child of God, lift up your head! Pa - tri - archs from
Saints shall stand be - fore the throne! O to en - ter

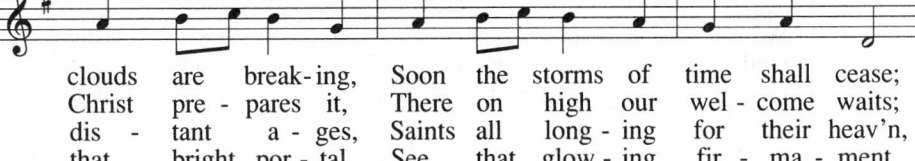

clouds are break - ing, Soon the storms of time shall cease;
Christ pre - pares it, There on high our wel - come waits;
dis - tant a - ges, Saints all long - ing for their heav'n,
that bright por - tal, See that glow - ing fir - ma - ment,

In God's like - ness, we a - wak - en, Know - ing ev - er - last - ing peace.
Ev - 'ry hum - ble spir - it shares it, Christ has passed the e - ter - nal gates.
Proph - ets, psalm - ists, seers, and sag - es, All a - wait the glo - ry giv'n.
Know, with you, O God im - mor - tal, Je - sus Christ whom you have sent!

Text: 1 Corinthians 15:20; William J. Irons, 1812-1883, alt.
Tune: HYMN TO JOY, 8 7 8 7 D; arr. from Ludwig van Beethoven, 1770-1827, by Edward Hodges, 1796-1867

443 Alleluia, Alleluia, Give Thanks

Refrain

Al - le - lu - ia, al - le - lu - ia, give
thanks to the ris - en Lord. Al - le - lu - ia, al - le -
lu - ia, give praise to his Name.

Verses

1. Je - sus is Lord of all the earth.
2. Spread the good news o'er all the earth:
3. We have been cru - ci - fied with Christ.
4. God has pro - claimed his gra - cious gift:
5. Come, let us praise the liv - ing God,

D.C.

He is the King of cre - a - tion.
Je - sus has died and has ris - en.
Now we shall live for ev - er.
Life e - ter - nal for all who be - lieve.
Joy - ful - ly sing to our Sav - ior.

Text: Donald Fishel, b.1950, © 1973, Word of God Music
Tune: ALLELUIA NO. 1, 8 8 with refrain; Donald Fishel, b.1950, © 1973, Word of God Music; descant harm. by Betty Pulkingham, b.1929,
   Charles Mallory, b.1953, and George Mims, b.1938, © 1979, Celebration

Now the Green Blade Rises   444

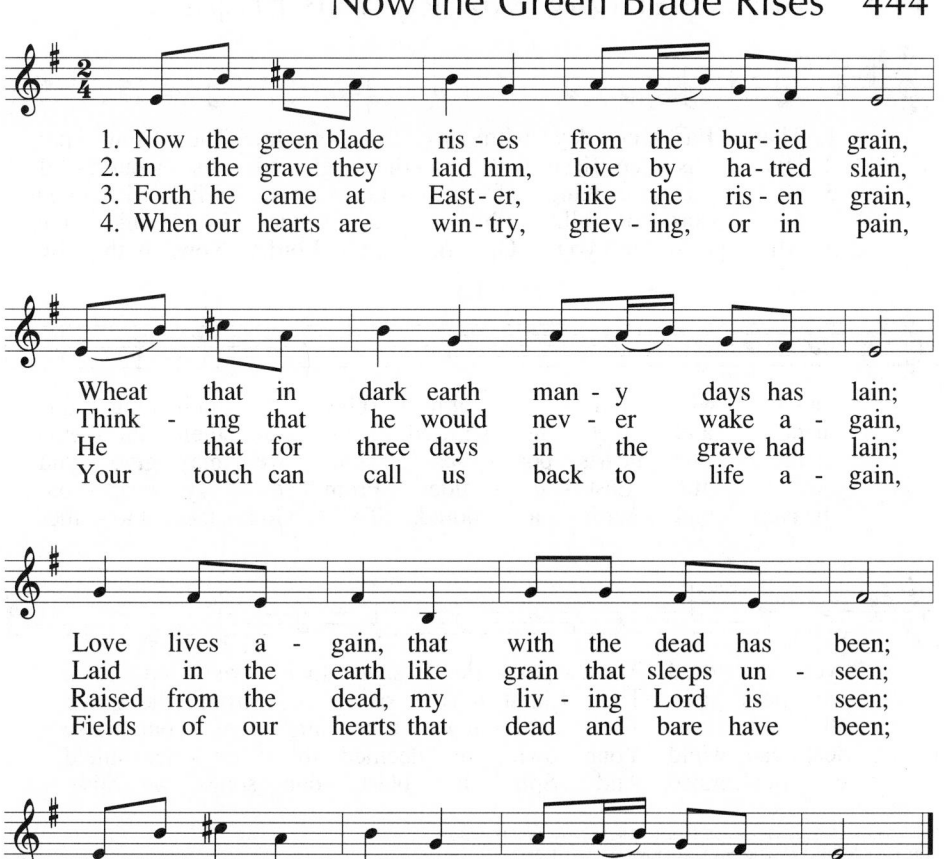

1. Now the green blade ris - es from the bur - ied grain,
2. In the grave they laid him, love by ha - tred slain,
3. Forth he came at East - er, like the ris - en grain,
4. When our hearts are win - try, griev - ing, or in pain,

Wheat that in dark earth man - y days has lain;
Think - ing that he would nev - er wake a - gain,
He that for three days in the grave had lain;
Your touch can call us back to life a - gain,

Love lives a - gain, that with the dead has been;
Laid in the earth like grain that sleeps un - seen;
Raised from the dead, my liv - ing Lord is seen;
Fields of our hearts that dead and bare have been;

Love is come a - gain like wheat a - ris - ing green.

Text: John M.C. Crum, 1872-1958, *Oxford Book of Carols,* © Oxford University Press
Tune: NOEL NOUVELET, 11 10   11 10; French Carol; acc. by Marty Haugen, b.1950, © 1987, GIA Publications, Inc.

445   That Easter Day with Joy Was Bright

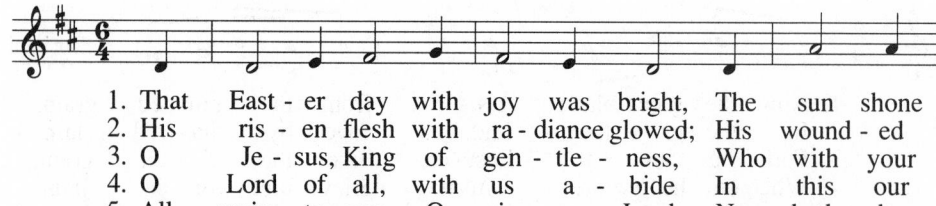

1. That   East - er day with joy was bright, The sun shone
2. His   ris - en flesh with ra - diance glowed; His wound - ed
3. O   Je - sus, King of   gen - tle - ness, Who with your
4. O   Lord of all, with us   a - bide   In   this our
5. All   praise, to you, O   ris - en Lord, Now both by

out   with   fair - er   light,   When   to   their long - ing
hands   and   feet he   showed; Those scars their sol - emn
grace   our   hearts pos - sess   That   we   may give you
joy -   ful   East - er - tide;   From   ev - 'ry weap - on
heaven   and   earth a - dored;   To   God   the Fa - ther

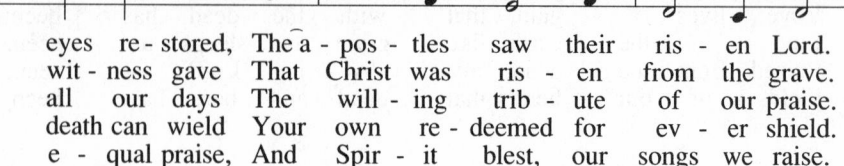

eyes re - stored, The a - pos - tles saw   their ris - en Lord.
wit - ness gave   That Christ was   ris - en from the grave.
all   our days   The will - ing   trib - ute of   our praise.
death can wield   Your own re - deemed for   ev - er shield.
e - qual praise,   And Spir - it blest, our songs we raise.

Text: *Claro paschali gaudio;* Latin 5th C.; tr. by John M. Neale, 1818-1866, alt.
Tune: PUER NOBIS, LM; adapt. by Michael Praetorius, 1571-1621

446   The Strife Is O'er

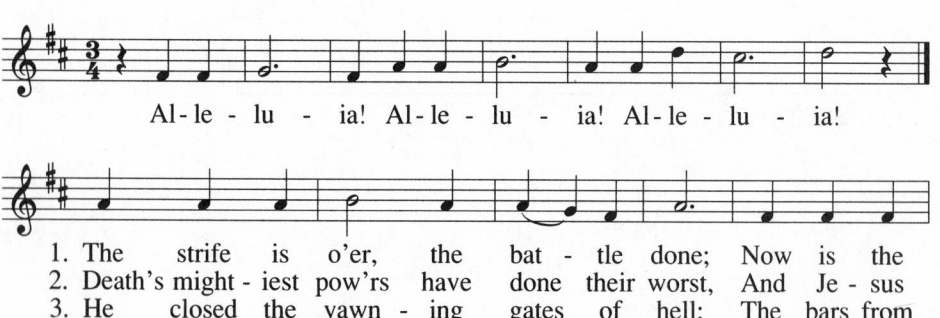

Al - le - lu - ia! Al - le - lu - ia! Al - le - lu - ia!

1. The   strife   is   o'er,   the   bat - tle done; Now is   the
2. Death's might - iest pow'rs have done their worst, And Je - sus
3. He   closed   the   yawn - ing gates of   hell; The bars from
4. On   the   third morn   he   rose a - gain, Glo - rious in

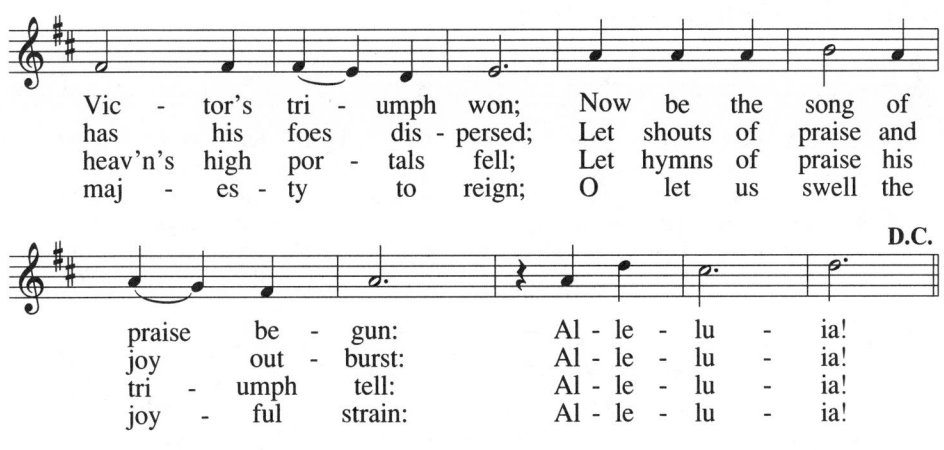

Vic - tor's tri - umph won; Now be the song of praise be - gun: Al - le - lu - ia!
has his foes dis - persed; Let shouts of praise and joy out - burst: Al - le - lu - ia!
heav'n's high por - tals fell; Let hymns of praise his tri - umph tell: Al - le - lu - ia!
maj - es - ty to reign; O let us swell the joy - ful strain: Al - le - lu - ia!

D.C.

Text: *Finita iam sunt praelia;* Latin, 12th C.; tr. by Francis Pott, 1832-1909, alt.
Tune: VICTORY, 888 with alleluias; Giovanni da Palestrina, 1525-1594; adapt. by William H. Monk, 1823-1889

Regina Caeli / O Queen of Heaven 447

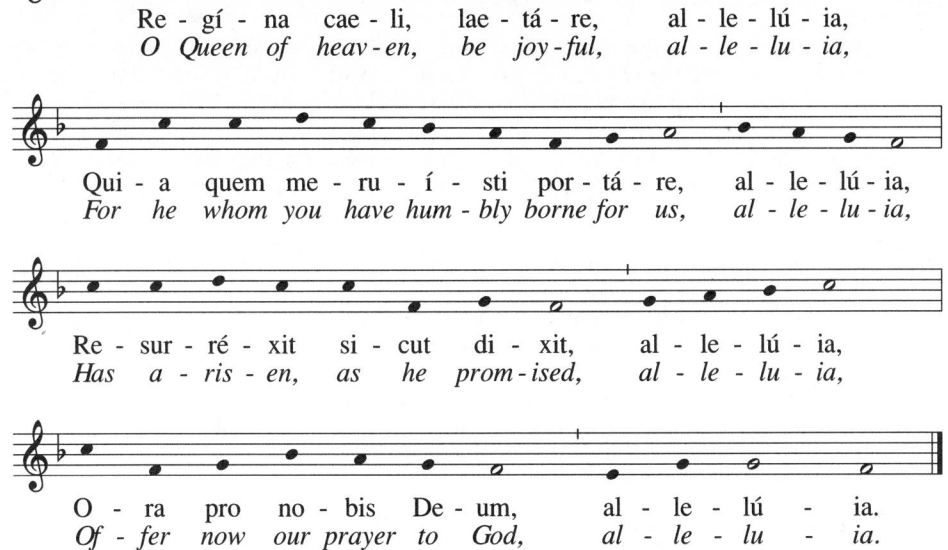

Re - gí - na cae - li, lae - tá - re, al - le - lú - ia,
O Queen of heav - en, be joy - ful, al - le - lu - ia,

Qui - a quem me - ru - í - sti por - tá - re, al - le - lú - ia,
For he whom you have hum - bly borne for us, al - le - lu - ia,

Re - sur - ré - xit si - cut di - xit, al - le - lú - ia,
Has a - ris - en, as he prom - ised, al - le - lu - ia,

O - ra pro no - bis De - um, al - le - lú - ia.
Of - fer now our prayer to God, al - le - lu - ia.

Text: Latin, 12th C.; tr. by C. Winfred Douglas, 1867-1944, alt.
Tune: REGINA CAELI, Irregular; Mode VI; acc. by Robert LeBlanc, OSB, b.1948, © 1986, GIA Publications, Inc.

448 Darkness Is Gone

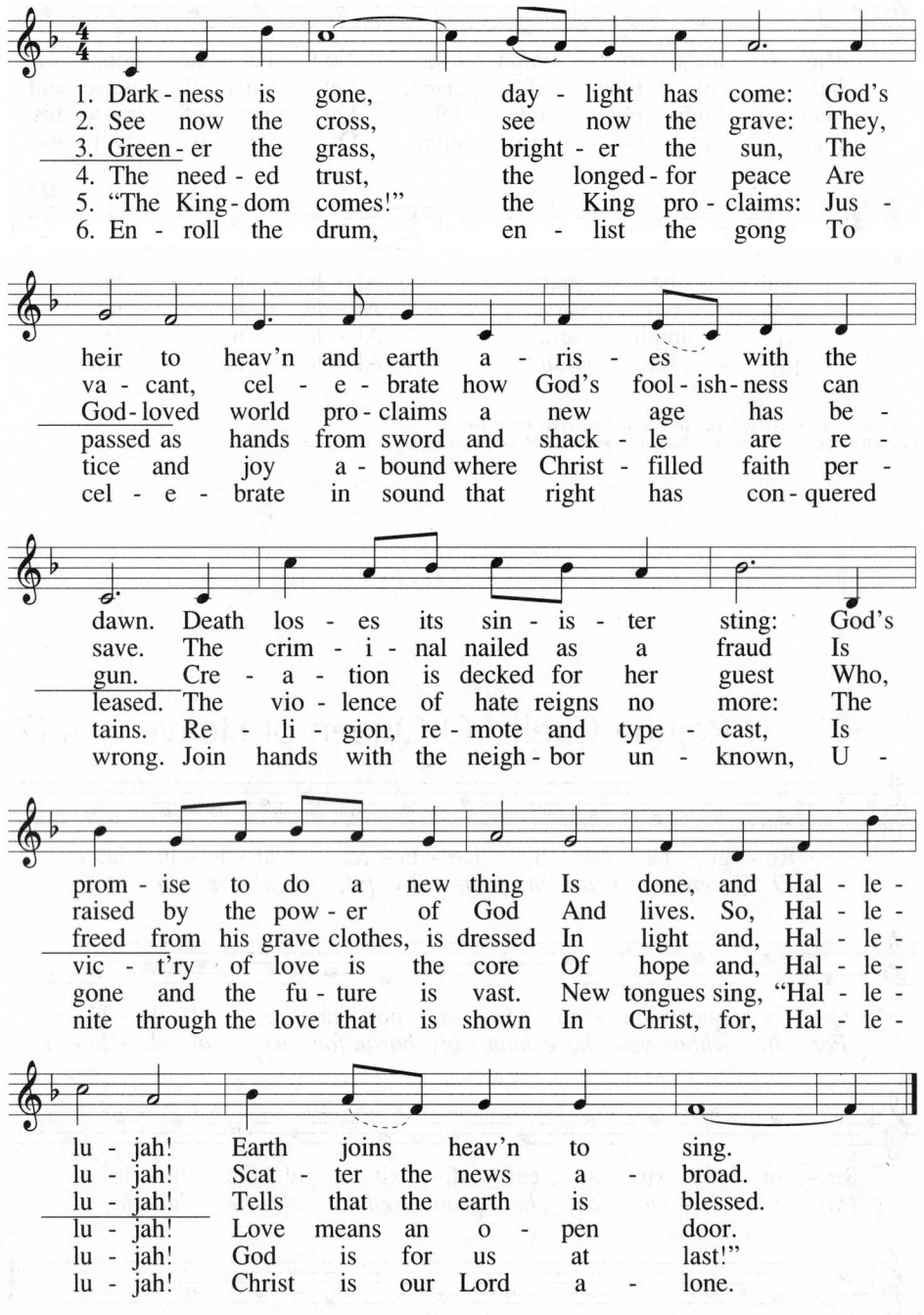

1. Dark - ness is gone, day - light has come: God's
2. See now the cross, see now the grave: They,
3. Green - er the grass, bright - er the sun, The
4. The need - ed trust, the longed - for peace Are
5. "The King - dom comes!" the King pro - claims: Jus -
6. En - roll the drum, en - list the gong To

heir to heav'n and earth a - ris - es with the
va - cant, cel - e - brate how God's fool - ish - ness can
God - loved world pro - claims a new age has be -
passed as hands from sword and shack - le are re -
tice and joy a - bound where Christ - filled faith per -
cel - e - brate in sound that right has con - quered

dawn. Death los - es its sin - is - ter sting: God's
save. The crim - i - nal nailed as a fraud Is
gun. Cre - a - tion is decked for her guest Who,
leased. The vio - lence of hate reigns no more: The
tains. Re - li - gion, re - mote and type - cast, Is
wrong. Join hands with the neigh - bor un - known, U -

prom - ise to do a new thing Is done, and Hal - le -
raised by the pow - er of God And lives. So, Hal - le -
freed from his grave clothes, is dressed In light and, Hal - le -
vic - t'ry of love is the core Of hope and, Hal - le -
gone and the fu - ture is vast. New tongues sing, "Hal - le -
nite through the love that is shown In Christ, for, Hal - le -

lu - jah! Earth joins heav'n to sing.
lu - jah! Scat - ter the news a - broad.
lu - jah! Tells that the earth is blessed.
lu - jah! Love means an o - pen door.
lu - jah! God is for us at last!"
lu - jah! Christ is our Lord a - lone.

Text: John L. Bell, b.1949
Tune: DAYLIGHT; Irregular; John L. Bell, b.1949
© 1988, Iona Community, GIA Publications, Inc. agent

This Is the Day 449

Refrain

This is the day that the Lord has made,

Let us re - joice and be glad, and be glad.

This is the day that the Lord has made, al - le -

lu - ia, al - le - lu - ia.

Verses

1. Let us sing un - to the Lord,
2. Let the heav - ens be glad,
3. Bring your gifts be - fore the Lord,

praise God's name with our joy - ful shouts,
let the earth now re - joice and sing,
bring your of - f'rings in - to his court;

en - ter in with our joy - ful hearts, to the
let the fields and the trees cry out and the
tell God's glo - ry to all the earth and God's

D.C.

God of our sal - va - tion.
o - ceans thun - der praise.
won- ders for all time.

Text: Psalm 95, 96; Marty Haugen, b.1950
Tune: Marty Haugen, b.1950
© 1980, GIA Publications, Inc.

450 Hail Thee, Festival Day

Text: *Salve festa dies;* Venantius Fortunatus, c.530-609; tr. composite
Tune: SALVE FESTA DIES. Irregular with refrain; Ralph Vaughan Williams, 1872-1958
© Oxford University Press

Christ Has Risen 451

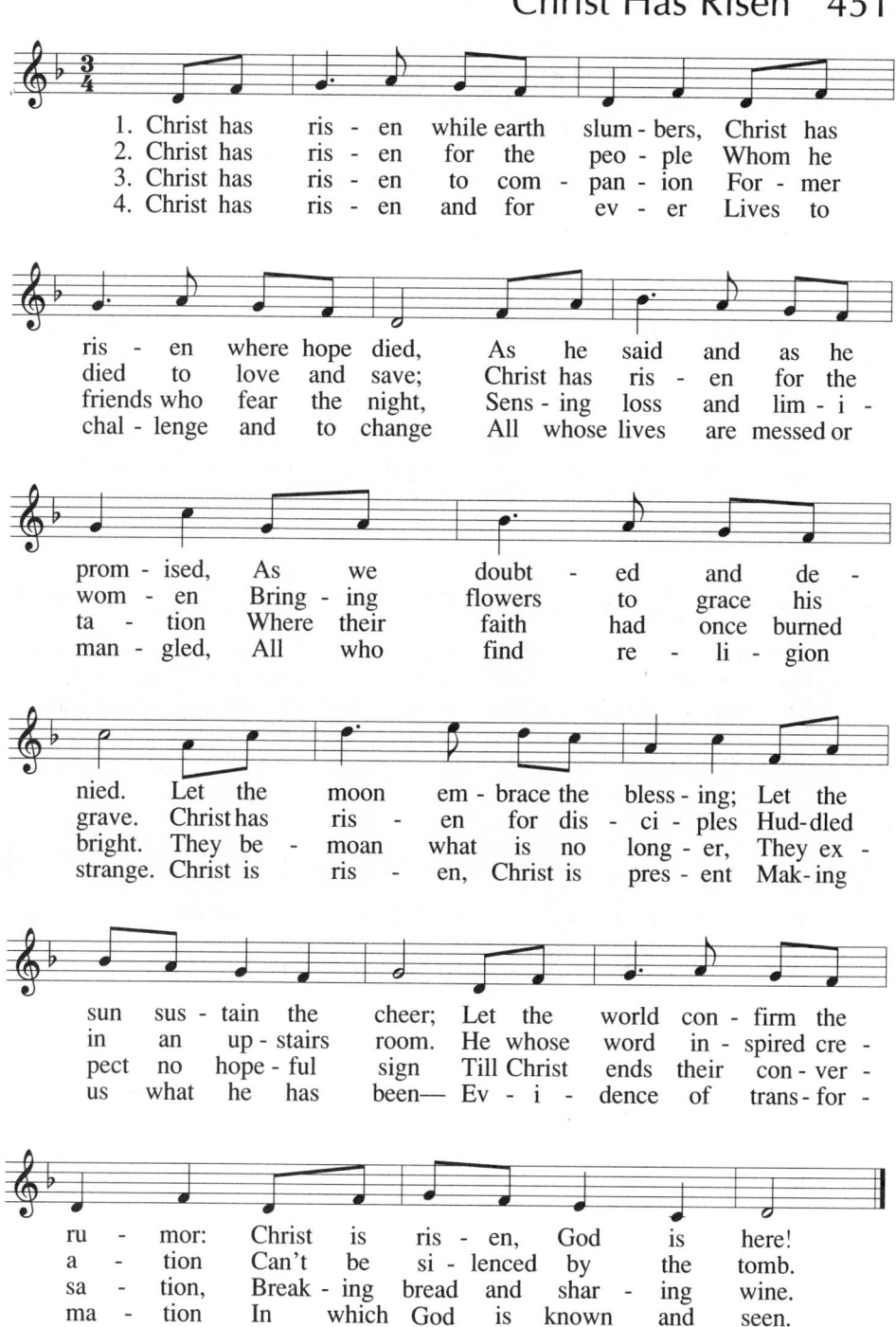

1. Christ has ris - en while earth slum - bers, Christ has
2. Christ has ris - en for the peo - ple Whom he
3. Christ has ris - en to com - pan - ion For - mer
4. Christ has ris - en and for ev - er Lives to

ris - en where hope died, As he said and as he
died to love and save; Christ has ris - en for the
friends who fear the night, Sens - ing loss and lim - i -
chal - lenge and to change All whose lives are messed or

prom - ised, As we doubt - ed and de -
wom - en Bring - ing flowers to grace his
ta - tion Where their faith had once burned
man - gled, All who find re - li - gion

nied. Let the moon em - brace the bless - ing; Let the
grave. Christ has ris - en for dis - ci - ples Hud - dled
bright. They be - moan what is no long - er, They ex -
strange. Christ is ris - en, Christ is pres - ent Mak - ing

sun sus - tain the cheer; Let the world con - firm the
in an up - stairs room. He whose word in - spired cre -
pect no hope - ful sign Till Christ ends their con - ver -
us what he has been— Ev - i - dence of trans - for -

ru - mor: Christ is ris - en, God is here!
a - tion Can't be si - lenced by the tomb.
sa - tion, Break - ing bread and shar - ing wine.
ma - tion In which God is known and seen.

Text: John L. Bell, b.1949
Tune: TRANSFORMATION, 8 7 8 7 D; John L. Bell, b.1949
© 1988, Iona Community, GIA Publications, Inc., agent

452 Up from the Earth

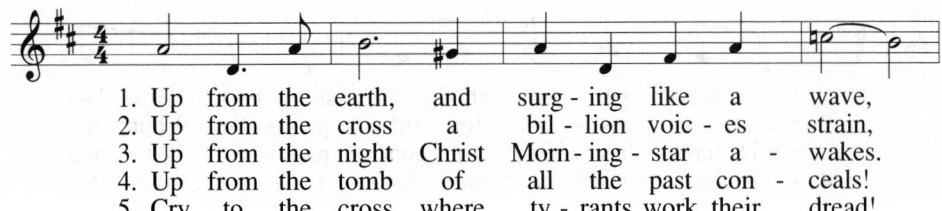

1. Up from the earth, and surg - ing like a wave,
2. Up from the cross a bil - lion voic - es strain,
3. Up from the night Christ Morn - ing - star a - wakes.
4. Up from the tomb of all the past con - ceals!
5. Cry to the cross where ty - rants work their dread!

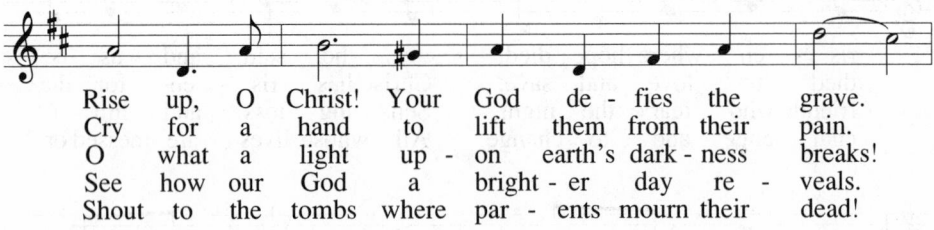

Rise up, O Christ! Your God de - fies the grave.
Cry for a hand to lift them from their pain.
O what a light up - on earth's dark - ness breaks!
See how our God a bright - er day re - veals.
Shout to the tombs where par - ents mourn their dead!

Up from the earth push blade and leaf and stem. They
Up from the cross but scarred in limbs and side, A
Up from the night Christ sows his life like wheat, And
Up from the tomb! Though death had bound us tight, Like
Sing to the earth, for God all new - ness gives! Al -

rise for Christ, and we shall rise with them!
wound - ed church brings heal - ing far and wide!
death it - self lies fal - low at his feet!
Laz - a - rus, we stum - ble in - to light!
le - lu - ia! Christ Lib - er - a - tor lives!

Text: Rory Cooney, b.1952
Tune: LIBERATOR, 10 10 10 10; Rory Cooney, b.1952
© 1987, North American Liturgy Resources

A Hymn of Glory Let Us Sing 453

1. A   hymn of glo - ry let us sing! New
2. The   ho - ly ap - os - tol - ic band Up -
3. To   whom the shin - ing an - gels cry, "Why
4. O   ris - en Christ, as - cend - ed Lord, All

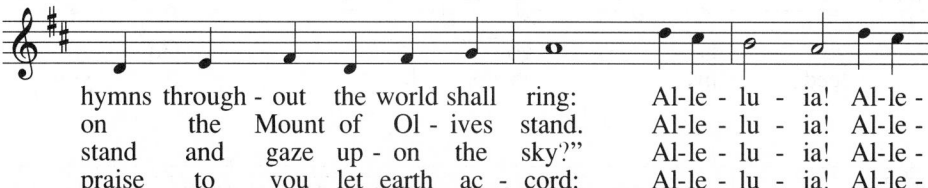

hymns through - out the world shall ring: Al-le - lu - ia! Al-le -
on   the Mount of Ol - ives stand. Al-le - lu - ia! Al-le -
stand and gaze up - on the sky?" Al-le - lu - ia! Al-le -
praise to you let earth ac - cord: Al-le - lu - ia! Al-le -

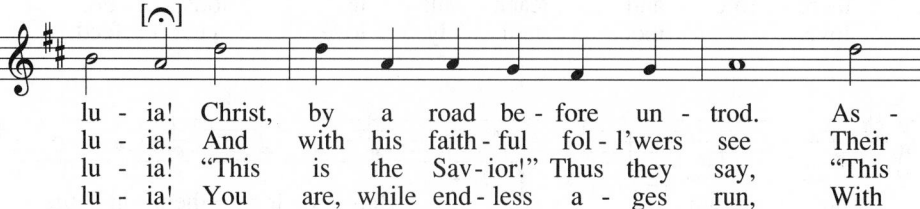

lu - ia! Christ, by a road be - fore un - trod. As -
lu - ia! And with his faith - ful fol - l'wers see Their
lu - ia! "This is the Sav - ior!" Thus they say, "This
lu - ia! You are, while end - less a - ges run, With

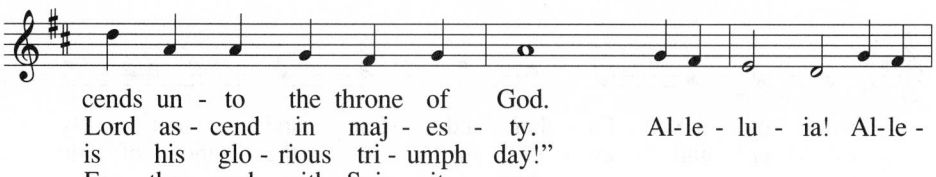

cends un - to the throne of God.
Lord as - cend in maj - es - ty.   Al-le - lu - ia! Al-le -
is   his glo - rious tri - umph day!"
Fa - ther and with Spir - it one.

lu - ia! Al - le - lu - ia! Al - le - lu - ia! Al - le - lu - ia!

Text: *Hymnum canamus gloria;* Venerable Bede, 673-735; tr. *Lutheran Book of Worship,* © 1978
Tune: LASST UNS ERFREUEN, LM; with alleluias; *Geistliche Kirchengasange,* Cologne, 1623; harm. by Ralph Vaughan Williams, 1872-1958,
© Oxford University Press

454 Go

1. Go ye there-fore and teach all na - tions,
2. If you love me, real - ly love me,

go, go, go. Go ye
feed my sheep. If you

there - fore and teach all na - tions, go,
love me, real - ly love me, feed

go, go. Bap - tiz - ing them in the
my sheep. And lo, I'll be with you for

name of the Fa - ther and Son and Ho - ly
ev - er and ev - er un - til the ends of the

Ghost. Go, go,
world, go, go,

go.
go.

Text: Leon Patillo
Tune: Leon Patillo
© 1981, 1982, Word Music, Inc.

I Will Be with You 455

Refrain

"I will be with you!" That is my prom-ise.

"I will be with you for ev - er - more."

Trust in my love. Bring me all your

cares, for I will be with you for ev - er - more.

Verses

1. You are my peo - ple, and I am your
2. You have re - ceived me, now go and spread my

God. I made you a prom-ise, to be with you al -
word. You are with-in me and I am in

ways, be-cause I real-ly love you. I real-ly
you,

D.S.

love you, and I will be with you for ev - er - more.

Text: James E. Moore, Jr., b.1951
Tune: James E. Moore, Jr., b.1951

456 Lord, You Give the Great Commission

1. Lord, you give the great com - mis-sion: "Heal the
2. Lord, you call us to your serv - ice: "In my
3. Lord, you make the com - mon ho - ly: "This my
4. Lord, you show us love's true meas-ure: "Fa - ther,
5. Lord, you bless with words as - sur - ing: "I am

sick and preach the word." Lest the Church ne -
name bap - tize and teach." That the world may
bod - y, this my blood." Let us all, for
what they do, for - give." Yet we hoard as
with you to the end." Faith and hope and

glect its mis-sion, And the Gos - pel go un -heard,
trust your prom-ise, Life a - bun - dant meant for each,
earth's true glo - ry, Dai - ly lift life heav - en -ward,
pri - vate treas-ure All that you so free - ly give.
love re - stor-ing, May we serve as you in - tend,

Help us wit - ness to your pur-pose With re -
Give us all new fer - vor, draw us Clos - er
Ask - ing that the world a - round us Share your
May your care and mer - cy lead us To a
And, a - mid the cares that claim us, Hold in

newed in - teg - ri - ty;
in com - mun - i - ty;
chil - dren's lib - er - ty; With the Spir - it's gifts em -
just so - ci - e - ty;
mind e - ter - ni - ty;

power us For the work of min - is - try.

Text: Jeffery Rowthorn, b.1934, © 1978, Hope Publishing Co.
Tune: ABBOT'S LEIGH, 8 7 8 7 D; Cyril V. Taylor, 1907-1991, © 1942, 1970, Hope Publishing Co.

Hail the Day That Sees Him Rise 457

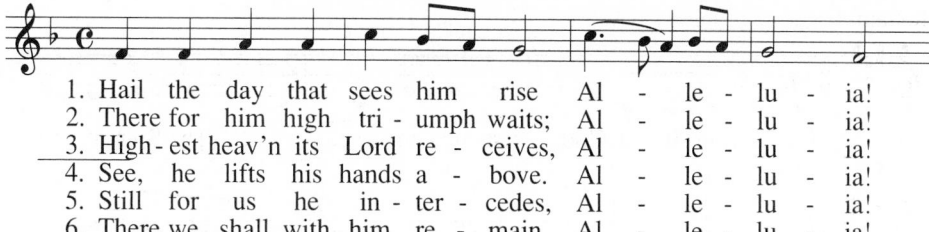

1. Hail the day that sees him rise   Al - le - lu - ia!
2. There for him high tri - umph waits;   Al - le - lu - ia!
3. High-est heav'n its Lord re - ceives,   Al - le - lu - ia!
4. See, he lifts his hands a - bove.   Al - le - lu - ia!
5. Still for us he in - ter - cedes,   Al - le - lu - ia!
6. There we shall with him re - main,   Al - le - lu - ia!

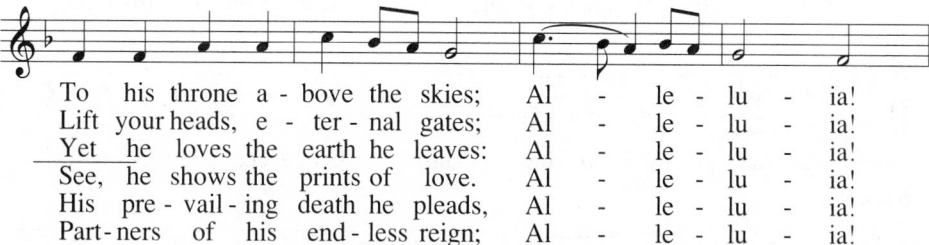

To his throne a - bove the skies;   Al - le - lu - ia!
Lift your heads, e - ter - nal gates;   Al - le - lu - ia!
Yet he loves the earth he leaves: Al - le - lu - ia!
See, he shows the prints of love.   Al - le - lu - ia!
His pre - vail - ing death he pleads,   Al - le - lu - ia!
Part-ners of his end - less reign;   Al - le - lu - ia!

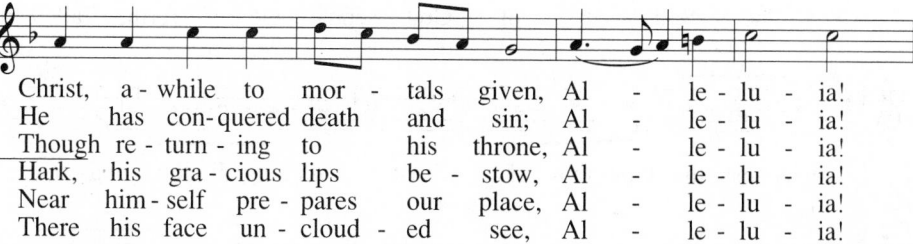

Christ, a - while to mor - tals given, Al - le - lu - ia!
He has con-quered death and sin; Al - le - lu - ia!
Though re - turn - ing to his throne, Al - le - lu - ia!
Hark, his gra - cious lips be - stow, Al - le - lu - ia!
Near him - self pre - pares our place, Al - le - lu - ia!
There his face un - cloud - ed see, Al - le - lu - ia!

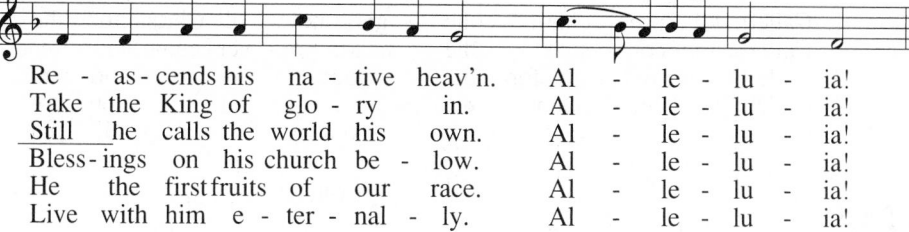

Re - as - cends his na - tive heav'n.   Al - le - lu - ia!
Take the King of glo - ry in.   Al - le - lu - ia!
Still he calls the world his own.   Al - le - lu - ia!
Bless-ings on his church be - low.   Al - le - lu - ia!
He the first fruits of our race.   Al - le - lu - ia!
Live with him e - ter - nal - ly.   Al - le - lu - ia!

Text: Charles Wesley, 1707-1788, alt.
Tune: LLANFAIR, 77 77 with alleluias; Robert Williams, 1781-1821

458 The Spirit of God

Refrain

The Spir-it of God rests up-on me, The Spir-it of God con-se-crates me, The Spir-it of God bids me go forth to pro-claim his peace, his joy.

Verses

1.-5. The Spir-it of God sends me forth, Called to wit-ness the king-dom of Christ a-mong all the na-tions;

1. Called to pro-claim the good news of Christ to the
2. Called to con-sole the hearts o-ver-come with great
3. Called to com-fort the poor who mourn and who
4. Called to an-nounce the grace of sal-va-tion to
5. Called to re-veal the glo-ry a-mong all the

D.C.

poor.
sor - row.
weep.   My spir-it re-joic-es in God, my Sav - ior.
all.
peo - ple.

Text: Isaiah 61:1, 2; Luke 4:18-19; Lucien Deiss, C S Sp, b.1921
Tune: Lucien Deiss, C S Sp, b.1921
© 1970, 1973, World Library Publications, Inc.

Envía Tu Espíritu 459

Refrain

En - ví - a tu Es-pí - ri - tu, en - ví - a tu Es-pí- ri - tu,

en - ví - a tu Es- pí - ri - tu, se - a re - no - va -

da la faz de la tie - rra. Se - a re-no- va -

da la faz de la tie - rra.

Verses

1. Spir - it of the liv - ing God,
2. Wind of prom - ise, wind of change,
3. Breath of life and ho - li - ness,

burn in our hearts, and make us a peo -
friend of the poor, em - pow - er your peo -
heal ev - 'ry wound, and lead us be - yond

D.C.

ple of hope and com - pas - sion.
ple to make peace and jus - tice.
ev - 'ry sin that di - vides us.

Text: *Send out your spirit and renew the face of the earth;* Psalm 104:30; the Sequence of Pentecost; Bob Hurd, b.1950, © 1988
Tune: Bob Hurd, b.1950, © 1988; acc. by Craig Kingsbury, b.1952, © 1988, OCP Publications; arr. © 1988, OCP Publications
Published by OCP Publications

460 Veni Creator Spiritus

1. Ve - ni Cre - á - tor Spí - ri - tus,
2. Qui dí - ce - ris Pa - rá - cli - tus,
3. Tu se - pti - fór - mis mú - ne - re,
4. Ac - cén - de lu - men sén - si - bus,
5. Hó - stem re - pél - las lón - gi - us,
6. Per te sci - á - mus da Pa - trem,
7. De - o Pa - tri sit gló - ri - a,

Men - tes tu - ó - rum ví - si - ta:
Al - tís - si - mi dó - num De - i,
Di - gi - tus pa - tér - nae déx - te - rae,
In - fun - de - a - mó - rem cór - di - bus,
Pa - cém - que do - nes pró - ti - nus:
No - scá - mus at - que Fí - li - um
Et Fí - li - o, qui a mór - tu - is

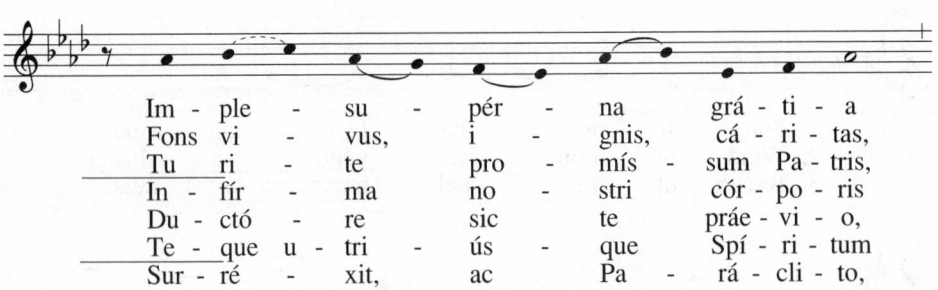

Im - ple - su - pér - na grá - ti - a
Fons vi - vus, i - gnis, cá - ri - tas,
Tu ri - te pro - mís - sum Pa - tris,
In - fír - ma no - stri cór - po - ris
Du - ctó - re sic te práe - vi - o,
Te - que u - tri - ús - que Spí - ri - tum
Sur - ré - xit, ac Pa - rá - cli - to,

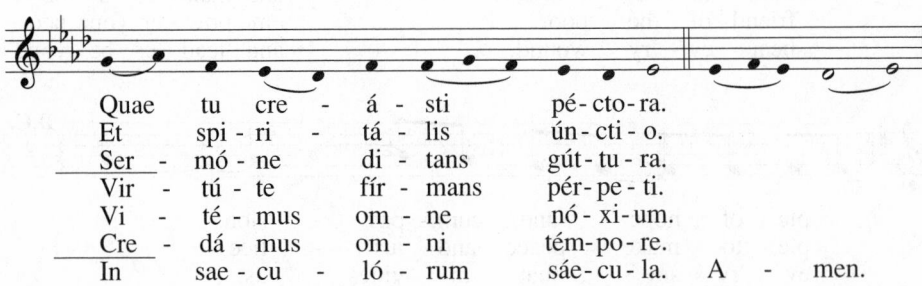

Quae tu cre - á - sti pé - cto - ra.
Et spi - ri - tá - lis ún - cti - o.
Ser - mó - ne di - tans gút - tu - ra.
Vir - tú - te fír - mans pér - pe - ti.
Vi - té - mus om - ne nó - xi - um.
Cre - dá - mus om - ni tém - po - re.
In sae - cu - ló - rum sáe - cu - la. A - men.

Text: Attr. to Rabanus Maurus, 776-856
Tune: VENI CREATOR SPIRITUS, LM; Mode VIII; acc. by Richard Proulx, b. 1937, © 1975, GIA Publications, Inc.

O Holy Spirit, by Whose Breath   461

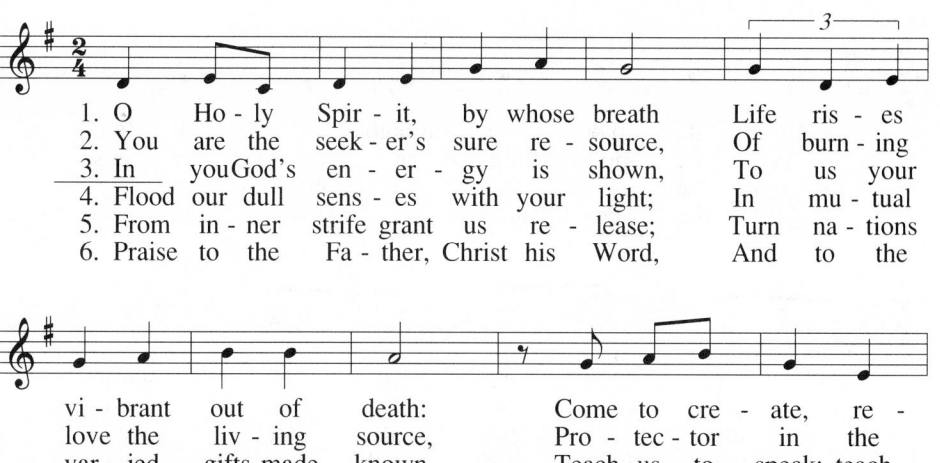

1. O   Ho - ly   Spir - it,   by whose breath   Life   ris - es
2. You   are the   seek - er's   sure re - source,   Of   burn - ing
3. In   you God's en - er - gy is   shown,   To   us   your
4. Flood our dull   sens - es   with your light;   In   mu - tual
5. From   in - ner   strife grant us   re - lease;   Turn   na - tions
6. Praise to the   Fa - ther,   Christ his Word,   And   to   the

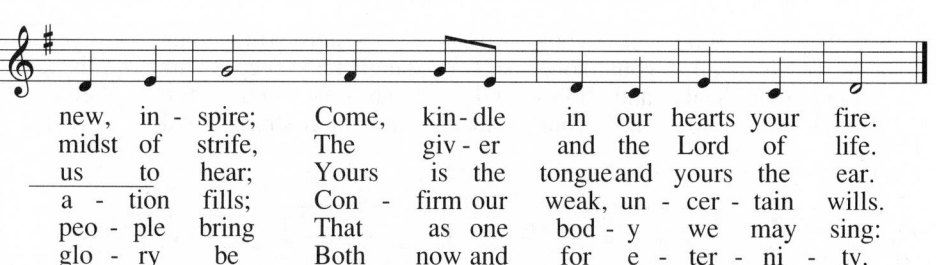

vi - brant   out of   death: Come to cre - ate,   re -
love the   liv - ing   source,   Pro - tec - tor in   the
var - ied   gifts made   known.   Teach us to   speak; teach
love our   hearts u -   nite.   Your pow'r the   whole cre -
to the   ways of   peace.   To   full - er   life your
Spir - it,   God the   Lord;   To   whom all   hon - or,

new, in - spire;   Come, kin - dle   in   our hearts your   fire.
midst of strife,   The   giv - er   and the Lord of   life.
us   to   hear;   Yours is   the   tongue and yours the   ear.
a - tion fills;   Con - firm our   weak, un - cer - tain   wills.
peo - ple bring   That   as   one   bod - y   we   may   sing:
glo - ry   be   Both   now and   for e - ter - ni -   ty.

Text: *Veni, Creator Spiritus;* attr. to Rabanus Maurus, 776-865; tr. by John W. Grant, b.1919, © 1971
Tune: VENI CREATOR SPIRITUS, LM; Mode VIII; setting by Richard J. Wojcik, b.1923, © 1975, GIA Publications, Inc.

462　Spirit Blowing through Creation

Verses

1. Spir - it blow - ing through cre - a - tion,
2. As you moved up - on the wa - ters,
3. Love that sends the riv - ers danc - ing,
4. All the crea - tures you have fash - ioned,

Spir - it burn - ing in the skies,
As you ride up - on the wind,
Love that wa - ters all that lives,
All that live and breathe in you,

Let the hope of your sal - va - tion fill our eyes;
Move us all, your sons and daugh-ters deep with - in;
Love that heals and holds and rous - es and for - gives;
Find their hope in your com - pas - sion, strong and true;

God of splen - dor, God of glo - ry,
As you shaped the hills and moun-tains,
You are food for all your crea - tures,
You, O Spir - it of sal - va - tion,

You who light the stars a - bove,
Formed the land and filled the deep,
You are hun - ger in the soul,
You a - lone, be - neath, a - bove,

All the heav - ens tell the sto - ry of your love. *(To verse 2)*
Let your hand re - new and wak - en all who sleep. *(To refrain)*
In your hands the bro - ken - heart-ed are made whole. *(To verse 4)*
Come, re - new your whole cre - a - tion in your love. *(To refrain)*

Refrain

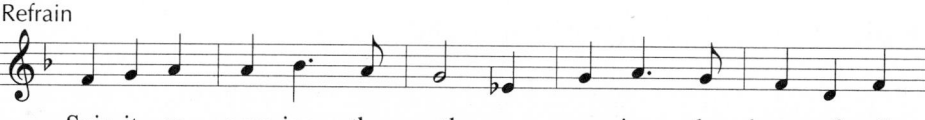

Spir-it re-new-ing the earth, re-new-ing the hearts of all

peo-ple; Burn in the wea-ry souls,

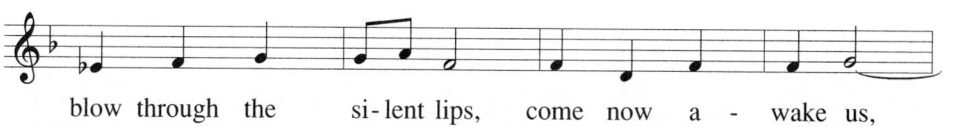

blow through the si-lent lips, come now a-wake us,

Spir-it of God.

Text: Marty Haugen, b.1950
Tune: Marty Haugen, b.1950
© 1987, GIA Publications, Inc.

Veni Sancte Spiritus 463

Ostinato Refrain

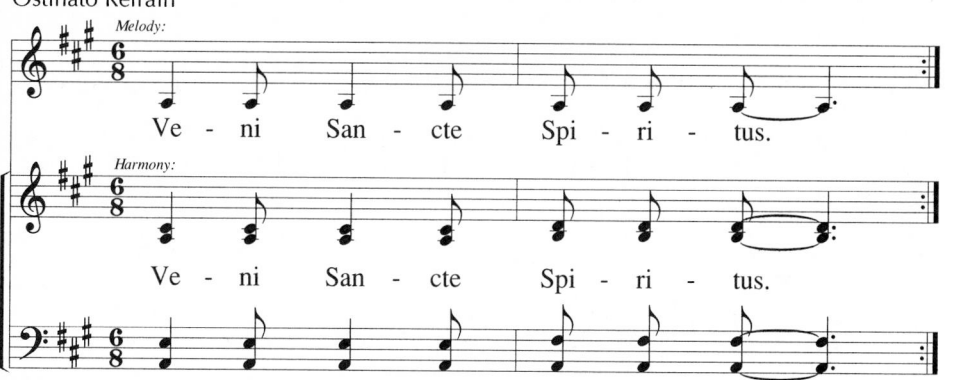

Melody:

Ve - ni San - cte Spi - ri - tus.

Harmony:

Ve - ni San - cte Spi - ri - tus.

Text: *Come Holy Spirit;* Verses drawn form the Pentecost Sequence; Taizé Community, 1978
Tune: Jacques Berthier, 1923-1994
© 1979, Les Presses de Taizé, GIA Publications, Inc., agent

464 Sequence for Pentecost

1. Ho - ly Spir - it, Lord Di - vine, Come, from heights of
2. Come, O Fa - ther of the poor, Come, whose treas - ured

heav'n and shine, Come with bless - ed ra - diance bright!
gifts en - dure, Come, our heart's un - fail - ing light!

3. Of con - so - lers, wis - est, best, And our soul's most
4. In our la - bor rest most sweet, Pleas - ant cool - ness

wel - come guest, Sweet re - fresh - ment sweet re - pose.
in the heat, Con - so - la - tion in our woes.

5. Light most bless - ed, shine with grace In our heart's most
6. Left with - out your pres - ence here, Life it - self would

se - cret place, Fill your faith - ful through and through.
dis - ap - pear, Noth - ing thrives a - part from you!

7. Cleanse our soil - ed hearts of sin, Ar - id souls re -
8. Bend the stub - born heart and will, Melt the fro - zen,

fresh with - in, Wound - ed lives to health re - store.
warm the chill, Guide the way - ward home once more!

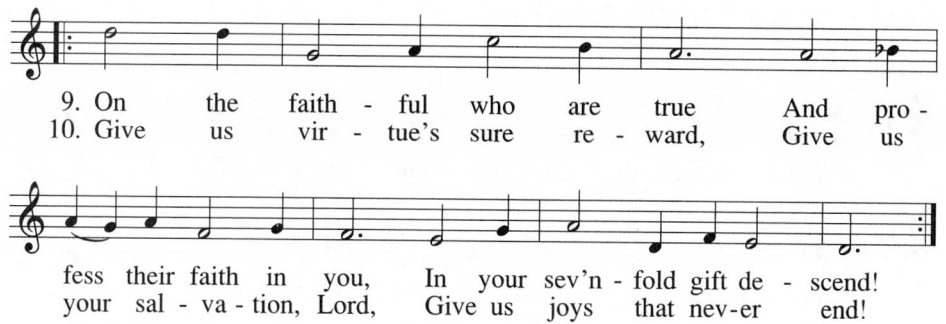

9. On the faith - ful who are true And pro -
10. Give us vir - tue's sure re - ward, Give us

fess their faith in you, In your sev'n - fold gift de - scend!
your sal - va - tion, Lord, Give us joys that nev-er end!

Text: Sequence for Pentecost, 13th. C.; tr. by Peter J. Scagnelli; b.1949, © 1983
Tune: Mode I; acc. by Adriaan Engels, b.1906, © Interkerkelijke Stichting voor het Kerklied Den Haag

Come Down, O Love Divine 465

1. Come down, O Love di - vine, Seek now this soul of
2. O let it free - ly burn, Till earth - ly pas - sions
3. And so the yearn - ing strong, With which the soul will

mine, And vis - it it with your own ar - dor glow - ing;
turn To dust and ash - es in its heat con - sum - ing;
long, Shall far out-pass the power of hu - man tell - ing;

O Com - fort - er, draw near, With - in my heart ap -
And let your glo - rious light Shine ev - er on my
For none can guess its grace, Till love cre - ates the

pear, And kin - dle it, your ho - ly flame be - stow - ing.
sight, And clothe me round, the while my path il - lum - ing.
place Where - in the Ho - ly Spir - it makes its dwell - ing.

Text: *Discendi, Amor Santo;* Bianco da Siena, d.c.1434; tr. by Richard F. Littledale, 1833-1890
Tune: DOWN AMPNEY, 66 11 D; Ralph Vaughan Williams, 1872-1958, © Oxford University Press

466 Send Down the Fire

Refrain

Send down the fire of your jus - tice,
Send down the rains of your love; Come,
send down the Spir - it, breathe life in your peo - ple, and
we shall be peo - ple of God.

Verses

1. Call us to be your com - pas - sion,
2. Call us to learn of your mer - cy,
3. Call us to an - swer op - pres - sion,
4. Call us to wit - ness your King - dom,

Teach us the song of your love; Give us
Teach us the way of your peace; Give us
Teach us the fire of your truth; Give us
Give us the pres - ence of Christ; May your

hearts that sing, Give us deeds that ring, Make us
hearts that feel, Give us hands that heal, Make us
right - eous souls, 'Til your jus - tice rolls, Make us
ho - ly light Keep us shin - ing bright, Ev - er

D.C.

ring with the song of your love.
walk in the way of your peace.
burn with the fire of your truth.
shine with the pres - ence of Christ.

Text: Marty Haugen, b.1950
Tune: Marty Haugen, b.1950
© 1989, GIA Publications, Inc.

Spirit-Friend 467

1. God sends us his Spir - it to be-friend and help us.
2. Dark-ened roads are clear - er, heav - y bur - dens light - er,
3. Now we are God's peo - ple, bond-ed by God's pres-ence,

Re - cre - ate and guide us, Spir - it - Friend.
When we're walk - ing with our Spir - it - Friend.
A - gents of God's pur - pose, Spir - it - Friend.

Spir - it who en - liv - ens, sanc - ti - fies, en - light - ens,
Now we need not fear the pow - ers of the dark - ness.
Lead us for-ward ev - er, slip - ping back-ward nev - er,

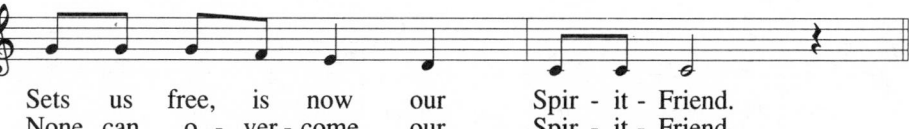

Sets us free, is now our Spir - it - Friend.
None can o - ver - come our Spir - it - Friend.
To your re - made world, our Spir - it - Friend.

Sing a., b., and c. after each stanza.   Hand claps

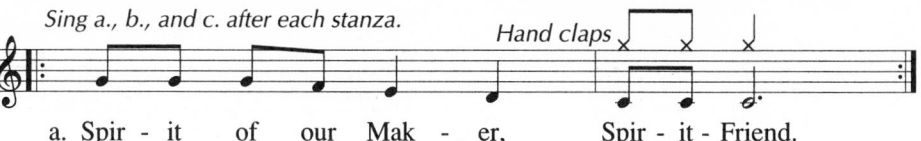

a. Spir - it of our Mak - er, Spir - it - Friend.
b. Spir - it of our Je - su, Spir - it - Friend.
c. Spir - it of God's peo - ple, Spir - it - Friend.

Text: Tom Colvin, b.1925
Tune: NATOMAH, 12 9 12 9 with refrain; Gonja folk song; adapt. by Tom Colvin, b.1925; acc. by Marty Haugen, b. 1950
© 1969, 1987, Hope Publishing Co.

468 Spirit of God within Me

1. Spir - it of God with - in me, Pos - sess my hu - man
2. Spir - it of truth with - in me, Pos - sess my thought and
3. Spir - it of love with - in me, Pos - sess my hands and
4. Spir - it of life with - in me, Pos - sess this life of

frame; Fan the dull em - bers of my heart, Stir
mind; Light - en a - new the in - ward eye By
heart; Break through the bonds of self - con - cern That
mine; Come as the wind of heav-en's breath, Come

up the liv - ing flame: Strive till that im - age
Sa - tan ren - dered blind: Shine on the words that
seeks to stand a - part: Grant me the love that
as the fire di - vine! Spir - it of Christ, the

A - dam lost, New mint - ed and re -
wis - dom speaks And grant me pow'r to
suf - fers long, That hopes, be - lieves and
liv - ing Lord, Reign in this house of

stored, In shin - ing splen - dor bright - ly
see The truth made known to all in
bears; The love ful - filled in sac - ri -
clay, Till from its dust with Christ I

bears The like - ness of the Lord.
Christ, And in that truth be free.
fice, That cares as Je - sus cares.
rise To ev - er - last - ing day.

Text: Timothy Dudley-Smith, b.1926, © 1968, Hope Publishing Co.
Tune: WILLOW RIVER, 7 6 8 7 8 6 8 6; Michael Joncas, b.1951, © 1985, 1988, GIA Publications, Inc.

Come, Holy Ghost   469

1. Come, Ho - ly Ghost, Cre - a - tor blest, And in our
2. O Com - fort - er, to thee we cry, Thou heav'n-ly
3. O Ho - ly Ghost, Through thee a - lone, Know we the
4. Praise we the Lord, Fa - ther and Son, And Ho - ly

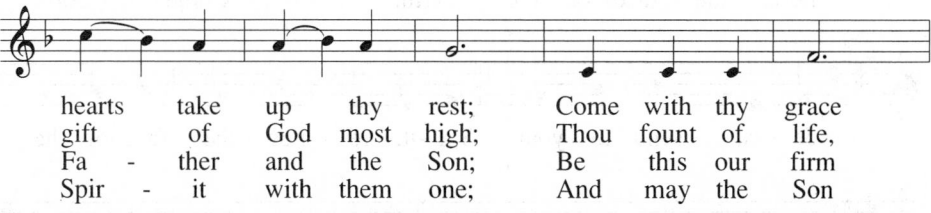

hearts take up thy rest; Come with thy grace
gift of God most high; Thou fount of life,
Fa - ther and the Son; Be this our firm
Spir - it with them one; And may the Son

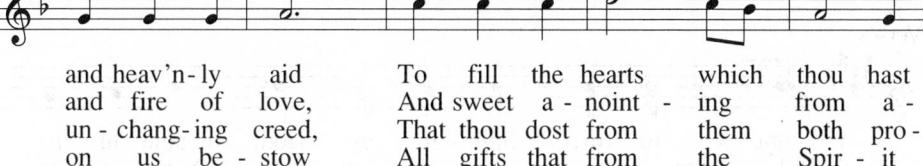

and heav'n-ly aid To fill the hearts which thou hast
and fire of love, And sweet a - noint - ing from a -
un - chang-ing creed, That thou dost from them both pro -
on us be - stow All gifts that from the Spir - it

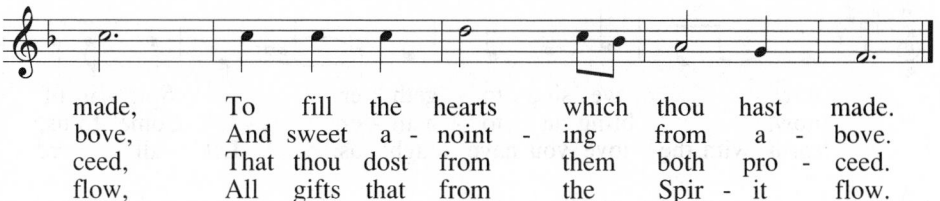

made, To fill the hearts which thou hast made.
bove, And sweet a - noint - ing from a - bove.
ceed, That thou dost from them both pro - ceed.
flow, All gifts that from the Spir - it flow.

Text: *Veni, Creator Spiritus;* attr. to Rabanus Maurus, 776-856; tr. by Edward Caswall, 1814-1878, alt.
Tune: LAMBILLOTTE, LM with repeat; Louis Lambillotte, SJ, 1796-1855, harm. by Richard Proulx, b. 1937. © 1986, GIA Publications, Inc.

470 Send Us Your Spirit

Refrain

*1.   2.

Come   Lord   Je-sus,   send   us   your   Spir-it,   re-

new   the   face   of   the   earth.   Come   Lord

Je-sus,   send   us   your   Spir-it,   re-new   the   face   of   the

earth.

Verses

1. Come   to   us,   Spir-it   of   God,   breathe   in   us
2. Fill us with   the   fire   of   your   love,   burn   in   us
3. Send   us   the   wings   of   new   birth,   fill   all   the

now,   we sing to-geth-er.   Spir-it of
now,   bring us to-geth-er.   Come to us,
earth with the   love you have taught us.   Let   all   cre-

hope   and   of   light,   fill   our   lives,
dwell   in   us,   change   our   lives,   O   Lord,
a - tion   now   be   shak-en   with   love,

D.C.

come   to   us,   Spir-it   of   God.
come   to   us,   Spir-it   of   God.
come   to   us,   Spir-it   of   God.

*May be sung in canon.

Text: David Haas, b.1957
Tune: David Haas, b.1957; acc. by Jeanne Cotter, b.1964
© 1981, 1982, 1987, GIA Publications, Inc.

Wa Wa Wa Emimimo / Come, O Holy Spirit 471

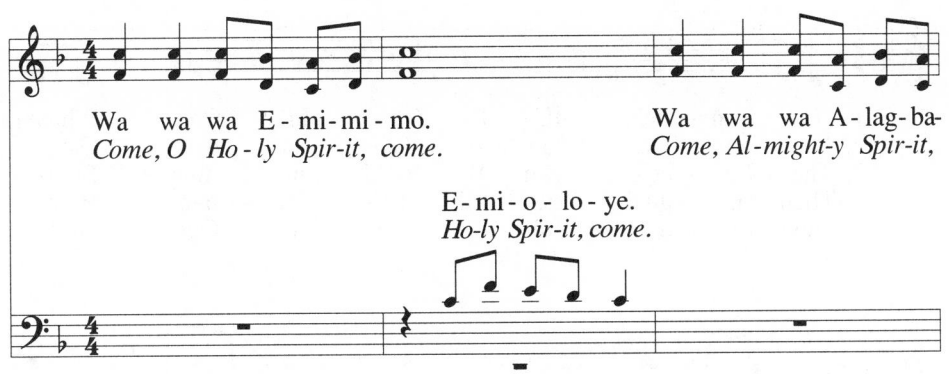

Wa   wa wa E - mi - mi - mo.
Come, O Ho - ly Spir-it, come.

Wa   wa   wa A - lag-ba-
Come, Al-might-y Spir-it,

E - mi - o - lo - ye.
Ho - ly Spir-it, come.

ra.
come.

A - lag - ba - ra - me - ta.
Al-might-y Spir-it, come.

Wa - o,   wa - o,   wa - o.
Come,   come,   come.

E - mi - mi - mo.
O Spir-it, come.

Text: Nigerian traditional
Tune: As taught by Samuel Solanke; transcription and paraphrase © 1990, I-to-Loh

472 How Wonderful the Three-in-One

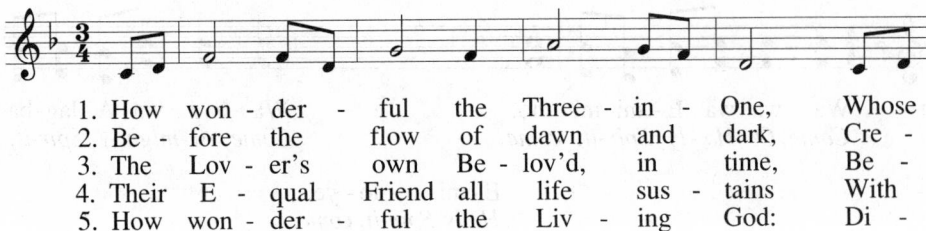

1. How won - der - ful the Three - in - One, Whose
2. Be - fore the flow of dawn and dark, Cre -
3. The Lov - er's own Be - lov'd, in time, Be -
4. Their E - qual Friend all life sus - tains With
5. How won - der - ful the Liv - ing God: Di -

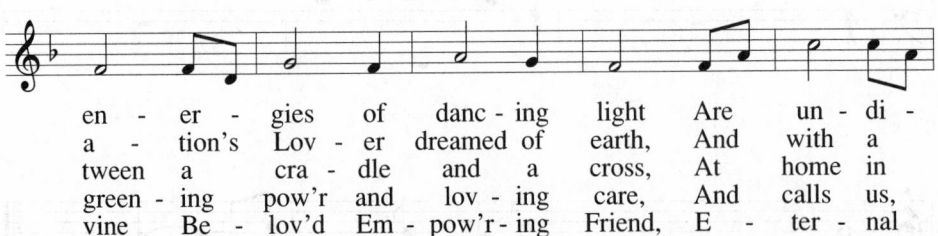

en - er - gies of danc - ing light Are un - di -
a - tion's Lov - er dreamed of earth, And with a
tween a cra - dle and a cross, At home in
green - ing pow'r and lov - ing care, And calls us,
vine Be - lov'd Em - pow'r - ing Friend, E - ter - nal

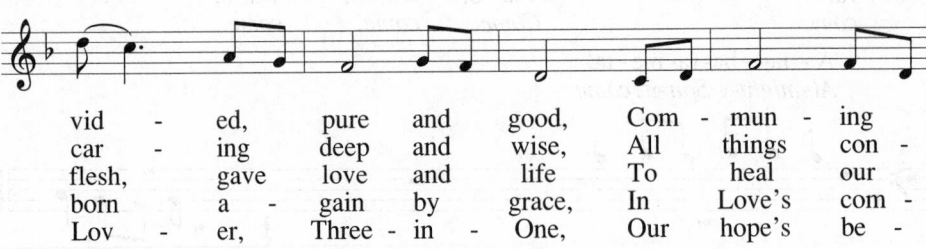

vid - ed, pure and good, Com - mun - ing
car - ing deep and wise, All things con -
flesh, gave love and life To heal our
born a - gain by grace, In Love's com -
Lov - er, Three - in - One, Our hope's be -

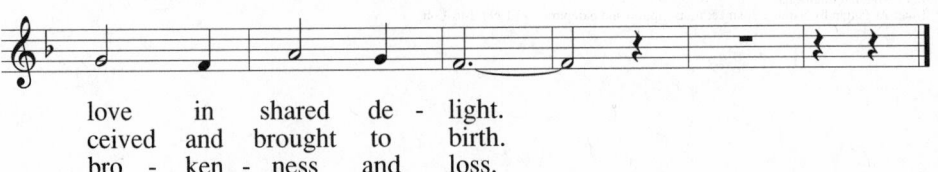

love in shared de - light.
ceived and brought to birth.
bro - ken - ness and loss.
mun - ing life to share.
gin - ning, way and end.

Text: Brian Wren, b.1936, © 1989, Hope Publishing Co.
Tune: PROSPECT, 8 8 8 8; *Southern Harmony*; arr. by Marty Haugen, b.1950, © 1991, GIA Publications, Inc.

Alleluia, Sing! 473

Cantor:

1. Bless - ed   be   our   God!   Bless - ed   be   our
2. Gift   of   love   and   peace!   Gift   of   love   and
3. Come,   O   Spir - it   of   truth!   Come,   O   Spir - it   of

All:

Cantor:

God!   Joy   of   our hearts,   source   of   all life   and
peace!   Je - sus   the Christ,   Je - sus   our hope   and
truth!   Prom - ise   of hope,   kind - ness   and   mer -

love!   God   of   heav - en   and
light!   A   flame   of   faith   in   our
cy!   Come   and   dwell   in   our

All:

earth!   God   of   heav - en   and   earth!
hearts!   A   flame   of   faith   in   our   hearts!   Pro -
hearts!   Come   and   dwell   in   our   hearts!

Cantor:

Dwell - ing with - in,   call - ing   us   all   by   name!
claim - ing   the   day,   shin - ing through - out   the   night!
Jus - tice and   peace,   the   king - dom   of   God   in   us!

Al - le - lu - ia,   sing!

All:

Al - le - lu - ia,   sing!

Text: David Haas, b.1957
Tune: David Haas, b.1957
© 1988, GIA Publications, Inc.

474 Holy, Holy, Holy! Lord God Almighty

1. Ho - ly, Ho - ly, Ho - ly! Lord God Al - might - y!
2. Ho - ly, Ho - ly, Ho - ly! all the saints a - dore thee,
3. Ho - ly, Ho - ly, Ho - ly! though the dark-ness hide thee,
4. Ho - ly, Ho - ly, Ho - ly! Lord God Al - might - y!

Ear - ly in the morn - ing our song shall rise to thee:
Cast - ing down their gold - en crowns a - round the glass - y sea;
Though the eye made blind by sin thy glo - ry may not see,
All thy works shall praise thy Name in earth, and sky, and sea;

Ho - ly, Ho - ly, Ho - ly! mer - ci - ful and might - y,
Cher - u - bim and ser - a - phim fall - ing down be - fore thee,
On - ly thou art ho - ly; there is none be - side thee,
Ho - ly, Ho - ly, Ho - ly! mer - ci - ful and might - y,

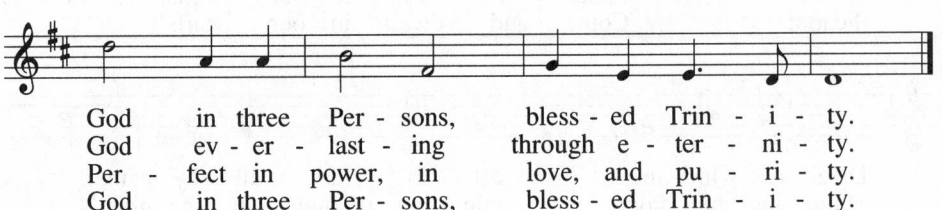

God in three Per - sons, bless - ed Trin - i - ty.
God ev - er - last - ing through e - ter - ni - ty.
Per - fect in power, in love, and pu - ri - ty.
God in three Per - sons, bless - ed Trin - i - ty.

Text: Reginald Heber, 1783-1826, alt.
Tune: NICAEA, 11 12 12 10; John Bacchus Dykes, 1823-1876

Come, Now Almighty King   475

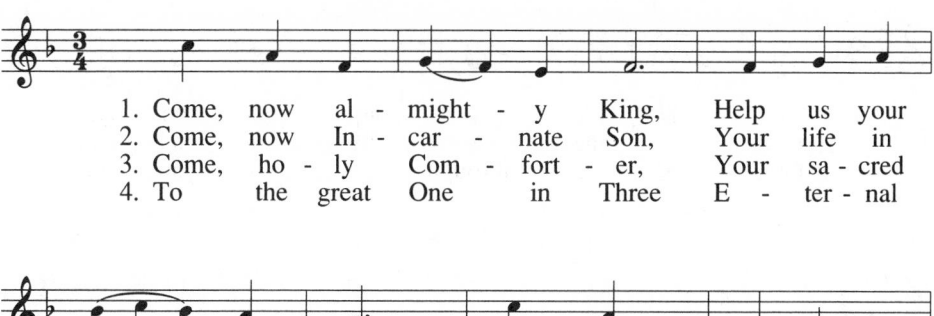

1. Come,   now   al - might - y   King,   Help   us   your
2. Come,   now   In - car - nate   Son,   Your   life   in
3. Come,   ho - ly   Com - fort - er,   Your   sa - cred
4. To   the   great   One   in   Three   E - ter - nal

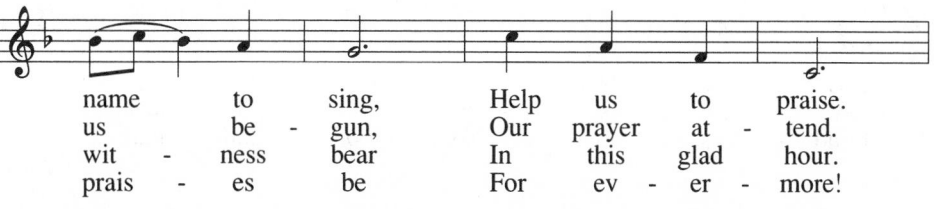

name   to   sing,   Help   us   to   praise.
us   be - gun,   Our   prayer   at - tend.
wit - ness   bear   In   this   glad   hour.
prais - es   be   For   ev - er - more!

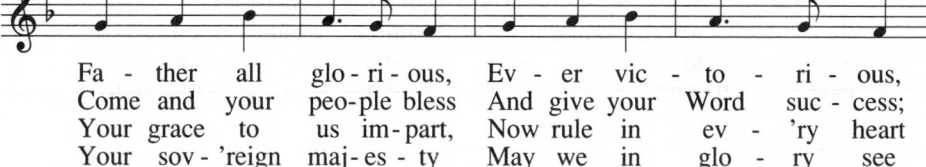

Fa - ther   all   glo - ri - ous,   Ev - er   vic - to - ri - ous,
Come and   your   peo-ple bless   And give your   Word   suc - cess;
Your grace   to   us im-part,   Now rule   in   ev - 'ry   heart
Your sov - 'reign   maj-es - ty   May we   in   glo - ry   see

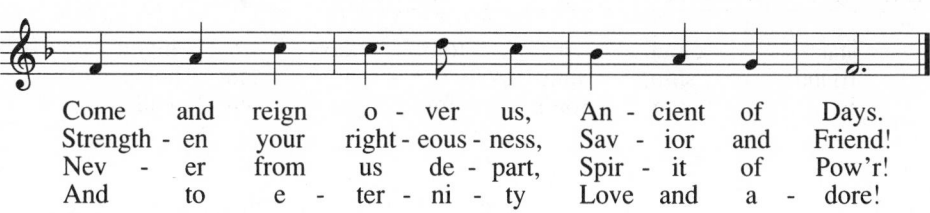

Come   and   reign   o - ver   us,   An - cient   of   Days.
Strength - en   your   right - eous - ness,   Sav - ior   and   Friend!
Nev - er   from   us   de - part,   Spir - it   of   Pow'r!
And   to   e - ter - ni - ty   Love   and   a - dore!

Text: Anon. c.1757
Tune: ITALIAN HYMN, 66 4 666 4; Felice de Giardini, 1716-1796

476 God Is One, Unique and Holy

1.,4. God is One, u - nique and ho - ly,
2. God is One - ness - by - Com - mun - ion,
3. God is One through des - o - la - tion—

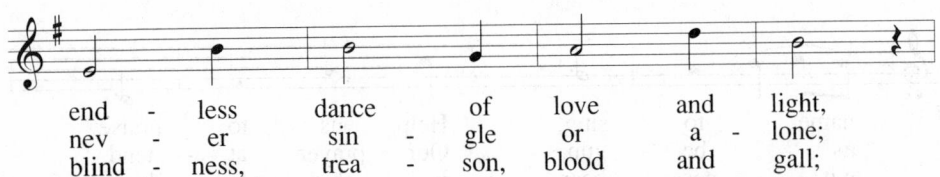

end - less dance of love and light,
nev - er sin - gle or a - lone;
blind - ness, trea - son, blood and gall;

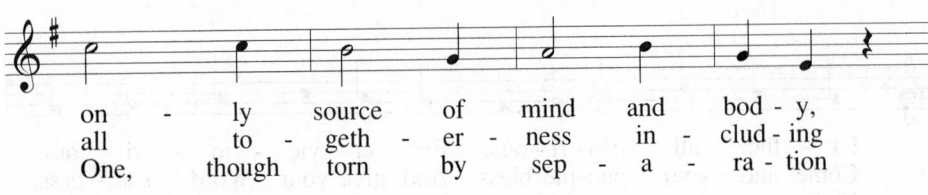

on - ly source of mind and bod - y,
all to - geth - er - ness in - clud - ing
One, though torn by sep - a - ra - tion

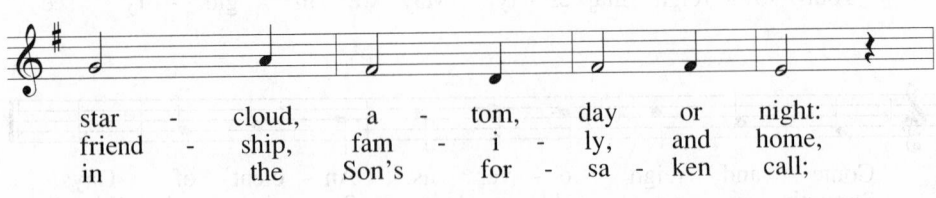

star - cloud, a - tom, day or night:
friend - ship, fam - i - ly, and home,
in the Son's for - sa - ken call;

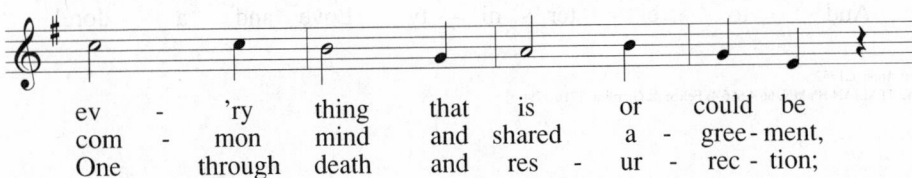

ev - 'ry thing that is or could be
com - mon mind and shared a - gree - ment,
One through death and res - ur - rec - tion;

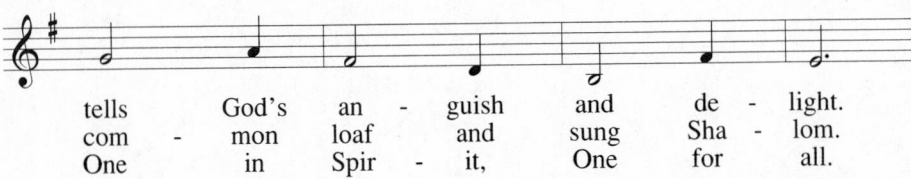

tells God's an - guish and de - light.
com - mon loaf and sung Sha - lom.
One in Spir - it, One for all.

Text: Brian Wren, b.1936, © 1983, Hope Publishing Co.
Tune: Gary Daigle, b.1957, © 1994, GIA Publications, Inc.

Blessed Be God 477

Refrain

Bless-ed be God.
Bless-ed be God's ho-ly name.

Bless-ed be Je-sus, the Lord, the Christ.

Bless-ed be the Spir-it, the com-fort-er.

Bless-ed be God in the an-gels and the saints.

Verses

1. You spread out the heav-ens and poured forth the seas, you
2. You pour out the wa-ter in clear run-ning springs which
3. Your moon marks the sea-sons of growth and de-cline and

trav-el on wings of the wind. The winds bring your mes-sage in
trav-el in streams to the sea. The moun-tains re-ply with a
bright-ens the dark - ness of night. Your sun brings the dawn-ing with

whis-per-ing breath and fire bright-ly glows with your word.
blan-ket of green and val - leys bear fruit in due time.
pow-er-ful light, a bea - con of life and of hope.

Text: Based on *The Divine Praises* and Psalm 103; Michael Connolly, b.1955
Tune: Michael Connolly, b.1955
© 1988, GIA Publications, Inc.

478 Stand Up, Friends

Verses

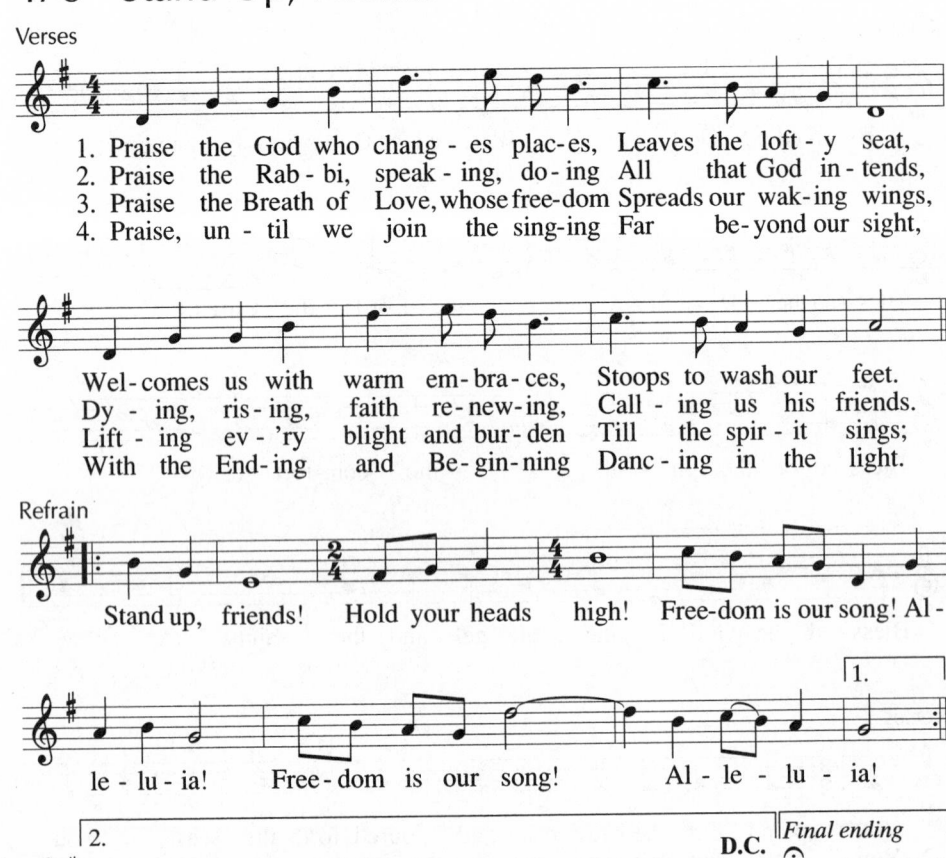

1. Praise the God who chang - es plac-es, Leaves the loft - y seat,
2. Praise the Rab - bi, speak - ing, do - ing All that God in - tends,
3. Praise the Breath of Love, whose free-dom Spreads our wak-ing wings,
4. Praise, un - til we join the sing-ing Far be-yond our sight,

Wel - comes us with warm em - bra - ces, Stoops to wash our feet.
Dy - ing, ris - ing, faith re - new-ing, Call - ing us his friends.
Lift - ing ev - 'ry blight and bur - den Till the spir - it sings;
With the End-ing and Be - gin-ning Danc - ing in the light.

Refrain

Stand up, friends! Hold your heads high! Free-dom is our song! Al -

le - lu - ia! Free-dom is our song! Al - le - lu - ia!

2. ia!   D.C.   Final ending

Text: Brian Wren, b. 1936, © 1986, Hope Publishing Co.
Tune: David Haas, b. 1957, © 1993, GIA Publications, Inc.

O God, Almighty Father 479

1. O God, al-might-y Fa-ther, Cre-a-tor of all things, The
2. O Je-sus, Word in-car-nate, Re-deem-er most a-dored, All
3. O God, the Ho-ly Spir-it, Who lives with-in our soul, Send

heav-ens stand in won-der, While earth your glo-ry sings.
glo-ry, praise, and hon-or Be yours, O sov-'reign Lord.
forth your light and lead us To our e-ter-nal goal.

O most ho-ly Trin-i-ty, Un-di-vid-ed u-ni-ty,

Ho-ly God, might-y God, God im-mor-tal be a-dored!

Text: *Gott Vater sei gepriesen;* anon; tr. by Irvin Udulutsch, OFM Cap., fl. 1959, alt. © 1959, The Liturgical Press
Tune: GOTT VATER SEI GEPRIESEN, 7 6 7 6 with refrain; *Limburg Gesangbuch,* 1838; harm. by Healey Willan, 1880-1968, © 1958,
Ralph Jusko Publications, Inc.

480 Jesus, My Lord, My God, My All

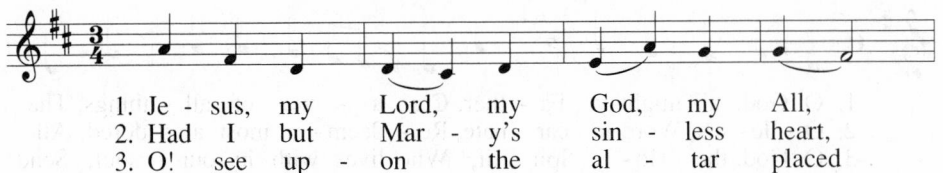

1. Je - sus, my Lord, my God, my All,
2. Had I but Mar - y's sin - less heart,
3. O! see up - on the al - tar placed

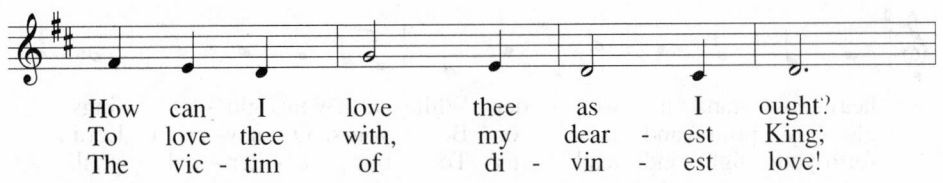

How can I love thee as I ought?
To love thee with, my dear - est King;
The vic - tim of di - vin - est love!

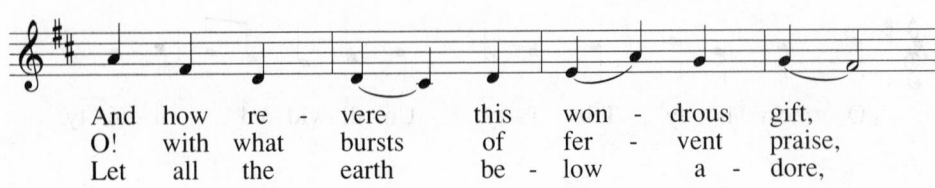

And how re - vere this won - drous gift,
O! with what bursts of fer - vent praise,
Let all the earth be - low a - dore,

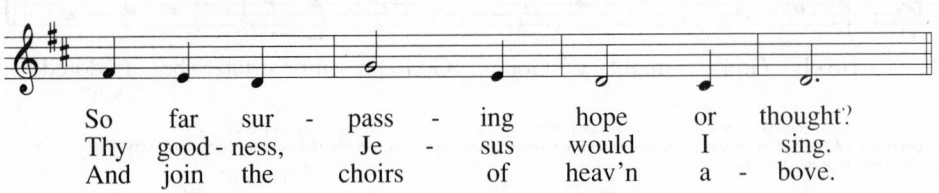

So far sur - pass - ing hope or thought?
Thy good - ness, Je - sus would I sing.
And join the choirs of heav'n a - bove.

Sweet Sac - ra - ment, we thee a - dore! O make us love thee

more and more! O make us love thee more and more.

Text: St. 1-2, Frederick W. Faber, 1814-1863; st. 3, *Mediator Dei Hymnal*, 1955. © 1955, GIA Publications, Inc.
Tune: SWEET SACRAMENT, LM with refrain; *Romischkatholisches Gesangbuchlein*, 1826

Christ Is the King 481

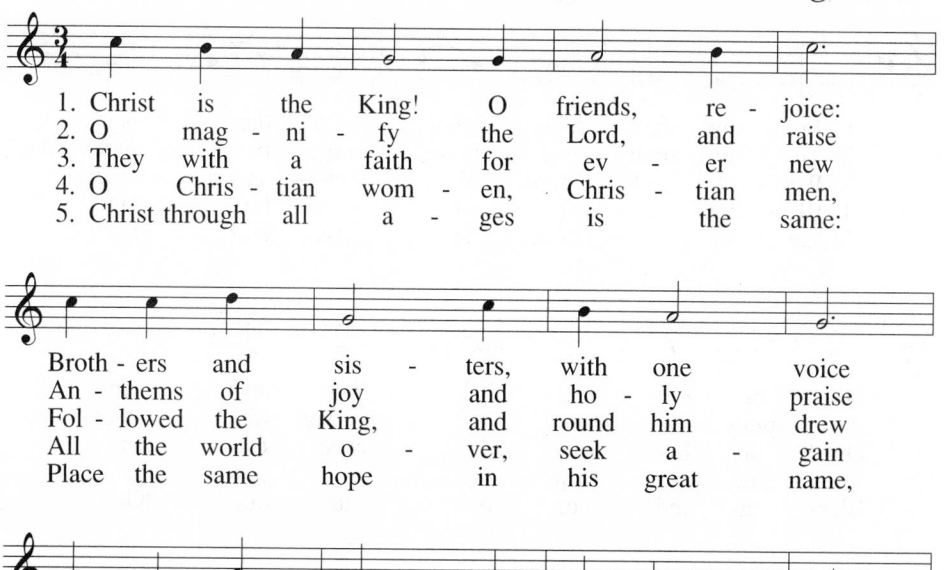

```
1. Christ    is     the    King!    O     friends,   re - joice:
2. O         mag - ni -  fy     the    Lord,      and   raise
3. They      with    a     faith    for    ev -      er    new
4. O         Chris - tian  wom - en,     Chris -    tian  men,
5. Christ through  all    a -   ges    is         the   same:
```

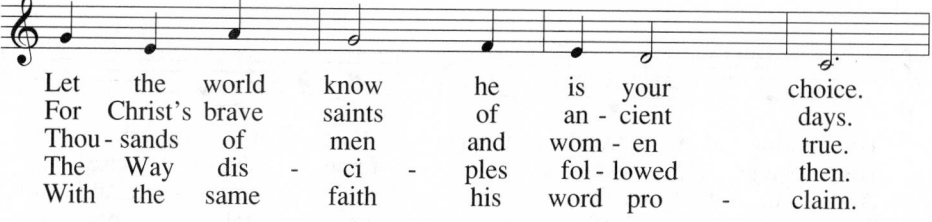

```
Broth - ers    and     sis  -  ters,    with    one        voice
An - thems     of      joy      and     ho - ly           praise
Fol - lowed    the     King,    and     round   him        drew
All      the   world    o  -   ver,     seek    a -        gain
Place    the   same    hope     in      his     great      name,
```

```
Let      the   world   know     he      is    your        choice.
For   Christ's brave   saints   of      an - cient        days.
Thou - sands   of      men      and     wom - en           true.
The   Way      dis -   ci -  ples      fol - lowed        then.
With     the   same    faith    his     word pro -        claim.
```

```
Al - le - lu - ia,        al - le - lu - ia,        al - le - lu - ia.
```

6. Let love's all reconciling might
Your scattered companies unite
In service to the Lord of light.
Alleluia, alleluia, alleluia.

7. So shall God's will on earth be done,
New lamps be lit, new tasks begun,
And the whole Church at last be one.
Alleluia, alleluia, alleluia.

Text: George K. A. Bell, 1883-1958, alt., © Oxford University Press
Tune: GELOBT SEI GOTT, 888 with alleluias; Melchior Vulpius, c. 1560-1616

482 Jesus Shall Reign

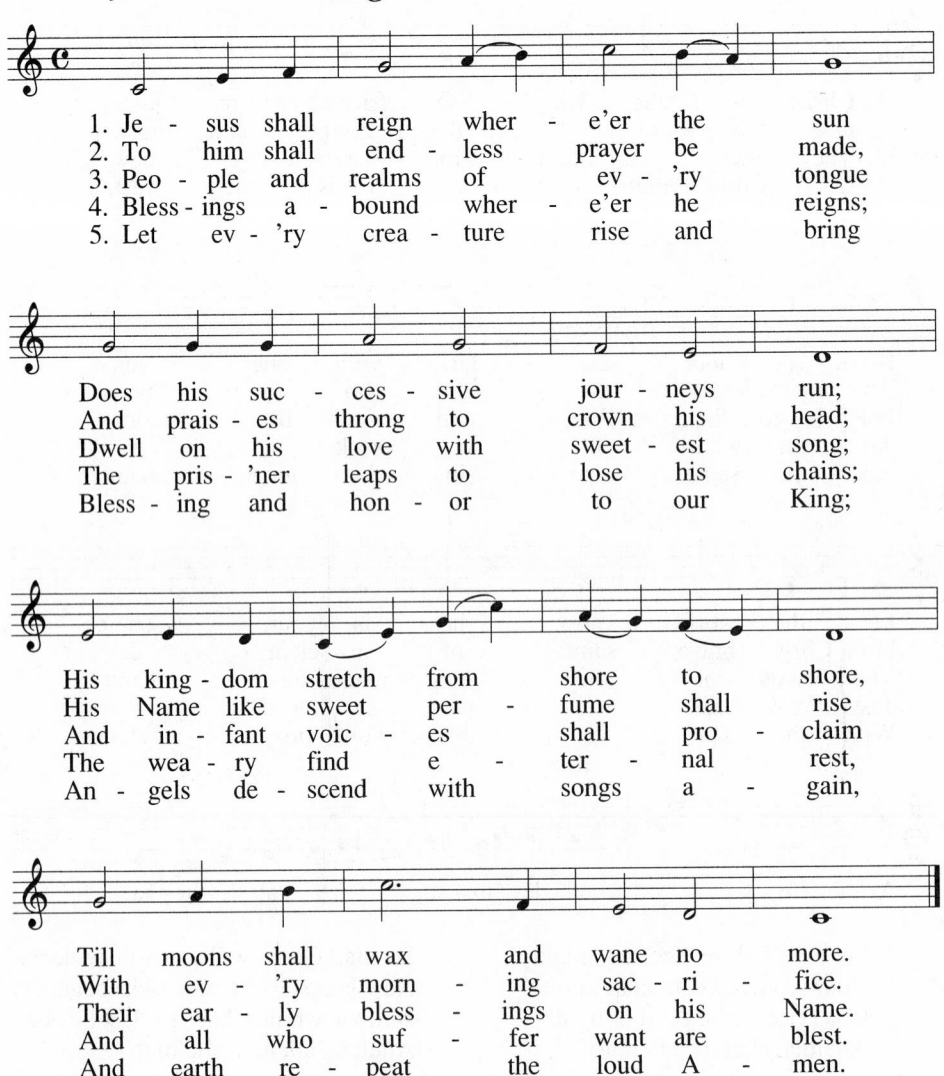

1. Je - sus shall reign wher - e'er the sun
2. To him shall end - less prayer be made,
3. Peo - ple and realms of ev - 'ry tongue
4. Bless - ings a - bound wher - e'er he reigns;
5. Let ev - 'ry crea - ture rise and bring

Does his suc - ces - sive jour - neys run;
And prais - es throng to crown his head;
Dwell on his love with sweet - est song;
The pris - 'ner leaps to lose his chains;
Bless - ing and hon - or to our King;

His king - dom stretch from shore to shore,
His Name like sweet per - fume shall rise
And in - fant voic - es shall pro - claim
The wea - ry find e - ter - nal rest,
An - gels de - scend with songs a - gain,

Till moons shall wax and wane no more.
With ev - 'ry morn - ing sac - ri - fice.
Their ear - ly bless - ings on his Name.
And all who suf - fer want are blest.
And earth re - peat the loud A - men.

Text: Isaac Watts, 1674-1748, alt.
Tune: DUKE STREET, LM; John Hatton, c.1710-1793

The Carpenter 483

Refrain

This   Je - sus Christ,   who   can he be,   what

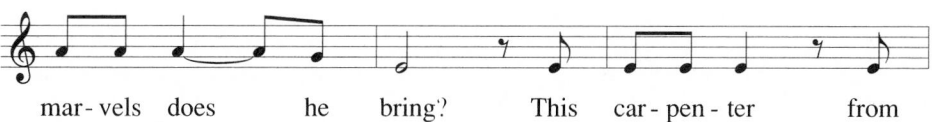

mar-vels does   he   bring?   This car-pen-ter   from

Gal - i - lee,   we   know him as   our   king.

Verses

1. They brought their sick, he made them well.
   He told their dead to rise.
   But on his cross few words he'd tell
   Till death announced its prize.

2. He brought glad tidings to the poor,
   And healed them in their fears.
   But Laz'rus died too soon for cure;
   And Jesus too shed tears.

3. He'd taken on our poverty,
   A migrant's life he led. But said to God,
   "All comes from thee.
   A banquet you have spread."

4. "O yes, a banquet's spread for me,
   In sight of ev'ry foe:
   For love has grown from death's high tree:
   O let that love now flow."

Text: John Foley, SJ, b.1939
Tune: John Foley, SJ, b.1939

484 All Hail the Power of Jesus' Name

1. All hail the power of Je - sus' name! Let
2. Crown him, ye mar - tyrs of our God, Who
3. Ye cho - sen seed of Is - rael's race, A
4. O that, with yon - der sa - cred throng, We

an - gels pros - trate fall; Bring forth the roy - al
from his al - tar call; Ex - tol the stem of
rem - nant weak and small, Hail him who saved you
at his feet may fall, Join in the ev - er -

di - a - dem And crown him Lord of
Jes - se's rod, And crown him Lord of
by his grace, And crown him Lord of
last - ing song, And crown him Lord of

all; And crown him Lord of all; And
all; And crown him Lord of all; And
all; And crown him Lord of all; And
all; And crown him Lord of all; And

crown him Lord of all; Bring forth the roy - al
crown him Lord of all; Ex - tol the stem of
crown him Lord of all; Hail him who saved you
crown him Lord of all; Join in the ev - er -

di - a - dem And crown him Lord of all.
Jes - se's rod, And crown him Lord of all.
by his grace, And crown him Lord of all.
last - ing song, And crown him Lord of all.

Text: Edward Perronet, 1726-1792; alt. by John Rippon, 1751-1836, alt.
Tune: DIADEM, CM with repeats; from the *Primitive Baptist Hymn and Tune Book*, 1902; harm. by Richard Proulx, b.1937, © 1975,
GIA Publications, Inc.

Crown Him with Many Crowns 485

1. Crown him with man - y crowns, The Lamb up - on his
2. Crown him the Lord of life, Who tri - umphed o'er the
3. Crown him the Lord of love, Be - hold his hands and
4. Crown him the Lord of peace, Whose power a scep - ter
5. Crown him the Lord of years, The ris - en Lord sub -

throne; Hark! how the heav'n - ly an - them drowns All
grave, And rose vic - to - rious in the strife For
side, Rich wounds yet vis - i - ble a - bove In
sways From pole to pole, that wars may cease, Ab -
lime, Cre - a - tor of the roll - ing spheres, The

mu - sic but its own. A - wake, my soul, and sing Of
those he came to save. His glo - ries now we sing, Who
beau - ty glo - ri - fied. No an - gel in the sky Can
sorbed in prayer and praise. His reign shall know no end, And
Mas - ter of all time. All hail, Re - deem - er, hail! For

him who set us free, And hail him as your
died and rose on high, Who died, e - ter - nal
ful - ly bear that sight, But down - ward bends his
round his pierc - ed feet Fair flow'rs of Par - a -
you have died for me; Your praise and glo - ry

heav'n - ly King Through all e - ter - ni - ty.
life to bring, And lives that death may die.
burn - ing eye At mys - ter - ies so bright.
dise ex - tend Their fra - grance ev - er sweet.
shall not fail Through - out e - ter - ni - ty.

Text: Revelation 19:12; St. 1, 3-5, Matthew Bridges, 1800-1894; St. 2, Godfrey Thring, 1823-1903
Tune: DIADEMATA, SMD.; George J. Elvey, 1816-1893

486 The King of Glory

The King of glo - ry comes, the na - tion re - joic - es.

O - pen the gates be - fore him, lift up your voic - es.

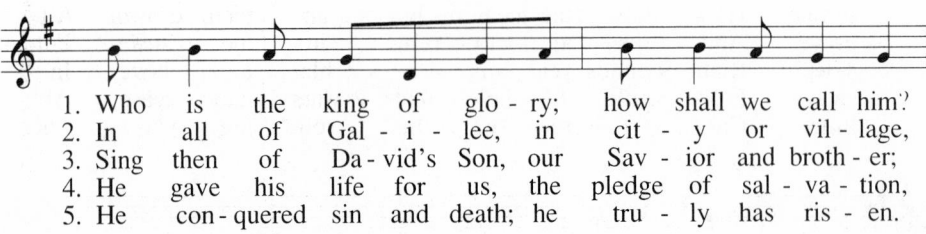

1. Who is the king of glo - ry; how shall we call him?
2. In all of Gal - i - lee, in cit - y or vil - lage,
3. Sing then of Da - vid's Son, our Sav - ior and broth - er;
4. He gave his life for us, the pledge of sal - va - tion,
5. He con - quered sin and death; he tru - ly has ris - en.

D.C.

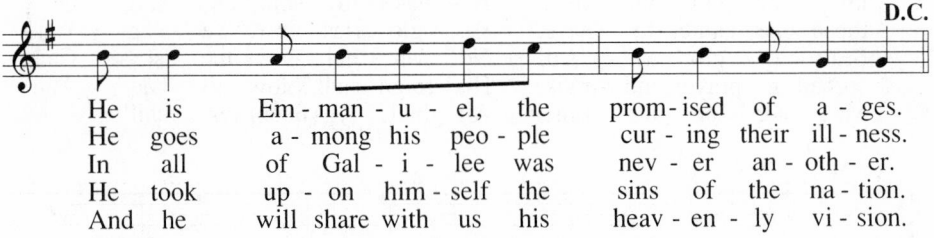

He is Em - man - u - el, the prom - ised of a - ges.
He goes a - mong his peo - ple cur - ing their ill - ness.
In all of Gal - i - lee was nev - er an - oth - er.
He took up - on him - self the sins of the na - tion.
And he will share with us his heav - en - ly vi - sion.

Text: Willard F. Jabusch, b. 1930, © 1966, 1984
Tune: KING OF GLORY, 12 12 with refrain; Israeli; harm. by Richard Proulx, b.1937, © 1986, GIA Publications, Inc.

Rejoice, the Lord Is King   487

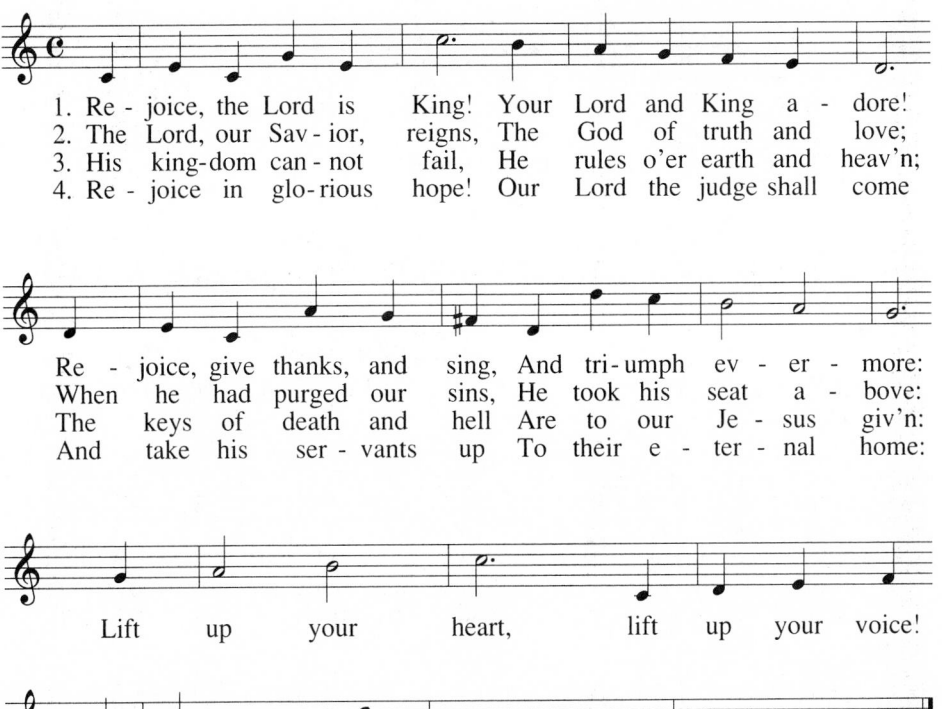

1. Re - joice, the Lord is King! Your Lord and King a - dore!
2. The Lord, our Sav - ior, reigns, The God of truth and love;
3. His king-dom can - not fail, He rules o'er earth and heav'n;
4. Re - joice in glo - rious hope! Our Lord the judge shall come

Re - joice, give thanks, and sing, And tri-umph ev - er - more:
When he had purged our sins, He took his seat a - bove:
The keys of death and hell Are to our Je - sus giv'n:
And take his ser - vants up To their e - ter - nal home:

Lift up your heart, lift up your voice!

Re - joice, a - gain I say, re - joice!

Text: Charles Wesley, 1707-1788
Tune: DARWALL'S 148TH, 6 6 6 6 88; John Darwall, 1731-1789; harm. from *The Hymnal 1940*

488　To Jesus Christ, Our Sovereign King

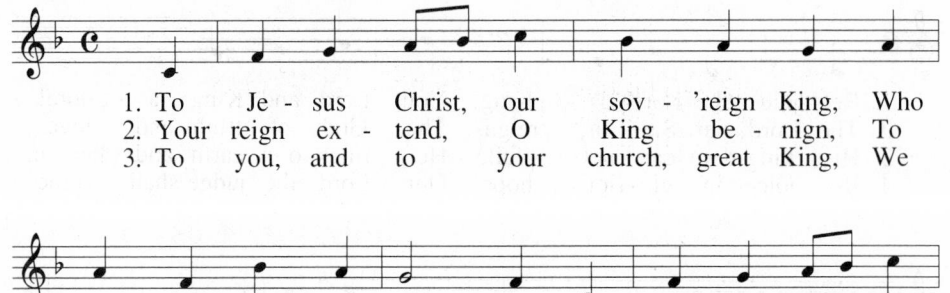

1. To Je - sus Christ, our sov - 'reign King, Who
2. Your reign ex - tend, O King be - nign, To
3. To you, and to your church, great King, We

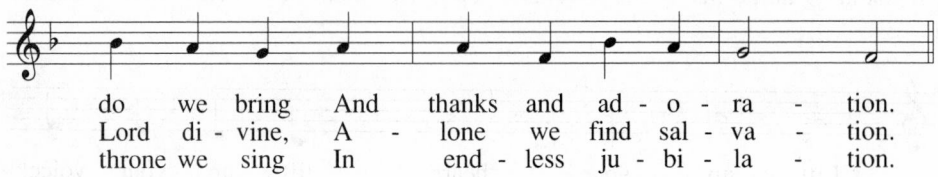

is the world's sal - va - tion, All praise and hom - age
ev - 'ry land and na - tion; For in your King - dom,
pledge our heart's ob - la - tion; Un - til be - fore your

do we bring And thanks and ad - o - ra - tion.
Lord di - vine, A - lone we find sal - va - tion.
throne we sing In end - less ju - bi - la - tion.

Christ Je - sus, Vic - tor! Christ Je - sus, Ru - ler!

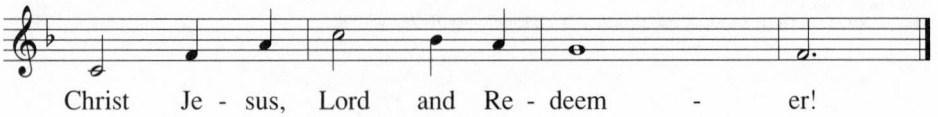

Christ Je - sus, Lord and Re - deem - er!

Text: Martin B. Hellrigel, 1891-1981, alt., © 1941, Irene C. Mueller
Tune: ICH GLAUB AN GOTT, 8 7 8 7 with refrain; *Mainz Gesangbuch*, 1870; harm. by Richard Proulx, b.1937, © 1986, GIA Publications, Inc.

The Stars Declare His Glory 489

1. The stars de - clare his glo - ry; The vault of heav - en
2. The dawn re - turns in splen - dor, The heav - ens burn and
3. So shine the Lord's com - mand - ments To make the sim - ple
4. So or - der too this life of mine, Di - rect it all my

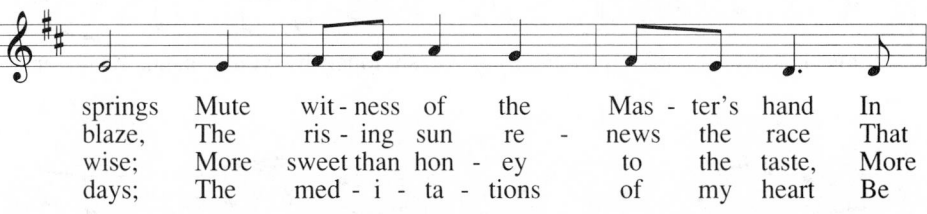

springs Mute wit - ness of the Mas - ter's hand In
blaze, The ris - ing sun re - news the race That
wise; More sweet than hon - ey to the taste, More
days; The med - i - ta - tions of my heart Be

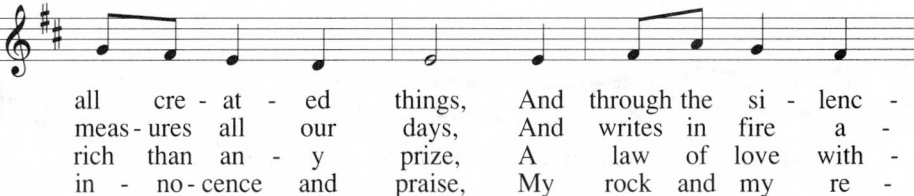

all cre - at - ed things, And through the si - lenc -
meas - ures all our days, And writes in fire a -
rich than an - y prize, A law of love with -
in - no - cence and praise, My rock and my re -

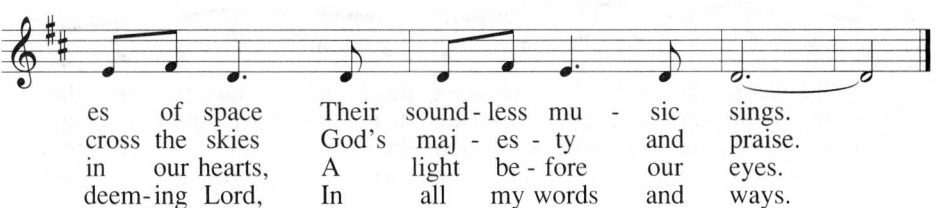

es of space Their sound - less mu - sic sings.
cross the skies God's maj - es - ty and praise.
in our hearts, A light be - fore our eyes.
deem - ing Lord, In all my words and ways.

Text: Psalm 19; Timothy Dudley-Smith, b.1926, © 1981, Hope Publishing Co.
Tune: DEERFIELD, 7 6 8 6 8 6; David Haas, b.1957, © 1986, GIA Publications, Inc.

490 Song at the Center

Refrain

From the cor-ners of cre - a - tion to the cen-ter where we stand, Let all

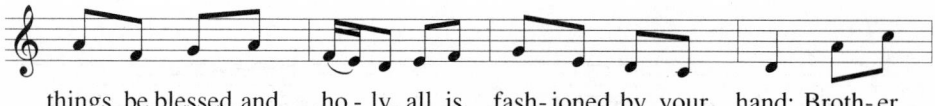

things be blessed and ho - ly, all is fash-ioned by your hand; Broth-er

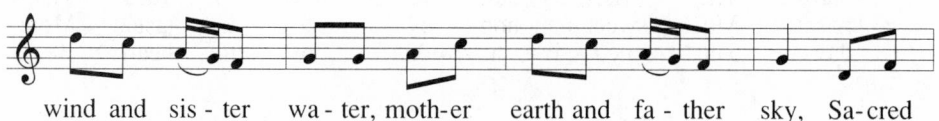

wind and sis - ter wa-ter, moth-er earth and fa - ther sky, Sa-cred

plants and sa-cred crea - tures, sa-cred peo - ple of the land.

Verses

1. In the east, the place of dawn-ing, there is beau - ty in the
2. In the south, the place of grow-ing, there is wis-dom in the
3. In the north, the place of wis - dom, there is ho - ly dark-ness
4. In the west, the place of see - ing, there is born a vi - sion

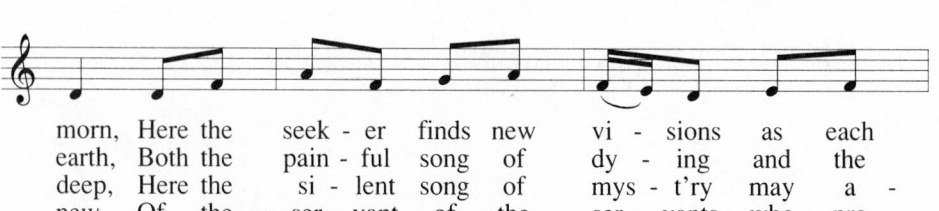

morn, Here the seek - er finds new vi - sions as each
earth, Both the pain - ful song of dy - ing and the
deep, Here the si - lent song of mys - t'ry may a -
new Of the ser - vant of the ser - vants, who pro -

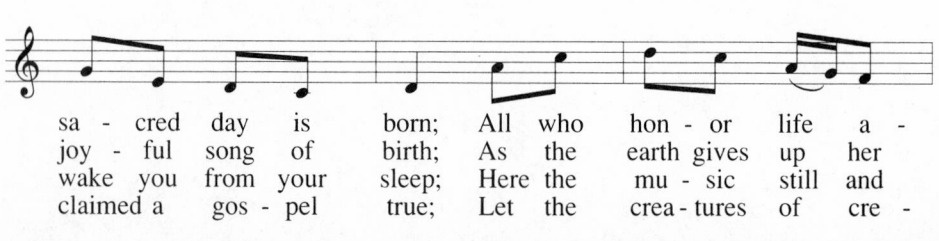

sa - cred day is born; All who hon - or life a -
joy - ful song of birth; As the earth gives up her
wake you from your sleep; Here the mu - sic still and
claimed a gos - pel true; Let the crea-tures of cre -

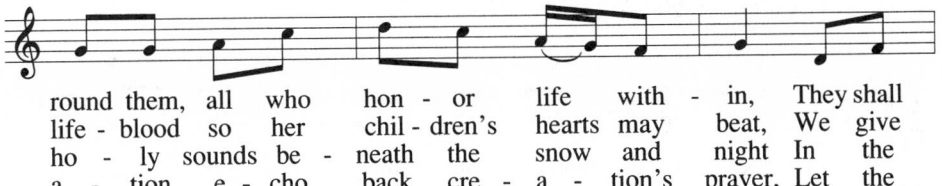

round them, all   who   hon - or   life   with - in,   They shall
life - blood so   her   chil - dren's hearts may beat, We give
ho - ly sounds be - neath the   snow and   night In   the
a   - tion e - cho back   cre - a - tion's prayer, Let   the

D.C.

shine with light and   glo - ry when the morn - ing breaks a - gain.
back to   her   our   rev - 'rence ho - ly ground be - neath our   feet.
ones who wait with   pa - tience for the com - ing of   the   light.
Spir - it now breathe through us and   re - store the   sa - cred there.

Text: Marty Haugen, b.1950
Tune: DEBORAH, 8 7 8 7 D with refrain; Marty Haugen, b.1950
© 1993, GIA Publications, Inc.

491 God, beyond All Names

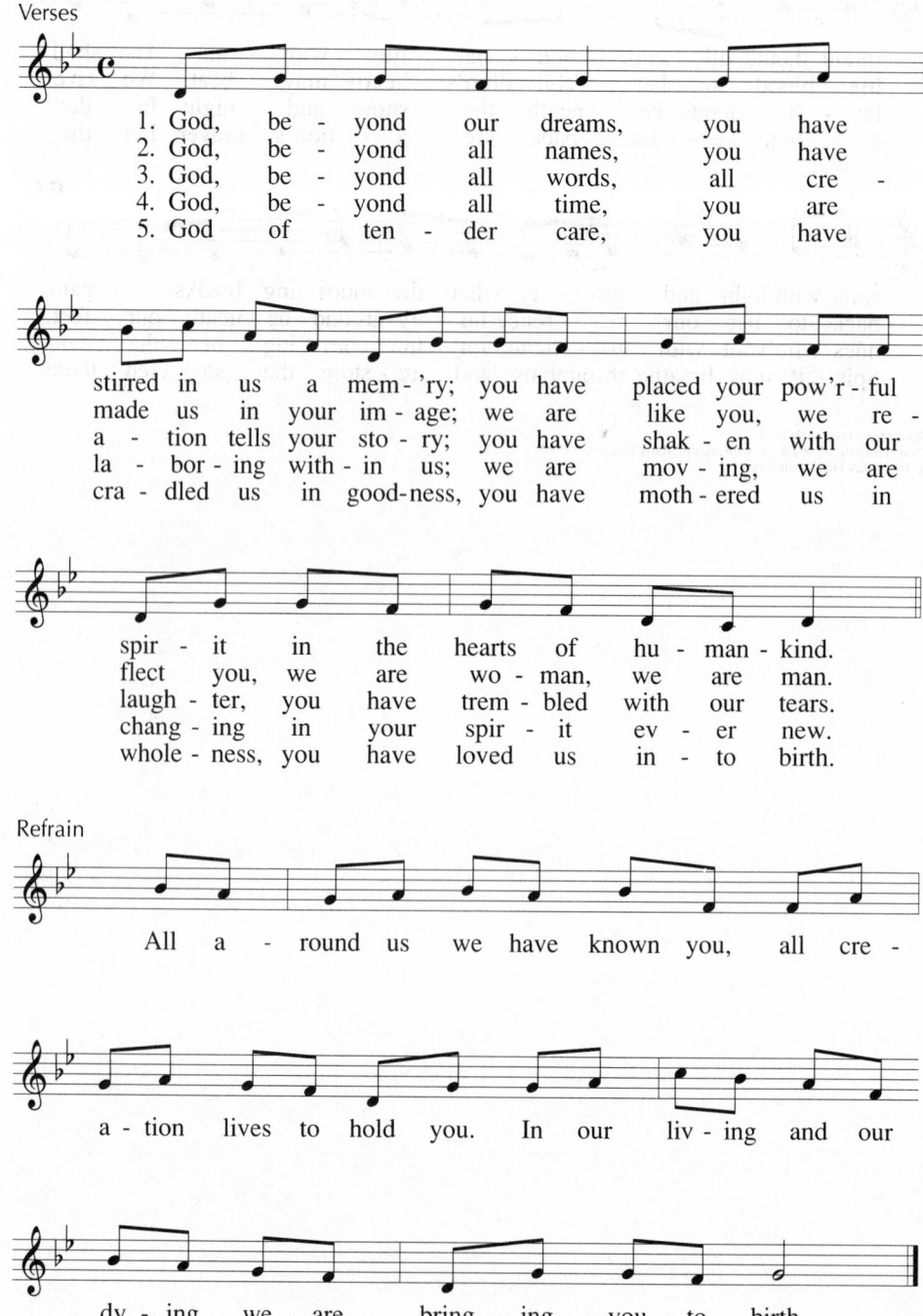

Verses

1. God, be - yond our dreams, you have
2. God, be - yond all names, you have
3. God, be - yond all words, all cre -
4. God, be - yond all time, you are
5. God of ten - der care, you have

stirred in us a mem - 'ry; you have placed your pow'r - ful
made us in your im - age; we are like you, we re -
a - tion tells your sto - ry; you have shak - en with our
la - bor - ing with - in us; we are mov - ing, we are
cra - dled us in good-ness, you have moth - ered us in

spir - it in the hearts of hu - man - kind.
flect you, we are wo - man, we are man.
laugh - ter, you have trem - bled with our tears.
chang - ing in your spir - it ev - er new.
whole - ness, you have loved us in - to birth.

Refrain

All a - round us we have known you, all cre -

a - tion lives to hold you. In our liv - ing and our

dy - ing we are bring - ing you to birth.

Text: Bernadette Farrell, b.1957
Tune: Bernadette Farrell, b.1957
© 1990, Bernadette Farrell, published by OCP Publications

All You Works of God   492

Refrain

All you works of God, ev-'ry moun-tain, star and tree, bless the One who shapes your beau-ty, who has caused you all to be one great song of love and grace, ev-er an - cient, ev-er new. Raise your voic-es, all you works of God!

Verses

Soloist: ... *All:* ... *Soloist:*

1. Sun and moon: Stars of heav-en:
2. Winds of God: Cold and win-ter:
3. Night and day: Light and dark-ness:
4. All the earth: Bless your Mak - er! Hills and moun-tains:
5. Wells and springs: Seas and riv-ers:
6. Fly - ing birds: Beasts and cat-tle:
7. All who live: Men and wom-en:

All: ... *Soloist:*

	Show - ers	and	dew:
Chant your praise!	Snow - storms	and	ice:
	Light - nings	and	clouds:
	Green things	that	grow:
	Whales in	the	deep:
	Chil - dren	at	play:
	Ser - vants	of	God:

All: **D.C.**

Raise up your joy - ful song.

Text: Marty Haugen, b.1950
Tune: Marty Haugen, b.1950

493 The Works of the Lord Are Created in Wisdom

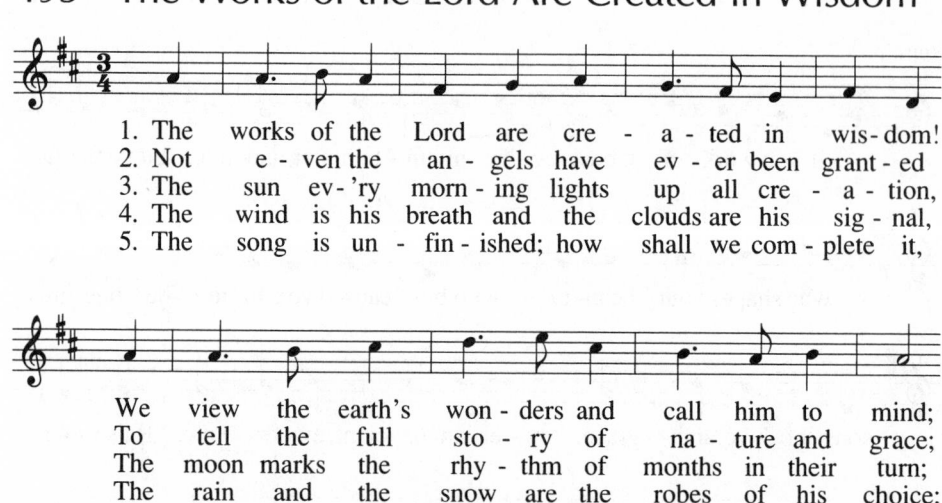

1. The works of the Lord are cre - a - ted in wis-dom!
2. Not e - ven the an - gels have ev - er been grant - ed
3. The sun ev- 'ry morn - ing lights up all cre - a - tion,
4. The wind is his breath and the clouds are his sig - nal,
5. The song is un - fin - ished; how shall we com - plete it,

We view the earth's won - ders and call him to mind;
To tell the full sto - ry of na - ture and grace;
The moon marks the rhy - thm of months in their turn;
The rain and the snow are the robes of his choice;
And where find the skill to per - fect all his praise?

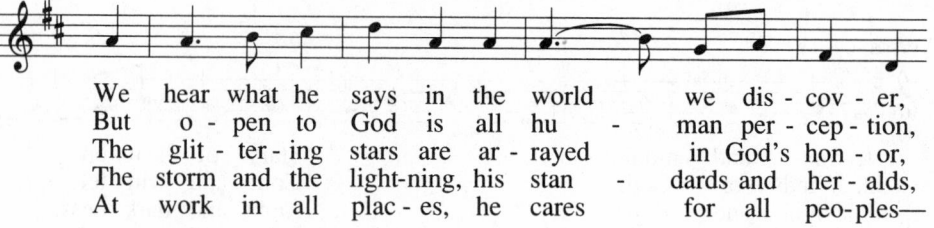

We hear what he says in the world we dis - cov - er,
But o - pen to God is all hu - man per - cep - tion,
The glit - ter - ing stars are ar - rayed in God's hon - or,
The storm and the light-ning, his stan - dards and her - alds,
At work in all plac - es, he cares for all peo-ples—

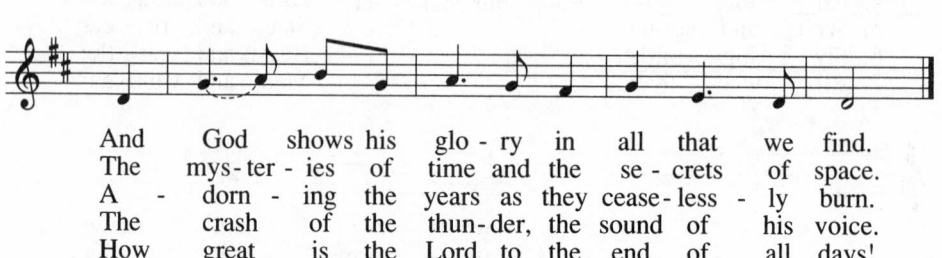

And God shows his glo - ry in all that we find.
The mys-ter - ies of time and the se - crets of space.
A - dorn - ing the years as they cease-less - ly burn.
The crash of the thun-der, the sound of his voice.
How great is the Lord to the end of all days!

Text: Ecclesiastes 42-43; Christopher Idle, b.1938, © 1982, Hope Publishing Co.
Tune: KREMSER, 12 11 12 11; *Neder-landtsch Gedanckclank*, 1626; harm. by Edward Kremser, 1838-1914

How Great Thou Art 494

1. O Lord my God, when I in awe-some won-der Con-sid-er all the worlds Thy hands have made, I see the stars, I hear the roll-ing thun-der, Thy pow'r thru-out the un-i-verse dis-played!

2. When thru the woods and for-est glades I wan-der And hear the birds sing sweet-ly in the trees, When I look down from loft-y moun-tain gran-deur And hear the brook and feel the gen-tle breeze.

3. And when I think that God, His Son not spar-ing, Sent Him to die, I scarce can take it in, That on the cross, my bur-den glad-ly bear-ing, He bled and died to take a-way my sin!

4. When Christ shall come with shout of ac-cla-ma-tion And take me home, what joy shall fill my heart! Then I shall bow in hum-ble ad-o-ra-tion And there pro-claim, my God, how great Thou art!

Then sings my soul, my Sav-ior God, to Thee; How great Thou art, how great Thou art! Then sings my soul, my Sav-ior God, to Thee; How great Thou art, How great Thou art!

Text: Stuart K. Hine, b.1899
Tune: O STORE GUD, 11 10 11 10 with refrain; Stuart K. Hine, b.1899

495 The Earth Is the Lord's

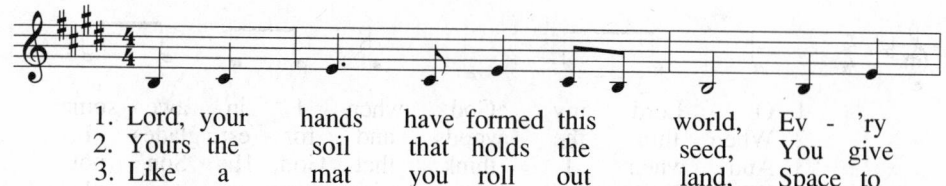

1. Lord, your hands have formed this world, Ev - 'ry
2. Yours the soil that holds the seed, You give
3. Like a mat you roll out land, Space to

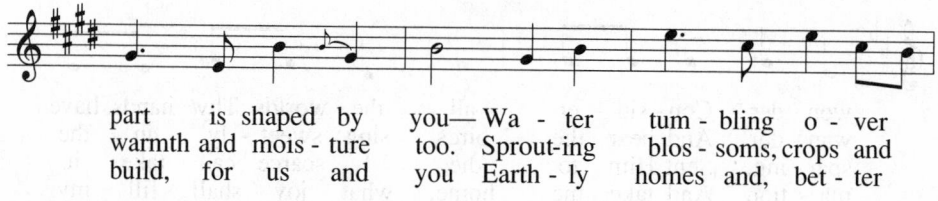

part is shaped by you— Wa - ter tum - bling o - ver
warmth and mois - ture too. Sprout-ing blos - soms, crops and
build, for us and you Earth - ly homes and, bet - ter

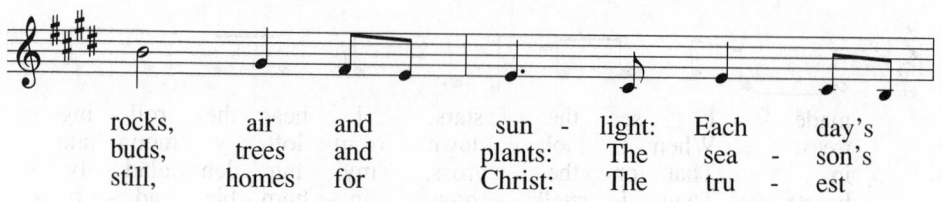

rocks, air and sun - light: Each day's
buds, trees and plants: The sea - son's
still, homes for Christ: The tru - est

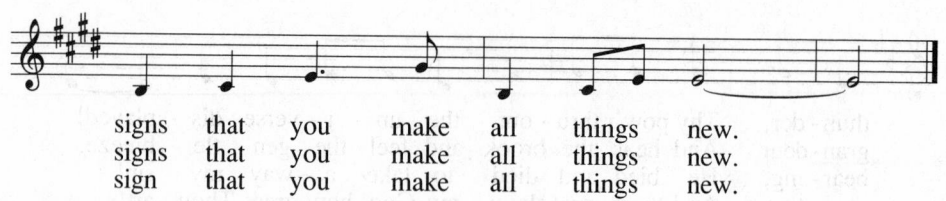

signs that you make all things new.
signs that you make all things new.
sign that you make all things new.

Text: Ramon and Sario Oliano; para. by James Minchin; trans. by Delebert Rice; © 1991, Ramon and Sario Oliano
Tune: GAYOM NI HIGAMI, 7 7 7 13; trad. Ikalahan melody; harm. © 1991, Iona Community, GIA Publications, Inc., agent

Canticle of the Sun   496

Refrain

The heav-ens are tell-ing the glo-ry of God, and all cre-a-tion is shout-ing for joy. Come, dance in the for-est, come, play in the field, and sing, sing to the glo-ry of the Lord.

Verses

1. Praise for the sun, the bring-er of day, He car-ries the light of the Lord in his rays; The moon and the stars who light up the way Un-to your throne.

2. Praise for the wind that blows through the trees, The seas might-y storms, the gen-tl-est breeze; They blow where they will, they blow where they please To please the Lord.

3. Praise for the rain that wa-ters our fields, And bless-es our crops so all the earth yields; From death un-to life her mys-t'ry re-vealed Springs forth in joy.

4. Praise for the fire who gives us his light, The warmth of the sun to bright-en our night; He danc-es with joy, his spir-it so bright, He sings of you.

5. Praise for the earth who makes life to grow, The crea-tures you made to let your life show; The flow-ers and trees that help us to know The heart of love.

6. Praise for our death that makes our life real, The knowl-edge of loss that helps us to feel; The gift of your-self, your pres-ence re-vealed To lead us home.

D.C.

Text: Marty Haugen, b.1950
Tune: Marty Haugen, b.1950
© 1980, GIA Publications, Inc.

497 God of All Creation

1. God of the o - cean and sea! Bathe us a - new with
2. God of the wind and the breeze! Breathe in our hearts the
3. God of the for - ests and trees! Col - or our lives with
4. God of the morn - ing and night! Gift all our days with
5. God of the plan - ets and stars! Pow - er our dreams and

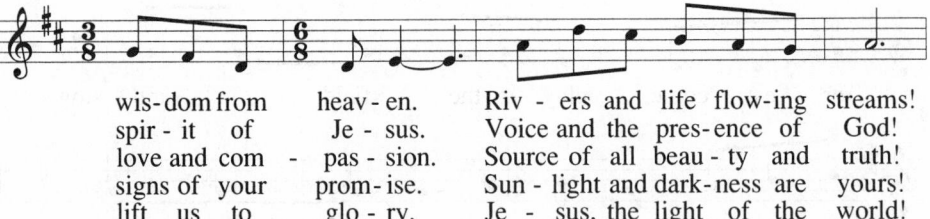

wis - dom from heav - en. Riv - ers and life flow-ing streams!
spir - it of Je - sus. Voice and the pres-ence of God!
love and com - pas - sion. Source of all beau - ty and truth!
signs of your prom - ise. Sun - light and dark-ness are yours!
lift us to glo - ry. Je - sus, the light of the world!

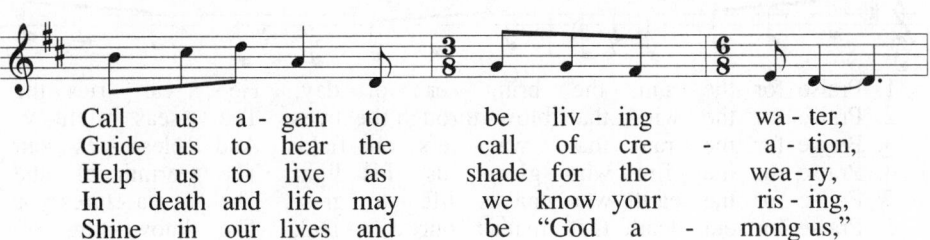

Call us a - gain to be liv - ing wa - ter,
Guide us to hear the call of cre - a - tion,
Help us to live as shade for the wea - ry,
In death and life may we know your ris - ing,
Shine in our lives and be "God a - mong us,"

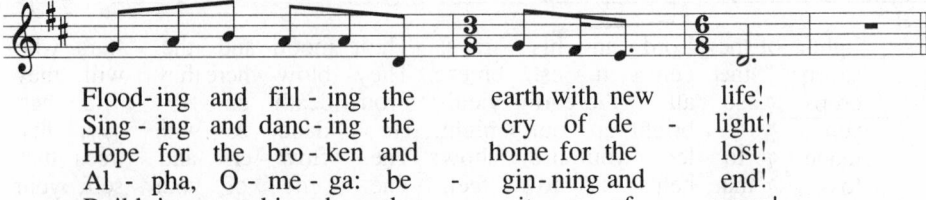

Flood - ing and fill - ing the earth with new life!
Sing - ing and danc - ing the cry of de - light!
Hope for the bro - ken and home for the lost!
Al - pha, O - me - ga: be - gin-ning and end!
Build - ing your king-dom, the cit - y of peace!

Text: David Haas, b.1957
Tune: CREATION, 7 10 7 10 10; David Haas, b. 1957; acc. by Jeanne Cotter, b.1964, alt.
© 1987, GIA Publications, Inc.

Many and Great 498

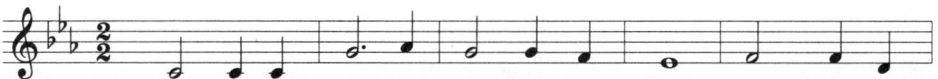

1. Man - y and great, O God, are your works, Mak - er of
2. Grant us com - mun- ion with you, our God, Though you tran -

earth and sky;   Your hands have set the
scend the stars.   Come close to us and

heav - ens with stars;   Your fin-gers spread the moun - tains and
stay by our side: With you are found the true gifts that

plains.   You mere - ly spoke and wa - ters were
last.   Bless us with life which nev - er shall

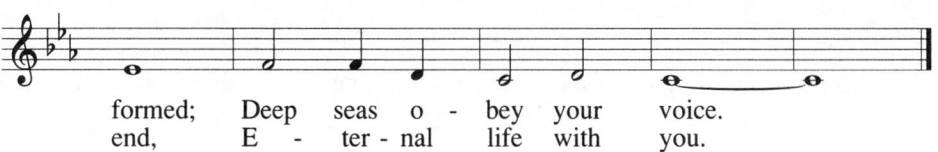

formed;   Deep seas o - bey your voice.
end,   E - ter - nal life with you.

Text: *Wakantanka tuku nitawa;* Dakota hymn; para. by Philip Frazier, 1892-1964, © 1916, Walton Music Corp.
Tune: LACQUIPARLE, 9 6 9 9 9 6; *Dakota Odowan,* 1879; acc. by John L. Bell, b.1949, © 1993, Iona Community, GIA Publications, Inc., agent

499 Sing Out, Earth and Skies

Verses

Cantor: *All:*

1. Come, O God of all the earth: Come to us, O
2. Come, O God of wind and flame: Fill the earth with
3. Come, O God of flash - ing light: Twin - kling star and
4. Come, O God of snow and rain: Show - er down up -
5. Come, O Jus - tice, Come, O Peace: Come and shape our

Cantor:

Right - eous One; Come, and bring our love to birth:
right - eous - ness; Teach us all to sing your name:
burn - ing sun; God of day and God of night:
on the earth; Come, O God of joy and pain:
hearts a - new; Come and make op - pres - sion cease:

All:

In the glo - ry of your Son.
May our lives your love con - fess.
In your light we all are one.
God of sor - row, God of mirth.
Bring us all to life in you.

Refrain

Sing out, earth and skies! Sing of the God who

loves you! Raise your joy - ful cries!

Dance to the life a - round you!

Text: Marty Haugen, b.1950
Tune: SING OUT, 7 7 7 7 with refrain; Marty Haugen, b.1950
© 1985, GIA Publications, Inc.

I Will Lift Up My Eyes 500

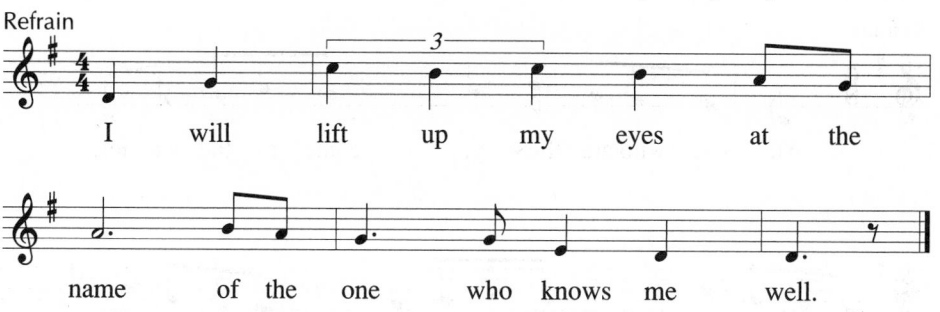

Refrain

I will lift up my eyes at the name of the one who knows me well.

Verses

1. You are my God, whom I seek with my life;
   for you I thirst, as the dry earth for water.
   Lifeless and parched,
   without you I am nowhere, no one at all.

2. Thus have I seen you in your holy house,
   with my own eyes, how faithful and sure.
   More than my life, your mercy endures
   longer than time.

3. Thus shall I bless you while I am alive;
   calling on you, my breath and my bread.
   And with a song through day and the darkness
   clinging to you.

4. And I shall see that day when his justice and pow'r
   will break the chains that bind me.
   And mine enemies' lies strewn broken and empty:
   his mighty hand, that awful grace.

Text: Psalm 63; Tom Conry, b.1951, alt.
Tune: Tom Conry, b.1951
© 1984, TEAM Publications, published by OCP Publications

501 All You Who Are Thirsty

Refrain

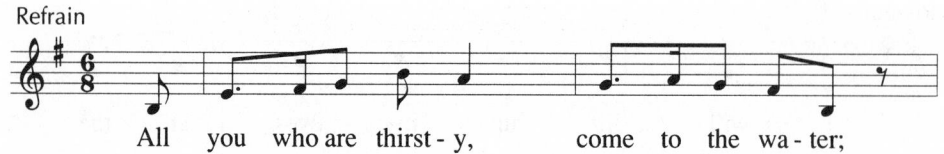

All you who are thirst-y, come to the wa-ter;

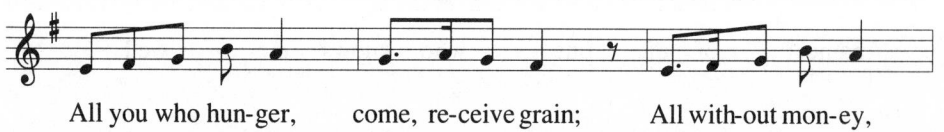

All you who hun-ger, come, re-ceive grain; All with-out mon-ey,

come with-out pay-ing; All you who heed me, come for rich fare.

Verses

Cantor or choir:

1. Come now and lis-ten that you may have life; my
2. Why spend your mon-ey for what is not bread, your
3. Drink of this wa-ter a - bun-dant with life and

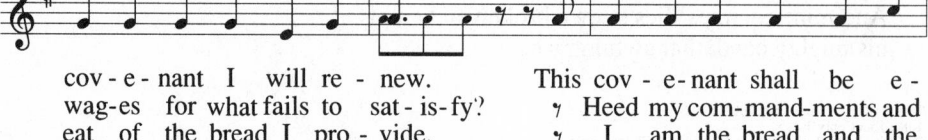

cov-e-nant I will re-new. This cov-e-nant shall be e-
wag-es for what fails to sat-is-fy? Heed my com-mand-ments and
eat of the bread I pro-vide. I am the bread, and the

D.C.

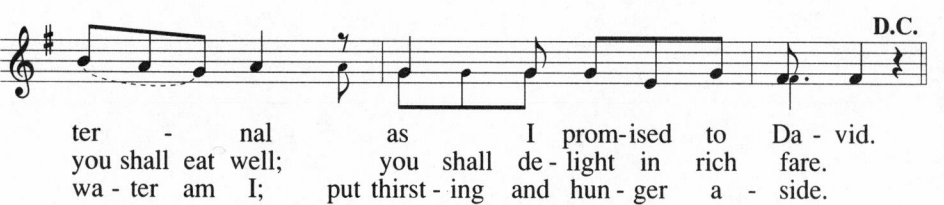

ter - nal as I prom-ised to Da-vid.
you shall eat well; you shall de-light in rich fare.
wa-ter am I; put thirst-ing and hun-ger a-side.

Text: Isaiah 55; adapt. by Michael Connolly, b.1955
Tune: Michael Connolly, b.1955
© 1982, 1988, GIA Publications, Inc.

Come to the Water 502

1. O let all who thirst, let them come to the
2. And let all who seek, let them come to the
3. And let all who toil, let them come to the
4. And let all the poor, let them come to the

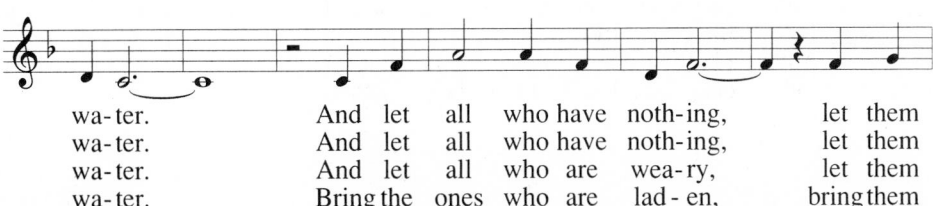

wa-ter. And let all who have noth-ing, let them
wa-ter. And let all who have noth-ing, let them
wa-ter. And let all who are wea-ry, let them
wa-ter. Bring the ones who are lad-en, bring them

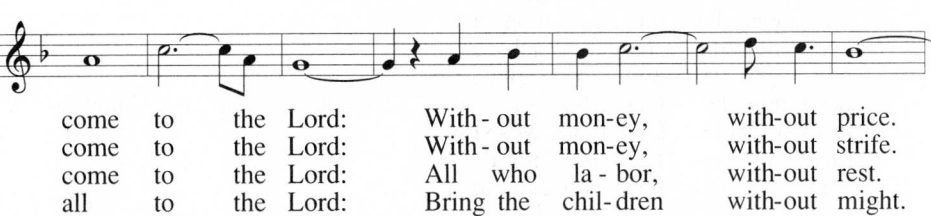

come to the Lord: With-out mon-ey, with-out price.
come to the Lord: With-out mon-ey, with-out strife.
come to the Lord: All who la-bor, with-out rest.
all to the Lord: Bring the chil-dren with-out might.

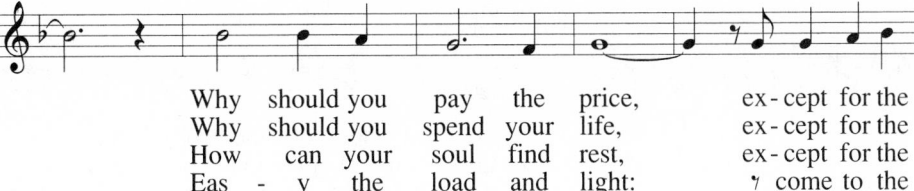

Why should you pay the price, ex-cept for the
Why should you spend your life, ex-cept for the
How can your soul find rest, ex-cept for the
Eas - y the load and light: come to the

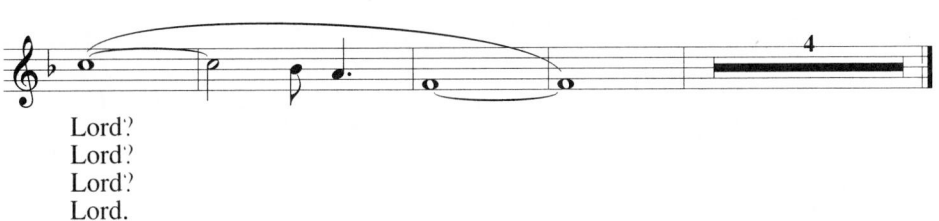

Lord?
Lord?
Lord?
Lord.

Text: Isaiah 55:1,2, Matthew 11:28-30; John Foley, SJ, b.1939
Tune: John Foley, SJ, b.1939
© 1978, John B. Foley, SJ, and New Dawn Music

503 Come to the Feast

1. Ho, ev - 'ry - one who thirsts:
   and ev - 'ry - one who la - bors:
2. Ho, ev - 'ry - one who seeks:
   and ev - 'ry - one who mourns:
3. Let all who seek their God: Come to the wa-ters!
   the ev - er - last - ing stream:
4. And you who are en - slaved:
   To all who live in fear:
5. And all who are op - pressed:
   and you, the lost and bro - ken:

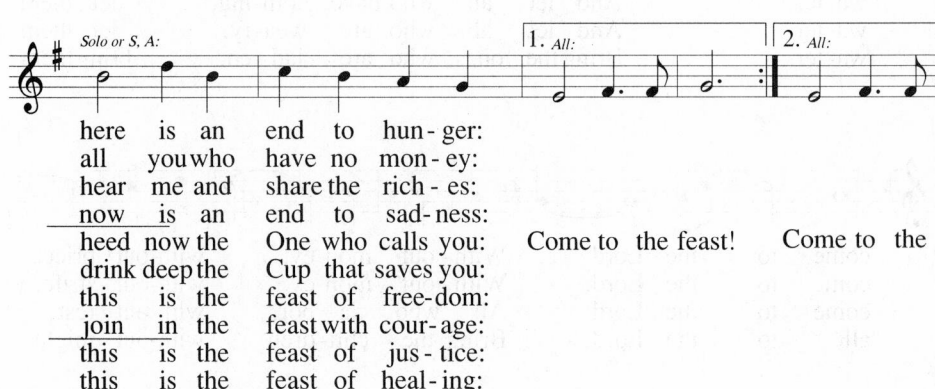

here is an end to hun-ger:
all you who have no mon-ey:
hear me and share the rich - es:
now is an end to sad-ness:
heed now the One who calls you: Come to the feast!   Come to the
drink deep the Cup that saves you:
this is the feast of free-dom:
join in the feast with cour-age:
this is the feast of jus - tice:
this is the feast of heal-ing:

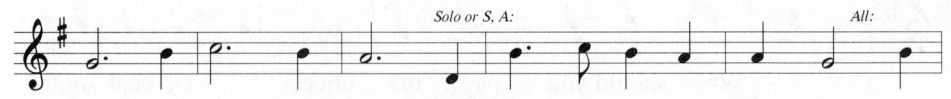

1. the wa - ters of the Jor - dan:
2. the streams of joy and glad - ness:
feast! For this is life: 3. the floods that o - ver-whelm you: For
4. the wa - ters that have freed you:
5. to die and rise in Je - sus:

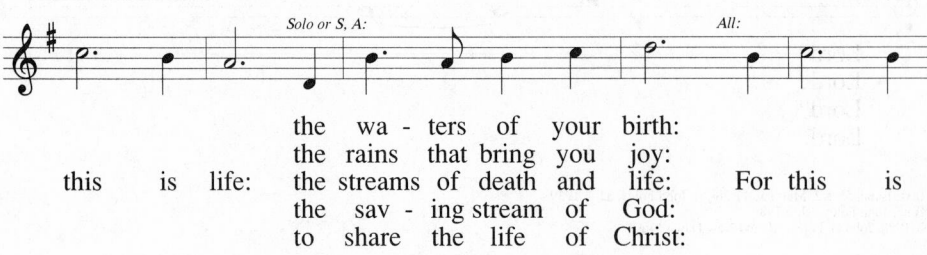

the wa - ters of your birth:
the rains that bring you joy:
this is life: the streams of death and life: For this is
the sav - ing stream of God:
to share the life of Christ:

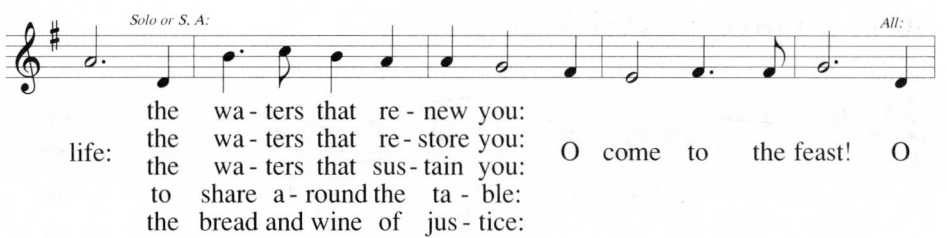

the wa - ters that re - new you:
life: the wa - ters that re - store you: O come to the feast! O
the wa - ters that sus - tain you:
to share a - round the ta - ble:
the bread and wine of jus - tice:

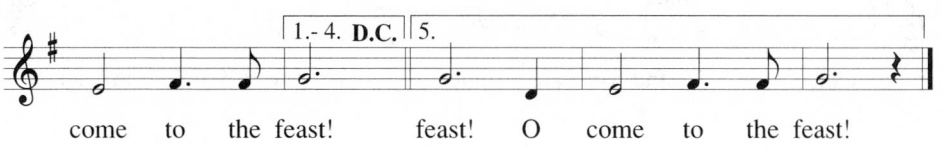

1.- 4. D.C. 5.

come to the feast! feast! O come to the feast!

Text: Isaiah 55; Marty Haugen, b.1950
Tune: Marty Haugen, b.1950
© 1991, GIA Publications, Inc.

504 I Have Loved You

Refrain

I have loved you with an ev-er-last-ing love, I have

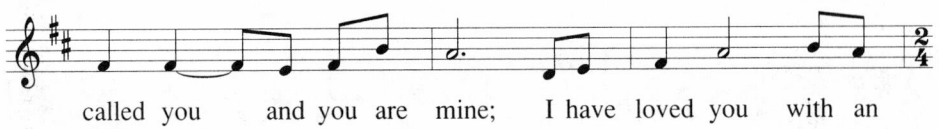

called you and you are mine; I have loved you with an

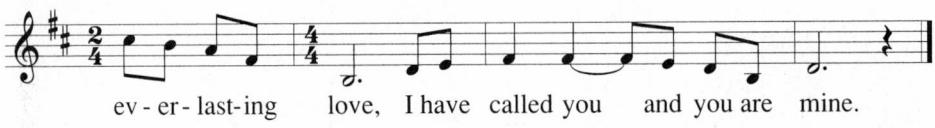

ev-er-last-ing love, I have called you and you are mine.

Verses

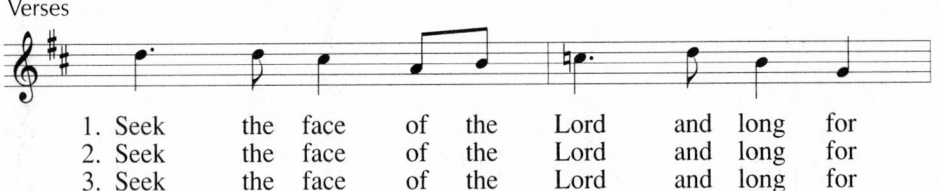

1. Seek the face of the Lord and long for
2. Seek the face of the Lord and long for
3. Seek the face of the Lord and long for

D.C.

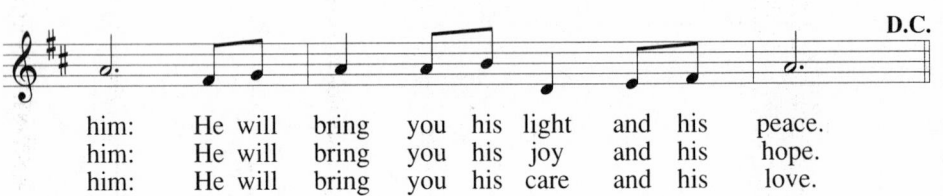

him: He will bring you his light and his peace.
him: He will bring you his joy and his hope.
him: He will bring you his care and his love.

Text: Jeremiah 31:3, Psalm 24:3; Michael Joncas, b.1951
Tune: Michael Joncas, b.1951
© 1979, New Dawn Music

You Are All We Have   505

Refrain

You are all we have. You give us what we need. Our

lives are in your hands, O Lord, our lives are in your hands.

Verses

1. Protect me, Lord; I come to you for safety.
   I say, "You are my God."
   All good things, Lord, all good things
   that I have come from you,
   the God of my salvation.

2. How wonderful are your gifts to me,
   how good they are!
   I praise the Lord who guides me
   and teaches me the way of truth and life.

3. You are near, the God I seek.
   Nothing can take me from your side.
   All my days I rest secure;
   you will show me the path that leads to life.

Text: Francis Patrick O'Brien, b.1958
Tune: Francis Patrick O'Brien, b.1958
© 1992, GIA Publications, Inc.

506 Immortal, Invisible, God Only Wise

1. Im - mor-tal, in - vis - i - ble, God on - ly wise,
2. Un - rest-ing, un - hast-ing, and si - lent as light,
3. Life - giv - ing Cre - a - tor of both great and small;
4. Great Fa - ther of glo - ry, pure Fa - ther of light,

In light in - ac - ces - si - ble hid from our eyes,
Nor want - ing, nor wast - ing, you rule day and night;
Of all life the mak - er, the true life of all;
Your an - gels a - dor - ing, all veil - ing their sight;

Most bless - ed, most glo - rious, the An - cient of Days,
Your jus - tice like moun - tains high soar - ing a - bove
We blos - som, then with - er as leaves on a tree,
We too, God in - vis - i - ble, of - fer our praise;

Al - might - y, vic - to - rious, your great name we praise.
Your clouds, which are foun-tains of good-ness and love.
But you live for ev - er, you are and will be.
O light in - ac - ces - si - ble, An - cient of Days!

Text: 1 Timothy 1:17; Walter C. Smith, 1824-1908, alt.
Tune: ST. DENIO, 11 11 11 11; Robert's *Canaidau y Cyssegr*, 1839

I Want to Walk as a Child of the Light   507

1. I want to walk as a child of the light.
2. I want to see the bright-ness of God.
3. I'm look-ing for the com-ing of Christ.

I want to fol - low Je - sus.
I want to look at Je - sus.
I want to be with Je - sus.

God set the stars to give light to the world. The
Clear sun of right-eous-ness shine on my path, And
When we have run with pa-tience the race, We

star of my life is Je - sus.
show me the way to the Fa - ther.
shall know the joy of Je - sus.

In him there is no dark - ness at all. The

night and the day are both a - like. The

Lamb is the light of the cit - y of God.

Shine in my heart, Lord Je - sus.

Text: Ephesians 5:8-10, Revelation 21:23, John 12: 46, 1 John 1:5, Hebrews 12:1; Kathleen Thomerson, b.1934, © 1970, 1975, Celebration
Tune: HOUSTON, 10 7 10 8 9 9 10 7; Kathleen Thomerson, b.1934, © 1970, 1975, Celebration; acc. by Robert J. Batastini, b.1942, © 1987, GIA
    Publications, Inc.

508 We Are the Light of the World

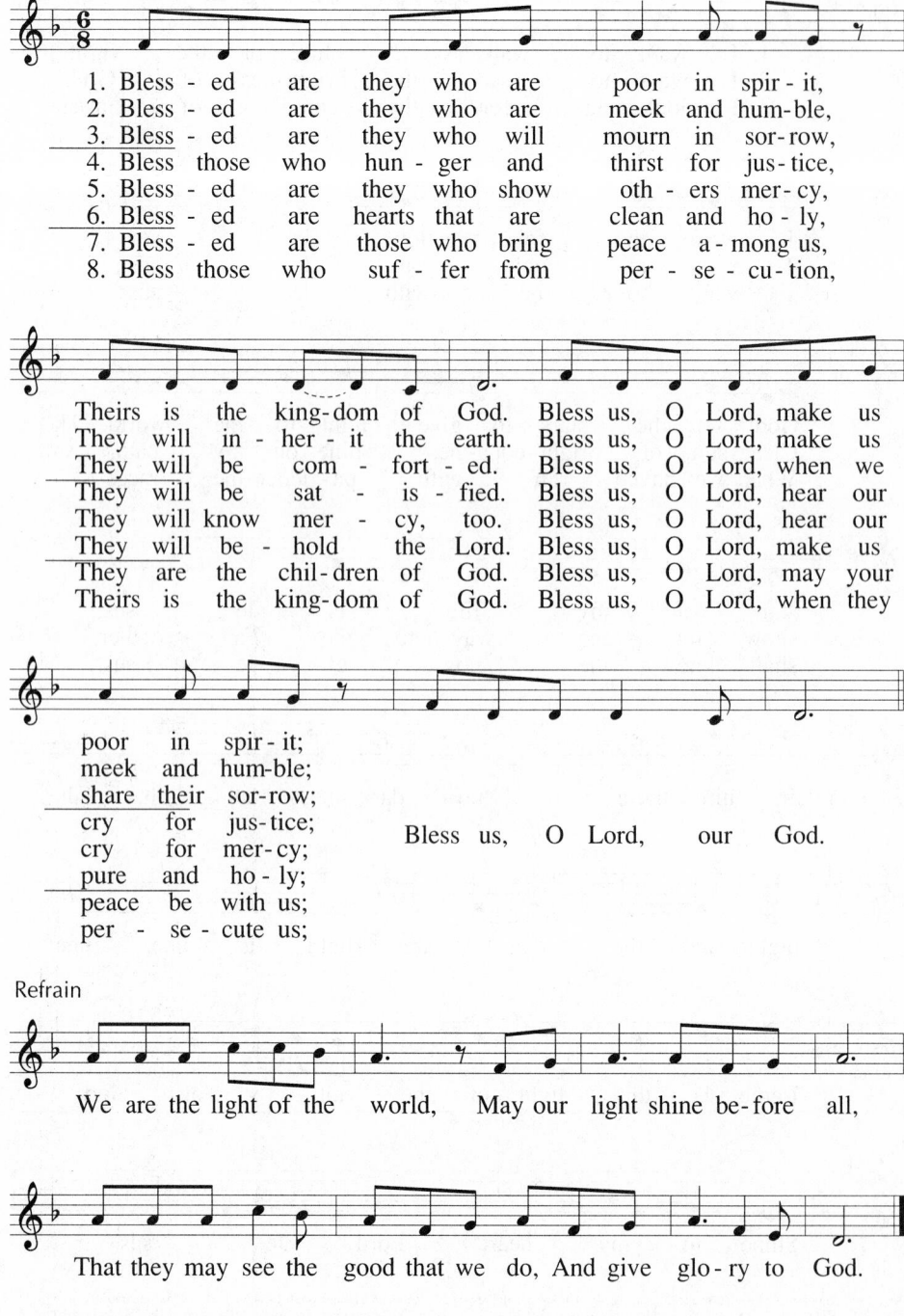

Verses

1. Bless - ed are they who are poor in spir - it,
2. Bless - ed are they who are meek and hum - ble,
3. Bless - ed are they who will mourn in sor - row,
4. Bless those who hun - ger and thirst for jus - tice,
5. Bless - ed are they who show oth - ers mer - cy,
6. Bless - ed are hearts that are clean and ho - ly,
7. Bless - ed are those who bring peace a - mong us,
8. Bless those who suf - fer from per - se - cu - tion,

Theirs is the king - dom of God. Bless us, O Lord, make us
They will in - her - it the earth. Bless us, O Lord, make us
They will be com - fort - ed. Bless us, O Lord, when we
They will be sat - is - fied. Bless us, O Lord, hear our
They will know mer - cy, too. Bless us, O Lord, hear our
They will be - hold the Lord. Bless us, O Lord, make us
They are the chil - dren of God. Bless us, O Lord, may your
Theirs is the king - dom of God. Bless us, O Lord, when they

poor in spir - it;
meek and hum - ble;
share their sor - row;
cry for jus - tice;
cry for mer - cy;   Bless us, O Lord, our God.
pure and ho - ly;
peace be with us;
per - se - cute us;

Refrain

We are the light of the world, May our light shine be - fore all,

That they may see the good that we do, And give glo - ry to God.

Text: Matthew 5:3-11, 14-16; Jean A. Greif, 1898-1981
Tune: Jean A. Greif, 1898-1981
© 1966, Vernacular Hymns Publishing Co.

Be Light for Our Eyes 509

Refrain

Come and be light for our eyes; be the air we
breathe, be the voice we speak! Come, be the song we
sing, be the path we seek!

Verses

1. Your life was giv - en; food for all peo - ple,
2. We hold your pres - ence, ris - en for ev - er!
3. Lead us to jus - tice, light in the dark - ness;

bod - y and blood, new life in our midst!
Your name now names us peo - ple of God!
sing - ing, pro - claim - ing Je - sus is Lord!

Death is no long - er, life is our fu - ture;
Filled with your vi - sion, peo - ple of mis - sion,
Teach us to speak, and help us to lis - ten

D.C.

Je - sus, Mes - si - ah, name of all names!
heal - ing, for - giv - ing; light for the world!
for when your truth and our dreams em - brace!

Text: David Haas, b.1957
Tune: David Haas, b.1957; keyboard arr. by David Haas, b.1957, and Marty Haugen, b.1950

510 I Am the Light of the World

Refrain

"I am the light of the world," says the Lord.

"They who fol-low me will have the light of life."

Verses

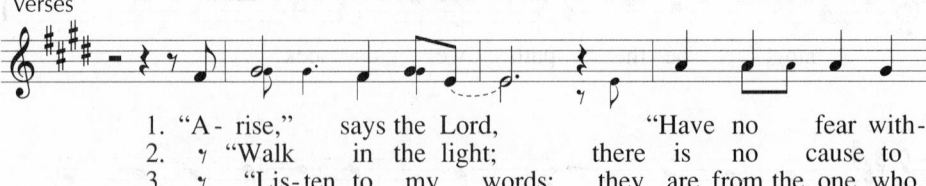

1. "A-rise," says the Lord, "Have no fear with-
2. ⁊ "Walk in the light; there is no cause to
3. ⁊ "Lis-ten to my words; they are from the one who

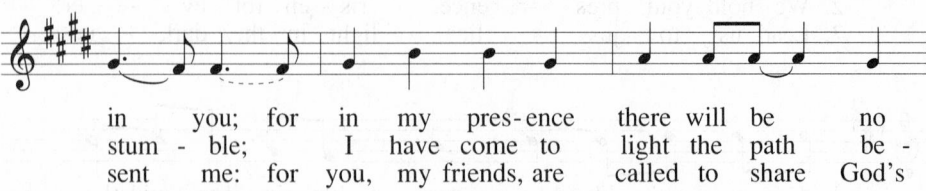

in you; for in my pres-ence there will be no
stum-ble; I have come to light the path be -
sent me: for you, my friends, are called to share God's

D.C.

dark - ness. I am the light of the world."
fore you. I am the light of the world."
glo - ry. You are the light of the world."

Text: John 8:12, Matthew 5:14; Ephesians 5:14, I John 2:10; Greg Hayakawa, b.1953, © 1978, 1979
Tune: Greg Hayakawa, b.1953, © 1978, 1979; acc. by Craig S. Kingsbury, b.1952, © 1985, OCP Publications
Published by OCP Publications

Light of Christ / Exsultet   511

Refrain

All:

The light of Christ sur- rounds us, the love of Christ en- folds us, the pow'r of Christ pro- tects us, the pres- ence of Christ watch- es o- ver us.

To verses

Last time

us, for ev-er, and ev-er, for ev-er, and ev-er. A - men.

Verses 1, 2, 3

Cantor or schola:

1. All the earth is a - blaze with the glo - ry of
2. Let us fill ev - 'ry space with the sound of our
3. As this can - dle shines out through the dark - ness of

D.C.

God, for the Light has come to burn a - way the dark - ness.
joy, prais - ing Christ, who is liv - ing now a - mong us.
night, may the love of Christ burn ev - er in our hearts.

Verse 4

4. In the east, the Morn-ing Star ris- es bright up - on you,

D.C.

in its peace-ful light shines the glo-ry of the Lord.

Text: Based on a prayer by James Dillet Freeman and the *Exsultet;* Marty Haugen, b.1950
Tune: Marty Haugen, b.1950
© 1987. GIA Publications, Inc.

512 We Are Marching

We are march - ing* in the light of God, we are
march-ing in the light of God.

1. march-ing in the light of God.

2. march-ing in the light of the
march-ing in the light of God,

we are march - ing,
light of God, we are march - ing, march - ing, we are

Oo we are
march - ing, march-ing, we are march-ing in the light of God.

Alternate text: dancing, singing, praying

Text: South African
Tune: South African
© 1984, Utryck, Walton Music Corporation, agent

This Little Light of Mine 513

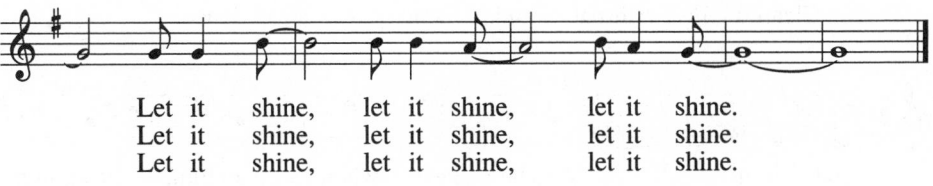

1. This lit - tle light of mine   I'm gon - na let it   shine,
2. Ev - 'ry - where I   go,   I'm gon - na let it   shine,
3. Je - sus gave it to   me,   I'm gon - na let it   shine,

This lit - tle light of   mine   I'm gon - na let it   shine;
Ev - 'ry - where I   go,   I'm gon - na let it   shine;
Je - sus gave it to   me,   I'm gon - na let it   shine;

This lit - tle light of   mine   I'm gon - na let it   shine,
Ev - 'ry - where I   go,   I'm gon - na let it   shine,
Je - sus gave it to   me,   I'm gon - na let it   shine,

Let it   shine,   let it   shine,   let it   shine.
Let it   shine,   let it   shine,   let it   shine.
Let it   shine,   let it   shine,   let it   shine.

Text: African-American spiritual
Tune: African-American spiritual; harm. by Horace Clarence Boyer, © 1992

514 The Word of Life

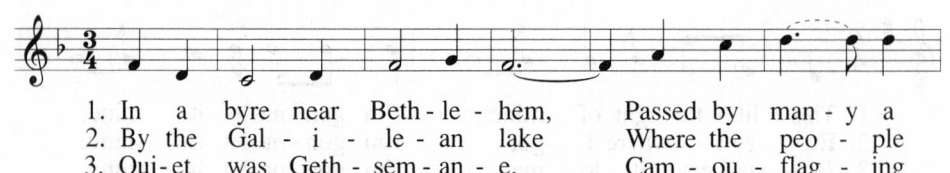

1. In a byre near Beth - le - hem,   Passed by man - y a
2. By the Gal - i - le - an lake   Where the peo - ple
3. Qui- et was Geth - sem - an - e,   Cam - ou - flag - ing
4. On the hill of Cal - va - ry—   Place to end all
5. In a gar - den, just at dawn,   Near the grave of

wand - 'ring stran- ger,
flocked for teach- ing,
priest and sol - dier;   The most pre - cious Word of Life
hope of liv - ing—
hu - man vio - lence,

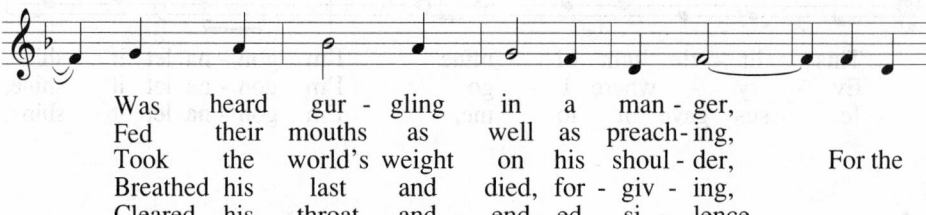

Was heard gur - gling in a man - ger,
Fed their mouths as well as preach- ing,
Took the world's weight on his shoul - der,   For the
Breathed his last and died, for - giv - ing,
Cleared his throat and end - ed si - lence,

good of us all. And he's here when we call him, bring-ing

health, love, and laugh - ter to life now and ev - er

af - ter, for the good of us all.

Text: John L. Bell, b.1949
Tune: WILD MOUNTAIN THYME, irregular; Irish traditional; arr. by John L. Bell, b.1949
© 1987, Iona Community, GIA Publications, Inc., agent

Praise to You, O Christ, Our Savior 515

Refrain

Praise to you, O Christ, our Sav-ior, Word of the Fa-ther,

call - ing us to life; Son of God who

leads us to free-dom: glo - ry to you, Lord Je-sus Christ!

Verses

1. You are the Word who calls us out of dark - ness;
2. You are the one whom proph-ets hoped and longed for;
3. You are the Word who calls us to be ser - vants;
4. You are the Word who binds us and u - nites us;

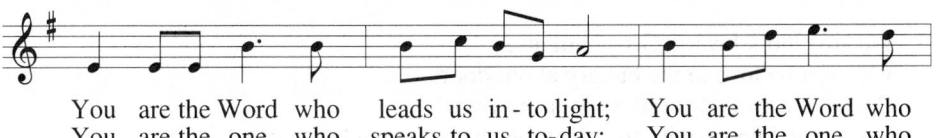

You are the Word who leads us in-to light; You are the Word who
You are the one who speaks to us to-day; You are the one who
You are the Word whose on - ly law is love; You are the Word made
You are the Word who calls us to be one; You are the Word who

D.C.

brings us through the des - ert: Glo - ry to you, Lord Je-sus Christ!
leads us to our fu - ture: Glo - ry to you, Lord Je-sus Christ!
flesh who lives a - mong us: Glo - ry to you, Lord Je-sus Christ!
teach-es us for-give-ness: Glo - ry to you, Lord Je-sus Christ!

Text: Bernadette Farrell, b.1957
Tune: Bernadette Farrell, b.1957
© 1986, Bernadette Farrell, published by OCP Publications

516 Sow the Word

Refrain

So the Word came to the world, so the

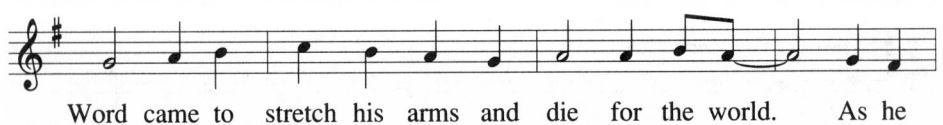

Word came to stretch his arms and die for the world. As he

loved, so we live to sow the Word.

Verses

1. As the rain and the snow come down from heaven
   and do not return without watering the earth,
   making it yield and giving it growth
   to provide seed for the sower and bread for the world:

2. This is the word that we have tasted with our eyes,
   and our lips speak the love in its passing on to you.
   God is light. If we live our love in light,
   we will reap the grain of the sower and be bread for the world.

3. We are God's lovers. Give it all away.
   We must be love to the hungry at our doors.
   Open the bread! Bring the robes and rings!
   Lavish the hungry with the plenty we have known in the word.

Text: Isaiah 55:10-11; J. Keith Zavelli, b.1958, Steven R. Janco, b.1961
Tune: J. Keith Zavelli, b.1958, Steven R. Janco, b.1961; harm. by Steven R. Janco, b.1961
© 1986, GIA Publications, Inc.

Not by Bread Alone 517

Refrain

We do not live by bread a - lone, but by ev - 'ry

word that comes from the mouth of God.

Verses 1, 3

1. Lead our hearts a - way from world- ly gain, turn our
3. When the snares of e - vil hem us in, _ and op -

eyes from see - ing what is vain, teach us your wis - dom.
pres - sion weighs us down, lib - er - a - tion

D.C.

Give us knowl- edge; in your word we hope and trust.
and sal - va - tion come as prom- ised through your word.

Verse 2

2. A lamp to our feet, a light to our path, sweet-er than

hon - ey, pre-cious as gold, your word is our de - light;

D.C.

it brings e - ter - nal life.

Text: Matthew 4:4, Psalm 119; Donald J. Reagan, b.1923
Tune: Donald J. Reagan, b.1923
© 1983, GIA Publications, Inc.

518 The Word Is in Your Heart

Refrain

The Word is near you, deep with - in you. The Word is

on your lips. The Word who made you yet will

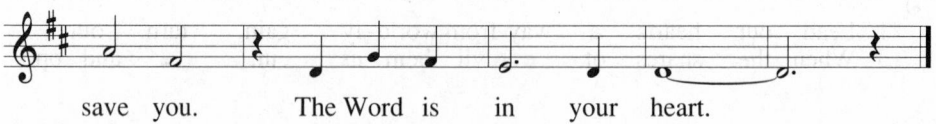

save you. The Word is in your heart.

Verses

1. Christ dwells in our hearts through faith, and by this
2. God's love sur - pass - es all we know. How rich are
3. God's Spir - it fills each faith - ful heart, and as God's

D.C.

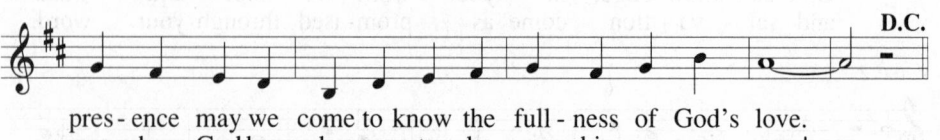

pres - ence may we come to know the full - ness of God's love.
we whom God has cho - sen to be - come his ve - ry own!
ves - sels we are called to live in ho - li - ness and love.

Text: Bob Moore, b. 1962
Tune: Bob Moore, b. 1962
© 1993, GIA Publications, Inc.

May We Praise You 519

1. May we praise you, O Lord, With heart and hand and
2. May our liv - ing be true. May all re - turn to
3. Let your step guide our path. Let shades of dark not
4. To the Fa - ther be praise; To Son and Spir - it,

voice. And since life it - self is your gift to us, Then may
you. And when life is done let our pass - ing be Like a
last. May the sun of jus - tice re - turn on high, And your
praise. Un - to God the one let all praise be done, Till the

1.- 3.

all that we are be yours.
birth in - to light of day.
love be our road and guide.
dawn of the last - ing

4.

day, may we praise.

Text: Vs. 1 from *The Liturgy of the Hours;* John Foley, SJ, b.1939
Tune: John Foley, SJ, b.1939
© 1981, John Foley, SJ, and New Dawn Music

520 All the Ends of the Earth

Refrain

All the ends of the earth, all you crea-tures of the sea, lift up your

eyes to the won - ders of the Lord. For the Lord of the earth, the

Mas - ter of the sea, has come with jus - tice for the world.

Verse 1

1. Break in - to song at the deeds of the Lord, the

D.C.

won - ders he has done in ev - 'ry age.

Verse 2

2. Heav - en and earth shall re - joice in his might; ev-'ry heart,

D.C.

ev - 'ry na - tion call him Lord.

Verse 3

3. The Lord has made sal - va-tion known, faith-ful to the prom-

is - es of old. Let the ends of the earth, let the

D.C.

sea and all it holds make mu-sic be - fore our King!

Text: Psalm 98; Bob Dufford, SJ, b.1943
Tune: Bob Dufford, SJ, b.1943; acc. by Bob Dufford and Chris Morash, alt.
© 1981, Robert J. Dufford, SJ, and New Dawn Music

Sing a New Song to the Lord 521

1. Sing a new song to the Lord,
2. Now to the ends of the earth
3. Sing a new song and re - joice,
4. Join with the hills and the sea

He to whom won - ders be - long! Re -
See his sal - va - tion is shown; And
Pub - lish his prais - es a - broad! Let
Thun - ders of praise to pro - long! In

joice in his tri - umph and
still he re - mem - bers his
voic - es in cho - rus, with
judge - ment and jus - tice he

tell of his power, O sing to the
mer - cy and truth, Un - chang - ing in
trum - pet and horn, Re - sound for the
comes to the earth, O sing to the

Lord a new song!
love to his own.
joy of the Lord!
Lord a new song!

Text: Psalm 98; Timothy Dudley-Smith, b.1926
Tune: CANTATE DOMINO (ONSLOW SQUARE), Irregular; David G. Wilson, b.1940
© 1973, Hope Publishing Co.

522 Glory and Praise to Our God

Refrain

Glo-ry and praise to our God, who a-lone gives light to our days. Man-y are the bless-ings he bears to those who trust in his ways.

Verses 1-3

1. We, the daugh-ters and sons of him who built the val-leys and plains, Praise the won-ders our God has done in ev-'ry heart that sings.

2. In his wis-dom he strength-ens us, like gold that's test-ed in fire. Though the pow-er of sin pre-vails, our God is there to save.

3. Ev-'ry mom-ent of ev-'ry day our God is wait-ing to save, Al-ways read-y to seek the lost, to an-swer those who pray.

D.C.

Verse 4

4. God has wa-tered our bar-ren land and spent his mer-ci-ful rain. Now the riv-ers of life run full for an-y-one to drink.

D.C.

Text: Psalm 65, 66; Dan Schutte, b. 1947
Tune: Dan Schutte, b. 1947; acc. by Sr. Theophane Hytrek, OSF, 1915-1992, alt.
© 1976, Daniel L. Schutte and New Dawn Music

Sing Our God Together 523

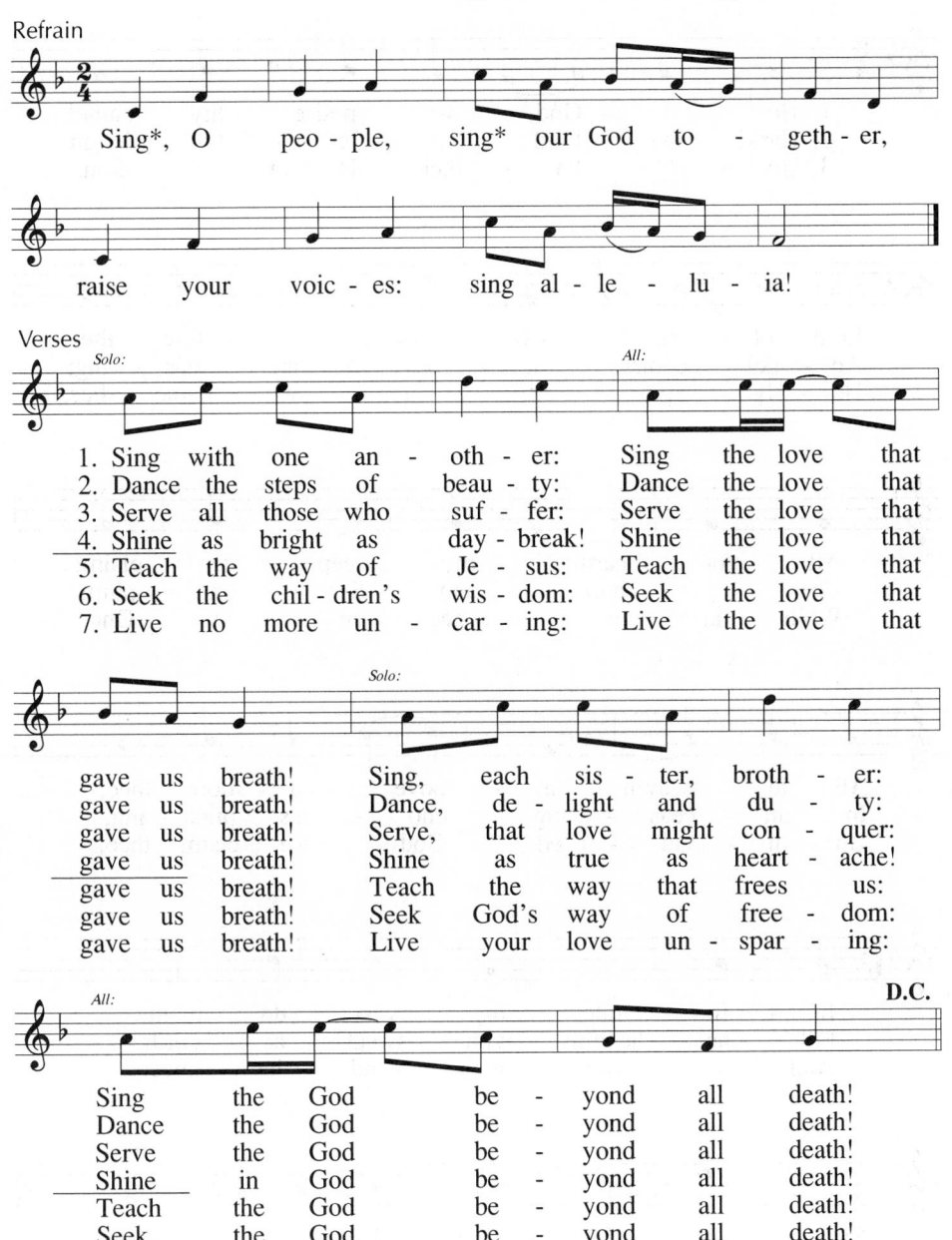

*After each verse, repeat key word in the refrain: (Dance/Dance our; Serve/Serve our;
Shine/Shine in; Teach/Teach our; Seek/ Seek our; Live/Live our)*

Text: David Haas, b. 1957, and Marty Haugen, b. 1950
Tune: David Haas, b. 1957, and Marty Haugen, b. 1950
© 1993, GIA Publications, Inc.

524 Holy God, We Praise Thy Name

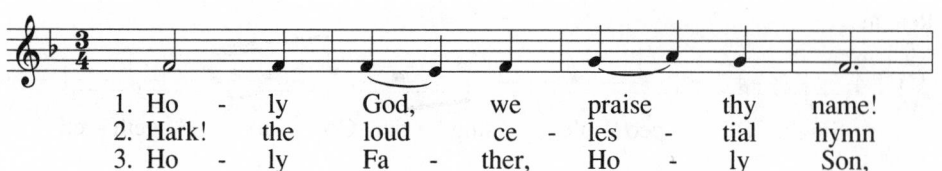

1. Ho - ly God, we praise thy name!
2. Hark! the loud ce - les - tial hymn
3. Ho - ly Fa - ther, Ho - ly Son,

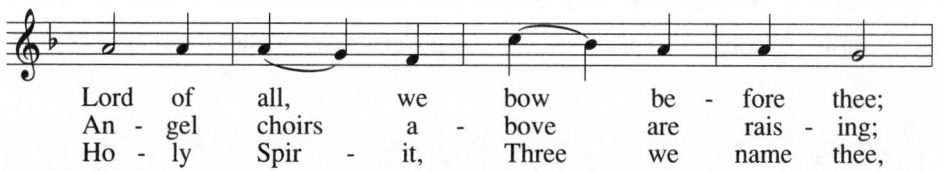

Lord of all, we bow be - fore thee;
An - gel choirs a - bove are rais - ing;
Ho - ly Spir - it, Three we name thee,

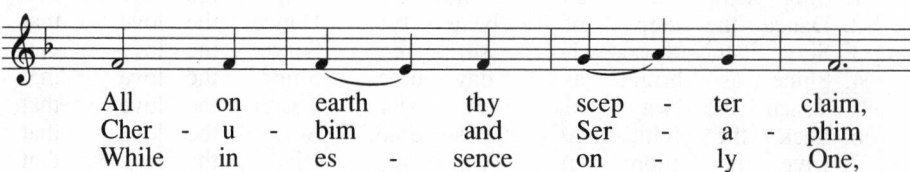

All on earth thy scep - ter claim,
Cher - u - bim and Ser - a - phim
While in es - sence on - ly One,

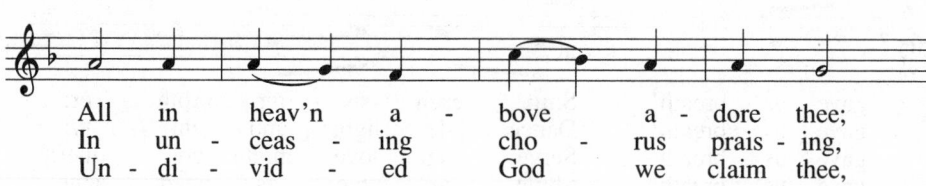

All in heav'n a - bove a - dore thee;
In un - ceas - ing cho - rus prais - ing,
Un - di - vid - ed God we claim thee,

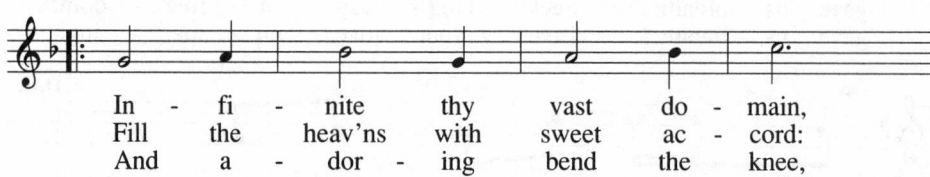

In - fi - nite thy vast do - main,
Fill the heav'ns with sweet ac - cord:
And a - dor - ing bend the knee,

Repeat ad lib.

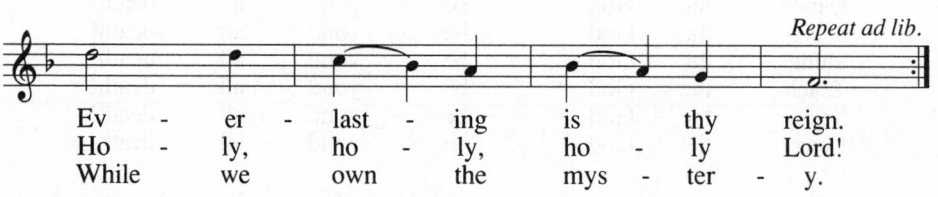

Ev - er - last - ing is thy reign.
Ho - ly, ho - ly, ho - ly Lord!
While we own the mys - ter - y.

Text: *Grosser Gott, wir loben dich;* ascr. to Ignaz Franz, 1719-1790; tr. by Clarence Walworth, 1820-1900
Tune: GROSSER GOTT. 7 8 7 8 77; *Katholisches Gesangbuch,* Vienna, c.1774

Laudate Dominum 525

Ostinato Refrain

Lau-da-te Do-mi-num, lau-da-te Do-mi-num om-nes

gen-tes,   al-le-lu - ia.   al-le-lu - ia.

Text: Psalm 117, *Praise the Lord, all you peoples;* Taizé Community, 1980
Tune: Jacques Berthier, 1923-1994
© 1980, Les Presses de Taizé, GIA Publications, Inc., agent

Cantai ao Senhor 526

Can - tai   ao Sen - hor um can - ti - co   no - vo, can - tai   ao Sen -
O   sing   to   the Lord, O sing God a   new song, O sing   to   the
Can - tar   al Se - ñor un can - ti - co   nue - vo, can - tar   al Se -

hor um can - ti - co   no - vo, can - tai ao Sen - hor um
Lord, O   sing God   a   new song, O   sing   to   the   Lord,   O
ñor un can - ti - co   nue - vo, can - tar al Se - ñor un

can - ti - co   no - vo, can - tai ao Sen - hor, can - tai ao Sen - hor.
sing God   a   new song, O sing   to   the   Lord, O sing   to   the Lord.
can - ti - co   nue - vo, can - tar al Se - ñor, can - tar al Se - ñor.

Text: Psalm 98; Anonymous
Tune: Tradtional Brazilian. © Editora Sinodal. Sao Leopoldo; arr. by John L. Bell. b. 1949. © 1991, Iona Community. GIA Publications. Inc., agent

527 Praise to the Lord, the Almighty

1. Praise to the Lord, the Al - might - y, the king of cre -
2. Praise to the Lord, a - bove all things so might - i - ly
3. Praise to the Lord, who shall pros - per our work and de -
4. Praise to the Lord— O let all that is in us a -

a - tion! O my soul, praise him, for
reign - ing; Keep - ing us safe at his
fend us; Sure - ly his good - ness and
dore him! All that has life and breath

he is your health and sal - va - tion!
side, and so gent - ly sus - tain - ing.
mer - cy shall dai - ly at - tend us.
come now with prais - es be - fore him!

Come, all who hear: Broth - ers and sis - ters, draw near,
Have you not seen All you have need - ed has been
Pon - der a - new What the Al - might - y can do,
Let the "A - men!" Sound from his peo - ple a - gain—.

Praise him in glad ad - o - ra - tion!
Met by his gra - cious or - dain - ing?
Who with his love will be - friend us.
Glad - ly with praise we a - dore him!

Text: *Lobe den Herren, den mächtigen König;* Joachim Neander, 1650-1680; tr. by Catherine Winkworth, 1827-1878, alt.
Tune: LOBE DEN HERREN, 14 14 47 8; *Stralsund Gesangbuch,* 1665; descant by C. S. Lang, 1891-1971. © 1953, Novello and Co. Ltd.

Joyful, Joyful, We Adore You   528

1. Joy - ful, joy - ful, we a - dore you, God of glo - ry,
2. All your works with joy sur-round you, Earth and heav'n re -
3. Al - ways giv - ing and for - giv - ing, Ev - er bless- ing,
4. Mor - tals join the might- y cho - rus, Which the morn- ing

Lord of love; Hearts un - fold like flowers be - fore you,
flect your rays, Stars and an - gels sing a - round you,
ev - er blest, Well - spring of the joy of liv - ing,
stars be - gan; God's own love is reign - ing o'er us,

Open - ing to the sun a - bove. Melt the clouds of
Cen - ter of un - bro - ken praise; Field and for - est,
O - cean depth of hap - py rest! Lov - ing Fa - ther,
Join - ing peo - ple hand in hand. Ev - er sing - ing,

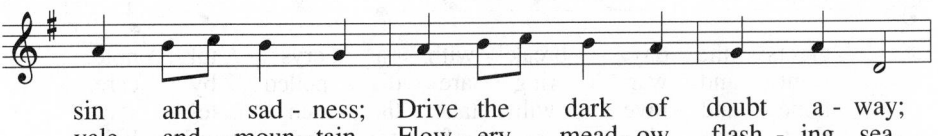

sin and sad - ness; Drive the dark of doubt a - way;
vale and moun - tain, Flow - ery mead - ow, flash - ing sea,
Christ our broth - er, Let your light up - on us shine;
march we on - ward, Vic - tors in the midst of strife;

Giv - er of im - mor - tal glad- ness, Fill us with the light of day!
Chant- ing bird and flow- ing foun - tain, Prais- ing you e - ter- nal- ly!
Teach us how to love each oth - er, Lift us to the joy di- vine.
Joy - ful mu - sic leads us sun - ward In the tri- umph song of life.

Text: Henry van Dyke, 1852-1933, alt., © Charles Scribner's Sons
Tune: HYMN TO JOY, 8 7 8 7 D; arr. from Ludwig van Beethoven, 1770-1827, by Edward Hodges, 1796-1867

529 Shake Up the Morning

1. Shake up the morn-ing, let the dawn un-dress, Let
2. Shake up the world and let the King-dom come, The
3. Shake up the Church and let all Chris-tians show That
4. Shake up the eve-ning, let the shad-ows range As

dew re-glis-ten na-ture's love-li-ness;
dumb be lis-tened to, the lost find home;
faith is real, that God is good to know;
clouds to cas-tles in the sun-set change;

Wak-en the song-bird and un-seal the throat That
Make earth-ly pol-i-tics the stuff of prayer Till
Fash-ion new sym-bols of the com-ing age When
Kin-dle the moon and stars which through each night Re-

greets the day-break with a crys-tal note.
want and war-ring are dis-pelled by care.
hope and love will take the cen-ter stage.
flect the glo-ry of to-mor-row's light.

Praise to the Lord, whose morn-ing we in-her-it;
Praise to the Lord, whose world we in-her-it;
Praise to the Lord, whose Gos-pel we in-her-it;
Praise to the Lord, whose eve-ning we in-her-it;

Praise cre-a-tion's fuse, the Ho-ly Spir-it;
Praise God's cat-a-lyst, the Ho-ly Spir-it;
Praise God's bird of love, the Ho-ly Spir-it;
Praise God's pres-ence in the Ho-ly Spir-it;

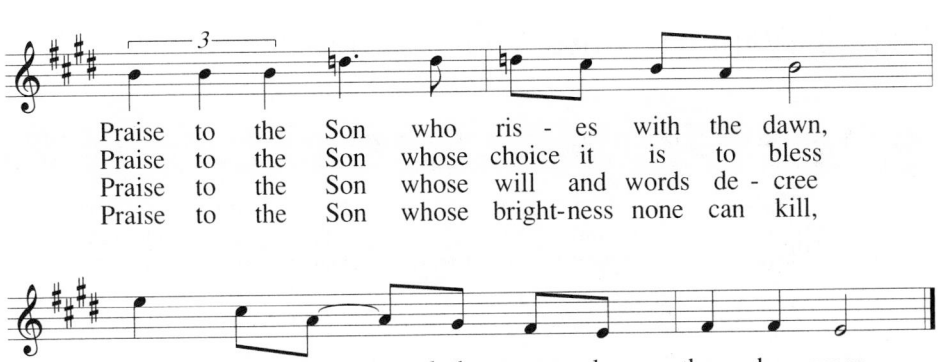

Praise to the Son who ris - es with the dawn,
Praise to the Son whose choice it is to bless
Praise to the Son whose will and words de - cree
Praise to the Son whose bright-ness none can kill,

Leav - ing grave - clothes scarce - ly three days worn.
Those who work for peace and live on less.
All are one in his com - mu - ni - ty.
Light - ing paths for those who seek his will.

Text: John L. Bell, b.1949
Tune: SHAKE UP, irregular; John L. Bell, b.1949
© 1987, Iona Community, GIA Publications, Inc., agent

A New Song   530

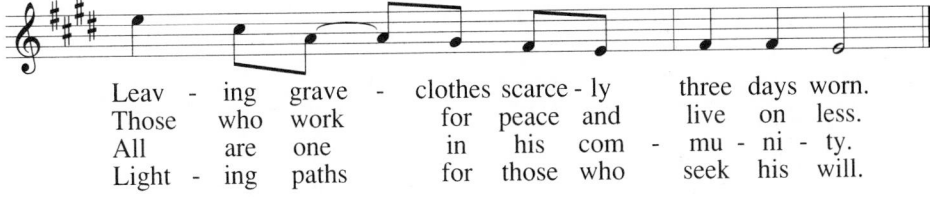

Refrain

I will sing the Lord a new song, a new song. I will sing his

prais - es while I live. I will sing his prais-es for ev - er more.

Verses

1. Sing God a new song,   Make it loud and clear.
2. Sing God a new song   ⁊ For all he's done.
3. Sing God a new song,   Spread his love a - round.

D.C.

Sing God a new song   For all the world to hear.
Sing God a new song,   ⁊ Help to make us one.
Sing God a new song,   ⁊ Make a joy - ful sound.

Text: James E. Moore, Jr., b.1951
Tune: James E. Moore, Jr., b.1951
© 1983, GIA Publications, Inc.

531 I Want to Praise Your Name

Verses

1. Praise with the trum-pet, Praise with the harp,
2. Moun-tains and val-leys, Riv-ers and seas,
3. Moth-ers and fa-thers, Daugh-ters and sons,

Praise with the tim-brel, the dance and the lyre; Let ev-'ry-
Stars in the heav-ens and fish in the deep; Let all cre-
All of God's peo-ple, the old and the young; Let all who

thing that has breath give praise to God.
a-tion give praise to God on high.
hun-ger to do God's will give praise.

Refrain

I want to praise your name. I want to sing your

1.,2.   D.C.

good-ness. Glo-ry, O God; Glo-ry.

3.

Glo - ry.

Text: Psalm 148, 149, 150; adapt. by Bob Hurd, b. 1950, © 1984
Tune: Bob Hurd, b. 1950, © 1984, acc. by Craig S. Kingsbury, b. 1952, © 1984, OCP Publications
Published by OCP Publications

World without End   532

1. Praise   to   the   Lord for   the   joys   of   the   earth:
2. Praise   to   the   Lord for   the   pro - gress   of   life:
3. Praise   to   the   Lord for   his   care   of   our   kind:
4. Praise   to   the   Lord for   the   peo - ple   we   meet,
5. Praise   to   the   Lord for   the   car - pen - ter's   son,

Cy - cles   of   sea - son   and   rea - son   and   birth,
Cra - dle   and   grave, bond   of   hus - band   and   wife,
Faith   for   the   faith - less   and   sight   for   the   blind,
Safe   in   our   homes   or   at   risk   in   the   street:
Dove - tail - ing   wor - ship   and   work   in - to   one:

Con - trasts   in   out - look   and   land - scape   and   need,
Pain   of   youth   grow - ing   and   wrin - kling   of   age,
Heal - ing,   ac - cep - tance, dis - tur - bance, and   change,
Kiss   of   a   lov - er   and   friend - ship's   em - brace,
Trades - man   and   teach - er   and   va - grant   and   friend,

Chal - lenge of   fam - ine,   pol - lu - tion,   and   greed.
Ques - tions in   step with   ex - pe - rience and   stage.
All   the   e - mo - tions through which   our   lives   range.
Smile   of   a   stran - ger   and   words   full   of   grace.
Source of   all   life   in   this   world with - out   end.

Text: John L. Bell, b.1949, © 1987, Iona Community, GIA Publications, Inc., agent
Tune: BONNIE GEORGE CAMPBELL, 10 10 10 10; Scottish Folk Song; acc. by John L. Bell, b.1949, © 1993, Iona Community,
    GIA Publications, Inc., agent

533 All Creatures of Our God and King

1. All crea - tures of our God and King, Lift
2. O rush - ing wind and breez - es soft, O
3. O flow - ing wa - ters, pure and clear, Make
4. Dear moth - er earth, who day by day Un -
5. O ev - 'ry one of ten - der heart, For -

up your voice and with us sing: Al-le - lu - ia! Al-le -
clouds that ride the winds a - loft: Al-le - lu - ia! Al-le -
mu - sic for your Lord to hear. Al-le - lu - ia! Al-le -
folds rich bless - ings on our way, Al-le - lu - ia! Al-le -
giv - ing oth - ers, take your part, Al-le - lu - ia! Al-le -

lu - ia! O burn - ing sun with gold - en beam And
lu - ia! O ris - ing morn, in praise re - joice, O
lu - ia! O fire so mas - ter - ful and bright, Pro -
lu - ia! The fruits and flow'rs that ver - dant grow, Let
lu - ia! All you who pain and sor - row bear, Praise

sil - ver moon with soft - er gleam:
lights of eve - ning, find a voice.
vid - ing us with warmth and light, Al - le -
them God's glo - ry al - so show.
God and cast on God your care.

lu - ia! Al - le - lu - ia! Al - le - lu - ia, al - le -

lu - ia, al - le - lu - ia!

6. And you, most kind and gentle death,
   Waiting to hush our final breath,
   Alleluia! Alleluia!
   You lead to heav'n the child of God,
   Where Christ our Lord the way has trod.
   Alleluia! Alleluia!
   Alleluia, alleluia, alleluia!

7. Let all things their Creator bless,
   And worship God in humbleness,
   Alleluia! Alleluia!
   Oh praise the Father, praise the Son,
   And praise the Spirit, Three in One!
   Alleluia! Alleluia!
   Alleluia, alleluia, alleluia!

Text: *Laudato si, mi Signor;* Francis of Assisi, 1182-1226; tr. by William H. Draper, 1855-1933, alt., © J. Curwen and Sons
Tune: LASST UNS ERFREUEN, LM with alleluias; *Geistliche Kirchengesänge,* 1623; harm. by Ralph Vaughan Williams, 1872-1958, © Oxford
University Press

Magnificat   534

Canon

Ma - gni - fi - cat,   ma - gni - fi - cat,   Ma - gni - fi - cat   a - ni - ma

me - a Do - mi - num.   Ma - gni - fi - cat,   ma - gni - fi - cat,

Ma - gni - fi - cat   a - ni - ma   me - a!

Text: Luke 1:46, *My soul magnifies the Lord;* Taizé Community, 1978
Tune: Jacques Berthier, 1923-1994
© 1979, Les Presses de Taizé, GIA Publications, Inc., agent

535 To God with Gladness Sing

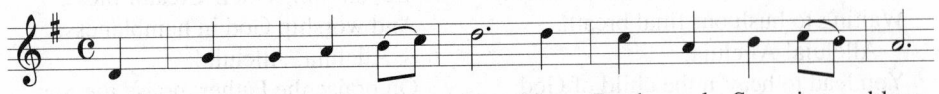

1. To God with glad-ness sing, Your Rock and Sav-ior bless;
2. God cra-dles in his hand The heights and depths of earth;
3. Your heav'n-ly Fa-ther praise, Ac-claim his on-ly Son,

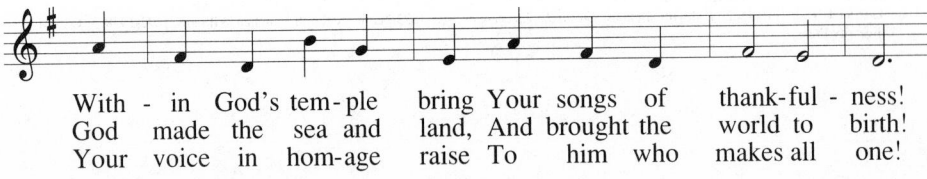

With-in God's tem-ple bring Your songs of thank-ful-ness!
God made the sea and land, And brought the world to birth!
Your voice in hom-age raise To him who makes all one!

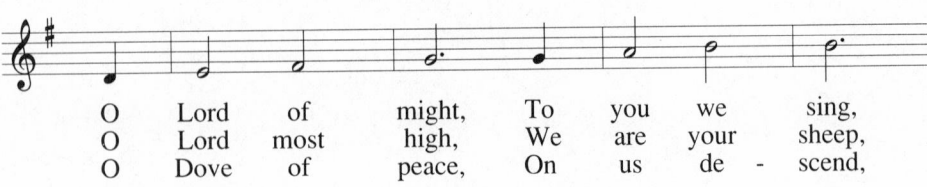

O Lord of might, To you we sing,
O Lord most high, We are your sheep,
O Dove of peace, On us de-scend,

En-throned as King On heav-en's height!
On us you keep Your Shep-herd's eye!
That strife may end And joy in-crease!

Text: Psalm 95; James Quinn, SJ, b.1919, © 1969. Used by permission of Selah Publishing., Inc., Kingston, N.Y.
Tune: CYMBALA, 6 6 6 6 4 44 4; Michael Joncas, b.1951, © 1979, GIA Publications, Inc.

Amen Siakudumisa 536

A-men si - a-ku-du-mi - sa. A-men si - a-ku-du-mi -

sa. A-men ba-wo, A-men ba-wo,

A - men si - a - ku - du - mi - sa.

Text: *Amen. Praise the name of the Lord.* South African traditional
Tune: Attributed to S.C. Molefe as taught by George Mxadana; arr. by John L. Bell, b.1949, © 1990, Iona Community, GIA Publications, Inc., agent

537 Sing a New Song

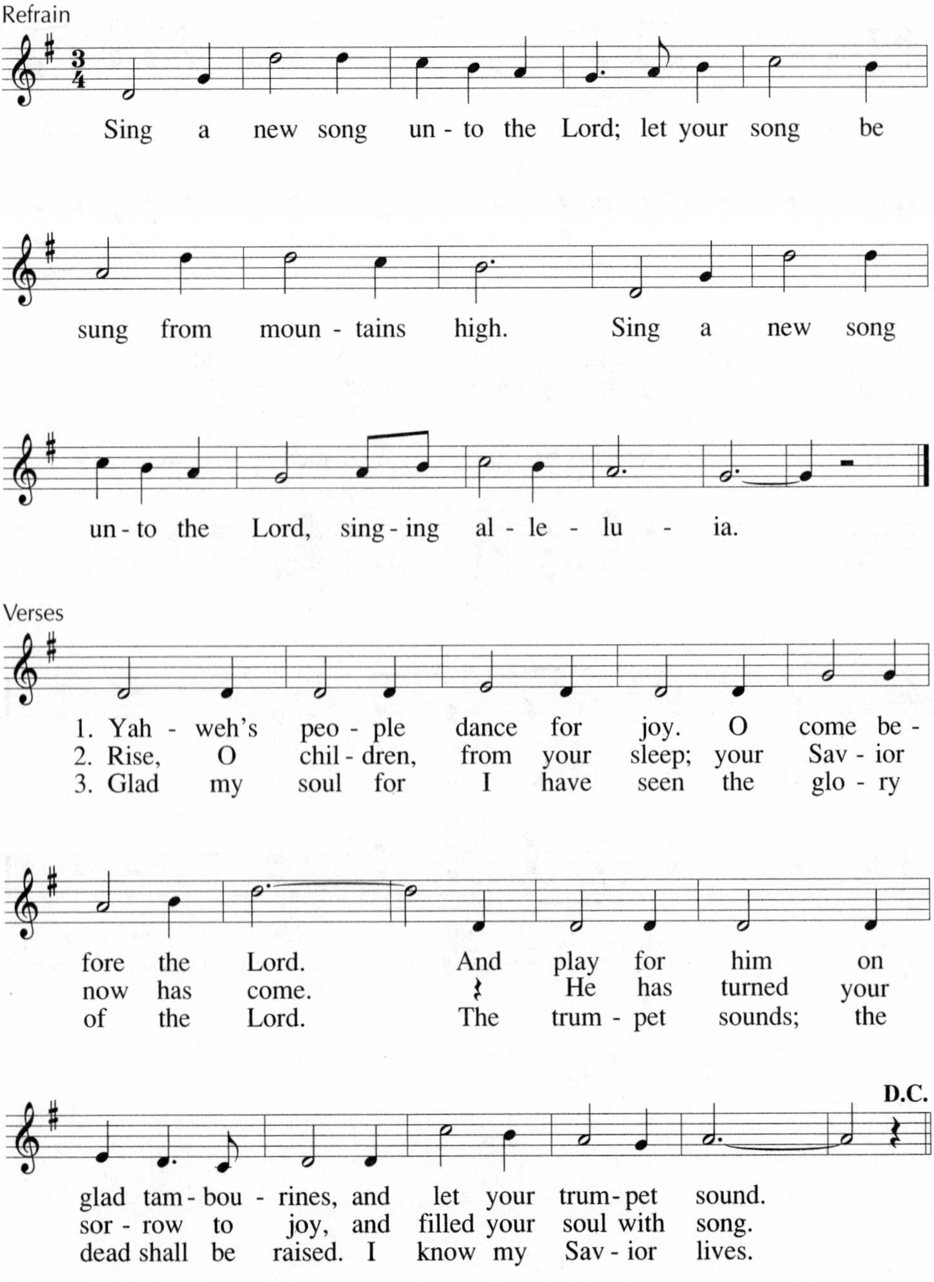

Refrain

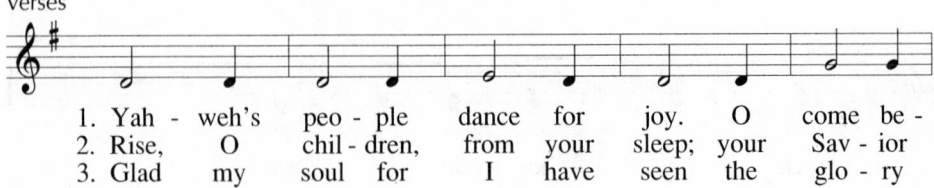

Sing a new song un-to the Lord; let your song be

sung from moun-tains high. Sing a new song

un-to the Lord, sing-ing al-le-lu - ia.

Verses

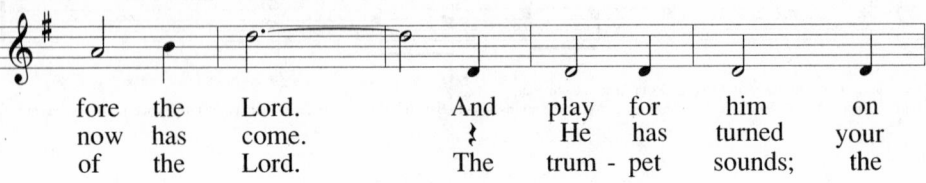

1. Yah - weh's peo-ple dance for joy. O come be -
2. Rise, O chil-dren, from your sleep; your Sav - ior
3. Glad my soul for I have seen the glo - ry

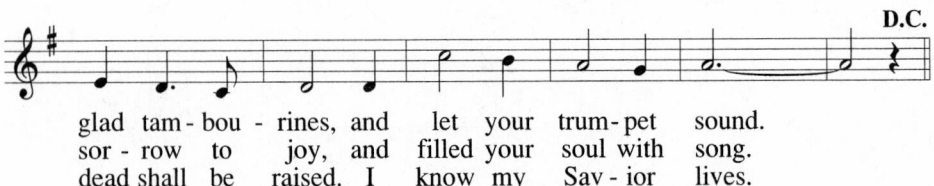

D.C.

fore the Lord. And play for him on
now has come. He has turned your
of the Lord. The trum - pet sounds; the

glad tam - bou - rines, and let your trum-pet sound.
sor - row to joy, and filled your soul with song.
dead shall be raised. I know my Sav - ior lives.

Text: Psalm 98; Dan Schutte, b. 1947
Tune: Dan Schutte, b. 1947
© 1972, Daniel L. Schutte, administered by New Dawn Music

Let Heaven Your Wonders Proclaim 538

1. Let heav - en your won - ders pro - claim, Let
an - gels your faith - ful - ness praise, For
who in the heights or the depths Can
e - qual your maj - es - ty, O God?

2. Your strength rules the rage of the sea, Your
faith - ful - ness calms its wild waves, You
quell ev - 'ry ter - ror of the deep And
scat - ter your en - e - mies a - far.

3. The heav - ens are yours and the earth: You
found - ed the world and its wealth; The
north and the south show your skill. The
east and the west at - test your fame.

4. { Tough - ness and val - or are yours, {
Strong is your hand lift - ed high; Yet
jus - tice is found at your throne And
love is for e - ver by your side.

5. So, glad are the peo - ple who praise you, Who
walk in the light of your love; In
you, God a - lone, is their strength, Their
hon - or, their jus - tice, and their joy.

Text: Psalm 89: 1-16; John L. Bell, b.1949, © 1991, Iona Community, GIA Publications, Inc., agent
Tune: Salvador T. Martinez, © 1989, Salvador T. Martinez; arr. by John L. Bell, b.1949, © 1991, Iona Community, GIA Publications, Inc., agent

539 Sing Praise to God Who Reigns Above

1. Sing praise to God who reigns a - bove, The
2. What God's al - might - y power has made, God's
3. Then all my glad - some way a - long, I
4. Let all who name Christ's ho - ly name, Give

God of all cre - a - tion, The God of pow'r, the
gra - cious mer - cy's keep - ing; By morn - ing glow or
sing a - loud your prais - es, That all may hear the
God all praise and glo - ry; All you who own his

God of love, The God of our sal - va - tion; With
eve - ning shade God's watch-ful eye ne'er sleep - ing; With-
grate - ful song My voice un - wea - ried rais - es; Be
pow'r, pro - claim A - loud the won - drous sto - ry! Cast

heal - ing balm my soul is filled, And ev - 'ry faith - less
in the king - dom of his might, Lo! all is just and
joy - ful in the Lord, my heart, Both soul and bod - y
each false i - dol from its throne, The Lord is God, the

mur - mur stilled: To God all praise and glo - ry.
all is right: To God all praise and glo - ry.
sing your part: To God all praise and glo - ry.
Lord a - lone: To God all praise and glo - ry.

Text: *Sei Lob und Ehr' dem höchsten Gut;* Johann J. Schütz, 1640-1690; tr. by Frances E. Cox. 1812-1897, alt.
Tune: MIT FREUDEN ZART, 8 7 8 7 88 7; Bohemian Brethren's *Kirchengesang,* 1566

Let All Mortal Flesh Keep Silence 540

1. Let all mor - tal flesh keep si - lence,
2. King of kings, yet born of Mar - y,
3. Rank on rank the host of heav - en
4. At his feet the six - winged ser - aph,

And with fear and trem - bling stand;
As of old on earth he stood,
Spreads its van - guard on the way,
Cher - u - bim with sleep - less eye,

Pon - der noth - ing earth - ly mind - ed,
Lord of lords in hu - man ves - ture,
As the Light of Light de - scend - ing
Veil their fac - es to the Pres - ence,

For with bless - ing in his hand
In the Bod - y and the Blood
From the realms of end - less day,
As with cease - less voice they cry,

Christ our God to earth de - scend -
He will give to all the faith -
That the pow'rs of hell may van -
"Al - le - lu - ia, al - le - lu -

ing, Our full hom - age to de - mand.
ful His own self for heav'n - ly food.
ish As the dark - ness clears a - way.
ia, Al - le - lu - ia, Lord, most high!"

Text: Liturgy of St. James 5th C.; para. by Gerard Moultrie, 1829-1885
Tune: PICARDY, 8 7 8 7 8 7; French Carol; harm. by Richard Proulx, b.1937, © 1986, GIA Publications, Inc.

541 We Praise You

Refrain

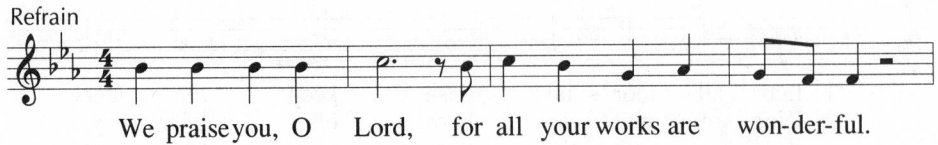

We praise you, O Lord, for all your works are won-der-ful.

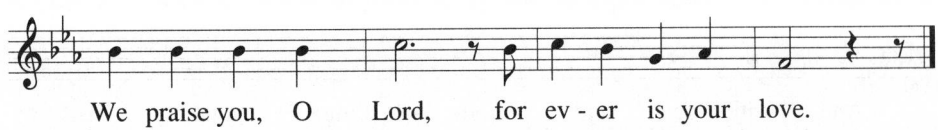

We praise you, O Lord, for ev - er is your love.

Verses

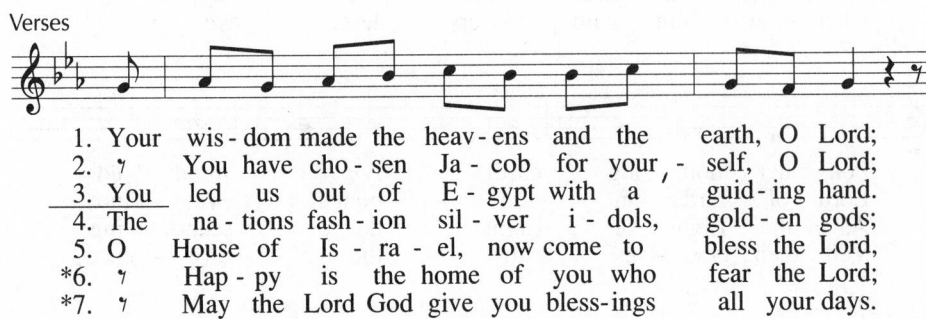

1. Your wis - dom made the heav - ens and the earth, O Lord;
2. ⅞ You have cho - sen Ja - cob for your - self, O Lord;
3. You led us out of E - gypt with a guid - ing hand.
4. The na - tions fash - ion sil - ver i - dols, gold - en gods;
5. O House of Is - ra - el, now come to bless the Lord,
*6. ⅞ Hap - py is the home of you who fear the Lord;
*7. ⅞ May the Lord God give you bless - ings all your days.

You formed the land then set the lights;
So ten - der - ly you spoke his name;
You raised your arm to set us free.
But none have hear - ing, speech or sight.
O House of Aar - on, bless God's name.
So fruit - ful shall your love be - come.
⅞ May you see God fill your land

And like your love the sun will rule the day,
Then called a ho - ly na - tion, Is - ra - el,
And like a ten - der vine you plant - ed us
Their mak - ers shall be like their emp - ty gods,
O bless the Lord, all you who hon - or God,
Your chil - dren flour - ish like the ol - ive plants,
Un - til your chil - dren bring their chil - dren home

wedding verses

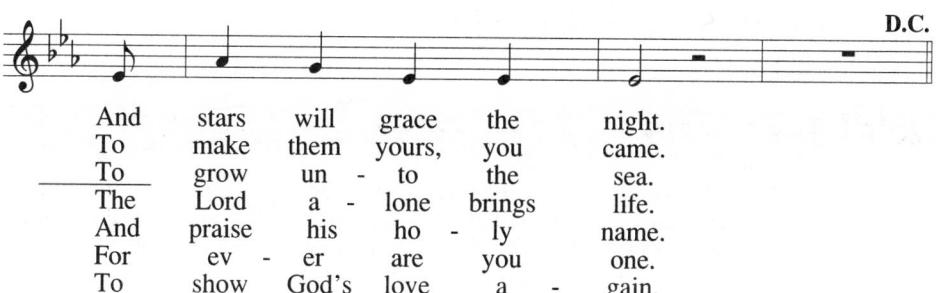

And stars will grace the night.
To make them yours, you came.
To grow un - to the sea.
The Lord a - lone brings life.
And praise his ho - ly name.
For ev - er are you one.
To show God's love a - gain.

Text: Mike Balhoff, b.1946
Tune: Darryl Ducote, b.1945, Gary Daigle, b.1957
© 1978, Damean Music. Distributed by GIA Publications, Inc.

Alabaré 542

Refrain

A-la-ba - ré, a-la-ba - ré, a - la - ba-ré a mi Se - ñor.

Verse

Juan vio el nú - me - ro, de los re - di - mi - dos, y
John saw the num - ber of all those re - deemed, and

to - dos a - la - ba - ban al Se - ñor. U - nos o - ra - ban, y
all were sing-ing prais-es to the Lord. Thou - sands were pray - ing, ten

o - tros can - ta - ban, y to - dos a - la - ba - ban al Se - ñor.
thou-sands, re - joic - ing, and all were sing-ing prais-es to the Lord.

Text: *I will praise the Lord;* Manuel José Alonso, José Pagán, © 1979 and Ediciones Musical PAX, published by OCP Publications;
trans. unknown
Tune: Manuel José Alonso, José Pagán, © 1979 and Ediciones Musical PAX, published by OCP Publications; acc. by Diana Kodner,
© 1994, GIA Publications, Inc.

543 I Will Sing, I Will Sing

Verses 1, 2, 3, 6

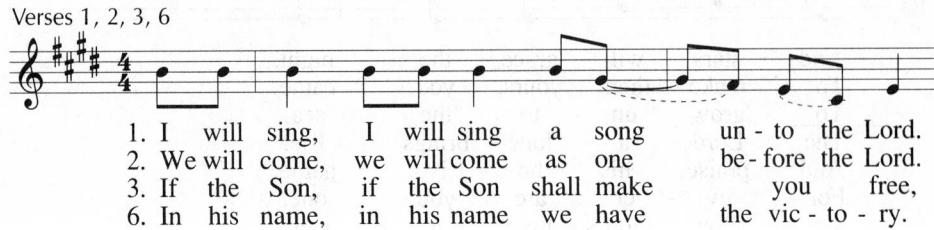

1. I will sing, I will sing a song un - to the Lord.
2. We will come, we will come as one be - fore the Lord.
3. If the Son, if the Son shall make you free,
6. In his name, in his name we have the vic - to - ry.

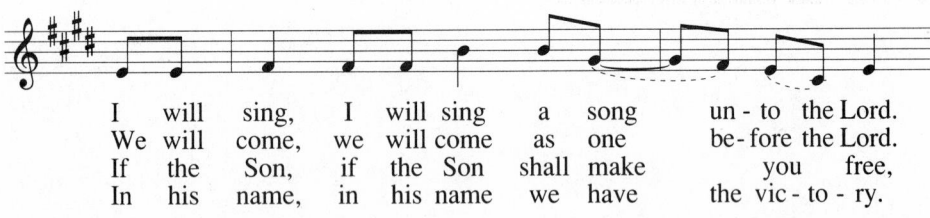

I will sing, I will sing a song un - to the Lord.
We will come, we will come as one be - fore the Lord.
If the Son, if the Son shall make you free,
In his name, in his name we have the vic - to - ry.

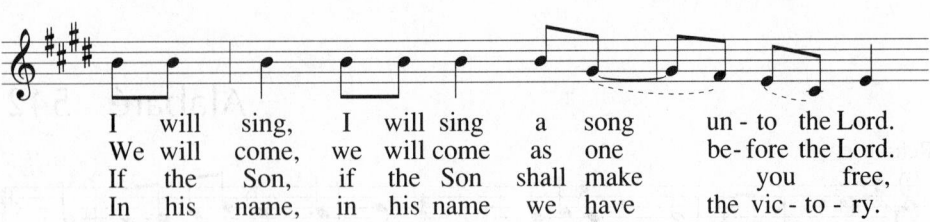

I will sing, I will sing a song un - to the Lord.
We will come, we will come as one be - fore the Lord.
If the Son, if the Son shall make you free,
In his name, in his name we have the vic - to - ry.

To refrain

Al - le - lu - ia, glo - ry to the Lord.
Al - le - lu - ia, glo - ry to the Lord.
You shall be free in - deed.
Al - le - lu - ia, glo - ry to the Lord.

Refrain

Al - le - lu, al - le - lu - ia, glo - ry to the Lord. Al - le -

lu, al-le-lu-ia, glo - ry to the Lord. Al-le-lu, al-le-lu-ia, glo

ry to the Lord. Al - le - lu - ia, glo - ry to the Lord.

To verses

Verses 4, 5

4. They that sow in tears shall reap in joy. They that
5. Ev - 'ry knee shall bow and ev-'ry tongue con - fess, Ev - 'ry

sow in tears shall reap in joy. They that
knee shall bow and ev-'ry tongue con - fess, Ev - 'ry

sow in tears shall reap in joy. Al - le -
knee shall bow and ev-'ry tongue con - fess, That

To refrain

lu - ia, glo - ry to the Lord.
Je - sus Christ is Lord.

Text: Max Dyer
Tune: PULKINGHAM. Irregular: Max Dyer

544 The God of Abraham Praise

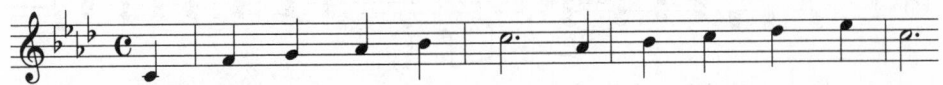

1. The God of A-braham praise, Who reigns en-throned a - bove;
2. The Lord, our God has sworn: I on that oath de-pend;
3. There dwells the Lord, our King, The Lord, our Right-eous-ness,
4. The God who reigns on high The great arch - an - gels sing,

The an - cient of e - ter - nal days, And God of love;
I shall, on ea - gle - wings up-borne, To heav'n as - cend:
Tri - umph-ant o'er the world and sin, The Prince of Peace;
And "Ho - ly, Ho-ly, Ho - ly," cry, "Al - might-y King!

The Lord, the great I AM, By earth and heav'n con - fessed
I shall be - hold God's face, I shall God's pow'r a - dore,
On Zi - on's sa - cred height The king-dom God main - tains,
Who was, and is, the same, For all e - ter - ni - ty,

We bow and bless the sa - cred name For ev - er blest.
And sing the won-ders of God's grace For ev - er - more.
And, glo - rious with the saints in light, For ev - er reigns.
Im - mor - tal God, the, great I AM, All glo - ry be."

Text: *Yigdal Elohim Hai;* ascr. to Daniel ben Judah Dayyan, fl.1400; para. by Thomas Olivers, 1725-1799, alt.
Tune: LEONI, 6 6 8 4 D; from the *Yigdal;* transcribed by Meyer Lyon, c.1751-1797

Sing Praise to the Lord 545

1. Sing praise to the Lord! praise God in the height;
2. Sing praise to the Lord! praise God up - on earth,
3. Sing praise to the Lord, all things that give sound;
4. Sing praise to the Lord! thanks - giv - ing and song

Re - joice in his word, you an - gels of light;
In tune - ful ac - cord, all you of new birth;
Each ju - bi - lant chord re - ech - o a - round;
To him be out - poured all a - ges a - long;

O heav - ens, a - dore him by whom you were made,
Praise him who has brought you his grace from a - bove,
Loud or - gans, his glo - ry tell forth in deep tone,
For love in cre - a - tion, for heav - en re - stored,

And wor - ship be - fore him in bright - ness ar - rayed.
Praise him who has taught you to sing of his love.
And trum - pets, the sto - ry of what God has done.
For grace of sal - va - tion, sing praise to the Lord!

Text: Psalm 150; Henry W. Baker, 1821-1877, alt.
Tune: LAUDATE DOMINUM, 10 10 11 11; Charles H. H. Parry, 1840-1918

546 O God of Matchless Glory

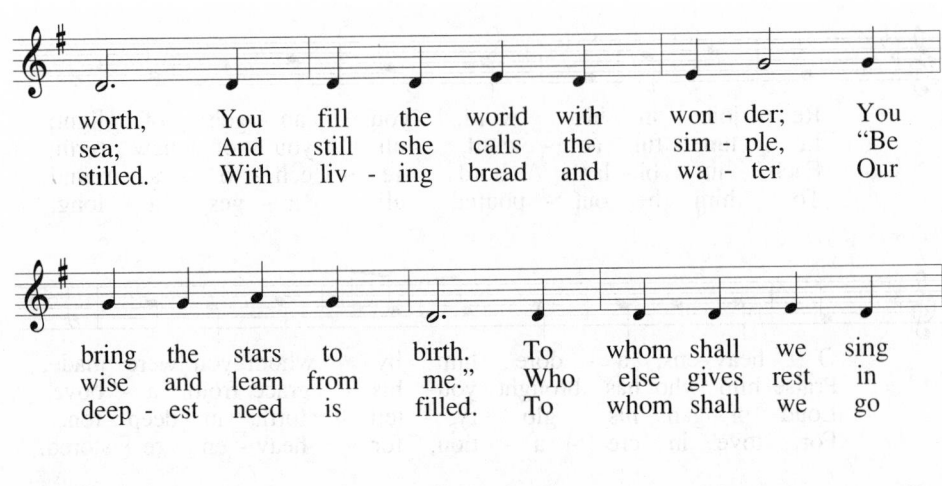

1. O God of match-less glo-ry, Of all-sur-pass-ing
2. With Wis-dom as your part-ner You formed the earth and
3. Your word gives life for - ev-er; Our fear of death is

worth, You fill the world with won - der; You
sea; And still she calls the sim - ple, "Be
stilled. With liv - ing bread and wa - ter Our

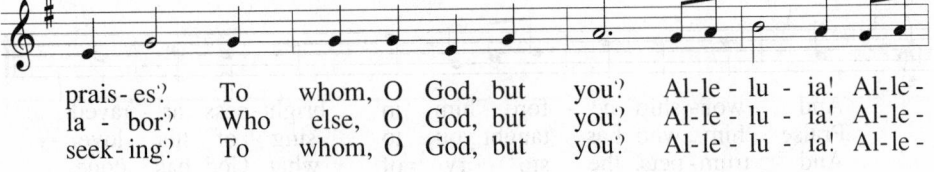

bring the stars to birth. To whom shall we sing
wise and learn from me." Who else gives rest in
deep - est need is filled. To whom shall we go

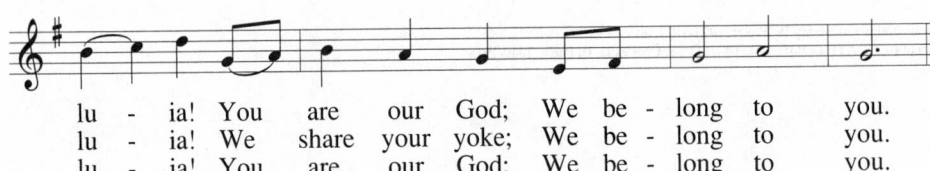

prais-es? To whom, O God, but you? Al-le-lu - ia! Al-le-
la - bor? Who else, O God, but you? Al-le-lu - ia! Al-le-
seek-ing? To whom, O God, but you? Al-le-lu - ia! Al-le-

lu - ia! You are our God; We be - long to you.
lu - ia! We share your yoke; We be - long to you.
lu - ia! You are our God; We be - long to you.

Text: Ruth Duck, b. 1947
Tune: MATCHLESS GLORY, 7 6 7 6 7 6 4 4 4 5; Ruth Duck, b. 1947; acc. by Randall Sensmeier, b.1948
© 1992, GIA Publications, Inc.

Sing of the Lord's Goodness 547

1. Sing of the Lord's good-ness, Fa - ther of all wis-dom,
2. Pow - er he has wield-ed, hon - or is his gar-ment,
3. Cour - age in our dark-ness, com-fort in our sor-row,
4. Praise him with your sing-ing, praise him with the trum-pet,

come to him and bless his name. Mer - cy he has shown us,
ris - en from the snares of death. His word he has spo - ken,
Spir - it of our God most high; sol - ace for the wea - ry,
praise God with the lute and harp; praise him with the cym-bals,

his love is for ev - er, faith - ful to the end of days.
one bread he has bro-ken, new life he now gives to all.
par - don for the sin - ner, splen-dor of the liv-ing God.
praise him with your danc-ing, praise God till the end of days.

Come, then, all you na - tions, sing of your Lord's good-ness,

mel - o - dies of praise and thanks to God.

Ring out the Lord's glo - ry, praise him with your mu - sic,

wor - ship him and bless his name.

Text: Ernest Sands, b.1949, © 1981
Tune: Ernest Sands, b.1949, © 1981; acc. by Paul Inwood, b.1947, © 1986
Published by OCP Publications

548 Joyfully Singing

Verses

1. Joy-ful-ly sing-ing to the Lord,
2. God, in your mer-cy, free our hearts to
3. Gath-er the na-tions to you, Lord,

prais-ing God on high, all of the earth in thank-
praise your ho-ly name, help-ing the poor and low-
draw them to your care, com-ing from all the dis-

ful-ness joins in glad re-ply.
ly ones faith-ful-ly pro-claim.
tant lands glad-ly to de-clare.

Refrain

Bless-ed are your days, ho-ly are your nights,

won-drous is your love all of our lives.

Lord, bring us to-geth-er from east and from the west.

Show us your moun-tain, your dwell-ing place, your

D.C.

life of ho-li-ness.

Text: Mike Balhoff, b. 1946, Gary Daigle, b.1957, Darryl Ducote, b.1945
Tune: Mike Balhoff, b. 1946, Gary Daigle, b.1957, Darryl Ducote, b.1945
© 1985, Damean Music. Distributed by GIA Publications, Inc.

You Are the Voice 549

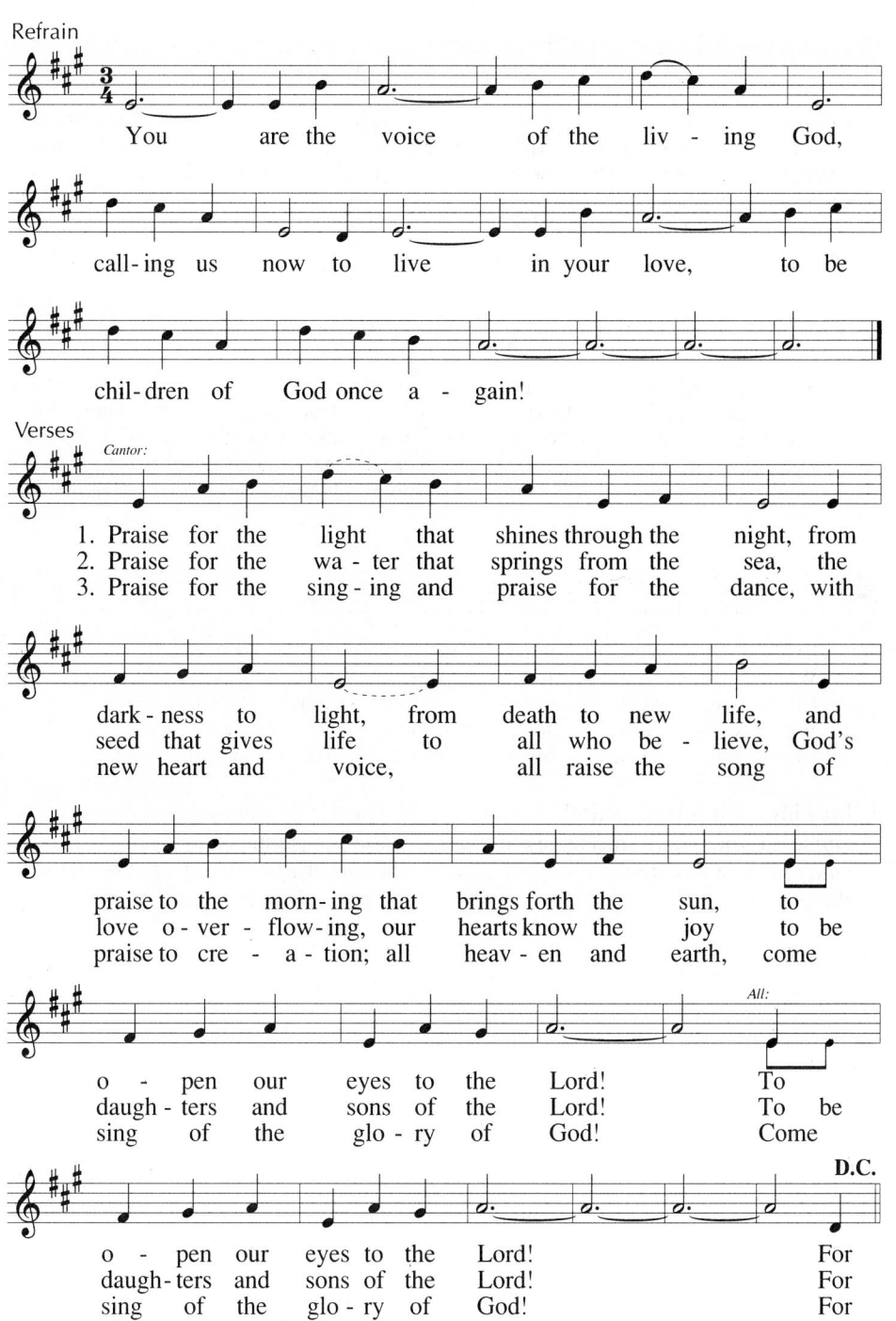

Refrain

You are the voice of the liv - ing God,

call-ing us now to live in your love, to be

chil-dren of God once a - gain!

Verses

Cantor:

1. Praise for the light that shines through the night, from
2. Praise for the wa - ter that springs from the sea, the
3. Praise for the sing - ing and praise for the dance, with

dark - ness to light, from death to new life, and
seed that gives life to all who be - lieve, God's
new heart and voice, all raise the song of

praise to the morn-ing that brings forth the sun, to
love o - ver - flow-ing, our hearts know the joy to be
praise to cre - a - tion; all heav - en and earth, come

All:

o - pen our eyes to the Lord! To
daugh - ters and sons of the Lord! To be
sing of the glo - ry of God! Come

D.C.

o - pen our eyes to the Lord! For
daugh-ters and sons of the Lord! For
sing of the glo - ry of God! For

Text: David Haas, b.1957
Tune: David Haas, b.1957; acc. by Jeanne Cotter, b.1964

550 There's a Spirit in the Air

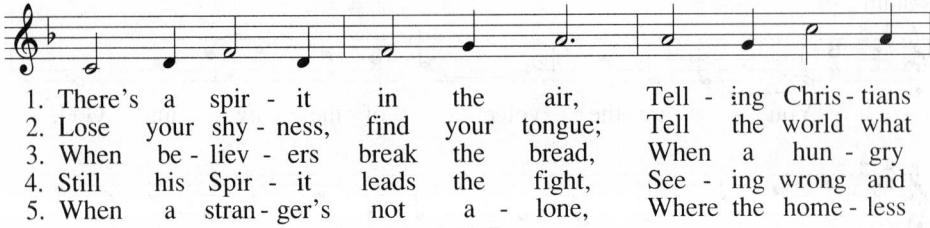

1. There's a spir - it in the air, Tell - ing Chris - tians
2. Lose your shy - ness, find your tongue; Tell the world what
3. When be - liev - ers break the bread, When a hun - gry
4. Still his Spir - it leads the fight, See - ing wrong and
5. When a stran - ger's not a - lone, Where the home - less

ev - 'ry - where, "Praise the love that Christ re - vealed,
God has done: God in Christ has come to stay,
child is fed: Praise the love that Christ re - vealed,
set - ting right: God in Christ has come to stay,
find a home, Praise the love that Christ re - vealed,

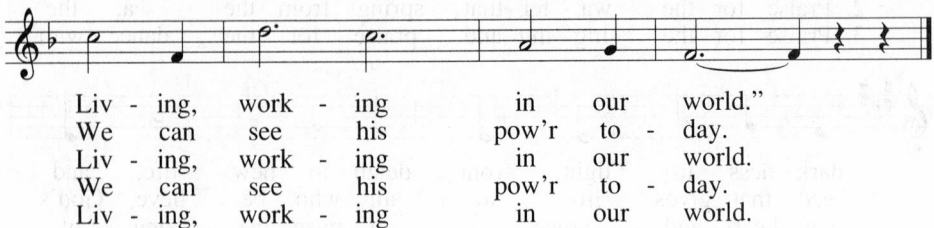

Liv - ing, work - ing in our world."
We can see his pow'r to - day.
Liv - ing, work - ing in our world.
We can see his pow'r to - day.
Liv - ing, work - ing in our world.

6. May his spirit fill our praise,
   Guide our thoughts and change our ways.
   God in Christ has come to stay,
   We can see his pow'r today.

7. There's a spirit in the air,
   Calling people ev'rywhere;
   Praise the love that Christ revealed;
   Living, working in our world.

Text: Brian Wren, b.1936
Tune: LAUDS, 77 77; John W. Wilson, b.1905
© 1979, Hope Publishing Co.

Praise, My Soul, the King of Heaven 551

1. Praise, my soul, the King of heav - en; To his
2. Praise him for his grace and fa - vor To his
3. Fa - ther - like he tends and spares us; Well our
4. Frail as sum-mer's flow'r we flour - ish, Blows the
5. An - gels, help us to a - dore him; You be -

feet your trib - ute bring; Ran - somed, healed, re - stored, for -
peo - ple in dis - tress; Praise him still the same as
fee - ble frame he knows; In his hands he gent - ly
wind and it is gone; But while mor - tals rise and
hold him face to face; Sun and moon, bow down be -

giv - en, Ev - er - more his prais - es sing: Al - le - lu - ia!
ev - er, Slow to chide, and swift to bless: Al - le - lu - ia!
bears us, Res - cues us from all our foes. Al - le - lu - ia!
per - ish, God en - dures un - chang-ing on; Al - le - lu - ia!
fore him, Dwell-ers all in time and space: Al - le - lu - ia!

Al - le - lu - ia! Praise the ev - er - last - ing King.
Al - le - lu - ia! Glo - rious in his faith - ful - ness.
Al - le - lu - ia! Wide - ly yet his mer - cy flows.
Al - le - lu - ia! Praise the high e - ter - nal one!
Al - le - lu - ia! Praise with us the God of grace.

Text: Psalm (102)103; Henry F. Lyte, 1793-1847, alt.
Tune: LAUDA ANIMA, 8 7 8 7 8 7; John Goss, 1800-1880

552 All the Earth, Proclaim God's Glory

Refrain

All the earth, pro - claim God's glo - ry. Sing with songs of

love. Mus - ic, danc - ing, new songs ris - ing, God of beau - ty,

God of splen - dor, God of won - der and love.

Verses 1, 2

1. Lov-ing kind-ness to all na - tions. Peace a - cross the land and sea.
2. For the God of liv-ing splen-dor, God of might - y deeds,

D.C.

Harps and cym-bals sound the mes-sage, blend in har - mo - ny.
keeps the prom-ise to the faith-ful, breath-ing Spir - it's peace.

Verse 3

3. Pour on us new clean wa-ter. Cleanse, re-fresh our souls.

D.C.

Give to us a will-ing spir-it. Heal us, make us whole.

Text: Mark Friedman and Bobby Fisher, b. 1952
Tune: Bobby Fisher, b.1952
© 1992, GIA Publications, Inc.

Cantemos al Señor / Let's Sing unto the Lord 553

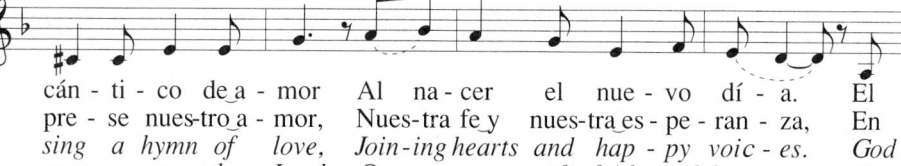

1. Can - te - mos al Se - ñor   Un him - no de a - le - grí - a,   Un
2. Can - te - mos al Se - ñor   Un him - no de a - la - ban - za   Que ex -
1. *Let's sing un-to the Lord*   *A hymn of glad re - joic-ing,*   *Let's*
2. *Let's sing un-to the Lord*   *A hymn of a - do - ra - tion,*   *Ex -*

cán - ti - co de a - mor   Al na - cer   el nue - vo dí - a.   El
pre - se nues-tro a - mor,   Nues-tra fe y   nues-tra es - pe - ran - za,   En
sing a hymn of love,   *Join-ing hearts and hap - py voic - es.*   *God*
press un - to the Lord   *Our   songs   of faith and hope.*   *Cre -*

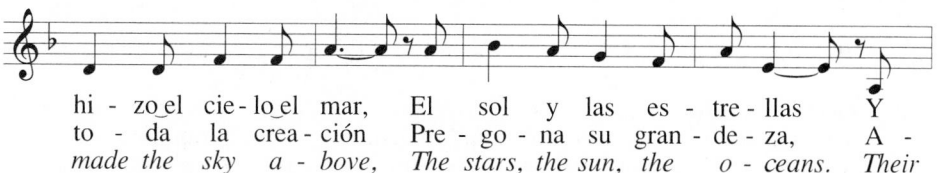

hi - zo el cie - lo el mar,   El sol y las es - tre - llas   Y
to - da   la crea - ción   Pre - go - na su gran - de - za,   A -
made the sky a - bove,   *The stars, the sun, the   o - ceans.*   *Their*
a - tion's broad dis - play   *Pro - claims the work of   gran-deur,*   *The*

vio en   e - llos bon - dad,   Pues sus   o - bras e - ran   be - llas.
sí   nues - tro can - tar   Va a-nun - cian - do su be - lle - za.
good - ness does pro - claim   *The   glo - ry of God's   name.*
bound - less love of One   *Who   bless - es us with   beau - ty.*

¡A - le - lu - ya!   ¡A - le - lu - ya!   Can - te - mos al Se -
Al - le - lu - ia!   *Al - le - lu - ia!*   *Let's sing un - to the*

1. | **2.**

ñor.   ¡A - le - lu   -   ya!   lu   -   ya!
Lord.   *Al - le - lu   -   ia!*   *lu   -   ia!*

Text: Based on Psalm 19; Carlos Rosas, b.1939; trans. by Roberto Escamilla, Elise Eslinger, and George Lockwood, 1983,
   © 1976, Resource Publications, Inc.
Tune: ROSAS, 6 7 6 8 D with refrain; Carlos Rosas, b.1939, © 1976, Resource Publications, Inc.; acc. by Diana Kodner, b.1957,
   © 1993, GIA Publications, Inc.

554 Praise the Lord, My Soul

Refrain

Praise the Lord, my soul! Sing al-le-lu-ia, bless God's name.

Verses 1, 3, 5, 7

1. All prais-es to the Fa-ther of our Lord, a
3. How great the sign of God's love for us in
5. And now we are God's work of art, a
7. We come to you with hearts full of faith, your

God so mer-ci-ful and kind, who gives to us a
giv-ing us his Son to be our bread: as prom-ised us so
new cre-a-tion formed in Christ the Lord. We know we are his
voice is call-ing us so deep with-in. We died with you as

new birth, who brings to us a new hope by
long a - go, re - vealed to us in these last days. How
chil-dren now. What we shall be in days to come, what
grain of wheat, we rise with you to fruit-ful lives, now

D.C.

rais - ing his Son from death to life!
hap - py we who put our faith in him!
tongue can tell? What ear has heard?
make us chil - dren of the light!

Verses 2, 4, 6

2. On this moun - tain God will pre - pare a ban - quet for all
4. Ev - 'ry tear shall be wiped a - way and shame shall be no
6. Taste and see the good-ness of God! Hap-py those who take their

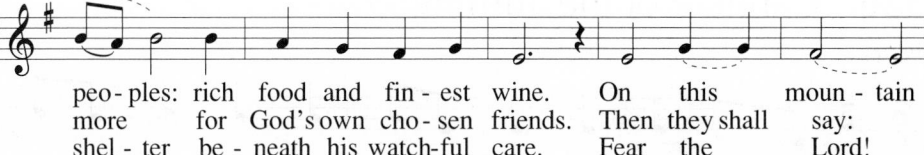

peo - ples: rich food and fin - est wine. On this moun - tain
more for God's own cho - sen friends. Then they shall say:
shel - ter be - neath his watch-ful care. Fear the Lord!

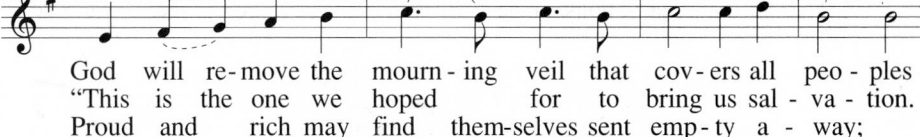

God will re - move the mourn - ing veil that cov - ers all peo - ples
"This is the one we hoped for to bring us sal - va - tion.
Proud and rich may find them-selves sent emp - ty a - way;

D.C.

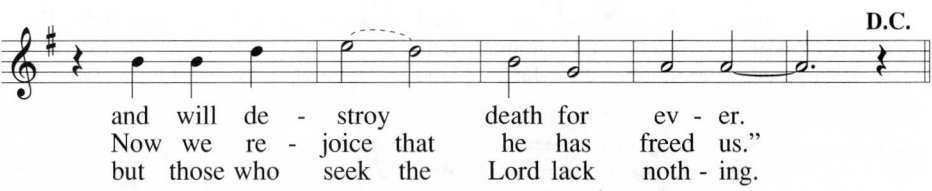

and will de - stroy death for ev - er.
Now we re - joice that he has freed us."
but those who seek the Lord lack noth - ing.

Text: Tom Parker, b.1947
Tune: Tom Parker, b.1947
© 1981, GIA Publications, Inc.

Jubilate Deo / In the Lord Rejoicing   555

Canon

Ju - bi - la - te De - o, ju - bi - la - te
In the Lord re - joic - ing! Christ is ris - en

De - o, al - le - lu - ia!
from the dead! Al - le - lu - ia!

Text: Psalm 100:1; tr. Taizé Community, 1990, © 1978, 1990, Les Presses de Taizé, GIA Publications, Inc., agent
Tune: Michael Praetorius, 1571-1621; acc. by Jacques Berthier, 1923-1994, © 1978, 1990, Les Presses de Taizé, GIA Publications, Inc., agent

556 Canticle of the Turning

Verses

1. My soul cries out with a joy - ful shout that the
2. Though I am small, my God, my all, you
3. From the halls of power to the for - tress tower, not a
4. Though the na - tions rage from age to age, we re -

God of my heart is great, And my spir - it sings of the
work great things in me, And your mer - cy will last from the
stone will be left on stone. Let the king be - ware for your
mem - ber who holds us fast: God's mer - cy must de -

won - drous things that you bring to the ones who wait. You
depths of the past to the end of the age to be. Your
jus - tice tears ev - 'ry ty - rant from his throne. The
liv - er us from the con - quer-or's crush-ing grasp. This

fixed your sight on your ser - vant's plight, and my
ver - y name puts the proud to shame, and to
hun - gry poor shall weep no more, for the
sav - ing word that our fore - bears heard is the

weak - ness you did not spurn, So from east to west shall my
those who would for you yearn, You will show your might, put the
food they can nev - er earn; There are ta - bles spread, ev - 'ry
prom - ise which holds us bound, 'Til the spear and rod can be

name be blest. Could the world be a - bout to turn?
strong to flight, for the world is a - bout to turn.
mouth be fed, for the world is a - bout to turn.
crushed by God, who is turn - ing the world a - round.

Refrain

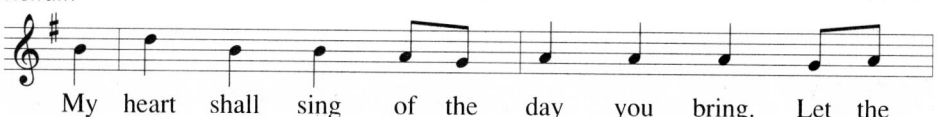

My heart shall sing of the day you bring. Let the

fires of your jus - tice burn. Wipe a - way all tears, for the

dawn draws near, and the world is a - bout to turn!

Text: Luke 1:46-58; Rory Cooney, b.1952
Tune: STAR OF THE COUNTY DOWN; Irish traditional; arr. by Rory Cooney, b.1952
© 1990, GIA Publications, Inc.

Jubilate Servite 557

Canon—*2 voices*

Ju - bi - la - te De - o om - nis ter - ra.

Ser - vi - te Do - mi - no in lae - ti - ti - a.

Al - le - lu - ia, al - le - lu - ia, in lae - ti - ti - a.

Al - le - lu - ia, al - le - lu - ia, in lae - ti - ti - a!

Text: Psalm 100, *Rejoice in God, all the earth, Serve the Lord with gladness;* Taizé Community, 1978
Tune: Jacques Berthier, 1923-1994
© 1979, Les Presses de Taizé, GIA Publications, Inc., agent

558 Lift Up Your Hearts

Refrain

Lift up your hearts to the Lord, praise God's gra-cious mer-cy!

Sing out your joy to the Lord, whose love is en - dur - ing.

Verses

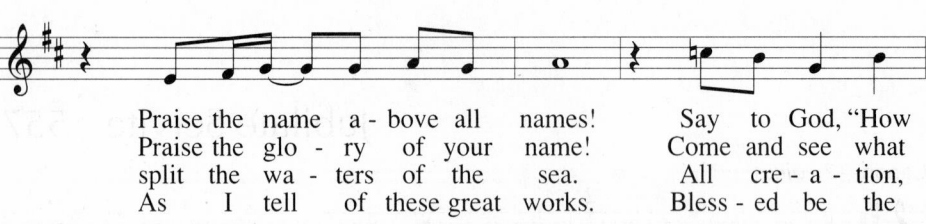

1. Shout with joy to the Lord, all the earth!
2. Let the earth wor - ship, sing - ing your praise.
3. God's right hand made a path through the night,
4. Lis - ten now, all you ser - vants of God,

Praise the name a - bove all names! Say to God, "How
Praise the glo - ry of your name! Come and see what
split the wa - ters of the sea. All cre - a - tion,
As I tell of these great works. Bless - ed be the

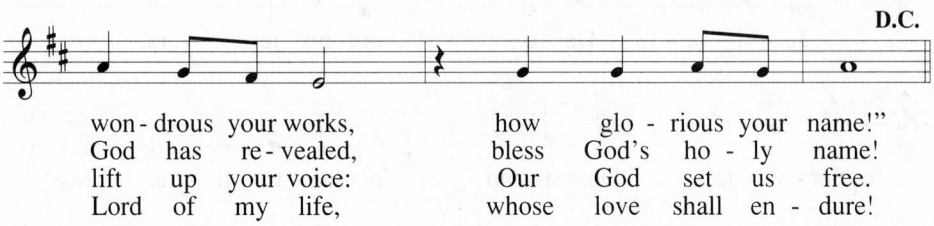

D.C.

won - drous your works, how glo - rious your name!"
God has re - vealed, bless God's ho - ly name!
lift up your voice: Our God set us free.
Lord of my life, whose love shall en - dure!

Text: Psalm 66; Roc O'Connor, SJ, b. 1949, © 1981, 1993, and New Dawn Music
Tune: Roc O'Connor, SJ, b. 1949, © 1981 and New Dawn Music; acc. by Robert J. Batastini, b. 1942, © 1994, GIA Publications, Inc.

Shout for Joy 559

Verses

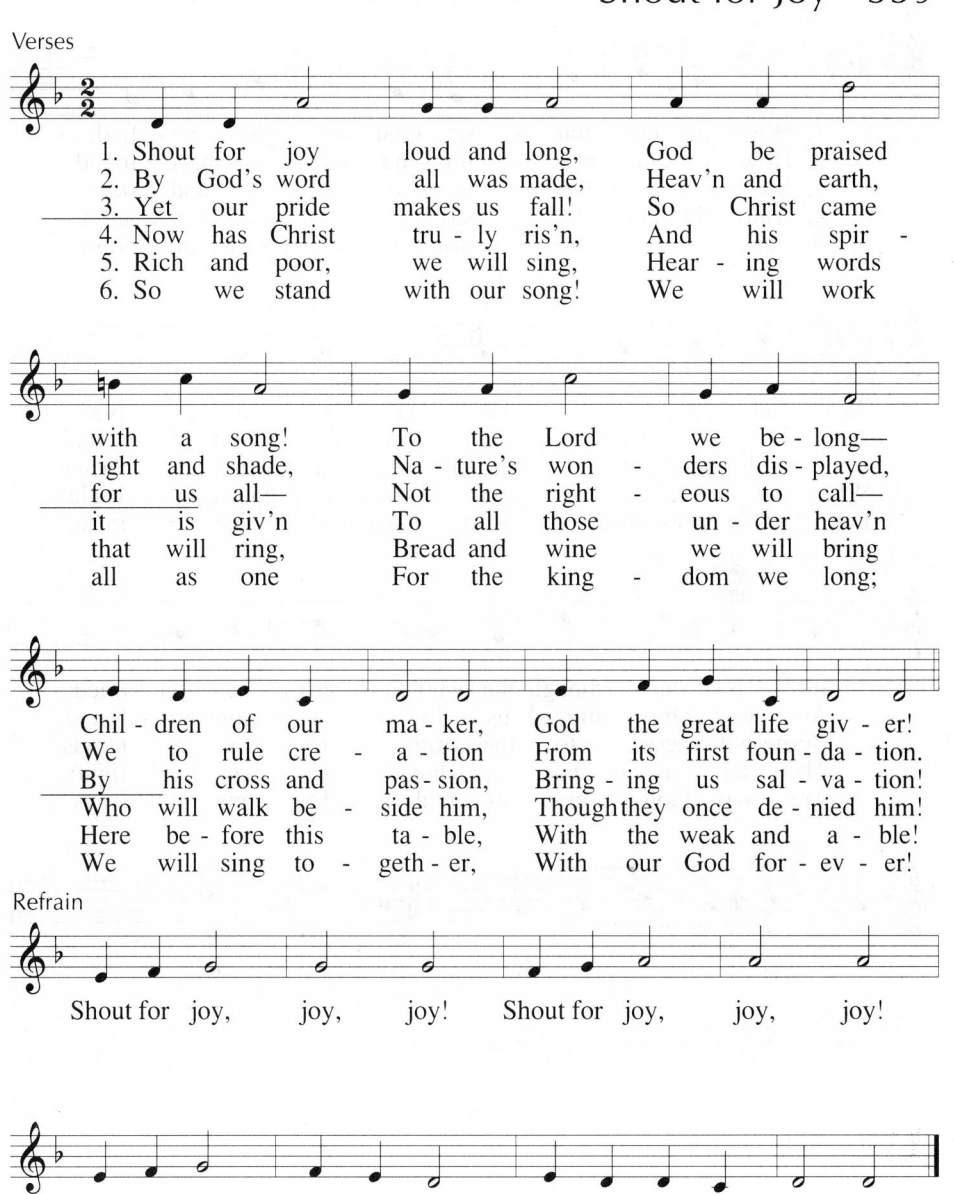

1. Shout for joy loud and long, God be praised
2. By God's word all was made, Heav'n and earth,
3. Yet our pride makes us fall! So Christ came
4. Now has Christ tru - ly ris'n, And his spir -
5. Rich and poor, we will sing, Hear - ing words
6. So we stand with our song! We will work

with a song! To the Lord we be - long—
light and shade, Na - ture's won - ders dis - played,
for us all— Not the right - eous to call—
it is giv'n To all those un - der heav'n
that will ring, Bread and wine we will bring
all as one For the king - dom we long;

Chil - dren of our ma - ker, God the great life giv - er!
We to rule cre - a - tion From its first foun - da - tion.
By his cross and pas - sion, Bring - ing us sal - va - tion!
Who will walk be - side him, Though they once de - nied him!
Here be - fore this ta - ble, With the weak and a - ble!
We will sing to - geth - er, With our God for - ev - er!

Refrain

Shout for joy, joy, joy! Shout for joy, joy, joy!

God is love, God is light, God is ev - er - last - ing!

Text: Stanzas 1-4, David Mowbray, © 1982, Hope Publishing Co.; stanzas 5-6, David Haas, b.1957, © 1993, GIA Publications, Inc.
Tune: PERSONET HODIE 666 66 with refrain, *Piae cantiones*, Griefswald, 1582; harm. by Diana Kodner, b.1957, © 1992, GIA Publications, Inc.

560 When, in Our Music, God Is Glorified

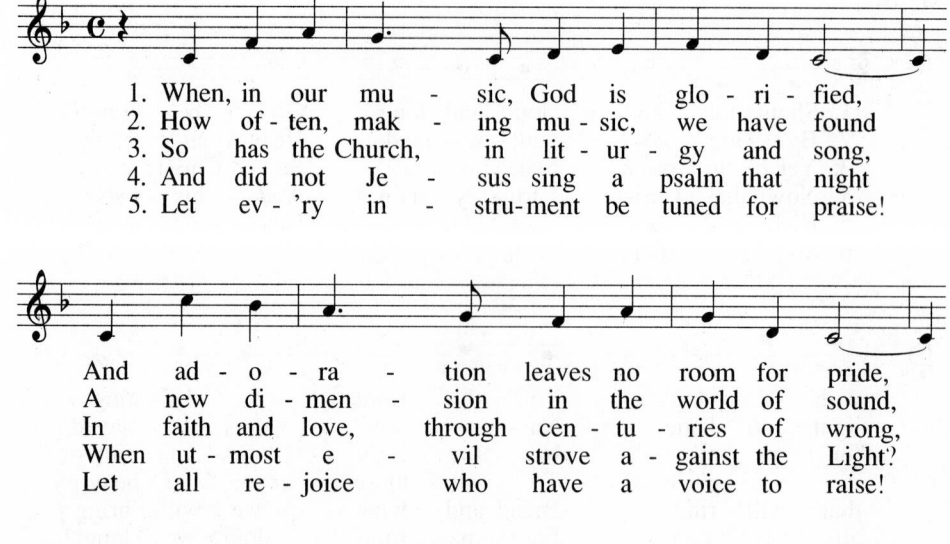

1. When, in our mu - sic, God is glo - ri - fied,
2. How of - ten, mak - ing mu - sic, we have found
3. So has the Church, in lit - ur - gy and song,
4. And did not Je - sus sing a psalm that night
5. Let ev - 'ry in - stru-ment be tuned for praise!

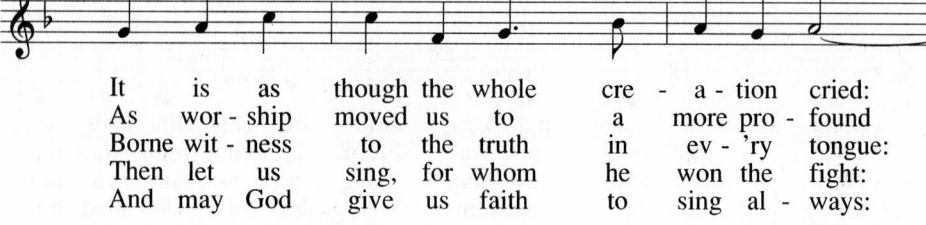

And ad - o - ra - tion leaves no room for pride,
A new di - men - sion in the world of sound,
In faith and love, through cen - tu - ries of wrong,
When ut - most e - vil strove a - gainst the Light?
Let all re - joice who have a voice to raise!

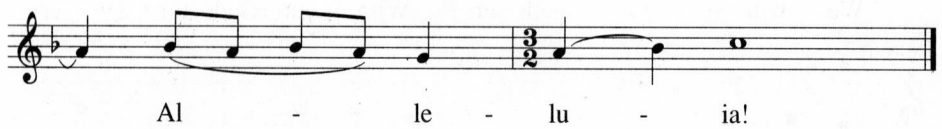

It is as though the whole cre - a - tion cried:
As wor - ship moved us to a more pro - found
Borne wit - ness to the truth in ev - 'ry tongue:
Then let us sing, for whom he won the fight:
And may God give us faith to sing al - ways:

Al - le - lu - ia!

Text: Mark 14:26; Fred Pratt Green, b.1903, © 1972, Hope Publishing Co.
Tune: ENGELBERG, 10 10 10 with alleluia; Charles V. Stanford, 1852-1924

When, in Our Music, God Is Glorified 561

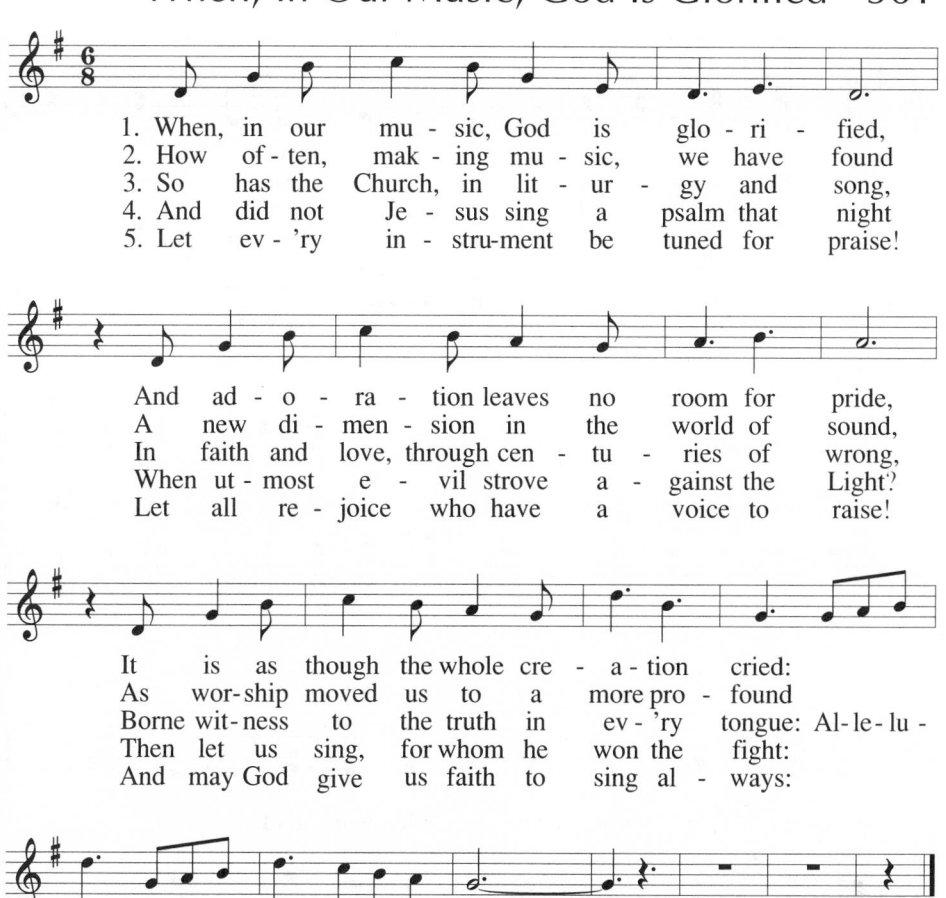

1. When, in our mu - sic, God is glo - ri - fied,
2. How of - ten, mak - ing mu - sic, we have found
3. So has the Church, in lit - ur - gy and song,
4. And did not Je - sus sing a psalm that night
5. Let ev - 'ry in - stru-ment be tuned for praise!

And ad - o - ra - tion leaves no room for pride,
A new di - men - sion in the world of sound,
In faith and love, through cen - tu - ries of wrong,
When ut - most e - vil strove a - gainst the Light?
Let all re - joice who have a voice to raise!

It is as though the whole cre - a - tion cried:
As wor-ship moved us to a more pro - found
Borne wit-ness to the truth in ev - 'ry tongue: Al-le-lu -
Then let us sing, for whom he won the fight:
And may God give us faith to sing al - ways:

ia! Al-le-lu - ia! Al-le-lu - ia!

Text: Fred Pratt Green, b.1903, © 1972, Hope Publishing Co.
Tune: MAYFLOWER, 10 10 10 with alleluias; Marty Haugen, b.1950, © 1989, GIA Publications, Inc.

562 Halleluya! We Sing Your Praises

Refrain

Hal - le - lu - ya! We sing your prais-es, all our

hearts are filled with glad - ness. Hal - le - lu - ya! We sing your

prais-es, all our hearts are filled with glad - ness.

Verses

1. Christ the Lord to us said: I am
2. Now he sends us all out, strong in

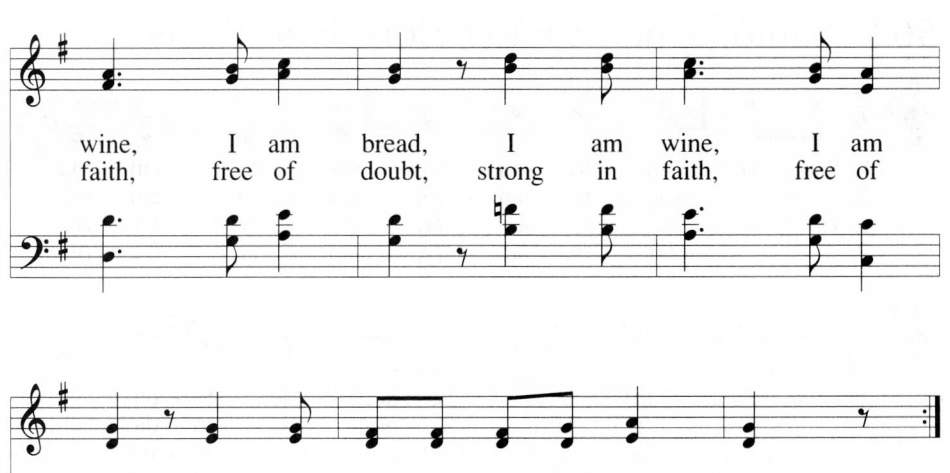

wine,   I   am   bread,   I   am   wine,   I   am
faith,   free   of   doubt,   strong   in   faith,   free   of

bread,   give   to   all   who thirst and   hun   -   ger.
doubt,   to   pro - claim the   joy - ful   Gos   -   pel.

Text: South African
Tune: South African
© 1984, Utryck, Walton Music Corporation, agent

563 Santo, Santo, Santo / Holy, Holy, Holy

1. San - to, san - to, san - to, san - to, san - to,
2.   san - to, san - to, san - to, san - to,
1. *Ho - ly, ho - ly, ho - ly, ho - ly, ho - ly,*
2.   *ho - ly, ho - ly, ho - ly, ho - ly,*

san - to_es nues - tro Dios, Se - ñor de to - da la
san - to_es nues - tro Dios, Se - ñor de to - da la_his -
ho - ly is our God, God, the Lord of earth and
ho - ly is our God, God, the Lord of all of

tie - rra. San-to, san - to_es nues - tro Dios. San-to,
to - ria. San-to, san - to_es nues - tro Dios.
heav - en. Ho-ly, ho - ly is our God. Ho-ly,
his - t'ry. Ho-ly, ho - ly is our God.

Que_a - com - pa - ña_a nues - tro pue - blo, que vi - ve_en
Ben - di - tos los que_en su nom - bre el e - van -
Who ac - com - pa - nies our peo - ple, who lives with -
Bless - ed those who in the Lord's name an - nounce the

nues - tras lu - chas, del u - ni - ver - so_en -
ge - lio_a - nun - cian, la bue - na_y gran no -
in our strug - gles, of all the earth and
ho - ly gos - pel, pro - claim - ing the good

te - ro el ú - ni - co Se - ñor.
ti - cia de la li - be - ra - ción.
heav - en the one and on - ly Lord.
news that our lib - er - a - tion comes.

Text: Guillermo Cuellar; trans. by Linda McCrae
Tune: Guillermo Cuellar; acc. by Diana Kodner, b.1957
© 1993, 1994, GIA Publications, Inc.

Come, Ye Thankful People, Come 564

1. Come, ye thank-ful peo-ple, come, Raise the song of
2. All the world is God's own field, Fruit un-to God's
3. For the Lord our God shall come, And shall take the
4. E-ven so, Lord, quick-ly come To your fi-nal

har-vest-home: All is safe-ly gath-ered in,
praise to yield; Wheat and tares to-geth-er sown,
har-vest home; From the field shall in that day
har-vest home; Gath-er all your peo-ple in,

Ere the win-ter storms be-gin; God, our Mak-er,
Un-to joy or sor-row grown; First the blade, and
All of-fens-es purge a-way, Giv-ing an-gels
Free from sor-row, free from sin; There, for ev-er

does pro-vide For our wants to be sup-plied;
then the ear, Then the full corn shall ap-pear:
charge at last In the fire the tares to cast,
pu-ri-fied, In your pres-ence to a-bide:

Come to God's own tem-ple, come,
Lord of har-vest, grant that we
But the fruit-ful ears to store
Come, with all your an-gels, come,

Raise the song of har-vest-home.
Whole-some grain and pure may be.
In God's gar-ner ev-er-more.
Raise the glo-rious har-vest-home.

Text: Henry Alford, 1810-1871, alt.
Tune: ST. GEORGE'S WINDSOR, 77 77 D; George J. Elvey, 1816-1893; harm. by Richard Proulx, b.1937. © 1986, GIA Publications, Inc.

565 Now Thank We All Our God

1. Now thank we all our God   With   hearts and hands and
2. O   may this gra-cious God   Through   all our life be
3. All praise and thanks to God   The   Fa-ther now be

voic - es, Who won-drous things has   done,   In
near   us,   With   ev - er joy - ful   hearts   And
giv - en,   The   Son, and Spir - it   blest,   Who

whom his world re - joic - es; Who, from our moth-ers'
bless-ed peace to cheer - us; Pre - serve us in his
reigns in high-est heav - en, E - ter - nal, Tri - une

arms,   Hath   blest   us   on   our   way   With
grace,   And   guide us   in   dis - tress,   And
God,   Whom earth and heav'n a - dore;   For

count-less gifts of love, And still is ours to - day.
free   us from all sin, Till heav - en we pos - sess.
thus   it was, is now, And shall be ev - er - more.

Text: *Nun danket alle Gott;* Martin Rinkart, 1586-1649; tr. by Catherine Winkworth, 1827-1878, alt.
Tune: NUN DANKET, 6 7 6 7 6 6 6 6; Johann Crüger, 1598-1662; harm. by A. Gregory Murray, OSB, b.1905

In the Lord I'll Be Ever Thankful   566

Ostinato Refrain

In the Lord I'll be ev - er thank - ful, in the Lord I will re - joice! Look to God, do not be a - fraid; lift up your voic - es, the Lord is near; lift up your voic - es, the Lord is near.

Text: Taizé Community
Tune: Jacques Berthier, 1923-1994
© 1986, 1991, Les Presses de Taizé, GIA Publications, Inc., agent

567 Let All Things Now Living

1. Let all things now liv-ing A song of thanks-giv-ing
2. His law he en-forc-es, The stars in their cours-es,

To God our Cre - a - tor tri - um-phant-ly raise;
The sun in its or - bit o - be-dient-ly shine,

Who fash-ioned and made us, Pro - tect-ed and stayed us,
The hills and the moun-tains, The riv - ers and foun-tains,

By guid - ing us on to the end of our days.
The depths of the o - cean pro - claim God di - vine.

God's ban - ners are o'er us, Pure light goes be - fore us,
We, too, should be voic - ing Our love and re - joic-ing

A pil - lar of fire shin-ing forth in the night:
With glad ad - o - ra - tion, a song let us raise:

Till shad-ows have van - ished And dark - ness is ban-ished,
Till all things now liv - ing U - nite in thanks-giv-ing,

As for - ward we trav - el from light in - to Light.
To God in the high-est, ho - san - na and praise.

Text: Katherine K. Davis, 1892-1980, © 1939, E.C. Schirmer Music Co.
Tune: ASH GROVE, 66 11 66 11 D; Welsh; harm. by Gerald H. Knight, 1908-1979, © The Royal School of Church Music

Father, We Thank Thee, Who Hast Planted 568

1. Fa - ther, we thank thee, who hast plant - ed
2. Watch o'er thy Church, O Lord, in mer - cy,

Thy ho - ly Name with - in our hearts.
Save it from e - vil, guard it still,

Knowl - edge and faith and life im - mor - tal
Per - fect it in thy love, u - nite it,

Je - sus, thy Son, to us im - parts.
Cleansed and con - formed un - to thy will.

Thou, Lord, didst make all for thy plea - sure,
As grain, once scat - ter'd on the hill - sides,

Didst give us food for all our days,
Was in this bro - ken bread made one,

Giv - ing in Christ the Bread e - ter - nal;
So from all lands thy Church be gath - er'd

Thine is the power, be thine the praise.
In - to thy king - dom by thy Son.

Text: From the *Didache*, c.110; tr. by F. Bland Tucker, 1895-1984, alt., © 1940, The Church Pension Fund
Tune: RENDEZ À DIEU, 9 8 9 8 D; *Genevan Psalter*, 1551; attr. to Louis Bourgeois, c.1510-1561

569 Thanks Be to You

1.,3. Praise to you, O God of mer-cy! Thanks be to you for
2. From of old you loved and sought us! Thanks be to you for

ev - er! Rais - ing high the weak and low - ly:
ev - er! Truth and jus - tice you have taught us:

1.
Thanks be to you for ev - er!
2., 3.
Thanks be to you for ev - er!

Strong is your faith - ful-ness, strong is your love, re -

D.C.
mem - b'ring your cov-e-nant of life with us.

Text: Marty Haugen, b.1950
Tune: Marty Haugen, b.1950
© 1990, GIA Publications, Inc.

Confitemini Domino / Come and Fill 570

Ostinato Refrain

Con - fi - te - mi - ni   Do - mi - no   quo - ni - am   bo - nus.
Come and fill our hearts with your peace. You a-lone, O Lord, are ho - ly.

Con - fi - te - mi - ni   Do - mi - no,   Al - le - lu - ia!
Come and fill our hearts   with your peace,   Al - le - lu - ia!

Text: Psalm 137, *Give thanks to the Lord for he is good;* Taizé Community, 1982
Tune: Jacques Berthier, 1923-1994
© 1982, 1991, Les Presses de Taizé, GIA Publications, Inc., agent

571　We Gather Together

1. We　gath - er　to - geth - er　to　ask　the Lord's　bless - ing;
2. Be - side　us　to　guide us,　our　God　with us　join - ing,
3. We　all　do ex - tol　you　our　lead - er　tri - um - phant,

He　chas - tens　and　has - tens　his　will　to　make　known;
Whose king - dom　calls　all　to　the　love　which en - dures.
And　pray　that　you　still　our　de - fend - er　will　be.

The　wick - ed　op - press - ing　now　cease　from dis - tress - ing:
So　from　the　be - gin - ning　the　fight　we were win - ning:
Let　your　con - gre - ga - tion　es - cape　trib - u - la - tion:

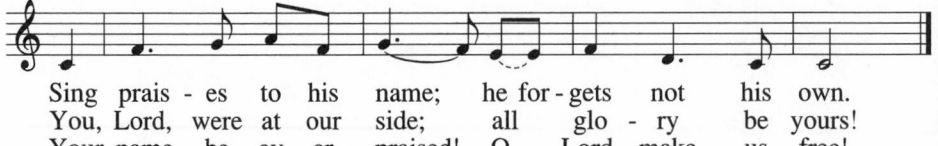

Sing　prais - es　to　his　name;　he for - gets　not　his　own.
You, Lord,　were　at　our　side;　all　glo - ry　be　yours!
Your name　be　ev - er　praised!　O　Lord, make　us　free!

Text: *Wilt heden nu treden*, Netherlands folk hymn; tr. by Theodore Baker, 1851-1934, alt.
Tune: KREMSER, 12 11 12 11; *Neder-landtsch Gedenckclanck*, 1626; harm. by Edward Kremser, 1838-1914

For the Beauty of the Earth   572

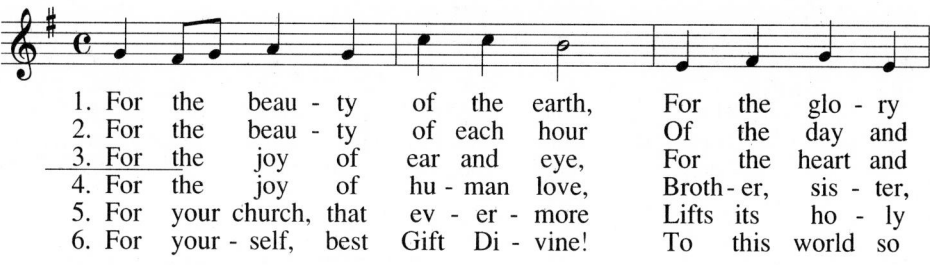

1. For   the   beau - ty   of   the   earth,   For   the   glo - ry
2. For   the   beau - ty   of   each   hour   Of   the   day   and
3. For   the   joy   of   ear   and   eye,   For   the   heart   and
4. For   the   joy   of   hu - man   love,   Broth - er,   sis - ter,
5. For   your church,   that   ev - er - more   Lifts   its   ho - ly
6. For   your - self,   best   Gift   Di - vine!   To   this   world   so

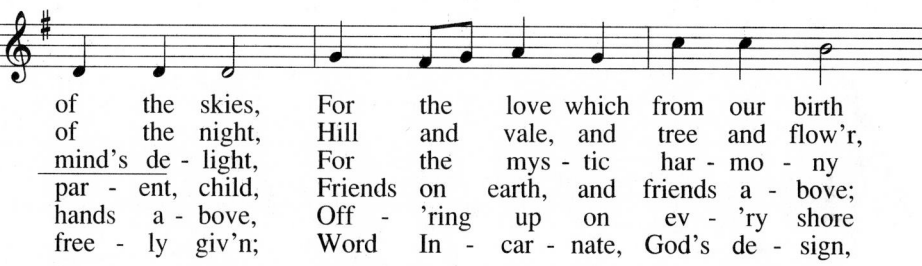

of   the   skies,   For   the   love which   from   our   birth
of   the   night,   Hill   and   vale,   and   tree   and   flow'r,
mind's   de - light,   For   the   mys - tic   har - mo - ny
par - ent,   child,   Friends   on   earth,   and   friends   a - bove;
hands   a - bove,   Off - 'ring   up   on   ev - 'ry   shore
free - ly   giv'n;   Word   In - car - nate,   God's   de - sign,

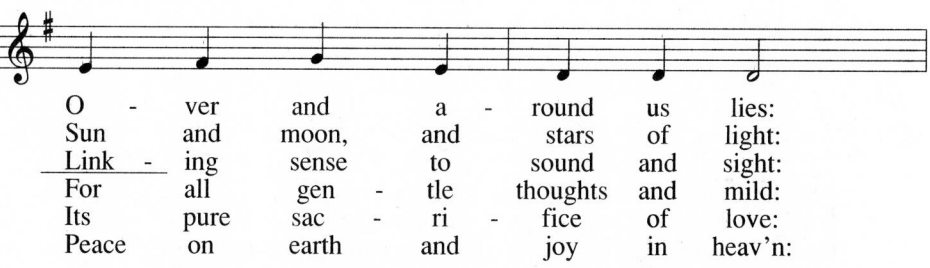

O - ver   and   a - round   us   lies:
Sun   and   moon,   and   stars   of   light:
Link - ing   sense   to   sound   and   sight:
For   all   gen - tle   thoughts   and   mild:
Its   pure   sac - ri - fice   of   love:
Peace   on   earth   and   joy   in   heav'n:

Lord   of   all,   to   you   we   raise   This our   hymn of   grate - ful praise.

Text: Folliot S. Pierpont, 1835-1917
Tune: DIX, 7 7 7 7 77; arr. from Conrad Kocher, 1786-1872, by William H. Monk, 1823-1889

573 Table Prayer

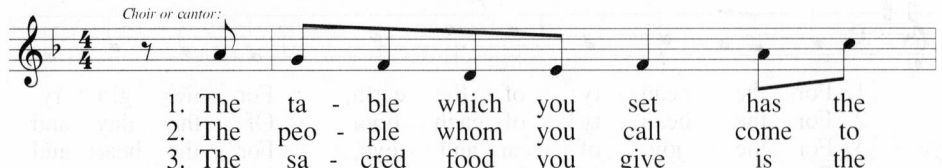

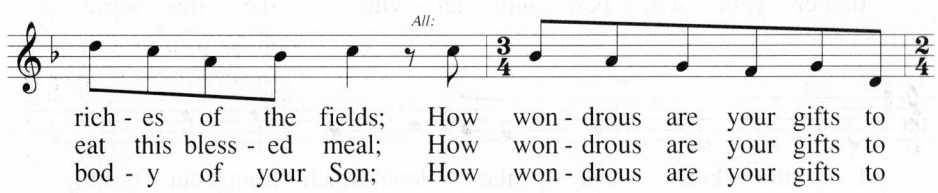

1. The   ta - ble   which   you   set   has   the
2. The   peo - ple   whom   you   call   come   to
3. The   sa - cred   food   you   give   is   the

rich - es of   the   fields; How won - drous are your gifts to
eat this bless - ed meal;   How won - drous are your gifts to
bod - y of your Son;   How won - drous are your gifts to

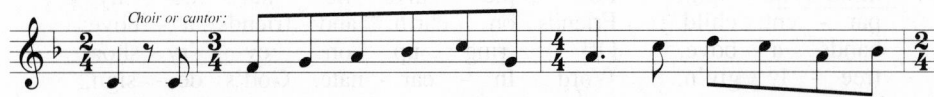

us. You share the fin - est por - tion, Lord, with rev - 'rence and with
us. We   raise our hearts in thanks to you, a   sin - gle prayer of
us. You nour - ish us with ho - ly wine to sat - is - fy our

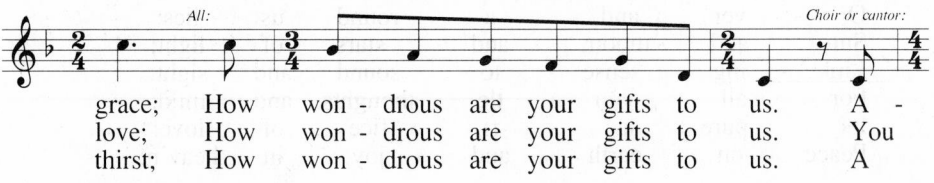

grace; How won - drous are your gifts to us.   A -
love;   How won - drous are your gifts to us.   You
thirst; How won - drous are your gifts to us.   A

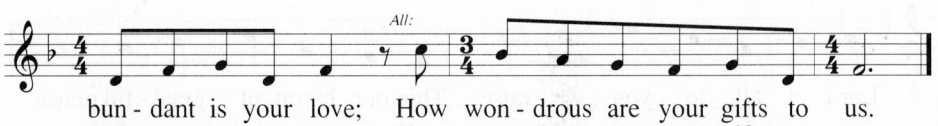

bun - dant is your love; How won - drous are your gifts to us.
gath - er us as one;   How won - drous are your gifts to us.
ban - quet for all time; How won - drous are your gifts to us.

Text: Mike Balhoff, b.1946, Gary Daigle, b.1957, Darryl Ducote, b.1945
Tune: Mike Balhoff, b.1946, Gary Daigle, b.1957, Darryl Ducote, b.1945
© 1985, Damean Music. Distributed by GIA Publications, Inc.

Lead Me, Guide Me 574

Refrain

Lead me, guide me, a - long the way, For if you
lead me, I can - not stray. Lord, let me walk each
day with thee. Lead me, oh Lord, lead me.

Verses

1. I am weak and I need thy strength and power to
2. Help me tread in the paths of right - eous - ness, Be my
3. I am lost if you take your hand from me, I am

help me o - ver my weak - est hour. Help me through the
aid when Sa - tan and sin op - press. I am put - ting
blind with - out thy Light to see, Lord, just al - ways

D.C.

dark-ness thy face to see, Lead me, oh Lord, lead me.
all my trust in thee. Lead me, oh Lord, lead me.
let me thy ser - vant be. Lead me, oh Lord, lead me.

Text: Doris M. Akers, b.1922
Tune: Doris M. Akers, b.1922, harm. by Richard Smallwood
© 1953, Doris M. Akers, All rights administered by Unichappell Music, Inc.

575 We Cannot Measure How You Heal

1. We can - not meas - ure how you heal Or
2. The pain that will not go a - way, The
3. So some have come who need your help And

an - swer ev - 'ry suf - f'rer's prayer, Yet
guilt that clings from things long past, The
some have come to make a - mends, As

we be - lieve your grace re - sponds Where faith and
fear of what the fu - ture holds, Are pres - ent
hands which shaped and saved the world Are pres - ent

doubt u - nite to care. Your hands, though blood - ied
as if meant to last. But pres - ent too is
in the touch of friends. Lord, let your Spir - it

on the cross, Sur - vive to hold and heal and
love which tends The hurt we nev - er hoped to
meet us here To mend the bod - y, mind, and

warn, To car - ry all through death to
find, The pri - vate ag - o - nies in -
soul, To dis - en - tan - gle peace from

life And cra - dle chil - dren yet un - born.
side, The mem - o - ries that haunt the mind.
pain, And make your bro - ken peo - ple whole.

Text: John L. Bell, b.1949
Tune: YE BANKS AND BRAES, 8 8 8 8 D; Scottish tradtional; arr. by John L. Bell, b.1949
© 1989, Iona Community, GIA Publications, Inc., agent

Come to Us, Creative Spirit 576

1. Come to us, cre - a - tive Spir - it, In our
2. Po - et, paint - er, mu - sic - mak - er, All your
3. Word from God e - ter - nal spring - ing, Fill our
4. In all plac - es and for ev - er Glo - ry

Fa - ther's house; Ev - 'ry hu - man tal - ent
treas - ures bring; Crafts - man, ac - tor, grace - ful
minds, we pray; And in all ar - tis - tic
be ex - pressed To the Son, with God the

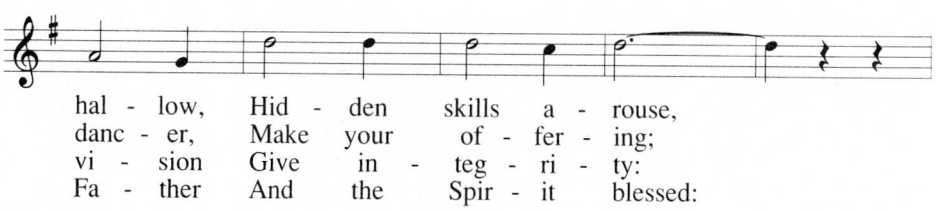

hal - low, Hid - den skills a - rouse,
danc - er, Make your of - fer - ing;
vi - sion Give in - teg - ri - ty:
Fa - ther And the Spir - it blessed:

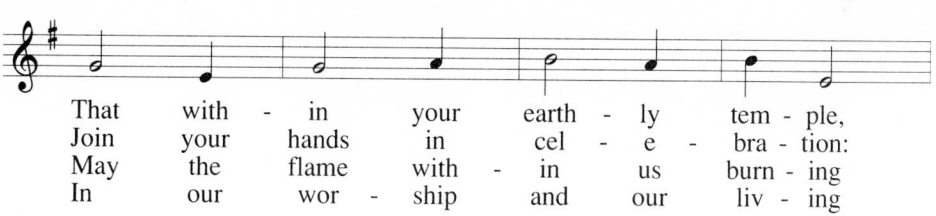

That with - in your earth - ly tem - ple,
Join your hands in cel - e - bra - tion:
May the flame with - in us burn - ing
In our wor - ship and our liv - ing

Wise and sim - ple, may re - joice.
Let cre - a - tion shout and sing!
Kin - dle yearn - ing day by day.
Keep us striv - ing for the best.

May be sung in canon.

Text: David Mowbray, b.1938, © 1979, Stainer and Bell Ltd., London, England
Tune: CREATOR SPIRITUS, 8 5 8 5 84 3; Thomas F. Savoy, b.1955, © 1987, GIA Publications, Inc.

577 Come, My Way, My Truth, My Life

1. Come, my Way, my Truth, my Life: Such a
2. Come, my Light, my Feast, my Strength: Such a
3. Come, my Joy, my Love, my Heart: Such a

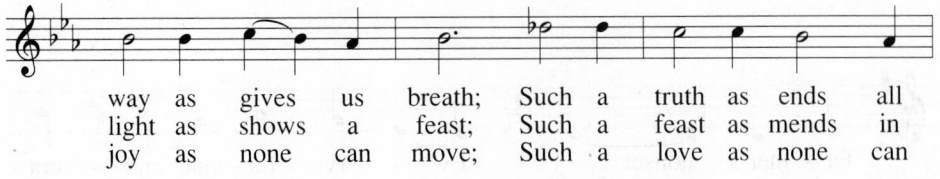

way as gives us breath; Such a truth as ends all
light as shows a feast; Such a feast as mends in
joy as none can move; Such a love as none can

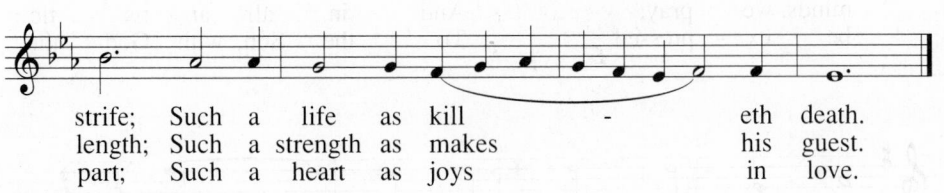

strife; Such a life as kill - eth death.
length; Such a strength as makes his guest.
part; Such a heart as joys in love.

Text: George Herbert, 1593-1632
Tune: THE CALL, 7 7 7 7; Ralph Vaughan Williams, 1872-1958. © Stainer and Bell Publications

Lord of All Hopefulness 578

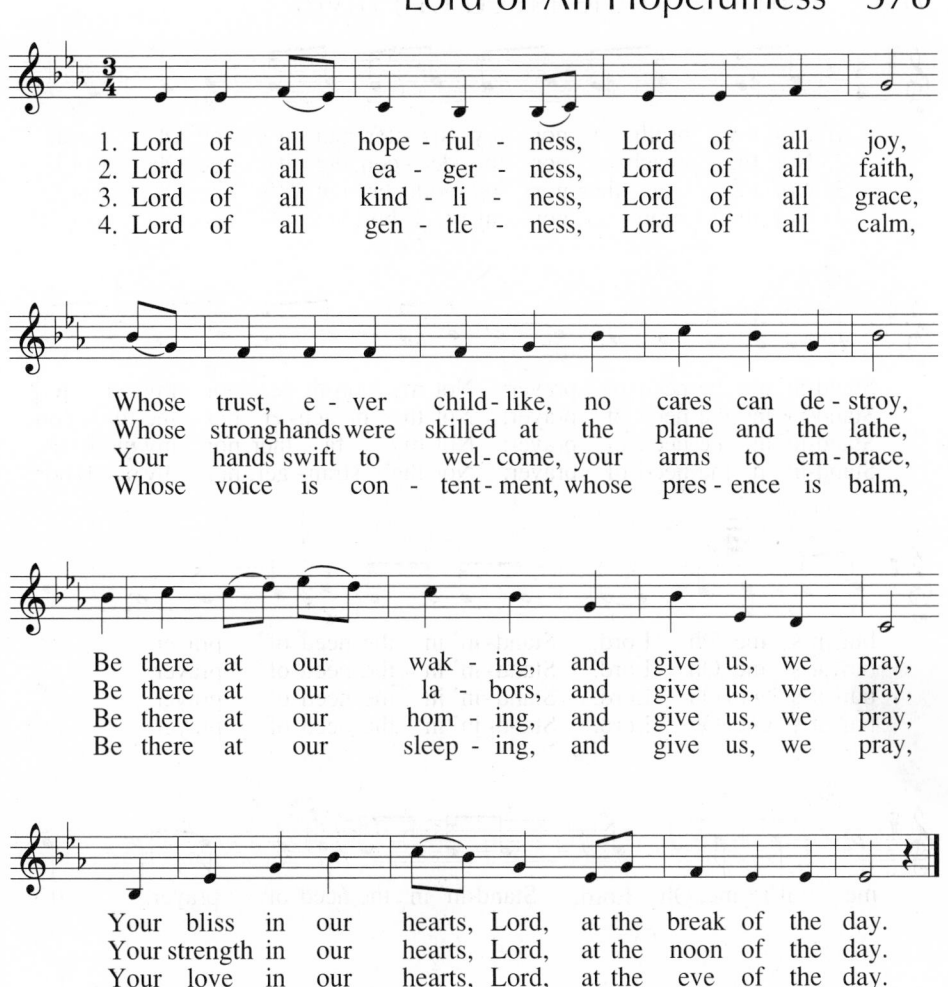

1. Lord of all hope - ful - ness, Lord of all joy,
2. Lord of all ea - ger - ness, Lord of all faith,
3. Lord of all kind - li - ness, Lord of all grace,
4. Lord of all gen - tle - ness, Lord of all calm,

Whose trust, e - ver child - like, no cares can de - stroy,
Whose strong hands were skilled at the plane and the lathe,
Your hands swift to wel - come, your arms to em - brace,
Whose voice is con - tent - ment, whose pres - ence is balm,

Be there at our wak - ing, and give us, we pray,
Be there at our la - bors, and give us, we pray,
Be there at our hom - ing, and give us, we pray,
Be there at our sleep - ing, and give us, we pray,

Your bliss in our hearts, Lord, at the break of the day.
Your strength in our hearts, Lord, at the noon of the day.
Your love in our hearts, Lord, at the eve of the day.
Your peace in our hearts, Lord, at the end of the day.

Text: Jan Struther, 1901-1953, © Oxford University Press
Tune: SLANE, 10 11 11 12; Gaelic; harm. by Erik Routley, 1917-1982, © 1985, Hope Publishing Co.

579 Standin' in the Need of Prayer

1. Not my broth-er, nor my sis-ter, but it's me, Oh Lord,
2. Not the preach-er, nor the dea-con, but it's me, Oh Lord,
3. Not my fa-ther, nor my moth-er, but it's me, Oh Lord,
4. Not the stran-ger, nor my neigh-bor, but it's me, Oh Lord,

Stand-in' in the need of prayer; Not my broth-er, nor my sis-ter,
Stand-in' in the need of prayer; Not the preach-er, nor the dea-con,
Stand-in' in the need of prayer; Not my fa-ther, nor my moth-er,
Stand-in' in the need of prayer; Not the stran-ger, nor my neigh-bor,

but it's me, Oh Lord, Stand-in' in the need of prayer.
but it's me, Oh Lord, Stand-in' in the need of prayer.
but it's me, Oh Lord, Stand-in' in the need of prayer. It's
but it's me, Oh Lord, Stand-in' in the need of prayer.

me, it's me, Oh Lord, Stand-in' in the need of prayer. It's

me, it's me, Oh Lord, Stand-in' in the need of prayer.

Text: African-American spiritual
Tune: African-American spiritual

Creating God 580

1. Cre - at - ing   God,   your   fin - gers
2. Sus - tain - ing   God,   your   hands   up -
3. Re - deem - ing   God,   your   arms   em -
4. In - dwel - ling   God,   your   gos - pel

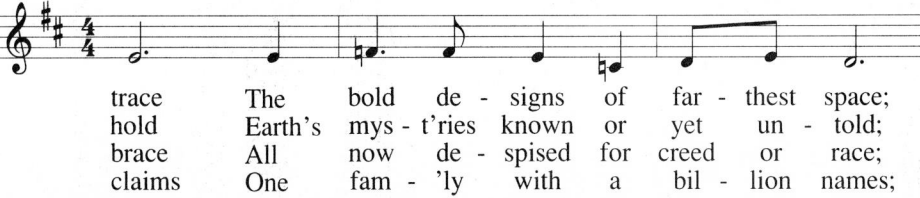

trace   The   bold   de - signs   of   far - thest   space;
hold   Earth's   mys - t'ries   known   or   yet   un - told;
brace   All   now   de - spised   for   creed   or   race;
claims   One   fam - 'ly   with   a   bil - lion   names;

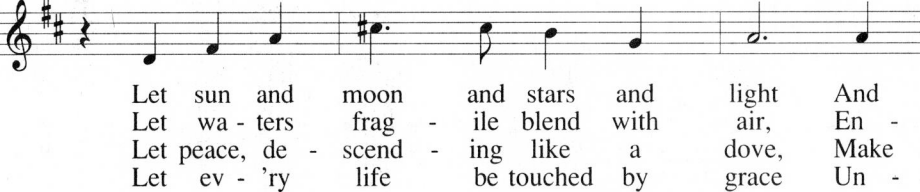

Let   sun   and   moon   and   stars   and   light   And
Let   wa - ters   frag - ile   blend   with   air,   En -
Let   peace,   de - scend - ing   like   a   dove,   Make
Let   ev - 'ry   life   be touched   by   grace   Un -

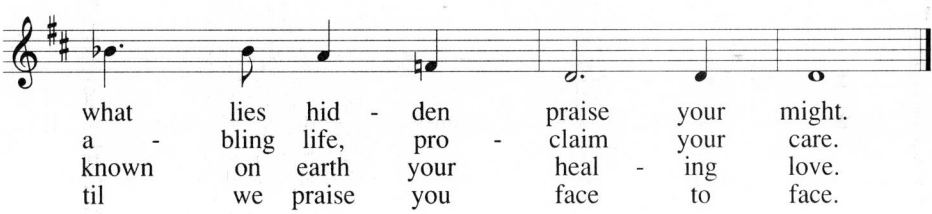

what   lies   hid - den   praise   your   might.
a - bling   life,   pro - claim   your   care.
known   on   earth   your   heal - ing   love.
til   we   praise   you   face   to   face.

Text: Jeffrey Rowthorn, b.1934, © 1979, Hymn Society of America, alt.
Tune: PRESENCE, LM; David Haas, b.1957, © 1989, GIA Publications, Inc.

581 Kyrie Guarany

1. O - ré mbo - ria - jú ve - re -
2. O - ré mbo - ria - jú ve - re -
1. On the poor, on the poor, show your
2. On the poor, on the poor, show your

kó Nan - de - ya - ra. O - ré mbo - ria -
kó Je - su - cris - to. O - ré mbo - ria -
mer - cy, O Lord. On the poor, on the
mer - cy, O Christ. On the poor, on the

jú ve - re - kó Nan - de - ya - ra.
jú ve - re - kó Je - su - cris - to.
poor, show your mer - cy, O Lord.
poor, show your mer - cy, O Christ.

Text: Adapt. liturgical text; traditional Paraguayan
Tune: As taught by Pablo Sosa; arr. by John L. Bell b.1949, © 1991, Iona Community, GIA Publications, Inc., agent

I Need You to Listen 582

Refrain

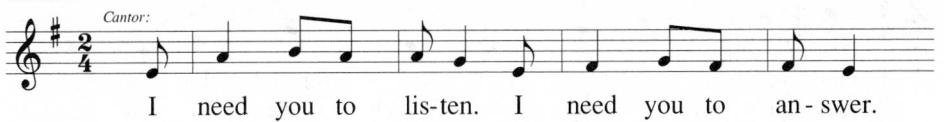

I need you to lis-ten. I need you to an-swer.

I need you to lis-ten. I need you to an - swer.

Verses

1. O God, I need you to. I want to see your face.
   It is this love I have. It makes me search for you.

2. Do not avoid my eyes or let me anger you.
   Do not toss me aside. O God, do not drop me.

3. You are the only hope I have; father, mother, they can leave me orphaned,
   but your love must never. Lead me to you, O God, along the smoothest road.

4. There are those who hate me. Do not leave me to them.
   They eat my life away by lying under oath or twisting evidence.

5. I trust your love. I will see your beauty after death in your land of life.
   My love will wait for you. It will be strong waiting. O God, my love will wait!

Text: Based on Psalm 27; Francis Patrick Sullivan, © 1983, The Pastoral Press
Tune: Marty Haugen, b.1950, © 1991, GIA Publications, Inc.

583 Gifts That Last

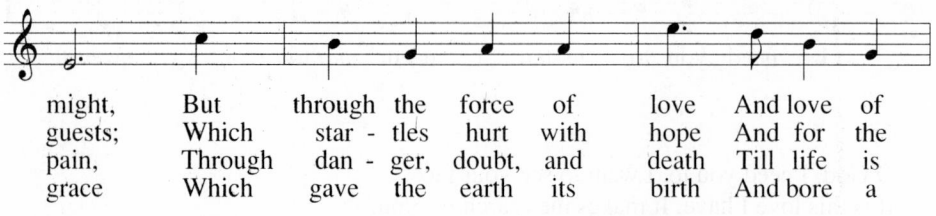

1. God, give us peace that lasts Not through the fear of
2. God, give us love that lasts, Which makes of stran - gers,
3. God, give us hope that lasts Through pas - sion and through
4. And all these things we ask In knowl - edge of your

might, But through the force of love And love of
guests; Which star - tles hurt with hope And for the
pain, Through dan - ger, doubt, and death Till life is
grace Which gave the earth its birth And bore a

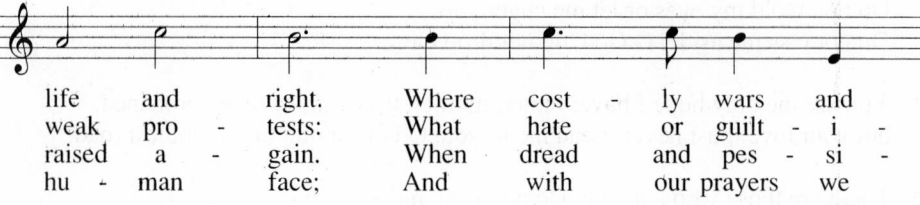

life and right. Where cost - ly wars and
weak pro - tests: What hate or guilt - i -
raised a - gain. When dread and pes - si -
hu - man face; And with our prayers we

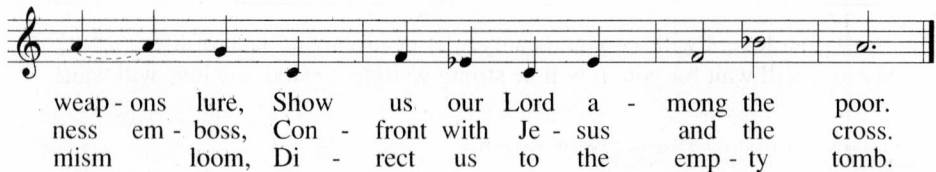

weap - ons lure, Show us our Lord a - mong the poor.
ness em - boss, Con - front with Je - sus and the cross.
mism loom, Di - rect us to the emp - ty tomb.
give our word To serve and fol - low Christ our Lord.

Text: John L. Bell, b.1949
Tune: ARKLET ROAD, 6 6 6 6 88; John L. Bell, b.1949
© 1989, Iona Community, GIA Publications, Inc., agent

Healing River 584

1. O heal - ing riv - er, send down your
2. This land is parch- ing, this land is
3. Let the seed of free - dom, a - wake and

wa - ters, Send down your wa - ters up - on this
burn- ing, No seed is grow- ing in the bar - ren
flour- ish, Let the deep roots nour- ish, let the tall stalks

land. O heal - ing riv - er, send down your
ground. O heal - ing riv - er, send down your
rise. O heal - ing riv - er, send down your

wa - ters, And wash the blood from off the sand.
wa - ters, O heal- ing riv- er, send your wa - ters down.
wa - ters, O heal- ing riv- er, from out of the skies.

The assembly echoes each phrase of the cantor at the interval of one half measure.

Text: Fran Minkoff.
Tune: Fred Hellerman; arr. by Michael Joncas, b.1951
© 1964, Appleseed Music, Inc.

585 Song over the Waters

Refrain

God, you have moved up-on the wa-ters, you have sung in the rush of wind and flame; and in your love, you have called us sons and daugh-ters, make us peo-ple of the wa-ter and your name.

Verses

1. Come fill our wait-ing hearts with the spir-it of Je-sus, let us shine with your light and peace.
2. Give us a thirst for love, give us a hun-ger for jus-tice, make us one with the mind of Christ.
3. You are the breath of life, you are the hope of the hope-less, come and fill us with light and peace.
4. Come, o-pen ev-'ry heart, come now and wake us to won-der, make us ves-sels of light and peace.

D.C.

Sprinkling Rite

Cantor: All:

(Invocation) Re-new us!

Cantor: All: D.C.

(Invocation) Re-new us!

Text: Marty Haugen, b.1950
Tune: Marty Haugen, b.1950
© 1987, GIA Publications, Inc.

O Lord, Hear My Prayer 586

Ostinato Chorale

O Lord, hear my prayer, O Lord, hear my prayer:
when I call an - swer me. O Lord, hear my prayer, O
Lord, hear my prayer. Come and lis - ten to me. O

Text: Psalm 102; Taizé Community, 1982
Tune: Jacques Berthier, 1923-1994
© 1982, Les Presses de Taizé, GIA Publications, Inc., agent

587 Bwana Awabariki / May God Grant You a Blessing

Bwa - na a - wa - ba - ri - ki, Bwa - na
May God grant you a bless-ing, may God

a - wa - ba - ri - ki, Bwa - na a - wa - ba - ri - ki
grant you a bless-ing, may God grant you a bless-ing

mi - le - le. U - ki - mcha Bwa - na.
ev - er - more. Re - vere the Lord.

Bwa - na a - wa - ba - ri - ki.
May God grant you a bless - ing.

Text: Swahili folk hymn
Tune: Swahili melody

Blest Are You 588

Cantor or choir:

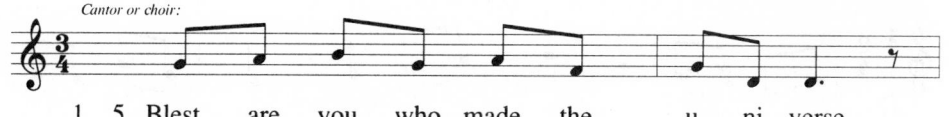

1., 5. Blest are you who made the u - ni - verse,
2. Through your good - ness we have bread to eat,
3. Through your good - ness we have wine to drink,
4. Here the stran - ger is a wel-come guest

You who see be - yond our death. Blest are you who dwells in
Seeds that died to bring life new. As the sep - 'rate grains be -
Fruit of vine-yard, work of hands. Let the fruits of all we
Here all hun - gers shall be fed. Come, and know the one who

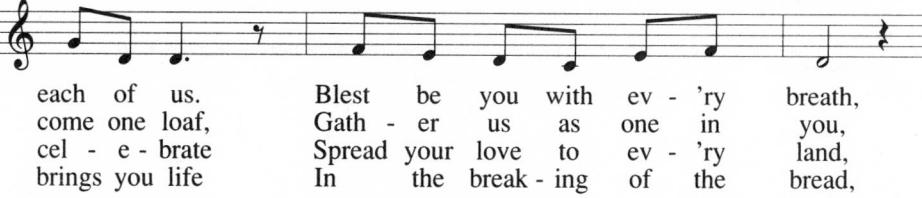

each of us. Blest be you with ev - 'ry breath,
come one loaf, Gath - er us as one in you,
cel - e - brate Spread your love to ev - 'ry land,
brings you life In the break - ing of the bread,

All:

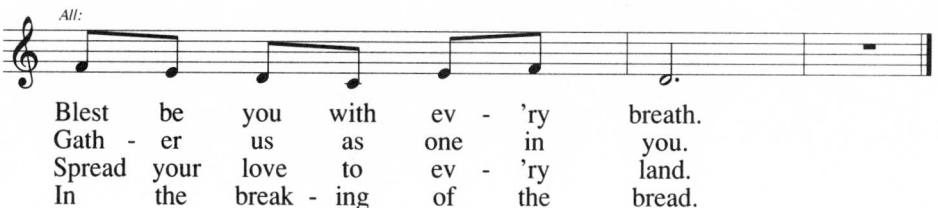

Blest be you with ev - 'ry breath.
Gath - er us as one in you.
Spread your love to ev - 'ry land.
In the break - ing of the bread.

Text: Berakhot and *Didache*; Marty Haugen, b.1950
Tune: Marty Haugen, b.1950
© 1993, GIA Publications, Inc.

589 May the Lord, Mighty God

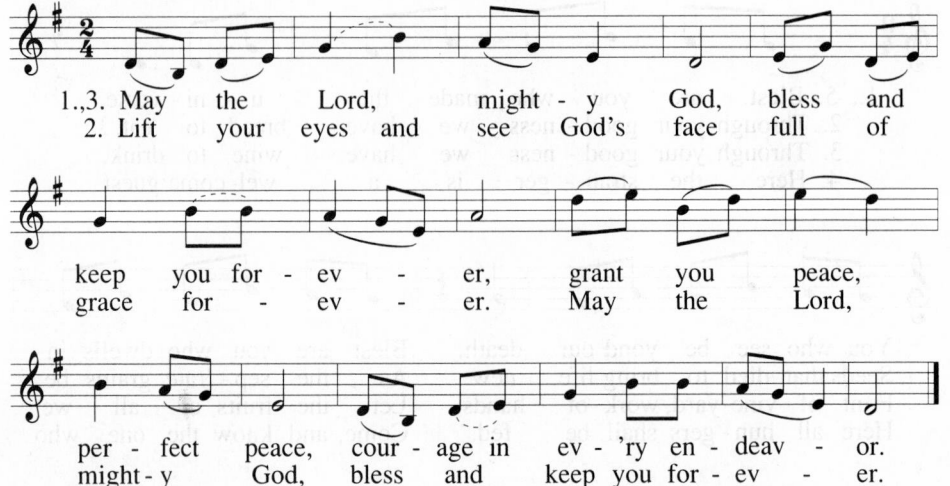

1.,3. May the Lord, might - y God, bless and
2. Lift your eyes and see God's face full of

keep you for - ev - er, grant you peace,
grace for - ev - er. May the Lord,

per - fect peace, cour - age in ev - 'ry en - deav - or.
might - y God, bless and keep you for - ev - er.

Text: Numbers 6:24-26; unknown
Tune: WEN-TI, Irregular; Chinese, Pao-chen Li; adapted by I-to Loh, © 1983, Abingdon Press; acc. by Diana Kodner, b.1957, © 1993,
    GIA Publications, Inc.

590 We Walk by Faith

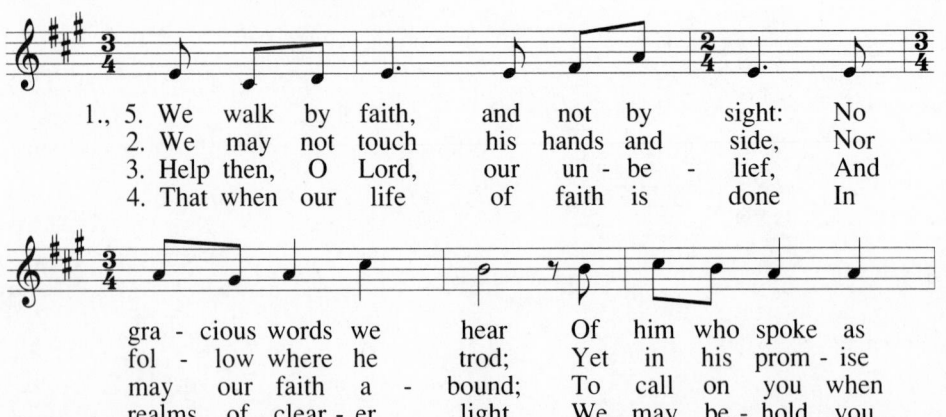

1., 5. We walk by faith, and not by sight: No
2. We may not touch his hands and side, Nor
3. Help then, O Lord, our un - be - lief, And
4. That when our life of faith is done In

gra - cious words we hear Of him who spoke as
fol - low where he trod; Yet in his prom - ise
may our faith a - bound; To call on you when
realms of clear - er light We may be - hold you

none e'er spoke, But we be-lieve him near.
we re-joice, And cry "My Lord and God!"
you are near, And seek where you are found:
as you are In full and end-less sight.

Text: Henry Alford, 1810-1871, alt.
Tune: SHANTI, CM; Marty Haugen, b.1950, © 1984, GIA Publications, Inc.

How Shall I Sing to God? 591

1. How shall I sing to God when life is filled with
2. How shall I sing to God when life is filled with
3. How shall I sing to God and tell my Sav-ior's

glad-ness, lov-ing and birth, won-der and worth? I'll
bleak-ness, emp-ty and chill, break-ing my will? I'll
sto-ry: pass-o-ver bread, life from the dead? I'll

sing from the heart, thank-ful-ly re-ceiv-ing, joy-ful in be-liev-ing.
sing through my pain, an-gri-ly or ach-ing, cry-ing or com-plain-ing.
sing with my life, wit-ness-ing and giv-ing, risk-ing and for-giv-ing.

This is my song, I'll sing it with love.
This is my song, I'll sing it with love.
This is my song, I'll sing it with love.

Text: Brian Wren, b.1936, © 1986, Hope Publishing Co.
Tune: HOPE, Irregular; David Haas, b.1957, © 1990, GIA Publications, Inc.

592 Mayenziwe / Your Will Be Done

Ma - ye - (Ma - ye) nzi - we 'nta - ndo ya - kho. Ma -
Your will (Your will) be done on earth, O Lord. Your

ye - (Ma - ye) nzi - we 'nta - ndo ya - kho. Ma - ye - nzi -
will (Your will) be done on earth, O Lord. Your will be

we 'nta - ndo ya - kho. Ma - ye - nzi - we 'nta -
done on earth, O Lord. Your will be done on

ndo ya - kho. Ma - ye - nzi - we 'nta - ndo ya - kho.
earth, O Lord. Your will be done on earth, O Lord.

Text: from the Lord's Prayer, South African
Tune: South African traditional, as taught by George Mxadana; transcribed by John L. Bell, b.1949; © 1990, Iona Community,
   GIA Publications, Inc., agent

We Remember 593

Refrain

We re - mem-ber how you loved us to your death, and still we cel-e-brate, for you are with us here; and we be-lieve that we will see you when you come in your glo - ry, Lord. We re - mem-ber, we cel-e-brate, we be - lieve.

Verses

1. Here, a mil - lion wound - ed souls are
2. Now we re - cre - ate your love, we
3. Christ, the Fa - ther's great "A - men" to
4. See the face of Christ re - vealed in

1. yearn - ing just to touch you and be healed.
2. bring the bread and wine to share a meal.
3. all the hopes and dreams of ev - 'ry heart,
4. ev - 'ry per - son stand - ing by your side,

D.C.

1. Gath - er all your peo - ple, and hold them to your heart.
2. Sign of grace and mer - cy, the pres - ence of the Lord.
3. Peace be - yond all tell - ing, and free - dom from all fear.
4. Gift to one an - oth - er, and tem - ples of your love.

Text: Marty Haugen, b.1950
Tune: Marty Haugen, b.1950
© 1980, GIA Publications, Inc.

594 Dwelling Place

Verses 1, 2, 4

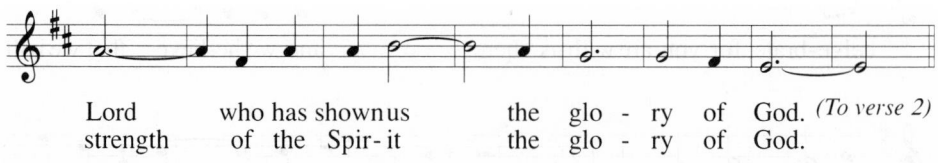

1.,4. I fall on my knees to the Fa - ther of Je-sus, the
2. May Christ in his love give us strength for our liv-ing, the

Lord who has shown us the glo - ry of God. *(To verse 2)*
strength of the Spir-it the glo - ry of God.

Refrain %

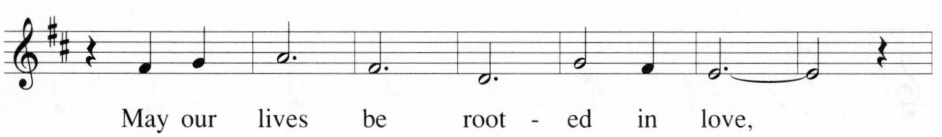

May Christ find a dwell-ing place of faith in our hearts.

May our lives be root - ed in love,

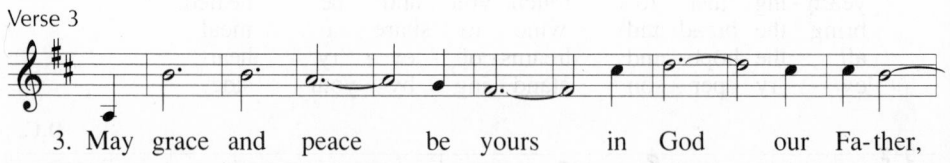

4

root-ed in love.

Verse 3

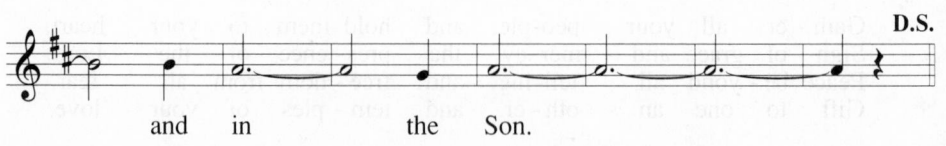

3. May grace and peace be yours in God our Fa-ther,

D.S.

and in the Son.

Text: Ephesians 3:14-17; 1:2; John Foley, SJ, b.1939
Tune: John Foley, SJ, b.1939
© 1976 by John B. Foley, SJ, administered by New Dawn Music

We Live a Mystery 595

Refrain

We live a mys-ter-y of ev-er - last-ing love:

Je - sus the liv-ing Lord, the God who came to earth to die and

rise a - gain; We live your mys - t'ry Lord.

Verses

1. This truth we car - ry, this faith we cling to:
2. He came as broth - er, he came as sav - ior.
3. No eye has seen it, no ear has heard it:

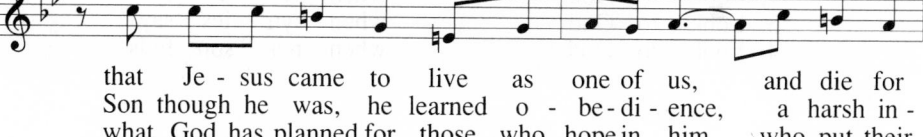

that Je - sus came to live as one of us, and die for
Son though he was, he learned o - be - di - ence, a harsh in -
what God has planned for those who hope in him, who put their

D.C.

all of us.
her - i - tance. We wait for your re - turn.
trust in him.

Text: Michael Connolly, b.1955
Tune: Michael Connolly, b.1955
© 1988, GIA Publications, Inc.

596 Do Not Fear to Hope

Refrain

Do not fear to hope tho' the wick-ed rage and rise, our

God sees not as we see, suc - cess is not the prize. Do not

fear to hope for tho' the night be long, the race shall not be

to the swift, the fight not to the strong.

Verses

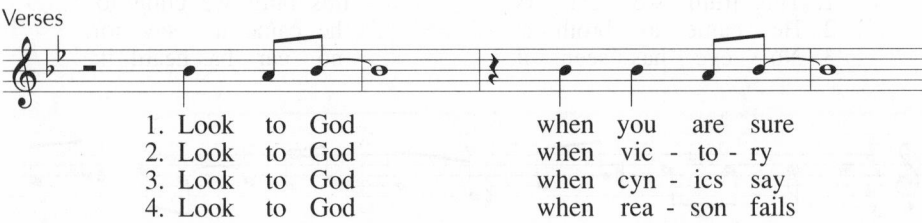

1. Look to God when you are sure
2. Look to God when vic - to - ry
3. Look to God when cyn - ics say
4. Look to God when rea - son fails

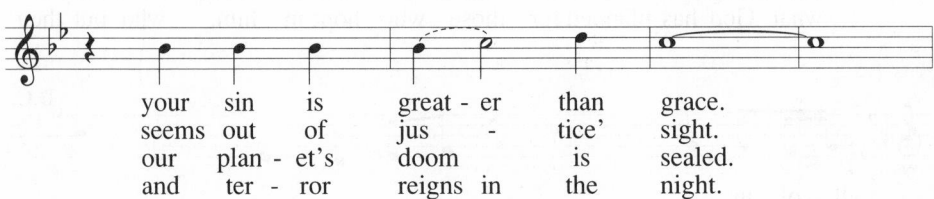

your sin is great - er than grace.
seems out of jus - tice' sight.
our plan - et's doom is sealed.
and ter - ror reigns in the night.

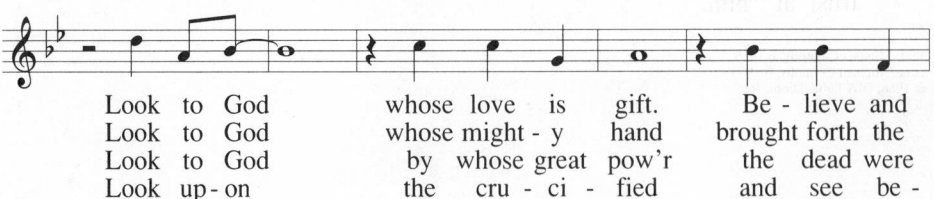

Look to God whose love is gift. Be - lieve and
Look to God whose might - y hand brought forth the
Look to God by whose great pow'r the dead were
Look up - on the cru - ci - fied and see be -

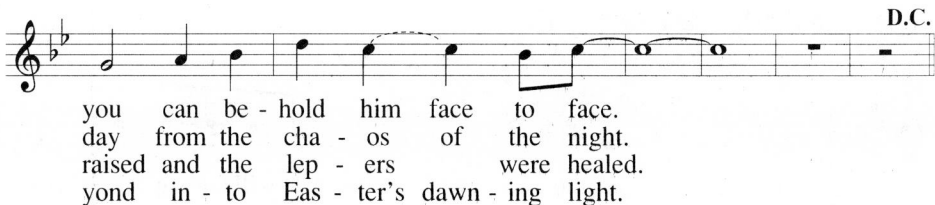

D.C.

you   can   be - hold   him   face   to   face.
day   from the   cha - os   of   the   night.
raised and the   lep - ers   were healed.
yond   in - to   Eas - ter's dawn - ing   light.

Text: Rory Cooney, b. 1952
Tune: Rory Cooney, b. 1952
© 1986, North American Liturgy Resources

I Say "Yes," Lord / Digo "Sí," Señor   597

Verses

(Invocation)   I say   "Yes," my Lord. I say "Yes," my Lord.
           Di - go   "Sí,"   Se - ñor. Di-go "Sí,"   Se-ñor.

Refrain

I   say   "Yes," my Lord,   in   all   the good times, through
Di - go   "Sí,"   Se - ñor,   en   tiem-pos mal - os,   en

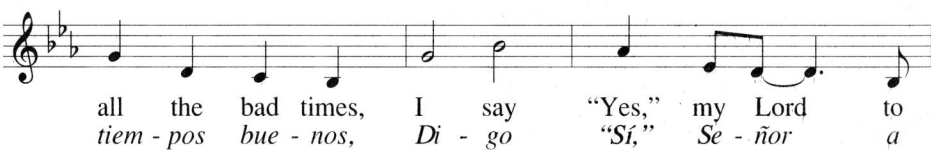

all   the   bad times,   I   say   "Yes," my   Lord   to
tiem - pos bue - nos,   Di - go   "Sí,"   Se - ñor   a

ev - 'ry   word   you   speak.
to - do   lo   que ha -   blas.

Text: Donna Peña, b.1955
Tune: Donna Peña, b.1955; arr. by Marty Haugen, b.1950
© 1989, GIA Publications, Inc.

598 Center of My Life

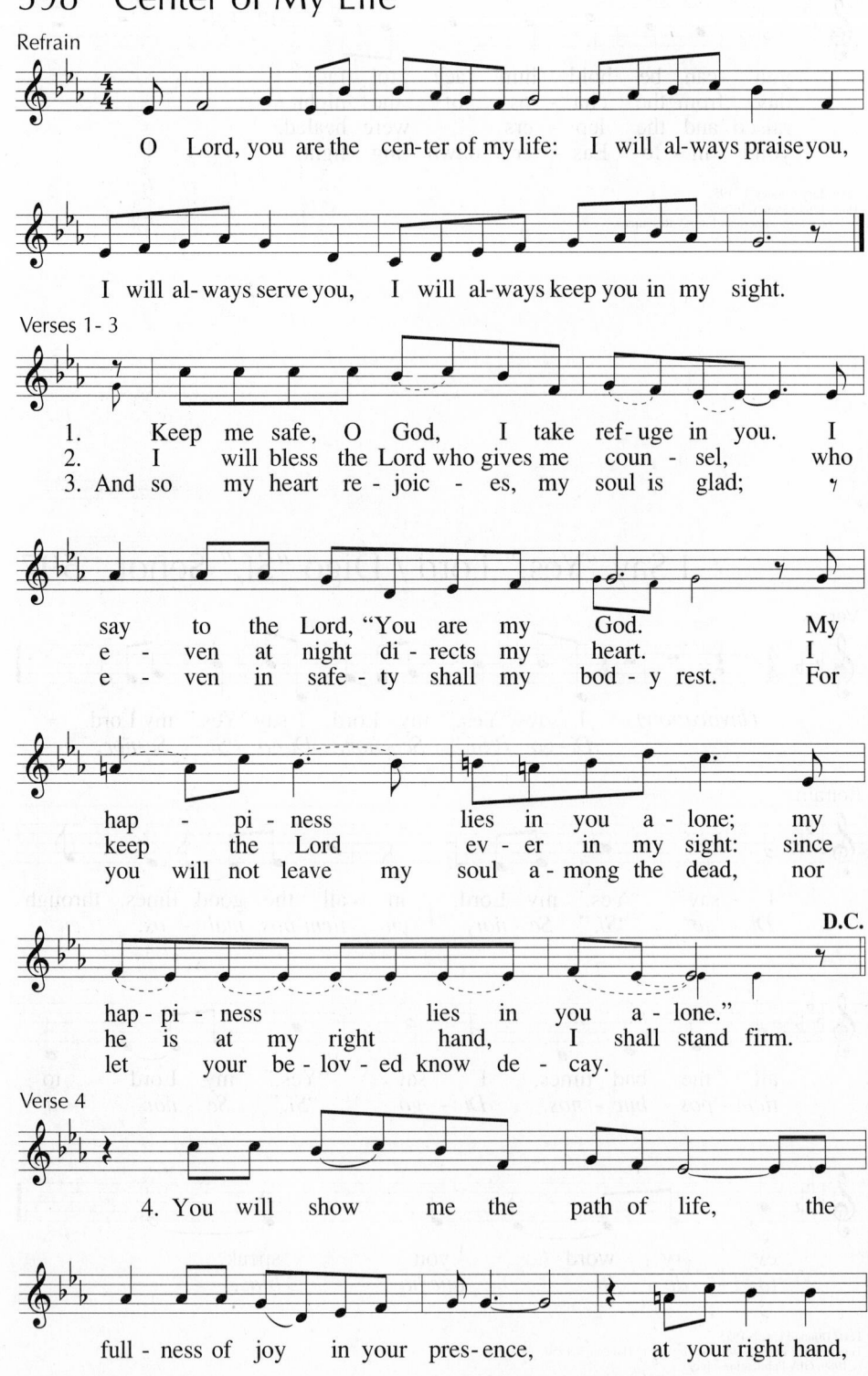

Refrain

O Lord, you are the cen-ter of my life: I will al-ways praise you,

I will al-ways serve you, I will al-ways keep you in my sight.

Verses 1-3

1. Keep me safe, O God, I take ref-uge in you. I
2. I will bless the Lord who gives me coun - sel, who
3. And so my heart re - joic - es, my soul is glad;

say to the Lord, "You are my God. My
e - ven at night di - rects my heart. I
e - ven in safe - ty shall my bod - y rest. For

hap - pi - ness lies in you a - lone; my
keep the Lord ev - er in my sight: since
you will not leave my soul a - mong the dead, nor

D.C.

hap - pi - ness lies in you a - lone."
he is at my right hand, I shall stand firm.
let your be - lov - ed know de - cay.

Verse 4

4. You will show me the path of life, the

full - ness of joy in your pres - ence, at your right hand,

D.C.

at your right hand   hap‑pi‑ness for ev‑er.

Text: Psalm 16; verses trans. © 1963, The Grail, GIA Publications, Inc., agent; refrain, Paul Inwood, b.1947, © 1985
Tune: Paul Inwood, b.1947, © 1985
Published by OCP Publications

Hold Me in Life   599

Refrain

Hold   me   in   life   for   you   are   my   safe - ty,

al - ways   my   eyes   are   look - ing   for   you.

Verses

1. Be - cause   you   are   just   who   you   are,
2. Are   you   the   one   who   is   to   come,
3. You   gave   your   Word   to   this,   our   world:

don't pass   me   by,   but   show   me   your   mer - cy;
or   must   we   wait   and   fol - low   some   oth - er?
you   are   my   song,   the   God   of   my   glad - ness;

D.C.

I   will   wait   for   you   all   my   life.
Lord,   my   God,   I   am   cer - tain   of   you.
my   de - sire   goes   out   to   you.

Text: Psalm 25; Huub Oosterhuis, b.1933; trans. by David Smith, b.1933, and Forrest Ingram
Tune: Bernard Huijbers, b.1922
© 1967, Gooi en Sticht, bv., Baarn, The Netherlands, Exclusive English-language agent: OCP Publications

600 Faith of Our Fathers

1. Faith of our fa - thers! Liv - ing still
2. The mar - tyrs, chained in pris - ons dark,
3. Faith of our moth - ers! Faith and pray'r
4. Faith of our fa - thers! We will love

In spite of dun - geon, fire and sword:
Were still in heart and con - science free:
Shall win all na - tions un - to thee;
Both friend and foe in all our strife:

O how our hearts beat high with joy,
And tru - ly blest would be our fate,
And through the truth that comes from God,
And preach thee, too, as love knows how,

When - e'er we hear that glo - rious word:
If we, like them, should die for thee.
We shall all then in - deed be free.
By kind - ly deeds and vir - tuous life.

Faith of our fa - thers, ho - ly faith!
Faith of the mar - tyrs, ho - ly faith!
Faith of our moth - ers, ho - ly faith!
Faith of our fa - thers, ho - ly faith!

We will be true to thee till death.
We will be true to thee till death.
We will be true to thee till death.
We will be true to thee till death.

Text: Frederick W. Faber, 1814-1863, alt.
Tune: ST. CATHERINE, LM with refrain; Henry F. Hemy, 1818-1888; adapt. by James G. Walton, 1821-1905

All That We Have 601

Refrain

All that we have and all that we of-fer Comes from a

heart both fright-ened and free. Take what we bring now and

give what we need, All done in his name.

Verses

1. Some would re - ly on their pow - er,
2. Some - times the road may be lone - some,
3. Some - times when trou - bles are man - y,

Oth - ers put trust in their gold.
Of - ten we may lose our way;
Life can seem emp - ty, it's true,

Some have on - ly their Sav - ior,
Take cour - age and al - ways re - mem - ber
But look at the life of the Mas - ter,

D.C.

Whose faith-ful-ness nev - er grows old.
Love is - n't just for a day.
Who lov - ing-ly suf - fered for you.

Text: Gary Ault, b.1944
Tune: Gary Ault b.1944; acc. by Gary Daigle, b.1957, alt.
© 1969, 1979, Damean Music. Distributed by GIA Publications, Inc.

602 Though the Mountains May Fall

Refrain

Though the mountains may fall and the hills turn to dust,
yet the love of the Lord will stand
as a shelter for all who will call on his name.
Sing the praise and the glory of God.

Verses

1. Could the Lord ever leave you? Could the Lord forget his love? Though a mother forsake her child, he will not abandon you.
2. Should you turn and forsake him, he will gently call your name. Should you wander away from him, he will always take you back.
3. Go to him when you're weary; he will give you eagle's wings. You will run, never tire, for your God will be your strength.
4. As he swore to your fathers, when the flood destroyed the land; He will never forsake you; he will swear to you again.

D.C.

Text: Isaiah 54:6-10, 49:15, 40:31-32; Dan Schutte, b.1947
Tune: Dan Schutte, b.1947; acc. by Michael Pope, SJ
© 1975, Daniel L. Schutte and New Dawn Music

How Can I Keep from Singing   603

Verses

1. My life flows on in end-less song A-
2. Through all the tu-mult and the strife, I
3. What though the tem-pest 'round me roar, I
4. When ty-rants trem-ble, sick with fear, And
5. The peace of Christ makes fresh my heart, A

bove earth's lam-en-ta-tion. I hear the real though
hear that mu-sic ring-ing; It sounds and ech-oes
hear the truth it liv-eth. What though the dark-ness
hear their death knells ring-ing; When friends re-joice both
foun-tain ev-er spring-ing. All things are mine since

far-off hymn That hails a new cre-a-tion.
in my soul; How can I keep from sing-ing?
'round me close, Songs in the night it giv-eth.
far and near, How can I keep from sing-ing?
I am his; How can I keep from sing-ing?

Refrain

No storm can shake my in-most calm, While to that rock I'm

cling-ing. Since love is Lord of heav-en and earth,

How can I keep from sing-ing?

Text: Robert Lowry, 1826-1899; adapted with additional text by Doris Plenn
Tune: HOW CAN I KEEP FROM SINGING, 8 7 8 7 with refrain; Robert Lowry, 1826-1899; harm. by Robert J. Batastini, b.1942
© 1957, 1964, Sanga Music, Inc.

604 You Are Near

Refrain

Yah-weh, I know you are near, stand-ing al - ways at my side. You guard me from the foe, and you lead me in ways ev - er - last - ing.

Verses

1. Lord, you have searched my heart, and you know when I sit and when I stand. Your hand is up - on me pro - tect - ing me from death, keep - ing me from harm.

2. Where can I run from your love? If I climb to the heav - ens you are there; if I fly to the sun - rise or sail be - yond the sea, still I'd find you there.

3. You know my heart and its ways, you who formed me be - fore I was born in the se - cret of dark - ness be - fore I saw the sun in my moth - er's womb.

4. Mar - vel - ous to me are your works; how pro - found are your thoughts, my Lord. E - ven if I could count them, they num - ber as the stars, you would still be there.

D.C.

Text: Psalm 139; Dan Schutte, b.1947
Tune: Dan Schutte, b.1947; acc. by Sr. Theophane Hytrek, OSF, 1915-1992
© 1971, Daniel L. Schutte, administered by New Dawn Music

The Lord Is My Light   605

Verses 1, 3

1. The Lord is my light and my sal-va-tion, the Lord is my
3. Wait on the Lord and be of good cour-age, O wait on the

light and my sal-va-tion, the Lord is my light and
Lord and be of good cour-age, wait on the Lord and

my sal-va-tion; whom shall I fear?
be of good cour-age. He shall strength-en thine heart.

Refrain

Whom shall I fear, whom shall I fear? The Lord is the

strength of my life; whom shall I fear?

Verse 2

2. In the time of trou-ble he shall hide me, O in the time of

trou-ble, he shall hide me, in the time of trou-ble,

D.S.

he shall hide me; whom shall I fear?

Text: Lillian Bouknight
Tune: Lillian Bouknight; arr. by Paul Gainer
© 1980, Savgos Music, Inc.

606 How Firm a Foundation

1. How firm a foun - da - tion, you saints of the
2. "Fear not, I am with you, O be not dis -
3. "When through the deep wa - ters I call you to
4. "The soul that on Je - sus still leans for re -

Lord, Is laid for your faith in this ex - cel - lent
mayed, For I am your God, and will still give you
go, The riv - ers of woe shall not you o - ver -
pose, I will not, I will not de - sert to its

Word! What more can God say than to you has been
aid; I'll strength - en you, help you, and cause you to
flow; For I will be with you, your trou - bles to
foes; That soul, though all hell should en - deav - or to

said, To you who for ref - uge to Je - sus have fled?
stand, Up - held by my right - eous, om - nip - o - tent hand.
bless, And sanc - ti - fy to you, your deep - est dis - tress.
shake, I'll nev - er, no nev - er, no nev - er for - sake!"

Text: 2 Peter 1:4; "K" in Rippon's *A Selection of Hymns*, 1787
Tune: FOUNDATION, 11 11 11 11; Funk's *Compilation of Genuine Church Music*, 1832; harm. by Richard Proulx, b.1937, GIA Publications, Inc.

A Mighty Fortress Is Our God   607

1. A might-y for-tress is our God, A sword and
2. No strength of ours can match his might! We would be
3. Though hordes of dev-ils fill the land All threat-n'ing
4. God's Word for-ev-er shall a - bide, No thanks to

shield vic-to-rious, Who breaks the cruel op-pres-sor's
lost, re-ject-ed. But now a cham-pion comes to
to de-vour us, We trem-ble not, un-moved we
foes, who fear it; For God, our Lord, fights by our

rod And wins sal-va-tion glo-rious. The old sa-
fight, Whom God a-lone e-lect-ed. You ask who
stand; They can-not o-ver-pow'r us. Let this world's
side With weap-ons of the Spir-it. Were they to

tan-ic foe Has sworn to work us woe!
this may be? The Lord of hosts is he!
ty-rant rage; In bat-tle we'll en-gage!
take our house, Goods, hon-or, child, or spouse,

With craft and dread-ful might He arms him-
Christ Je-sus, might-y Lord, God's on-ly
His might is doomed to fail; God's judge-ment
Though life be wrenched a-way, They can-not

self to fight. On earth he has no e - qual.
Son, a-dored. He holds the field vic-to - rious.
must pre-vail! One lit-tle word sub-dues him.
win the day. The King-dom's ours for-ev - er!

Text: Psalm (45) 46; *Ein'feste Burg ins unser Gott;* Martin Luther. 1483-1546: tr. © 1978. *Lutheran Book of Worship*
Tune: EIN' FESTE BURG. 8 7 8 7 66 66 7; Martin Luther. 1483-1546: harm by J.S. Bach. 1685-1750

608 Be Not Afraid

pow'r of hell and death is at your side, know that I am

with you through it all.

Verse 3

3. Bless-ed are your poor, for the king-dom shall be theirs.

Blest are you that weep and mourn, for one day you shall

laugh. And if wick-ed tongues in - sult and hate you

all be - cause of me, bless-ed,

bless - ed are you!

609 The Lord Is Near

Refrain

The Lord is near to all who call, rest in

God a - lone, rest in God a - lone.

Verses

1. God will guard your com - ing and your go - ing;
2. God has seen a thou - sand years go past;
3. Lord, in you I come to take my ref - uge;
4. Trust in God for ev - er, O my peo - ple;

And will be the one to guard your life. The
Swift - ly as a morn - ing fades to night. So
Through the night you ev - er coun - sel me. O
Pour out all your hearts be - fore the Lord. Your

sun will not harm you in the day - light, And the
come, and be filled with God's wis - dom, To
Lord, you have formed me to be ho - ly And to
God is a rock of strength, your glo - ry; In the

D.C.

Lord will watch you through the night.
num - ber all your days a - right.
rest with - in you peace - ful - ly.
Lord is all your hope re - stored.

Text: Psalm 62; Mike Balhoff, b.1946
Tune: Darryl Ducote, b.1945, Gary Daigle, b.1957
© 1978, Damean Music. Distributed by GIA Publications, Inc.

My Refuge 610

Refrain

In you, O God, my re-fuge I take;

I will not be a - fraid.

Verses

1. In your jus - tice save me;
2. You, O God, are my rock, my
3. I will re - joice in the Lord, be
4. You will free me, O Lord, from
5. In - to your hands, O Lord, I com -

turn your ear to me. O
for - tress, and my strength; for
glad of your kind - ness to me.
out of my cap - tor's snares; for
mend my spir - it to you. For

Lord make haste to an -
your name's sake you will lead
Lord, let your face shine up -
you are my ref - uge
you will re - deem me,

D.C.

swer me.
and guide me.
on me, your ser - vant.
you are my hope.
faith - ful God.

Text: Psalm 31; Dennis Vessels, b.1953
Tune: Dennis Vessels, b.1953; arr. by Sheryl Soderberg
© 1982, Dennis Vessels

611 On Eagle's Wings

Verse 1

1. You who dwell in the shel-ter of the Lord, who a-

bide in his shad-ow for life, say to the Lord: "My

ref-uge, my rock in whom I trust!"

Refrain 𝄋

And he will raise you up on ea-gle's wings,

bear you on the breath of dawn, make you to shine like the sun, and

Last time to coda ⊕   *To verses*

hold you in the palm of his hand.   2. The

Verse 2

snare of the fowl-er will nev-er cap-ture you, and

3

fam-ine will bring you no fear: un-der his wings your

D.S.

ref - uge, his faith - ful - ness your shield.

Verse 3

3. You need not fear the ter - ror of the night, nor the

ar - row that flies by day; though thou - sands fall a -

D.S.

bout you, near you it shall not come.

Verse 4

4. For to his an - gels he's giv - en a com-mand to

guard you in all of your ways; up - on their hands they will

D.S.

bear you up, lest you dash your foot a- gainst a stone.

Coda

And hold you, hold you in the palm of his hand.

Text: Psalm 91: Michael Joncas. b.1951
Tune: Michael Joncas. b.1951
© 1979, New Dawn Music

612 Amazing Grace

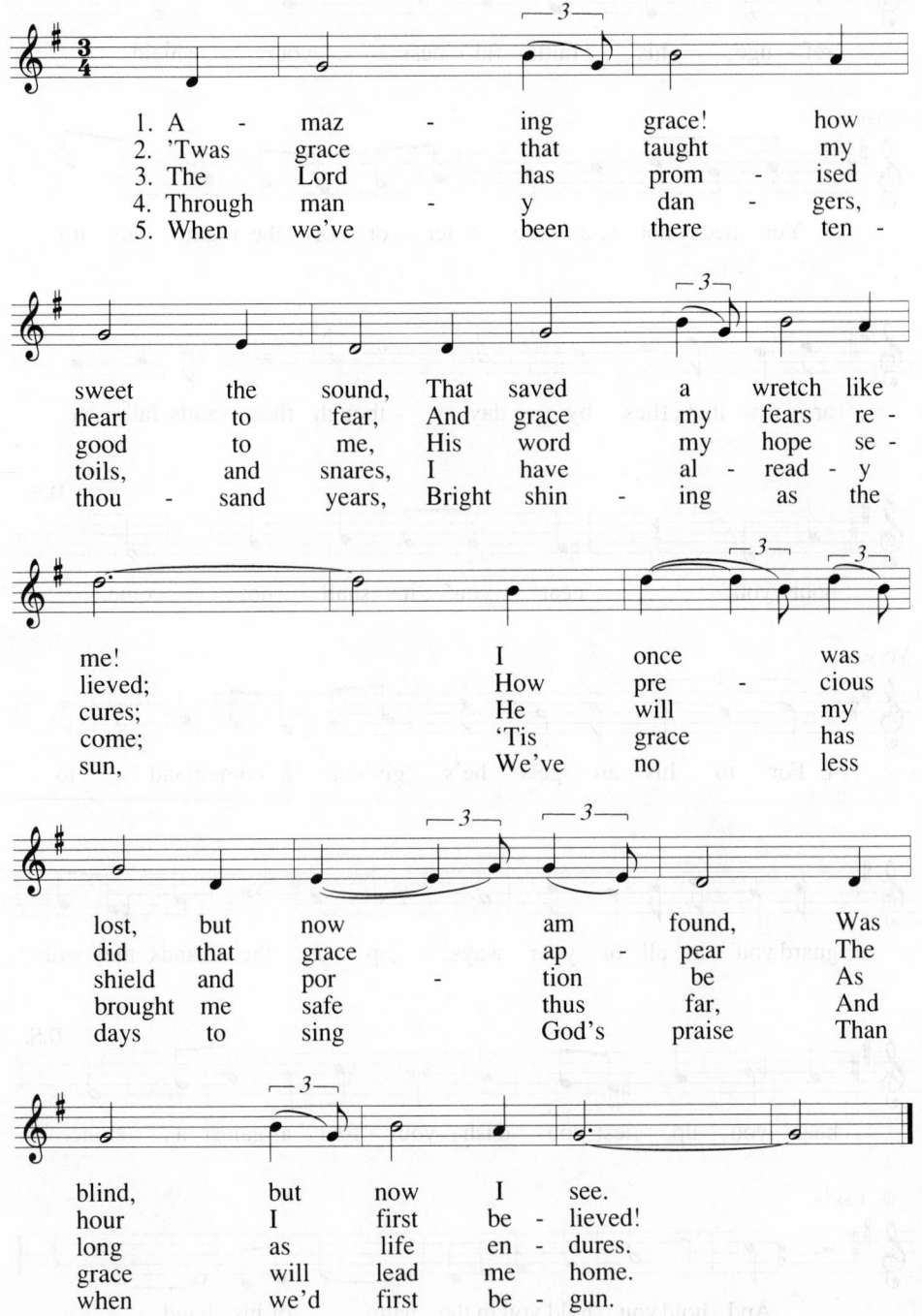

1. A - maz - ing grace! how sweet the sound, That saved a wretch like me! I once was lost, but now am found, Was blind, but now I see.
2. 'Twas grace that taught my heart to fear, And grace my fears re - lieved; How pre - cious did that grace ap - pear The hour I first be - lieved!
3. The Lord has prom - ised good to me, His word my hope se - cures; He will my shield and por - tion be, As long as life en - dures.
4. Through man - y dan - gers, toils, and snares, I have al - read - y come; 'Tis grace has brought me safe thus far, And grace will lead me home.
5. When we've been there ten - thou - sand years, Bright shin - ing as the sun, We've no less days to sing God's praise Than when we'd first be - gun.

Text: St. 1-4 John Newton, 1725-1807; st. 5 attr. to John Rees, fl.1859
Tune: NEW BRITAIN, CM; *Virginia Harmony*, 1831; acc. by Diana Kodner, b.1957, © 1993, GIA Publications, Inc.

The Lord Is My Hope   613

Refrain

The Lord is my hope and my glo-ry. The Lord is the song that I sing: so ten-der and lov-ing a shep-herd, so root-ed in jus-tice, a king. When shad-ow con-fus-es my vi-sion, when sor-row lays claim to my heart, God is my re-fuge, my rock and my shield. I will re-ly on the Lord.

Verses

1. Near to death, I cried "Save me!" and you heard.
2. King-doms fall; na-tions trem-ble at your pow'r.
3. Jus-tice reigns, and the wick-ed are cast down.
4. All who trust in your prom-ise will be saved,
5. Morn-ing comes: I will praise you with my life,

D.C.

You are God, and you lift up the poor.
None can stand with-out you at their side.
In your love is our safe-ty and strength.
for your word has been test-ed in fire.
ev - er faith-ful and true to your word.

Text: 2 Samuel 22; M. D. Ridge, b.1938. © 1989
Tune: M. D. Ridge, b.1938. © 1989; acc. by Patrick Loomis, 1951-1990, © 1990, OCP Publications
Published by OCP Publications

614 O God, Our Help in Ages Past

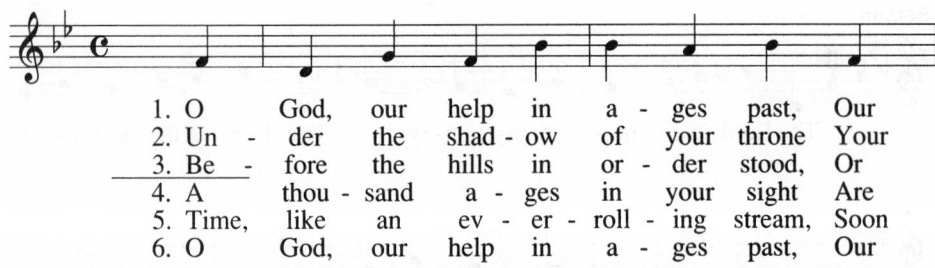

1. O God, our help in a - ges past, Our
2. Un - der the shad - ow of your throne Your
3. Be - fore the hills in or - der stood, Or
4. A thou - sand a - ges in your sight Are
5. Time, like an ev - er - roll - ing stream, Soon
6. O God, our help in a - ges past, Our

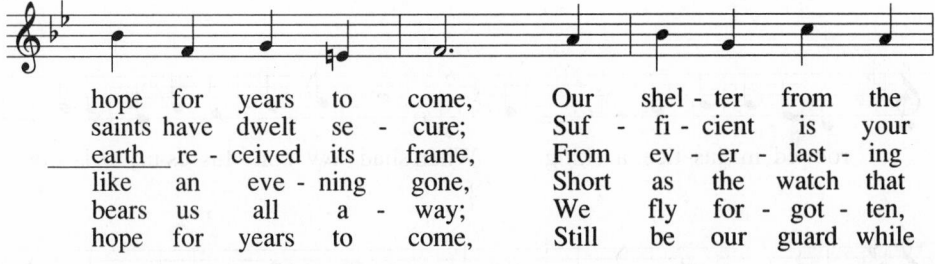

hope for years to come, Our shel - ter from the
saints have dwelt se - cure; Suf - fi - cient is your
earth re - ceived its frame, From ev - er - last - ing
like an eve - ning gone, Short as the watch that
bears us all a - way; We fly for - got - ten,
hope for years to come, Still be our guard while

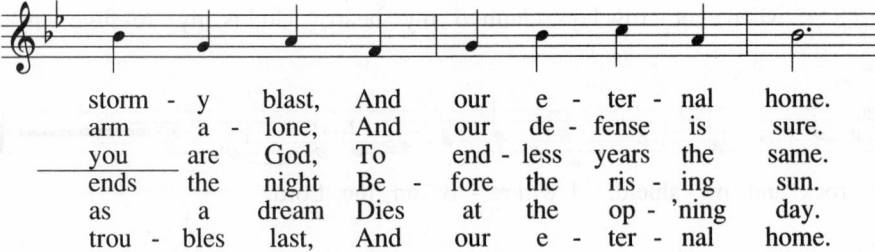

storm - y blast, And our e - ter - nal home.
arm a - lone, And our de - fense is sure.
you are God, To end - less years the same.
ends the night Be - fore the ris - ing sun.
as a dream Dies at the op - 'ning day.
trou - bles last, And our e - ter - nal home.

Text: Psalm (89)90; Isaac Watts, 1674-1748
Tune: ST. ANNE, CM; attr. to William Croft, 1678-1727; harm. composite from 18th C. versions

Seek Ye First the Kingdom of God 615

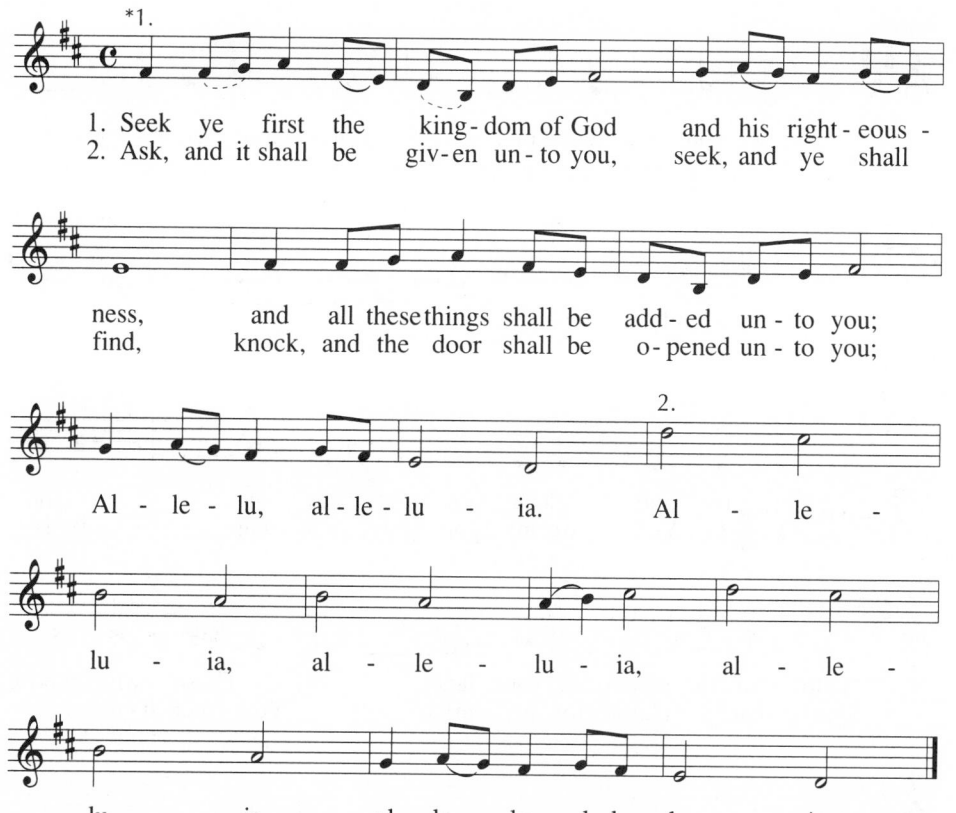

1. Seek ye first the king-dom of God and his right-eous -
2. Ask, and it shall be giv-en un-to you, seek, and ye shall

ness, and all these things shall be add-ed un-to you;
find, knock, and the door shall be o-pened un-to you;

Al - le - lu, al-le-lu - ia. Al - le -

lu - ia, al - le - lu - ia, al - le -

lu - ia, al - le - lu, al-le-lu - ia.

*May be sung as a two voice canon.

Text: Matthew 6:33, 7:7; St. 1, adapt, by Karen Lafferty, b.1948; St. 2, anon.
Tune: SEEK YE FIRST, Irregular; Karen Lafferty, b.1948
© 1972, Maranatha! Music

616 For You Are My God

Refrain

For you are my God; you a-lone are my joy.

Last time

De-fend me, O Lord.

Verses 1,2

1. You give mar - vel-ous com-rades to me: the
2. You are my por - tion and cup; it is

faith - ful who dwell in your land. Those who choose
you that I claim for my prize. Your her-it-age

a - li-en gods have cho - sen an
is my de - light, the lot you have

D.C.

a - li - en band.
giv-en to me.

Verses 3, 4

3. Glad are my heart and my soul;
4. You show me the path for my life;

se - cure - ly my bod - y shall rest.
in your pres-ence the full - ness of joy.

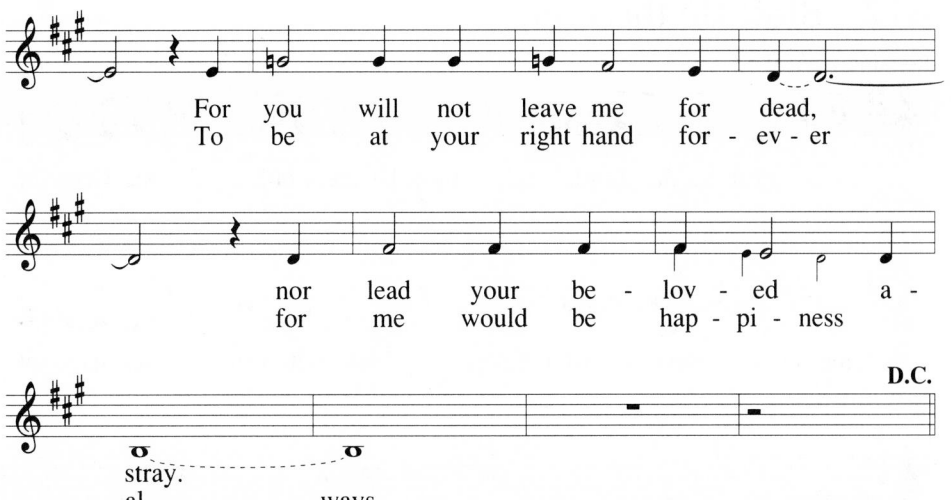

For you will not leave me for dead,
To be at your right hand for - ev - er

nor lead your be - lov - ed a -
for me would be hap - pi - ness

D.C.

stray.
al - ways.

Text: Psalm 16; John Foley, SJ, b.1939
Tune: John Foley, SJ, b.1939
© 1970, John B. Foley, SJ, administered by New Dawn Music

617　Blest Be the Lord

Refrain

Blest be the Lord; blest be the Lord, the God of
mer-cy, the God who saves. I shall not fear the dark of
night, nor the ar-row that flies by day.

Verses

1. He will re - lease me from the
2. I need not shrink be - fore the
3. Al - though a thou - sand strong have

nets of all my foes. He will pro -
ter - rors of the night nor stand a -
fall - en at my side, I'll not be

tect me from their wick-ed hands.
lone be - fore the light of day.
shak - en with the Lord at hand.

Be - neath the shad - ow of his wings
No harm shall come to me, no
His faith - ful love is all the

I will re - joice
ar - row strike me down,
ar - mor that I need

D.C.

to find a dwell - ing place se - cure.
no e - vil set - tle in my soul.
to wage my bat - tle with the foe.

Text: Psalm 91; Dan Schutte, b.1947, alt.
Tune: Dan Schutte, b.1947; arr. by Sr. Theophane Hytrek, OSF, 1915-1992
© 1976, 1979, Daniel L. Schutte and New Dawn Music

Be Still, and Know That I Am God 618

Be still and know that I am God. Be still and
know that I am God.

Text: Psalm 46:10; John L. Bell, b.1949
Tune: John L. Bell, b.1949
© 1989, Iona Community, GIA Publications, Inc., agent

619 The Lord Is Near

*Refrain

O the Lord is near to all who call on him; he is
** May the an - gels lead you in - to par - a - dise; may the

close to all who seek his face, slow to an - ger and full of com -
mar - tyrs come to wel - come you, and take you to the ho - ly

pas - sion and a - bound - ing in mer - ci - ful love.
cit - y, the new and e - ter - nal Je - ru - sa - lem.

Verse 1

1. The Lord is my light and my sal - va - tion, there is

noth - ing at all I fear; the Lord is the

D.C.

ref - uge of my life; of whom should I be a - fraid?

Verse 2

2. One thing I ask of the Lord; there is

on - ly one thing I seek: to dwell in the

D.C.

house of the Lord all the days of my life.

Verse 3

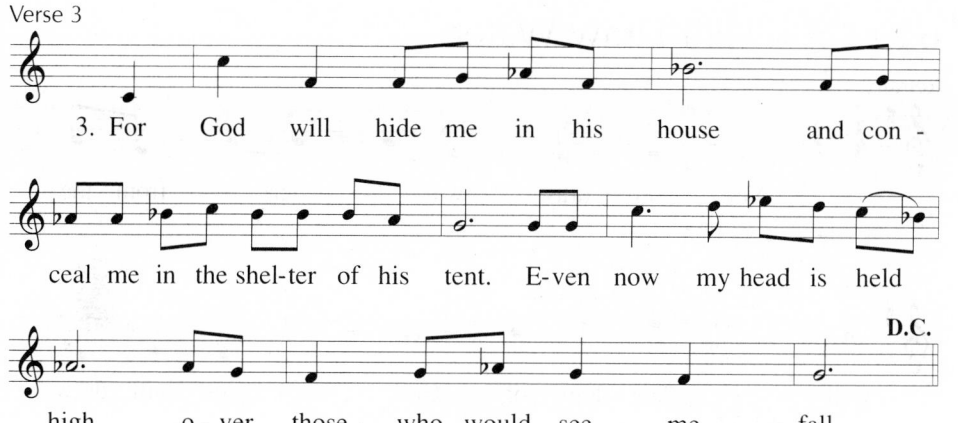

3. For God will hide me in his house and con-

ceal me in the shel-ter of his tent. E-ven now my head is held

D.C.

high o-ver those who would see me fall.

The refrain may be sung in a two-voice canon at a distance of one measure, or a three-voice canon at a distance of one-half measure.

** *Alternate refrain for funerals*

Text: Psalm 27; Michael Joncas, b.1951
Tune: Michael Joncas, b.1951
© 1979, New Dawn Music

620 You Will Draw Water

Refrain

You will draw wa - ter from the

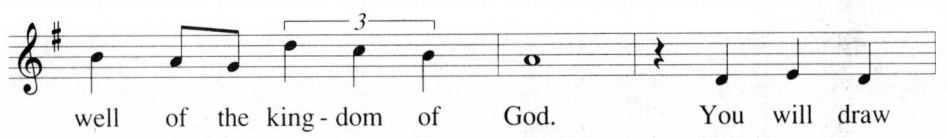

well of the king-dom of God. You will draw

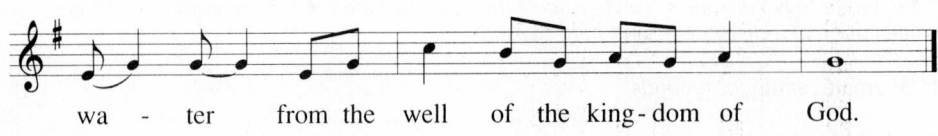

wa - ter from the well of the king-dom of God.

Verses

1. God alone is my rock;
   how then should I be afraid?

2. God alone is my strength;
   who then can stand before me?

3. God alone is my rest;
   the Lord God is my safety.

4. God alone is my peace;
   God shatters steel and nations.

5. God alone is my day;
   God's name will shine before me.

6. God alone is my prize;
   though mountains fall to pieces.

7. God alone is my life,
   living, now and for ever.

Text: Tom Conry, b.1951, © 1981, New Dawn Music
Tune: Tom Conry, b.1951, © 1981, New Dawn Music; acc. by Robert J. Batastini, b.1942, © 1994, GIA Publications, Inc.

Only in God   621

Refrain

On - ly in God will my soul be at rest. From him comes my

hope, my sal - va - tion. He a - lone is my rock of

safe - ty, my strength, my glo - ry, my God.

Verses

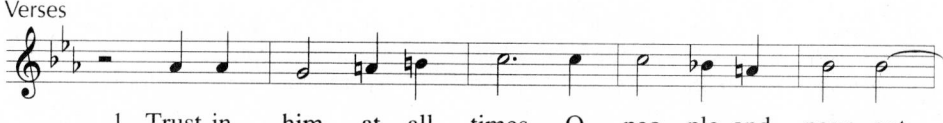

1. Trust in him at all times, O peo - ple, and pour out
2. Man - y times have I heard him tell of his long last -

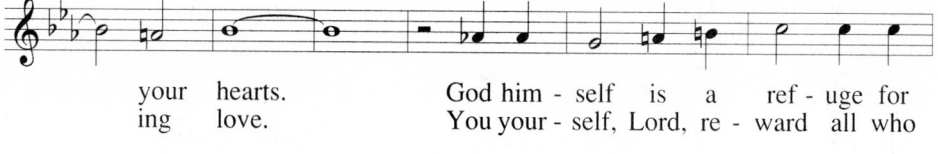

your hearts. God him - self is a ref - uge for
ing love. You your - self, Lord, re - ward all who

D.C.

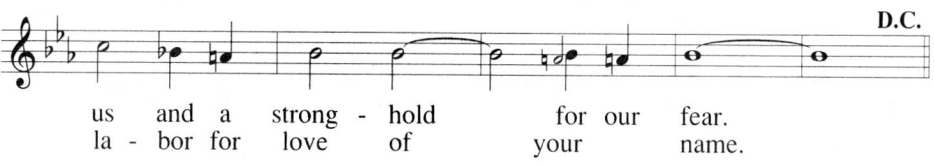

us and a strong - hold for our fear.
la - bor for love of your name.

Text: Psalm 62:1, 2 8, 11, 12: John Foley, SJ, b.1939
Tune: John Foley, SJ, b.1939
© 1976, John B. Foley, SJ and New Dawn Music

622 Love Divine, All Loves Excelling

1. Love di - vine, all loves ex - cel - ling,
2. Come, al - might - y to de - liv - er,
3. Fin - ish then your new cre - a - tion,

Joy of heav'n to earth come down!
Let us all your life re - ceive;
Pure and spot - less, gra - cious Lord,

Fix in us your hum - ble dwell - ing,
Sud - den - ly re - turn and nev - er,
Let us see your great sal - va - tion

All your faith - ful mer - cies crown.
Nev - er more your tem - ples leave.
Per - fect - ly in you re - stored.

Je - sus, source of all com - pas - sion,
Lord, we would be al - ways bless - ing,
Changed from glo - ry in - to glo - ry,

Love un - bound - ed, love all pure!
Serve you as your hosts a - bove,
Till in heav'n we take our place,

Vis - it us with your sal - va - tion,
Pray, and praise you with - out ceas - ing,
Till we sing be - fore the al - might - y

Let your love in us en - dure.
Glo - ry in your pre - cious love.
Lost in won - der, love and praise.

Text: Charles Wesley, 1707-1788, alt.
Tune: HYFRYDOL. 8 7 8 7 D; Rowland H. Prichard, 1811-1887

Not for Tongues of Heaven's Angels   623

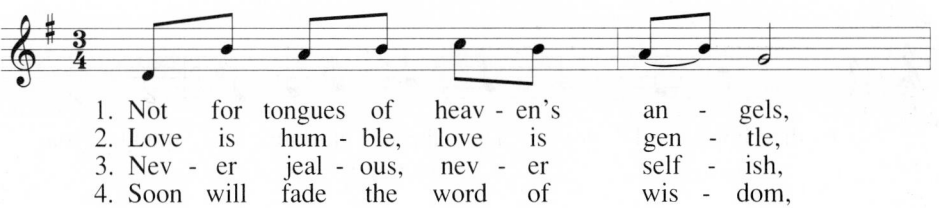

1. Not for tongues of heav - en's an - gels,
2. Love is hum - ble, love is gen - tle,
3. Nev - er jeal - ous, nev - er self - ish,
4. Soon will fade the word of wis - dom,

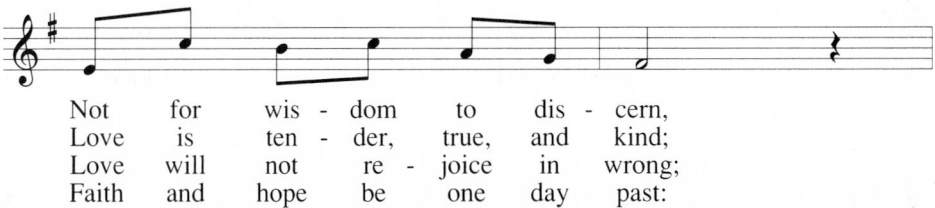

Not for wis - dom to dis - cern,
Love is ten - der, true, and kind;
Love will not re - joice in wrong;
Faith and hope be one day past:

Not for faith that mas - ters moun - tains,
Love is gra - cious, ev - er pa - tient,
Nev - er boast - ful nor re - sent - ful,
When we see our Sav - ior clear - ly,

For this bet - ter gift we yearn:
Gen - er - ous of heart and mind—
Love be - lieves and suf - fers long—
Love it is a - lone will last

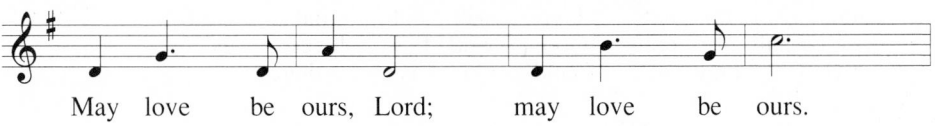

May love be ours, Lord; may love be ours.

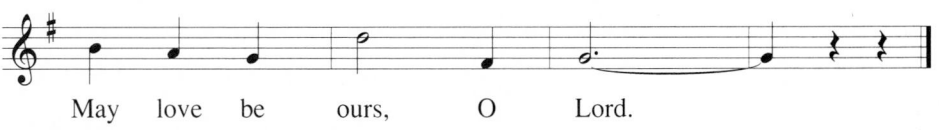

May love be ours, O Lord.

Text: Timothy Dudley-Smith, b.1926. © 1985, Hope Publishing Co.
Tune: COMFORT, 8 7 8 7 with refrain; Michael Joncas, b.1951, © 1988, GIA Publications, Inc.

624 Faith, Hope and Love

Refrain

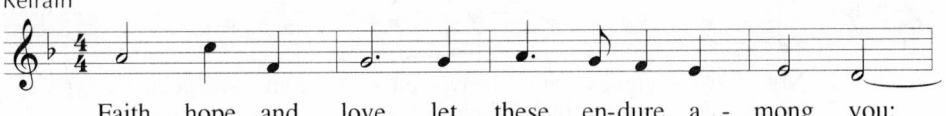

Faith, hope and love, let these en-dure a - mong you;

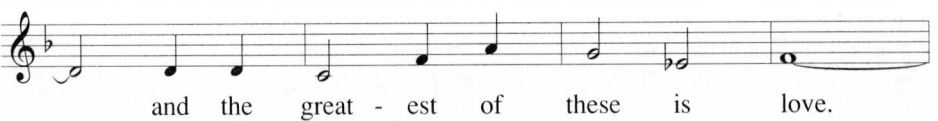

and the great - est of these is love.

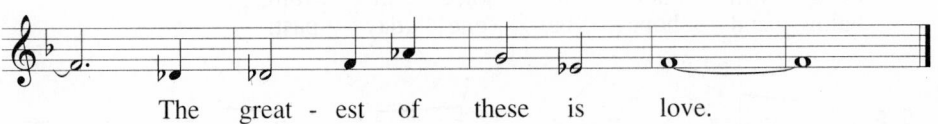

The great - est of these is love.

Verses

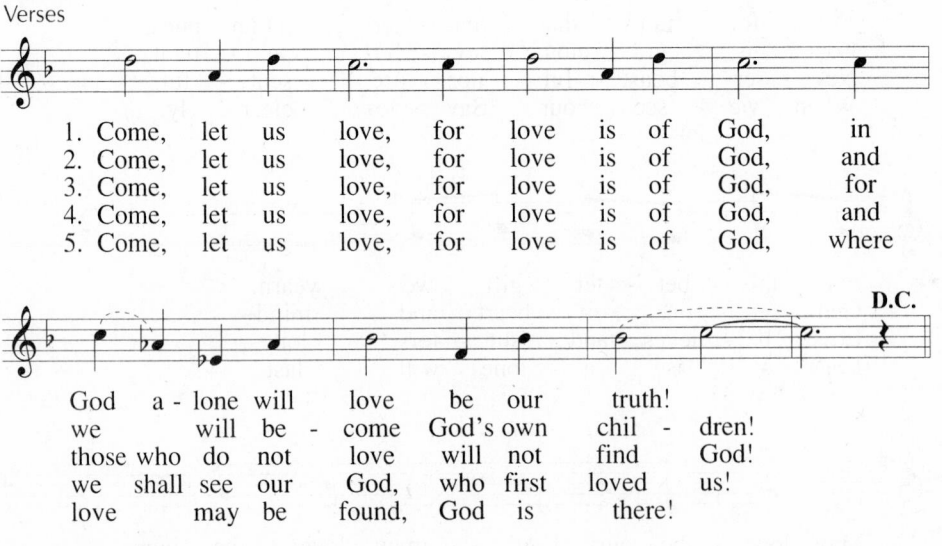

1. Come, let us love, for love is of God, in
2. Come, let us love, for love is of God, and
3. Come, let us love, for love is of God, for
4. Come, let us love, for love is of God, and
5. Come, let us love, for love is of God, where

God a - lone will love be our truth!
we will be - come God's own chil - dren!
those who do not love will not find God!
we shall see our God, who first loved us!
love may be found, God is there!

Text: 1 Corinthians 13:13, 1 John 4:7; David Haas, b. 1957
Tune: David Haas, b. 1957
© 1992, GIA Publications, Inc.

Where Charity and Love Prevail   625

1. Where char - i - ty and love pre - vail,
2. With grate - ful joy and ho - ly fear
3. For - give we now each oth - er's faults
4. Let strife a - mong us be un - known,
5. Let us re - call that in our midst
6. No race nor creed can love ex - clude,

There God is ev - er found; Brought here to - geth - er
God's char - i - ty we learn; Let us with heart and
As we our faults con - fess; And let us love each
Let all con - ten - tion cease; Be God's the glo - ry
Dwells God's be - got - ten Son; As mem - bers of his
If hon - ored be God's name; Our fam - i - ly em -

by Christ's love, By love are we thus bound.
mind and soul Now love him in re - turn.
oth - er well In Chris - tian ho - li - ness.
that we seek, Be ours God's ho - ly peace.
bod - y joined, We are in him made one.
brac - es all Whose Fa - ther is the same.

Text: *Ubi caritas;* trans. by Omer Westendorf, b.1916
Tune: CHRISTIAN LOVE, CM; Paul Benoit, OSB, 1893-1979
© 1961, 1962, World Library Publications, Inc.

626 There's a Wideness in God's Mercy

1. There's a wide-ness in God's mer - cy Like the wide-ness
2. For the love of God is broad - er Than the meas - ures
3. Trou - bled souls, why will you scat - ter Like a crowd of

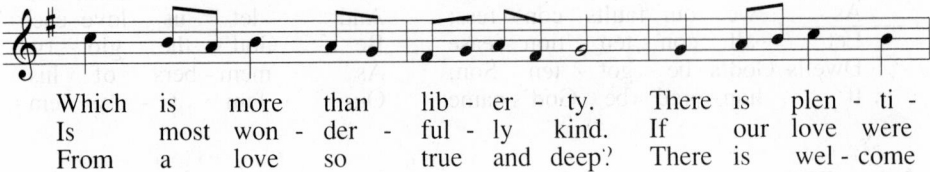

of the sea; There's a kind-ness in God's jus - tice
of our mind, And the heart of the E - ter - nal
fright - ened sheep? Fool - ish hearts, why will you wan - der

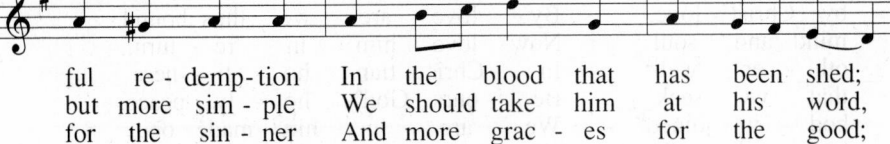

Which is more than lib - er - ty. There is plen - ti -
Is most won - der - ful - ly kind. If our love were
From a love so true and deep? There is wel - come

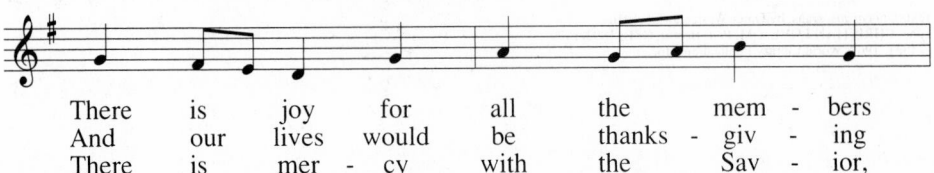

ful re - demp-tion In the blood that has been shed;
but more sim - ple We should take him at his word,
for the sin - ner And more grac - es for the good;

There is joy for all the mem - bers
And our lives would be thanks - giv - ing
There is mer - cy with the Sav - ior,

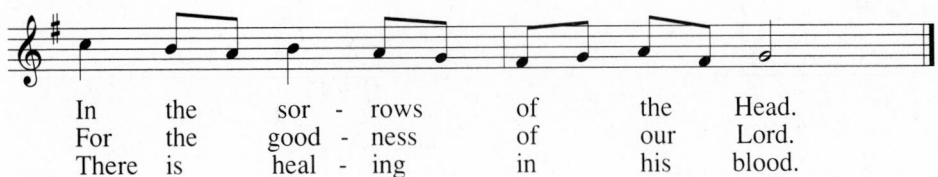

In the sor - rows of the Head.
For the good - ness of our Lord.
There is heal - ing in his blood.

Text: Frederick W. Faber, 1814-1863, alt.
Tune: IN BABILONE, 8 7 8 7 D; *Oude en Nieuwe Hollanste Boerenlities*, c.1710

What Wondrous Love Is This   627

1. What won-drous love is this, O my soul, O my soul?
2. To God and to the Lamb I will sing, I will sing;
3. And when from death I'm free, I'll sing on, I'll sing on;

What won-drous love is this, O my soul?
To God and to the Lamb, I will sing;
And when from death I'm free, I'll sing on;

What won-drous love is this that caused the Lord of bliss
To God and to the Lamb who is the great I Am,
And when from death I'm free, I'll sing and joy-ful be,

To bear the dread-ful curse for my soul, for my soul;
While mil-lions join the theme, I will sing, I will sing;
And through e-ter-ni-ty I'll sing on, I'll sing on!

To bear the dread-ful curse for my soul?
While mil-lions join the theme, I will sing.
And through e-ter-ni-ty I'll sing on.

Text: Alexander Means, 1801-1853
Tune: WONDROUS LOVE, 12 9 12 12 9; *Southern Harmony*, 1835; harm. from *Cantate Domino*, 1980. © 1980, World Council of Churches

628 No Greater Love

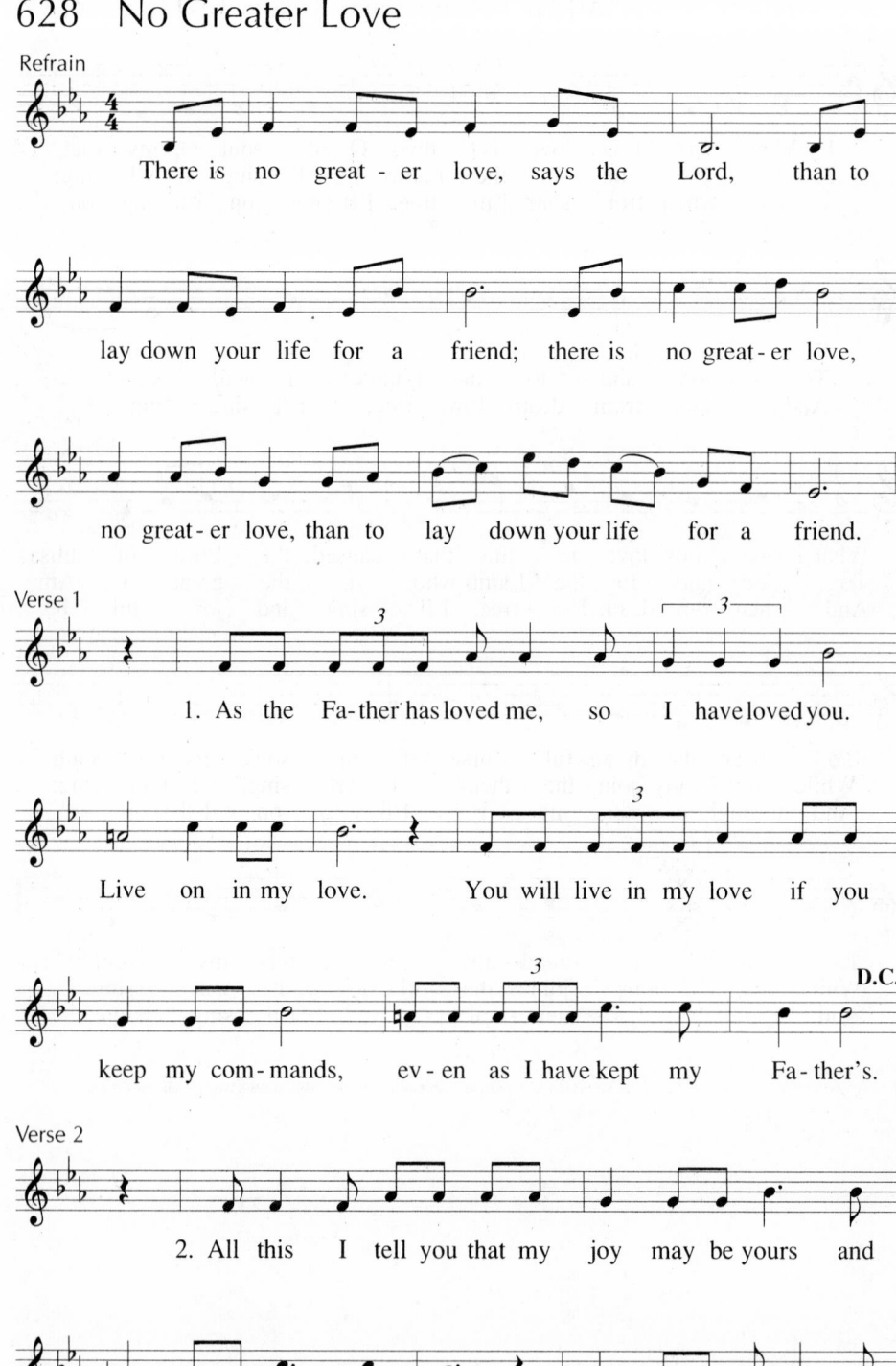

Refrain

There is no great-er love, says the Lord, than to lay down your life for a friend; there is no great-er love, no great-er love, than to lay down your life for a friend.

Verse 1

1. As the Fa-ther has loved me, so I have loved you. Live on in my love. You will live in my love if you keep my com-mands, ev-en as I have kept my Fa-ther's.

Verse 2

2. All this I tell you that my joy may be yours and your joy may be com-plete. Love one an-oth-er as

I have loved you: This is my com - mand.

Verse 3

3. You are my friends if you keep my com-mands;

no long-er slaves but friends to me. All I heard from my Fa-ther,

I have made known to you: Now I call you friends.

Verse 4

4. It was not you who chose me, it was I who chose you, chose

you to go forth and bear fruit. Your fruit must en-dure, so

you will re-ceive all you ask the Fa-ther in my name.

Text: John 15: 9-17; Michael Joncas, b.1951
Tune: Michael Joncas, b. 1951
© 1988, GIA Publications, Inc.

629 God Is Love

Refrain

God is love, and all who live in love, live in God.

Verse 1

1. God is light, in God there is no dark - ness. Come

D.C.

live in the love of the Lord.

Verse 2

2. Come to the Lord, re - ceive the light, and

D.C.

live in the love of the Lord.

Verse 3

3. We are called to be God's own chil - dren, to

D.C.

live in the love of the Lord.

Verse 4

4. All of you are one, u - nit - ed in Je - sus, to

D.C.

live in the love of the Lord.

Text: 1 John 1:5, 3:2, 4:15, Psalm 33:6, Galatians, 3:28; David Haas, b.1957
Tune: David Haas, b.1957
© 1987, GIA Publications, Inc.

Love One Another 630

Refrain

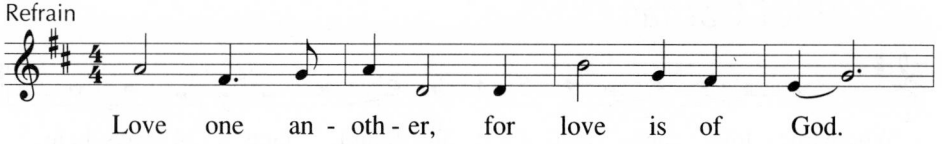

Love   one   an - oth - er,   for   love   is   of   God.

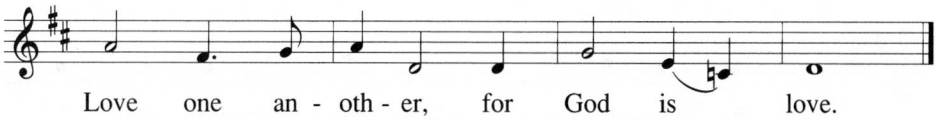

Love   one   an - oth - er,   for   God   is   love.

Verses

1. God loved the world so much he sent us his only son,
   that all who believe in him might have eternal life.

2. Since God has given his love to us, therefore let us love one another.
   If we love one another, God will love us, and live in us in perfect love.

3. Ev'ryone who loves is begotten of God and knows him as the Father.
   But they who do not love do not know God, for God is love.

4. Let not your hearts be troubled, for love has no room for fear.
   In love all fear is forgotten, for God is here with us.

5. God is love, and they who abide in love,
   abide in God, and God in them.

Text:1 John 4; James J. Chepponis, b.1956
Tune: James J. Chepponis, b.1956
© 1983, GIA Publications, Inc.

631 Where True Love and Charity Are Found / Ubi Caritas

Where true love and char-i-ty are found, God is al-ways there.
U - bi cá - ri - tas et a - mor De-us i - bi est.

1. Since the love of Christ has brought us
2. There-fore when we gath - er as one
3. Bring us with your saints to be - hold
1. Con - gre - gá - vit nos in u - num
2. Si - mul er - go cum in u - num
3. Si - mul quo - que cum be - á - tis

all to - geth - er, Let us all re -
in Christ Je - sus, Let our love en -
your great beau - ty, There to see you,
Chri - sti a - mor. Ex - sul - té - mus
con - gre - gá - mur: Ne nos men - te
vi - de - á - mus. Glo - ri - án - ter

joice and be glad, now and al - ways.
fold each race, creed, ev - 'ry per - son.
Christ our God, throned in great glo - ry;
et in ip - so iu - cun - dé - mur.
di - vi - dá - mur, ca - ve - á - mus.
vul - tum tu - um, Chri - ste De - us:

Let ev - 'ry one love the Lord God,
Let en - vy, di - vi - sion and strife
There to pos - sess heav - en's peace and joy,
Ti - me - á - mus et a - mé - mus
Ces - sent iúr - gi - a ma - líg - na,
Gáu - di - um, quod est im - mén - sum

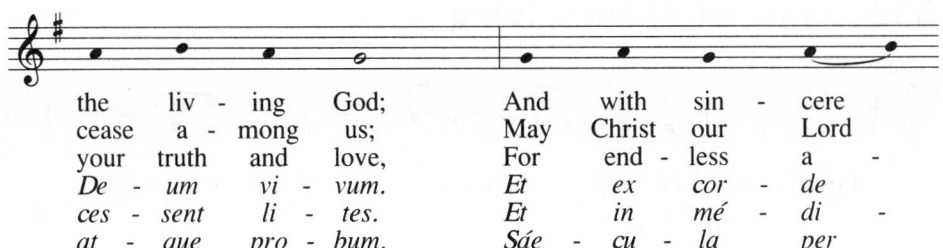

the	liv - ing	God;	And	with	sin -	cere
cease	a - mong	us;	May	Christ	our	Lord
your	truth and	love,	For	end - less	a -
De -	*um*	*vi -*	*vum.*	*Et*	*ex*	*cor -*	*de*
ces -	*sent*	*li -*	*tes.*	*Et*	*in*	*mé -*	*di -*
at -	*que*	*pro -*	*bum.*	*Sáe -*	*cu -*	*la*	*per*

D.C.

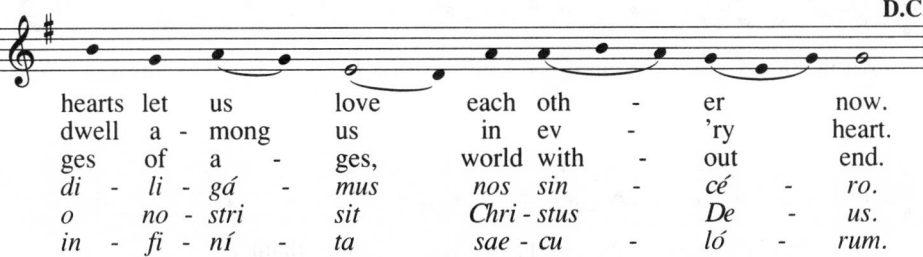

hearts let	us	love	each oth -	er	now.
dwell a -	mong	us	in ev -	'ry	heart.
ges of a -	ges,	world with -	out	end.
di - li - gá -	*mus*	*nos sin -*	*cé -*	*ro.*
o no - stri	*sit*	*Chri - stus*	*De -*	*us.*
in - fi - ní -	*ta*	*sae - cu -*	*ló -*	*rum.*

Text: Latin, 9th C.; tr. by Richard Proulx, b.1937. © 1975, 1986, GIA Publications, Inc.
Tune: UBI CARITAS, 12 12 12 12 with refrain; Mode VI; acc. by Richard Proulx, b.1937, © 1986, GIA Publications, Inc.

632 Song of Thanksgiving

Refrain

Love that's free-ly giv - en wants to free-ly be re - ceived.

All the love you've poured on us can hard-ly be be - lieved, And

all that we can of - fer you is thanks.

All that we can of - fer you is thanks.

Verses

1. Cre - a - tion tells a sto - ry that be -
2. Your care called out a peo - ple; Your
3. Our hearts for - got your sto - ry, So your
4. So now we stand in won - der of

1. gan so long a - go, of love that longed to
2. love made them your own. You freed their hearts and
3. Son be - came its Word and gave a sign in
4. all your love has done: to hear your tale and

1. share its life in hope that love would grow. The
2. calmed their fears and fi - nally brought them home. It's
3. bread and wine to be sure that we had heard. We
4. of - fer thanks that we are not a - lone. Just

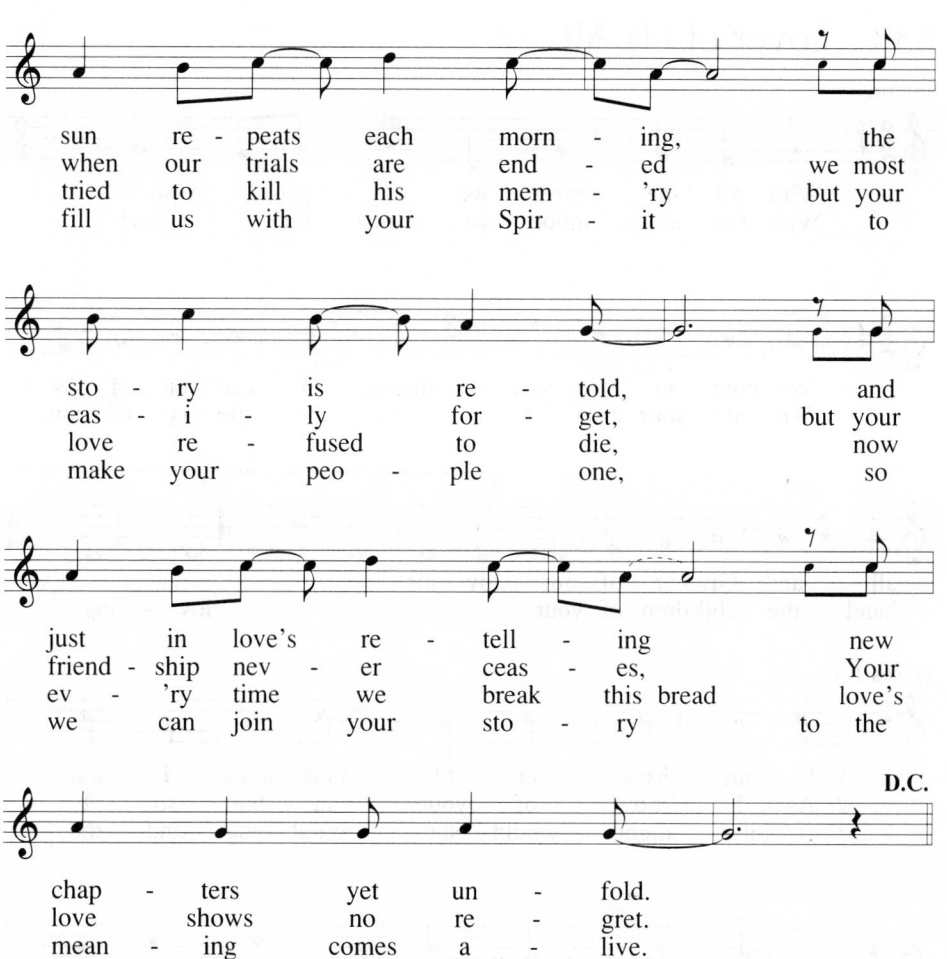

sun	re -	peats	each	morn -	ing,		the
when	our	trials	are	end -	ed		we most
tried	to	kill	his	mem -	'ry		but your
fill	us	with	your	Spir -	it		to

sto -	ry	is	re -	told,			and
eas -	i -	ly	for -	get,			but your
love	re -	fused	to	die,			now
make	your	peo -	ple	one,			so

just	in	love's	re -	tell -	ing		new
friend -	ship	nev -	er	ceas -	es,		Your
ev -	'ry	time	we	break	this bread		love's
we	can	join	your	sto -	ry		to the

D.C.

chap -	ters	yet	un -	fold.
love	shows	no	re -	gret.
mean -	ing	comes	a -	live.
one	told	through	your	son.

Text: Darryl Ducote, b.1945, © 1973, Damean Music, Distributed by GIA Publications, Inc.
Tune: Darryl Ducote, b.1945, © 1973, Damean Music, Distributed by GIA Publications, Inc.; acc. by Diana Kodner, b.1957, © 1993,
    GIA Publications, Inc.

633 Lover of Us All

Refrain

With all the earth we sing your praise!
With sun and moon we dance for joy!

We come to give you thanks, O Lov - er of us
We are your work of art, the glo - ry of your

1.
all, and Giv - er of our lov - ing.
hand, the chil-dren of your

2.
lov - ing.

Verses 1-3

1. I am Mak - er of moun - tains; I am
2. As I know of your la - bor, so I
3. If the night would sur - round you and the

God of the earth. Like a moth - er in
watch while you sleep. Ev - er close at your
sun fall from sight, yet my hand will pro -

D.C.

la - bor I bring all to birth.
call - ing so my love will be.
tect you; I will be your light.

Verses 4-6

4. Long be - fore there were mead - ows, or
5. If you trav - el the heav - ens, or
6. In the womb of my wis - dom, I

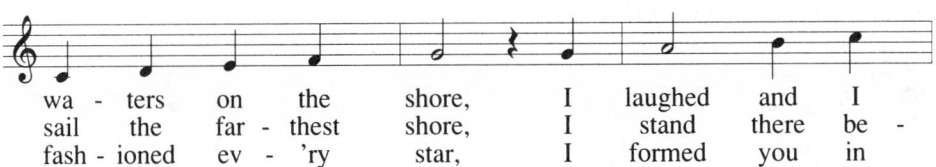

wa - ters on the shore, I laughed and I
sail the far - thest shore, I stand there be -
fash - ioned ev - 'ry star, I formed you in

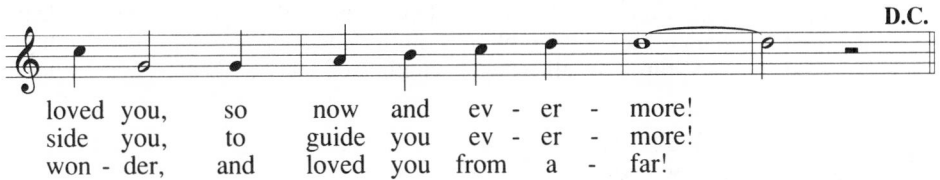

D.C.

loved you, so now and ev - er - more!
side you, to guide you ev - er - more!
won - der, and loved you from a - far!

Text: Ephesians 2:7-10; 5:19-20; Dan Schutte, b.1947
Tune: Dan Schutte, b.1947; acc. alt.
© 1987, 1989, Daniel L. Schutte, published by OCP Publications

Lord of All Nations, Grant Me Grace 634

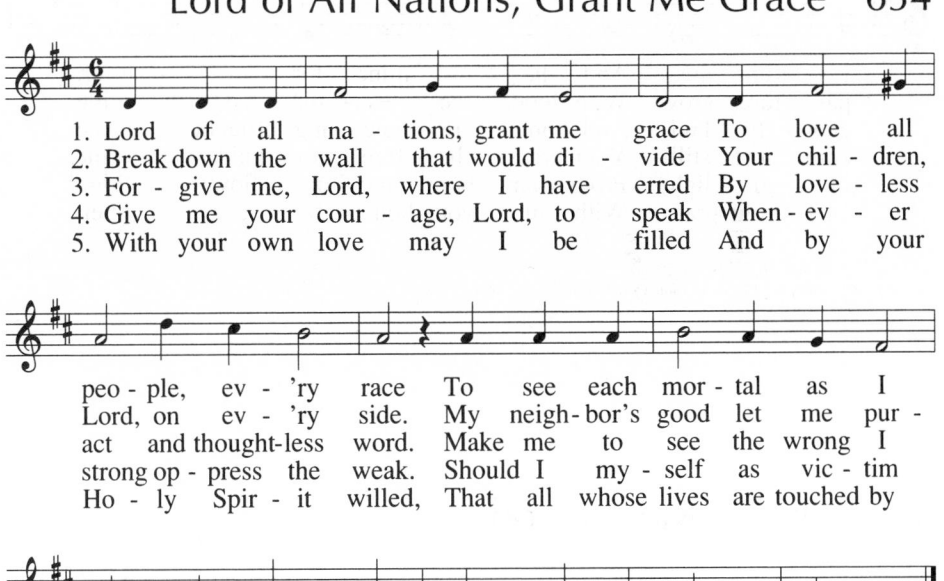

1. Lord of all na - tions, grant me grace To love all
2. Break down the wall that would di - vide Your chil - dren,
3. For - give me, Lord, where I have erred By love - less
4. Give me your cour - age, Lord, to speak When - ev - er
5. With your own love may I be filled And by your

peo - ple, ev - 'ry race To see each mor - tal as I
Lord, on ev - 'ry side. My neigh - bor's good let me pur -
act and thought - less word. Make me to see the wrong I
strong op - press the weak. Should I my - self as vic - tim
Ho - ly Spir - it willed, That all whose lives are touched by

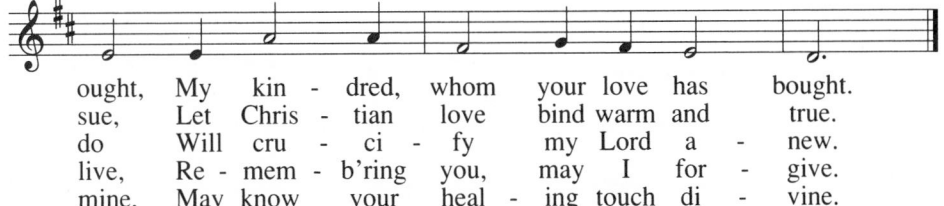

ought, My kin - dred, whom your love has bought.
sue, Let Chris - tian love bind warm and true.
do Will cru - ci - fy my Lord a - new.
live, Re - mem - b'ring you, may I for - give.
mine, May know your heal - ing touch di - vine.

Text: Philippians 2:1-18; Olive W. Spannaus, b.1916. © 1969. Concordia Publishing House
Tune: BEATUS VIR, LM; Slovak; harm. by Richard Hillert, b.1923. © 1969. Concordia Publishing House

635 The King of Love My Shepherd Is

1. The King of love my shep - herd is, Whose good - ness
2. Where streams of liv - ing wa - ter flow My ran - somed
3. Con - fused and fool - ish oft I strayed, But yet in
4. In death's dark vale I fear no ill With you, dear
5. You spread a ta - ble in my sight; Your sav - ing
6. And so through all the length of days Your good - ness

fails me nev - er; I noth - ing lack if
soul he's lead - ing, And where the ver - dant
love he sought me; And on his shoul - der
Lord, be - side me, Your rod and staff my
grace be - stow - ing; And O what trans - port
fails me nev - er; Good Shep - herd, may I

I am his, And he is mine for ev - er.
pas - tures grow With food ce - les - tial feed - ing.
gent - ly laid, And home, re - joic - ing, brought me.
com - fort still, Your cross be - fore to guide me.
of de - light From your pure chal - ice flow - ing!
sing your praise With - in your house for ev - er.

Text: Psalm 23; Henry W. Baker, 1821-1877, alt.
Tune: ST. COLUMBA, 8 7 8 7; Gaelic; harm. by A. Gregory Murray, OSB, b. 1905, ©

636 Shelter Me, O God

Refrain

Shel - ter me, O God; hide me in the shad - ow of your

wings. You a - lone are my hope.

Verses

1. When my foes sur - round me, set me high a - bove their
2. As a moth - er gath - ers her young be - neath her
3. Though I walk in dark - ness, through the nee - dle's eye of

D.C.

reach. Hear me when I call your name.
care, gath - er me in - to your arms.
death, you will nev - er leave my side.

Text: Psalm 16, 61, Luke 13:34; Bob Hurd, b. 1950. © 1984
Tune: Bob Hurd, b. 1950, © 1984; harm. by Craig S. Kingsbury, b. 1952. © 1984. OCP Publications
Published by OCP Publications

Come to Me, O Weary Traveler   637

1. Come to me, O wea - ry trav - 'ler; Come to me with
2. Do not fear, my yoke is eas - y; Do not fear, my
3. Take my yoke and leave your trou - bles; Take my yoke and
4. Rest in me, O wea - ry trav - 'ler; Rest in me and

your dis - tress; Come to me, you heav - y bur-dened;
bur - den's light; Do not fear the path be - fore you;
come with me. Take my yoke, I am be - side you;
do not fear. Rest in me, my heart is gen - tle;

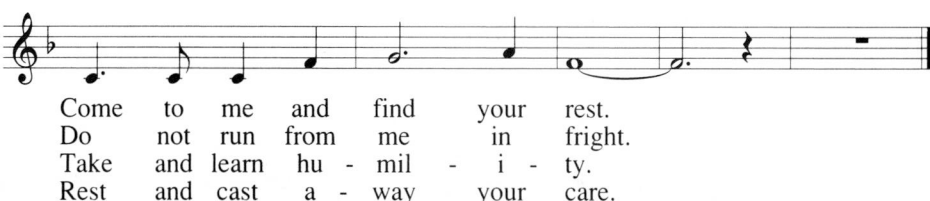

Come to me and find your rest.
Do not run from me in fright.
Take and learn hu - mil - i - ty.
Rest and cast a - way your care.

Text: Matthew 11:28-30; Sylvia G. Dunstan, 1955-1993, © 1991, GIA Publications, Inc.
Tune: DUNSTAN, 8 7 8 7; Bob Moore, b.1962, © 1993. GIA Publications, Inc.

638 Eye Has Not Seen

Refrain

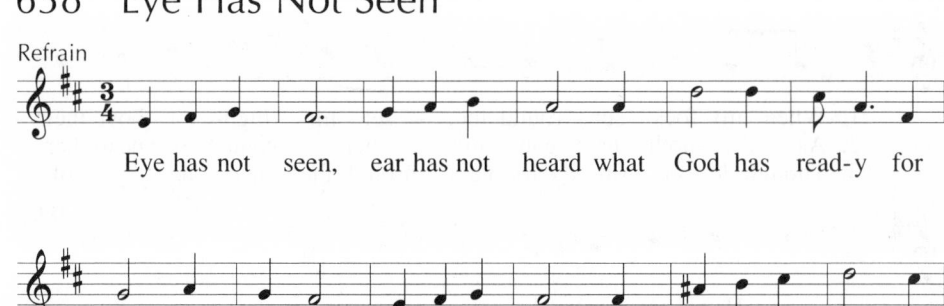

Eye has not seen, ear has not heard what God has read-y for

those who love him; Spir-it of love, come, give us the mind of

Je - sus, teach us the wis-dom of God.

Verses 1-3

1. When pain and sor-row weigh us down, be near to us, O
2. Our lives are but a sin-gle breath, we flow-er and we
3. To those who see with eyes of faith, the Lord is ev-er

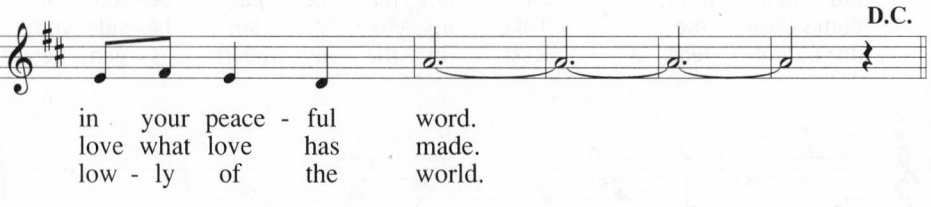

Lord, for-give the weak-ness of our faith, and bear us up with-
fade, yet all our days are in your hands, so we re-turn in
near, re-flect-ed in the fac - es of all the poor and

D.C.

in your peace - ful word.
love what love has made.
low - ly of the world.

Verse 4

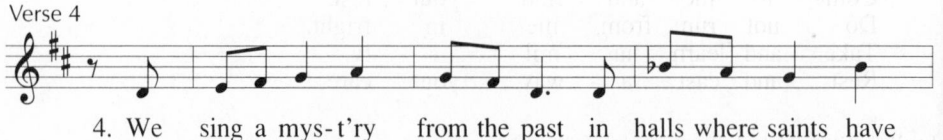

4. We sing a mys-t'ry from the past in halls where saints have

trod,   yet   ev-er   new   the   mu-sic rings   to   Je-sus, Liv - ing

D.C.

Song   of   God.

Text: 1 Corinthians 2:9-10; Marty Haugen, b.1950
Tune: Marty Haugen, b.1950
© 1982, GIA Publications, Inc.

Nada Te Turbe / Nothing Can Trouble   639

Ostinato Refrain

Na - da   te   tur - be,   na - da   te es-pan - te.   Quien   a   Dios   tie - ne
Noth-ing   can trou-ble,   noth-ing   can fright-en.   Those who   seek   God shall

na - da   le   fal - ta.   So - lo   Dios   bas - ta.
nev-er   go   want - ing.   God   a - lone   fills   us.

Text: St. Teresa of Jesus; Taizé Community, 1986, 1991
Tune: Jacques Berthier, 1923-1994
© 1986, 1991, Les Presses de Taizé, GIA Publications, Inc., agent

640   A Touching Place

1. Christ's is the world in which we move,
2. Feel for the peo - ple we most a - void,
3. Feel for the par - ents who've lost their child,
4. Feel for the lives by life con - fused,

Christ's are the folk we're sum - moned to love,
Strange or be - reaved or nev - er em - ployed;
Feel for the wom - en whom men have de - filed,
Rid - dled with doubt, in lov - ing a - bused;

Christ's is the voice which calls us to care, And
Feel for the wom - en, and feel for the men Who
Feel for the ba - by for whom there's no breast, And
Feel for the lone - ly heart, con - scious of sin, Which

Christ is the one who meets us here.
fear that their liv - ing is all in vain.
feel for the wea - ry who find no rest.
longs to be pure but fears to be - gin.

To the lost Christ shows his face; To the un - loved he

gives his em - brace; To those who cry in pain or dis -

grace, Christ makes, with his friends, a touch - ing place.

Text: John L. Bell, b.1949, © 1989, Iona Community, GIA Publications, Inc., agent
Tune: DREAM ANGUS, Irregular; Scottish folk song; acc. by John L. Bell, b.1949, © 1993, Iona Community, GIA Publications, Inc., agent

Shepherd of My Heart   641

Verses

1. My   shep-herd   is   the Lord,   for noth-ing shall I   want;
2. If   I   should walk one   day   in - to   the vale of dark-ness,
3. You a-noint my   head with oil;   my cup is   o - ver-flow-ing;

green are the   pas - tures where I'm   led   to   re - pose.
no   e - vil   shall I   fear with God   at my side.
good - ness and kind - ness crown the   days   of my life.

Near wa - ters still and deep   God will re - fresh my soul.
There with your crook and staff   you give me strength and com - fort;
With - in   the Lord's own house   I dwell in peace for ev - er;

I   am led   on-ward in ways   true   to the   Name.
you spread a   ban-quet in   the   sight   of my   foes.
with - in   the house of God my   soul   is at   rest.

Refrain

Guide me,   O shep-herd of my heart; lead me home-ward through the

dark, in - to ev - er-last-ing, day.   Show me   the way of truth and

light; keep me   al - ways in your   sight. May my life   nev - er

D.C.

part   from   the shep - herd   of   my   heart.

Text: Psalm 23: Francis Patrick O'Brien, b.1958
Tune: Francis Patrick O'Brien, b.1958
© 1992, GIA Publications, Inc.

642 Jesus, Lead the Way

1. Je - sus, lead the way Through our life's long day,
2. Je - sus be our light, In the midst of night,
3. When in deep - est grief, Strength - en our be - lief.
4. Je - sus, still lead on 'Til our rest be won:

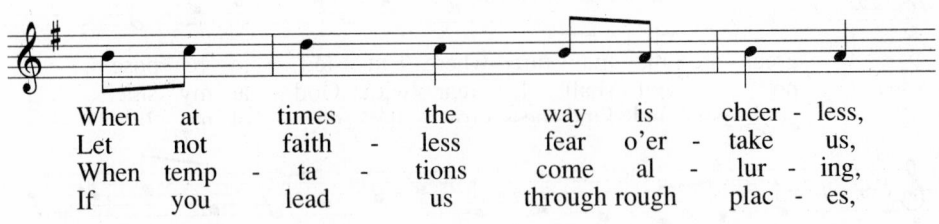

When at times the way is cheer - less,
Let not faith - less fear o'er - take us,
When temp - ta - tions come al - lur - ing,
If you lead us through rough plac - es,

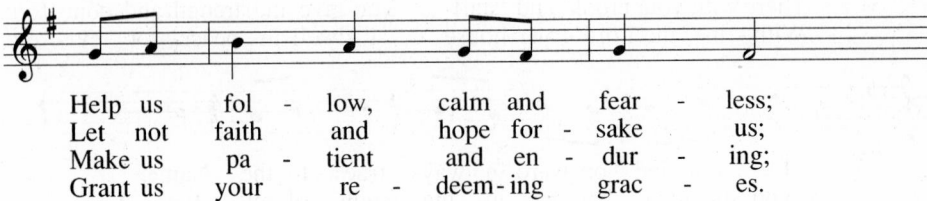

Help us fol - low, calm and fear - less;
Let not faith and hope for - sake us;
Make us pa - tient and en - dur - ing;
Grant us your re - deem - ing grac - es.

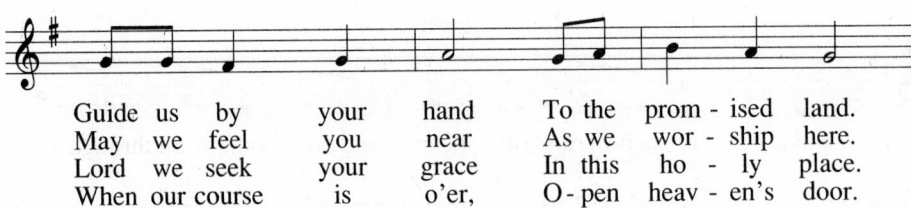

Guide us by your hand To the prom - ised land.
May we feel you near As we wor - ship here.
Lord we seek your grace In this ho - ly place.
When our course is o'er, O - pen heav - en's door.

Text: *Jesu, geh voran;* Nicholas L. von Zinzendorf, 1700-1760; tr. by Jane Borthwick, 1813-1897, alt.
Tune: ROCHELLE, 55 88 55; Adam Drese, 1620-1701; harm. alt.

The Lord Is My Shepherd 643

Verses

1. The Lord is my shep-herd, my shield and my strong-hold, de - fend - ing me sound - ly, re - deem-ing my shame. He will an - swer my call 'til the fall of the moun - tains, the fall of the cit - ies; he's true to his name.

2. If I walk in the val - ley of dark - ness, the shad - ow of death, then no fear will I have, you are there with your staff and your rod, O my God, give me com - fort, O God give me com - fort, as al - ways you have.

3. Sure-ly good-ness and kind - ness will al - ways pur - sue me. My ta - ble is full now; my cup o - ver - flows. While my head is a - noint-ed the time is ap - point - ed; for - ev - er I live in the house of the Lord.

4. The Lord is my shep-herd, green pas - tures, cool wa - ter; He ten - ders me al - ways, love ev - er the same. He will an - swer my call 'til the fall of the moun - tains, the fall of the cit - ies; he's true to his name.

Refrain

Al - le - lu - ia, al - le - lu - ia, the Lord is my shep-herd and ev-er the same. Al - le - lu - ia, al - le - lu - ia, the Lord is my shep-herd; he's true to his name.

Text: Psalm 23; Joe Wise, b.1939
Tune: Joe Wise, b.1939; acc. by Marty Haugen, b.1950
© 1979, 1987, GIA Publications, Inc.

644 Within Our Darkest Night

With - in our dark - est night, you kin - dle the
fire that nev - er dies a - way, nev - er dies a -
way. With - in our dark - est night, you kin - dle the
fire that nev - er dies a - way, nev - er dies a - way.

Text: Taizé Community, 1991
Tune: Jacques Berthier, 1923-1994
© 1991, Les Presses de Taizé, GIA Publications, Inc., agent

Show Us the Path of Life 645

Refrain

Lord, come show us the path of life, we will
walk ev - er joy - ful, near to your side.

Verse 1

1. Keep me safe, O Lord, with - out you I am noth-ing,
run-ning af-ter shad-ows, fol-low-ing an emp-ty dream.

Verse 2

2. Let us tell the sto-ry of how our God has loved us.
God has been our cup of life, for ev-er true and faith-ful.

Verses 3, 4

3. Glo-ry in God's coun-sel, the wis-dom of e-ter-ni-ty,
4. I re-joice in you, Lord, your love and light sur-round me;

lead-ing us through dark-ness, sing-ing in each si-lent heart.
nev-er shall you leave me, ev-er will I trust in you.

Text: Psalm 16; Marty Haugen, b.1950
Tune: Marty Haugen, b.1950
© 1982, GIA Publications, Inc.

646 I Heard the Voice of Jesus Say

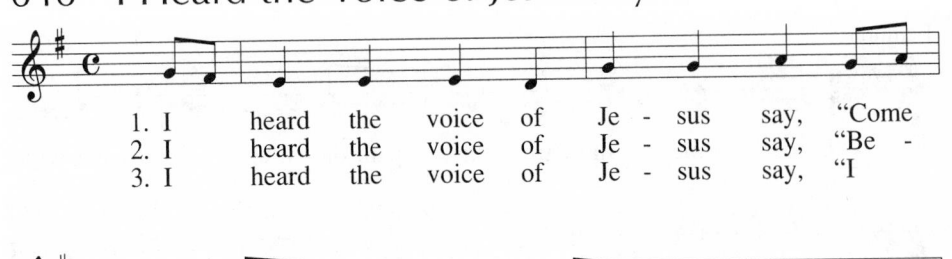

1. I heard the voice of Je - sus say, "Come
2. I heard the voice of Je - sus say, "Be -
3. I heard the voice of Je - sus say, "I

un - to me and rest; Lay down, O wear - y
hold, I free - ly give The liv - ing wa - ter;
am this dark world's light; Look un - to me, your

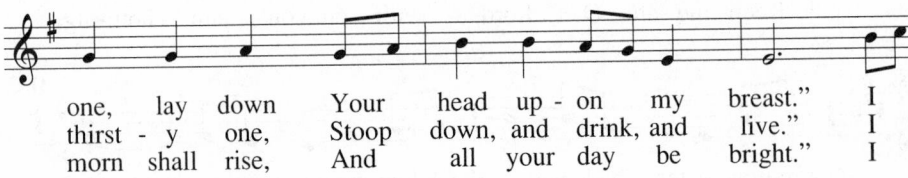

one, lay down Your head up - on my breast." I
thirst - y one, Stoop down, and drink, and live." I
morn shall rise, And all your day be bright." I

came to Je - sus as I was, So
came to Je - sus, and I drank Of
looked to Je - sus, and I found In

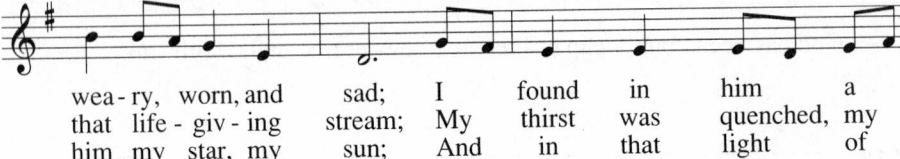

wea - ry, worn, and sad; I found in him a
that life - giv - ing stream; My thirst was quenched, my
him my star, my sun; And in that light of

rest - ing place, And he has made me glad.
soul re - vived, And now I live in him.
life I'll walk Till trav - 'ling days are done.

Text: Horatius Bonar, 1808-1889
Tune: KINGSFOLD, CMD; English; harm. by Ralph Vaughan Williams, 1872-1958, © Oxford University Press

Come to Me   647

Refrain

Come to me, come to me, come when you are wea - ry;

come to me, come to me, and I will give you rest.

Verses 1,2

1. All who la - bor and are bur - dened,
2. Take my yoke up - on your shoul - ders,

all who la - bor and are bur - dened, let them come to me,
take my yoke up - on your shoul-ders, come and learn from me,

D.C.

come to me, and I will give them rest.
learn from me, for I am gen - tle of heart.

Verse 3

3. For the heart I hold is hum - ble,

yes, the heart I hold is hum-ble, and my yoke is eas-y, my

D.C.

bur - den light, and you will find rest for your souls.

Text: Matthew 11:28-30; Michael Joncas, b.1951
Tune: Michael Joncas, b.1951
© 1989, GIA Publications, Inc.

648 There Is a Balm in Gilead

Refrain

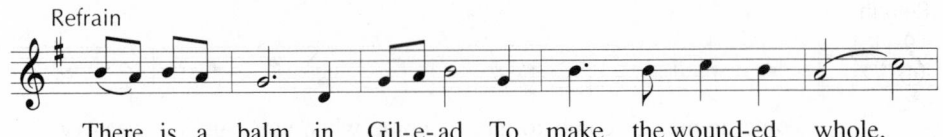

There is a balm in Gil-e-ad To make the wound-ed whole,

There is a balm in Gil-e-ad To heal the sin-sick soul.

Verses

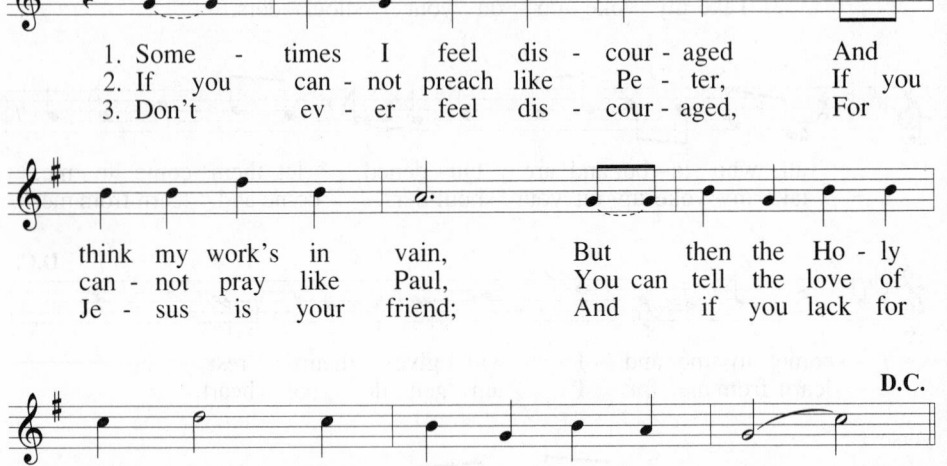

1. Some - times I feel dis - cour - aged And
2. If you can - not preach like Pe - ter, If you
3. Don't ev - er feel dis - cour - aged, For

think my work's in vain, But then the Ho - ly
can - not pray like Paul, You can tell the love of
Je - sus is your friend; And if you lack for

D.C.

Spir - it Re - vives my soul a - gain.
Je - sus, And say, "He died for all!"
knowl - edge He'll ne'er re - fuse to lend.

Text: Jeremiah 8:22, African-American spiritual
Tune: BALM IN GILEAD, Irregular; African-American spiritual; acc. by Robert J. Batastini, b.1942, © 1987, GIA Publications, Inc.

You Are Mine 649

Verses

1. I will come to you in the si-lence,
2. I am hope for all who are hope-less,
3. I am strength for all the des - pair-ing,
4. am the Word that leads all to free-dom, I

I will lift you from all your fear.
I am eyes for all who long to see. In the
heal - ing for the ones who dwell in shame.
am the peace the world can - not give.

You will hear my voice, I claim you as my choice, be
shad-ows of the night, I will be your light,
All the blind will see, the lame will all run free, and
I will call your name, em - brac-ing all your pain, stand

still and know I am here. *(To verse 2)*
come and rest in me. *(To refrain)*
all will know my name. *(To refrain)*
up, now walk, and live! *(To refrain)*

Refrain

Do not be a-fraid, I am with you. I have called you each by

name. Come and fol-low me, I will bring you home; I

D.C.

love you and you are mine.

4. I

650 Come to Me

Refrain

Come to me, all you wea - ry.
I will re - fresh you, learn from me.
My yoke is eas - y, my bur - den light.

Verses

1. Ask and you shall receive; seek and you shall find.
   Knock, it shall be opened, the goodness of the Lord.
   For the one who asks, receives, the one who seeks shall find.
   The one who knocks will enter, and see the face of God.

2. See the birds in the sky, they neither sow nor reap,
   and still our God cares for them, will not the Lord care for you?
   See the lilies of the field, they do not work or spin;
   if they are clothed in splendor, God will provide for you.

3. Do not worry about your life, what to eat or wear.
   Is not your life for greater things?
   Is not your life for the Lord?
   Seek the one who knows your need, and all things will be yours.
   Worry not of tomorrow, let tomorrow find its way.

Text: Matthew 6:26, 28, 30-31, 33-34; 7: 7-8; David Haas, b.1957
Tune: David Haas, b.1957
© 1989, GIA Publications, Inc.

So the Day Dawn for Me 651

1. So the day dawn for me, so the day
2. Be the day shine to me, be the day
3. Be the day dark to me, be the day
4. Be the day swift to me, be the day
5. So the day close for me, so the night

break, Christ watch-ing o - ver me,
bright, Christ my com - pan - ion be,
drear, Christ shall my com - fort be,
long, Christ my con - tent - ment be,
fall, Christ watch-ing o - ver me,

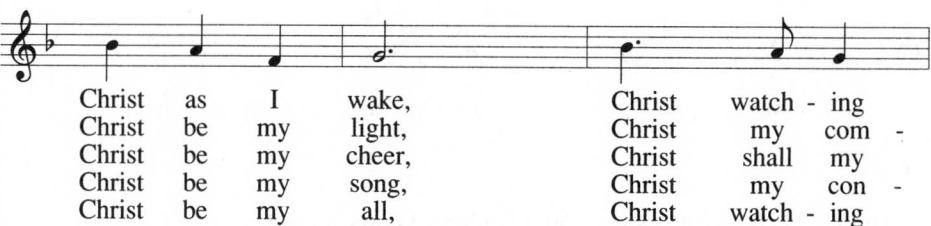

Christ as I wake, Christ watch - ing
Christ be my light, Christ my com -
Christ be my cheer, Christ shall my
Christ be my song, Christ my con -
Christ be my all, Christ watch - ing

o - ver me, Christ as I wake.
pan - ion be, Christ be my light.
com - fort be, Christ be my cheer.
tent - ment be, Christ be my song.
o - ver me, Christ be my all.

Text: Timothy Dudley-Smith, b.1926, © 1993, Hope Publishing Co.
Tune: NEW FREEDOM, 6 4 6 4 6 4; David Haas, b.1957, © 1994, GIA Publications, Inc.

652 Our God Is Rich in Love

Refrain

Our God is ten-der, ten-der and car-ing,

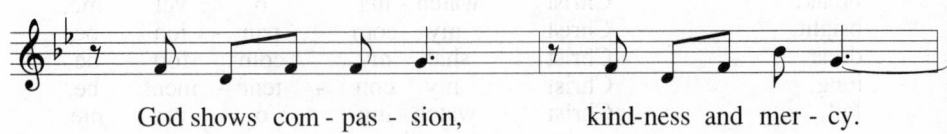

slow to an-ger so rich in love.

God shows com-pas-sion, kind-ness and mer-cy.

God is gen-tle. Our God is rich in love.

Verses

1. Our God is merciful. God's gentle kindness knows no end.
   And though our sins be great or small, God's love is our reward.

2. Our God is tender as a parent to a child.
   God remembers how we were made, remembers that we are dust.

3. God's love is eternal for those who live the law;
   for those who live the covenant; for those who keep the faith.

Text: Psalm 103: Bob Moore, b. 1962
Tune: Bob Moore, b. 1962
© 1993, GIA Publications, Inc.

The People of God 653

Refrain

Come to me all who are bur - dened;

come and rest in my love. Re -

joice and be glad, your hope lies in heav - en, your

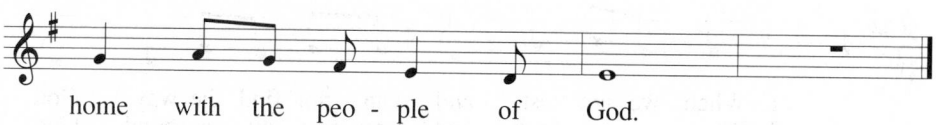

home with the peo - ple of God.

Verses

1. Blessed, blessed are the poor in spirit, blessed be the Lord's own children,
   theirs is the kingdom of God.
   Blessed, blessed are they who walk in sorrow, blessed be the Lord's own children;
   they are embraced by God.

2. Blessed, blessed the ones who are lowly, blessed be the Lord's own children;
   they shall inherit the land.
   Blessed, blessed the ones who thirst for righteousness,
   blessed be the Lord's own children; all of their dreams will come true.

3. Blessed, blessed are they who show mercy, blessed be the Lord's own children;
   mercy from God shall be theirs.
   Blessed, blessed the ones with a pure heart, blessed be the Lord's own children;
   for they shall see God.

4. Blessed, blessed the ones who make peace. Blessed are they who know pain
   for the sake of righteousness.
   Blessed, blessed are you who know suff'ring, blessed are you who know insult
   because of your God.

Text: Matthew 5:3-12; Francis Patrick O'Brien, b.1958
Tune: Francis Patrick O'Brien, b.1958
© 1992, GIA Publications, Inc.

654 With a Shepherd's Care

Refrain

With a shep-herd's care, God leads us. With a fa-ther's strength, God guides us. With a moth-er's love, God nur-tures us, and cra-dles us in gen-tle arms.

Verses

1. When we are lost, and can-not find the way, God cares for us and keeps us safe. For
2. When we are weak, and cares press all a-round, God strength-ens us to face each day. For
3. When we are scared, and feel so all a-lone, God loves us and is by our side. For

God is our light and our faith-ful guide, and
God is our rock and our sav-ing help, and
God is our hope and our con-stant friend, and

D.C.

leads us with a shep-herd's care.
guides us with a fa-ther's strength.
nur-tures with a moth-er's love.

Text: James J. Chepponis, b.1956
Tune: James J. Chepponis, b.1956
© 1992, GIA Publications, Inc.

The Kingdom of God   655

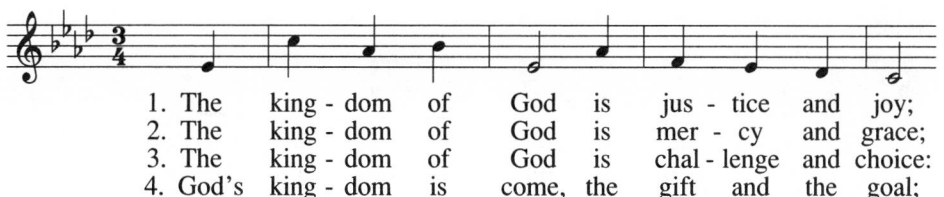

1. The king - dom of God is jus - tice and joy;
2. The king - dom of God is mer - cy and grace;
3. The king - dom of God is chal - lenge and choice:
4. God's king - dom is come, the gift and the goal;

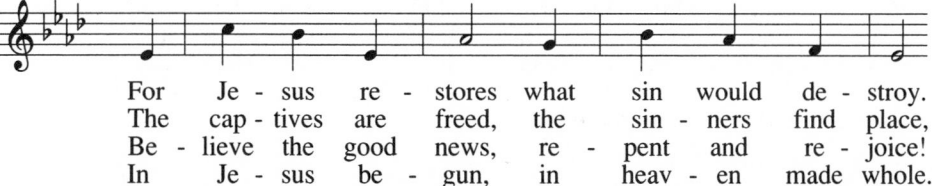

For Je - sus re - stores what sin would de - stroy.
The cap - tives are freed, the sin - ners find place,
Be - lieve the good news, re - pent and re - joice!
In Je - sus be - gun, in heav - en made whole.

God's pow - er and glo - ry in Je - sus we know;
The out - cast are wel - comed God's ban - quet to share;
God's love for us sin - ners brought Christ to his cross:
The heirs of the king - dom shall an - swer his call;

And here and here - af - ter the king - dom shall grow.
And hope is a - wak - ened in place of de - spair.
Our cri - sis of judge - ment for gain or for loss.
And all things cry "Glo - ry!" to God all in all.

Text: Bryn A. Rees, b.1911, © Mrs. M. Rees
Tune: LAUDATE DOMINUM, 10 10 11 11; Charles H. H. Parry, 1848-1918

656 Thy Kingdom Come

Verses

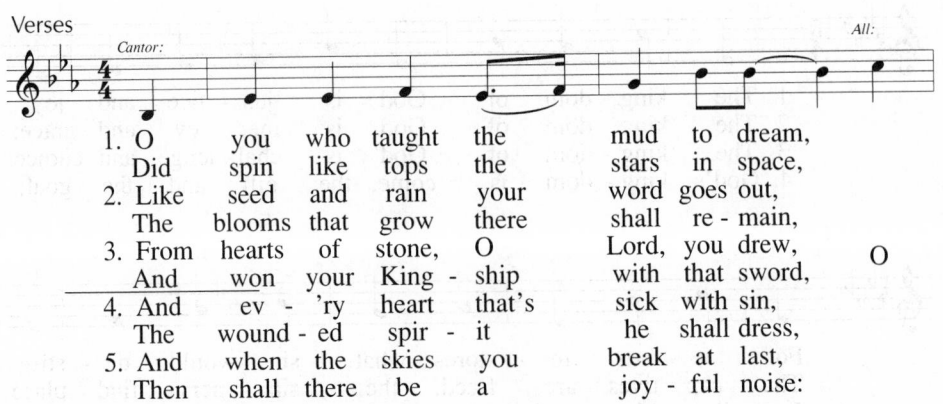

Cantor: *All:*

1. O you who taught the mud to dream,
   Did spin like tops the stars in space,
2. Like seed and rain your word goes out,
   The blooms that grow there shall re - main,
3. From hearts of stone, O Lord, you drew,   O
   And won your King - ship with that sword,
4. And ev - 'ry heart that's sick with sin,
   The wound - ed spir - it he shall dress,
5. And when the skies you break at last,
   Then shall there be a joy - ful noise:

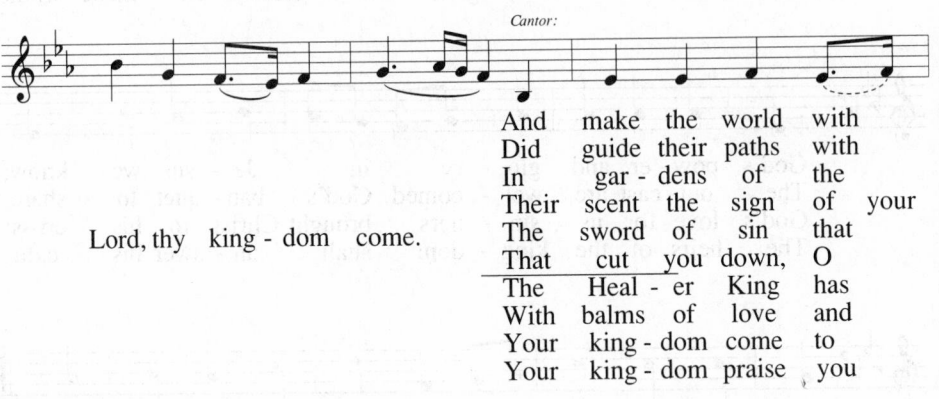

Cantor:

                          And make the world with
                          Did guide their paths with
                          In gar - dens of the
Lord, thy king - dom come.   Their scent the sign of your
                          The sword of sin that
                          That cut you down, O
                          The Heal - er King has
                          With balms of love and
                          Your king - dom come to
                          Your king - dom praise you

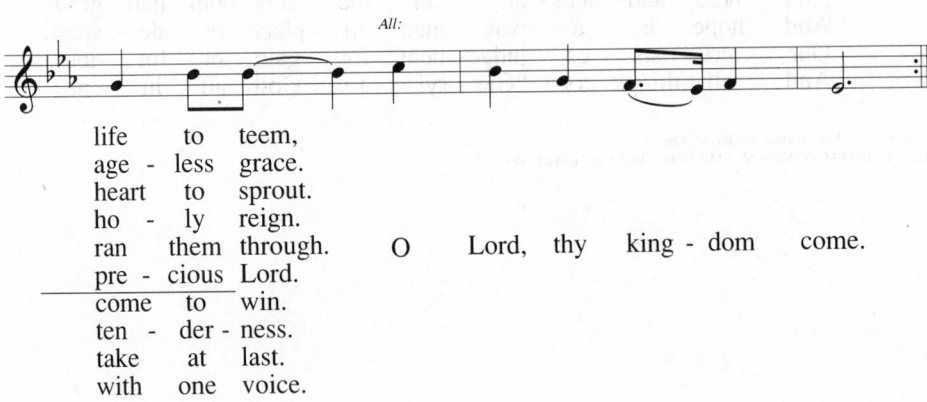

All:

life to teem,
age - less grace.
heart to sprout.
ho - ly reign.
ran them through.   O Lord, thy king - dom come.
pre - cious Lord.
come to win.
ten - der - ness.
take at last.
with one voice.

Refrain

We wait in joy, we wait in joy,

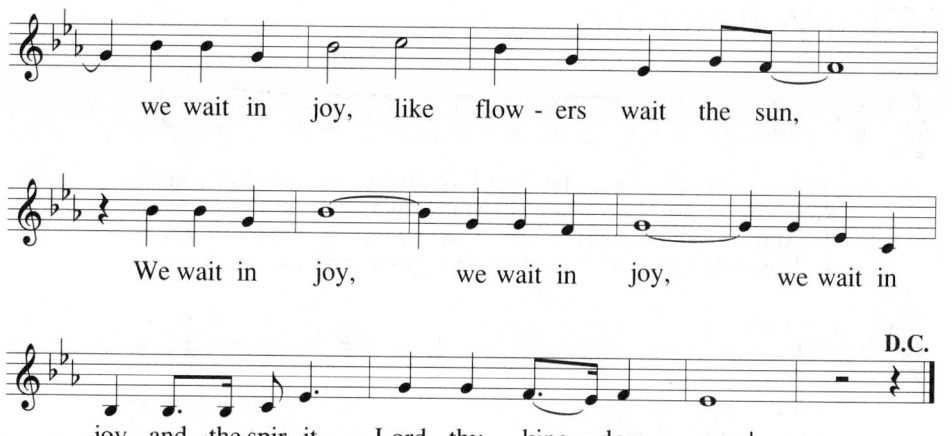

we wait in joy, like flow - ers wait the sun,

We wait in joy, we wait in joy, we wait in

joy and the spir - it, Lord, thy king - dom come!

Text: Rory Cooney, b.1952
Tune: Rory Cooney, b.1952
© 1984, North American Liturgy Resources

657　I Will Not Die

Verses

1., 5. I will not die be-fore I've lived to see that land;
2. I will not rest un-til your dawn is in my eyes;
3. And I will breathe in that might-y wind of jus-tice;
4. You will stand up for the poor and the need-y;

firm as the earth, your own prom-ise.
that frag-ile light, new like morn-ing.
I'll know my name and rise up sing-ing.
you'll break the chains that bind your peo-ple.

I'll not let go un-til I've held it in my hand;
I will not sleep be-fore I've wak-ened to that sun-rise;
And I will call un-til my words bring on the thun-der;
For you are home for the lost and the des-p'rate;

that word of hope, and gen-tle laugh-ter.
and all the world knows your glo-ry.
washed in that rain, then I'll know you.
your strong right hand goes be-fore us.

Refrain

For your right hand has de-liv-ered us from death;

You have re-gard-ed our tears,

D.C.

you who are good-ness and grace.

Text: Tom Conry, b.1951
Tune: Tom Conry, b.1951
© 1984, 1990, TEAM Publications, published by OCP Publications

Bring Forth the Kingdom 658

Verses

Cantor:

1. You are salt for the earth, O peo-ple:
2. You are a light on the hill, O peo-ple:
3. You are a seed of the Word, O peo-ple:
4. We are a blest and a pil - grim peo-ple:

All:

Salt for the King-dom of God!
Light for the Cit - y of God!
Bring forth the King-dom of God!
Bound for the King-dom of God!

Cantor:

Share the fla - vor of
Shine so ho - ly and
Seeds of mer - cy and
Love our jour-ney and

All:

life, O peo - ple: Life in the King-dom of God!
bright, O peo - ple: Shine for the King-dom of God!
seeds of jus - tice, Grow in the King-dom of God!
love our home - land: Love is the King-dom of God!

Refrain

Bring forth the King-dom of mer - cy, Bring forth the

King-dom of peace; Bring forth the King-dom of jus - tice,

Bring forth the Cit - y of God!

Text: Marty Haugen, b.1950
Tune: Marty Haugen, b.1950
© 1986, GIA Publications, Inc.

659　Blest Are They

Verses 1-3

1. Blest are they, the poor in spir - it,
2. Blest are they, the low - ly ones,
3. Blest are they who show mer - cy,

theirs is the king - dom of God.
they shall in - her - it the earth.
mer - cy shall be theirs.

Blest are they, full of sor - row,
Blest are they who hun - ger and thirst,
Blest are they, the pure of heart,

they shall be con - soled.
they shall have their fill.
they shall see God!

Refrain %

Re - joice and be glad! Bless-ed are you,

ho - ly are you! Re - joice and be glad!

Yours is the king-dom of God!

Verses 4, 5

4. Blest are they who seek peace;
5. Blest are you who suf - fer hate,

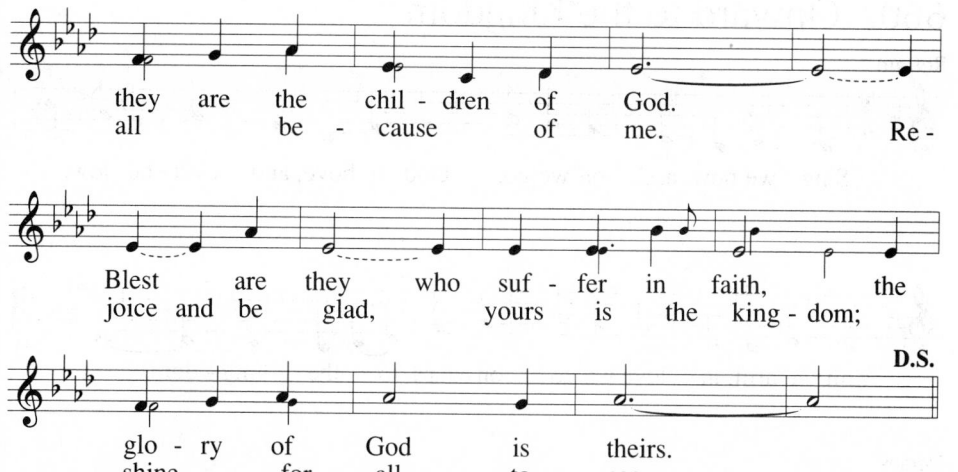

they   are   the   chil - dren   of   God.
all   be - cause   of   me.   Re -

Blest   are   they   who   suf - fer   in   faith,   the
joice and   be   glad,   yours   is   the   king - dom;

D.S.

glo - ry   of   God   is   theirs.
shine   for   all   to   see.

Text: Matthew 5:3-12; David Haas, b.1957
Tune: David Haas, b.1957; vocal arr. by David Haas, b.1957, Michael Joncas, b.1951
© 1985, GIA Publications, Inc.

660 Onward to the Kingdom

Refrain

Sing we now, and on we go; God a-bove, and God be-low;

Arm in arm, in love we go on-ward to the king - dom.

Verses

1. Star a-bove to show the way, through the night and
2. Come now sis - ters, broth - ers all, time to heed the
3. In the prom - ised land we'll be, one with God, where

in - to day, with the light we won't
Lord's call, we will tra - vel stand -
all are free, the deaf will hear, the blind

D.C.

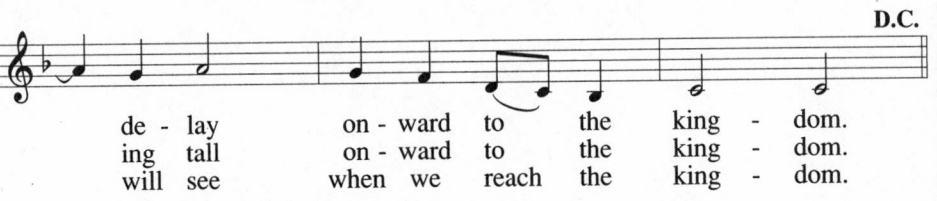

de - lay on - ward to the king - dom.
ing tall on - ward to the king - dom.
will see when we reach the king - dom.

Text: David Haas, b. 1957, © 1993, GIA Publications, Inc.
Tune: MARIE'S WEDDING, 7 7 7 6 with refrain; Irish traditional; arr. by David Haas, b. 1957, © 1993, GIA Publications, Inc.

The Church's One Foundation 661

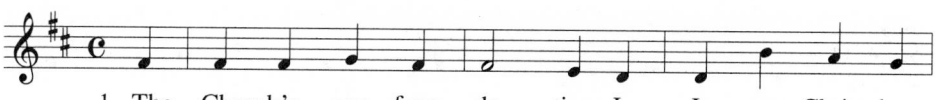

1. The Church's one foun - da - tion Is Je - sus Christ her
2. E - lect from ev - 'ry na - tion, Yet one o'er all the
3. 'Mid toil and trib - u - la - tion, And tu - mult of her
4. Yet she on earth hath un - ion With God, the Three in

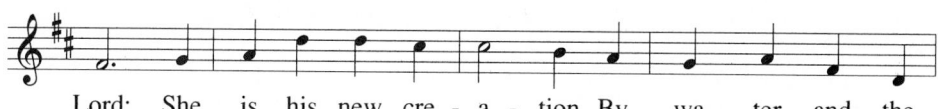

Lord; She is his new cre - a - tion By wa - ter and the
earth, Her char - ter of sal - va - tion, One Lord, one faith, one
war, She waits the con - sum - ma - tion Of peace for ev - er -
One, And mys - tic sweet com - mun - ion With those whose rest is

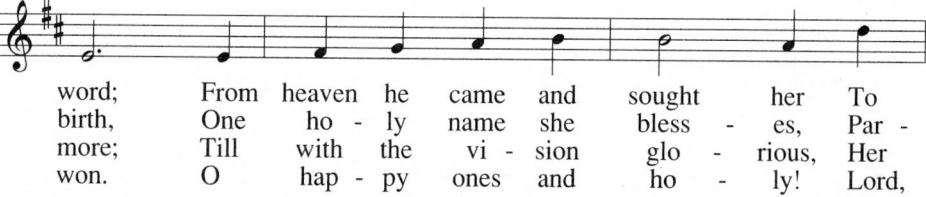

word; From heaven he came and sought her To
birth, One ho - ly name she bless - es, Par -
more; Till with the vi - sion glo - rious, Her
won. O hap - py ones and ho - ly! Lord,

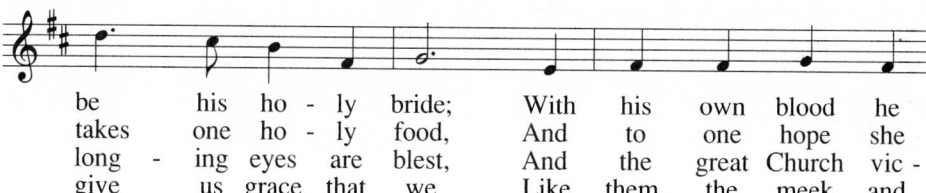

be his ho - ly bride; With his own blood he
takes one ho - ly food, And to one hope she
long - ing eyes are blest, And the great Church vic -
give us grace that we Like them, the meek and

bought her, And for her life he died.
press - es, With ev - 'ry grace en - dued.
to - rious Shall be the Church at rest.
low - ly, On high may dwell with thee.

Text: Samuel J. Stone, 1839-1900
Tune: AURELIA 7 6 7 6 D; Samuel S. Wesley, 1810-1876

662 Christ Is Made the Sure Foundation

1. Christ is made the sure foun - da - tion, Christ the head and
2. To this tem - ple where we call you, Come, O Lord of
3. Grant, we pray, to all your peo - ple, All the grace they

cor - ner-stone; Cho - sen of the Lord, and pre - cious,
hosts, to - day; With your wont - ed lov - ing kind - ness
ask to gain; What they gain from you for ev - er

Bind - ing all the Church in one; Ho - ly Zi - on's
Hear your ser - vants as they pray, And your full - est
With the bless - ed to re - tain, And here - af - ter

help for ev - er, And her con - fi - dence a - lone.
ben - e - dic - tion Shed in all its bright ar - ray.
in your glo - ry Ev - er - more with you to reign.

Text: *Angularis fundamentum;* 11th C.; tr. by John M. Neale, 1818-1866, alt.
Tune: ST. THOMAS, 8 7 8 7 8 7; John Wade, 1711-1786

As a Fire Is Meant for Burning 663

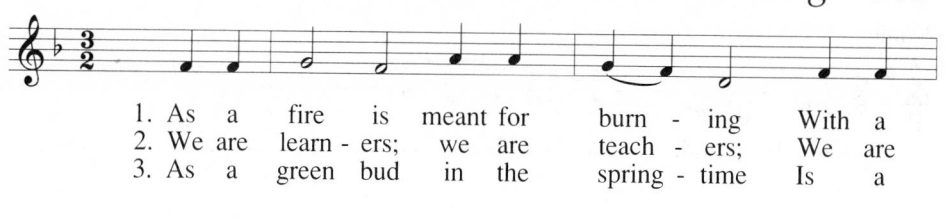

1. As a fire is meant for burn - ing With a
2. We are learn - ers; we are teach - ers; We are
3. As a green bud in the spring - time Is a

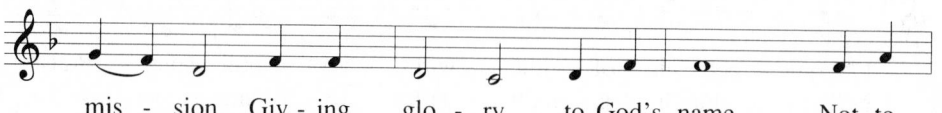

bright and warm - ing flame, So the church is meant for
pil - grims on the way. We are seek - ers; we are
sign of life re - newed, So may we be signs of

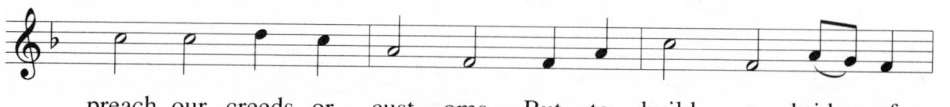

mis - sion, Giv - ing glo - ry to God's name. Not to
giv - ers; We are ves - sels made of clay. By our
one - ness 'Mid earth's peo - ples, man - y hued. As a

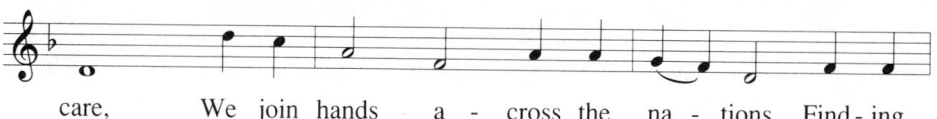

preach our creeds or cust - oms, But to build a bridge of
gen - tle, lov - ing ac - tions, We would show that Christ is
rain - bow lights the heav - ens When a storm is past and

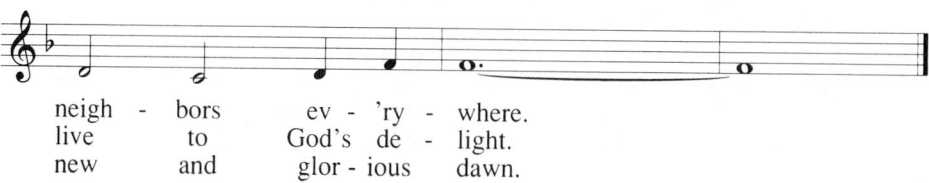

care, We join hands a - cross the na - tions, Find - ing
light. In a hum - ble, lis - t'ning Spir - it, We would
gone, May our lives re - flect the ra - diance Of God's

neigh - bors ev - 'ry - where.
live to God's de - light.
new and glor - ious dawn.

Text: Ruth Duck, b.1947. © 1992. GIA Publications, Inc.
Tune: BEACH SPRING, 8 7 8 7 D: *The Sacred Harp*, 1844; harm. by Marty Haugen, b.1950. © 1985. GIA Publications, Inc.

664 Church of God

Refrain

Church of God, cho - sen peo - ple, sing your praise to God.

He has called you out of dark-ness in - to his mar-vel-ous light.

Verses

1. Come,	peo - ple	of	God,	with	joy -	ful	song,	Praise
2. The	church	is	built	with	liv -	ing	stones	With
3. As	heirs	of	Christ,	re - deemed	by	love	We
4. As	wa -	ter	spring - ing	from	the	rock	Once
5. We	gath -	er	here	to	wor -	ship	God,	Our
6. May	fra -	grant smoke	of	in -	cense	rise	To
7. The	light	of	Christ	has	come	to	us	Dis -

God	the	Fa - ther	of	all.	Bap -
Christ	as	cor -	ner - stone.	In
wait	for	his	re - turn;	A
brought	God's	peo -	ple	life,	The
eu -	cha - rist	to	share.	We
fill	this	house	of	prayer.	May
pel -	ling	all	our	fears.	His

tized	in	Christ,	re - born	in	him,	Our
him	we	trust	who	makes	us	one,	U -
priest - ly	peo -	ple	of - f'ring	praise	To
liv - ing	wa -	ter	giv'n	by	Christ	Cre -
give	him	thanks	and	cel - e - brate	The
we	who	gath -	er	find	true	peace,	God's
light	re - veals	the	path	of	life.	We

hearts	are	filled	with	joy.	He	cleans	-	es	our
nit -	ing	us	in	love.	We	build		on	the
God,	the	source	of	hope.	For	Je -		sus	is
ates	our	lives	a -	new.	So	come		you	who
mys -	t'ry	of	his	love;	The	Word		is	made
pres -	ence	fill - ing	our	lives.	Our	hearts		lift	with
fol -	low	him	with	joy,	The	glo -		ry	of

D.C.

sin,	Re -	new -	ing	our	lives.
rock	Of	faith		in	Christ.
Lord,	Our	Sav -	ior	and	God.
thirst	To	springs	of	new	life.
flesh	And	giv -	en	for	us.
praise,	Our	lips	sing	in	joy.
God,	The	light	of	the	world.

Text: Sr. Pamela Stotter
Tune: Margaret Daly
© 1980, International Commission on English in the Liturgy, Inc.

665 We Will Serve the Lord

Verses

1. Wealth can be an i - dol built of gleam-ing gold,
2. Plea - sure is a si - ren, prom-is - ing the flesh
3. Pow - er is a hun-ger, burn-ing in the breast, to
4. Fath - er of all mer-cy, Giv - er of all life,

bring-ing dreams of par - a - dise, fu - tures bought and sold.
brief re - lief from emp - ti - ness, a hid - ing place from death.
walk a - mong the might-y and tram - ple on the rest.
here we speak our cov - e - nant a - bove the nois - y strife.

Some will choose to gath-er it, all that they can hoard, but
Some will choose to chase it, un - til it leaves them bored, but
Some will choose to gain it by lie or guile, or sword, but
Hear us shout in glo-ry a - bove the pa - gan horde,

1.

2.- 4.

as for me and my house, we will serve the Lord!
as for me and my house, we will serve the Lord!
as for me and my house, we will serve the Lord!
as for me and my house, we will serve the Lord!

Refrain

Melody:

As for me and my house, we will serve the Lord,

we will serve the Lord, we will serve the Lord!

Text: Rory Cooney, b.1952
Tune: Rory Cooney, b.1952
© 1986, North American Liturgy Resources

Pues Si Vivimos / If We Are Living 666

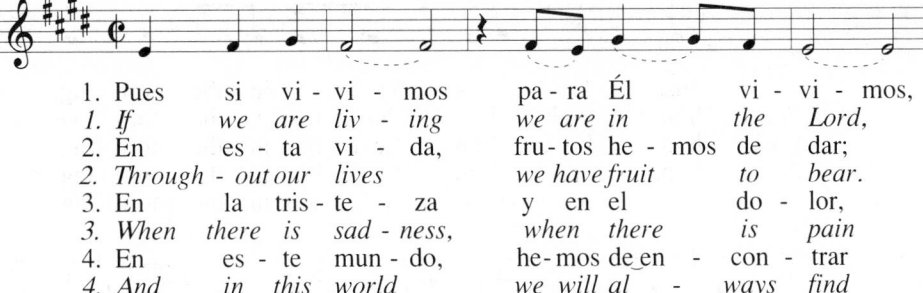

1. Pues si vi - vi - mos pa - ra Él vi - vi - mos,
1. If we are liv - ing we are in the Lord,
2. En es - ta vi - da, fru - tos he - mos de dar;
2. Through - out our lives we have fruit to bear.
3. En la tris - te - za y en el do - lor,
3. When there is sad - ness, when there is pain
4. En es - te mun - do, he - mos de en - con - trar
4. And in this world we will al - ways find

y si mo - ri - mos pa - ra Él Mo - ri - mos.
and if we die we are in the Lord,
las o - bras bue - nas son pa - ra of - ren - dar.
All of our good works are for us to share.
en la be - lle - za y en el a - mor
in Christ the Lord, we have love to gain.
gen - te que llo - ra y sin con - so - lar.
those who are weep - ing, sick in heart and mind.

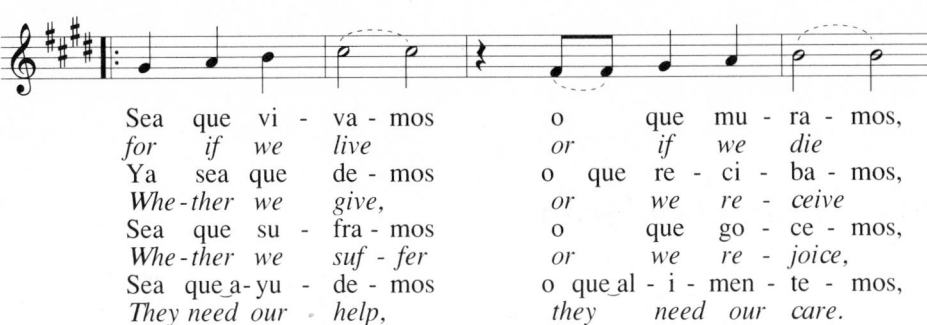

Sea que vi - va - mos o que mu - ra - mos,
for if we live or if we die
Ya sea que de - mos o que re - ci - ba - mos,
Whe - ther we give, or we re - ceive
Sea que su - fra - mos o que go - ce - mos,
Whe - ther we suf - fer, or we re - joice,
Sea que a - yu - de - mos o que al - i - men - te - mos,
They need our help, they need our care.

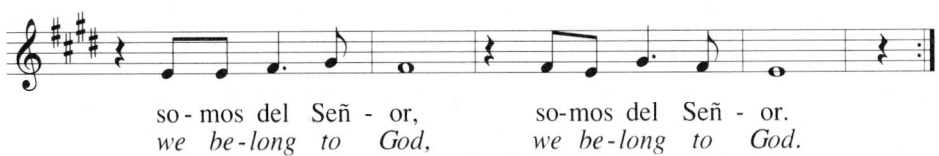

so - mos del Señ - or, so - mos del Señ - or.
we be - long to God, we be - long to God.

Text: Verse 1, Romans; 14:8; traditional Spanish; translation by Deborah L. Schmitz, b.1969, © 1994, GIA Publications, inc.
Tune: Traditional Spanish; arr. by Diana Kodner, b.1957. © 1994, GIA Publications, Inc.

667 Jesus in the Morning

1. Je - sus, Je - sus, Je - sus in the morn - ing,
2. Praise him, Praise him, Praise him in the morn - ing,
3. Love him, Love him, Love him in the morn - ing,
4. Serve him, Serve him, Serve him in the morn - ing,
5. Je - sus, Je - sus, Je - sus in the morn - ing,

Je - sus in the noon - time; Je - sus, Je - sus,
Praise him in the noon - time; Praise him, Praise him,
Love him in the noon - time; Love him, Love him,
Serve him in the noon - time; Serve him, Serve him,
Je - sus in the noon - time; Je - sus, Je - sus,

Je - sus when the sun goes down!
Praise him when the sun goes down!
Love him when the sun goes down!
Serve him when the sun goes down!
Je - sus when the sun goes down!

Text: African-American folk song
Tune: African-American folk song

668 I Bind My Heart

1. I bind my heart this tide, To the
2. I bind my soul this day, To the
3. I bind my heart in thrall, To the
4. I bind my - self to peace, To make

Gal - i - le - an's side, To the wounds of Cal - va -
broth - er far a - way, To the sis - ter near at
God, the Lord of all, To the God, the poor one's
strife and en - vy cease; O God, knit thou sure the

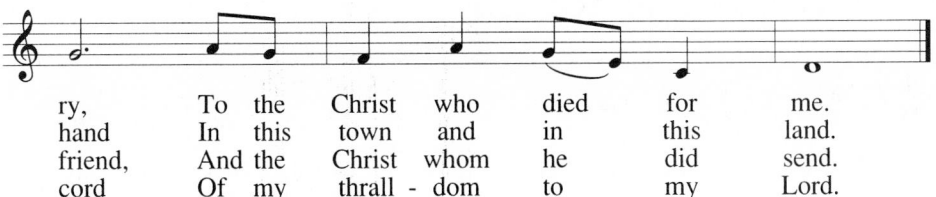

ry,	To	the	Christ	who	died	for	me.
hand	In	this	town	and	in	this	land.
friend,	And	the	Christ	whom	he	did	send.
cord	Of	my	thrall - dom	to	my	Lord.

Text: "Thraldom," *The Tryst*, 1907, Lauchlan McLean Watt, 1853-1931
Tune: Suzanne Toolan, SM, b.1927, © 1979, Resource Publications, Inc.

The Servant Song 669

1.,6. Will	you	let	me	be	your	ser - vant,
2. We	are	pil - grims	on	a	jour - ney,
3. I	will	hold	the	Christ - light	for	you
4. I	will	weep	when	you	are	weep - ing;
5. When	we	sing	to	God	in	heav - en

Let	me	be	as	Christ to	you;	Pray	that	I	may
We	are	trav - 'lers	on	the	road;	We	are	here	to
In	the	night - time	of	your	fear;	I	will	hold	my
When you	laugh	I'll	laugh with	you.	I	will	share	your
We	shall	find	such	har - mo - ny,	Born	of	all	we've

have	the grace to	Let	you	be	my	ser - vant,	too.
help	each oth - er	Walk	the	mile and	bear	the	load.
hand	out to you,	Speak	the	peace you	long	to	hear.
joy	and sor - row	'Til	we've	seen this	jour - ney	through.
known	to - geth - er	Of	Christ's love and	ag - o - ny.

Text: Richard Gillard
Tune: Richard Gillard; harm. by Betty Pulkingham, b.1929
© 1977, Scripture in Song

670 Whatsoever You Do

Refrain

What-so-ev-er you do to the least of my

peo-ple, that you do un-to me.

Verses

1. When I was hun-gry, you gave me to eat;
2. When I was home-less, you o-pened your door;
3. When I was wea-ry, you helped me find rest;
4. When I was lit-tle, you taught me to read;
5. When in a pris-on, you came to my cell;
6. In a strange coun-try, you made me at home;
7. Hurt in a bat-tle, you bound up my wounds;
8. When I was Black, or La-ti-no, or white;
9. When I was a-ged, you both-ered to smile;
10. You saw me cov-ered with spit-tle and blood;
11. When I was laughed at, you stood by my side;

When I was thirst-y, you gave me to drink.
When I was na-ked, you gave me your coat.
When I was anx-ious, you calmed all my fears.
When I was lone-ly, you gave me your love.
When on a sick-bed, you cared for my needs.
Seek-ing em-ploy-ment, you found me a job.
Search-ing for kind-ness, you held out your hand.
Mocked and in-sult-ed, you car-ried my cross.
When I was rest-less, you lis-tened and cared.
You knew my fea-tures, though grim-y with sweat.
When I was hap-py, you shared in my joy.

D.C.

Now en-ter in-to the home of my Fa-ther.

Text: Matthew 5:3-12; Willard F. Jabusch, b.1930, © 1966, 1979
Tune: WHATSOEVER YOU DO, 10 10 11 with refrain; Willard F. Jabusch, b.1930, © 1966, 1979; harm. by Robert J. Batastini, b.1942, © 1975, GIA Publications, Inc.

Glorious in Majesty 671

Verses

1. Glo - ri - ous in maj - es - ty, Ho - ly in his prais - es,
2. Vic - to - ry he won for us, Free-ing us from dark - ness,
3. One in love, as fam - i - ly, Liv - ing with each oth - er,

Je - sus, our Sav - ior and our King. Born a man, yet God of old,
Dy - ing and ris - ing from the dead. Liv-ing with the Fa-ther now,
Glad-ly we share each oth-er's pain. Yet he will not leave us so,

Let us all a - dore him: Filled with his Spir - it, let us sing.
Yet he is a-mong us: We are the bod - y, he the head.
Soon he is re - turn - ing, Tak - ing us back with him to reign.

Refrain

Liv - ing is to love him, serv - ing him to know his free-dom.

Come a - long with us to join the praise of Je - sus.

Come to Je - sus now, Go to live his word re - joic - ing.

Text: Jeff Cothran, fl.1972, © 1972, GIA Publications, Inc.
Tune: SHIBBOLET BASADEH, 7 6 7 8 D with refrain; Jewish melody; harm. by Jeff Cothran, fl.1972. © 1972, GIA Publications, Inc.

672 I Am the Vine

Refrain

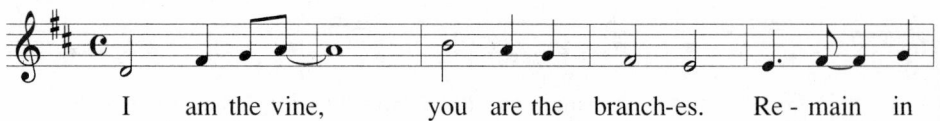

I am the vine, you are the branch-es. Re - main in

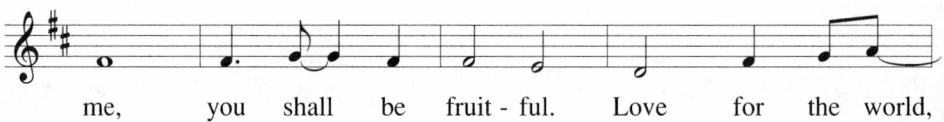

me, you shall be fruit - ful. Love for the world,

hope for the hope - less.

Verses

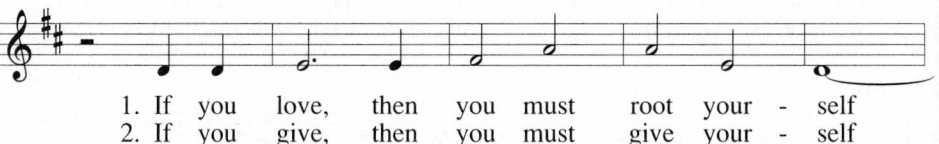

1. If you love, then you must root your - self
2. If you give, then you must give your - self

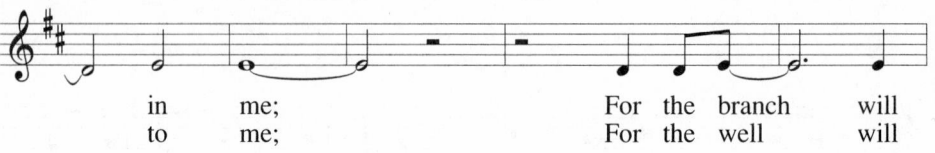

in me; For the branch will
to me; For the well will

D.C.

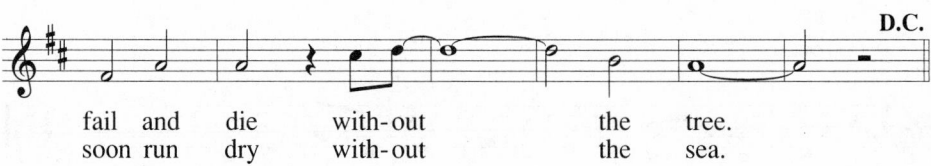

fail and die with-out the tree.
soon run dry with-out the sea.

Text: John 15:1-10; Bob Hurd, b.1950, © 1979
Tune: Bob Hurd, b.1950, © 1979; acc. by Craig Kingsbury, b.1952, © 1983, OCP Publications
Published by OCP Publications

Take This Moment 673

1. Take this mo - ment, sign, and space;
2. Take the time to call my name,
3. Take the tired - ness of my days,
4. Take the lit - tle child in me,
5. Take my tal - ents, take my skills,

Take my friends a - round; Here a -
Take the time to mend Who I
Take my past re - gret, Let - ting
Scared of grow - ing old; Help him/her
Take what's yet to be; Let my

mong us make the place Where your
am and what I've been, All I've
your for - give - ness touch All I
here to find his/her worth Made in
life be yours, and yet, Let it

love is found.
failed to tend.
can't for - get.
Christ's own mold.
still be me.

Text: John L. Bell, b.1949
Tune: TAKE THIS MOMENT, 7 5 7 5; John L. Bell, b.1949
© 1989, Iona Community, GIA Publications, agent

674 Keep in Mind

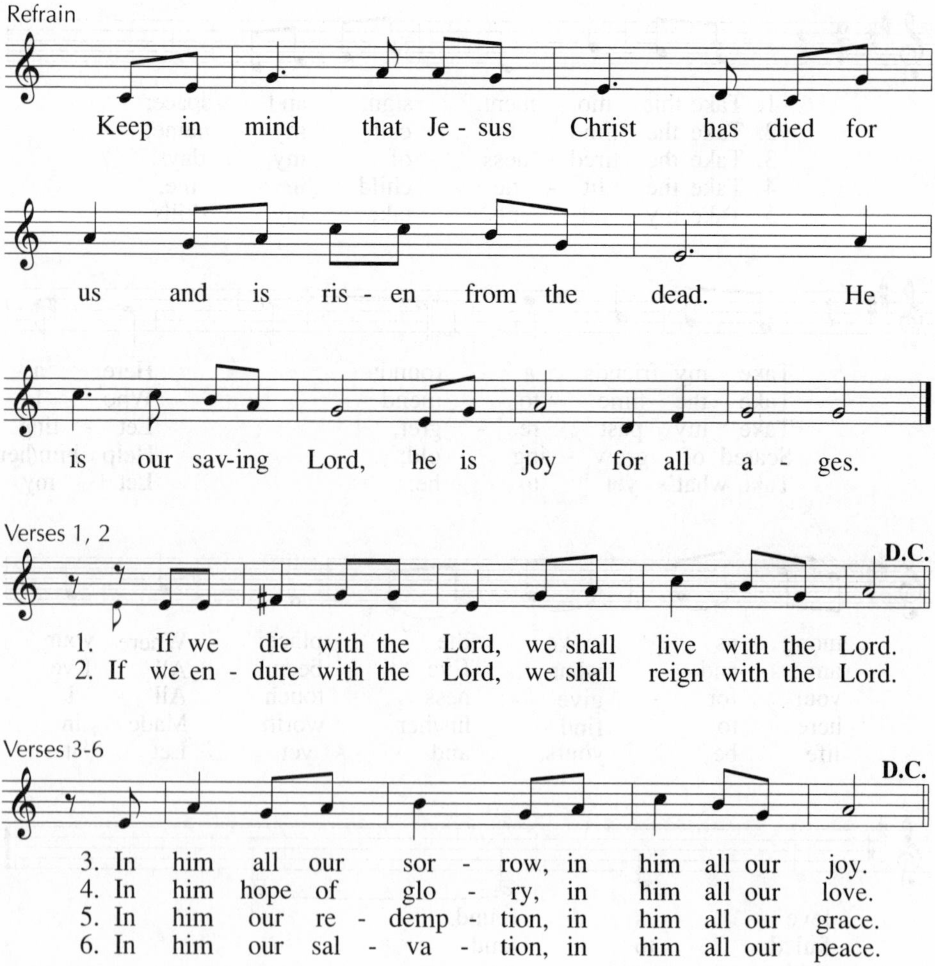

Refrain

Keep in mind that Je - sus Christ has died for

us and is ris - en from the dead. He

is our sav-ing Lord, he is joy for all a - ges.

Verses 1, 2

D.C.

1. If we die with the Lord, we shall live with the Lord.
2. If we en - dure with the Lord, we shall reign with the Lord.

Verses 3-6

D.C.

3. In him all our sor - row, in him all our joy.
4. In him hope of glo - ry, in him all our love.
5. In him our re - demp - tion, in him all our grace.
6. In him our sal - va - tion, in him all our peace.

Text: 2 Timothy 2:8-12, Lucien Deiss, CSSp, b.1921
Tune: Lucien Deiss, CSSp, b.1921
© 1965, 1966, World Library Publications, Inc.

The God Who Sends Us Forth   675

1. The God who sends us forth, u - nit - ed
2. The road a - head is filled by trav - 'lers
3. So let us bless our God, the send - er

in our pray'r, Has strength - ened us and
with - out end: The way - ward and the
and the one, And let us bless the

tend - ed us with shep - herd's care.
wan - der - er, the mi - grant friend.
ser - vant, Je - sus Christ the Son.

God's Je - sus makes us bold, his bod - y
And we are Je - sus' flesh, his wel - come
The Spir - it let us thank, whose love is

is our bread; His wine of life is
and his home We go from here to
bright in - deed, Who lights a gen - tle

full - ness for the road a - head.
love and serve, to tend God's own.
path - way for a world in need.

Text: John Foley, SJ, b.1939
Tune: John Foley, SJ, b.1939
© 1993, GIA Publications, Inc.

676 You Have Anointed Me

Verse 1

1. To bring glad tid - ings to the low - ly, to heal the bro - ken heart, You have a - noint - ed me. To pro - claim lib - er - ty to cap - tives, re - lease to pris - on - ers, You have a - noint - ed me.

Refrain

Your Spir - it, O God, is up - on me, You have a - noint - ed me.

Verse 2

2. To an - nounce a year of fa - vor, to com - fort those who mourn, You have a - noint - ed me. To give to them the oil of glad-ness, and

D.S.

share a man-tle of joy, You have a - noint - ed me.

Text: Mike Balhoff, b.1946, Gary Daigle, b.1957, Darryl Ducote, b.1945
Tune: Mike Balhoff, b.1946, Gary Daigle, b.1957, Darryl Ducote, b.1945; acc. by Gary Daigle, b.1945
© 1981, Damean Music. Distributed by GIA Publications, Inc.

Thuma Mina / Send Me, Jesus 677

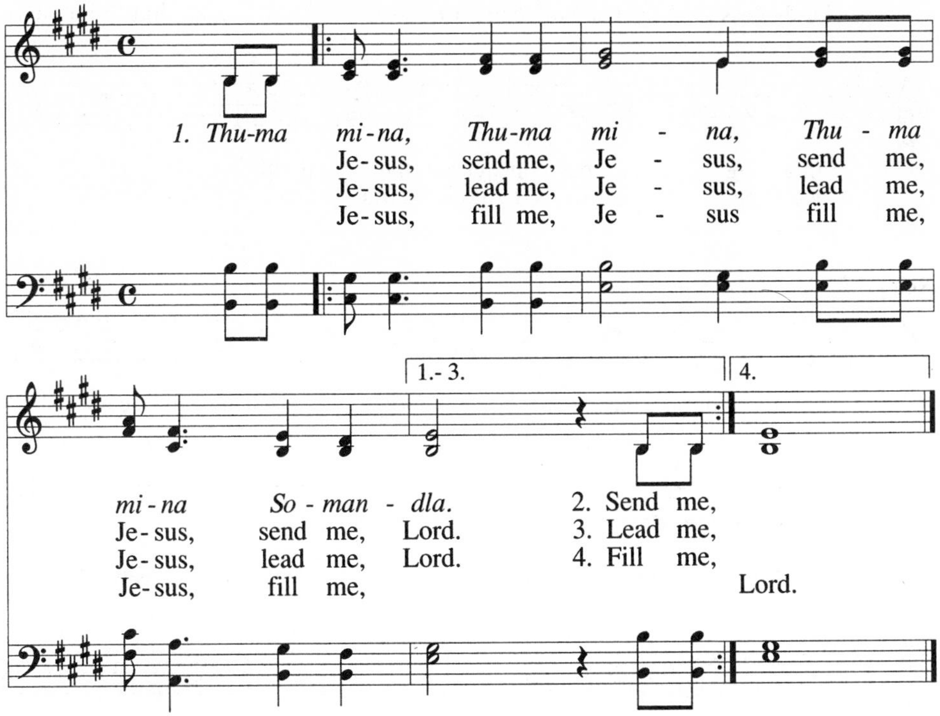

1. Thu-ma mi-na, Thu-ma mi - na, Thu - ma
   Je- sus, send me, Je - sus, send me,
   Je- sus, lead me, Je - sus, lead me,
   Je- sus, fill me, Je - sus fill me,

1.- 3.   **4.**

mi - na So - man - dla. 2. Send me,
Je- sus, send me, Lord. 3. Lead me,
Je- sus, lead me, Lord. 4. Fill me,
Je- sus, fill me, Lord.

Text: South African
Tune: THUMA MINA, South African
© 1984, Utryck

678　City of God

Verses 1, 2

1. A-wake from your slum-ber! A - rise from your
2. We are sons of the morn-ing; we are daugh-ters of

sleep! A new day is dawn - ing
day. The One who has loved us

for all those who weep. The peo - ple in
has bright-ened our way. The Lord of all

dark - ness have seen a great light. The Lord of our
kind - ness has called us to be a light for his

long - ing has con-quered the night.
peo - ple to set their hearts free.

Refrain 𝄋

Let us build the cit-y of God. May our tears be

turned in - to danc - ing! For the Lord, our light and our

love, has turned the night in - to day!

Verse 3

3. God is light; in him there is no dark - ness. Let us walk in his light, his chil - dren, one and all.

O com-fort my peo - ple; make gen-tle your words. Pro - claim to my cit-y the day of her birth.

Verse 4

4. O cit-y of glad-ness, now lift up your voice. Pro - claim the good tid - ings that all may re - joice!

Text: Dan Schutte, b.1947
Tune: Dan Schutte, b.1947; acc. by Robert J. Batastini, b. 1942
© 1981, Daniel L. Schutte and New Dawn Music. Published by OCP Publications.

679 Good News

Verses

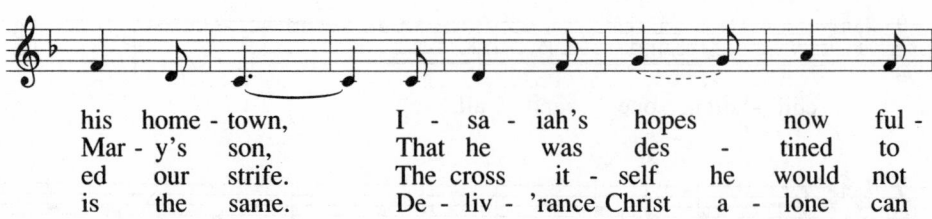

1. When Je - sus worked here on earth he preached in
2. The eld - ers of the syn - a - gogue were shocked by
3. The way he lived was proof of it: he qui - et -
4. So pass it on to - day, good friend: the mes - sage

his home - town, I - sa - iah's hopes now ful -
Mar - y's son, That he was des - tined to
ed our strife. The cross it - self he would not
is the same. De - liv - 'rance Christ a - lone can

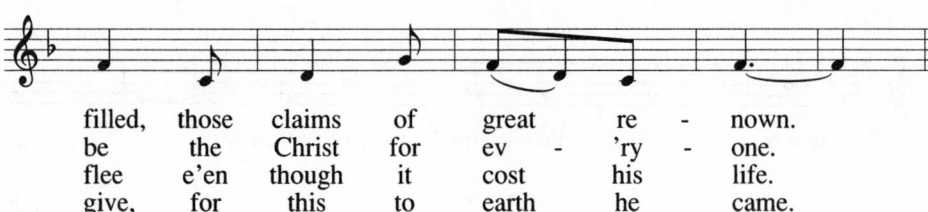

filled, those claims of great re - nown.
be the Christ for ev - 'ry - one.
flee e'en though it cost his life.
give, for this to earth he came.

Refrain

To bring good news to the need - y, to make the blind to

see, the bro - ken hearts healed a - gain, to

|1.

set the cap - tive free.

|2.

cap - tive free.

Text: Howard S. Olson
Tune: Almaz Belihu; Yemissrach Dimts Literature Program, Ethiopia
© 1993, Howard S. Olson

You Are Called to Tell the Story   680

1. You are called to tell the sto - ry, pass - ing
2. You are called to teach the rhy - thm of the
3. You are called to set the ta - ble, bless - ing
4. May the One whose love is broad - er than the

words of life a - long, Then to
dance that nev - er ends, Then to
bread as Je - sus blessed, Then to
meas - ure of all space Give us

blend your voice with oth - ers as you
move with - in the cir - cle, hand in
come with thirst and hun - ger, need - ing
words to sing the sto - ry, move a -

sing the sa - cred song. Christ be
hand with stran - gers, friends. Christ be
care like all the rest, Christ be
mong us in this place. Christ be

known in all our sing - ing,
known in all our danc - ing,
known in all our shar - ing,
known in all our liv - ing,

fill - ing all with songs of love.
touch - ing all with hands of love.
feed - ing all with signs of love.
fill - ing all with gifts of love.

Text: Ruth Duck, b.1947, © 1992, GIA Publications, Inc.
Tune: GHENT, 8 7 8 7 8 7; M.D. Ridge, b.1938; acc. by Patrick Loomis, 1951-1990, © 1987, GIA Publications, Inc.

681 Lord, Whose Love in Humble Service

1. Lord, whose love in hum - ble ser - vice
2. Still your chil - dren wan - der home - less;
3. As we wor - ship, grant us vi - sion,
4. Called from wor - ship in - to ser - vice

Bore the weight of hu - man need,
Still the hun - gry cry for bread;
Till your love's re - veal - ing light,
Forth in your great name we go,

Who did on the Cross for - sak - en,
Still the cap - tives long for free - dom;
Till the height and depth and great - ness
To the child, the youth, the a - ged,

Show us mer - cy's per - fect deed;
Still in grief we mourn our dead.
Dawns up - on our hu - man sight:
Love in liv - ing deeds to show;

We, your ser - vants, bring the wor - ship
As, O Lord, your deep com - pas - sion
Mak - ing known the needs and bur - dens
Hope and health, good - will and com - fort,

Not of voice a - lone, but heart:
Healed the sick and freed the soul,
Your com - pas - sion bids us bear,
Coun - sel, aid, and peace we give

Con - se - crat - ing to your pur - pose
Use the love your Spir - it kin - dles
Stir - ring us to faith - ful ser - vice,
That your chil - dren, Lord, in free - dom,

Ev - 'ry gift which you im - part.
Still to save and make us whole.
Your a - bun - dant life to share.
May your mer - cy know and live.

Text: Albert F. Bayly, 1901-1984, © Oxford University Press
Tune: IN BABILONE 8 7 8 7 D; *Oude en Nieuwe Hollanste Boerenlities,* © c.1710

682 God Has Chosen Me

Servant Song   683

Refrain

Be fair and just. Be mer-ci-ful and true.

These are the things I am ask-ing of you. Walk

hum-bly with your God, in ev-'ry-thing you do.

This is the way that will lead you to the truth.

Verses

1. To you, O Lord, we lift our souls. To
2. Lead us on the path of truth.
3. Breathe in us the spir-it of life. A -
4. Mold our hearts for all that is good. Let

you, O Lord, we pray. For we
Guide us a - long the way. Re -
wak - en our sens - es this day to
kind - ness be our guide. May

o - pen our hearts to you, O God, a -
mem - ber your kind - ness and mer - cy, O God.
feel your pres - ence in all of the earth.
we be your voice to oth - ers in need, your

D.C.

wak - en us, show us the way.
Give us your wis - dom to - day.
Move in us, lead us to you.
shel - ter where friends can a - bide.

Text: Micah 6:8, Psalm 25; Ziggy Stardust and Bobby Fisher, b.1952
Tune: Bobby Fisher, b.1952
© 1992, GIA Publications, Inc.

684   Great Is the Lord

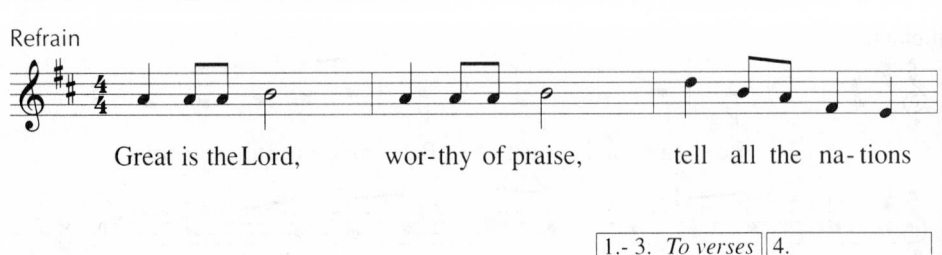

Refrain

Great is the Lord,   wor-thy of praise,   tell all the na-tions

God is King!   Spread the news of God's love!   love!

Verses

1. The   Spir-it   of the Lord   is up - on   me   be-cause the
2. How   beau-ti - ful   up - on the moun - tains,   the feet of
3. Give   glo - ry   to the   Fa - ther,   the Son and

Lord   has a-noint - ed   me.   God has
those   who   bring   glad   tid - ings,   an-nounc-ing
Ho - ly   Spir - it   blest,   the God who

sent   me to bring   glad   tid - ings   to the
peace,   bear - ing   good   news   that the
is,   who   was,   who   will   be,   for

D.C.

low - ly,   to   the   low - ly.
Lord   God   is   King!
ev - er,   A - men.

Text: Isaiah 61:1 - 4; 52:7; Suzanne Toolan, SM, b.1927
Tune: Suzanne Toolan, SM, b.1927
© 1974, GIA Publications, Inc.

Moved by the Gospel, Let Us Move 685

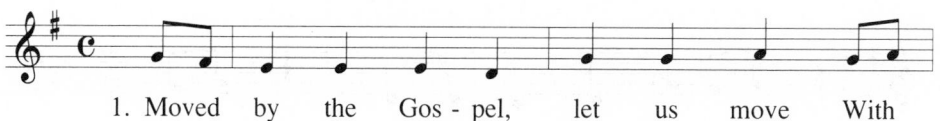

1. Moved by the Gos - pel, let us move With
2. Let weav - ers form from bro - ken strands A
3. O Spir - it, breathe a - mong us here; In -

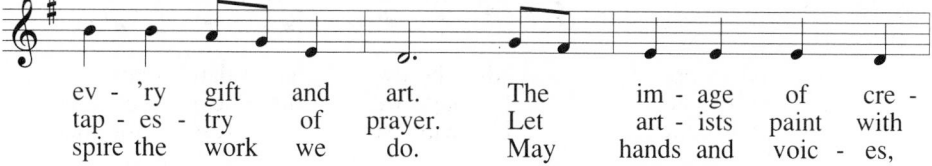

ev - 'ry gift and art. The im - age of cre -
tap - es - try of prayer. Let art - ists paint with
spire the work we do. May hands and voic - es,

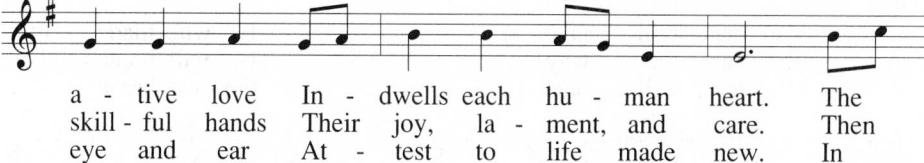

a - tive love In - dwells each hu - man heart. The
skill - ful hands Their joy, la - ment, and care. Then
eye and ear At - test to life made new. In

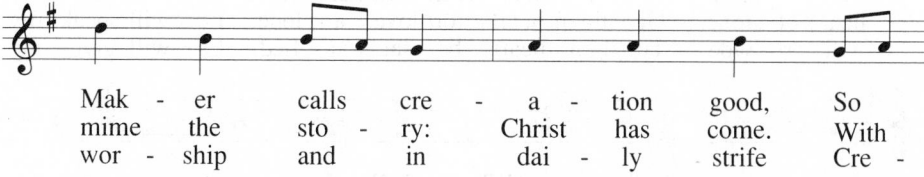

Mak - er calls cre - a - tion good, So
mime the sto - ry: Christ has come. With
wor - ship and in dai - ly strife Cre -

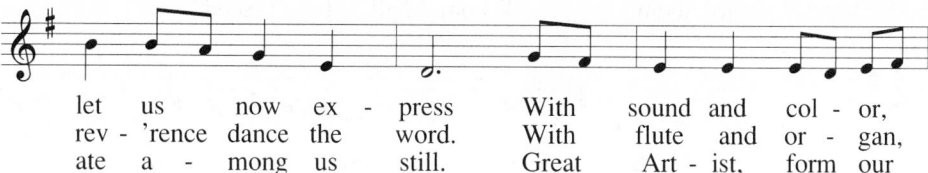

let us now ex - press With sound and col - or,
rev - 'rence dance the word. With flute and or - gan,
ate a - mong us still. Great Art - ist, form our

stone and wood, The shape of ho - li - ness.
ching and drum God's praise be ev - er heard.
com - mon life Ac - cord - ing to your will.

Text: Ruth Duck, b. 1947. © 1992, GIA Publications, Inc.
Tune: KINGSFOLD, CMD; English: harm. by Ralph Vaughan Williams, 1872-1958

686 Here I Am, Lord

Verses

1. I, the Lord of sea and sky, I have heard my
2. I, the Lord of snow and rain, I have borne my
3. I, the Lord of wind and flame, I will tend the

peo - ple cry. All who dwell in dark and sin
peo - ple's pain. I have wept for love of them.
poor and lame. I will set a feast for them.

My hand will save. I who made the
They turn a - way. I will break their
My hand will save. Fin - est bread I

stars of night, I will make their dark-ness bright. Who will bear my
hearts of stone, Give them hearts for love a - lone. I will speak my
will pro - vide Till their hearts be sat - is - fied. I will give my

light to them? Whom shall I send?
word to them. Whom shall I send?
life to them. Whom shall I send?

Refrain

Here I am, Lord. Is it I, Lord? I have heard you

call-ing in the night. I will go, Lord, if you lead me.

I will hold your peo - ple in my heart.

Text: Isaiah 6; Dan Schutte. b.1947
Tune: Dan Schutte. b.1947; arr. by Michael Pope, SJ, John Weissrock
© 1981, Daniel L. Schutte and New Dawn Music

Go Make of All Disciples 687

1. "Go make of all dis - ci - ples:" We hear the call, O
2. "Go make of all dis - ci - ples:" Bap - tiz - ing in the
3. "Go make of all dis - ci - ples:" We at your feet would
4. "Go make of all dis - ci - ples:" We wel - come your com -

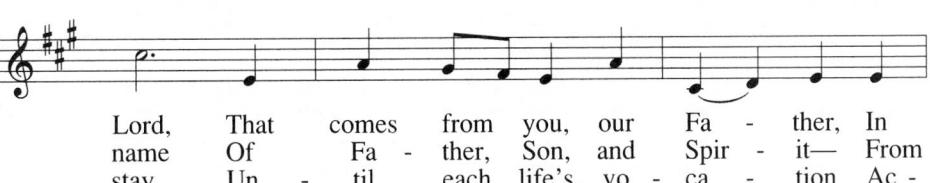

Lord, That comes from you, our Fa - ther, In
name Of Fa - ther, Son, and Spir - it— From
stay Un - til each life's vo - ca - tion Ac -
mand; "Lo, I am with you al - ways:" We

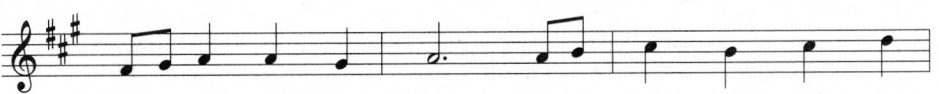

your e - ter - nal Word. In - spire our ways of
age to age the same. We call each new dis -
cents your ho - ly way. We cul - ti - vate the
take your guid - ing hand. The task looms large be -

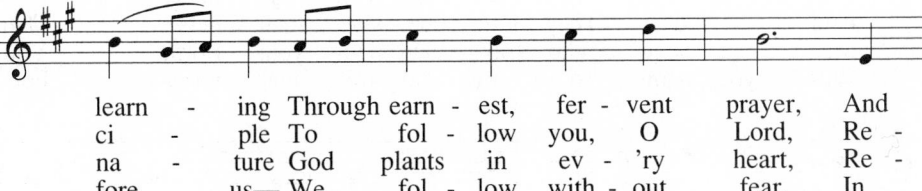

learn - ing Through earn - est, fer - vent prayer, And
ci - ple To fol - low you, O Lord, Re -
na - ture God plants in ev - 'ry heart, Re -
fore us— We fol - low with - out fear. In

let our dai - ly liv - ing Re - veal you ev - 'ry - where.
deem - ing soul and bod - y By wa - ter and the Word.
veal - ing in our wit - ness The Mas - ter Teach-er's art.
heav'n and earth your pow - er Shall bring God's king - dom here.

Text: Matthew 28:19-20; Leon M. Adkins, b.1896, alt., © 1955,1964, Abingdon Press
Tune: ELLACOMBE, 7 6 7 6 D; *Gesangbuch der Herzogl, Wirtemberg*, 1784

688 Two Fishermen

1. Two fish-er-men, who lived a-long The Sea of Gal-i-
2. And as he walked a-long the shore 'Twas James and John he'd
3. O Si-mon Pe-ter, An-drew, James And John be-lov-ed
4. And you, good Chris-tians, one and all Who'd fol-low Je-sus'

lee, Stood by the shore to cast their nets In -
find, And these two sons of Zeb - e-dee Would
one, You heard Christ's call to speak good news Re -
way, Come leave be-hind what keeps you bound To

to an age-less sea. Now Je - sus watched them
leave their boats be-hind. Their work and all they
vealed to God's own Son. Su - san - na, Mar - y,
trap-pings of our day, And lis - ten as he

from a - far Then called them each by name; It
held so dear They left be-side their nets. Their
Mag - da-lene Who trav-eled with your Lord, You
calls your name To come and fol - low near, For

changed their lives, these sim - ple men; They'd nev - er be the same.
names they'd heard as Je - sus called; They came with-out re - gret.
min - is-tered to him with joy For he is God a - dored.
still he speaks in var - ied ways To those his call will hear.

Leave all things you have And come and fol - low

me, And come and fol - low me.

Text: Suzanne Toolan, SM, b.1927, © 1986, GIA Publications, Inc.
Tune: LEAVE ALL THINGS, CMD with refrain; Suzanne Toolan, SM, b.1927, © 1970, GIA Publications, Inc.

Out of Darkness 689

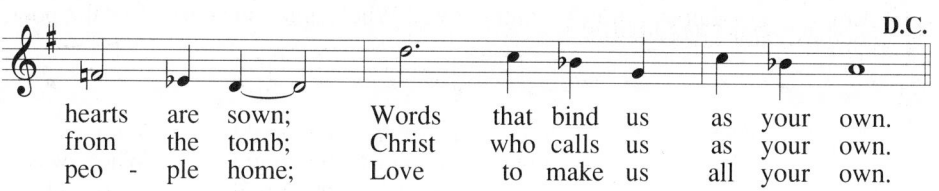

Refrain

Out of dark - ness God has called us, claimed by Christ as

God's own peo - ple. Ho - ly na - tion, roy - al priest - hood,

1.- 3. *To verse* | *Last time*

walk-ing in God's marv'-lous light. A - men.

Verses

1. Let us take the words you give,
2. Let us take the Christ you give,
3. Let us take the love you give,

Strong and faith - ful words to live. Words that in our
Bro - ken Bod - y Christ we live. Christ the ris - en
That the way of love we live. Love to bring your

D.C.

hearts are sown; Words that bind us as your own.
from the tomb; Christ who calls us as your own.
peo - ple home; Love to make us all your own.

Text: Christopher Walker, b.1947
Tune: Christopher Walker, b.1947
© 1989, Christopher Walker, published by OCP Publications

690 Anthem

Refrain

We are called, we are cho-sen. We are Christ for one an-oth-er. We are
prom-ised to to-mor-row, while we are for him to-day. We are
sign, we are won-der. We are sow-er, we are seed. We are
har-vest, we are hun-ger. We are ques-tion, we are creed.

Verses

1. Then where can we stand jus-ti-fied? In what can we be-
2. Then how are we to stand at all, this world of bend-ed
3. Then shall we not stand emp-ty at the al-tar of our

lieve? In no one else but Christ who suf-fered, noth-ing
knee? In noth-ing more than bar-ren shad-ows. No one
dreams? When Christ prom-ised us our-selves. Who mark

more than Christ who rose. Who was jus-tice for the poor.
else but Christ could save us. Who was jus-tice for the poor.
time a-gainst to-mor-row. Who are jus-tice for the poor.

Who was rage a-gainst the night. Who was
Who was rage a-gainst the night. Who was
Who are rage a-gainst the night. Who are

D.C.

hope for peace-ful peo-ple. Who was light.
hope for peace-ful peo-ple. Who was light.
hope for peace-ful peo-ple. Who are light.

Text: Tom Conry, b.1951, © 1978, New Dawn Music
Tune: Tom Conry, b.1951, © 1978, New Dawn Music; acc. by Robert J. Batastini, b.1942, © 1994, GIA Publications, Inc.

Now Go Forward   691

Now go   for-ward,   press toward the goal.   Plen-ti-ful har - vest

waits for you.   Faith-ful   ser - vants,   fear   not death,

toil and   la - bor   for   the Lord.   Come,   be-hold, your

days   pass a - way.   Look   a - head,   the

cross   leads the way.   While   you have breath

on   this day,   give your - self.   For - ward   go!

Text: Unknown; trans. © 1986, Evelyn Chiu
Tune: Traditional Chinese melody; acc. by Diana Kodner, b. 1957. © 1994, GIA Publications, Inc.

692 Sing Hey for the Carpenter

Verses

1. Come with me, come wan - der, come wel - come the
2. Come walk in my com - p'ny, come sleep by my
3. Come share in my laugh - ter, come close to my
4. Come leave your pos - ses - sions, come share out your

world Where stran - gers might smile or where
side, Come sa - vor a life - style with
fears, Come find your - self washed with the
treas - ure. Come give and re - ceive with - out

stones may be hurled; Come leave what you
noth - ing to hide; Come sit at my
kiss of my tears; Come stand close at
meth - od or meas - ure; Come loose ev - 'ry

cling to, lay down what you clutch And
ta - ble and eat with my friends, Dis -
hand while I suf - fer and die And
bond that's re - sist - ing the Spir - it, En -

find, with hands emp - ty, that hearts can hold much.
cov - 'ring that love which the world nev - er ends.
find in three days how I nev - er will lie.
a - bling the earth to be yours to in - her - it.

Refrain

Sing hey for the car - pen - ter leav - ing his

tools! Sing hey for the Phar - i - sees leav - ing their

rules! Sing hey for the fish - er - men leav - ing their

nets! Sing hey for the peo-ple who leave their re - grets!

Text: John L. Bell, b.1949
Tune: SING HEY, Irregular; John L. Bell, b.1949
© 1987, The Iona Community, GIA Publications, Inc., agent

We Are Climbing Jacob's Ladder   693

1. We are climb-ing Ja - cob's lad - der, We are
2. Ev - 'ry round goes high - er, high - er, Ev - 'ry
3. Sin - ner, do you love my Je - sus? Sin - ner,
4. If you love him, why not serve him? If you
5. We are climb-ing high - er, high - er, We are

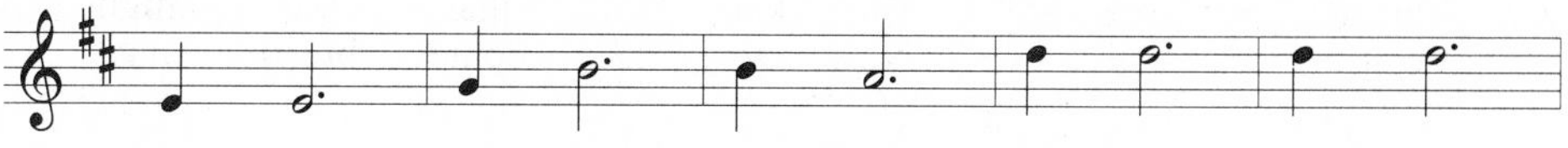

climb - ing Ja - cob's lad - der, We are climb - ing
round goes high - er, high - er, Ev - 'ry round goes
do you love my Je - sus? Sin - ner, do you
love him, why not serve him? If you love him,
climb - ing high - er, high - er, We are climb - ing

Ja - cob's lad - der, Sol - diers of the cross.
high - er, high - er, Sol - diers of the cross.
love my Je - sus? Sol - diers of the cross.
why not serve him? Sol - diers of the cross.
high - er, high - er, Sol - diers of the cross.

Text: African-American spiritual
Tune: JACOB'S LADDER, 8 8 8 5; African-American spiritual

694 Now We Remain

Refrain

We hold the death of the Lord deep in our hearts.
Liv-ing; now we re-main with Je - sus the Christ.

Verses

1. Once we were peo - ple a - fraid, lost in the
2. Some-thing which we have known, some-thing we've
3. He chose to give of him - self, be - came our
4. We are the pres - ence of God; this is our

night. Then by your cross we were
touched, What we have seen with our
bread. Bro - ken, that we might
call. Now to be - come bread and

saved; Dead be - came liv - ing, Life from your
eyes: This we have heard; Life giv - ing
live. Love be - yond love, Pain for our
wine: Food for the hun-gry, Life for the

1.- 3.   D.C.   4.

giv - ing.   for to live with the
word.
pain.
wea - ry,

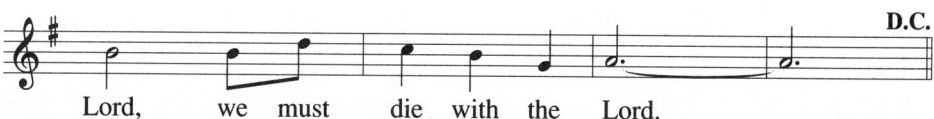

D.C.

Lord, we must die with the Lord.

Text: Corinthians, 1 John, 2 Timothy; David Haas, b.1957
Tune: David Haas, b.1957
© 1983, GIA Publications, Inc.

Only This I Want 695

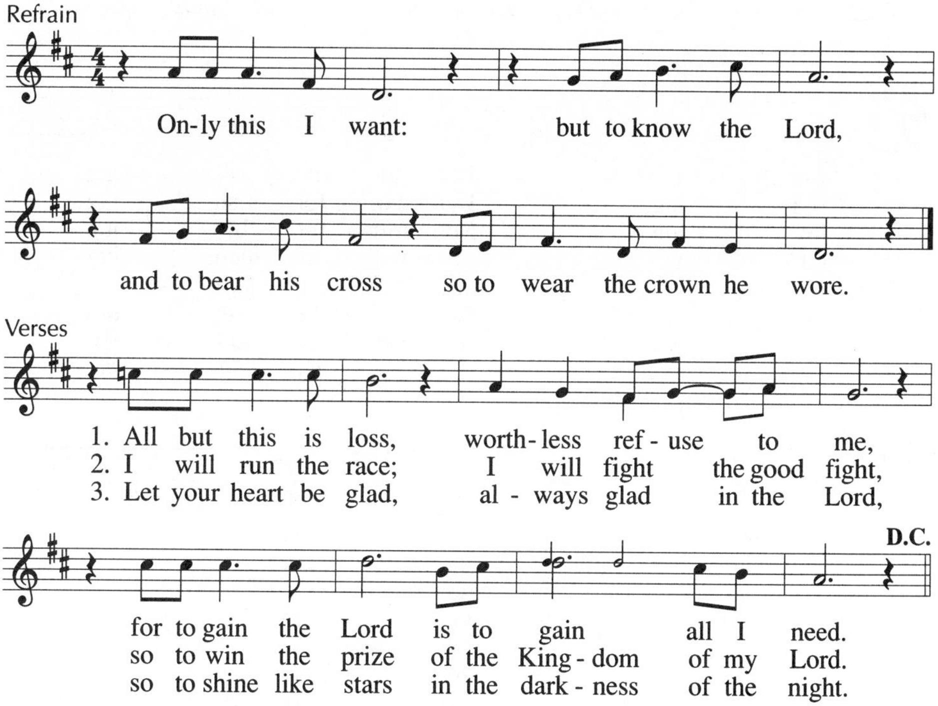

Refrain

On-ly this I want: but to know the Lord,

and to bear his cross so to wear the crown he wore.

Verses

1. All but this is loss, worth-less ref-use to me,
2. I will run the race; I will fight the good fight,
3. Let your heart be glad, al-ways glad in the Lord,

D.C.

for to gain the Lord is to gain all I need.
so to win the prize of the King-dom of my Lord.
so to shine like stars in the dark-ness of the night.

Text: Philippians 3:7-16; 2:15, 18; Dan Schutte, b.1947
Tune: Dan Schutte, b.1947; arr. by Michael Pope, SJ
© 1981, Daniel L. Schutte and New Dawn Music

696 Lord, When You Came / Pescador de Hombres

Verses

1. Lord, when you came to the sea - shore
2. Lord, you knew what my boat car - ried:
3. Lord, have you need of my la - bor,
4. Lord, send me where you would have me,

1. Tú has ve - ni - do_a la_o - ri - lla,
2. Tú sa - bes bien lo que ten - go,
3. Tú ne - ce - si - tas mis ma - nos,
4. Tú pes - ca - dor de_o-tros, ma - res,

You weren't seek - ing the wise or the
Nei - ther mon - ey nor weap - ons for
Hands for ser - vice, a heart made for
To a vil - lage, or heart of the

no_has bus - ca - do ni_a sa - bios, ni_a
en mi bar - ca no_hay o - ro ni_es-
mi can - san - cio que_a o - tros des -
an - sia_e - ter - na, al - mas que es -

wealth - y, But on - ly ask - ing
fight - ing, But nets for fish - ing,
lov - ing, My arms for lift - ing
cit - y; I will re - mem - ber

ri - cos, tan só - lo quie - res
pa - das, tan só - lo re - des
can - se, a - mor que quie - ra
pe - ran. A - mi - go bue - no,

that I might fol - low.
my dai - ly la - bor.
the poor and bro - ken?
that you are with me.

que yo te si - ga.
y mi tra - ba - jo.
se - guir a - man - do.
que_a - sí me lla - mas.

Refrain

O Lord,   in my eyes you were gaz - ing,
Se - ñor   me has mi - ra - do a los   o - jos,

Kind-ly   smil - ing,   my name you were
son - ri - en - do   has   di - cho mi

say - ing;   All I   treas - ured,
nom - bre,   en la a - re - na

I have left on the   sand   there;   Close to
he de - ja - do mi   bar - ca,   jun - to a

you,   I will find oth - er   seas.
ti   bus - ca - ré o - tro   mar.

Text: *Pescador de Hombres*, Cesáreo Gabaráin; trans. by Willard Francis Jabusch, b.1930, © 1979, published by OCP Publications
Tune: Cesáreo Gabaráin, © 1979, published by OCP Publications; acc. by Diana Kodner, b.1957, © 1994, GIA Publications, Inc.

697 Unless a Grain of Wheat

Refrain

Un - less a grain of wheat shall fall up - on the ground

and die, it re - mains but a sin - gle grain

|1.- 6. *To verses* || *Last time*

with no life.   2. If

Verses

1. If   we   have   died   with   him   then   we   shall
2. an - y - one   serves   me   then   they   must
3. ♪ Make   your   home   in   me   as   I   make
4. If   you   re - main   in   me   and   my   word
5. ♪ Those   who   love   me   are   loved   by   my
6. ♪ Peace   I   leave   with   you,   my   peace   I

live   with   him;   if   we   hold   firm   we   shall
fol - low   me;   where - ev - er   I   am   my
mine in   you;   those   who   re -   main   in   me
lives   in   you,   then   you   will   be   my   dis -
Fa -   ther;   we   shall   be   with   them   and
give   to   you;   peace   which   the   world   can - not

D.C.

reign   with   him.
ser - vants   will   be.
bear   much   fruit.
ci - ples.
dwell   in   them.
give   is   my   gift.

Text: John 12:24; Bernadette Farrell, b.1957
Tune: Bernadette Farrell, b.1957
© 1983, Bernadette Farrell, published by OCP Publications

Take Up Your Cross 698

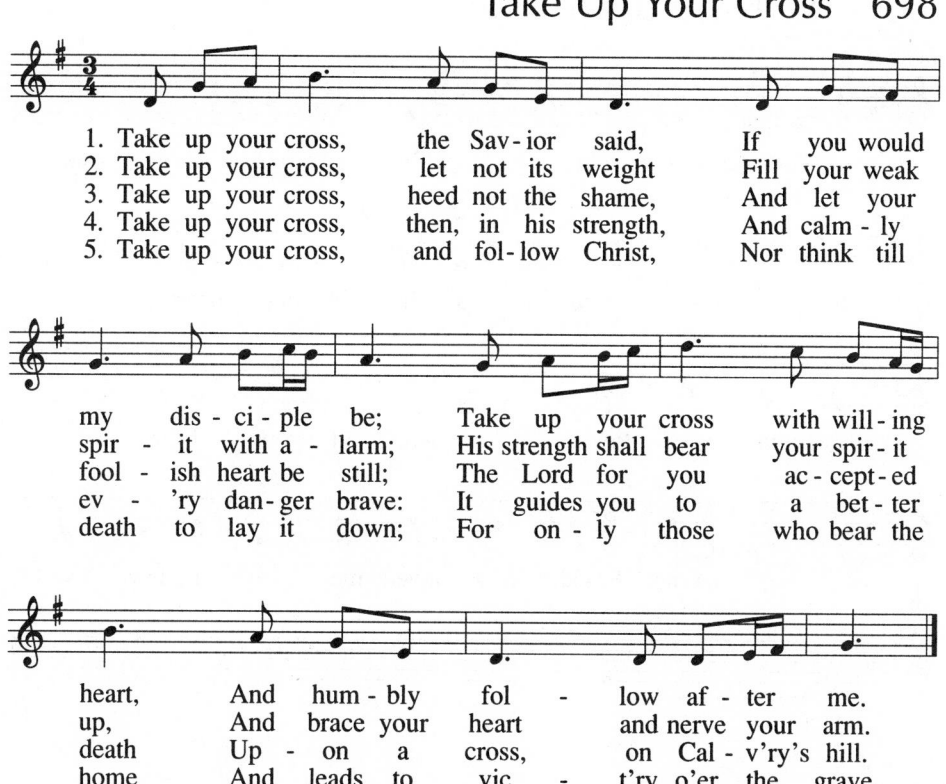

1. Take up your cross, the Sav-ior said,   If you would
2. Take up your cross, let not its weight   Fill your weak
3. Take up your cross, heed not the shame,   And let your
4. Take up your cross, then, in his strength,   And calm - ly
5. Take up your cross, and fol-low Christ,   Nor think till

my   dis - ci - ple   be;   Take up   your cross   with will- ing
spir - it   with a - larm;   His strength shall bear   your spir - it
fool - ish   heart be   still;   The Lord   for   you   ac - cept- ed
ev - 'ry   dan- ger   brave: It   guides you   to   a   bet - ter
death   to   lay it   down;   For   on - ly   those   who bear the

heart,   And   hum - bly   fol - low   af - ter   me.
up,   And   brace your   heart   and nerve   your   arm.
death   Up - on   a   cross,   on   Cal - v'ry's   hill.
home   And   leads   to   vic - t'ry   o'er   the   grave.
cross   May   hope   to   wear   the   glo - rious crown.

Text: Charles W. Everest, 1814-1877, alt.
Tune: O WALY WALY, LM; English; harm. by Martin West, b.1929, © 1983, Hope Publishing Co.

699 We Have Been Told

Refrain

We have been told, we've seen his face, and heard his voice a - live in our hearts; "Live in my love with all your heart, as the Fa - ther has loved me, so I have loved you."

Verse 1

1. "I am the vine, you are the branch-es, and all who live in me will bear great fruit."

Verses 2, 3

2. "You are my friends, if you keep my com - mands, no long - er slaves, I call you friends."

3. "No great-er love is there than this: to lay down one's life, for a friend."

Text: David Haas, b.1957
Tune: David Haas, b.1957; vocal arr. by David Haas, b.1957, Marty Haugen, b.1950
© 1983, GIA Publications, Inc.

The Summons 700

1. Will you come and fol - low me If I but
2. Will you leave your - self be - hind If I but
3. Will you let the blind - ed see If I but
4. Will you love the 'you' you hide If I but
5. Lord, your sum - mons ech - oes true When you but

call your name? Will you go where you don't
call your name? Will you care for cruel and
call your name? Will you set the pris - 'ners
call your name? Will you quell the fear in -
call my name. Let me turn and fol - low

know And nev - er be the same? Will you
kind And nev - er be the same? Will you
free And nev - er be the same? Will you
side And nev - er be the same? Will you
you And nev - er be the same. In your

let my love be shown, Will you let my
risk the hos - tile stare Should your life at -
kiss the lep - er clean, And do such as
use the faith you've found To re - shape the
com - pa - ny I'll go Where your love and

name be known, Will you let my life be
tract or scare? Will you let me an - swer
this un - seen, And ad - mit to what I
world a - round, Through my sight and touch and
foot - steps show. Thus I'll move and live and

grown In you and you in me?
pray'r In you and you in me?
mean In you and you in me?
sound In you and you in me?
grow In you and you in me.

Text: John L. Bell, b.1949, © 1987, Iona Community, GIA Publications, Inc., agent
Tune: KELVINGROVE, 7 6 7 6 777 6; Scottish traditional; arr. by John L. Bell, b.1949, © 1987, Iona Community, GIA Publications, Inc., agent

701   God It Was

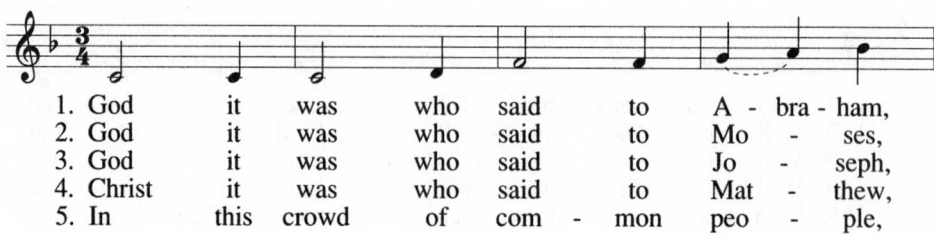

1. God   it   was   who   said   to A - bra - ham,
2. God   it   was   who   said   to Mo - ses,
3. God   it   was   who   said   to Jo - seph,
4. Christ it   was   who   said   to Mat - thew,
5. In   this crowd of com - mon peo - ple,

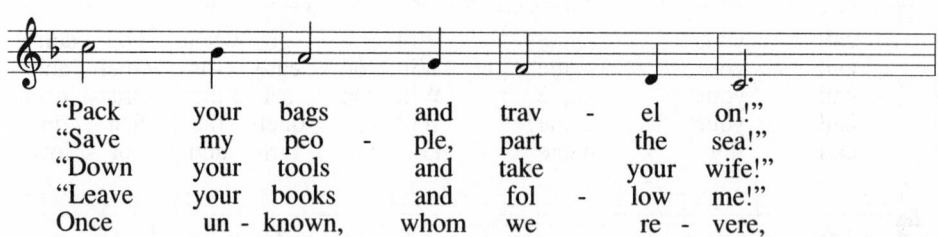

"Pack your bags   and trav - el   on!"
"Save my   peo - ple, part the sea!"
"Down your tools and take your wife!"
"Leave your books and fol - low me!"
Once un - known, whom we   re - vere,

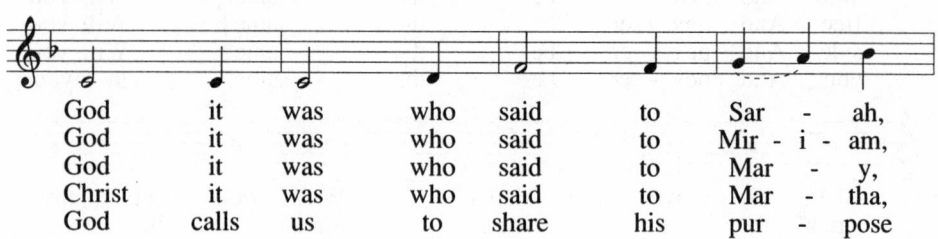

God   it   was   who said to Sar - ah,
God   it   was   who said to Mir - i - am,
God   it   was   who said to Mar - y,
Christ it   was   who said to Mar - tha,
God   calls us   to share his pur - pose

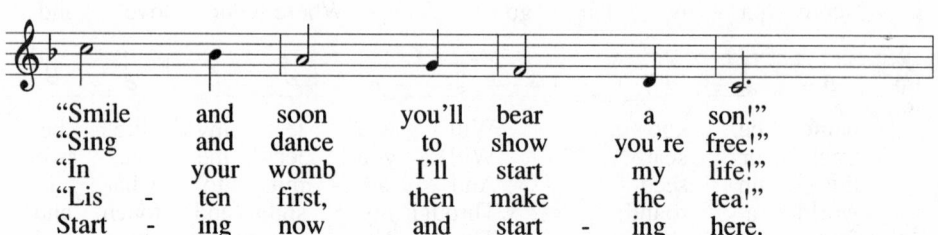

"Smile and   soon you'll bear   a   son!"
"Sing   and   dance to   show you're free!"
"In   your   womb I'll start my   life!"
"Lis - ten   first, then make the tea!"
Start - ing   now   and start - ing here.

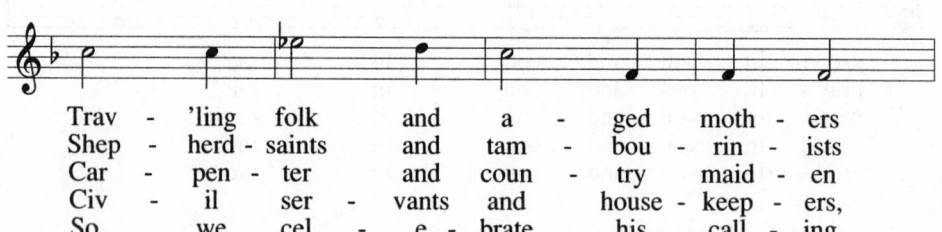

Trav - 'ling folk   and   a - ged   moth - ers
Shep - herd - saints and   tam - bou - rin - ists
Car - pen - ter   and   coun - try maid - en
Civ - il   ser - vants and   house - keep - ers,
So   we   cel - e - brate his call - ing,

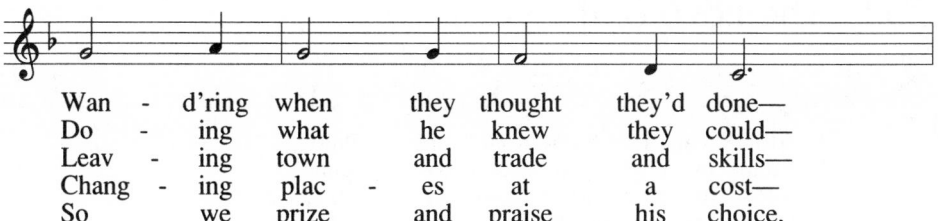

Wan - d'ring when they thought they'd done—
Do - ing what he knew they could—
Leav - ing town and trade and skills—
Chang - ing plac - es at a cost—
So we prize and praise his choice,

This is how God calls his peo - ple,
This is how God calls his peo - ple,
This is how God calls his peo - ple,
This is how Christ calls dis - ci - ples,
As we pray that through this com - pa - ny

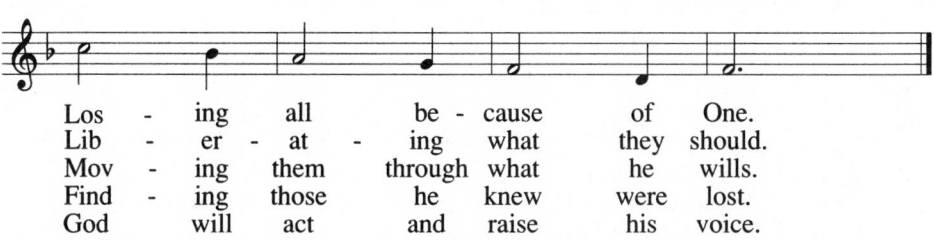

Los - ing all be - cause of One.
Lib - er - at - ing what they should.
Mov - ing them through what he wills.
Find - ing those he knew were lost.
God will act and raise his voice.

Text: John L. Bell, b.1949
Tune: JESUS CALLS US, Irregular; adapt. from a Gaelic Air by John L. Bell, b.1949
© 1989, Iona Community, GIA Publications, Inc., agent

702 The Love of the Lord

1. All that I count-ed as gain
2. Rich-es and hon-ors will fade,
3. Sil-ver and gold have I none,
4. Faith is the wealth I pos - sess

now I con-sid-er as loss,
earth-ly de-light dis-ap - pear,
no land to count as my home, yet
Find-ing its source in my God:

emp-ty and worth-less to me in the
fade like the grass of the field in the
wealth be-yond meas-ure I own in the
faith in the prom-ise of Christ is my

1., 3.
light of the love of the Lord.
light of the love of the
light of the love of the Lord.
life and my love of the

2., 4.
Lord.
Lord.

What more could bring us hope than to know the pow'r of his

life? What more could bring us peace than to

share in his suf-f'ring and death? What more could be our

fi - nal wish than to live in the love of the Lord?

Text: Philippians 3:7-11; Michael Joncas, b.1951
Tune: Michael Joncas, b.1951
© 1988, GIA Publications, Inc.

Song of St. Patrick   703

Refrain

May the Spir-it of Christ be our hope through the day, be our guard through the night, our com-pan-ion on the way.

Verse 1

1. Christ be ev-er be-fore us, Christ be ev-er be-hind us, Christ be ev-er with-in.

D.C.

Verses 2-5

2. Christ up-on our left hand watch-ing, At our right hand
3. Christ be in each ho-ly si-lence, Christ be in our
4. Let us be God's light in the dark-ness, Let us be God's
5. God Cre-a-tor, bless and keep us, Christ, be ev-er

guid-ing, Christ a-bove, be-neath us guard-ing,
speak-ing, Christ in ev-'ry work we of-fer,
kind-ness; Let us be God's jus-tice and mer-cy,
near us; Spir-it be the light be-fore us,

D.C.

Near to us a-bid-ing.
Ev-er in our seek-ing.
Hands and feet of Christ.
Gen-tle be our path-way.

Text: Based on *St. Patrick's Breastplate;* Marty Haugen, b.1950
Tune: Marty Haugen, b.1950
© 1986, GIA Publications, Inc.

704   I Am for You

1. There is a moun - tain   there   is   a   sea.
2. There was a wom - an   small   as   a   star,
3. There was a man   who walked in   the storm,
4. We   are a - noint - ed,   ser - vants of God;
5. There is a world   that waits in   the womb;

There is   a   wind with - in   all breath - ing,
Full of   the pa - tient dreams of   her na - tion,
Caught in be - tween the waves   and the light - ning,
We   have been born a - gain   of   Spir - it.
There is   a   hope un - born   God is bear - ing,

There is   an   arm   to   break ev - 'ry chain,
Wel - com - ing   in   an   an - gel of God,
Shar - ing his   bread with those cast a - side,
We   are the word God speaks to the world,
Though the powers of   death prowl the night,

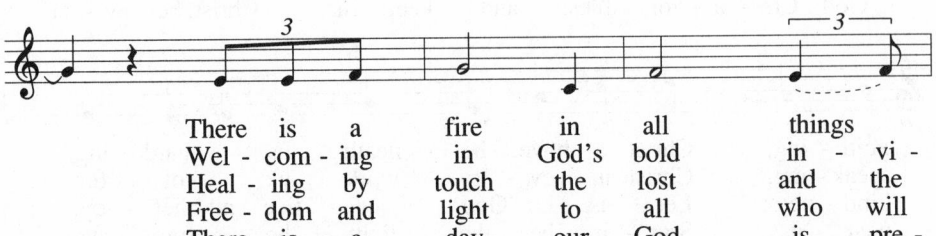

There is   a   fire   in   all   things
Wel - com - ing   in   God's bold   in - vi -
Heal - ing by   touch the lost   and the
Free - dom and light to   all   who will
There is   a   day   our God   is   pre -

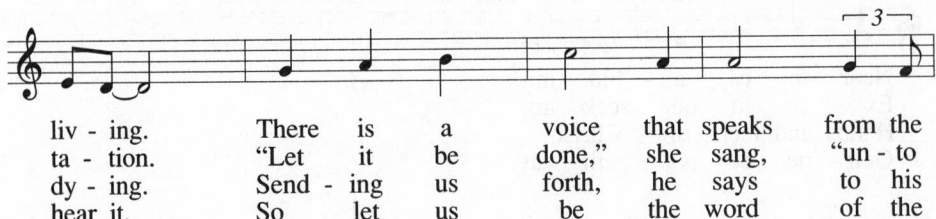

liv - ing.   There is   a   voice that speaks from the
ta - tion.   "Let it   be   done," she sang, "un - to
dy - ing.   Send - ing us   forth, he says   to his
hear it.   So   let   us   be   the word   of the
par - ing.   Sing 'round the fire   to wa - ken the

flame:	"I	am	for	you,		I	am	for
me.		I	am	for	you,	I	am	for
friends:	"I	am	for	you,		I	am	for
Lord:		I	am	for	you,	I	am	for
dawn:		I	am	for	you,	I	am	for

you,	I	am	for	you	is		my	name."
you,	I	am	for	you:	let		it	be."
you,	I	am	for	you	to		the	end."
you,	I	am	for	you	ev	-	er -	more.
you,	I	am	for	you:	We		are	one.

Text: Rory Cooney, b.1952
Tune: Rory Cooney, b.1952
© 1993, GIA Publications, Inc.

Jesu Tawa Pano / Jesus, We Are Here 705

Je - su ta - wa pa - no; Je - su ta - wa pa - no;
Je - sus, we are here; Je - sus, we are here;

Je - su ta - wa pa - no; ta - wa pa - no, mu zi - ta re - nyu.
Je - sus, we are here; we are here for you.

Text: Zimbabwean; Patrick Matsikenyiri
Tune: Patrick Matsikenyiri
© 1990, Patrick Matsikenyiri

706 Never the Blade Shall Rise

Verse 1

1. Un-less a grain of wheat falls to the earth,

falls to the earth and dies, it re - mains on - ly a

grain of wheat and nev - er the blade shall rise.

Refrain 𝄋

For the grain of wheat pro - duc - es much fruit, but

on - ly if it dies. Un-less a grain of wheat

falls to the earth, nev - er the blade shall rise.

Verse 2

2. The one who loves the world - ly life

los - es the life so lived, while the one who hates the

life in this world pre - serves it to life e - ter - nal.

D.S.

Verse 3

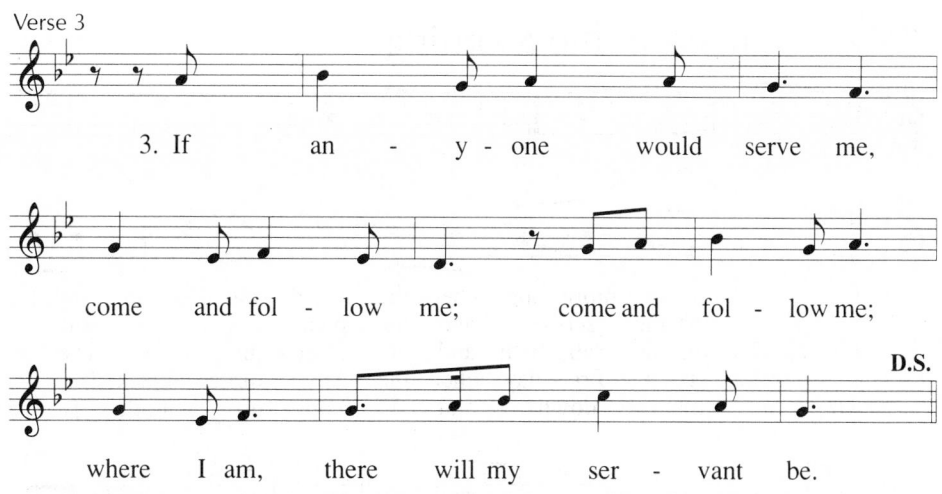

3. If an - y - one would serve me,

come and fol - low me; come and fol - low me;

D.S.

where I am, there will my ser - vant be.

Text: John 12; Kathy Powell, b. 1942
Tune: Kathy Powell, b. 1942
©1993, GIA Publications, Inc.

Guide My Feet 707

1., 6. Guide my feet while I run this race,

Guide my feet while I run this race,

Guide my feet while I run this race, for I

don't want to run this race in vain!

2. Hold my hand... 3. Stand by me... 4. I'm your child... 5. Search my heart...

Text: African-American spiritual
Tune: African-American spiritual; harm. by Diana Kodner, b. 1957. © 1994, GIA Publications, Inc.

708   I Danced in the Morning

1. I danced in the morn - ing when the world was be - gun, And I
2. I danced for the scribe and the phar - i - see, But
3. I danced on the Sab - bath and I cured the lame: The
4. I danced on a Fri - day when the sky turned black; It's
5. They cut me down and I leapt up high;

danced in the moon and the stars and the sun, And I
they would-n't dance, and they would-n't fol - low me; I
ho - ly peo - ple said it was a shame. They
hard to dance with the dev - il on your back. They
I am the life that - 'll nev - er, nev - er die; I'll

came down from heav - en and I danced on the earth; At
danced for the fish - er - men, for James and John; They
whipped and they stripped and they hung me high, And
bur - ied my bod - y and they thought I'd gone; But
live in you if you'll live in me:

Beth - le - hem I had my birth.
came with me and the dance went on.
left me there on a cross to die.
I am the dance and I still go on.
I am the Lord of the Dance, said he.

Dance then wher - ev - er you may be; I am the

Lord of the dance, said he, And I'll lead you all, wher-

ev-er you may be, And I'll lead you all in the dance, said he.

Text: Sydney Carter, b.1915, © Stainer and Bell Ltd., London, England
Tune: SHAKER SONG, Irregular; American Shaker; harm. by Sydney Carter, b.1915, © Stainer and Bell Ltd., London, England

We Will Drink the Cup   709

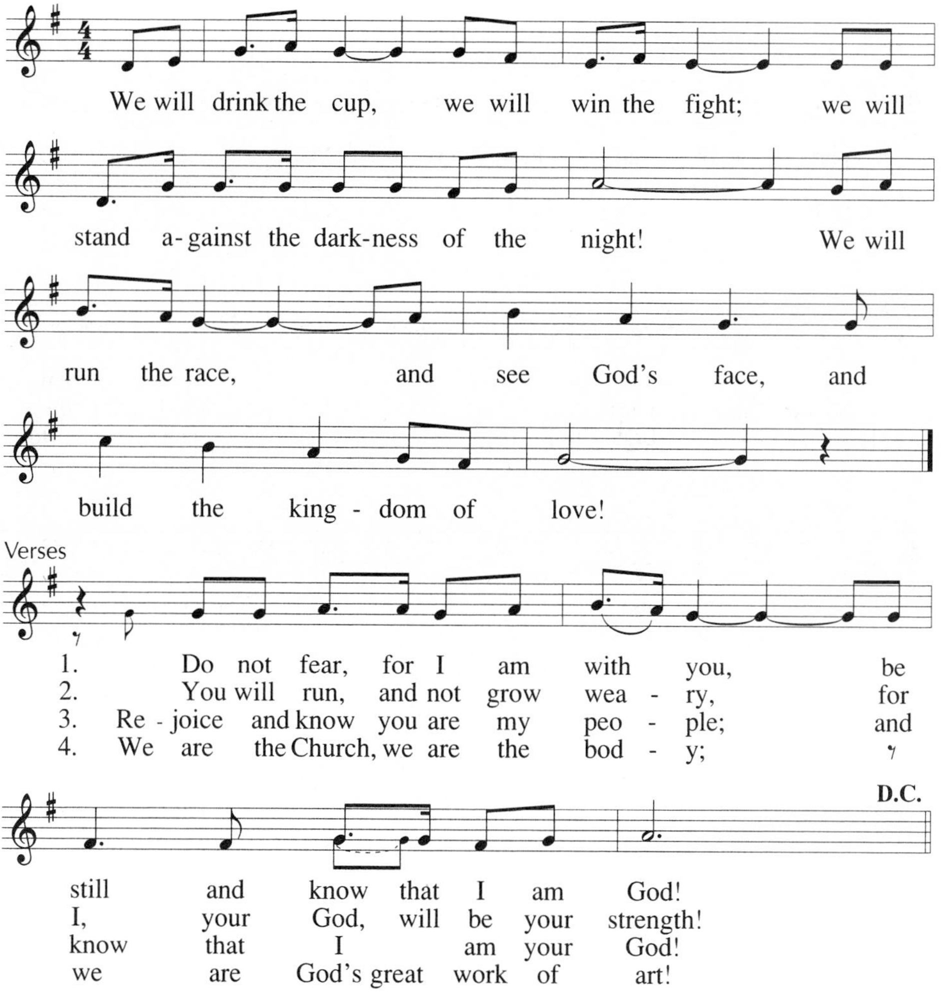

Refrain

We will drink the cup,   we will   win the   fight;   we will

stand a- gainst the dark-ness of the   night!   We will

run   the race,   and   see   God's   face,   and

build   the   king - dom of   love!

Verses

1.   Do not fear, for I   am   with   you,   be
2.   You will run,   and not grow   wea - ry,   for
3.   Re - joice and know you are   my   peo - ple;   and
4.   We   are   the Church, we are   the   bod - y;

D.C.

still   and   know   that   I   am   God!
I,   your   God,   will   be   your   strength!
know   that   I   am   your   God!
we   are   God's great   work   of   art!

Text: David Haas, b.1957
Tune: David Haas, b.1957
© 1991, GIA Publications, Inc.

710 Abundant Life

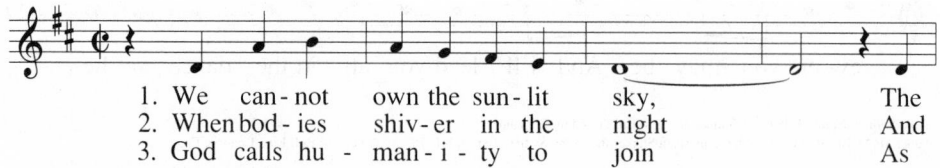

1. We can-not own the sun-lit sky, The
2. When bod-ies shiv-er in the night And
3. God calls hu - man-i - ty to join As

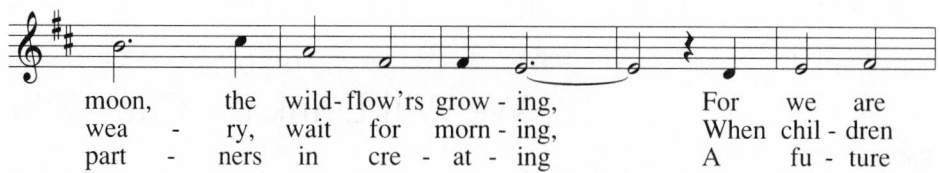

moon, the wild-flow'rs grow - ing, For we are
wea - ry, wait for morn - ing, When chil - dren
part - ners in cre - at - ing A fu - ture

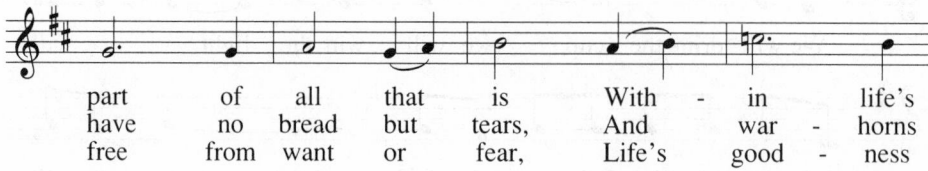

part of all that is With - in life's
have no bread but tears, And war - horns
free from want or fear, Life's good - ness

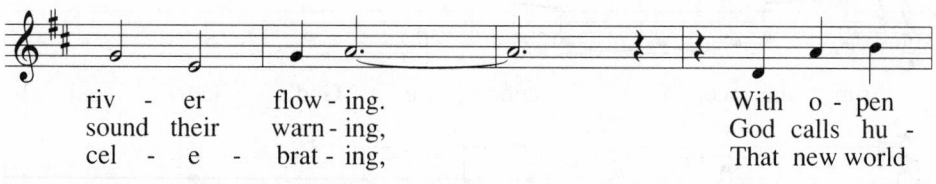

riv - er flow - ing. With o - pen
sound their warn - ing, God calls hu -
cel - e - brat - ing, That new world

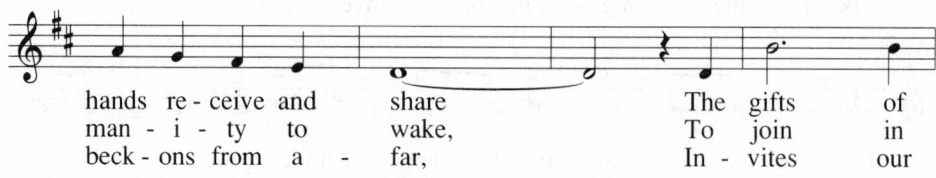

hands re - ceive and share The gifts of
man - i - ty to wake, To join in
beck - ons from a - far, In - vites our

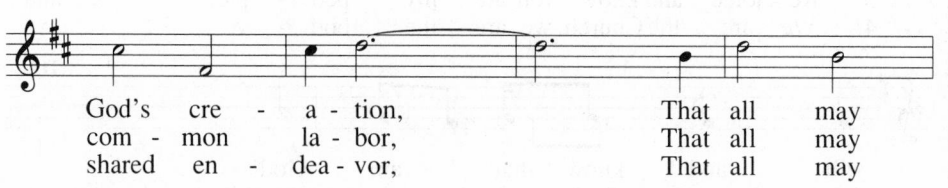

God's cre - a - tion, That all may
com - mon la - bor, That all may
shared en - dea - vor, That all may

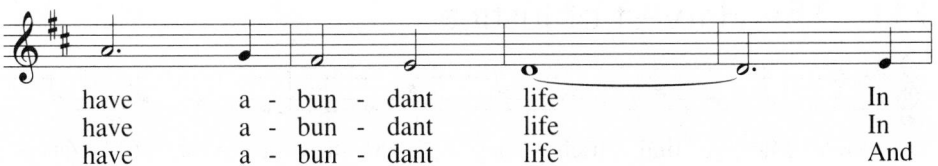

have   a - bun - dant   life   In
have   a - bun - dant   life   In
have   a - bun - dant   life   And

ev - 'ry earth - ly   na - tion.
one - ness with their   neigh - bor.
peace en - dure for - ev - er.

Text: Ruth Duck, b.1947, © 1992, GIA Publications, Inc.
Tune: LA GRANGE, 8 7 8 7 D; Marty Haugen, b.1950, © 1994, GIA Publications, Inc.

711 The Harvest of Justice

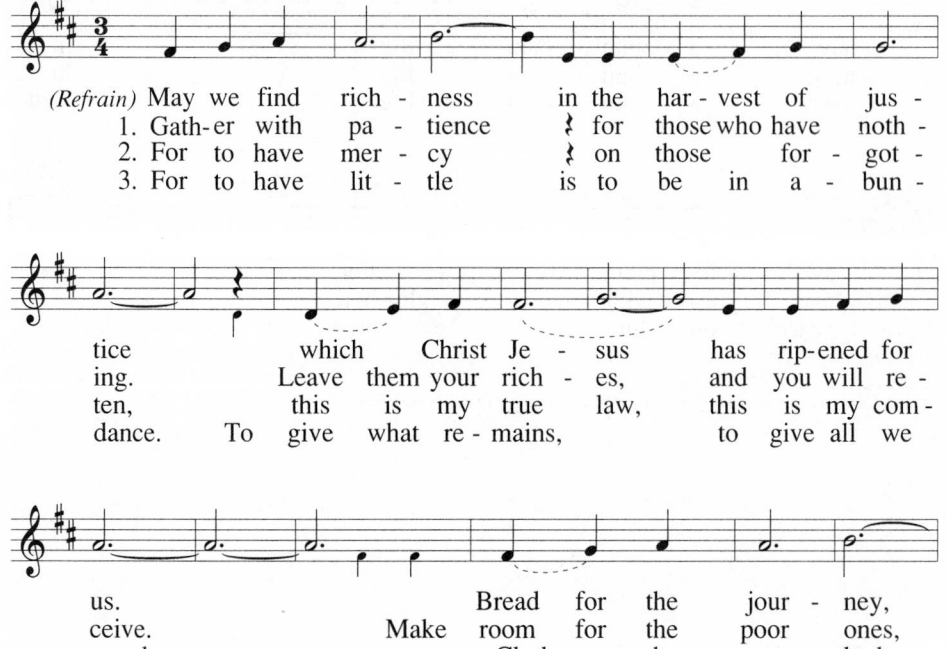

(Refrain) May we find rich - ness in the har - vest of jus -
1. Gath-er with pa - tience for those who have noth -
2. For to have mer - cy on those for - got -
3. For to have lit - tle is to be in a - bun -

tice which Christ Je - sus has rip-ened for
ing. Leave them your rich - es, and you will re -
ten, this is my true law, this is my com -
dance. To give what re - mains, to give all we

us. Bread for the jour - ney,
ceive. Make room for the poor ones,
mand: Clothe the na - ked,
have, is to walk with the poor ones,

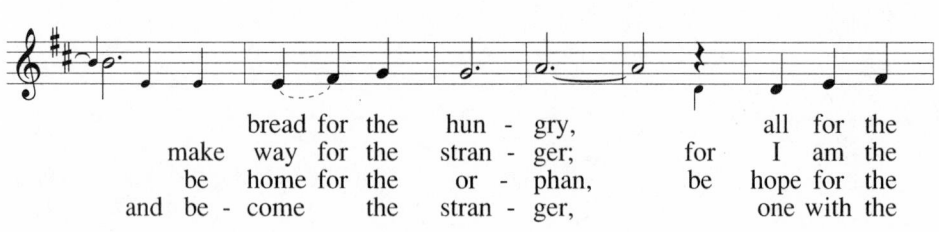

bread for the hun - gry, all for the
make way for the stran - ger; for I am the
be home for the or - phan, be hope for the
and be - come the stran - ger, one with the

glo - ry and praise of God.
Lord, the Lord your God.
wid - ow, and wel - come the lost.
Lord, the Lord our God.

Text: Philippians 1:11, Leviticus 19:9, 23:22, Deuteronomy 24:19; David Haas, b.1957
Tune: David Haas, b.1957
© 1985, GIA Publications, Inc.

On Holy Ground 712

Verses

1. The heav-ens em-brace the earth, then they
2. A - bran - se los cie - los, en el
3. Let heav-en and earth sing praise to the
4. Bless earth, wa - ter, fire, and wind. Bless your
5. La his - to - ria de los Pue - blos se - rá
6. U - nit - ed we join the light. We are

sing of the new birth. The earth ech - oes and re -
nom - bre de Cris - to Dios. Trans - for - men la tie - rra cau -
one who from death was raised. Let hearts ut - ter words pro -
peo - ple with - out, with - in. Let beau - ty and birth sur -
li - bre por la ver - dad. La cau - sa es ju - ti - fi -
born of the same right. We've come to re - lease what's

sounds that we are on ho - ly ground.
ti - va a u - na tie - rra con li - ber - tad.
found in pro - claim-ing this ho - ly ground.
round in re - claim-ing this ho - ly ground.
ca - da. San - ta tie - rra nues - tra se - rá.
bound, for we are on ho - ly ground.

Refrain

Assembly: Do you be-lieve in free-dom? **Yes, we do Lord!** *Assembly:* Do you be-lieve in jus-tice? **Jus-tice for all!**

Assembly: ¿Y en la nue-va vi-da? **¡En su es-pí-ri-tu!** *Assembly:* ¿Quién es su li-be-ra-ción? **¡Tú, Se - ñor!**

¡A - rri - ba! **¡Pro - cla - men!** **¡San - ta Tie - rra!**

We are on ho - ly ground!

Text: Donna Peña, b.1955
Tune: Donna Peña, b.1955; acc. by Diana Kodner, b.1957
© 1992, 1994, GIA Publications, Inc.

713 Your Love, O God, Has All the World Created

1. Your love, O God, has all the world cre - a - ted,
2. We bring you, Lord, in fer - vent in - ter - ces - sion
3. From out the dark - ness of our hope's frus - tra - tion,
4. In pit - y look up - on your chil - dren's striv - ing
5. In - spire your church, mid earth's dis - cord - ant voic - es,

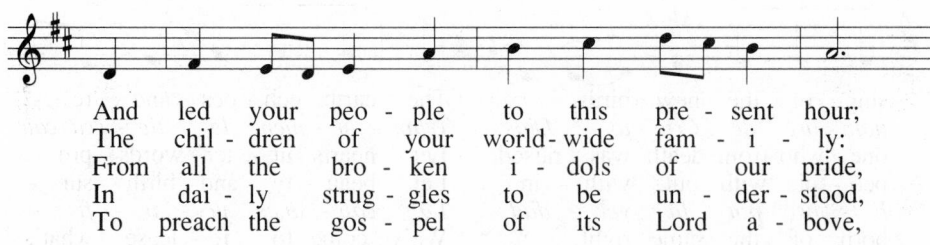

And led your peo - ple to this pre - sent hour;
The chil - dren of your world - wide fam - i - ly:
From all the bro - ken i - dols of our pride,
In dai - ly strug - gles to be un - der - stood,
To preach the gos - pel of its Lord a - bove,

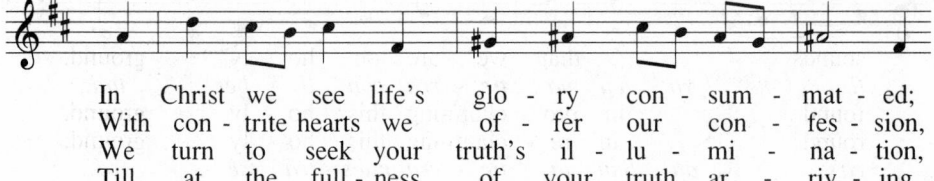

In Christ we see life's glo - ry con - sum - mat - ed;
With con - trite hearts we of - fer our con - fes - sion,
We turn to seek your truth's il - lu - mi - na - tion,
Till at the full - ness of your truth ar - riv - ing,
Un - til the day this war - ring world re - joic - es

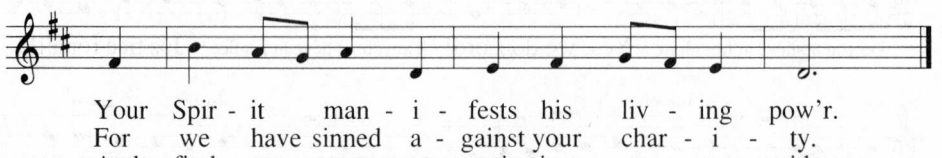

Your Spir - it man - i - fests his liv - ing pow'r.
For we have sinned a - gainst your char - i - ty.
And find your mer - cy wait - ing at our side.
We find in Christ the crown of ev - 'ry good.
To hear the might - y har - mo - nies of love.

Text: Albert F. Bayly, 1901-1984 alt.
Tune: NORTHBROOK, 11 10 11 10; Reginald S. Thatcher, 1888-1957. © Oxford University Press

God, Whose Purpose Is to Kindle   714

1. God, whose pur-pose is to kin-dle: Now ig-nite us
2. God, who in your ho-ly gos-pel Wills that all should
3. God, who still a sword de-liv-ers Rath-er than a

with your fire; While the earth a-waits your burn-ing,
tru-ly live, Make us sense our share of fail-ure,
plac-id peace, With your sharp-ened word dis-turb us,

With your pas-sion us in-spire. O-ver-come our
Our tran-quil-li-ty for-give. Teach us cour-age
From com-pla-cen-cy re-lease! Save us now from

sin-ful calm-ness, Stir us with your sav-ing name;
as we strug-gle In all lib-er-at-ing strife;
sat-is-fac-tion, When we pri-vate-ly are free,

Bap-tize with your fi-ery Spir-it,
Lift the small-ness of our vi-sion
Yet are un-dis-turbed in spir-it

Crown our lives with tongues of flame.
By your own a-bun-dant life.
By our neigh-bor's mis-er-y.

Text: Luke 12:49; David E. Trueblood, b.1900, © 1967, David Elton Trueblood
Tune: HYMN TO JOY, 8 7 8 7 D; arr. from Ludwig van Beethoven, 1770-1827, by Edward Hodges, 1796-1867

715 Go Down, Moses

1. When Is - rael was in E - gypt's land:
2. The Lord told Mo - ses what to do,
3. As Is - rael stood by the wa - ter side,
4. When they had reached the oth - er shore,
5. Oh, let us all from bond - age flee,

Let my peo - ple go:
Op - pressed so hard they
To lead the chil - dren of
At God's com - mand it
They sang the song of
And let us all in

could not stand,
Is - rael through,
did di - vide, Let my peo - ple go. Go down,
tri - umph o'er,
Christ be free,

Mo - ses, 'Way down in E - gypt land,

Tell ol' Phar - aoh, to let my peo - ple go.

Text: Exodus; African-American spiritual
Tune: African-American spiritual

Let Justice Roll Like a River   716

Refrain

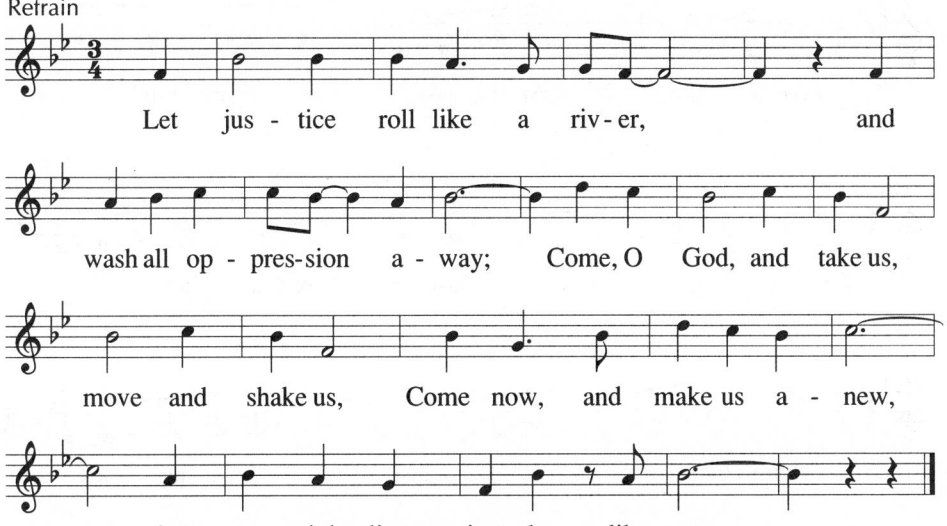

Let jus-tice roll like a riv-er, and
wash all op-pres-sion a-way; Come, O God, and take us,
move and shake us, Come now, and make us a-new,
that we might live just-ly like you.

Verses

1. Take from me your holy feasts, all your off'rings and your music;
   Let justice flow like waters, and integrity like an ever-flowing stream.

2. How long shall we wait, O God, for the day of your mercy to dawn,
   the day we beat our swords into ploughs, when your peace reigns over the earth?

3. Hear this, all of you who use the poor in your thirst of power and riches:
   the Lord will turn your laughter to tears, on the wondrous Day of our God.

4. Even now return to me, let your hearts be broken and humble,
   for I am gracious, gen'rous and kind; come and seek the mercies of God.

5. You have been told the way of life, the way of justice and peace;
   to act justly, to love gently, and walk humbly with God.

Text: Amos 5:21-24, 8:4, Micah 4:3-4, 6:8, Joel 2:12-14; Marty Haugen, b.1950
Tune: Marty Haugen, b.1950
© 1991, GIA Publications, Inc.

717 Free at Last

Free at last, free at last, I thank God I'm free at last;

Free at last, free at last, I thank God I'm free at last. (O) free at last.

1. 'Way down yon-der in the grave - yard walk,
2. On a my knees when the light passed by,
3. Some of these morn - ings, bright and fair,

I thank God I'm free at last,
I thank God I'm free at last,
I thank God I'm free at last, Goin'

Me and my Je - sus goin' to meet and talk,
Thought my soul would rise and fly,
meet King Je - sus in the air,

I thank God I'm free at last. (O)

Text: African-American spiritual
Tune: African-American spiritual

We Are Called 718

Verses

1. Come! Live in the light!
2. Come! O - pen your heart!
3. Sing! Sing a new song!

Shine with the joy and the love of the Lord! We are
Show your mer - cy to all those in fear! We are
Sing of that great day when all will be one! God will

called to be light for the king - dom, to
called to be hope for the hope - less so all
reign, and we'll walk with each oth - er as

live in the free - dom of the cit - y of God!
ha - tred and blind - ness will be no more!
sis - ters and broth - ers u - ni - ted in love!

Refrain

We are called to act with jus - tice, we are called to

love ten - der - ly, we are called to serve one an - oth - er;

to walk hum - bly with God!

Text: Micah 6:8; David Haas, b.1957
Tune: David Haas, b.1957
© 1988, GIA Publications, Inc.

719 For the Healing of the Nations

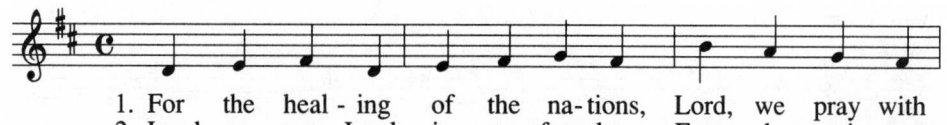

1. For the heal - ing of the na-tions, Lord, we pray with
2. Lead us now, Lord, in - to free-dom, From de - spair your
3. All that kills a - bun-dant liv - ing, Let it from the
4. You, cre - a - tor God, have writ-ten Your great name on

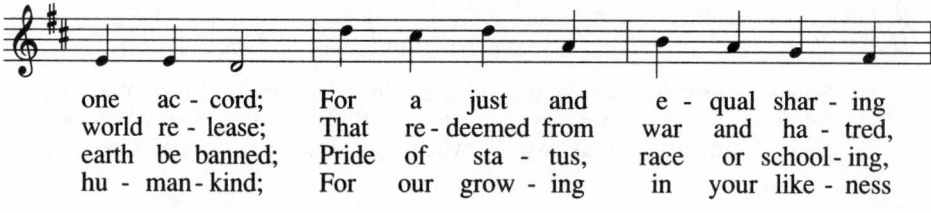

one ac - cord; For a just and e - qual shar - ing
world re - lease; That re - deemed from war and ha - tred,
earth be banned; Pride of sta - tus, race or school-ing,
hu - man-kind; For our grow - ing in your like - ness

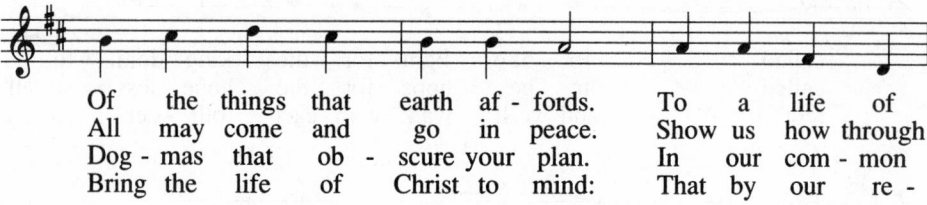

Of the things that earth af - fords. To a life of
All may come and go in peace. Show us how through
Dog - mas that ob - scure your plan. In our com - mon
Bring the life of Christ to mind: That by our re -

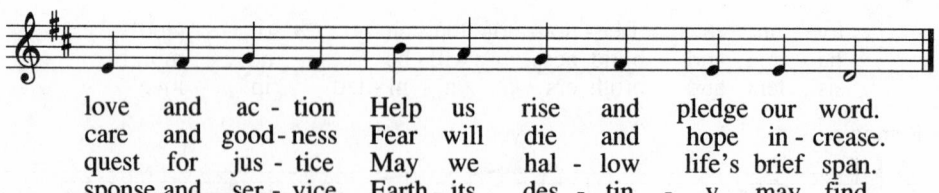

love and ac - tion Help us rise and pledge our word.
care and good-ness Fear will die and hope in - crease.
quest for jus - tice May we hal - low life's brief span.
sponse and ser - vice Earth its des - tin - y may find.

Text: Fred Kaan, b. 1929, alt., © 1968, Hope Publishing Co.
Tune: ST. THOMAS, 8 7 8 7 8 7; John Wade, 1711-1786

Now Join We to Praise the Creator   720

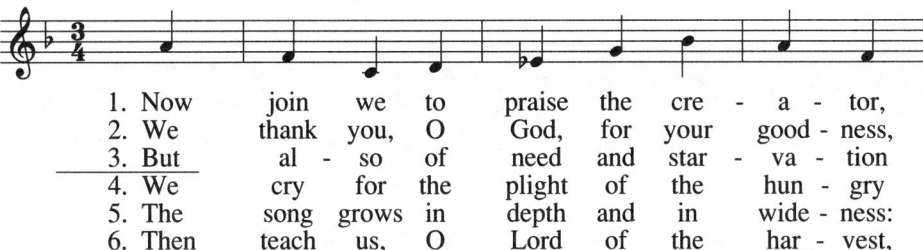

1. Now   join   we   to   praise   the   cre - a - tor,
2. We   thank   you,   O   God,   for   your   good - ness,
3. But   al - so   of   need   and   star - va - tion
4. We   cry   for   the   plight   of   the   hun - gry
5. The   song   grows   in   depth   and   in   wide - ness:
6. Then   teach   us,   O   Lord   of   the   har - vest,

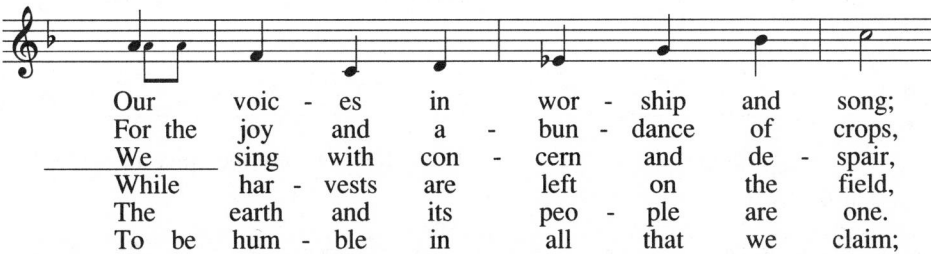

Our   voic - es   in   wor - ship   and   song;
For the   joy   and   a - bun - dance   of   crops,
We   sing   with   con - cern   and   de - spair,
While   har - vests   are   left   on   the   field,
The   earth   and   its   peo - ple   are   one.
To be   hum - ble   in   all   that   we   claim;

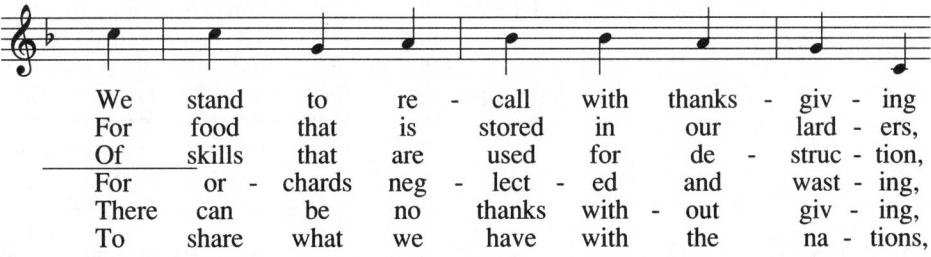

We   stand   to   re - call   with   thanks - giv - ing
For   food   that   is   stored   in   our   lard - ers,
Of   skills   that   are   used   for   de - struc - tion,
For   or - chards   neg - lect - ed   and   wast - ing,
There   can   be   no   thanks   with - out   giv - ing,
To   share   what   we   have   with   the   na - tions,

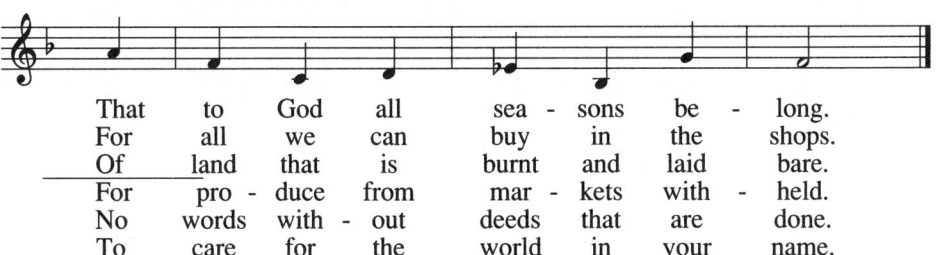

That   to   God   all   sea - sons   be - long.
For   all   we   can   buy   in   the   shops.
Of   land   that   is   burnt   and   laid   bare.
For   pro - duce   from   mar - kets   with - held.
No   words   with - out   deeds   that   are   done.
To   care   for   the   world   in   your   name.

Text: Fred Kaan, b.1929, © 1968, Hope Publishing Co.
Tune: HARVEST, 9 8 9 8; Geoffrey Laycock, b.1927, © 1971, Faber Music Ltd.

721　Voices That Challenge

Refrain

Call us to hear the　voic-es that chal-lenge, deep in the hearts of all

peo - ple! By　serv-ing your world　as　lov - ers and dream-ers,

we be-come voic-es that　chal-lenge, for　we are the voice of　God!

Verses 1, 2

All:　　　　　　　　　　　　Cantor:

1. Voic-es that chal-lenge: the　　chil - dren who long to be
　　　　　　　　　　　　the　　low - ly and bro-ken de -
　　　　　　　　　　　　the　　old　and the　fear-ful who
2. Voic-es that chal-lenge: the　　lives　and the　cries of the
　　　　　　　　　　　　the　　young ones who dream of　a
　　　　　　　　　　　　the　　sick　and the　dy - ing who

|1., 2., 4., 5.|　|3., 6.|　　　　D.C.|

heard　　and re　spec-ted!
stroyed　by op -　pres-sion!
hope　　for　a　　　　　new day!
poor　　and the　si - lenced!
world　　free of　ha - tred!
cry　　for com　　-　　pas - sion!

Verse 3

All:　　　　　　　　　　　　Cantor:

3. Voic-es that chal-lenge: the　ones　who seek peace　by their
　　　　　　　　　　　　the　wo - men who suf - fer　the
　　　　　　　　　　　　the　peo - ple with AIDS　and those
　　　　　　　　　　　　the　pro - phets and　he - roes who
　　　　　　　　　　　　the　hea - lers who teach　us　for -
　　　　　　　　　　　　the　vic - tims of　vio - lent　a -
　　　　　　　　　　　　the　Christ　who　gave　　his

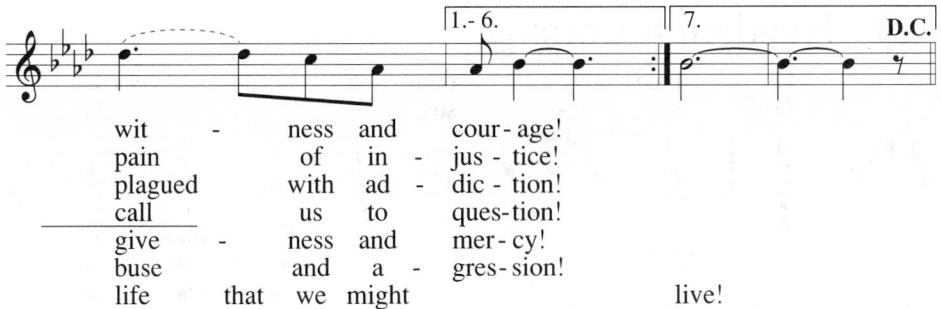

| 1.- 6. | | 7. | D.C. |

wit - ness and cour - age!
pain of in - jus - tice!
plagued with ad - dic - tion!
call us to ques - tion!
give - ness and mer - cy!
buse and a - gres - sion!
life that we might live!

Text: David Haas, b.1957
Tune: David Haas, b.1957
© 1990, GIA Publications, Inc.

If You Believe and I Believe 722

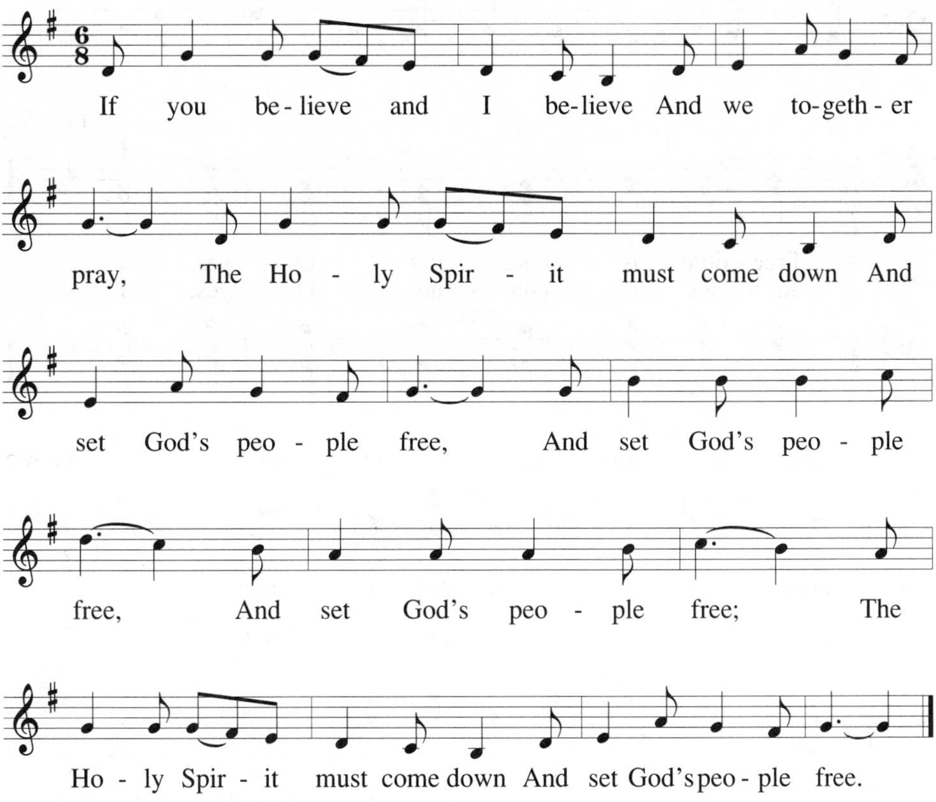

If you be-lieve and I be-lieve And we to-geth-er pray, The Ho - ly Spir - it must come down And set God's peo - ple free, And set God's peo - ple free, And set God's peo - ple free; The Ho - ly Spir - it must come down And set God's peo - ple free.

Text: Zimbabwean traditional
Tune: Zimbabwean traditional; adapt. of English traditional; as taught by Tarasai; arr. by John L. Bell, b.1949, © 1991, Iona Community,
    GIA Publications, Inc., agent

723 Freedom Is Coming

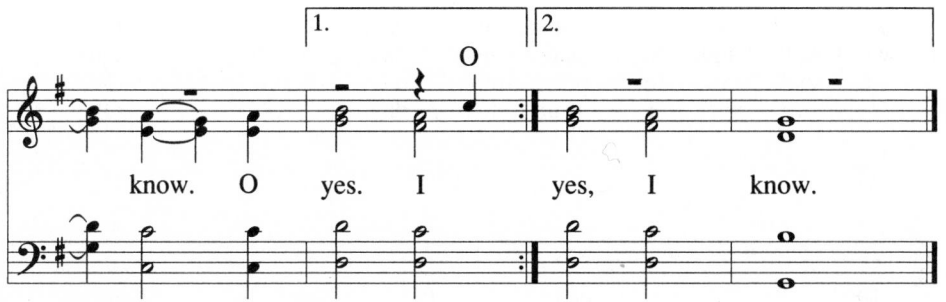

724 We Shall Overcome

1. We shall o - ver - come, we shall o - ver - come,
2. We'll walk hand in hand, we'll walk hand in hand,
3. We shall live in peace, we shall live in peace,
4. We are not a - fraid, we are not a - fraid,

we shall o - ver - come some - day. Oh,
we'll walk hand in hand some - day. Oh,
we shall live in peace some - day. Oh,
we are not a - fraid to - day. Oh,

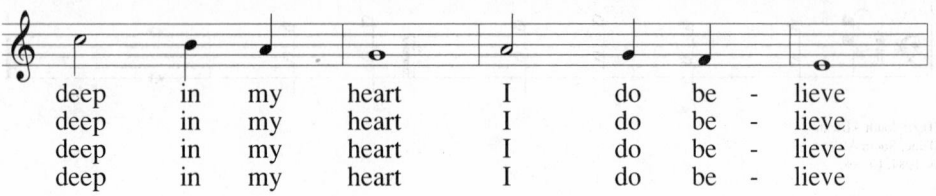

deep in my heart I do be - lieve
deep in my heart I do be - lieve
deep in my heart I do be - lieve
deep in my heart I do be - lieve

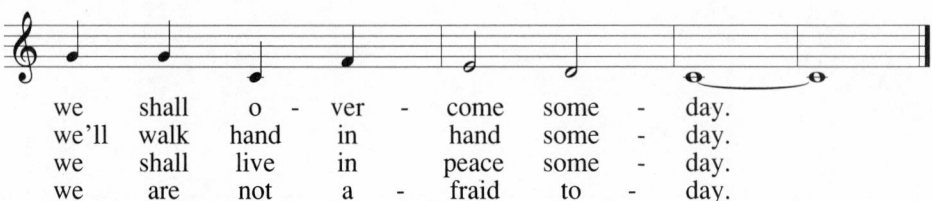

we shall o - ver - come some - day.
we'll walk hand in hand some - day.
we shall live in peace some - day.
we are not a - fraid to - day.

5. We shall stand together...
6. The truth will make us free...
7. The Lord will see us through...
8. We shall be like him...
9. The whole wide world around...

Text: adapt. by Zilphia Horton, Frank Hamilton, Guy Carawan, and Pete Seeger, © 1960, 1963, Ludlow Music.
Tune: adapt. by Zilphia Horton, Frank Hamilton, Guy Carawan, and Pete Seeger, © 1960, 1963, Ludlow Music;
    harm. by J. Jefferson Cleveland, b.1937, from *Songs of Zion*, harm. © 1981, by Abingdon Press

Jesus, Shepherd of Our Souls 725

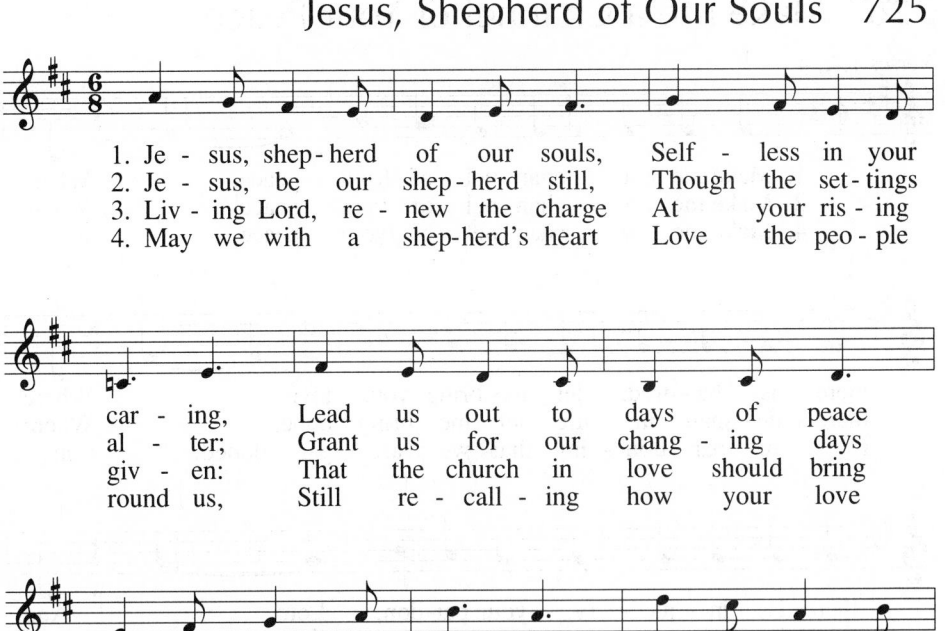

1. Je - sus, shep - herd of our souls, Self - less in your
2. Je - sus, be our shep - herd still, Though the set - tings
3. Liv - ing Lord, re - new the charge At your ris - ing
4. May we with a shep-herd's heart Love the peo - ple

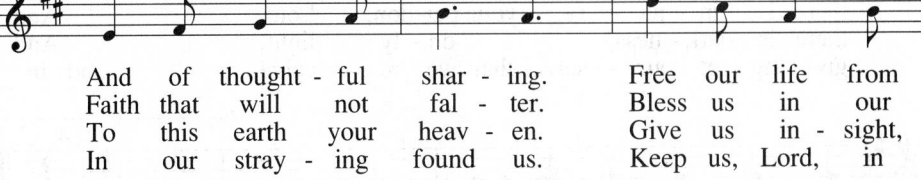

car - ing, Lead us out to days of peace
al - ter; Grant us for our chang - ing days
giv - en: That the church in love should bring
round us, Still re - call - ing how your love

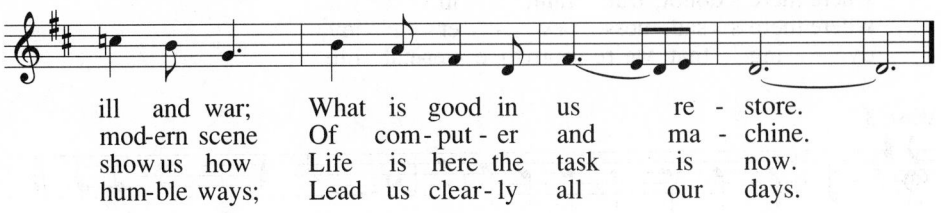

And of thought - ful shar - ing. Free our life from
Faith that will not fal - ter. Bless us in our
To this earth your heav - en. Give us in - sight,
In our stray - ing found us. Keep us, Lord, in

ill and war; What is good in us re - store.
mod-ern scene Of com - put - er and ma - chine.
show us how Life is here the task is now.
hum-ble ways; Lead us clear - ly all our days.

Text: Fred Kaan, b.1929, © 1968, Hope Publishing Co.
Tune: GOOD SHEPHERD, 7 6 7 6 77; Alexander Peloquin, b.1918, © 1975, GIA Publications, Inc.

726 Make Me a Channel of Your Peace

Verses 1, 2, 4

1. Make me a chan-nel of your peace. Where
2. Make me a chan-nel of your peace. Where
4. Make me a chan-nel of your peace. It

there is ha-tred, let me bring your love. Where
there's de-spair in life, let me bring hope. Where
is in par-don-ing that we are par-doned, in

there is in-ju-ry, your par-don, Lord, And
there is dark-ness, on-ly light, And
giv-ing of our-selves that we re-ceive, and in

where there's doubt, true faith in you.
where there's sad-ness, ev-er joy.
dy-ing that we're born to e-ter-nal life.

Verse 3

3. Oh, Mas-ter, grant that I may nev-er seek So much to be con-

soled as to con-sole. To be un-der-stood as to un-der-

stand. To be loved as to love with all my soul.

Text: *Prayer of St. Francis;* adapt. by Sebastian Temple, b. 1928, ©1967, 1975, 1980, Franciscan Communications
Tune: Sebastian Temple, b. 1928, © 1967, 1975, 1980, Franciscan Communications; acc. by Diana Kodner, b. 1957, © 1993, GIA Publications, Inc.
Dedicated to Mrs. Frances Tracy. Reprinted with permission.

How Good It Is 727

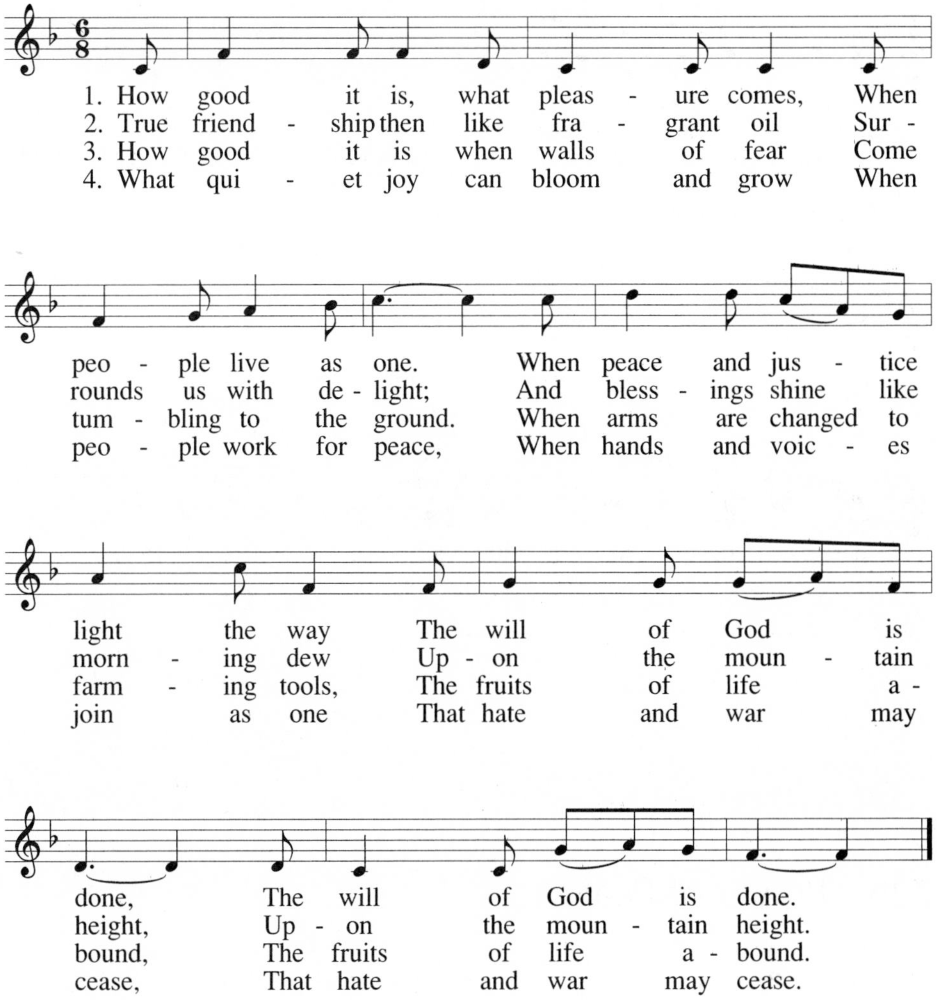

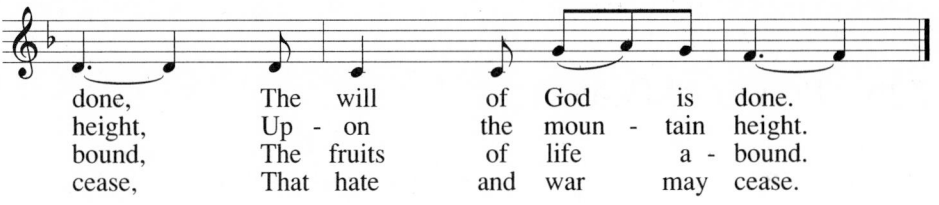

1. How good   it is,   what pleas - ure comes,   When
2. True friend - ship then   like fra - grant oil   Sur -
3. How good   it is   when walls   of fear   Come
4. What qui - et joy   can bloom   and grow   When

peo - ple live as one. When peace and jus - tice
rounds us with de - light; And bless - ings shine like
tum - bling to the ground. When arms are changed to
peo - ple work for peace, When hands and voic - es

light the way The will of God is
morn - ing dew Up - on the moun - tain
farm - ing tools, The fruits of life a -
join as one That hate and war may

done, The will of God is done.
height, Up - on the moun - tain height.
bound, The fruits of life a - bound.
cease, That hate and war may cease.

Text: Psalm 133, Isaiah 2:1-4; Ruth Duck, b.1947, © 1992, GIA Publications, Inc.
Tune: DOVE OF PEACE, CM; American; harm. by Charles H. Webb, b.1933, © 1989, The United Methodist Publishing House

728 Peace Is Flowing Like a River

1. Peace is flow-ing like a riv - er,
2. Joy is flow-ing like a riv - er,
3. Faith is flow-ing like a riv - er, Flow - ing out through you and
4. Hope is flow-ing like a riv - er,
5. Love is flow-ing like a riv - er,

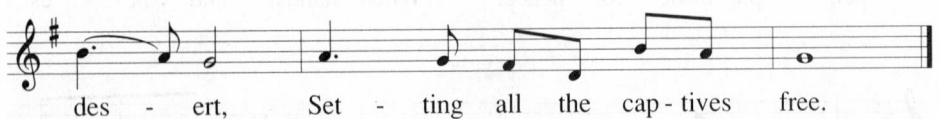

me; Flow - ing out in - to the

des - ert, Set - ting all the cap - tives free.

Text: Unknown
Tune: Unknown; acc. by Diana Kodner, b.1957, © 1993, GIA Publications, Inc.

729 Prayer of Peace

1. Peace be - fore us, peace be - hind us, peace
2. Love be - fore us, love be - hind us, love
3. Light be - fore us, light be - hind us, light
4. Christ be - fore us, Christ be - hind us, Christ
5. Al - le - lu-ia, al - le - lu - ia, al - le -
6. Peace be - fore us, peace be - hind us, peace

un - der our feet. Peace with - in us, peace
un - der our feet. Love with - in us, love
un - der our feet. Light with - in us, light
un - der our feet. Christ with - in us, Christ
lu - ia, Al - le - lu - ia, al - le -
un - der our feet. Peace with - in us, peace

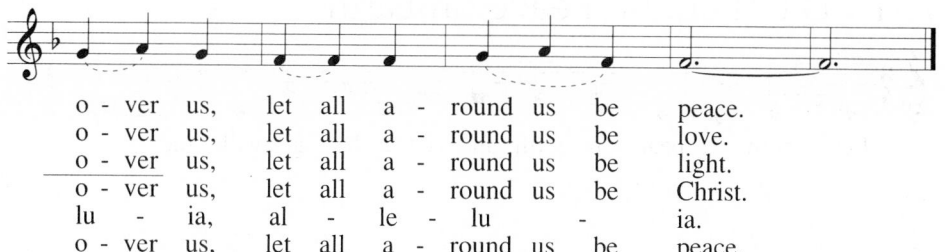

o - ver us, let all a - round us be peace.
o - ver us, let all a - round us be love.
o - ver us, let all a - round us be light.
o - ver us, let all a - round us be Christ.
lu - ia, al - le - lu - ia.
o - ver us, let all a - round us be peace.

Text: Based on a Navajo prayer; David Haas, b.1957
Tune: David Haas, b.1957
© 1987, GIA Publications, Inc.

Dona Nobis Pacem   730

Canon

Do - na no - bis pa - cem, pa - cem.

Do - na no - bis pa - cem.

Do - na no - bis pa - cem.

Do - na no - bis pa - cem.

Do - na no - bis pa - cem.

Do - na no - bis pa - cem.

Text: *Grant us peace;* Unknown
Tune: Traditional; acc. by Diana Kodner, b.1957. © 1994, GIA Publications, Inc.

731 Let There Be Peace on Earth

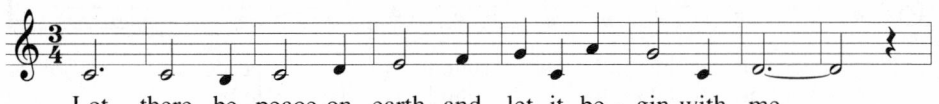

Let there be peace on earth, and let it be - gin with me.

Let there be peace on earth, the peace that was meant to be. With

God as our Fa - ther, broth - ers / fam - 'ly all are we.

Let me / us walk with my broth-er / each oth - er in per-fect har-mo - ny.

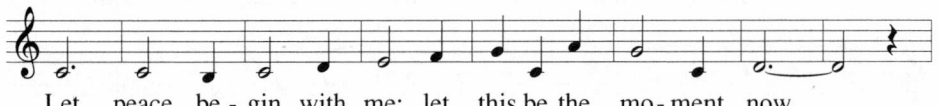

Let peace be - gin with me; let this be the mo - ment now.

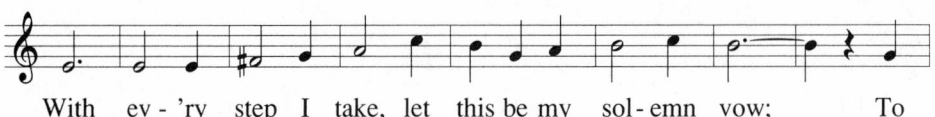

With ev - 'ry step I take, let this be my sol-emn vow; To

take each mo-ment, and live each mo-ment in peace e - ter-nal - ly!

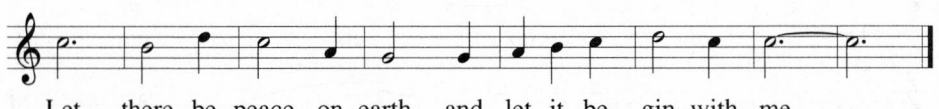

Let there be peace on earth, and let it be - gin with me.

Text: Sy Miller, 1908-1941, Jill Jackson, © 1955, 1983, Jan-Lee Music
Tune: Sy Miller, 1908-1941, Jill Jackson © 1955, 1983, Jan-Lee Music; acc. by Diana Kodner, b.1957, © 1993 GIA Publications, Inc.
Used with permission

World Peace Prayer 732

Refrain

Lead us from death to life, from false-hood to truth, from des -
pair to hope, from fear to trust. Lead us from
hate to love, from war to peace; let peace fill our
hearts, let peace fill our world, let peace fill our u - ni - verse.

Verses

1. Still all the an - gry cries, still all the an - gry guns,
2. So man - y lone - ly hearts, so man - y bro - ken lives,
3. Let jus - tice ev - er roll, let mer - cy fill the earth,

still now your peo - ple die, earth's sons and daugh-ters.
long - ing for love to break in - to their dark - ness.
let us be - gin to grow in - to your peo - ple.

Let jus - tice roll, let mer - cy pour down,
Come, teach us love, come, teach us peace,
We can be love, we can bring peace,

D.C.

come and teach us your way of com - pas - sion.
come and teach us your way of com - pas - sion.
we can still be your way of com - pas - sion.

Text: Refrain, Upanishads, Satish Kumar; verses, Marty Haugen, b.1950, © 1985, GIA Publications, Inc.
Tune: Marty Haugen, b.1950, © 1985, GIA Publications, Inc.

733 We Are Many Parts

Refrain

We are man-y parts, we are all one bod-y,
and the gifts we have we are giv-en to share.
May the Spir-it of love make us one in-deed;
one, the love that we share, one, our hope in de-spair,
one, the cross that we bear.

Verses

1. God of all, we look to you, we would be your
2. So my pain is pain for you, in your joy is
3. All you seek-ers, great and small, seek the great-est

D.C.

ser-vants true, let us be your love to all the world.
my joy, too; all is brought to-geth-er in the Lord.
gift of all; if you love, then you will know the Lord.

Text: 1 Corinthians 12, 13; Marty Haugen, b.1950
Tune: Marty Haugen, b.1950
© 1980, 1986, GIA Publications, Inc.

No Longer Strangers 734

Verses

1. We once were lost; with-out
2. We once were cut off; but now
3. We who once were dead, now we

hope, with - out God; but now in Christ
we are brought near, for Christ is our
live in the light, we fol - low Christ

Je - sus, we have been found!
peace, we were bro - ken, now whole! One
Je - sus, a - bun - dant in grace! Who

Saved by the prom-ise of God!
spir - it, one Bod - y of Christ!
saved us, who raised us to life!

Refrain

No long - er stran-gers, no long-er lost and a - lone!

No long - er stran-gers, now we are saints! We are

one in the house of God!

Text: David Haas, b.1957
Tune: David Haas, b.1957, vocal arr. by Jeanne Cotter, b.1964
© 1993, GIA Publications, Inc.

735 They'll Know We Are Christians

1. We are one in the Spir - it, we are
2. We will walk with each oth - er, we will
3. We will work with each oth - er, we will
4. All praise to the Fa - ther, from

one in the Lord, We are one in the
walk hand in hand, We will walk with each
work side by side, We will work with each
whom all things come, And all praise to Christ

Spir - it, we are one in the Lord, And we
oth - er, we will walk hand in hand, And to -
oth - er, we will work side by side, And we'll
Je - sus, his on - ly Son, And all

pray that all u - ni - ty may one day be re -
geth - er we'll spread the news that God is in our
guard hu - man's dig - ni - ty and save hu - man's
praise to the Spir - it, who makes us

stored:
land: And they'll know we are Chris - tians by our
pride:
one:

love, by our love, Yes, they'll know we are

Chris - tians by our love.

Text: Peter Scholtes, b.1938
Tune: ST. BRENDAN'S, 7 6 7 6 8 6 with refrain; Peter Scholtes, b.1938
© 1966, F.E.L. Publications, assigned to The Lorenz Corp., 1991

Many Are the Lightbeams 736

1. Man - y are the light - beams from the one light.
2. Man - y are the branch - es of the one tree.
3. Man - y are the gifts giv'n, love is all one.
4. Man - y ways to serve God, the Spir - it is one;
5. Man - y are the mem - bers, the bod - y is one;

Our   one   light   is   Je - sus.
Our   one   tree   is   Je - sus.
Love's   the   gift   of   Je - sus.
ser -   vant   spir - it   of   Je - sus.
mem -   bers   all   of   Je - sus.

Man - y are the light - beams from the one
Man - y are the branch - es of the one
Man - y are the gifts giv'n, love is all
Man - y ways to serve God, the Spir - it is
Man - y are the mem - bers, the bod - y is

light; we are one   in   Christ.
tree; we are one   in   Christ.
one;   we are one   in   Christ.
one;   we are one   in   Christ.
one;   we are one   in   Christ.

Text: *De unitate ecclesiae*, Cyprian of Carthage, 252 A.D.; trans. by Anders Frostenson © Verbum Forlong AB
Tune: Olle Widestrand ©; acc. by Marty Haugen, b.1950, © 1987, GIA Publications, Inc.

737 The Broken Body

1. How can we live as Chris - tians here, Un -
2. Christ is the one who calls us one, Who
3. One is the wa - ter by which sign Our
4. But not in bread and wine as yet Are
5. If our still hands no bod - y take, Still
6. O Christ of vi - sion and of hope, With -

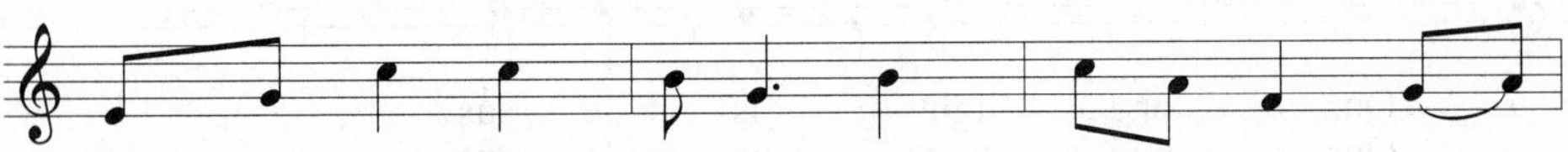

touched by one an - oth - er, Lip ser - vice pay - ing
leads us to each oth - er; His voice we hear, his
lives for God are cho - sen; One is the grace with
hearts and hands u - nit - ed, Though each can hear the
bind us in in - ten - tion: Com - mun - ion must come
out whose food we per - ish, Show us the way by

to the name Of sis - ter or of broth - er.
word we read And yet his will we smoth - er.
which our Lord From sin our - selves can loos - en;
ban - quet song To which all are in - vit - ed.
first through you And not by our in - ven - tion,
which, as one, We'll share the One we cher - ish.

Text: John L. Bell b.1949, © 1993, Iona Community, GIA Publications, Inc., agent
Tune: BARBARA ALLEN, 8 7 8 7; English folk song; acc. by John Bell, b.1949, © 1993, Iona Community, GIA Publications, Inc., agent

738 In Christ There Is No East or West

1. In Christ there is no east or west, In
2. In him shall true hearts ev - 'ry - where Their
3. Join hands, dis - ci - ples in the faith, What -
4. In Christ now meet both east and west, In

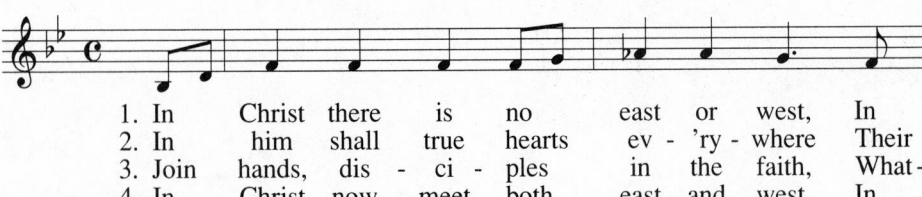

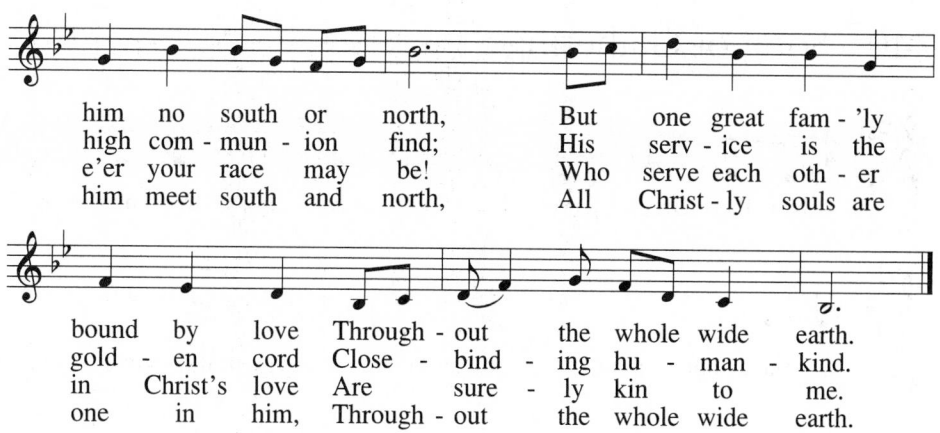

him   no   south   or   north,   But   one great   fam - 'ly
high com - mun - ion   find;   His   serv - ice   is   the
e'er   your   race   may   be!   Who   serve each   oth - er
him   meet   south   and   north,   All   Christ - ly   souls are

bound   by   love   Through - out   the   whole   wide   earth.
gold - en   cord   Close - bind - ing   hu - man - kind.
in   Christ's   love   Are   sure - ly   kin   to   me.
one   in   him,   Through - out   the   whole   wide   earth.

Text: Galatians 3:23; John Oxenham, 1852-1941
Tune: MC KEE, CM; African-American; adapt. by Harry T. Burleigh, 1866-1949

Diverse in Culture, Nation, Race   739

*1.   2.   3.

1. Di - verse   in   cul - ture,   na - tion,   race,   We
2. God,   let   us   be   a   bridge   of   care   Con -
3. When   cha - sms   wid - en,   storms   a - rise,   O
4. God,   let   us   be   a   ta - ble   spread   With

4.

come to - geth - er   by   your grace. God,   let   us   be   a
nect - ing   peo - ple   ev - 'ry - where. Help   us   con - front all
Ho - ly   Spir - it,   make   us   wise. Let   our   re - solve, like
gifts   of   love and   bro - ken bread, Where   all   find wel - come,

meet - ing ground Where   hope   and   heal - ing   love   are   found.
fear   and   hate   And   lust   for   pow'r that   sep - a - rate.
steel,   be   strong   To   stand with those who   suf - fer wrong.
grace   at - tends,   And   en - e - mies a - rise   as   friends.

* May be sung as a two or four-voice canon.

Text: Ruth Duck, b.1947, © 1992, GIA Publications, Inc.
Tune: TALLIS' CANON, LM; Thomas Tallis, c.1510-1583

740 Song of Gathering

Refrain

Nei-ther Greek, nor Jew, nor slave, nor free, nei-ther wo-man, nor man, but chil-dren are we, of the same God, the one Lord, the Fa-ther of all, let it be.

Verses 1, 3

1. From the four winds, and the high seas, from the low-lands, and the val-leys we come to the ta-ble, to the Sav-ior, to the call.

3. From the one cup, from the one bread, at the one meal, we are all fed once more in the bod-y, in the Spir-it, in the dream.

D.C.

Verse 2

2. Your sons and your daugh-ters, young brides and old lov-ers, we come from the wa-ters that spring from your side.

D.C.

Text: Joe Wise
Tune: Joe Wise; acc. by David Barrickman, alt.
© 1982, GIA Publications, Inc.

God Is Here! As We His People 741

1. God is here! As we his peo - ple, Meet to of - fer praise and prayer, May we find in ful - ler meas-ure What it is in Christ we share: Here, as in the world a - round us, All our var - ied skills and arts Wait the com - ing of his Spir - it In - to o - pen minds and hearts.

2. Here are sym - bols to re - mind us Of our life - long need of grace; Here are ta - ble, font and pul - pit, Here the cross has cen - tral place: Here in hon - es - ty of preach-ing, Here in si - lence as in speech, Here in new - ness and re - new - al God the Spir - it comes to each.

3. Here our chil - dren find a wel - come In the Shep - herd's flock and fold; Here, as bread and wine are tak - en, Christ sus - tains us as of old: Here the ser - vants of the Ser - vant Seek in wor - ship to ex - plore What it means in dai - ly liv - ing To be - lieve and to a - dore.

4. Lord of all, of church and king-dom, In an age of change and doubt, Keep us faith - ful to the gos - pel, Help us work your pur - pose out: Here, in this day's ded - i - ca - tion, All we have to give, re - ceive; We who can - not live with - out you, We a - dore you! We be - lieve!

Text: Fred Pratt Green, b.1903, © 1979, Hope Publishing Co.
Tune: ABBOT'S LEIGH, 8 7 8 7 D; Cyril V. Taylor, 1907-1991, © 1942, 1970, Hope Publishing Co.

742 Now the Feast and Celebration

Refrain

Now the feast and cel - e - bra-tion, all of cre - a-tion

sings for joy, to the God of life and love and free-dom;

praise and glo - ry for - ev - er - more!

Verse 1

1. Now is the feast of the Lamb once slain,

whose blood has freed and u - nit - ed us

D.C.

to be one great peo - ple of God.

Verse 2

2. Pow - er and rich-es, wis-dom and might, all hon - or and

D.C.

glo - ry to Christ for - ev - er.

Verse 3

3. For God has come to dwell with us, to make us

peo-ple of God; to make all things new.

Text: Marty Haugen, b.1950
Tune: Marty Haugen, b.1950
© 1990, GIA Publications, Inc.

Come to Us   743

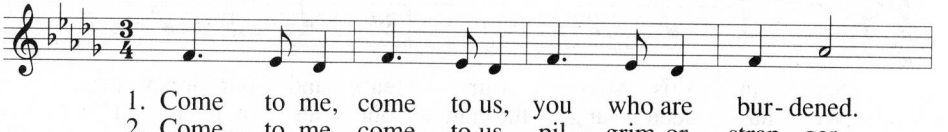

1. Come   to me, come   to us,   you   who are   bur-dened.
2. Come   to me, come   to us,   pil - grim or   stran - ger,
3. Come   to me, come   to us,   bro - ken or   build - ing,

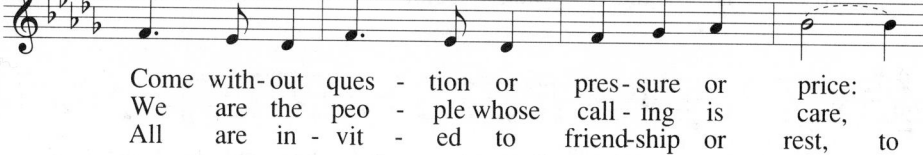

Come   to   the   word,   and   come   to   the   meal.
look - ing for   change,   or   chal - lenge, or   light.
Come   with your   chil-dren, your   choic - es, your   chains.

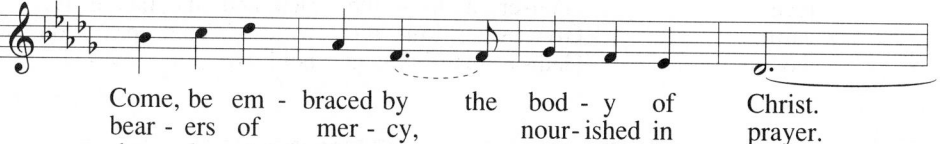

Come with-out   ques - tion or   pres - sure or   price:
We   are   the   peo - ple whose   call - ing   is   care,
All   are   in - vit - ed   to   friend-ship or   rest,   to

Come, be em - braced by   the   bod - y   of   Christ.
bear - ers   of   mer - cy,   nour - ished in   prayer.
share   in   our   strug-gle,   our   call   and our   quest.

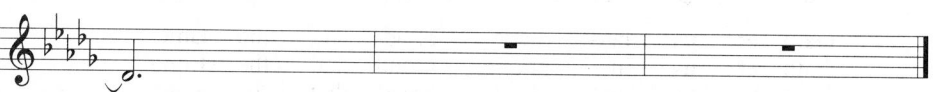

Text: Rory Cooney, b.1952
Tune: Rory Cooney, b.1952
© 1986, North American Liturgy Resources

744 Gather Us In

1. Here in this place new light is stream - ing,
2. We are the young— our lives are a mys - t'ry,
3. Here we will take the wine and the wa - ter,
4. Not in the dark of build - ings con - fin - ing,

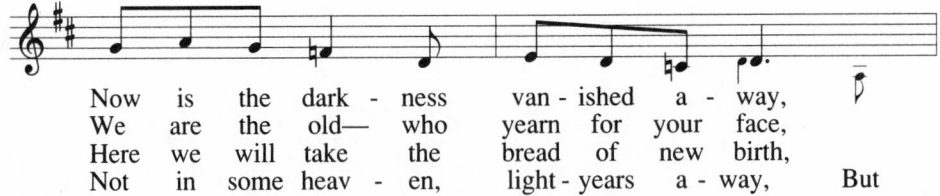

Now is the dark - ness van - ished a - way,
We are the old— who yearn for your face,
Here we will take the bread of new birth,
Not in some heav - en, light - years a - way, But

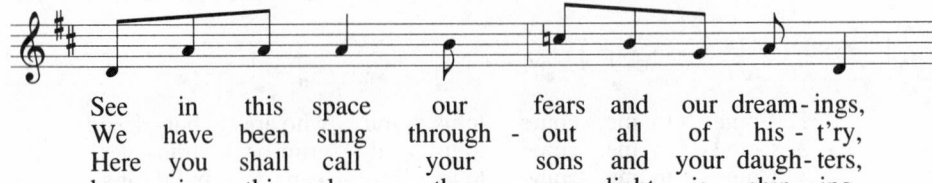

See in this space our fears and our dream - ings,
We have been sung through - out all of his - t'ry,
Here you shall call your sons and your daugh - ters,
here in this place the new light is shin - ing,

Brought here to you in the light of this
Called to be light to the whole hu - man
Call us a - new to be salt for the
Now is the King - dom, now is the

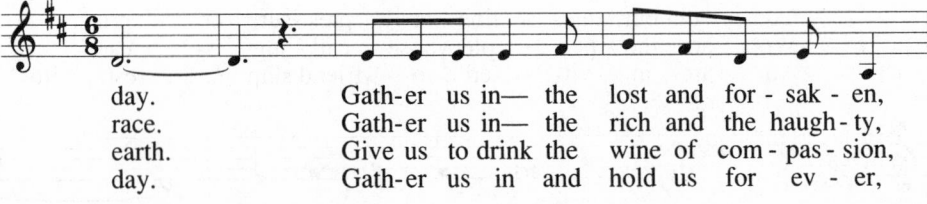

day. Gath-er us in— the lost and for - sak - en,
race. Gath-er us in— the rich and the haugh - ty,
earth. Give us to drink the wine of com - pas - sion,
day. Gath-er us in and hold us for - ev - er,

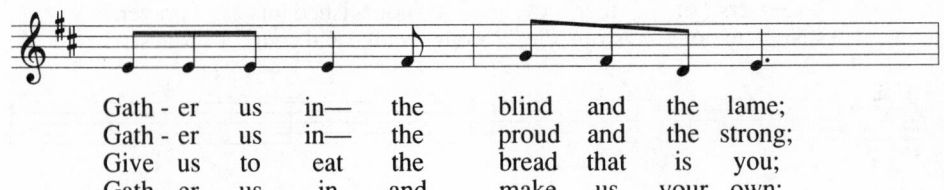

Gath - er us in— the blind and the lame;
Gath - er us in— the proud and the strong;
Give us to eat the bread that is you;
Gath - er us in and make us your own;

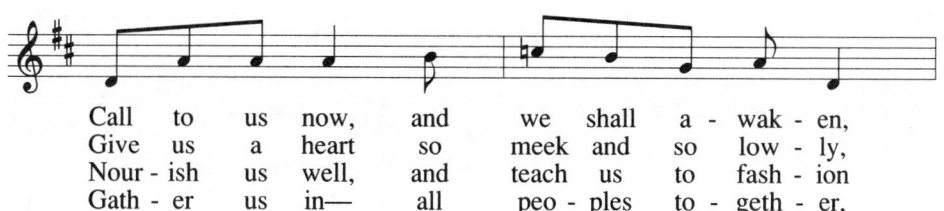

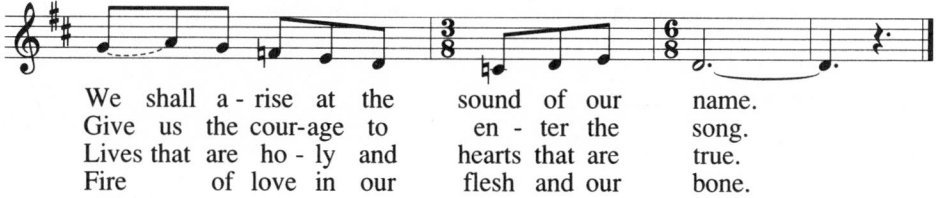

Call	to	us	now,	and		we	shall	a -	wak -	en,
Give	us	a	heart	so		meek	and	so	low -	ly,
Nour -	ish	us	well,	and		teach	us	to	fash -	ion
Gath -	er	us	in—	all		peo -	ples	to -	geth -	er,

We	shall	a - rise	at	the	sound	of	our	name.
Give	us	the cour-age	to		en -	ter	the	song.
Lives	that	are ho - ly	and		hearts	that	are	true.
Fire		of love	in	our	flesh	and	our	bone.

Text: Marty Haugen, b.1950
Tune: GATHER US IN, Irregular; Marty Haugen, b.1950
© 1982, GIA Publications, Inc.

Jesus Christ, Yesterday, Today and for Ever   745

Ostinato Refrain

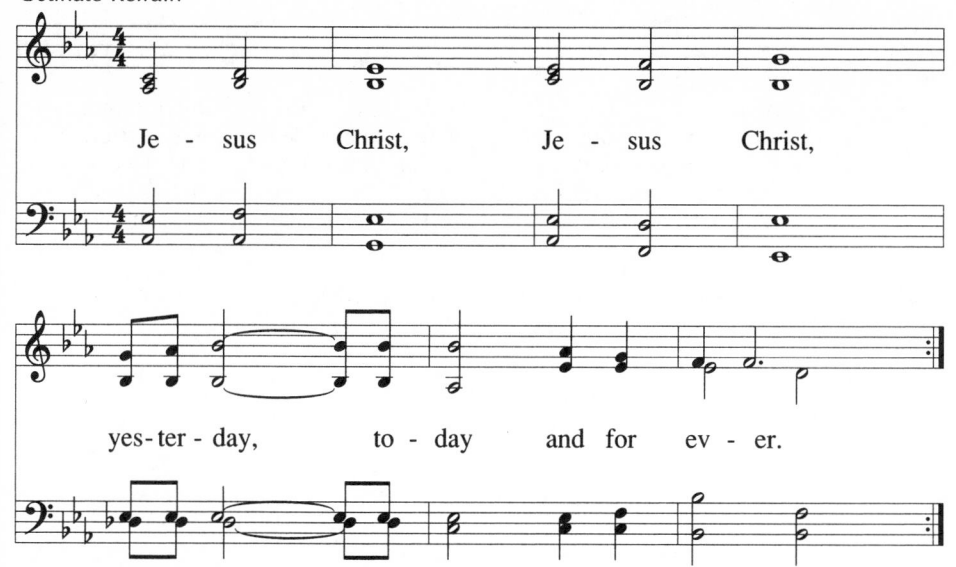

Je - sus   Christ,   Je - sus   Christ,

yes-ter - day,   to - day   and for   ev - er.

Text: Suzanne Toolan, SM, b.1927
Tune: Suzanne Toolan, SM, b.1927
© 1988, GIA Publications, Inc.

746   This Is the Day When Light Was First Created

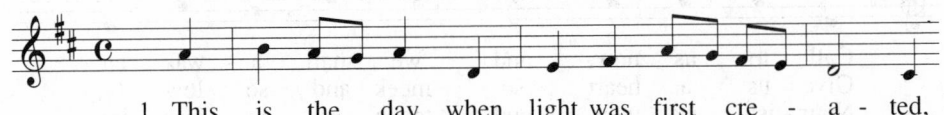

1. This   is   the   day   when   light was   first   cre - a - ted,
2. This   is   the   day   of   our com - plete   sur - pris - ing,
3. We   join   to   praise, with   ev - 'ry   race   and   na - tion,
4. This   is   the   day   of   wor-ship   and   of   vi - sion,
5. We   pray that   this,   the   day of   re - cre - a - tion,

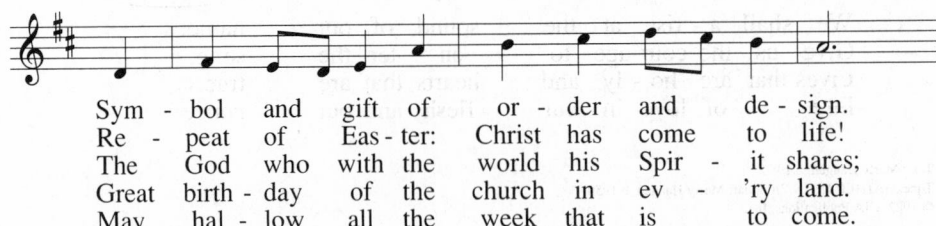

Sym - bol   and   gift   of   or - der   and   de - sign.
Re - peat   of   Eas-ter: Christ   has   come   to   life!
The   God   who   with the   world   his   Spir - it   shares;
Great   birth - day   of   the   church   in   ev - 'ry   land.
May   hal - low   all   the   week   that   is   to   come.

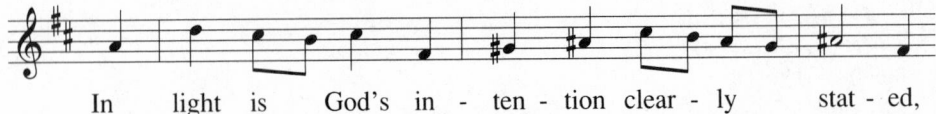

In   light   is   God's   in - ten - tion clear - ly   stat - ed,
Now   is   the   feast   of   love's   re - volt   and   ris - ing
Strong wind   of   change and   earth's   il - lu - mi - na - tion,
Let   Chris - tians   all   con - fess   their sad   di - vi - sion,
Help   us,   O   Lord,   to   lay   a   good   foun - da - tion

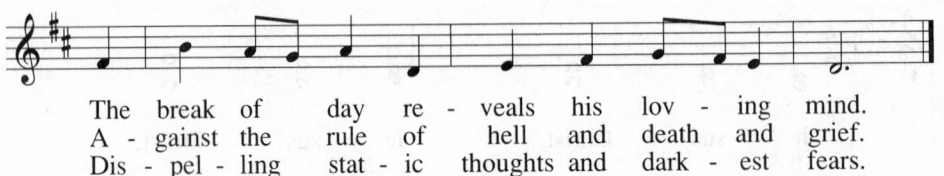

The   break   of   day   re - veals   his   lov - ing   mind.
A - gainst   the   rule   of   hell   and   death   and   grief.
Dis - pel - ling   stat - ic   thoughts and   dark - est   fears.
And   seek   the   strength a - gain   as   one   to   stand.
For   all   we   do   at   work,   at   school,   at   home.

Text: Fred Kaan, b.1929, © 1968, Hope Publishing Co.
Tune: NORTHBROOK. 11 10 11 10; Reginald S. Thatcher, 1888-1957. © Oxford University Press

All People That on Earth Do Dwell 747

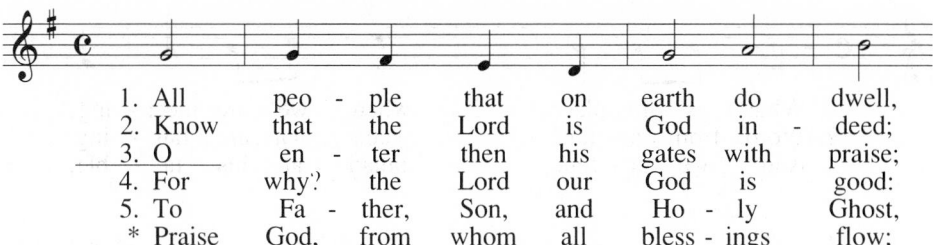

1. All peo - ple that on earth do dwell,
2. Know that the Lord is God in - deed;
3. O en - ter then his gates with praise;
4. For why? the Lord our God is good:
5. To Fa - ther, Son, and Ho - ly Ghost,
* Praise God, from whom all bless - ings flow;

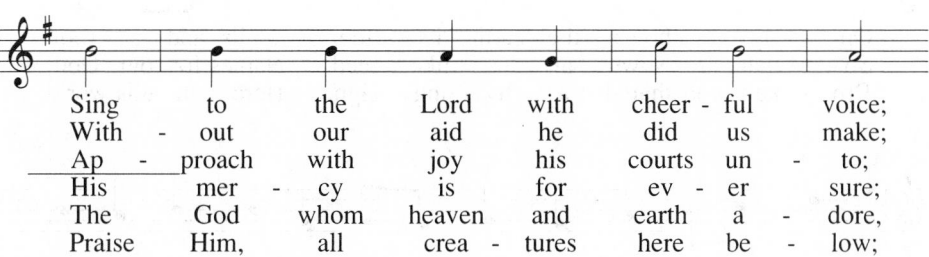

Sing to the Lord with cheer - ful voice;
With - out our aid he did us make;
Ap - proach with joy his courts un - to;
His mer - cy is for ev - er sure;
The God whom heaven and earth a - dore,
Praise Him, all crea - tures here be - low;

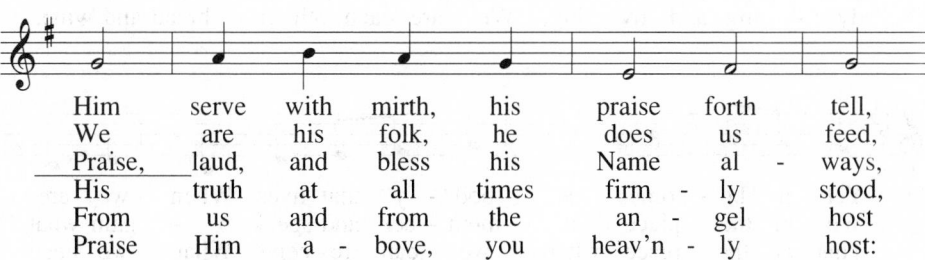

Him serve with mirth, his praise forth tell,
We are his folk, he does us feed,
Praise, laud, and bless his Name al - ways,
His truth at all times firm - ly stood,
From us and from the an - gel host
Praise Him a - bove, you heav'n - ly host:

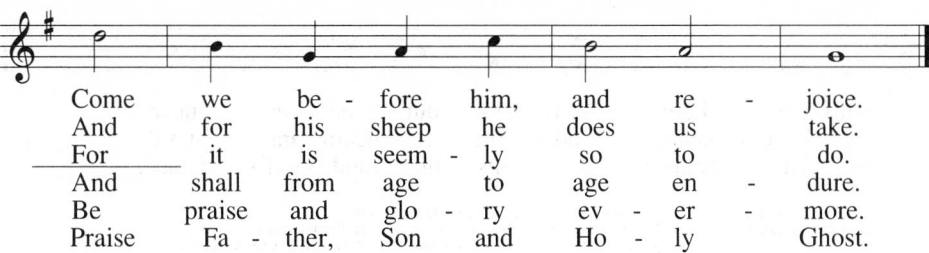

Come we be - fore him, and re - joice.
And for his sheep he does us take.
For it is seem - ly so to do.
And shall from age to age en - dure.
Be praise and glo - ry ev - er - more.
Praise Fa - ther, Son and Ho - ly Ghost.

* May be sung alone or as an alternate to stanza 5.

Text: Psalm (99)100; William Kethe, d. c.1593; Doxology, Thomas Ken, 1637-1711
Tune: OLD HUNDREDTH, LM; Louis Bourgeois, c.1510-1561

748 What Is This Place

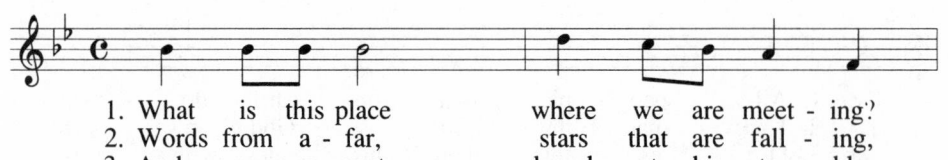

1. What is this place where we are meet - ing?
2. Words from a - far, stars that are fall - ing,
3. And we ac - cept bread at his ta - ble,

On - ly a house, the earth its floor, Walls and a roof
Sparks that are sown in us like seed. Names for our God,
Bro - ken and shared, a liv - ing sign. Here in this world,

shel - ter - ing peo - ple, Win - dows for light, an o - pen door.
dreams, signs and won - ders Sent from the past are all we need.
dy - ing and liv - ing, We are each oth - er's bread and wine.

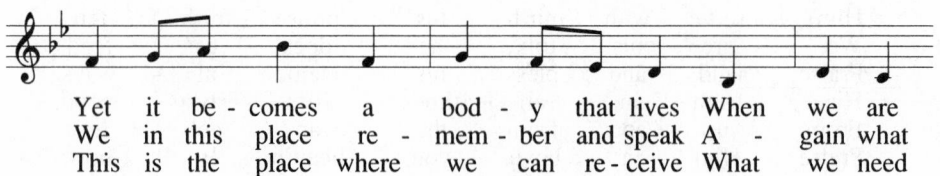

Yet it be - comes a bod - y that lives When we are
We in this place re - mem - ber and speak A - gain what
This is the place where we can re - ceive What we need

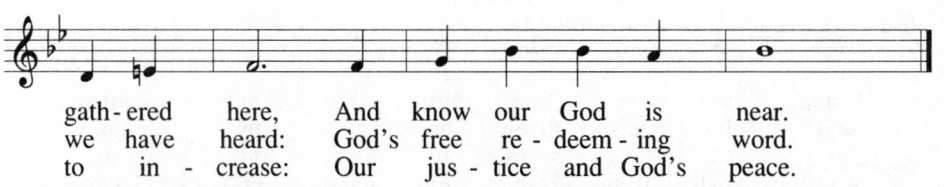

gath - ered here, And know our God is near.
we have heard: God's free re - deem - ing word.
to in - crease: Our jus - tice and God's peace.

Text: *Zomaar een dak boven wat hoofen;* Huub Oosterhuis, b.1933; trans. by David Smith, b.1933,
© 1967, Gooi en Sticht, bv., Baarn, The Netherlands. Exclusive English language agent: OCP Publications
Tune: KOMT NU MET ZANG, 9 8 9 8 9 66; Valerius' *Neder-landtsche gedenck-klanck;* acc. by Robert J. Batastini, b.1942,
© 1987, GIA Publications, Inc.

In Christ There Is a Table Set for All 749

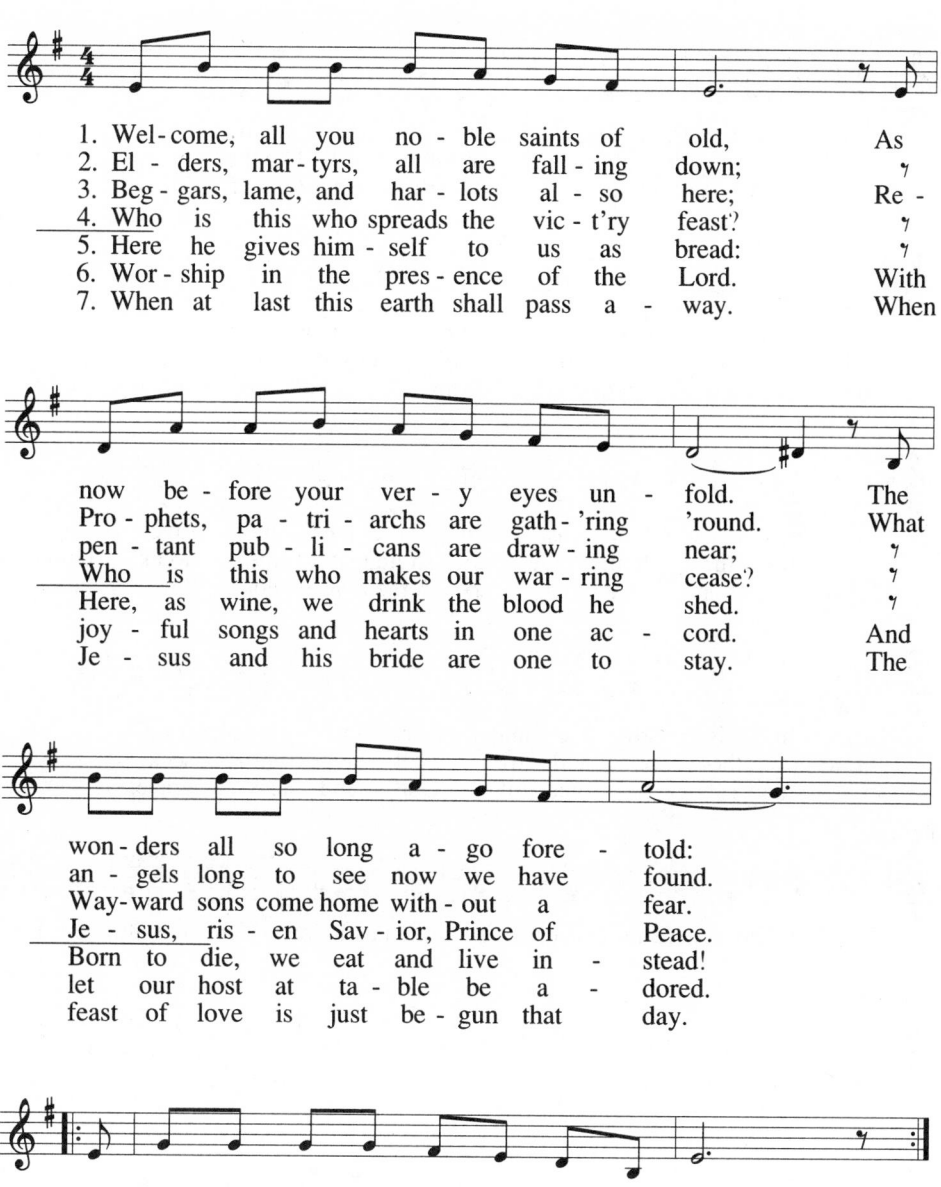

1. Wel-come, all you no - ble saints of old, As
2. El - ders, mar - tyrs, all are fall - ing down; 7
3. Beg - gars, lame, and har - lots al - so here; Re -
4. Who is this who spreads the vic - t'ry feast? 7
5. Here he gives him - self to us as bread: 7
6. Wor - ship in the pres - ence of the Lord. With
7. When at last this earth shall pass a - way. When

now be - fore your ver - y eyes un - fold. The
Pro - phets, pa - tri - archs are gath - 'ring 'round. What
pen - tant pub - li - cans are draw - ing near; 7
Who is this who makes our war - ring cease? 7
Here, as wine, we drink the blood he shed. 7
joy - ful songs and hearts in one ac - cord. And
Je - sus and his bride are one to stay. The

won - ders all so long a - go fore - told:
an - gels long to see now we have found.
Way-ward sons come home with - out a fear.
Je - sus, ris - en Sav - ior, Prince of Peace.
Born to die, we eat and live in - stead!
let our host at ta - ble be a - dored.
feast of love is just be - gun that day.

In Christ there is a ta - ble set for all.

Text: Robert J. Stamps
Tune: CENÉDIUS, Irregular, Robert J. Stamps

750 We Gather in Worship

Verses

1. We gath-er in wor-ship, in prayer and in praise; The
2. We gath-er that jus-tice may roll like the streams, From
3. We gath-er to-geth-er, the Bod-y of Christ; No

bread here we break and the cup now we raise, For
all of our pris-ons, God's mer-cy re-deems; A
one is ex-clud-ed from Cal-va-ry's price. No

Je-sus lives in us and loves us and saves! We
home for the home-less, a strength for the weak, Good
class, sex, nor sta-tus, no creed, age nor race Is

trust in this prom-ise and are not a-fraid.
news for the poor and for all those who seek.
out-side as-sur-ance of God's end-less grace.

Refrain

Here in hope, here in peace, ev-'ry-one has a part. Here in faith, here in

grace, now we lift up our hearts. God's love is a riv-er that

Last time to coda ✛

does not run dry; God's faith-ful-ness lifts like a full ris-ing tide.

✛ Coda

tide. We gath-er in wor-ship, the Bod-y of Christ.

Text: Sylvia G. Dunstan, 1955-1993, © 1991, GIA Publications, Inc.
Tune: Bob Moore, b.1962, © 1993, GIA Publications, Inc.

Come, Host of Heaven's High Dwelling Place 751

1. Come, Host of Heav'n's high dwell - ing place, Come,
2. Sur - round these walls with faith and love That
3. Bless and in - spire those gath - ered here With
4. Here may the los - er find his worth, The
5. Build, from the hu - man fab - ric, signs Of
6. So, to the Lord whose care en - folds The

earth's dis - put - ed guest; Find where we meet a
through the nights and days, When hu - man tongues from
pa - tience, hope, and peace, And all the joys that
stran - ger find a friend; Here may the hope - less
how your king - dom thrives, Of how the Ho - ly
world held in his hands, Be glo - ry, hon - or,

wel - come home, Stay here and take your rest.
speak - ing cease, These stones may ech - o praise.
know the depth In which all sor - rows cease.
find their faith And aim - less find an end.
Spir - it chang - es life By chang - ing lives.
pow'r and praise For which this com - p'ny stands.

Text: John L. Bell, b.1949, © 1989, Iona Community, GIA Publications, Inc., agent
Tune: ST. COLUMBA, 8 6 8 6; Irish traditional; arr. by John L. Bell, b.1949, © 1989, Iona Community, GIA Publications, Inc., agent

752 Bless the Feast

1. Wel - come this mo - ment, this day of sweet
2. Here in this pres - ence, come to be
3. Free - dom to cap - tives, good news to the
4. Come to re - mem - ber who is the

grace, wel - come and en - ter this gath - er - ing
one, come to be gath - ered, eld - ers and
poor, light - ing the dark - ling, un - sight - ed, un -
one, come to re - mem - ber what has been

place. Wel - come these sym - bols, feast - ing and
young. Here in this pres - ence, gath - er - ing
sure. Tell - ing the sto - ry: love with - out
done. What name do we call you? From where is our

tell - ing; signs of thanks - giv - ing, signs of in -
force, pres - ent on pur - pose, life - giv - ing
end, breath of cre - a - tion, all life to de -
breath? Come to re - mem - ber life wrest - ed from

dwell - ing. Wel - come a priv - i - lege, sis - ter and
source. Now is this peo - ple, now to the
fend. Tell - ing the cov - e - nant sto - ry a -
death. Come to re - mem - ber in Euch - ar - ist

broth - er, shar - ing this in - break - ing light with each
last, fus - ing the fu - ture with pres - ent and
gain; ex - o - dus jour - ney for wom - en and
faith, this is the ban - quet, the cup we pro -

oth - er. Wel - come the stran - ger be - yond and a -
past. Now is this peo - ple here to re -
men. Tell - ing once more and hear - ing the
claim: Weav - ing the gar - ment of jus - tice on

bove; here on - ly friends,
veal pres - ence in Word,
Word whose shin - ing con - clu - sion,
earth, come to cre - ate,

here on - ly friends and be - gin - ning of love.
pres - ence in Word and pres - ence in meal.
whose shin - ing con - clu - sion has yet to be heard.
come to cre - ate a - new, cel - e - brate birth.

Text: James Hansen
Tune: James Hansen
© 1989, OCP Publications

753 All Are Welcome

1. Let us build a house where love can dwell And
2. Let us build a house where proph - ets speak, And
3. Let us build a house where love is found In
4. Let us build a house where hands will reach Be -
5. Let us build a house where all are named, Their

all can safe - ly live, A place where saints and
words are strong and true, Where all God's chil - dren
wa - ter, wine and wheat: A ban - quet hall on
yond the wood and stone To heal and strength- en,
songs and vi - sions heard And loved and treas - ured,

chil - dren tell How hearts learn to for -
dare to seek To dream God's reign a -
ho - ly ground, Where peace and jus - tice
serve and teach, And live the Word they've
taught and claimed As words with - in the

give. Built of hopes and dreams and vi - sions, Rock of
new. Here the cross shall stand as wit - ness And as
meet. Here the love of God, through Je - sus, Is re -
known. Here the out - cast and the stran - ger Bear the
Word. Built of tears and cries and laugh - ter, Prayers of

faith and vault of grace; Here the
sym - bol of God's grace; Here as
vealed in time and space; As we
im - age of God's face; Let us
faith and songs of grace, Let this

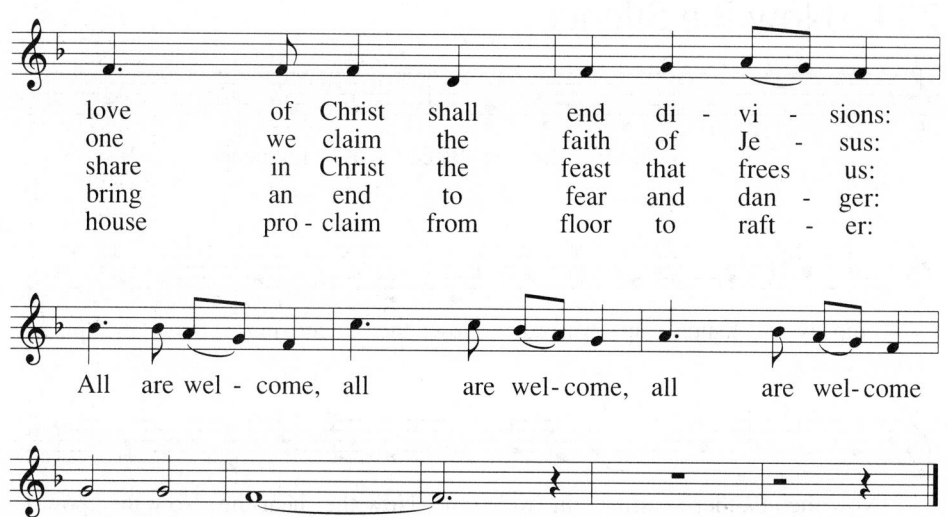

love	of	Christ	shall	end	di -	vi -	sions:
one	we	claim	the	faith	of	Je -	sus:
share	in	Christ	the	feast	that	frees	us:
bring	an	end	to	fear	and	dan -	ger:
house	pro - claim	from	floor	to	raft -	er:

All are wel - come, all are wel-come, all are wel-come

in this place.

Text: Marty Haugen, b. 1950
Tune: TWO OAKS, 9 6 8 6 8 7 10 with refrain; Marty Haugen, b. 1950
© 1994, GIA Publications, Inc.

754 Now the Silence

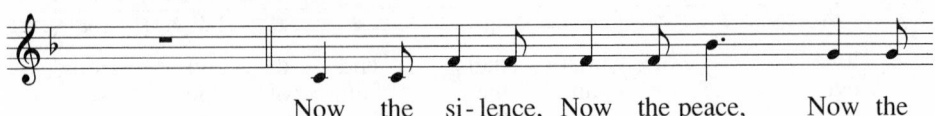

Now the si-lence, Now the peace, Now the

emp-ty hands up-lift-ed; Now the kneel-ing, Now the plea,

Now the Fa-ther's arms in wel-come; Now the hear-ing, Now the pow'r,

Now the ves-sel brimmed for pour-ing; Now the bod-y, Now the

blood, Now the joy-ful cel - e - bra - tion;

Now the wed-ding, Now the songs, Now the heart for - giv - en leap-ing;

Now the Spir-it's vis - i - ta - tion, Now the Son's e - piph - a - ny,

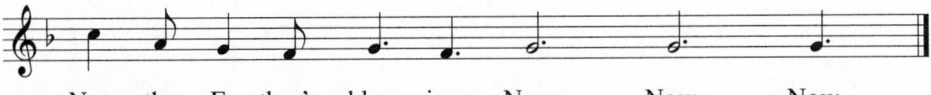

Now the Fa-ther's bless - ing. Now. Now. Now.

Text: Jaroslav J. Vajda, b.1919
Tune: NOW, 4 3 8 4 3 8 D with refrain; Carl Schalk, b.1929
© 1969, Hope Publishing Co.

Today I Awake 755

1. To - day I a - wake and God is be - fore me. At
2. To - day I a - rise and Christ is be - side me. He
3. To - day I af - firm the Spir- it with - in me At
4. To - day I en - joy the Trin - i - ty round me, A -

night, as I dreamt, he sum-moned the day; For
walked through the dark to scat - ter new light. Yes,
wor - ship and work, in strug - gle and rest. The
bove and be - neath, be-fore and be - hind; The

God nev - er sleeps but pat - terns the morn - ing With
Christ is a - live, and beck-ons his peo - ple To
Spir - it in - spires all life which is chang - ing From
Mak - er, the Son, the Spir - it to - geth - er— They

slith - ers of gold or glo - ry in gray.
hope and to heal, re - sist and in - vite.
fear - ing to faith, from bro - ken to blest.
called me to life and call me their friend.

Text: John L. Bell, b.1949
Tune: SLITHERS OF GOLD, 11 10 11 10; John L. Bell, b.1949
© 1989, Iona Community, GIA Publications, Inc., agent

756 Morning Has Broken

1. Morn-ing has bro-ken Like the first morn-ing, Black-bird has
2. Sweet the rain's new fall Sun-lit from heav-en, Like the first
3. Mine is the sun-light! Mine is the morn-ing Born of the

spo-ken Like the first bird. Praise for the sing-ing! Praise for the
dew-fall On the first grass. Praise for the sweet-ness Of the wet
one light E-den saw play! Praise with e - la-tion, Praise ev-'ry

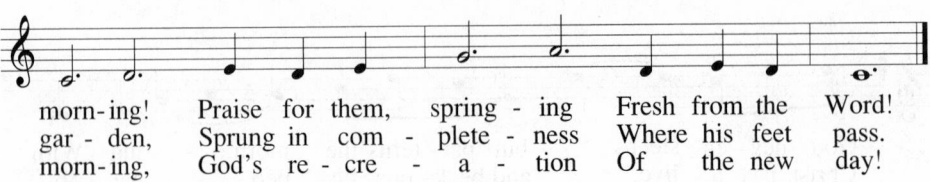

morn-ing! Praise for them, spring-ing Fresh from the Word!
gar-den, Sprung in com - plete-ness Where his feet pass.
morn-ing, God's re-cre - a-tion Of the new day!

Text: Eleanor Farjeon, 1881-1965, *The Children's Bells,* © David Higham Assoc., Ltd.
Tune: BUNESSAN, 5 5 5 4 D; Gaelic; acc. by Marty Haugen, b.1950, © 1987, GIA Publications, Inc.

This Day God Gives Me 757

1. This day God gives me Strength of high
2. This day God sends me Strength as my
3. God's way is my way, God's shield is
4. Ris - ing I thank you, Might - y and

heav - en, Sun and moon shin - ing,
guar - dian, Might to up - hold me,
'round me, God's host de - fends me,
strong One, King of cre - a - tion,

Flame in my hearth, Flash - ing of light - ning,
Wis - dom as guide. Your eyes are watch - ful,
Sav - ing from ill. An - gels of heav - en,
Giv - er of rest, Firm - ly con - fess - ing

Wind in its swift - ness, Depths of the
Your ears are lis - t'ning, Your lips are
Drive from me al - ways All that would
God in three Per - sons, One - ness of

o - cean, Firm - ness of earth.
speak - ing, Friend at my side.
harm me, Stand by me still.
God - head, Trin - i - ty blest.

Text: Ascribed to St. Patrick; James Quinn, SJ, b.1919, © 1969. Used by permission of Selah Publishing Co., Inc., Kingston, N.Y.
Tune: ANDREA, 5 5 5 4 D; David Haas, b.1957, © 1993, GIA Publications, Inc.

758 Day Is Done

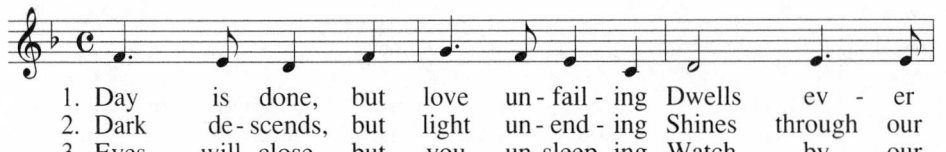

1. Day is done, but love un-fail-ing Dwells ev - er
2. Dark de-scends, but light un-end-ing Shines through our
3. Eyes will close, but you un-sleep-ing Watch by our

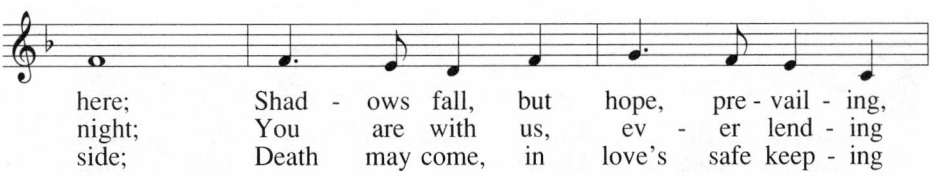

here; Shad - ows fall, but hope, pre - vail - ing,
night; You are with us, ev - er lend - ing
side; Death may come, in love's safe keep - ing

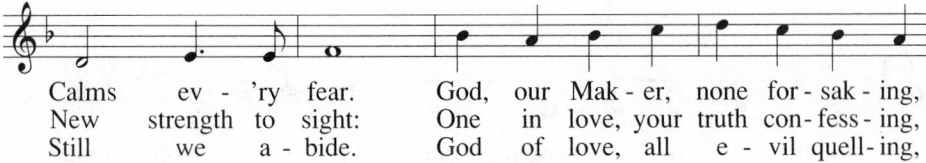

Calms ev - 'ry fear. God, our Mak - er, none for - sak - ing,
New strength to sight: One in love, your truth con - fess - ing,
Still we a - bide. God of love, all e - vil quell - ing,

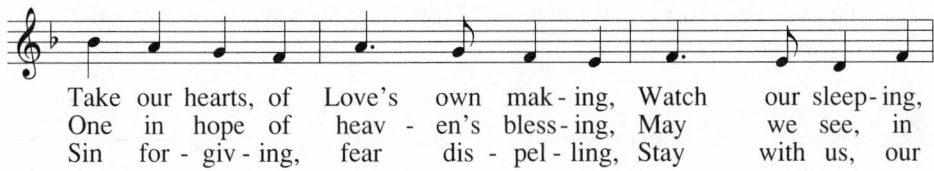

Take our hearts, of Love's own mak - ing, Watch our sleep-ing,
One in hope of heav - en's bless-ing, May we see, in
Sin for - giv - ing, fear dis - pel - ling, Stay with us, our

guard our wak - ing, Be al - ways near.
love's pos - sess - ing, Love's end - less light!
hearts in - dwell - ing, This e - ven - tide.

Text: James Quinn, SJ, b.1919, © 1969, Used by permission of Selah Publishing, Inc., Kingston, N.Y.
Tune: AR HYD Y NOS, 8 4 8 4 888 4; Welsh

At Evening 759

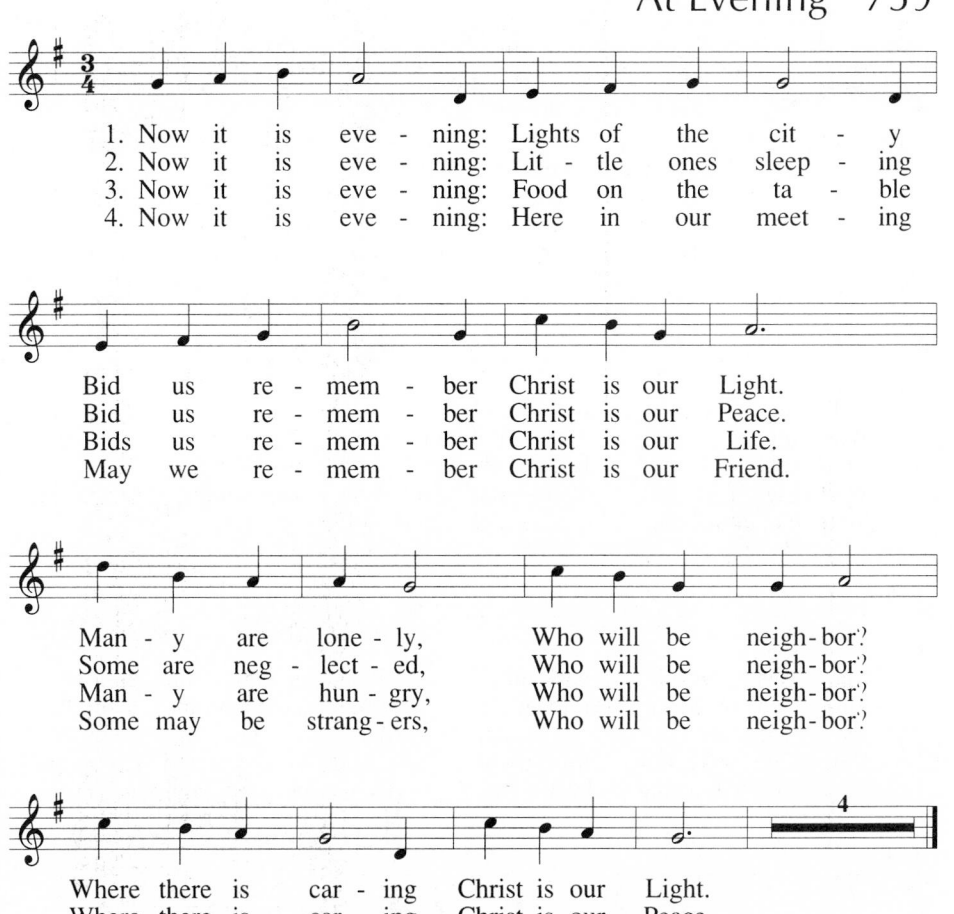

1. Now it is eve - ning: Lights of the cit - y
2. Now it is eve - ning: Lit - tle ones sleep - ing
3. Now it is eve - ning: Food on the ta - ble
4. Now it is eve - ning: Here in our meet - ing

Bid us re - mem - ber Christ is our Light.
Bid us re - mem - ber Christ is our Peace.
Bids us re - mem - ber Christ is our Life.
May we re - mem - ber Christ is our Friend.

Man - y are lone - ly, Who will be neigh-bor?
Some are neg - lect - ed, Who will be neigh-bor?
Man - y are hun - gry, Who will be neigh-bor?
Some may be strang - ers, Who will be neigh-bor?

Where there is car - ing Christ is our Light.
Where there is car - ing Christ is our Peace.
Where there is shar - ing Christ is our Life.
Where there's a wel - come Christ is our Friend.

Text: Fred Pratt Green, b.1903, © 1974, Hope Publishing Co.
Tune: EVENING HYMN, 5 5 5 4 D; David Haas, b.1957, © 1985, GIA Publications, Inc.

760 Joyful Is the Dark

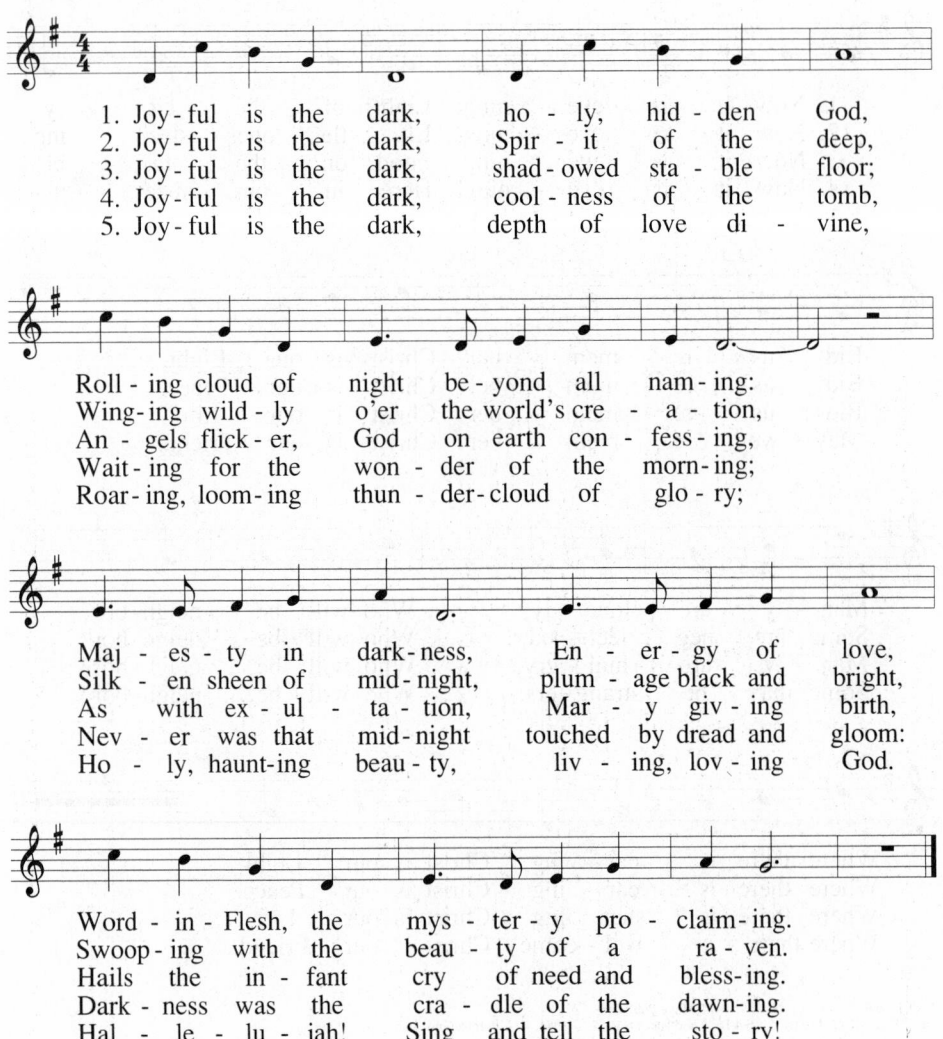

1. Joy - ful is the dark, ho - ly, hid - den God,
2. Joy - ful is the dark, Spir - it of the deep,
3. Joy - ful is the dark, shad - owed sta - ble floor;
4. Joy - ful is the dark, cool - ness of the tomb,
5. Joy - ful is the dark, depth of love di - vine,

Roll - ing cloud of night be - yond all nam - ing:
Wing - ing wild - ly o'er the world's cre - a - tion,
An - gels flick - er, God on earth con - fess - ing,
Wait - ing for the won - der of the morn - ing;
Roar - ing, loom - ing thun - der - cloud of glo - ry;

Maj - es - ty in dark - ness, En - er - gy of love,
Silk - en sheen of mid - night, plum - age black and bright,
As with ex - ul - ta - tion, Mar - y giv - ing birth,
Nev - er was that mid - night touched by dread and gloom:
Ho - ly, haunt - ing beau - ty, liv - ing, lov - ing God.

Word - in - Flesh, the mys - ter - y pro - claim - ing.
Swoop - ing with the beau - ty of a ra - ven.
Hails the in - fant cry of need and bless - ing.
Dark - ness was the cra - dle of the dawn - ing.
Hal - le - lu - jah! Sing and tell the sto - ry!

Text: Brian Wren, b.1936, © 1989, Hope Publishing Co.
Tune: JOYFUL DARKNESS, 10 10 11 10; Bob Moore, b.1962, © 1993, GIA Publications, Inc.

God of Day and God of Darkness   761

1. God of day and God of darkness, Now we
2. Still the na-tions curse the darkness, Still the
3. Show us Christ in one an-oth-er, Make us
4. You shall be the path that guides us, You the
5. Praise to you in day and darkness, You our

stand be-fore the night; As the shad-ows stretch and
rich op-press the poor; Still the earth is bruised and
ser-vants strong and true; Give us all your love of
light that in us burns; Shin-ing deep with-in all
source and you our end; Praise to you who love and

deep-en, Come and make our dark-ness bright. All cre-
bro-ken By the ones who still want more. Come and
jus-tice So we do what you would do. Let us
peo-ple, Yours the love that we must learn, For our
nur-ture us As a fa-ther, moth-er, friend. Grant us

a-tion still is groan-ing For the dawn-ing of your
wake us from our sleep-ing, So our hearts can-not ig-
call all peo-ple ho-ly, Let us pledge our lives a-
hearts shall wan-der rest-less 'Til they safe to you re-
all a peace-ful rest-ing, Let each mind and bod-y

might, When the Sun of peace and jus-tice
nore All your peo-ple lost and bro-ken,
new, Make us one with all the low-ly,
turn; Find-ing you in one an-oth-er,
mend, So we rise re-freshed to-mor-row,

Fills the earth with ra-diant light.
All your chil-dren at our door.
Let us all be one in you.
We shall all your face dis-cern.
Hearts re-newed to King-dom tend.

Text: Marty Haugen, b.1950, © 1985, 1994, GIA Publications, Inc.
Tune: BEACH SPRING, 8 7 8 7 D; The Sacred Harp, 1844; harm. by Marty Haugen, b.1950, © 1985, GIA Publications, Inc.

762 Joyous Light of Heavenly Glory

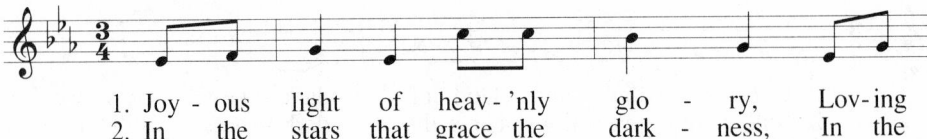

1. Joy - ous light of heav - 'nly glo - ry, Lov-ing
2. In the stars that grace the dark - ness, In the
3. You who made the heav-en's splen - dor, Ev - 'ry

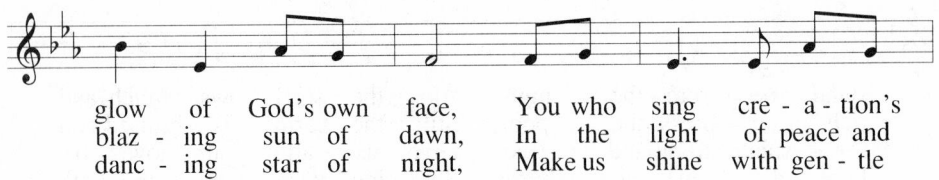

glow of God's own face, You who sing cre - a - tion's
blaz - ing sun of dawn, In the light of peace and
danc - ing star of night, Make us shine with gen - tle

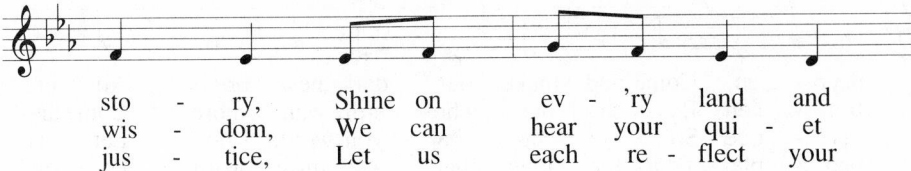

sto - ry, Shine on ev - 'ry land and
wis - dom, We can hear your qui - et
jus - tice, Let us each re - flect your

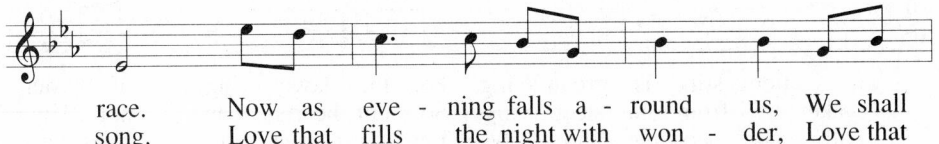

race. Now as eve - ning falls a - round us, We shall
song. Love that fills the night with won - der, Love that
light. Might-y God of all cre - a - tion, Gen-tle

raise our songs to you, God of day - break, God of
warms the wea - ry soul, Love that bursts all chains a -
Christ who lights our way, Lov - ing Spir - it of sal -

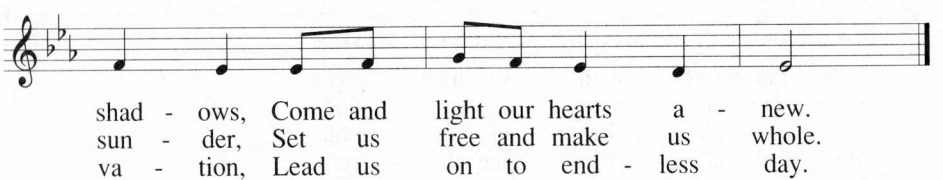

shad - ows, Come and light our hearts a - new.
sun - der, Set us free and make us whole.
va - tion, Lead us on to end - less day.

Text: Marty Haugen, b.1950
Tune: JOYOUS LIGHT, 8 7 8 7 D; Marty Haugen, b.1950
© 1987, GIA Publications, Inc.

Our Darkness / La Ténèbre 763

Our dark - ness is nev - er dark-ness in your sight: the
La té - nè - bre n'est point té - nè - bre de - vant toi: la

deep - est night is clear as the day - light.
nuit com - me le jour est lu - miè - re.

Text: Taizé Community
Tune: Jacques Berthier, 1923-1994
© 1991, Les Presses de Taizé, GIA Publications, Inc., agent

764 Praise and Thanksgiving

1. Praise and thanks - giv - ing, Fa - ther, we of - fer,
2. Lord, bless the la - bor We bring to serve you,
3. Fa - ther, pro - vid - ing Food for your chil - dren,
4. Then will your bless - ing Reach ev - 'ry peo - ple,

For all things liv - ing You have made good.
That with our neigh - bor We may be fed.
Your wis - dom guid - ing Teach - es us share
Free - ly con - fess - ing Your gra - cious hand.

Har - vest of sown fields, Fruits of the or - chard,
Sow - ing or till - ing, We would work with you,
One with an - oth - er, So that re - joic - ing
Where you are reign - ing No one will hun - ger,

Hay from the mown fields, Blos - som and wood.
Har - vest - ing, mill - ing, For dai - ly bread.
With us, all oth - ers May know your care.
Your love sus - tain - ing, Fruit - ful the land.

Text: Albert F. Bayly, 1901-1984, © 1988, Oxford University Press
Tune: BUNESSAN, 5 5 5 4 D; Gaelic; harm. by A. Gregory Murray, OSB, 1905-1992, © Downside Abbey

When the Lord in Glory Comes   765

1. When the Lord in glo-ry comes not the trum-pets, not the
   shout the heav-ens raise, not the cho-rus, not the
2. When the Lord is seen a - gain not the glo-ries of his
   pomp and pow'r a - lone, not the splen-dors of his
3. When the Lord to hu-man eyes shall be-stride our nar-row
   man by all de - nied, not the vic-tim cru-ci-

drums, not the an - them, not the psalm, not the
praise, not the si - lenc - es sub - lime, not the
reign, not the light - nings through the storm, not the
throne, not his robe and di - a - dems, not the
skies, not the child of hum - ble birth, not the
fied, but the God who died to save, but the

[1., 3., 5.]

thun - der, not the calm, not the
ra - diance of his form, not his
car - pen - ter of earth, not the

[2., 4., 6.]

sounds of space and time,
gold and not the gems,
vic - tor of the grave,

but his voice when he ap - pears shall be
but his face up - on my sight shall be
he it is to whom I fall, Je - sus

All:

mu - sic to my ears— but his voice when he ap -
dark - ness in - to light— but his face up - on my
Christ, my All in all— he it is to whom I

pears shall be mu - sic to my ears.
sight shall be dark - ness in - to light.
fall, Je - sus Christ, my All in all.

Text: Timothy Dudley-Smith, b.1926, © 1967, Hope Publishing Co.
Tune: ST. JOHN'S, 77 77 77 D; Bob Moore, b.1962, © 1993, GIA Publications, Inc.

766 Mine Eyes Have Seen the Glory

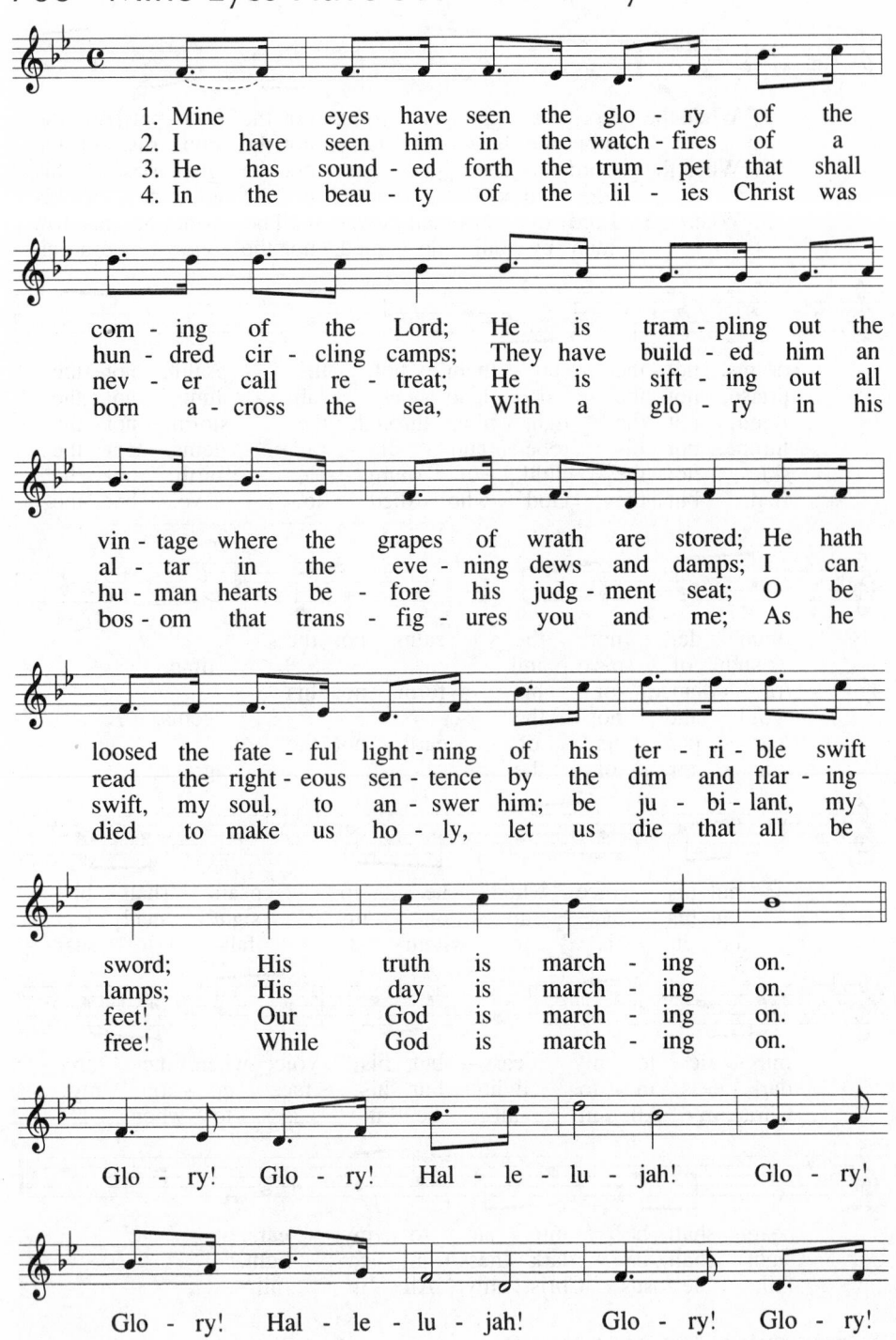

1. Mine eyes have seen the glo - ry of the
2. I have seen him in the watch - fires of a
3. He has sound - ed forth the trum - pet that shall
4. In the beau - ty of the lil - ies Christ was

com - ing of the Lord; He is tram - pling out the
hun - dred cir - cling camps; They have build - ed him an
nev - er call re - treat; He is sift - ing out all
born a - cross the sea, With a glo - ry in his

vin - tage where the grapes of wrath are stored; He hath
al - tar in the eve - ning dews and damps; I can
hu - man hearts be - fore his judg - ment seat; O be
bos - om that trans - fig - ures you and me; As he

loosed the fate - ful light - ning of his ter - ri - ble swift
read the right - eous sen - tence by the dim and flar - ing
swift, my soul, to an - swer him; be ju - bi - lant, my
died to make us ho - ly, let us die that all be

sword; His truth is march - ing on.
lamps; His day is march - ing on.
feet! Our God is march - ing on.
free! While God is march - ing on.

Glo - ry! Glo - ry! Hal - le - lu - jah! Glo - ry!

Glo - ry! Hal - le - lu - jah! Glo - ry! Glo - ry!

Hal - le - lu - jah! His truth is march - ing on.

Text: Julia W. Howe, 1819-1910
Tune: BATTLE HYMN OF THE REPUBLIC, 15 15 15 6 with refrain; attr. to William Steffe, d.1911

O Holy City, Seen of John 767

1. O	Ho - ly	Cit - y,	seen	of	John,	Where
2. O	shame to	us who	rest	con -	tent	While
3. Give us,	O God,	the strength to	build	The
4. Al - read - y	in the	mind	of	God	That

Christ,	the	Lamb,	does	reign,	With - in	those	four - square
lust	and	greed	for	gain	In	street and	shop	and
Cit - y	that has	stood	Too	long a	dream, whose
Cit - y	ris - es	fair:	Lo,	how its	splen - dor

walls shall	come	No	night,	nor	need, nor	pain,	And
ten - e - ment	Wring	gold	from	hu - man	pain,	And
laws are	love,	Whose ways,	the	com - mon	good,	And
chal - leng - es	The	souls	that	great - ly	dare:	Yea,

where the tears are	wiped from eyes	That shall	not weep	a - gain.
bit - ter lips in	blind de - spair	Cry, "Christ has died	in vain."
where the shin - ing	sun be - comes	God's grace	for hu - man good.
bids us seize the	whole of	life	And build	its glo - ry there.

Text: Revelation 21; W. Russell Bowie, 1882-1969, © Harper and Row
Tune: MORNING SONG, 8 6 8 6 8 6; *Kentucky Harmony*, 1816; harm. by C. Winfred Douglas, 1867-1944, © 1940, The Church Pension Fund

768 The Day Is Near

1. For words and deeds en-shrined in gran - ite tombs, For
2. The word of God or - dains the day is near That
3. For all who dare re - ly on words and bread, A

all en - throned in re - gal splen - dor; For
all who weep should turn to laugh - ter; That
dwin - dling flame nev - er ex - tin - guished; Who

pow'r that lives on fear and clash of arms, Whose
home - less peo - ple find a dwell - ing place, That
cling to dreams and an - cient prom - is - es, How -

faith a - bides in steel and sil - ver. All things held in es - ti -
thirst and hun - ger should be end - ed. Then the bar - ren shall be
ev - er hard the task to do so. They may groan be-neath their

ma - tion: God's word leaves them all con -
fruit - ful; Or - phans shall them - selves be
bur - dens, And their strug - gle waged in

found - ed. In our weak - ness he may
fa - thers. Truth and mer - cy shall em -
se - cret. They may yet a - wake to

lend his strength And face the might - y with his jus - tice.
brace at last And peace will reign the whole world o - ver.
greet the dawn And not be - lieve what they are see - ing.

Text: Huub Oosterhuis, b.1933; trans. by Tony Barr, b.1945; rev. by Tom Conry
Tune: Bernard Huijbers, b.1922
© 1973, Gooi en Sticht, bv., Baarn, The Netherlands
Exclusive English-language agent: OCP Publications

My Lord Will Come Again   769

Refrain

My Lord will come a-gain, my Lord, my Lord will come a-gain, My Lord will come a-gain, my Lord will come a-gain! My Lord will come a-gain, my Lord, and the king-dom will have no end! A - men! A - men! My Lord will come a-gain!

Verses

1. I will bless the Lord at all times! I will praise God with all my life!
   For the Lord our God is risen, and death will be no more!
   Amen, Amen, My Lord will come again!

2. I will sing to God a new song: Make music to my God while I live!
   For the Lord our God is with us, and death will be no more!
   Amen, Amen, My Lord will come again!

3. I will see a new heaven and new earth! God will make a home within our hearts!
   And we will be God's people, and death will be no more!
   Amen, Amen, My Lord will come again!

4. God will wipe all tears from our eyes! The world of the past will be gone!
   Sadness, pain, and mourning: these will be no more!
   Amen, Amen, My Lord will come again!

Text: David Haas, b.1957
Tune: David Haas, b.1957
© 1991, GIA Publications, Inc.

770 Soon and Very Soon

1. Soon and ver - y soon   we are goin' to see the King,
2. No   more cry - in' there   we are goin' to see the King,
3. No   more dy - in' there   we are goin' to see the King,
4. Soon and ver - y soon   we are goin' to see the King,

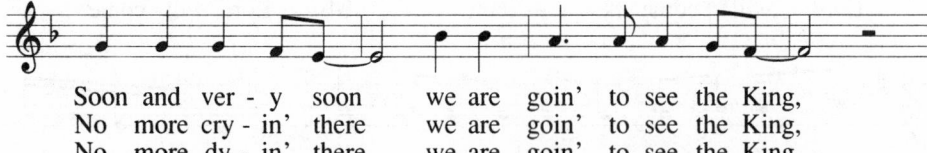

Soon and ver - y soon   we are goin' to see the King,
No   more cry - in' there   we are goin' to see the King,
No   more dy - in' there   we are goin' to see the King,
Soon and ver - y soon   we are goin' to see the King,

Soon and ver - y soon   we are goin' to see the King,
No   more cry - in' there   we are goin' to see the King,   Hal-le -
No   more dy - in' there   we are goin' to see the King,
Soon and ver - y soon   we are goin' to see the King,

1., 2.

lu - jah, Hal-le - lu - jah, we're goin' to see the King!

3., 4.

Hal - le - lu - jah, Hal - le - lu -

jah, Hal - le - lu - jah, Hal - le - lu - jah.

Text: Andraé Crouch
Tune: Andraé Crouch
© 1976, Bud John Songs, Inc./Crouch Music/ASCAP

Jerusalem, My Happy Home 771

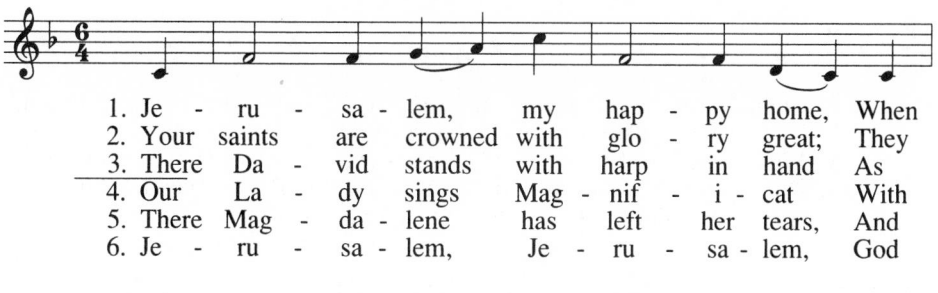

1. Je - ru - sa - lem, my hap - py home, When
2. Your saints are crowned with glo - ry great; They
3. There Da - vid stands with harp in hand As
4. Our La - dy sings Mag - nif - i - cat With
5. There Mag - da - lene has left her tears, And
6. Je - ru - sa - lem, Je - ru - sa - lem, God

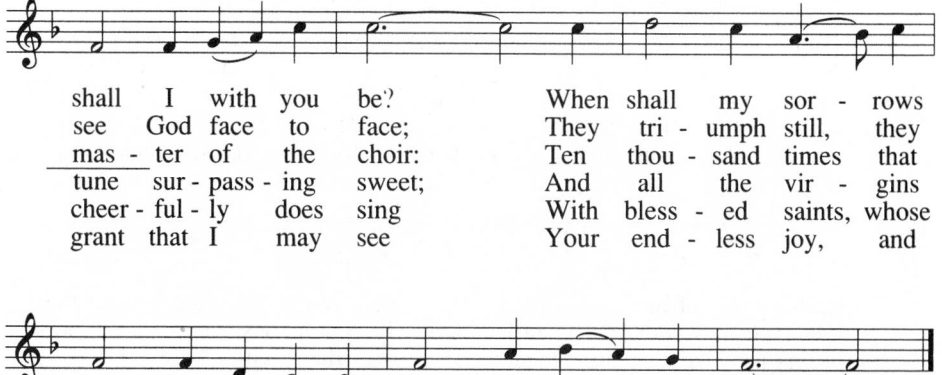

shall I with you be? When shall my sor - rows
see God face to face; They tri - umph still, they
mas - ter of the choir: Ten thou - sand times that
tune sur - pass - ing sweet; And all the vir - gins
cheer - ful - ly does sing With bless - ed saints, whose
grant that I may see Your end - less joy, and

have an end? Your joys when shall I see?
still re - joice: In that most ho - ly place.
we were blest That might this mu - sic hear.
join the song While sit - ting at her feet.
har - mo - ny In ev - 'ry street does ring.
of the same Par - tak - er ev - er be!

Text: Joseph Bromehead, 1747-1826, alt.
Tune: LAND OF REST, CM; American; harm. by Richard Proulx, b.1937, © 1975, GIA Publications, Inc.

772 We Shall Rise Again

1. Come to me, all you wea-ry, with your bur-dens and
2. Though we walk through the dark-ness, e-vil we do not
3. We de-pend on God's mer-cy, mer-cy which nev-er
4. Do not fear death's do-min-ion, look be-yond earth and
5. At the door there to greet us, mar-tyrs, an-gels, and

pain. Take my yoke on your shoul - ders and
fear. You are walk - ing be - side us with your
fades. We re - mem - ber our cov - e - nant and the
grave. See the bright - ness of Je - sus shin - ing
saints, And our fam - 'ly and loved ones, ev - 'ry -

learn from me: I am gen - tle and hum - ble,
rod and your staff. On - ly good - ness and kind - ness
prom - ise Je - sus made: If we die with Christ Je - sus,
out to light our way. Lov - ing Fa - ther and Spir - it,
one freed from their chains. We shall feel their ac - cep - tance,

and your soul will find rest, For my yoke is
fol - low us all our lives. We shall dwell in the
we shall live with him, And if we are
lov - ing Je - sus the Son, All God's peo - ple to -
and the joy of new life. We shall join in the

eas - y and my bur - den is light.
Lord's house for so man - y years to come!
faith - ful, we shall reign with him!
geth - er, we shall live on as one!
gath - er - ing, re - u - nit - ed in God's love!

We shall rise a-gain on the last day with the faith - ful, rich and

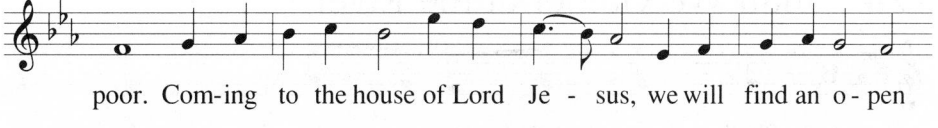

poor. Com-ing to the house of Lord Je - sus, we will find an o - pen

door there, we will find an o - pen door.

Text: Matthew 11:29-30, Psalm 23, John 11, 2 Timothy 2; Jeremy Young, b.1948
Tune: RESURRECTION; Irregular with refrain; Jeremy Young, b.1948
©1987, GIA Publications, Inc.

Steal Away to Jesus   773

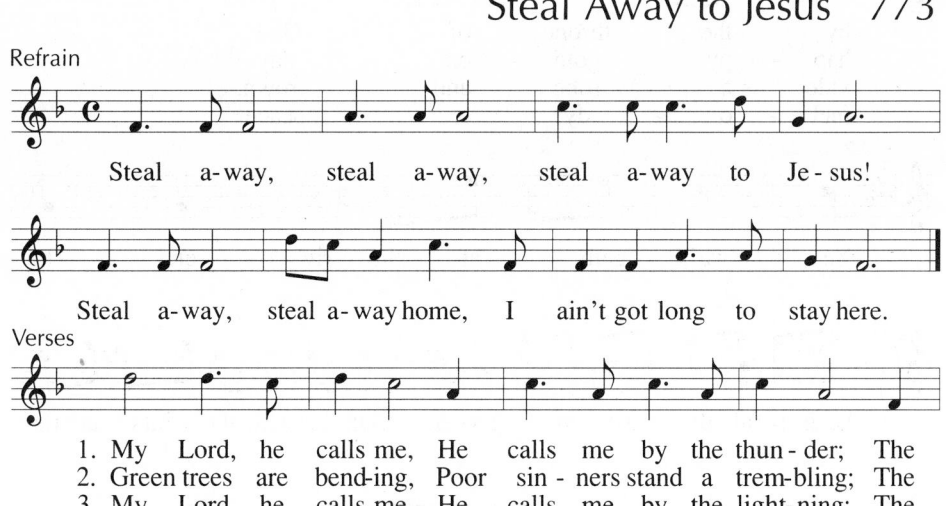

Refrain

Steal a-way, steal a-way, steal a-way to Je-sus!

Steal a-way, steal a-way home, I ain't got long to stay here.

Verses

1. My Lord, he calls me, He calls me by the thun - der; The
2. Green trees are bend-ing, Poor sin - ners stand a trem-bling; The
3. My Lord, he calls me, He calls me by the light-ning; The

D.C.

trum-pet sounds with - in my soul; I ain't got long to stay here.

Text: African-American spiritual
Tune: African-American spiritual

774 Shall We Gather at the River

1. Shall we gath - er at the riv - er,
2. On the mar - gin of the riv - er,
3. Ere we reach the shin - ing riv - er,
4. Soon we'll reach the shin - ing riv - er,

Where bright an - gel feet have trod;
Wash - ing up its sil - ver spray,
Lay we ev - 'ry bur - den down;
Soon our pil - grim-age will cease,

With its crys - tal tide for ev - er Flow-ing
We will walk and wor - ship ev - er, All the
Grace our spir - its will de - liv - er, And pro -
Soon our hap - py hearts will quiv - er With the

by the throne of God?
hap - py gold - en day.
vide a robe and crown.
mel - o - dy of peace.

Yes, we'll gath - er at the riv - er, The

beau- ti-ful, the beau-ti- ful riv-er; Gath- er with the saints at the

riv - er That flows by the throne of God.

Text: Robert Lowry, 1826-1899
Tune: Robert Lowry, 1826-1899

Canticle of Zachary   775

1. Now bless the God of Is - ra - el, Who
2. Re - mem - ber - ing the cov - e - nant, God
3. In ten - der mer - cy, God will send The

comes in love and pow'r, Who rais - es from the
res - cues us from fear, That we might serve in
day - spring from on high, Our ris - ing sun, the

roy - al house De - liv - 'rance in this hour. Through
ho - li - ness And peace from year to year; And
light of life For those who sit and sigh. God

ho - ly proph - ets God has sworn To
you, my child, shall go be - fore To
comes to guide our way to peace, That

free us from a - larm, To save us from the
preach, to proph - e - sy, That all may know the
death shall reign no more. Sing prais - es to the

heav - y hand Of all who wish us harm.
ten - der love, The grace of God most high.
Ho - ly One! O wor - ship and a - dore!

Text: *Benedictus*, Luke 1:68-79; Ruth Duck, b.1947, © 1992, GIA Publications, Inc.
Tune: FOREST GREEN, CMD; English; harm. by Michael Joncas, b.1951, © 1987, GIA Publications, Inc.

776   Now Let Your Servant Go

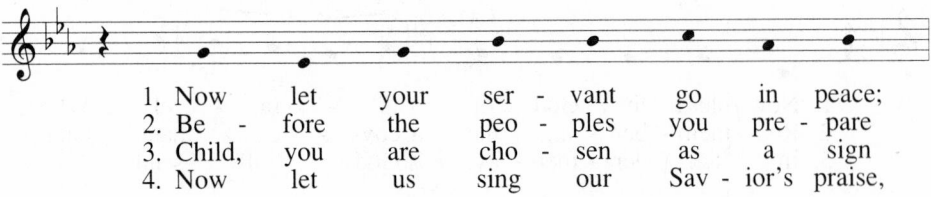

1. Now let your ser - vant go in peace;
2. Be - fore the peo - ples you pre - pare
3. Child, you are cho - sen as a sign
4. Now let us sing our Sav - ior's praise,

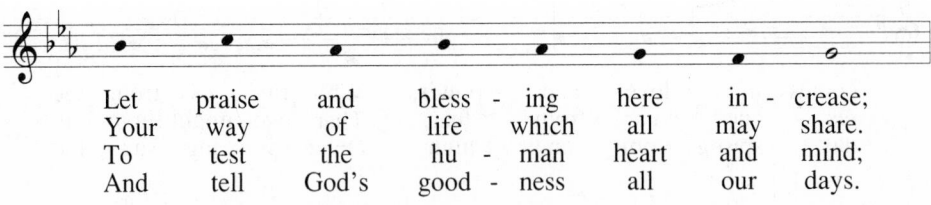

Let praise and bless - ing here in - crease;
Your way of life which all may share.
To test the hu - man heart and mind;
And tell God's good - ness all our days.

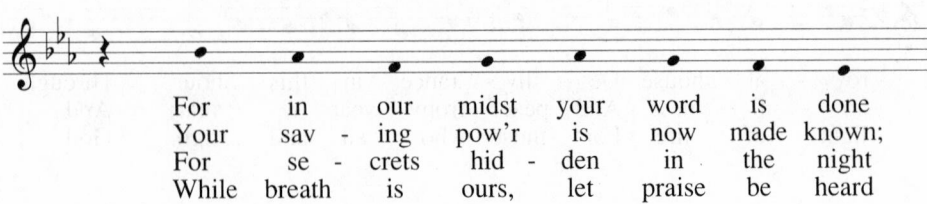

For in our midst your word is done
Your sav - ing pow'r is now made known;
For se - crets hid - den in the night
While breath is ours, let praise be heard

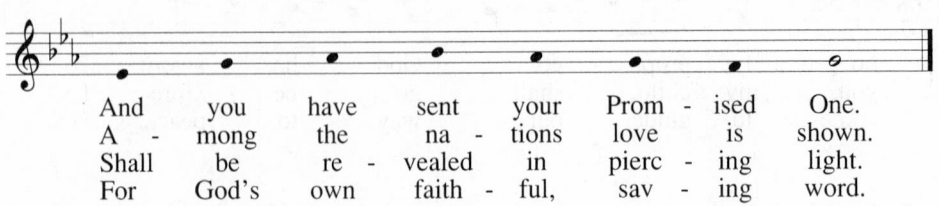

And you have sent your Prom - ised One.
A - mong the na - tions love is shown.
Shall be re - vealed in pierc - ing light.
For God's own faith - ful, sav - ing word.

Text: *Nunc dimittis*, Luke 2:29-35; Ruth Duck, b. 1947, © 1992 GIA Publications, Inc.
Tune: CONDITOR ALME SIDERUM, LM; Mode IV; acc. by Gerard Farrell, OSB, b. 1919, © 1986, GIA Publications, Inc.

Praise We the Lord This Day   777

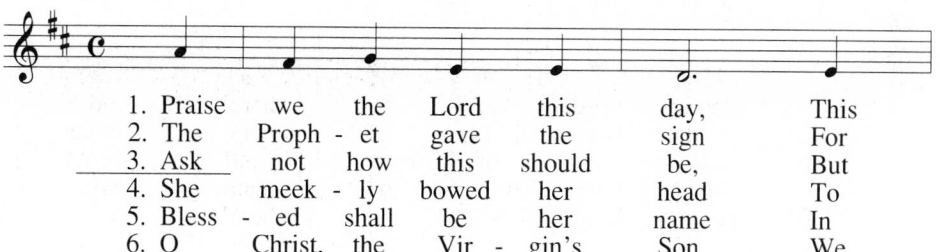

1. Praise we the Lord this day, This
2. The Proph - et gave the sign For
3. Ask not how this should be, But
4. She meek - ly bowed her head To
5. Bless - ed shall be her name In
6. O Christ, the Vir - gin's Son, We

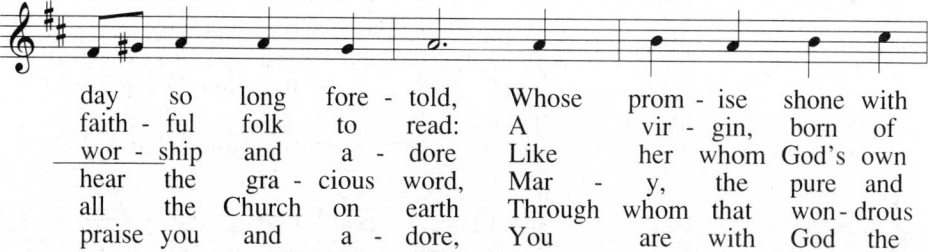

day so long fore - told, Whose prom - ise shone with
faith - ful folk to read: A vir - gin, born of
wor - ship and a - dore Like her whom God's own
hear the gra - cious word, Mar - y, the pure and
all the Church on earth Through whom that won - drous
praise you and a - dore, You are with God the

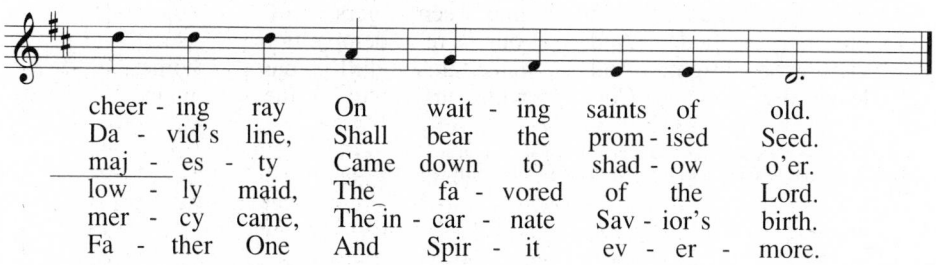

cheer - ing ray On wait - ing saints of old.
Da - vid's line, Shall bear the prom - ised Seed.
maj - es - ty Came down to shad - ow o'er.
low - ly maid, The fa - vored of the Lord.
mer - cy came, The in - car - nate Sav - ior's birth.
Fa - ther One And Spir - it ev - er - more.

Text: Matthew 1:23; *Hymns for the Festivals and Saints' Days*, 1846
Tune: SWABIA, SM; Johann M. Speiss, 1715-1772; adapt. by William H. Havergal, 1793-1870

778 'Tis Good, Lord, to Be Here

1. 'Tis good, Lord, to be here! Your
2. 'Tis good, Lord, to be here, Your
3. Ful - fill - er of the past! Prom -
4. Be - fore we taste of death, We
5. 'Tis good, Lord, to be here! Yet

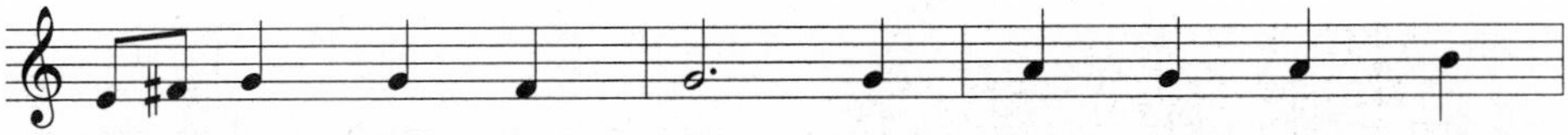

glo - ry fills the night; Your face and gar - ments,
beau - ty to be - hold, Where Mo - ses and E -
ise of things to be! We hail your bod - y
see your king - dom come; We long to hold the
we may not re - main; But since you bid us

like the sun, Shine with un - bor - rowed light.
li - jah stand, Your mes - sen - gers of old.
glo - ri - fied, And our re - demp - tion see.
vi - sion bright, And make this hill our home.
leave the mount, Come with us to the plain.

Text: Luke 9:32-33; Joseph A. Robinson, 1858-1933, alt., © Esme. D. E. Bird
Tune: SWABIA, SM; Johann M. Speiss, 1715-1772; adapt. by William H. Havergal, 1793-1870

779 Salve, Regina / Hail, Queen of Heaven

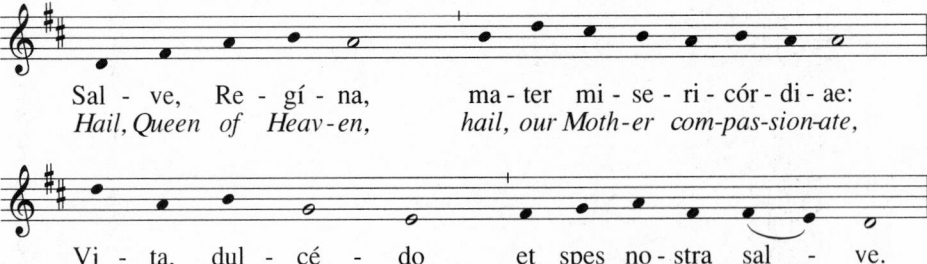

Sal - ve, Re - gí - na, ma - ter mi - se - ri - cór - di - ae:
Hail, Queen of Heav - en, hail, our Moth - er com - pas - sion - ate,

Vi - ta, dul - cé - do et spes no - stra sal - ve.
True life and com - fort and our hope, we greet you!

Ad te cla-má-mus, éx-su-les fí-li-i He-vae.
To you we ex-iles, chil-dren of Eve, raise our voic-es.

Ad te sus-pi-rá-mus, ge-mén-tes et flen-tes
We send up sighs to you, as mourn-ing and weep-ing,

in hac la-cri-má-rum val-le. E-ia er-go,
we pass through this vale of sor-row. Then turn to us,

ad-vo-cá-ta no-stra, il-los tu-os mi-se-ri-
O most gra-cious Wom-an, those eyes of yours, so full of

cór-des ó-cu-los ad nos con-vér-te.
love and ten-der-ness, so full of pit-y.

Et Je-sum, be-ne-dí-ctum fru-ctum ven-tris tu-i,
And grant us af-ter these, our days of lone-ly ex-ile,

no-bis post hoc ex-sí-li-um o-stén-de.
the sight of your blest Son and Lord, Christ Je-sus.

O cle-mens, O pi-a,
O gen-tle, O lov-ing,

O dul-cis Vir-go Ma-rí-a.
O ho-ly, sweet Vir-gin Mar-y.

Text: Latin, c.1080, tr. by John C. Selner, SS, b.1904, © 1954, GIA Publications, Inc.
Tune: SALVE REGINA, Irregular; Mode V; acc. by Gerard Farrell, OSB, b.1919, © 1986, GIA Publications, Inc.

780 O Sanctissima / O Most Virtuous

1. O   san - ctís - si - ma,   O   pi - ís - si - ma,
2. Tu   so - lá - ti - um   Et   re - fú - gi - um,
3. Ec - ce   dé - bi - les,   Per - quam   flé - bi - les,
4. Vir - go   ré - spi - ce,   Ma - ter,   ád - spi - ce,
1. O   most   vir - tu - ous   And   most   pi - ous,
2. Our   pro - tec - tion and   Con - so - la - tion,
3. See   us   pow - er - less   In   our   hope - less - ness:
4. Maid - en,   look   on us,   Moth - er,   care   for us.

Dul - cis   vir - go   Ma - rí - a!
Vir - go   ma - ter   Ma - rí - a!
Sal - va   nos,   Ma - rí - a!
Au - di   nos,   Ma - rí - a!
Dear - est   maid - en,   sweet   Mar - y,
Vir - gin   moth - er,   good   Mar - y,
Aid   us,   save   us,   Mar - y!
Hear   our   pleas,   O   Mar - y!

Ma - ter a - má - ta,   In - te - me - rá - ta,
Quid - quid op - tá - mus,   Per   te spe - rá - mus,
Tol - le lan - guó - res,   Sa - na do - ló - res,
Tu   me - di - cí - nam,   Por - tas di - ví - nam;
Moth - er af - fec - tion-ate,   Vir - gin in - vi - o - late,
What - e'er our souls de-sire,   May you help us   to   ac - quire.
Wipe a - way the tears   we shed,   Heal us   of   our grief and dread.
Balm   and our sur - e - ty,   Gate-way to   di - vin - i - ty,

O - ra,   o - ra pro   no - bis.
O - ra,   o - ra pro   no - bis.
O - ra,   o - ra pro   no - bis.
O - ra,   o - ra pro   no - bis.
In - ter - cede   and   pray   for   us,   O   Mar - y!
In - ter - cede   and   pray   for   us,   O   Mar - y!
In - ter - cede   and   pray   for   us,   O   Mar - y!
In - ter - cede   and   pray   for   us,   O   Mar - y!

Text: St. 1, *Stimmen der Völker in Liedern*, 1807; st. 2, *Arundel Hymnal*, 1902; tr. Neil Borgstrom, b.1953, © 1994, GIA Publications, Inc.
Tune: O DU FRÖLICHE, 55 7 55 7; Tattersall's *Improved Psalmody*, 1794

I Sing a Maid 781

1. I sing a maid of ten - der years To
2. She watched him grow to man - hood's strength To
3. And if the song had end - ed then, Our

whom an an - gel came, And knelt, as to a
meet his des - tin - y, And when the dan - ger
eyes would fill with tears, But ah! the song had

might - y queen, And bowed bright wings of
of his truth Brought him to Cal - va -
just be - gun To ech - o down the

flame: A na - tion's hope in her re - ply, This
ry, She stood by him all pow - er - less To
years! Now lift your voic - es, hearts and souls, To

maid of match-less grace; For God's own son be -
ease his dy - ing pain, 'Til in the dark - est
sing with one ac - cord To hon - or Mar - y,

came her child, And she his rest - ing place.
hour of all, She held her son a - gain.
Moth - er of The Christ, the Ris - en Lord!

Text: M. D. Ridge, b.1938, © 1987, GIA Publications, Inc.
Tune: THE FLIGHT OF THE EARLS; 14 14 14 14; trad. Celtic melody; harm. by Michael Joncas, b.1951, © 1987, GIA Publications, Inc.

782   Hail Mary: Gentle Woman

Hail Mar - y, full of grace, the Lord is with you. Bless-ed are you a - mong wo - men, and blest is the fruit of your womb, Je - sus.

Ho-ly Mar - y, Moth-er of God, pray for us sin - ners now and at the hour of death. A - men.

Refrain 𝄋

Gen - tle wom-an, qui-et light, morn-ing star, so strong and bright, gen - tle Moth-er, peace - ful dove, teach us wis - dom; teach us love.

Verse 1

1. You were cho - sen by the Fa - ther;
you were cho - sen for the Son.
You were cho - sen from all wom-en and for
wom - an, shin - ing one.

Verse 2

2. Bless - ed are you a-mong wom-en,
blest in turn all wom-en, too. Bless-ed
they with peace - ful spir - its.
Bless-ed they with gen - tle hearts.

Text: *Hail Mary*, alt; Carey Landry
Tune: Carey Landry; arr. by Martha Lesinski, alt.
© 1975, Carey Landry and North American Liturgy Resources

783 Sing of Mary, Pure and Lowly

1. Sing of Mar - y pure and low - ly, Vir - gin - moth - er
2. Sing of Je - sus, son of Mar - y, In the home at
3. Glo - ry be to God the Fa - ther; Glo - ry be to

un - de - filed, Sing of God's own Son most ho - ly,
Naz - a - reth. Toil and la - bor can - not wea - ry
God the Son; Glo - ry be to God the Spir - it;

Who be - came her lit - tle child. Fair - est child of
Love en - dur - ing un - to death. Con - stant was the
Glo - ry to the Three in One. From the heart of

fair - est moth-er, God the Lord who came to earth,
love he gave her, Though he went forth from her side,
bless - ed Mar - y, From all saints the song as - cends,

Word made flesh, our ver - y broth - er,
Forth to preach, and heal, and suf - fer,
And the church the strain re - ech - oes

Takes our na - ture by his birth.
Till on Cal - va - ry he died.
Un - to earth's re - mot - est ends.

Text: Roland F. Palmer, 1891-1985
Tune: PLEADING SAVIOR, 8 7 8 7 D; *Christian Lyre*, 1830; harm. by Richard Proulx, b.1937, © 1986, GIA Publications, Inc.

Hail, Holy Queen Enthroned Above   784

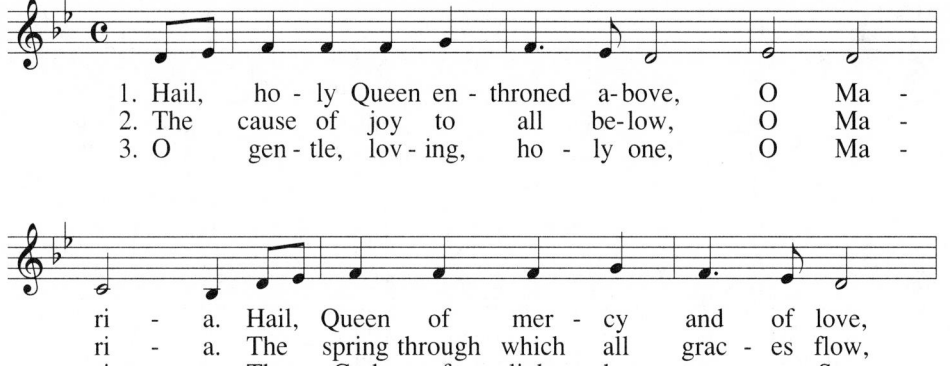

1. Hail, ho - ly Queen en - throned a-bove, O Ma -
2. The cause of joy to all be-low, O Ma -
3. O gen - tle, lov - ing, ho - ly one, O Ma -

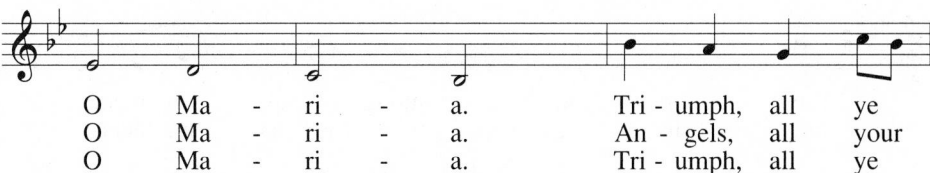

ri - a. Hail, Queen of mer - cy and of love,
ri - a. The spring through which all grac - es flow,
ri - a. The God of light be - came your Son,

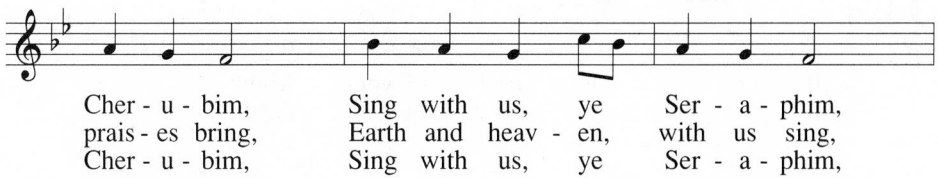

O Ma - ri - a. Tri - umph, all ye
O Ma - ri - a. An - gels, all your
O Ma - ri - a. Tri - umph, all ye

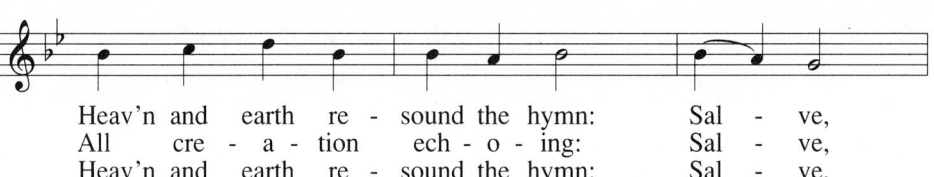

Cher - u - bim, Sing with us, ye Ser - a - phim,
prais - es bring, Earth and heav - en, with us sing,
Cher - u - bim, Sing with us, ye Ser - a - phim,

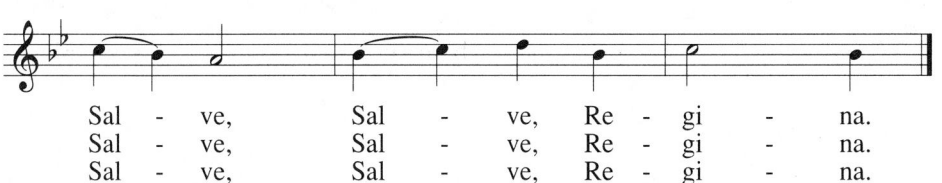

Heav'n and earth re - sound the hymn: Sal - ve,
All cre - a - tion ech - o - ing: Sal - ve,
Heav'n and earth re - sound the hymn: Sal - ve,

Sal - ve, Sal - ve, Re - gi - na.
Sal - ve, Sal - ve, Re - gi - na.
Sal - ve, Sal - ve, Re - gi - na.

Text: *Salve, Regina, mater misericordia;* c.1080; tr. *Roman Hymnal*, 1884; st. 2-3 adapt. by M. Owen Lee, CSB, b.1930
Tune: SALVE REGINA COELITUM, 8 4 8 4 777 4 5; *Choralmelodien zum Heiligen Gesänge*, 1808; harm. by Healey Willan, 1880-1968, © Willis Music Co.

785 Ave Maria

Verses

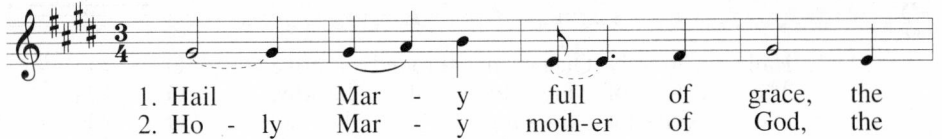

1. Hail Mar - y full of grace, the
2. Ho - ly Mar - y moth-er of God, the

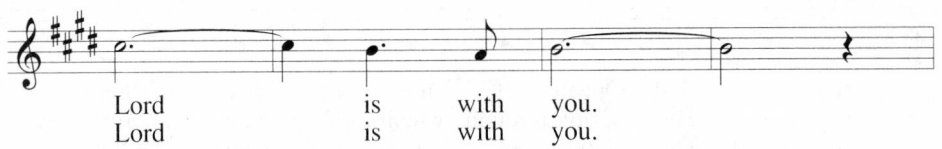

Lord is with you.
Lord is with you.

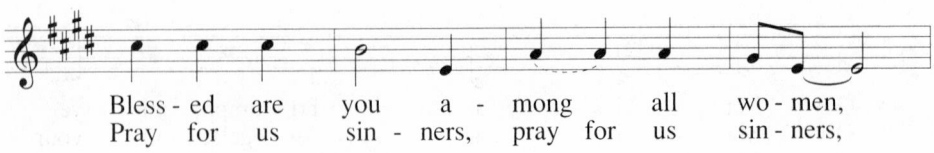

Bless - ed are you a - mong all wo - men,
Pray for us sin - ners, pray for us sin - ners,

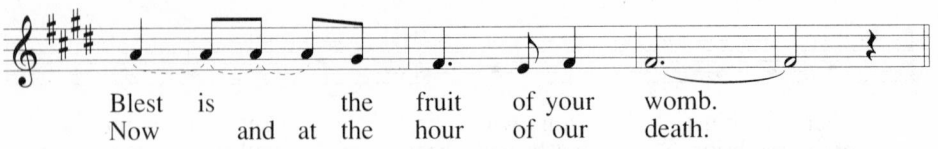

Blest is the fruit of your womb.
Now and at the hour of our death.

Refrain

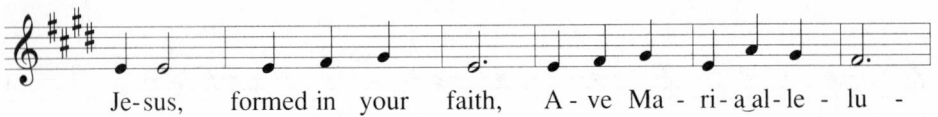

Je-sus, formed in your faith, A - ve Ma - ri-a al-le - lu -

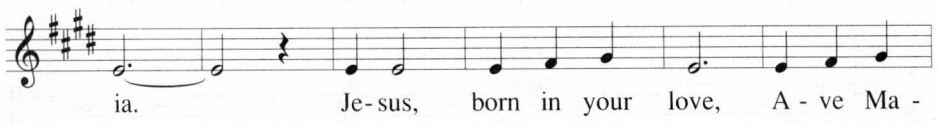

ia. Je-sus, born in your love, A - ve Ma -

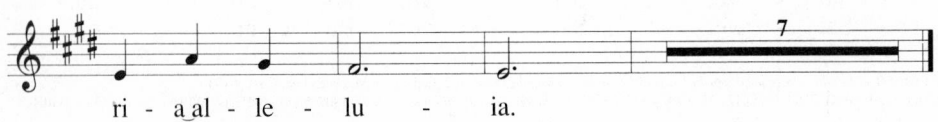

ri - a al - le - lu - ia.

Text: Hail Mary; additional text by Dan Kantor, b.1960
Tune: Dan Kantor, b.1960; arr. by Rob Glover
© 1993, GIA Publications, Inc.

Sing We of the Blessed Mother 786

1. Sing we of the bless-ed Moth-er Who re - ceived the
2. Sing we, too, of Mar-y's sor-rows, Of the sword that
3. Sing a - gain the joys of Mar - y When she saw the
4. Sing the great-est joy of Mar - y When on earth her

an - gel's word, And o - be - dient to the sum-mons
pierced her through, When be - neath the cross of Je - sus
ris - en Lord, And in prayer with Christ's a - pos - tles,
work was done, And the Lord of all cre - a - tion

Bore in love the in - fant Lord; Sing we of the
She his weight of suf - f'ring knew, Looked up - on her
Wait - ed on his prom - ised word: From on high the
Brought her to his heav'n - ly home: Vir - gin Moth - er,

joys of Mar - y At whose breast that child was fed
Son and Sav - ior Reign-ing from the aw - ful tree,
blaz - ing glo - ry Of the Spir - it's pres - ence came,
Mar - y bless-ed, Raised on high and crowned with grace,

Who is Son of God e - ter - nal
Saw the price of our re - demp - tion
Heav'n - ly breath of God's own be - ing,
May your Son, the world's re - deem - er,

And the ev - er - last - ing Bread.
Paid to set the sin - ner free.
To - kened in the wind and flame.
Grant us all to see his face.

Text: George B. Timms, b.1910, © 1975, Oxford University Press
Tune: OMNE DIE, 8 7 8 7 D; *Trier Gesängbuch*, 1695

787 All Who Claim the Faith of Jesus

1. All who claim the faith of Je - sus Sing the
2. Bless - ed were the cho - sen peo - ple Out of
3. There - fore let all faith - ful peo - ple Sing the
4. "Mag - ni - fy, my soul, God's great - ness; In my

won - ders that were done When the love of God the
whom the Lord did come; Bless - ed was the land of
hon - or of her name; Let the Church, in her fore -
Sav - ior I re - joice; All the ag - es call me

Fa - ther O'er our sins the vic - t'ry
prom - ise Fash - ioned for his earth - ly
shad - owed, Part in her thanks - giv - ing
bless - ed, In his praise I lift my

won, When God made the Vir - gin
home; But more bless - ed far the
claim; What Christ's moth - er sang in
voice; God has cast down all the

Mar - y Moth - er of the on - ly Son.
moth - er, She who bore him in her womb.
glad - ness Let Christ's peo - ple sing the same:
might - y, And the low - ly are his choice."

Text: Vincent Stuckey Stratton Coles, 1845-1929, alt.; St. 4, F. Bland Tucker, 1895-1984
Tune: TILLFLYKT, 87 87 87; *Sionstoner*, 1889; harm. by Marty Haugen, b.1950, © 1987, GIA Publications, Inc.

Magnificat 788

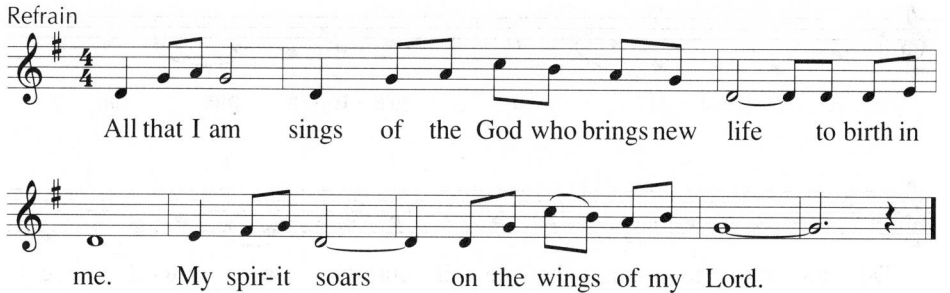

Refrain

All that I am sings of the God who brings new life to birth in me. My spir-it soars on the wings of my Lord.

Verses

1. My soul gives glory to the Lord, rejoicing in my saving God,
   Who looks upon me in my state, and all the world will call me blest;
   For God works marvels in my sight, and holy, holy is God's name!

2. God's mercy is from age to age, on those who follow in fear;
   Whose arm is power and strength, and scatters all the proud of heart;
   Who casts the mighty from their thrones and raises up the lowly ones!

3. God fills the starving with good things, the rich are left with empty hands;
   Protecting all the faithful ones, rememb'ring Israel with mercy,
   The promise known to those before and to their children for ever!

Text: Luke 1:46-55; David Haas, b.1957
Tune: David Haas, b.1957
© 1990, GIA Publications, Inc.

789 Ave Maria

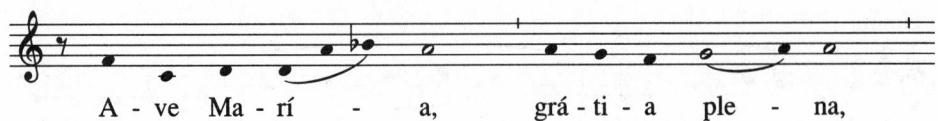

A - ve Ma - rí - a, grá - ti - a ple - na,

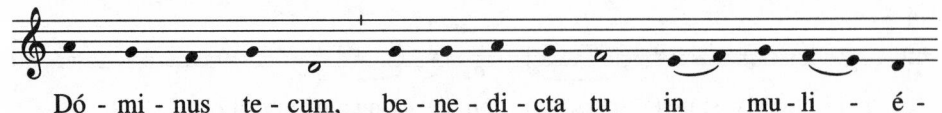

Dó - mi - nus te - cum, be - ne - di - cta tu in mu - li - é -

ri - bus, et be - ne - dí - ctus fru - ctus ven - tris tu - i, Je - sus.

San - cta Ma - rí - a, Ma - ter De - i, o - ra pro no - bis pec - ca -

tó - ri - bus, nunc et in ho - ra mor - tis no - strae. A - men.

Text: *Hail, Mary, full of grace,* Luke 1:29; Latin, 13th C.
Tune: AVE MARÍA, Irregular; Mode I; acc. by Robert LeBlanc, b.1948, © 1986, GIA Publications, Inc.

Immaculate Mary 790

1. Im - ma - cu - late Mar - y, your prais - es we sing;
2. Pre - des - tined for Christ by e - ter - nal de - cree,
3. To you by an an - gel, the Lord God made known
4. Most blest of all wom - en, you heard and be - lieved,
5. The an - gels re - joiced when you brought forth God's Son;

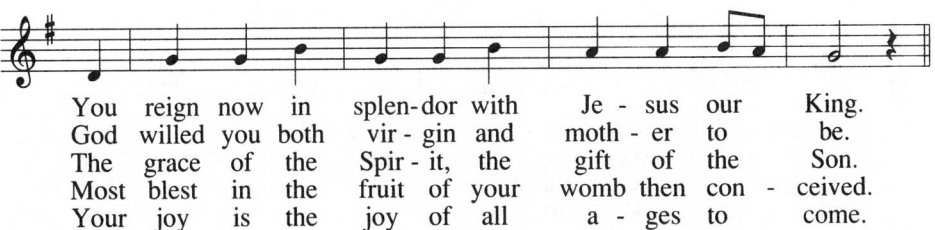

You reign now in splen-dor with Je - sus our King.
God willed you both vir - gin and moth - er to be.
The grace of the Spir - it, the gift of the Son.
Most blest in the fruit of your womb then con - ceived.
Your joy is the joy of all a - ges to come.

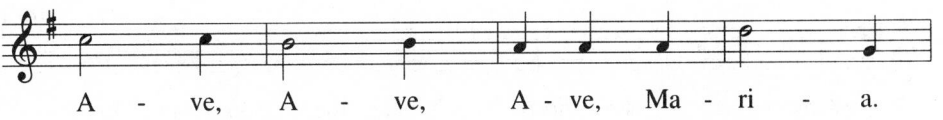

A - ve, A - ve, A - ve, Ma - ri - a.

A - ve, A - ve, Ma - ri - a.

6. Your child is the Savior, all hope lies in him:
   He gives us new life and redeems us from sin.

7. In glory for ever now close to your Son,
   All ages will praise you for all God has done.

Text: St. 1 Jeremiah Cummings, 1814-1866, alt.; St. 2-7, Brian Foley, b.1919, © 1971, Faber Music Ltd.
Tune: LOURDES HYMN, 11 11 with refrain; Grenoble, 1882

791 Lift High the Cross

Lift high the cross, the love of Christ pro - claim till
all the world a - dore his sa - cred name.

1. Come, Chris - tians, fol - low where the Mas - ter trod, our
2. Led on their way by this tri - um - phant sign, the
3. Each new - born fol - l'wer of the Cru - ci - fied bears
4. O Lord, once lift - ed on the glo - rious tree, your
5. So shall our song of tri - umph ev - er be: praise

D.C.

King vic - to - rious, Christ, the Son of God.
hosts of God in con - quering ranks com - bine.
on the brow the seal of him who died.
death has bought us life e - ter - nal - ly.
to the Cru - ci - fied for vic - to - ry!

Text: 1 Corinthians 1:18; George W. Kitchin, 1827-1912, and Michael R. Newbolt, 1874-1956, alt.
Tune: CRUCIFER, 10 10 with refrain; Sydney H. Nicholson, 1875-1947
© 1978, Hope Publishing Co.

Give Thanks to God on High   792

1. Give   thanks   to God   on   high   For   saints   of
2. Their   vi -   sion long   ful - filled,   Our   prayer   is
3. New   tasks   to - day   are   ours   Who   serve   a
4. Give   thanks   to God   on   high   For   all   the

oth - er   days,   Whose   hope   it   was   to
still   the   same;   Up - on   their   work   of
world   of   pain,   New   calls   to   chal - lenge
fu - ture   sends,   In   praise   of   Christ   to

live   and   die   In   love's   con - sum - ing   blaze,
faith   to   build,   Their   word   of   truth   pro - claim,
all   our pow'rs   Of   heart   and hand   and   brain,
live   and   die   Who   calls   his   ser - vants   friends,

For Christ and his king-dom,   His   glo - ry and his   praise.
For Christ and his king-dom,   And   for his   ho - ly   name.
For Christ and his king-dom,   While   life and breath re - main.
For Christ and his king-dom,   Whose glo - ry nev - er   ends.

Text: Timothy Dudley-Smith, b.1926, © 1985, Hope Publishing Co.
Tune: BALDWIN, 6 6 8 6 6 6; James J. Chepponis, b.1956, © 1987, GIA Publications, Inc.

793 For All the Saints

1. For all the saints who from their la - bors
2. You were their rock, their for - tress and their
3. O may your sol - diers, faith - ful, true and
4. O blest com - mun - ion, fam - i - ly di -
5. And when the strife is fierce, the war - fare
6. The gold - en eve - ning bright - ens in the

rest, All who by faith be - fore the world con-
might; You, Lord, their Cap - tain in the well - fought
bold, Fight as the saints who no - bly fought of
vine! We fee - bly strug - gle, they in glo - ry
long, Steals on the ear the dis - tant tri - umph
west; Soon, soon to faith - ful war - riors comes their

fessed, Your name, O Je - sus, be for ev - er blest.
fight; You in the dark - ness drear, their one true light.
old, And win with them, the vic - tor's crown of gold.
shine; Yet all are one with - in your great de - sign.
song, And hearts are brave a - gain, and arms are strong.
rest; Sweet is the calm of par - a - dise the blest.

Al - le - lu - ia! Al - le - lu - ia!

7. But then there breaks a yet more glorious day:
The saints triumphant rise in bright array;
The King of glory passes on his way.
Alleluia! Alleluia!

8. From earth's wide bounds, from ocean's farthest coast,
Through gates of pearl streams in the countless host,
Singing to Father, Son, and Holy Ghost:
Alleluia! Alleluia!

Text: William W. How, 1823-1897
Tune: SINE NOMINE, 10 10 10 with alleluias; Ralph Vaughan Williams, 1872-1958, © Oxford University Press

Ye Watchers and Ye Holy Ones 794

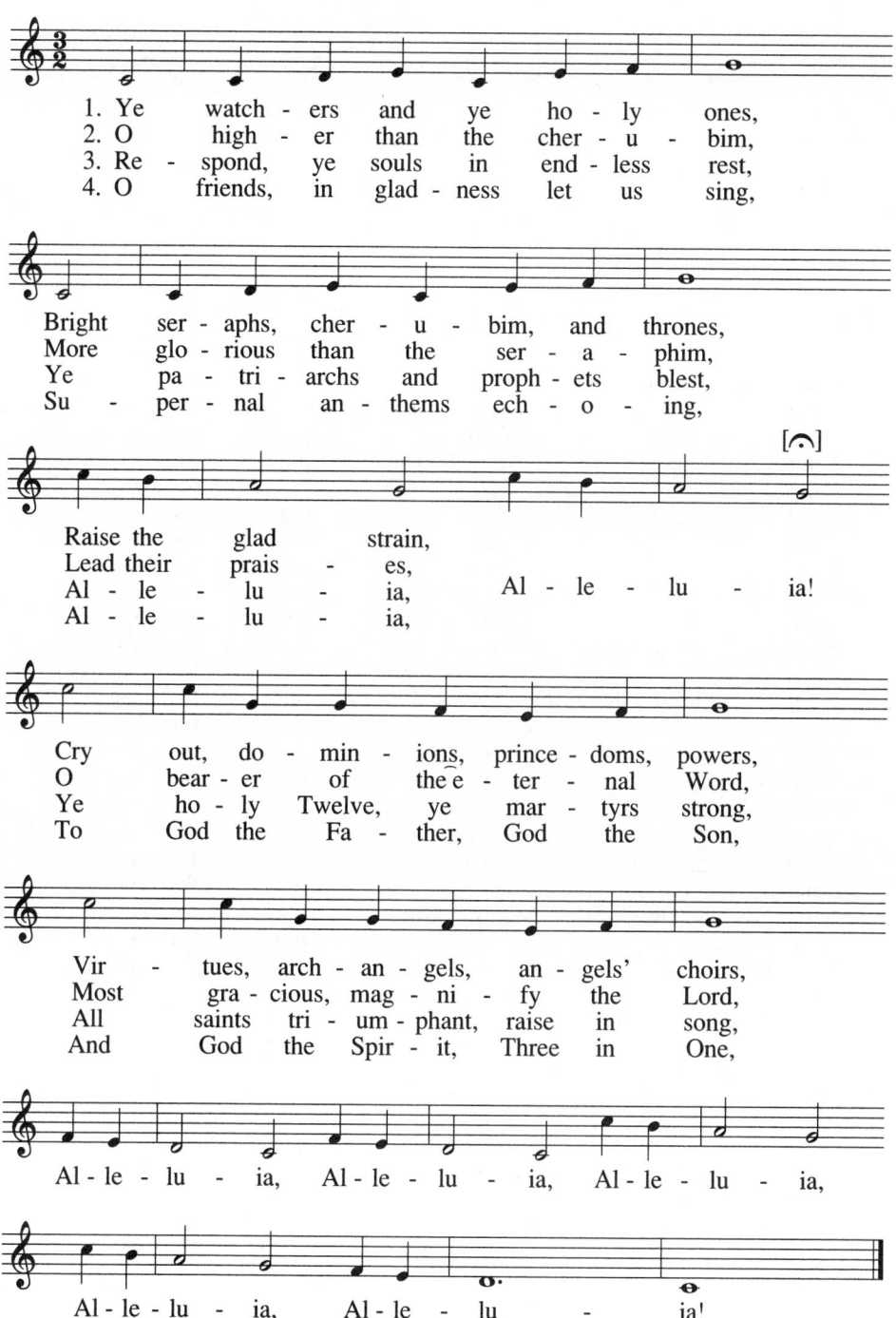

1. Ye watch - ers and ye ho - ly ones,
2. O high - er than the cher - u - bim,
3. Re - spond, ye souls in end - less rest,
4. O friends, in glad - ness let us sing,

Bright ser - aphs, cher - u - bim, and thrones,
More glo - rious than the ser - a - phim,
Ye pa - tri - archs and proph - ets blest,
Su - per - nal an - thems ech - o - ing,

[⌃]

Raise the glad strain,
Lead their prais - es,
Al - le - lu - ia, Al - le - lu - ia!
Al - le - lu - ia,

Cry out, do - min - ions, prince - doms, powers,
O bear - er of the e - ter - nal Word,
Ye ho - ly Twelve, ye mar - tyrs strong,
To God the Fa - ther, God the Son,

Vir - tues, arch - an - gels, an - gels' choirs,
Most gra - cious, mag - ni - fy the Lord,
All saints tri - um - phant, raise in song,
And God the Spir - it, Three in One,

Al - le - lu - ia, Al - le - lu - ia, Al - le - lu - ia,

Al - le - lu - ia, Al - le - lu - ia!

Text: John A. Riley, 1858-1945, © Oxford University Press
Tune: LASST UNS ERFREUEN, LM with alleluias; *Geistliche Kirchengasänge*, Cologne, 1623; harm. by Ralph Vaughan Williams, 1872-1958,
© Oxford University Press

795 Litany of the Saints

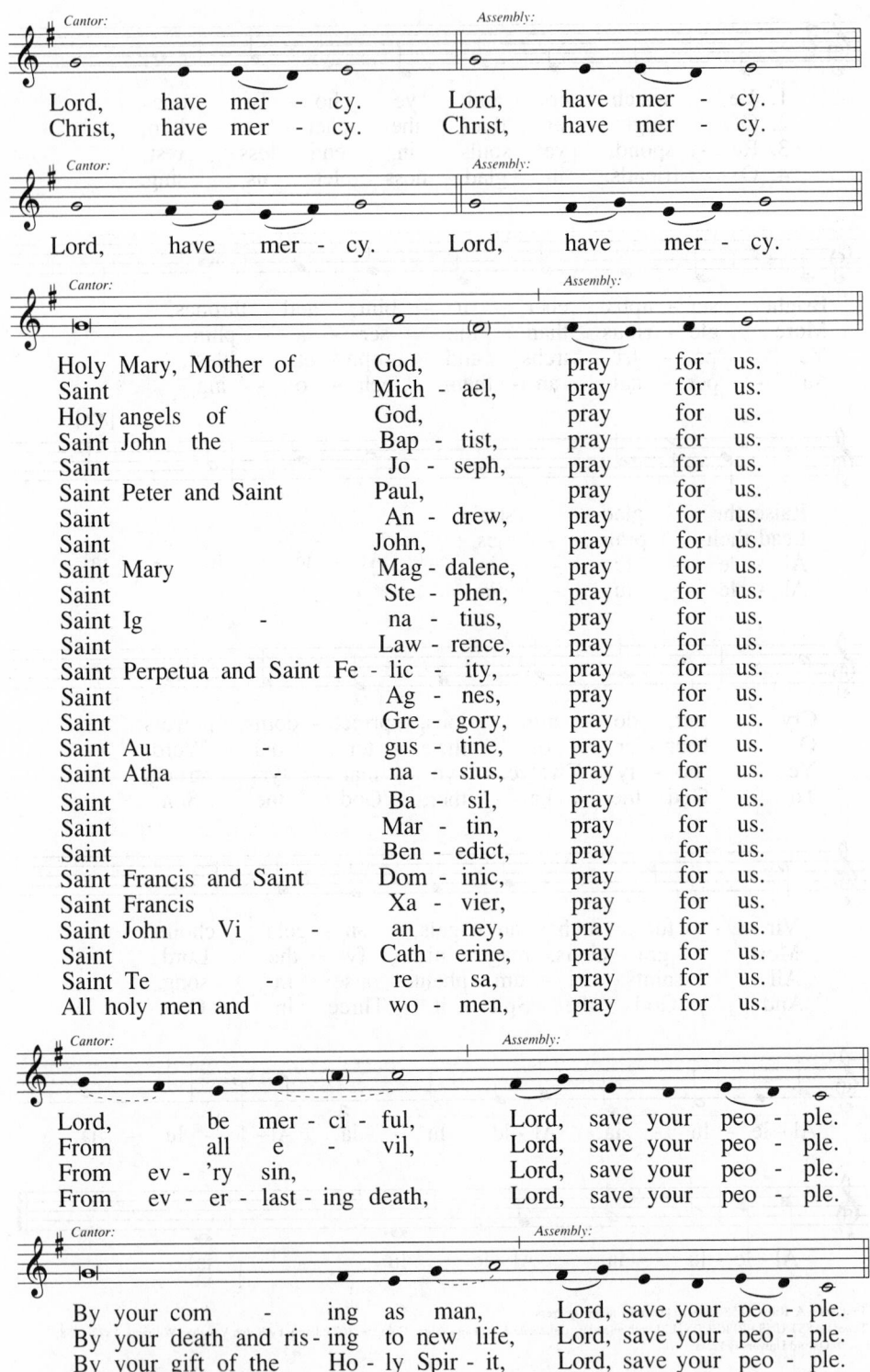

Cantor: Lord, have mer - cy. *Assembly:* Lord, have mer - cy.
Christ, have mer - cy. Christ, have mer - cy.

Cantor: Lord, have mer - cy. *Assembly:* Lord, have mer - cy.

Cantor: / *Assembly:*

		pray	for us.
Holy Mary, Mother of	God,	pray	for us.
Saint	Mich - ael,	pray	for us.
Holy angels of	God,	pray	for us.
Saint John the	Bap - tist,	pray	for us.
Saint	Jo - seph,	pray	for us.
Saint Peter and Saint	Paul,	pray	for us.
Saint	An - drew,	pray	for us.
Saint	John,	pray	for us.
Saint Mary	Mag - dalene,	pray	for us.
Saint	Ste - phen,	pray	for us.
Saint Ig -	na - tius,	pray	for us.
Saint	Law - rence,	pray	for us.
Saint Perpetua and Saint Fe - lic -	ity,	pray	for us.
Saint	Ag - nes,	pray	for us.
Saint	Gre - gory,	pray	for us.
Saint Au -	gus - tine,	pray	for us.
Saint Atha -	na - sius,	pray	for us.
Saint	Ba - sil,	pray	for us.
Saint	Mar - tin,	pray	for us.
Saint	Ben - edict,	pray	for us.
Saint Francis and Saint	Dom - inic,	pray	for us.
Saint Francis	Xa - vier,	pray	for us.
Saint John Vi -	an - ney,	pray	for us.
Saint	Cath - erine,	pray	for us.
Saint Te -	re - sa,	pray	for us.
All holy men and	wo - men,	pray	for us.

Cantor: / *Assembly:*

Lord,	be mer - ci - ful,	Lord, save your	peo - ple.
From	all e - vil,	Lord, save your	peo - ple.
From	ev - 'ry sin,	Lord, save your	peo - ple.
From	ev - er - last - ing death,	Lord, save your	peo - ple.

Cantor: / *Assembly:*

By your com -	ing as man,	Lord, save your	peo - ple.
By your death and ris -	ing to new life,	Lord, save your	peo - ple.
By your gift of the	Ho - ly Spir - it,	Lord, save your	peo - ple.

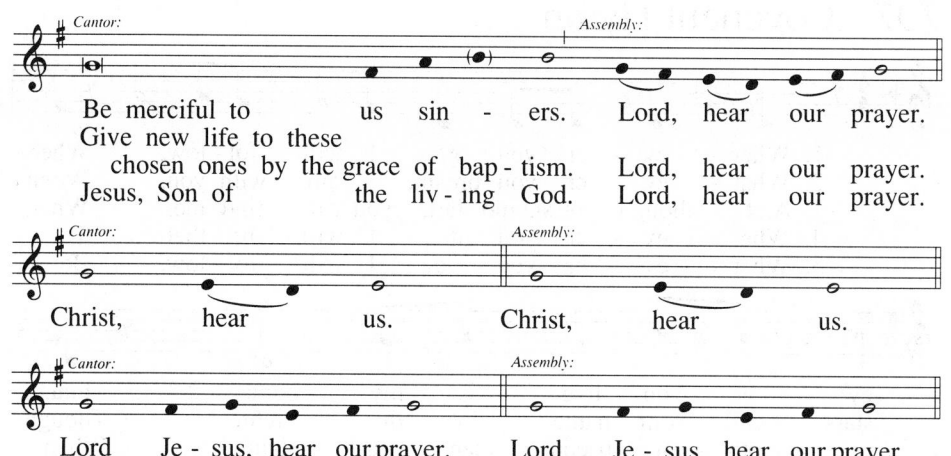

Be merciful to us sin - ers. Lord, hear our prayer.
Give new life to these
  chosen ones by the grace of bap - tism. Lord, hear our prayer.
Jesus, Son of the liv - ing God. Lord, hear our prayer.

Christ, hear us. Christ, hear us.

Lord Je - sus, hear our prayer. Lord Je - sus, hear our prayer.

Text: *Litany of the Saints, Roman Missal*
Music: *Litany of the Saints, Roman Missal*

Litany of the Saints 796

Repeat each invocation immediately after the priest or cantor:

Lord, have mer-cy. Christ, have mer-cy. Lord, have mer-cy.

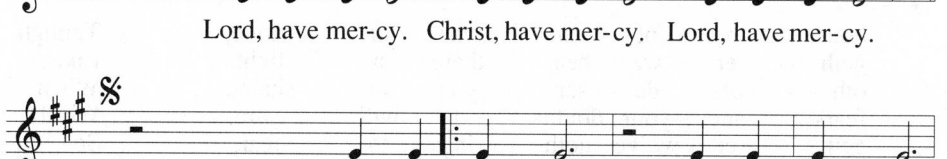

(*Saint Invocation*) 1.- 4. Pray for us, Pray for us.
("*Lord, be merciful.*") 5. Save your peo - ple. Save your peo - ple.
("*Lord, give new life.*") 6. Hear our prayer. Hear our prayer.

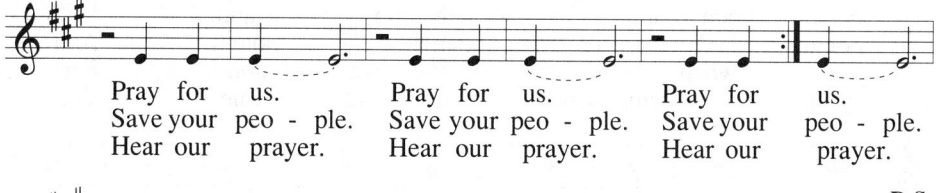

Pray for us. Pray for us. Pray for us.
Save your peo - ple. Save your peo - ple. Save your peo - ple.
Hear our prayer. Hear our prayer. Hear our prayer.

D.S.

1.- 4. All you ho - ly men and wo - men, pray for us.
5.- 6. Christ, hear us; Lord Je - sus, hear our prayer.

Text: Litany of the Saints
Tune: John D. Becker, © 1987, published by OCP Publications

797 Covenant Hymn

1. Wher - ev - er you go, I will fol - low, Wher -
2. What - ev - er you dream, I am with you, When
3. And though you should fall, you will find me, When
4. Wher - ev - er you die, I will be there To
5. Wher - ev - er you go, I will fol - low, Be -

ev - er you live is my home. Though
stars call your name in the night. Though
no oth - er friend can you claim, When
sing you to sleep with a psalm, To
hold! The ho - ri - zon shines clear. The

days be of bless - ing or sor - row, Though
shad - ows and mist cloud the fu - ture, To -
foes beat you down or be - tray you And
soothe you with tales of our jour - ney, Your
pos - si - ble gleams like a cit - y: To -

house be of can - vas or stone, Though
geth - er we bear there a light. Like
oth - ers de - sert you in shame. When
fears and your doubts I will calm. We'll
geth - er we've noth - ing to fear. So

E - den be lost to the past, Though
A - bram and Sar - ah we stand, With
home and dreams aren't e - nough, And
live when jour - neys are done For -
speak with words bold and true The

moun - tains be - fore us be vast, Wher -
on - ly a prom - ise in hand. But
you run a - way from my love, I'll
ev - er in mem - 'ry as one. And
mes - sage my heart speaks to you. You

ev - er	you	go,	I	am	with you,	I
lead	where	you dream:	I	will	fol - low.	To
raise	you	from where	you	have	fall - en.	
we	will	be bur - ied	to -		geth - er,	And
won't	be	a - lone,	I	have	prom - ised.	Wher -

nev - er	will	leave	you	a -	lone.
dream	with	you	is	my	de -	light.
Faith - ful	to	you	is	my	name.
wak - en	to	greet	a	new	dawn.
ev - er	you	go,	I	am	here.

Text: Ruth 1:16; Rory Cooney, b.1952
Tune: Gary Daigle, b.1957
© 1993, GIA Publications, Inc.

Baptized in Water 798

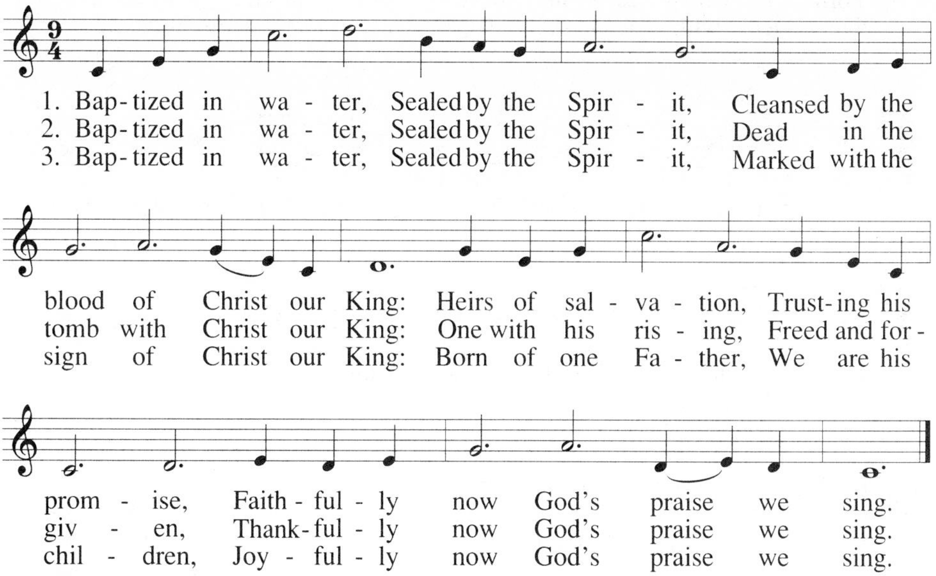

1. Bap- tized in wa - ter, Sealed by the Spir - it, Cleansed by the
2. Bap- tized in wa - ter, Sealed by the Spir - it, Dead in the
3. Bap- tized in wa - ter, Sealed by the Spir - it, Marked with the

blood of Christ our King: Heirs of sal - va - tion, Trust- ing his
tomb with Christ our King: One with his ris - ing, Freed and for -
sign of Christ our King: Born of one Fa - ther, We are his

prom - ise, Faith - ful - ly now God's praise we sing.
giv - en, Thank - ful - ly now God's praise we sing.
chil - dren, Joy - ful - ly now God's praise we sing.

Text: Michael Saward, b.1932, © 1982, Hope Publishing Co.
Tune: BUNESSAN, 5 5 8 D; Gaelic melody; acc. by Marty Haugen, b.1950, © 1987, GIA Publications, Inc.

799 Alive in Christ Jesus

Refrain

A - live! A - live in Christ Je - sus! A - live!

New life from the dead! A - live! For death has no

pow - er! We are a - live with God!

Verse 1

All: 1. Are you not a - ware? *Cantor:* We who were
We were

born in Christ Je - sus were born in - to his death.
bur - ied with Je - sus that we too might live?

All: Are you not a - ware? *Cantor:* We are u - nit - ed with

him, so that we will rise now with him. **D.C.**

Verse 2

All: 2. This we know: *Cantor:* That our
If we have
The

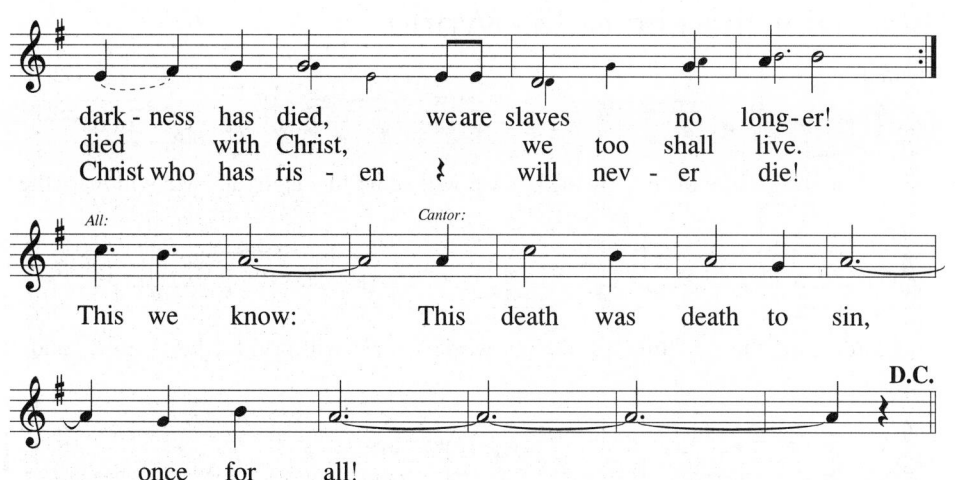

dark - ness has died, we are slaves no long - er!
died with Christ, we too shall live.
Christ who has ris - en 〉 will nev - er die!

All: *Cantor:*

This we know: This death was death to sin,

D.C.

once for all!

Text: Romans 8; David Haas, b.1957
Tune: David Haas, b.1957
© 1991, GIA Publications, Inc.

O Breathe on Me, O Breath of God   800

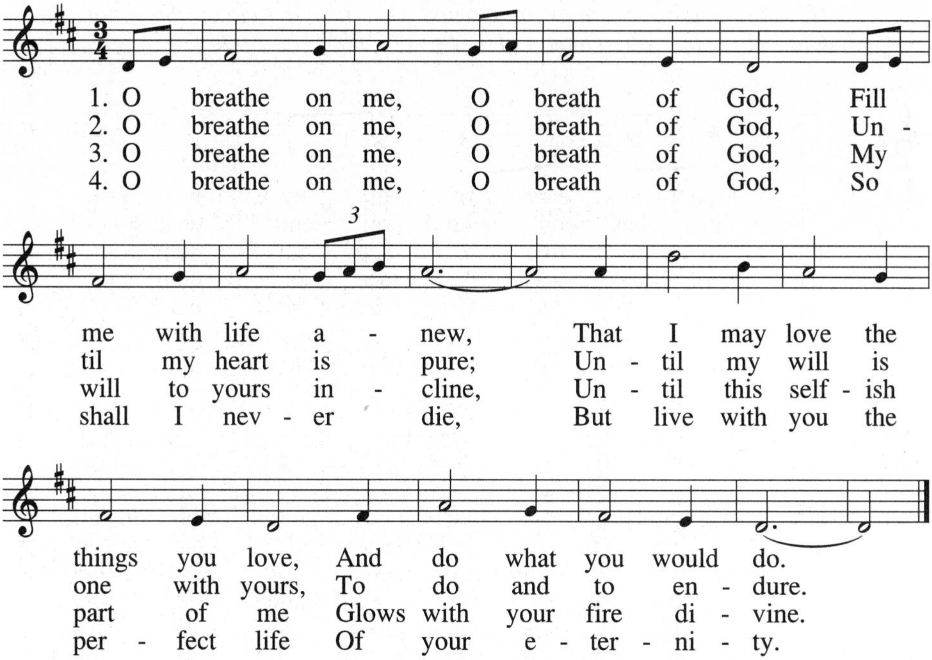

1. O breathe on me, O breath of God, Fill
2. O breathe on me, O breath of God, Un -
3. O breathe on me, O breath of God, My
4. O breathe on me, O breath of God, So

me with life a - new, That I may love the
til my heart is pure; Un - til my will is
will to yours in - cline, Un - til this self - ish
shall I nev - er die, But live with you the

things you love, And do what you would do.
one with yours, To do and to en - dure.
part of me Glows with your fire di - vine.
per - fect life Of your e - ter - ni - ty.

Text: Edwin Hatch, 1835-1889
Tune: ST. COLUMBA, CM; Gaelic; harm. by A. Gregory Murray, OSB, 1905-1992, © Downside Abbey

801 For the Life of the World

Refrain

For the life of the world, we will stand to-geth-er, we will serve the

Lord. For the life of the world, we will cry for jus-tice, and

ev-'ry heart will sing that Je-sus Christ is Lord!

Verses

1. We walk to-geth-er to be chil-dren of light,
2. We are em-pow-ered by the love of Christ,
3. We are the cho-sen peo-ple God has called,
4. The lost and bro-ken will be healed from their shame,
1. *Nos da la fuer-za el a - mor de Dios.*
2. *Hoy lu-char - e - mos por jus - ti - cia, Se - ñor.*
3. *Glo-ri - fi - que-mos al Se - ñor, Je - sus.*

our God calls each of us by name!
whose life has con-quered sin and death!
the life we live is not our own!
the poor will see the face of God!
Su vi - da qui - ta nues - tro mal.
Te ser - vir - e - mos y por fin.
Can - tan - do le - van - té - mos - nos,

Christ moves with-in us, we are God's work of art!
There is no oth-er name but Je - sus the Lord!
If we will die with Christ, then we will be free!
Sent by the Spir-it, we are called to serve!
No que - da na - die me - nos el Se - ñor.
Ten - dre-mos paz sin ham - bre ni do - lor.
Por - que él vie - ne ¡a - le - gré - mo - nos!

D.C.

1.-4. We live no long - er for our - selves!
1.-3. ¡So - mos el pueb - lo de Dios!

Text: David Haas, b.1957; Spanish verses by Jeffrey Judge
Tune: David Haas, b.1957; acc. by Jeanne Cotter, b.1964
© 1993, GIA Publications, Inc.

I've Just Come from the Fountain   802

I've just come from the foun-tain, I've just come from the

foun - tain, Lord, I've just come from the foun - tain, His

name's so sweet.   O broth-ers, I love Je - sus, O
        O sis - ters, I love Je - sus, O
        Been drink - ing from the foun - tain, Been

broth-ers, I love Je - sus, O broth-ers, I love
sis - ters, I love Je - sus, O sis - ters, I love
drink - ing from the foun-tain, Been drink - ing from the

Je - sus,
Je - sus, His name's so sweet.
foun-tain,

Text: African-American spiritual
Tune: African-American spiritual

803   Awake, O Sleeper

Refrain

A - wake, O sleep-er, a - rise from death, a - ban-don the shad-ows of

night;   the wind of the spir - it shall be your breath, and

Christ will fill you with light.

Verses 1, 2

1. Once you were dark - ness, once you were lost in the
2. Live as God's peo - ple, live as God's jus - tice and

shad - ows.   Once you were dark - ness,
mer - cy,   filled with com - pas - sion,

D.C.

now you are chil - dren of light.
filled with the pow - er of love.

Verse 3

3. Shine out with the splen-dor of love, shine with

jus-tice and right-eous-ness.   Sing the mu-sic your spir-it has

D.C.

heard, the songs of glo - ry and light.

Text: Ephesians 5; Marty Haugen, b.1950
Tune: Marty Haugen, b.1950
© 1987, GIA Publications, Inc.

Little Heart of Ages   804

1. Lit - tle heart of a - ges, spir - it child;
2. Ev - 'ry lamb is yours, Lord, ev - 'ry one,
3. Wel-come to the chil - dren on their way,

Heav - en - ly our dream - er, here you lie;
Leap - ing out of time now, to the sun;
Bless-ings to all pil - grims on this day;

Light is all a - bout you, Pet - al now e - ter -
Nev - er was a soul born that was not a treas -
Glo - ry to the light that leads us to the king -

nal; Lit - tle heart of a - ges,
ure; Ev - 'ry lamb is yours, Lord,
dom; Wel - come to the chil - dren

spir - it child.
ev - 'ry one.
on their way.

Text: Michael Dennis Browne
Tune: John Foley, SJ, b. 1939
© 1993, GIA Publications, Inc.

805 Sign Me Up

Refrain

Sign me up, Sign me up for the Chris-tian ju-bi-lee,

Write my name, Write my name on the roll

For, I've been changed, I've been changed since the

Lord has lift-ed me, I want to be

ready when Je-sus comes.

Verse 1

1. When Je-sus comes, oh, the trum-pet will sound

loud, When my Sav-ior comes, all the

saints in Christ shall rise, Oh, I'm glad I've been

changed since he lift-ed me, I

want to be read-y when Je-sus comes.

Verse 2

2. You know not the day nor the hour he shall ap-

pear, But we know in our hearts that he's

com-ing back a - gain, My heart is fixed

and my mind's made up. I want to be

D.C.

read - y when Je - sus comes.

Text: Kevin Yancy and Jerome Metcalfe
Tune: Kevin Yancy and Jerome Metcalfe; harm. by Kenneth Morris
© 1979, Kevin Yancy and Jerome Metcalfe

806 I Come with Joy to Meet My Lord

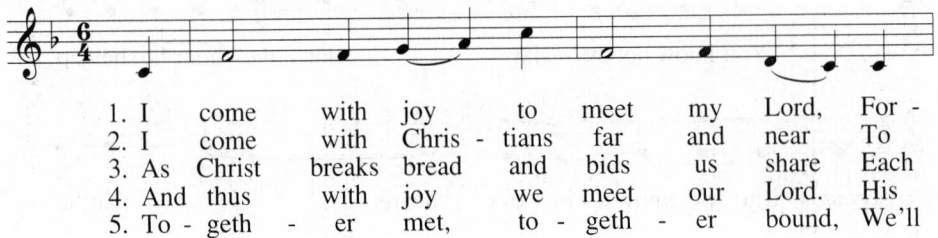

1. I come with joy to meet my Lord, For -
2. I come with Chris - tians far and near To
3. As Christ breaks bread and bids us share Each
4. And thus with joy we meet our Lord. His
5. To - geth - er met, to - geth - er bound, We'll

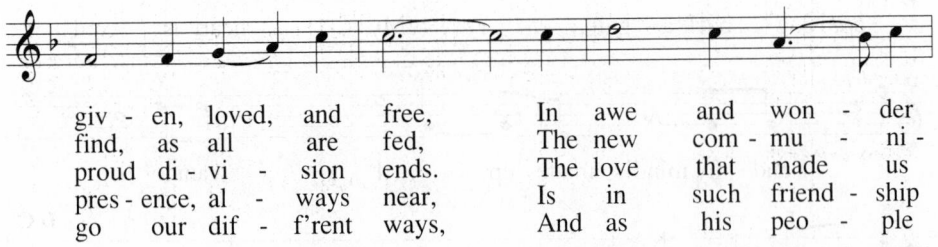

giv - en, loved, and free, In awe and won - der
find, as all are fed, The new com - mu - ni -
proud di - vi - sion ends. The love that made us
pres - ence, al - ways near, Is in such friend - ship
go our dif - f'rent ways, And as his peo - ple

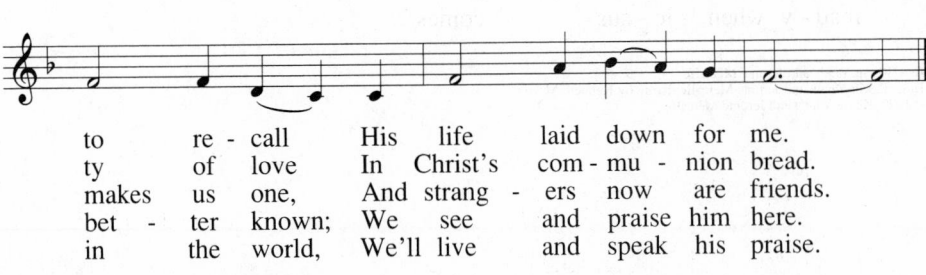

to re - call His life laid down for me.
ty of love In Christ's com - mu - nion bread.
makes us one, And strang - ers now are friends.
bet - ter known; We see and praise him here.
in the world, We'll live and speak his praise.

Text: Brian Wren, b.1936, © 1971, Hope Publishing Co.
Tune: LAND OF REST, CM; American; harm. by Annabel M. Buchanan, b. 1888, © 1938, 1966, J. Fisher and Bro.

Come and Let Us Drink of That New River 807

1. Come and let us drink of that new riv - er,
2. Now the world has bright il - lu - mi - na - tion,
3. Yes - ter - day with you in bur - ial ly - ing,

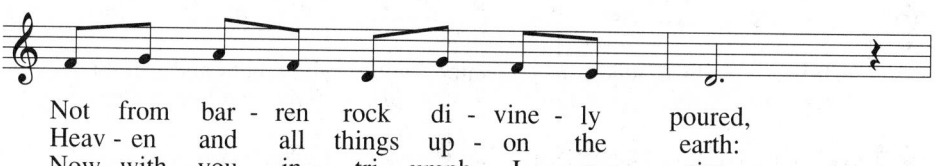

Not from bar - ren rock di - vine - ly poured,
Heav - en and all things up - on the earth:
Now with you in tri - umph I a - rise,

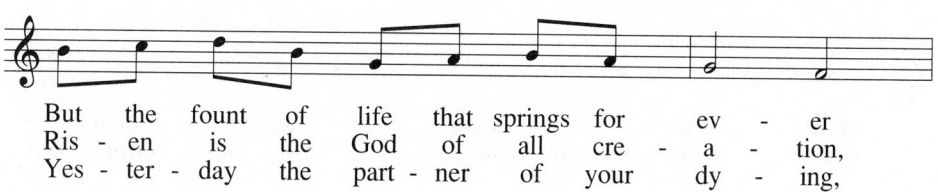

But the fount of life that springs for ev - er
Ris - en is the God of all cre - a - tion,
Yes - ter - day the part - ner of your dy - ing,

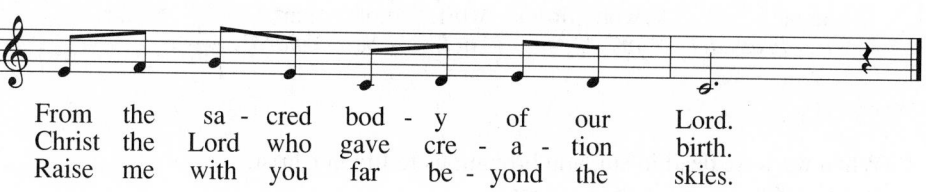

From the sa - cred bod - y of our Lord.
Christ the Lord who gave cre - a - tion birth.
Raise me with you far be - yond the skies.

Text: John of Damascus, c.675-746; tr. by John M. Neale, 1818-1866, adapt. by Anthony G. Petti, 1932-1985, © 1971, Faber Music Ltd.
Tune: NEW RIVER, 10 9 10 9; Kenneth D. Smith, b.1928

808 We Are God's Work of Art / Somos la Creación de Dios

Refrain

We are God's work of art, fash-ioned in
So-mos la crea - ción de Dios, co - mo en

Christ, fash-ioned to shine with good-ness and light.
Cris - to, el nos hi - zo bri - llar con su luz.

As it was from the start— formed by this
A - sí fue al co - men - zar, con gran a -

great, great love, we are God's
mor, el nos for - mó, so - mos gran - des

great, won - drous work of art.
o - bras del ar - te del Se - ñor.

Verses

1. When we were dead in sin, you brought us to life in Christ,
   and raised us up, up to the heavens.

1. *Cuando en pecado morimos,*
   nos trajo la vida en Cristo y nos llevó a las alturas.

2. How rich is the grace of God, how strong is the love of God,
   to send us Christ for our salvation.

2. *Qué rica es la gracia de Dios qué fuerte es su amor,*
   envió a Cristo para nuestra salvacion.

3. We are strangers no longer, outcasts no longer,
   we are saints in the house of God.

3. *No somos extranjeros, no mas desterrados,*
   somos santos en la casa del Señor.

4. We are the temple that our God has fashioned,
   in Christ we are the dwelling place of love.

4. Somos el templo que_el Señor hizo,
   en Cristo somos morada de su_amor.

5. From the foundation of the world you have chosen us,
   destined in love to be your sons and daughters.
   You have revealed to us the myst'ry of grace, to unite all things in Christ.

5. Desde_el principio del mundo nos escogiste el destino de ser tus hijos y tus hijas.
   Nos reveló el misterio de gracia, para unir todas las cosas en Cristo.

Text: Ephesians 2:1, 4-7, 10, 19, 21-22; Marty Haugen, b.1950; Spanish trans. by Donna Peña, b.1955
Tune: Marty Haugen, b.1950
© 1991, GIA Publications, Inc.

There Is One Lord   809

Ostinato Refrain

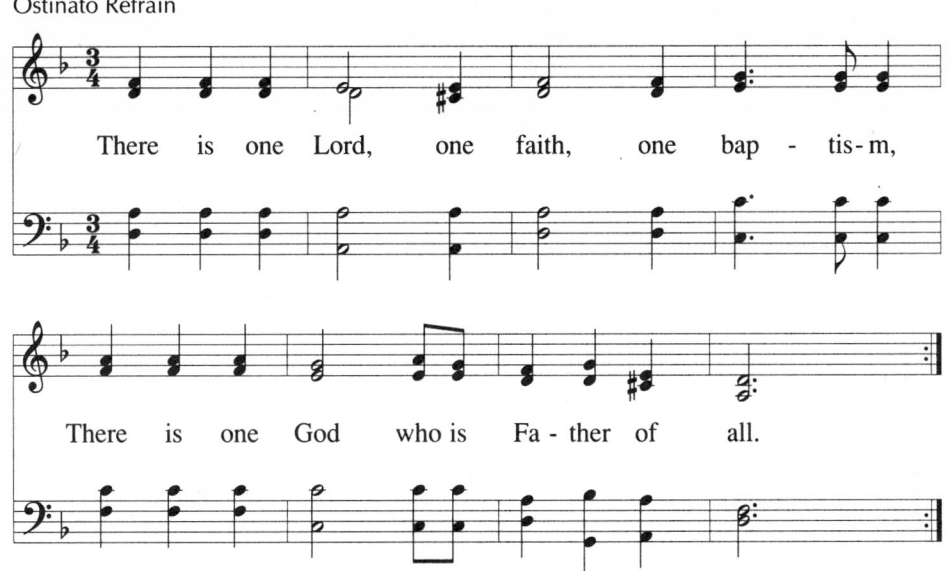

There is one Lord, one faith, one bap - tis-m,

There is one God who is Fa - ther of all.

Text: Ephesians 4. Taizé Community, 1984
Tune: Jacques Berthier, 1923-1994
© 1984, Les Presses de Taizé, GIA Publications, Inc., agent

810 You Are God's Work of Art

Refrain

You are God's work of art, cre -

at - ed in Je - sus the Christ.

Verses

1. You have been en - light-ened by the Lord.
2. Keep the flame of faith in your heart, and
3. Bless - ed be our God, who

D.C.

Walk as chil - dren of the light.
may you meet him when he comes.
chose you in the light of Christ.

Text: Ephesians 1:4, 2:10, *Rite of Baptism*, David Haas, b.1957
Tune: David Haas, b.1957
© 1988, GIA Publications, Inc.

811 Christ Will Be Your Strength

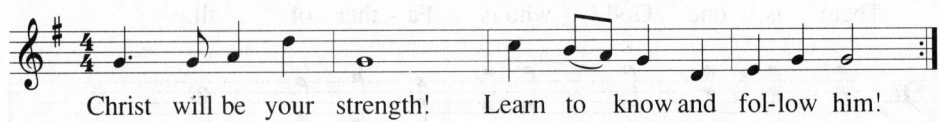

Christ will be your strength! Learn to know and fol-low him!

Text: David Haas, b.1957
Tune: David Haas, b.1957
© 1988, GIA Publications, Inc.

Wade in the Water 812

Refrain

Wade in the wa-ter, wade in the wa-ter, chil-dren, wade in the wa-ter, God's a gon-na trou-ble the wa-ter.

Verses

Cantor:

1. See that host all dressed in white,
2. See that band all dressed in red,
3. Look o-ver yon-der, what do I see?
4. If you don't be-lieve I've been re-deemed,

All:

God's a gon-na trou-ble the wa-ter; The
God's a gon-na trou-ble the wa-ter; Looks
God's a gon-na trou-ble the wa-ter; The
God's a gon-na trou-ble the wa-ter; Just

Cantor:

lead-er looks like the Is-ra-el-ite,
like the band that Mo-ses led,
Ho-ly Ghost a com-in' on me,
fol-low me down to Jor-dan's stream,

All:

D.C.

God's a gon-na trou-ble the wa-ter.
God's a gon-na trou-ble the wa-ter.
God's a gon-na trou-ble the wa-ter.
God's a gon-na trou-ble the wa-ter.

Text: African-American spiritual
Tune: African-American spiritual; harm. by Diana Kodner, b.1957. © 1994, GIA Publications, Inc.

813 Song of the Chosen

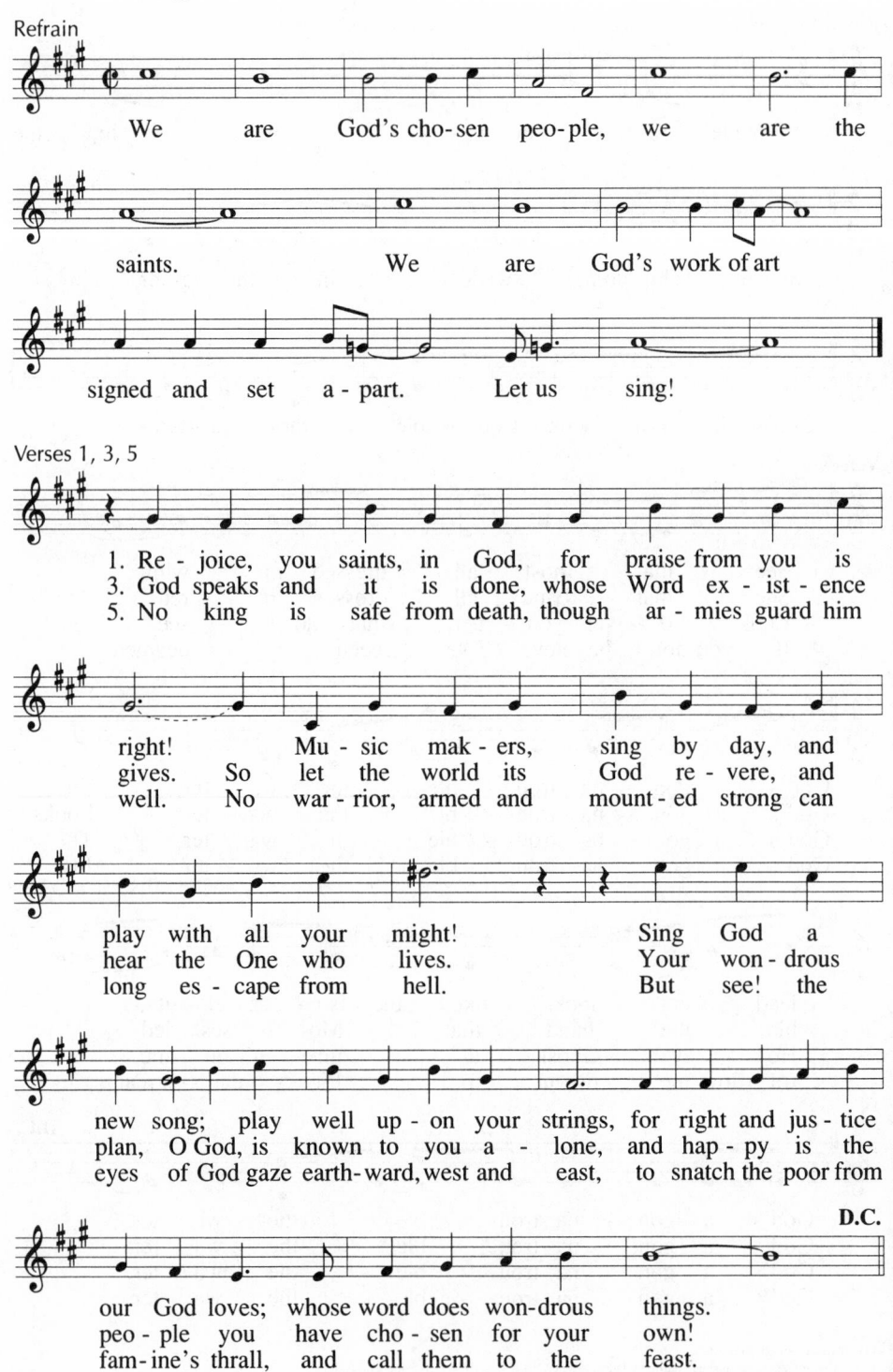

Refrain

We are God's cho-sen peo-ple, we are the saints. We are God's work of art signed and set a - part. Let us sing!

Verses 1, 3, 5

1. Re - joice, you saints, in God, for praise from you is right! Mu - sic mak - ers, sing by day, and play with all your might! Sing God a new song; play well up - on your strings, for right and jus - tice our God loves; whose word does won-drous things.

3. God speaks and it is done, whose Word ex - ist - ence gives. So let the world its God re - vere, and hear the One who lives. Your won - drous plan, O God, is known to you a - lone, and hap - py is the peo - ple you have cho - sen for your own!

5. No king is safe from death, though ar - mies guard him well. No war - rior, armed and mount - ed strong can long es - cape from hell. But see! the eyes of God gaze earth-ward, west and east, to snatch the poor from fam - ine's thrall, and call them to the feast.

D.C.

Verses 2, 4, 6

2. God's kind-ness fills our world, whose word the
4. From heav-en, our God sees the ways of
6. So wait up - on the One who is our

heav-ens forms, Whose sing - ing mouth, to
hu - man - kind. God knows the dwell-ers
help and shield. Re - joice, you saints, in

north and south, has spo - ken stars and storms, Whose
of our globe, and probes the heart and mind. No,
that great name, pro - claim God's might re - vealed.

might for-bids the waves to tres-pass on the land
none es-capes the glance of God who reigns on high,
May your kind-ness, God, be on us all our days,

And gath - ers all the o - ceans up to
No se - cret can cre - a - tion keep on
We hope in you, we trust in you, to

cup them in a hand, Who
earth or sea or sky, No
you be end - less praise, We

gath - ers all the o - ceans up to
se - cret can cre - a - tion keep on
hope in you, we trust in you, to

D.C.

cup them in a hand.
earth or sea or sky.
you be end - less praise.

Text: Psalm 33; Rory Cooney, b.1952
Tune: Rory Cooney, b.1952
© 1986, North American Liturgy Resources

814 Taste and See

Text: Psalm 34; James E. Moore, Jr., b.1951
Tune: James E. Moore, Jr., b.1951
© 1983, GIA Publications, Inc.

You Satisfy the Hungry Heart 815

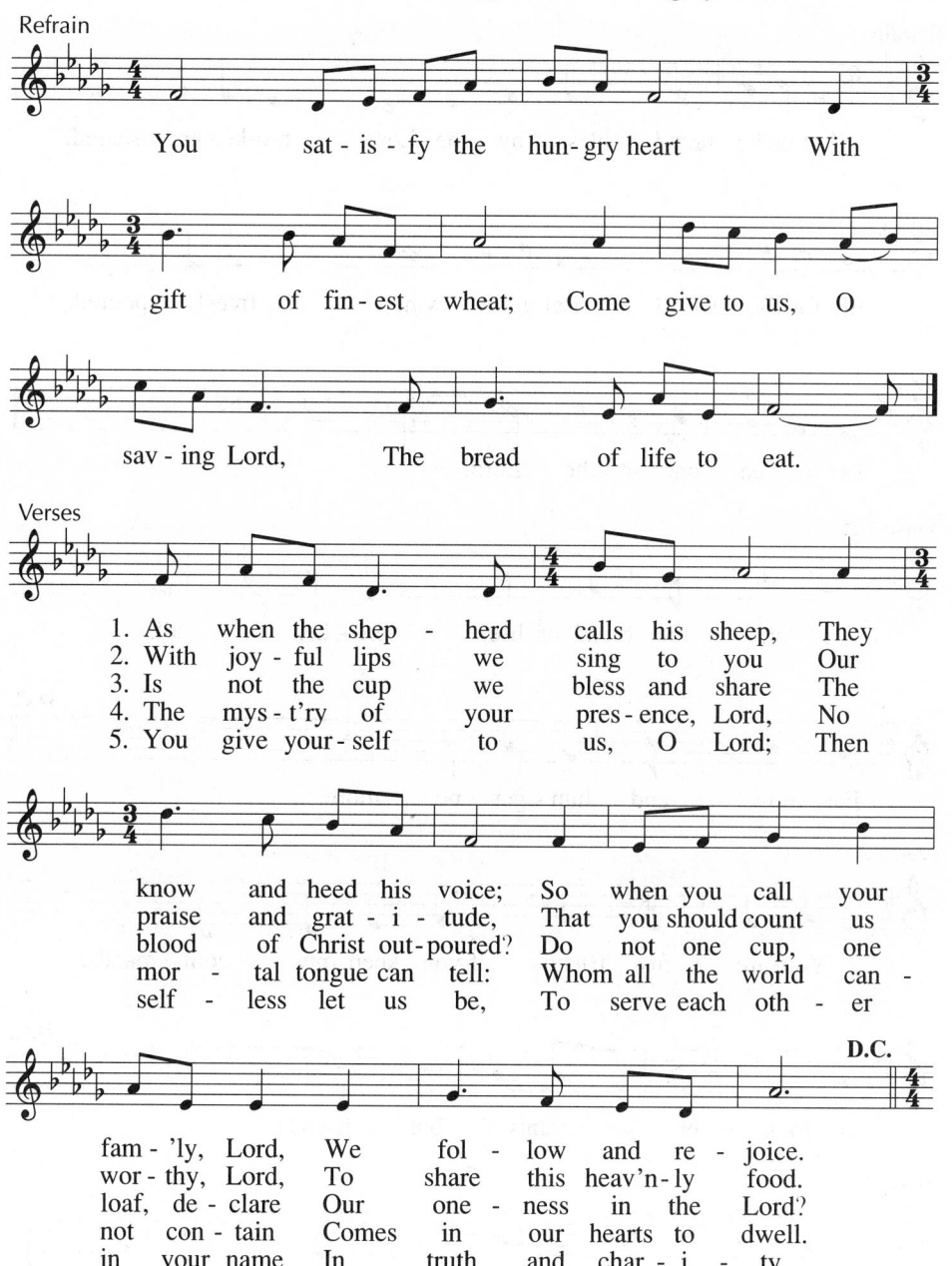

Refrain

You sat - is - fy the hun- gry heart With gift of fin - est wheat; Come give to us, O sav - ing Lord, The bread of life to eat.

Verses

1. As when the shep - herd calls his sheep, They
2. With joy - ful lips we sing to you Our
3. Is not the cup we bless and share The
4. The mys - t'ry of your pres - ence, Lord, No
5. You give your - self to us, O Lord; Then

know and heed his voice; So when you call your
praise and grat - i - tude, That you should count us
blood of Christ out- poured? Do not one cup, one
mor - tal tongue can tell: Whom all the world can -
self - less let us be, To serve each oth - er

D.C.

fam - 'ly, Lord, We fol - low and re - joice.
wor - thy, Lord, To share this heav'n - ly food.
loaf, de - clare Our one - ness in the Lord?
not con - tain Comes in our hearts to dwell.
in your name In truth and char - i - ty.

Text: Omer Westendorf, b.1916
Tune: BICENTENNIAL, CM, with refrain; Robert E. Kreutz, b.1922
© 1977, Archdiocese of Philadelphia

816   Let Us Be Bread

Refrain

Let us be bread, blessed by the Lord, bro-ken and shared, life for the world. Let us be wine, love free-ly poured. Let us be one in the Lord.

Verse 1

1. I am the bread of life, bro-ken for all. Eat now and hun-ger no more.

D.C.

Verse 2

2. You are my friends if you keep my com-mands, no long - er ser - vants but friends.

D.C.

Verse 3

3. See how my peo-ple have noth-ing to eat. Give them the bread that is you.

D.C.

Verse 4

4. As God has loved me so I have loved you.

D.C.

Go and live on in my love.

Text: Thomas J. Porter, b.1958
Tune: Thomas J. Porter, b.1958
© 1990, GIA Publications, Inc.

Jesus, Wine of Peace 817

Refrain

Je - sus, wine of peace, wine of love, may we drink of

you; may we taste your pres-ence, your prom-ise, our fu-ture.

Verses

1. I will be the path that guides you, I will save you.
2. You will nev - er be a - lone, I am with you.
3. You will nev - er thirst a - gain, I will fill you.
4. You will laugh and sing a - gain in my pres - ence.
5. You will live in fear no more, peace be with you.
6. I have come that you may live, I am with you.
7. You will rise and live a - new in my king - dom.
8. I will be your one true shep - herd, I will guide you.
9. I will be your light in dark - ness, I will save you.
10. No more weep - ing, no more pain in my king - dom.

D.C.

Drink well, drink and live.

Text: David Haas, b.1957
Tune: David Haas, b.1957
© 1985, GIA Publications, Inc.

818 As We Remember

Refrain

As we re - mem-ber,   we are be - com-ing;   what we see

bro-ken,   we hope to be.   Show us your mer-cy,   show us your

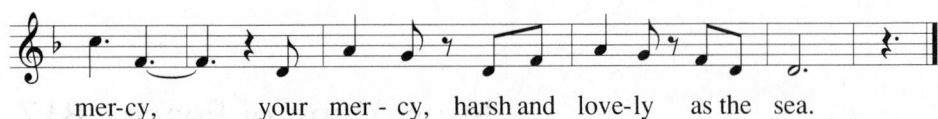

mer-cy,   your mer - cy,   harsh and love-ly   as the sea.

Verses 1, 2, 4, 5, 7, 8

1. Wind-fall	of	way -	bread		scat-tered on	sand,
2. Pass - o - ver		Lamb,			slain and con -	sumed
4. No	one	re - joic -	es	or	suf - fers a -	lone:
5. Each	has	been	washed,		each is a -	noint-ed,
7. Cup	of	for - give -	ness,		bread of our	peace;
8. Feast	of	be - long -	ing,		feast for the	lost;

D.C.

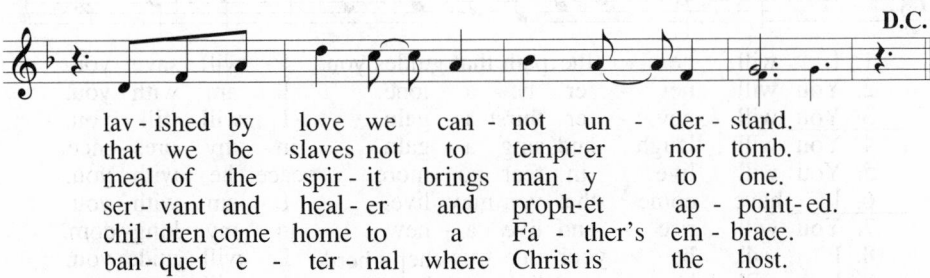

lav - ished by   love we   can - not   un - der - stand.
that we   be   slaves not   to   tempt-er   nor   tomb.
meal of the   spir - it   brings   man - y   to   one.
ser - vant and   heal - er   and   proph-et   ap - point-ed.
chil-dren come   home to   a   Fa - ther's   em - brace.
ban-quet   e - ter - nal   where   Christ is   the   host.

Verses 3, 6, 9, 10

3. Here	are our	hearts	marked with	blood	of	the	lamb:
6. Tem -	ple not	built	by	mus - cle	and	bone:
9. Christ	in the	meal	to	which	we	are	called
10. Love	of the	Fa - ther,		Spir - it	of	Christ,

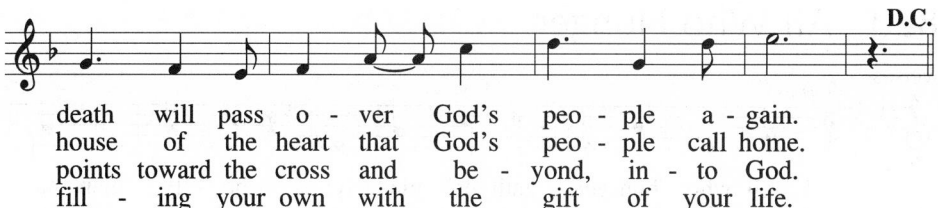

D.C.

death will pass o - ver God's peo - ple a - gain.
house of the heart that God's peo - ple call home.
points toward the cross and be - yond, in - to God.
fill - ing your own with the gift of your life.

Text: Rory Cooney, b.1952
Tune: Rory Cooney, b.1952, acc. alt.
© 1987, North American Liturgy Resources

You Are Our Living Bread 819

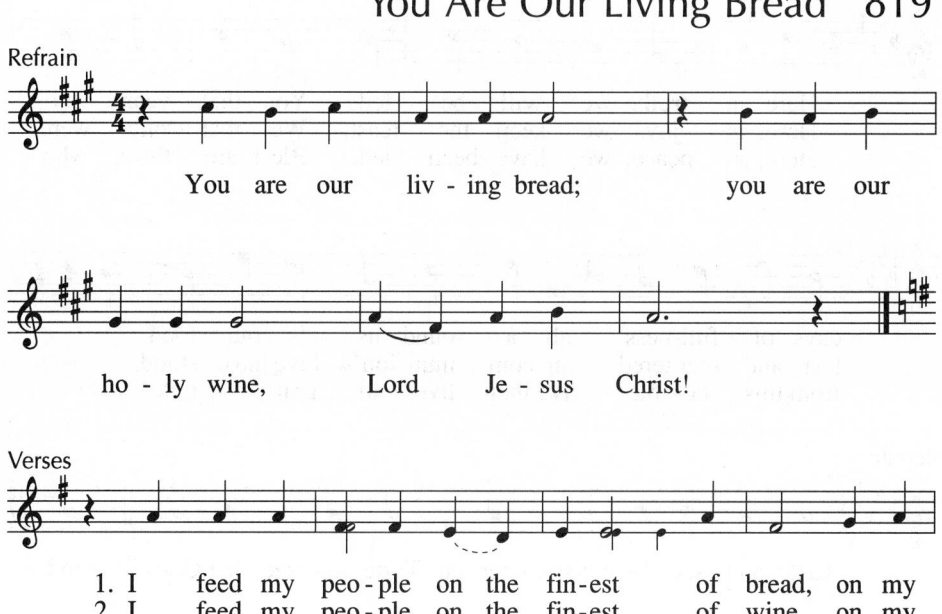

Refrain

You are our liv - ing bread; you are our

ho - ly wine, Lord Je - sus Christ!

Verses

1. I feed my peo - ple on the fin - est of bread, on my
2. I feed my peo - ple on the fin - est of wine, on my
3. Where two or three have gath-ered in my name, there am

D.C.

bod - y bro - ken for them.
blood of suf - f'ring and shame.
I in the midst— of—— them.

Text: Michael Joncas, b.1955
Tune: Michael Joncas, b.1955
© 1979, New Dawn Music

820 All Who Hunger

Verses

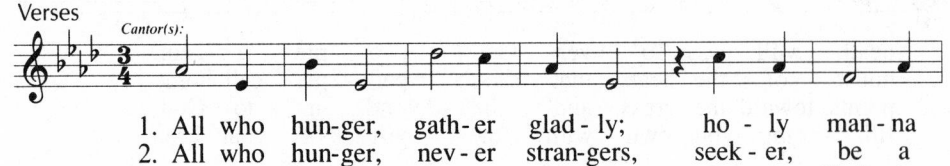

1. All who hun-ger, gath-er glad-ly; ho - ly man-na
2. All who hun-ger, nev-er stran-gers, seek - er, be a
3. All who hun-ger, sing to - geth-er; Je - sus Christ is

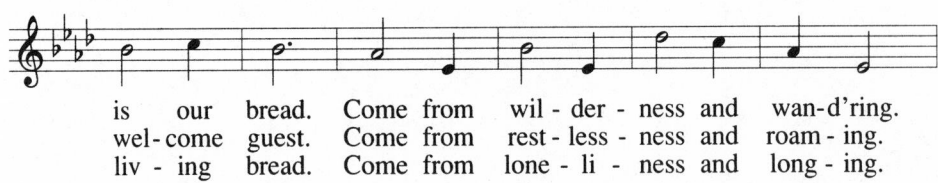

is our bread. Come from wil - der - ness and wan-d'ring.
wel - come guest. Come from rest - less - ness and roam - ing.
liv - ing bread. Come from lone - li - ness and long - ing.

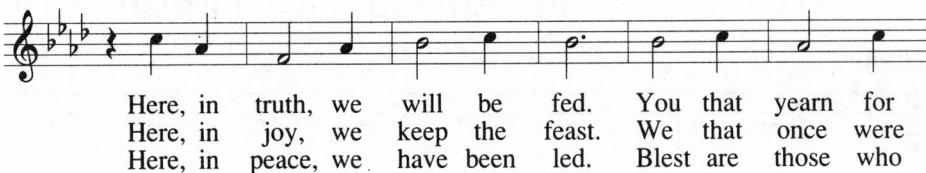

Here, in truth, we will be fed. You that yearn for
Here, in joy, we keep the feast. We that once were
Here, in peace, we have been led. Blest are those who

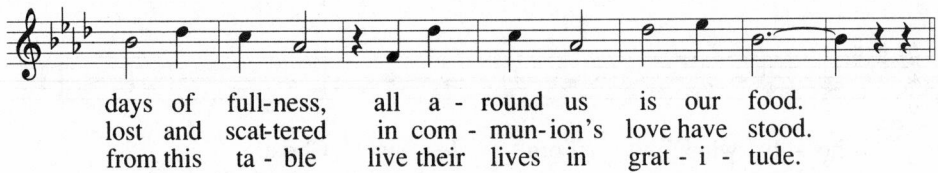

days of full-ness, all a - round us is our food.
lost and scat-tered in com - mun-ion's love have stood.
from this ta - ble live their lives in grat - i - tude.

Refrain

Taste and see the grace e - ter-nal. Taste and see that God is good.

Text: Sylvia G. Dunstan, 1955-1993, © 1991, GIA Publications, Inc.
Tune: Bob Moore, b. 1962, © 1993, GIA Publications, Inc.

Bread of Life, Hope of the World   821

Refrain

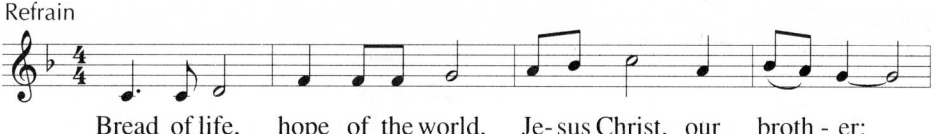

Bread of life,   hope of the world,   Je-sus Christ, our   broth-er:

Last time

feed us now,   give us life,   lead us   to   one an-oth-er.

Verses

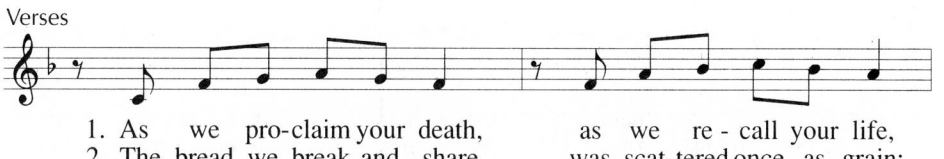

1. As   we   pro-claim your death,   as   we   re-call your life,
2. The bread we break and   share   was scat-tered once as grain:
3. We   eat   this   liv-ing bread,   we drink this sav-ing cup:
4. Hold   us   in   u-ni-ty,   in love for   all   to   see;
5. You   are   the bread of peace,   you are   the wine of   joy,

D.C.

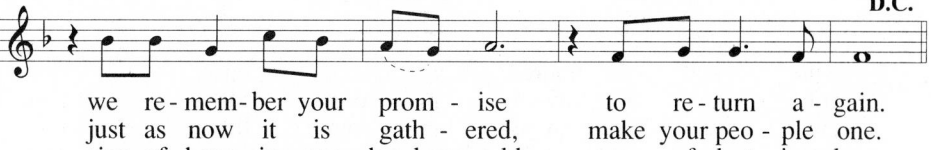

we   re-mem-ber your   prom-ise   to   re-turn   a-gain.
just   as   now   it   is   gath-ered,   make your peo-ple one.
sign   of   hope   in   our   bro-ken world,   source of last-ing love.
that the world may be-lieve in   you,   God   of   all   who live.
bro-ken now for your   peo-ple,   poured in   end-less love.

Text: Bernadette Farrell, b.1957
Tune: Bernadette Farrell, b.1957
© 1982, 1987, Bernadette Farrell, published by OCP Publications

822 Life-Giving Bread, Saving Cup

Refrain

Life-giv-ing bread, sav-ing cup, we of-fer in thanks-giv-ing, O God.

Life-giv-ing bread sav-ing cup, we of-fer as a sign of our love.

Verses

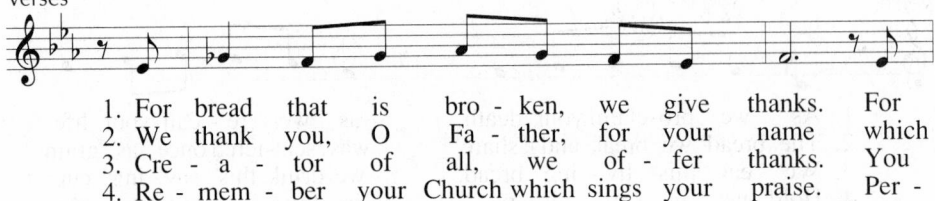

1. For bread that is bro - ken, we give thanks. For
2. We thank you, O Fa - ther, for your name which
3. Cre - a - tor of all, we of - fer thanks. You
4. Re - mem - ber your Church which sings your praise. Per -

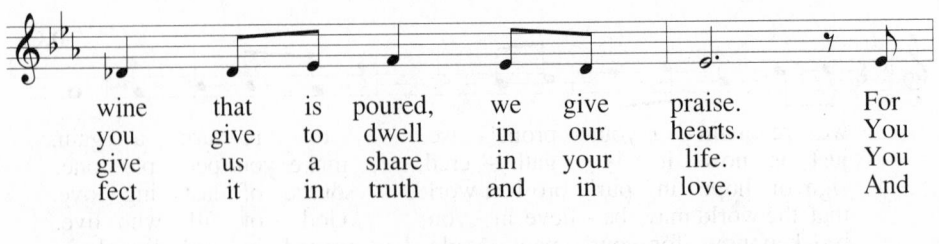

wine that is poured, we give praise. For
you give to dwell in our hearts. You
give us a share in your life. You
fect it in truth and in love. And

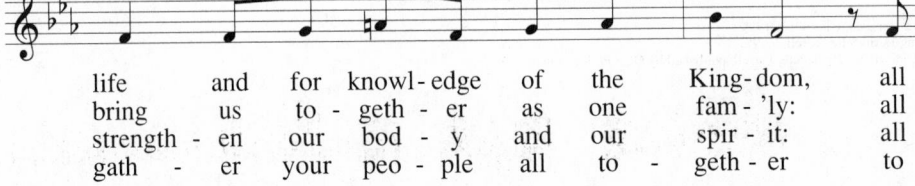

life and for knowl-edge of the King-dom, all
bring us to - geth - er as one fam - 'ly: all
strength - en our bod - y and our spir - it: all
gath - er your peo - ple all to - geth - er to

D.C.

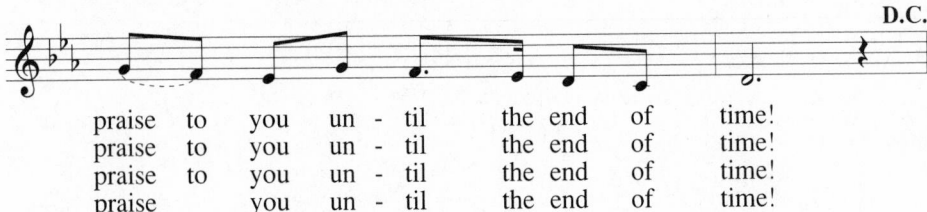

praise to you un - til the end of time!
praise to you un - til the end of time!
praise to you un - til the end of time!
praise you un - til the end of time!

Text: Adapted from the *Didache*, 2nd C.; James J. Chepponis, b.1956
Tune: James J. Chepponis, b.1956
© 1987, GIA Publications, Inc.

Behold the Lamb 823

Verses

1. Those who were in the dark are thank-ful for the
2. Peace-ful now, those whose hearts are blessed with un-der-
3. Gen-tle one, Child of God, join with us at this
4. Lord of all, give us light. De-liv-er us from

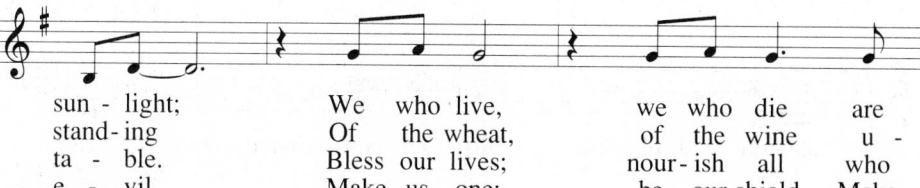

sun-light; We who live, we who die are
stand-ing Of the wheat, of the wine u-
ta-ble. Bless our lives; nour-ish all who
e-vil. Make us one; be our shield. Make

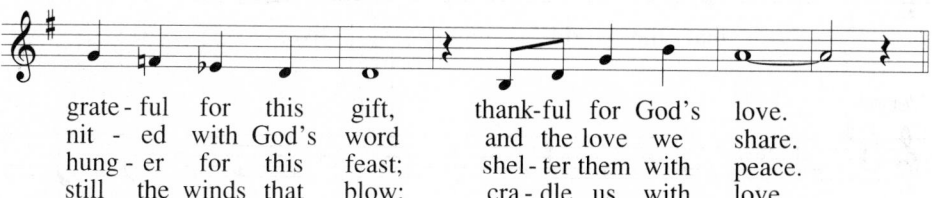

grate-ful for this gift, thank-ful for God's love.
nit-ed with God's word and the love we share.
hung-er for this feast; shel-ter them with peace.
still the winds that blow; cra-dle us with love.

Refrain

Be-hold, be-hold the Lamb of God. All who eat,

all who drink shall live; and all, all who dwell in

God, shall come to know God's glo-ry!

Text: Martin Willett
Tune: Martin Willett; acc. by Craig S. Kingsbury, b.1952
© 1984, OCP Publications

824 I Myself Am the Bread of Life

Refrain

I my-self am the bread of life.

You and I are the bread of life,

tak - en and blessed, bro - ken and shared by Christ

that the world might live.

Verses

1. This bread is spir - it, gift of the Mak - er's
2. Here is God's king-dom giv - en to us as
3. Lives bro - ken o - pen, sto - ries shared a -

love, and we who share it know that we can be
food. This is our bod - y, this is our
loud, be - come a ban - quet, a shel - ter for the

D.C.

one:
blood: a liv-ing sign of God in Christ.
world:

Text: Rory Cooney, b.1952
Tune: Rory Cooney, b.1952
© 1987, North American Liturgy Resources

As the Grains of Wheat   825

Refrain

As the grains of wheat once scat-tered on the hill were

gath-ered in-to one to be-come our bread;

so may all your peo-ple from all the ends of earth be

gath-ered in-to one in you.

Verses

1. As this cup of bless-ing is shared with-in our midst,
2. Let this be a fore-taste of all that is to come when

D.C.

    may we share the pres-ence of your love.
    all cre-a-tion shares this feast with you.

Text: Marty Haugen, b.1950
Tune: Marty Haugen, b.1950
© 1990, GIA Publications, Inc.

826 The Living Bread of God

Refrain

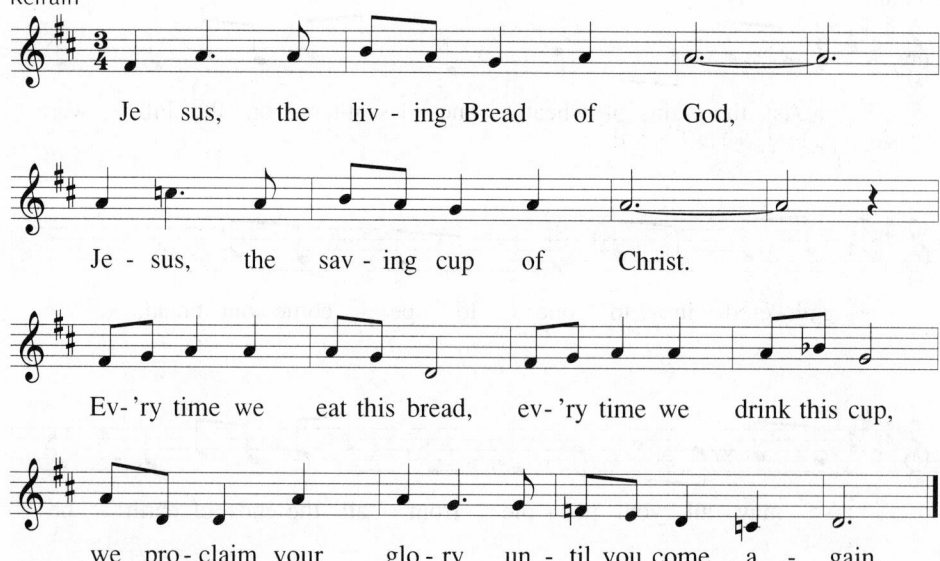

Je - sus, the liv - ing Bread of God,

Je - sus, the sav - ing cup of Christ.

Ev-'ry time we eat this bread, ev-'ry time we drink this cup,

we pro - claim your glo - ry un - til you come a - gain.

Verses

1. You are the bread of life.
   If we come to you, we will never be in need.
   If we believe in you, we will never thirst, and we will live for ever.

2. You are the life of the world.
   If we come to you, we will never know death.
   If we eat of this bread, we will be renewed, and and we will live for ever.

3. You are the living bread,
   our bread from heaven, our food from above.
   If we eat and drink, we will be like you, and we will live for ever.

4. You are the living Christ.
   If we follow you, we will see the face of God.
   If we die with you, we will rise again, and we will live for ever.

Text: 1 Corinthians 11:26; David Haas, b.1957
Tune: Kate Cuddy
© 1992, GIA Publications, Inc.

Bread for the World 827

Refrain

Bread for the world: a world of hun - ger.

Wine for all peo - ples: peo - ple who thirst. May we who eat

be bread for oth - ers. May we who drink pour out our love.

Verses

1. Lord Je - sus Christ, you are the bread of life, bro - ken to
2. Lord Je - sus Christ, you are the wine of peace, poured in - to
3. Lord Je - sus Christ, you call us to your feast, at which the

reach and heal the wounds of hu - man pain. Where we di -
hearts once bro - ken and where dry - ness sleeps. Where we are
rich and pow'r - ful have be - come the least. Where we sur -

vide your peo - ple you are wait - ing there on bend - ed
tired and wea - ry you are wait - ing there to be the
vive on oth - ers in our hu - man greed you walk a -

D.C.

knee to wash our feet with end - less care.
way which beck - ons us be - yond des - pair.
mong us beg - ging for your ev - 'ry need.

Text: Bernadette Farrell, b.1957
Tune: Bernadette Farrell, b.1957
© 1990, Bernadette Farrell, published by OCP Publications

828 I Am the Bread of Life / Yo Soy el Pan de Vida

Verses

1. ___ I am the Bread of life. You who
2. The bread that___ I will give is my
3. Un - less___ you___ eat of the
4. ___ I am the Res - ur - rec - tion, ___
5. Yes, Lord, ___ I be - lieve that___

1. ___ Yo soy el pan de vi - da. El que
2. El pan que___ yo da - ré___ es mi
3. ___ Mien - tras no co - mas el___
4. ___ Yo soy la re - su - rrec - ción. ___
5. ___ Sí, Se - ñor, yo cre - o que___

come to me shall not hun - ger; and who be -
flesh for the life of the world, ___ and if you
flesh of the Son of Man ___ and___
I ___ am the life. ___ If you be -
you ___ are the Christ, ___ the___

vie - ne a mí no ten - drá ham - bre. ___ El que
cuer - po ___ vi - da del mun - do, y el que
cuer - po del hi - jo del hom - bre, ___ y ___
Yo ___ soy la vi - da. ___ El que
tú e - res el Cris - to, ___ El___

lieve in me shall not thirst. ___ No one can come to
eat ___ of this bread, ___ you shall___ live for
drink ___ of his blood, ___ and drink ___ of his
lieve ___ in ___ me, ___ e - ven ___ though you
Son ___ of ___ God, ___ Who ___ has___

cree en mí no ten - drá sed. ___ Na - die ___ vie - ne a
co - ma ___ de mi car - ne ___ ten - drá ___ vi - da e -
be - bas ___ de su san - gre, y be - bas ___ de su
cree ___ en ___ mí, ___ aun - que ___ mu - rie -
Hi - jo de Dios, ___ que vi - no al

me   un - less   the___   Fa - ther___   beck-ons.
ev - er,___   you   shall___   live   for___   ev - er.
blood,   you   shall   not have life   with - in you.
die,___   you   shall___   live   for___   ev - er.
come   in - to___   the___   world.___
mí___   mien - tras el   Pa - dre nos   lla - me.
ter - na,___   ten - drá___   vi - da e - ter - na.
san - gre,   no   ten - drá___   vi - da___   en ti.
ra,___   ten - drá vi - da   e - ter - na.
mun - do___   pa - ra   sal - var-nos.

Refrain

And I will   raise   you   up,   and I will   raise   you
Yo le re - su - ci - ta - ré,   Yo le re - su - ci - ta -

up,   and I will raise   you up   on the last   day.
ré,   Yo le re - su - ci - ta - ré   el   di - a   de El.

Text: John 6; Suzanne Toolan, SM, b.1927; translator unknown
Tune: BREAD OF LIFE, Irregular with refrain; Suzanne Toolan, SM, b.1927; acc. by Diana Kodner, b.1957
© 1966, 1970, 1986, 1993, GIA Publications, Inc.

829 Shepherd of Our Hearts

Refrain

Shep-herd of our hearts, re - ceive our song of praise. Lead us to the King-dom, and guide us all our days.

Verses

1. Shep - herd of souls, re - fresh and bless your
2. We would not live by bread a - lone, but
3. Be known to us in break - ing bread, but
4. Lord, sup with us in love di - vine; your

cho - sen pil - grim flock with
by your word of grace, in
do not then de - part; O
Bod - y and your Blood, that

man - na in the wil - der - ness, with
strength of which we trav - el on to
Lord, a - bide with us, and spread your
liv - ing bread, that heav'n - ly wine be

D.C.

wa - ter from the rock.
our a - bid - ing place.
ta - ble in our heart.
our im - mor - tal food.

Text: Verses by James Montgomery, 1771-1854, alt; refrain by James J. Chepponis, b.1956
Tune: James J. Chepponis, b.1956
© 1988, GIA Publications, Inc.

One Bread, One Body   830

Refrain

One bread, one bod-y, one Lord of all, one cup of bless - ing which we bless. And we, though man-y, through-out the earth, we are one bod - y in this one Lord.

Verses

1. Gen - tile or Jew, ser - vant or free, wom - an or man no more.
2. Man - y the gifts, man - y the works, one in the Lord of all.
3. Grain for the fields, scat-tered and grown, gath-ered to one for all.

D.C.

Text: I Corinthians 10:16; 17, 12:4, Galatians 3:28; the *Didache* 9; John Foley, SJ, b.1939
Tune: John Foley, SJ, b.1939
©1978, John B. Foley, SJ, and New Dawn Music

831 Take and Eat

Refrain

Take and eat; take and eat: this is my bod - y
giv-en up for you. Take and drink; take and drink:
this is my blood giv - en up for you.

Verses

1. I am the Word that spoke and light was made;
2. I am the way that leads the ex - ile home;
3. I am the Lamb that takes a - way your sin;
4. I am the cor - ner-stone that God has laid;
5. I am the light that came in - to the world;
6. I am the first and last, the Liv - ing One;

I am the seed that died to be re - born;
I am the truth that sets the cap - tive free;
I am the gate that guards you night and day;
A cho-sen stone and pre - cious in his eyes;
I am the light that dark - ness can - not hide;
I am the Lord who died that you might live;

I am the bread that comes from heav'n a - bove;
I am the life that rais - es up the dead;
You are my flock: you know the shep-herd's voice;
You are God's dwell - ing place, on me you rest;
I am the morn - ing star that nev - er sets;
I am the bride-groom, this my wed - ding song;

D.C.

I am the vine that fills your cup with joy.
I am your peace, true peace my gift to you.
You are my own: your ran - som is my blood.
Like liv - ing stones, a tem - ple for God's praise.
Lift up your face, in you my light will shine.
You are my bride, come to the mar - riage feast.

Text: Verse text, James Quinn, SJ, b.1919, © 1989. Used by permission of Selah Publishing., Inc., Kingston, N.Y.; refrain text,
    Michael Joncas, b.1951, © 1989, GIA Publications, Inc.
Tune: Michael Joncas, b.1951, © 1989, GIA Publications, Inc.

Let Us Break Bread Together 832

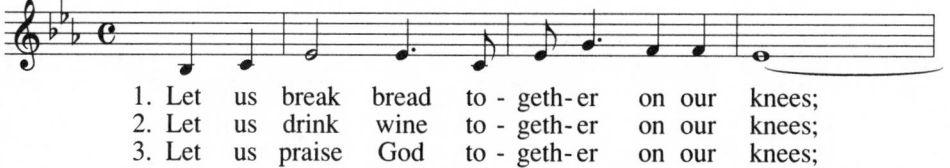

1. Let us break bread to - geth-er on our knees;
2. Let us drink wine to - geth-er on our knees;
3. Let us praise God to - geth-er on our knees;

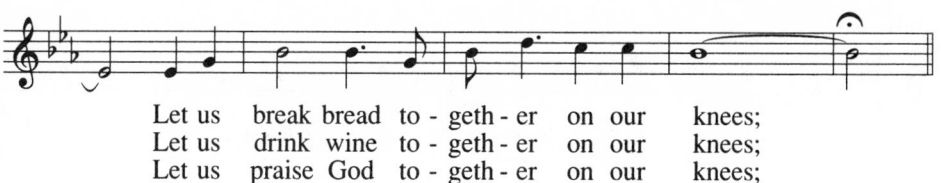

Let us break bread to - geth - er on our knees;
Let us drink wine to - geth - er on our knees;
Let us praise God to - geth - er on our knees;

When I fall on my knees, With my face to the ris - ing

sun, O Lord, have mer - cy on me.

Text: American folk hymn
Tune: LET US BREAK BREAD, 10 10 6 8 7; American folk hymn; harm. by David Hurd, b.1950, © 1968, GIA Publications, Inc.

833 Now in This Banquet

Refrain

1.*
Now in this ban - quet,
Advent: God of our jour - neys,
Lent: Lord, you can o - pen

2.
Christ is our bread;
day - break to night;
hearts that are stone;

Here shall all hun - gers be fed.
Lead us to jus - tice and light.
Live in our flesh and our bone;

Bread that is bro - ken, wine that is poured,
Grant us com - pas - sion, strength for the day,
Lead us to won - der, mys - t'ry and grace,

Love is the sign of our Lord.
Wis - dom to walk in your way.
One in your lov - ing em - brace.

Verses 1, 2

1. You who have touched us and graced us with love,
2. Let our hearts burn with the fire of your love;

D.C.

make us your peo - ple of good - ness and light.
o - pen our eyes to the glo - ry of God.

Verse 3

3. God who makes the blind to see, God who makes the lame to walk,

*May be sung in canon.

bring us danc-ing in-to day, lead your peo-ple in your way.

Verse 4

4. Hope for the hope-less, light for the blind,

"Strong" is your name, Lord, "Gen-tle" and "Kind."

Verse 5

5. Call us to be your light, call us to be your love,

make us your peo-ple a - gain.

Verse 6

6. Come, O Spir - it! re - new our hearts!

We shall a - rise to be chil-dren of light.

Text: Marty Haugen, b.1950
Tune: Marty Haugen, b.1950
© 1986, GIA Publications, Inc.

834 Seed, Scattered and Sown

Refrain

Seed, scat-tered and sown, wheat, gath-ered and grown, bread, bro-ken and shared as one, the Liv-ing Bread of God.

Vine, fruit of the land, wine, work of our hands, one cup that is shared by all; the Liv-ing Cup, the Liv-ing Bread of God.

Verses

1. Is not the bread we break a
2. The seed which falls on rock will
3. As wheat up - on the hills was

shar - ing in our Lord? Is not the
with - er and will die. The seed with -
gath - ered and was grown, So may the

D.C.

cup we bless the blood of Christ out - poured?
in good ground will flow - er and have life.
church of God be gath - ered in - to one.

Text: *Didache* 9, 1 Corinthians 10:16-17, Mark 4:3-6; Dan Feiten
Tune: Dan Feiten; keyboard arr. by Eric Gunnison, R.J. Miller
© 1987, Ekklesia Music, Inc.

O Taste and See   835

Refrain

O   taste,   taste and   see   the

good-ness of   God,   the   bless-ings of   God.

Verses

1. I will sing God's praises all the days that I shall live.
   My soul will glory in my God, the lowly will hear and be glad.
   O glorify God's name with me, together let us rejoice.

2. For God has heard my anguished cries, and delivered me from all my foes.
   O look to God that you might shine, your faces be radiant with joy.

3. When the poor cry out, God hears and saves them,
   rescues them from their distress.
   God's angel watches near to those who look to their God to save them.

4. O taste and see that God is good, how happy the ones who find refuge.
   The mighty shall grow weak and hungry, those who seek God lack nothing.

5. Come, my children, hear me, I will teach you the fear of God.
   Come, all of you who thirst for life and seek joy in all of your days.

6. For God is close to the brokenhearted, near to those crushed in spirit.
   The hand of God redeems your life, a refuge for all those who seek.

Text: Psalm 34:2-4, 5-6, 7-8, 9, 11, 12-13, 19; Marty Haugen, b.1950
Tune: Marty Haugen, b.1950
© 1993, GIA Publications, Inc.

836 We Know and Believe

Refrain

We know and be - lieve in God's love for us.

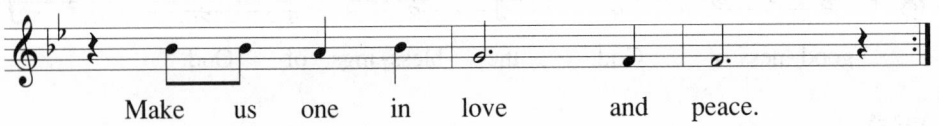

Make us one in love and peace.

Verses

1. Nourish us well with this bread of the kingdom,
   the gift of yourself so freely given.
   To make us all one you call us to the table,
   to eat and drink of your flesh and blood.

2. Happy are we who eat at your table.
   Happy are we who drink of this cup.
   Your blood once shed, your body once broken,
   now call us to rise again daily with you.

3. God's love we embrace in each brother and sister.
   The signs of your presence are constantly new.
   Though many we are we become one in Jesus,
   one body, one bread, we are sign of you.

4. Neither Jew nor Greek, male nor female,
   We are all one in your presence, O Lord.
   All fighting and discord will melt in your mercy.
   We are one in your Spirit and one in your peace.

Text: Rob Glover, b.1950
Tune: Rob Glover, b.1950
© 1992, GIA Publications, Inc.

Taste and See 837

Refrain

Taste and see, taste and see the good-ness of the Lord.

Taste and see, taste and see the good-ness of the Lord.

Verses

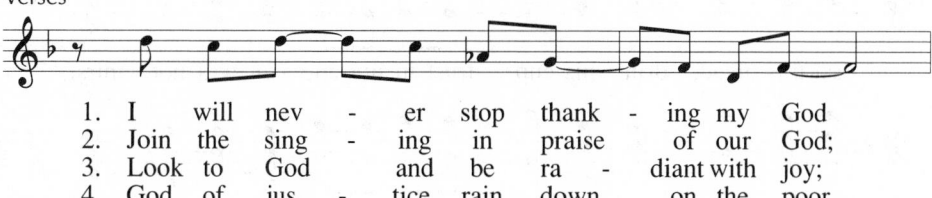

1. I will nev - er stop thank - ing my God
2. Join the sing - ing in praise of our God;
3. Look to God and be ra - diant with joy;
4. God of jus - tice, rain down on the poor,

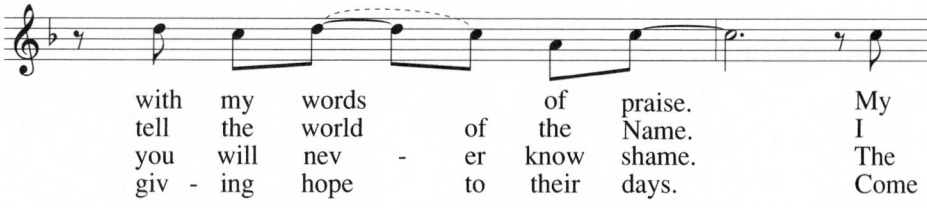

with my words of praise. My
tell the world of the Name. I
you will nev - er know shame. The
giv - ing hope to their days. Come

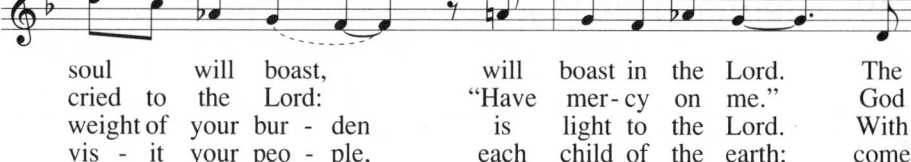

soul will boast, will boast in the Lord. The
cried to the Lord: "Have mer-cy on me." God
weight of your bur - den is light to the Lord. With
vis - it your peo - ple, each child of the earth; come

D.C.

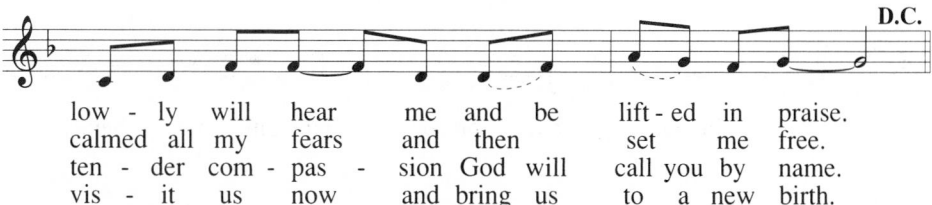

low - ly will hear me and be lift - ed in praise.
calmed all my fears and then set me free.
ten - der com - pas - sion God will call you by name.
vis - it us now and bring us to a new birth.

Text: Psalm 34:1-3; Francis Patrick O'Brien, b.1958
Tune: Francis Patrick O'Brien, b.1958

838 Eat This Bread

Refrain

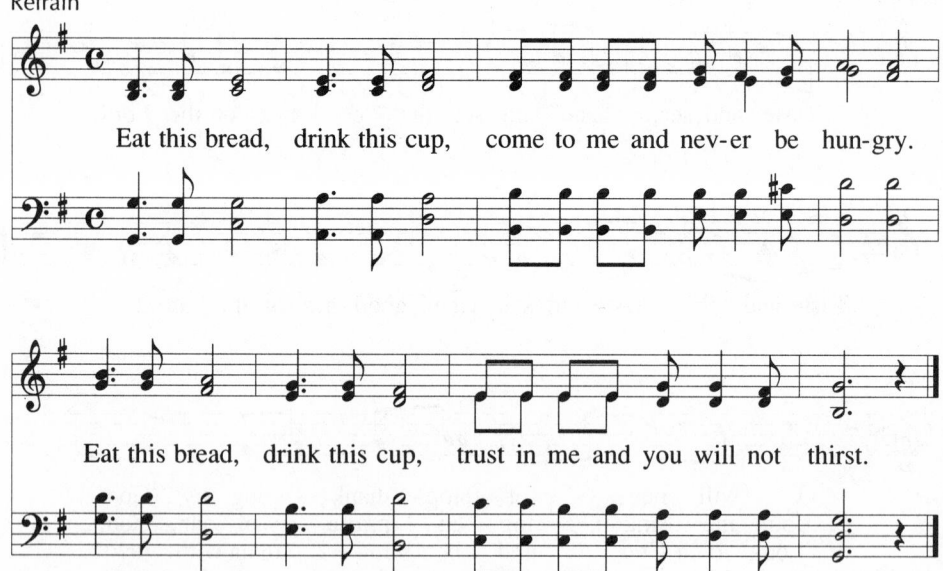

Eat this bread, drink this cup, come to me and nev-er be hun-gry.

Eat this bread, drink this cup, trust in me and you will not thirst.

Text: John 6; adapt. by Robert J. Batastini, b.1942, and the Taizé Community
Tune: Jacques Berthier, 1923-1994
© 1984, Les Presses de Taizé, GIA Publications, Inc., agent

839 Here in This Place

Refrain

Are not our hearts burn - ing with - in us? Are not our

lives shared as one bread? Here in our hands,

here in this place: Je-sus, our hope, life from the dead.

Verses

1. In the breaking of the bread, may we know the Lord.
   We were lost, and now are found, home again with God!

2. You are food for all our hunger, you are all we need.
   You are our promise and our hope, life for the world.

3. As grain, once scattered on the hill, was gathered all as one,
   may we be one in this bread: Behold the Lamb of God!

4. As this bread is broken, as this cup is shared, we give our lives,
   broken and outpoured. We will serve the Lord!

Text: Luke 24:13-35; David Haas, b.1957
Tune: David Haas, b.1957
© 1992, GIA Publications, Inc.

Shepherd of Souls   840

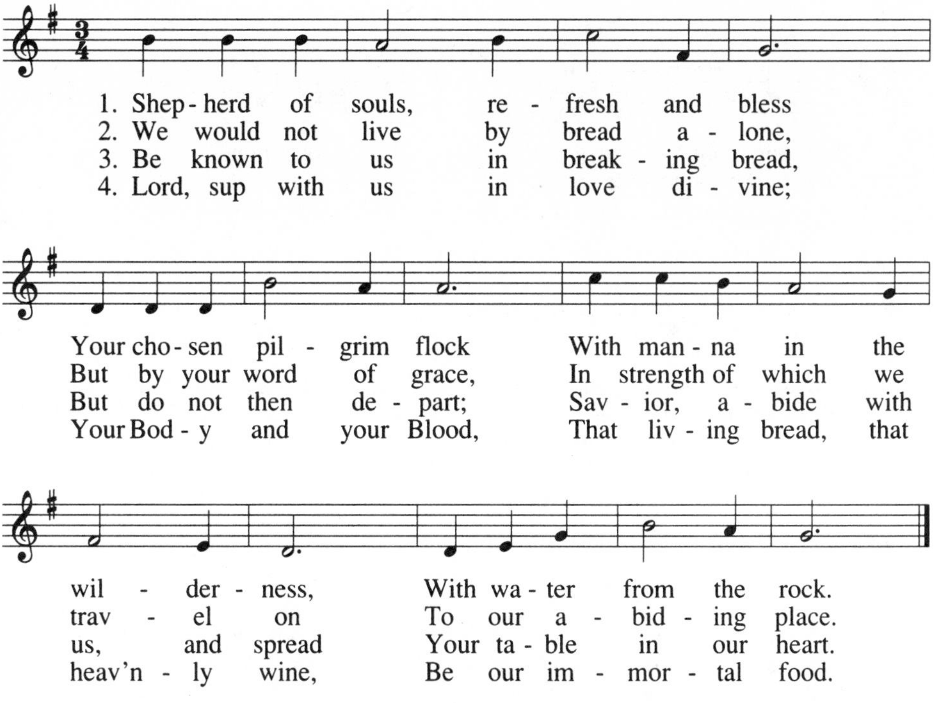

1. Shep-herd of souls, re - fresh and bless
2. We would not live by bread a - lone,
3. Be known to us in break - ing bread,
4. Lord, sup with us in love di - vine;

Your cho-sen pil - grim flock   With man - na in the
But by your word of grace,   In strength of which we
But do not then de - part;   Sav - ior, a - bide with
Your Bod - y and your Blood,   That liv - ing bread, that

wil - der - ness,   With wa - ter from the rock.
trav - el on   To our a - bid - ing place.
us, and spread   Your ta - ble in our heart.
heav'n - ly wine,   Be our im - mor - tal food.

Text: James Montgomery, 1771-1854, alt.
Tune: ST. AGNES. CM; John B. Dykes, 1823-1876; harm. by Richard Proulx, b.1937. © 1986, GIA Publications, Inc.

841 In the Breaking of the Bread /
Cuando Partimos el Pan del Señor

Refrain

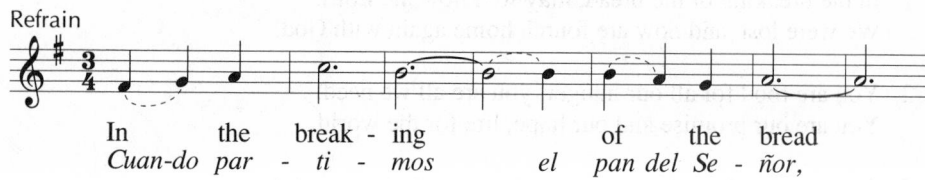

In   the   break - ing   of   the   bread
Cuan-do par   -   ti - mos   el   pan del Se - ñor,

We   have   known   him;   we have been   fed.
lo   co - no - ce   -   mos, nos   da   de   co - mer.   Je -

Je - sus the   stran - ger,   Je - sus the Lord,
sús des-co - no   -   ci - do,   Je - sús,   Se - ñor,

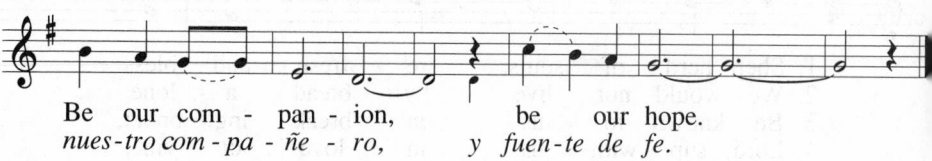

Be   our com - pan - ion,   be   our hope.
nues-tro com - pa - ñe - ro,   y   fuen-te de fe.

Verses

1. Bread for   the   jour - ney,   strength for   our years,
1. *Pan   pa - ra el   via - je,   Pan   de   la   vi - da,*
2. Bread of   the   prom - ise,   peo - ple   of   hope,
2. *Pan   del   pro - me - sa,   Pan de es - pe - ran - za,*

Man - na   of   ag   -   es, of strug - gle   and tears.
Pan de los   si   -   glos de   lu - cha y do - lor,
Wine of com - pas -   sion,   life   for   the world
Vi - no   de   vi   -   da, de   su   com - pa - sión,

Cup of sal - va - tion,   fruit of the land,
y   es - te   vi - no,   fru - to   de   la   tie - rra   ben -
Gath-ered at   ta - ble,   joined as   his   bod - y,
En   es - ta   me - sa   un   so - lo   cuer - po

D.C.

Bless and re - ceive   now,   the work of our   hands.
dí - ce - lo,   Pa - dre,   es   tu - yo,   mi   Dios.
Sealed in   the   Spir - it,   sent by the   Word.
en   un   es - pí - ri - tu,   con   u - na   mi - sión.

Original Verses:

1. Once I was helpless, sad and confused; darkness surrounded me, courage removed.
   And then I saw him by my side. Carry my burden, open my eyes.

2. There is no sorrow, pain or woe; there is no suffering he did not know.
   He did not waver; he did not bend. He is the victor. He is my friend.

842 Take and Eat This Bread

Refrain

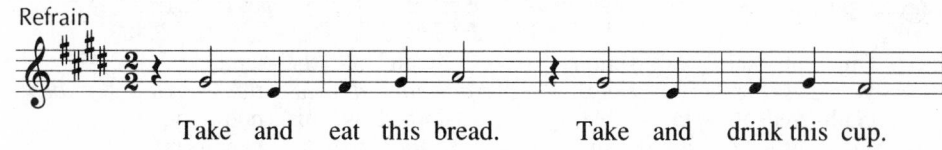

Take and eat this bread. Take and drink this cup.

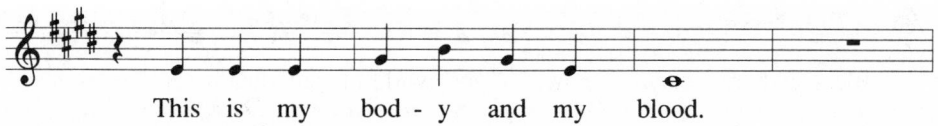

This is my bod - y and my blood.

When you eat this bread, when you drink this cup,

you live in me and I in you.

Verses

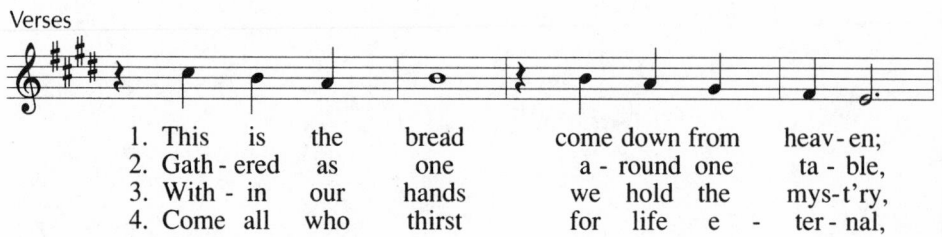

1. This is the bread come down from heav-en;
2. Gath - ered as one a - round one ta - ble,
3. With - in our hands we hold the mys-t'ry,
4. Come all who thirst for life e - ter - nal,

D.C.

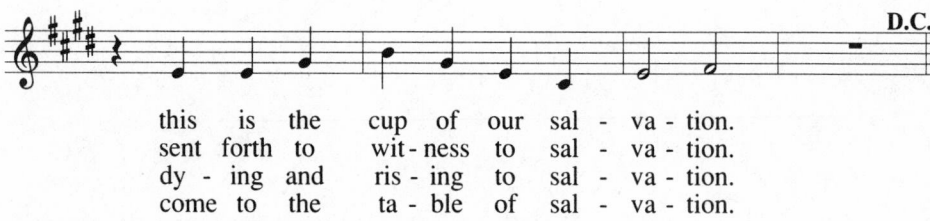

this is the cup of our sal - va - tion.
sent forth to wit-ness to sal - va - tion.
dy - ing and ris - ing to sal - va - tion.
come to the ta - ble of sal - va - tion.

Text: Francis Patrick O'Brien, b.1958
Tune: Francis Patrick O'Brien, b.1958
© 1992, GIA Publications, Inc.

Look Beyond 843

Refrain

Look be-yond the bread you eat; See your Sav-ior and your Lord. Look be-yond the cup you drink; See his love poured out as blood.

To verses | *Final ending*

See his life poured out as blood.

Verses

1. Give us a sign that we might be-lieve in you. Mos-es had man-na from the sky.
2. I am the bread which from the heav-ens came; Those who eat this bread will nev-er die.
3. The bread I give you will be my ver-y flesh; My blood will tru-ly be your drink.
4. This man speaks harsh-ly; who can lis-ten to his word? We shall no long-er fol-low him.
5. You, my dis-ci-ples, will you al-so leave? Lord whom can we go?

D.C.

Text: Darryl Ducote, b.1945
Tune: Darryl Ducote, b.1945
© 1969, 1979, Damean Music. Distributed by GIA Publications, Inc.

844 Without Seeing You

Refrain

With - out see - ing you, we love you; with - out

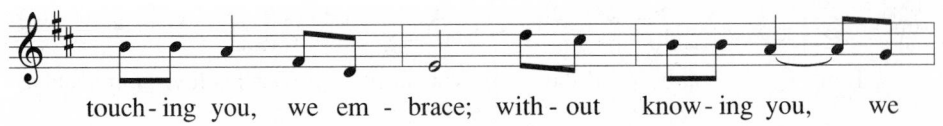

touch - ing you, we em - brace; with - out know - ing you, we

fol - low; with - out see-ing you, we be - lieve.

Verses

1. We re - turn to you deep with - in, leave the
2. The spar - row will find a home, near to
3. For ev - er we sing to you of your
4. For you are our shep - herd, there is

past to the dust; turn to you with tears and
you, O God; how hap - py, we who
good - ness, O God; pro - claim-ing to
noth - ing that we need; in green pas - tures we will

D.C.

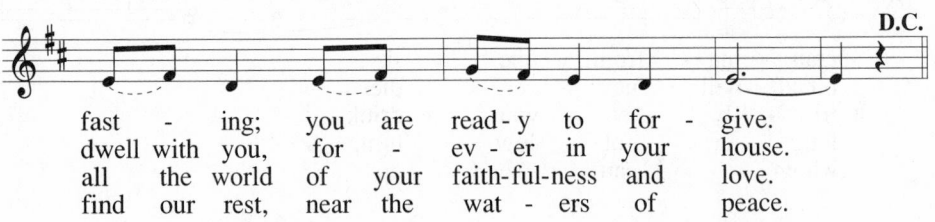

fast - ing; you are read - y to for - give.
dwell with you, for - ev - er in your house.
all the world of your faith-ful-ness and love.
find our rest, near the wat - ers of peace.

Text: Inspired by 1 Peter 1:8; David Haas, b. 1957
Tune: David Haas, b. 1957
© 1993, GIA Publications, Inc.

The Song of the Supper 845

Verses

1. The time was ear - ly eve - ning, The
2. The com - pa - ny of Je - sus Had
3. "The bread and bod - y bro - ken The
4. On both sides of the ta - ble, On
5. Lord, Je - sus, now a - mong us, Con -

place a room up - stairs; The guests were the dis -
met to share a meal, But he, who made them
wine and blood out - poured, The cross and kitch - en
both sides of the grave, The Lord joins those who
firm our faith's in - tent, As, with your words and

ci - ples, Few in num - ber and few in prayers.
wel - come, Had much more to re - veal.
ta - ble Are one by my sign and word."
love him To serve them and to save.
ac - tions, We u - nite in this sac - ra - ment.

Refrain

Oh, the food comes from the bak - er, the

drink comes from the vine, the words come from the

sav - ior, "I will meet you in bread and wine."

Text: John L. Bell, b.1949, © 1988, Iona Community, GIA Publications, Inc., agent
Tune: AFTON WATERS, Irregular; Scottish folk song; acc. by John L. Beil, b.1949, © 1993, Iona Community, GIA Publications, Inc., agent

846 One Is the Body

Refrain

One is the bod-y, one is the bread, one are the liv-ing, the un-born, the dead. One is the cup, one blood in us flows, one is the breath of the star and the rose. One is the Spir-it with Mak-er and Son, just as the source and the riv-er are one; one are the stran-ger, my foe and my friend. To this I will say, "A-men."

Verses

1. Gath-er, dis-ci-ples, your mas-ter to meet.
2. Now split the tim-ber, now turn the stone;
3. I am the hun-gry, you are the poor;

1. Learn to for-give from the bread that you eat;
2. look where you will, you are nev-er a-lone.
3. God is the stran-ger who waits at the door.

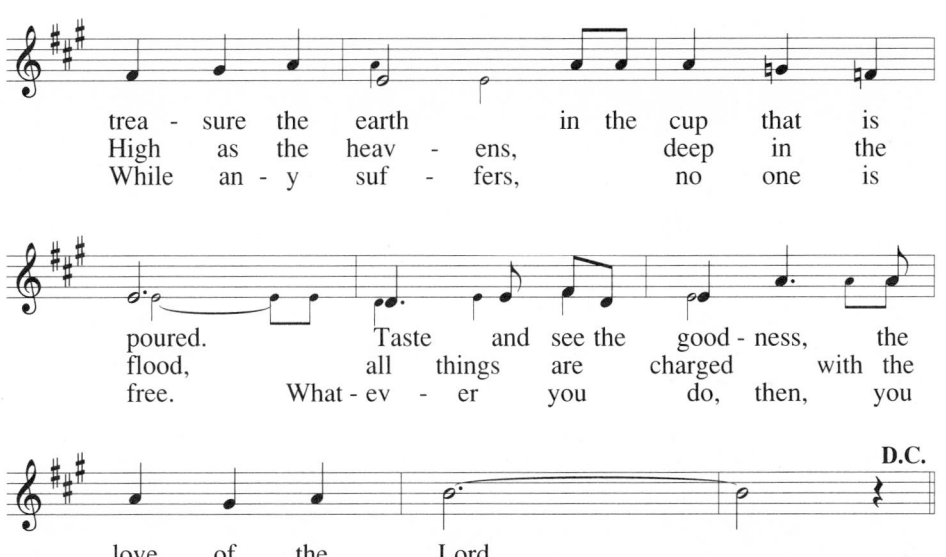

trea - sure the earth   in the cup that is
High as the heav - ens,   deep in the
While an - y suf - fers,   no one is

poured.   Taste and see the good - ness, the
flood,   all things are charged with the
free.   What - ev - er you do, then, you

D.C.

love of the Lord.
pres - ence of God.
do it to me.

Text: Rory Cooney, b.1952
Tune: Rory Cooney, b.1952
© 1993, GIA Publications, Inc.

847 Song of the Body of Christ / Canción del Cuerpo de Cristo

Refrain

We come to share our sto - ry, we
Ve - ni-mos a de-cir del mis - te - rio, y par -

come to break the bread, We come to know our
tir el pan de vi - da. Ve - ni - mos a sa - ber de

ris - ing from the dead.
nues - tra e - ter - ni - dad.

Verses

1. We come as your peo - ple, we
2. We are called to heal the bro - ken, to be
3. Bread of life and cup of prom - ise, in this
4. You will lead and we shall fol - low, you will
5. We will live and sing: "A - lo - ha," "Al - le -
   (live and sing your prais - es,)

come as your own, u - nit - ed with each
hope for the poor, we are called to feed the
meal we all are one. In our dy - ing and our
be the breath of life; liv-ing wa - ter, we are
lu - ia" is our song. May we live in love and

D.C.

oth - er, love finds a home.
hun - gry at our door.
ris - ing, may your king-dom come.
thirst - ing for your light.
peace our whole life long.

Verses

1. Ve - ni - mos, co - mo   su pueb - lo   en es -
2. Nos lla - ma pa - ra cu - rar   y
3. Pan de vi - da y co - pa de pro - me - sa,   so - mos
4. Nos guia - rás y te se - gui - re - mos,   por - que
5. Vi - vi - re - mos can - tan - do "A - lo - ha."   "A - le -

pí - ri - tu de ver - dad.   U - ni - dos en su a-
ser su es - per - an - za.   So - mos su - yos pa - ra a - li - men-
u - no en es - ta co - mi - da.   Ven - drá su rei - no en
e - res la luz que bus - ca - mos.   En el di - a o en la
lu - ya" es nues - tra can - ción.   Por siem - pre vi - vi -

D.C.

mor, so - mos un cor - a - zón.
tar a los po - bres.
nues - tra trans - for - ma - ción.
no - che, bri - lla - rás.
re - mos en su paz.

Text: David Haas, b.1957, Spanish translation by Donna Peña, b. 1955
Tune: NO KE ANO' AHI AHI, Irregular, Hawaiian traditional, arr. by David Haas, b.1957
© 1989, GIA Publications, Inc.

848 Pan de Vida

Refrain

* Pan de Vi - da, cuer-po del Se - ñor,

cup of bless - ing, blood of Christ the Lord.

At this ta - ble the last shall be first, ** po-

der es ser - vir, por-que Dios es a - mor.

Verses

1. We are the dwell-ing of God,
*** 2. Us - te - des me lla - man "Se - ñor," me in-
3. There is no Jew or Greek,

fra - gile and wound-ed and weak. We are the
cli - no_a la - var - les los pies: Ha - gan lo
there is no slave or free: there is no

bod - y of Christ, called to be the com -
mis - mo, hu - mil - des, sir - vién - do - se
wom-an or man; on - ly heirs of the

D.C.

pas - sion of God.
u - nos a o - tros.
prom - ise of God.

* Bread of Life, body of the Lord, **power is for service, because God is Love.
***You call me "Lord," and I bow to wash your feet:
you must do the same, humbly serving each other.

Text: John 13:1-15, Galatians 3:28-29; Bob Hurd, b.1950, and Pia Moriarty, © 1988, Bob Hurd
Tune: Bob Hurd, b.1950, © 1988; acc. by Craig Kingsbury, b.1952, © 1988, OCP Publications; arr. © 1988, OCP Publications
Published by OCP Publications

Table Song 849

Refrain

We are the bod-y of Christ, Bro-ken and

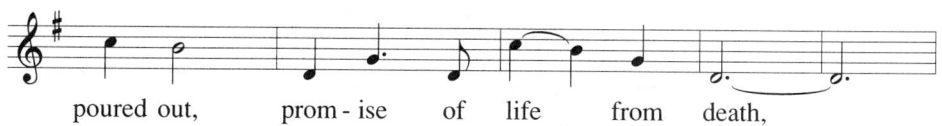

poured out, prom-ise of life from death,

we are the bod-y of Christ.

Verses

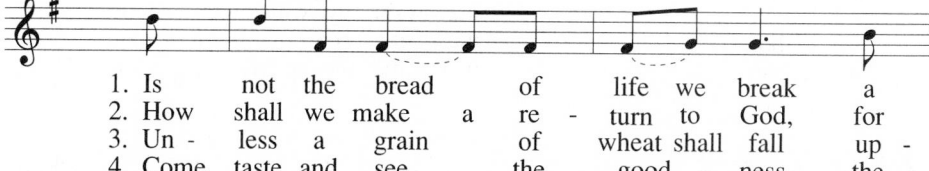

1. Is not the bread of life we break a
2. How shall we make a re - turn to God, for
3. Un - less a grain of wheat shall fall up -
4. Come taste and see the good - ness, the

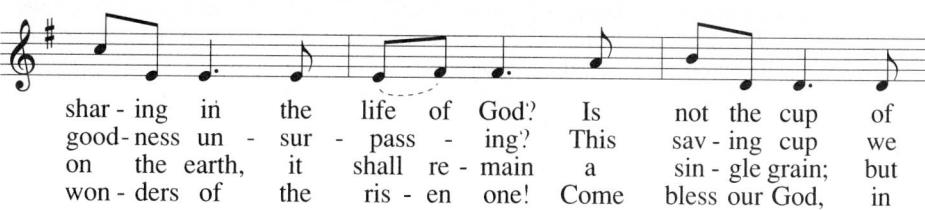

shar - ing in the life of God? Is not the cup of
good - ness un - sur - pass - ing? This sav - ing cup we
on the earth, it shall re - main a sin - gle grain; but
won - ders of the ris - en one! Come bless our God, in

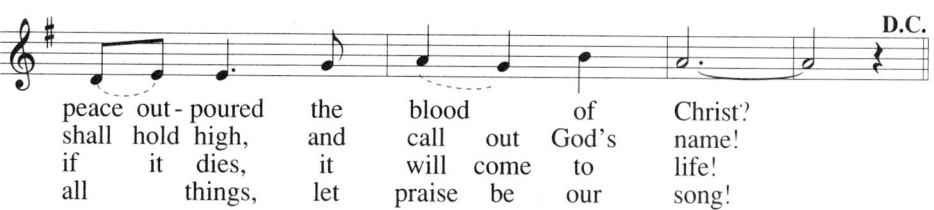

peace out - poured the blood of Christ?
shall hold high, and call out God's name!
if it dies, it will come to life!
all things, let praise be our song!

Text: David Haas, b. 1957
Tune: David Haas, b. 1957
© 1991, GIA Publications, Inc.

850 We Come to Your Feast

Verses

Cantor or choir:

1. We place up - on your ta - ble
2. We place up - on your ta - ble
3. We place up - on your ta - ble
4. We ga - ther 'round your ta - ble,

a gleam-ing cloth of white: the weav-ing of our
a hum - ble loaf of bread: the gift of field and
a sim - ple cup of wine: the fruit of hu - man
we pause with - in our quest, we stand be-side our

sto - ries, the fab - ric of our lives;
hill - side, the grain by which we're fed;
la - bor, the gift of sun and vine;
neigh-bors, we name the stran - ger "guest."

the dreams of those be - fore us, the an-cient hope - ful
we come to taste the pres-ence of him on whom we
we come to taste the pres-ence of him we claim as
The feast is spread be - fore us; you bid us come and

cries, the prom - ise of our
feed, to strength - en and con -
Lord, his dy - ing and his
dine: in bless - ing we'll un -

fu - ture: our need-ing and our nur-ture lie here be - fore our eyes.
nect us, to chal-lenge and cor - rect us, to love in word and deed.
liv - ing, his lead-ing and his giv-ing, his love in cup out-poured.
cov - er, in shar-ing we'll dis - cov - er your sub-stance and your sign.

Refrain

We come to your feast, we come to your feast: the young and the old, the fright-ened, the bold, the great-est and the least. We come to your feast, we come to your feast with the fruit of our lands and the work of our hands, we come to your feast.

Text: Michael Joncas, b.1951
Tune: Michael Joncas, b.1951
© 1994, GIA Publications, Inc.

851 I Received the Living God

Refrain

I re - ceived the liv - ing God, and my heart is full of joy. I re - ceived the liv - ing God, and my heart is full of joy.

Verses

1. Je - sus said: "I am the Bread Knead - ed
2. Je - sus said: "I am the Way, And my
3. Je - sus said: "I am the Truth; If you
4. Je - sus said: "I am the Life Far from

long to give you life; You who will par - take of
Fa - ther longs for you; So I come to bring you
fol - low close to me, You will know me in your
whom no thing can grow, But re - ceive this liv - ing

D.C.

me   Need not ev - er fear to die."
home   To be one with him a - new."
heart, And my word shall make you free."
bread, And my Spir - it you shall know."

Text: Anonymous
Tune: LIVING GOD, 7 7 7 7 with refrain; Anonymous; harm. by Richard Proulx, b.1937, © 1986, GIA Publications, Inc.

At That First Eucharist 852

1. At that first Eu - cha - rist be - fore you died,
2. For all your church, O Lord, we in - ter - cede;
3. We pray for those who wan - der from the fold;

O Lord, you prayed that all be one in you;
O make our lack of char - i - ty to cease;
O bring them back, Good Shep - herd of the sheep,

At this our Eu - cha - rist a - gain pre - side,
Draw us the near - er each to each we plead,
Back to the faith which saints be - lieved of old,

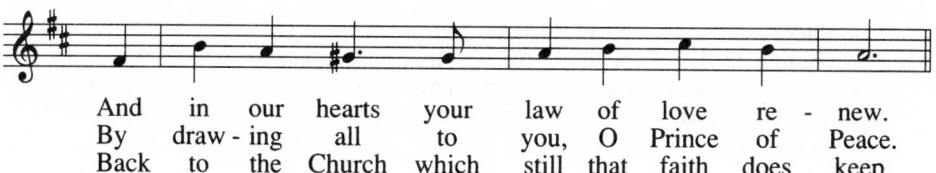

And in our hearts your law of love re - new.
By draw - ing all to you, O Prince of Peace.
Back to the Church which still that faith does keep.

Thus may we all one Bread, one Bod - y be;

Through this blest Sac - ra - ment of U - ni - ty.

Text: William H. Turton, 1859-1938, alt.
Tune: UNDE ET MEMORES, 10 10 10 10 with refrain; William H. Monk, 1823-1889, alt.

853 Alleluia! Sing to Jesus

1. Al - le - lu - ia! sing to Je - sus! His the scep - ter, his the throne; Al - le - lu - ia! his the tri - umph, His the vic - to - ry a - lone; Hark! the songs of peace - ful Zi - on Thun - der like a might - y flood; ev - 'ry na - tion Has re - deemed us by his blood.

2. Al - le - lu - ia! not as or - phans Are we left in sor - row now; Al - le - lu - ia! he is near us, Faith be - lieves, nor ques - tions how: Though the cloud from sight re - ceived him, When the for - ty days were o'er, get his prom - ise, "I am with you ev - er - more"?

3. Al - le - lu - ia! Bread of An - gels, Here on earth our food, our stay! Al - le - lu - ia! here the sin - ful Flee to you from day to day: In - ter - ces - sor, friend of sin - ners, Earth's re - deem - er, plead for me, all the sin - less Sweep a - cross the crys - tal sea.

4. Al - le - lu - ia! King e - ter - nal, You the Lord of lords we own; Al - le - lu - ia! born of Mar - y, Earth your foot - stool, heav'n your throne: You, with - in the veil, have en - tered, Robed in flesh, our great high priest; Where the songs of priest and vic - tim In the eu - cha - ris - tic feast.

Text: Revelation 5:9; William C. Dix, 1837-1898
Tune: HYFRYDOL, 8 7 8 7 D; Rowland H. Prichard, 1811-1887

I Know That My Redeemer Lives   854

Refrain

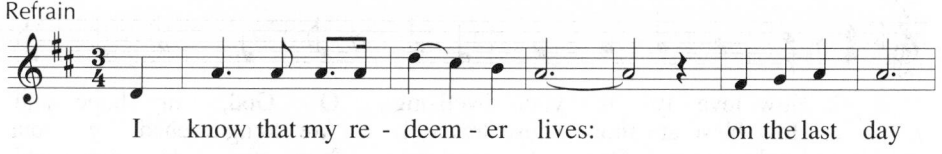

I know that my re - deem - er lives: on the last day

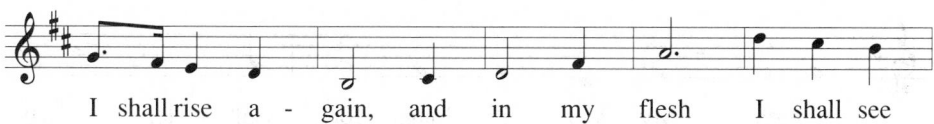

I shall rise a - gain, and in my flesh I shall see

God.   On the last day   I shall rise a - gain!

Verses

Cantor:

1. I   shall   see   my   Sav - ior's   face;   and my own
2. With- in   my   heart   this hope   I   hold;   that in my

All:

eyes   shall be- hold   my   God.   On the last day
flesh   shall see   my   God.   On the last day

D.C.

I shall rise   a - gain!
I shall rise   a - gain!

Text: Job 19:25-27; David Haas, b.1957
Tune: David Haas, b.1957
© 1990, GIA Publications, Inc.

855 How Lovely Is Your Dwelling

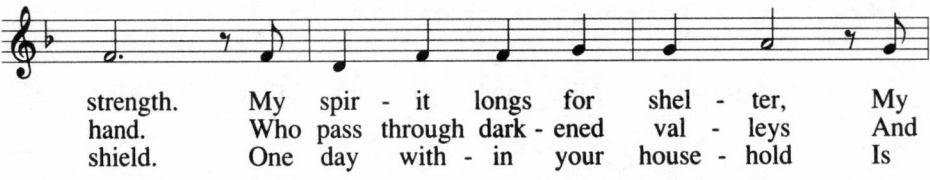

1. How love - ly is your dwell-ing, O God, my hope and
2. How blest are those whose trav - els Are strength-ened by your
3. Look on me, God of good-ness, You are my sun and

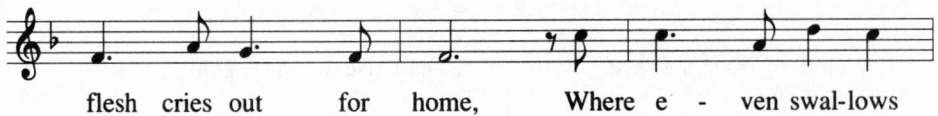

strength. My spir - it longs for shel - ter, My
hand. Who pass through dark - ened val - leys And
shield. One day with - in your house - hold Is

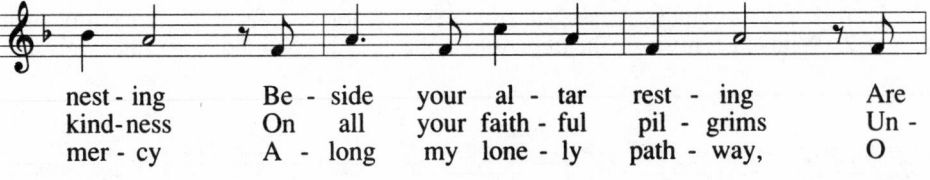

flesh cries out for home, Where e - ven swal-lows
find re - fresh - ing springs. Your rains fall soft as
what I most de - sire. O guide me in your

nest - ing Be - side your al - tar rest - ing Are
kind-ness On all your faith - ful pil - grims Un -
mer - cy A - long my lone - ly path - way, O

ev - er prais-ing you, Are ev - er prais - ing you.
til they come to you, Un - til they come to you.
bring me safe - ly home. O bring me safe - ly home.

Text: Psalm 84; Jean Janzen, © 1991
Tune: GILMAN, 7 6 7 6 77 6; John Foley, SJ, b.1939, © 1993, GIA Publications, Inc.

I Shall See My God 856

Text: Kevin Keil, b.1965
Tune: Kevin Keil, b.1965
© 1993, GIA Publications, Inc.

857 I Know That My Redeemer Lives

Cantor:

I know that my Re-deem-er lives, and on the

last day I shall rise a-gain; in my bod-y I shall

All:

look on God, my Sav-ior, in my bod-y I shall look on God, my

Cantor:

Sav - ior. I my-self shall see him; my own eyes will

gaze on him, my own eyes will gaze on him; in my bod-y I shall

All:

look on God, my Sav-ior, in my bod-y I shall look on God, my

Cantor:

Sav - ior. This is the hope I cher-ish, this is the hope I

cher - ish in my heart; in my bod - y I shall

look on God, my Sav - ior, in my bod - y I shall

look on God, my Sav - ior.

Text: *Rite of Funerals*, © 1970, ICEL
Music: *Music for Rite of Funerals and Rite of Baptism for Children*, Howard Hughes, SM, © 1977, ICEL

May the Angels Lead You into Paradise 858

Cantor, then all:

May the an - gels lead you in - to par - a - dise;

may the mar - tyrs come to wel - come you and

take you to the ho - ly cit - y, the

new and e - ter - nal Je - ru - sa - lem.

Text: *In paradisum; Rite of Funerals*, © 1970, ICEL
Tune: *Music for Rite of Funerals and Rite of Baptism for Children*, Howard Hughes, SM, © 1977, ICEL

859 The Hand of God Shall Hold You

Refrain

The hand of God shall hold you, the peace of God en -

fold you, the love that dreamed and formed you still sur -

rounds you here to - day; The light of God be - side you, a -

bove, be - neath, in - side you, the light that shines to

guide you home to the lov - ing hand of God.

Verses

1. May God's light shine ever upon you, may you rest in the arms of God;
   may you dwell for evermore in communion with all the blessed.

2. May the angels lead you into paradise; may the martyrs come to welcome you
   and take you to the holy city, the new and eternal Jerusalem.

Text: Marty Haugen, b.1950, © 1994, GIA Publications, Inc.; verse 2 from *In paradisum; Rite of Funerals,* © 1970, ICEL
Tune: Marty Haugen, b.1950, © 1994, GIA Publications, Inc.

I, the Lord   860

Refrain

I, the Lord am with you, al - ways by your side.

Come and take my hand, for I will lead you home. Fol-low

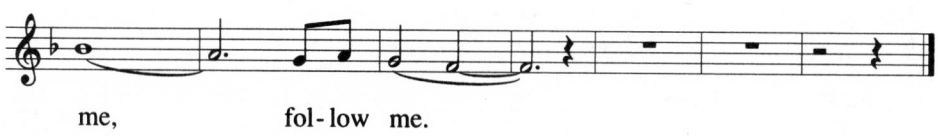

me, fol-low me.

Verse 1

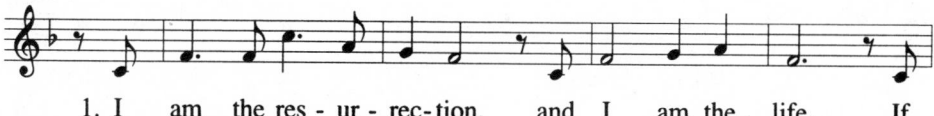

1. I am the res - ur - rec-tion, and I am the life. If

D.C.

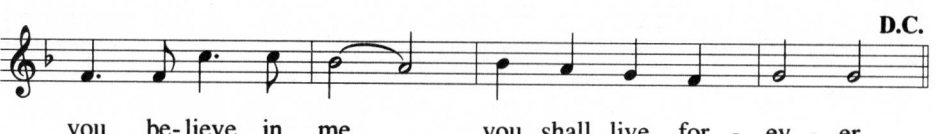

you be-lieve in me you shall live for - ev - er.

Verse 2

2. You shall have new life and live it to the full.

D.C.

Turn your sor - row in - to joy, for life has just be - gun.

861 Song of the Exile

Refrain

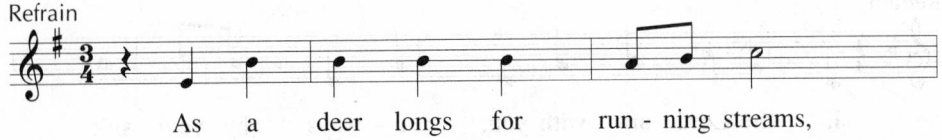

As a deer longs for run - ning streams,

so my soul longs for you, and my

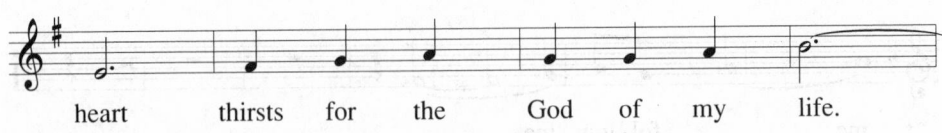

heart thirsts for the God of my life.

When shall I go to see the

face of God?

Verses

1. I remember, and my soul melts within me:
   I am on my way to your wonderful tent,
   to the house of God, singing my songs of joy and thanksgiving.

2. I am broken, so I call to my Savior;
   as the waves roar down, sweeping over my head,
   and I call to you, be with me now, O God of my life.

3. In the daytime may the Lord's love be with me;
   in the night your song will be still on my lips.
   I will sing to you, sing prayers to you, the God of my life.

Text: Psalm 42:2-3, 5, 7-9; para. by Marty Haugen, b.1950
Tune: Marty Haugen, b.1950
© 1980, GIA Publications, Inc.

Saints of God   862

Refrain

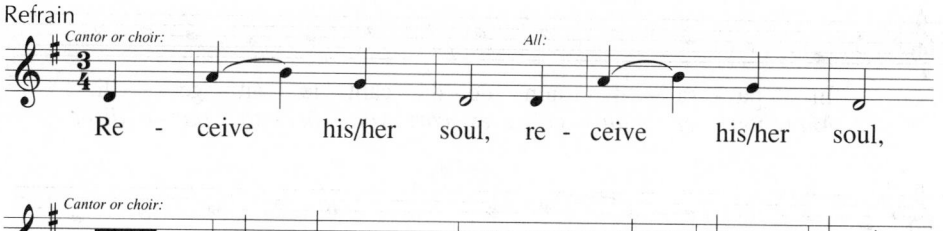

Re - ceive his/her soul, re - ceive his/her soul,

and pre - sent him/her to God the Most High,

and pre - sent him/her to God the Most High.

Verses

1. Saints of God, come to his/her aid!
   Hasten to meet him/her, angels of the Lord!

2. May Christ, who called you, take you to himself;
   may angels lead you to the bosom of Abraham.

3. Eternal rest grant unto him/her, O Lord, and let
   perpetual light shine upon him/her.

Text: *Order of Christian Funerals,* © 1985, ICEL
Tune: Steven R. Janco, b. 1961, © 1990, GIA Publications, Inc.

863 In Paradisum / May Choirs of Angels

In pa - ra - dí - sum de - dú - cant te án - ge - li:
May choirs of an - gels es - cort you in - to par - a - dise:

in tu - o ad - vén - tu su - scí - pi - ant te
and at your ar - ri - val may the mar - tyrs re - ceive

már - ty - res, et per - dú - cant te in
and wel - come you; may they bring you home in -

ci - vi - tá - tem san - ctam Je - rú - sa - lem.
to the ho - ly cit - y, Je - ru - sa - lem.

Cho - rus an - ge - ló - rum te su -
May the ho - ly an - gels wel -

scí - pi - at, et cum Lá - za - ro quon - dam
come you, and with Laz - a - rus, who lived in

páu - pe - re ae - tér - nam
pov - er - ty, may you have

há - be - as ré - qui - em.
ev - er - last - ing rest.

Text: *In Paradisum*, tr. © 1986, GIA Publications, Inc.
Tune: Mode VII; acc. by Richard Proulx, b.1937, © 1986, GIA Publications, Inc.

Song of Farewell 864

Refrain

Dy-ing you de - stroyed our death! Ris-ing you re - stored our life!

Lord Je - sus,   Lord Je - sus,   come in   glo - ry!

Verses

1. May Christ who died for you lead you into his kingdom;
   may Christ who died for you lead you this day into paradise.

2. May Christ, the Good Shepherd, lead you home today
   and give you a place within his flock.

Alternate children's verse:
2. May Christ, the Good Shepherd, take you on his shoulders
   and bring you home, bring you home today.

3. May the angels lead you into paradise;
   may the martyrs come to welcome you
   and take you to the Holy City, the new and eternal Jerusalem.

4. May the choirs of angels come to meet you,
   may the choirs of angels come to meet you;
   where Lazarus is poor no longer may you have eternal life in Christ.

Alternate children's verse:
4. May the choirs of angels come to meet you,
   may the choirs of angels come to meet you;
   and with all God's children may you have eternal life in Christ.

Text: Memorial Acclamation © 1973, ICEL; *In paradisum;* Michael Marchal, © 1988, GIA Publications, Inc.
Tune: Michael Joncas, b.1951, © 1988, GIA Publications, Inc.

865 When Love Is Found

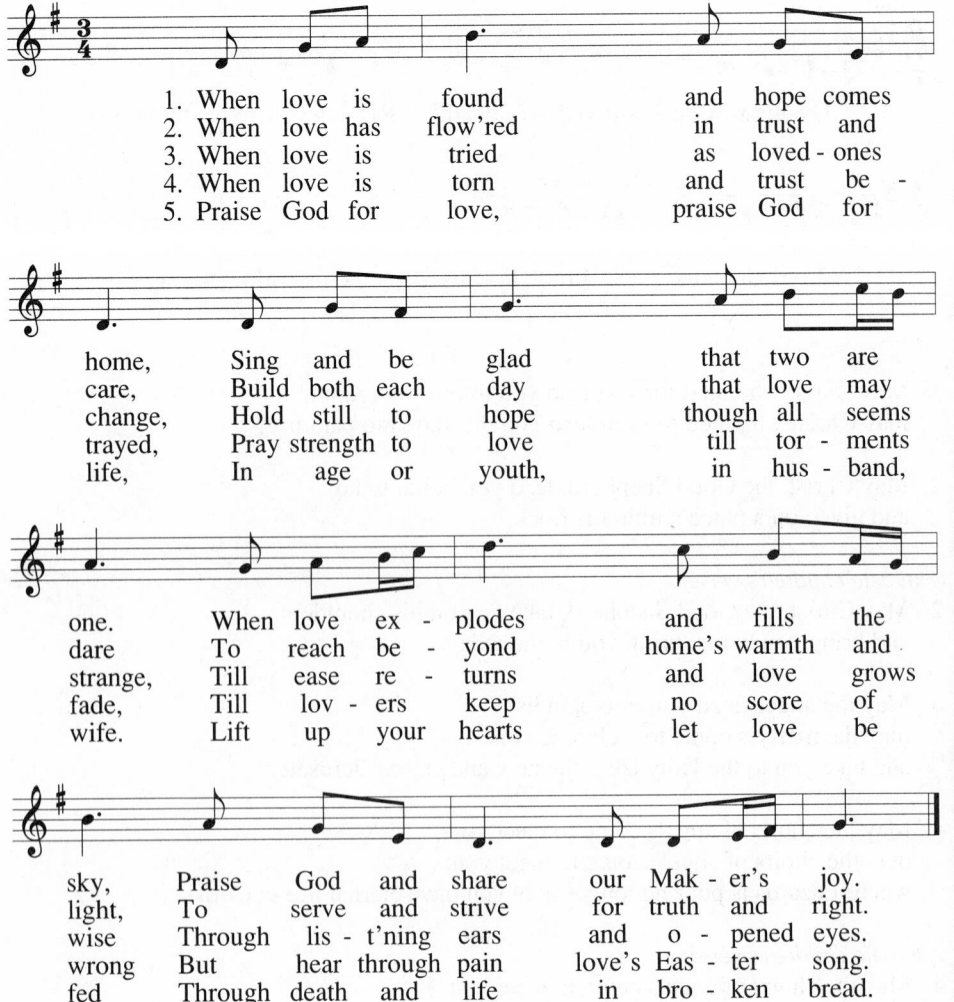

1. When love is found and hope comes
2. When love has flow'red in trust and
3. When love is tried as loved - ones
4. When love is torn and trust be -
5. Praise God for love, praise God for

home, Sing and be glad that two are
care, Build both each day that love may
change, Hold still to hope though all seems
trayed, Pray strength to love till tor - ments
life, In age or youth, in hus - band,

one. When love ex - plodes and fills the
dare To reach be - yond home's warmth and
strange, Till ease re - turns and love grows
fade, Till lov - ers keep no score of
wife. Lift up your hearts let love be

sky, Praise God and share our Mak - er's joy.
light, To serve and strive for truth and right.
wise Through lis - t'ning ears and o - pened eyes.
wrong But hear through pain love's Eas - ter song.
fed Through death and life in bro - ken bread.

Text: Brian Wren, b.1936
Tune: O WALY WALY, LM; English; harm. by Martin West, b.1929
© 1983, Hope Publishing Co.

Love Is the Sunlight   866

1. Love is the sun - light Shaped of your splen - dor,
2. Love is the spa - cious Qui - et of shad - ows,
3. May we in glad - ness Grow in your sun - shine,

Love is the star bright Born of your hand,
Love is the gra - cious Shade of re - lease,
May we in sad - ness Rest in your shade,

Bless - ing of heav - en Gra - cious - ly giv - en,
Mist of the morn - ing, Mid - day a - dorn - ing,
Giv - ing and gain - ing, Ev - er re - main - ing,

Ra - diant with glo - ry From your com -
Cool with the twi - light Breath of your
One in the mar - riage Your love has

mand.
peace.
made.

Text: Borghild Jacobson, © 1981, Concordia Publishing House
Tune: SHADE, 5 5 5 4 D; David Haas, b.1957, © 1993, GIA Publications, Inc.

867 Wherever You Go

Refrain

Wher-ev - er you go, I will go; wher - ev - er you

live, I'll be with you. Wher - ev - er you lie, I'll

be there be - side you. Wher-ev - er you go,

I'll be there.

Verses

1. Come, set me like a seal upon your heart; a seal protecting your arm.
   Deep waters cannot quench this love; the ocean will not sweep it away.

2. Arise my beloved, come to me; the rains are gone, the winter is past.
   The flowers appear, the vines are pruned, and the dove's song is heard in our land.

3. Wherever you stay, I will stay; your people will be my people.
   Wherever you die, so will I die with you in the arms of God!

Text: Ruth 1:16-17; Song of Songs 2:10-12, 7:6-7; David Haas, b.1957
Tune: David Haas, b.1957
© 1993, GIA Publications, Inc.

God, in the Planning   868

1. God,   in   the   plan - ning   and   pur-pose   of   life,
2. Je - sus   was   found,   at   a   sim - i - lar   feast,
3. There-fore   we   pray   that   his   spir - it   pre - side
4. Praise then   the   Mak - er,   the   Spir - it,   the   Son,

Hal - lowed   the   un - ion   of   hus - band   and   wife:
Tak - ing   the   roles   of   both   wait - er   and   priest,
O - ver   the   wed - ding   of   bride - groom   and   bride,
Source of   the   love through which   two   are   made   one.

This   we   em - bod - y   where   love   is   dis - played,
Turn - ing   the   world - ly   to - wards the   di - vine,
Ful - fill - ing   all   that they've hoped will   come   true,
God's   is   the   glo - ry,   the   good-ness, and   grace

Rings   are   pre - sent - ed   and   prom - is - es   made.
Tears   in - to   laugh - ter   and   wa - ter   to   wine.
Light - ing   with   love   all   they   dream of   and   do.
Seen   in   this   mar - riage   and   known in   this   place.

Text: John L. Bell, b.1949, © 1989, Iona Community, GIA Publication, Inc., agent
Tune: SLANE, 10 10 10 10; Irish traditional; harm. by Erik Routley, 1917-1982, © 1985, Hope Publishing Co.

869 We Will Serve the Lord

Refrain

As for me and my house, we will serve the Lord; To -

geth-er on our jour - ney, we'll walk with our God.

As for me and my house, we will serve the Lord.

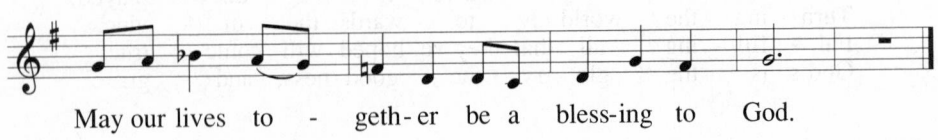

May our lives to - geth-er be a bless-ing to God.

Verses

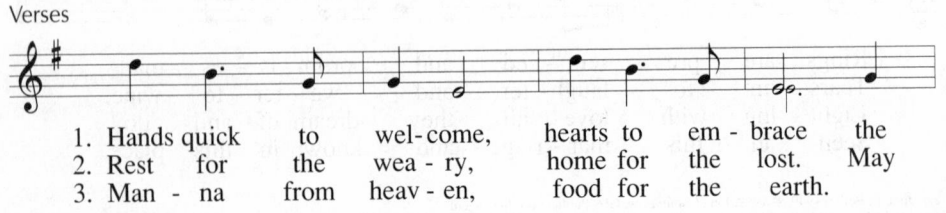

1. Hands quick to wel-come, hearts to em - brace the
2. Rest for the wea - ry, home for the lost. May
3. Man - na from heav - en, food for the earth.

D.C.

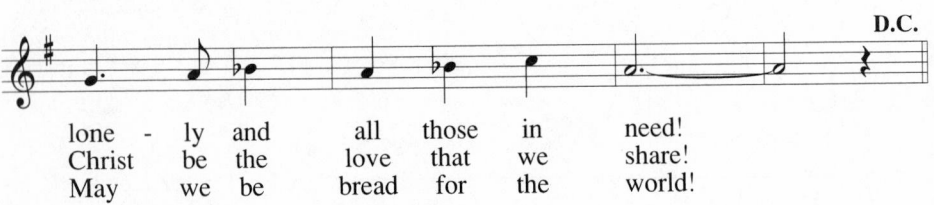

lone - ly and all those in need!
Christ be the love that we share!
May we be bread for the world!

Text: David Haas, b.1957
Tune: David Haas, b.1957
© 1993, GIA Publications, Inc.

A Nuptial Blessing 870

Refrain

May God bless you, hold and keep you;

may God's mer - cy shine on you,

guide your work and guard your rest - ing,

keep your love for ev - er new.

Verses

1. May God satisfy your longing, be refreshment at your table,
   and provide your daily bread,
   guard your going and your coming, be the solace in your silence:
   life within the lives you wed.

2. May God join your hopeful spirits, fill your hearts with truth and courage,
   trust to share both joy and tears,
   teach love to your children's children; may your household learn to witness
   living faith through all your years.

3. May God make your home a refuge where you warmly welcome strangers
   and the lowly find a place;
   make you caring, kind companions, help you meet the needs of neighbors,
   finding Christ in ev'ry face.

Text: Vicki Klima; adapt. by Michael Joncas, b.1951, and George Szews
Tune: Michael Joncas, b.1951
© 1989, GIA Publications, Inc.

871 Blessing the Marriage

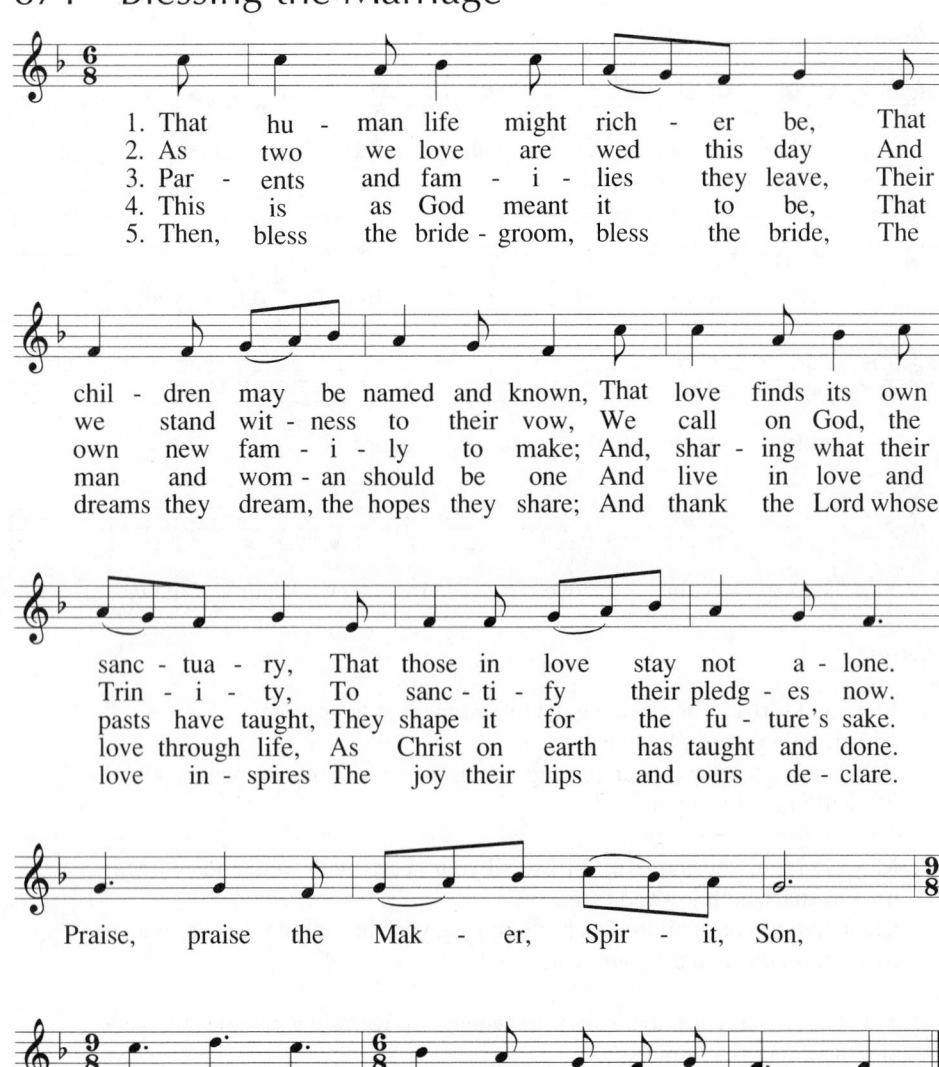

1. That hu - man life might rich - er be, That
2. As two we love are wed this day And
3. Par - ents and fam - i - lies they leave, Their
4. This is as God meant it to be, That
5. Then, bless the bride - groom, bless the bride, The

chil - dren may be named and known, That love finds its own
we stand wit - ness to their vow, We call on God, the
own new fam - i - ly to make; And, shar - ing what their
man and wom - an should be one And live in love and
dreams they dream, the hopes they share; And thank the Lord whose

sanc - tua - ry, That those in love stay not a - lone.
Trin - i - ty, To sanc - ti - fy their pledg - es now.
pasts have taught, They shape it for the fu - ture's sake.
love through life, As Christ on earth has taught and done.
love in - spires The joy their lips and ours de - clare.

Praise, praise the Mak - er, Spir - it, Son,

bless - ing this mar - riage now be - gun.

Text: John L. Bell, b.1949, © 1989, Iona Community, GIA Publications, Inc., agent
Tune: SUSSEX CAROL, 8 8 8 8 88; harm. by Ralph Vaughan Williams, 1872-1958

Wherever You Go   872

1. Wher - ev - er you go   I shall go.
Wher - ev - er you live   so shall I
live.   Your peo - ple will
be   my peo - ple,   and your   God   will
be   my God   too.
2. Wher - ev - er you die   I shall die
and   there   shall   I   be bur - ied be -
side   you.   We will be to - geth - er   for
ev - er,   and our   love   will be the
gift   of   our   life.

Text: Ruth 1:16, 17; Gregory Norbet, b.1940
Tune: Gregory Norbet, b.1940; arr. by Mary David Callahan, b.1923
© 1972, 1980, The Benedictine Foundation of the State of Vermont, Inc.

873　In Love We Choose to Live

Refrain

Love is pa - tient, love is kind.

Love is read- y to for - give,

In our love new hope is found. In

love we choose to live.

Verses

1. May love be our home; rest to soothe tired bones.
   May love be healing for our wounds.
   May love speak the truth; free us from our fear.
   May love be the heart of our anger!
   For…

2. May love be the sun shining in our darkness.
   May love fill the lives of our children.
   May love be our strength, to live a life of justice.
   May love be our call to live the Kingdom!
   For…

Text: 1 Corinthians 13; Jeanne Cotter, b.1964
Tune: Jeanne Cotter, b.1964
© 1993, GIA Publications, Inc.

Precious Lord, Take My Hand 874

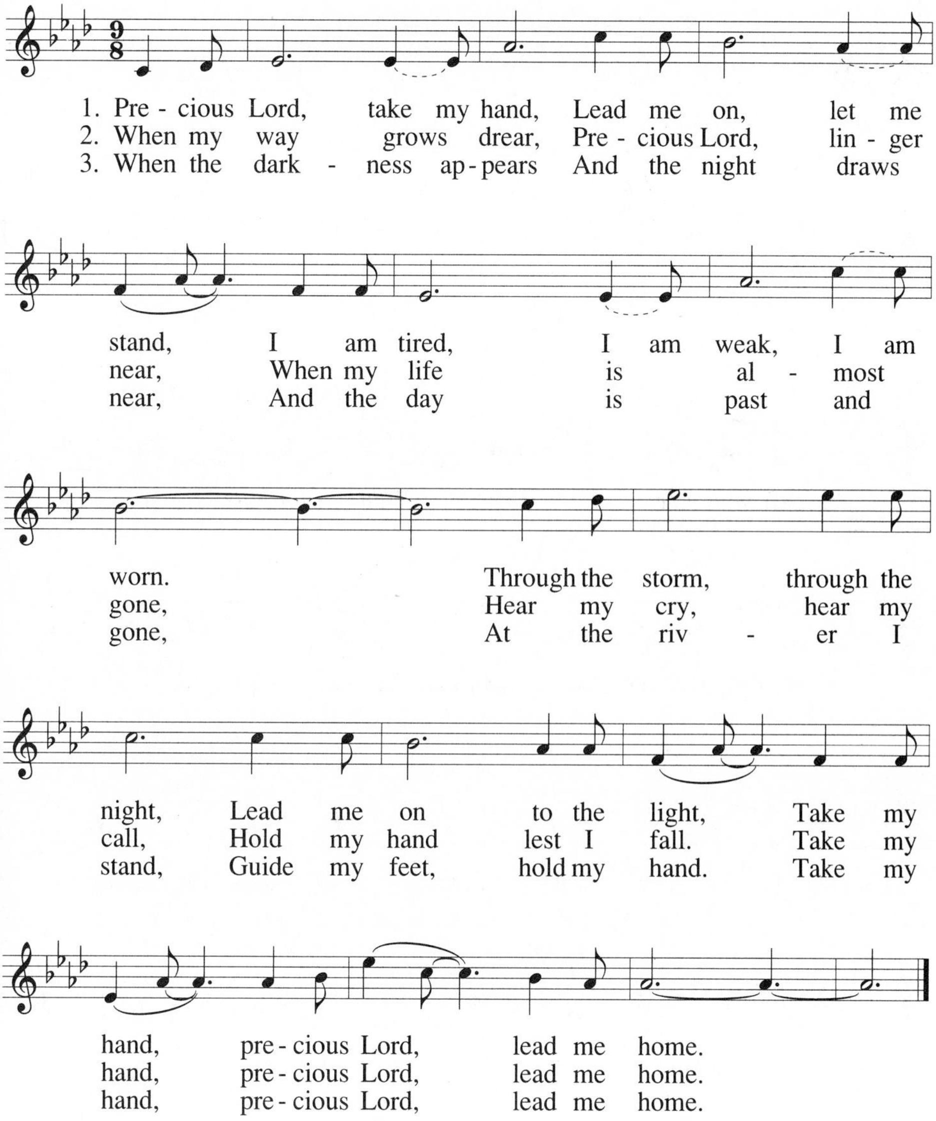

1. Pre - cious Lord, take my hand, Lead me on, let me
2. When my way grows drear, Pre - cious Lord, lin - ger
3. When the dark - ness ap - pears And the night draws

stand, I am tired, I am weak, I am
near, When my life is al - most
near, And the day is past and

worn. Through the storm, through the
gone, Hear my cry, hear my
gone, At the riv - er I

night, Lead me on to the light, Take my
call, Hold my hand lest I fall. Take my
stand, Guide my feet, hold my hand. Take my

hand, pre - cious Lord, lead me home.
hand, pre - cious Lord, lead me home.
hand, pre - cious Lord, lead me home.

Text: Thomas A. Dorsey, 1899-1993, © 1938, Unichappell Music, Inc.
Tune: PRECIOUS LORD 66 9 D; George N. Allen, © 1938, Unichappell Music, Inc.; arr. by Kelly Dobbs Mickus, b. 1966,
© 1994, GIA Publications, Inc.

875   Jesus, Heal Us

Refrain

Je - sus, heal us; Je - sus.

Je - sus, hear us now.

Verse 1

1. All who fear the Lord: Wait for God's mer - cy.

D.C.

All who love the Lord: Come, he will fill you.

Verse 2

2. All who fear the Lord: Fol - low the way.

D.C.

All who love the Lord: Hope in God's good - ness.

Verse 3

3. All who fear the Lord: Keep your hearts pre - pared.

D.C.

All who love the Lord: Be hum - bled in God's pres - ence.

Verse 4

4. All who trust the Lord: God will up -

hold you. Let us cling to our God; let us

D.C.

fall in the arms of the Lord!

Text: David Haas, b.1957
Tune: David Haas, b.1957
© 1988, GIA Publications, Inc.

He Healed the Darkness of My Mind 876

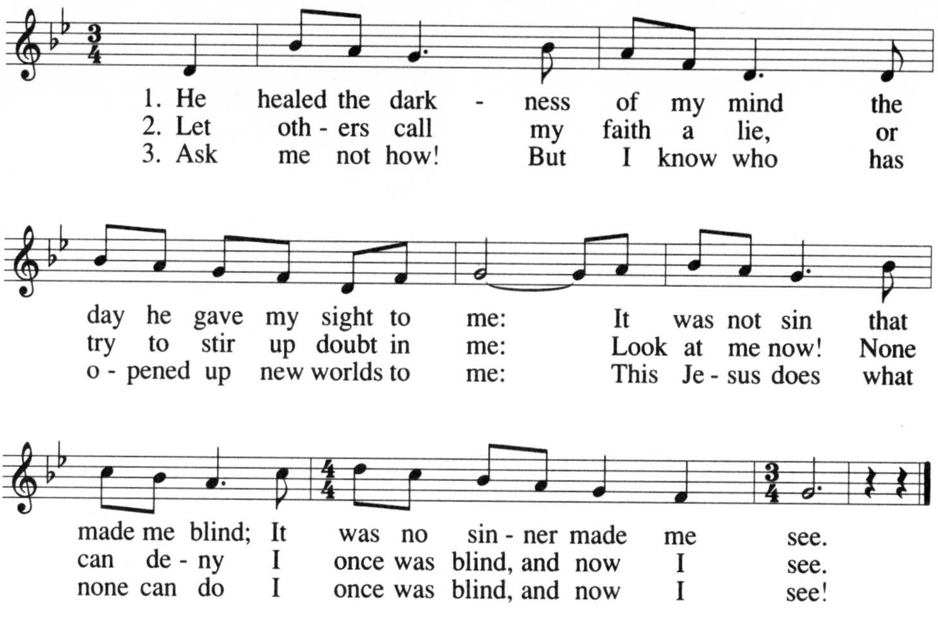

1. He   healed the dark - ness of my mind   the
2. Let   oth - ers call   my   faith a lie,   or
3. Ask   me not how!   But   I   know who   has

day he gave my sight to   me: It was not sin   that
try to stir up doubt in me: Look at me now! None
o - pened up new worlds to me: This Je - sus does what

made me blind; It   was no   sin - ner made   me   see.
can de - ny I   once was blind, and now   I   see.
none can do I   once was blind, and now   I   see!

Text: John 9; Fred Pratt Green, b.1903, © 1982, Hope Publishing Co.
Tune: ARLINGTON, LM: David Haas, b.1957, © 1988, GIA Publications, Inc.

877   Out of the Depths

1. Out   of   the depths, O   God, we call   to   you.
2. Out   of   the depths of   fear, O God, we speak.
3. God   of   the lov - ing   heart, we praise your name.

Wounds of   the   past re - main, af - fect - ing all we do.
Break - ing   the   si - len - ces, the   sear - ing truth we seek.
Dance through our lives and loves; a - noint with Spir - it flame.

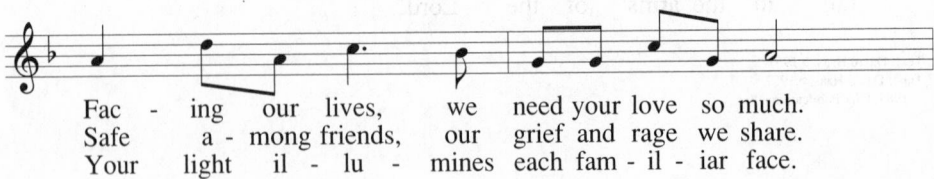

Fac -   ing   our lives,   we   need your love so much.
Safe   a - mong friends, our   grief and rage we share.
Your   light   il - lu -   mines each fam - il - iar face.

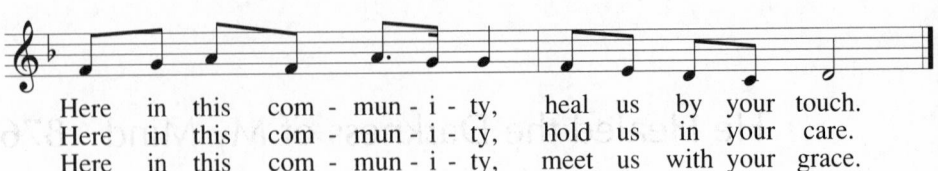

Here   in   this   com - mun - i - ty,   heal us   by your touch.
Here   in   this   com - mun - i - ty,   hold us   in your care.
Here   in   this   com - mun - i - ty,   meet us   with your grace.

Text: Psalm 130:1; Ruth Duck, b.1947, © 1992, GIA Publications, Inc.
Tune: FENNVILLE, 10 12 10 12; Robert J. Batastini, b.1942, © 1994, GIA Publications, Inc.

The Master Came to Bring Good News 878

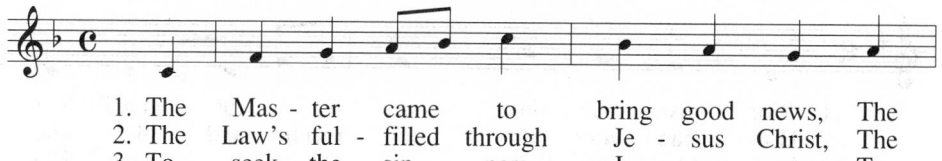

1. The Mas - ter came to bring good news, The
2. The Law's ful - filled through Je - sus Christ, The
3. To seek the sin - ners Je - sus came, To
4. For - give us, Lord, as we for - give And

news of love and free - dom, To heal the sick and
man who lived for oth - ers, The law of Christ is:
live a - mong the friend - less, To show them love that
seek to help each oth - er. For - give us, Lord, and

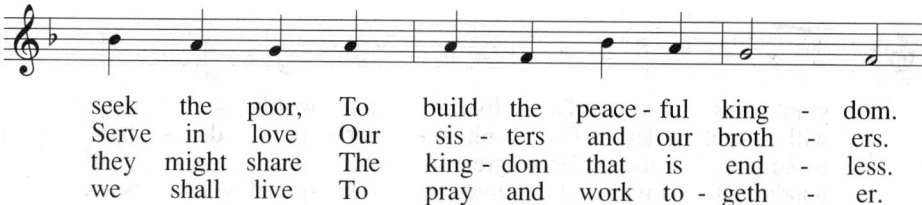

seek the poor, To build the peace - ful king - dom.
Serve in love Our sis - ters and our broth - ers.
they might share The king - dom that is end - less.
we shall live To pray and work to - geth - er.

Fa - ther, for - give us! Through Je - sus hear us!

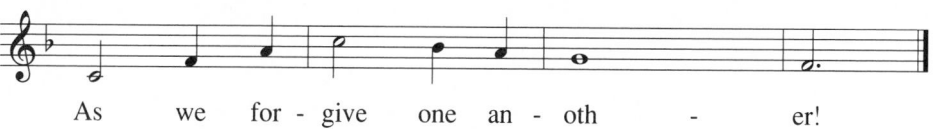

As we for - give one an - oth - er!

Text: Ralph Finn b.1941, © 1965, GIA Publications, Inc.
Tune: ICH GLAUB AN GOTT, 8 7 8 7 with refrain; *Mainz Gesangbuch*, 1870; harm. by Richard Proulx, b.1937, © 1986, GIA Publications, Inc.

879 Forgive Our Sins

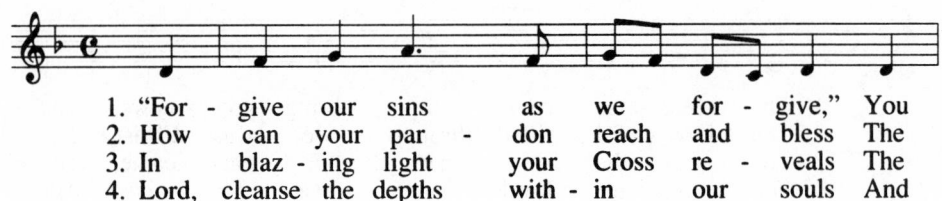

1. "For - give our sins as we for - give," You
2. How can your par - don reach and bless The
3. In blaz - ing light your Cross re - veals The
4. Lord, cleanse the depths with - in our souls And

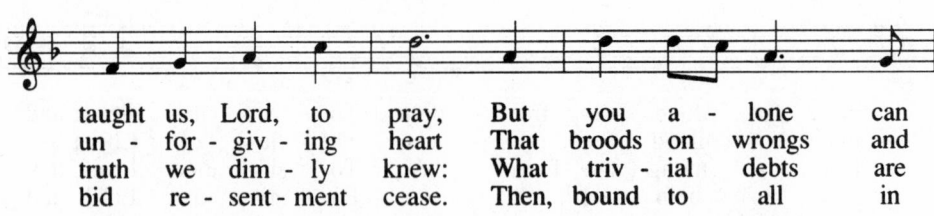

taught us, Lord, to pray, But you a - lone can
un - for - giv - ing heart That broods on wrongs and
truth we dim - ly knew: What triv - ial debts are
bid re - sent - ment cease. Then, bound to all in

grant us grace To live the words we say.
will not let Old bit - ter - ness de - part?
owed to us, How great our debt to you!
bonds of love, Our lives will spread your peace.

Text: Rosamund Herklots, b.1905, © Oxford University Press
Tune: DETROIT, CM; Supplement to *Kentucky Harmony*, 1820; harm. by Gerald H. Knight, 1908-1979, © The Royal School of Church Music

Deep Down in My Soul 880

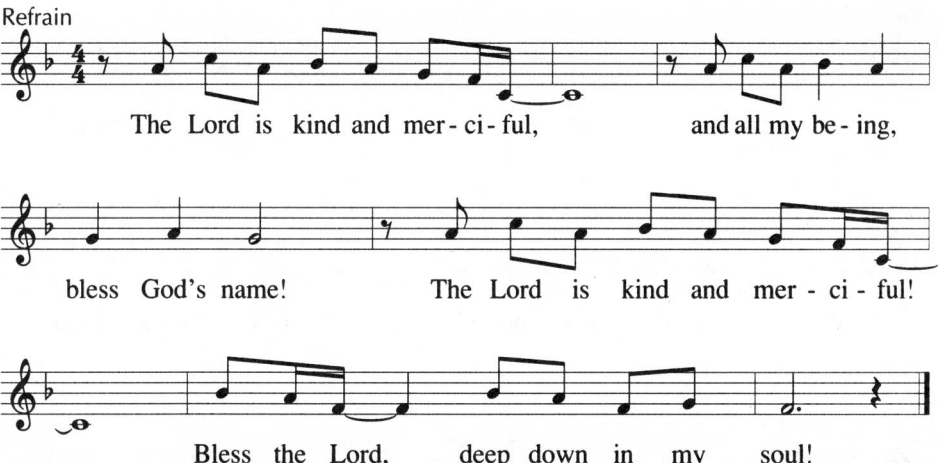

Refrain

The Lord is kind and mer-ci-ful,   and all my be-ing,

bless God's name!   The Lord is kind and mer-ci-ful!

Bless the Lord,   deep down in my   soul!

Verses

1. O my soul; bless the Lord, and now with all my being, bless God's holy name!
   O my soul: I will bless the Lord,
   forgetting not the benefits, rememb'ring God's faithfulness!

2. O my soul: bless the Lord, forgiving our offenses, healing all our ills!
   O my soul: I will bless the Lord,
   who redeems us from destruction, and crowns us with compassion!

3. Merciful, and gracious; Our God is slow to anger, abounding in love!
   Our tender God will not haunt us with our sins;
   no longer abandoned! Our God is here to save us!

4. As the east is from the west, God will come and cast away all guilt and shame!
   With tenderness, as parents to their children
   healing and compassion, for those who fear the Lord!

Text: Psalm 103; David Haas, b.1957
Tune: David Haas, b.1957; arr. by David Haas and Rob Glover, b.1950
© 1993, GIA Publications, Inc.

881 Remember Your Love

Refrain

Re - mem- ber   your   love   and your faith- ful- ness, O

Lord. Re - mem-ber   your peo-ple   and have mer-cy on us, Lord.

Verses

1. The Lord is my light and my sal - va - tion, whom should I
2. If you dwelt, O Lord, up - on our sin - ful-ness, then who could
3. O Lord, hear the sound of my call and an - swer
4. As watch-man who waits up - on the day - light, wait for the
5. Be - fore all the moun - tains were be - got - ten and earth took

fear?   The Lord is my life and my
stand?   But with you there is mer - cy and for -
me.   My heart cries out for your
Lord.   I trust in your kind - ness and re -
shape,   e - ven then, O Lord, you were our

D.C.

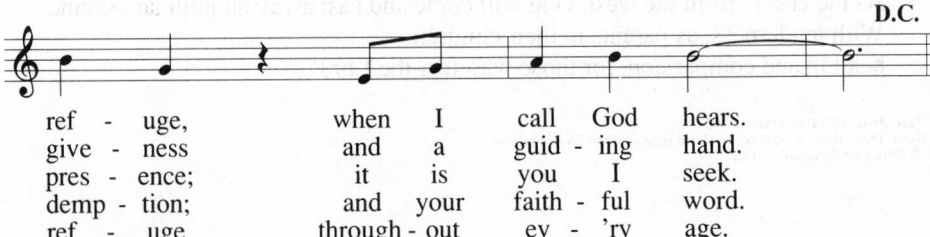

ref - uge, when I call God hears.
give - ness and a guid - ing hand.
pres - ence; it is you I seek.
demp - tion; and your faith - ful word.
ref - uge through - out ev - 'ry age.

Text: Psalm 27; Mike Balhoff, b.1946
Tune: Darryl Ducote, b.1945, and Gary Daigle, b.1957
© 1978, Damean Music. Distributed by GIA Publications, Inc.

Healer of Our Every Ill 882

Refrain

Heal-er of our ev-'ry ill, light of each to - mor-row,

give us peace be - yond our fear, and hope be-yond our sor - row.

Verses

1. You who know our fears and sad - ness,
2. In the pain and joy be - hold - ing,
3. Give us strength to love each oth - er,
4. You who know each thought and feel - ing,

Grace us with your peace and glad - ness,
How your grace is still un - fold - ing,
Ev - 'ry sis - ter, ev - 'ry broth - er,
Teach us all your way of heal - ing,

D.C.

Spir - it of all com - fort: fill our hearts.
Give us all your vi - sion: God of love.
Spir - it of all kind - ness: be our guide.
Spir - it of com-pas - sion: fill each heart.

883 Ashes

1. We rise a-gain from ash - es, from the
2. We of - fer you our fail - ures, we
3. Then rise a - gain from ash - es, let
4. Thanks be to the Fa - ther, who

good we've failed to do. We rise a - gain from
of - fer you at - tempts, The gifts not ful - ly
heal - ing come to pain, Though spring has turned to
made us like him - self. Thanks be to the

ash - es, to cre - ate our-selves a - new. If
giv - en, the dreams not ful - ly dreamt. Give our
win - ter, and sun - shine turned to rain. The
Son, who saved us by his death.

all our world is ash - es, then
stum - bl - ings di - rec - tion, give our
rain we'll use for grow - ing, and cre -
Thanks be to the Spir - it, who cre -

must our lives be true, An of - fer-ing of
vi - sions wid - er view, An of - fer-ing of
ate the world a - new From an of - fer-ing of
ates the world a - new From an of - fer-ing of

ash - es, an of - fer - ing to you.
ash - es, an of - fer - ing to you.
ash - es, an of - fer - ing to you.
ash - es, an of - fer - ing to you.

Text: Tom Conry, b.1951
Tune: Tom Conry, b.1951; acc. by Michael Joncas, b.1951
© 1978, New Dawn Music

I Want to Call You 884

Refrain

I want to call you by your name while I live.

I will call you: "My God." I will

thank you, I will sing my praise to you.

Verses

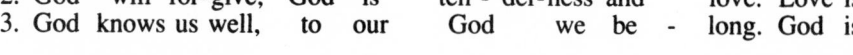

1. God calls to me: "Come forth from your grave." Like an
2. God will for-give, God is ten - der-ness and love. Love is
3. God knows us well, to our God we be - long. God is

D.C.

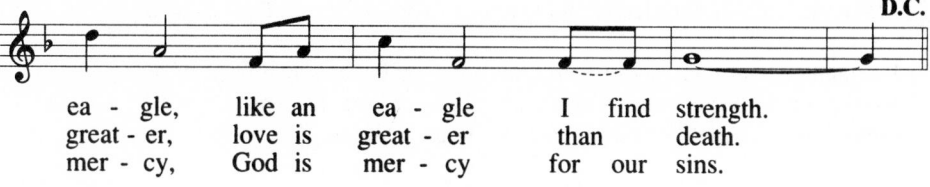

ea - gle, like an ea - gle I find strength.
great - er, love is great - er than death.
mer - cy, God is mer - cy for our sins.

Text: David Haas, b.1957
Tune: David Haas, b.1957

885 Remember Your Mercy, Lord

Refrain

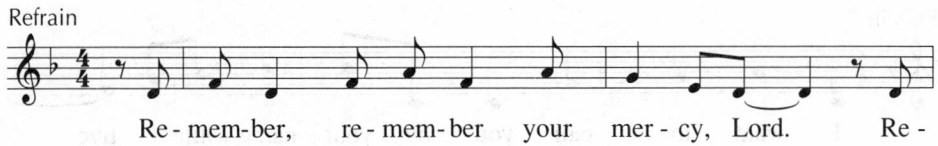

Re - mem-ber, re - mem-ber your mer - cy, Lord. Re -

mem - ber, re - mem - ber your mer - cy, Lord.

Hear your peo - ple's prayer as they call to you: re -

mem - ber, re - mem - ber your mer - cy, Lord.

Verses

1. Lord, make me know your ways. Lord, teach me your paths.
   Make me walk in your truth, and teach me: for you are God my Savior.

2. Remember your mercy, Lord, and the love you have shown from of old.
   Do not remember the sins of my youth. In your love, remember me,
   in your love, remember me, because of your goodness, O Lord.

3. The Lord is good and upright. He shows the path to all who stray,
   he guides the humble in the right path; he teaches his way to the poor.

Text: Psalm 25:4-9; © 1963, The Grail, GIA Publications, Inc., agent; refrain, Paul Inwood, b.1947, © 1987
Tune: Paul Inwood, b.1947, © 1987
Published by OCP Publications

O Food of Exiles Lowly 886

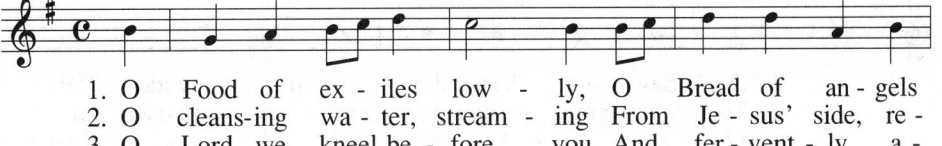

1. O Food of ex - iles low - ly, O Bread of an - gels
2. O cleans-ing wa - ter, stream - ing From Je - sus' side, re -
3. O Lord, we kneel be - fore you And fer - vent - ly a -

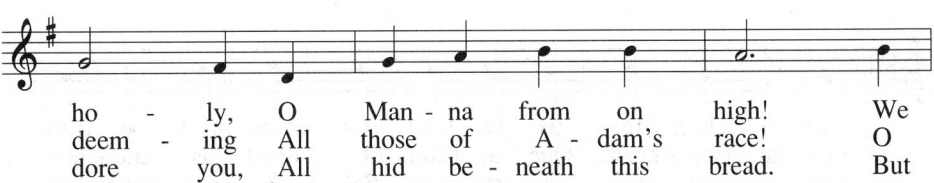

ho - ly, O Man - na from on high! We
deem - ing All those of A - dam's race! O
dore you, All hid be - neath this bread. But

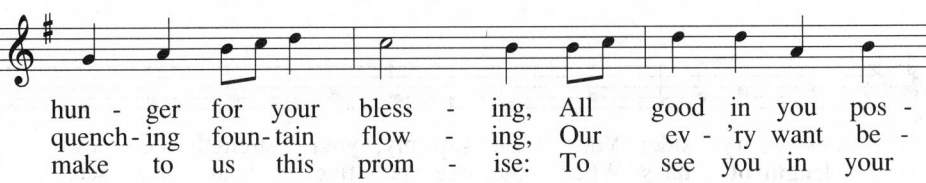

hun - ger for your bless - ing, All good in you pos -
quench - ing foun - tain flow - ing, Our ev - 'ry want be -
make to us this prom - ise: To see you in your

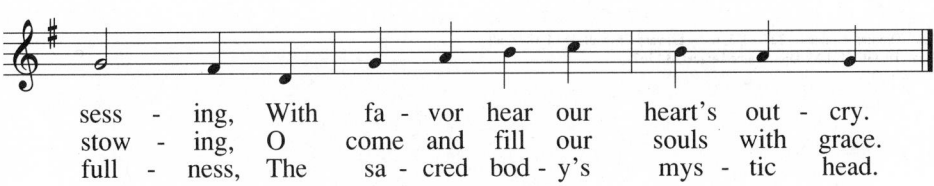

sess - ing, With fa - vor hear our heart's out - cry.
stow - ing, O come and fill our souls with grace.
full - ness, The sa - cred bod - y's mys - tic head.

Text: *O esca viatorum; Mainz Gesangbuch,* 1661; tr. by M. Owen Lee, CSB, b.1930
Tune: INNSBRUCK, 77 6 77 8; Heinrich Isaak, c.1460-c.1527; harm. by J.S. Bach, 1685-1750

887 O Saving Victim / O Salutaris

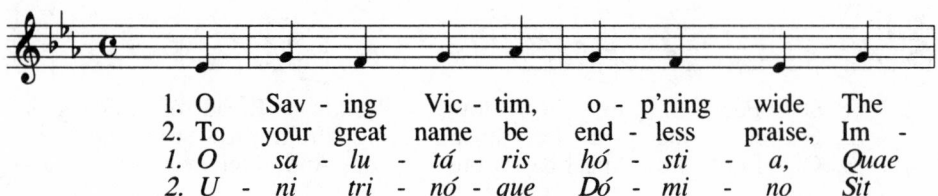

1. O   Sav - ing   Vic - tim,   o - p'ning   wide   The
2. To   your great   name   be   end - less   praise,   Im -
1. O   sa - lu - tá - ris   hó - sti - a,   Quae
2. U - ni   tri - nó - que   Dó - mi - no   Sit

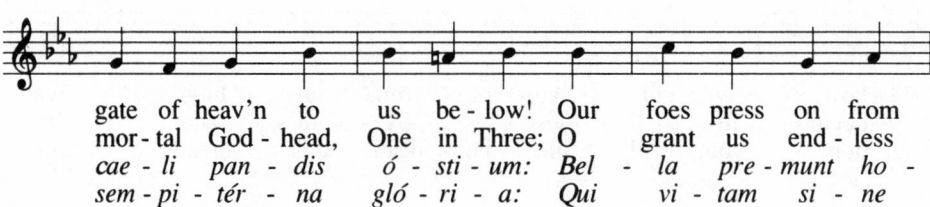

gate of heav'n   to   us   be - low!   Our   foes press   on from
mor - tal   God - head,   One   in Three;   O   grant   us   end - less
cae - li   pan - dis   ó - sti - um: Bel - la   pre - munt ho -
sem - pi - tér - na   gló - ri - a: Qui   vi - tam   si - ne

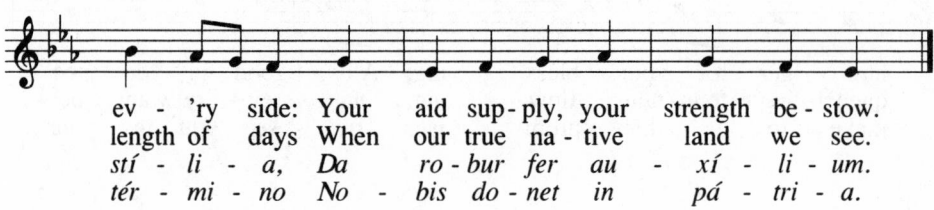

ev - 'ry   side: Your   aid sup - ply, your   strength be - stow.
length of   days When   our true na - tive   land   we   see.
stí - li - a,   Da   ro - bur fer au - xí - li - um.
tér - mi - no   No - bis do - net   in   pá - tri - a.

Text: Thomas Aquinas, 1227-1275; tr. by Edward Caswall, 1814-1878, alt.
Tune: DUGUET, LM: Dieu donne Duguet, d.1767

Come Adore / Tantum Ergo   888

1. Come a - dore this won-drous pres - ence, Bow to Christ the
2. Glo - ry be to God the Fa - ther, Praise to his co -
1. *Tan - tum er - go Sa - cra - mén - tum Ve - ne - ré - mur*
2. *Ge - ni - tó - ri, Ge - ni - tó - que Laus et ju - bi -*

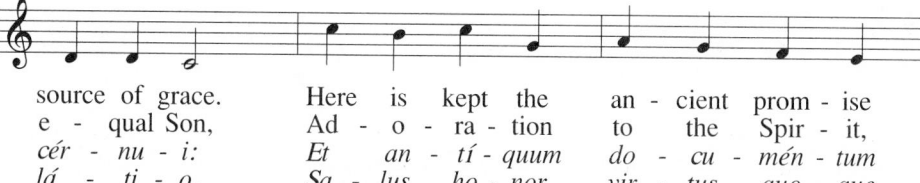

source of grace. Here is kept the an - cient prom - ise
e - qual Son, Ad - o - ra - tion to the Spir - it,
cér - nu - i: Et an - tí - quum do - cu - mén - tum
lá - ti - o, Sa - lus, ho - nor, vir - tus quo - que

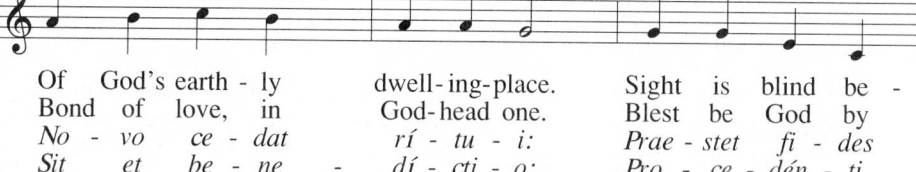

Of God's earth - ly dwell-ing-place. Sight is blind be -
Bond of love, in God-head one. Blest be God by
No - vo ce - dat rí - tu - i: Prae - stet fi - des
Sit et be - ne - dí - cti - o: Pro - ce - dén - ti

fore God's glo - ry, Faith a - lone may see his face.
all cre - a - tion Joy - ous - ly while a - ges run.
sup - ple - mén - tum Sén - su - um de - fé - ctu - i.
ab u - tró - que Com - par sit lau - dá - ti - o.

Text: Thomas Aquinas, 1227-1274; tr. by James Quinn, SJ, b.1919, © 1969
Tune: ST. THOMAS, 8 7 8 7 8 7; John F. Wade, 1711-1786

889 My Country, 'Tis of Thee

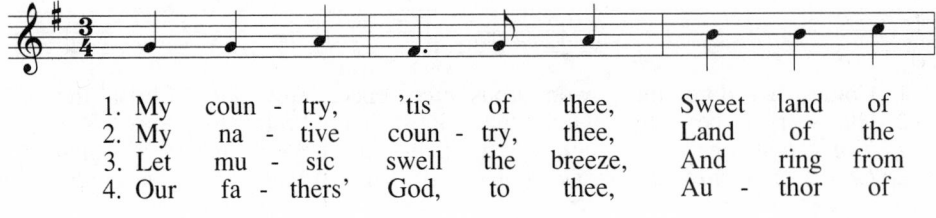

1. My coun - try, 'tis of thee, Sweet land of
2. My na - tive coun - try, thee, Land of the
3. Let mu - sic swell the breeze, And ring from
4. Our fa - thers' God, to thee, Au - thor of

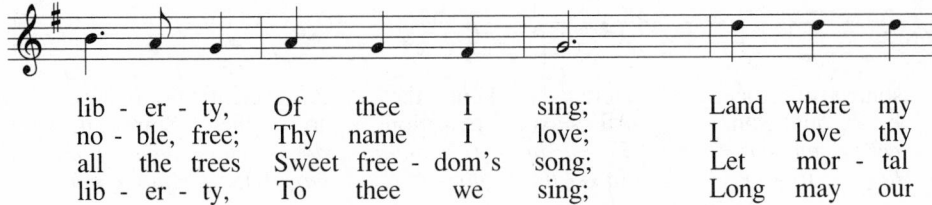

lib - er - ty, Of thee I sing; Land where my
no - ble, free; Thy name I love; I love thy
all the trees Sweet free - dom's song; Let mor - tal
lib - er - ty, To thee we sing; Long may our

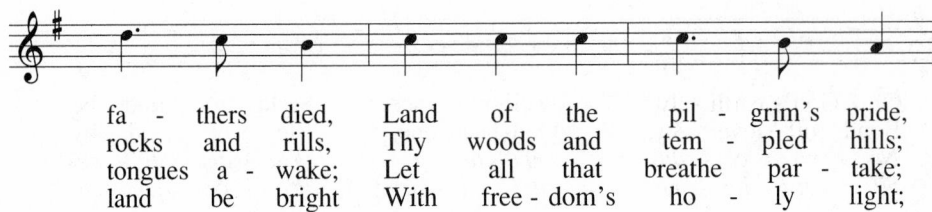

fa - thers died, Land of the pil - grim's pride,
rocks and rills, Thy woods and tem - pled hills;
tongues a - wake; Let all that breathe par - take;
land be bright With free - dom's ho - ly light;

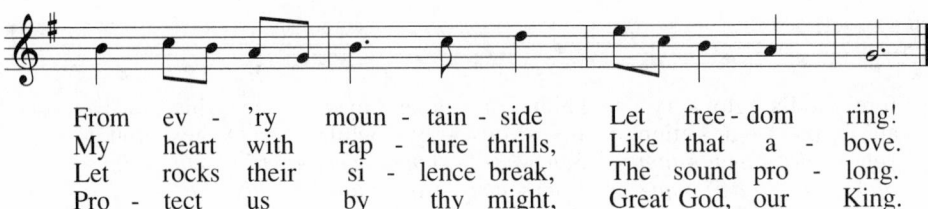

From ev - 'ry moun - tain - side Let free - dom ring!
My heart with rap - ture thrills, Like that a - bove.
Let rocks their si - lence break, The sound pro - long.
Pro - tect us by thy might, Great God, our King.

Text: Samuel F. Smith, 1808-1895
Tune: AMERICA, 66 4 666 4; *Thesaurus Musicus*, 1744

America the Beautiful 890

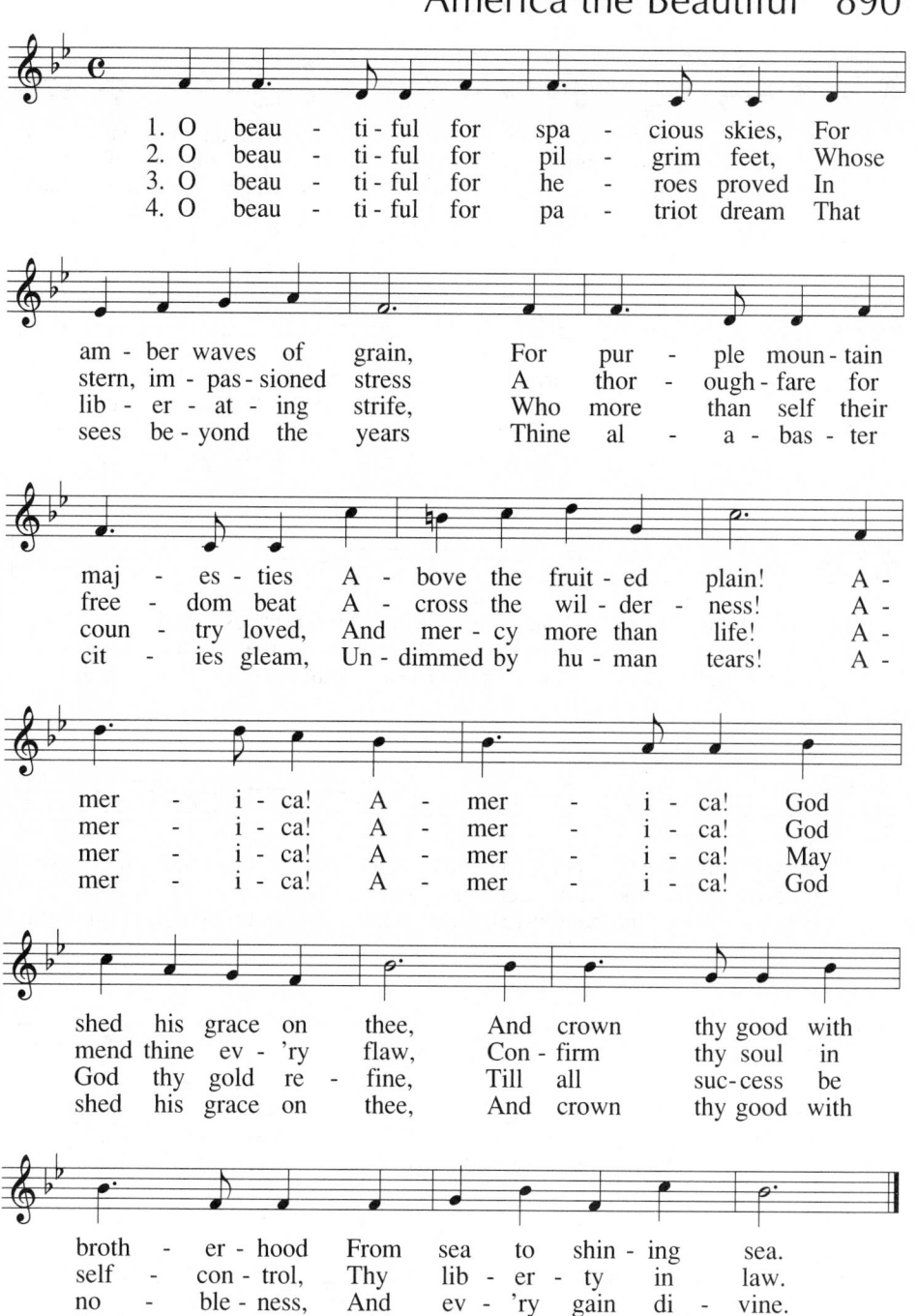

1. O beau - ti - ful for spa - cious skies, For
2. O beau - ti - ful for pil - grim feet, Whose
3. O beau - ti - ful for he - roes proved In
4. O beau - ti - ful for pa - triot dream That

am - ber waves of grain, For pur - ple moun - tain
stern, im - pas - sioned stress A thor - ough - fare for
lib - er - at - ing strife, Who more than self their
sees be - yond the years Thine al - a - bas - ter

maj - es - ties A - bove the fruit - ed plain! A -
free - dom beat A - cross the wil - der - ness! A -
coun - try loved, And mer - cy more than life! A -
cit - ies gleam, Un - dimmed by hu - man tears! A -

mer - i - ca! A - mer - i - ca! God
mer - i - ca! A - mer - i - ca! God
mer - i - ca! A - mer - i - ca! May
mer - i - ca! A - mer - i - ca! God

shed his grace on thee, And crown thy good with
mend thine ev - 'ry flaw, Con - firm thy soul in
God thy gold re - fine, Till all suc - cess be
shed his grace on thee, And crown thy good with

broth - er - hood From sea to shin - ing sea.
self - con - trol, Thy lib - er - ty in law.
no - ble - ness, And ev - 'ry gain di - vine.
broth - er - hood From sea to shin - ing sea.

Text: Katherine L. Bates, 1859-1929
Tune: MATERNA, CMD; Samuel A. Ward, 1848-1903

891 Star-Spangled Banner

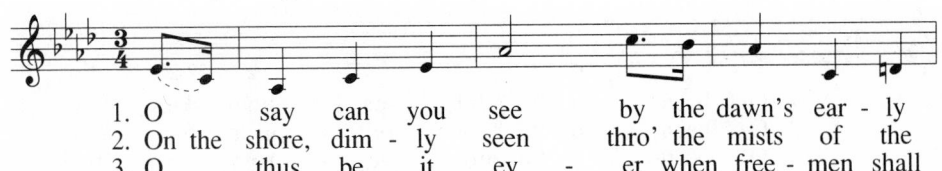

1. O   say   can   you   see   by the dawn's ear - ly
2. On the shore, dim - ly   seen   thro' the mists   of   the
3. O   thus   be   it   ev -   er when free - men shall

light,   What   so   proud -   ly   we   hailed   at the
deep,   Where the foe's   haugh - ty   host   in dead
stand   Be - tween   their loved   homes   and the

twi - light's last   gleam - ing, Whose broad stripes and   bright
si - lence re - pos - es,   What   is   that which the
war's des - o - la - tion! Blest   with   vic - t'ry   and

stars, through the   per - il - ous fight, O'er the ram - parts we
breeze, o'er the   tow - er - ing steep, As   it   fit - ful - ly
peace,   may the heav'n-res-cued land Praise the Pow'r that hath

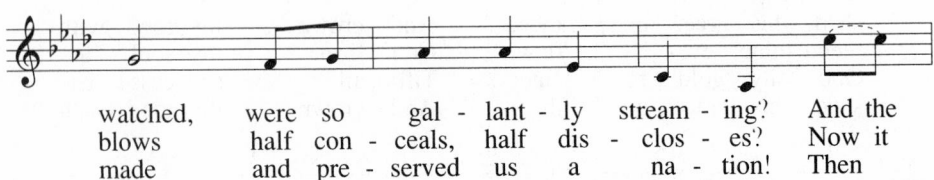

watched,   were so   gal - lant - ly stream - ing? And the
blows   half con - ceals, half dis - clos - es? Now it
made   and pre - served us   a   na - tion! Then

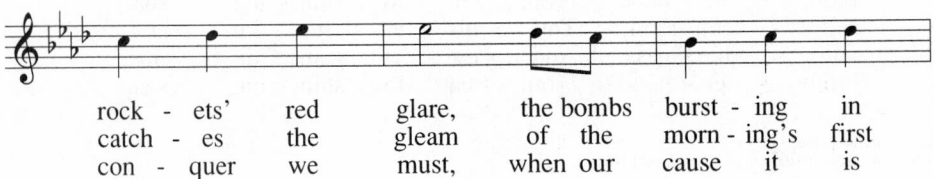

rock - ets' red   glare,   the bombs burst - ing in
catch - es   the   gleam   of the   morn - ing's first
con - quer   we   must,   when our cause   it   is

air,	Gave	proof	through the	night	that our
beam,	In full	glo -	ry re -	flect - ed	now
just,	And	this	be our	mot - to,	"In

flag	was	still	there.	O	say	does	that
shined	on	the	stream,	'Tis the	Star - Span -	gled
God	is	our	trust."	And the	Star - Span -	gled

Star - Span - gled	Ban - ner	yet	wave	O'er the
Ban - ner	O	long	may	it	wave	O'er the
Ban - ner	in	tri - umph	shall	wave	O'er the

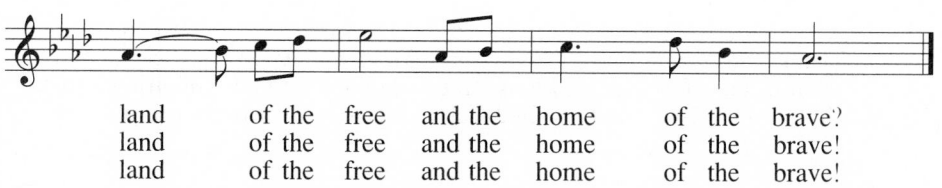

land	of the	free	and the	home	of	the	brave?
land	of the	free	and the	home	of	the	brave!
land	of the	free	and the	home	of	the	brave!

Text: Francis S. Key, 1779-1843
Tune: STAR SPANGLED BANNER; Irregular, John S. Smith, 1750-1836

892 God of Eve and God of Mary

Refrain

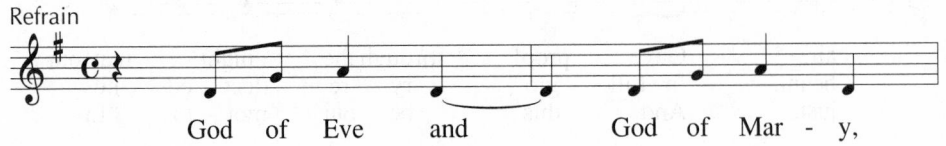

God of Eve and God of Mar - y,

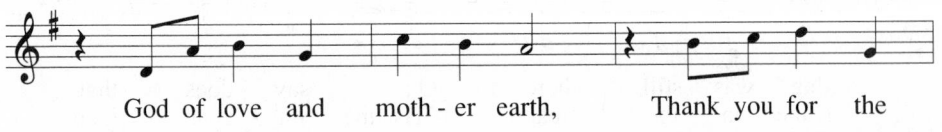

God of love and moth - er earth, Thank you for the

ones who with us Shared their life and gave us birth.

Verses

1. As you came to earth in Je - sus, So you come to
2. Thank you, that the Church, our Moth-er, Gives us bread and
3. Thank you for be - long - ing, shel-ter, Bonds of friend-ship,
4. God of Eve and God of Mar - y, Christ our broth - er,

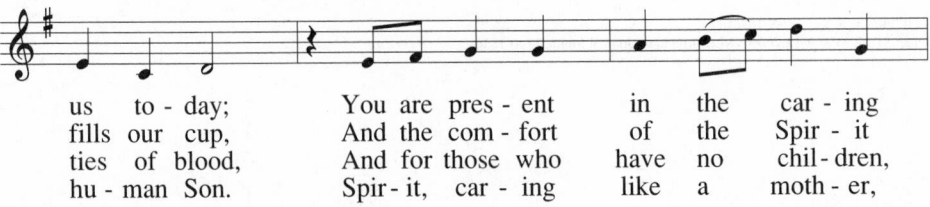

us to - day; You are pres - ent in the car - ing
fills our cup, And the com - fort of the Spir - it
ties of blood, And for those who have no chil-dren,
hu - man Son. Spir-it, car - ing like a moth - er,

D.C.

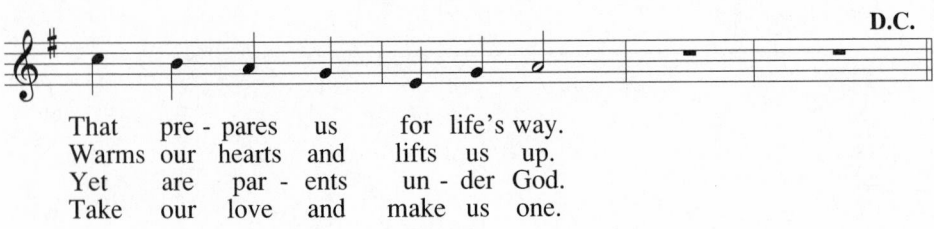

That pre - pares us for life's way.
Warms our hearts and lifts us up.
Yet are par - ents un - der God.
Take our love and make us one.

Text: Fred Kaan, b.1929, © 1989, Hope Publishing Co.
Tune: FARRELL, 8 7 8 7 with refrain; Thomas J. Porter, b.1958, © 1994, GIA Publications, Inc.

God of Adam, God of Joseph 893

Refrain

God of A - dam, God of Jo - seph,

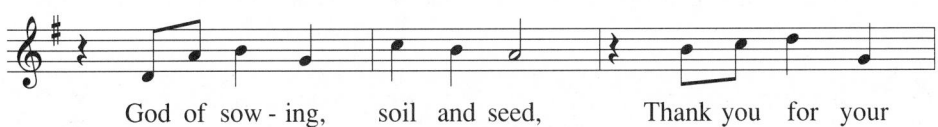

God of sow - ing, soil and seed, Thank you for your

world of prom - ise: Milk and hon - ey, wine and bread.

Verses

1. God, you make us your com - pan - ions, Shar - ers of your
2. May your pas - sion for cre - a - tion Be re - flect - ed
3. Thank you for all men en - trust - ed With the charge of
4. Ab - ba (Fa - ther), God of Jo - seph, Hu - man Christ whose

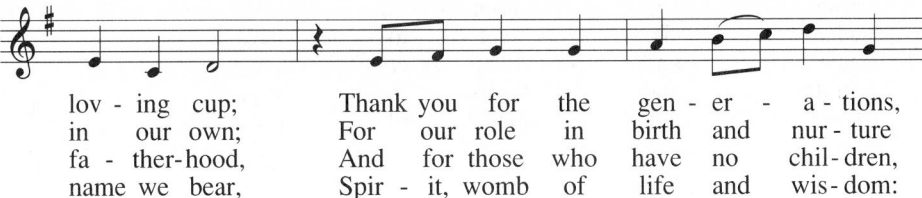

lov - ing cup; Thank you for the gen - er - a - tions,
in our own; For our role in birth and nur - ture
fa - ther - hood, And for those who have no chil - dren,
name we bear, Spir - it, womb of life and wis - dom:

D.C.

Weave of names and threads of hope.
Make through us your pres - ence known.
Yet are par - ents un - der God.
Thank you, God, for who we are!

Text: Fred Kaan, b.1929, © 1989, Hope Publishing Co.
Tune: FARRELL, 8 7 8 7 with refrain; Thomas J. Porter, b.1958, © 1994, GIA Publications, Inc.

894 The God of All Eternity

1. The God of all e - ter - ni - ty, Un - bound by
2. What shall we of - fer God to - day— Our dreams of
3. God does not share our doubts and fears, Nor shrinks from
4. Let faith or for - tune rise or fall, Let dreams and
5. God grant that we, in this new year, May show the

space yet al - ways near, Is pres - ent
what we can - not see, Or, with eyes
the un - known or strange: The one who
dread both have their day; Those whom God
world the King - dom's face, And let our

where his peo - ple meet To cel - e -
fas - tened to the past, Our dread of
fash - ioned heav'n and earth Makes all things
loves walk un - a - fraid With Christ their
work and wor - ship thrive As signs of

brate the com - ing year.
what is yet to be?
new and ush - ers change.
guide and Christ their way.
hope and means of grace.

Text: John L. Bell, b.1949, © 1989, Iona Community, GIA Publications, Inc., agent
Tune: O WALY WALY 8 8 8 8; English traditional; arr. by John L. Bell, b.1949, © 1989, Iona Community, GIA Publications, Inc., agent

Greet Now the Swiftly Changing Year 895

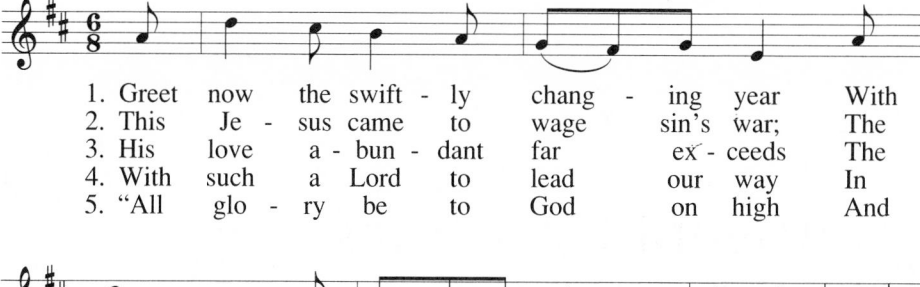

1. Greet now the swift - ly chang - ing year With
2. This Je - sus came to wage sin's war; The
3. His love a - bun - dant far ex - ceeds The
4. With such a Lord to lead our way In
5. "All glo - ry be to God on high And

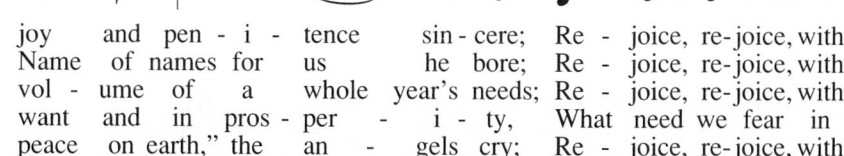

joy and pen - i - tence sin - cere; Re - joice, re-joice, with
Name of names for us he bore; Re - joice, re-joice, with
vol - ume of a whole year's needs; Re - joice, re-joice, with
want and in pros - per - i - ty, What need we fear in
peace on earth," the an - gels cry; Re - joice, re-joice, with

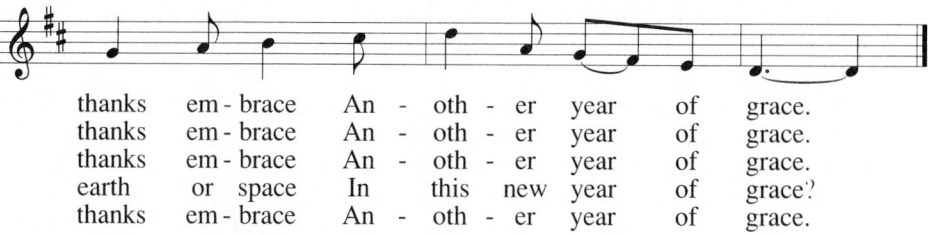

thanks em - brace An - oth - er year of grace.
thanks em - brace An - oth - er year of grace.
thanks em - brace An - oth - er year of grace.
earth or space In this new year of grace?
thanks em - brace An - oth - er year of grace.

Text: Slovak, 17th C.; tr. Jaroslav J. Vajda, b.1919, alt. © 1969, Concordia Publishing House
Tune: SIXTH NIGHT, 88 86; Alfred V. Fedak, © 1989, Selah Publishing Co.

Advent/Christmas

896 In various ways and various places the churches have marked the days around the winter solstice (adapting when possible in the southern hemisphere when December and January surround the summer solstice). Christians have quite naturally kept from their former religions and traditions all manner of customs and rituals, giving these a home around the many-faceted celebration of the Word-made-flesh, the manifestation of God-with-us.

The present Roman calendar has a period of three to four weeks before December 25. This is called Advent and it is filled with beautiful scriptures, songs, prayers and gestures. These have no single focus but abound with images: of God's promise and human longing, of the beauty in both darkness and light, of the earth's sorrows and its fullness, of the goodness and mystery of time. The spirit of the church's Advent is in the silence and song that arise from constant attention to the human condition.

At Christmas this spirit blossoms in acclamation: the stories of nativity and epiphany, of Mary and of the Innocents, of Jesus baptized and of water become wine. Until well into January the songs and sights and smells of Christmas surround the church not with sentimental fantasies but with everyday faith in a gracious God. The festivals of the Christmas season bear their own reflection of what is proclaimed on every Sunday of the year and in every baptism: our lives are caught up now in Jesus who was born of the virgin Mary, who suffered, died and has been raised.

The lectionary of Advent/Christmas is the foundation of these winter days. These scriptures, read and pondered year after year, turn the Christian and the church toward that peace and glory we name but do not yet know.

FIRST SUNDAY OF ADVENT / A 897

READING I
Isaiah 2:1-5 / 1

This is what Isaiah, son of Amoz,
saw concerning Judah and Jerusalem.
   In days to come,
the mountain of the LORD's house
   shall be established as
      the highest mountain
   and raised above the hills.
All nations shall stream toward it;
   many peoples shall come and say:
"Come, let us climb the LORD's
      mountain,
   to the house of the God of Jacob,
that he may instruct us in his ways,
   and we may walk in his paths."

For from Zion shall go forth
      instruction,
   and the word of the LORD from
      Jerusalem.
He shall judge between the nations,
   and impose terms on many peoples.
They shall beat their swords into
      plowshares
   and their spears into pruning hooks;
one nation shall not raise the sword
      against another,
   nor shall they train for war again.
O house of Jacob, come,
   let us walk in the light of the Lord!

RESPONSORIAL PSALM
Psalm 122:1-2, 3-4, 4-5, 6-7, 8-9

℟. **Let us go rejoicing to the house of the Lord.**

I rejoiced because they said to me,
   "We will go up to the house of the
      LORD."
And now we have set foot
   within your gates, O Jerusalem. ℟.

Jerusalem, built as a city
   with compact unity.
To it the tribes go up,
   the tribes of the LORD. ℟.

According to the decree for Israel,
   to give thanks to the name of the
      LORD.

In it are set up judgment seats,
   seats for the house of David. ℟.

Pray for the peace of Jerusalem!
   May those who love you prosper!
May peace be within your walls,
   prosperity in your buildings. ℟.

Because of my brothers and friends
   I will say, "Peace be within you!"
Because of the house of the LORD, our
      God,
   I will pray for your good. ℟.

READING II
Romans 13:11-14

Brothers and sisters: You know the time; it is the hour now for you to awake from sleep. For our salvation is nearer now than when we first believed; the night is advanced, the day is at hand. Let us then throw off the works of darkness and put on the armor of light; let us conduct ourselves properly as in the day, not in orgies and drunkenness, not in promiscuity and lust, not in rivalry and jealousy. But put on the Lord Jesus Christ, and make no provision for the desires of the flesh.

GOSPEL
Matthew 24:37-44

Jesus said to his disciples: "As it was in the days of Noah, so it will be at the coming of the Son of Man. In those days before the flood, they were eating and drinking, marrying and giving in marriage, up to the day that Noah entered the ark. They did not know until the flood came and carried them all away. So will it be also at the coming of the Son of Man. Two men will be out in the field; one will be taken, and one will be left. Two women will be grinding at the mill; one will be taken, and one will be left. Therefore, stay awake! For you do not know on which day your Lord will come. Be sure of this: if the master of the house had known the hour of night when the thief was coming, he would have stayed awake and not let his house be broken into. So too, you also must be prepared, for at an hour you do not expect, the Son of Man will come."

898   FIRST SUNDAY OF ADVENT / B

READING I
Isaiah 63:16b-17, 19b; 64:2-7 / 2

You, Lord, are our father,
    our redeemer you are named forever.
Why do you let us wander, O Lord, from
    your ways,
    and harden our hearts so that we fear
    you not?
Return for the sake of your servants,
    the tribes of your heritage.
Oh, that you would rend the heavens and
    come down,
    with the mountains quaking before
    you,
while you wrought awesome deeds we
    could not hope for,
    such as they had not heard of from
    of old.
No ear has ever heard, no eye ever seen,
    any God but you
    doing such deeds for those who
    wait for him.

Would that you might meet us doing
    right,
    that we were mindful of you in our
    ways!
Behold, you are angry, and we are sinful;
    all of us have become like unclean
    people,
    all our good deeds are like polluted
    rags;
we have all withered like leaves,
    and our guilt carries us away like
    the wind.
There is none who calls upon your name,
    who rouses himself to cling to you;
for you have hidden your face from us
    and have delivered us up to our guilt.
Yet, O Lord, you are our father;
    we are the clay and you the potter:
    we are all the work of your hands.

RESPONSORIAL PSALM
Psalm 80:2-3, 15-16, 18-19

℟. **Lord, make us turn to you; let us see your face and we shall be saved.**

O shepherd of Israel, hearken,
    from your throne upon the cherubim,
    shine forth.
Rouse your power,
    and come to save us. ℟.

Once again, O Lord of hosts,
    look down from heaven, and see;
take care of this vine,
    and protect what your right hand has
    planted,

the son of man whom you yourself
    made strong. ℟.

May your help be with the man of your
    right hand,
    with the son of man whom you
    yourself made strong.
Then we will no more withdraw from
    you;
    give us new life, and we will call
    upon your name. ℟.

READING II
1 Corinthians 1:3-9

Brothers and sisters: Grace to you and peace from God our Father and the Lord Jesus Christ.

I give thanks to my God always on your account for the grace of God bestowed on you in Christ Jesus, that in him you were enriched in every way, with all discourse and all knowledge, as the testimony to Christ was confirmed among you, so that you are not lacking in any spiritual gift as you wait for the revelation of our Lord Jesus Christ. He will keep you firm to the end, irreproachable on the day of our Lord Jesus Christ. God is faithful, and by him you were called to fellowship with his Son, Jesus Christ our Lord.

GOSPEL
Mark 13:33-37

Jesus said to his disciples: "Be watchful! Be alert! You do not know when the time will come. It is like a man traveling abroad. He leaves home and places his servants in charge, each with his own work, and orders the gatekeeper to be on the watch. Watch, therefore; you do not know when the lord of the house is coming, whether in the evening, or at midnight, or at cockcrow, or in the morning. May he not come suddenly and find you sleeping. What I say to you, I say to all: 'Watch!'"

FIRST SUNDAY OF ADVENT / C   899

READING I   *Jeremiah 33:14-16 / 3*

The days are coming, says the Lord,
    when I will fulfill the promise
    I made to the house of Israel and
        Judah.
In those days, in that time,
    I will raise up for David a just shoot;

he shall do what is right and just in
    the land.
In those days Judah shall be safe
    and Jerusalem shall dwell secure;
    this is what they shall call her:
    "The Lord our justice."

RESPONSORIAL PSALM   *Psalm 25:4-5, 8-9, 10, 14*

℟. To you, O Lord, I lift my soul.

Your ways, O Lord, make known to me;
    teach me your paths,
guide me in your truth and teach me,
    for you are God my savior,
    and for you I wait all the day. ℟.

Good and upright is the Lord;
    thus he shows sinners the way.
He guides the humble to justice,
    and teaches the humble his way. ℟.

All the paths of the Lord are kindness
    and constancy
    toward those who keep his covenant
    and his decrees.
The friendship of the Lord is with those
    who fear him,
    and his covenant, for their
    instruction. ℟.

READING II   *1 Thessalonians 3:12—4:2*

Brothers and sisters: May the Lord make you increase and abound in love for one another and for all, just as we have for you, so as to strengthen your hearts, to be blameless in holiness before our God and Father at the coming of our Lord Jesus with all his holy ones. Amen.

    Finally, brothers and sisters, we earnestly ask and exhort you in the Lord Jesus that, as you received from us how you should conduct yourselves to please God—and as you are conducting yourselves—you do so even more. For you know what instructions we gave you through the Lord Jesus.

GOSPEL   *Luke 21:25-28, 34-36*

Jesus said to his disciples: "There will be signs in the sun, the moon, and the stars, and on earth nations will be in dismay, perplexed by the roaring of the sea and the waves. People will die of fright in anticipation of what is coming upon the world, for the powers of the heavens will be shaken. And then they will see the Son of Man coming in a cloud with power and great glory. But when these signs begin to happen, stand erect and raise your heads because your redemption is at hand.

    "Beware that your hearts do not become drowsy from carousing and drunkenness and the anxieties of daily life, and that day catch you by surprise like a trap. For that day will assault everyone who lives on the face of the earth. Be vigilant at all times and pray that you have the strength to escape the tribulations that are imminent and to stand before the Son of Man."

900 SECOND SUNDAY OF ADVENT / A

READING I
Isaiah 11:1-10 / 4

On that day, a shoot shall sprout from the
stump of Jesse,
and from his roots a bud shall
blossom.
The spirit of the Lord shall rest upon him:
a spirit of wisdom and of
understanding,
a spirit of counsel and of strength,
a spirit of knowledge and of fear of
the Lord,
and his delight shall be the fear of
the Lord.
Not by appearance shall he judge,
nor by hearsay shall he decide,
but he shall judge the poor with justice,
and decide aright for the land's
afflicted.
He shall strike the ruthless with the rod
of his mouth,
and with the breath of his lips he shall
slay the wicked.
Justice shall be the band around his waist,
and faithfulness a belt upon his hips.

Then the wolf shall be a guest of the
lamb,
and the leopard shall lie down with
the kid;
the calf and the young lion shall browse
together,
with a little child to guide them.
The cow and the bear shall be neighbors,
together their young shall rest;
the lion shall eat hay like the ox.
The baby shall play by the cobra's den,
and the child lay his hand on the
adder's lair.
There shall be no harm or ruin on all my
holy mountain;
for the earth shall be filled with
knowledge of the Lord,
as water covers the sea.
On that day, the root of Jesse,
set up as a signal for the nations,
the Gentiles shall seek out,
for his dwelling shall be glorious.

RESPONSORIAL PSALM
Psalm 72:1-2, 7-8, 12-13, 17

℟. **Justice shall flourish in his time, and fullness of peace for ever.**

O God, with your judgment endow the
king,
and with your justice, the king's son;
he shall govern your people with justice
and your afflicted ones with
judgment. ℟.

Justice shall flower in his days,
and profound peace, till the moon be
no more.
May he rule from sea to sea,
and from the River to the ends of the
earth. ℟.

For he shall rescue the poor when he cries
out,
and the afflicted when he has no
one to help him.
He shall have pity for the lowly and the
poor;
the lives of the poor he shall save. ℟.

May his name be blessed forever;
as long as the sun his name shall
remain.
In him shall all the tribes of the earth be
blessed;
all the nations shall proclaim his
happiness. ℟.

READING II
Romans 15:4-9

Brothers and sisters: Whatever was written previously was written for our instruction,
that by endurance and by the encouragement of the Scriptures we might have hope. May
the God of endurance and encouragement grant you to think in harmony with one another, in keeping with Christ Jesus, that with one accord you may with one voice glorify the
God and Father of our Lord Jesus Christ.

Welcome one another, then, as Christ welcomed you, for the glory of God. For I say that Christ became a minister of the circumcised to show God's truthfulness, to confirm the promises to the patriarchs, but so that the Gentiles might glorify God for his mercy. As it is written:

"Therefore, I will praise you among the Gentiles
and sing praises to your name."

GOSPEL
Matthew 3:1-12

John the Baptist appeared, preaching in the desert of Judea and saying, "Repent, for the kingdom of heaven is at hand!" It was of him that the prophet Isaiah had spoken when he said:

"A voice of one crying out in the desert,
'Prepare the way of the Lord,
make straight his paths.'"

John wore clothing made of camel's hair and had a leather belt around his waist. His food was locusts and wild honey. At that time Jerusalem, all Judea, and the whole region around the Jordan were going out to him and were being baptized by him in the Jordan River as they acknowledged their sins.

When he saw many of the Pharisees and Sadducees coming to his baptism, he said to them, "You brood of vipers! Who warned you to flee from the coming wrath? Produce good fruit as evidence of your repentance. And do not presume to say to yourselves, 'We have Abraham as our father.' For I tell you, God can raise up children to Abraham from these stones. Even now the ax lies at the root of the trees. Therefore every tree that does not bear good fruit will be cut down and thrown into the fire. I am baptizing you with water, for repentance, but the one who is coming after me is mightier than I. I am not worthy to carry his sandals. He will baptize you with the Holy Spirit and fire. His winnowing fan is in his hand. He will clear his threshing floor and gather his wheat into his barn, but the chaff he will burn with unquenchable fire."

SECOND SUNDAY OF ADVENT / B   901

READING I
Isaiah 40:1-5, 9-11 / 5

Comfort, give comfort to my people,
   says your God.
Speak tenderly to Jerusalem, and proclaim
   to her
   that her service is at an end,
   her guilt is expiated;
indeed, she has received from the hand of
   the LORD
   double for all her sins.

A voice cries out:
In the desert prepare the way of the LORD!
   Make straight in the wasteland a
     highway for our God!
Every valley shall be filled in,
   every mountain and hill shall be made
     low;
the rugged land shall be made a plain,
   the rough country, a broad valley.
Then the glory of the LORD shall be
   revealed,

and all people shall see it together;
   for the mouth of the LORD has
     spoken.

Go up on to a high mountain,
   Zion, herald of glad tidings;
cry out at the top of your voice,
   Jerusalem, herald of good news!
Fear not to cry out
   and say to the cities of Judah:
   Here is your God!
Here comes with power
   the Lord GOD,
   who rules by his strong arm;
here is his reward with him,
   his recompense before him.
Like a shepherd he feeds his flock;
   in his arms he gathers the lambs,
carrying them in his bosom,
   and leading the ewes with care.

RESPONSORIAL PSALM　　　　　　　*Psalm 85:9-10, 11-12, 13-14*
℟. Lord, let us see your kindness, and grant us your salvation.

I will hear what God proclaims;
　　the Lord—for he proclaims peace to
　　his people.
Near indeed is his salvation to those who
　　fear him,
　　glory dwelling in our land. ℟.

Kindness and truth shall meet;
　　justice and peace shall kiss.

Truth shall spring out of the earth,
　　and justice shall look down from
　　heaven. ℟.

The Lord himself will give his benefits;
　　our land shall yield its increase.
Justice shall walk before him,
　　and prepare the way of his steps. ℟.

READING II　　　　　　　　　　　　*2 Peter 3:8-14*

Do not ignore this one fact, beloved, that with the Lord one day is like a thousand years and a thousand years like one day. The Lord does not delay his promise, as some regard "delay," but he is patient with you, not wishing that any should perish but that all should come to repentance. But the day of the Lord will come like a thief, and then the heavens will pass away with a mighty roar and the elements will be dissolved by fire, and the earth and everything done on it will be found out.

Since everything is to be dissolved in this way, what sort of persons ought you to be, conducting yourselves in holiness and devotion, waiting for and hastening the coming of the day of God, because of which the heavens will be dissolved in flames and the elements melted by fire. But according to his promise we await new heavens and a new earth in which righteousness dwells. Therefore, beloved, since you await these things, be eager to be found without spot or blemish before him, at peace.

GOSPEL　　　　　　　　　　　　　　*Mark 1:1-8*

The beginning of the gospel of Jesus Christ the Son of God.
As it is written in Isaiah the prophet:
　　"Behold, I am sending my messenger ahead of you;
　　he will prepare your way.
　　A voice of one crying out in the desert:
　　'Prepare the way of the Lord,
　　make straight his paths.'"
John the Baptist appeared in the desert proclaiming a baptism of repentance for the forgiveness of sins. People of the whole Judean countryside and all the inhabitants of Jerusalem were going out to him and were being baptized by him in the Jordan River as they acknowledged their sins. John was clothed in camel's hair, with a leather belt around his waist. He fed on locusts and wild honey. And this is what he proclaimed: "One mightier than I is coming after me. I am not worthy to stoop and loosen the thongs of his sandals. I have baptized you with water; he will baptize you with the Holy Spirit."

902　SECOND SUNDAY OF ADVENT / C

READING I　　　　　　　　　　　　*Baruch 5:1-9 / 6*

Jerusalem, take off your robe of
　　mourning and misery;
　　put on the splendor of glory from
　　God forever:
wrapped in the cloak of justice from God,
　　bear on your head the mitre
　　that displays the glory of the eternal

name.
For God will show all the earth your
　　splendor:
　　you will be named by God forever
　　the peace of justice, the glory of
　　God's worship.

Up, Jerusalem! stand upon the heights;
   look to the east and see your children
gathered from the east and the west
   at the word of the Holy One,
   rejoicing that they are remembered
     by God.
Led away on foot by their enemies they
   left you:
but God will bring them back to you
borne aloft in glory as on royal
   thrones.
For God has commanded
   that every lofty mountain be made

low,
and that the age-old depths and gorges
   be filled to level ground,
   that Israel may advance secure in
     the glory of God.
The forests and every fragrant kind of
   tree
   have overshadowed Israel at God's
     command;
for God is leading Israel in joy
   by the light of his glory,
   with his mercy and justice for
     company.

RESPONSORIAL PSALM

Psalm 126:1-2, 2-3, 4-5, 6

℟. **The Lord has done great things for us; we are filled with joy.**

When the Lord brought back the captives
   of Zion,
we were like men dreaming.
Then our mouth was filled with laughter,
   and our tongue with rejoicing. ℟.

Then they said among the nations,
   "The Lord has done great things for
     them."
The Lord has done great things for us;
   we are glad indeed. ℟.

Restore our fortunes, O Lord,
   like the torrents in the southern
     desert.
Those who sow in tears
   shall reap rejoicing. ℟.

Although they go forth weeping,
   carrying the seed to be sown,
they shall come back rejoicing,
   carrying their sheaves. ℟.

READING II

Philippians 1:4-6, 8-11

Brothers and sisters: I pray always with joy in my every prayer for all of you, because of your partnership for the gospel from the first day until now. I am confident of this, that the one who began a good work in you will continue to complete it until the day of Christ Jesus. God is my witness, how I long for all of you with the affection of Christ Jesus. And this is my prayer: that your love may increase ever more and more in knowledge and every kind of perception, to discern what is of value, so that you may be pure and blameless for the day of Christ, filled with the fruit of righteousness that comes through Jesus Christ for the glory and praise of God.

GOSPEL

Luke 3:1-6

In the fifteenth year of the reign of Tiberius Caesar, when Pontius Pilate was governor of Judea, and Herod was tetrarch of Galilee, and his brother Philip tetrarch of the region of Ituraea and Trachonitis, and Lysanias was tetrarch of Abilene, during the high priesthood of Annas and Caiaphas, the word of God came to John the son of Zechariah in the desert. John went throughout the whole region of the Jordan, proclaiming a baptism of repentance for the forgiveness of sins, as it is written in the book of the words of the prophet Isaiah:
   "A voice of one crying out in the desert:
   'Prepare the way of the Lord,
   make straight his paths.
   Every valley shall be filled
   and every mountain and hill shall be made low.
   The winding roads shall be made straight,
   and the rough ways made smooth,
   and all flesh shall see the salvation of God.'"

903 THIRD SUNDAY OF ADVENT / A

READING I
Isaiah 35:1-6a, 10 / 7

The desert and the parched land will
    exult;
the steppe will rejoice and bloom.
They will bloom with abundant flowers,
    and rejoice with joyful song.
The glory of Lebanon will be given to
    them,
    the splendor of Carmel and Sharon;
they will see the glory of the Lord,
    the splendor of our God.
Strengthen the hands that are feeble,
    make firm the knees that are weak,
say to those whose hearts are frightened:
Be strong, fear not!
Here is your God,

he comes with vindication;
with divine recompense
he comes to save you.
Then will the eyes of the blind be
    opened,
    the ears of the deaf be cleared;
then will the lame leap like a stag,
    then the tongue of the mute will sing.

Those whom the Lord has ransomed
    will return
    and enter Zion singing,
    crowned with everlasting joy;
they will meet with joy and gladness,
    sorrow and mourning will flee.

RESPONSORIAL PSALM
Psalm 146:6-7, 8-9, 9-10

℟. **Lord, come and save us.**
    or:
Alleluia.

The Lord God keeps faith forever,
    secures justice for the oppressed,
    gives food to the hungry.
The Lord sets captives free. ℟.

The Lord gives sight to the blind;
    the Lord raises up those who were
        bowed down.

The Lord loves the just;
    the Lord protects strangers. ℟.

The fatherless and the widow he sustains,
    but the way of the wicked he thwarts.
The Lord shall reign forever;
    your God, O Zion, through all
        generations. ℟.

READING II
James 5:7-10

Be patient, brothers and sisters, until the coming of the Lord. See how the farmer waits
for the precious fruit of the earth, being patient with it until it receives the early and the
late rains. You too must be patient. Make your hearts firm, because the coming of the
Lord is at hand. Do not complain, brothers and sisters, about one another, that you may
not be judged. Behold, the Judge is standing before the gates. Take as an example of
hardship and patience, brothers and sisters, the prophets who spoke in the name of the
Lord.

GOSPEL
Matthew 11:2-11

When John the Baptist heard in prison of the works of the Christ, he sent his disciples
to Jesus with this question, "Are you the one who is to come, or should we look for
another?" Jesus said to them in reply, "Go and tell John what you hear and see: the blind
regain their sight, the lame walk, lepers are cleansed, the deaf hear, the dead are raised,
and the poor have the good news proclaimed to them. And blessed is the one who takes
no offense at me."

As they were going off, Jesus began to speak to the crowds about John, "What did
you go out to the desert to see? A reed swayed by the wind? Then what did you go out
to see? Someone dressed in fine clothing? Those who wear fine clothing are in royal
palaces. Then why did you go out? To see a prophet? Yes, I tell you, and more than a
prophet. This is the one about whom it is written:

'Behold, I am sending my messenger ahead of you;
he will prepare your way before you.'
Amen, I say to you, among those born of women there has been none greater than John
the Baptist; yet the least in the kingdom of heaven is greater than he."

THIRD SUNDAY OF ADVENT / B   904

READING I
Isaiah 61:1-2a, 10-11 / 8

The spirit of the Lord GOD is upon me,
  because the LORD has anointed me;
he has sent me to bring glad tidings to
  the poor,
  to heal the brokenhearted,
to proclaim liberty to the captives
  and release to the prisoners,
to announce a year of favor from the
  LORD
  and a day of vindication by our God.

I rejoice heartily in the LORD,
  in my God is the joy of my soul;

for he has clothed me with a robe of
  salvation
  and wrapped me in a mantle of
  justice,
like a bridegroom adorned with a diadem,
like a bride bedecked with her jewels.
As the earth brings forth its plants,
  and a garden makes its growth spring
  up,
so will the Lord GOD make justice and
  praise
spring up before all the nations.

RESPONSORIAL PSALM
Luke 1:46-48, 49-50, 53-54

℟. My soul rejoices in my God.

My soul proclaims the greatness of the
  Lord;
  my spirit rejoices in God my Savior,
for he has looked upon his lowly servant.
From this day all generations will call me
  blessed: ℟.

The Almighty has done great things for
  me,
  and holy is his Name.

He has mercy on those who fear him
  in every generation. ℟.

He has filled the hungry with good
  things,
  and the rich he has sent away empty.
He has come to the help of his servant
  Israel
  for he has remembered his promise
  of mercy. ℟.

READING II
1 Thessalonians 5:16-24

Brothers and sisters: Rejoice always. Pray without ceasing. In all circumstances give
thanks, for this is the will of God for you in Christ Jesus. Do not quench the Spirit. Do
not despise prophetic utterances. Test everything; retain what is good. Refrain from
every kind of evil.
    May the God of peace make you perfectly holy and may you entirely, spirit, soul,
and body, be preserved blameless for the coming of our Lord Jesus Christ. The one who
calls you is faithful, and he will also accomplish it.

GOSPEL
John 1:6-8, 19-28

A man named John was sent from God. He came for testimony, to testify to the light, so
that all might believe through him. He was not the light, but came to testify to the light.
    And this is the testimony of John. When the Jews from Jerusalem sent priests and
Levites to him to ask him, "Who are you?" he admitted and did not deny it, but admitted, "I am not the Christ." So they asked him, "What are you then? Are you Elijah?" And
he said, "I am not." "Are you the Prophet?" He answered, "No." So they said to him,

"Who are you, so we can give an answer to those who sent us? What do you have to say for yourself?" He said:
"I am 'the voice of one crying out in the desert,
"make straight the way of the Lord,'"
as Isaiah the prophet said." Some Pharisees were also sent. They asked him, "Why then do you baptize if you are not the Christ or Elijah or the Prophet?" John answered them, "I baptize with water; but there is one among you whom you do not recognize, the one who is coming after me, whose sandal strap I am not worthy to untie." This happened in Bethany across the Jordan, where John was baptizing.

905 THIRD SUNDAY OF ADVENT / C

READING I
Zephaniah 3:14-18a / 9

Shout for joy, O daughter Zion!
Sing joyfully, O Israel!
Be glad and exult with all your heart,
O daughter Jerusalem!
The LORD has removed the judgment
against you
he has turned away your enemies;
the King of Israel, the LORD, is in your
midst,
you have no further misfortune to
fear.
On that day, it shall be said to Jerusalem:
Fear not, O Zion, be not discouraged!
The LORD, your God, is in your midst,
a mighty savior;
he will rejoice over you with gladness,
and renew you in his love,
he will sing joyfully because of you,
as one sings at festivals.

RESPONSORIAL PSALM
Isaiah 12:2-3, 4, 5-6

℟. Cry out with joy and gladness: for among you is the great
and Holy One of Israel.

God indeed is my savior;
I am confident and unafraid.
My strength and my courage is the LORD,
and he has been my savior.
With joy you will draw water
at the fountain of salvation. ℟.

Give thanks to the LORD, acclaim his
name;
among the nations make known his
deeds,
proclaim how exalted is his name. ℟.

Sing praise to the LORD for his glorious
achievement;
let this be known throughout all the
earth.
Shout with exultation, O city of Zion,
for great in your midst
is the Holy One of Israel! ℟.

READING II
Philippians 4:4-7

Brothers and sisters: Rejoice in the Lord always. I shall say it again: rejoice! Your kindness should be known to all. The Lord is near. Have no anxiety at all, but in everything, by prayer and petition, with thanksgiving, make your requests known to God. Then the peace of God that surpasses all understanding will guard your hearts and minds in Christ Jesus.

GOSPEL
Luke 3:10-18

The crowds asked John the Baptist, "What should we do?" He said to them in reply, "Whoever has two cloaks should share with the person who has none. And whoever has food should do likewise." Even tax collectors came to be baptized and they said to him, "Teacher, what should we do?" He answered them, "Stop collecting more than what is prescribed." Soldiers also asked him, "And what is it that we should do?" He told them, "Do not practice extortion, do not falsely accuse anyone, and be satisfied with your wages."

Now the people were filled with expectation, and all were asking in their hearts whether John might be the Christ. John answered them all, saying, "I am baptizing you with water, but one mightier than I is coming. I am not worthy to loosen the thongs of his sandals. He will baptize you with the Holy Spirit and fire. His winnowing fan is in his hand to clear his threshing floor and to gather the wheat into his barn, but the chaff he will burn with unquenchable fire." Exhorting them in many other ways, he preached good news to the people.

FOURTH SUNDAY OF ADVENT / A 906

READING I
Isaiah 7:10-14 / 10

The LORD spoke to Ahaz, saying: Ask for a sign from the LORD, your God; let it be deep as the netherworld, or high as the sky! But Ahaz answered, "I will not ask! I will not tempt the LORD!" Then Isaiah said: Listen, O house of David! Is it not enough for you to weary people, must you also weary my God? Therefore the Lord himself will give you this sign: the virgin shall conceive, and bear a son, and shall name him Emmanuel.

RESPONSORIAL PSALM
Psalm 24:1-2, 3-4, 5-6

℞. Let the Lord enter; he is king of glory.

The LORD's are the earth and its fullness;
    the world and those who dwell in it.
For he founded it upon the seas
    and established it upon the rivers. ℞.

Who can ascend the mountain of the
    LORD?
    or who may stand in his holy place?
One whose hands are sinless, whose heart

is clean,
    who desires not what is vain. ℞.

He shall receive a blessing from the
    LORD,
    a reward from God his savior.
Such is the race that seeks for him,
    that seeks the face of the God of
    Jacob. ℞.

READING II
Romans 1:1-7

Paul, a slave of Christ Jesus, called to be an apostle and set apart for the gospel of God, which he promised previously through his prophets in the holy Scriptures, the gospel about his Son, descended from David according to the flesh, but established as Son of God in power according to the Spirit of holiness through resurrection from the dead, Jesus Christ our Lord. Through him we have received the grace of apostleship, to bring about the obedience of faith, for the sake of his name, among all the Gentiles, among whom are you also, who are called to belong to Jesus Christ; to all the beloved of God in Rome, called to be holy. Grace to you and peace from God our Father and the Lord Jesus Christ.

GOSPEL
Matthew 1:18-24

This is how the birth of Jesus Christ came about. When his mother Mary was betrothed to Joseph, but before they lived together, she was found with child through the Holy Spirit. Joseph her husband, since he was a righteous man, yet unwilling to expose her to shame, decided to divorce her quietly. Such was his intention when, behold, the angel of the Lord appeared to him in a dream and said, "Joseph, son of David, do not be afraid to take Mary your wife into your home. For it is through the Holy Spirit that this child has been conceived in her. She will bear a son and you are to name him Jesus, because he will save his people from their sins." All this took place to fulfill what the Lord had said through the prophet:
    "Behold, the virgin shall conceive and bear a son,
    and they shall name him Emmanuel,"
which means "God is with us." When Joseph awoke, he did as the angel of the Lord had commanded him and took his wife into his home.

907 FOURTH SUNDAY OF ADVENT / B

READING I   *2 Samuel 7:1-5, 8b-12, 14a, 16 / 11*

When King David was settled in his palace, and the LORD had given him rest from his enemies on every side, he said to Nathan the prophet, "Here I am living in a house of cedar, while the ark of God dwells in a tent!" Nathan answered the king, "Go, do whatever you have in mind, for the LORD is with you." But that night the LORD spoke to Nathan and said: "Go, tell my servant David, 'Thus says the LORD: Should you build me a house to dwell in?'

"It was I who took you from the pasture and from the care of the flock to be commander of my people Israel. I have been with you wherever you went, and I have destroyed all your enemies before you. And I will make you famous like the great ones of the earth. I will fix a place for my people Israel; I will plant them so that they may dwell in their place without further disturbance. Neither shall the wicked continue to afflict them as they did of old, since the time I first appointed judges over my people Israel. I will give you rest from all your enemies. The LORD also reveals to you that he will establish a house for you. And when your time comes and you rest with your ancestors, I will raise up your heir after you, sprung from your loins, and I will make his kingdom firm. I will be a father to him, and he shall be a son to me. Your house and your kingdom shall endure forever before me; your throne shall stand firm forever."

RESPONSORIAL PSALM   *Psalm 89:2-3, 4-5, 27, 29*

℟. **For ever I will sing the goodness of the Lord.**

The promises of the LORD I will sing
　　forever;
　　through all generations my mouth
　　　shall proclaim your faithfulness.
For you have said, "My kindness is
　　established forever";
　　in heaven you have confirmed your
　　　faithfulness. ℟.

"I have made a covenant with my chosen
　　one,

I have sworn to David my servant:
　　forever will I confirm your posterity
　　and establish your throne for all
　　　generations." ℟.

"He shall say of me, 'You are my father,
　　my God, the Rock, my savior.'
Forever I will maintain my kindness
　　toward him,
　　and my covenant with him stands
　　　firm." ℟.

READING II   *Romans 16:25-27*

Brothers and sisters: To him who can strengthen you, according to my gospel and the proclamation of Jesus Christ, according to the revelation of the mystery kept secret for long ages but now manifested through the prophetic writings and, according to the command of the eternal God, made known to all nations to bring about the obedience of faith, to the only wise God, through Jesus Christ be glory forever and ever. Amen.

GOSPEL   *Luke 1:26-38*

The angel Gabriel was sent from God to a town of Galilee called Nazareth, to a virgin betrothed to a man named Joseph, of the house of David, and the virgin's name was Mary. And coming to her, he said, "Hail, full of grace! The Lord is with you." But she was greatly troubled at what was said and pondered what sort of greeting this might be. Then the angel said to her, "Do not be afraid, Mary, for you have found favor with God.

"Behold, you will conceive in your womb and bear a son, and you shall name him Jesus. He will be great and will be called Son of the Most High, and the Lord God will give him the throne of David his father, and he will rule over the house of Jacob forever, and of his kingdom there will be no end." But Mary said to the angel, "How can this be, since I have no relations with a man?" And the angel said to her in reply, "The Holy Spirit will come upon you, and the power of the Most High will overshadow you. Therefore the child to be born will be called holy, the Son of God. And behold, Elizabeth, your relative, has also conceived a son in her old age, and this is the sixth month for her who was called barren; for nothing will be impossible for God." Mary said, "Behold, I am the handmaid of the Lord. May it be done to me according to your word." Then the angel departed from her.

FOURTH SUNDAY OF ADVENT / C   908

READING I   *Micah 5:1-4a / 12*

Thus says the LORD:
You, Bethlehem-Ephrathah
  too small to be among the clans of
    Judah,
from you shall come forth for me
  one who is to be ruler in Israel;
whose origin is from of old,
  from ancient times.
Therefore the Lord will give them up,
    until the time
  when she who is to give birth has
    borne,

and the rest of his kindred shall return
  to the children of Israel.
He shall stand firm and shepherd his
    flock
  by the strength of the LORD,
  in the majestic name of the LORD,
    his God;
and they shall remain, for now his
    greatness
  shall reach to the ends of the earth;
  he shall be peace.

RESPONSORIAL PSALM   *Psalm 80:2-3, 15-16, 18-19*

℟. **Lord, make us turn to you; let us see your face and we shall be saved.**

O shepherd of Israel, hearken,
  from your throne upon the cherubim,
    shine forth.
Rouse your power,
  and come to save us. ℟.

Once again, O Lord of hosts,
  look down from heaven, and see;
take care of this vine,
  and protect what your right hand has
    planted

the son of man whom you yourself
    made strong. ℟.

May your help be with the man of your
    right hand,
  with the son of man whom you
    yourself made strong.
Then we will no more withdraw from
    you;
  give us new life, and we will call
    upon your name. ℟.

READING II   *Hebrews 10:5-10*

Brothers and sisters: When Christ came into the world, he said:
  "Sacrifice and offering you did not desire,
  but a body you prepared for me;
  in holocausts and sin offerings you took no delight.
  Then I said, 'As is written of me in the scroll,
  behold, I come to do your will, O God.'"
First he says, "Sacrifices and offerings, holocausts and sin offerings, you neither desired nor delighted in." These are offered according to the law. Then he says, "Behold, I come to do your will." He takes away the first to establish the second. By this "will," we have been consecrated through the offering of the body of Jesus Christ once for all.

GOSPEL *Luke 1:39-45*

Mary set out and traveled to the hill country in haste to a town of Judah, where she entered the house of Zechariah and greeted Elizabeth. When Elizabeth heard Mary's greeting, the infant leaped in her womb, and Elizabeth, filled with the Holy Spirit, cried out in a loud voice and said, "Blessed are you among women, and blessed is the fruit of your womb. And how does this happen to me, that the mother of my Lord should come to me? For at the moment the sound of your greeting reached my ears, the infant in my womb leaped for joy. Blessed are you who believed that what was spoken to you by the Lord would be fulfilled."

909 DECEMBER 25: CHRISTMAS—VIGIL / ABC

READING I *Isaiah 62:1-5 / 13*

For Zion's sake I will not be silent,
    for Jerusalem's sake I will not be
    quiet,
until her vindication shines forth like
    the dawn
and her victory like a burning torch.

Nations shall behold your vindication,
    and all the kings your glory;
you shall be called by a new name
    pronounced by the mouth of the
    LORD.
You shall be a glorious crown in the

hand of the LORD,
    a royal diadem held by your God.
No more shall people call you
    "Forsaken,"
    or your land "Desolate,"
but you shall be called "My Delight,"
    and your land "Espoused."
For the LORD delights in you
    and makes your land his spouse.
As a young man marries a virgin,
    your Builder shall marry you;
and as a bridegroom rejoices in his bride
    so shall your God rejoice in you.

RESPONSORIAL PSALM *Psalm 89:4-5, 16-17, 27, 29*

℟. **For ever I will sing the goodness of the Lord.**

I have made a covenant with my chosen
    one,
    I have sworn to David my servant:
forever will I confirm your posterity
    and establish your throne for all
    generations. ℟.

Blessed the people who know the joyful
    shout;
    in the light of your countenance, O
    LORD, they walk.

At your name they rejoice all the day,
    and through your justice they are
    exalted. ℟.

He shall say of me, "You are my father,
    my God, the rock, my savior."
Forever I will maintain my kindness
    toward him,
    and my covenant with him stands
    firm. ℟.

READING II *Acts 13:16-17, 22-25*

When Paul reached Antioch in Pisidia and entered the synagogue, he stood up, motioned with his hand, and said, "Fellow Israelites and you others who are God-fearing, listen. The God of this people Israel chose our ancestors and exalted the people during their sojourn in the land of Egypt. With uplifted arm he led them out of it. Then he removed Saul and raised up David as king; of him he testified, 'I have found David, son of Jesse, a man after my own heart; he will carry out my every wish.' From this man's descendants God, according to his promise, has brought to Israel a savior, Jesus. John heralded his coming by proclaiming a baptism of repentance to all the people of Israel; and as

John was completing his course, he would say, 'What do you suppose that I am? I am not he. Behold, one is coming after me; I am not worthy to unfasten the sandals of his feet.'"

GOSPEL   *Matthew 1:1-25 or 1:18-25*
For short form read only the part in brackets.

The book of the genealogy of Jesus Christ, the son of David, the son of Abraham.

Abraham became the father of Isaac, Isaac the father of Jacob, Jacob the father of Judah and his brothers. Judah became the father of Perez and Zerah, whose mother was Tamar. Perez became the father of Hezron, Hezron the father of Ram, Ram the father of Amminadab. Amminadab became the father of Nahshon, Nahshon the father of Salmon, Salmon the father of Boaz, whose mother was Rahab. Boaz became the father of Obed, whose mother was Ruth. Obed became the father of Jesse, Jesse the father of David the king.

David became the father of Solomon, whose mother had been the wife of Uriah. Solomon became the father of Rehoboam, Rehoboam the father of Abijah, Abijah the father of Asaph. Asaph became the father of Jehoshaphat, Jehoshaphat the father of Joram, Joram the father of Uzziah. Uzziah became the father of Jotham, Jotham the father of Ahaz, Ahaz the father of Hezekiah. Hezekiah became the father of Manasseh, Manasseh the father of Amos, Amos the father of Josiah. Josiah became the father of Jechoniah and his brothers at the time of the Babylonian exile.

After the Babylonian exile, Jechoniah became the father of Shealtiel, Shealtiel the father of Zerubbabel, Zerubbabel the father of Abiud. Abiud became the father of Eliakim, Eliakim the father of Azor, Azor the father of Zadok. Zadok became the father of Achim, Achim the father of Eliud, Eliud the father of Eleazar. Eleazar became the father of Matthan, Matthan the father of Jacob, Jacob the father of Joseph, the husband of Mary. Of her was born Jesus who is called the Christ.

Thus the total number of generations from Abraham to David is fourteen generations; from David to the Babylonian exile, fourteen generations; from the Babylonian exile to the Christ, fourteen generations.

Now [this is how the birth of Jesus Christ came about. When his mother Mary was betrothed to Joseph, but before they lived together, she was found with child through the Holy Spirit. Joseph her husband, since he was a righteous man, yet unwilling to expose her to shame, decided to divorce her quietly. Such was his intention when, behold, the angel of the Lord appeared to him in a dream and said, "Joseph, son of David, do not be afraid to take Mary your wife into your home. For it is through the Holy Spirit that this child has been conceived in her. She will bear a son and you are to name him Jesus, because he will save his people from their sins." All this took place to fulfill what the Lord had said through the prophet:
"Behold, the virgin shall conceive and bear a son,
    and they shall name him Emmanuel,"
which means "God is with us." When Joseph awoke, he did as the angel of the Lord had commanded him and took his wife into his home. He had no relations with her until she bore a son, and he named him Jesus.]

DECEMBER 25: CHRISTMAS—MASS AT MIDNIGHT / ABC   910

READING I   *Isaiah 9:1-6 / 14*
The people who walked in darkness   a light has shone.
    have seen a great light;   You have brought them abundant joy
upon those who dwelt in the land of   and great rejoicing,
    gloom

as they rejoice before you as at the
harvest,
as people make merry when dividing
spoils.
For the yoke that burdened them,
the pole on their shoulder,
and the rod of their taskmaster
you have smashed, as on the day of
Midian.
For every boot that tramped in battle,
every cloak rolled in blood,
will be burned as fuel for flames.
For a child is born to us, a son is given
us;

upon his shoulder dominion rests
They name him Wonder-Counselor,
God-Hero,
Father-Forever, Prince of Peace.
His dominion is vast
and forever peaceful,
from David's throne, and over his
kingdom,
which he confirms and sustains
by judgment and justice,
both now and forever.
The zeal of the LORD of hosts will do
this!

RESPONSORIAL PSALM   *Psalm 96:1-2, 2-3, 11-12, 13*
℟. **Today is born our Savior, Christ the Lord.**

Sing to the LORD a new song;
sing to the LORD, all you lands.
Sing to the LORD; bless his name. ℟.

Announce his salvation, day after day.
Tell his glory among the nations;
among all peoples, his wondrous
deeds. ℟.

Let the heavens be glad and the earth
rejoice;
let the sea and what fills it resound;

let the plains be joyful and all that is
in them!
Then shall all the trees of the forest
exult. ℟.

They shall exult before the LORD, for he
comes;
for he comes to rule the earth.
He shall rule the world with justice
and the peoples with his
constancy. ℟.

READING II   *Titus 2:11-14*
Beloved: The grace of God has appeared, saving all and training us to reject godless ways and worldly desires and to live temperately, justly, and devoutly in this age, as we await the blessed hope, the appearance of the glory of our great God and savior Jesus Christ, who gave himself for us to deliver us from all lawlessness and to cleanse for himself a people as his own, eager to do what is good.

GOSPEL   *Luke 2:1-14*
In those days a decree went out from Caesar Augustus that the whole world should be enrolled. This was the first enrollment, when Quirinius was governor of Syria. So all went to be enrolled, each to his own town. And Joseph too went up from Galilee from the town of Nazareth to Judea, to the city of David that is called Bethlehem, because he was of the house and family of David, to be enrolled with Mary, his betrothed, who was with child. While they were there, the time came for her to have her child, and she gave birth to her firstborn son. She wrapped him in swaddling clothes and laid him in a manger, because there was no room for them in the inn.

Now there were shepherds in that region living in the fields and keeping the night watch over their flock. The angel of the Lord appeared to them and the glory of the Lord shone around them, and they were struck with great fear. The angel said to them, "Do not be afraid; for behold, I proclaim to you good news of great joy that will be for all the people. For today in the city of David a savior has been born for you who is Christ and Lord. And this will be a sign for you: you will find an infant wrapped in swaddling clothes and lying in a manger." And suddenly there was a multitude of the heavenly host

with the angel, praising God and saying:
    "Glory to God in the highest
        and on earth peace to those on whom his favor rests."

DECEMBER 25: CHRISTMAS—MASS AT DAWN / ABC   911

READING I   *Isaiah 62:11-12 / 15*

See, the LORD proclaims
    to the ends of the earth:
say to daughter Zion,
    your savior comes!
Here is his reward with him,

his recompense before him.
They shall be called the holy people,
    the redeemed of the LORD,
and you shall be called "Frequented,"
    a city that is not forsaken.

RESPONSORIAL PSALM   *Psalm 97:1, 6, 11-12*

℟. **A light will shine on us this day: the Lord is born for us.**

The LORD is king; let the earth rejoice;
    let the many islands be glad.
The heavens proclaim his justice,
    and all peoples see his glory. ℟.

Light dawns for the just;
    and gladness, for the upright of heart.
Be glad in the LORD, you just,
    and give thanks to his holy name. ℟.

READING II   *Titus 3:4-7*

Beloved:
    When the kindness and generous love
        of God our savior appeared,
    not because of any righteous deeds
        we had done
    but because of his mercy,
he saved us through the bath of
    rebirth

and renewal by the Holy Spirit,
    whom he richly poured out on us
        through Jesus Christ our savior,
so that we might be justified by his
    grace
and become heirs in hope of
    eternal life.

GOSPEL   *Luke 2:15-20*

When the angels went away from them to heaven, the shepherds said to one another,
"Let us go, then, to Bethlehem to see this thing that has taken place, which the Lord has
made known to us." So they went in haste and found Mary and Joseph, and the infant
lying in the manger. When they saw this, they made known the message that had been
told them about this child. All who heard it were amazed by what had been told them by
the shepherds. And Mary kept all these things, reflecting on them in her heart. Then the
shepherds returned, glorifying and praising God for all they had heard and seen, just as
it had been told to them.

DECEMBER 25: CHRISTMAS   912
MASS DURING THE DAY / ABC

READING I   *Isaiah 52:7-10 / 16*

How beautiful upon the mountains
    are the feet of him who brings glad
        tidings,
announcing peace, bearing good news,
    announcing salvation, and saying to
        Zion,

    "Your God is King!"

Hark! Your sentinels raise a cry,
    together they shout for joy,
for they see directly, before their eyes,
    the Lord restoring Zion.

Break out together in song,
   O ruins of Jerusalem!
For the LORD comforts his people,
   he redeems Jerusalem.

The LORD has bared his holy arm
   in the sight of all the nations;
all the ends of the earth will behold
   the salvation of our God.

RESPONSORIAL PSALM
Psalm 98:1, 2-3, 3-4, 5-6
℟. **All the ends of the earth have seen the saving power of God.**

Sing to the LORD a new song,
   for he has done wondrous deeds;
his right hand has won victory for him,
   his holy arm. ℟.

The LORD has made his salvation known:
   in the sight of the nations he has
      revealed his justice.
He has remembered his kindness and his
   faithfulness
   toward the house of Israel. ℟.

All the ends of the earth have seen
   the salvation by our God.
Sing joyfully to the LORD, all you lands;
   break into song; sing praise. ℟.

Sing praise to the LORD with the harp,
   with the harp and melodious song.
With trumpets and the sound of the horn
   sing joyfully before the King, the
   LORD. ℟.

READING II
Hebrews 1:1-6
Brothers and sisters: In times past, God spoke in partial and various ways to our ancestors through the prophets; in these last days, he has spoken to us through the Son, whom
he made heir of all things and through whom he created the universe,
   who is the refulgence of his glory,
      the very imprint of his being,
   and who sustains all things by his mighty word.
When he had accomplished purification from sins,
   he took his seat at the right hand of the Majesty on high,
   as far superior to the angels
   as the name he has inherited is more excellent than theirs.

For to which of the angels did God ever say:
   "You are my son; this day I have begotten you"?
Or again:
   "I will be a father to him, and he shall be a son to me"?
And again, when he leads the firstborn into the world, he says:
   "Let all the angels of God worship him."

GOSPEL
John 1:1-18 or 1:1-5, 9-14
For short form read only the parts in brackets.

   [In the beginning was the Word,
      and the Word was with God,
      and the Word was God.
   He was in the beginning with God.
   All things came to be through him,
      and without him nothing came to be.
   What came to be through him was life,
      and this life was the light of the human race;
   the light shines in the darkness,
      and the darkness has not overcome it.]
A man named John was sent from God. He came for testimony, to testify to the light, so

that all might believe through him. He was not the light, but came to testify to the light. [The true light, which enlightens everyone, was coming into the world.

He was in the world,
and the world came to be through him,
but the world did not know him.
He came to what was his own,
but his own people did not accept him.

But to those who did accept him he gave power to become children of God, to those who believe in his name, who were born not by natural generation nor by human choice nor by a man's decision but of God.

And the Word became flesh
and made his dwelling among us,
and we saw his glory,
the glory as of the Father's only Son,
full of grace and truth.]
John testified to him and cried out, saying, "This was he of whom I said, 'The one who is coming after me ranks ahead of me because he existed before me.'" From his fullness we have all received, grace in place of grace, because while the law was given through Moses, grace and truth came through Jesus Christ. No one has ever seen God. The only Son, God, who is at the Father's side, has revealed him.

SUNDAY IN THE OCTAVE OF CHRISTMAS   913
HOLY FAMILY OF JESUS, MARY, AND JOSEPH / ABC

READING I   *Sirach 3:2-7, 12-14 / 17*

God sets a father in honor over his
children;
a mother's authority he confirms
over her sons.
Whoever honors his father atones for sins,
and preserves himself from them.
When he prays, he is heard;
he stores up riches who reveres his
mother.
Whoever honors his father is gladdened
by children,
and, when he prays, is heard.
Whoever reveres his father will live a
long life;

he who obeys his father brings
comfort to his mother.

My son, take care of your father when
he is old;
grieve him not as long as he lives.
Even if his mind fail, be considerate of
him;
revile him not all the days of his life;
kindness to a father will not be forgotten,
firmly planted against the debt of
your sins
—a house raised in justice to you.

RESPONSORIAL PSALM   *Psalm 128:1-2, 3, 4-5*

℟. **Blessed are those who fear the Lord and walk in his ways.**

Blessed is everyone who fears the LORD,
who walks in his ways!
For you shall eat the fruit of your
handiwork;
blessed shall you be, and favored. ℟.

Your wife shall be like a fruitful vine
in the recesses of your home;
your children like olive plants

around your table. ℟.

Behold, thus is the man blessed
who fears the LORD.
The LORD bless you from Zion:
may you see the prosperity of
Jerusalem
all the days of your life. ℟.

READING II
Colossians 3:12-21 or 3:12-17

For short form read only the part in brackets.

[Brothers and sisters: Put on, as God's chosen ones, holy and beloved, heartfelt compassion, kindness, humility, gentleness, and patience, bearing with one another and forgiving one another, if one has a grievance against another; as the Lord has forgiven you, so must you also do. And over all these put on love, that is, the bond of perfection. And let the peace of Christ control your hearts, the peace into which you were also called in one body. And be thankful. Let the word of Christ dwell in you richly, as in all wisdom you teach and admonish one another, singing psalms, hymns, and spiritual songs with gratitude in your hearts to God. And whatever you do, in word or in deed, do everything in the name of the Lord Jesus, giving thanks to God the Father through him.]

Wives, be subordinate to your husbands, as is proper in the Lord. Husbands, love your wives, and avoid any bitterness toward them. Children, obey your parents in everything, for this is pleasing to the Lord. Fathers, do not provoke your children, so they may not become discouraged.

GOSPEL / A
Matthew 2:13-15, 19-23

When the magi had departed, behold, the angel of the Lord appeared to Joseph in a dream and said, "Rise, take the child and his mother, flee to Egypt, and stay there until I tell you. Herod is going to search for the child to destroy him." Joseph rose and took the child and his mother by night and departed for Egypt. He stayed there until the death of Herod, that what the Lord had said through the prophet might be fulfilled, "Out of Egypt I called my son."

When Herod had died, behold, the angel of the Lord appeared in a dream to Joseph in Egypt and said, "Rise, take the child and his mother and go to the land of Israel, for those who sought the child's life are dead." He rose, took the child and his mother, and went to the land of Israel. But when he heard that Archelaus was ruling over Judea in place of his father Herod, he was afraid to go back there. And because he had been warned in a dream, he departed for the region of Galilee. He went and dwelt in a town called Nazareth, so that what had been spoken through the prophets might be fulfilled, "He shall be called a Nazorean."

GOSPEL / B
Luke 2:22-40 or 2:22, 39-40

For short form read only the parts in brackets.

[When the days were completed for their purification according to the law of Moses, they took him up to Jerusalem to present him to the Lord,] just as it is written in the law of the Lord, "Every male that opens the womb shall be consecrated to the Lord," and to offer the sacrifice of "a pair of turtledoves or two young pigeons," in accordance with the dictate in the law of the Lord.

Now there was a man in Jerusalem whose name was Simeon. This man was righteous and devout, awaiting the consolation of Israel, and the Holy Spirit was upon him. It had been revealed to him by the Holy Spirit that he should not see death before he had seen the Christ of the Lord. He came in the Spirit into the temple; and when the parents brought in the child Jesus to perform the custom of the law in regard to him, he took him into his arms and blessed God, saying:

"Now, Master, you may let your servant go
    in peace, according to your word,
for my eyes have seen your salvation,
    which you prepared in sight of all the peoples,
a light for revelation to the Gentiles,
    and glory for your people Israel."

The child's father and mother were amazed at what was said about him; and Simeon blessed them and said to Mary his mother, "Behold, this child is destined for the fall and rise of many in Israel, and to be a sign that will be contradicted (and you yourself a sword will pierce) so that the thoughts of many hearts may be revealed." There was also a prophetess, Anna, the daughter of Phanuel, of the tribe of Asher. She was advanced in years, having lived seven years with her husband after her marriage, and then as a widow until she was eighty-four. She never left the temple, but worshiped night and day with fasting and prayer. And coming forward at that very time, she gave thanks to God and spoke about the child to all who were awaiting the redemption of Jerusalem.

[When they had fulfilled all the prescriptions of the law of the Lord, they returned to Galilee, to their own town of Nazareth. The child grew and became strong, filled with wisdom; and the favor of God was upon him.]

GOSPEL / C

Luke 2:41-52

Each year Jesus' parents went to Jerusalem for the feast of Passover, and when he was twelve years old, they went up according to festival custom. After they had completed its days, as they were returning, the boy Jesus remained behind in Jerusalem, but his parents did not know it. Thinking that he was in the caravan, they journeyed for a day and looked for him among their relatives and acquaintances, but not finding him, they returned to Jerusalem to look for him. After three days they found him in the temple, sitting in the midst of the teachers, listening to them and asking them questions, and all who heard him were astounded at his understanding and his answers. When his parents saw him, they were astonished, and his mother said to him, "Son, why have you done this to us? Your father and I have been looking for you with great anxiety." And he said to them, "Why were you looking for me? Did you not know that I must be in my Father's house?" But they did not understand what he said to them. He went down with them and came to Nazareth, and was obedient to them; and his mother kept all these things in her heart. And Jesus advanced in wisdom and age and favor before God and man.

IN YEAR B, THESE READINGS MAY BE USED

914

READING I

Genesis 15:1-6; 21:1-3

The word of the LORD came to Abram in a vision, saying:
"Fear not, Abram!
  I am your shield;
  I will make your reward very great."
But Abram said, "O Lord GOD, what good will your gifts be, if I keep on being childless and have as my heir the steward of my house, Eliezer?" Abram continued, "See, you have given me no offspring, and so one of my servants will be my heir." Then the word of the LORD came to him: "No, that one shall not be your heir; your own issue shall be your heir." The Lord took Abram outside and said, "Look up at the sky and count the stars, if you can. Just so, " he added, "shall your descendants be." Abram put his faith in the LORD, who credited it to him as an act of righteousness.

The LORD took note of Sarah as he had said he would; he did for her as he had promised. Sarah became pregnant and bore Abraham a son in his old age, at the set time that God had stated. Abraham gave the name Isaac to this son of his whom Sarah bore him.

RESPONSORIAL PSALM

Psalm 105:1-2, 3-4, 6-7, 8-9

℞. The Lord remembers his covenant for ever.

Give thanks to the LORD, invoke his name;
  make known among the nations his
    deeds.
Sing to him, sing his praise,
  proclaim all his wondrous deeds. ℞.

Glory in his holy name;
  rejoice, O hearts that seek the LORD!
Look to the LORD in his strength;
  constantly seek his face. ℞.

You descendants of Abraham, his
    servants,
    sons of Jacob, his chosen ones!
He, the LORD, is our God;
    throughout the earth his judgments
    prevail. ℟.

He remembers forever his covenant
    which he made binding for a
    thousand generations
    which he entered into with Abraham
    and by his oath to Isaac. ℟.

READING II   *Hebrews 11:8, 11-12, 17-19*

Brothers and sisters: By faith Abraham obeyed when he was called to go out to a place
that he was to receive as an inheritance; he went out, not knowing where he was to go.
By faith he received power to generate, even though he was past the normal age—and
Sarah herself was sterile—for he thought that the one who had made the promise was
trustworthy. So it was that there came forth from one man, himself as good as dead,
descendants as numerous as the stars in the sky and as countless as the sands on the
seashore.

    By faith Abraham, when put to the test, offered up Isaac, and he who had received
the promises was ready to offer his only son, of whom it was said, "Through Isaac
descendants shall bear your name." He reasoned that God was able to raise even from
the dead, and he received Isaac back as a symbol.

915   IN YEAR C, THESE READINGS MAY BE USED

READING I   *1 Samuel 1:20-22, 24-28*

In those days Hannah conceived, and at the end of her term bore a son whom she called
Samuel, since she had asked the LORD for him. The next time her husband Elkanah was
going up with the rest of his household to offer the customary sacrifice to the LORD and
to fulfill his vows, Hannah did not go, explaining to her husband, "Once the child is
weaned, I will take him to appear before the LORD and to remain there forever; I will
offer him as a perpetual nazirite."

    Once Samuel was weaned, Hannah brought him up with her, along with a three-
year-old bull, an ephah of flour, and a skin of wine, and presented him at the temple of
the LORD in Shiloh. After the boy's father had sacrificed the young bull, Hannah, his
mother, approached Eli and said: "Pardon, my lord! As you live, my lord, I am the
woman who stood near you here, praying to the LORD. I prayed for this child, and the
LORD granted my request. Now I, in turn, give him to the LORD; as long as he lives, he
shall be dedicated to the LORD." Hannah left Samuel there.

RESPONSORIAL PSALM   *Psalm 84:2-3, 5-6, 9-10*

℟. Blessed are they who dwell in your house, O Lord.

How lovely is your dwelling place, O
    LORD of hosts!
My soul yearns and pines for the
    courts of the LORD.
My heart and my flesh cry out for the
    living God. ℟.

Happy they who dwell in your house!
    Continually they praise you.

Happy the men whose strength you are!
    Their hearts are set upon the
    pilgrimage. ℟.

O LORD of hosts, hear our prayer;
    hearken, O God of Jacob!
O God, behold our shield,
    and look upon the face of your
    anointed. ℟.

READING II
John 3:1-2, 21-24

Beloved: See what love the Father has bestowed on us that we may be called the children of God. And so we are. The reason the world does not know us is that it did not know him. Beloved, we are God's children now; what we shall be has not yet been revealed. We do know that when it is revealed we shall be like him, for we shall see him as he is.

Beloved, if our hearts do not condemn us, we have confidence in God and receive from him whatever we ask, because we keep his commandments and do what pleases him. And his commandment is this: we should believe in the name of his Son, Jesus Christ, and love one another just as he commanded us. Those who keep his commandments remain in him, and he in them, and the way we know that he remains in us is from the Spirit he gave us.

JANUARY 1: SOLEMNITY OF MARY, THE MOTHER OF GOD / ABC
916

READING I
Numbers 6:22-27 / 18

The LORD said to Moses: "Speak to Aaron and his sons and tell them: This is how you shall bless the Israelites. Say to them: The LORD bless you and keep you! The LORD let his face shine upon you, and be gracious to you! The LORD look upon you kindly and give you peace! So shall they invoke my name upon the Israelites, and I will bless them."

RESPONSORIAL PSALM
Psalm 67:2-3, 5, 6, 8

℟. **May God bless us in his mercy.**

May God have pity on us and bless us;
　　may he let his face shine upon us.
So may your way be known upon earth;
　　among all nations, your salvation. ℟.

May the nations be glad and exult
　　because you rule the peoples in
　　equity;

the nations on the earth you guide. ℟.

May the peoples praise you, O God;
　　may all the peoples praise you!
May God bless us,
　　and may all the ends of the earth fear
　　him! ℟.

READING II
Galatians 4:4-7

Brothers and sisters: When the fullness of time had come, God sent his Son, born of a woman, born under the law, to ransom those under the law, so that we might receive adoption as sons. As proof that you are sons, God sent the Spirit of his Son into our hearts, crying out, "Abba, Father!" So you are no longer a slave but a son, and if a son then also an heir, through God.

GOSPEL
Luke 2:16-21

The shepherds went in haste to Bethlehem and found Mary and Joseph, and the infant lying in the manger. When they saw this, they made known the message that had been told them about this child. All who heard it were amazed by what had been told them by the shepherds. And Mary kept all these things, reflecting on them in her heart. Then the shepherds returned, glorifying and praising God for all they had heard and seen, just as it had been told to them. When eight days were completed for his circumcision, he was named Jesus, the name given him by the angel before he was conceived in the womb.

917 THE EPIPHANY OF THE LORD / ABC

READING I
Isaiah 60:1-6 / 20

Rise up in splendor, Jerusalem! Your
light has come,
the glory of the Lord shines upon
you.
See, darkness covers the earth,
and thick clouds cover the
peoples;
but upon you the LORD shines,
and over you appears his glory.
Nations shall walk by your light,
and kings by your shining radiance.
Raise your eyes and look about;
they all gather and come to you:
your sons come from afar,
and your daughters in the arms of
their nurses.

Then you shall be radiant at what you see,
your heart shall throb and overflow,
for the riches of the sea shall be emptied
out before you,
the wealth of nations shall be
brought to you.
Caravans of camels shall fill you,
dromedaries from Midian and Ephah;
all from Sheba shall come
bearing gold and frankincense,
and proclaiming the praises of the
LORD.

RESPONSORIAL PSALM
Psalm 72:1-2, 7-8, 10-11, 12-13

℟. **Lord, every nation on earth will adore you.**

O God, with your judgment endow the
king,
and with your justice, the king's son;
he shall govern your people with
justice
and your afflicted ones with
judgment. ℟.

Justice shall flower in his days,
and profound peace, till the moon be
no more.
May he rule from sea to sea,
and from the River to the ends of the
earth. ℟.

The kings of Tarshish and the Isles shall
offer gifts;
the kings of Arabia and Seba shall
bring tribute.
All kings shall pay him homage,
all nations shall serve him. ℟.

For he shall rescue the poor when he
cries out,
and the afflicted when he has no one
to help him.
He shall have pity for the lowly and the
poor;
the lives of the poor he shall save. ℟.

READING II
Ephesians 3:2-3a, 5-6

Brothers and sisters: You have heard of the stewardship of God's grace that was given
to me for your benefit, namely, that the mystery was made known to me by revelation.
It was not made known to people in other generations as it has now been revealed to his
holy apostles and prophets by the Spirit: that the Gentiles are coheirs, members of the
same body, and copartners in the promise in Christ Jesus through the gospel.

GOSPEL
Matthew 2:1-12

When Jesus was born in Bethlehem of Judea, in the days of King Herod, behold, magi
from the east arrived in Jerusalem, saying, "Where is the newborn king of the Jews? We
saw his star at its rising and have come to do him homage." When King Herod heard
this, he was greatly troubled, and all Jerusalem with him. Assembling all the chief priests
and the scribes of the people, he inquired of them where the Christ was to be born. They
said to him, "In Bethlehem of Judea, for thus it has been written through the prophet:
'And you, Bethlehem, land of Judah,
are by no means least among the rulers of Judah;
since from you shall come a ruler,
who is to shepherd my people Israel.'"

Then Herod called the magi secretly and ascertained from them the time of the star's appearance. He sent them to Bethlehem and said, "Go and search diligently for the child. When you have found him, bring me word, that I too may go and do him homage." After their audience with the king they set out. And behold, the star that they had seen at its rising preceded them, until it came and stopped over the place where the child was. They were overjoyed at seeing the star, and on entering the house they saw the child with Mary his mother. They prostrated themselves and did him homage. Then they opened their treasures and offered him gifts of gold, frankincense, and myrrh. And having been warned in a dream not to return to Herod, they departed for their country by another way.

BAPTISM OF THE LORD / ABC 918

READING I
Isaiah 42:1-4, 6-7 / 21

Thus says the LORD:
Here is my servant whom I uphold,
   my chosen one with whom I am
      pleased,
upon whom I have put my spirit;
   he shall bring forth justice to the
      nations,
not crying out, not shouting,
   not making his voice heard in the
      street.
A bruised reed he shall not break,
   and a smoldering wick he shall not
      quench,
until he establishes justice on the earth;

the coastlands will wait for his
   teaching.

I, the LORD, have called you for the
   victory of justice,
   I have grasped you by the hand;
I formed you, and set you
   as a covenant of the people,
   a light for the nations,
to open the eyes of the blind,
   to bring out prisoners from
      confinement,
   and from the dungeon, those who
      live in darkness.

RESPONSORIAL PSALM
Psalm 29:1-2, 3-4, 3, 9-10

℟. **The Lord will bless his people with peace.**

Give to the LORD, you sons of God,
   give to the LORD glory and praise,
Give to the LORD the glory due his name;
   adore the LORD in holy attire. ℟.

The voice of the LORD is over the waters,
   the LORD, over vast waters.
The voice of the LORD is mighty;

the voice of the LORD is majestic. ℟.

The God of glory thunders,
   and in his temple all say, "Glory!"
The LORD is enthroned above the flood;
   the LORD is enthroned as king
      forever. ℟.

READING II
Acts 10:34-38

Peter proceeded to speak to those gathered in the house of Cornelius, saying: "In truth, I see that God shows no partiality. Rather, in every nation whoever fears him and acts uprightly is acceptable to him. You know the word that he sent to the Israelites as he proclaimed peace through Jesus Christ, who is Lord of all, what has happened all over Judea, beginning in Galilee after the baptism that John preached, how God anointed Jesus of Nazareth with the Holy Spirit and power. He went about doing good and healing all those oppressed by the devil, for God was with him."

GOSPEL / A
Matthew 3:13-17

Jesus came from Galilee to John at the Jordan to be baptized by him. John tried to prevent him, saying, "I need to be baptized by you, and yet you are coming to me?" Jesus said to him in reply, "Allow it now, for thus it is fitting for us to fulfill all righteousness."

Then he allowed him. After Jesus was baptized, he came up from the water and behold, the heavens were opened for him, and he saw the Spirit of God descending like a dove and coming upon him. And a voice came from the heavens, saying, "This is my beloved Son, with whom I am well pleased."

GOSPEL / B *Mark 1:7-11*

This is what he proclaimed:

"One mightier than I is coming after me. I am not worthy to stoop and loosen the thongs of his sandals. I have baptized you with water; he will baptize you with the Holy Spirit."

It happened in those days that Jesus came from Nazareth of Galilee and was baptized in the Jordan by John. On coming up out of the water he saw the heavens being torn open and the Spirit, like a dove, descending upon him. And a voice came from the heavens, "You are my beloved Son; with you I am well pleased."

GOSPEL / C *Luke 3:15-16, 21-22*

The people were filled with expectation, and all were asking in their hearts whether John might be the Christ. John answered them all, saying, "I am baptizing you with water, but one mightier than I is coming. I am not worthy to loosen the thongs of his sandals. He will baptize you with the Holy Spirit and fire."

After all the people had been baptized and Jesus also had been baptized and was praying, heaven was opened and the Holy Spirit descended upon him in bodily form like a dove. And a voice came from heaven, "You are my beloved Son; with you I am well pleased."

919 IN YEAR B, THESE READINGS MAY BE USED

READING I *Isaiah 55:1-11*

Thus says the LORD:
All you who are thirsty,
   come to the water!
You who have no money,
   come, receive grain and eat;
come, without paying and without cost,
   drink wine and milk!
Why spend your money for what is not
   bread,
   your wages for what fails to satisfy?
Heed me, and you shall eat well,
   you shall delight in rich fare.
Come to me heedfully,
   listen, that you may have life.
I will renew with you the everlasting
   covenant,
   the benefits assured to David.
As I made him a witness to the peoples,
   a leader and commander of nations,
so shall you summon a nation you knew
   not,
   and nations that knew you not shall
     run to you,

because of the LORD, your God
   the Holy One of Israel, who has
   glorified you.

Seek the LORD while he may be found,
   call him while he is near.
Let the scoundrel forsake his way,
   and the wicked man his thoughts;
let him turn to the LORD for mercy;
   to our God, who is generous in
   forgiving.
For my thoughts are not your thoughts,
   nor are your ways my ways, says
   the LORD.
As high as the heavens are above the
   earth
   so high are my ways above your
   ways
   and my thoughts above your
   thoughts.

For just as from the heavens
   the rain and snow come down

and do not return there
till they have watered the earth,
making it fertile and fruitful,
giving seed to the one who sows
and bread to the one who eats,

so shall my word be
that goes forth from my mouth;
my word shall not return to me void,
but shall do my will,
achieving the end for which I sent it.

RESPONSORIAL PSALM   *Isaiah 12:2-3, 4bcd, 5-6*

℟. **You will draw water joyfully from the springs of salvation.**

God indeed is my savior;
    I am confident and unafraid.
My strength and my courage is the LORD,
    and he has been my savior.
With joy you will draw water
    at the fountain of salvation. ℟.

Give thanks to the LORD, acclaim his
        name;
    among the nations make known his

deeds,
proclaim how exalted is his name. ℟.

Sing praise to the LORD for his glorious
    achievement;
    let this be known throughout all the
        earth.
Shout with exultation, O city of Zion,
    for great in your midst
    is the Holy One of Israel! ℟.

READING II   *1 John 5:1-9*

Beloved: Everyone who believes that Jesus is the Christ is begotten by God, and everyone who loves the Father loves also the one begotten by him. In this way we know that
we love the children of God when we love God and obey his commandments. For the
love of God is this, that we keep his commandments. And his commandments are not
burdensome, for whoever is begotten by God conquers the world. And the victory that
conquers the world is our faith. Who indeed is the victor over the world but the one who
believes that Jesus is the Son of God? This is the one who came through water and
blood, Jesus Christ, not by water alone, but by water and blood. The Spirit is the one
who testifies, and the Spirit is truth. So there are three that testify, the Spirit, the water,
and the blood, and the three are of one accord. If we accept human testimony, the testimony of God is surely greater. Now the testimony of God is this, that he has testified on
behalf of his Son.

IN YEAR C, THESE READINGS MAY BE USED   920

READING I   *Isaiah 40:1-5, 9-11*

Comfort, give comfort to my people,
    says your God.
Speak tenderly to Jerusalem, and proclaim
        to her
    that her service is at an end,
    her guilt is expiated;
indeed, she has received from the hand of
        the LORD
    double for all her sins.

A voice cries out:
In the desert prepare the way of the LORD!
    Make straight in the wasteland a
        highway for our God!
Every valley shall be filled in,
    every mountain and hill shall be made

low;
the rugged land shall be made a plain,
    the rough country, a broad valley.
Then the glory of the LORD shall be
        revealed,
    and all people shall see it together;
    for the mouth of the LORD has
        spoken.

Go up onto a high mountain,
    Zion, herald of glad tidings;
cry out at the top of your voice,
    Jerusalem, herald of good news!
Fear not to cry out
    and say to the cities of Judah:
    Here is your God!

Here comes with power
the Lord GOD,
who rules by a strong arm;
here is his reward with him,
his recompense before him.

Like a shepherd he feeds his flock;
in his arms he gathers the lambs,
carrying them in his bosom,
and leading the ewes with care.

RESPONSORIAL PSALM

Psalm 104:1b-2, 3-4, 24-25, 27-28, 29-30

℟. **O bless the Lord, my soul.**

O LORD, my God, you are great indeed!
you are clothed with majesty and
glory,
robed in light as with a cloak.
You have spread out the heavens like
a tent-cloth. ℟.

You have constructed your palace upon
the waters.
You make the clouds your chariot;
you travel on the wings of the wind.
You make the winds your
messengers,
and flaming fire your ministers. ℟.

How manifold are your works, O LORD!
In wisdom you have wrought them
all—

the earth is full of your creatures;
the sea also, great and wide,
in which are schools without number
of living things both small and
great. ℟.

They look to you to give them food in
due time.
When you give it to them, they
gather it;
when you open your hand, they are filled
with good things. ℟.

If you take away their breath, they perish
and return to the dust.
When you send forth your spirit, they
are created,
and you renew the face of the earth. ℟.

READING II

Titus 2:11-14; 3:4-7

Beloved: The grace of God has appeared, saving all and training us to reject godless ways and worldly desires and to live temperately, justly, and devoutly in this age, as we await the blessed hope, the appearance of the glory of our great God and savior Jesus Christ, who gave himself for us to deliver us from all lawlessness and to cleanse for himself a people as his own, eager to do what is good.
When the kindness and generous love
of God our savior appeared,
not because of any righteous deeds we had done
but because of his mercy,
He saved us through the bath of rebirth
and renewal by the Holy Spirit,
whom he richly poured out on us
through Jesus Christ our savior,
so that we might be justified by his grace
and become heirs in hope of eternal life.

Lent/Easter

On a Wednesday in February or early March the church enters into prayer and fasting and almsgiving, attending with great seriousness to its calling. Forty days later on a Thursday evening, that season of Lent ends. From Holy Thursday night until Easter Sunday afternoon, the church keeps the Paschal Triduum, the "Easter Three Days." Good Friday and Holy Saturday find Christians fasting, keeping vigil, remembering the passion, death and resurrection of the Lord until, at the great Vigil liturgy, the church celebrates this paschal mystery in baptism, confirmation and eucharist. Then, for the fifty days of Eastertime the church again sings the alleluia and rejoices to bring God's peace to the world.

The origins of Lent are bound up with the final stages in the initiation of those seeking to be baptized. After months or years of learning gradually the Christian way of life, the catechumens were called to spend the last weeks before baptism in fasting and prayer. The whole church stayed by the catechumens in these days. The lenten season was also kept intensely by those doing penance for their sins. Today both catechumens and penitents keep Lent with the whole church. Lent's scriptures, prayers and rites give clarity and strength to the life-long struggle against evil. That struggle is waged with many forms of prayer and fasting and practices of charity.

The origins of the fifty days of Eastertime are even more ancient. This is the springtime rejoicing of people who know their dependence on fields and flocks. It is the rejoicing of Israel remembering the exodus from slavery to freedom. It became the rejoicing of the church in the resurrection of Jesus and the presence of that risen life in the newly baptized. The Eastertime lectionary is filled with a lively peace and the quiet exuberance of those who believe that evil is not finally triumphant. When the fifty days conclude at Pentecost the church knows again how disturbing, how restless, how strong is the Spirit given by Christ.

922 FIRST SUNDAY OF LENT / A

READING I   *Genesis 2:7-9; 3:1-7 / 22*

The Lord God formed man out of the clay of the ground and blew into his nostrils the breath of life, and so man became a living being.

Then the Lord God planted a garden in Eden, in the east, and placed there the man whom he had formed. Out of the ground the Lord God made various trees grow that were delightful to look at and good for food, with the tree of life in the middle of the garden and the tree of the knowledge of good and evil.

Now the serpent was the most cunning of all the animals that the Lord God had made. The serpent asked the woman, "Did God really tell you not to eat from any of the trees in the garden?" The woman answered the serpent: "We may eat of the fruit of the trees in the garden; it is only about the fruit of the tree in the middle of the garden that God said, 'You shall not eat it or even touch it, lest you die.'" But the serpent said to the woman: "You certainly will not die! No, God knows well that the moment you eat of it your eyes will be opened and you will be like gods who know what is good and what is evil." The woman saw that the tree was good for food, pleasing to the eyes, and desirable for gaining wisdom. So she took some of its fruit and ate it; and she also gave some to her husband, who was with her, and he ate it. Then the eyes of both of them were opened, and they realized that they were naked; so they sewed fig leaves together and made loincloths for themselves.

RESPONSORIAL PSALM   *Psalm 51:3-4, 5-6, 12-13, 14, 17*
℟. **Be merciful, O Lord, for we have sinned.**

Have mercy on me, O God, in your
     goodness;
   in the greatness of your compassion
     wipe out my offense.
Thoroughly wash me from my guilt
   and of my sin cleanse me. ℟.

For I acknowledge my offense,
   and my sin is before me always:
"Against you only have I sinned,
   and done what is evil in your
     sight." ℟.

A clean heart create for me, O God,
   and a steadfast spirit renew within
     me.
Cast me not out from your presence,
   and your Holy Spirit take not from
     me. ℟.

Give me back the joy of your salvation,
   and a willing spirit sustain in me.
O Lord, open my lips,
   and my mouth shall proclaim your
     praise. ℟.

READING II   *Romans 5:12-19 or 5:12, 17-19*
For short form read only the parts in brackets.

[Brothers and sisters: Through one man sin entered the world, and through sin, death, and thus death came to all men, inasmuch as all sinned—] for up to the time of the law, sin was in the world, though sin is not accounted when there is no law. But death reigned from Adam to Moses, even over those who did not sin after the pattern of the trespass of Adam, who is the type of the one who was to come.

But the gift is not like the transgression. For if by the transgression of the one, the many died, how much more did the grace of God and the gracious gift of the one man Jesus Christ overflow for the many. And the gift is not like the result of the one who sinned. For after one sin there was the judgment that brought condemnation; but the gift, after many transgressions, brought acquittal. [For if, by the transgression of the one, death came to reign through that one, how much more will those who receive the abundance of grace and of the gift of justification come to reign in life through the one Jesus Christ. In conclusion, just as through one transgression condemnation came upon all, so, through one righteous act, acquittal and life came to all. For just as through the disobedience of the one man the many were made sinners, so, through the obedience of the one, the many will be made righteous.]

GOSPEL   *Matthew 4:1-11*
At that time Jesus was led by the Spirit into the desert to be tempted by the devil. He fasted for forty days and forty nights, and afterwards he was hungry. The tempter approached and said to him, "If you are the Son of God, command that these stones become loaves of bread."
He said in reply, "It is written:
'One does not live on bread alone,
but on every word that comes forth
from the mouth of God.'"

Then the devil took him to the holy city, and made him stand on the parapet of the temple, and said to him, "If you are the Son of God, throw yourself down. For it is written:
'He will command his angels concerning you'
and 'with their hands they will support you,
lest you dash your foot against a stone.'"
Jesus answered him, "Again it is written, 'You shall not put the Lord, your God, to the test.'" Then the devil took him up to a very high mountain, and showed him all the kingdoms of the world in their magnificence, and he said to him, "All these I shall give to you, if you will prostrate yourself and worship me." At this, Jesus said to him, "Get away, Satan! It is written:
'The Lord, your God, shall you worship
and him alone shall you serve.'"
Then the devil left him and, behold, angels came and ministered to him.

RITE OF ELECTION
At the beginning of Lent, it is the responsibility of the bishop to call those who are judged ready to prepare for the sacraments of initiation at Easter. The bishop is to consult first with the pastors, catechists and others. The rite may take place at the cathedral. If the rite takes place in the parish church, the bishop may designate the pastor to act in his place.
This rite is also called the "Enrollment of Names." Each candidate now gives his/her name, or writes it down. When all have been enrolled, the bishop says: "You have been chosen to be initiated into the sacred mysteries at the Easter Vigil." He then speaks to them and to their sponsors about their lenten preparation for baptism.
The faithful join in prayers of intercession for the elect, as the catechumens are now called. If the eucharist is to be celebrated, the elect are first dismissed.

FIRST SUNDAY OF LENT / B   923

READING I   *Genesis 9:8-15 / 23*
God said to Noah and to his sons with him: "See, I am now establishing my covenant with you and your descendants after you and with every living creature that was with you: all the birds, and the various tame and wild animals that were with you and came out of the ark. I will establish my covenant with you, that never again shall all bodily creatures be destroyed by the waters of a flood; there shall not be another flood to devastate the earth."
God added: "This is the sign that I am giving for all ages to come, of the covenant between me and you and every living creature with you: I set my bow in the clouds to serve as a sign of the covenant between me and the earth.

When I bring clouds over the earth, and the bow appears in the clouds, I will recall the covenant I have made between me and you and all living beings, so that the waters shall never again become a flood to destroy all mortal beings."

RESPONSORIAL PSALM
Psalm 25:4-5, 6-7, 8-9

℞. **Your ways, O Lord, are love and truth to those who keep your covenant.**

Your ways, O LORD, make known to me;
    teach me your paths,
Guide me in your truth and teach me,
    for you are God my savior. ℞.

Remember that your compassion, O LORD,
    and your love are from of old.

In your kindness remember me,
    because of your goodness, O
    LORD. ℞.

Good and upright is the LORD,
    thus he shows sinners the way.
He guides the humble to justice,
    and he teaches the humble his way. ℞.

READING II
1 Peter 3:18-22

Beloved: Christ suffered for sins once, the righteous for the sake of the unrighteous, that he might lead you to God. Put to death in the flesh, he was brought to life in the Spirit. In it he also went to preach to the spirits in prison, who had once been disobedient while God patiently waited in the days of Noah during the building of the ark, in which a few persons, eight in all, were saved through water. This prefigured baptism, which saves you now. It is not a removal of dirt from the body but an appeal to God for a clear conscience, through the resurrection of Jesus Christ, who has gone into heaven and is at the right hand of God, with angels, authorities, and powers subject to him.

GOSPEL
Mark 1:12-15

The Spirit drove Jesus out into the desert, and he remained in the desert for forty days, tempted by Satan. He was among wild beasts, and the angels ministered to him.

After John had been arrested, Jesus came to Galilee proclaiming the gospel of God: "This is the time of fulfillment. The kingdom of God is at hand. Repent, and believe in the gospel."

RITE OF ELECTION
See no. 922

924   FIRST SUNDAY OF LENT / C

READING I
Deuteronomy 26:4-10 / 24

Moses spoke to the people, saying: "The priest shall receive the basket from you and shall set it in front of the altar of the LORD, your God. Then you shall declare before the Lord, your God, 'My father was a wandering Aramean who went down to Egypt with a small household and lived there as an alien. But there he became a nation great, strong, and numerous. When the Egyptians maltreated and oppressed us, imposing hard labor upon us, we cried to the LORD, the God of our fathers, and he heard our cry and saw our affliction, our toil, and our oppression. He brought us out of Egypt with his strong hand and outstretched arm, with terrifying power, with signs and wonders; and bringing us into this country, he gave us this land flowing with milk and honey. Therefore, I have now brought you the firstfruits of the products of the soil which you, O LORD, have given me.' And having set them before the Lord, your God, you shall bow down in his presence."

RESPONSORIAL PSALM

Psalm 91:1-2, 10-11, 12-13, 14-15

℞. **Be with me, Lord, when I am in trouble.**

You who dwell in the shelter of the Most
High,
who abide in the shadow of the
Almighty,
say to the LORD, "My refuge and
fortress,
my God in whom I trust." ℞.

No evil shall befall you,
nor shall affliction come near your
tent,
for to his angels he has given command
about you,
that they guard you in all your
ways. ℞.

Upon their hands they shall bear you up,
lest you dash your foot against a
stone.
You shall tread upon the asp and the
viper;
you shall trample down the lion and
the dragon. ℞.

Because he clings to me, I will deliver
him;
I will set him on high because he
acknowledges my name.
He shall call upon me, and I will
answer him;
I will be with him in distress;
I will deliver him and glorify him. ℞.

READING II

Romans 10:8-13

Brothers and sisters: What does Scripture say?
"The word is near you,
in your mouth and in your heart"
(that is, the word of faith that we preach), for, if you confess with your mouth that Jesus
is Lord and believe in your heart that God raised him from the dead, you will be saved.
For one believes with the heart and so is justified, and one confesses with the mouth and
so is saved. For the Scripture says, "No one who believes in him will be put to shame."
For there is no distinction between Jew and Greek; the same Lord is Lord of all, enrich-
ing all who call upon him. For "everyone who calls on the name of the Lord will be
saved."

GOSPEL

Luke 4:1-13

Filled with the Holy Spirit, Jesus returned from the Jordan and was led by the Spirit into
the desert for forty days, to be tempted by the devil. He ate nothing during those days,
and when they were over he was hungry. The devil said to him, "If you are the Son of
God, command this stone to become bread." Jesus answered him, "It is written, 'One
does not live on bread alone.'" Then he took him up and showed him all the kingdoms
of the world in a single instant. The devil said to him, "I shall give to you all this power
and glory; for it has been handed over to me, and I may give it to whomever I wish. All
this will be yours, if you worship me." Jesus said to him in reply, "It is written:
'You shall worship the Lord, your God,
and him alone shall you serve.'"
Then he led him to Jerusalem, made him stand on the parapet of the temple, and said to
him, "If you are the Son of God, throw yourself down from here, for it is written:
'He will command his angels concerning you, to guard you,'
and:
'With their hands they will support you,
lest you dash your foot against a stone.'"
Jesus said to him in reply, "It also says, 'You shall not put the Lord, your God, to the
test.'" When the devil had finished every temptation, he departed from him for a time.

RITE OF ELECTION
See no. 922

925 SECOND SUNDAY OF LENT / A

READING I
Genesis 12:1-4a / 25

The LORD said to Abram: "Go forth from the land of your kinsfolk and from your father's house to a land that I will show you.

"I will make of you a great nation,
    and I will bless you;
I will make your name great,
    so that you will be a blessing.
I will bless those who bless you
    and curse those who curse you.
All the communities of the earth
    shall find blessing in you."

Abram went as the LORD directed him.

RESPONSORIAL PSALM
Psalm 33:4-5, 18-19, 20, 22

℟. Lord, let your mercy be on us, as we place our trust in you.

Upright is the word of the LORD,
    and all his works are trustworthy.
He loves justice and right;
    of the kindness of the LORD the earth
    is full. ℟.

See, the eyes of the LORD are upon those
    who fear him,
    upon those who hope for his
kindness,
to deliver them from death
    and preserve them in spite of
    famine. ℟.

Our soul waits for the LORD,
    who is our help and our shield.
May your kindness, O LORD, be upon us
    who have put our hope in you. ℟.

READING II
2 Timothy 1:8b-10

Beloved: Bear your share of hardship for the gospel with the strength that comes from God.

He saved us and called us to a holy life, not according to our works but according to his own design and the grace bestowed on us in Christ Jesus before time began, but now made manifest through the appearance of our savior Christ Jesus, who destroyed death and brought life and immortality to light through the gospel.

GOSPEL
Matthew 17:1-9

Jesus took Peter, James, and John his brother, and led them up a high mountain by themselves. And he was transfigured before them; his face shone like the sun and his clothes became white as light. And behold, Moses and Elijah appeared to them, conversing with him. Then Peter said to Jesus in reply, "Lord, it is good that we are here. If you wish, I will make three tents here, one for you, one for Moses, and one for Elijah." While he was still speaking, behold, a bright cloud cast a shadow over them, then from the cloud came a voice that said, "This is my beloved Son, with whom I am well pleased; listen to him." When the disciples heard this, they fell prostrate and were very much afraid. But Jesus came and touched them, saying, "Rise, and do not be afraid." And when the disciples raised their eyes, they saw no one else but Jesus alone.

As they were coming down from the mountain, Jesus charged them, "Do not tell the vision to anyone until the Son of Man has been raised from the dead."

SECOND SUNDAY OF LENT / B 926

READING I
Genesis 22:1-2, 9a, 10-13, 15-18 / 26

God put Abraham to the test. He called to him, "Abraham!" "Here I am!" he replied. Then God said: "Take your son Isaac, your only one, whom you love, and go to the land of Moriah. There you shall offer him up as a holocaust on a height that I will point out to you."

When they came to the place of which God had told him, Abraham built an altar there and arranged the wood on it. Then he reached out and took the knife to slaughter his son. But the LORD's messenger called to him from heaven, "Abraham, Abraham!" "Here I am!" he answered. "Do not lay your hand on the boy," said the messenger. "Do not do the least thing to him. I know now how devoted you are to God, since you did not withhold from me your own beloved son." As Abraham looked about, he spied a ram caught by its horns in the thicket. So he went and took the ram and offered it up as a holocaust in place of his son.

Again the LORD's messenger called to Abraham from heaven and said: "I swear by myself, declares the LORD, that because you acted as you did in not withholding from me your beloved son, I will bless you abundantly and make your descendants as countless as the stars of the sky and the sands of the seashore; your descendants shall take possession of the gates of their enemies, and in your descendants all the nations of the earth shall find blessing—all this because you obeyed my command."

RESPONSORIAL PSALM
Psalm 116:10, 15, 16-17, 18-19

℟. I will walk before the Lord, in the land of the living.

I believed, even when I said,
  "I am greatly afflicted."
Precious in the eyes of the LORD
  is the death of his faithful ones. ℟.

O LORD, I am your servant;
  I am your servant, the son of your
    handmaid;
you have loosed my bonds.

To you will I offer sacrifice of
  thanksgiving,
and I will call upon the name of the
  LORD. ℟.

My vows to the LORD I will pay
  in the presence of all his people,
in the courts of the house of the LORD,
  in your midst, O Jerusalem. ℟.

READING II
Romans 8:31b-34

Brothers and sisters: If God is for us, who can be against us? He who did not spare his own Son but handed him over for us all, how will he not also give us everything else along with him? Who will bring a charge against God's chosen ones? It is God who acquits us, who will condemn? Christ Jesus it is who died - or, rather, was raised - who also is at the right hand of God, who indeed intercedes for us.

GOSPEL
Mark 9:2-10

Jesus took Peter, James, and John and led them up a high mountain apart by themselves. And he was transfigured before them, and his clothes became dazzling white, such as no fuller on earth could bleach them. Then Elijah appeared to them along with Moses, and they were conversing with Jesus. Then Peter said to Jesus in reply, "Rabbi, it is good that we are here! Let us make three tents: one for you, one for Moses, and one for Elijah." He hardly knew what to say, they were so terrified. Then a cloud came, casting a shadow over them; from the cloud came a voice, "This is my beloved Son. Listen to him." Suddenly, looking around, they no longer saw anyone but Jesus alone with them.

As they were coming down from the mountain, he charged them not to relate what they had seen to anyone, except when the Son of Man had risen from the dead. So they kept the matter to themselves, questioning what rising from the dead meant.

927 SECOND SUNDAY OF LENT / C

READING I
Genesis 15:5-12, 17-18 / 27

The Lord God took Abram outside and said, "Look up at the sky and count the stars, if you can. Just so," he added, "shall your descendants be." Abram put his faith in the LORD, who credited it to him as an act of righteousness.

He then said to him, "I am the LORD who brought you from Ur of the Chaldeans to give you this land as a possession." "O Lord GOD," he asked, "how am I to know that I shall possess it?" He answered him, "Bring me a three-year-old heifer, a three-year-old she-goat, a three-year-old ram, a turtledove, and a young pigeon." Abram brought him all these, split them in two, and placed each half opposite the other; but the birds he did not cut up. Birds of prey swooped down on the carcasses, but Abram stayed with them. As the sun was about to set, a trance fell upon Abram, and a deep, terrifying darkness enveloped him.

When the sun had set and it was dark, there appeared a smoking fire pot and a flaming torch, which passed between those pieces. It was on that occasion that the LORD made a covenant with Abram, saying: "To your descendants I give this land, from the Wadi of Egypt to the Great River, the Euphrates."

RESPONSORIAL PSALM
Psalm 27:1, 7-8, 8-9, 13-14

℟. The Lord is my light and my salvation.

The LORD is my light and my salvation;
  whom should I fear?
The LORD is my life's refuge;
  of whom should I be afraid? ℟.

Hear, O LORD, the sound of my call;
  have pity on me, and answer me.
Of you my heart speaks; you my glance
  seeks. ℟.

Your presence, O LORD, I seek.

Hide not your face from me;
do not in anger repel your servant.
You are my helper: cast me not
  off. ℟.

I believe that I shall see the bounty of the
  LORD
  in the land of the living.
Wait for the LORD with courage;
  be stouthearted, and wait for the
  LORD. ℟.

READING II
Philippians 3:17—4:1 or 3:20—4:1

For short form read only the parts in brackets.

Join with others in being imitators of me, [brothers and sisters,] and observe those who thus conduct themselves according to the model you have in us. For many, as I have often told you and now tell you even in tears, conduct themselves as enemies of the cross of Christ. Their end is destruction. Their God is their stomach; their glory is in their "shame." Their minds are occupied with earthly things. But [our citizenship is in heaven, and from it we also await a savior, the Lord Jesus Christ. He will change our lowly body to conform with his glorified body by the power that enables him also to bring all things into subjection to himself.

Therefore, my brothers and sisters, whom I love and long for, my joy and crown, in this way stand firm in the Lord, beloved.]

GOSPEL
Luke 9:28b-36

Jesus took Peter, John, and James and went up the mountain to pray. While he was praying his face changed in appearance and his clothing became dazzling white. And behold, two men were conversing with him, Moses and Elijah, who appeared in glory and spoke of his exodus that he was going to accomplish in Jerusalem. Peter and his companions had been overcome by sleep, but becoming fully awake, they saw his glory and the two men standing with him. As they were about to part from him, Peter said to Jesus, "Master, it is good that we are here; let us make three tents, one for you, one for Moses, and one for Elijah." But he did not know what he was saying. While he was still speaking, a cloud came and cast a shadow over them, and they became frightened when they entered the cloud. Then from the cloud came a voice that said, "This is my chosen Son; listen to him." After the voice had spoken, Jesus was found alone. They fell silent and did not at that time tell anyone what they had seen.

THIRD SUNDAY OF LENT / A 928

READING I
Exodus 17:3-7 / 28

In those days, in their thirst for water, the people grumbled against Moses, saying, "Why did you ever make us leave Egypt? Was it just to have us die here of thirst with our children and our livestock?" So Moses cried out to the LORD, "What shall I do with this people? A little more and they will stone me!" The LORD answered Moses, "Go over there in front of the people, along with some of the elders of Israel, holding in your hand, as you go, the staff with which you struck the river. I will be standing there in front of you on the rock in Horeb. Strike the rock, and the water will flow from it for the people to drink." This Moses did, in the presence of the elders of Israel. The place was called Massah and Meribah, because the Israelites quarreled there and tested the LORD, saying, "Is the LORD in our midst or not?"

RESPONSORIAL PSALM
Psalm 95:1-2, 6-7, 8-9

℟. **If today you hear his voice, harden not your hearts.**

Come, let us sing joyfully to the LORD;
    let us acclaim the Rock of our
        salvation.
Let us come into his presence with
    thanksgiving;
    let us joyfully sing psalms to him. ℟.

Come, let us bow down in worship;
    let us kneel before the LORD who
        made us.
For he is our God,

and we are the people he shepherds,
    the flock he guides. ℟.

Oh, that today you would hear his
    voice:
    "Harden not your hearts as at
        Meribah,
as in the day of Massah in the desert,
    where your fathers tempted me;
they tested me though they had seen my
        works." ℟.

READING II
Romans 5:1-2, 5-8

Brothers and sisters: Since we have been justified by faith, we have peace with God through our Lord Jesus Christ, through whom we have gained access by faith to this grace in which we stand, and we boast in hope of the glory of God.

And hope does not disappoint, because the love of God has been poured out into our hearts through the Holy Spirit who has been given to us. For Christ, while we were still helpless, died at the appointed time for the ungodly. Indeed, only with difficulty does one die for a just person, though perhaps for a good person one might even find courage to die. But God proves his love for us in that while we were still sinners Christ died for us.

GOSPEL
John 4:5-42 or 4:5-15, 19b-26, 39a, 40-42

For short form read only the parts in brackets.

[Jesus came to a town of Samaria called Sychar, near the plot of land that Jacob had given to his son Joseph. Jacob's well was there. Jesus, tired from his journey, sat down there at the well. It was about noon.

A woman of Samaria came to draw water. Jesus said to her, "Give me a drink." His disciples had gone into the town to buy food. The Samaritan woman said to him, "How can you, a Jew, ask me, a Samaritan woman, for a drink?" (For Jews use nothing in common with Samaritans.) Jesus answered and said to her, "If you knew the gift of God and who is saying to you, 'Give me a drink,' you would have asked him and he would have given you living water." The woman said to him, "Sir, you do not even have a bucket and the cistern is deep; where then can you get this living water? Are you greater than our father Jacob, who gave us this cistern and drank from it himself with his children and his flocks?" Jesus answered and said to her, "Everyone who drinks this water will be thirsty again; but whoever drinks the water I shall give will never thirst; the water I shall give will become in him a spring of water welling up to eternal life." The woman said to him, "Sir, give me this water, so that I may not be thirsty or have to keep coming here to draw water."]

Jesus said to her, "Go call your husband and come back." The woman answered and said to him, "I do not have a husband." Jesus answered her, "You are right in saying, 'I do not have a husband.' For you have had five husbands, and the one you have now is not your husband. What you have said is true." The woman said to him, "Sir, [I can see that you are a prophet. Our ancestors worshiped on this mountain; but you people say that the place to worship is in Jerusalem." Jesus said to her, "Believe me, woman, the hour is coming when you will worship the Father neither on this mountain nor in Jerusalem. You people worship what you do not understand; we worship what we understand, because salvation is from the Jews. But the hour is coming, and is now here, when true worshipers will worship the Father in Spirit and truth; and indeed the Father seeks such people to worship him. God is Spirit, and those who worship him must worship in Spirit and truth." The woman said to him, "I know that the Messiah is coming, the one called the Christ; when he comes, he will tell us everything." Jesus said to her, "I am he, the one speaking with you."]

At that moment his disciples returned, and were amazed that he was talking with a woman, but still no one said, "What are you looking for?" or "Why are you talking with her?" The woman left her water jar and went into the town and said to the people, "Come see a man who told me everything I have done. Could he possibly be the Christ?" They went out of the town and came to him. Meanwhile, the disciples urged him, "Rabbi, eat." But he said to them, "I have food to eat of which you do not know." So the disciples said to one another, "Could someone have brought him something to eat?" Jesus said to them, "My food is to do the will of the one who sent me and to finish his work. Do you not say, 'In four months the harvest will be here'? I tell you, look up and see the fields ripe for the harvest. The reaper is already receiving payment and gathering crops for eternal life, so that the sower and reaper can rejoice together. For here the saying is verified that 'One sows and another reaps.' I sent you to reap what you have not worked for; others have done the work, and you are sharing the fruits of their work."

[Many of the Samaritans of that town began to believe in him] because of the word of the woman who testified, "He told me everything I have done." [When the Samaritans came to him, they invited him to stay with them; and he stayed there two days. Many more began to believe in him because of his word, and they said to the woman, "We no longer believe because of your word; for we have heard for ourselves, and we know that this is truly the savior of the world."]

FIRST SCRUTINY

During Lent, the elect (those catechumens who have been called to prepare for baptism at Easter) are called to come before the community for exorcisms and prayers. This takes place after the liturgy of the word on the Third, Fourth, and Fifth Sundays of Lent. These rites are intended to purify the hearts and minds

of the elect, to strengthen them against temptation, to help them progress in the love of God.
  The presider asks the assembly to pray in silence for the elect, then to join in intercessions for them. The presider lays hands on each of the elect and prays that the elect be delivered from the power of evil and become witnesses to the gospel. A song or psalm may be sung, then the elect are dismissed as usual and the faithful continue with the liturgy of the eucharist.

THIRD SUNDAY OF LENT / B   929

READING I   *Exodus 20:1-17 or 20:1-3, 7-8, 12-17 / 29*
For short form read only the parts in brackets.

[In those days, God delivered all these commandments: "I, the LORD, am your God, who brought you out of the land of Egypt, that place of slavery. You shall not have other gods besides me.] You shall not carve idols for yourselves in the shape of anything in the sky above or on the earth below or in the waters beneath the earth; you shall not bow down before them or worship them. For I, the LORD, your God, am a jealous God, inflicting punishment for their fathers' wickedness on the children of those who hate me, down to the third and fourth generation; but bestowing mercy down to the thousandth generation on the children of those who love me and keep my commandments.
  ["You shall not take the name of the LORD, your God, in vain. For the LORD will not leave unpunished the one who takes his name in vain.
  "Remember to keep holy the sabbath day.] Six days you may labor and do all your work, but the seventh day is the sabbath of the LORD, your God. No work may be done then either by you, or your son or daughter, or your male or female slave, or your beast, or by the alien who lives with you. In six days the Lord made the heavens and the earth, the sea and all that is in them; but on the seventh day he rested. That is why the LORD has blessed the sabbath day and made it holy.
  ["Honor your father and your mother, that you may have a long life in the land which the LORD, your God, is giving you.
  "You shall not kill.
  "You shall not commit adultery.
  "You shall not steal.
  "You shall not bear false witness against your neighbor.
  "You shall not covet your neighbor's house. You shall not covet your neighbor's wife, nor his male or female slave, nor his ox or ass, nor anything else that belongs to him."]

RESPONSORIAL PSALM   *Psalm 19:8, 9, 10, 11*
℟. **Lord, you have the words of everlasting life.**

The law of the LORD is perfect,
  refreshing the soul;
the decree of the LORD is trustworthy,
  giving wisdom to the simple. ℟.

The precepts of the LORD are right,
  rejoicing the heart;
the command of the LORD is clear,
  enlightening the eye. ℟.

The fear of the LORD is pure,
  enduring forever;
the ordinances of the LORD are true,
  all of them just. ℟.

They are more precious than gold,
  than a heap of purest gold;
sweeter also than syrup
  or honey from the comb. ℟.

READING II   *1 Corinthians 1:22-25*

Brothers and sisters: Jews demand signs and Greeks look for wisdom, but we proclaim Christ crucified, a stumbling block to Jews and foolishness to Gentiles, but to those who are called, Jews and Greeks alike, Christ the power of God and the wisdom of God. For the foolishness of God is wiser than human wisdom, and the weakness of God is stronger than human strength.

GOSPEL   *John 2:13-25*

Since the Passover of the Jews was near, Jesus went up to Jerusalem. He found in the temple area those who sold oxen, sheep, and doves, as well as the money changers seated there. He made a whip out of cords and drove them all out of the temple area, with the sheep and oxen, and spilled the coins of the money changers and overturned their tables, and to those who sold doves he said, "Take these out of here, and stop making my Father's house a marketplace." His disciples recalled the words of Scripture, "Zeal for your house will consume me." At this the Jews answered and said to him, "What sign can you show us for doing this?" Jesus answered and said to them, "Destroy this temple and in three days I will raise it up." The Jews said, "This temple has been under construction for forty-six years, and you will raise it up in three days?" But he was speaking about the temple of his body. Therefore, when he was raised from the dead, his disciples remembered that he had said this, and they came to believe the Scripture and the word Jesus had spoken.

While he was in Jerusalem for the feast of Passover, many began to believe in his name when they saw the signs he was doing. But Jesus would not trust himself to them because he knew them all, and did not need anyone to testify about human nature. He himself understood it well.

FIRST SCRUTINY

See no. 928

---

930   **THIRD SUNDAY OF LENT / C**

READING I   *Exodus 3:1-8a, 13-15 / 30*

Moses was tending the flock of his father-in-law Jethro, the priest of Midian. Leading the flock across the desert, he came to Horeb, the mountain of God. There an angel of the LORD appeared to Moses in fire flaming out of a bush. As he looked on, he was surprised to see that the bush, though on fire, was not consumed. So Moses decided, "I must go over to look at this remarkable sight, and see why the bush is not burned."

When the LORD saw him coming over to look at it more closely, God called out to him from the bush, "Moses! Moses!" He answered, "Here I am." God said, "Come no nearer! Remove the sandals from your feet, for the place where you stand is holy ground. I am the God of your fathers," he continued, "the God of Abraham, the God of Isaac, the God of Jacob." Moses hid his face, for he was afraid to look at God. But the LORD said, "I have witnessed the affliction of my people in Egypt and have heard their cry of complaint against their slave drivers, so I know well what they are suffering. Therefore I have come down to rescue them from the hands of the Egyptians and lead them out of that land into a good and spacious land, a land flowing with milk and honey."

Moses said to God, "But when I go to the Israelites and say to them, 'The God of your fathers has sent me to you,' if they ask me, 'What is his name?' what am I to tell them?" God replied, "I am who am." Then he added, "This is what you shall tell the Israelites: I AM sent me to you." God spoke further to Moses, "Thus shall you say to the Israelites: The LORD, the God of your fathers, the God of Abraham, the God of Isaac, the

God of Jacob, has sent me to you.
"This is my name forever;
    thus am I to be remembered through all generations."

RESPONSORIAL PSALM
Psalm 103:1-2, 3-4, 6-7, 8, 11

℞. **The Lord is kind and merciful.**

Bless the LORD, O my soul;
    and all my being, bless his holy name.
Bless the LORD, O my soul,
    and forget not all his benefits. ℞.

He pardons all your iniquities,
    heals all your ills.
He redeems your life from destruction,
    crowns you with kindness and
        compassion. ℞.

The LORD secures justice
and the rights of all the oppressed.
He has made known his ways to Moses,
    and his deeds to the children of
        Israel. ℞.

Merciful and gracious is the LORD,
    slow to anger and abounding in
        kindness.
For as the heavens are high above the
        earth,
    so surpassing is his kindness toward
        those who fear him. ℞.

READING II
1 Corinthians 10:1-6, 10-12

I do not want you to be unaware, brothers and sisters, that our ancestors were all under the cloud and all passed through the sea, and all of them were baptized into Moses in the cloud and in the sea. All ate the same spiritual food, and all drank the same spiritual drink, for they drank from a spiritual rock that followed them, and the rock was the Christ. Yet God was not pleased with most of them, for they were struck down in the desert.

These things happened as examples for us, so that we might not desire evil things, as they did. Do not grumble as some of them did, and suffered death by the destroyer. These things happened to them as an example, and they have been written down as a warning to us, upon whom the end of the ages has come. Therefore, whoever thinks he is standing secure should take care not to fall.

GOSPEL
Luke 13:1-9

Some people told Jesus about the Galileans whose blood Pilate had mingled with the blood of their sacrifices. Jesus said to them in reply, "Do you think that because these Galileans suffered in this way they were greater sinners than all other Galileans? By no means! But I tell you, if you do not repent, you will all perish as they did! Or those eighteen people who were killed when the tower at Siloam fell on them—do you think they were more guilty than everyone else who lived in Jerusalem? By no means! But I tell you, if you do not repent, you will all perish as they did!"

And he told them this parable: "There once was a person who had a fig tree planted in his orchard, and when he came in search of fruit on it but found none, he said to the gardener, 'For three years now I have come in search of fruit on this fig tree but have found none. So cut it down. Why should it exhaust the soil?' He said to him in reply, 'Sir, leave it for this year also, and I shall cultivate the ground around it and fertilize it; it may bear fruit in the future. If not you can cut it down.'"

FIRST SCRUTINY
See no. 928

931 FOURTH SUNDAY OF LENT / A

READING I   *1 Samuel 16:1b, 6-7, 10-13a / 31*

The LORD said to Samuel: "Fill your horn with oil, and be on your way. I am sending you to Jesse of Bethlehem, for I have chosen my king from among his sons."

As Jesse and his sons came to the sacrifice, Samuel looked at Eliab and thought, "Surely the Lord's anointed is here before him." But the LORD said to Samuel: "Do not judge from his appearance or from his lofty stature, because I have rejected him. Not as man sees does God see, because man sees the appearance but the LORD looks into the heart." In the same way Jesse presented seven sons before Samuel, but Samuel said to Jesse, "The LORD has not chosen any one of these." Then Samuel asked Jesse, "Are these all the sons you have?" Jesse replied, "There is still the youngest, who is tending the sheep." Samuel said to Jesse, "Send for him; we will not begin the sacrificial banquet until he arrives here." Jesse sent and had the young man brought to them. He was ruddy, a youth handsome to behold and making a splendid appearance. The LORD said, "There—anoint him, for this is the one!" Then Samuel, with the horn of oil in hand, anointed David in the presence of his brothers; and from that day on, the spirit of the LORD rushed upon David.

RESPONSORIAL PSALM   *Psalm 23:1-3a, 3b-4, 5, 6*

℟. **The Lord is my shepherd; there is nothing I shall want.**

The LORD is my shepherd; I shall not
    want.
    In verdant pastures he gives me
    repose;
beside restful waters he leads me;
    he refreshes my soul. ℟.

He guides me in right paths
    for his name's sake.
Even though I walk in the dark valley
    I fear no evil; for you are at my side
with your rod and your staff

that give me courage. ℟.

You spread the table before me
    in the sight of my foes;
you anoint my head with oil;
    my cup overflows. ℟.

Only goodness and kindness follow me
    all the days of my life;
and I shall dwell in the house of the
    LORD
    for years to come. ℟.

READING II   *Ephesians 5:8-14*

Brothers and sisters: You were once darkness, but now you are light in the Lord. Live as children of light, for light produces every kind of goodness and righteousness and truth. Try to learn what is pleasing to the Lord. Take no part in the fruitless works of darkness; rather expose them, for it is shameful even to mention the things done by them in secret; but everything exposed by the light becomes visible, for everything that becomes visible is light. Therefore, it says:
    "Awake, O sleeper,
    and arise from the dead,
    and Christ will give you light."

GOSPEL   *John 9:1-41 or 9:1, 6-9, 13-17, 34-38*

For short form read only the parts in brackets.

[As Jesus passed by he saw a man blind from birth.]
His disciples asked him, "Rabbi, who sinned, this man or his parents, that he was born blind?" Jesus answered, "Neither he nor his parents sinned; it is so that the works of God

might be made visible through him. We have to do the works of the one who sent me while it is day. Night is coming when no one can work. While I am in the world, I am the light of the world." When he had said this, [he spat on the ground and made clay with the saliva, and smeared the clay on his eyes, and said to him, "Go wash in the Pool of Siloam" (which means Sent). So he went and washed, and came back able to see.

His neighbors and those who had seen him earlier as a beggar said, "Isn't this the one who used to sit and beg?" Some said, "It is, " but others said, "No, he just looks like him." He said, "I am."] So they said to him, "How were your eyes opened?" He replied, "The man called Jesus made clay and anointed my eyes and told me, 'Go to Siloam and wash.' So I went there and washed and was able to see." And they said to him, "Where is he?" He said, "I don't know."

[They brought the one who was once blind to the Pharisees. Now Jesus had made clay and opened his eyes on a sabbath. So then the Pharisees also asked him how he was able to see. He said to them, "He put clay on my eyes, and I washed, and now I can see." So some of the Pharisees said, "This man is not from God, because he does not keep the sabbath." But others said, "How can a sinful man do such signs?" And there was a division among them. So they said to the blind man again, "What do you have to say about him, since he opened your eyes?" He said, "He is a prophet."]

Now the Jews did not believe that he had been blind and gained his sight until they summoned the parents of the one who had gained his sight. They asked them, "Is this your son, who you say was born blind? How does he now see?" His parents answered and said, "We know that this is our son and that he was born blind. We do not know how he sees now, nor do we know who opened his eyes. Ask him, he is of age; he can speak for himself." His parents said this because they were afraid of the Jews, for the Jews had already agreed that if anyone acknowledged him as the Christ, he would be expelled from the synagogue. For this reason his parents said, "He is of age; question him."

So a second time they called the man who had been blind and said to him, "Give God the praise! We know that this man is a sinner." He replied, "If he is a sinner, I do not know. One thing I do know is that I was blind and now I see." So they said to him, "What did he do to you? How did he open your eyes?" He answered them, "I told you already and you did not listen. Why do you want to hear it again? Do you want to become his disciples, too?" They ridiculed him and said, "You are that man's disciple; we are disciples of Moses! We know that God spoke to Moses, but we do not know where this one is from." The man answered and said to them, "This is what is so amazing, that you do not know where he is from, yet he opened my eyes. We know that God does not listen to sinners, but if one is devout and does his will, he listens to him. It is unheard of that anyone ever opened the eyes of a person born blind. If this man were not from God, he would not be able to do anything." [They answered and said to him, "You were born totally in sin, and are you trying to teach us?" Then they threw him out.

When Jesus heard that they had thrown him out, he found him and said, "Do you believe in the Son of Man?" He answered and said, "Who is he, sir, that I may believe in him?" Jesus said to him, "You have seen him, the one speaking with you is he." He said, "I do believe, Lord," and he worshiped him.] Then Jesus said, "I came into this world for judgment, so that those who do not see might see, and those who do see might become blind."

Some of the Pharisees who were with him heard this and said to him, "Surely we are not also blind, are we?" Jesus said to them, "If you were blind, you would have no sin; but now you are saying, 'We see,' so your sin remains.

SECOND SCRUTINY

During Lent, the elect (those catechumens who have been called to prepare for baptism at Easter) are called to come before the community for exorcisms and prayers. This takes place after the liturgy of the word on the Third, Fourth, and Fifth Sundays of Lent. These rites are intended to purify the hearts and minds of the elect, to strengthen them against temptation, to help them progress in the love of God.

The presider asks the assembly to pray in silence for the elect, then to join in intercessions for them. The presider lays hands on each of the elect and prays that the elect be delivered from the power of evil and become witnesses to the gospel. A song or psalm may be sung, then the elect are dismissed as usual and the faithful continue with the liturgy of the eucharist.

932 FOURTH SUNDAY OF LENT / B

READING I   *2 Chronicles 36:14-16, 19-23 / 32*

In those days, all the princes of Judah, the priests, and the people added infidelity to infidelity, practicing all the abominations of the nations and polluting the LORD's temple which he had consecrated in Jerusalem.

Early and often did the LORD, the God of their fathers, send his messengers to them, for he had compassion on his people and his dwelling place. But they mocked the messengers of God, despised his warnings, and scoffed at his prophets, until the anger of the LORD against his people was so inflamed that there was no remedy. Their enemies burnt the house of God, tore down the walls of Jerusalem, set all its palaces afire, and destroyed all its precious objects. Those who escaped the sword were carried captive to Babylon, where they became servants of the king of the Chaldeans and his sons until the kingdom of the Persians came to power. All this was to fulfill the word of the Lord spoken by Jeremiah: "Until the land has retrieved its lost sabbaths, during all the time it lies waste it shall have rest while seventy years are fulfilled."

In the first year of Cyrus, king of Persia, in order to fulfill the word of the LORD spoken by Jeremiah, the LORD inspired King Cyrus of Persia to issue this proclamation throughout his kingdom, both by word of mouth and in writing: "Thus says Cyrus, king of Persia: All the kingdoms of the earth the LORD, the God of heaven, has given to me, and he has also charged me to build him a house in Jerusalem, which is in Judah. Whoever, therefore, among you belongs to any part of his people, let him go up, and may his God be with him!"

RESPONSORIAL PSALM   *Psalm 137:1-2, 3, 4-5, 6*

℟. Let my tongue be silenced, if I ever forget you!

By the streams of Babylon
    we sat and wept
when we remembered Zion.
    On the aspens of that land
we hung up our harps. ℟.

For there our captors asked of us
    the lyrics of our songs,
and our despoilers urged us to be joyous:
    "Sing for us the songs of Zion!" ℟.

How could we sing a song of the LORD
    in a foreign land?
If I forget you, Jerusalem,
    may my right hand be forgotten! ℟.

May my tongue cleave to my palate
    if I remember you not,
if I place not Jerusalem
    ahead of my joy. ℟.

READING II   *Ephesians 2:4-10*

Brothers and sisters: God, who is rich in mercy, because of the great love he had for us, even when we were dead in our transgressions, brought us to life with Christ (by grace you have been saved), raised us up with him, and seated us with him in the heavens in Christ Jesus, that in the ages to come he might show the immeasurable riches of his grace in his kindness to us in Christ Jesus. For by grace you have been saved through faith, and this is not from you; it is the gift of God; it is not from works, so no one may boast. For we are his handiwork, created in Christ Jesus for the good works that God has prepared in advance, that we should live in them.

GOSPEL
John 3:14-21

Jesus said to Nicodemus: "Just as Moses lifted up the serpent in the desert, so must the Son of Man be lifted up, so that everyone who believes in him may have eternal life."

For God so loved the world that he gave his only Son, so that everyone who believes in him might not perish but might have eternal life. For God did not send his Son into the world to condemn the world, but that the world might be saved through him. Whoever believes in him will not be condemned, but whoever does not believe has already been condemned, because he has not believed in the name of the only Son of God. And this is the verdict, that the light came into the world, but people preferred darkness to light, because their works were evil. For everyone who does wicked things hates the light and does not come toward the light, so that his works might not be exposed. But whoever lives the truth comes to the light, so that his works may be clearly seen as done in God.

SECOND SCRUTINY
See no. 931

FOURTH SUNDAY OF LENT / C
933

READING I
Joshua 5:9a, 10-12 / 33

The LORD said to Joshua, "Today I have removed the reproach of Egypt from you."

While the Israelites were encamped at Gilgal on the plains of Jericho, they celebrated the Passover on the evening of the fourteenth of the month. On the day after the Passover, they ate of the produce of the land in the form of unleavened cakes and parched grain. On that same day after the Passover, on which they ate of the produce of the land, the manna ceased. No longer was there manna for the Israelites, who that year ate of the yield of the land of Canaan.

RESPONSORIAL PSALM
Psalm 34:2-3, 4-5, 6-7

℟. **Taste and see the goodness of the Lord.**

I will bless the LORD at all times;
    his praise shall be ever in my mouth.
Let my soul glory in the LORD;
    the lowly will hear me and be
    glad. ℟.

Glorify the LORD with me,
    let us together extol his name.
I sought the LORD, and he answered me
    and delivered me from all my

fears. ℟.

Look to him that you may be radiant
    with joy,
    and your faces may not blush with
    shame.
When the poor one called out, the LORD
    heard,
    and from all his distress he saved
    him. ℟.

READING II
2 Corinthians 5:17-21

Brothers and sisters: Whoever is in Christ is a new creation: the old things have passed away; behold, new things have come. And all this is from God, who has reconciled us to himself through Christ and given us the ministry of reconciliation, namely, God was reconciling the world to himself in Christ, not counting their trespasses against them and entrusting to us the message of reconciliation. So we are ambassadors for Christ, as if God were appealing through us. We implore you on behalf of Christ, be reconciled to God. For our sake he made him to be sin who did not know sin, so that we might become the righteousness of God in him.

GOSPEL   *Luke 15:1-3, 11-32*

Tax collectors and sinners were all drawing near to listen to Jesus, but the Pharisees and scribes began to complain, saying, "This man welcomes sinners and eats with them." So to them Jesus addressed this parable: "A man had two sons, and the younger son said to his father, 'Father give me the share of your estate that should come to me.' So the father divided the property between them. After a few days, the younger son collected all his belongings and set off to a distant country where he squandered his inheritance on a life of dissipation. When he had freely spent everything, a severe famine struck that country, and he found himself in dire need. So he hired himself out to one of the local citizens who sent him to his farm to tend the swine. And he longed to eat his fill of the pods on which the swine fed, but nobody gave him any. Coming to his senses he thought, 'How many of my father's hired workers have more than enough food to eat, but here am I, dying from hunger. I shall get up and go to my father and I shall say to him, "Father, I have sinned against heaven and against you. I no longer deserve to be called your son; treat me as you would treat one of your hired workers."' So he got up and went back to his father. While he was still a long way off, his father caught sight of him, and was filled with compassion. He ran to his son, embraced him and kissed him. His son said to him, 'Father, I have sinned against heaven and against you; I no longer deserve to be called your son.' But his father ordered his servants, 'Quickly bring the finest robe and put it on him; put a ring on his finger and sandals on his feet. Take the fattened calf and slaughter it. Then let us celebrate with a feast, because this son of mine was dead, and has come to life again; he was lost, and has been found.' Then the celebration began. Now the older son had been out in the field and, on his way back, as he neared the house, he heard the sound of music and dancing. He called one of the servants and asked what this might mean. The servant said to him, 'Your brother has returned and your father has slaughtered the fattened calf because he has him back safe and sound.' He became angry, and when he refused to enter the house, his father came out and pleaded with him. He said to his father in reply, 'Look, all these years I served you and not once did I disobey your orders; yet you never gave me even a young goat to feast on with my friends. But when your son returns who swallowed up your property with prostitutes, for him you slaughter the fattened calf.' He said to him, 'My son, you are here with me always; everything I have is yours. But now we must celebrate and rejoice, because your brother was dead and has come to life again; he was lost and has been found.'"

SECOND SCRUTINY
See no. 931

934 FIFTH SUNDAY OF LENT / A

READING I   *Ezekiel 37:12-14 / 34*

Thus says the Lord GOD: O my people, I will open your graves and have you rise from them, and bring you back to the land of Israel. Then you shall know that I am the LORD, when I open your graves and have you rise from them, O my people! I will put my spirit in you that you may live, and I will settle you upon your land; thus you shall know that I am the LORD. I have promised, and I will do it, says the LORD.

RESPONSORIAL PSALM   *Psalm 130:1-2, 3-4, 5-6, 7-8*
℟. **With the Lord there is mercy and fullness of redemption.**

Out of the depths I cry to you, O LORD;
   LORD, hear my voice!
Let your ears be attentive
   to my voice in supplication. ℟.

If you, O LORD, mark iniquities,
   LORD, who can stand?
But with you is forgiveness,
   that you may be revered. ℟.

I trust in the LORD;
  my soul trusts in his word.
More than sentinels wait for the dawn,
  let Israel wait for the LORD. ℟.

For with the LORD is kindness
  and with him is plenteous
    redemption;
  and he will redeem Israel
    from all their iniquities. ℟.

READING II   *Romans 8:8-11*

Brothers and sisters: Those who are in the flesh cannot please God. But you are not in the flesh; on the contrary, you are in the spirit, if only the Spirit of God dwells in you. Whoever does not have the Spirit of Christ does not belong to him. But if Christ is in you, although the body is dead because of sin, the spirit is alive because of righteousness. If the Spirit of the one who raised Jesus from the dead dwells in you, the one who raised Christ from the dead will give life to your mortal bodies also, through his Spirit dwelling in you.

GOSPEL   *John 11:1-45 or 11:3-7, 17, 20-27, 33b-45*
For short form read only the parts in brackets.

Now a man was ill, Lazarus from Bethany, the village of Mary and her sister Martha. Mary was the one who had anointed the Lord with perfumed oil and dried his feet with her hair; it was her brother Lazarus who was ill. So [the sisters sent word to Jesus saying, "Master, the one you love is ill." When Jesus heard this he said, "This illness is not to end in death, but is for the glory of God, that the Son of God may be glorified through it." Now Jesus loved Martha and her sister and Lazarus. So when he heard that he was ill, he remained for two days in the place where he was. Then after this he said to his disciples, "Let us go back to Judea."] The disciples said to him, "Rabbi, the Jews were just trying to stone you, and you want to go back there?" Jesus answered, "Are there not twelve hours in a day? If one walks during the day, he does not stumble, because he sees the light of this world. But if one walks at night, he stumbles, because the light is not in him." He said this, and then told them, "Our friend Lazarus is asleep, but I am going to awaken him." So the disciples said to him, "Master, if he is asleep, he will be saved." But Jesus was talking about his death, while they thought that he meant ordinary sleep. So then Jesus said to them clearly, "Lazarus has died. And I am glad for you that I was not there, that you may believe. Let us go to him." So Thomas, called Didymus, said to his fellow disciples, "Let us also go to die with him."

[When Jesus arrived, he found that Lazarus had already been in the tomb for four days.] Now Bethany was near Jerusalem, only about two miles away. And many of the Jews had come to Martha and Mary to comfort them about their brother. [When Martha heard that Jesus was coming, she went to meet him; but Mary sat at home. Martha said to Jesus, "Lord, if you had been here, my brother would not have died. But even now I know that whatever you ask of God, God will give you." Jesus said to her, "Your brother will rise." Martha said to him, "I know he will rise, in the resurrection on the last day." Jesus told her, "I am the resurrection and the life; whoever believes in me, even if he dies, will live, and everyone who lives and believes in me will never die. Do you believe this?" She said to him, "Yes, Lord. I have come to believe that you are the Christ, the Son of God, the one who is coming into the world."]

When she had said this, she went and called her sister Mary secretly, saying, "The teacher is here and is asking for you." As soon as she heard this, she rose quickly and went to him. For Jesus had not yet come into the village, but was still where Martha had met him. So when the Jews who were with her in the house comforting her saw Mary get up quickly and go out, they followed her, presuming that she was going to the tomb to weep there. When Mary came to where Jesus was and saw him, she fell at his feet and said to him, "Lord, if you had been here, my brother would not have died." When Jesus saw her weeping and the Jews who had come with her weeping, [he became perturbed and deeply troubled, and said, "Where have you laid him?" They said to him, "Sir, come and see." And Jesus wept. So the Jews said, "See how he loved him." But some of them said, "Could not the one who opened the eyes of the blind man have done something so that this man would not have died?"

So Jesus, perturbed again, came to the tomb. It was a cave, and a stone lay across it. Jesus said, "Take away the stone." Martha, the dead man's sister, said to him, "Lord, by now there will be a stench; he has been dead for four days." Jesus said to her, "Did I not tell you that if you believe you will see the glory of God?" So they took away the stone. And Jesus raised his eyes and said, "Father, I thank you for hearing me. I know that you always hear me; but because of the crowd here I have said this, that they may believe that you sent me." And when he had said this, he cried out in a loud voice, "Lazarus, come out!" The dead man came out, tied hand and foot with burial bands, and his face was wrapped in a cloth. So Jesus said to them, "Untie him and let him go."

Now many of the Jews who had come to Mary and seen what he had done began to believe in him.]

THIRD SCRUTINY

During Lent, the elect (those catechumens who have been called to prepare for baptism at Easter) are called to come before the community for exorcisms and prayers. This takes place after the liturgy of the word on the Third, Fourth, and Fifth Sundays of Lent. These rites are intended to purify the hearts and minds of the elect, to strengthen them against temptation, to help them progress in the love of God.

The presider asks the assembly to pray in silence for the elect, then to join in intercessions for them. The presider lays hands on each of the elect and prays that the elect be delivered from the power of evil and become witnesses to the gospel. A song or psalm may be sung, then the elect are dismissed as usual and the faithful continue with the liturgy of the eucharist.

935 FIFTH SUNDAY OF LENT / B

READING I   *Jeremiah 31:31-34 / 35*

The days are coming, says the LORD, when I will make a new covenant with the house of Israel and the house of Judah. It will not be like the covenant I made with their fathers the day I took them by the hand to lead them forth from the land of Egypt; for they broke my covenant, and I had to show myself their master, says the LORD. But this is the covenant that I will make with the house of Israel after those days, says the LORD. I will place my law within them and write it upon their hearts; I will be their God, and they shall be my people. No longer will they have need to teach their friends and relatives how to know the LORD. All, from least to greatest, shall know me, says the LORD, for I will forgive their evildoing and remember their sin no more.

RESPONSORIAL PSALM   *Psalm 51:3-4, 12-13, 14-15*
℟. **Create a clean heart in me, O God.**

Have mercy on me, O God, in your
    goodness;
    in the greatness of your compassion
    wipe out my offense.
Thoroughly wash me from my guilt
    and of my sin cleanse me. ℟.

A clean heart create for me, O God,
    and a steadfast spirit renew within

me.
Cast me not out from your presence,
    and your Holy Spirit take not from
    me. ℟.

Give me back the joy of your salvation,
    and a willing spirit sustain in me.
I will teach transgressors your ways,
    and sinners shall return to you. ℟.

READING II
Hebrews 5:7-9

In the days when Christ Jesus was in the flesh, he offered prayers and supplications with loud cries and tears to the one who was able to save him from death, and he was heard because of his reverence. Son though he was, he learned obedience from what he suffered; and when he was made perfect, he became the source of eternal salvation for all who obey him.

GOSPEL
John 12:20-33

Some Greeks who had come to worship at the Passover Feast came to Philip, who was from Bethsaida in Galilee, and asked him, "Sir, we would like to see Jesus." Philip went and told Andrew; then Andrew and Philip went and told Jesus. Jesus answered them, "The hour has come for the Son of Man to be glorified. Amen, amen, I say to you, unless a grain of wheat falls to the ground and dies, it remains just a grain of wheat; but if it dies, it produces much fruit. Whoever loves his life loses it, and whoever hates his life in this world will preserve it for eternal life. Whoever serves me must follow me, and where I am, there also will my servant be. The Father will honor whoever serves me. "I am troubled now. Yet what should I say? 'Father, save me from this hour'? But it was for this purpose that I came to this hour. Father, glorify your name." Then a voice came from heaven, "I have glorified it and will glorify it again." The crowd there heard it and said it was thunder; but others said, "An angel has spoken to him." Jesus answered and said, "This voice did not come for my sake but for yours. Now is the time of judgment on this world; now the ruler of this world will be driven out. And when I am lifted up from the earth, I will draw everyone to myself." He said this indicating the kind of death he would die.

THIRD SCRUTINY
See no. 934

FIFTH SUNDAY OF LENT / C
936

READING I
Isaiah 43:16-21 / 36

Thus says the LORD,
 who opens a way in the sea
 and a path in the mighty waters,
who leads out chariots and horsemen,
 a powerful army,
till they lie prostrate together, never to
 rise,
 snuffed out and quenched like a wick.
Remember not the events of the past,
 the things of long ago consider not;
see, I am doing something new!

Now it springs forth, do you not
 perceive it?
In the desert I make a way,
 in the wasteland, rivers.
Wild beasts honor me,
 jackals and ostriches,
for I put water in the desert
 and rivers in the wasteland
 for my chosen people to drink,
the people whom I formed for myself,
 that they might announce my praise.

RESPONSORIAL PSALM
Psalm 126:1-2, 2-3, 4-5, 6

℟. **The Lord has done great things for us; we are filled with joy.**

When the LORD brought back the captives
 of Zion,
 we were like men dreaming.
Then our mouth was filled with laughter,
 and our tongue with rejoicing. ℟.

Then they said among the nations,
 "The LORD has done great things for
 them."
The LORD has done great things for us;
 we are glad indeed. ℟.

Restore our fortunes, O LORD,
like the torrents in the southern
desert.
Those that sow in tears
shall reap rejoicing. ℟.

Although they go forth weeping,
carrying the seed to be sown,
They shall come back rejoicing,
carrying their sheaves. ℟.

READING II   *Philippians 3:8-14*
Brothers and sisters: I consider everything as a loss because of the supreme good of knowing Christ Jesus my Lord. For his sake I have accepted the loss of all things and I consider them so much rubbish, that I may gain Christ and be found in him, not having any righteousness of my own based on the law but that which comes through faith in Christ, the righteousness from God, depending on faith to know him and the power of his resurrection and the sharing of his sufferings by being conformed to his death, if somehow I may attain the resurrection from the dead.
It is not that I have already taken hold of it or have already attained perfect maturity, but I continue my pursuit in hope that I may possess it, since I have indeed been taken possession of by Christ Jesus. Brothers and sisters, I for my part do not consider myself to have taken possession. Just one thing: forgetting what lies behind but straining forward to what lies ahead, I continue my pursuit toward the goal, the prize of God's upward calling, in Christ Jesus.

GOSPEL   *John 8:1-11*
Jesus went to the Mount of Olives. But early in the morning he arrived again in the temple area, and all the people started coming to him, and he sat down and taught them. Then the scribes and the Pharisees brought a woman who had been caught in adultery and made her stand in the middle. They said to him, "Teacher, this woman was caught in the very act of committing adultery. Now in the law, Moses commanded us to stone such women. So what do you say?" They said this to test him, so that they could have some charge to bring against him. Jesus bent down and began to write on the ground with his finger. But when they continued asking him, he straightened up and said to them, "Let the one among you who is without sin be the first to throw a stone at her." Again he bent down and wrote on the ground. And in response, they went away one by one, beginning with the elders. So he was left alone with the woman before him. Then Jesus straightened up and said to her, "Woman, where are they? Has no one condemned you?" She replied, "No one, sir." Then Jesus said, "Neither do I condemn you. Go, and from now on do not sin any more."

THIRD SCRUTINY
See no. 934

937 PASSION SUNDAY (PALM SUNDAY)

Passion or Palm Sunday is the last Sunday in Lent. Its closeness to the end of Lent has given this liturgy two distinct features: the procession with palms and the gospel reading of the Lord's passion. The blessing and carrying of palms celebrates Jesus' entrance into Jerusalem to accomplish his paschal mystery. The reading of the passion comes as a conclusion to all the gospel readings of the lenten Sundays: these scriptures yearly prepare catechumens and the faithful to approach the celebration of Christ's death and resurrection. That celebration takes place most especially in the sacraments of initiation at the Easter Vigil.

COMMEMORATION OF THE LORD'S ENTRANCE INTO JERUSALEM

This rite may be very simple or may involve the entire assembly in a procession with the blessing of palms and the gospel reading of Jesus' entrance into Jerusalem. Depending on the local church, then, some of the following hymns, psalms and readings will be used.

OPENING ANTIPHON 938

The following or another appropriate acclamation may be sung.

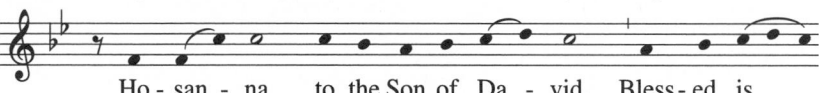

Ho - san - na   to the Son of Da - vid.   Bless- ed is

he   who comes in   the   name   of   the   Lord.

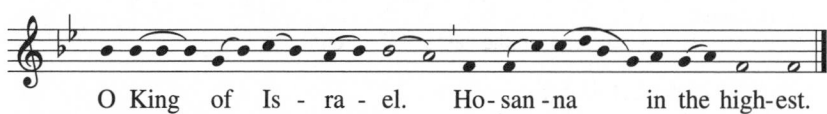

O King   of   Is - ra - el.   Ho- san -na   in the high- est.

Music: Mode VII; adapt. by Richard Proulx, © 1986, GIA Publications, Inc.

BLESSING OF BRANCHES 939

All hold branches as these are blessed. The branches may be of palm or from a tree that is native to the area. The green or flowering branches signify the victory of life.

GOSPEL / A   *Matthew 21:1-11 / 37*

When Jesus and the disciples drew near Jerusalem and came to Bethphage on the Mount of Olives, Jesus sent two disciples, saying to them, "Go into the village opposite you, and immediately you will find an ass tethered, and a colt with her. Untie them and bring them here to me. And if anyone should say anything to you, reply, 'The master has need of them.' Then he will send them at once." This happened so that what had been spoken through the prophet might be fulfilled:
"Say to daughter Zion,
'Behold, your king comes to you,
meek and riding on an ass,
and on a colt, the foal of a beast of burden.'"
The disicples went and did as Jesus had ordered them. They brought the ass and the colt and laid their cloaks over them, and he sat upon them. The very large crowd spread their cloaks on the road, while others cut branches from the trees and strewed them on the road. The crowds preceding him and those following kept crying out and saying:
"Hosanna to the Son of David;
blessed is he who comes in the name of the Lord;
hosanna in the highest."
And when he entered Jerusalem the whole city was shaken and asked, "Who is this?" And the crowds replied, "This is Jesus the prophet, from Nazareth in Galilee."

GOSPEL / B *Mark 11:1-10*

When Jesus and his disciples drew near to Jerusalem, to Bethphage and Bethany at the Mount of Olives, he sent two of his disciples and said to them, "Go into the village opposite you, and immediately on entering it, you will find a colt tethered on which no one has ever sat. Untie it and bring it here. If anyone should say to you, 'Why are you doing this?' reply, 'The Master has need of it and will send it back here at once.'" So they went off and found a colt tethered at a gate outside on the street, and they untied it. Some of the bystanders said to them, "What are you doing, untying the colt?" They answered them just as Jesus had told them to, and they permitted them to do it. So they brought the colt to Jesus and put their cloaks over it. And he sat on it. Many people spread their cloaks on the road, and others spread leafy branches that they had cut from the fields. Those preceding him as well as those following kept crying out:

"Hosanna!
Blessed is he who comes in the name of the Lord!
Blessed is the kingdom of our father David that is to come!
Hosanna in the highest!"

Or:

GOSPEL / B *John 12:12-16*

When the great crowd that had come to the feast heard that Jesus was coming to Jerusalem, they took palm branches and went out to meet him, and cried out:

"Hosanna!
"Blessed is he who comes in the name of the Lord,
the king of Israel."

Jesus found an ass and sat upon it, as is written:

"Fear no more, O daughter Zion;
see, your king comes, seated upon an ass's colt."

His disciples did not understand this at first, but when Jesus had been glorified they remembered that these things were written about him and that they had done this for him.

GOSPEL / C *Luke 19:28-40*

Jesus proceeded on his journey up to Jerusalem. As he drew near to Bethphage and Bethany at the place called the Mount of Olives, he sent two of his disciples. He said, "Go into the village opposite you, and as you enter it you will find a colt tethered on which no one has ever sat. Untie it and bring it here. And if anyone should ask you, 'Why are you untying it?' you will answer, 'The Master has need of it.'" So those who had been sent off and found everything just as he had told them. And as they were untying the colt, its owners said to them, "Why are you untying this colt?" They answered, "The Master has need of it." So they brought it to Jesus, threw their cloaks over the colt, and helped Jesus to mount. As he rode along, the people were spreading their cloaks on the road; and now as he was approaching the slope of the Mount of Olives, the whole multitude of his disciples began to praise God aloud with joy for all the mighty deeds they had seen. They proclaimed:

"Blessed is the king who comes
in the name of the Lord.
Peace in heaven
and glory in the highest."

Some of the Pharisees in the crowd said to him, "Teacher, rebuke your disciples." He said in reply, "I tell you, if they keep silent, the stones will cry out!"

940 **PROCESSION**

All join in the procession or at least in the song. Such a movement of people expresses the experience of Lent: the church has been called to move on, to go ever further toward the paschal mystery of death and resurrection. Hymn no. 402, or another appropriate song is sung.

The commemoration of the Lord's entrance into Jerusalem, whether this is done in a simple or solemn manner, concludes with the opening prayer of the Mass.

LITURGY OF THE WORD / ABC   941

READING I   *Isaiah 50:4-7 / 38*

The Lord GOD has given me
  a well-trained tongue,
that I might know how to speak to the
    weary
  a word that will rouse them.
Morning after morning
  he opens my ear that I may hear;
and I have not rebelled,
  have not turned back.
I gave my back to those who beat me,

my cheeks to those who plucked my
    beard;
my face I did not shield
  from buffets and spitting.

The Lord GOD is my help,
  therefore I am not disgraced;
I have set my face like flint,
  knowing that I shall not be put to
    shame.

RESPONSORIAL PSALM   *Psalm 22:8-9, 17-18, 19-20, 23-24*
℟. My God, my God, why have you abandoned me?

All who see me scoff at me;
  they mock me with parted lips, they
    wag their heads:
"He relied on the LORD; let him deliver
    him,
  let him rescue him, if he loves
    him." ℟.

Indeed, many dogs surround me,
  a pack of evildoers closes in upon
    me;
They have pierced my hands and my feet;
  I can count all my bones. ℟.

They divide my garments among them,
  and for my vesture they cast lots.
But you, O LORD, be not far from me;
  O my help, hasten to aid me. ℟.

I will proclaim your name to my
    brethren;
  in the midst of the assembly I will
    praise you:
"You who fear the LORD, praise him;
  all you descendants of Jacob, give
    glory to him;
revere him, all you descendants of
    Israel!" ℟.

READING II   *Philippians 2:6-11*

Christ Jesus, though he was in the form
    of God,
  did not regard equality with God
    something to be grasped.
Rather, he emptied himself,
  taking the form of a slave,
  coming in human likeness;
and found human in appearance,
  he humbled himself,
  becoming obedient to the point of
    death,

even death on a cross.
Because of this, God greatly exalted him
  and bestowed on him the name
  which is above every name,
that at the name of Jesus
  every knee should bend,
  of those in heaven and on earth and
    under the earth,
and every tongue confess that
  Jesus Christ is Lord,
  to the glory of God the Father.

GOSPEL / A   *Matthew 26:14—27:66 or 27:11-54*   942
For short form read only the part in brackets.

One of the Twelve, who was called Judas Iscariot, went to the chief priests and said,
"What are you willing to give me if I hand him over to you?" They paid him thirty pieces

of silver, and from that time on he looked for an opportunity to hand him over.

On the first day of the Feast of Unleavened Bread, the disciples approached Jesus and said, "Where do you want us to prepare for you to eat the Passover?" He said, "Go into the city to a certain man and tell him, 'The teacher says, "My appointed time draws near; in your house I shall celebrate the Passover with my disciples."'" The disciples then did as Jesus had ordered, and prepared the Passover.

When it was evening, he reclined at table with the Twelve. And while they were eating, he said, "Amen, I say to you, one of you will betray me." Deeply distressed at this, they began to say to him one after another, "Surely it is not I, Lord?" He said in reply, "He who has dipped his hand into the dish with me is the one who will betray me. The Son of Man indeed goes, as it is written of him, but woe to that man by whom the Son of Man is betrayed. It would be better for that man if he had never been born." Then Judas, his betrayer, said in reply, "Surely it is not I, Rabbi?" He answered, "You have said so."

While they were eating, Jesus took bread, said the blessing, broke it, and giving it to his disciples said, "Take and eat; this is my body." Then he took a cup, gave thanks, and gave it to them, saying, "Drink from it, all of you, for this is my blood of the covenant, which will be shed on behalf of many for the forgiveness of sins. I tell you, from now on I shall not drink this fruit of the vine until the day when I drink it with you new in the kingdom of my Father." Then, after singing a hymn, they went out to the Mount of Olives.

Then Jesus said to them, "This night all of you will have your faith in me shaken, for it is written:

'I will strike the shepherd,
   and the sheep of the flock will be dispersed;'

but after I have been raised up, I shall go before you to Galilee." Peter said to him in reply, "Though all may have their faith in you shaken, mine will never be." Jesus said to him, "Amen, I say to you, this very night before the cock crows, you will deny me three times." Peter said to him, "Even though I should have to die with you, I will not deny you." And all the disciples spoke likewise.

Then Jesus came with them to a place called Gethsemane, and he said to his disciples, "Sit here while I go over there and pray." He took along Peter and the two sons of Zebedee, and began to feel sorrow and distress. Then he said to them, "My soul is sorrowful even to death. Remain here and keep watch with me." He advanced a little and fell prostrate in prayer, saying, "My Father, if it is possible, let this cup pass from me; yet, not as I will, but as you will." When he returned to his disciples he found them asleep. He said to Peter, "So you could not keep watch with me for one hour? Watch and pray that you may not undergo the test. The spirit is willing, but the flesh is weak." Withdrawing a second time, he prayed again, "My Father, if it is not possible that this cup pass without my drinking it, your will be done!" Then he returned once more and found them asleep, for they could not keep their eyes open. He left them and withdrew again and prayed a third time, saying the same thing again. Then he returned to his disciples and said to them, "Are you still sleeping and taking your rest? Behold, the hour is at hand when the Son of Man is to be handed over to sinners. Get up, let us go. Look, my betrayer is at hand."

While he was still speaking, Judas, one of the Twelve, arrived, accompanied by a large crowd, with swords and clubs, who had come from the chief priests and the elders of the people. His betrayer had arranged a sign with them, saying, "The man I shall kiss is the one; arrest him." Immediately he went over to Jesus and said, "Hail, Rabbi!" and he kissed him. Jesus answered him, "Friend, do what you have come for." Then stepping forward they laid hands on Jesus and arrested him. And behold, one of those who accompanied Jesus put his hand to his sword, drew it, and struck the high priest's servant, cutting off his ear. Then Jesus said to him, "Put your sword back into its sheath, for all who take the sword will perish by the sword. Do you think that I cannot call upon my Father and he will not provide me at this moment with more than twelve legions of angels? But then how would the Scriptures be fulfilled which say that it must come to pass in this way?" At that hour Jesus said to the crowds, "Have you come out as against a robber, with swords and clubs to seize me? Day after day I sat teaching in the temple area, yet you did not arrest me. But all this has come to pass that the writings of the prophets may be fulfilled." Then all the disciples left him and fled.

Those who had arrested Jesus led him away to Caiaphas the high priest, where the scribes and the elders were assembled. Peter was following him at a distance as far as the high priest's courtyard, and going inside he sat down with the servants to see the outcome. The chief priests and the entire Sanhedrin kept trying to obtain false testimony against Jesus in order to put him to death, but they found none, though many false witnesses came forward. Finally two came forward who stated, "This man said, 'I can destroy the temple of God and within three days rebuild it.'" The high priest rose and addressed him, "Have you no answer? What are these men testifying against you?" But Jesus was silent. Then the high priest said to him, "I order you to tell us under oath before the living God whether you are the Christ, the Son of God." Jesus said to him in reply, "You have said so. But I tell you:

> From now on you will see 'the Son of Man
> seated at the right hand of the Power'
> and 'coming on the clouds of heaven.'"

Then the high priest tore his robes and said, "He has blasphemed! What further need have we of witnesses? You have now heard the blasphemy; what is your opinion?" They said in reply, "He deserves to die!" Then they spat in his face and struck him, while some slapped him, saying, "Prophesy for us, Christ: who is it that struck you?"

Now Peter was sitting outside in the courtyard. One of the maids came over to him and said, "You too were with Jesus the Galilean." But he denied it in front of everyone, saying, "I do not know what you are talking about!" As he went out to the gate, another girl saw him and said to those who were there, "This man was with Jesus the Nazorean." Again he denied it with an oath, "I do not know the man!" A little later the bystanders came over and said to Peter, "Surely you too are one of them; even your speech gives you away." At that he began to curse and to swear, "I do not know the man." And immediately a cock crowed. Then Peter remembered the word that Jesus had spoken: "Before the cock crows you will deny me three times." He went out and began to weep bitterly.

When it was morning, all the chief priests and the elders of the people took counsel against Jesus to put him to death. They bound him, led him away, and handed him over to Pilate, the governor.

Then Judas, his betrayer, seeing that Jesus had been condemned, deeply regretted what he had done. He returned the thirty pieces of silver to the chief priests and elders, saying, "I have sinned in betraying innocent blood." They said, "What is that to us? Look to it yourself." Flinging the money into the temple, he departed and went off and hanged himself. The chief priests gathered up the money, but said, "It is not lawful to deposit this in the temple treasury, for it is the price of blood." After consultation, they used it to buy the potter's field as a burial place for foreigners. That is why that field even today is called the Field of Blood. Then was fulfilled what had been said through Jeremiah the prophet, "And they took the thirty pieces of silver, the value of a man with a price on his head, a price set by some of the Israelites, and they paid it out for the potter's field just as the Lord had commanded me."

[Now Jesus stood before the governor, and he questioned him, "Are you the king of the Jews?" Jesus said, "You say so." And when he was accused by the chief priests and elders, he made no answer. Then Pilate said to him, "Do you not hear how many things they are testifying against you?" But he did not answer him one word, so that the governor was greatly amazed.

Now on the occasion of the feast the governor was accustomed to release to the crowd one prisoner whom they wished. And at that time they had a notorious prisoner called Barabbas. So when they had assembled, Pilate said to them, "Which one do you want me to release to you, Barabbas, or Jesus called Christ?" For he knew that it was out of envy that they had handed him over. While he was still seated on the bench, his wife sent him a message, "Have nothing to do with that righteous man. I suffered much in a dream today because of him." The chief priests and the elders persuaded the crowds to ask for Barabbas but to destroy Jesus. The governor said to them in reply, "Which of the two do you want me to release to you?" They answered, "Barabbas!" Pilate said to them, "Then what shall I do with Jesus called Christ?" They all said, "Let him be crucified!" But he said, "Why? What evil has he done?" They only shouted the louder, "Let him be crucified!" When Pilate saw that he was not succeeding at all, but that a riot was breaking out instead, he took water and washed his hands in the sight of the crowd, saying, "I am innocent of this man's blood. Look to it yourselves." And the whole people said in reply, "His blood be upon us and upon our children." Then he released Barabbas to them, but after he had Jesus scourged, he handed him over to be crucified.

Then the soldiers of the governor took Jesus inside the praetorium and gathered the whole cohort around him. They stripped off his clothes and threw a scarlet military cloak about him. Weaving a crown out of thorns, they placed it on his head, and a reed in his right hand. And kneeling before him, they mocked him, saying, "Hail, King of the Jews!" They spat upon him and took the reed and kept striking him on the head. And when they had mocked him, they stripped him of the cloak, dressed him in his own clothes, and led him off to crucify him.

As they were going out, they met a Cyrenian named Simon; this man they pressed into service to carry his cross.

And when they came to a place called Golgotha (which means Place of the Skull), they gave Jesus wine to drink mixed with gall. But when he had tasted it, he refused to drink. After they had crucified him, they divided his garments by casting lots; then they sat down and kept watch over him there. And they placed over his head the written charge against him: This is Jesus, the King of the Jews. Two revolutionaries were crucified with him, one on his right and the other on his left. Those passing by reviled him, shaking their heads and saying, "You who would destroy the temple and rebuild it in three days, save yourself, if you are the Son of God, and come down from the cross!" Likewise the chief priests with the scribes and elders mocked him and said, "He saved others; he cannot save himself. So he is the king of Israel! Let him come down from the cross now, and we will believe in him. He trusted in God; let him deliver him now if he wants him. For he said, 'I am the Son of God.'" The revolutionaries who were crucified with him also kept abusing him in the same way.

From noon onward, darkness came over the whole land until three in the afternoon. And about three o'clock Jesus cried out in a loud voice, *"Eli, Eli, lema sabachthani?"* which means, "My God, my God, why have you forsaken me?" Some of the bystanders who heard it said, "This one is calling for Elijah." Immediately one of them ran to get a sponge; he soaked it in wine, and putting it on a reed, gave it to him to drink. But the rest said, "Wait, let us see if Elijah comes to save him." But Jesus cried out again in a loud voice, and gave up his spirit.

Here all kneel and pause for a short time.

And behold, the veil of the sanctuary was torn in two from top to bottom. The earth quaked, rocks were split, tombs were opened, and the bodies of many saints who had fallen asleep were raised. And coming forth from their tombs after his resurrection, they entered the holy city and appeared to many. The centurion and the men with him who were keeping watch over Jesus feared greatly when they saw the earthquake and all that was happening, and they said, "Truly, this was the Son of God!"] There were many women there, looking on from a distance, who had followed Jesus from Galilee, ministering to him. Among them were Mary Magdalene and Mary the mother of James and Joseph, and the mother of the sons of Zebedee.

When it was evening, there came a rich man from Arimathea named Joseph, who was himself a disciple of Jesus. He went to Pilate and asked for the body of Jesus; then Pilate ordered it to be handed over. Taking the body, Joseph wrapped it in clean linen and laid it in his new tomb that he had hewn in the rock. Then he rolled a huge stone across the entrance to the tomb and departed. But Mary Magdalene and the other Mary remained sitting there, facing the tomb. The next day, the one following the day of preparation, the chief priests and the Pharisees gathered before Pilate and said, "Sir, we remember that this impostor while still alive said, 'After three days I will be raised up.' Give orders, then, that the grave be secured until the third day, lest his disciples come and steal him and say to the people, 'He has been raised from the dead.' This last imposture would be worse than the first." Pilate said to them, "The guard is yours; go, secure it as best you can." So they went and secured the tomb by fixing a seal to the stone and setting the guard.

GOSPEL / B   *Mark 14:1—15:47 or 15:1-39* 943
For short form read only the part in brackets.

The Passover and the Feast of Unleavened Bread were to take place in two days' time. So the chief priests and the scribes were seeking a way to arrest him by treachery and put him to death. They said, "Not during the festival, for fear that there may be a riot among the people."

When he was in Bethany reclining at table in the house of Simon the leper, a woman came with an alabaster jar of perfumed oil, costly genuine spikenard. She broke the alabaster jar and poured it on his head. There were some who were indignant. "Why has there been this waste of perfumed oil? It could have been sold for more than three hundred days' wages and the money given to the poor." They were infuriated with her. Jesus said, "Let her alone. Why do you make trouble for her? She has done a good thing for me. The poor you will always have with you, and whenever you wish you can do good to them, but you will not always have me. She has done what she could. She has anticipated anointing my body for burial. Amen, I say to you, wherever the gospel is proclaimed to the whole world, what she has done will be told in memory of her."

Then Judas Iscariot, one of the Twelve, went off to the chief priests to hand him over to them. When they heard him they were pleased and promised to pay him money. Then he looked for an opportunity to hand him over.

On the first day of the Feast of Unleavened Bread, when they sacrificed the Passover lamb, his disciples said to him, "Where do you want us to go and prepare for you to eat the Passover?" He sent two of his disciples and said to them, "Go into the city and a man will meet you, carrying a jar of water. Follow him. Wherever he enters, say to the master of the house, 'The Teacher says, "Where is my guest room where I may eat the Passover with my disciples?"' Then he will show you a large upper room furnished and ready. Make the preparations for us there." The disciples then went off, entered the city, and found it just as he had told them; and they prepared the Passover.

When it was evening, he came with the Twelve. And as they reclined at table and were eating, Jesus said, "Amen, I say to you, one of you will betray me, one who is eating with me." They began to be distressed and to say to him, one by one, "Surely it is not I?" He said to them, "One of the Twelve, the one who dips with me into the dish. For the Son of Man indeed goes, as it is written of him, but woe to that man by whom the Son of Man is betrayed. It would be better for that man if he had never been born."

While they were eating, he took bread, said the blessing, broke it, and gave it to them, and said, "Take it; this is my body." Then he took a cup, gave thanks, and gave it to them, and they all drank from it. He said to them, "This is my blood of the covenant, which will be shed for many. Amen, I say to you, I shall not drink again the fruit of the vine until the day when I drink it new in the kingdom of God." Then, after singing a hymn, they went out to the Mount of Olives.

Then Jesus said to them, "All of you will have your faith shaken, for it is written:
'I will strike the shepherd,
      and the sheep will be dispersed.'
But after I have been raised up, I shall go before you to Galilee." Peter said to him, "Even though all should have their faith shaken, mine will not be." Then Jesus said to him, "Amen, I say to you, this very night before the cock crows twice you will deny me three times." But he vehemently replied, "Even though I should have to die with you, I will not deny you." And they all spoke similarly. Then they came to a place named Gethsemane, and he said to his disciples, "Sit here while I pray." He took with him Peter, James, and John, and began to be troubled and distressed. Then he said to them, "My soul is sorrowful even to death. Remain here and keep watch." He advanced a little and fell to the ground and prayed that if it were possible the hour might pass by him; he said, "Abba, Father, all things are possible to you. Take this cup away from me, but not what

I will but what you will." When he returned he found them asleep. He said to Peter, "Simon, are you asleep? Could you not keep watch for one hour? Watch and pray that you may not undergo the test. The spirit is willing but the flesh is weak." Withdrawing again, he prayed, saying the same thing. Then he returned once more and found them asleep, for they could not keep their eyes open and did not know what to answer him. He returned a third time and said to them, "Are you still sleeping and taking your rest? It is enough. The hour has come. Behold, the Son of Man is to be handed over to sinners. Get up, let us go. See, my betrayer is at hand."

Then, while he was still speaking, Judas, one of the Twelve, arrived, accompanied by a crowd with swords and clubs who had come from the chief priests, the scribes, and the elders. His betrayer had arranged a signal with them, saying, "The man I shall kiss is the one; arrest him and lead him away securely." He came and immediately went over to him and said, "Rabbi." And he kissed him. At this they laid hands on him and arrested him. One of the bystanders drew his sword, struck the high priest's servant, and cut off his ear. Jesus said to them in reply, "Have you come out as against a robber, with swords and clubs, to seize me? Day after day I was with you teaching in the temple area, yet you did not arrest me; but that the Scriptures may be fulfilled." And they all left him and fled. Now a young man followed him wearing nothing but a linen cloth about his body. They seized him, but he left the cloth behind and ran off naked.

They led Jesus away to the high priest, and all the chief priests and the elders and the scribes came together. Peter followed him at a distance into the high priest's courtyard and was seated with the guards, warming himself at the fire. The chief priests and the entire Sanhedrin kept trying to obtain testimony against Jesus in order to put him to death, but they found none. Many gave false witness against him, but their testimony did not agree. Some took the stand and testified falsely against him, alleging, "We heard him say, 'I will destroy this temple made with hands and within three days I will build another not made with hands.'" Even so their testimony did not agree. The high priest rose before the assembly and questioned Jesus, saying, "Have you no answer? What are these men testifying against you?" But he was silent and answered nothing. Again the high priest asked him and said to him, "Are you the Christ, the son of the Blessed One?" Then Jesus answered, "I am;

and 'you will see the Son of Man
seated at the right hand of the Power
and coming with the clouds of heaven.'"

At that the high priest tore his garments and said, "What further need have we of witnesses? You have heard the blasphemy. What do you think?" They all condemned him as deserving to die. Some began to spit on him. They blindfolded him and struck him and said to him, "Prophesy!" And the guards greeted him with blows. While Peter was below in the courtyard, one of the high priest's maids came along. Seeing Peter warming himself, she looked intently at him and said, "You too were with the Nazorean, Jesus." But he denied it saying, "I neither know nor understand what you are talking about." So he went out into the outer court. Then the cock crowed. The maid saw him and began again to say to the bystanders, "This man is one of them." Once again he denied it. A little later the bystanders said to Peter once more, "Surely you are one of them; for you too are a Galilean." He began to curse and to swear, "I do not know this man about whom you are talking." And immediately a cock crowed a second time. Then Peter remembered the word that Jesus had said to him, "Before the cock crows twice you will deny me three times." He broke down and wept.

[As soon as morning came, the chief priests with the elders and the scribes, that is, the whole Sanhedrin held a council. They bound Jesus, led him away, and handed him over to Pilate. Pilate questioned him, "Are you the king of the Jews?" He said to him in reply, "You say so." The chief priests accused him of many things. Again Pilate questioned him, "Have you no answer? See how many things they accuse you of." Jesus gave him no further answer, so that Pilate was amazed.

Now on the occasion of the feast he used to release to them one prisoner whom they requested. A man called Barabbas was then in prison along with the rebels who had committed murder in a rebellion. The crowd came forward and began to ask him to do for them as he was accustomed. Pilate answered, "Do you want me to release to you the king of the Jews?" For he knew that it was out of envy that the chief priests had handed him over. But the chief priests stirred up the crowd to have him release Barabbas for them instead. Pilate again said to them in reply, "Then what do you want me to do with the man you call the king of the Jews?" They shouted again, "Crucify him." Pilate said to them, "Why? What evil has he done?" They only shouted the louder, "Crucify him." So Pilate, wishing to satisfy the crowd, released Barabbas to them and, after he had Jesus scourged, handed him over to be crucified.

The soldiers led him away inside the palace, that is, the praetorium, and assembled the whole cohort. They clothed him in purple and, weaving a crown of thorns, placed it on him. They began to salute him with, "Hail, King of the Jews!" and kept striking his head with a reed and spitting upon him. They knelt before him in homage. And when they had mocked him, they stripped him of the purple cloak, dressed him in his own clothes, and led him out to crucify him.

They pressed into service a passer-by, Simon, a Cyrenian, who was coming in from the country, the father of Alexander and Rufus, to carry his cross.

They brought him to the place of Golgotha (which is translated Place of the Skull). They gave him wine drugged with myrrh, but he did not take it. Then they crucified him and divided his garments by casting lots for them to see what each should take. It was nine o'clock in the morning when they crucified him. The inscription of the charge against him read, "The King of the Jews." With him they crucified two revolutionaries, one on his right and one on his left. Those passing by reviled him, shaking their heads and saying, "Aha! You who would destroy the temple and rebuild it in three days, save yourself by coming down from the cross." Likewise the chief priests, with the scribes, mocked him among themselves and said, "He saved others; he cannot save himself. Let the Christ, the King of Israel, come down now from the cross that we may see and believe." Those who were crucified with him also kept abusing him.

At noon darkness came over the whole land until three in the afternoon. And at three o'clock Jesus cried out in a loud voice, *"Eloi, Eloi, lema sabachthani?"* which is translated, "My God, my God, why have you forsaken me?" Some of the bystanders who heard it said, "Look, he is calling Elijah." One of them ran, soaked a sponge with wine, put it on a reed and gave it to him to drink saying, "Wait, let us see if Elijah comes to take him down." Jesus gave a loud cry and breathed his last.

Here all kneel and pause for a short time.

The veil of the sanctuary was torn in two from top to bottom. When the centurion who stood facing him saw how he breathed his last he said, "Truly this man was the Son of God!"] There were also women looking on from a distance. Among them were Mary Magdalene, Mary the mother of the younger James and of Joses, and Salome. These women had followed him when he was in Galilee and ministered to him. There were also many other women who had come up with him to Jerusalem.

When it was already evening, since it was the day of preparation, the day before the sabbath, Joseph of Arimathea, a distinguished member of the council, who was himself awaiting the kingdom of God, came and courageously went to Pilate and asked for the body of Jesus. Pilate was amazed that he was already dead. He summoned the centurion and asked him if Jesus had already died. And when he learned of it from the centurion, he gave the body to Joseph. Having bought a linen cloth, he took him down, wrapped him in the linen cloth, and laid him in a tomb that had been hewn out of the rock. Then he rolled a stone against the entrance to the tomb. Mary Magdalene and Mary the mother of Joses watched where he was laid.

944 GOSPEL / C *Luke 22:14—23:56 or 23:1-49*
For short form read only the part in brackets.

When the hour came, Jesus took his place at table with the apostles. He said to them, "I have eagerly desired to eat this Passover with you before I suffer, for, I tell you, I shall not eat it again until there is fulfillment in the kingdom of God." Then he took a cup, gave thanks, and said, "Take this and share it among yourselves; for I tell you that from this time on I shall not drink of the fruit of the vine until the kingdom of God comes." Then he took the bread, said the blessing, broke it, and gave it to them, saying, "This is my body, which will be given for you; do this in memory of me." And likewise the cup after they had eaten, saying, "This cup is the new covenant in my blood, which will be shed for you.

"And yet behold, the hand of the one who is to betray me is with me on the table; for the Son of Man indeed goes as it has been determined; but woe to that man by whom he is betrayed." And they began to debate among themselves who among them would do such a deed.

Then an argument broke out among them about which of them should be regarded as the greatest. He said to them, "The kings of the Gentiles lord it over them and those in authority over them are addressed as 'Benefactors'; but among you it shall not be so. Rather, let the greatest among you be as the youngest, and the leader as the servant. For who is greater: the one seated at table or the one who serves? Is it not the one seated at table? I am among you as the one who serves. It is you who have stood by me in my trials; and I confer a kingdom on you, just as my Father has conferred one on me, that you may eat and drink at my table in my kingdom; and you will sit on thrones judging the twelve tribes of Israel.

"Simon, Simon, behold Satan has demanded to sift all of you like wheat, but I have prayed that your own faith may not fail; and once you have turned back, you must strengthen your brothers." He said to him, "Lord, I am prepared to go to prison and to die with you." But he replied, "I tell you, Peter, before the cock crows this day, you will deny three times that you know me."

He said to them, "When I sent you forth without a money bag or a sack or sandals, were you in need of anything?" "No, nothing," they replied. He said to them, "But now one who has a money bag should take it, and likewise a sack, and one who does not have a sword should sell his cloak and buy one. For I tell you that this Scripture must be fulfilled in me, namely, 'He was counted among the wicked;' and indeed what is written about me is coming to fulfillment." Then they said, "Lord, look, there are two swords here." But he replied, "It is enough!"

Then going out, he went, as was his custom, to the Mount of Olives, and the disciples followed him. When he arrived at the place he said to them, "Pray that you may not undergo the test." After withdrawing about a stone's throw from them and kneeling, he prayed, saying, "Father, if you are willing, take this cup away from me; still, not my will but yours be done." And to strengthen him an angel from heaven appeared to him. He was in such agony and he prayed so fervently that his sweat became like drops of blood falling on the ground. When he rose from prayer and returned to his disciples, he found them sleeping from grief. He said to them, "Why are you sleeping? Get up and pray that you may not undergo the test."

While he was still speaking, a crowd approached and in front was one of the Twelve, a man named Judas. He went up to Jesus to kiss him. Jesus said to him, "Judas, are you betraying the Son of Man with a kiss?" His disciples realized what was about to happen, and they asked, "Lord, shall we strike with a sword?" And one of them struck the high priest's servant and cut off his right ear. But Jesus said in reply, "Stop, no more of this!" Then he touched the servant's ear and healed him. And Jesus said to the chief priests and temple guards and elders who had come for him, "Have you come out as against a robber, with swords and clubs? Day after day I was with you in the temple area, and you did not seize me; but this is your hour, the time for the power of darkness."

After arresting him they led him away and took him into the house of the high priest; Peter was following at a distance. They lit a fire in the middle of the courtyard and sat around it, and Peter sat down with them. When a maid saw him seated in the light, she looked intently at him and said, "This man too was with him." But he denied it saying, "Woman, I do not know him." A short while later someone else saw him and said, "You too are one of them"; but Peter answered, "My friend, I am not." About an hour later, still another insisted, "Assuredly, this man too was with him, for he also is a Galilean." But Peter said, "My friend, I do not know what you are talking about." Just as he was saying this, the cock crowed, and the Lord turned and looked at Peter; and Peter remembered the word of the Lord, how he had said to him, "Before the cock crows today, you will deny me three times." He went out and began to weep bitterly. The men who held Jesus in custody were ridiculing and beating him. They blindfolded him and questioned him, saying, "Prophesy! Who is it that struck you?" And they reviled him in saying many other things against him.

When day came the council of elders of the people met, both chief priests and scribes, and they brought him before their Sanhedrin. They said, "If you are the Christ, tell us," but he replied to them, "If I tell you, you will not believe, and if I question, you will not respond. But from this time on the Son of Man will be seated at the right hand of the power of God." They all asked, "Are you then the Son of God?" He replied to them, "You say that I am." Then they said, "What further need have we for testimony? We have heard it from his own mouth."

[Then the whole assembly of them arose and brought him before Pilate. They brought charges against him, saying, "We found this man misleading our people; he opposes the payment of taxes to Caesar and maintains that he is the Christ, a king." Pilate asked him, "Are you the king of the Jews?" He said to him in reply, "You say so." Pilate then addressed the chief priests and the crowds, "I find this man not guilty." But they were adamant and said, "He is inciting the people with his teaching throughout all Judea, from Galilee where he began even to here."

On hearing this Pilate asked if the man was a Galilean; and upon learning that he was under Herod's jurisdiction, he sent him to Herod who was in Jerusalem at that time. Herod was very glad to see Jesus; he had been wanting to see him for a long time, for he had heard about him and had been hoping to see him perform some sign. He questioned him at length, but he gave him no answer. The chief priests and scribes, meanwhile, stood by accusing him harshly. Herod and his soldiers treated him contemptuously and mocked him, and after clothing him in resplendent garb, he sent him back to Pilate. Herod and Pilate became friends that very day, even though they had been enemies formerly. Pilate then summoned the chief priests, the rulers, and the people and said to them, "You brought this man to me and accused him of inciting the people to revolt. I have conducted my investigation in your presence and have not found this man guilty of the charges you have brought against him, nor did Herod, for he sent him back to us. So no capital crime has been committed by him. Therefore I shall have him flogged and then release him."

But all together they shouted out, "Away with this man! Release Barabbas to us." (Now Barabbas had been imprisoned for a rebellion that had taken place in the city and for murder.) Again Pilate addressed them, still wishing to release Jesus, but they continued their shouting, "Crucify him! Crucify him!" Pilate addressed them a third time, "What evil has this man done? I found him guilty of no capital crime. Therefore I shall have him flogged and then release him." With loud shouts, however, they persisted in calling for his crucifixion, and their voices prevailed. The verdict of Pilate was that their demand should be granted. So he released the man who had been imprisoned for rebellion and murder, for whom they asked, and he handed Jesus over to them to deal with as they wished.

As they led him away they took hold of a certain Simon, a Cyrenian, who was coming in from the country; and after laying the cross on him, they made him carry it behind Jesus. A large crowd of people followed Jesus, including many women who mourned and lamented him. Jesus turned to them and said, "Daughters of Jerusalem, do not weep for me; weep instead for yourselves and for your children for indeed, the days are coming when people will say, 'Blessed are the barren, the wombs that never bore and the breasts that never nursed.' At that time people will say to the mountains, 'Fall upon us!'

and to the hills, 'Cover us!' for if these things are done when the wood is green what will happen when it is dry?" Now two others, both criminals, were led away with him to be executed.

When they came to the place called the Skull, they crucified him and the criminals there, one on his right, the other on his left. Then Jesus said, "Father, forgive them, they know not what they do." They divided his garments by casting lots. The people stood by and watched; the rulers, meanwhile, sneered at him and said, "He saved others, let him save himself if he is the chosen one, the Christ of God." Even the soldiers jeered at him. As they approached to offer him wine they called out, "If you are King of the Jews, save yourself." Above him there was an inscription that read, "This is the King of the Jews."

Now one of the criminals hanging there reviled Jesus, saying, "Are you not the Christ? Save yourself and us." The other, however, rebuking him, said in reply, "Have you no fear of God, for you are subject to the same condemnation? And indeed, we have been condemned justly, for the sentence we received corresponds to our crimes, but this man has done nothing criminal." Then he said, "Jesus, remember me when you come into your kingdom." He replied to him, "Amen, I say to you, today you will be with me in Paradise."

It was now about noon and darkness came over the whole land until three in the afternoon because of an eclipse of the sun. Then the veil of the temple was torn down the middle. Jesus cried out in a loud voice, "Father, into your hands I commend my spirit"; and when he had said this he breathed his last.

Here all kneel and pause for a short time.

The centurion who witnessed what had happened glorified God and said, "This man was innocent beyond doubt." When all the people who had gathered for this spectacle saw what had happened, they returned home beating their breasts; but all his acquaintances stood at a distance, including the women who had followed him from Galilee and saw these events.]

Now there was a virtuous and righteous man named Joseph who, though he was a member of the council, had not consented to their plan of action. He came from the Jewish town of Arimathea and was awaiting the kingdom of God. He went to Pilate and asked for the body of Jesus. After he had taken the body down, he wrapped it in a linen cloth and laid him in a rock-hewn tomb in which no one had yet been buried. It was the day of preparation, and the sabbath was about to begin. The women who had come from Galilee with him followed behind, and when they had seen the tomb and the way in which his body was laid in it, they returned and prepared spices and perfumed oils. Then they rested on the sabbath according to the commandment.

Easter Triduum

945

"The Easter Triduum of the passion and resurrection of Christ is...the culmination of the entire liturgical year. What Sunday is to the week, the solemnity of Easter is to the liturgical year." (General Norms for the Liturgical Year, #18)

Lent ends quietly on Thursday afternoon. The church enters the Triduum ("three days"). On Thursday night the church begins a time of prayer and fasting, a time of keeping watch, that lasts into the great Vigil between Saturday and Sunday. The church emphasizes that the fasting of Good Friday and, if possible, of Holy Saturday are integral to the keeping of these days and the preparation for the sacraments of initiation celebrated at the Vigil. On Thursday night and on Friday afternoon or evening the church gathers to pray and to remember the many facets of the single mystery.

HOLY THURSDAY: EVENING MASS OF THE LORD'S SUPPER 946

On Thursday night Lent has ended and the church, at this Mass of the Lord's Supper, enters into the Easter Triduum. From the very first moment the all-embracing experience of these three days is proclaimed: "We should glory in the cross of our Lord Jesus Christ. For he is our salvation, our life, and our resurrection. Through him we are saved and made free." This is the whole of the great Triduum. On Thursday night, the liturgy draws us toward this through the scriptures, through the mandatum or washing of the feet which is the direct expression of our service to one another and the world, through the eucharistic banquet itself.

LITURGY OF THE WORD / ABC

READING I   *Exodus 12:1-8, 11-14 / 39*

The LORD said to Moses and Aaron in the land of Egypt, "This month shall stand at the head of your calendar; you shall reckon it the first month of the year. Tell the whole community of Israel: On the tenth of this month every one of your families must procure for itself a lamb, one apiece for each household. If a family is too small for a whole lamb, it shall join the nearest household in procuring one and shall share in the lamb in proportion to the number of persons who partake of it. The lamb must be a year-old male and without blemish. You may take it from either the sheep or the goats. You shall keep it until the fourteenth day of this month, and then, with the whole assembly of Israel present, it shall be slaughtered during the evening twilight. They shall take some of its blood and apply it to the two doorposts and the lintel of every house in which they partake of the lamb. That same night they shall eat its roasted flesh with unleavened bread and bitter herbs.

"This is how you are to eat it: with your loins girt, sandals on your feet and your staff in hand, you shall eat like those who are in flight. It is the Passover of the LORD. For on this same night I will go through Egypt, striking down every firstborn of the land, both man and beast, and executing judgment on all the gods of Egypt—I, the LORD! But the blood will mark the houses where you are. Seeing the blood, I will pass over you; thus, when I strike the land of Egypt, no destructive blow will come upon you.

"This day shall be a memorial feast for you, which all your generations shall celebrate with pilgrimage to the LORD, as a perpetual institution."

RESPONSORIAL PSALM
Psalm 116:12-13, 15-16bc, 17-18

℟. **Our blessing-cup is a communion with the Blood of Christ.**

How shall I make a return to the LORD
for all the good he has done for me?
The cup of salvation I will take up,
and I will call upon the name of the
LORD. ℟.

Precious in the eyes of the LORD
is the death of his faithful ones.
I am your servant, the son of your
handmaid;
you have loosed my bonds. ℟.

To you will I offer sacrifice of
thanksgiving,
and I will call upon the name of the
LORD.
My vows to the LORD I will pay
in the presence of all his people. ℟.

READING II
I Corinthians 11:23-26

Brothers and sisters: I received from the Lord what I also handed on to you, that the Lord Jesus, on the night he was handed over, took bread, and, after he had given thanks, broke it and said, "This is my body that is for you. Do this in remembrance of me." In the same way also the cup, after supper, saying, "This cup is the new covenant in my blood. Do this, as often as you drink it, in remembrance of me." For as often as you eat this bread and drink the cup, you proclaim the death of the Lord until he comes.

GOSPEL
John 13:1-15

Before the feast of Passover, Jesus knew that his hour had come to pass from this world to the Father. He loved his own in the world and he loved them to the end. The devil had already induced Judas, son of Simon the Iscariot, to hand him over. So, during supper, fully aware that the Father had put everything into his power and that he had come from God and was returning to God, he rose from supper and took off his outer garments. He took a towel and tied it around his waist. Then he poured water into a basin and began to wash the disciples' feet and dry them with the towel around his waist. He came to Simon Peter, who said to him, "Master, are you going to wash my feet?" Jesus answered and said to him, "What I am doing, you do not understand now, but you will understand later." Peter said to him, "You will never wash my feet." Jesus answered him, "Unless I wash you, you will have no inheritance with me." Simon Peter said to him, "Master, then not only my feet, but my hands and head as well." Jesus said to him, "Whoever has bathed has no need except to have his feet washed, for he is clean all over; so you are clean, but not all." For he knew who would betray him; for this reason, he said, "Not all of you are clean."

So when he had washed their feet and put his garments back on and reclined at table again, he said to them, "Do you realize what I have done for you? You call me 'teacher' and 'master,' and rightly so, for indeed I am. If I, therefore, the master and teacher, have washed your feet, you ought to wash one another's feet. I have given you a model to follow, so that as I have done for you, you should also do."

WASHING OF FEET 947

The homily is followed by the washing of feet, the mandatum (from the Latin word for "command": "A new commandment I give to you..."). This is a simple gesture of humble service: the presider and others wash the feet of various members of the assembly. Such a gesture, with the song which accompanies it, speaks directly of the way of life Christians seek. Appropriate songs are nos. 414, 409, 410, 408, 625, 631.

The Mass continues with the general intercessions.

TRANSFER OF THE HOLY EUCHARIST 948

When the communion rite is concluded, the eucharistic bread that remains is solemnly carried from the altar. Hymn no. 407, or another appropriate selection, accompanies the procession.

The liturgy has no concluding rite, no dismissal. Rather, the church continues to watch and pray throughout the Triduum.

GOOD FRIDAY / ABC 949

In Good Friday's liturgy of the word and veneration of the cross there is great solemnity: a pondering of the "mystery of our faith," the passion, death and resurrection of our Lord Jesus Christ. Fasting and praying during these days, the catechumens and the baptized assemble on Good Friday in the afternoon or evening for a time of prayer together. This begins a time of silence.

LITURGY OF THE WORD

READING I   Isaiah 52:13—53:12 / 40

See, my servant shall prosper,
  he shall be raised high and greatly
    exalted.
Even as many were amazed at him—
  so marred was his look beyond
    human semblance
and his appearance beyond that of
    the sons of man—
so shall he startle many nations,
  because of him kings shall stand
    speechless;
for those who have not been told shall
    see,
  those who have not heard shall
    ponder it.

Who would believe what we have heard?
  To whom has the arm of the LORD
    been revealed?
He grew up like a sapling before him,
  like a shoot from the parched earth;
there was in him no stately bearing to
    make us look at him,
  nor appearance that would attract us
    to him.
He was spurned and avoided by people,
  a man of suffering, accustomed to
    infirmity,
one of those from whom people hide
    their faces,
  spurned, and we held him in no
    esteem.

Yet it was our infirmities that he bore,
  our sufferings that he endured,
while we thought of him as stricken,
  as one smitten by God and afflicted.
But he was pierced for our offenses,
  crushed for our sins;
upon him was the chastisement that
    makes us whole,
  by his stripes we were healed.
We had all gone astray like sheep,
  each following his own way;
but the LORD laid upon him
  the guilt of us all.

Though he was harshly treated, he
    submitted
  and opened not his mouth;
like a lamb led to the slaughter
  or a sheep before the shearers,
  he was silent and opened not his
    mouth.
Oppressed and condemned, he was taken
    away,
  and who would have thought any
    more of his destiny?
When he was cut off from the land of the
    living,
  and smitten for the sin of his people,

a grave was assigned him among the
    wicked
  and a burial place with evildoers,
though he had done no wrong
  nor spoken any falsehood.
But the LORD was pleased
  to crush him in infirmity.

If he gives his life as an offering for sin,
  he shall see his descendants in a
    long life,
  and the will of the LORD shall be
    accomplished through him.

Because of his affliction
  he shall see the light
    in fullness of days;
through his suffering, my servant shall
    justify many,
  and their guilt he shall bear.
Therefore I will give him his portion
    among the great,
  and he shall divide the spoils with
    the mighty,
because he surrendered himself to death
  and was counted among the wicked;
and he shall take away the sins of many,
  and win pardon for their offenses.

RESPONSORIAL PSALM

Psalm 31:2, 6, 12-13, 15-16, 17, 25

℟. **Father, into your hands I commend my spirit.**

In you, O LORD, I take refuge;
  let me never be put to shame.
In your justice rescue me.
    Into your hands I commend my
      spirit;
  you will redeem me, O LORD, O faithful
    God. ℟.

For all my foes I am an object of
    reproach,
  a laughingstock to my neighbors,
    and a dread to my friends;
they who see me abroad flee from me.
  I am forgotten like the

unremembered dead;
  I am like a dish that is broken. ℟.

But my trust is in you, O LORD;
  I say, "You are my God."
In your hands is my destiny; rescue me
    from the clutches of my enemies and
    my persecutors." ℟.

Let your face shine upon your servant;
  save me in your kindness.
Take courage and be stouthearted,
  all you who hope in the LORD. ℟.

READING II

Hebrews 4:14-16; 5:7-9

Brothers and sisters: Since we have a great high priest who has passed through the heavens, Jesus, the Son of God, let us hold fast to our confession. For we do not have a high priest who is unable to sympathize with our weaknesses, but one who has similarly been tested in every way, yet without sin. So let us confidently approach the throne of grace to receive mercy and to find grace for timely help.

In the days when Christ was in the flesh, he offered prayers and supplications with loud cries and tears to the one who was able to save him from death, and he was heard because of his reverence. Son though he was, he learned obedience from what he suffered; and when he was made perfect, he became the source of eternal salvation for all who obey him.

GOSPEL
John 18:1—19:42

Jesus went out with his disciples across the Kidron valley to where there was a garden, into which he and his disciples entered. Judas his betrayer also knew the place, because Jesus had often met there with his disciples. So Judas got a band of soldiers and guards from the chief priests and the Pharisees and went there with lanterns, torches, and weapons. Jesus, knowing everything that was going to happen to him, went out and said to them, "Whom are you looking for?" They answered him, "Jesus the Nazorean." He said to them, "I AM." Judas his betrayer was also with them. When he said to them, "I AM, " they turned away and fell to the ground. So he again asked them, "Whom are you looking for?" They said, "Jesus the Nazorean." Jesus answered, "I told you that I AM. So if you are looking for me, let these men go." This was to fulfill what he had said, "I have not lost any of those you gave me." Then Simon Peter, who had a sword, drew it, struck the high priest's slave, and cut off his right ear. The slave's name was Malchus. Jesus said to Peter, "Put your sword into its scabbard. Shall I not drink the cup that the Father gave me?"

So the band of soldiers, the tribune, and the Jewish guards seized Jesus, bound him, and brought him to Annas first. He was the father-in-law of Caiaphas, who was high priest that year. It was Caiaphas who had counseled the Jews that it was better that one man should die rather than the people.

Simon Peter and another disciple followed Jesus. Now the other disciple was known to the high priest, and he entered the courtyard of the high priest with Jesus. But Peter stood at the gate outside. So the other disciple, the acquaintance of the high priest, went out and spoke to the gatekeeper and brought Peter in. Then the maid who was the gatekeeper said to Peter, "You are not one of this man's disciples, are you?" He said, "I am not." Now the slaves and the guards were standing around a charcoal fire that they had made, because it was cold, and were warming themselves. Peter was also standing there keeping warm.

The high priest questioned Jesus about his disciples and about his doctrine. Jesus answered him, "I have spoken publicly to the world. I have always taught in a synagogue or in the temple area where all the Jews gather, and in secret I have said nothing. Why ask me? Ask those who heard me what I said to them. They know what I said." When he had said this, one of the temple guards standing there struck Jesus and said, "Is this the way you answer the high priest?" Jesus answered him, "If I have spoken wrongly, testify to the wrong; but if I have spoken rightly, why do you strike me?" Then Annas sent him bound to Caiaphas the high priest.

Now Simon Peter was standing there keeping warm. And they said to him, "You are not one of his disciples, are you?" He denied it and said, "I am not." One of the slaves of the high priest, a relative of the one whose ear Peter had cut off, said, "Didn't I see you in the garden with him?" Again Peter denied it. And immediately the cock crowed.

Then they brought Jesus from Caiaphas to the praetorium. It was morning. And they themselves did not enter the praetorium, in order not to be defiled so that they could eat the Passover. So Pilate came out to them and said, "What charge do you bring against this man?" They answered and said to him, "If he were not a criminal, we would not have handed him over to you." At this, Pilate said to them, "Take him yourselves, and judge him according to your law." The Jews answered him, "We do not have the right to execute anyone," in order that the word of Jesus might be fulfilled that he said indicating the kind of death he would die. So Pilate went back into the praetorium and summoned Jesus and said to him, "Are you the King of the Jews?" Jesus answered, "Do you say this on your own or have others told you about me?" Pilate answered, "I am not a Jew, am I? Your own nation and the chief priests handed you over to me. What have you done?" Jesus answered, "My kingdom does not belong to this world. If my kingdom did belong to this world, my attendants would be fighting to keep me from being handed over to the Jews. But as it is, my kingdom is not here." So Pilate said to him, "Then you are a king?" Jesus answered, "You say I am a king. For this I was born and for this I came into the world, to testify to the truth. Everyone who belongs to the truth listens to my voice." Pilate said to him, "What is truth?"

When he had said this, he again went out to the Jews and said to them, "I find no guilt in him. But you have a custom that I release one prisoner to you at Passover. Do you want me to release to you the King of the Jews?" They cried out again, "Not this one but Barabbas!" Now Barabbas was a revolutionary.

Then Pilate took Jesus and had him scourged. And the soldiers wove a crown out of thorns and placed it on his head, and clothed him in a purple cloak, and they came to him and said, "Hail, King of the Jews!" And they struck him repeatedly. Once more Pilate went out and said to them, "Look, I am bringing him out to you, so that you may know that I find no guilt in him." So Jesus came out, wearing the crown of thorns and the purple cloak. And he said to them, "Behold, the man!" When the chief priests and the guards saw him they cried out, "Crucify him, crucify him!" Pilate said to them, "Take him yourselves and crucify him. I find no guilt in him." The Jews answered, "We have a law, and according to that law he ought to die, because he made himself the Son of God." Now when Pilate heard this statement, he became even more afraid, and went back into the praetorium and said to Jesus, "Where are you from?" Jesus did not answer him. So Pilate said to him, "Do you not speak to me? Do you not know that I have power to release you and I have power to crucify you?" Jesus answered him, "You would have no power over me if it had not been given to you from above. For this reason the one who handed me over to you has the greater sin." Consequently, Pilate tried to release him; but the Jews cried out, "If you release him, you are not a Friend of Caesar. Everyone who makes himself a king opposes Caesar."

When Pilate heard these words he brought Jesus out and seated him on the judge's bench in the place called Stone Pavement, in Hebrew, Gabbatha. It was preparation day for Passover, and it was about noon. And he said to the Jews, "Behold, your king!" They cried out, "Take him away, take him away! Crucify him!" Pilate said to them, "Shall I crucify your king?" The chief priests answered, "We have no king but Caesar." Then he handed him over to them to be crucified.

So they took Jesus, and, carrying the cross himself, he went out to what is called the Place of the Skull, in Hebrew, Golgotha. There they crucified him, and with him two others, one on either side, with Jesus in the middle. Pilate also had an inscription written and put on the cross. It read, "Jesus the Nazorean, the King of the Jews." Now many of the Jews read this inscription, because the place where Jesus was crucified was near the city; and it was written in Hebrew, Latin, and Greek. So the chief priests of the Jews said to Pilate, "Do not write 'The King of the Jews,' but that he said, 'I am the King of the Jews'." Pilate answered, "What I have written, I have written."

When the soldiers had crucified Jesus, they took his clothes and divided them into four shares, a share for each soldier. They also took his tunic, but the tunic was seamless, woven in one piece from the top down. So they said to one another, "Let's not tear it, but cast lots for it to see whose it will be," in order that the passage of Scripture might be fulfilled that says:

"They divided my garments among them,
  and for my vesture they cast lots."

This is what the soldiers did. Standing by the cross of Jesus were his mother and his mother's sister, Mary the wife of Clopas, and Mary of Magdala. When Jesus saw his mother and the disciple there whom he loved he said to his mother, "Woman, behold, your son." Then he said to the disciple, "Behold, your mother." And from that hour the disciple took her into his home.

After this, aware that everything was now finished, in order that the Scripture might be fulfilled, Jesus said, "I thirst." There was a vessel filled with common wine. So they put a sponge soaked in wine on a sprig of hyssop and put it up to his mouth. When Jesus had taken the wine, he said, "It is finished." And bowing his head, he handed over the spirit.

Here all kneel and pause for a short time.

Now since it was preparation day, in order that the bodies might not remain on the cross on the sabbath, for the sabbath day of that week was a solemn one, the Jews asked Pilate that their legs be broken and that they be taken down. So the soldiers came and broke the legs of the first and then of the other one who was crucified with Jesus. But when they came to Jesus and saw that he was already dead, they did not break his legs, but one soldier thrust his lance into his side, and immediately blood and water flowed out. An eyewitness has testified, and his testimony is true; he knows that he is speaking the truth, so that you also may come to believe. For this happened so that the Scripture passage might be fulfilled:

"Not a bone of it will be broken."

And again another passage says:

"They will look upon him whom they have pierced."

After this, Joseph of Arimathea, secretly a disciple of Jesus for fear of the Jews, asked Pilate if he could remove the body of Jesus. And Pilate permitted it. So he came and took his body. Nicodemus, the one who had first come to him at night, also came bringing a mixture of myrrh and aloes weighing about one hundred pounds. They took the body of Jesus and bound it with burial cloths along with the spices, according to the Jewish burial custom. Now in the place where he had been crucified there was a garden, and in the garden a new tomb, in which no one had yet been buried. So they laid Jesus there because of the Jewish preparation day; for the tomb was close by.

GENERAL INTERCESSIONS

As at Sunday liturgy, the word service concludes with prayers of intercession. Today these prayers take a more solemn form as the church lifts up to God its own needs and those of the world.

VENERATION OF THE CROSS   950

An ancient liturgical text reads: "See here the true and most revered Tree. Hasten to kiss it and to cry out with faith: You are our help, most revered Cross." For many centuries the church has solemnly venerated the relic or image of the cross on Good Friday. It is not present as a picture of suffering only but as a symbol of Christ's passover, where "dying he destroyed our death and rising restored our life." It is the glorious, the life-giving cross that the faithful venerate with song, prayer, kneeling and a kiss.

As the cross is shown to the assembly, the following is sung.

This is the wood of the cross, on which hung the Sav-ior of the world.

Come, let us wor - ship.

As the assembly comes forward to venerate the cross, appropriate chants and hymns may be sung, e.g., nos. 396, 421, 420, 416.

951 HOLY COMMUNION

This liturgy concludes with a simple communion rite. All recite the Lord's Prayer and receive holy communion. There is no concluding rite or dismissal for the church continues to be at prayer throughout the Triduum.

952 HOLY SATURDAY

The church continues to fast and pray and to make ready for this night's great Vigil. Saturday is a day of great quiet and reflection. Catechumens, sponsors and some of the faithful may assemble during the day for prayer, the recitation of the Creed, and for the rite of Ephpheta (opening of ears and mouth).

953 EASTER VIGIL

The long preparation of the catechumens, the lenten disciplines and fast of the faithful, the vigiling and fasting and prayer that have gone on since Thursday night—all culminate in the great liturgy of this night. On this night the church assembles to spend much time listening to scriptures, praying psalms, acclaiming the death and resurrection of the Lord. Only then are the catechumens called forward and prayed over, challenged to renounce evil and affirm their faith in God, led to the font and baptized in the blessed water. The newly baptized are then anointed with chrism and the entire assembly joins in intercession and finally in the eucharist.

INTRODUCTORY RITE

BLESSING OF THE FIRE AND LIGHTING OF THE PASCHAL CANDLE
The night vigil begins with the kindling of new fire and the lighting of the assembly's paschal candle.

PROCESSION
The ministers and assembly go in procession to the place where the scriptures will be read. The following is sung during the procession.

Deacon or Priest: All:

Christ   our   light.   Thanks   be   to   God.

EASTER PROCLAMATION: THE EXSULTET
In this ancient text the church gives thanks and praise to God for all that is recalled this night: Adam's fall, the deliverance from Egypt, the passover of Christ, the wedding of earth and heaven, our reconciliation.

LITURGY OF THE WORD

At the Vigil, the liturgy of the word is an extended time of readings, silence and the chanting of psalms. On this night when the faithful know the death and resurrection of the Lord in baptism and eucharist, the church needs first to hear these scriptures which are the foundation of our life together: the creation story, Abraham and Isaac, the dividing of the sea, the poetry of Isaiah and Baruch and Ezekiel, the proclamation of Paul to the Romans and the gospel account of Jesus' resurrection.

READING I   *Genesis 1:1—2:2 or 1:1, 26-31a / 41*   954
For short form read only the parts in brackets.

[In the beginning, when God created the heavens and the earth,] the earth was a formless wasteland, and darkness covered the abyss, while a mighty wind swept over the waters.

Then God said, "Let there be light," and there was light. God saw how good the light was. God then separated the light from the darkness. God called the light "day," and the darkness he called "night." Thus evening came, and morning followed—the first day.

Then God said, "Let there be a dome in the middle of the waters, to separate one body of water from the other." And so it happened: God made the dome, and it separated the water above the dome from the water below it. God called the dome "the sky." Evening came, and morning followed—the second day.

Then God said, "Let the water under the sky be gathered into a single basin, so that the dry land may appear." And so it happened: the water under the sky was gathered into its basin, and the dry land appeared. God called the dry land "the earth," and the basin of the water he called "the sea." God saw how good it was. Then God said, "Let the earth bring forth vegetation: every kind of plant that bears seed and every kind of fruit tree on earth that bears fruit with its seed in it." And so it happened: the earth brought forth every kind of plant that bears seed and every kind of fruit tree on earth that bears fruit with its seed in it. God saw how good it was. Evening came, and morning followed—the third day.

Then God said: "Let there be lights in the dome of the sky, to separate day from night. Let them mark the fixed times, the days and the years, and serve as luminaries in the dome of the sky, to shed light upon the earth." And so it happened: God made the two great lights, the greater one to govern the day, and the lesser one to govern the night; and he made the stars. God set them in the dome of the sky, to shed light upon the earth, to govern the day and the night, and to separate the light from the darkness. God saw how good it was. Evening came, and morning followed—the fourth day.

Then God said, "Let the water teem with an abundance of living creatures, and on the earth let birds fly beneath the dome of the sky." And so it happened: God created the great sea monsters and all kinds of swimming creatures with which the water teems, and all kinds of winged birds. God saw how good it was, and God blessed them, saying, "Be fertile, multiply, and fill the water of the seas; and let the birds multiply on the earth." Evening came, and morning followed—the fifth day.

Then God said, "Let the earth bring forth all kinds of living creatures: cattle, creeping things, and wild animals of all kinds." And so it happened: God made all kinds of wild animals, all kinds of cattle, and all kinds of creeping things of the earth. God saw how good it was. Then [God said: "Let us make man in our image, after our likeness. Let them have dominion over the fish of the sea, the birds of the air, and the cattle, and over all the wild animals and all the creatures that crawl on the ground."

God created man in his image;
in the image of God he created him;
male and female he created them.

God blessed them, saying: "Be fertile and multiply; fill the earth and subdue it. Have dominion over the fish of the sea, the birds of the air, and all the living things that move on the earth." God also said: "See, I give you every seed-bearing plant all over the earth and every tree that has seed-bearing fruit on it to be your food; and to all the animals of the land, all the birds of the air, and all the living creatures that crawl on the ground, I give all the green plants for food." And so it happened. God looked at everything he had made, and he found it very good.] Evening came, and morning followed—the sixth day.

Thus the heavens and the earth and all their array were completed. Since on the seventh day God was finished with the work he had been doing, he rested on the seventh day from all the work he had undertaken.

RESPONSORIAL PSALM   *1. Psalm 104:1-2, 5-6, 10, 12, 13-14, 24, 35*

℟. **Lord, send out your Spirit, and renew the face of the earth.**

Bless the LORD, O my soul!
   O LORD, my God, you are great
      indeed!
You are clothed with majesty and
      glory,
   robed in light as with a cloak. ℟.

You fixed the earth upon its foundation,
   not to be moved forever;
with the ocean, as with a garment, you
      covered it;
   above the mountains the waters
      stood. ℟.

You send forth springs into the
      watercourses
   that wind among the mountains.

Beside them the birds of heaven dwell;
   from among the branches they send
      forth their song. ℟.

You water the mountains from your
      palace;
   the earth is replete with the fruit of
      your works.
You raise grass for the cattle,
   and vegetation for man's use,
producing bread from the earth. ℟.

How manifold are your works, O LORD!
   In wisdom you have wrought them
      all —
the earth is full of your creatures.
   Bless the LORD, O my soul! ℟.

Or:

2. Psalm 33:4-5, 6-7, 12-13, 20, 22

℟. **The earth is full of the goodness of the Lord.**

Upright is the word of the LORD,
   and all his works are trustworthy.
He loves justice and right;
   of the kindness of the LORD the earth
      is full. ℟.

By the word of the LORD the heavens
      were made;
   by the breath of his mouth all their
      host.
He gathers the waters of the sea as in a
      flask;
   in cellars he confines the deep. ℟.

Blessed the nation whose God is the
      LORD,
   the people he has chosen for his
      own inheritance.
From heaven the LORD looks down;
   he sees all mankind. ℟.

Our soul waits for the LORD,
   who is our help and our shield.
May your kindness, O LORD, be upon us
   who have put our hope in you. ℟.

955   **READING II**   *Genesis 22:1-18 or 22:1-2, 9a, 10-13, 15-18*
For short form read only the parts in brackets.

[God put Abraham to the test. He called to him, "Abraham!" "Here I am," he replied. Then God said: "Take your son Isaac, your only one, whom you love, and go to the land of Moriah. There you shall offer him up as a holocaust on a height that I will point out to you."]
   Early the next morning Abraham saddled his donkey, took with him his son Isaac and two of his servants as well, and with the wood that he had cut for the holocaust, set out for the place of which God had told him.
   On the third day Abraham got sight of the place from afar. Then he said to his servants: "Both of you stay here with the donkey, while the boy and I go on over yonder. We will worship and then come back to you." Thereupon Abraham took the wood for the holocaust and laid it on his son Isaac's shoulders, while he himself carried the fire

and the knife. As the two walked on together, Isaac spoke to his father Abraham: "Father!" Isaac said. "Yes, son," he replied. Isaac continued, "Here are the fire and the wood, but where is the sheep for the holocaust?" "Son," Abraham answered, "God himself will provide the sheep for the holocaust." Then the two continued going forward.

[When they came to the place of which God had told him, Abraham built an altar there and arranged the wood on it.] Next he tied up his son Isaac, and put him on top of the wood on the altar. [Then he reached out and took the knife to slaughter his son. But the LORD's messenger called to him from heaven, "Abraham, Abraham!" "Here I am," he answered. "Do not lay your hand on the boy," said the messenger. "Do not do the least thing to him. I know now how devoted you are to God, since you did not withhold from me your own beloved son." As Abraham looked about, he spied a ram caught by its horns in the thicket. So he went and took the ram and offered it up as a holocaust in place of his son.] Abraham named the site Yahweh-yireh; hence people now say, "On the mountain the LORD will see."

[Again the LORD's messenger called to Abraham from heaven and said: "I swear by myself, declares the LORD, that because you acted as you did in not withholding from me your beloved son, I will bless you abundantly and make your descendants as countless as the stars of the sky and the sands of the seashore; your descendants shall take possession of the gates of their enemies, and in your descendants all the nations of the earth shall find blessing—all this because you obeyed my command."]

RESPONSORIAL PSALM
℟. You are my inheritance, O Lord.

Psalm 16:5, 8, 9-10, 11

O LORD, my allotted portion and my cup,
    you it is who hold fast my lot.
I set the LORD ever before me;
    with him at my right hand I shall not
    be disturbed. ℟.

Therefore my heart is glad and my soul
    rejoices,
    my body, too, abides in confidence;

because you will not abandon my soul to
    the netherworld,
nor will you suffer your faithful one
    to undergo corruption. ℟.

You will show me the path to life,
    fullness of joys in your presence,
    the delights at your right hand forever. ℟.

READING III

Exodus 14:15—15:1   956

The LORD said to Moses, "Why are you crying out to me? Tell the Israelites to go forward. And you, lift up your staff and, with hand outstretched over the sea, split the sea in two, that the Israelites may pass through it on dry land. But I will make the Egyptians so obstinate that they will go in after them. Then I will receive glory through Pharaoh and all his army, his chariots and charioteers. The Egyptians shall know that I am the LORD, when I receive glory through Pharaoh and his chariots and charioteers."

The angel of God, who had been leading Israel's camp, now moved and went around behind them. The column of cloud also, leaving the front, took up its place behind them, so that it came between the camp of the Egyptians and that of Israel. But the cloud now became dark, and thus the night passed without the rival camps coming any closer together all night long. Then Moses stretched out his hand over the sea, and the LORD swept the sea with a strong east wind throughout the night and so turned it into dry land. When the water was thus divided, the Israelites marched into the midst of the sea on dry land, with the water like a wall to their right and to their left.

The Egyptians followed in pursuit; all Pharaoh's horses and chariots and charioteers went after them right into the midst of the sea. In the night watch just before dawn the LORD cast through the column of the fiery cloud upon the Egyptian force a glance that threw it into a panic; and he so clogged their chariot wheels that they could hardly drive. With that the Egyptians sounded the retreat before Israel, because the LORD was fighting for them against the Egyptians.

Then the LORD told Moses, "Stretch out your hand over the sea, that the water may flow back upon the Egyptians, upon their chariots and their charioteers." So Moses stretched out his hand over the sea, and at dawn the sea flowed back to its normal depth. The Egyptians were fleeing head on toward the sea, when the LORD hurled them into its midst. As the water flowed back, it covered the chariots and the charioteers of Pharaoh's whole army which had followed the Israelites into the sea. Not a single one of them escaped. But the Israelites had marched on dry land through the midst of the sea, with the water like a wall to their right and to their left. Thus the LORD saved Israel on that day from the power of the Egyptians. When Israel saw the Egyptians lying dead on the seashore and beheld the great power that the LORD had shown against the Egyptians, they feared the LORD and believed in him and in his servant Moses.

Then Moses and the Israelites sang this song to the LORD:
I will sing to the LORD, for he is gloriously triumphant;
horse and chariot he has cast into the sea.

RESPONSORIAL PSALM
Exodus 15:1-2, 3-4, 5-6, 17-18

℟. **Let us sing to the Lord; he has covered himself in glory.**

I will sing to the LORD, for he is
gloriously triumphant;
horse and chariot he has cast into the
sea.
My strength and my courage is the LORD,
and he has been my savior.
He is my God, I praise him;
the God of my father, I extol him. ℟.

The LORD is a warrior,
LORD is his name!
Pharaoh's chariots and army he hurled
into the sea;
the elite of his officers were
submerged in the Red Sea. ℟.

The flood waters covered them,
they sank into the depths like a stone.
Your right hand, O LORD, magnificent in
power,
your right hand, O LORD, has
shattered the enemy. ℟.

You brought in the people you redeemed
and planted them on the mountain
of your inheritance—
the place where you made your seat, O
LORD,
the sanctuary, Lord, which your
hands established.
The LORD shall reign forever and ever. ℟.

957   **READING IV**
Isaiah 54:5-14

The One who has become your husband
is your Maker;
his name is the LORD of hosts;
your redeemer is the Holy One of Israel,
called God of all the earth.
The LORD calls you back,
like a wife forsaken and grieved in
spirit,
a wife married in youth and then
cast off,
says your God.
For a brief moment I abandoned you,
but with great tenderness I will take
you back.
In an outburst of wrath, for a moment
I hid my face from you;
but with enduring love I take pity on you,
says the LORD, your redeemer.
This is for me like the days of Noah,
when I swore that the waters of Noah
should never again deluge the earth;
so I have sworn not to be angry with you,

or to rebuke you.
Though the mountains leave their place
and the hills be shaken,
my love shall never leave you
nor my covenant of peace be shaken,
says the LORD, who has mercy on
you.
O afflicted one, storm-battered and
unconsoled,
I lay your pavements in carnelians,
and your foundations in sapphires;
I will make your battlements of rubies,
your gates of carbuncles,
and all your walls of precious stones.
All your children shall be taught by the
LORD,
and great shall be the peace of your
children.
In justice shall you be established,
far from the fear of oppression,
where destruction cannot come near
you.

RESPONSORIAL PSALM
Psalm 30:2, 4, 5-6, 11-12, 13

℟. I will praise you, Lord, for you have rescued me.

I will extol you, O LORD, for you drew me
    clear
  and did not let my enemies rejoice
    over me.
O LORD, you brought me up from the
  netherworld;
  you preserved me from among those
  going down into the pit. ℟.

Sing praise to the LORD, you his faithful
    ones,
  and give thanks to his holy

name.
For his anger lasts but a moment;
  a lifetime, his good will.
At nightfall, weeping enters in,
  but with the dawn, rejoicing. ℟.

Hear, O LORD, and have pity on me;
  O LORD, be my helper.
You changed my mourning into
  dancing;
  O LORD, my God, forever will I
  give you thanks. ℟.

READING V
Isaiah 55:1-11   **958**

Thus says the LORD:
All you who are thirsty,
  come to the water!
You who have no money,
  come, receive grain and eat;
come, without paying and without cost,
  drink wine and milk!
Why spend your money for what is not
  bread,
  your wages for what fails to satisfy?
Heed me, and you shall eat well,
  you shall delight in rich fare.
Come to me heedfully,
  listen, that you may have life.
I will renew with you the everlasting
  covenant,
  the benefits assured to David.
As I made him a witness to the peoples,
  a leader and commander of nations,
so shall you summon a nation you knew
  not,
  and nations that knew you not shall
  run to you,
because of the LORD, your God,
  the Holy One of Israel, who has
  glorified you.

Seek the LORD while he may be found,

call him while he is near.
Let the scoundrel forsake his way,
  and the wicked man his thoughts;
let him turn to the LORD for mercy;
  to our God, who is generous in
  forgiving.
For my thoughts are not your thoughts,
  nor are your ways my ways, says the
  LORD.
As high as the heavens are above the
  earth,
  so high are my ways above your
  ways
  and my thoughts above your
  thoughts.

For just as from the heavens
  the rain and snow come down
and do not return there
  till they have watered the earth,
  making it fertile and fruitful,
giving seed to the one who sows
  and bread to the one who eats,
so shall my word be
  that goes forth from my mouth;
my word shall not return to me void,
  but shall do my will,
  achieving the end for which I sent it.

RESPONSORIAL PSALM
Isaiah 12:2-3, 4bcd, 5-6

℟. You will draw water joyfully from the springs of salvation.

God indeed is my savior;
  I am confident and unafraid.
My strength and my courage is the LORD,
  and he has been my savior.
With joy you will draw water
  at the fountain of salvation. ℟.

Give thanks to the LORD, acclaim his
  name;
  among the nations make known his
  deeds,
proclaim how exalted is his name. ℟.

Sing praise to the LORD for his glorious
achievement;
let this be known throughout all the
earth.

959 **READING VI** *Baruch 3:9-15, 32—4:4*

Hear, O Israel, the commandments of
life:
listen, and know prudence!
How is it, Israel,
that you are in the land of your foes,
grown old in a foreign land,
defiled with the dead,
accounted with those destined for
the netherworld?
You have forsaken the fountain of
wisdom!
Had you walked in the way of God,
you would have dwelt in enduring
peace.
Learn where prudence is,
where strength, where understanding;
that you may know also
where are length of days, and life,
where light of the eyes, and peace.
Who has found the place of wisdom,
who has entered into her treasures?

The One who knows all things knows
her;
he has probed her by his
knowledge—
the One who established the earth for
all time,
and filled it with four-footed beasts;

Shout with exultation, O city of Zion,
for great in your midst
is the Holy One of Israel! ℟.

he who dismisses the light, and it
departs,
calls it, and it obeys him trembling;
before whom the stars at their posts
shine and rejoice;
when he calls them, they answer, "Here
we are!"
shining with joy for their Maker.
Such is our God;
no other is to be compared to him:
he has traced out the whole way of
understanding,
and has given her to Jacob, his
servant,
to Israel, his beloved son.

Since then she has appeared on earth,
and moved among people.
She is the book of the precepts of God,
the law that endures forever;
all who cling to her will live,
but those will die who forsake her.
Turn, O Jacob, and receive her:
walk by her light toward splendor.
Give not your glory to another,
your privileges to an alien race.
Blessed are we, O Israel;
for what pleases God is known to us!

RESPONSORIAL PSALM *Psalm 19:8, 9, 10, 11*

℟. **Lord, you have the words of everlasting life.**

The law of the LORD is perfect,
refreshing the soul;
the decree of the LORD is trustworthy,
giving wisdom to the simple. ℟.

The precepts of the LORD are right,
rejoicing the heart;
the command of the LORD is clear,
enlightening the eye. ℟.

The fear of the LORD is pure,
enduring forever;
the ordinances of the LORD are true,
all of them just. ℟.

They are more precious than gold,
than a heap of purest gold;
sweeter also than syrup
or honey from the comb. ℟.

960 **READING VII** *Ezekiel 36:16-17a, 18-28*

The word of the LORD came to me, saying: Son of man, when the house of Israel lived
in their land, they defiled it by their conduct and deeds. Therefore I poured out my fury
upon them because of the blood that they poured out on the ground, and because they
defiled it with idols. I scattered them among the nations, dispersing them over foreign
lands; according to their conduct and deeds I judged them. But when they came among
the nations wherever they came, they served to profane my holy name, because it was
said of them: "These are the people of the LORD, yet they had to leave their land." So I

have relented because of my holy name which the house of Israel profaned among the nations where they came. Therefore say to the house of Israel: Thus says the Lord GOD: Not for your sakes do I act, house of Israel, but for the sake of my holy name, which you profaned among the nations to which you came. I will prove the holiness of my great name, profaned among the nations, in whose midst you have profaned it. Thus the nations shall know that I am the LORD, says the Lord GOD, when in their sight I prove my holiness through you. For I will take you away from among the nations, gather you from all the foreign lands, and bring you back to your own land. I will sprinkle clean water upon you to cleanse you from all your impurities, and from all your idols I will cleanse you. I will give you a new heart and place a new spirit within you, taking from your bodies your stony hearts and giving you natural hearts. I will put my spirit within you and make you live by my statutes, careful to observe my decrees. You shall live in the land I gave your fathers; you shall be my people, and I will be your God.

RESPONSORIAL PSALM

1. When baptism is celebrated   Psalm 42:3, 5; 43:3, 4

℟. **Like a deer that longs for running streams, my soul longs for you, my God.**

Athirst is my soul for God, the living
   God.
   When shall I go and behold the
      face of God? ℟.

I went with the throng
   and led them in procession to the
      house of God,
amid loud cries of joy and thanksgiving,
   with the multitude keeping
      festival. ℟.

Send forth your light and your fidelity;
   they shall lead me on
and bring me to your holy mountain,
   to your dwelling-place. ℟.

Then will I go in to the altar of God,
   the God of my gladness and joy;
then will I give you thanks upon the harp,
   O God, my God! ℟.

2. When baptism is not celebrated   Isaiah 12:2-3, 4bcd, 5-6

℟. **You will draw water joyfully from the springs of salvation.**

God indeed is my savior;
   I am confident and unafraid.
My strength and my courage is the LORD,
   and he has been my savior.
With joy you will draw water
   at the fountain of salvation. ℟.

Give thanks to the LORD, acclaim his
      name;
   among the nations make known his

   deeds,
proclaim how exalted is his name. ℟.

Sing praise to the LORD for his glorious
      achievement;
   let this be known throughout all the
      earth.
Shout with exultation, O city of Zion,
   for great in your midst
is the Holy One of Israel! ℟.

3. When baptism is not celebrated   Psalm 51:12-13, 14-15, 18-19

℟. **Create a clean heart in me, O God.**

A clean heart create for me, O God,
   and a steadfast spirit renew within
      me.
Cast me not out from your presence,
   and your Holy Spirit take not from
      me. ℟.

Give me back the joy of your salvation,
   and a willing spirit sustain in me.

I will teach transgressors your ways,
   and sinners shall return to you. ℟.

For you are not pleased with sacrifices;
   should I offer a holocaust, you
      would not accept it.
My sacrifice, O God, is a contrite spirit;
   a heart contrite and humbled, O God,
      you will not spurn. ℟.

GLORIA

PRAYER

961   **EPISTLE**   *Romans 6:3-11*

Brothers and sisters: Are you unaware that we who were baptized into Christ Jesus were baptized into his death? We were indeed buried with him through baptism into death, so that, just as Christ was raised from the dead by the glory of the Father, we too might live in newness of life.

For if we have grown into union with him through a death like his, we shall also be united with him in the resurrection. We know that our old self was crucified with him, so that our sinful body might be done away with, that we might no longer be in slavery to sin. For a dead person has been absolved from sin. If, then, we have died with Christ, we believe that we shall also live with him. We know that Christ, raised from the dead, dies no more; death no longer has power over him. As to his death, he died to sin once and for all; as to his life, he lives for God. Consequently, you too must think of your-selves as being dead to sin and living for God in Christ Jesus.

RESPONSORIAL PSALM   *Psalm 118:1-2, 16-17, 22-23*

Al- le - lu - ia.

Music: Chant Mode VIII

Give thanks to the LORD, for he is good,
    for his mercy endures forever.
Let the house of Israel say,
    "His mercy endures forever." ℟.

The right hand of the LORD has struck
    with power;
    the right hand of the LORD is exalted.

I shall not die, but live,
    and declare the works of the
    LORD. ℟.

The stone which the builders rejected
    has become the cornerstone.
By the LORD has this been done;
    it is wonderful in our eyes. ℟.

GOSPEL / A   *Matthew 28:1-10*

After the sabbath, as the first day of the week was dawning, Mary Magdalene and the other Mary came to see the tomb. And behold, there was a great earthquake; for an angel of the Lord descended from heaven, approached, rolled back the stone, and sat upon it. His appearance was like lightning and his clothing was white as snow. The guards were shaken with fear of him and became like dead men. Then the angel said to the women in reply, "Do not be afraid! I know that you are seeking Jesus the crucified. He is not here, for he has been raised just as he said. Come and see the place where he lay. Then go quickly and tell his disciples, 'He has been raised from the dead, and he is going before you to Galilee; there you will see him.' Behold, I have told you." Then they went away quickly from the tomb, fearful yet overjoyed, and ran to announce this to his disciples. And behold, Jesus met them on their way and greeted them. They approached, embraced his feet, and did him homage. Then Jesus said to them, "Do not be afraid. Go tell my brothers to go to Galilee, and there they will see me."

GOSPEL / B   *Mark 16:1-7*

When the sabbath was over, Mary Magdalene, Mary, the mother of James, and Salome bought spices so that they might go and anoint him. Very early when the sun had risen, on the first day of the week, they came to the tomb. They were saying to one another, "Who will roll back the stone for us from the entrance to the tomb?" When they looked up, they saw that the stone had been rolled back; it was very large. On entering the tomb they saw a young man sitting on the right side, clothed in a white robe, and they were utterly amazed. He said to them, "Do not be amazed! You seek Jesus of Nazareth, the crucified. He has been raised; he is not here. Behold the place where they laid him. But go and tell his disciples and Peter, 'He is going before you to Galilee; there you will see him, as he told you.'"

GOSPEL / C
Luke 24:1-12

At daybreak on the first day of the week the women who had come from Galilee with Jesus took the spices they had prepared and went to the tomb. They found the stone rolled away from the tomb; but when they entered, they did not find the body of the Lord Jesus. While they were puzzling over this, behold, two men in dazzling garments appeared to them. They were terrified and bowed their faces to the ground. They said to them, "Why do you seek the living one among the dead? He is not here, but he has been raised. Remember what he said to you while he was still in Galilee, that the Son of Man must be handed over to sinners and be crucified, and rise on the third day." And they remembered his words. Then they returned from the tomb and announced all these things to the eleven and to all the others. The women were Mary Magdalene, Joanna, and Mary the mother of James; the others who accompanied them also told this to the apostles, but their story seemed like nonsense and they did not believe them. But Peter got up and ran to the tomb, bent down, and saw the burial cloths alone; then he went home amazed at what had happened.

LITURGY OF BAPTISM
962

After the homily the catechumens are called forward. The assembly chants the litany of the saints (no. 795), invoking the holy women and men of all centuries. Patron saints of the church and of the catechumens and the faithful may be included in the litany.

BLESSING OF WATER
963

The presider gives thanks and praise to God over the waters of baptism. This acclamation is sung by all.

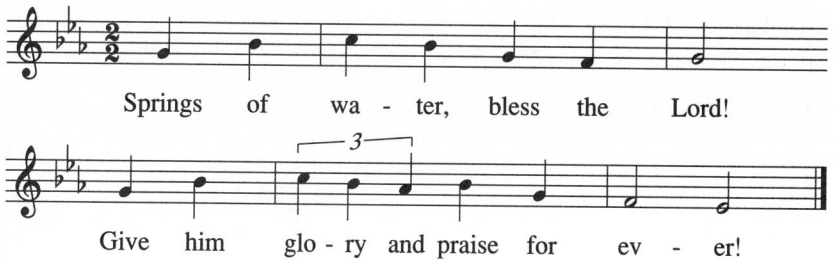

Springs of wa - ter, bless the Lord!

Give him glo - ry and praise for ev - er!

Text: Refrain trans. © 1973, ICEL
Music: Marty Haugen, © 1994, GIA Publications, Inc.

RENUNCIATION OF SIN AND PROFESSION OF FAITH
964

Each candidate for baptism is asked to reject sin and the ways of evil and to testify to faith in Father, Son and Holy Spirit. All join to affirm this faith.

THE BAPTISMS
965

One by one the candidates are led into the waters, or they bend over the font, and water is poured over them as the presider says: "N., I baptize you in the name of the Father, and of the Son, and of the Holy Spirit." After each baptism, the assembly sings an acclamation.

You have put on Christ, in him you have been bap - tized.

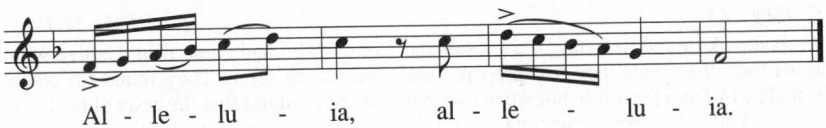

Al - le - lu - ia, al - le - lu - ia.

Music: Howard Hughes, SM, © 1977, ICEL

Each of the newly baptized is then clothed in a baptismal garment.

966 RECEPTION INTO FULL COMMUNION
Those who have been previously baptized are now called forward to profess their faith and to be received into the full communion of the Roman Catholic Church.

967 CONFIRMATION
Infants who have been baptized are anointed with chrism. Children and adults are usually confirmed: the presider prays and lays hands on them, then anoints each of the newly baptized with chrism saying: "N., be sealed with the Gift of the Holy Spirit."

968 RENEWAL OF BAPTISMAL PROMISES
All of the faithful repeat and affirm the rejection of sin made at baptism and profess faith in the Father, Son and Holy Spirit. The assembly is sprinkled with the baptismal water. The newly baptized then take their places in the assembly and, for the first time, join in the prayer of the faithful, the prayers of intercession.

969 LITURGY OF THE EUCHARIST
The gifts and table are prepared and the eucharist is celebrated in the usual way.

970 CONCLUDING RITE
The dismissal is sung with "alleluia", and all respond.

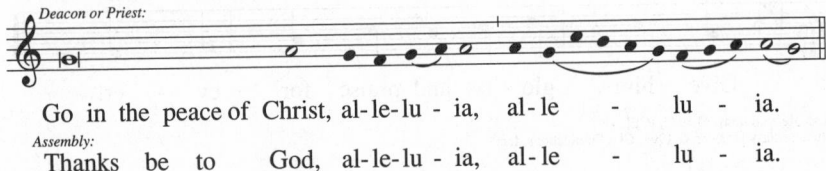

Deacon or Priest:
Go in the peace of Christ, al-le-lu - ia, al-le - lu - ia.
Assembly:
Thanks be to God, al-le-lu-ia, al-le - lu - ia.

971 EASTER SUNDAY / ABC

READING I   *Acts 10:34a, 37-43 / 42*
Peter proceeded to speak and said: "You know what has happened all over Judea, beginning in Galilee after the baptism that John preached, how God anointed Jesus of Nazareth with the Holy Spirit and power. He went about doing good and healing all those oppressed by the devil, for God was with him. We are witnesses of all that he did both in the country of the Jews and in Jerusalem. They put him to death by hanging him

on a tree. This man God raised on the third day and granted that he be visible, not to all the people, but to us, the witnesses chosen by God in advance, who ate and drank with him after he rose from the dead. He commissioned us to preach to the people and testify that he is the one appointed by God as judge of the living and the dead. To him all the prophets bear witness, that everyone who believes in him will receive forgiveness of sins through his name.

RESPONSORIAL PSALM
Psalm 118:1-2, 16-17, 22-23

℟. **This is the day the Lord has made; let us rejoice and be glad.**
  or:
Alleluia.

Give thanks to the LORD, for he is good,
  for his mercy endures forever.
Let the house of Israel say,
  "His mercy endures forever." ℟.

"The right hand of the LORD has struck
  with power;
  the right hand of the LORD is exalted.

I shall not die, but live,
  and declare the works of the LORD. ℟.

The stone which the builders rejected
  has become the cornerstone.
By the LORD has this been done;
  it is wonderful in our eyes. ℟.

READING II
Colossians 3:1-4

Brothers and sisters: If then you were raised with Christ, seek what is above, where Christ is seated at the right hand of God. Think of what is above, not of what is on earth. For you have died, and your life is hidden with Christ in God. When Christ your life appears, then you too will appear with him in glory.

Or:

READING II
1 Corinthians 5:6b-8

Brothers and sisters: Do you not know that a little yeast leavens all the dough? Clear out the old yeast, so that you may become a fresh batch of dough, inasmuch as you are unleavened. For our paschal lamb, Christ, has been sacrificed. Therefore, let us celebrate the feast, not with the old yeast, the yeast of malice and wickedness, but with the unleavened bread of sincerity and truth.

SEQUENCE
See no. 438

GOSPEL
John 20:1-9

On the first day of the week, Mary of Magdala came to the tomb early in the morning, while it was still dark, and saw the stone removed from the tomb. So she ran and went to Simon Peter and to the other disciple whom Jesus loved, and told them, "They have taken the Lord from the tomb, and we don't know where they put him." So Peter and the other disciple went out and came to the tomb. They both ran, but the other disciple ran faster than Peter and arrived at the tomb first; he bent down and saw the burial cloths there, but did not go in. When Simon Peter arrived after him, he went into the tomb and saw the burial cloths there, and the cloth that had covered his head, not with the burial cloths but rolled up in a separate place. Then the other disciple also went in, the one who had arrived at the tomb first, and he saw and believed. For they did not yet understand the Scripture that he had to rise from the dead.

972 SECOND SUNDAY OF EASTER / ABC

READING I / A   Acts 2:42-47 / 43

They devoted themselves to the teaching of the apostles and to the communal life, to the breaking of bread and to the prayers. Awe came upon everyone, and many wonders and signs were done through the apostles. All who believed were together and had all things in common; they would sell their property and possessions and divide them among all according to each one's need. Every day they devoted themselves to meeting together in the temple area and to breaking bread in their homes. They ate their meals with exultation and sincerity of heart, praising God and enjoying favor with all the people. And every day the Lord added to their number those who were being saved.

READING I / B   Acts 4:32-35 / 44

The community of believers was of one heart and mind, and no one claimed that any of his possessions was his own, but they had everything in common. With great power the apostles bore witness to the resurrection of the Lord Jesus, and great favor was accorded them all. There was no needy person among them, for those who owned property or houses would sell them, bring the proceeds of the sale, and put them at the feet of the apostles, and they were distributed to each according to need.

READING I / C   Acts 5:12-16 / 45

Many signs and wonders were done among the people at the hands of the apostles. They were all together in Solomon's portico. None of the others dared to join them, but the people esteemed them. Yet more than ever, believers in the Lord, great numbers of men and women, were added to them. Thus they even carried the sick out into the streets and laid them on cots and mats so that when Peter came by, at least his shadow might fall on one or another of them. A large number of people from the towns in the vicinity of Jerusalem also gathered, bringing the sick and those disturbed by unclean spirits, and they were all cured.

RESPONSORIAL PSALM   Psalm 118:2-4, 13-15, 22-24

℟. Give thanks to the Lord, for he is good, his love is everlasting.
or:
Alleluia.

Let the house of Israel say,
  "His mercy endures forever."
Let the house of Aaron say,
  "His mercy endures forever."
Let those who fear the LORD say,
  "His mercy endures forever." ℟.

I was hard pressed and was falling,
  but the LORD helped me.
My strength and my courage is the LORD,

and he has been my savior.
The joyful shout of victory
  in the tents of the just. ℟.

The stone which the builders rejected
  has become the cornerstone.
By the LORD has this been done;
  it is wonderful in our eyes.
This is the day the LORD has made;
  let us be glad and rejoice in it. ℟.

READING II / A   1 Peter 1:3-9

Blessed be the God and Father of our Lord Jesus Christ, who in his great mercy gave us a new birth to a living hope through the resurrection of Jesus Christ from the dead, to an inheritance that is imperishable, undefiled, and unfading, kept in heaven for you who by the power of God are safeguarded through faith, to a salvation that is ready to be revealed in the final time. In this you rejoice, although now for a little while you may have to suffer through various trials, so that the genuineness of your faith, more precious than gold that is perishable even though tested by fire, may prove to be for praise, glory, and honor at the revelation of Jesus Christ. Although you have not seen him you love him; even though you do not see him now yet believe in him, you rejoice with an indescribable and glorious joy, as you attain the goal of your faith, the salvation of your souls.

READING II / B   *1 John 5:1-6*

Beloved: Everyone who believes that Jesus is the Christ is begotten by God, and everyone who loves the Father loves also the one begotten by him. In this way we know that we love the children of God when we love God and obey his commandments. For the love of God is this, that we keep his commandments. And his commandments are not burdensome, for whoever is begotten by God conquers the world. And the victory that conquers the world is our faith. Who indeed is the victor over the world but the one who believes that Jesus is the Son of God?

This is the one who came through water and blood, Jesus Christ, not by water alone, but by water and blood. The Spirit is the one that testifies, and the Spirit is truth.

READING II / C   *Revelation 1:9-11a, 12-13, 17-19*

I, John, your brother, who share with you the distress, the kingdom, and the endurance we have in Jesus, found myself on the island called Patmos because I proclaimed God's word and gave testimony to Jesus. I was caught up in spirit on the Lord's day and heard behind me a voice as loud as a trumpet, which said, "Write on a scroll what you see." Then I turned to see whose voice it was that spoke to me, and when I turned, I saw seven gold lampstands and in the midst of the lampstands one like a son of man, wearing an ankle-length robe, with a gold sash around his chest.

When I caught sight of him, I fell down at his feet as though dead. He touched me with his right hand and said, "Do not be afraid. I am the first and the last, the one who lives. Once I was dead, but now I am alive forever and ever. I hold the keys to death and the netherworld. Write down, therefore, what you have seen, and what is happening, and what will happen afterwards."

GOSPEL   *John 20:19-31*

On the evening of that first day of the week, when the doors were locked, where the disciples were, for fear of the Jews, Jesus came and stood in their midst and said to them, "Peace be with you." When he had said this, he showed them his hands and his side. The disciples rejoiced when they saw the Lord. Jesus said to them again, "Peace be with you. As the Father has sent me, so I send you." And when he had said this, he breathed on them and said to them, "Receive the Holy Spirit. Whose sins you forgive are forgiven them, and whose sins you retain are retained."

Thomas, called Didymus, one of the Twelve, was not with them when Jesus came. So the other disciples said to him, "We have seen the Lord." But he said to them, "Unless I see the mark of the nails in his hands and put my finger into the nailmarks and put my hand into his side, I will not believe."

Now a week later his disciples were again inside and Thomas was with them. Jesus came, although the doors were locked, and stood in their midst and said, "Peace be with you." Then he said to Thomas, "Put your finger here and see my hands, and bring your hand and put it into my side, and do not be unbelieving, but believe." Thomas answered and said to him, "My Lord and my God!" Jesus said to him, "Have you come to believe because you have seen me? Blessed are those who have not seen and have believed."

Now, Jesus did many other signs in the presence of his disciples that are not written in this book. But these are written that you may come to believe that Jesus is the Christ, the Son of God, and that through this belief you may have life in his name.

973 THIRD SUNDAY OF EASTER / A

READING I *Acts 2:14, 22-33 / 46*

Then Peter stood up with the Eleven, raised his voice, and proclaimed: "You who are Jews, indeed all of you staying in Jerusalem. Let this be known to you, and listen to my words. You who are Israelites, hear these words. Jesus the Nazorean was a man commended to you by God with mighty deeds, wonders, and signs, which God worked through him in your midst, as you yourselves know. This man, delivered up by the set plan and foreknowledge of God, you killed, using lawless men to crucify him. But God raised him up, releasing him from the throes of death, because it was impossible for him to be held by it. For David says of him:

'I saw the Lord ever before me,
with him at my right hand I shall not be disturbed.
Therefore my heart has been glad and my tongue has exulted;
my flesh, too, will dwell in hope,
because you will not abandon my soul to the netherworld,
nor will you suffer your holy one to see corruption.
You have made known to me the paths of life;
you will fill me with joy in your presence.'

"My brothers, one can confidently say to you about the patriarch David that he died and was buried, and his tomb is in our midst to this day. But since he was a prophet and knew that God had sworn an oath to him that he would set one of his descendants upon his throne, he foresaw and spoke of the resurrection of the Christ, that neither was he abandoned to the netherworld nor did his flesh see corruption. God raised this Jesus; of this we are all witnesses. Exalted at the right hand of God, he received the promise of the Holy Spirit from the Father and poured him forth, as you see and hear."

RESPONSORIAL PSALM *Psalm 16:1-2, 5, 7-8, 9-10, 11*

℟. **Lord, you will show us the path of life.**
   or:
Alleluia.

Keep me, O God, for in you I take refuge;
   I say to the LORD, "My LORD are you."
O LORD, my allotted portion and my cup,
   you it is who hold fast my lot. ℟.

I bless the LORD who counsels me;
   even in the night my heart exhorts me.
I set the LORD ever before me;
   with him at my right hand I shall not be disturbed. ℟.

Therefore my heart is glad and my soul rejoices,
   my body, too, abides in confidence;
because you will not abandon my soul to the netherworld,
   nor will you suffer your faithful one to undergo corruption. ℟.

You will show me the path to life,
   abounding joy in your presence,
   the delights at your right hand forever. ℟.

READING II *1 Peter 1:17-21*

Beloved: If you invoke as Father him who judges impartially according to each one's works, conduct yourselves with reverence during the time of your sojourning, realizing that you were ransomed from your futile conduct, handed on by your ancestors, not with perishable things like silver or gold but with the precious blood of Christ as of a spotless unblemished lamb. He was known before the foundation of the world but revealed in the final time for you, who through him believe in God who raised him from the dead and gave him glory, so that your faith and hope are in God.

GOSPEL   *Luke 24:13-35*

That very day, the first day of the week, two of Jesus' disciples were going to a village seven miles from Jerusalem called Emmaus, and they were conversing about all the things that had occurred. And it happened that while they were conversing and debating, Jesus himself drew near and walked with them, but their eyes were prevented from recognizing him. He asked them, "What are you discussing as you walk along?" They stopped, looking downcast. One of them, named Cleopas, said to him in reply, "Are you the only visitor to Jerusalem who does not know of the things that have taken place there in these days?" And he replied to them, "What sort of things?" They said to him, "The things that happened to Jesus the Nazarene, who was a prophet mighty in deed and word before God and all the people, how our chief priests and rulers both handed him over to a sentence of death and crucified him. But we were hoping that he would be the one to redeem Israel; and besides all this, it is now the third day since this took place. Some women from our group, however, have astounded us: they were at the tomb early in the morning and did not find his body; they came back and reported that they had indeed seen a vision of angels who announced that he was alive. Then some of those with us went to the tomb and found things just as the women had described, but him they did not see." And he said to them, "Oh, how foolish you are! How slow of heart to believe all that the prophets spoke! Was it not necessary that the Christ should suffer these things and enter into his glory?" Then beginning with Moses and all the prophets, he interpreted to them what referred to him in all the Scriptures. As they approached the village to which they were going, he gave the impression that he was going on farther. But they urged him, "Stay with us, for it is nearly evening and the day is almost over." So he went in to stay with them. And it happened that, while he was with them at table, he took bread, said the blessing, broke it, and gave it to them. With that their eyes were opened and they recognized him, but he vanished from their sight. Then they said to each other, "Were not our hearts burning within us while he spoke to us on the way and opened the Scriptures to us?" So they set out at once and returned to Jerusalem where they found gathered together the eleven and those with them who were saying, "The Lord has truly been raised and has appeared to Simon!" Then the two recounted what had taken place on the way and how he was made known to them in the breaking of bread.

THIRD SUNDAY OF EASTER / B   974

READING I   *Acts 3:13-15, 17-19 / 47*

Peter said to the people: "The God of Abraham, the God of Isaac, and the God of Jacob, the God of our fathers, has glorified his servant Jesus, whom you handed over and denied in Pilate's presence when he had decided to release him. You denied the Holy and Righteous One and asked that a murderer be released to you. The author of life you put to death, but God raised him from the dead; of this we are witnesses. Now I know, brothers, that you acted out of ignorance, just as your leaders did; but God has thus brought to fulfillment what he had announced beforehand through the mouth of all the prophets, that his Christ would suffer. Repent, therefore, and be converted, that your sins may be wiped away."

RESPONSORIAL PSALM   *Psalm 4:2, 4, 7-8, 9*
℟. **Lord, let your face shine on us.**
   or:
Alleluia.

When I call, answer me, O my just God,
   you who relieve me when I am in
      distress;
have pity on me, and hear my prayer! ℟.

Know that the LORD does wonders for
   his faithful one;
   the LORD will hear me when I call
      upon him. ℟.

O LORD, let the light of your
    countenance shine upon us!
    You put gladness into my heart. ℞.

As soon as I lie down, I fall peacefully
    asleep,
    for you alone, O LORD,
    bring security to my dwelling. ℞.

READING II   *1 John 2:1-5a*

My children, I am writing this to you so that you may not commit sin. But if anyone does sin, we have an Advocate with the Father, Jesus Christ the righteous one. He is expiation for our sins, and not for our sins only but for those of the whole world. The way we may be sure that we know him is to keep his commandments. Those who say, "I know him," but do not keep his commandments are liars, and the truth is not in them. But whoever keeps his word, the love of God is truly perfected in him.

GOSPEL   *Luke 24:35-48*

The two disciples recounted what had taken place on the way, and how Jesus was made known to them in the breaking of bread.

While they were still speaking about this, he stood in their midst and said to them, "Peace be with you." But they were startled and terrified and thought that they were seeing a ghost. Then he said to them, "Why are you troubled? And why do questions arise in your hearts? Look at my hands and my feet, that it is I myself. Touch me and see, because a ghost does not have flesh and bones as you can see I have." And as he said this, he showed them his hands and his feet. While they were still incredulous for joy and were amazed, he asked them, "Have you anything here to eat?" They gave him a piece of baked fish; he took it and ate it in front of them.

He said to them, "These are my words that I spoke to you while I was still with you, that everything written about me in the law of Moses and in the prophets and psalms must be fulfilled." Then he opened their minds to understand the Scriptures. And he said to them, "Thus it is written that the Christ would suffer and rise from the dead on the third day and that repentance, for the forgiveness of sins, would be preached in his name to all the nations, beginning from Jerusalem. You are witnesses of these things."

975   THIRD SUNDAY OF EASTER / C

READING I   *Acts 5:27-32, 40b-41 / 48*

When the captain and the court officers had brought the apostles in and made them stand before the Sanhedrin, the high priest questioned them, "We gave you strict orders, did we not, to stop teaching in that name? Yet you have filled Jerusalem with your teaching and want to bring this man's blood upon us." But Peter and the apostles said in reply, "We must obey God rather than men. The God of our ancestors raised Jesus, though you had him killed by hanging him on a tree. God exalted him at his right hand as leader and savior to grant Israel repentance and forgiveness of sins. We are witnesses of these things, as is the Holy Spirit whom God has given to those who obey him."

The Sanhedrin ordered the apostles to stop speaking in the name of Jesus, and dismissed them. So they left the presence of the Sanhedrin, rejoicing that they had been found worthy to suffer dishonor for the sake of the name.

RESPONSORIAL PSALM   *Psalm 30:2, 4, 5-6, 11-12, 13*

℞. I will praise you, Lord, for you have rescued me.
    or:
Alleluia.

I will extol you, O LORD, for you drew
    me clear
    and did not let my enemies rejoice
    over me.

O LORD, you brought me up from the
    netherworld;
    you preserved me from among those
    going down into the pit. ℞.

Sing praise to the LORD, you his faithful
  ones,
  and give thanks to his holy name.
For his anger lasts but a moment;
  a lifetime, his good will.
At nightfall, weeping enters in,
  but with the dawn, rejoicing. ℟.

Hear, O LORD, and have pity on me;
  O LORD, be my helper.
You changed my mourning into
  dancing;
  O LORD, my God, forever will I give
  you thanks. ℟.

READING II
Revelation 5:11-14

I, John, looked and heard the voices of many angels who surrounded the throne and the living creatures and the elders. They were countless in number, and they cried out in a loud voice:
"Worthy is the Lamb that was slain
to receive power and riches, wisdom and strength,
honor and glory and blessing."
Then I heard every creature in heaven and on earth and under the earth and in the sea, everything in the universe, cry out:
"To the one who sits on the throne and to the Lamb
be blessing and honor, glory and might,
forever and ever."
The four living creatures answered, "Amen," and the elders fell down and worshiped.

GOSPEL
John 21:1-19 or 21:1-14

For short form read only the part in brackets.

[At that time, Jesus revealed himself again to his disciples at the Sea of Tiberias. He revealed himself in this way. Together were Simon Peter, Thomas called Didymus, Nathanael from Cana in Galilee, Zebedee's sons, and two others of his disciples. Simon Peter said to them, "I am going fishing." They said to him, "We also will come with you." So they went out and got into the boat, but that night they caught nothing. When it was already dawn, Jesus was standing on the shore; but the disciples did not realize that it was Jesus. Jesus said to them, "Children, have you caught anything to eat?" They answered him, "No." So he said to them, "Cast the net over the right side of the boat and you will find something." So they cast it, and were not able to pull it in because of the number of fish. So the disciple whom Jesus loved said to Peter, "It is the Lord." When Simon Peter heard that it was the Lord, he tucked in his garment, for he was lightly clad, and jumped into the sea. The other disciples came in the boat, for they were not far from shore, only about a hundred yards, dragging the net with the fish. When they climbed out on shore, they saw a charcoal fire with fish on it and bread. Jesus said to them, "Bring some of the fish you just caught." So Simon Peter went over and dragged the net ashore full of one hundred fifty-three large fish. Even though there were so many, the net was not torn. Jesus said to them, "Come, have breakfast." And none of the disciples dared to ask him, "Who are you?" because they realized it was the Lord. Jesus came over and took the bread and gave it to them, and in like manner the fish. This was now the third time Jesus was revealed to his disciples after being raised from the dead.]

When they had finished breakfast, Jesus said to Simon Peter, "Simon, son of John, do you love me more than these?" Simon Peter answered him, "Yes, Lord, you know that I love you." Jesus said to him, "Feed my lambs." He then said to Simon Peter a second time, "Simon, son of John, do you love me?" Simon Peter answered him, "Yes, Lord, you know that I love you." Jesus said to him, "Tend my sheep." Jesus said to him the third time, "Simon, son of John, do you love me?" Peter was distressed that Jesus had said to him a third time, "Do you love me?" and he said to him, "Lord, you know everything; you know that I love you." Jesus said to him, "Feed my sheep. Amen, amen, I say to you, when you were younger, you used to dress yourself and go where you wanted; but when you grow old, you will stretch out your hands, and someone else will dress you and lead you where you do not want to go." He said this signifying by what kind of death he would glorify God. And when he had said this, he said to him, "Follow me."

976 FOURTH SUNDAY OF EASTER / A

READING I
Acts 2:14a, 36-41 / 49

Then Peter stood up with the Eleven, raised his voice, and proclaimed: "Let the whole house of Israel know for certain that God has made both Lord and Christ, this Jesus whom you crucified."

Now when they heard this, they were cut to the heart, and they asked Peter and the other apostles, "What are we to do, my brothers?" Peter said to them, "Repent and be baptized, every one of you, in the name of Jesus Christ for the forgiveness of your sins; and you will receive the gift of the Holy Spirit. For the promise is made to you and to your children and to all those far off, whomever the Lord our God will call." He testified with many other arguments, and was exhorting them, "Save yourselves from this corrupt generation." Those who accepted his message were baptized, and about three thousand persons were added that day.

RESPONSORIAL PSALM
Psalm 23:1-3a, 3b-4, 5, 6

℟. **The Lord is my shepherd; there is nothing I shall want.**
or:
Alleluia.

The LORD is my shepherd; I shall not
    want.
  In verdant pastures he gives me
    repose;
beside restful waters he leads me;
  he refreshes my soul. ℟.

He guides me in right paths
  for his name's sake.
Even though I walk in the dark valley
  I fear no evil; for you are at my side;
with your rod and your staff

that give me courage. ℟.

You spread the table before me
  in the sight of my foes;
you anoint my head with oil;
  my cup overflows. ℟.

Only goodness and kindness follow me
  all the days of my life;
and I shall dwell in the house of the
  LORD
  for years to come. ℟.

READING II
1 Peter 2:20b-25

Beloved: If you are patient when you suffer for doing what is good, this is a grace before God. For to this you have been called, because Christ also suffered for you, leaving you an example that you should follow in his footsteps.

"He committed no sin,
  and no deceit was found in his mouth."

When he was insulted, he returned no insult; when he suffered, he did not threaten; instead, he handed himself over to the one who judges justly. He himself bore our sins in his body upon the cross, so that, free from sin, we might live for righteousness. By his wounds you have been healed. For you had gone astray like sheep, but you have now returned to the shepherd and guardian of your souls.

GOSPEL
John 10:1-10

Jesus said: "Amen, amen, I say to you, whoever does not enter a sheepfold through the gate but climbs over elsewhere is a thief and a robber. But whoever enters through the gate is the shepherd of the sheep. The gatekeeper opens it for him, and the sheep hear his voice, as the shepherd calls his own sheep by name and leads them out. When he has driven out all his own, he walks ahead of them, and the sheep follow him, because they recognize his voice. But they will not follow a stranger; they will run away from him, because they do not recognize the voice of strangers." Although Jesus used this figure of speech, the Pharisees did not realize what he was trying to tell them.

So Jesus said again, "Amen, amen, I say to you, I am the gate for the sheep. All who came before me are thieves and robbers, but the sheep did not listen to them. I am the gate. Whoever enters through me will be saved, and will come in and go out and find pasture. A thief comes only to steal and slaughter and destroy; I came so that they might have life and have it more abundantly."

FOURTH SUNDAY OF EASTER / B   977

READING I   *Acts 4:8-12 / 50*
Peter, filled with the Holy Spirit, said: "Leaders of the people and elders: If we are being examined today about a good deed done to a cripple, namely, by what means he was saved, then all of you and all the people of Israel should know that it was in the name of Jesus Christ the Nazarene whom you crucified, whom God raised from the dead; in his name this man stands before you healed. He is 'the stone rejected by you, the builders, which has become the cornerstone.' There is no salvation through anyone else, nor is there any other name under heaven given to the human race by which we are to be saved."

RESPONSORIAL PSALM   *Psalm 118:1, 8-9, 21-23, 26, 28, 29*
℟. The stone rejected by the builders has become the cornerstone.
   or:
Alleluia.

Give thanks to the LORD, for he is good,
   for his mercy endures forever.
It is better to take refuge in the LORD
   than to trust in man.
It is better to take refuge in the LORD
   than to trust in princes. ℟.

I will give thanks to you, for you have
   answered me
   and have been my savior.
The stone which the builders rejected
   has become the cornerstone.

By the LORD has this been done;
   it is wonderful in our eyes. ℟.

Blessed is he who comes in the name of
   the LORD;
   we bless you from the house of the
   LORD.
I will give thanks to you, for you have
   answered me
   and have been my savior.
Give thanks to the LORD, for he is good;
   for his kindness endures forever. ℟.

READING II   *1 John 3:1-2*
Beloved: See what love the Father has bestowed on us that we may be called the children of God. Yet so we are. The reason the world does not know us is that it did not know him. Beloved, we are God's children now; what we shall be has not yet been revealed. We do know that when it is revealed we shall be like him, for we shall see him as he is.

GOSPEL   *John 10:11-18*
Jesus said: "I am the good shepherd. A good shepherd lays down his life for the sheep. A hired man, who is not a shepherd and whose sheep are not his own, sees a wolf coming and leaves the sheep and runs away, and the wolf catches and scatters them. This is because he works for pay and has no concern for the sheep. I am the good shepherd, and I know mine and mine know me, just as the Father knows me and I know the Father; and I will lay down my life for the sheep. I have other sheep that do not belong to this fold. These also I must lead, and they will hear my voice, and there will be one flock, one shepherd. This is why the Father loves me, because I lay down my life in order to take it up again. No one takes it from me, but I lay it down on my own. I have power to lay it down, and power to take it up again. This command I have received from my Father."

978 FOURTH SUNDAY OF EASTER / C

READING I
Acts 13:14, 43-52 / 51

Paul and Barnabas continued on from Perga and reached Antioch in Pisidia. On the sabbath they entered the synagogue and took their seats. Many Jews and worshipers who were converts to Judaism followed Paul and Barnabas, who spoke to them and urged them to remain faithful to the grace of God.

On the following sabbath almost the whole city gathered to hear the word of the Lord. When the Jews saw the crowds, they were filled with jealousy and with violent abuse contradicted what Paul said. Both Paul and Barnabas spoke out boldly and said, "It was necessary that the word of God be spoken to you first, but since you reject it and condemn yourselves as unworthy of eternal life, we now turn to the Gentiles. For so the Lord has commanded us, 'I have made you a light to the Gentiles, that you may be an instrument of salvation to the ends of the earth.'"

The Gentiles were delighted when they heard this and glorified the word of the Lord. All who were destined for eternal life came to believe, and the word of the Lord continued to spread through the whole region. The Jews, however, incited the women of prominence who were worshipers and the leading men of the city, stirred up a persecution against Paul and Barnabas, and expelled them from their territory. So they shook the dust from their feet in protest against them, and went to Iconium. The disciples were filled with joy and the Holy Spirit.

RESPONSORIAL PSALM
Psalm 100:1-2, 3, 5

℟. **We are his people, the sheep of his flock.**
> *or:*

Alleluia.

Sing joyfully to the LORD, all you lands;
> serve the LORD with gladness;
come before him with joyful song. ℟.

Know that the LORD is God;
> he made us, his we are;

his people, the flock he tends. ℟.

The LORD is good:
> his kindness endures forever,
and his faithfulness, to all generations. ℟.

READING II
Revelation 7:9, 14b-17

I, John, had a vision of a great multitude, which no one could count, from every nation, race, people, and tongue. They stood before the throne and before the Lamb, wearing white robes and holding palm branches in their hands.

Then one of the elders said to me, "These are the ones who have survived the time of great distress; they have washed their robes and made them white in the blood of the Lamb.

"For this reason they stand before God's throne
> and worship him day and night in his temple.
The one who sits on the throne will shelter them.
They will not hunger or thirst anymore,
> nor will the sun or any heat strike them.
For the Lamb who is in the center of the throne
> will shepherd them
> and lead them to springs of life-giving water,
> and God will wipe away every tear from their eyes."

GOSPEL
John 10:27-30

Jesus said: "My sheep hear my voice; I know them, and they follow me. I give them eternal life, and they shall never perish. No one can take them out of my hand. My Father, who has given them to me, is greater than all, and no one can take them out of the Father's hand. The Father and I are one."

FIFTH SUNDAY OF EASTER / A   979

READING I   *Acts 6:1-7 / 52*

As the number of disciples continued to grow, the Hellenists complained against the Hebrews because their widows were being neglected in the daily distribution. So the Twelve called together the community of the disciples and said, "It is not right for us to neglect the word of God to serve at table. Brothers, select from among you seven reputable men, filled with the Spirit and wisdom, whom we shall appoint to this task, whereas we shall devote ourselves to prayer and to the ministry of the word." The proposal was acceptable to the whole community, so they chose Stephen, a man filled with faith and the Holy Spirit, also Philip, Prochorus, Nicanor, Timon, Parmenas, and Nicholas of Antioch, a convert to Judaism. They presented these men to the apostles who prayed and laid hands on them. The word of God continued to spread, and the number of the disciples in Jerusalem increased greatly; even a large group of priests were becoming obedient to the faith.

RESPONSORIAL PSALM   *Psalm 33:1-2, 4-5, 18-19*

℟. Lord, let your mercy be on us, as we place our trust in you.
  or:
Alleluia.

Exult, you just, in the LORD;
  praise from the upright is fitting.
Give thanks to the LORD on the harp;
  with the ten-stringed lyre chant his
    praises. ℟.

Upright is the word of the LORD,
  and all his works are trustworthy.
He loves justice and right;

of the kindness of the LORD the earth
  is full. ℟.

See, the eyes of the LORD are upon those
    who fear him,
  upon those who hope for his
    kindness,
to deliver them from death
  and preserve them in spite of
    famine. ℟.

READING II   *1 Peter 2:4-9*

Beloved: Come to him, a living stone, rejected by human beings but chosen and precious in the sight of God, and, like living stones, let yourselves be built into a spiritual house to be a holy priesthood to offer spiritual sacrifices acceptable to God through Jesus Christ. For it says in Scripture:
  "Behold, I am laying a stone in Zion,
  a cornerstone, chosen and precious,
  and whoever believes in it shall not be put to shame."
Therefore, its value is for you who have faith, but for those without faith:
  "The stone that the builders rejected
  has become the cornerstone,"
and
  "A stone that will make people stumble,
  and a rock that will make them fall."
They stumble by disobeying the word, as is their destiny.
  You are "a chosen race, a royal priesthood, a holy nation, a people of his own, so that you may announce the praises" of him who called you out of darkness into his wonderful light.

GOSPEL   *John 14:1-12*

Jesus said to his disciples: "Do not let your hearts be troubled. You have faith in God; have faith also in me. In my Father's house there are many dwelling places. If there were not, would I have told you that I am going to prepare a place for you? And if I go and prepare a place for you, I will come back again and take you to myself, so that where I am you also may be. Where I am going you know the way." Thomas said to him, "Master, we do not know where you are going; how can we know the way?" Jesus said to him, "I am the way and the truth and the life. No one comes to the Father except through me. If you know me, then you will also know my Father. From now on you do know him and have seen him." Philip said to him, "Master, show us the Father, and that will be enough for us." Jesus said to him, "Have I been with you for so long a time and you still do not know me, Philip? Whoever has seen me has seen the Father. How can you say, 'Show us the Father'? Do you not believe that I am in the Father and the Father is in me? The words that I speak to you I do not speak on my own. The Father who dwells in me is doing his works. Believe me that I am in the Father and the Father is in me, or else, believe because of the works themselves. Amen, amen, I say to you, whoever believes in me will do the works that I do, and will do greater ones than these, because I am going to the Father."

980 FIFTH SUNDAY OF EASTER / B

READING I   *Acts 9:26-31 / 53*

When Saul arrived in Jerusalem he tried to join the disciples, but they were all afraid of him, not believing that he was a disciple. Then Barnabas took charge of him and brought him to the apostles, and he reported to them how he had seen the Lord, and that he had spoken to him, and how in Damascus he had spoken out boldly in the name of Jesus. He moved about freely with them in Jerusalem, and spoke out boldly in the name of the Lord. He also spoke and debated with the Hellenists, but they tried to kill him. And when the brothers learned of this, they took him down to Caesarea and sent him on his way to Tarsus. The church throughout all Judea, Galilee, and Samaria was at peace. It was being built up and walked in the fear of the Lord, and with the consolation of the Holy Spirit it grew in numbers.

RESPONSORIAL PSALM   *Psalm 22:26-27, 28, 30, 31-32*

℟. I will praise you, Lord, in the assembly of your people.
or:
Alleluia.

I will fulfill my vows before those who
    fear the LORD.
The lowly shall eat their fill;
they who seek the LORD shall praise him:
    "May your hearts live forever!" ℟.

All the ends of the earth
    shall remember and turn to the LORD;
all the families of the nations
    shall bow down before him. ℟.

To him alone shall bow down

all who sleep in the earth;
before him shall bend
    all who go down into the dust. ℟.

And to him my soul shall live;
    my descendants shall serve him.
Let the coming generation be told of the
    LORD
that they may proclaim to a people
    yet to be born
the justice he has shown. ℟.

READING II   *1 John 3:18-24*

Children, let us love not in word or speech but in deed and truth. Now this is how we shall know that we belong to the truth and reassure our hearts before him in whatever our hearts condemn, for God is greater than our hearts and knows everything. Beloved, if our hearts do not condemn us, we have confidence in God and receive from him whatever we ask, because we keep his commandments and do what pleases him. And his commandment is this: we should believe in the name of his Son, Jesus Christ, and love one another just as he commanded us. Those who keep his commandments remain in him, and he in them, and the way we know that he remains in us is from the Spirit he gave us.

GOSPEL   *John 15:1-8*

Jesus said to his disciples: "I am the true vine, and my Father is the vine grower. He takes away every branch in me that does not bear fruit, and every one that does he prunes so that it bears more fruit. You are already pruned because of the word that I spoke to you. Remain in me, as I remain in you. Just as a branch cannot bear fruit on its own unless it remains on the vine, so neither can you unless you remain in me. I am the vine, you are the branches. Whoever remains in me and I in him will bear much fruit, because without me you can do nothing. Anyone who does not remain in me will be thrown out like a branch and wither; people will gather them and throw them into a fire and they will be burned. If you remain in me and my words remain in you, ask for whatever you want and it will be done for you. By this is my Father glorified, that you bear much fruit and become my disciples."

FIFTH SUNDAY OF EASTER / C   981

READING I   *Acts 14:21-27 / 54*

After Paul and Barnabas had proclaimed the good news to that city and made a considerable number of disciples, they returned to Lystra and to Iconium and to Antioch. They strengthened the spirits of the disciples and exhorted them to persevere in the faith, saying, "It is necessary for us to undergo many hardships to enter the kingdom of God." They appointed elders for them in each church and, with prayer and fasting, commended them to the Lord in whom they had put their faith. Then they traveled through Pisidia and reached Pamphylia. After proclaiming the word at Perga they went down to Attalia. From there they sailed to Antioch, where they had been commended to the grace of God for the work they had now accomplished. And when they arrived, they called the church together and reported what God had done with them and how he had opened the door of faith to the Gentiles.

RESPONSORIAL PSALM   *Psalm 145:8-9, 10-11, 12-13*

℟. **I will praise your name for ever, my king and my God.**
  or:
Alleluia.

The LORD is gracious and merciful,
  slow to anger and of great kindness.
The LORD is good to all
  and compassionate toward all his
  works. ℟.

Let all your works give you thanks, O
  LORD,
  and let your faithful ones bless you.
Let them discourse of the glory of your

kingdom
  and speak of your might. ℟.

Let them make known your might to the
  children of Adam,
  and the glorious splendor of your
  kingdom.
Your kingdom is a kingdom for all ages,
  and your dominion endures through
  all generations. ℟.

READING II   *Revelation 21:1-5a*

Then I, John, saw a new heaven and a new earth. The former heaven and the former earth had passed away, and the sea was no more. I also saw the holy city, a new Jerusalem, coming down out of heaven from God, prepared as a bride adorned for her husband. I heard a loud voice from the throne saying, "Behold, God's dwelling is with the human race. He will dwell with them and they will be his people and God himself will always be with them as their God. He will wipe every tear from their eyes, and there shall be no more death or mourning, wailing or pain, for the old order has passed away." The One who sat on the throne said, "Behold, I make all things new."

GOSPEL   *John 13:31-33a, 34-35*

When Judas had left them, Jesus said, "Now is the Son of Man glorified, and God is glorified in him. If God is glorified in him, God will also glorify him in himself, and God will glorify him at once. My children, I will be with you only a little while longer. I give you a new commandment: love one another. As I have loved you, so you also should love one another. This is how all will know that you are my disciples, if you have love for one another."

982 SIXTH SUNDAY OF EASTER / A

READING I   *Acts 8:5-8, 14-17 / 55*

Philip went down to the city of Samaria and proclaimed the Christ to them. With one accord, the crowds paid attention to what was said by Philip when they heard it and saw the signs he was doing. For unclean spirits, crying out in a loud voice, came out of many possessed people, and many paralyzed or crippled people were cured. There was great joy in that city.

Now when the apostles in Jerusalem heard that Samaria had accepted the word of God, they sent them Peter and John, who went down and prayed for them, that they might receive the Holy Spirit, for it had not yet fallen upon any of them; they had only been baptized in the name of the Lord Jesus. Then they laid hands on them and they received the Holy Spirit.

RESPONSORIAL PSALM   *Psalm 66:1-3, 4-5, 6-7, 16, 20*

℟. **Let all the earth cry out to God with joy.**
>   *or:*
Alleluia.

Shout joyfully to God, all the earth,
>   sing praise to the glory of his name;
proclaim his glorious praise.
>   Say to God, "How tremendous are
>   your deeds! ℟.

Let all on earth worship and sing praise
>   to you,
>   sing praise to your name!"
Come and see the works of God,
>   his tremendous deeds among the
>   children of Adam. ℟.

He has changed the sea into dry land;
>   through the river they passed on foot;
therefore let us rejoice in him.
>   He rules by his might forever. ℟.

Hear now, all you who fear God, while
>   I declare
>   what he has done for me.
Blessed be God who refused me not
>   my prayer or his kindness! ℟.

READING II   *1 Peter 3:15-18*

Beloved: Sanctify Christ as Lord in your hearts. Always be ready to give an explanation to anyone who asks you for a reason for your hope, but do it with gentleness and reverence, keeping your conscience clear, so that, when you are maligned, those who defame your good conduct in Christ may themselves be put to shame. For it is better to suffer for doing good, if that be the will of God, than for doing evil. For Christ also suffered for sins once, the righteous for the sake of the unrighteous, that he might lead you to God. Put to death in the flesh, he was brought to life in the Spirit.

GOSPEL   *John 14:15-21*

Jesus said to his disciples: "If you love me, you will keep my commandments. And I will ask the Father, and he will give you another Advocate to be with you always, the Spirit of truth, whom the world cannot accept, because it neither sees nor knows him. But you know him, because he remains with you, and will be in you. I will not leave you orphans; I will come to you. In a little while the world will no longer see me, but you will see me, because I live and you will live. On that day you will realize that I am in my Father and you are in me and I in you. Whoever has my commandments and observes them is the one who loves me. And whoever loves me will be loved by my Father, and I will love him and reveal myself to him."

SIXTH SUNDAY OF EASTER / B   983

READING I   *Acts 10:25-26, 34-35, 44-48 / 56*

When Peter entered, Cornelius met him and, falling at his feet, paid him homage. Peter, however, raised him up, saying, "Get up. I myself am also a human being."

Then Peter proceeded to speak and said, "In truth, I see that God shows no partiality. Rather, in every nation whoever fears him and acts uprightly is acceptable to him."

While Peter was still speaking these things, the Holy Spirit fell upon all who were listening to the word. The circumcised believers who had accompanied Peter were astounded that the gift of the Holy Spirit should have been poured out on the Gentiles also, for they could hear them speaking in tongues and glorifying God. Then Peter responded, "Can anyone withhold the water for baptizing these people, who have received the Holy Spirit even as we have?" He ordered them to be baptized in the name of Jesus Christ.

RESPONSORIAL PSALM   *Psalm 98:1, 2-3, 3-4*

℟. **The Lord has revealed to the nations his saving power.**
    or:
Alleluia.

Sing to the LORD a new song,
    for he has done wondrous deeds;
His right hand has won victory for him,
    his holy arm. ℟.

The LORD has made his salvation known:
    in the sight of the nations he has
        revealed his justice.

He has remembered his kindness and his
        faithfulness
    toward the house of Israel. ℟.

All the ends of the earth have seen
    the salvation by our God.
Sing joyfully to the LORD, all you lands;
    break into song; sing praise. ℟.

READING II   *1 John 4:7-10*

Beloved, let us love one another, because love is of God; everyone who loves is begotten by God and knows God. Whoever is without love does not know God, for God is love. In this way the love of God was revealed to us: God sent his only Son into the world so that we might have life through him. In this is love: not that we have loved God, but that he loved us and sent his Son as expiation for our sins.

GOSPEL   *John 15:9-17*

Jesus said to his disciples: "As the Father loves me, so I also love you. Remain in my love. If you keep my commandments, you will remain in my love, just as I have kept my Father's commandments and remain in his love.

"I have told you this so that my joy may be in you and your joy might be complete.

This is my commandment: love one another as I love you. No one has greater love than this, to lay down one's life for one's friends. You are my friends if you do what I command you. I no longer call you slaves, because a slave does not know what his master is doing. I have called you friends, because I have told you everything I have heard from my Father. It was not you who chose me, but I who chose you and appointed you to go and bear fruit that will remain, so that whatever you ask the Father in my name he may give you. This I command you: love one another."

984 SIXTH SUNDAY OF EASTER / C

READING I
Acts 15:1-2, 22-29 / 57

Some who had come down from Judea were instructing the brothers, "Unless you are circumcised according to the Mosaic practice, you cannot be saved." Because there arose no little dissension and debate by Paul and Barnabas with them, it was decided that Paul, Barnabas, and some of the others should go up to Jerusalem to the apostles and elders about this question.

The apostles and elders, in agreement with the whole church, decided to choose representatives and to send them to Antioch with Paul and Barnabas. The ones chosen were Judas, who was called Barsabbas, and Silas, leaders among the brothers. This is the letter delivered by them:

"The apostles and the elders, your brothers, to the brothers in Antioch, Syria, and Cilicia of Gentile origin: greetings. Since we have heard that some of our number who went out without any mandate from us have upset you with their teachings and disturbed your peace of mind, we have with one accord decided to choose representatives and to send them to you along with our beloved Barnabas and Paul, who have dedicated their lives to the name of our Lord Jesus Christ. So we are sending Judas and Silas who will also convey this same message by word of mouth: 'It is the decision of the Holy Spirit and of us not to place on you any burden beyond these necessities, namely, to abstain from meat sacrificed to idols, from blood, from meats of strangled animals, and from unlawful marriage. If you keep free of these, you will be doing what is right. Farewell.'"

RESPONSORIAL PSALM
Psalm 67:2-3, 5, 6, 8

℟. **O God, let all the nations praise you!**
or:
Alleluia.

May God have pity on us and bless us;
    may he let his face shine upon us.
So may your way be known upon earth;
    among all nations, your salvation. ℟.

May the nations be glad and exult
    because you rule the peoples in
      equity;

the nations on the earth you guide. ℟.

May the peoples praise you, O God;
    may all the peoples praise you!
May God bless us,
    and may all the ends of the earth
      fear him! ℟.

READING II
Revelation 21:10-14, 22-23

The angel took me in spirit to a great, high mountain and showed me the holy city Jerusalem coming down out of heaven from God. It gleamed with the splendor of God. Its radiance was like that of a precious stone, like jasper, clear as crystal. It had a massive, high wall, with twelve gates where twelve angels were stationed and on which names were inscribed, the names of the twelve tribes of the Israelites. There were three gates facing east, three north, three south, and three west. The wall of the city had twelve courses of stones as its foundation, on which were inscribed the twelve names of the twelve apostles of the Lamb.

I saw no temple in the city for its temple is the Lord God almighty and the Lamb. The city had no need of sun or moon to shine on it, for the glory of God gave it light, and its lamp was the Lamb.

GOSPEL   *John 14:23-29*

Jesus said to his disciples: "Whoever loves me will keep my word, and my Father will love him, and we will come to him and make our dwelling with him. Whoever does not love me does not keep my words; yet the word you hear is not mine but that of the Father who sent me.

"I have told you this while I am with you. The Advocate, the Holy Spirit, whom the Father will send in my name, will teach you everything and remind you of all that I told you. Peace I leave with you; my peace I give to you. Not as the world gives do I give it to you. Do not let your hearts be troubled or afraid. You heard me tell you, 'I am going away and I will come back to you.' If you loved me, you would rejoice that I am going to the Father; for the Father is greater than I. And now I have told you this before it happens, so that when it happens you may believe."

THE ASCENSION OF THE LORD / ABC   985

READING I   *Acts 1:1-11 / 58*

In the first book, Theophilus, I dealt with all that Jesus did and taught until the day he was taken up, after giving instructions through the Holy Spirit to the apostles whom he had chosen. He presented himself alive to them by many proofs after he had suffered, appearing to them during forty days and speaking about the kingdom of God. While meeting with them, he enjoined them not to depart from Jerusalem, but to wait for "the promise of the Father about which you have heard me speak; for John baptized with water, but in a few days you will be baptized with the Holy Spirit."

When they had gathered together they asked him, "Lord, are you at this time going to restore the kingdom to Israel?" He answered them, "It is not for you to know the times or seasons that the Father has established by his own authority. But you will receive power when the Holy Spirit comes upon you, and you will be my witnesses in Jerusalem, throughout Judea and Samaria, and to the ends of the earth." When he had said this, as they were looking on, he was lifted up, and a cloud took him from their sight. While they were looking intently at the sky as he was going, suddenly two men dressed in white garments stood beside them. They said, "Men of Galilee, why are you standing there looking at the sky? This Jesus who has been taken up from you into heaven will return in the same way as you have seen him going into heaven."

RESPONSORIAL PSALM   *Psalm 47:2-3, 6-7, 8-9*

℟. **God mounts his throne to shouts of joy: a blare of trumpets for the Lord.**
   or:
Alleluia.

All you peoples, clap your hands,
   shout to God with cries of gladness,
For the LORD, the Most High, the
   awesome,
   is the great king over all the earth. ℟.

God mounts his throne amid shouts of
   joy;
   the LORD, amid trumpet blasts.

Sing praise to God, sing praise;
   sing praise to our king, sing praise. ℟.

For king of all the earth is God;
   sing hymns of praise.
God reigns over the nations,
   God sits upon his holy throne. ℟.

READING II
Ephesians 1:17-23

Brothers and sisters: May the God of our Lord Jesus Christ, the Father of glory, give you a Spirit of wisdom and revelation resulting in knowledge of him. May the eyes of your hearts be enlightened, that you may know what is the hope that belongs to his call, what are the riches of glory in his inheritance among the holy ones, and what is the surpassing greatness of his power for us who believe, in accord with the exercise of his great might, which he worked in Christ, raising him from the dead and seating him at his right hand in the heavens, far above every principality, authority, power, and dominion, and every name that is named not only in this age but also in the one to come. And he put all things beneath his feet and gave him as head over all things to the church, which is his body, the fullness of the one who fills all things in every way.

Or:

READING II / B
Ephesians 4:1-13 or 4:1-7, 11-13
For short form read only the parts in brackets.

[Brothers and sisters, I, a prisoner for the Lord, urge you to live in a manner worthy of the call you have received, with all humility and gentleness, with patience, bearing with one another through love, striving to preserve the unity of the spirit through the bond of peace: one body and one Spirit, as you were also called to the one hope of your call; one Lord, one faith, one baptism; one God and Father of all, who is over all and through all and in all.

But grace was given to each of us according to the measure of Christ's gift.]
Therefore, it says:
"He ascended on high and took prisoners captive;
he gave gifts to men."
What does "he ascended" mean except that he also descended into the lower regions of the earth? The one who descended is also the one who ascended far above all the heavens, that he might fill all things.

[And he gave some as apostles, others as prophets, others as evangelists, others as pastors and teachers, to equip the holy ones for the work of ministry, for building up the body of Christ, until we all attain to the unity of faith and knowledge of the Son of God, to mature manhood, to the extent of the full stature of Christ.]

Or:

READING II / C
Hebrews 9:24-28; 10:19-23

Christ did not enter into a sanctuary made by hands, a copy of the true one, but heaven itself, that he might now appear before God on our behalf. Not that he might offer himself repeatedly, as the high priest enters each year into the sanctuary with blood that is not his own; if that were so, he would have had to suffer repeatedly from the foundation of the world. But now once for all he has appeared at the end of the ages to take away sin by his sacrifice. Just as it is appointed that men and women die once, and after this the judgment, so also Christ, offered once to take away the sins of many, will appear a second time, not to take away sin but to bring salvation to those who eagerly await him.

Therefore, brothers and sisters, since through the blood of Jesus we have confidence of entrance into the sanctuary by the new and living way he opened for us through the veil, that is, his flesh, and since we have "a great priest over the house of God," let us approach with a sincere heart and in absolute trust, with our hearts sprinkled clean from an evil conscience and our bodies washed in pure water. Let us hold unwaveringly to our confession that gives us hope, for he who made the promise is trustworthy.

GOSPEL / A
Matthew 28:16-20

The eleven disciples went to Galilee, to the mountain to which Jesus had ordered them. When they saw him, they worshiped, but they doubted. Then Jesus approached and said to them, "All power in heaven and on earth has been given to me. Go, therefore, and make disciples of all nations, baptizing them in the name of the Father, and of the Son, and of the Holy Spirit, teaching them to observe all that I have commanded you. And behold, I am with you always, until the end of the age."

GOSPEL / B   *Mark 16:15-20*

Jesus said to his disciples: "Go into the whole world and proclaim the gospel to every creature. Whoever believes and is baptized will be saved; whoever does not believe will be condemned. These signs will accompany those who believe: in my name they will drive out demons, they will speak new languages. They will pick up serpents with their hands, and if they drink any deadly thing, it will not harm them. They will lay hands on the sick, and they will recover."

So then the Lord Jesus, after he spoke to them, was taken up into heaven and took his seat at the right hand of God. But they went forth and preached everywhere, while the Lord worked with them and confirmed the word through accompanying signs.

GOSPEL / C   *Luke 24:46-53*

Jesus said to his disciples: "Thus it is written that the Christ would suffer and rise from the dead on the third day and that repentance, for the forgiveness of sins, would be preached in his name to all the nations, beginning from Jerusalem. You are witnesses of these things. And behold I am sending the promise of my Father upon you; but stay in the city until you are clothed with power from on high."

Then he led them out as far as Bethany, raised his hands, and blessed them. As he blessed them he parted from them and was taken up to heaven. They did him homage and then returned to Jerusalem with great joy, and they were continually in the temple praising God.

SEVENTH SUNDAY OF EASTER / A   986

READING I   *Acts 1:12-14 / 59*

After Jesus had been taken up to heaven the apostles returned to Jerusalem from the mount called Olivet, which is near Jerusalem, a sabbath day's journey away.

When they entered the city they went to the upper room where they were staying, Peter and John and James and Andrew, Philip and Thomas, Bartholomew and Matthew, James son of Alphaeus, Simon the Zealot, and Judas son of James. All these devoted themselves with one accord to prayer, together with some women, and Mary the mother of Jesus, and his brothers.

RESPONSORIAL PSALM   *Psalm 27:1, 4, 7-8*

℟. I believe that I shall see the good things of the Lord in the land of the living.
  or:
Alleluia.

The LORD is my light and my salvation;
  whom should I fear?
The LORD is my life's refuge;
  of whom should I be afraid? ℟.

One thing I ask of the LORD; this I seek:
  To dwell in the house of the LORD
all the days of my life,

That I may gaze on the loveliness of
  the LORD
and contemplate his temple. ℟.

Hear, O Lord, the sound of my call;
  have pity on me, and answer me.
Of you my heart speaks; you my glance
  seeks. ℟.

READING II   *1 Peter 4:13-16*

Beloved: Rejoice to the extent that you share in the sufferings of Christ, so that when his glory is revealed you may also rejoice exultantly. If you are insulted for the name of Christ, blessed are you, for the Spirit of glory and of God rests upon you. But let no one among you be made to suffer as a murderer, a thief, an evildoer, or as an intriguer. But whoever is made to suffer as a Christian should not be ashamed but glorify God because of the name.

GOSPEL   *John 17:1-11a*
Jesus raised his eyes to heaven and said, "Father, the hour has come. Give glory to your son, so that your son may glorify you, just as you gave him authority over all people, so that your son may give eternal life to all you gave him. Now this is eternal life, that they should know you, the only true God, and the one whom you sent, Jesus Christ. I glorified you on earth by accomplishing the work that you gave me to do. Now glorify me, Father, with you, with the glory that I had with you before the world began.

"I revealed your name to those whom you gave me out of the world. They belonged to you, and you gave them to me, and they have kept your word. Now they know that everything you gave me is from you, because the words you gave to me I have given to them, and they accepted them and truly understood that I came from you, and they have believed that you sent me. I pray for them. I do not pray for the world but for the ones you have given me, because they are yours, and everything of mine is yours and everything of yours is mine, and I have been glorified in them. And now I will no longer be in the world, but they are in the world, while I am coming to you."

987   SEVENTH SUNDAY OF EASTER / B

READING I   *Acts 1:15-17, 20a, 20c-26 / 60*
Peter stood up in the midst of the brothers (there was a group of about one hundred and twenty persons in the one place). He said, "My brothers, the Scripture had to be fulfilled which the Holy Spirit spoke beforehand through the mouth of David, concerning Judas, who was the guide for those who arrested Jesus. He was numbered among us and was allotted a share in this ministry. "For it is written in the Book of Psalms:
'May another take his office.'

"Therefore, it is necessary that one of the men who accompanied us the whole time the Lord Jesus came and went among us, beginning from the baptism of John until the day on which he was taken up from us, become with us a witness to his resurrection." So they proposed two, Judas called Barsabbas, who was also known as Justus, and Matthias. Then they prayed, "You, Lord, who know the hearts of all, show which one of these two you have chosen to take the place in this apostolic ministry from which Judas turned away to go to his own place." Then they gave lots to them, and the lot fell upon Matthias, and he was counted with the eleven apostles.

RESPONSORIAL PSALM   *Psalm 103:1-2, 11-12, 19-20*
℟. **The Lord has set his throne in heaven.**
or:
Alleluia.

Bless the LORD, O my soul;
and all my being, bless his holy name.
Bless the LORD, O my soul,
and forget not all his benefits. ℟.

For as the heavens are high above the earth,
so surpassing is his kindness toward those who fear him.

As far as the east is from the west,
so far has he put our transgressions from us. ℟.

The LORD has established his throne in heaven,
and his kingdom rules over all.
Bless the LORD, all you his angels,
you mighty in strength, who do his bidding. ℟.

READING II   *1 John 4:11-16*

Beloved, if God so loved us, we also must love one another. No one has ever seen God. Yet, if we love one another, God remains in us, and his love is brought to perfection in us. This is how we know that we remain in him and he in us, that he has given us of his Spirit. Moreover, we have seen and testify that the Father sent his Son as savior of the world. Whoever acknowledges that Jesus is the Son of God, God remains in him and he in God. We have come to know and to believe in the love God has for us.

God is love, and whoever remains in love remains in God and God in him.

GOSPEL   *John 17:11b-19*

Lifting up his eyes to heaven, Jesus prayed saying: "Holy Father, keep them in your name that you have given me, so that they may be one just as we are one. When I was with them I protected them in your name that you gave me, and I guarded them, and none of them was lost except the son of destruction, in order that the Scripture might be fulfilled. But now I am coming to you. I speak this in the world so that they may share my joy completely. I gave them your word, and the world hated them, because they do not belong to the world any more than I belong to the world. I do not ask that you take them out of the world but that you keep them from the evil one. They do not belong to the world any more than I belong to the world. Consecrate them in the truth. Your word is truth. As you sent me into the world, so I sent them into the world. And I consecrate myself for them, so that they also may be consecrated in truth."

SEVENTH SUNDAY OF EASTER / C   988

READING I   *Acts 7:55-60 / 61*

Stephen, filled with the Holy Spirit, looked up intently to heaven and saw the glory of God and Jesus standing at the right hand of God, and Stephen said, "Behold, I see the heavens opened and the Son of Man standing at the right hand of God." But they cried out in a loud voice, covered their ears, and rushed upon him together. They threw him out of the city, and began to stone him. The witnesses laid down their cloaks at the feet of a young man named Saul. As they were stoning Stephen, he called out, "Lord Jesus, receive my spirit." Then he fell to his knees and cried out in a loud voice, "Lord, do not hold this sin against them;" and when he said this, he fell asleep.

RESPONSORIAL PSALM   *Psalm 97:1-2, 6-7, 9*

℞. **The Lord is king, the most high over all the earth.**
   or:
Alleluia.

The LORD is king; let the earth rejoice;
   let the many islands be glad.
Justice and judgment are the foundation
   of his throne. ℞.

The heavens proclaim his justice,

and all peoples see his glory.
All gods are prostrate before him. ℞.

You, O LORD, are the Most High over
   all the earth,
exalted far above all gods. ℞.

READING II   *Revelation 22:12-14, 16-17, 20*

I, John, heard a voice saying to me: "Behold, I am coming soon. I bring with me the recompense I will give to each according to his deeds. I am the Alpha and the Omega, the first and the last, the beginning and the end."

Blessed are they who wash their robes so as to have the right to the tree of life and enter the city through its gates.

"I, Jesus, sent my angel to give you this testimony for the churches. I am the root and offspring of David, the bright morning star."

The Spirit and the bride say, "Come." Let the hearer say, "Come." Let the one who thirsts come forward, and the one who wants it receive the gift of life-giving water.

The one who gives this testimony says, "Yes, I am coming soon." Amen! Come, Lord Jesus!

GOSPEL   *John 17:20-26*

Lifting up his eyes to heaven, Jesus prayed saying: "Holy Father, I pray not only for them, but also for those who will believe in me through their word, so that they may all be one, as you, Father, are in me and I in you, that they also may be in us, that the world may believe that you sent me. And I have given them the glory you gave me, so that they may be one, as we are one, I in them and you in me, that they may be brought to perfection as one, that the world may know that you sent me, and that you loved them even as you loved me. Father, they are your gift to me. I wish that where I am they also may be with me, that they may see my glory that you gave me, because you loved me before the foundation of the world. Righteous Father, the world also does not know you, but I know you, and they know that you sent me. I made known to them your name and I will make it known, that the love with which you loved me may be in them and I in them."

989   PENTECOST / VIGIL / ABC

READING I   *Genesis 11:1-9 / 62*

The whole world spoke the same language, using the same words. While the people were migrating in the east, they came upon a valley in the land of Shinar and settled there. They said to one another, "Come, let us mold bricks and harden them with fire." They used bricks for stone, and bitumen for mortar. Then they said, "Come, let us build ourselves a city and a tower with its top in the sky, and so make a name for ourselves; otherwise we shall be scattered all over the earth."

The LORD came down to see the city and the tower that the people had built. Then the LORD said: "If now, while they are one people, all speaking the same language, they have started to do this, nothing will later stop them from doing whatever they presume to do. Let us then go down there and confuse their language, so that one will not understand what another says." Thus the LORD scattered them from there all over the earth, and they stopped building the city. That is why it was called Babel, because there the LORD confused the speech of all the world. It was from that place that he scattered them all over the earth.

Or:

READING I   *Exodus 19:3-8a, 16-20b*

Moses went up the mountain to God. Then the LORD called to him and said, "Thus shall you say to the house of Jacob; tell the Israelites: You have seen for yourselves how I treated the Egyptians and how I bore you up on eagle wings and brought you here to myself. Therefore, if you hearken to my voice and keep my covenant, you shall be my special possession, dearer to me than all other people, though all the earth is mine. You shall be to me a kingdom of priests, a holy nation. That is what you must tell the Israelites." So Moses went and summoned the elders of the people. When he set before them all that the LORD had ordered him to tell them, the people all answered together, "Everything the LORD has said, we will do."

On the morning of the third day there were peals of thunder and lightning, and a heavy cloud over the mountain, and a very loud trumpet blast, so that all the people in the camp trembled. But Moses led the people out of the camp to meet God, and they stationed themselves at the foot of the mountain. Mount Sinai was all wrapped in smoke, for the LORD came down upon it in fire. The smoke rose from it as though from a furnace, and the whole mountain trembled violently. The trumpet blast grew louder and louder, while Moses was speaking, and God answering him with thunder.

When the LORD came down to the top of Mount Sinai, he summoned Moses to the top of the mountain.

Or:

READING I *Ezekiel 37:1-14*

The hand of the LORD came upon me, and he led me out in the spirit of the LORD and set me in the center of the plain, which was now filled with bones. He made me walk among the bones in every direction so that I saw how many they were on the surface of the plain. How dry they were! He asked me: Son of man, can these bones come to life? I answered, "Lord GOD, you alone know that." Then he said to me: Prophesy over these bones, and say to them: Dry bones, hear the word of the LORD! Thus says the Lord GOD to these bones: See! I will bring spirit into you, that you may come to life. I will put sinews upon you, make flesh grow over you, cover you with skin, and put spirit in you so that you may come to life and know that I am the LORD. I, Ezekiel, prophesied as I had been told, and even as I was prophesying I heard a noise; it was a rattling as the bones came together, bone joining bone. I saw the sinews and the flesh come upon them, and the skin cover them, but there was no spirit in them. Then the LORD said to me: Prophesy to the spirit, prophesy, son of man, and say to the spirit: Thus says the Lord GOD: From the four winds come, O spirit, and breathe into these slain that they may come to life. I prophesied as he told me, and the spirit came into them; they came alive and stood upright, a vast army. Then he said to me: Son of man, these bones are the whole house of Israel. They have been saying, "Our bones are dried up, our hope is lost, and we are cut off." Therefore, prophesy and say to them: Thus says the Lord GOD: O my people, I will open your graves and have you rise from them, and bring you back to the land of Israel. Then you shall know that I am the LORD, when I open your graves and have you rise from them, O my people! I will put my spirit in you that you may live, and I will settle you upon your land; thus you shall know that I am the LORD. I have promised, and I will do it, says the LORD.

Or:

READING I *Joel 3:1-5*

Thus says the Lord: I will pour out my spirit upon all flesh. Your sons and daughters shall prophesy, your old men shall dream dreams, your young men shall see visions; even upon the servants and the handmaids, in those days, I will pour out my spirit. And I will work wonders in the heavens and on the earth, blood, fire, and columns of smoke; the sun will be turned to darkness, and the moon to blood, at the coming of the day of the LORD, the great and terrible day. Then everyone shall be rescued who calls on the name of the LORD; for on Mount Zion there shall be a remnant, as the LORD has said, and in Jerusalem survivors whom the LORD shall call.

RESPONSORIAL PSALM *Psalm 104:1-2, 24, 35, 27-28, 29, 30*

℞. **Lord, send out your Spirit, and renew the face of the earth.**
  or:
Alleluia.

Bless the LORD, O my soul!
  O LORD, my God, you are great
    indeed!
You are clothed with majesty and glory,
  robed in light as with a cloak. ℞.

How manifold are your works, O LORD!
  In wisdom you have wrought them
    all—
the earth is full of your creatures;
  bless the LORD, O my soul!
    Alleluia. ℞.

Creatures all look to you
  to give them food in due time.
When you give it to them, they gather it;
  when you open your hand, they are
    filled with good things. ℞.

If you take away their breath, they
    perish
  and return to their dust.
When you send forth your spirit, they
    are created,
  and you renew the face of the
    earth. ℞.

READING II
Romans 8:22-27

Brothers and sisters: We know that all creation is groaning in labor pains even until now; and not only that, but we ourselves, who have the firstfruits of the Spirit, we also groan within ourselves as we wait for adoption, the redemption of our bodies. For in hope we were saved. Now hope that sees is not hope. For who hopes for what one sees? But if we hope for what we do not see, we wait with endurance.

In the same way, the Spirit too comes to the aid of our weakness; for we do not know how to pray as we ought, but the Spirit himself intercedes with inexpressible groanings. And the one who searches hearts knows what is the intention of the Spirit, because he intercedes for the holy ones according to God's will.

GOSPEL
John 7:37-39

On the last and greatest day of the feast, Jesus stood up and exclaimed, "Let anyone who thirsts come to me and drink. As Scripture says:

'Rivers of living water will flow from within him' who believes in me."

He said this in reference to the Spirit that those who came to believe in him were to receive. There was, of course, no Spirit yet, because Jesus had not yet been glorified.

990 PENTECOST SUNDAY / ABC

READING I
Acts 2:1-11 / 63

When the time for Pentecost was fulfilled, they were all in one place together. And suddenly there came from the sky a noise like a strong driving wind, and it filled the entire house in which they were. Then there appeared to them tongues as of fire, which parted and came to rest on each one of them. And they were all filled with the Holy Spirit and began to speak in different tongues, as the Spirit enabled them to proclaim.

Now there were devout Jews from every nation under heaven staying in Jerusalem. At this sound, they gathered in a large crowd, but they were confused because each one heard them speaking in his own language. They were astounded, and in amazement they asked, "Are not all these people who are speaking Galileans? Then how does each of us hear them in his native language? We are Parthians, Medes, and Elamites, inhabitants of Mesopotamia, Judea and Cappadocia, Pontus and Asia, Phrygia and Pamphylia, Egypt and the districts of Libya near Cyrene, as well as travelers from Rome, both Jews and converts to Judaism, Cretans and Arabs, yet we hear them speaking in our own tongues of the mighty acts of God."

RESPONSORIAL PSALM
Psalm 104:1, 24, 29-30, 31, 34

℟. Lord, send out your Spirit, and renew the face of the earth.
or:
Alleluia.

Bless the LORD, O my soul!
O LORD, my God, you are great
indeed!
How manifold are your works, O Lord!
the earth is full of your creatures. ℟.

May the glory of the LORD endure
forever;
may the LORD be glad in his works!

Pleasing to him be my theme;
I will be glad in the LORD. ℟.

If you take away their breath, they perish
and return to their dust.
When you send forth your spirit, they are
created,
and you renew the face of the
earth. ℟.

READING II / ABC
1 Corinthians 12:3b-7, 12-13

Brothers and sisters: No one can say, "Jesus is Lord," except by the Holy Spirit. There are different kinds of spiritual gifts but the same Spirit; there are different forms of service but the same Lord; there are different workings but the same God who produces all of them in everyone. To each individual the manifestation of the Spirit is given for some benefit.

As a body is one though it has many parts, and all the parts of the body, though many, are one body, so also Christ. For in one Spirit we were all baptized into one body, whether Jews or Greeks, slaves or free persons, and we were all given to drink of one Spirit.

Or:

READING II / B
Galatians 5:16-25

Brothers and sisters, live by the Spirit and you will certainly not gratify the desire of the flesh. For the flesh has desires against the Spirit, and the Spirit against the flesh; these are opposed to each other, so that you may not do what you want. But if you are guided by the Spirit, you are not under the law. Now the works of the flesh are obvious: immorality, impurity, lust, idolatry, sorcery, hatreds, rivalry, jealousy, outbursts of fury, acts of selfishness, dissensions, factions, occasions of envy, drinking bouts, orgies, and the like. I warn you, as I warned you before, that those who do such things will not inherit the kingdom of God. In contrast, the fruit of the Spirit is love, joy, peace, patience, kindness, generosity, faithfulness, gentleness, self-control. Against such there is no law. Now those who belong to Christ Jesus have crucified their flesh with its passions and desires. If we live in the Spirit, let us also follow the Spirit.

Or:

READING II / C
Romans 8:8-17

Brothers and sisters: Those who are in the flesh cannot please God. But you are not in the flesh; on the contrary, you are in the spirit, if only the Spirit of God dwells in you. Whoever does not have the Spirit of Christ does not belong to him. But if Christ is in you, although the body is dead because of sin, the spirit is alive because of righteousness. If the Spirit of the one who raised Jesus from the dead dwells in you, the one who raised Christ from the dead will give life to your mortal bodies also, through his Spirit that dwells in you. Consequently, brothers and sisters, we are not debtors to the flesh, to live according to the flesh. For if you live according to the flesh, you will die, but if by the Spirit you put to death the deeds of the body, you will live.

For those who are led by the Spirit of God are sons of God. For you did not receive a spirit of slavery to fall back into fear, but you received a Spirit of adoption, through whom we cry, "Abba, Father!" The Spirit himself bears witness with our spirit that we are children of God, and if children, then heirs, heirs of God and joint heirs with Christ, if only we suffer with him so that we may also be glorified with him.

SEQUENCE
See no. 464

GOSPEL / ABC
John 20:19-23

On the evening of that first day of the week, when the doors were locked, where the disciples were, for fear of the Jews, Jesus came and stood in their midst and said to them, "Peace be with you." When he had said this, he showed them his hands and his side. The disciples rejoiced when they saw the Lord. Jesus said to them again, "Peace be with you. As the Father has sent me, so I send you." And when he had said this, he breathed on them and said to them, "Receive the Holy Spirit. Whose sins you forgive are forgiven them, and whose sins you retain are retained."

Or:

GOSPEL / B *John 15:26-27; 16:12-15*

Jesus said to his disciples: "When the Advocate comes whom I will send you from the Father, the Spirit of truth that proceeds from the Father, he will testify to me. And you also testify, because you have been with me from the beginning.

"I have much more to tell you, but you cannot bear it now. But when he comes, the Spirit of truth, he will guide you to all truth. He will not speak on his own, but he will speak what he hears, and will declare to you the things that are coming. He will glorify me, because he will take from what is mine and declare it to you. Everything that the Father has is mine; for this reason I told you that he will take from what is mine and declare it to you."

Or:

GOSPEL / C *John 14:15-16, 23b-26*

Jesus said to his disciples: "If you love me, you will keep my commandments. And I will ask the Father, and he will give you another Advocate to be with you always. "Whoever loves me will keep my word, and my Father will love him, and we will come to him and make our dwelling with him. Those who do not love me do not keep my words; yet the word you hear is not mine but that of the Father who sent me. "I have told you this while I am with you. The Advocate, the Holy Spirit whom the Father will send in my name, will teach you everything and remind you of all that I told you."

Ordinary Time

When the church assembles, there is always time to read from the scriptures. This is the book the church carries: the Law and the prophets, the
books of wisdom and psalms, the letters and writings of Paul and of the
other apostles, the gospels themselves. In various places and times the
readings from scripture have been arranged so that the various Sundays
have their assigned texts. This book of assigned scriptures is the lectionary.
In the present Roman lectionary the scriptures are marked for reading
through a cycle of three years.

Most of each year is called "Ordinary Time" or "Sundays of the Year."
These are the weeks between the Christmas season and Lent, and the long
period between Pentecost (the conclusion of the Easter season) and
Advent (usually the first Sunday in December). On the Sundays of
Ordinary Time, the lectionary has us read in order through the letters of
the New Testament and the gospels. In the first year of the cycle, the
gospel of Matthew is read from beginning to end; in the second year,
Mark; in the third, Luke. Likewise, each Sunday finds the church picking
up the reading of one of the letters of the New Testament roughly where
the previous week's reading concluded. At present, the first reading at
Sunday Mass in Ordinary Time is chosen from the Hebrew Scriptures;
these texts show the richness and the continuity of faith.

Sunday by Sunday, year after year, the church reads through its book
in the weeks of Ordinary Time. Each Christian, each local church, each
generation listens and so finds its own life in God's word.

The Church assembles around the scriptures and around the Lord's
table on Sunday. This day is called by Christians the Lord's Day. Whether
the church is in Ordinary Time or in the seasons of Advent/Christmas or
Lent/Easter, the Lord's Day is kept holy; it is the original feast day. The
rhythm of the weekdays and the Sunday is the basic rhythm of life in
Christian churches. The practices with which a church keeps the Lord's
Day vary, but always and everywhere Christians assemble on this day so
that the church may listen to God's word. Through the days of the week,
the Sunday's scriptures are to be for reflection and nourishment as they are
repeated and pondered in the households of the assembly.

992 SUNDAY AFTER PENTECOST—TRINITY SUNDAY / A

READING I
Exodus 34:4b-6, 8-9 / 164

Early in the morning Moses went up Mount Sinai as the LORD had commanded him, taking along the two stone tablets.

Having come down in a cloud, the LORD stood with Moses there and proclaimed his name, "LORD." Thus the LORD passed before him and cried out, "The LORD, the LORD, a merciful and gracious God, slow to anger and rich in kindness and fidelity." Moses at once bowed down to the ground in worship. Then he said, "If I find favor with you, O Lord, do come along in our company. This is indeed a stiff-necked people; yet pardon our wickedness and sins, and receive us as your own."

RESPONSORIAL PSALM
Daniel 3:52, 53, 54, 55

℞. **Glory and praise for ever!**

Blessed are you, O Lord, the God of our fathers,
praiseworthy and exalted above all forever;
and blessed is your holy and glorious name,
praiseworthy and exalted above all for all ages. ℞.

Blessed are you in the temple of your holy glory,
praiseworthy and glorious above all forever. ℞.

Blessed are you on the throne of your kingdom,
praiseworthy and exalted above all forever. ℞.

Blessed are you who look into the depths from your throne upon the cherubim,
praiseworthy and exalted above all forever. ℞.

READING II
2 Corinthians 13:11-13

Brothers and sisters, rejoice. Mend your ways, encourage one another, agree with one another, live in peace, and the God of love and peace will be with you. Greet one another with a holy kiss. All the holy ones greet you.

The grace of the Lord Jesus Christ and the love of God and the fellowship of the Holy Spirit be with all of you.

GOSPEL
John 3:16-18

God so loved the world that he gave his only Son, so that everyone who believes in him might not perish but might have eternal life. For God did not send his Son into the world to condemn the world, but that the world might be saved through him. Whoever believes in him will not be condemned, but whoever does not believe has already been condemned, because he has not believed in the name of the only Son of God.

993 SUNDAY AFTER PENTECOST—TRINITY SUNDAY / B

READING I
Deuteronomy 4:32-34, 39-40 / 165

Moses said to the people: "Ask now of the days of old, before your time, ever since God created man upon the earth; ask from one end of the sky to the other: Did anything so great ever happen before? Was it ever heard of? Did a people ever hear the voice of God speaking from the midst of fire, as you did, and live? Or did any god venture to go and take a nation for himself from the midst of another nation, by testings, by signs and wonders, by war, with strong hand and outstretched arm, and by great terrors, all of which the LORD, your God, did for you in Egypt before your very eyes? This is why you must now know, and fix in your heart, that the LORD is God in the heavens above and on earth below, and that there is no other. You must keep his statutes and commandments that I enjoin on you today, that you and your children after you may prosper, and that you may have long life on the land which the LORD, your God, is giving you forever."

RESPONSORIAL PSALM *Psalm 33:4-5, 6, 9, 18-19, 20, 22*
℟. **Blessed the people the Lord has chosen to be his own.**

Upright is the word of the LORD,
and all his works are trustworthy.
He loves justice and right;
of the kindness of the Lord the earth
is full. ℟.

By the word of the Lord the heavens
were made;
by the breath of his mouth all their
host.
For he spoke, and it was made;
he commanded, and it stood forth. ℟.

See, the eyes of the Lord are upon those
who fear him,
upon those who hope for his
kindness,
to deliver them from death
and preserve them in spite of
famine. ℟.

Our soul waits for the Lord,
who is our help and our shield.
May your kindness, O Lord, be upon us
who have put our hope in you. ℟.

READING II *Romans 8:14-17*
Brothers and sisters: those who are led by the Spirit of God are sons of God. For you did not receive a spirit of slavery to fall back into fear, but you received a Spirit of adoption, through whom we cry, "Abba, Father!" The Spirit himself bears witness with our spirit that we are children of God, and if children, then heirs, heirs of God and joint heirs with Christ, if only we suffer with him so that we may also be glorified with him.

GOSPEL *Matthew 28:16-20*
The eleven disciples went to Galilee, to the mountain to which Jesus had ordered them. When they all saw him, they worshiped, but they doubted. Then Jesus approached and said to them, "All power in heaven and on earth has been given to me. Go, therefore, and make disciples of all nations, baptizing them in the name of the Father, and of the Son, and of the Holy Spirit, teaching them to observe all that I have commanded you. And behold, I am with you always, until the end of the age."

SUNDAY AFTER PENTECOST—TRINITY SUNDAY / C   994

READING I *Proverbs 8:22-31 / 166*
Thus says the wisdom of God:
"The LORD possessed me, the beginning
of his ways,
the forerunner of his prodigies of
long ago;
from of old I was poured forth,
at the first, before the earth.
When there were no depths I was brought
forth,
when there were no fountains or
springs of water;
before the mountains were settled into
place,
before the hills, I was brought forth;
while as yet the earth and fields were not
made,
nor the first clods of the world.

"When the Lord established the heavens
I was there,
when he marked out the vault over
the face of the deep;
when he made firm the skies above,
when he fixed fast the foundations
of the earth;
when he set for the sea its limit,
so that the waters should not
transgress his command;
then was I beside him as his craftsman,
and I was his delight day by day,
playing before him all the while,
playing on the surface of his earth;
and I found delight in the human
race."

RESPONSORIAL PSALM *Psalm 8:4-5, 6-7, 8-9*
℞. O Lord, our God, how wonderful your name in all the earth!

When I behold your heavens, the work
  of your fingers,
the moon and the stars which you
  set in place—
what is man that you should be mindful
  of him,
  or the son of man that you should
  care for him? ℞.

You have made him little less than the
  angels,

and crowned him with glory and
  honor.
You have given him rule over the works
  of your hands,
putting all things under his feet. ℞.

All sheep and oxen,
  yes, and the beasts of the field,
the birds of the air, the fishes of the sea,
  and whatever swims the paths of
  the seas. ℞.

READING II *Romans 5:1-5*
Brothers and sisters: Therefore, since we have been justified by faith, we have peace with God through our Lord Jesus Christ, through whom we have gained access by faith to this grace in which we stand, and we boast in hope of the glory of God. Not only that, but we even boast of our afflictions, knowing that affliction produces endurance, and endurance, proven character, and proven character, hope, and hope does not disappoint, because the love of God has been poured out into our hearts through the Holy Spirit that has been given to us.

GOSPEL *John 16:12-15*
Jesus said to his disciples: "I have much more to tell you, but you cannot bear it now. But when he comes, the Spirit of truth, he will guide you to all truth. He will not speak on his own, but he will speak what he hears, and will declare to you the things that are coming. He will glorify me, because he will take from what is mine and declare it to you. Everything that the Father has is mine; for this reason I told you that he will take from what is mine and declare it to you."

995 BODY AND BLOOD OF CHRIST / A

READING I *Deuteronomy 8:2-3, 14b-16a / 167*
Moses said to the people: "Remember how for forty years now the LORD, your God, has directed all your journeying in the desert, so as to test you by affliction and find out whether or not it was your intention to keep his commandments. He therefore let you be afflicted with hunger, and then fed you with manna, a food unknown to you and your fathers, in order to show you that not by bread alone does one live, but by every word that comes forth from the mouth of the LORD.

"Do not forget the LORD, your God, who brought you out of the land of Egypt, that place of slavery; who guided you through the vast and terrible desert with its saraph serpents and scorpions, its parched and waterless ground; who brought forth water for you from the flinty rock and fed you in the desert with manna, a food unknown to your fathers."

RESPONSORIAL PSALM *Psalm 147:12-13, 14-15, 19-20*
℞. Praise the Lord, Jerusalem.
  or:
Alleluia.

Glorify the LORD, O Jerusalem;
  praise your God, O Zion.
For he has strengthened the bars of your

gates;
he has blessed your children within
  you. ℞.

He has granted peace in your borders;
 with the best of wheat he fills you.
He sends forth his command to the earth;
 swiftly runs his word! ℟.

He has proclaimed his word to Jacob,

his statutes and his ordinances to
 Israel.
He has not done thus for any other
 nation;
his ordinances he has not made
 known to them. Alleluia. ℟.

READING II   *1 Corinthians 10:16-17*

Brothers and sisters: The cup of blessing that we bless, is it not a participation in the blood of Christ? The bread that we break, is it not a participation in the body of Christ? Because the loaf of bread is one, we, though many, are one body, for we all partake of the one loaf.

GOSPEL   *John 6:51-58*

Jesus said to the Jewish crowds: "I am the living bread that came down from heaven; whoever eats this bread will live forever; and the bread that I will give is my flesh for the life of the world."

 The Jews quarreled among themselves, saying, "How can this man give us his flesh to eat?" Jesus said to them, "Amen, amen, I say to you, unless you eat the flesh of the Son of Man and drink his blood, you do not have life within you. Whoever eats my flesh and drinks my blood has eternal life, and I will raise him on the last day. For my flesh is true food, and my blood is true drink. Whoever eats my flesh and drinks my blood remains in me and I in him. Just as the living Father sent me and I have life because of the Father, so also the one who feeds on me will have life because of me. This is the bread that came down from heaven. Unlike your ancestors who ate and still died, whoever eats this bread will live forever."

BODY AND BLOOD OF CHRIST / B   996

READING I   *Exodus 24:3-8 / 168*

When Moses came to the people and related all the words and ordinances of the LORD, they all answered with one voice, "We will do everything that the LORD has told us." Moses then wrote down all the words of the LORD and, rising early the next day, he erected at the foot of the mountain an altar and twelve pillars for the twelve tribes of Israel. Then, having sent certain young men of the Israelites to offer holocausts and sacrifice young bulls as peace offerings to the LORD, Moses took half of the blood and put it in large bowls; the other half he splashed on the altar. Taking the book of the covenant, he read it aloud to the people, who answered, "All that the LORD has said, we will heed and do." Then he took the blood and sprinkled it on the people, saying, "This is the blood of the covenant that the LORD has made with you in accordance with all these words of his."

RESPONSORIAL PSALM   *Psalm 116:12-13, 15-16, 17-18*

℟. **I will take the cup of salvation, and call on the name of the Lord.**
 or:
Alleluia.

How shall I make a return to the LORD
 for all the good he has done for me?
The cup of salvation I will take up,
 and I will call upon the name of the
 LORD. ℟.

Precious in the eyes of the LORD
 is the death of his faithful ones.
I am your servant, the son of your

handmaid;
you have loosed my bonds. ℟.

To you will I offer sacrifice of
 thanksgiving,
 and I will call upon the name of the
 LORD.
My vows to the LORD I will pay
 in the presence of all his people. ℟.

READING II *Hebrews 9:11-15*

Brothers and sisters: When Christ came as high priest of the good things that have come to be, passing through the greater and more perfect tabernacle not made by hands, that is, not belonging to this creation, he entered once for all into the sanctuary, not with the blood of goats and calves but with his own blood, thus obtaining eternal redemption. For if the blood of goats and bulls and the sprinkling of a heifer's ashes can sanctify those who are defiled so that their flesh is cleansed, how much more will the blood of Christ, who through the eternal Spirit offered himself unblemished to God, cleanse our consciences from dead works to worship the living God.

For this reason he is mediator of a new covenant: since a death has taken place for deliverance from transgressions under the first covenant, those who are called may receive the promised eternal inheritance.

GOSPEL *Mark 14:12-16, 22-26*

On the first day of the Feast of Unleavened Bread, when they sacrificed the Passover lamb, Jesus' disciples said to him, "Where do you want us to go and prepare for you to eat the Passover?" He sent two of his disciples and said to them, "Go into the city and a man will meet you, carrying a jar of water. Follow him. Wherever he enters, say to the master of the house, 'The Teacher says, "Where is my guest room where I may eat the Passover with my disciples?"'" Then he will show you a large upper room furnished and ready. Make the preparations for us there." The disciples then went off, entered the city, and found it just as he had told them; and they prepared the Passover.

While they were eating, he took bread, said the blessing, broke it, gave it to them, and said, "Take it; this is my body." Then he took a cup, gave thanks, and gave it to them, and they all drank from it. He said to them, "This is my blood of the covenant, which will be shed for many. Amen, I say to you, I shall not drink again the fruit of the vine until the day when I drink it new in the kingdom of God." Then, after singing a hymn, they went out to the Mount of Olives.

997 BODY AND BLOOD OF CHRIST / C

READING I *Genesis 14:18-20 / 169*

In those days, Melchizedek, king of Salem, brought out bread and wine, and being a priest of God Most High, he blessed Abram with these words:
"Blessed be Abram by God Most High,
the creator of heaven and earth;
and blessed be God Most High,
who delivered your foes into your hand."
Then Abram gave him a tenth of everything.

RESPONSORIAL PSALM *Psalm 110:1, 2, 3, 4*

℟. **You are a priest for ever, in the line of Melchizedek.**

The LORD said to my Lord: "Sit at my
    right hand
till I make your enemies your
    footstool." ℟.

The scepter of your power the LORD will
    stretch forth from Zion:
"Rule in the midst of your
    enemies." ℟.

"Yours is princely power in the day of
    your birth, in holy splendor;
before the daystar, like the dew, I
    have begotten you." ℟.

The LORD has sworn, and he will not
    repent:
"You are a priest forever,
    according to the order of
    Melchizedek." ℟.

READING II
1 Corinthians 11:23-26

Brothers and sisters: I received from the Lord what I also handed on to you, that the Lord Jesus, on the night he was handed over, took bread, and, after he had given thanks, broke it and said, "This is my body that is for you. Do this in remembrance of me." In the same way also the cup, after supper, saying, "This cup is the new covenant in my blood. Do this, as often as you drink it, in remembrance of me." For as often as you eat this bread and drink the cup, you proclaim the death of the Lord until he comes.

GOSPEL
Luke 9:11b-17

Jesus spoke to the crowds about the kingdom of God, and he healed those who needed to be cured. As the day was drawing to a close, the Twelve approached him and said, "Dismiss the crowd so that they can go to the surrounding villages and farms and find lodging and provisions; for we are in a deserted place here." He said to them, "Give them some food yourselves." They replied, "Five loaves and two fish are all we have, unless we ourselves go and buy food for all these people." Now the men there numbered about five thousand. Then he said to his disciples, "Have them sit down in groups of about fifty." They did so and made them all sit down. Then taking the five loaves and the two fish, and looking up to heaven, he said the blessing over them, broke them, and gave them to the disciples to set before the crowd. They all ate and were satisfied. And when the leftover fragments were picked up, they filled twelve wicker baskets.

SACRED HEART / A
998

READING I
Deuteronomy 7:6-11 / 170

Moses said to the people: "You are a people sacred to the LORD, your God; he has chosen you from all the nations on the face of the earth to be a people peculiarly his own. It was not because you are the largest of all nations that the LORD set his heart on you and chose you, for you are really the smallest of all nations. It was because the LORD loved you and because of his fidelity to the oath he had sworn to your fathers, that he brought you out with his strong hand from the place of slavery, and ransomed you from the hand of Pharaoh, king of Egypt. Understand, then, that the LORD, your God, is God indeed, the faithful God who keeps his merciful covenant down to the thousandth generation toward those who love him and keep his commandments, but who repays with destruction a person who hates him; he does not dally with such a one, but makes them personally pay for it. You shall therefore carefully observe the commandments, the statutes and the decrees that I enjoin on you today."

RESPONSORIAL PSALM
Psalm 103:1-2, 3-4, 6-7, 8, 10

℟. The Lord's kindness is everlasting to those who fear him.

Bless the LORD, O my soul;
    all my being, bless his holy name.
Bless the LORD, O my soul;
    and forget not all his benefits. ℟.

He pardons all your iniquities,
    heals all your ills.
He redeems your life from destruction,
    crowns you with kindness and

compassion. ℟.

Merciful and gracious is the Lord,
    slow to anger and abounding in
    kindness.
Not according to our sins does he deal
    with us,
    nor does he requite us according to
    our crimes. ℟.

READING II
1 John 4:7-16

Beloved, let us love one another, because love is of God; everyone who loves is begotten by God and knows God. Whoever is without love does not know God, for God is love. In this way the love of God was revealed to us: God sent his only Son into the world so that we might have life through him. In this is love: not that we have loved God, but that he loved us and sent his Son as expiation for our sins. Beloved, if God so loved us, we also must love one another. No one has ever seen God. Yet, if we love one another, God remains in us, and his love is brought to perfection in us.

This is how we know that we remain in him and he in us, that he has given us of his Spirit. Moreover, we have seen and testify that the Father sent his Son as savior of the world. Whoever acknowledges that Jesus is the Son of God, God remains in him and he in God. We have come to know and to believe in the love God has for us.

God is love, and whoever remains in love remains in God and God in him.

GOSPEL
Matthew 11:25-30

At that time Jesus exclaimed: "I give praise to you, Father, Lord of heaven and earth, for although you have hidden these things from the wise and the learned you have revealed them to little ones. Yes, Father, such has been your gracious will. All things have been handed over to me by my Father. No one knows the Son except the Father, and no one knows the Father except the Son and anyone to whom the Son wishes to reveal him."

"Come to me, all you who labor and are burdened, and I will give you rest. Take my yoke upon you and learn from me, for I am meek and humble of heart; and you will find rest for yourselves. For my yoke is easy, and my burden light."

999 SACRED HEART / B

READING I
Hosea 11:1, 3-4, 8c-9 / 171

Thus says the LORD:
When Israel was a child I loved him,
   out of Egypt I called my son.
Yet it was I who taught Ephraim to walk,
   who took them in my arms;
I drew them with human cords,
   with bands of love;
I fostered them like one
   who raises an infant to his cheeks;
Yet, though I stooped to feed my child,

they did not know that I was their
   healer.

My heart is overwhelmed,
   my pity is stirred.
I will not give vent to my blazing anger,
   I will not destroy Ephraim again;
For I am God and not a man,
   the Holy One present among you;
I will not let the flames consume you.

RESPONSORIAL PSALM
Isaiah 12:2-3, 4bcd, 5-6

℟. You will draw water joyfully from the springs of salvation.

God indeed is my savior;
   I am confident and unafraid.
My strength and my courage is the LORD,
   and he has been my savior.
With joy you will draw water
   at the fountain of salvation. ℟.

Give thanks to the LORD, acclaim his
   name;
   among the nations make known his

deeds,
proclaim how exalted is his name. ℟.

Sing praise to the LORD for his glorious
   achievement;
   let this be known throughout all the
     earth.
Shout with exultation, O city of Zion,
   for great in your midst
   is the Holy One of Israel! ℟.

READING II
Ephesians 3:8-12, 14-19

Brothers and sisters: To me, the very least of all the holy ones, this grace was given, to preach to the Gentiles the inscrutable riches of Christ, and to bring to light for all what is the plan of the mystery hidden from ages past in God who created all things, so that the manifold wisdom of God might now be made known through the church to the principalities and authorities in the heavens. This was according to the eternal purpose that he accomplished in Christ Jesus our Lord, in whom we have boldness of speech and confidence of access through faith in him.

For this reason I kneel before the Father, from whom every family in heaven and on earth is named, that he may grant you in accord with the riches of his glory to be strengthened with power through his Spirit in the inner self, and that Christ may dwell in your hearts through faith; that you, rooted and grounded in love, may have strength to comprehend with all the holy ones what is the breadth and length and height and depth, and to know the love of Christ which surpasses knowledge, so that you may be filled with all the fullness of God.

GOSPEL

John 19:31-37

Since it was preparation day, in order that the bodies might not remain on the cross on the sabbath, for the sabbath day of that week was a solemn one, the Jews asked Pilate that their legs be broken and they be taken down. So the soldiers came and broke the legs of the first and then of the other one who was crucified with Jesus. But when they came to Jesus and saw that he was already dead, they did not break his legs, but one soldier thrust his lance into his side, and immediately blood and water flowed out. An eyewitness has testified, and his testimony is true; he knows that he is speaking the truth, so that you also may come to believe. For this happened so that the Scripture passage might be fulfilled:

'Not a bone of it will be broken.'
And again another passage says:
'They will look upon him whom they have pierced.'

SACRED HEART / C   1000

READING I

Ezekiel 34:11-16 / 172

Thus says the Lord GOD: I myself will look after and tend my sheep. As a shepherd tends his flock when he finds himself among his scattered sheep, so will I tend my sheep. I will rescue them from every place where they were scattered when it was cloudy and dark. I will lead them out from among the peoples and gather them from the foreign lands; I will bring them back to their own country and pasture them upon the mountains of Israel in the land's ravines and all its inhabited places. In good pastures will I pasture them, and on the mountain heights of Israel shall be their grazing ground. There they shall lie down on good grazing ground, and in rich pastures shall they be pastured on the mountains of Israel. I myself will pasture my sheep; I myself will give them rest, says the Lord GOD. The lost I will seek out, the strayed I will bring back, the injured I will bind up, the sick I will heal, but the sleek and the strong I will destroy, shepherding them rightly.

RESPONSORIAL PSALM

Psalm 23:1-3a, 3b-4, 5, 6

℞. The Lord is my shepherd; there is nothing I shall want.

The LORD is my shepherd; I shall not
    want.
  In verdant pastures he gives me
    repose;
beside restful waters he leads me;
  he refreshes my soul. ℞.

He guides me in right paths
  for his name's sake.
Even though I walk in the dark valley
  I fear no evil; for you are at my side
with your rod and your staff

that give me courage. ℞.

You spread the table before me
  in the sight of my foes;
you anoint my head with oil;
  my cup overflows. ℞.

Only goodness and kindness follow me
  all the days of my life;
and I shall dwell in the house of the LORD
  for years to come. ℞.

READING II   *Romans 5:5b-11*

Brothers and sisters: The love of God has been poured out into our hearts through the Holy Spirit that has been given to us. For Christ, while we were still helpless, died at the appointed time for the ungodly. Indeed, only with difficulty does one die for a just person, though perhaps for a good person one might even find courage to die. But God proves his love for us in that while we were still sinners Christ died for us. How much more then, since we are now justified by his blood, will we be saved through him from the wrath. Indeed, if, while we were enemies, we were reconciled to God through the death of his Son, how much more, once reconciled, will we be saved by his life. Not only that, but we also boast of God through our Lord Jesus Christ, through whom we have now received reconciliation.

GOSPEL   *Luke 15:3-7*

Jesus addressed this parable to the Pharisees and scribes: "What man among you having a hundred sheep and losing one of them would not leave the ninety-nine in the desert and go after the lost one until he finds it? And when he does find it, he sets it on his shoulders with great joy and, upon his arrival home, he calls together his friends and neighbors and says to them, 'Rejoice with me because I have found my lost sheep.' I tell you, in just the same way there will be more joy in heaven over one sinner who repents than over ninety-nine righteous people who have no need of repentance."

1001   **SECOND SUNDAY IN ORDINARY TIME / A**

READING I   *Isaiah 49:3, 5-6 / 64*

The LORD said to me: You are my
   servant,
   Israel, through whom I show my
      glory.
Now the LORD has spoken
   who formed me as his servant from
      the womb,
   that Jacob may be brought back to
      him
   and Israel gathered to him;

and I am made glorious in the sight
   of the LORD,
   and my God is now my strength!
It is too little, the LORD says, for you to
      be my servant,
   to raise up the tribes of Jacob,
   and restore the survivors of Israel;
I will make you a light to the nations,
   that my salvation may reach to the
      ends of the earth.

RESPONSORIAL PSALM   *Psalm 40:2, 4, 7-8, 8-9, 10*

℟. **Here am I, Lord; I come to do your will.**

I have waited, waited for the LORD,
   and he stooped toward me and heard
      my cry.
And he put a new song into my mouth,
   a hymn to our God. ℟.

Sacrifice or offering you wished not,
   but ears open to obedience you gave
      me.
Holocausts or sin-offerings you sought
      not;
   then said I, "Behold I come." ℟.

"In the written scroll it is prescribed for
      me,
   to do your will, O my God, is my
      delight,
and your law is within my heart!" ℟.

I announced your justice in the vast
      assembly;
   I did not restrain my lips, as you, O
      LORD, know. ℟.

READING II
1 Corinthians 1:1-3

Paul, called to be an apostle of Christ Jesus by the will of God, and Sosthenes our brother, to the church of God that is in Corinth, to you who have been sanctified in Christ Jesus, called to be holy, with all those everywhere who call upon the name of our Lord Jesus Christ, their Lord and ours. Grace to you and peace from God our Father and the Lord Jesus Christ.

GOSPEL
John 1:29-34

John the Baptist saw Jesus coming toward him and said, "Behold, the Lamb of God, who takes away the sin of the world. He is the one of whom I said, 'A man is coming after me who ranks ahead of me because he existed before me.' I did not know him, but the reason why I came baptizing with water was that he might be made known to Israel." John testified further, saying, "I saw the Spirit come down like a dove from heaven and remain upon him. I did not know him, but the one who sent me to baptize with water told me, 'On whomever you see the Spirit come down and remain, he is the one who will baptize with the Holy Spirit.' Now I have seen and testified that he is the Son of God."

SECOND SUNDAY IN ORDINARY TIME / B   1002

READING I
1 Samuel 3:3b-10, 19 / 65

Samuel was sleeping in the temple of the LORD where the ark of God was. The LORD called to Samuel, who answered, "Here I am." Samuel ran to Eli and said, "Here I am. You called me." "I did not call you," Eli said. "Go back to sleep." So he went back to sleep. Again the LORD called Samuel, who rose and went to Eli. "Here I am," he said. "You called me." But Eli answered, "I did not call you, my son. Go back to sleep."

At that time Samuel was not familiar with the LORD, because the LORD had not revealed anything to him as yet. The LORD called Samuel again, for the third time. Getting up and going to Eli, he said, "Here I am. You called me." Then Eli understood that the LORD was calling the youth. So he said to Samuel, "Go to sleep, and if you are called, reply, 'Speak, LORD, for your servant is listening.'" When Samuel went to sleep in his place, the LORD came and revealed his presence, calling out as before, "Samuel, Samuel!" Samuel answered, "Speak, for your servant is listening."

Samuel grew up, and the LORD was with him, not permitting any word of his to be without effect.

RESPONSORIAL PSALM
Psalm 40:2, 4, 7-8, 8-9, 10

℞. Here am I, Lord; I come to do your will.

I have waited, waited for the LORD,
    and he stooped toward me and heard
        my cry.
And he put a new song into my mouth,
    a hymn to our God. ℞.

Sacrifice or offering you wished not,
    but ears open to obedience you gave
        me.
Holocausts or sin-offerings you sought
        not;
    then said I, "Behold I come." ℞.

"In the written scroll it is prescribed for
        me,
    to do your will, O my God, is my
        delight,
And your law is within my heart!" ℞.

I announced your justice in the vast
        assembly;
    I did not restrain my lips, as you,
        O LORD, know. ℞.

READING II   *1 Corinthians 6:13c-15a, 17-20*

Brothers and sisters: The body is not for immorality, but for the Lord, and the Lord is for the body; God raised the Lord and will also raise us by his power.

Do you not know that your bodies are members of Christ? But whoever is joined to the Lord becomes one Spirit with him. Avoid immorality. Every other sin a person commits is outside the body, but the immoral person sins against his own body. Do you not know that your body is a temple of the Holy Spirit within you, whom you have from God, and that you are not your own? For you have been purchased at a price. Therefore glorify God in your body.

GOSPEL   *John 1:35-42*

John was standing with two of his disciples, and as he watched Jesus walk by, he said, "Behold, the Lamb of God." The two disciples heard what he said and followed Jesus. Jesus turned and saw them following him and said to them, "What are you looking for?" They said to him, "Rabbi" (which translated means Teacher), "where are you staying?" He said to them, "Come, and you will see." So they went and saw where Jesus was staying, and they stayed with him that day. It was about four in the afternoon. Andrew, the brother of Simon Peter, was one of the two who heard John and followed Jesus. He first found his own brother Simon and told him, "We have found the Messiah" (which is translated Christ). Then he brought him to Jesus. Jesus looked at him and said, "You are Simon the son of John; you will be called Cephas" (which is translated Peter).

1003 SECOND SUNDAY IN ORDINARY TIME / C

READING I   *Isaiah 62:1-5 / 66*

For Zion's sake I will not be silent,
  for Jerusalem's sake I will not be
    quiet,
until her vindication shines forth like
    the dawn
  and her victory like a burning torch.

Nations shall behold your vindication,
  and all the kings your glory;
you shall be called by a new name
  pronounced by the mouth of the
    LORD.
You shall be a glorious crown in the
    hand of the LORD,
  a royal diadem held by your God.
No more shall people call you
  "Forsaken,"
  or your land "Desolate,"
but you shall be called "My Delight,"
  and your land "Espoused."
For the LORD delights in you
  and makes your land his spouse.
As a young man marries a virgin,
  your Builder shall marry you;
and as a bridegroom rejoices in his bride
  so shall your God rejoice in you.

RESPONSORIAL PSALM   *Psalm 96:1-2, 2-3, 7-8, 9-10*

℟. **Proclaim his marvelous deeds to all the nations.**

Sing to the LORD a new song;
  sing to the LORD, all you lands.
Sing to the LORD; bless his name. ℟.

Announce his salvation, day after day.
  Tell his glory among the nations;
among all peoples, his wondrous
    deeds. ℟.

Give to the LORD, you families of
    nations,
  give to the LORD glory and praise;
give to the LORD the glory due his
    name! ℟.

Worship the LORD in holy attire.
Tremble before him, all the earth;
say among the nations: The LORD is
king.
He governs the peoples with
equity. ℟.

READING II

1 Corinthians 12:4-11

Brothers and sisters: There are different kinds of spiritual gifts but the same Spirit; there are different forms of service but the same Lord; there are different workings but the same God who produces all of them in everyone. To each individual the manifestation of the Spirit is given for some benefit. To one is given through the Spirit the expression of wisdom; to another, the expression of knowledge according to the same Spirit; to another, faith by the same Spirit; to another, gifts of healing by the one Spirit; to another, mighty deeds; to another, prophecy; to another, discernment of spirits; to another, varieties of tongues; to another, interpretation of tongues. But one and the same Spirit produces all of these, distributing them individually to each person as he wishes.

GOSPEL

John 2:1-11

There was a wedding at Cana in Galilee, and the mother of Jesus was there. Jesus and his disciples were also invited to the wedding. When the wine ran short, the mother of Jesus said to him, "They have no wine." And Jesus said to her, "Woman, how does your concern affect me? My hour has not yet come." His mother said to the servers, "Do whatever he tells you." Now there were six stone water jars there for Jewish ceremonial washings, each holding twenty to thirty gallons. Jesus told them, "Fill the jars with water." So they filled them to the brim. Then he told them, "Draw some out now and take it to the headwaiter." So they took it. And when the headwaiter tasted the water that had become wine, without knowing where it came from (although the servers who had drawn the water knew), the headwaiter called the bridegroom and said to him, "Everyone serves good wine first, and then when people have drunk freely, an inferior one; but you have kept the good wine until now." Jesus did this as the beginning of his signs at Cana in Galilee and so revealed his glory, and his disciples began to believe in him.

THIRD SUNDAY IN ORDINARY TIME / A   1004

READING I

Isaiah 8:23—9:3 / 67

First the Lord degraded the land of Zebulun and the land of Naphtali; but in the end he has glorified the seaward road, the land west of the Jordan, the District of the Gentiles.

Anguish has taken wing, dispelled is darkness:
    for there is no gloom where but now there was distress.

The people who walked in darkness
    have seen a great light;
    upon those who dwelt in the land of gloom a light has shone.
You have brought them abundant joy
    and great rejoicing,
    as they rejoice before you as at the harvest,
    as people make merry when dividing spoils.
For the yoke that burdened them,

the pole on their shoulder,
and the rod of their taskmaster
you have smashed, as on the day of Midian.

RESPONSORIAL PSALM   *Psalm 27:1, 4, 13-14*
℟. **The Lord is my light and my salvation.**

The LORD is my light and my salvation;
    whom should I fear?
The LORD is my life's refuge;
    of whom should I be afraid? ℟.

One thing I ask of the LORD;
    this I seek:
to dwell in the house of the LORD
    all the days of my life,
that I may gaze on the loveliness of the
    LORD
    and contemplate his temple. ℟.

I believe that I shall see the bounty of the
    LORD
    in the land of the living.
Wait for the LORD with courage;
    be stouthearted, and wait for the
    LORD. ℟.

READING II   *1 Corinthians 1:10-13, 17*
I urge you, brothers and sisters, in the name of our Lord Jesus Christ, that all of you
agree in what you say, and that there be no divisions among you, but that you be united
in the same mind and in the same purpose. For it has been reported to me about you, my
brothers and sisters, by Chloe's people, that there are rivalries among you. I mean that
each of you is saying, "I belong to Paul," or "I belong to Apollos," or "I belong to
Cephas," or "I belong to Christ." Is Christ divided? Was Paul crucified for you? Or were
you baptized in the name of Paul? For Christ did not send me to baptize but to preach
the gospel, and not with the wisdom of human eloquence, so that the cross of Christ
might not be emptied of its meaning.

GOSPEL   *Matthew 4:12-23 or 4:12-17*
For short form read only the part in brackets.

[When Jesus heard that John had been arrested, he withdrew to Galilee. He left Nazareth
and went to live in Capernaum by the sea, in the region of Zebulun and Naphtali, that
what had been said through Isaiah the prophet might be fulfilled:
    "Land of Zebulun and land of Naphtali,
        the way to the sea, beyond the Jordan,
        Galilee of the Gentiles,
        the people who sit in darkness have seen a great light,
        on those dwelling in a land overshadowed by death
            light has arisen."
From that time on, Jesus began to preach and say, "Repent, for the kingdom of heaven
is at hand."]
    As he was walking by the Sea of Galilee, he saw two brothers, Simon who is called
Peter, and his brother Andrew, casting a net into the sea; they were fishermen. He said
to them, "Come after me, and I will make you fishers of men." At once they left their
nets and followed him. He walked along from there and saw two other brothers, James,
the son of Zebedee, and his brother John. They were in a boat, with their father Zebedee,

mending their nets. He called them, and immediately they left their boat and their father and followed him. He went around all of Galilee, teaching in their synagogues, proclaiming the gospel of the kingdom, and curing every disease and illness among the people.

THIRD SUNDAY IN ORDINARY TIME / B 1005

READING I
Jonah 3:1-5, 10 / 68

The word of the LORD came to Jonah, saying: "Set out for the great city of Nineveh, and announce to it the message that I will tell you." So Jonah made ready and went to Nineveh, according to the LORD's bidding. Now Nineveh was an enormously large city; it took three days to go through it. Jonah began his journey through the city, and had gone but a single day's walk announcing, "Forty days more and Nineveh shall be destroyed," when the people of Nineveh believed God; they proclaimed a fast and all of them, great and small, put on sackcloth.

When God saw by their actions how they turned from their evil way, he repented of the evil that he had threatened to do to them; he did not carry it out.

RESPONSORIAL PSALM
Psalm 25:4-5, 6-7, 8-9

℟. **Teach me your ways, O Lord.**

Your ways, O LORD, make known to me;
　　teach me your paths,
Guide me in your truth and teach me,
　　for you are God my savior. ℟.

Remember that your compassion, O
　　LORD,
　　and your love are from of old.

In your kindness remember me,
　　because of your goodness, O
　　LORD. ℟.

Good and upright is the LORD;
　　thus he shows sinners the way.
He guides the humble to justice
　　and teaches the humble his way. ℟.

READING II
1 Corinthians 7:29-31

I tell you, brothers and sisters, the time is running out. From now on, let those having wives act as not having them, those weeping as not weeping, those rejoicing as not rejoicing, those buying as not owning, those using the world as not using it fully. For the world in its present form is passing away.

GOSPEL
Mark 1:14-20

After John had been arrested, Jesus came to Galilee proclaiming the gospel of God: "This is the time of fulfillment. The kingdom of God is at hand. Repent, and believe in the gospel."

As he passed by the Sea of Galilee, he saw Simon and his brother Andrew casting their nets into the sea; they were fishermen. Jesus said to them, "Come after me, and I will make you fishers of men." Then they abandoned their nets and followed him. He walked along a little farther and saw James, the son of Zebedee, and his brother John. They too were in a boat mending their nets. Then he called them. So they left their father Zebedee in the boat along with the hired men and followed him.

1006 THIRD SUNDAY IN ORDINARY TIME / C

READING I   *Nehemiah 8:2-4a, 5-6, 8-10 / 69*

Ezra the priest brought the law before the assembly, which consisted of men, women, and those children old enough to understand. Standing at one end of the open place that was before the Water Gate, he read out of the book from daybreak till midday, in the presence of the men, the women, and those children old enough to understand; and all the people listened attentively to the book of the law. Ezra the scribe stood on a wooden platform that had been made for the occasion. He opened the scroll so that all the people might see it (for he was standing higher up than any of the people); and, as he opened it, all the people rose. Ezra blessed the LORD, the great God, and all the people, their hands raised high, answered, "Amen, amen!" Then they bowed down and prostrated themselves before the LORD, their faces to the ground. Ezra read plainly from the book of the law of God, interpreting it so that all could understand what was read. Then Nehemiah, that is, His Excellency, and Ezra the priest-scribe and the Levites who were instructing the people said to all the people: "Today is holy to the LORD your God. Do not be sad, and do not weep"— for all the people were weeping as they heard the words of the law. He said further: "Go, eat rich foods and drink sweet drinks, and allot portions to those who had nothing prepared; for today is holy to our LORD. Do not be saddened this day, for rejoicing in the LORD must be your strength!"

RESPONSORIAL PSALM   *Psalm 19:8, 9, 10, 15*

℞. **Your words, Lord, are Spirit and life.**

The law of the LORD is perfect,
  refreshing the soul;
the decree of the LORD is trustworthy,
  giving wisdom to the simple. ℞.

the precepts of the LORD are right,
  rejoicing the heart;
the command of the LORD is clear,
  enlightening the eye. ℞.

The fear of the Lord is pure,
  enduring forever;
the ordinances of the Lord are true,
  all of them just. ℞.

Let the words of my mouth and the
    thought of my heart
  find favor before you,
O Lord, my rock and my redeemer. ℞.

READING II   *1 Corinthians 12:12-30 or 12:12-14, 27*

For short form read only the parts in brackets.

[Brothers and sisters: As a body is one though it has many parts, and all the parts of the body, though many, are one body, so also Christ. For in one Spirit we were all baptized into one body, whether Jews or Greeks, slaves or free persons, and we were all given to drink of one Spirit.

Now the body is not a single part, but many.] If a foot should say, "Because I am not a hand I do not belong to the body," it does not for this reason belong any less to the body. Or if an ear should say, "Because I am not an eye I do not belong to the body," it does not for this reason belong any less to the body. If the whole body were an eye, where would the hearing be? If the whole body were hearing, where would the sense of smell be? But as it is, God placed the parts, each one of them, in the body as he intended. If they were all one part, where would the body be? But as it is, there are many parts, yet one body. The eye cannot say to the hand, "I do not need you," nor again the head to the feet, "I do not need you." Indeed, the parts of the body that seem to be weaker are all the more necessary, and those parts of the body that we consider less honorable we surround with greater honor, and our less presentable parts are treated with greater propriety, whereas our more presentable parts do not need this. But God has so constructed the body as to give greater honor to a part that is without it, so that there may be no division in the body, but that the parts may have the same concern for one another. If one part suffers, all the parts suffer with it; if one part is honored, all the parts share its joy.

Now [you are Christ's body, and individually parts of it.] Some people God has designated in the church to be, first, apostles; second, prophets; third, teachers; then, mighty deeds; then gifts of healing, assistance, administration, and varieties of tongues. Are all apostles? Are all prophets? Are all teachers? Do all work mighty deeds? Do all have gifts of healing? Do all speak in tongues? Do all interpret?

GOSPEL   *Luke 1:1-4; 4:14-21*

Since many have undertaken to compile a narrative of the events that have been fulfilled among us, just as those who were eyewitnesses from the beginning and ministers of the word have handed them down to us, I too have decided, after investigating everything accurately anew, to write it down in an orderly sequence for you, most excellent Theophilus, so that you may realize the certainty of the teachings you have received.

Jesus returned to Galilee in the power of the Spirit, and news of him spread throughout the whole region. He taught in their synagogues and was praised by all.

He came to Nazareth, where he had grown up, and went according to his custom into the synagogue on the sabbath day. He stood up to read and was handed a scroll of the prophet Isaiah. He unrolled the scroll and found the passage where it was written:
"The Spirit of the Lord is upon me,
    because he has anointed me
    to bring glad tidings to the poor.
He has sent me to proclaim liberty to captives
    and recovery of sight to the blind,
    to let the oppressed go free,
    and to proclaim a year acceptable to the Lord."
Rolling up the scroll, he handed it back to the attendant and sat down, and the eyes of all in the synagogue looked intently at him. He said to them, "Today this Scripture passage is fulfilled in your hearing."

FOURTH SUNDAY IN ORDINARY TIME / A   1007

READING I   *Zephaniah 2:3; 3:12-13 / 70*

Seek the LORD, all you humble of the
    earth,
    who have observed his law;
seek justice, seek humility;
    perhaps you may be sheltered
    on the day of the LORD's anger.

But I will leave as a remnant in your
    midst
    a people humble and lowly,

who shall take refuge in the name of the
    LORD:
    the remnant of Israel.
They shall do no wrong
    and speak no lies;
nor shall there be found in their mouths
    a deceitful tongue;
they shall pasture and couch their flocks
    with none to disturb them.

RESPONSORIAL PSALM   *Psalm 146:6-7, 8-9, 9-10*

℞. **Blessed are the poor in spirit; the kingdom of heaven is theirs!**
    or:
Alleluia.

The LORD keeps faith forever,
    secures justice for the oppressed,

gives food to the hungry.
    The LORD sets captives free. ℞.

The L ORD gives sight to the blind;
the L ORD raises up those who were
bowed down.
The L ORD loves the just;
the L ORD protects strangers. ℟.

The fatherless and the widow the L ORD
sustains,
but the way of the wicked he thwarts.
The L ORD shall reign forever;
your God, O Zion, through all
generations.
Alleluia. ℟.

READING II
1 Corinthians 1:26-31

Consider your own calling, brothers and sisters. Not many of you were wise by human standards, not many were powerful, not many were of noble birth. Rather, God chose the foolish of the world to shame the wise, and God chose the weak of the world to shame the strong, and God chose the lowly and despised of the world, those who count for nothing, to reduce to nothing those who are something, so that no human being might boast before God. It is due to him that you are in Christ Jesus, who became for us wisdom from God, as well as righteousness, sanctification, and redemption, so that, as it is written, "Whoever boasts, should boast in the Lord."

GOSPEL
Matthew 5:1-12a

When Jesus saw the crowds, he went up the mountain, and after he had sat down, his disciples came to him. He began to teach them, saying:
"Blessed are the poor in spirit,
for theirs is the kingdom of heaven.
Blessed are they who mourn,
for they will be comforted.
Blessed are the meek,
for they will inherit the land.
Blessed are they who hunger and thirst for righteousness,
for they will be satisfied.
Blessed are the merciful,
for they will be shown mercy.
Blessed are the clean of heart,
for they will see God.
Blessed are the peacemakers,
for they will be called children of God.
Blessed are they who are persecuted for the sake of
righteousness,
for theirs is the kingdom of heaven.
Blessed are you when they insult you and persecute you and utter every kind of evil against you falsely because of me. Rejoice and be glad, for your reward will be great in heaven."

1008 FOURTH SUNDAY IN ORDINARY TIME / B

READING I
Deuteronomy 18:15-20 / 71

Moses spoke to all the people, saying: "A prophet like me will the L ORD, your God, raise up for you from among your own kin; to him you shall listen. This is exactly what you requested of the L ORD, your God, at Horeb on the day of the assembly, when you said, 'Let us not again hear the voice of the L ORD, our God, nor see this great fire any more, lest we die.' And the L ORD said to me, 'This was well said. I will raise up for them a prophet like you from among their kin, and will put my words into his mouth; he shall tell them all that I command him.'" Whoever will not listen to my words which he speaks in my name, I myself will make him answer for it. But if a prophet presumes to speak in my name an oracle that I have not commanded him to speak, or speaks in the name of other gods, he shall die."

RESPONSORIAL PSALM   *Psalm 95:1-2, 6-7, 7-9*
℟. **If today you hear his voice, harden not your hearts.**

Come, let us sing joyfully to the LORD;
    let us acclaim the rock of our
      salvation.
Let us come into his presence with
    thanksgiving;
    let us joyfully sing psalms to him. ℟.

Come, let us bow down in worship;
    let us kneel before the LORD who
      made us.
For he is our God,

and we are the people he shepherds,
    the flock he guides. ℟.

Oh, that today you would hear his voice:
    "Harden not your hearts as at
      Meribah,
as in the day of Massah in the desert,
    where your fathers tempted me;
they tested me though they had seen my
    works." ℟.

READING II   *1 Corinthians 7:32-35*
Brothers and sisters: I should like you to be free of anxieties. An unmarried man is anxious about the things of the Lord, how he may please the Lord. But a married man is anxious about the things of the world, how he may please his wife, and he is divided. An unmarried woman or a virgin is anxious about the things of the Lord, so that she may be holy in both body and spirit. A married woman, on the other hand, is anxious about the things of the world, how she may please her husband. I am telling you this for your own benefit, not to impose a restraint upon you, but for the sake of propriety and adherence to the Lord without distraction.

GOSPEL   *Mark 1:21-28*
Then they came to Capernaum, and on the sabbath Jesus entered the synagogue and taught. The people were astonished at his teaching, for he taught them as one having authority and not as the scribes. In their synagogue was a man with an unclean spirit; he cried out, "What have you to do with us, Jesus of Nazareth? Have you come to destroy us? I know who you are—the Holy One of God!" Jesus rebuked him and said, "Quiet! Come out of him!" The unclean spirit convulsed him and with a loud cry came out of him. All were amazed and asked one another, "What is this? A new teaching with authority. He commands even the unclean spirits and they obey him." His fame spread everywhere throughout the whole region of Galilee.

FOURTH SUNDAY IN ORDINARY TIME / C   1009

READING I   *Jeremiah 1:4-5, 17-19 / 72*
The word of the LORD came to me, saying:
    Before I formed you in the womb I
      knew you,
    before you were born I dedicated
      you,
    a prophet to the nations I
      appointed you.

    But do you gird your loins;
      stand up and tell them
      all that I command you.
    Be not crushed on their account,
      as though I would leave you

      crushed before them;
    for it is I this day
      who have made you a fortified
      city,
    a pillar of iron, a wall of brass,
      against the whole land:
    against Judah's kings and princes,
      against its priests and people.
    They will fight against you but not
      prevail over you,
    for I am with you to deliver you,
      says the LORD.

RESPONSORIAL PSALM
Psalm 71:1-2, 3-4, 5-6, 15, 17

℟. **I will sing of your salvation.**

In you, O LORD, I take refuge;
    let me never be put to shame.
In your justice rescue me, and deliver me;
    incline your ear to me, and save
    me. ℟.

Be my rock of refuge,
    a stronghold to give me safety,
for you are my rock and my fortress.
    O my God, rescue me from the hand
    of the wicked. ℟.

For you are my hope, O Lord;
    my trust, O God, from my youth.
On you I depend from birth;
    from my mother's womb you are my
    strength. ℟.

My mouth shall declare your justice,
    day by day your salvation.
O God, you have taught me from my
    youth,
and till the present I proclaim your
    wondrous deeds. ℟.

READING II
1 Corinthians 12:31—13:13 or 13:4-13

For short form read only the parts in brackets.

[Brothers and sisters:] Strive eagerly for the greatest spiritual gifts. But I shall show you a still more excellent way.

If I speak in human and angelic tongues, but do not have love, I am a resounding gong or a clashing cymbal. And if I have the gift of prophecy, and comprehend all mysteries and all knowledge; if I have all faith so as to move mountains, but do not have love, I am nothing. If I give away everything I own, and if I hand my body over so that I may boast, but do not have love, I gain nothing.

[Love is patient, love is kind. It is not jealous, it is not pompous, it is not inflated, it is not rude, it does not seek its own interests, it is not quick-tempered, it does not brood over injury, it does not rejoice over wrongdoing but rejoices with the truth. It bears all things, believes all things, hopes all things, endures all things. Love never fails. If there are prophecies, they will be brought to nothing; if tongues, they will cease; if knowledge, it will be brought to nothing. For we know partially and we prophesy partially, but when the perfect comes, the partial will pass away. When I was a child, I used to talk as a child, think as a child, reason as a child; when I became a man, I put aside childish things. At present we see indistinctly, as in a mirror, but then face to face. At present I know partially; then I shall know fully, as I am fully known. So faith, hope, love remain, these three; but the greatest of these is love.]

GOSPEL
Luke 4:21-30

Jesus began speaking in the synagogue, saying: "Today this Scripture passage is fulfilled in your hearing." And all spoke highly of him and were amazed at the gracious words that came from his mouth. They also asked, "Isn't this the son of Joseph?" He said to them, "Surely you will quote me this proverb, 'Physician, cure yourself,' and say, 'Do here in your native place the things that we heard were done in Capernaum.'" And he said, "Amen, I say to you, no prophet is accepted in his own native place. Indeed, I tell you, there were many widows in Israel in the days of Elijah when the sky was closed for three and a half years and a severe famine spread over the entire land. It was to none of these that Elijah was sent, but only to a widow in Zarephath in the land of Sidon. Again, there were many lepers in Israel during the time of Elisha the prophet; yet not one of them was cleansed, but only Naaman the Syrian." When the people in the synagogue heard this, they were all filled with fury. They rose up, drove him out of the town, and led him to the brow of the hill on which their town had been built, to hurl him down headlong. But Jesus passed through the midst of them and went away.

FIFTH SUNDAY IN ORDINARY TIME / A 1010

READING I *Isaiah 58:7-10 / 73*

Thus says the LORD:
Share your bread with the hungry,
  shelter the oppressed and the homeless;
clothe the naked when you see them,
  and do not turn your back on your own.
Then your light shall break forth like the dawn,
  and your wound shall quickly be healed;
your vindication shall go before you,
  and the glory of the LORD shall be your rear guard.
Then you shall call, and the LORD will answer,
  you shall cry for help, and he will say: Here I am!
If you remove from your midst
  oppression, false accusation and malicious speech;
if you bestow your bread on the hungry
  and satisfy the afflicted;
then light shall rise for you in the darkness,
  and the gloom shall become for you like midday.

RESPONSORIAL PSALM *Psalm 112:4-5, 6-7, 8-9*

℞. **The just man is a light in darkness to the upright.**
  or:
Alleluia.

Light shines through the darkness for the
    upright;
  he is gracious and merciful and just.
Well for the man who is gracious and
    lends,
  who conducts his affairs with
    justice. ℞.

He shall never be moved;
  the just one shall be in everlasting
remembrance.
An evil report he shall not fear;
  his heart is firm, trusting in the
    LORD. ℞.

His heart is steadfast; he shall not fear.
  Lavishly he gives to the poor;
His justice shall endure forever;
  his horn shall be exalted in glory. ℞.

READING II *1 Corinthians 2:1-5*

When I came to you, brothers and sisters, proclaiming the mystery of God, I did not come with sublimity of words or of wisdom. For I resolved to know nothing while I was with you except Jesus Christ, and him crucified. I came to you in weakness and fear and much trembling, and my message and my proclamation were not with persuasive words of wisdom, but with a demonstration of Spirit and power, so that your faith might rest not on human wisdom but on the power of God.

GOSPEL *Matthew 5:13-16*

Jesus said to his disciples: "You are the salt of the earth. But if salt loses its taste, with what can it be seasoned? It is no longer good for anything but to be thrown out and trampled underfoot. You are the light of the world. A city set on a mountain cannot be hidden. Nor do they light a lamp and then put it under a bushel basket; it is set on a lamp stand, where it gives light to all in the house. Just so, your light must shine before others, that they may see your good deeds and glorify your heavenly Father."

1011 FIFTH SUNDAY IN ORDINARY TIME / B

READING I
Job 7:1-4, 6-7 / 74

Job spoke, saying:
Is not man's life on earth a drudgery?
    Are not his days those of hirelings?
He is a slave who longs for the shade,
    a hireling who waits for his wages.
So I have been assigned months of
        misery,
    and troubled nights have been
        allotted to me.

If in bed I say, "When shall I arise?"
    then the night drags on;
    I am filled with restlessness until the
        dawn.
My days are swifter than a weaver's
        shuttle;
    they come to an end without hope.
Remember that my life is like the wind;
    I shall not see happiness again.

RESPONSORIAL PSALM
Psalm 147:1-2, 3-4, 5-6

℟. **Praise the Lord, who heals the brokenhearted.**
    or:
Alleluia.

Praise the LORD, for he is good;
    sing praise to our God, for he is
        gracious;
it is fitting to praise him.
The LORD rebuilds Jerusalem;
the dispersed of Israel he gathers. ℟.

He heals the brokenhearted

and binds up their wounds.
He tells the number of the stars;
    he calls each by name. ℟.

Great is our Lord and mighty in power;
    to his wisdom there is no limit.
The LORD sustains the lowly;
    the wicked he casts to the ground. ℟.

READING II
1 Corinthians 9:16-19, 22-23

Brothers and sisters: If I preach the gospel, this is no reason for me to boast, for an obligation has been imposed on me, and woe to me if I do not preach it! If I do so willingly, I have a recompense, but if unwillingly, then I have been entrusted with a stewardship. What then is my recompense? That, when I preach, I offer the gospel free of charge so as not to make full use of my right in the gospel. Although I am free in regard to all, I have made myself a slave to all so as to win over as many as possible. To the weak I became weak, to win over the weak. I have become all things to all, to save at least some. All this I do for the sake of the gospel, so that I too may have a share in it.

GOSPEL
Mark 1:29-39

On leaving the synagogue Jesus entered the house of Simon and Andrew with James and John. Simon's mother-in-law lay sick with a fever. They immediately told him about her. He approached, grasped her hand, and helped her up. Then the fever left her and she waited on them.

When it was evening, after sunset, they brought to him all who were ill or possessed by demons. The whole town was gathered at the door. He cured many who were sick with various diseases, and he drove out many demons, not permitting them to speak because they knew him.

Rising very early before dawn, he left and went off to a deserted place, where he prayed. Simon and those who were with him pursued him and on finding him said, "Everyone is looking for you." He told them, "Let us go on to the nearby villages that I may preach there also. For this purpose have I come." So he went into their synagogues, preaching and driving out demons throughout the whole of Galilee.

FIFTH SUNDAY IN ORDINARY TIME / C   1012

READING I   *Isaiah 6:1-2a, 3-8 / 75*

In the year King Uzziah died, I saw the Lord seated on a high and lofty throne, with the train of his garment filling the temple. Seraphim were stationed above.

They cried one to the other, "Holy, holy, holy is the LORD of hosts! All the earth is filled with his glory!" At the sound of that cry, the frame of the door shook and the house was filled with smoke.

Then I said, "Woe is me, I am doomed! For I am a man of unclean lips, living among a people of unclean lips; yet my eyes have seen the King, the LORD of hosts!" Then one of the seraphim flew to me, holding an ember that he had taken with tongs from the altar.

He touched my mouth with it, and said, "See, now that this has touched your lips, your wickedness is removed, your sin purged."

Then I heard the voice of the Lord saying, "Whom shall I send? Who will go for us?" "Here I am," I said; "send me!"

RESPONSORIAL PSALM   *Psalm 138:1-2, 2-3, 4-5, 7-8*

℟. **In the sight of the angels I will sing your praises, Lord.**

I will give thanks to you, O LORD, with
    all my heart,
    for you have heard the words of my
    mouth;
in the presence of the angels I will sing
    your praise;
    I will worship at your holy temple
and give thanks to your name. ℟.

Because of your kindness and your truth;
    for you have made great above all
    things
your name and your promise.
    When I called, you answered me;
you built up strength within me. ℟.

All the kings of the earth shall give
    thanks to you, O LORD,
    when they hear the words of your
    mouth;
and they shall sing of the ways of the
    LORD:
    "Great is the glory of the LORD." ℟.

Your right hand saves me.
    The LORD will complete what he
    has done for me;
your kindness, O LORD, endures forever;
    forsake not the work of your
    hands. ℟.

READING II   *1 Corinthians 15:1-11 or 15:3-8, 11*

For short form read only the parts in brackets.

I am reminding you, [brothers and sisters,] of the gospel I preached to you, which you indeed received and in which you also stand. Through it you are also being saved, if you hold fast to the word I preached to you, unless you believed in vain. For [I handed on to you as of first importance what I also received: that Christ died for our sins in accordance with the Scriptures; that he was buried; that he was raised on the third day in accordance with the Scriptures; that he appeared to Cephas, then to the Twelve. After that, he appeared to more than five hundred brothers at once, most of whom are still living, though some have fallen asleep. After that he appeared to James, then to all the apostles. Last of all, as to one born abnormally, he appeared to me.] For I am the least of the apostles, not fit to be called an apostle, because I persecuted the church of God. But by the grace of God I am what I am, and his grace to me has not been ineffective. Indeed, I have toiled harder than all of them; not I, however, but the grace of God that is with me. [Therefore, whether it be I or they, so we preach and so you believed.]

GOSPEL *Luke 5:1-11*

While the crowd was pressing in on Jesus and listening to the word of God, he was standing by the Lake of Gennesaret. He saw two boats there alongside the lake; the fishermen had disembarked and were washing their nets. Getting into one of the boats, the one belonging to Simon, he asked him to put out a short distance from the shore. Then he sat down and taught the crowds from the boat. After he had finished speaking, he said to Simon, "Put out into deep water and lower your nets for a catch." Simon said in reply, "Master, we have worked hard all night and have caught nothing, but at your command I will lower the nets." When they had done this, they caught a great number of fish and their nets were tearing. They signaled to their partners in the other boat to come to help them. They came and filled both boats so that the boats were in danger of sinking. When Simon Peter saw this, he fell at the knees of Jesus and said, "Depart from me, Lord, for I am a sinful man." For astonishment at the catch of fish they had made seized him and all those with him, and likewise James and John, the sons of Zebedee, who were partners of Simon. Jesus said to Simon, "Do not be afraid; from now on you will be catching men." When they brought their boats to the shore, they left everything and followed him.

1013 SIXTH SUNDAY IN ORDINARY TIME / A

READING I *Sirach 15:15-20 / 76*

If you choose you can keep the
    commandments, they will save
        you;
    if you trust in God, you too shall
        live;
he has set before you fire and water;
    to whichever you choose, stretch
        forth your hand.
Before man are life and death, good and
    evil,

whichever he chooses shall be given
    him.
Immense is the wisdom of the Lord;
    he is mighty in power, and all-seeing.
The eyes of God are on those who fear
    him;
    he understands man's every deed.
No one does he command to act unjustly,
    to none does he give license to sin.

RESPONSORIAL PSALM *Psalm 119:1-2, 4-5, 17-18, 33-34*

℟. **Blessed are they who follow the law of the Lord!**

Blessed are they whose way is
    blameless,
    who walk in the law of the LORD.
Blessed are they who observe his
    decrees,
    who seek him with all their heart. ℟.

You have commanded that your precepts
    be diligently kept.
Oh, that I might be firm in the ways
    of keeping your statutes! ℟.

Be good to your servant, that I may live
    and keep your words.
Open my eyes, that I may consider
    the wonders of your law. ℟.

Instruct me, O LORD, in the way of
    your statutes,
    that I may exactly observe them.
Give me discernment, that I may observe
    your law
    and keep it with all my heart. ℟.

READING II *1 Corinthians 2:6-10*

Brothers and sisters: We speak a wisdom to those who are mature, not a wisdom of this age, nor of the rulers of this age who are passing away. Rather, we speak God's wisdom, mysterious, hidden, which God predetermined before the ages for our glory, and which none of the rulers of this age knew; for, if they had known it, they would not have crucified the Lord of glory. But as it is written:

"What eye has not seen, and ear has not heard,
    and what has not entered the human heart,
      what God has prepared for those who love him,"
this God has revealed to us through the Spirit.

For the Spirit scrutinizes everything, even the depths of God.

GOSPEL   *Matthew 5:17-37 or 5:20-22a, 27-28, 33-34a, 37*
For short form read only the parts in brackets.

[Jesus said to his disciples:] "Do not think that I have come to abolish the law or the prophets. I have come not to abolish but to fulfill. Amen, I say to you, until heaven and earth pass away, not the smallest letter or the smallest part of a letter will pass from the law, until all things have taken place. Therefore, whoever breaks one of the least of these commandments and teaches others to do so will be called least in the kingdom of heaven. But whoever obeys and teaches these commandments will be called greatest in the kingdom of heaven. [I tell you, unless your righteousness surpasses that of the scribes and Pharisees, you will not enter the kingdom of heaven.

"You have heard that it was said to your ancestors 'You shall not kill; and whoever kills will be liable to judgment.' But I say to you, whoever is angry with brother will be liable to judgment;] and whoever says to brother, 'Raqa,' will be answerable to the Sanhedrin; and whoever says, 'You fool,' will be liable to fiery Gehenna. Therefore, if you bring your gift to the altar, and there recall that your brother has anything against you, leave your gift there at the altar, go first and be reconciled with your brother, and then come and offer your gift. Settle with your opponent quickly while on the way to court. Otherwise your opponent will hand you over to the judge, and the judge will hand you over to the guard, and you will be thrown into prison. Amen, I say to you, you will not be released until you have paid the last penny.

["You have heard that it was said, 'You shall not commit adultery.' But I say to you, everyone who looks at a woman with lust has already committed adultery with her in his heart.] If your right eye causes you to sin, tear it out and throw it away. It is better for you to lose one of your members than to have your whole body thrown into Gehenna. And if your right hand causes you to sin, cut it off and throw it away. It is better for you to lose one of your members than to have your whole body go into Gehenna.

"It was also said, 'Whoever divorces his wife must give her a bill of divorce.' But I say to you, whoever divorces his wife (unless the marriage is unlawful) causes her to commit adultery, and whoever marries a divorced woman commits adultery.

["Again you have heard that it was said to your ancestors, 'Do not take a false oath, but make good to the Lord all that you vow.' But I say to you, do not swear at all;] not by heaven, for it is God's throne; nor by the earth, for it is his footstool; nor by Jerusalem, for it is the city of the great King. Do not swear by your head, for you cannot make a single hair white or black. [Let your 'Yes' mean 'Yes,' and your 'No' mean 'No.' Anything more is from the evil one."]

SIXTH SUNDAY IN ORDINARY TIME / B   1014

READING I   *Leviticus 13:1-2, 44-46 / 77*

The Lord said to Moses and Aaron, "If someone has on his skin a scab or pustule or blotch which appears to be the sore of leprosy, he shall be brought to Aaron, the priest, or to one of the priests among his descendants. If the man is leprous and unclean, the priest shall declare him unclean by reason of the sore on his head.

"The one who bears the sore of leprosy shall keep his garments rent and his head bare, and shall muffle his beard; he shall cry out, 'Unclean, unclean!' As long as the sore is on him he shall declare himself unclean, since he is in fact unclean. He shall dwell apart, making his abode outside the camp."

RESPONSORIAL PSALM   *Psalm 32:1-2, 5, 11*
℞. I turn to you, Lord, in time of trouble, and you fill me with the joy of salvation.

Blessed is he whose fault is taken away,
  whose sin is covered.
Blessed the man to whom the LORD
  imputes not guilt,
  in whose spirit there is no guile. ℞.

Then I acknowledged my sin to you,

my guilt I covered not.
I said, "I confess my faults to the LORD,"
  and you took away the guilt of my
  sin. ℞.

Be glad in the LORD and rejoice, you just;
  exult, all you upright of heart. ℞.

READING II   *1 Corinthians 10:31—11:1*
Brothers and sisters, Whether you eat or drink, or whatever you do, do everything for the glory of God. Avoid giving offense, whether to the Jews or Greeks or the church of God, just as I try to please everyone in every way, not seeking my own benefit but that of the many, that they may be saved. Be imitators of me, as I am of Christ.

GOSPEL   *Mark 1:40-45*
A leper came to Jesus and kneeling down begged him and said, "If you wish, you can make me clean." Moved with pity, he stretched out his hand, touched him, and said to him, "I do will it. Be made clean." The leprosy left him immediately, and he was made clean. Then, warning him sternly, he dismissed him at once.

He said to him, "See that you tell no one anything, but go, show yourself to the priest and offer for your cleansing what Moses prescribed; that will be proof for them."

The man went away and began to publicize the whole matter. He spread the report abroad so that it was impossible for Jesus to enter a town openly. He remained outside in deserted places, and people kept coming to him from everywhere.

1015 SIXTH SUNDAY IN ORDINARY TIME / C

READING I   *Jeremiah 17:5-8 / 78*
Thus says the LORD:
  Cursed is the one who trusts in
    human beings,
  who seeks his strength in flesh,
  whose heart turns away from the
    LORD.
He is like a barren bush in the desert
  that enjoys no change of season,
but stands in a lava waste,
  a salt and empty earth.
Blessed is the one who trusts in the

LORD.
  whose hope is the LORD.
He is like a tree planted beside the
  waters
  that stretches out its roots to the
    stream:
it fears not the heat when it comes;
  its leaves stay green;
in the year of drought it shows no
  distress,
but still bears fruit.

RESPONSORIAL PSALM   *Psalm 1:1-2, 3, 4, 6*
℞. Blessed are they who hope in the Lord.

Blessed the man who follows not
  the counsel of the wicked,
nor walks in the way of sinners,
  nor sits in the company of the
    insolent,

but delights in the law of the
  LORD
and meditates on his law day and
  night. ℞.

He is like a tree
    planted near running water,
that yields its fruit in due season,
    and whose leaves never fade.
Whatever he does, prospers. ℟.

Not so the wicked, not so;

they are like chaff which the wind
    drives away.
For the LORD watches over the way of
    the just,
but the way of the wicked
    vanishes. ℟.

READING II
1 Corinthians 15:12, 16-20

Brothers and sisters: If Christ is preached as raised from the dead, how can some among you say there is no resurrection of the dead? If the dead are not raised, neither has Christ been raised, and if Christ has not been raised, your faith is vain; you are still in your sins. Then those who have fallen asleep in Christ have perished. If for this life only we have hoped in Christ, we are the most pitiable people of all.
    But now Christ has been raised from the dead, the firstfruits of those who have fallen asleep.

GOSPEL
Luke 6:17, 20-26

Jesus came down with the Twelve and stood on a stretch of level ground with a great crowd of his disciples and a large number of the people from all Judea and Jerusalem and the coastal region of Tyre and Sidon. And raising his eyes toward his disciples he said:
"Blessed are you who are poor,
    for the kingdom of God is yours.
Blessed are you who are now hungry,
    for you will be satisfied.
Blessed are you who are now weeping,
    for you will laugh.
Blessed are you when people hate you,
    and when they exclude and insult you,
    and denounce your name as evil
    on account of the Son of Man.

Rejoice and leap for joy on that day! Behold, your reward will be great in heaven. For their ancestors treated the prophets in the same way.
    But woe to you who are rich,
    for you have received your consolation.
Woe to you who are filled now,
    for you will be hungry.
Woe to you who laugh now,
    for you will grieve and weep.
Woe to you when all speak well of you,
    for their ancestors treated the false
    prophets in this way."

SEVENTH SUNDAY IN ORDINARY TIME / A
1016

READING I
Leviticus 19:1-2, 17-18 / 79

The LORD said to Moses, "Speak to the whole Israelite community and tell them: Be holy, for I, the LORD, your God, am holy.
    "You shall not bear hatred for your brother or sister in your heart. Though you may have to reprove your fellow citizen, do not incur sin because of him. Take no revenge and cherish no grudge against any of your people. You shall love your neighbor as yourself. I am the LORD."

RESPONSORIAL PSALM

Psalm 103:1-2, 3-4, 8, 10, 12-13

℟. The Lord is kind and merciful.

Bless the LORD, O my soul;
and all my being, bless his holy
name.
Bless the LORD, O my soul,
and forget not all his benefits. ℟.

He pardons all your iniquities,
heals all your ills.
He redeems your life from destruction,
crowns you with kindness and
compassion. ℟.

Merciful and gracious is the LORD,
slow to anger and abounding in
kindness.
Not according to our sins does he deal
with us,
nor does he requite us according to
our crimes. ℟.

As far as the east is from the west,
so far has he put our transgressions
from us.
As a father has compassion on his
children,
so the LORD has compassion on
those who fear him. ℟.

READING II

1 Corinthians 3:16-23

Brothers and sisters: Do you not know that you are the temple of God, and that the Spirit of God dwells in you? If anyone destroys God's temple, God will destroy that person; for the temple of God, which you are, is holy.

Let no one deceive himself. If any one among you considers himself wise in this age, let him become a fool, so as to become wise. For the wisdom of this world is foolishness in the eyes of God, for it is written:
"God catches the wise in their own ruses,"
and again:
"The Lord knows the thoughts of the wise,
that they are vain."

So let no one boast about human beings, for everything belongs to you, Paul or Apollos or Cephas, or the world or life or death, or the present or the future: all belong to you, and you to Christ, and Christ to God.

GOSPEL

Matthew 5:38-48

Jesus said to his disciples: "You have heard that it was said, 'An eye for an eye and a tooth for a tooth.' But I say to you, offer no resistance to one who is evil. When someone strikes you on your right cheek, turn the other one as well. If anyone wants to go to law with you over your tunic, hand over your cloak as well. Should anyone press you into service for one mile, go for two miles. Give to the one who asks of you, and do not turn your back on one who wants to borrow.

"You have heard that it was said, 'You shall love your neighbor and hate your enemy.' But I say to you, love your enemies and pray for those who persecute you, that you may be children of your heavenly Father, for he makes his sun rise on the bad and the good, and causes rain to fall on the just and the unjust. For if you love those who love you, what recompense will you have? Do not the tax collectors do the same? And if you greet your brothers only, what is unusual about that? Do not the pagans do the same? So be perfect, just as your heavenly Father is perfect."

1017 SEVENTH SUNDAY IN ORDINARY TIME / B

READING I

Isaiah 43:18-19, 21-22, 24b-25 / 80

Thus says the LORD:
Remember not the events of the past,
the things of long ago consider not;
see, I am doing something new!
Now it springs forth, do you not
perceive it?

In the desert I make a way,
in the wasteland, rivers.
The people I formed for myself,
that they might announce my praise.
Yet you did not call upon me, O Jacob,
for you grew weary of me, O Israel.

You burdened me with your sins,
and wearied me with your crimes.
It is I, I, who wipe out,
for my own sake, your offenses;
your sins I remember no more.

RESPONSORIAL PSALM
Psalm 41:2-3, 4-5, 13-14

℟. **Lord, heal my soul, for I have sinned against you.**

Blessed is the one who has regard for the
lowly and the poor;
in the day of misfortune the LORD
will deliver him.
The LORD will keep and preserve him;
and make him blessed on earth,
and not give him over to the will of his
enemies. ℟.

The LORD will help him on his sickbed,
he will take away all his ailment

when he is ill.
Once I said, "O LORD, have pity on me;
heal me, though I have sinned against
you." ℟.

But because of my integrity you sustain
me
and let me stand before you forever.
Blessed be the LORD, the God of Israel,
from all eternity. Amen. Amen. ℟.

READING II
2 Corinthians 1:18-22

Brothers and sisters: As God is faithful, our word to you is not "yes" and "no." For the Son of God, Jesus Christ, who was proclaimed to you by us, Silvanus and Timothy and me, was not "yes" and "no," but "yes" has been in him. For however many are the promises of God, their Yes is in him; therefore, the Amen from us also goes through him to God for glory. But the one who gives us security with you in Christ and who anointed us is God; he has also put his seal upon us and given the Spirit in our hearts as a first installment.

GOSPEL
Mark 2:1-12

When Jesus returned to Capernaum after some days, it became known that he was at home. Many gathered together so that there was no longer room for them, not even around the door, and he preached the word to them. They came bringing to him a paralytic carried by four men. Unable to get near Jesus because of the crowd, they opened up the roof above him. After they had broken through, they let down the mat on which the paralytic was lying. When Jesus saw their faith, he said to the paralytic, "Child, your sins are forgiven." Now some of the scribes were sitting there asking themselves, "Why does this man speak that way? He is blaspheming. Who but God alone can forgive sins?" Jesus immediately knew in his mind what they were thinking to themselves, so he said, "Why are you thinking such things in your hearts? Which is easier, to say to the paralytic, 'Your sins are forgiven,' or to say, 'Rise, pick up your mat and walk?' But that you may know that the Son of Man has authority to forgive sins on earth" —he said to the paralytic, "I say to you, rise, pick up your mat, and go home." He rose, picked up his mat at once, and went away in the sight of everyone. They were all astounded and glorified God, saying, "We have never seen anything like this."

SEVENTH SUNDAY IN ORDINARY TIME / C
1018

READING I
1 Samuel 26:2, 7-9, 12-13, 22-23 / 81

In those days, Saul went down to the desert of Ziph with three thousand picked men of Israel, to search for David in the desert of Ziph. So David and Abishai went among Saul's soldiers by night and found Saul lying asleep within the barricade, with his spear thrust into the ground at his head and Abner and his men sleeping around him.

Abishai whispered to David: "God has delivered your enemy into your grasp this day. Let me nail him to the ground with one thrust of the spear; I will not need a second thrust!" But David said to Abishai, "Do not harm him, for who can lay hands on the LORD's anointed and remain unpunished?" So David took the spear and the water jug from their place at Saul's head, and they got away without anyone's seeing or knowing or awakening. All remained asleep, because the LORD had put them into a deep slumber.

Going across to an opposite slope, David stood on a remote hilltop at a great distance from Abner, son of Ner, and the troops. He said: "Here is the king's spear. Let an attendant come over to get it. The LORD will reward each man for his justice and faithfulness. Today, though the LORD delivered you into my grasp, I would not harm the LORD's anointed."

RESPONSORIAL PSALM
Psalm 103:1-2, 3-4, 8, 10, 12-13

℟. **The Lord is kind and merciful.**

Bless the LORD, O my soul;
  and all my being, bless his holy
    name.
Bless the LORD, O my soul,
  and forget not all his benefits. ℟.

He pardons all your iniquities,
  heals all your ills.
He redeems your life from destruction,
  crowns you with kindness and
    compassion. ℟.

Merciful and gracious is the LORD,
  slow to anger and abounding in
    kindness.
Not according to our sins does he deal
    with us,
  nor does he requite us according to
    our crimes. ℟.

As far as the east is from the west,
  so far has he put our transgressions
    from us.
As a father has compassion on his
    children,
  so the LORD has compassion on those
    who fear him. ℟.

READING II
1 Corinthians 15:45-49

Brothers and sisters: It is written, "The first man, Adam, became a living being," the last Adam a life-giving spirit. But the spiritual was not first; rather the natural and then the spiritual. The first man was from the earth, earthly; the second man, from heaven. As was the earthly one, so also are the earthly, and as is the heavenly one, so also are the heavenly. Just as we have borne the image of the earthly one, we shall also bear the image of the heavenly one.

GOSPEL
Luke 6:27-38

Jesus said to his disciples: "To you who hear I say, love your enemies, do good to those who hate you, bless those who curse you, pray for those who mistreat you. To the person who strikes you on one cheek, offer the other one as well, and from the person who takes your cloak, do not withhold even your tunic. Give to everyone who asks of you, and from the one who takes what is yours do not demand it back. Do to others as you would have them do to you. For if you love those who love you, what credit is that to you? Even sinners love those who love them. And if you do good to those who do good to you, what credit is that to you? Even sinners do the same. If you lend money to those from whom you expect repayment, what credit is that to you? Even sinners lend to sinners, and get back the same amount. But rather, love your enemies and do good to them, and lend expecting nothing back; then your reward will be great and you will be children of the Most High, for he himself is kind to the ungrateful and the wicked. Be merciful, just as your Father is merciful.

"Stop judging and you will not be judged. Stop condemning and you will not be condemned. Forgive and you will be forgiven. Give, and gifts will be given to you; a good measure, packed together, shaken down, and overflowing, will be poured into your lap. For the measure with which you measure will in return be measured out to you."

EIGHTH SUNDAY IN ORDINARY TIME / A   1019

READING I   *Isaiah 49:14-15 / 82*

Zion said, "The Lord has forsaken me;
  my Lord has forgotten me."
Can a mother forget her infant,
  be without tenderness for the child
of her womb?
Even should she forget,
  I will never forget you.

RESPONSORIAL PSALM   *Psalm 62:2-3, 6-7, 8-9*
℟. **Rest in God alone, my soul.**

Only in God is my soul at rest;
  from him comes my salvation.
He only is my rock and my salvation,
  my stronghold; I shall not be
  disturbed at all. ℟.

Only in God be at rest, my soul,
  for from him comes my hope.
He only is my rock and my salvation,

my stronghold; I shall not be
  disturbed. ℟.

With God is my safety and my glory,
  he is the rock of my strength; my
  refuge is in God.
Trust in him at all times, O my people!
Pour out your hearts before him. ℟.

READING II   *1 Corinthians 4:1-5*

Brothers and sisters: Thus should one regard us: as servants of Christ and stewards of the mysteries of God. Now it is of course required of stewards that they be found trustworthy. It does not concern me in the least that I be judged by you or any human tribunal; I do not even pass judgment on myself; I am not conscious of anything against me, but I do not thereby stand acquitted; the one who judges me is the Lord. Therefore do not make any judgment before the appointed time, until the Lord comes, for he will bring to light what is hidden in darkness and will manifest the motives of our hearts, and then everyone will receive praise from God.

GOSPEL   *Matthew 6:24-34*

Jesus said to his disciples: "No one can serve two masters. He will either hate one and love the other, or be devoted to one and despise the other. You cannot serve God and mammon.

"Therefore I tell you, do not worry about your life, what you will eat or drink, or about your body, what you will wear. Is not life more than food and the body more than clothing? Look at the birds in the sky; they do not sow or reap, they gather nothing into barns, yet your heavenly Father feeds them. Are not you more important than they? Can any of you by worrying add a single moment to your life-span? Why are you anxious about clothes? Learn from the way the wild flowers grow. They do not work or spin. But I tell you that not even Solomon in all his splendor was clothed like one of them. If God so clothes the grass of the field, which grows today and is thrown into the oven tomorrow, will he not much more provide for you, O you of little faith? So do not worry and say, 'What are we to eat?' or 'What are we to drink?' or 'What are we to wear?' All these things the pagans seek. Your heavenly Father knows that you need them all. But seek first the kingdom of God and his righteousness, and all these things will be given you besides. Do not worry about tomorrow; tomorrow will take care of itself. Sufficient for a day is its own evil."

EIGHTH SUNDAY IN ORDINARY TIME / B   1020

READING I   *Hosea 2:16b, 17b, 21-22 / 83*

Thus says the Lord:
I will lead her into the desert
and speak to her heart.
She shall respond there as in the days of

her youth,
when she came up from the land of
Egypt.
I will espouse you to me forever:
I will espouse you in right and in

justice,
in love and in mercy;
I will espouse you in fidelity,
and you shall know the Lord.

RESPONSORIAL PSALM   *Psalm 103:1-2, 3-4, 8, 10, 12-13*
℟. **The Lord is kind and merciful.**

Bless the Lord, O my soul;
  and all my being, bless his holy
  name.
Bless the Lord, O my soul,
  and forget not all his benefits. ℟.

He pardons all your iniquities,
  heals all your ills.
He redeems your life from destruction,
  crowns you with kindness and
  compassion. ℟.

Merciful and gracious is the Lord,
  slow to anger and abounding in

kindness.
Not according to our sins does he deal
  with us,
  nor does he requite us according to
  our crimes. ℟.

As far as the east is from the west,
  so far has he put our transgressions
  from us.
As a father has compassion on his
  children,
  so the Lord has compassion on those
  who fear him. ℟.

READING II   *2 Corinthians 3:1b-6*
Brothers and sisters: Do we need, as some do, letters of recommendation to you or from you? You are our letter, written on our hearts, known and read by all, shown to be a letter of Christ ministered by us, written not in ink but by the Spirit of the living God, not on tablets of stone but on tablets that are hearts of flesh.

Such confidence we have through Christ toward God. Not that of ourselves we are qualified to take credit for anything as coming from us; rather, our qualification comes from God, who has indeed qualified us as ministers of a new covenant, not of letter but of spirit; for the letter brings death, but the Spirit gives life.

GOSPEL   *Mark 2:18-22*
The disciples of John and of the Pharisees were accustomed to fast. People came to him and objected, "Why do the disciples of John and the disciples of the Pharisees fast, but your disciples do not fast?" Jesus answered them, "Can the wedding guests fast while the bridegroom is with them? As long as they have the bridegroom with them they cannot fast. But the days will come when the bridegroom is taken away from them, and then they will fast on that day. No one sews a piece of unshrunken cloth on an old cloak. If he does, its fullness pulls away, the new from the old, and the tear gets worse. Likewise, no one pours new wine into old wineskins. Otherwise, the wine will burst the skins, and both the wine and the skins are ruined. Rather, new wine is poured into fresh wineskins."

1021 EIGHTH SUNDAY IN ORDINARY TIME / C

READING I   *Sirach 27:4-7 / 84*
When a sieve is shaken, the husks
  appear;
  so do one's faults when one speaks.
As the test of what the potter molds is in
  the furnace,
  so in tribulation is the test of the just.

The fruit of a tree shows the care it has
  had;
  so too does one's speech disclose the
  bent of one's mind.
Praise no one before he speaks,
  for it is then that people are tested.

RESPONSORIAL PSALM

Psalm 92:2-3, 13-14, 15-16

℟. **Lord, it is good to give thanks to you.**

It is good to give thanks to the Lord,
  to sing praise to your name, Most
    High,
To proclaim your kindness at dawn
  and your faithfulness throughout the
    night. ℟.

The just one shall flourish like the palm
    tree,
  like a cedar of Lebanon shall he grow.

They that are planted in the house of the
    Lord
  shall flourish in the courts of our
    God. ℟.

They shall bear fruit even in old age;
    vigorous and sturdy shall they be,
Declaring how just is the Lord,
  my rock, in whom there is no
    wrong. ℟.

READING II

1 Corinthians 15:54-58

Brothers and sisters: When this which is corruptible clothes itself with incorruptibility and this which is mortal clothes itself with immortality, then the word that is written shall come about:
  "Death is swallowed up in victory.
  Where, O death, is your victory?
  Where, O death, is your sting?"
The sting of death is sin, and the power of sin is the law. But thanks be to God who gives us the victory through our Lord Jesus Christ.

Therefore, my beloved brothers and sisters, be firm, steadfast, always fully devoted to the work of the Lord, knowing that in the Lord your labor is not in vain.

GOSPEL

Luke 6:39-45

Jesus told his disciples a parable, "Can a blind person guide a blind person? Will not both fall into a pit? No disciple is superior to the teacher; but when fully trained, every disciple will be like his teacher. Why do you notice the splinter in your brother's eye, but do not perceive the wooden beam in your own? How can you say to your brother, 'Brother, let me remove that splinter in your eye,' when you do not even notice the wooden beam in your own eye? You hypocrite! Remove the wooden beam from your eye first; then you will see clearly to remove the splinter in your brother's eye.

"A good tree does not bear rotten fruit, nor does a rotten tree bear good fruit. For every tree is known by its own fruit. For people do not pick figs from thornbushes, nor do they gather grapes from brambles. A good person out of the store of goodness in his heart produces good, but an evil person out of a store of evil produces evil; for from the fullness of the heart the mouth speaks."

NINTH SUNDAY IN ORDINARY TIME / A
1022

READING I

Deuteronomy 11:18, 26-28, 32 / 85

Moses told the people, "Take these words of mine into your heart and soul. Bind them at your wrist as a sign, and let them be a pendant on your forehead.

"I set before you here, this day, a blessing and a curse: a blessing for obeying the commandments of the Lord, your God, which I enjoin on you today; a curse if you do not obey the commandments of the Lord, your God, but turn aside from the way I ordain for you today, to follow other gods, whom you have not known. Be careful to observe all the statutes and decrees that I set before you today."

RESPONSORIAL PSALM

Psalm 31:2-3, 3-4, 17, 25

℟. **Lord, be my rock of safety.**

In you, O Lord, I take refuge;
  let me never be put to shame.
In your justice rescue me,

incline your ear to me,
  make haste to deliver me! ℟.

Be my rock of refuge,
    a stronghold to give me safety.
You are my rock and my fortress;
    for your name's sake you will lead
    and guide me. ℟.

Let your face shine upon your servant;
    save me in your kindness.
Take courage and be stouthearted,
    all you who hope in the Lord. ℟.

READING II
Romans 3:21-25, 28

Brothers and sisters, Now the righteousness of God has been manifested apart from the law, though testified to by the law and the prophets, the righteousness of God through faith in Jesus Christ for all who believe. For there is no distinction; all have sinned and are deprived of the glory of God. They are justified freely by his grace through the redemption in Christ Jesus, whom God set forth as an expiation, through faith, by his blood. For we consider that a person is justified by faith apart from works of the law.

GOSPEL
Matthew 7:21-27

Jesus said to his disciples: "Not everyone who says to me, 'Lord, Lord,' will enter the kingdom of heaven, but only the one who does the will of my Father in heaven. Many will say to me on that day, 'Lord, Lord, did we not prophesy in your name? Did we not drive out demons in your name? Did we not do mighty deeds in your name?' Then I will declare to them solemnly, 'I never knew you. Depart from me, you evildoers.' "Everyone who listens to these words of mine and acts on them will be like a wise man who built his house on rock. The rain fell, the floods came, and the winds blew and buffeted the house. But it did not collapse; it had been set solidly on rock. And everyone who listens to these words of mine but does not act on them will be like a fool who built his house on sand. The rain fell, the floods came, and the winds blew and buffeted the house. And it collapsed and was completely ruined."

1023   NINTH SUNDAY IN ORDINARY TIME / B

READING I
Deuteronomy 5:12-15 / 86

Thus says the Lord: "Take care to keep holy the sabbath day as the Lord, your God, commanded you. Six days you may labor and do all your work; but the seventh day is the sabbath of the Lord, your God. No work may be done then, whether by you, or your son or daughter, or your male or female slave, or your ox or ass or any of your beasts, or the alien who lives with you. Your male and female slave should rest as you do. For remember that you too were once a slave in Egypt, and the Lord, your God, brought you from there with his strong hand and outstretched arm. That is why the Lord, your God, has commanded you to observe the sabbath day."

RESPONSORIAL PSALM
Psalm 81:3-4, 5-6, 6-8, 10-11

℟. Sing with joy to God our help.

Take up a melody, and sound the timbrel,
    the pleasant harp and the lyre.
Blow the trumpet at the new moon,
    at the full moon, on our solemn
    feast. ℟.

For it is a statute in Israel,
    an ordinance of the God of Jacob,
who made it a decree for Joseph
    when he came forth from the land of
    Egypt. ℟.

An unfamiliar speech I hear:

"I relieved his shoulder of the
    burden;
his hands were freed from the basket.
    In distress you called, and I rescued
    you." ℟.

"There shall be no strange god among
    you
nor shall you worship any alien god.
I, the Lord, am your God
    who led you forth from the land of
    Egypt." ℟.

READING II
2 Corinthians 4:6-11

Brothers and sisters: God who said, "Let light shine out of darkness," has shone in our hearts to bring to light the knowledge of the glory of God on the face of Jesus Christ. But we hold this treasure in earthen vessels, that the surpassing power may be of God and not from us. We are afflicted in every way, but not constrained; perplexed, but not driven to despair; persecuted, but not abandoned; struck down, but not destroyed; always carrying about in the body the dying of Jesus, so that the life of Jesus may also be manifested in our body. For we who live are constantly being given up to death for the sake of Jesus, so that the life of Jesus may be manifested in our mortal flesh.

GOSPEL
Mark 2:23—3:6 or 2:23-28

For short form read only the part in brackets.

[As Jesus was passing through a field of grain on the sabbath, his disciples began to make a path while picking the heads of grain. At this the Pharisees said to him, "Look, why are they doing what is unlawful on the sabbath?" He said to them, "Have you never read what David did when he was in need and he and his companions were hungry? How he went into the house of God when Abiathar was high priest and ate the bread of offering that only the priests could lawfully eat, and shared it with his companions?" Then he said to them, "The sabbath was made for man, not man for the sabbath. That is why the Son of Man is lord even of the sabbath."]

Again he entered the synagogue. There was a man there who had a withered hand. They watched him closely to see if he would cure him on the sabbath so that they might accuse him. He said to the man with the withered hand, "Come up here before us." Then he said to them, "Is it lawful to do good on the sabbath rather than to do evil, to save life rather than to destroy it?" But they remained silent. Looking around at them with anger and grieved at their hardness of heart, he said to the man, "Stretch out your hand." He stretched it out and his hand was restored. The Pharisees went out and immediately took counsel with the Herodians against him to put him to death.

NINTH SUNDAY IN ORDINARY TIME / C
1024

READING I
1 Kings 8:41-43 / 87

In those days, Solomon prayed in the temple, saying, "To the foreigner, who is not of your people Israel, but comes from a distant land to honor you (since they will learn of your great name and your mighty hand and your outstretched arm) when he comes and prays toward this temple, listen from your heavenly dwelling. Do all that foreigner asks of you, that all the peoples of the earth may know your name, may fear you as do your people Israel, and may acknowledge that this temple which I have built is dedicated to your honor."

RESPONSORIAL PSALM
Psalm 117:1, 2

℟. **Go out to all the world and tell the good news.**
or:
Alleluia.

Praise the Lord, all you nations;
glorify him, all you peoples! ℟.

For steadfast is his kindness toward us,
and the fidelity of the Lord endures forever. ℟.

READING II
Galatians 1:1-2, 6-10

Paul, an apostle not from human beings nor through a human being but through Jesus Christ and God the Father who raised him from the dead, and all the brothers who are with me, to the churches of Galatia.

I am amazed that you are so quickly forsaking the one who called you by the grace of Christ for a different gospel (not that there is another). But there are some who are disturbing you and wish to pervert the gospel of Christ. But even if we or an angel from heaven should preach to you a gospel other than the one that we preached to you, let that one be accursed! As we have said before, and now I say again, if anyone preaches to you a gospel other than what you have received, let that one be accursed!

Am I now currying favor with humans or with God? Or am I seeking to please people? If I were still trying to please people, I would not be a slave of Christ.

GOSPEL   *Luke 7:1-10*

When Jesus had finished all his words to the people, he entered Capernaum. A centurion there had a slave who was ill and about to die, and he was valuable to him. When he heard about Jesus, he sent elders of the Jews to him, asking him to come and save the life of his slave. They approached Jesus and strongly urged him to come, saying, "He deserves to have you do this for him, for he loves our nation and built the synagogue for us." And Jesus went with them, but when he was only a short distance from the house, the centurion sent friends to tell him, "Lord, do not trouble yourself, for I am not worthy to have you enter under my roof. Therefore, I did not consider myself worthy to come to you; but say the word and let my servant be healed. For I too am a person subject to authority, with soldiers subject to me. And I say to one, 'Go,' and he goes; and to another, 'Come here,' and he comes; and to my slave, 'Do this,' and he does it." When Jesus heard this he was amazed at him and, turning, said to the crowd following him, "I tell you, not even in Israel have I found such faith." When the messengers returned to the house, they found the slave in good health.

1025 TENTH SUNDAY IN ORDINARY TIME / A

READING I   *Hosea 6:3-6 / 88*

In their affliction, people will say:
"Let us know, let us strive to know the
    Lord;
as certain as the dawn is his coming,
and his judgment shines forth like
    the light of day!
He will come to us like the rain,
    like spring rain that waters the earth."
What can I do with you, Ephraim?
    What can I do with you, Judah?

Your piety is like a morning cloud,
    like the dew that early passes away.
For this reason I smote them through the
    prophets,
I slew them by the words of my
    mouth;
for it is love that I desire, not sacrifice,
    and knowledge of God rather than
    holocausts.

RESPONSORIAL PSALM   *Psalm 50:1, 8, 12-13, 14-15*
℟. **To the upright I will show the saving power of God.**

God the Lord has spoken and summoned
    the earth,
from the rising of the sun to its
    setting.
"Not for your sacrifices do I rebuke you,
    for your holocausts are before me
    always." ℟.

"If I were hungry, I would not tell you,
    for mine are the world and its
    fullness.

Do I eat the flesh of strong bulls,
    or is the blood of goats my
    drink?" ℟.

"Offer to God praise as your sacrifice
    and fulfill your vows to the Most
    High;
then call upon me in time of distress;
    I will rescue you, and you shall
    glorify me." ℟.

READING II
Romans 4:18-25

Brothers and sisters: Abraham believed, hoping against hope, that he would become "the father of many nations," according to what was said, "Thus shall your descendants be." He did not weaken in faith when he considered his own body as already dead (for he was almost a hundred years old) and the dead womb of Sarah. He did not doubt God's promise in unbelief; rather, he was strengthened by faith and gave glory to God and was fully convinced that what he had promised he was also able to do. That is why "it was credited to him as righteousness." But it was not for him alone that it was written that "it was credited to him;" it was also for us, to whom it will be credited, who believe in the one who raised Jesus our Lord from the dead, who was handed over for our transgressions and was raised for our justification.

GOSPEL
Matthew 9:9-13

As Jesus passed on from there, he saw a man named Matthew sitting at the customs post. He said to him, "Follow me." And he got up and followed him. While he was at table in his house, many tax collectors and sinners came and sat with Jesus and his disciples. The Pharisees saw this and said to his disciples, "Why does your teacher eat with tax collectors and sinners?" He heard this and said, "Those who are well do not need a physician, but the sick do. Go and learn the meaning of the words, 'I desire mercy, not sacrifice.' I did not come to call the righteous but sinners."

TENTH SUNDAY IN ORDINARY TIME / B   1026

READING I
Genesis 3:9-15 / 89

After the man, Adam, had eaten of the tree, the Lord God called to the man and asked him, "Where are you?" He answered, "I heard you in the garden; but I was afraid, because I was naked, so I hid myself." Then he asked, "Who told you that you were naked? You have eaten, then, from the tree of which I had forbidden you to eat!" The man replied, "The woman whom you put here with me— she gave me fruit from the tree, and so I ate it." The Lord God then asked the woman, "Why did you do such a thing?" The woman answered, "The serpent tricked me into it, so I ate it."

Then the Lord God said to the serpent:
  "Because you have done this, you
    shall be banned from
    all the animals
    and from all the wild creatures;
  on your belly shall you crawl,
    and dirt shall you eat

all the days of your life.
  I will put enmity between you and
    the woman,
    and between your offspring and
      hers;
  he will strike at your head,
    while you strike at his heel."

RESPONSORIAL PSALM
Psalm 130:1-2, 3-4, 5-6, 7-8

℞. **With the Lord there is mercy, and fullness of redemption.**

Out of the depths I cry to you, O Lord;
  Lord, hear my voice!
Let your ears be attentive
  to my voice in supplication. ℞.

If you, O Lord, mark iniquities,
  Lord, who can stand?
But with you is forgiveness,
  that you may be revered. ℞.

I trust in the Lord;
  my soul trusts in his word.
More than sentinels wait for the dawn,
  let Israel wait for the Lord. ℞.

For with the Lord is kindness
  and with him is plenteous redemption;
and he will redeem Israel
  from all their iniquities. ℞.

READING II   *2 Corinthians 4:13—5:1*

Brothers and sisters: Since we have the same spirit of faith, according to what is written, "I believed, therefore I spoke," we too believe and therefore we speak, knowing that the one who raised the Lord Jesus will raise us also with Jesus and place us with you in his presence. Everything indeed is for you, so that the grace bestowed in abundance on more and more people may cause the thanksgiving to overflow for the glory of God. Therefore, we are not discouraged; rather, although our outer self is wasting away, our inner self is being renewed day by day. For this momentary light affliction is producing for us an eternal weight of glory beyond all comparison, as we look not to what is seen but to what is unseen; for what is seen is transitory, but what is unseen is eternal. For we know that if our earthly dwelling, a tent, should be destroyed, we have a building from God, a dwelling not made with hands, eternal in heaven.

GOSPEL   *Mark 3:20-35*

Jesus came home with his disciples. Again the crowd gathered, making it impossible for them even to eat. When his relatives heard of this they set out to seize him, for they said, "He is out of his mind." The scribes who had come from Jerusalem said, "He is possessed by Beelzebul," and "By the prince of demons he drives out demons."

Summoning them, he began to speak to them in parables, "How can Satan drive out Satan? If a kingdom is divided against itself, that kingdom cannot stand. And if a house is divided against itself, that house will not be able to stand. And if Satan has risen up against himself and is divided, he cannot stand; that is the end of him. But no one can enter a strong man's house to plunder his property unless he first ties up the strong man. Then he can plunder the house. Amen, I say to you, all sins and all blasphemies that people utter will be forgiven them. But whoever blasphemes against the Holy Spirit will never have forgiveness, but is guilty of an everlasting sin." For they had said, "He has an unclean spirit." His mother and his brothers arrived. Standing outside they sent word to him and called him. A crowd seated around him told him, "Your mother and your brothers and your sisters are outside asking for you." But he said to them in reply, "Who are my mother and my brothers?" And looking around at those seated in the circle he said, "Here are my mother and my brothers. For whoever does the will of God is my brother and sister and mother."

1027 **TENTH SUNDAY IN ORDINARY TIME / C**

READING I   *1 Kings 17:17-24 / 90*

Elijah went to Zarephath of Sidon to the house of a widow. The son of the mistress of the house fell sick, and his sickness grew more severe until he stopped breathing. So she said to Elijah, "Why have you done this to me, O man of God? Have you come to me to call attention to my guilt and to kill my son?" Elijah said to her, "Give me your son." Taking him from her lap, he carried the son to the upper room where he was staying, and put him on his bed. Elijah called out to the Lord: "O Lord, my God, will you afflict even the widow with whom I am staying by killing her son?" Then he stretched himself out upon the child three times and called out to the Lord: "O Lord, my God, let the life breath return to the body of this child." The Lord heard the prayer of Elijah; the life breath returned to the child's body and he revived. Taking the child, Elijah brought him down into the house from the upper room and gave him to his mother. Elijah said to her, "See! Your son is alive." The woman replied to Elijah, "Now indeed I know that you are a man of God. The word of the Lord comes truly from your mouth."

RESPONSORIAL PSALM   *Psalm 30:2, 4, 5-6, 11, 12, 13*

℟. **I will praise you, Lord, for you have rescued me.**

I will extol you, O Lord, for you drew
    me clear

and did not let my enemies rejoice
over me.

O Lord, you brought me up from the
    nether world;
    you preserved me from among those
    going down into the pit. ℟.

Sing praise to the Lord, you his faithful
    ones,
    and give thanks to his holy name.
For his anger lasts but a moment;

a lifetime, his good will.
At nightfall, weeping enters in,
    but with the dawn, rejoicing. ℟.

Hear, O Lord, and have pity on me;
    O Lord, be my helper.
You changed my mourning into dancing;
    O Lord, my God, forever will I give
    you thanks. ℟.

READING II   *Galatians 1:11-19*

I want you to know, brothers and sisters, that the gospel preached by me is not of human origin. For I did not receive it from a human being, nor was I taught it, but it came through a revelation of Jesus Christ.

For you heard of my former way of life in Judaism, how I persecuted the church of God beyond measure and tried to destroy it, and progressed in Judaism beyond many of my contemporaries among my race, since I was even more a zealot for my ancestral traditions. But when God, who from my mother's womb had set me apart and called me through his grace, was pleased to reveal his Son to me, so that I might proclaim him to the Gentiles, I did not immediately consult flesh and blood, nor did I go up to Jerusalem to those who were apostles before me; rather, I went into Arabia and then returned to Damascus.

Then after three years I went up to Jerusalem to confer with Cephas and remained with him for fifteen days. But I did not see any other of the apostles, only James the brother of the Lord.

GOSPEL   *Luke 7:11-17*

Jesus journeyed to a city called Nain, and his disciples and a large crowd accompanied him. As he drew near to the gate of the city, a man who had died was being carried out, the only son of his mother, and she was a widow. A large crowd from the city was with her. When the Lord saw her, he was moved with pity for her and said to her, "Do not weep." He stepped forward and touched the coffin; at this the bearers halted, and he said, "Young man, I tell you, arise!" The dead man sat up and began to speak, and Jesus gave him to his mother. Fear seized them all, and they glorified God, exclaiming, "A great prophet has arisen in our midst," and "God has visited his people." This report about him spread through the whole of Judea and in all the surrounding region.

ELEVENTH SUNDAY IN ORDINARY TIME / A   1028

READING I   *Exodus 19:2-6a / 91*

In those days, the Israelites came to the desert of Sinai and pitched camp. While Israel was encamped here in front of the mountain, Moses went up the mountain to God. Then the Lord called to him and said, "Thus shall you say to the house of Jacob; tell the Israelites: You have seen for yourselves how I treated the Egyptians and how I bore you up on eagle wings and brought you here to myself. Therefore, if you hearken to my voice and keep my covenant, you shall be my special possession, dearer to me than all other people, though all the earth is mine. You shall be to me a kingdom of priests, a holy nation."

RESPONSORIAL PSALM   *Psalm 100:1-2, 3, 5*

℟. **We are his people: the sheep of his flock.**

Sing joyfully to the Lord, all you lands;
    serve the Lord with gladness;
    come before him with joyful song. ℟.

Know that the Lord is God;
    he made us, his we are;
    his people, the flock he tends. ℟.

The Lord is good: and his faithfulness to all
his kindness endures forever, generations. ℟.

READING II
Romans 5:6-11

Brothers and sisters: Christ, while we were still helpless, yet died at the appointed time for the ungodly. Indeed, only with difficulty does one die for a just person, though perhaps for a good person one might even find courage to die. But God proves his love for us in that while we were still sinners Christ died for us. How much more then, since we are now justified by his blood, will we be saved through him from the wrath. Indeed, if, while we were enemies, we were reconciled to God through the death of his Son, how much more, once reconciled, will we be saved by his life. Not only that, but we also boast of God through our Lord Jesus Christ, through whom we have now received reconciliation.

GOSPEL
Matthew 9:36—10:8

At the sight of the crowds, Jesus' heart was moved with pity for them because they were troubled and abandoned, like sheep without a shepherd. Then he said to his disciples, "The harvest is abundant but the laborers are few; so ask the master of the harvest to send out laborers for his harvest."

Then he summoned his twelve disciples and gave them authority over unclean spirits to drive them out and to cure every disease and every illness. The names of the twelve apostles are these: first, Simon called Peter, and his brother Andrew; James, the son of Zebedee, and his brother John; Philip and Bartholomew, Thomas and Matthew the tax collector; James, the son of Alphaeus, and Thaddeus; Simon from Cana, and Judas Iscariot who betrayed him.

Jesus sent out these twelve after instructing them thus, "Do not go into pagan territory or enter a Samaritan town. Go rather to the lost sheep of the house of Israel. As you go, make this proclamation: 'The kingdom of heaven is at hand.' Cure the sick, raise the dead, cleanse lepers, drive out demons. Without cost you have received; without cost you are to give."

1029 ELEVENTH SUNDAY IN ORDINARY TIME / B

READING I
Ezekiel 17:22-24 / 92

Thus says the Lord GOD:
  I, too, will take from the crest of the
    cedar,
    from its topmost branches tear
     off a tender shoot,
  and plant it on a high and lofty
    mountain;
    on the mountain heights of Israel
     I will plant it.
  It shall put forth branches and bear
    fruit,
    and become a majestic cedar.
Birds of every kind shall dwell

beneath it,
    every winged thing in the shade
     of its boughs.
And all the trees of the field shall
    know
    that I, the Lord,
  bring low the high tree,
    lift high the lowly tree,
  wither up the green tree,
    and make the withered tree
     bloom.
As I, the Lord, have spoken, so will I do.

RESPONSORIAL PSALM
Psalm 92:2-3, 13-14, 15-16

℟. **Lord, it is good to give thanks to you.**

It is good to give thanks to the Lord,
  to sing praise to your name, Most
    High,

To proclaim your kindness at dawn
  and your faithfulness throughout the
    night. ℟.

The just one shall flourish like the palm tree,
like a cedar of Lebanon shall he grow.
They that are planted in the house of the Lord
shall flourish in the courts of our

God. ℟.

They shall bear fruit even in old age;
vigorous and sturdy shall they be,
Declaring how just is the Lord,
my rock, in whom there is no wrong. ℟.

READING II
2 Corinthians 5:6-10

Brothers and sisters: We are always courageous, although we know that while we are at home in the body we are away from the Lord, for we walk by faith, not by sight. Yet we are courageous, and we would rather leave the body and go home to the Lord. Therefore, we aspire to please him, whether we are at home or away. For we must all appear before the judgment seat of Christ, so that each may receive recompense, according to what he did in the body, whether good or evil.

GOSPEL
Mark 4:26-34

Jesus said to the crowds: "This is how it is with the kingdom of God; it is as if a man were to scatter seed on the land and would sleep and rise night and day and through it all the seed would sprout and grow, he knows not how. Of its own accord the land yields fruit, first the blade, then the ear, then the full grain in the ear. And when the grain is ripe, he wields the sickle at once, for the harvest has come."

He said, "To what shall we compare the kingdom of God, or what parable can we use for it? It is like a mustard seed that, when it is sown in the ground, is the smallest of all the seeds on the earth. But once it is sown, it springs up and becomes the largest of plants and puts forth large branches, so that the birds of the sky can dwell in its shade." With many such parables he spoke the word to them as they were able to understand it. Without parables he did not speak to them, but to his own disciples he explained everything in private.

ELEVENTH SUNDAY IN ORDINARY TIME / C
1030

READING I
2 Samuel 12:7-10, 13 / 93

Nathan said to David: "Thus says the Lord God of Israel: 'I anointed you king of Israel. I rescued you from the hand of Saul. I gave you your lord's house and your lord's wives for your own. I gave you the house of Israel and of Judah. And if this were not enough, I could count up for you still more. Why have you spurned the Lord and done evil in his sight? You have cut down Uriah the Hittite with the sword; you took his wife as your own, and him you killed with the sword of the Ammonites. Now, therefore, the sword shall never depart from your house, because you have despised me and have taken the wife of Uriah to be your wife.' Then David said to Nathan, "I have sinned against the Lord." Nathan answered David: "The Lord on his part has forgiven your sin: you shall not die."

RESPONSORIAL PSALM
Psalm 32:1-2, 5, 7, 11

℟. **Lord, forgive the wrong I have done.**

Blessed is the one whose fault is taken away,
whose sin is covered.
Blessed the man to whom the Lord imputes not guilt,
in whose spirit there is no guile. ℟.

I acknowledged my sin to you,
my guilt I covered not.
I said, "I confess my faults to the Lord,"
and you took away the guilt of my sin. ℟.

You are my shelter; from distress you
    will preserve me;
with glad cries of freedom you will
    ring me round. ℟.

Be glad in the Lord and rejoice, you just;
    exult, all you upright of heart. ℟.

READING II   *Galatians 2:16, 19-21*

Brothers and sisters: We who know that a person is not justified by works of the law but through faith in Jesus Christ, even we have believed in Christ Jesus that we may be justified by faith in Christ and not by works of the law, because by works of the law no one will be justified. For through the law I died to the law, that I might live for God. I have been crucified with Christ; yet I live, no longer I, but Christ lives in me; insofar as I now live in the flesh, I live by faith in the Son of God who has loved me and given himself up for me. I do not nullify the grace of God; for if justification comes through the law, then Christ died for nothing.

GOSPEL   *Luke 7:36—8:3 or 7:36-50*

For short form read only the part in brackets.

[A Pharisee invited Jesus to dine with him, and he entered the Pharisee's house and reclined at table. Now there was a sinful woman in the city who learned that he was at table in the house of the Pharisee. Bringing an alabaster flask of ointment, she stood behind him at his feet weeping and began to bathe his feet with her tears. Then she wiped them with her hair, kissed them, and anointed them with the ointment. When the Pharisee who had invited him saw this he said to himself, "If this man were a prophet, he would know who and what sort of woman this is who is touching him, that she is a sinner." Jesus said to him in reply, "Simon, I have something to say to you." "Tell me, teacher," he said. "Two people were in debt to a certain creditor; one owed five hundred days' wages and the other owed fifty. Since they were unable to repay the debt, he forgave it for both. Which of them will love him more?" Simon said in reply, "The one, I suppose, whose larger debt was forgiven." He said to him, "You have judged rightly."

Then he turned to the woman and said to Simon, "Do you see this woman? When I entered your house, you did not give me water for my feet, but she has bathed them with her tears and wiped them with her hair. You did not give me a kiss, but she has not ceased kissing my feet since the time I entered. You did not anoint my head with oil, but she anointed my feet with ointment. So I tell you, her many sins have been forgiven because she has shown great love. But the one to whom little is forgiven, loves little." He said to her, "Your sins are forgiven." The others at table said to themselves, "Who is this who even forgives sins?" But he said to the woman, "Your faith has saved you; go in peace."]

Afterward he journeyed from one town and village to another, preaching and proclaiming the good news of the kingdom of God. Accompanying him were the Twelve and some women who had been cured of evil spirits and infirmities, Mary, called Magdalene, from whom seven demons had gone out, Joanna, the wife of Herod's steward Chuza, Susanna, and many others who provided for them out of their resources.

1031   **TWELFTH SUNDAY IN ORDINARY TIME / A**

READING I   *Jeremiah 20:10-13 / 94*

Jeremiah said:
    "I hear the whisperings of many:
        'Terror on every side!

Denounce! let us denounce him!'
All those who were my friends
    are on the watch for any misstep

of mine.
'Perhaps he will be trapped; then we
 can prevail,
 and take our vengeance on him.'
But the LORD is with me, like a
 mighty champion:
 my persecutors will stumble,
 they will not triumph.
In their failure they will be put to
 utter shame,
 to lasting, unforgettable
 confusion.

O LORD of hosts, you who test the
 just,
 who probe mind and heart,
let me witness the vengeance you
 take on them,
 for to you I have entrusted my
 cause.
Sing to the LORD,
 praise the LORD,
for he has rescued the life of the poor
 from the power of the wicked!"

RESPONSORIAL PSALM

Psalm 69:8-10, 14, 17, 33-35

℟. **Lord, in your great love, answer me.**

For your sake I bear insult,
 and shame covers my face.
I have become an outcast to my brothers,
 a stranger to my children,
because zeal for your house consumes
 me,
 and the insults of those who
 blaspheme you fall upon me. ℟.

I pray to you, O Lord,
 for the time of your favor, O God!
In your great kindness answer me
 with your constant help.
Answer me, O Lord, for bounteous is

your kindness;
in your great mercy turn toward
 me. ℟.

"See, you lowly ones, and be glad;
 you who seek God, may your hearts
 revive!
For the Lord hears the poor,
 and his own who are in bonds he
 spurns not.
Let the heavens and the earth praise him,
 the seas and whatever moves in
 them!" ℟.

READING II

Romans 5:12-15

Brothers and sisters: Through one man sin entered the world, and through sin, death, and thus death came to all men, inasmuch as all sinned—for up to the time of the law, sin was in the world, though sin is not accounted when there is no law. But death reigned from Adam to Moses, even over those who did not sin after the pattern of the trespass of Adam, who is the type of the one who was to come.

But the gift is not like the transgression. For if by the transgression of the one the many died, how much more did the grace of God and the gracious gift of the one man Jesus Christ overflow for the many.

GOSPEL

Matthew 10:26-33

Jesus said to the Twelve: "Fear no one. Nothing is concealed that will not be revealed, nor secret that will not be known. What I say to you in the darkness, speak in the light; what you hear whispered, proclaim on the housetops. And do not be afraid of those who kill the body but cannot kill the soul; rather, be afraid of the one who can destroy both soul and body in Gehenna. Are not two sparrows sold for a small coin? Yet not one of them falls to the ground without your Father's knowledge. Even all the hairs of your head are counted. So do not be afraid; you are worth more than many sparrows. Everyone who acknowledges me before others I will acknowledge before my heavenly Father. But whoever denies me before others, I will deny before my heavenly Father."

1032 TWELFTH SUNDAY IN ORDINARY TIME / B

READING I
Job 38:1, 8-11 / 95

The Lord addressed Job out of the storm
and said:
Who shut within doors the sea,
    when it burst forth from the womb;
when I made the clouds its garment
    and thick darkness its swaddling
    bands?

When I set limits for it
    and fastened the bar of its door,
and said: Thus far shall you come but no
    farther,
    and here shall your proud waves be
    stilled!

RESPONSORIAL PSALM
Psalm 107:23-24, 25-26, 28-29, 30-31

℟. **Give thanks to the Lord, his love is everlasting.**
    or:
Alleluia.

They who sailed the sea in ships,
    trading on the deep waters,
these saw the works of the Lord
    and his wonders in the abyss. ℟.

His command raised up a storm wind
    which tossed its waves on high.
They mounted up to heaven; they sank
    to the depths;
    their hearts melted away in their
    plight. ℟.

They cried to the Lord in their distress;

from their straits he rescued them,
He hushed the storm to a gentle breeze,
    and the billows of the sea were
    stilled. ℟.

They rejoiced that they were calmed,
    and he brought them to their desired
    haven.
Let them give thanks to the Lord for his
    kindness
    and his wondrous deeds to the
    children of men. ℟.

READING II
2 Corinthians 5:14-17

Brothers and sisters: The love of Christ impels us, once we have come to the conviction
that one died for all; therefore, all have died. He indeed died for all, so that those who
live might no longer live for themselves but for him who for their sake died and was
raised.
    Consequently, from now on we regard no one according to the flesh; even if we once
knew Christ according to the flesh, yet now we know him so no longer. So whoever is
in Christ is a new creation: the old things have passed away; behold, new things have
come.

GOSPEL
Mark 4:35-41

On that day, as evening drew on, Jesus said to his disciples: "Let us cross to the other
side." Leaving the crowd, they took Jesus with them in the boat just as he was. And other
boats were with him. A violent squall came up and waves were breaking over the boat,
so that it was already filling up. Jesus was in the stern, asleep on a cushion. They woke
him and said to him, "Teacher, do you not care that we are perishing?" He woke up,
rebuked the wind, and said to the sea, "Quiet! Be still!" The wind ceased and there was
great calm. Then he asked them, "Why are you terrified? Do you not yet have faith?"
They were filled with great awe and said to one another, "Who then is this whom even
wind and sea obey?"

TWELFTH SUNDAY IN ORDINARY TIME / C   1033

READING I
Zechariah 12:10-11; 13:1 / 96

Thus says the Lord: I will pour out on the house of David and on the inhabitants of Jerusalem a spirit of grace and petition; and they shall look on him whom they have pierced, and they shall mourn for him as one mourns for an only son, and they shall grieve over him as one grieves over a firstborn.

On that day the mourning in Jerusalem shall be as great as the mourning of Hadadrimmon in the plain of Megiddo.

On that day there shall be open to the house of David and to the inhabitants of Jerusalem, a fountain to purify from sin and uncleanness.

RESPONSORIAL PSALM
Psalm 63:2, 3-4, 5-6, 8-9

℟. **My soul is thirsting for you, O Lord my God.**

O God, you are my God whom I seek;
for you my flesh pines and my soul thirsts
like the earth, parched, lifeless and without water. ℟.

Thus have I gazed toward you in the sanctuary
to see your power and your glory,
for your kindness is a greater good than life;
my lips shall glorify you. ℟.

Thus will I bless you while I live;
lifting up my hands, I will call upon your name.
As with the riches of a banquet shall my soul be satisfied,
and with exultant lips my mouth shall praise you. ℟.

You are my help,
and in the shadow of your wings I shout for joy.
My soul clings fast to you;
your right hand upholds me. ℟.

READING II
Galatians 3:26-29

Brothers and sisters: Through faith you are all children of God in Christ Jesus. For all of you who were baptized into Christ have clothed yourselves with Christ. There is neither Jew nor Greek, there is neither slave nor free person, there is not male and female; for you are all one in Christ Jesus. And if you belong to Christ, then you are Abraham's descendant, heirs according to the promise.

GOSPEL
Luke 9:18-24

Once when Jesus was praying in solitude, and the disciples were with him, he asked them, "Who do the crowds say that I am?" They said in reply, "John the Baptist; others, Elijah; still others, 'One of the ancient prophets has arisen.'" Then he said to them, "But who do you say that I am?" Peter said in reply, "The Christ of God." He rebuked them and directed them not to tell this to anyone.

He said, "The Son of Man must suffer greatly and be rejected by the elders, the chief priests, and the scribes, and be killed and on the third day be raised."

Then he said to all, "If anyone wishes to come after me, he must deny himself and take up his cross daily and follow me. For whoever wishes to save his life will lose it, but whoever loses his life for my sake will save it."

1034 THIRTEENTH SUNDAY IN ORDINARY TIME / A

READING I *2 Kings 4:8-11, 14-16a / 97*

One day Elisha came to Shunem, where there was a woman of influence, who urged him to dine with her. Afterward, whenever he passed by, he used to stop there to dine. So she said to her husband, "I know that Elisha is a holy man of God. Since he visits us often, let us arrange a little room on the roof and furnish it for him with a bed, table, chair, and lamp, so that when he comes to us he can stay there." Sometime later Elisha arrived and stayed in the room overnight.

Later Elisha asked, "Can something be done for her?" His servant Gehazi answered, "Yes! She has no son, and her husband is getting on in years." Elisha said, "Call her." When the woman had been called and stood at the door, Elisha promised, "This time next year you will be fondling a baby son."

RESPONSORIAL PSALM *Psalm 89:2-3, 16-17, 18-19*

℟. **For ever I will sing the goodness of the Lord.**

The promises of the Lord I will sing
　forever,
　　through all generations my mouth
　　　shall proclaim your faithfulness.
For you have said, "My kindness is
　established forever;"
　in heaven you have confirmed your
　　faithfulness. ℟.

Blessed the people who know the joyful
　shout;

in the light of your countenance, O
　Lord, they walk.
At your name they rejoice all the day,
　and through your justice they are
　　exalted. ℟.

You are the splendor of their strength,
　and by your favor our horn is
　　exalted.
For to the Lord belongs our shield,
　and to the Holy One of Israel, our
　　king. ℟.

READING II *Romans 6:3-4, 8-11*

Brothers and sisters: Are you unaware that we who were baptized into Christ Jesus were baptized into his death? We were indeed buried with him through baptism into death, so that, just as Christ was raised from the dead by the glory of the Father, we too might live in newness of life.

If, then, we have died with Christ, we believe that we shall also live with him. We know that Christ, raised from the dead, dies no more; death no longer has power over him. As to his death, he died to sin once and for all; as to his life, he lives for God. Consequently, you too must think of yourselves as dead to sin and living for God in Christ Jesus.

GOSPEL *Matthew 10:37-42*

Jesus said to his apostles: "Whoever loves father or mother more than me is not worthy of me, and whoever loves son or daughter more than me is not worthy of me; and whoever does not take up his cross and follow after me is not worthy of me. Whoever finds his life will lose it, and whoever loses his life for my sake will find it. Whoever receives you receives me, and whoever receives me receives the one who sent me. Whoever receives a prophet because he is a prophet will receive a prophet's reward, and whoever receives a righteous man because he is a righteous man will receive a righteous man's reward. And whoever gives only a cup of cold water to one of these little ones to drink because the little one is a disciple—amen, I say to you, he will surely not lose his reward."

THIRTEENTH SUNDAY IN ORDINARY TIME / B   1035

READING I

Wisdom 1:13-15; 2:23-24 / 98

God did not make death,
  nor does he rejoice in the destruction
    of the living.
For he fashioned all things that they
  might have being;
  and the creatures of the world are
    wholesome,
and there is not a destructive drug among
  them
  nor any domain of the netherworld
on earth,
  for justice is undying.
For God formed man to be imperishable;
  the image of his own nature he made
    him.
But by the envy of the devil, death
  entered the world,
  and they who belong to his company
    experience it.

RESPONSORIAL PSALM

Psalm 30:2, 4, 5-6, 11, 12, 13

℟. I will praise you, Lord, for you have rescued me.

I will extol you, O Lord, for you drew
  me clear
  and did not let my enemies rejoice
    over me.
O Lord, you brought me up from the
  netherworld;
  you preserved me from among those
    going down into the pit. ℟.

Sing praise to the Lord, you his faithful
  ones,
and give thanks to his holy name.
For his anger lasts but a moment;
  a lifetime, his good will.
At nightfall, weeping enters in,
  but with the dawn, rejoicing. ℟.

Hear, O Lord, and have pity on me;
  O Lord, be my helper.
You changed my mourning into dancing;
  O Lord, my God, forever will I give
    you thanks. ℟.

READING II

2 Corinthians 8:7, 9, 13-15

Brothers and sisters: As you excel in every respect, in faith, discourse, knowledge, all earnestness, and in the love we have for you, may you excel in this gracious act also.
  For you know the gracious act of our Lord Jesus Christ, that though he was rich, for your sake he became poor, so that by his poverty you might become rich. Not that others should have relief while you are burdened, but that as a matter of equality your abundance at the present time should supply their needs, so that their abundance may also supply your needs, that there may be equality. As it is written:
  "Whoever had much did not have more,
    and whoever had little did not have less."

GOSPEL

Mark 5:21-43 or 5:21-24, 35b-43

For short form read only the parts in brackets.

[When Jesus had crossed again in the boat to the other side, a large crowd gathered around him, and he stayed close to the sea. One of the synagogue officials, named Jairus, came forward. Seeing him he fell at his feet and pleaded earnestly with him, saying, "My daughter is at the point of death. Please, come lay your hands on her that she may get well and live." He went off with him, and a large crowd followed him and pressed upon him.]

There was a woman afflicted with hemorrhages for twelve years. She had suffered greatly at the hands of many doctors and had spent all that she had. Yet she was not helped but only grew worse. She had heard about Jesus and came up behind him in the crowd and touched his cloak. She said, "If I but touch his clothes, I shall be cured." Immediately her flow of blood dried up. She felt in her body that she was healed of her affliction. Jesus, aware at once that power had gone out from him, turned around in the crowd and asked, "Who has touched my clothes?" But his disciples said to Jesus, "You see how the crowd is pressing upon you, and yet you ask, 'Who touched me?'" And he looked around to see who had done it. The woman, realizing what had happened to her, approached in fear and trembling. She fell down before Jesus and told him the whole truth. He said to her, "Daughter, your faith has saved you. Go in peace and be cured of your affliction."

[While he was still speaking, people from the synagogue official's house arrived and said, "Your daughter has died; why trouble the teacher any longer?" Disregarding the message that was reported, Jesus said to the synagogue official, "Do not be afraid; just have faith." He did not allow anyone to accompany him inside except Peter, James, and John, the brother of James. When they arrived at the house of the synagogue official, he caught sight of a commotion, people weeping and wailing loudly. So he went in and said to them, "Why this commotion and weeping? The child is not dead but asleep." And they ridiculed him. Then he put them all out. He took along the child's father and mother and those who were with him and entered the room where the child was. He took the child by the hand and said to her, "Talitha koum," which means, "Little girl, I say to you, arise!" The girl, a child of twelve, arose immediately and walked around. At that they were utterly astounded. He gave strict orders that no one should know this and said that she should be given something to eat.]

1036 THIRTEENTH SUNDAY IN ORDINARY TIME / C

READING I   *Kings 19:16b, 19-21 / 99*

The Lord said to Elijah: "You shall anoint Elisha, son of Shaphat of Abel-Meholah, as prophet to succeed you."

Elijah set out and came upon Elisha, son of Shaphat, as he was plowing with twelve yoke of oxen; he was following the twelfth. Elijah went over to him and threw his cloak over him. Elisha left the oxen, ran after Elijah, and said, "Please, let me kiss my father and mother goodbye, and I will follow you." Elijah answered, "Go back! Have I done anything to you?" Elisha left him and, taking the yoke of oxen, slaughtered them; he used the plowing equipment for fuel to boil their flesh, and gave it to his people to eat. Then Elisha left and followed Elijah as his attendant.

RESPONSORIAL PSALM   *Psalm 16:1-2, 5, 7-8, 9-10, 11*

℟. You are my inheritance, O Lord.

Keep me, O God, for in you I take refuge;
I say to the Lord, "My Lord are you.
O Lord, my allotted portion and my cup,
you it is who hold fast my lot." ℟.

I bless the Lord who counsels me;
even in the night my heart exhorts me.
I set the Lord ever before me;
with him at my right hand I shall not be disturbed. ℟.

Therefore my heart is glad and my soul rejoices,
my body, too, abides in confidence
because you will not abandon my soul to the netherworld,
nor will you suffer your faithful one to undergo corruption. ℟.

You will show me the path to life,
fullness of joys in your presence,
the delights at your right hand forever. ℟.

READING II
Galatians 5:1, 13-18

Brothers and sisters: For freedom Christ set us free; so stand firm and do not submit again to the yoke of slavery.

For you were called for freedom, brothers and sisters. But do not use this freedom as an opportunity for the flesh; rather, serve one another through love. For the whole law is fulfilled in one statement, namely, "You shall love your neighbor as yourself." But if you go on biting and devouring one another, beware that you are not consumed by one another.

I say, then: live by the Spirit and you will certainly not gratify the desire of the flesh. For the flesh has desires against the Spirit, and the Spirit against the flesh; these are opposed to each other, so that you may not do what you want. But if you are guided by the Spirit, you are not under the law.

GOSPEL
Luke 9:51-62

When the days for Jesus' being taken up were fulfilled, he resolutely determined to journey to Jerusalem, and he sent messengers ahead of him. On the way they entered a Samaritan village to prepare for his reception there, but they would not welcome him because the destination of his journey was Jerusalem. When the disciples James and John saw this they asked, "Lord, do you want us to call down fire from heaven to consume them?" Jesus turned and rebuked them, and they journeyed to another village.

As they were proceeding on their journey someone said to him, "I will follow you wherever you go." Jesus answered him, "Foxes have dens and birds of the sky have nests, but the Son of Man has nowhere to rest his head."

And to another he said, "Follow me." But he replied, "Lord, let me go first and bury my father." But he answered him, "Let the dead bury their dead. But you, go and proclaim the kingdom of God." And another said, "I will follow you, Lord, but first let me say farewell to my family at home." To him Jesus said, "No one who sets a hand to the plow and looks to what was left behind is fit for the kingdom of God."

FOURTEENTH SUNDAY IN ORDINARY TIME / A   1037

READING I
Zechariah 9:9-10 / 100

Thus says the LORD:
Rejoice heartily, O daughter Zion,
  shout for joy, O daughter Jerusalem!
See, your king shall come to you;
  a just savior is he,
meek, and riding on an ass,
  on a colt, the foal of an ass.
He shall banish the chariot from Ephraim,

and the horse from Jerusalem;
the warrior's bow shall be banished,
  and he shall proclaim peace to the
    nations.
His dominion shall be from sea to sea,
  and from the River to the ends of
    the earth.

RESPONSORIAL PSALM
Psalm 145:1-2, 8-9, 10-11, 13-14

℟. **I will praise your name for ever, my king and my God.**
  or:
Alleluia.

I will extol you, O my God and King,
  and I will bless your name forever
    and ever.
Every day will I bless you,
  and I will praise your name forever
    and ever. ℟.

The Lord is gracious and merciful,
  slow to anger and of great kindness.
The Lord is good to all
  and compassionate toward all his
    works. ℟.

Let all your works give you thanks, O
   Lord,
   and let your faithful ones bless you.
Let them discourse of the glory of your
   kingdom
   and speak of your might. ℟.

The Lord is faithful in all his words
   and holy in all his works.
The Lord lifts up all who are falling
   and raises up all who are bowed
   down. ℟.

READING II   *Romans 8:9, 11-13*

Brothers and sisters: You are not in the flesh; on the contrary, you are in the spirit, if only the Spirit of God dwells in you. Whoever does not have the Spirit of Christ does not belong to him. If the Spirit of the one who raised Jesus from the dead dwells in you, the one who raised Christ from the dead will give life to your mortal bodies also, through his Spirit that dwells in you. Consequently, brothers and sisters, we are not debtors to the flesh, to live according to the flesh. For if you live according to the flesh, you will die, but if by the Spirit you put to death the deeds of the body, you will live.

GOSPEL   *Matthew 11:25-30*

At that time Jesus exclaimed: "I give praise to you, Father, Lord of heaven and earth, for although you have hidden these things from the wise and the learned you have revealed them to little ones. Yes, Father, such has been your gracious will. All things have been handed over to me by my Father. No one knows the Son except the Father, and no one knows the Father except the Son and anyone to whom the Son wishes to reveal him."

"Come to me, all you who labor and are burdened, and I will give you rest. Take my yoke upon you and learn from me, for I am meek and humble of heart; and you will find rest for yourselves. For my yoke is easy, and my burden light."

1038   FOURTEENTH SUNDAY IN ORDINARY TIME / B

READING I   *Ezekiel 2:2-5 / 101*

As the LORD spoke to me, the spirit entered into me and set me on my feet, and I heard the one who was speaking say to me: Son of man, I am sending you to the Israelites, rebels who have rebelled against me; they and their ancestors have revolted against me to this very day. Hard of face and obstinate of heart are they to whom I am sending you. But you shall say to them: Thus says the LORD God! And whether they heed or resist— for they are a rebellious house—they shall know that a prophet has been among them.

RESPONSORIAL PSALM   *Psalm 123:1-2, 2, 3-4*

℟. Our eyes are fixed on the Lord, pleading for his mercy.

To you I lift up my eyes
   who are enthroned in heaven —
As the eyes of servants
   are on the hands of their masters. ℟.

As the eyes of a maid
   are on the hands of her mistress,
So are our eyes on the Lord, our God,

till he have pity on us. ℟.

Have pity on us, O Lord, have pity on us,
   for we are more than sated with
     contempt;
our souls are more than sated
   with the mockery of the arrogant,
   with the contempt of the proud. ℟.

READING II   *2 Corinthians 12:7-10*

Brothers and sisters: That I, Paul, might not become too elated, because of the abundance of the revelations, a thorn in the flesh was given to me, an angel of Satan, to beat me, to keep me from being too elated. Three times I begged the Lord about this, that it might leave me, but he said to me, "My grace is sufficient for you, for power is made perfect in weakness." I will rather boast most gladly of my weaknesses, in order that the power of Christ may dwell with me. Therefore, I am content with weaknesses, insults, hardships, persecutions, and constraints, for the sake of Christ; for when I am weak, then I am strong.

GOSPEL
Mark 6:1-6

Jesus departed from there and came to his native place, accompanied by his disciples. When the sabbath came he began to teach in the synagogue, and many who heard him were astonished. They said, "Where did this man get all this? What kind of wisdom has been given him? What mighty deeds are wrought by his hands! Is he not the carpenter, the son of Mary, and the brother of James and Joses and Judas and Simon? And are not his sisters here with us?" And they took offense at him. Jesus said to them, "A prophet is not without honor except in his native place and among his own kin and in his own house." So he was not able to perform any mighty deed there, apart from curing a few sick people by laying his hands on them. He was amazed at their lack of faith.

FOURTEENTH SUNDAY IN ORDINARY TIME / C
1039

READING I
Isaiah 66:10-14c / 102

Thus says the LORD:
Rejoice with Jerusalem and be glad
　　because of her,
　　all you who love her;
exult, exult with her,
　　all you who were mourning over her!
Oh, that you may suck fully
　　of the milk of her comfort,
that you may nurse with delight
　　at her abundant breasts!
For thus says the LORD:
Lo, I will spread prosperity over
　　Jerusalem like a river,
and the wealth of the nations like an
　　overflowing torrent.

As nurslings, you shall be carried in her
　　arms,
　　and fondled in her lap;
as a mother comforts her child,
　　so will I comfort you;
in Jerusalem you shall find your
　　comfort.

When you see this, your heart shall
　　rejoice
and your bodies flourish like the
　　grass;
the LORD's power shall be known to
　　his servants.

RESPONSORIAL PSALM
Psalm 66:1-3, 4-5, 6-7, 16, 20

℟. Let all the earth cry out to God with joy.

Shout joyfully to God, all the earth,
　　sing praise to the glory of his name;
　　proclaim his glorious praise.
Say to God, "How tremendous are your
　　deeds!" ℟.

"Let all on earth worship and sing praise
　　to you,
　　sing praise to your name!"
Come and see the works of God,
　　his tremendous deeds among the
　　children of Adam. ℟.

He has changed the sea into dry land;
　　through the river they passed on foot;
　　therefore let us rejoice in him.
He rules by his might forever. ℟.

Hear now, all you who fear God,
　　while I declare what he has done for
　　me.
Blessed be God who refused me not
　　my prayer or his kindness! ℟.

READING II
Galatians 6:14-18

Brothers and sisters: May I never boast except in the cross of our Lord Jesus Christ, through which the world has been crucified to me, and I to the world. For neither does circumcision mean anything, nor does uncircumcision, but only a new creation. Peace and mercy be to all who follow this rule and to the Israel of God.

From now on, let no one make troubles for me; for I bear the marks of Jesus on my body.

The grace of our Lord Jesus Christ be with your spirit, brothers and sisters. Amen.

GOSPEL
Luke 10:1-12, 17-20 or 10:1-9

For short form read only the part in brackets.

[At that time the Lord appointed seventy-two others whom he sent ahead of him in pairs to every town and place he intended to visit. He said to them, "The harvest is abundant but the laborers are few; so ask the master of the harvest to send out laborers for his harvest. Go on your way; behold, I am sending you like lambs among wolves. Carry no money bag, no sack, no sandals; and greet no one along the way. Into whatever house you enter, first say, 'Peace to this household.' If a peaceful person lives there, your peace will rest on him; but if not, it will return to you. Stay in the same house and eat and drink what is offered to you, for the laborer deserves his payment. Do not move about from one house to another. Whatever town you enter and they welcome you, eat what is set before you, cure the sick in it and say to them, 'The kingdom of God is at hand for you.'] Whatever town you enter and they do not receive you, go out into the streets and say, 'The dust of your town that clings to our feet, even that we shake off against you.' Yet know this: the kingdom of God is at hand. I tell you, it will be more tolerable for Sodom on that day than for that town."

The seventy-two returned rejoicing, and said, "Lord, even the demons are subject to us because of your name." Jesus said, "I have observed Satan fall like lightning from the sky. Behold, I have given you the power to 'tread upon serpents' and scorpions and upon the full force of the enemy and nothing will harm you. Nevertheless, do not rejoice because the spirits are subject to you, but rejoice because your names are written in heaven."

1040 FIFTEENTH SUNDAY IN ORDINARY TIME / A

READING I
Isaiah 55:10-11 / 103

Thus says the LORD:
Just as from the heavens
    the rain and snow come down
and do not return there
    till they have watered the earth,
    making it fertile and fruitful,
giving seed to the one who sows

and bread to the one who eats,
so shall my word be
    that goes forth from my mouth;
my word shall not return to me void,
    but shall do my will,
    achieving the end for which I sent it.

RESPONSORIAL PSALM
Psalm 65:10, 11, 12-13, 14

℟. **The seed that falls on good ground will yield a fruitful harvest.**

You have visited the land and watered it;
    greatly have you enriched it.
God's watercourses are filled;
    you have prepared the grain. ℟.

Thus have you prepared the land:
    drenching its furrows,

    breaking up its clods,
softening it with showers,
    blessing its yield. ℟.

You have crowned the year with your
    bounty,
and your paths overflow with a rich

harvest;
the untilled meadows overflow with it,
and rejoicing clothes the hills. ℟.

The fields are garmented with flocks
and the valleys blanketed with grain.
They shout and sing for joy. ℟.

READING II
Romans 8:18-23

Brothers and sisters: I consider that the sufferings of this present time are as nothing compared with the glory to be revealed for us. For creation awaits with eager expectation the revelation of the children of God; for creation was made subject to futility, not of its own accord but because of the one who subjected it, in hope that creation itself would be set free from slavery to corruption and share in the glorious freedom of the children of God. We know that all creation is groaning in labor pains even until now; and not only that, but we ourselves, who have the firstfruits of the Spirit, we also groan within ourselves as we wait for adoption, the redemption of our bodies.

GOSPEL
Matthew 13:1-23 or 13:1-9

For short form read only the part in brackets.

[On that day, Jesus went out of the house and sat down by the sea. Such large crowds gathered around him that he got into a boat and sat down, and the whole crowd stood along the shore. And he spoke to them at length in parables, saying: "A sower went out to sow. And as he sowed, some seed fell on the path, and birds came and ate it up. Some fell on rocky ground, where it had little soil. It sprang up at once because the soil was not deep, and when the sun rose it was scorched, and it withered for lack of roots. Some seed fell among thorns, and the thorns grew up and choked it. But some seed fell on rich soil, and produced fruit, a hundred or sixty or thirtyfold. Whoever has ears ought to hear."]
The disciples approached him and said, "Why do you speak to them in parables?" He said to them in reply, "Because knowledge of the mysteries of the kingdom of heaven has been granted to you, but to them it has not been granted. To anyone who has, more will be given and he will grow rich; from anyone who has not, even what he has will be taken away. This is why I speak to them in parables, because 'they look but do not see and hear but do not listen or understand.' Isaiah's prophecy is fulfilled in them, which says:
'You shall indeed hear but not understand,
    you shall indeed look but never see.
Gross is the heart of this people,
    they will hardly hear with their ears,
        they have closed their eyes,
        lest they see with their eyes
    and hear with their ears
and understand with their hearts and be converted,
    and I heal them.'

"But blessed are your eyes, because they see, and your ears, because they hear. Amen, I say to you, many prophets and righteous people longed to see what you see but did not see it, and to hear what you hear but did not hear it.
"Hear then the parable of the sower. The seed sown on the path is the one who hears the word of the kingdom without understanding it, and the evil one comes and steals away what was sown in his heart. The seed sown on rocky ground is the one who hears the word and receives it at once with joy. But he has no root and lasts only for a time. When some tribulation or persecution comes because of the word, he immediately falls away. The seed sown among thorns is the one who hears the word, but then worldly anxiety and the lure of riches choke the word and it bears no fruit. But the seed sown on rich soil is the one who hears the word and understands it, who indeed bears fruit and yields a hundred or sixty or thirtyfold."

1041 FIFTEENTH SUNDAY IN ORDINARY TIME / B

READING I   *Amos 7:12-15 / 104*

Amaziah, priest of Bethel, said to Amos, "Off with you, visionary, flee to the land of Judah! There earn your bread by prophesying, but never again prophesy in Bethel; for it is the king's sanctuary and a royal temple." Amos answered Amaziah, "I was no prophet, nor have I belonged to a company of prophets; I was a shepherd and a dresser of sycamores. The LORD took me from following the flock, and said to me, Go, prophesy to my people Israel."

RESPONSORIAL PSALM   *Psalm 85:9-10, 11-12, 13-14*

℟. Lord, let us see your kindness, and grant us your salvation.

I will hear what God proclaims;
  the Lord—for he proclaims peace.
Near indeed is his salvation to those who
    fear him,
  glory dwelling in our land. ℟.

Kindness and truth shall meet;
  justice and peace shall kiss.

Truth shall spring out of the earth,
  and justice shall look down from
    heaven. ℟.

The Lord himself will give his benefits;
  our land shall yield its increase.
Justice shall walk before him,
  and prepare the way of his steps. ℟.

READING II   *Ephesians 1:3-14 or 1:3-10*

For short form read only the part in brackets.

[Blessed be the God and Father of our Lord Jesus Christ, who has blessed us in Christ with every spiritual blessing in the heavens, as he chose us in him, before the foundation of the world, to be holy and without blemish before him. In love he destined us for adoption to himself through Jesus Christ, in accord with the favor of his will, for the praise of the glory of his grace that he granted us in the beloved. In him we have redemption by his blood, the forgiveness of transgressions, in accord with the riches of his grace that he lavished upon us. In all wisdom and insight, he has made known to us the mystery of his will in accord with his favor that he set forth in him as a plan for the fullness of times, to sum up all things in Christ, in heaven and on earth.] In him we were also chosen, destined in accord with the purpose of the One who accomplishes all things according to the intention of his will, so that we might exist for the praise of his glory, we who first hoped in Christ. In him you also, who have heard the word of truth, the gospel of your salvation, and have believed in him, were sealed with the promised holy Spirit, which is the first installment of our inheritance toward redemption as God's possession, to the praise of his glory.

GOSPEL   *Mark 6:7-13*

Jesus summoned the Twelve and began to send them out two by two and gave them authority over unclean spirits. He instructed them to take nothing for the journey but a walking stick—no food, no sack, no money in their belts. They were, however, to wear sandals but not a second tunic. He said to them, "Wherever you enter a house, stay there until you leave. Whatever place does not welcome you or listen to you, leave there and shake the dust off your feet in testimony against them." So they went off and preached repentance. The Twelve drove out many demons, and they anointed with oil many who were sick and cured them.

FIFTEENTH SUNDAY IN ORDINARY TIME / C   1042

READING I   *Deuteronomy 30:10-14 / 105*

Moses said to the people: "If only you would heed the voice of the LORD, your God, and keep his commandments and statutes that are written in this book of the law, when you return to the LORD, your God, with all your heart and all your soul.

"For this command that I enjoin on you today is not too mysterious and remote for you. It is not up in the sky, that you should say, 'Who will go up in the sky to get it for us and tell us of it, that we may carry it out?' Nor is it across the sea, that you should say, 'Who will cross the sea to get it for us and tell us of it, that we may carry it out?' No, it is something very near to you, already in your mouths and in your hearts; you have only to carry it out."

RESPONSORIAL PSALM   *Psalm 69:14, 17, 30-31, 33-34, 36, 37*
℟. **Turn to the Lord in your need, and you will live.**

I pray to you, O Lord,
   for the time of your favor, O God!
In your great kindness answer me
   with your constant help.
Answer me, O Lord, for bounteous is
   your kindness:
   in your great mercy turn toward
     me. ℟.

I am afflicted and in pain;
   let your saving help, O God, protect
   me.
I will praise the name of God in song,
   and I will glorify him with
     thanksgiving. ℟.

"See, you lowly ones, and be glad;
   you who seek God, may your hearts
     revive!
For the Lord hears the poor,
   and his own who are in bonds he
     spurns not." ℟.

For God will save Zion
   and rebuild the cities of Judah.
The descendants of his servants shall
   inherit it,
   and those who love his name shall
   inhabit it. ℟.

Or:

RESPONSORIAL PSALM   *Psalm 19:8, 9, 10, 11*
℟. **Your words, Lord, are Spirit and life.**

The law of the Lord is perfect,
   refreshing the soul;
the decree of the Lord is trustworthy,
   giving wisdom to the simple. ℟.

The precepts of the Lord are right,
   rejoicing the heart;
the command of the Lord is clear,
   enlightening the eye. ℟.

The fear of the Lord is pure,
   enduring forever;
the ordinances of the Lord are true,
   all of them just. ℟.

They are more precious than gold,
   than a heap of purest gold;
sweeter also than syrup
   or honey from the comb. ℟.

READING II   *Colossians 1:15-20*

Christ Jesus is the image of the invisible
   God,
   the firstborn of all creation.
For in him were created all things in
   heaven and on earth,
   the visible and the invisible,
   whether thrones or dominions or
   principalities or powers;
all things were created through him
   and for him.
He is before all things,
   and in him all things hold together.
He is the head of the body, the church.
He is the beginning, the firstborn from

the dead,
that in all things he himself might
be preeminent.
For in him all the fullness was pleased to
dwell,
and through him to reconcile all
things for him,
making peace by the blood of his
cross
through him, whether those on earth
or those in heaven.

GOSPEL   *Luke 10:25-37*

There was a scholar of the law who stood up to test him and said, "Teacher, what must I do to inherit eternal life?" Jesus said to him, "What is written in the law? How do you read it?" He said in reply, 'You shall love the Lord, your God, with all your heart, with all your being, with all your strength, and with all your mind, and your neighbor as yourself.'" He replied to him, "You have answered correctly; do this and you will live."

But because he wished to justify himself, he said to Jesus, "And who is my neighbor?" Jesus replied, "A man fell victim to robbers as he went down from Jerusalem to Jericho. They stripped and beat him and went off leaving him half-dead. A priest happened to be going down that road, but when he saw him, he passed by on the opposite side. Likewise a Levite came to the place, and when he saw him, he passed by on the opposite side. But a Samaritan traveler who came upon him was moved with compassion at the sight. He approached the victim, poured oil and wine over his wounds and bandaged them. Then he lifted him up on his own animal, took him to an inn, and cared for him. The next day he took out two silver coins and gave them to the innkeeper with the instruction, 'Take care of him. If you spend more than what I have given you, I shall repay you on my way back.' Which of these three, in your opinion, was neighbor to the robbers' victim?" He answered, "The one who treated him with mercy." Jesus said to him, "Go and do likewise."

1043   SIXTEENTH SUNDAY IN ORDINARY TIME / A

READING I   *Wisdom 12:13, 16-19 / 106*

There is no god besides you who have the care of all,
    that you need show you have not unjustly condemned.
For your might is the source of justice;
    your mastery over all things makes you lenient to all.
For you show your might when the perfection of your power is disbelieved;
    and in those who know you, you rebuke temerity.
But though you are master of might, you judge with clemency,
    and with much lenience you govern us;
    for power, whenever you will, attends you.
And you taught your people, by these deeds,
    that those who are just must be kind;
and you gave your children good ground for hope
    that you would permit repentance for their sins.

RESPONSORIAL PSALM   *Psalm 86:5-6, 9-10, 15-16*

℞. Lord, you are good and forgiving.

You, O Lord, are good and forgiving,
    abounding in kindness to all who
    call upon you.
Hearken, O Lord, to my prayer
    and attend to the sound of my
    pleading. ℞.

All the nations you have made shall come
    and worship you, O Lord,
    and glorify your name.
For you are great, and you do wondrous
    deeds;
    you alone are God. ℞.

You, O Lord, are a God merciful and gracious, slow to anger, abounding in kindness and fidelity. Turn toward me, and have pity on me; give your strength to your servant. ℟.

READING II
Romans 8:26-27

Brothers and sisters: The Spirit comes to the aid of our weakness; for we do not know how to pray as we ought, but the Spirit himself intercedes with inexpressible groanings. And the one who searches hearts knows what is the intention of the Spirit, because he intercedes for the holy ones according to God's will.

GOSPEL
Matthew 13:24-43 or 13:24-30

For short form read only the part in brackets.

[Jesus proposed another parable to the crowds, saying: "The kingdom of heaven may be likened to a man who sowed good seed in his field. While everyone was asleep his enemy came and sowed weeds all through the wheat, and then went off. When the crop grew and bore fruit, the weeds appeared as well. The slaves of the householder came to him and said, 'Master, did you not sow good seed in your field? Where have the weeds come from?' He answered, 'An enemy has done this.' His slaves said to him, 'Do you want us to go and pull them up?' He replied, 'No, if you pull up the weeds you might uproot the wheat along with them. Let them grow together until harvest; then at harvest time I will say to the harvesters, "First collect the weeds and tie them in bundles for burning; but gather the wheat into my barn."'"]

He proposed another parable to them. "The kingdom of heaven is like a mustard seed that a person took and sowed in a field. It is the smallest of all the seeds, yet when full-grown it is the largest of plants. It becomes a large bush, and the 'birds of the sky come and dwell in its branches.'"

He spoke to them another parable. "The kingdom of heaven is like yeast that a woman took and mixed with three measures of wheat flour until the whole batch was leavened."

All these things Jesus spoke to the crowds in parables. He spoke to them only in parables, to fulfill what had been said through the prophet:

"I will open my mouth in parables,
I will announce what has lain hidden from the foundation
of the world."

Then, dismissing the crowds, he went into the house. His disciples approached him and said, "Explain to us the parable of the weeds in the field." He said in reply, "He who sows good seed is the Son of Man, the field is the world, the good seed the children of the kingdom. The weeds are the children of the evil one, and the enemy who sows them is the devil. The harvest is the end of the age, and the harvesters are angels. Just as weeds are collected and burned up with fire, so will it be at the end of the age. The Son of Man will send his angels, and they will collect out of his kingdom all who cause others to sin and all evildoers. They will throw them into the fiery furnace, where there will be wailing and grinding of teeth. Then the righteous will shine like the sun in the kingdom of their Father. Whoever has ears ought to hear."

SIXTEENTH SUNDAY IN ORDINARY TIME / B
1044

READING I
Jeremiah 23:1-6 / 107

Woe to the shepherds who mislead and scatter the flock of my pasture, says the LORD. Therefore, thus says the LORD, the God of Israel, against the shepherds who shepherd my people: You have scattered my sheep and driven them away. You have not cared for them, but I will take care to punish your evil deeds. I myself will gather the remnant of my flock from all the lands to which I have driven them and bring them back to their meadow; there they shall increase and multiply. I will appoint shepherds for them who will shepherd them so that they need no longer fear and tremble; and none shall be missing, says the LORD.

Behold, the days are coming, says the LORD,
when I will raise up a righteous shoot to David;
as king he shall reign and govern wisely,
he shall do what is just and right in the land.
In his days Judah shall be saved,
Israel shall dwell in security.
This is the name they give him:
"The LORD our justice."

RESPONSORIAL PSALM   *Psalm 23:1-3, 3-4, 5, 6*
℟. **The Lord is my shepherd; there is nothing I shall want.**

The Lord is my shepherd; I shall not
  want.
In verdant pastures he gives me
  repose;
beside restful waters he leads me;
  he refreshes my soul. ℟.

He guides me in right paths
  for his name's sake.
Even though I walk in the dark valley
  I fear no evil; for you are at my side

with your rod and your staff
  that give me courage. ℟.

You spread the table before me
  in the sight of my foes;
you anoint my head with oil;
  my cup overflows. ℟.

Only goodness and kindness follow me
  all the days of my life;
and I shall dwell in the house of the Lord
  for years to come. ℟.

READING II   *Ephesians 2:13-18*
Brothers and sisters: In Christ Jesus you who once were far off have become near by the blood of Christ.

For he is our peace, he who made both one and broke down the dividing wall of enmity, through his flesh, abolishing the law with its commandments and legal claims, that he might create in himself one new person in place of the two, thus establishing peace, and might reconcile both with God, in one body, through the cross, putting that enmity to death by it. He came and preached peace to you who were far off and peace to those who were near, for through him we both have access in one Spirit to the Father.

GOSPEL   *Mark 6:30-34*
The apostles gathered together with Jesus and reported all they had done and taught. He said to them, "Come away by yourselves to a deserted place and rest a while." People were coming and going in great numbers, and they had no opportunity even to eat. So they went off in the boat by themselves to a deserted place. People saw them leaving and many came to know about it. They hastened there on foot from all the towns and arrived at the place before them.

When he disembarked and saw the vast crowd, his heart was moved with pity for them, for they were like sheep without a shepherd; and he began to teach them many things.

1045 # SIXTEENTH SUNDAY IN ORDINARY TIME / C

READING I   *Genesis 18:1-10a / 108*
The LORD appeared to Abraham by the terebinth of Mamre, as he sat in the entrance of his tent, while the day was growing hot. Looking up, Abraham saw three men standing nearby. When he saw them, he ran from the entrance of the tent to greet them; and

bowing to the ground, he said: "Sir, if I may ask you this favor, please do not go on past your servant. Let some water be brought, that you may bathe your feet, and then rest yourselves under the tree. Now that you have come this close to your servant, let me bring you a little food, that you may refresh yourselves; and afterward you may go on your way." The men replied, "Very well, do as you have said."

Abraham hastened into the tent and told Sarah, "Quick, three measures of fine flour! Knead it and make rolls." He ran to the herd, picked out a tender, choice steer, and gave it to a servant, who quickly prepared it. Then Abraham got some curds and milk, as well as the steer that had been prepared, and set these before the three men; and he waited on them under the tree while they ate.

They asked Abraham, "Where is your wife Sarah?" He replied, "There in the tent." One of them said, "I will surely return to you about this time next year, and Sarah will then have a son."

RESPONSORIAL PSALM
Psalm 15:2-3, 3-4, 5

℟. **He who does justice will live in the presence of the Lord.**

One who walks blamelessly and does
    justice;
  who thinks the truth in his heart
  and slanders not with his tongue. ℟.

Who harms not his fellow man,
    nor takes up a reproach against his
    neighbor;
by whom the reprobate is despised,

while he honors those who fear the
  Lord. ℟.

Who lends not his money at usury
  and accepts no bribe against the
  innocent.
One who does these things
  shall never be disturbed. ℟.

READING II
Colossians 1:24-28

Brothers and sisters: Now I rejoice in my sufferings for your sake, and in my flesh I am filling up what is lacking in the afflictions of Christ on behalf of his body, which is the church, of which I am a minister in accordance with God's stewardship given to me to bring to completion for you the word of God, the mystery hidden from ages and from generations past. But now it has been manifested to his holy ones, to whom God chose to make known the riches of the glory of this mystery among the Gentiles; it is Christ in you, the hope for glory. It is he whom we proclaim, admonishing everyone and teaching everyone with all wisdom, that we may present everyone perfect in Christ.

GOSPEL
Luke 10:38-42

Jesus entered a village where a woman whose name was Martha welcomed him. She had a sister named Mary who sat beside the Lord at his feet listening to him speak. Martha, burdened with much serving, came to him and said, "Lord, do you not care that my sister has left me by myself to do the serving? Tell her to help me." The Lord said to her in reply, "Martha, Martha, you are anxious and worried about many things. There is need of only one thing. Mary has chosen the better part and it will not be taken from her."

SEVENTEENTH SUNDAY IN ORDINARY TIME / A   1046

READING I
1 Kings 3:5, 7-12 / 109

The LORD appeared to Solomon in a dream at night. God said, "Ask something of me and I will give it to you." Solomon answered: "O LORD, my God, you have made me, your servant, king to succeed my father David; but I am a mere youth, not knowing at all how to act. I serve you in the midst of the people whom you have chosen, a people so vast that it cannot be numbered or counted. Give your servant, therefore, an understanding heart to judge your people and to distinguish right from wrong. For who is able to govern this vast people of yours?"

The LORD was pleased that Solomon made this request. So God said to him: "Because you have asked for this— not for a long life for yourself, nor for riches, nor for the life of your enemies, but for understanding so that you may know what is right— I do as you requested. I give you a heart so wise and understanding that there has never been anyone like you up to now, and after you there will come no one to equal you."

RESPONSORIAL PSALM　　　　　　　　　*Psalm 119:57, 72, 76-77, 127-128, 129-130*
℟. **Lord, I love your commands.**

I have said, O Lord, that my part
　　is to keep your words.
The law of your mouth is to me more
　　precious
　　than thousands of gold and silver
　　pieces. ℟.

Let your kindness comfort me
　　according to your promise to your
　　servants.
Let your compassion come to me that I
　　may live,

for your law is my delight. ℟.

For I love your commands
　　more than gold, however fine.
For in all your precepts I go forward;
　　every false way I hate. ℟.

Wonderful are your decrees;
　　therefore I observe them.
The revelation of your words sheds light,
　　giving understanding to the
　　simple. ℟.

READING II　　　　　　　　　　　　　　　*Romans 8:28-30*
Brothers and sisters: We know that all things work for good for those who love God, who are called according to his purpose. For those he foreknew he also predestined to be conformed to the image of his Son, so that he might be the firstborn among many brothers and sisters. And those he predestined he also called; and those he called he also justified; and those he justified he also glorified.

GOSPEL　　　　　　　　　　　　　　*Matthew 13:44-52 or 13:44-46*
For short form read only the part in brackets.

[Jesus said to his disciples: "The kingdom of heaven is like a treasure buried in a field, which a person finds and hides again, and out of joy goes and sells all that he has and buys that field. Again, the kingdom of heaven is like a merchant searching for fine pearls. When he finds a pearl of great price, he goes and sells all that he has and buys it.] Again, the kingdom of heaven is like a net thrown into the sea, which collects fish of every kind. When it is full they haul it ashore and sit down to put what is good into buckets. What is bad they throw away. Thus it will be at the end of the age. The angels will go out and separate the wicked from the righteous and throw them into the fiery furnace, where there will be wailing and grinding of teeth.
　　"Do you understand all these things?" They answered, "Yes." And he replied, "Then every scribe who has been instructed in the kingdom of heaven is like the head of a household who brings from his storeroom both the new and the old."

1047　**SEVENTEENTH SUNDAY IN ORDINARY TIME / B**

READING I　　　　　　　　　　　　　　*2 Kings 4:42-44 / 110*
A man came from Baal-shalishah bringing to Elisha, the man of God, twenty barley loaves made from the firstfruits, and fresh grain in the ear. Elisha said, "Give it to the people to eat." But his servant objected, "How can I set this before a hundred people?" Elisha insisted, "Give it to the people to eat. For thus says the LORD, 'They shall eat and there shall be some left over.'" And when they had eaten, there was some left over, as the LORD had said.

RESPONSORIAL PSALM *Psalm 145:10-11, 15-16, 17-18*

℟. **The hand of the Lord feeds us; he answers all our needs.**

Let all your works give you thanks, O
  Lord,
  and let your faithful ones bless you.
Let them discourse of the glory of your
  kingdom
  and speak of your might. ℟.

The eyes of all look hopefully to you,
  and you give them their food in due
  season;

you open your hand
  and satisfy the desire of every living
  thing. ℟.

The Lord is just in all his ways
  and holy in all his works.
The Lord is near to all who call upon
  him,
  to all who call upon him in truth. ℟.

READING II *Ephesians 4:1-6*

Brothers and sisters: I, a prisoner for the Lord, urge you to live in a manner worthy of the call you have received, with all humility and gentleness, with patience, bearing with one another through love, striving to preserve the unity of the spirit through the bond of peace: one body and one Spirit, as you were also called to the one hope of your call; one Lord, one faith, one baptism; one God and Father of all, who is over all and through all and in all.

GOSPEL *John 6:1-15*

Jesus went across the Sea of Galilee. A large crowd followed him, because they saw the signs he was performing on the sick. Jesus went up on the mountain, and there he sat down with his disciples. The Jewish feast of Passover was near. When Jesus raised his eyes and saw that a large crowd was coming to him, he said to Philip, "Where can we buy enough food for them to eat?" He said this to test him, because he himself knew what he was going to do. Philip answered him, "Two hundred days' wages worth of food would not be enough for each of them to have a little." One of his disciples, Andrew, the brother of Simon Peter, said to him, "There is a boy here who has five barley loaves and two fish; but what good are these for so many?" Jesus said, "Have the people recline." Now there was a great deal of grass in that place. So the men reclined, about five thousand in number. Then Jesus took the loaves, gave thanks, and distributed them to those who were reclining, and also as much of the fish as they wanted. When they had had their fill, he said to his disciples, "Gather the fragments left over, so that nothing will be wasted." So they collected them, and filled twelve wicker baskets with fragments from the five barley loaves that had been more than they could eat. When the people saw the sign he had done, they said, "This is truly the Prophet, the one who is to come into the world." Since Jesus knew that they were going to come and carry him off to make him king, he withdrew again to the mountain alone.

SEVENTEENTH SUNDAY IN ORDINARY TIME / C 1048

READING I *Genesis 18:20-32 / 111*

In those days, the LORD said: "The outcry against Sodom and Gomorrah is so great, and their sin so grave, that I must go down and see whether or not their actions fully correspond to the cry against them that comes to me. I mean to find out."

While Abraham's visitors walked on farther toward Sodom, the LORD remained standing before Abraham. Then Abraham drew nearer and said: "Will you sweep away the innocent with the guilty? Suppose there were fifty innocent people in the city; would you wipe out the place, rather than spare it for the sake of the fifty innocent people within it? Far be it from you to do such a thing, to make the innocent die with the guilty so that the innocent and the guilty would be treated alike! Should not the judge of all the world act with justice?" The LORD replied, "If I find fifty innocent people in the city of Sodom, I will spare the whole place for their sake." Abraham spoke up again: "See how I am presuming to speak to my Lord, though I am but dust and ashes! What if there are five less than fifty innocent people? Will you destroy the whole city because of those five?" He answered, "I will not destroy it, if I find forty-five there." But Abraham persisted, saying "What if only forty are found there?" He replied, "I will forbear doing it for the sake of the forty." Then Abraham said, "Let not my Lord grow impatient if I go on. What if only thirty are found there?" He replied, "I will forbear doing it if I can find but thirty there." Still Abraham went on, "Since I have thus dared to speak to my Lord, what if there are no more than twenty?" The LORD answered, "I will not destroy it, for the sake of the twenty." But he still persisted: "Please, let not my Lord grow angry if I speak up this last time. What if there are at least ten there?" He replied, "For the sake of those ten, I will not destroy it."

RESPONSORIAL PSALM
Psalm 138:1-2, 2-3, 6-7, 7-8

℞. **Lord, on the day I called for help, you answered me.**

I will give thanks to you, O Lord, with
    all my heart,
    for you have heard the words of my
      mouth;
    in the presence of the angels I will
      sing your praise;
I will worship at your holy temple
    and give thanks to your name. ℞.

Because of your kindness and your truth;
    for you have made great above all
      things
    your name and your promise.
When I called you answered me;
    you built up strength within me. ℞.

The Lord is exalted, yet the lowly he
    sees,
    and the proud he knows from afar.
Though I walk amid distress, you
    preserve me;
    against the anger of my enemies you
    raise your hand. ℞.

Your right hand saves me.
    The Lord will complete what he has
      done for me;
your kindness, O Lord, endures forever;
    forsake not the work of your
      hands. ℞.

READING II
Colossians 2:12-14

Brothers and sisters: You were buried with him in baptism, in which you were also raised with him through faith in the power of God, who raised him from the dead. And even when you were dead in transgressions and the uncircumcision of your flesh, he brought you to life along with him, having forgiven us all our transgressions; obliterating the bond against us, with its legal claims, which was opposed to us, he also removed it from our midst, nailing it to the cross.

GOSPEL
Luke 11:1-13

Jesus was praying in a certain place, and when he had finished, one of his disciples said to him, "Lord, teach us to pray just as John taught his disciples." He said to them, "When you pray, say:
    "Father, hallowed be your name,
      your kingdom come.
      Give us each day our daily bread
      and forgive us our sins
      for we ourselves forgive everyone in debt to us,
      and do not subject us to the final test."

And he said to them, "Suppose one of you has a friend to whom he goes at midnight and says, 'Friend, lend me three loaves of bread, for a friend of mine has arrived at my house from a journey and I have nothing to offer him,' and he says in reply from within, 'Do not bother me; the door has already been locked and my children and I are already in bed. I cannot get up to give you anything.' I tell you, if he does not get up to give the visitor the loaves because of their friendship, he will get up to give him whatever he needs because of his persistence.

"And I tell you, ask and you will receive; seek and you will find; knock and the door will be opened to you. For everyone who asks, receives; and the one who seeks, finds; and to the one who knocks, the door will be opened. What father among you would hand his son a snake when he asks for a fish? Or hand him a scorpion when he asks for an egg? If you then, who are wicked, know how to give good gifts to your children, how much more will the Father in heaven give the Holy Spirit to those who ask him?"

EIGHTEENTH SUNDAY IN ORDINARY TIME / A   1049

READING I
Isaiah 55:1-3 / 112

Thus says the LORD:
All you who are thirsty,
    come to the water!
You who have no money,
    come, receive grain and eat;
Come, without paying and without cost,
    drink wine and milk!
Why spend your money for what is not
    bread;
your wages for what fails to satisfy?
Heed me, and you shall eat well,
    you shall delight in rich fare.
Come to me heedfully,
    listen, that you may have life.
I will renew with you the everlasting
    covenant,
    the benefits assured to David.

RESPONSORIAL PSALM
Psalm 145:8-9, 15-16, 17-18

℞. The hand of the Lord feeds us; he answers all our needs.

The Lord is gracious and merciful,
    slow to anger and of great kindness.
The Lord is good to all
    and compassionate toward all his
        works. ℞.

The eyes of all look hopefully to you,
    and you give them their food in due
        season;
you open your hand
    and satisfy the desire of every living
        thing. ℞.

The Lord is just in all his ways
    and holy in all his works.
The Lord is near to all who call upon
    him,
    to all who call upon him in truth. ℞.

READING II
Romans 8:35, 37-39

Brothers and sisters: What will separate us from the love of Christ? Will anguish, or distress, or persecution, or famine, or nakedness, or peril, or the sword? No, in all these things we conquer overwhelmingly through him who loved us. For I am convinced that neither death, nor life, nor angels, nor principalities, nor present things, nor future things, nor powers, nor height, nor depth, nor any other creature will be able to separate us from the love of God in Christ Jesus our Lord.

GOSPEL
Matthew 14:13-21

When Jesus heard of the death of John the Baptist, he withdrew in a boat to a deserted place by himself. The crowds heard of this and followed him on foot from their towns. When he disembarked and saw the vast crowd, his heart was moved with pity for them, and he cured their sick. When it was evening, the disciples approached him and said,

"This is a deserted place and it is already late; dismiss the crowds so that they can go to the villages and buy food for themselves." Jesus said to them, "There is no need for them to go away; give them some food yourselves." But they said to him, "Five loaves and two fish are all we have here." Then he said, "Bring them here to me," and he ordered the crowds to sit down on the grass. Taking the five loaves and the two fish, and looking up to heaven, he said the blessing, broke the loaves, and gave them to the disciples, who in turn gave them to the crowds. They all ate and were satisfied, and they picked up the fragments left over— twelve wicker baskets full. Those who ate were about five thousand men, not counting women and children.

1050 EIGHTEENTH SUNDAY IN ORDINARY TIME / B

READING I
Exodus 16:2-4, 12-15 / 113

The whole Israelite community grumbled against Moses and Aaron. The Israelites said to them, "Would that we had died at the Lord's hand in the land of Egypt, as we sat by our fleshpots and ate our fill of bread! But you had to lead us into this desert to make the whole community die of famine!"

Then the Lord said to Moses, "I will now rain down bread from heaven for you. Each day the people are to go out and gather their daily portion; thus will I test them, to see whether they follow my instructions or not.

"I have heard the grumbling of the Israelites. Tell them: In the evening twilight you shall eat flesh, and in the morning you shall have your fill of bread, so that you may know that I, the Lord am your God."

In the evening quail came up and covered the camp. In the morning a dew lay all about the camp, and when the dew evaporated, there on the surface of the desert were fine flakes like hoarfrost on the ground. On seeing it, the Israelites asked one another, "What is this?" for they did not know what it was. But Moses told them, "This is the bread that the Lord has given you to eat."

RESPONSORIAL PSALM
Psalm 78:3-4, 23-24, 25, 54

℟. **The Lord gave them bread from heaven.**

What we have heard and know,
   and what our fathers have declared
     to us,
We will declare to the generation to come
   the glorious deeds of the Lord and
     his strength
   and the wonders that he wrought. ℟.

He commanded the skies above

and opened the doors of heaven;
he rained manna upon them for food
   and gave them heavenly bread. ℟.

Man ate the bread of angels,
   food he sent them in abundance.
And he brought them to his holy land,
   to the mountains his right hand had
     won. ℟.

READING II
Ephesians 4:17, 20-24

Brothers and sisters: I declare and testify in the Lord that you must no longer live as the Gentiles do, in the futility of their minds; that is not how you learned Christ, assuming that you have heard of him and were taught in him, as truth is in Jesus, that you should put away the old self of your former way of life, corrupted through deceitful desires, and be renewed in the spirit of your minds, and put on the new self, created in God's way in righteousness and holiness of truth.

GOSPEL
John 6:24-35

When the crowd saw that neither Jesus nor his disciples were there, they themselves got into boats and came to Capernaum looking for Jesus. And when they found him across the sea they said to him, "Rabbi, when did you get here?" Jesus answered them and said

"Amen, amen, I say to you, you are looking for me not because you saw signs but because you ate the loaves and were filled. Do not work for food that perishes but for the food that endures for eternal life, which the Son of Man will give you. For on him the Father, God, has set his seal." So they said to him, "What can we do to accomplish the works of God?" Jesus answered and said to them, "This is the work of God, that you believe in the one he sent." So they said to him, "What sign can you do, that we may see and believe in you? What can you do? Our ancestors ate manna in the desert, as it is written:

'He gave them bread from heaven to eat.'"

So Jesus said to them, "Amen, amen, I say to you, it was not Moses who gave the bread from heaven; my Father gives you the true bread from heaven. For the bread of God is that which comes down from heaven and gives life to the world."

So they said to him, "Sir, give us this bread always." Jesus said to them, "I am the bread of life; whoever comes to me will never hunger, and whoever believes in me will never thirst."

EIGHTEENTH SUNDAY IN ORDINARY TIME / C 1051

READING I
Ecclesiastes 1:2; 2:21-23 / 114

Vanity of vanities, says Qoheleth,
vanity of vanities! All things are vanity!
Here is one who has labored with wisdom and knowledge and skill, and yet to another who has not labored over it, he must leave property. This also is vanity and a great misfortune. For what profit comes to man from all the toil and anxiety of heart with which he has labored under the sun? All his days sorrow and grief are his occupation; even at night his mind is not at rest. This also is vanity.

RESPONSORIAL PSALM
Psalm 90:3-4, 5-6, 12-13, 14, 17

℟. If today you hear his voice, harden not your hearts.

You turn man back to dust,
saying, "Return, O children of men."
For a thousand years in your sight
are as yesterday, now that it is past,
or as a watch of the night. ℟.

You make an end of them in their sleep;
the next morning they are like the
changing grass,
which at dawn springs up anew,
but by evening wilts and fades. ℟.

Teach us to number our days aright,
that we may gain wisdom of heart.
Return, O Lord! How long?
Have pity on your servants! ℟.

Fill us at daybreak with your kindness,
that we may shout for joy and gladness
all our days.
And may the gracious care of the Lord
our God be ours;
prosper the work of our hands for us!
Prosper the work of our hands! ℟.

READING II
Colossians 3:1-5, 9-11

Brothers and sisters: If you were raised with Christ, seek what is above, where Christ is seated at the right hand of God. Think of what is above, not of what is on earth. For you have died, and your life is hidden with Christ in God. When Christ your life appears, then you too will appear with him in glory.

Put to death, then, the parts of you that are earthly: immorality, impurity, passion, evil desire, and the greed that is idolatry. Stop lying to one another, since you have taken off the old self with its practices and have put on the new self, which is being renewed, for knowledge, in the image of its creator. Here there is not Greek and Jew, circumcision and uncircumcision, barbarian, Scythian, slave, free; but Christ is all and in all.

GOSPEL *Luke 12:13-21*

Someone in the crowd said to Jesus, "Teacher, tell my brother to share the inheritance with me." He replied to him, "Friend, who appointed me as your judge and arbitrator?" Then he said to the crowd, "Take care to guard against all greed, for though one may be rich, one's life does not consist of possessions."

Then he told them a parable. "There was a rich man whose land produced a bountiful harvest. He asked himself, 'What shall I do, for I do not have space to store my harvest?' And he said, 'This is what I shall do: I shall tear down my barns and build larger ones. There I shall store all my grain and other goods and I shall say to myself, "Now as for you, you have so many good things stored up for many years, rest, eat, drink, be merry!"' But God said to him, 'You fool, this night your life will be demanded of you; and the things you have prepared, to whom will they belong?' Thus will it be for all who store up treasure for themselves but are not rich in what matters to God."

1052 NINETEENTH SUNDAY IN ORDINARY TIME / A

READING I *1 Kings 19:9a, 11-13a / 115*

At the mountain of God, Horeb, Elijah came to a cave where he took shelter. Then the LORD said to him, "Go outside and stand on the mountain before the LORD; the LORD will be passing by." A strong and heavy wind was rending the mountains and crushing rocks before the LORD— but the LORD was not in the wind. After the wind there was an earthquake— but the LORD was not in the earthquake. After the earthquake there was fire— but the LORD was not in the fire. After the fire there was a tiny whispering sound. When he heard this, Elijah hid his face in his cloak and went and stood at the entrance of the cave.

RESPONSORIAL PSALM *Psalm 85:9, 10, 11-12, 13-14*

℟. **Lord, let us see your kindness, and grant us your salvation.**

I will hear what God proclaims;
the Lord — for he proclaims peace.
Near indeed is his salvation to those who
fear him,
glory dwelling in our land. ℟.

Kindness and truth shall meet;
justice and peace shall kiss.

Truth shall spring out of the earth,
and justice shall look down from
heaven. ℟.

The Lord himself will give his benefits;
our land shall yield its increase.
Justice shall walk before him,
and prepare the way of his steps. ℟.

READING II *Romans 9:1-5*

Brothers and sisters: I speak the truth in Christ, I do not lie; my conscience joins with the Holy Spirit in bearing me witness that I have great sorrow and constant anguish in my heart. For I could wish that I myself were accursed and cut off from Christ for the sake of my own people, my kindred according to the flesh. They are Israelites; theirs the adoption, the glory, the covenants, the giving of the law, the worship, and the promises; theirs the patriarchs, and from them, according to the flesh, is the Christ, who is over all, God blessed forever. Amen.

GOSPEL *Matthew 14:22-33*

After he had fed the people, Jesus made the disciples get into a boat and precede him to the other side, while he dismissed the crowds. After doing so, he went up on the mountain by himself to pray. When it was evening he was there alone. Meanwhile the boat, already a few miles offshore, was being tossed about by the waves, for the wind was against it. During the fourth watch of the night, he came toward them walking on the sea. When the disciples saw him walking on the sea they were terrified. "It is a ghost," they said, and they cried out in fear. At once Jesus spoke to them, "Take courage, it is I; do not be afraid." Peter said to him in reply, "Lord, if it is you, command me to come to you on the water." He said, "Come." Peter got out of the boat and began to walk on the water toward Jesus. But when he saw how strong the wind was he became frightened; and, beginning to sink, he cried out, "Lord, save me!" Immediately Jesus stretched out his hand and caught Peter, and said to him, "O you of little faith, why did you doubt?" After they got into the boat, the wind died down. Those who were in the boat did him homage, saying, "Truly, you are the Son of God."

NINETEENTH SUNDAY IN ORDINARY TIME / B   1053

READING I   *1 Kings 19:4-8 / 116*

Elijah went a day's journey into the desert, until he came to a broom tree and sat beneath it. He prayed for death, saying: "This is enough, O LORD! Take my life, for I am no better than my fathers." He lay down and fell asleep under the broom tree, but then an angel touched him and ordered him to get up and eat. Elijah looked and there at his head was a hearth cake and a jug of water. After he ate and drank, he lay down again, but the angel of the LORD came back a second time, touched him, and ordered, "Get up and eat, else the journey will be too long for you!" He got up, ate, and drank; then strengthened by that food, he walked forty days and forty nights to the mountain of God, Horeb.

RESPONSORIAL PSALM   *Psalm 34:2-3, 4-5, 6-7, 8-9*
℟. Taste and see the goodness of the Lord.

I will bless the Lord at all times;
   his praise shall be ever in my mouth.
Let my soul glory in the Lord;
   the lowly will hear me and be glad. ℟.

Glorify the Lord with me,
   let us together extol his name.
I sought the Lord, and he answered me
   and delivered me from all my
     fears. ℟.

Look to him that you may be radiant
   with joy.

And your faces may not blush with
   shame.
When the afflicted man called out, the
   Lord heard,
And from all his distress he saved
   him. ℟.

The angel of the Lord encamps
   around those who fear him and
   delivers them.
Taste and see how good the Lord is;
   blessed the man who takes refuge in
   him. ℟.

READING II   *Ephesians 4:30—5:2*

Brothers and sisters: Do not grieve the Holy Spirit of God, with which you were sealed for the day of redemption. All bitterness, fury, anger, shouting, and reviling must be removed from you, along with all malice. And be kind to one another, compassionate, forgiving one another as God has forgiven you in Christ.
    So be imitators of God, as beloved children, and live in love, as Christ loved us and handed himself over for us as a sacrificial offering to God for a fragrant aroma.

GOSPEL   *John 6:41-51*

The Jews murmured about Jesus because he said, "I am the bread that came down from heaven," and they said, "Is this not Jesus, the son of Joseph? Do we not know his father and mother? Then how can he say, 'I have come down from heaven'?" Jesus answered and said to them, "Stop murmuring among yourselves. No one can come to me unless the Father who sent me draw him, and I will raise him on the last day. It is written in the prophets:

'They shall all be taught by God.'
Everyone who listens to my Father and learns from him comes to me. Not that anyone has seen the Father except the one who is from God; he has seen the Father. Amen, amen, I say to you, whoever believes has eternal life. I am the bread of life. Your ancestors ate the manna in the desert, but they died; this is the bread that comes down from heaven so that one may eat it and not die. I am the living bread that came down from heaven; whoever eats this bread will live forever; and the bread that I will give is my flesh for the life of the world."

1054 NINETEENTH SUNDAY IN ORDINARY TIME / C

READING I *Wisdom 18:6-9 / 117*

The night of the passover was known beforehand to our fathers,
    that, with sure knowledge of the oaths in which they put their faith,
    they might have courage.
Your people awaited the salvation of the just
    and the destruction of their foes.
For when you punished our adversaries,
    in this you glorified us whom you had summoned.
For in secret the holy children of the good were offering sacrifice
    and putting into effect with one accord the divine institution.

RESPONSORIAL PSALM *Psalm 33:1, 12, 18-19, 20, 22*

℟. Blessed the people the Lord has chosen to be his own.

Exult, you just, in the Lord;
    praise from the upright is fitting.
Blessed the nation whose God is the
    Lord,
    the people he has chosen for his own
    inheritance. ℟.

See, the eyes of the Lord are upon those
    who fear him,
    upon those who hope for his
kindness,
to deliver them from death
    and preserve them in spite of
    famine. ℟.

Our soul waits for the Lord,
    who is our help and our shield.
May your kindness, O Lord, be upon us
    who have put our hope in you. ℟.

READING II *Hebrews 11:1-2, 8-19 or 11:1-2, 8-12*

For short form read only the part in brackets.

[Brothers and sisters: Faith is the realization of what is hoped for and evidence of things not seen. Because of it the ancients were well attested.

By faith Abraham obeyed when he was called to go out to a place that he was to receive as an inheritance; he went out, not knowing where he was to go. By faith he sojourned in the promised land as in a foreign country, dwelling in tents with Isaac and Jacob, heirs of the same promise; for he was looking forward to the city with foundations, whose architect and maker is God. By faith he received power to generate, even though he was past the normal age —and Sarah herself was sterile— for he thought that the one who had made the promise was trustworthy. So it was that there came forth from one man, himself as good as dead, descendants as numerous as the stars in the sky and as countless as the sands on the seashore.]

All these died in faith. They did not receive what had been promised but saw it and greeted it from afar and acknowledged themselves to be strangers and aliens on earth, for those who speak thus show that they are seeking a homeland. If they had been thinking of the land from which they had come, they would have had opportunity to return. But now they desire a better homeland, a heavenly one. Therefore, God is not ashamed to be called their God, for he has prepared a city for them.

By faith Abraham, when put to the test, offered up Isaac, and he who had received the promises was ready to offer his only son, of whom it was said, "Through Isaac descendants shall bear your name." He reasoned that God was able to raise even from the dead, and he received Isaac back as a symbol.

GOSPEL
Luke 12:32-48 or 12:35-40

For short form read only the parts in brackets.

[Jesus said to his disciples:] "Do not be afraid any longer, little flock, for your Father is pleased to give you the kingdom. Sell your belongings and give alms. Provide money bags for yourselves that do not wear out, an inexhaustible treasure in heaven that no thief can reach nor moth destroy. For where your treasure is, there also will your heart be.

["Gird your loins and light your lamps and be like servants who await their master's return from a wedding, ready to open immediately when he comes and knocks. Blessed are those servants whom the master finds vigilant on his arrival. Amen, I say to you, he will gird himself, have them recline at table, and proceed to wait on them. And should he come in the second or third watch and find them prepared in this way, blessed are those servants. Be sure of this: if the master of the house had known the hour when the thief was coming, he would not have let his house be broken into. You also must be prepared, for at an hour you do not expect, the Son of Man will come."]

Then Peter said, "Lord, is this parable meant for us or for everyone?" And the Lord replied, "Who, then, is the faithful and prudent steward whom the master will put in charge of his servants to distribute the food allowance at the proper time? Blessed is that servant whom his master on arrival finds doing so. Truly, I say to you, the master will put the servant in charge of all his property. But if that servant says to himself, 'My master is delayed in coming,' and begins to beat the menservants and the maidservants, to eat and drink and get drunk, then that servant's master will come on an unexpected day and at an unknown hour and will punish the servant severely and assign him a place with the unfaithful. That servant who knew his master's will but did not make preparations nor act in accord with his will shall be beaten severely; and the servant who was ignorant of his master's will but acted in a way deserving of a severe beating shall be beaten only lightly. Much will be required of the person entrusted with much, and still more will be demanded of the person entrusted with more."

TWENTIETH SUNDAY IN ORDINARY TIME / A
1055

READING I
Isaiah 56:1, 6-7 / 118

Thus says the LORD:
Observe what is right, do what is just;
    for my salvation is about to come,
    my justice, about to be revealed.

The foreigners who join themselves to
    the LORD,
    ministering to him,
loving the name of the LORD,
    and becoming his servants—

all who keep the sabbath free from
    profanation
    and hold to my covenant,
them I will bring to my holy mountain
    and make joyful in my house of
    prayer;
their burnt offerings and sacrifices
    will be acceptable on my altar,
for my house shall be called
    a house of prayer for all peoples.

RESPONSORIAL PSALM *Psalm 67:2-3, 5, 6, 8*

℟. **O God, let all the nations praise you!**

May God have pity on us and bless us;
may he let his face shine upon us.
So may your way be known upon earth;
among all nations, your salvation. ℟.

May the nations be glad and exult
because you rule the peoples in
equity;

the nations on the earth you guide. ℟.

May the peoples praise you, O God;
may all the peoples praise you!
May God bless us,
and may all the ends of the earth
fear him! ℟.

READING II *Romans 11:13-15, 29-32*

Brothers and sisters: I am speaking to you Gentiles. Inasmuch as I am the apostle to the Gentiles, I glory in my ministry in order to make my race jealous and thus save some of them. For if their rejection is the reconciliation of the world, what will their acceptance be but life from the dead?

For the gifts and the call of God are irrevocable. Just as you once disobeyed God but have now received mercy because of their disobedience, so they have now disobeyed in order that, by virtue of the mercy shown to you, they too may now receive mercy. For God delivered all to disobedience, that he might have mercy upon all.

GOSPEL *Matthew 15:21-28*

At that time, Jesus withdrew to the region of Tyre and Sidon. And behold, a Canaanite woman of that district came and called out, "Have pity on me, Lord, Son of David! My daughter is tormented by a demon." But Jesus did not say a word in answer to her. Jesus' disciples came and asked him, "Send her away, for she keeps calling out after us." He said in reply, "I was sent only to the lost sheep of the house of Israel." But the woman came and did Jesus homage, saying, "Lord, help me." He said in reply, "It is not right to take the food of the children and throw it to the dogs." She said, "Please, Lord, for even the dogs eat the scraps that fall from the table of their masters." Then Jesus said to her in reply, "O woman, great is your faith! Let it be done for you as you wish." And the woman's daughter was healed from that hour.

1056 TWENTIETH SUNDAY IN ORDINARY TIME / B

READING I *Proverbs 9:1-6 / 119*

Wisdom has built her house,
she has set up her seven columns;
she has dressed her meat, mixed her wine,
yes, she has spread her table.
She has sent out her maidens; she calls
from the heights out over the city:
"Let whoever is simple turn in here;

To the one who lacks understanding,
she says,
Come, eat of my food,
and drink of the wine I have mixed!
Forsake foolishness that you may live;
advance in the way of
understanding."

RESPONSORIAL PSALM *Psalm 34:2-3, 4-5, 6-7*

℟. **Taste and see the goodness of the Lord.**

I will bless the Lord at all times;
his praise shall be ever in my mouth.
Let my soul glory in the Lord;
the lowly will hear me and be
glad. ℟.

Glorify the Lord with me,
let us together extol his name.
I sought the Lord, and he answered me
and delivered me from all my
fears. ℟.

Look to him that you may be radiant
    with joy,
and your faces may not blush with
    shame.

When the poor one called out, the Lord
    heard,
and from all his distress he saved
    him. ℟.

READING II
Ephesians 5:15-20

Brothers and sisters: Watch carefully how you live, not as foolish persons but as wise, making the most of the opportunity, because the days are evil. Therefore, do not continue in ignorance, but try to understand what is the will of the Lord. And do not get drunk on wine, in which lies debauchery, but be filled with the Spirit, addressing one another in psalms and hymns and spiritual songs, singing and playing to the Lord in your hearts, giving thanks always and for everything in the name of our Lord Jesus Christ to God the Father.

GOSPEL
John 6:51-58

Jesus said to the crowds: "I am the living bread that came down from heaven; whoever eats this bread will live forever; and the bread that I will give is my flesh for the life of the world."

    The Jews quarreled among themselves, saying, "How can this man give us his flesh to eat?" Jesus said to them, "Amen, amen, I say to you, unless you eat the flesh of the Son of Man and drink his blood, you do not have life within you. Whoever eats my flesh and drinks my blood has eternal life, and I will raise him on the last day. For my flesh is true food, and my blood is true drink. Whoever eats my flesh and drinks my blood remains in me and I in him. Just as the living Father sent me and I have life because of the Father, so also the one who feeds on me will have life because of me. This is the bread that came down from heaven. Unlike your ancestors who ate and still died, whoever eats this bread will live forever."

TWENTIETH SUNDAY IN ORDINARY TIME / C
1057

READING I
Jeremiah 38:4-6, 8-10 / 120

In those days, the princes said to the king: "Jeremiah ought to be put to death; he is demoralizing the soldiers who are left in this city, and all the people, by speaking such things to them; he is not interested in the welfare of our people, but in their ruin." King Zedekiah answered: "He is in your power"; for the king could do nothing with them. And so they took Jeremiah and threw him into the cistern of Prince Malchiah, which was in the quarters of the guard, letting him down with ropes. There was no water in the cistern, only mud, and Jeremiah sank into the mud.

    Ebed-melech, a court official, went there from the palace and said to him: "My lord king, these men have been at fault in all they have done to the prophet Jeremiah, casting him into the cistern. He will die of famine on the spot, for there is no more food in the city." Then the king ordered Ebed-melech the Cushite to take three men along with him, and draw the prophet Jeremiah out of the cistern before he should die.

RESPONSORIAL PSALM
Psalm 40:2, 3, 4, 18

℟. Lord, come to my aid!

I have waited, waited for the Lord,
    and he stooped toward me. ℟.

The Lord heard my cry.
He drew me out of the pit of destruction,
    out of the mud of the swamp;

he set my feet upon a crag;
    he made firm my steps. ℟.

And he put a new song into my mouth,
    a hymn to our God.
Many shall look on in awe
    and trust in the Lord. ℟.

Though I am afflicted and poor,
yet the Lord thinks of me.

You are my help and my deliverer;
O my God, hold not back! ℟.

READING II
Hebrews 12:1-4

Brothers and sisters: Since we are surrounded by so great a cloud of witnesses, let us rid ourselves of every burden and sin that clings to us and persevere in running the race that lies before us while keeping our eyes fixed on Jesus, the leader and perfecter of faith. For the sake of the joy that lay before him he endured the cross, despising its shame, and has taken his seat at the right of the throne of God. Consider how he endured such opposition from sinners, in order that you may not grow weary and lose heart. In your struggle against sin you have not yet resisted to the point of shedding blood.

GOSPEL
Luke 12:49-53

Jesus said to his disciples: "I have come to set the earth on fire, and how I wish it were already blazing! There is a baptism with which I must be baptized, and how great is my anguish until it is accomplished! Do you think that I have come to establish peace on the earth? No, I tell you, but rather division. From now on a household of five will be divided, three against two and two against three; a father will be divided against his son and a son against his father, a mother against her daughter and a daughter against her mother, a mother-in-law against her daughter-in-law and a daughter-in-law against her mother-in-law."

1058 TWENTY-FIRST SUNDAY IN ORDINARY TIME / A

READING I
Isaiah 22:19-23 / 121

Thus says the Lord to Shebna, master of the palace:
"I will thrust you from your office
    and pull you down from your station.
On that day I will summon my servant
    Eliakim, son of Hilkiah;
I will clothe him with your robe,
    and gird him with your sash,
    and give over to him your authority.

He shall be a father to the inhabitants of
        Jerusalem,
    and to the House of Judah.
I will place the key of the House of
        David on Eliakim's shoulder;
    when he opens, no one shall shut,
    when he shuts, no one shall open.
I will fix him like a peg in a sure spot,
    to be a place of honor for his family."

RESPONSORIAL PSALM
Psalm 138:1-2, 2-3, 6, 8

℟. Lord, your love is eternal; do not forsake the work of your hands.

I will give thanks to you, O Lord, with
        all my heart,
    for you have heard the words of my
        mouth;
in the presence of the angels I will sing
        your praise;
    I will worship at your holy temple. ℟.

I will give thanks to your name,
    because of your kindness and your

truth:
when I called, you answered me;
    you built up strength within me. ℟.

The Lord is exalted, yet the lowly he
        sees,
    and the proud he knows from afar.
Your kindness, O Lord, endures forever;
    forsake not the work of your
        hands. ℟.

READING II
Romans 11:33-36

Oh, the depth of the riches and wisdom and knowledge of God! How inscrutable are his judgments and how unsearchable his ways!

'For who has known the mind of the Lord
    or who has been his counselor?
Or who has given the Lord anything
    that he may be repaid?'

For from him and through him and for him are all things. To him be glory forever. Amen.

GOSPEL
Matthew 16:13-20

Jesus went into the region of Caesarea Philippi and he asked his disciples, "Who do people say that the Son of Man is?" They replied, "Some say John the Baptist, others Elijah, still others Jeremiah or one of the prophets." He said to them, "But who do you say that I am?" Simon Peter said in reply, "You are the Christ, the Son of the living God." Jesus said to him in reply, "Blessed are you, Simon son of Jonah. For flesh and blood has not revealed this to you, but my heavenly Father. And so I say to you, you are Peter, and upon this rock I will build my church, and the gates of the netherworld shall not prevail against it. I will give you the keys to the kingdom of heaven. Whatever you bind on earth shall be bound in heaven; and whatever you loose on earth shall be loosed in heaven." Then he strictly ordered his disciples to tell no one that he was the Christ.

TWENTY-FIRST SUNDAY IN ORDINARY TIME / B   1059

READING I
Joshua 24:1-2a, 15-17, 18b / 122

Joshua gathered together all the tribes of Israel at Shechem, summoning their elders, their leaders, their judges, and their officers. When they stood in ranks before God, Joshua addressed all the people: "If it does not please you to serve the LORD, decide today whom you will serve, the gods your fathers served beyond the River or the gods of the Amorites in whose country you are now dwelling. As for me and my household, we will serve the LORD."

But the people answered, "Far be it from us to forsake the LORD for the service of other gods. For it was the LORD, our God, who brought us and our fathers up out of the land of Egypt, out of a state of slavery. He performed those great miracles before our very eyes and protected us along our entire journey and among the peoples through whom we passed. Therefore we also will serve the LORD, for he is our God."

RESPONSORIAL PSALM
Psalm 34:2-3, 16-17, 18-19, 20-21

℟. Taste and see the goodness of the Lord.

I will bless the Lord at all times;
    his praise shall be ever in my mouth.
Let my soul glory in the Lord;
    the lowly will hear me and be glad. ℟.

The Lord has eyes for the just,
    and ears for their cry.
The Lord confronts the evildoers,
    to destroy remembrance of them
        from the earth. ℟.

When the just cry out, the Lord hears them,
    and from all their distress he rescues them.
The Lord is close to the brokenhearted;
    and those who are crushed in spirit
        he saves. ℟.

Many are the troubles of the just one,
    but out of them all the Lord delivers him;
he watches over all his bones;
    not one of them shall be broken. ℟.

READING II   *Ephesians 5:21-32 or 5:2a, 25-32*
For long form, omit the phrase in double brackets; for short form read only the parts in brackets.

[Brothers and sisters:] [[Live in love, as Christ loved us.]] Be subordinate to one another out of reverence for Christ. Wives should be subordinate to their husbands as to the Lord. For the husband is head of his wife just as Christ is head of the church, he himself the savior of the body. As the church is subordinate to Christ, so wives should be subordinate to their husbands in everything. [Husbands, love your wives, even as Christ loved the church and handed himself over for her to sanctify her, cleansing her by the bath of water with the word, that he might present to himself the church in splendor, without spot or wrinkle or any such thing, that she might be holy and without blemish. So also husbands should love their wives as their own bodies. He who loves his wife loves himself. For no one hates his own flesh but rather nourishes and cherishes it, even as Christ does the church, because we are members of his body.
    'For this reason a man shall leave his father and his mother
        and be joined to his wife,
    and the two shall become one flesh.'
This is a great mystery, but I speak in reference to Christ and the church.]

GOSPEL   *John 6:60-69*
Many of Jesus' disciples who were listening said, "This saying is hard; who can accept it?" Since Jesus knew that his disciples were murmuring about this, he said to them, "Does this shock you? What if you were to see the Son of Man ascending to where he was before? It is the spirit that gives life, while the flesh is of no avail. The words I have spoken to you are Spirit and life. But there are some of you who do not believe." Jesus knew from the beginning the ones who would not believe and the one who would betray him. And he said, "For this reason I have told you that no one can come to me unless it is granted him by my Father."
    As a result of this, many of his disciples returned to their former way of life and no longer accompanied him. Jesus then said to the Twelve, "Do you also want to leave?" Simon Peter answered him, "Master, to whom shall we go? You have the words of eternal life. We have come to believe and are convinced that you are the Holy One of God."

1060 TWENTY-FIRST SUNDAY IN ORDINARY TIME / C

READING I   *Isaiah 66:18-21 / 123*
Thus says the LORD: I know their works and their thoughts, and I come to gather nations of every language; they shall come and see my glory. I will set a sign among them; from them I will send fugitives to the nations: to Tarshish, Put and Lud, Mosoch, Tubal and Javan, to the distant coastlands that have never heard of my fame, or seen my glory; and they shall proclaim my glory among the nations. They shall bring all your brothers and sisters from all the nations as an offering to the LORD, on horses and in chariots, in carts, upon mules and dromedaries, to Jerusalem, my holy mountain, says the LORD, just as the Israelites bring their offering to the house of the LORD in clean vessels. Some of these I will take as priests and Levites, says the LORD.

RESPONSORIAL PSALM   *Psalm 117:1-2*
℟. **Go out to all the world and tell the Good News.**
    or:
Alleluia.

Praise the Lord, all you nations;   For steadfast is his kindness toward us,
    glorify him, all you peoples! ℟.   and the fidelity of the Lord endures
                                                   forever. ℟.

READING II   *Hebrews 12:5-7, 11-13*

Brothers and sisters, You have forgotten the exhortation addressed to you as children:
"My son, do not disdain the discipline of the Lord
   or lose heart when reproved by him;
for whom the Lord loves, he disciplines;
   he scourges every son he acknowledges."
Endure your trials as "discipline"; God treats you as sons. For what "son" is there whom
his father does not discipline? At the time, all discipline seems a cause not for joy but
for pain, yet later it brings the peaceful fruit of righteousness to those who are trained
by it.
   So strengthen your drooping hands and your weak knees. Make straight paths for
your feet, that what is lame may not be disjointed but healed.

GOSPEL   *Luke 13:22-30*

Jesus passed through towns and villages, teaching as he went and making his way to
Jerusalem. Someone asked him, "Lord, will only a few people be saved?" He answered
them, "Strive to enter through the narrow gate, for many, I tell you, will attempt to enter
but will not be strong enough. After the master of the house has arisen and locked the
door, then will you stand outside knocking and saying, 'Lord, open the door for us.' He
will say to you in reply, 'I do not know where you are from.' And you will say, 'We ate
and drank in your company and you taught in our streets.' Then he will say to you, 'I do
not know where you are from. Depart from me, all you evildoers!' And there will be
wailing and grinding of teeth when you see Abraham, Isaac, and Jacob and all the
prophets in the kingdom of God and you yourselves cast out. And people will come from
the east and the west and from the north and the south and will recline at table in the
kingdom of God. For behold, some are last who will be first, and some are first who will
be last."

TWENTY-SECOND SUNDAY IN ORDINARY TIME / A   1061

READING I   *Jeremiah 20:7-9 / 124*

You duped me, O LORD, and I let myself
   be duped;
   you were too strong for me, and you
      triumphed.
All the day I am an object of laughter;
   everyone mocks me.

Whenever I speak, I must cry out,
   violence and outrage is my message;

the word of the LORD has brought me
   derision and reproach all the day.

I say to myself, I will not mention him,
   I will speak in his name no more.
But then it becomes like fire burning in
      my heart,
   imprisoned in my bones;
I grow weary holding it in, I cannot
   endure it.

RESPONSORIAL PSALM   *Psalm 63:2, 3-4, 5-6, 8-9*

℟. My soul is thirsting for you, O Lord my God.

O God, you are my God whom I seek;
   for you my flesh pines and my soul
      thirsts
like the earth, parched, lifeless and
   without water. ℟.

Thus have I gazed toward you in the
   sanctuary

to see your power and your glory,
for your kindness is a greater good than
   life;
my lips shall glorify you. ℟.

Thus will I bless you while I live;
   lifting up my hands, I will call upon
      your name.

As with the riches of a banquet shall my
  soul be satisfied,
and with exultant lips my mouth
  shall praise you. ℟.

You are my help,
  and in the shadow of your wings I
  shout for joy.
My soul clings fast to you;
  your right hand upholds me. ℟.

READING II   *Romans 12:1-2*

I urge you, brothers and sisters, by the mercies of God, to offer your bodies as a living sacrifice, holy and pleasing to God, your spiritual worship. Do not conform yourselves to this age but be transformed by the renewal of your mind, that you may discern what is the will of God, what is good and pleasing and perfect.

GOSPEL   *Matthew 16:21-27*

Jesus began to show his disciples that he must go to Jerusalem and suffer greatly from the elders, the chief priests, and the scribes, and be killed and on the third day be raised. Then Peter took Jesus aside and began to rebuke him, "God forbid, Lord! No such thing shall ever happen to you." He turned and said to Peter, "Get behind me, Satan! You are an obstacle to me. You are thinking not as God does, but as human beings do."

Then Jesus said to his disciples, "Whoever wishes to come after me must deny himself, take up his cross, and follow me. For whoever wishes to save his life will lose it, but whoever loses his life for my sake will find it. What profit would there be for one to gain the whole world and forfeit his life? Or what can one give in exchange for his life? For the Son of Man will come with his angels in his Father's glory, and then he will repay all according to his conduct."

1062 TWENTY-SECOND SUNDAY IN ORDINARY TIME / B

READING I   *Deuteronomy 4:1-2, 6-8 / 125*

Moses said to the people: "Now, Israel, hear the statutes and decrees which I am teaching you to observe, that you may live, and may enter in and take possession of the land which the LORD, the God of your fathers, is giving you. In your observance of the commandments of the LORD, your God, which I enjoin upon you, you shall not add to what I command you nor subtract from it. Observe them carefully, for thus will you give evidence of your wisdom and intelligence to the nations, who will hear of all these statutes and say, 'This great nation is truly a wise and intelligent people.' For what great nation is there that has gods so close to it as the LORD, our God, is to us whenever we call upon him? Or what great nation has statutes and decrees that are as just as this whole law which I am setting before you today?"

RESPONSORIAL PSALM   *Psalm 15:2-3, 3-4, 4-5*

℟. One who does justice will live in the presence of the Lord.

Whoever walks blamelessly and does
  justice;
who thinks the truth in his heart
and slanders not with his tongue. ℟.

Who harms not his fellow man,
  nor takes up a reproach against his
  neighbor;
by whom the reprobate is despised,

while he honors those who fear the
  Lord. ℟.

Who lends not his money at usury
  and accepts no bribe against the
  innocent.
Whoever does these things
  shall never be disturbed. ℟.

READING II   *James 1:17-18, 21b-22, 27*

Dearest brothers and sisters: All good giving and every perfect gift is from above, coming down from the Father of lights, with whom there is no alteration or shadow caused by change. He willed to give us birth by the word of truth that we may be a kind of first-fruits of his creatures.

Humbly welcome the word that has been planted in you and is able to save your souls.

Be doers of the word and not hearers only, deluding yourselves.

Religion that is pure and undefiled before God and the Father is this: to care for orphans and widows in their affliction and to keep oneself unstained by the world.

GOSPEL   *Mark 7:1-8, 14-15, 21-23*

When the Pharisees with some scribes who had come from Jerusalem gathered around Jesus, they observed that some of his disciples ate their meals with unclean, that is, unwashed, hands. (For the Pharisees and, in fact, all Jews, do not eat without carefully washing their hands, keeping the tradition of the elders. And on coming from the marketplace they do not eat without purifying themselves. And there are many other things that they have traditionally observed, the purification of cups and jugs and kettles [and beds].) So the Pharisees and scribes questioned him, "Why do your disciples not follow the tradition of the elders but instead eat a meal with unclean hands?" He responded, "Well did Isaiah prophesy about you hypocrites, as it is written:

'This people honors me with their lips,
     but their hearts are far from me;
in vain do they worship me,
     teaching as doctrines human precepts.'
You disregard God's commandment but cling to human tradition."

He summoned the crowd again and said to them, "Hear me, all of you, and understand. Nothing that enters one from outside can defile that person; but the things that come out from within are what defile.

"From within people, from their hearts, come evil thoughts, unchastity, theft, murder, adultery, greed, malice, deceit, licentiousness, envy, blasphemy, arrogance, folly. All these evils come from within and they defile."

TWENTY-SECOND SUNDAY IN ORDINARY TIME / C   1063

READING I   *Sirach 3:17-18, 20, 28-29 / 126*

My child, conduct your affairs with
     humility,
     and you will be loved more than a
     giver of gifts.
Humble yourself the more, the greater
     you are,
     and you will find favor with God.
What is too sublime for you, seek not,
into things beyond your strength
     search not.
The mind of a sage appreciates proverbs,
     and an attentive ear is the joy of the
     wise.
Water quenches a flaming fire,
     and alms atone for sins.

RESPONSORIAL PSALM   *Psalm 68:4-5, 6-7, 10-11*

℟. **God, in your goodness, you have made a home for the poor.**

The just rejoice and exult before God;
     they are glad and rejoice.
Sing to God, chant praise to his name;
     whose name is the Lord. ℟.

The father of orphans and the defender
     of widows
     is God in his holy dwelling.
God gives a home to the forsaken;

he leads forth prisoners to
prosperity. ℟.

A bountiful rain you showered down, O
God, upon your inheritance;

you restored the land when it
languished;
your flock settled in it;
in your goodness, O God, you
provided it for the needy. ℟.

READING II
Hebrews 12:18-19, 22-24a

Brothers and sisters: You have not approached that which could be touched and a blazing fire and gloomy darkness and storm and a trumpet blast and a voice speaking words such that those who heard begged that no message be further addressed to them. No, you have approached Mount Zion and the city of the living God, the heavenly Jerusalem, and countless angels in festal gathering, and the assembly of the firstborn enrolled in heaven, and God the judge of all, and the spirits of the just made perfect, and Jesus, the mediator of a new covenant, and the sprinkled blood that speaks more eloquently than that of Abel.

GOSPEL
Luke 14:1, 7-14

On a sabbath Jesus went to dine at the home of one of the leading Pharisees, and the people there were observing him carefully.

He told a parable to those who had been invited, noticing how they were choosing the places of honor at the table. "When you are invited by someone to a wedding banquet, do not recline at table in the place of honor. A more distinguished guest than you may have been invited by him, and the host who invited both of you may approach you and say, 'Give your place to this man,' and then you would proceed with embarrassment to take the lowest place. Rather, when you are invited, go and take the lowest place so that when the host comes to you he may say, 'My friend, move up to a higher position.' Then you will enjoy the esteem of your companions at the table. For everyone who exalts himself will be humbled, but the one who humbles himself will be exalted." Then he said to the host who invited him, "When you hold a lunch or a dinner, do not invite your friends or your brothers or your relatives or your wealthy neighbors, in case they may invite you back and you have repayment. Rather, when you hold a banquet, invite the poor, the crippled, the lame, the blind; blessed indeed will you be because of their inability to repay you. For you will be repaid at the resurrection of the righteous."

1064 TWENTY-THIRD SUNDAY IN ORDINARY TIME / A

READING I
Ezekiel 33:7-9 / 127

Thus says the LORD: You, son of man, I have appointed watchman for the house of Israel; when you hear me say anything, you shall warn them for me. If I tell the wicked, "O wicked one, you shall surely die," and you do not speak out to dissuade the wicked from his way, the wicked shall die for his guilt, but I will hold you responsible for his death. But if you warn the wicked, trying to turn him from his way, and he refuses to turn from his way, he shall die for his guilt, but you shall save yourself.

RESPONSORIAL PSALM
Psalm 95:1-2, 6-7, 8-9

℟. If today you hear his voice, harden not your hearts.

Come, let us sing joyfully to the Lord;
let us acclaim the rock of our
salvation.
Let us come into his presence with
thanksgiving;
let us joyfully sing psalms to him. ℟.

Come, let us bow down in worship;
let us kneel before the Lord who
made us.
For he is our God,
and we are the people he shepherds,
the flock he guides. ℟.

Oh, that today you would hear his voice:
"Harden not your hearts as at
Meribah,
as in the day of Massah in the desert,

Where your fathers tempted me;
they tested me though they had seen my
works." ℟.

READING II
Romans 13:8-10

Brothers and sisters: Owe nothing to anyone, except to love one another; for the one who loves another has fulfilled the law. The commandments, "You shall not commit adultery; you shall not kill; you shall not steal; you shall not covet," and whatever other commandment there may be, are summed up in this saying, namely, "You shall love your neighbor as yourself." Love does no evil to the neighbor; hence, love is the fulfillment of the law.

GOSPEL
Matthew 18:15-20

Jesus said to his disciples: "If your brother sins against you, go and tell him his fault between you and him alone. If he listens to you, you have won over your brother. If he does not listen, take one or two others along with you, so that 'every fact may be established on the testimony of two or three witnesses.' If he refuses to listen to them, tell the church. If he refuses to listen even to the church, then treat him as you would a Gentile or a tax collector. Amen, I say to you, whatever you bind on earth shall be bound in heaven, and whatever you loose on earth shall be loosed in heaven. Again, amen, I say to you, if two of you agree on earth about anything for which they are to pray, it shall be granted to them by my heavenly Father. For where two or three are gathered together in my name, there am I in the midst of them."

TWENTY-THIRD SUNDAY IN ORDINARY TIME / B   1065

READING I
Isaiah 35:4-7a / 128

Thus says the LORD:
Say to those whose hearts are
frightened:
Be strong, fear not!
Here is your God,
he comes with vindication;
with divine recompense
he comes to save you.
Then will the eyes of the blind be
opened,

the ears of the deaf be cleared;
then will the lame leap like a stag,
then the tongue of the mute will
sing.
Streams will burst forth in the desert,
and rivers in the steppe.
The burning sands will become
pools,
and the thirsty ground, springs of
water.

RESPONSORIAL PSALM
Psalm 146:7, 8-9, 9-10

℟. **Praise the Lord, my soul!**
or:
Alleluia.

The God of Jacob keeps faith forever,
secures justice for the oppressed,
gives food to the hungry.
The Lord sets captives free. ℟.

The Lord gives sight to the blind;
the Lord raises up those who were
bowed down.
The Lord loves the just;

the Lord protects strangers. ℟.

The fatherless and the widow the Lord
sustains,
but the way of the wicked he
thwarts.
The Lord shall reign forever;
your God, O Zion, through all
generations. Alleluia. ℟.

READING II *James 2:1-5*

My brothers and sisters, show no partiality as you adhere to the faith in our glorious Lord Jesus Christ. For if a man with gold rings and fine clothes comes into your assembly, and a poor person in shabby clothes also comes in, and you pay attention to the one wearing the fine clothes and say, "Sit here, please," while you say to the poor one, "Stand there," or "Sit at my feet," have you not made distinctions among yourselves and become judges with evil designs?

Listen, my beloved brothers and sisters. Did not God choose those who are poor in the world to be rich in faith and heirs of the kingdom that he promised to those who love him?

GOSPEL *Mark 7:31-37*

Again Jesus left the district of Tyre and went by way of Sidon to the Sea of Galilee, into the district of the Decapolis. And people brought to him a deaf man who had a speech impediment and begged him to lay his hand on him. He took him off by himself away from the crowd. He put his finger into the man's ears and, spitting, touched his tongue; then he looked up to heaven and groaned, and said to him, "*Ephphatha!*" (that is, "Be opened!") And immediately the man's ears were opened, his speech impediment was removed, and he spoke plainly. He ordered them not to tell anyone. But the more he ordered them not to, the more they proclaimed it. They were exceedingly astonished and they said, "He has done all things well. He makes the deaf hear and the mute speak."

1066 TWENTY-THIRD SUNDAY IN ORDINARY TIME / C

READING I *Wisdom 9:13-18b / 129*

Who can know God's counsel,
or who can conceive what the LORD intends?
For the deliberations of mortals are timid,
and unsure are our plans.
For the corruptible body burdens the soul
and the earthen shelter weighs down the mind
that has many concerns.
And scarce do we guess the things on earth,
and what is within our grasp we find with difficulty;
but when things are in heaven, who can search them out?
Or who ever knew your counsel, except you had given wisdom
and sent your holy spirit from on high?
And thus were the paths of those on earth made straight.

RESPONSORIAL PSALM *Psalm 90:3-4, 5-6, 12-13, 14-17*

℞. In every age, O Lord, you have been our refuge.

You turn man back to dust,
saying, "Return, O children of men."
For a thousand years in your sight
are as yesterday, now that it is past,
or as a watch of the night. ℞.

You make an end of them in their sleep;
the next morning they are like the changing grass,
Which at dawn springs up anew,
but by evening wilts and fades. ℞.

Teach us to number our days aright,
that we may gain wisdom of heart.
Return, O Lord! How long?
Have pity on your servants! ℞.

Fill us at daybreak with your kindness,
that we may shout for joy and gladness all our days.
And may the gracious care of the Lord our God be ours;
prosper the work of our hands for us!
Prosper the work of our hands! ℞.

READING II   *Philemon 9-10, 12-17*

I, Paul, an old man, and now also a prisoner for Christ Jesus, urge you on behalf of my child Onesimus, whose father I have become in my imprisonment; I am sending him, that is, my own heart, back to you. I should have liked to retain him for myself, so that he might serve me on your behalf in my imprisonment for the gospel, but I did not want to do anything without your consent, so that the good you do might not be forced but voluntary. Perhaps this is why he was away from you for a while, that you might have him back forever, no longer as a slave but more than a slave, a brother, beloved especially to me, but even more so to you, as a man and in the Lord. So if you regard me as a partner, welcome him as you would me.

GOSPEL   *Luke 14:25-33*

Great crowds were traveling with Jesus, and he turned and addressed them, "If anyone comes to me without hating his father and mother, wife and children, brothers and sisters, and even his own life, he cannot be my disciple. Whoever does not carry his own cross and come after me cannot be my disciple. Which of you wishing to construct a tower does not first sit down and calculate the cost to see if there is enough for its completion? Otherwise, after laying the foundation and finding himself unable to finish the work the onlookers should laugh at him and say, 'This one began to build but did not have the resources to finish.' Or what king marching into battle would not first sit down and decide whether with ten thousand troops he can successfully oppose another king advancing upon him with twenty thousand troops? But if not, while he is still far away, he will send a delegation to ask for peace terms. In the same way, anyone of you who does not renounce all his possessions cannot be my disciple."

TWENTY-FOURTH SUNDAY IN ORDINARY TIME / A   1067

READING I   *Sirach 27:30—28:9 / 130*

Wrath and anger are hateful things,
    yet the sinner hugs them tight.
The vengeful will suffer the LORD's
    vengeance,
    for he remembers their sins in detail.
Forgive your neighbor's injustice;
    then when you pray, your own sins
      will be forgiven.
Could anyone nourish anger against
    another
    and expect healing from the LORD?
Could anyone refuse mercy to another

like himself,
    can he seek pardon for his own sins?
If one who is but flesh cherishes wrath,
    who will forgive his sins?
Remember your last days, set enmity
    aside;
    remember death and decay, and cease
      from sin!
Think of the commandments, hate not
    your neighbor;
    remember the Most High's covenant,
    and overlook faults.

RESPONSORIAL PSALM   *Psalm 103:1-2, 3-4, 9-10, 11-12*

℟. **The Lord is kind and merciful, slow to anger, and rich in compassion.**

Bless the Lord, O my soul;
    and all my being, bless his holy
      name.
Bless the Lord, O my soul,
    and forget not all his benefits. ℟.

He pardons all your iniquities,
    heals all your ills.
redeems your life from destruction,
    he crowns you with kindness and
      compassion. ℟.

He will not always chide,
  nor does he keep his wrath forever.
Not according to our sins does he deal
  with us,
  nor does he requite us according to
  our crimes. ℟.

For as the heavens are high above the
  earth,
  so surpassing is his kindness toward
  those who fear him.
As far as the east is from the west,
  so far has he put our transgressions
  from us. ℟.

READING II   *Romans 14:7-9*

Brothers and sisters: None of us lives for oneself, and no one dies for oneself. For if we live, we live for the Lord, and if we die, we die for the Lord; so then, whether we live or die, we are the Lord's. For this is why Christ died and came to life, that he might be Lord of both the dead and the living.

GOSPEL   *Matthew 18:21-35*

Peter approached Jesus and asked him, "Lord, if my brother sins against me, how often must I forgive? As many as seven times?" Jesus answered, "I say to you, not seven times but seventy-seven times. That is why the kingdom of heaven may be likened to a king who decided to settle accounts with his servants. When he began the accounting, a debtor was brought before him who owed him a huge amount. Since he had no way of paying it back, his master ordered him to be sold, along with his wife, his children, and all his property, in payment of the debt. At that, the servant fell down, did him homage, and said, 'Be patient with me, and I will pay you back in full.' Moved with compassion the master of that servant let him go and forgave him the loan. When that servant had left, he found one of his fellow servants who owed him a much smaller amount. He seized him and started to choke him, demanding, 'Pay back what you owe.' Falling to his knees, his fellow servant begged him, 'Be patient with me, and I will pay you back.' But he refused. Instead, he had the fellow servant put in prison until he paid back the debt. Now when his fellow servants saw what had happened, they were deeply disturbed, and went to their master and reported the whole affair. His master summoned him and said to him, 'You wicked servant! I forgave you your entire debt because you begged me to. Should you not have had pity on your fellow servant, as I had pity on you?' Then in anger his master handed him over to the torturers until he should pay back the whole debt. So will my heavenly Father do to you, unless each of you forgives your brother from your heart."

1068 TWENTY-FOURTH SUNDAY IN ORDINARY TIME / B

READING I   *Isaiah 50:5-9a / 131*

The Lord GOD opens my ear that I
  may hear;
and I have not rebelled,
  have not turned back.
I gave my back to those who beat me,
  my cheeks to those who plucked my
  beard;
my face I did not shield
  from buffets and spitting.

The Lord GOD is my help,

therefore I am not disgraced;
I have set my face like flint,
  knowing that I shall not be put to
  shame.
He is near who upholds my right;
  if anyone wishes to oppose me,
  let us appear together.
Who disputes my right?
  Let that man confront me.
See, the Lord GOD is my help;
  who will prove me wrong?

RESPONSORIAL PSALM   *Psalm 116:1-2, 3-4, 5-6, 8-9*

℟. **I will walk before the Lord, in the land of the living.**
or:
Alleluia.

I love the Lord because he has heard
    my voice in supplication,
because he has inclined his ear to me
    the day I called. ℟.

The cords of death encompassed me;
    the snares of the netherworld seized
      upon me;
I fell into distress and sorrow,
and I called upon the name of the Lord,
    "O Lord, save my life!" ℟.

Gracious is the Lord and just;
    yes, our God is merciful.
The Lord keeps the little ones;
    I was brought low, and he saved
      me. ℟.

For he has freed my soul from death,
    my eyes from tears, my feet from
      stumbling.
I shall walk before the Lord
    in the land of the living. ℟.

READING II   *James 2:14-18*

What good is it, my brothers and sisters, if someone says he has faith but does not have works? Can that faith save him? If a brother or sister has nothing to wear and has no food for the day, and one of you says to them, "Go in peace, keep warm, and eat well," but you do not give them the necessities of the body, what good is it? So also faith of itself, if it does not have works, is dead. Indeed someone might say, "You have faith and I have works." Demonstrate your faith to me without works, and I will demonstrate my faith to you from my works.

GOSPEL   *Mark 8:27-35*

Jesus and his disciples set out for the villages of Caesarea Philippi. Along the way he asked his disciples, "Who do people say that I am?" They said in reply, "John the Baptist, others Elijah, still others one of the prophets." And he asked them, "But who do you say that I am?" Peter said to him in reply, "You are the Christ." Then he warned them not to tell anyone about him.

He began to teach them that the Son of Man must suffer greatly and be rejected by the elders, the chief priests, and the scribes, and be killed, and rise after three days. He spoke this openly. Then Peter took him aside and began to rebuke him. At this he turned around and, looking at his disciples, rebuked Peter and said, "Get behind me, Satan. You are thinking not as God does, but as human beings do."

He summoned the crowd with his disciples and said to them, "Whoever wishes to come after me must deny himself, take up his cross, and follow me. For whoever wishes to save his life will lose it, but whoever loses his life for my sake and that of the gospel will save it."

TWENTY-FOURTH SUNDAY IN ORDINARY TIME / C   1069

READING I   *Exodus 32:7-11, 13-14 / 132*

The LORD said to Moses, "Go down at once to your people, whom you brought out of the land of Egypt, for they have become depraved. They have soon turned aside from the way I pointed out to them, making for themselves a molten calf and worshiping it, sacrificing to it and crying out, 'This is your God, O Israel, who brought you out of the land of Egypt!' I see how stiff-necked this people is," continued the LORD to Moses. "Let me alone, then, that my wrath may blaze up against them to consume them. Then I will make of you a great nation."

But Moses implored the LORD, his God, saying, "Why, O LORD, should your wrath blaze up against your own people, whom you brought out of the land of Egypt with such great power and with so strong a hand? Remember your servants Abraham, Isaac, and Israel, and how you swore to them by your own self, saying, 'I will make your descendants as numerous as the stars in the sky; and all this land that I promised, I will give your descendants as their perpetual heritage.'" So the LORD relented in the punishment he had threatened to inflict on his people.

RESPONSORIAL PSALM

Psalm 51:3-4, 12-13, 17, 19

℟. **I will rise and go to my father.**

Have mercy on me, O God, in your
  goodness;
  in the greatness of your compassion
  wipe out my offense.
Thoroughly wash me from my guilt
  and of my sin cleanse me. ℟.

A clean heart create for me, O God,
  and a steadfast spirit renew within
  me.

Cast me not out from your presence,
  and your holy spirit take not from
  me. ℟.

O Lord, open my lips,
  and my mouth shall proclaim your
  praise.
My sacrifice, O God, is a contrite spirit;
  a heart contrite and humbled, O God,
  you will not spurn. ℟.

READING II

1 Timothy 1:12-17

Beloved: I am grateful to him who has strengthened me, Christ Jesus our Lord, because he considered me trustworthy in appointing me to the ministry. I was once a blasphemer and a persecutor and arrogant, but I have been mercifully treated because I acted out of ignorance in my unbelief. Indeed, the grace of our Lord has been abundant, along with the faith and love that are in Christ Jesus. This saying is trustworthy and deserves full acceptance: Christ Jesus came into the world to save sinners. Of these I am the foremost. But for that reason I was mercifully treated, so that in me, as the foremost, Christ Jesus might display all his patience as an example for those who would come to believe in him for everlasting life. To the king of ages, incorruptible, invisible, the only God, honor and glory forever and ever. Amen.

GOSPEL

Luke 15:1-32 or 15:1-10

For short form read only the part in brackets.

[Tax collectors and sinners were all drawing near to listen to Jesus, but the Pharisees and scribes began to complain, saying, "This man welcomes sinners and eats with them." So to them he addressed this parable. "What man among you having a hundred sheep and losing one of them would not leave the ninety-nine in the desert and go after the lost one until he finds it? And when he does find it, he sets it on his shoulders with great joy and, upon his arrival home, he calls together his friends and neighbors and says to them, 'Rejoice with me because I have found my lost sheep.' I tell you, in just the same way there will be more joy in heaven over one sinner who repents than over ninety-nine righteous people who have no need of repentance.

"Or what woman having ten coins and losing one would not light a lamp and sweep the house, searching carefully until she finds it? And when she does find it, she calls together her friends and neighbors and says to them, 'Rejoice with me because I have found the coin that I lost.' In just the same way, I tell you, there will be rejoicing among the angels of God over one sinner who repents."]

Then he said, "A man had two sons, and the younger son said to his father, 'Father give me the share of your estate that should come to me.' So the father divided the property between them. After a few days, the younger son collected all his belongings and set off to a distant country where he squandered his inheritance on a life of dissipation. When he had freely spent everything, a severe famine struck that country, and he found himself in dire need. So he hired himself out to one of the local citizens who sent him to his farm to tend the swine. And he longed to eat his fill of the pods on which the swine fed, but nobody gave him any. Coming to his senses he thought, 'How many of my father's hired workers have more than enough food to eat, but here am I, dying from hunger. I shall get up and go to my father and I shall say to him, "Father, I have sinned against heaven and against you. I no longer deserve to be called your son; treat me as you would treat one of your hired workers."' So he got up and went back to his father. While he was still a long way off, his father caught sight of him, and was filled with compassion. He ran to his son, embraced him and kissed him. His son said to him, 'Father, I have sinned against heaven and against you; I no longer deserve to be called your son.' But his father ordered his servants, 'Quickly bring the finest robe and put it on him; put a ring on his finger and sandals on his feet. Take the fattened calf and slaughter it. Then let us celebrate with a feast, because this son of mine was dead, and has come to life again; he was lost, and has been found.' Then the celebration began. Now the older son had been out in the field and, on his way back, as he neared the house, he heard the sound of music and dancing. He called one of the servants and asked what this might mean. The servant said to him, 'Your brother has returned and your father has slaughtered the fattened calf because he has him back safe and sound.' He became angry, and when he refused to enter the house, his father came out and pleaded with him. He said to his father in reply, 'Look, all these years I served you and not once did I disobey your orders; yet you never gave me even a young goat to feast on with my friends. But when your son returns, who swallowed up your property with prostitutes, for him you slaughter the fattened calf.' He said to him, 'My son, you are here with me always; everything I have is yours. But now we must celebrate and rejoice, because your brother was dead and has come to life again; he was lost and has been found.'"

TWENTY-FIFTH SUNDAY IN ORDINARY TIME / A ·   1070

READING I
Isaiah 55:6-9 / 133

Seek the LORD while he may be found,
   call him while he is near.
Let the scoundrel forsake his way,
   and the wicked his thoughts;
let him turn to the LORD for mercy;
   to our God, who is generous in
      forgiving.
For my thoughts are not your thoughts,

nor are your ways my ways, says the
   LORD.
As high as the heavens are above the
   earth,
so high are my ways above your
   ways
and my thoughts above your
   thoughts.

RESPONSORIAL PSALM
Psalm 145:2-3, 8-9, 17-18

℟. **The Lord is near to all who call upon him.**

Every day will I bless you,
   and I will praise your name forever
      and ever.
Great is the Lord and highly to be
      praised;
   his greatness is unsearchable. ℟.

The Lord is gracious and merciful,
   slow to anger and of great kindness.

The Lord is good to all
   and compassionate toward all his
      works. ℟.

The Lord is just in all his ways
   and holy in all his works.
The Lord is near to all who call upon
   him,
   to all who call upon him in truth. ℟.

READING II   *Philippians 1:20c-24, 27a*

Brothers and sisters: Christ will be magnified in my body, whether by life or by death.
For to me life is Christ, and death is gain. If I go on living in the flesh, that means fruitful labor for me. And I do not know which I shall choose. I am caught between the two.
I long to depart this life and be with Christ, for that is far better. Yet that I remain in the
flesh is more necessary for your benefit.

Only, conduct yourselves in a way worthy of the gospel of Christ.

GOSPEL   *Matthew 20:1-16a*

Jesus told his disciples this parable: "The kingdom of heaven is like a landowner who
went out at dawn to hire laborers for his vineyard. After agreeing with them for the usual
daily wage, he sent them into his vineyard. Going out about nine o'clock, the landowner saw others standing idle in the marketplace, and he said to them, 'You too go into my
vineyard, and I will give you what is just.' So they went off. And he went out again
around noon, and around three o'clock, and did likewise. Going out about five o'clock,
the landowner found others standing around, and said to them, 'Why do you stand here
idle all day?' They answered, 'Because no one has hired us.' He said to them, 'You too
go into my vineyard.' When it was evening the owner of the vineyard said to his fore-
man, 'Summon the laborers and give them their pay, beginning with the last and ending
with the first.' When those who had started about five o'clock came, each received the
usual daily wage. So when the first came, they thought that they would receive more,
but each of them also got the usual wage. And on receiving it they grumbled against the
landowner, saying, 'These last ones worked only one hour, and you have made them
equal to us, who bore the day's burden and the heat.' He said to one of them in reply,
'My friend, I am not cheating you. Did you not agree with me for the usual daily wage?
Take what is yours and go. What if I wish to give this last one the same as you? Or am
I not free to do as I wish with my own money? Are you envious because I am generous?' Thus, the last will be first, and the first will be last."

1071 **TWENTY-FIFTH SUNDAY IN ORDINARY TIME / B**

READING I   *Wisdom 2:12, 17-20 / 134*

The wicked say:
  Let us beset the just one, because he is obnoxious to us;
    he sets himself against our doings,
  reproaches us for transgressions of the law
    and charges us with violations of our training.
  Let us see whether his words be true;
    let us find out what will happen to him.
  For if the just one be the son of God, God will defend him
    and deliver him from the hand of his foes.
  With revilement and torture let us put the just one to the test
    that we may have proof of his gentleness
    and try his patience.
  Let us condemn him to a shameful death;
    for according to his own words, God will take care of him.

RESPONSORIAL PSALM   *Psalm 54:3-4, 5, 6-8*

℟. **The Lord upholds my life.**

O God, by your name save me,
  and by your might defend my cause.
O God, hear my prayer;
  hearken to the words of my mouth. ℟.

For the haughty men have risen up
    against me,
  the ruthless seek my life;
  they set not God before their eyes. ℟.

Behold, God is my helper;
    the Lord sustains my life.

Freely will I offer you sacrifice;
    I will praise your name, O Lord, for
        its goodness. ℟.

READING II
James 3:16—4:3

Beloved: Where jealousy and selfish ambition exist, there is disorder and every foul practice. But the wisdom from above is first of all pure, then peaceable, gentle, compliant, full of mercy and good fruits, without inconstancy or insincerity. And the fruit of righteousness is sown in peace for those who cultivate peace.

Where do the wars and where do the conflicts among you come from? Is it not from your passions that make war within your members? You covet but do not possess. You kill and envy but you cannot obtain; you fight and wage war. You do not possess because you do not ask. You ask but do not receive, because you ask wrongly, to spend it on your passions.

GOSPEL
Mark 9:30-37

Jesus and his disciples left from there and began a journey through Galilee, but he did not wish anyone to know about it. He was teaching his disciples and telling them, "The Son of Man is to be handed over to men and they will kill him, and three days after his death the Son of Man will rise." But they did not understand the saying, and they were afraid to question him.

They came to Capernaum and, once inside the house, he began to ask them, "What were you arguing about on the way?" But they remained silent. They had been discussing among themselves on the way who was the greatest. Then he sat down, called the Twelve, and said to them, "If anyone wishes to be first, he shall be the last of all and the servant of all." Taking a child, he placed it in the their midst, and putting his arms around it, he said to them, "Whoever receives one child such as this in my name, receives me; and whoever receives me, receives not me but the One who sent me."

TWENTY-FIFTH SUNDAY IN ORDINARY TIME / C   1072

READING I
Amos 8:4-7 / 135

Hear this, you who trample upon the
    needy
    and destroy the poor of the land!
"When will the new moon be over," you
    ask,
    "that we may sell our grain,
and the sabbath, that we may display
    the wheat?
We will diminish the ephah,

add to the shekel,
    and fix our scales for cheating!
We will buy the lowly for silver,
    and the poor for a pair of sandals;
    even the refuse of the wheat we will
        sell!"
The LORD has sworn by the pride of
    Jacob:
    Never will I forget a thing they have
        done!

RESPONSORIAL PSALM
Psalm 113:1-2, 4-6, 7-8

℟. **Praise the Lord who lifts up the poor.**
    or:
Alleluia.

Praise, you servants of the Lord,
    praise the name of the Lord.
Blessed be the name of the Lord
    both now and forever. ℟.

High above all nations is the Lord;

above the heavens is his glory.
Who is like the Lord, our God, who is
    enthroned on high
    and looks upon the heavens and the
        earth below? ℟.

He raises up the lowly from the dust;
   from the dunghill he lifts up the
     poor

to seat them with princes,
   with the princes of his own
     people. ℟.

READING II
1 Timothy 2:1-8

Beloved: First of all, I ask that supplications, prayers, petitions, and thanksgivings be offered for everyone, for kings and for all in authority, that we may lead a quiet and tranquil life in all devotion and dignity. This is good and pleasing to God our savior, who wills everyone to be saved and to come to knowledge of the truth.
   'For there is one God.
   There is also one mediator between God and men,
     the man Christ Jesus,
   who gave himself as ransom for all.'
This was the testimony at the proper time. For this I was appointed preacher and apostle (I am speaking the truth, I am not lying), teacher of the Gentiles in faith and truth.
   It is my wish, then, that in every place the men should pray, lifting up holy hands, without anger or argument.

GOSPEL
Luke 16:1-13 or 16:10-13

For short form read only the parts in brackets.

[Jesus said to his disciples,] "A rich man had a steward who was reported to him for squandering his property. He summoned him and said, 'What is this I hear about you? Prepare a full account of your stewardship, because you can no longer be my steward.' The steward said to himself, 'What shall I do, now that my master is taking the position of steward away from me? I am not strong enough to dig and I am ashamed to beg. I know what I shall do so that, when I am removed from the stewardship, they may welcome me into their homes.' He called in his master's debtors one by one. To the first he said, 'How much do you owe my master?' He replied, 'One hundred measures of olive oil.' He said to him, 'Here is your promissory note. Sit down and quickly write one for fifty.' Then to another the steward said, 'And you, how much do you owe?' He replied, 'One hundred kors of wheat.' The steward said to him, 'Here is your promissory note; write one for eighty.' And the master commended that dishonest steward for acting prudently. "For the children of this world are more prudent in dealing with their own generation than are the children of light. I tell you, make friends for yourselves with dishonest wealth, so that when it fails, you will be welcomed into eternal dwellings. [The person who is trustworthy in very small matters is also trustworthy in great ones; and the person who is dishonest in very small matters is also dishonest in great ones. If, therefore, you are not trustworthy with dishonest wealth, who will trust you with true wealth? If you are not trustworthy with what belongs to another, who will give you what is yours? No servant can serve two masters. He will either hate one and love the other, or be devoted to one and despise the other. You cannot serve both God and mammon."]

1073 TWENTY-SIXTH SUNDAY IN ORDINARY TIME / A

READING I
Ezekiel 18:25-28 / 136

Thus says the LORD: You say, "The LORD's way is not fair!" Hear now, house of Israel: Is it my way that is unfair, or rather, are not your ways unfair? When someone virtuous turns away from virtue to commit iniquity, and dies, it is because of the iniquity he committed that he must die. But if he turns from the wickedness he has committed, and does what is right and just, he shall preserve his life; since he has turned away from all the sins that he has committed, he shall surely live, he shall not die.

RESPONSORIAL PSALM   *Psalm 25:4-5, 6-7, 8-9*
℟. **Remember your mercies, O Lord.**

Your ways, O LORD, make known to me;
   teach me your paths,
guide me in your truth and teach me,
   for you are God my savior. ℟.

Remember that your compassion, O
   LORD,
and your love are from of old.
The sins of my youth and my frailties

remember not;
in your kindness remember me,
because of your goodness, O
   LORD. ℟.

Good and upright is the LORD;
   thus he shows sinners the way.
He guides the humble to justice,
   and teaches the humble his way. ℟.

READING II   *Philippians 2:1-11 or 2:1-5*
For short form read only the part in brackets.

[Brothers and sisters: If there is any encouragement in Christ, any solace in love, any participation in the Spirit, any compassion and mercy, complete my joy by being of the same mind, with the same love, united in heart, thinking one thing. Do nothing out of selfishness or out of vainglory; rather, humbly regard others as more important than yourselves, each looking out not for his own interests, but also for those of others.
   Have in you the same attitude that is also in Christ Jesus,]
     Who, though he was in the form of God,
       did not regard equality with God
       something to be grasped.
     Rather, he emptied himself,
       taking the form of a slave,
       coming in human likeness;
       and found human in appearance,
       he humbled himself,
       becoming obedient to the point of death,
     even death on a cross.
     Because of this, God greatly exalted him
       and bestowed on him the name
       which is above every name,
       that at the name of Jesus
       every knee should bend,
       of those in heaven and on earth and under the earth,
       and every tongue confess that
       Jesus Christ is Lord,
       to the glory of God the Father.

GOSPEL   *Matthew 21:28-32*
Jesus said to the chief priests and elders of the people: "What is your opinion? A man had two sons. He came to the first and said, 'Son, go out and work in the vineyard today.' He said in reply, 'I will not,' but afterwards changed his mind and went. The man came to the other son and gave the same order. He said in reply, 'Yes, sir,' but did not go. Which of the two did his father's will?" They answered, "The first." Jesus said to them, "Amen, I say to you, tax collectors and prostitutes are entering the kingdom of God before you. When John came to you in the way of righteousness, you did not believe him; but tax collectors and prostitutes did. Yet even when you saw that, you did not later change your minds and believe him."

1074 TWENTY-SIXTH SUNDAY IN ORDINARY TIME / B

READING I *Numbers 11:25-29 / 137*

The LORD came down in the cloud and spoke to Moses. Taking some of the spirit that was on Moses, the Lord bestowed it on the seventy elders; and as the spirit came to rest on them, they prophesied.

Now two men, one named Eldad and the other Medad, were not in the gathering but had been left in the camp. They too had been on the list, but had not gone out to the tent; yet the spirit came to rest on them also, and they prophesied in the camp. So, when a young man quickly told Moses, "Eldad and Medad are prophesying in the camp," Joshua, son of Nun, who from his youth had been Moses' aide, said, "Moses, my lord, stop them." But Moses answered him, "Are you jealous for my sake? Would that all the people of the LORD were prophets! Would that the LORD might bestow his spirit on them all!"

RESPONSORIAL PSALM *Psalm 19:8, 10, 12-13, 14*

℟. **The precepts of the Lord give joy to the heart.**

The law of the LORD is perfect,
    refreshing the soul;
the decree of the LORD is trustworthy,
    giving wisdom to the simple. ℟.

The fear of the LORD is pure,
    enduring forever;
the ordinances of the LORD are true,
    all of them just. ℟.

Though your servant is careful of them,

very diligent in keeping them,
yet who can detect failings?
    Cleanse me from my unknown
    faults! ℟.

From wanton sin especially, restrain your
    servant;
let it not rule over me.
Then shall I be blameless and innocent
    of serious sin. ℟.

READING II *James 5:1-6*

Come now, you rich, weep and wail over your impending miseries. Your wealth has rotted away, your clothes have become moth-eaten, your gold and silver have corroded, and that corrosion will be a testimony against you; it will devour your flesh like a fire. You have stored up treasure for the last days. Behold, the wages you withheld from the workers who harvested your fields are crying aloud; and the cries of the harvesters have reached the ears of the Lord of hosts. You have lived on earth in luxury and pleasure; you have fattened your hearts for the day of slaughter. You have condemned; you have murdered the righteous one; he offers you no resistance.

GOSPEL *Mark 9:38-43, 45, 47-48*

At that time, John said to Jesus, "Teacher, we saw someone driving out demons in your name, and we tried to prevent him because he does not follow us." Jesus replied, "Do not prevent him. There is no one who performs a mighty deed in my name who can at the same time speak ill of me. For whoever is not against us is for us. Anyone who gives you a cup of water to drink because you belong to Christ, amen, I say to you, will surely not lose his reward.

"Whoever causes one of these little ones who believe in me to sin, it would be better for him if a great millstone were put around his neck and he were thrown into the sea. If your hand causes you to sin, cut it off. It is better for you to enter into life maimed than with two hands to go into Gehenna, into the unquenchable fire. And if your foot causes you to sin, cut if off. It is better for you to enter into life crippled than with two feet to be thrown into Gehenna. And if your eye causes you to sin, pluck it out. Better for you to enter into the kingdom of God with one eye than with two eyes to be thrown into Gehenna, where 'their worm does not die, and the fire is not quenched.'"

TWENTY-SIXTH SUNDAY IN ORDINARY TIME / C   1075

READING I   *Amos 6:1a, 4-7 / 138*

Thus says the Lord the God of hosts:
Woe to the complacent in Zion!
Lying upon beds of ivory,
　stretched comfortably on their
　couches,
they eat lambs taken from the flock,
　and calves from the stall!
Improvising to the music of the harp,
　like David, they devise their own
　accompaniment.

They drink wine from bowls
　and anoint themselves with the best
　oils;
yet they are not made ill by the
　collapse of Joseph!
Therefore, now they shall be the first to
　go into exile,
　and their wanton revelry shall be
　done away with.

RESPONSORIAL PSALM   *Psalm 146:7, 8-9, 9-10*
℟. **Praise the Lord, my soul!**
　or:
Alleluia.

Blessed is he who keeps faith forever,
　secures justice for the oppressed,
　gives food to the hungry.
The LORD sets captives free. ℟.

The LORD gives sight to the blind.
　The LORD raises up those who were
　bowed down;

the LORD loves the just.
　The LORD protects strangers. ℟.

The fatherless and the widow he sustains,
　but the way of the wicked he thwarts.
The LORD shall reign forever;
　your God, O Zion, through all
　generations. Alleluia. ℟.

READING II   *1 Timothy 6:11-16*

But you, man of God, pursue righteousness, devotion, faith, love, patience, and
gentleness. Compete well for the faith. Lay hold of eternal life, to which you were called
when you made the noble confession in the presence of many witnesses. I charge you
before God, who gives life to all things, and before Christ Jesus, who gave testimony
under Pontius Pilate for the noble confession, to keep the commandment without stain
or reproach until the appearance of our Lord Jesus Christ that the blessed and only ruler
will make manifest at the proper time, the King of kings and Lord of lords, who alone
has immortality, who dwells in unapproachable light, and whom no human being has
seen or can see. To him be honor and eternal power. Amen.

GOSPEL   *Luke 16:19-31*

Jesus said to the Pharisees: "There was a rich man who dressed in purple garments and
fine linen and dined sumptuously each day. And lying at his door was a poor man named
Lazarus, covered with sores, who would gladly have eaten his fill of the scraps that fell
from the rich man's table. Dogs even used to come and lick his sores. When the poor
man died, he was carried away by angels to the bosom of Abraham. The rich man also
died and was buried, and from the netherworld, where he was in torment, he raised his
eyes and saw Abraham far off and Lazarus at his side. And he cried out, 'Father
Abraham, have pity on me. Send Lazarus to dip the tip of his finger in water and cool
my tongue, for I am suffering torment in these flames.' Abraham replied, 'My child,
remember that you received what was good during your lifetime while Lazarus likewise
received what was bad; but now he is comforted here, whereas you are tormented.
Moreover, between us and you a great chasm is established to prevent anyone from
crossing who might wish to go from our side to yours or from your side to ours.' He said,

'Then I beg you, father, send him to my father's house, for I have five brothers, so that he may warn them, lest they too come to this place of torment.' But Abraham replied, 'They have Moses and the prophets. Let them listen to them.' He said, 'Oh no, father Abraham, but if someone from the dead goes to them, they will repent.' Then Abraham said, 'If they will not listen to Moses and the prophets, neither will they be persuaded if someone should rise from the dead.'"

1076 TWENTY-SEVENTH SUNDAY IN ORDINARY TIME / A

READING I
Isaiah 5:1-7 / 139

Let me now sing of my friend,
, my friend's song concerning his
vineyard.
My friend had a vineyard
on a fertile hillside;
he spaded it, cleared it of stones,
and planted the choicest vines;
within it he built a watchtower,
and hewed out a wine press.
Then he looked for the crop of grapes,
but what it yielded was wild grapes.

Now, inhabitants of Jerusalem and people
of Judah,
judge between me and my vineyard:
What more was there to do for my
vineyard
that I had not done?
Why, when I looked for the crop of
grapes,

did it bring forth wild grapes?
Now, I will let you know
what I mean to do with my vineyard:
take away its hedge, give it to grazing,
break through its wall, let it be
trampled!
Yes, I will make it a ruin:
it shall not be pruned or hoed,
but overgrown with thorns and
briers;
I will command the clouds
not to send rain upon it.
The vineyard of the LORD of hosts is the
house of Israel,
and the people of Judah are his
cherished plant;
he looked for judgment, but see,
bloodshed!
for justice, but hark, the outcry!

RESPONSORIAL PSALM
Psalm 80:9, 12, 13-14, 15-16, 19-20

℟. The vineyard of the Lord is the house of Israel.

A vine from Egypt you transplanted;
you drove away the nations and
planted it.
It put forth its foliage to the Sea,
its shoots as far as the River. ℟.

Why have you broken down its walls,
so that every passer-by plucks its
fruit,
The boar from the forest lays it waste,
and the beasts of the field feed upon
it? ℟.

Once again, O LORD of hosts,

look down from heaven, and see;
take care of this vine,
and protect what your right hand has
planted
the son of man whom you yourself
made strong. ℟.

Then we will no more withdraw from
you;
give us new life, and we will call
upon your name.
O LORD, God of hosts, restore us;
if your face shine upon us, then we
shall be saved. ℟.

READING II
Philippians 4:6-9

Brothers and sisters: Have no anxiety at all, but in everything, by prayer and petition, with thanksgiving, make your requests known to God. Then the peace of God that surpasses all understanding will guard your hearts and minds in Christ Jesus.

Finally, brothers and sisters, whatever is true, whatever is honorable, whatever is just, whatever is pure, whatever is lovely, whatever is gracious, if there is any excellence and if there is anything worthy of praise, think about these things. Keep on doing what you have learned and received and heard and seen in me. Then the God of peace will be with you.

GOSPEL   *Matthew 21:33-43*

Jesus said to the chief priests and the elders of the people: "Hear another parable. There was a landowner who planted a vineyard, put a hedge around it, dug a wine press in it, and built a tower. Then he leased it to tenants and went on a journey. When vintage time drew near, he sent his servants to the tenants to obtain his produce. But the tenants seized the servants and one they beat, another they killed, and a third they stoned. Again he sent other servants, more numerous than the first ones, but they treated them in the same way. Finally, he sent his son to them, thinking, 'They will respect my son.' But when the tenants saw the son, they said to one another, 'This is the heir. Come, let us kill him and acquire his inheritance.' They seized him, threw him out of the vineyard, and killed him. What will the owner of the vineyard do to those tenants when he comes?" They answered him, "He will put those wretched men to a wretched death and lease his vineyard to other tenants who will give him the produce at the proper times." Jesus said to them, "Did you never read in the Scriptures:

'The stone that the builders rejected
    has become the cornerstone;
by the Lord has this been done,
    and it is wonderful in our eyes?'

Therefore, I say to you, the kingdom of God will be taken away from you and given to a people that will produce its fruit."

TWENTY-SEVENTH SUNDAY IN ORDINARY TIME / B   1077

READING I   *Genesis 2:18-24 / 140*

The Lord God said: "It is not good for the man to be alone. I will make a suitable partner for him." So the Lord God formed out of the ground various wild animals and various birds of the air, and he brought them to the man to see what he would call them; whatever the man called each of them would be its name. The man gave names to all the cattle, all the birds of the air, and all wild animals; but none proved to be the suitable partner for the man.

So the Lord God cast a deep sleep on the man, and while he was asleep, he took out one of his ribs and closed up its place with flesh. The Lord God then built up into a woman the rib that he had taken from the man. When he brought her to the man, the man said:

"This one, at last, is bone of my bones
    and flesh of my flesh;
this one shall be called 'woman,'
    for out of 'her man' this one has been taken."

That is why a man leaves his father and mother and clings to his wife, and the two of them become one flesh.

RESPONSORIAL PSALM   *Psalm 128:1-2, 3, 4-5, 6*

℟. **May the Lord bless us all the days of our lives.**

Blessed are you who fear the Lord,
    who walk in his ways!
For you shall eat the fruit of your
    handiwork;
    blessed shall you be, and favored. ℟.

Your wife shall be like a fruitful vine
    in the recesses of your home;
your children like olive plants
    around your table. ℟.

Behold, thus is the man blessed
  who fears the LORD.
The LORD bless you from Zion:
  may you see the prosperity of
  Jerusalem

all the days of your life. ℟.

May you see your children's children.
  Peace be upon Israel! ℟.

READING II
Hebrews 2:9-11

Brothers and sisters: He "for a little while" was made "lower than the angels," that by the grace of God he might taste death for everyone.

For it was fitting that he, for whom and through whom all things exist, in bringing many children to glory, should make the leader to their salvation perfect through suffering. He who consecrates and those who are being consecrated all have one origin. Therefore, he is not ashamed to call them "brothers."

GOSPEL
Mark 10:2-16 or 10:2-12

For short form read only the part in brackets.

[The Pharisees approached Jesus and asked, "Is it lawful for a husband to divorce his wife?" They were testing him. He said to them in reply, "What did Moses command you?" They replied, "Moses permitted a husband to write a bill of divorce and dismiss her." But Jesus told them, "Because of the hardness of your hearts he wrote you this commandment. But from the beginning of creation, 'God made them male and female. For this reason a man shall leave his father and mother and be joined to his wife, and the two shall become one flesh.' So they are no longer two but one flesh. Therefore what God has joined together, no human being must separate." In the house the disciples again questioned Jesus about this. He said to them, "Whoever divorces his wife and marries another commits adultery against her; and if she divorces her husband and marries another, she commits adultery."]

And people were bringing children to him that he might touch them, but the disciples rebuked them. When Jesus saw this he became indignant and said to them, "Let the children come to me; do not prevent them, for the kingdom of God belongs to such as these. Amen, I say to you, whoever does not accept the kingdom of God like a child will not enter it." Then he embraced them and blessed them, placing his hands on them.

1078 TWENTY-SEVENTH SUNDAY IN ORDINARY TIME / C

READING I
Habakkuk 1:2-3; 2:2-4 / 141

How long, O LORD? I cry for help
  but you do not listen!
I cry out to you, "Violence!"
  but you do not intervene.
Why do you let me see ruin;
  why must I look at misery?
Destruction and violence are before me;
  there is strife, and clamorous discord.
Then the LORD answered me and said:
  Write down the vision clearly upon

the tablets,
  so that one can read it readily.
For the vision still has its time,
  presses on to fulfillment, and will
    not disappoint;
if it delays, wait for it,
  it will surely come, it will not be late.
The rash one has no integrity;
  but the just one, because of his faith,
    shall live.

RESPONSORIAL PSALM
Psalm 95:1-2, 6-7, 8-9

℟. **If today you hear his voice, harden not your hearts.**

Come, let us sing joyfully to the LORD;
  let us acclaim the Rock of our
    salvation.

Let us come into his presence with
    thanksgiving;
  let us joyfully sing psalms to him. ℟.

Come, let us bow down in worship;
    let us kneel before the LORD who
    made us.
For he is our God,
    and we are the people he shepherds,
    the flock he guides. ℟.

Oh, that today you would hear his voice:
    "Harden not your hearts as at
    Meribah,
    as in the day of Massah in the desert,
Where your fathers tempted me;
    they tested me though they had seen
    my works." ℟.

READING II
2 Timothy 1:6-8, 13-14

Beloved: I remind you to stir into flame the gift of God that you have through the imposition of my hands. For God did not give us a spirit of cowardice but rather of power and love and self-control. So do not be ashamed of your testimony to our Lord, nor of me, a prisoner for his sake; but bear your share of hardship for the gospel with the strength that comes from God.

Take as your norm the sound words that you heard from me, in the faith and love that are in Christ Jesus. Guard this rich trust with the help of the Holy Spirit that dwells within us.

GOSPEL
Luke 17:5-10

The apostles said to the Lord, "Increase our faith." The Lord replied, "If you have faith the size of a mustard seed, you would say to this mulberry tree, 'Be uprooted and planted in the sea,' and it would obey you.

"Who among you would say to your servant who has just come in from plowing or tending sheep in the field, 'Come here immediately and take your place at table'? Would he not rather say to him, 'Prepare something for me to eat. Put on your apron and wait on me while I eat and drink. You may eat and drink when I am finished'? Is he grateful to that servant because he did what was commanded? So should it be with you. When you have done all you have been commanded, say, 'We are unprofitable servants; we have done what we were obliged to do.'"

TWENTY-EIGHTH SUNDAY IN ORDINARY TIME / A   1079

READING I
Isaiah 25:6-10a / 142

On this mountain the LORD of hosts
    will provide for all peoples
a feast of rich food and choice wines,
    juicy, rich food and pure, choice
    wines.
On this mountain he will destroy
    the veil that veils all peoples,
the web that is woven over all nations;
    he will destroy death forever.
The Lord GOD will wipe away
    the tears from every face;
    the reproach of his people he will

remove
    from the whole earth; for the LORD
    has spoken.
    On that day it will be said:
"Behold our God, to whom we looked to
    save us!
This is the LORD for whom we
    looked;
let us rejoice and be glad that he has
    saved us!"
For the hand of the LORD will rest on
    this mountain.

RESPONSORIAL PSALM
Psalm 23:1-3a, 3b-4, 5, 6

℟. I shall live in the house of the Lord all the days of my life.

The LORD is my shepherd; I shall not
    want.
    In verdant pastures he gives me
    repose;

beside restful waters he leads me;
    he refreshes my soul. ℟.

He guides me in right paths
  for his name's sake.
Even though I walk in the dark valley
  I fear no evil; for you are at my side
with your rod and your staff
  that give me courage. ℟.

You spread the table before me
  in the sight of my foes;

you anoint my head with oil;
  my cup overflows. ℟.

Only goodness and kindness follow me
  all the days of my life;
and I shall dwell in the house of the
  LORD
  for years to come. ℟.

READING II
Philippians 4:12-14, 19-20

Brothers and sisters: I know how to live in humble circumstances; I know also how to live with abundance. In every circumstance and in all things I have learned the secret of being well fed and of going hungry, of living in abundance and of being in need. I can do all things in him who strengthens me. Still, it was kind of you to share in my distress.

My God will fully supply whatever you need, in accord with his glorious riches in Christ Jesus. To our God and Father, glory forever and ever. Amen.

GOSPEL
Matthew 22:1-14 or 22:1-10

For short form read only the part in brackets.

[Jesus again in reply spoke to the chief priests and elders of the people in parables, saying, "The kingdom of heaven may be likened to a king who gave a wedding feast for his son. He dispatched his servants to summon the invited guests to the feast, but they refused to come. A second time he sent other servants, saying, 'Tell those invited: "Behold, I have prepared my banquet, my calves and fattened cattle are killed, and everything is ready; come to the feast."' Some ignored the invitation and went away, one to his farm, another to his business. The rest laid hold of his servants, mistreated them, and killed them. The king was enraged and sent his troops, destroyed those murderers, and burned their city. Then he said to his servants, 'The feast is ready, but those who were invited were not worthy to come. Go out, therefore, into the main roads and invite to the feast whomever you find.' The servants went out into the streets and gathered all they found, bad and good alike, and the hall was filled with guests.] But when the king came in to meet the guests, he saw a man there not dressed in a wedding garment. The king said to him, 'My friend, how is it that you came in here without a wedding garment?' But he was reduced to silence. Then the king said to his attendants, 'Bind his hands and feet, and cast him into the darkness outside, where there will be wailing and grinding of teeth.' Many are invited, but few are chosen."

1080 TWENTY-EIGHTH SUNDAY IN ORDINARY TIME / B

READING I
Wisdom 7:7-11 / 143

I prayed, and prudence was given me;
  I pleaded, and the spirit of wisdom came to me.
I preferred her to scepter and throne,
and deemed riches nothing in comparison with her,
  nor did I liken any priceless gem to her;
because all gold, in view of her, is a little sand,
  and before her, silver is to be accounted mire.
Beyond health and comeliness I loved her,
and I chose to have her rather than the light,
  because the splendor of her never yields to sleep.
Yet all good things together came to me in her company,
  and countless riches at her hands.

RESPONSORIAL PSALM   *Psalm 90:12-13, 14-15, 16-17*
℟. **Fill us with your love, O Lord, and we will sing for joy!**

Teach us to number our days aright,
   that we may gain wisdom of heart.
Return, O LORD! How long?
   Have pity on your servants! ℟.

Fill us at daybreak with your kindness,
   that we may shout for joy and
      gladness all our days.
Make us glad, for the days when you

afflicted us,
   for the years when we saw evil. ℟.

Let your work be seen by your servants
   and your glory by their children;
and may the gracious care of the Lord
   our God be ours;
prosper the work of our hands for us!
Prosper the work of our hands! ℟.

READING II   *Hebrews 4:12-13*
Brothers and sisters: Indeed the word of God is living and effective, sharper than any
two-edged sword, penetrating even between soul and spirit, joints and marrow, and able
to discern reflections and thoughts of the heart. No creature is concealed from him, but
everything is naked and exposed to the eyes of him to whom we must render an account.

GOSPEL   *Mark 10:17-30 or 10:17-27*
For short form read only the part in brackets.

[As Jesus was setting out on a journey, a man ran up, knelt down before him, and asked
him, "Good teacher, what must I do to inherit eternal life?" Jesus answered him, "Why
do you call me good? No one is good but God alone. You know the commandments:
'You shall not kill; you shall not commit adultery; you shall not steal; you shall not bear
false witness; you shall not defraud; honor your father and your mother.'" He replied and
said to him, "Teacher, all of these I have observed from my youth." Jesus, looking at
him, loved him and said to him, "You are lacking in one thing. Go, sell what you have,
and give to the poor and you will have treasure in heaven; then come, follow me." At
that statement his face fell, and he went away sad, for he had many possessions.
   Jesus looked around and said to his disciples, "How hard it is for those who have
wealth to enter the kingdom of God!" The disciples were amazed at his words. So Jesus
again said to them in reply, "Children, how hard it is to enter the kingdom of God! It is
easier for a camel to pass through the eye of a needle than for one who is rich to enter
the kingdom of God." They were exceedingly astonished and said among themselves,
"Then who can be saved?" Jesus looked at them and said, "For human beings it is
impossible, but not for God. All things are possible for God."] Peter began to say to him,
"We have given up everything and followed you." Jesus said, "Amen, I say to you, there
is no one who has given up house or brothers or sisters or mother or father or children
or lands for my sake and for the sake of the gospel who will not receive a hundred times
more now in this present age: houses and brothers and sisters and mothers and children
and lands, with persecutions, and eternal life in the age to come."

TWENTY-EIGHTH SUNDAY IN ORDINARY TIME / C   1081

READING I   *2 Kings 5:14-17 / 144*
Naaman went down and plunged into the Jordan seven times at the word of Elisha, the
man of God. His flesh became again like the flesh of a little child, and he was clean of
his leprosy.
   Naaman returned with his whole retinue to the man of God. On his arrival he stood
before Elisha and said, "Now I know that there is no God in all the earth, except in
Israel. Please accept a gift from your servant."
   Elisha replied, "As the LORD lives whom I serve, I will not take it;" and despite

Naaman's urging, he still refused. Naaman said: "If you will not accept, please let me, your servant, have two mule-loads of earth, for I will no longer offer holocaust or sacrifice to any other god except to the LORD."

RESPONSORIAL PSALM
Psalm 98:1, 2-3, 3-4

℟. **The Lord has revealed to the nations his saving power.**

Sing to the LORD a new song,
for he has done wondrous deeds;
his right hand has won victory for him,
his holy arm. ℟.

The LORD has made his salvation known:
in the sight of the nations he has
revealed his justice.

He has remembered his kindness and his
faithfulness
toward the house of Israel. ℟.

All the ends of the earth have seen
the salvation by our God.
Sing joyfully to the LORD, all you lands:
break into song; sing praise. ℟.

READING II
2 Timothy 2:8-13

Beloved: Remember Jesus Christ, raised from the dead, a descendant of David: such is my gospel, for which I am suffering, even to the point of chains, like a criminal. But the word of God is not chained. Therefore, I bear with everything for the sake of those who are chosen, so that they too may obtain the salvation that is in Christ Jesus, together with eternal glory. This saying is trustworthy:
If we have died with him
we shall also live with him;
if we persevere
we shall also reign with him.
But if we deny him
he will deny us.
If we are unfaithful
he remains faithful,
for he cannot deny himself.

GOSPEL
Luke 17:11-19

As Jesus continued his journey to Jerusalem, he traveled through Samaria and Galilee. As he was entering a village, ten lepers met him. They stood at a distance from him and raised their voices, saying, "Jesus, Master! Have pity on us!" And when he saw them, he said, "Go show yourselves to the priests." As they were going they were cleansed. And one of them, realizing he had been healed, returned, glorifying God in a loud voice; and he fell at the feet of Jesus and thanked him. He was a Samaritan. Jesus said in reply, "Ten were cleansed, were they not? Where are the other nine? Has none but this foreigner returned to give thanks to God?" Then he said to him, "Stand up and go; your faith has saved you."

1082 TWENTY-NINTH SUNDAY IN ORDINARY TIME / A

READING I
Isaiah 45:1, 4-6 / 145

Thus says the LORD to his anointed,
Cyrus,
whose right hand I grasp,
subduing nations before him,
and making kings run in his service,
opening doors before him
and leaving the gates unbarred:

For the sake of Jacob, my servant,
of Israel, my chosen one,
I have called you by your name,
giving you a title, though you knew
me not.
I am the LORD and there is no other,
there is no God besides me.

It is I who arm you, though you know
  me not,
    so that toward the rising and the
    setting of the sun

people may know that there is none
  besides me.
I am the LORD, there is no other.

RESPONSORIAL PSALM

Psalm 96:1, 3, 4-5, 7-8, 9-10

℟. Give the Lord glory and honor.

Sing to the LORD a new song;
  sing to the LORD, all you lands.
Tell his glory among the nations;
  among all peoples, his wondrous
  deeds. ℟.

For great is the LORD and highly to be
  praised;
    awesome is he, beyond all gods.
For all the gods of the nations are things
  of nought,
    but the LORD made the heavens. ℟.

Give to the LORD, you families of
  nations,
    give to the LORD glory and praise;
    give to the LORD the glory due his
    name!
Bring gifts, and enter his courts. ℟.

Worship the LORD, in holy attire;
  tremble before him, all the earth;
say among the nations: The LORD is king,
  he governs the peoples with
  equity. ℟.

READING II

1 Thessalonians 1:1-5b

Paul, Silvanus, and Timothy to the church of the Thessalonians in God the Father and the Lord Jesus Christ: grace to you and peace. We give thanks to God always for all of you, remembering you in our prayers, unceasingly calling to mind your work of faith and labor of love and endurance in hope of our Lord Jesus Christ, before our God and Father, knowing, brothers and sisters loved by God, how you were chosen. For our gospel did not come to you in word alone, but also in power and in the Holy Spirit and with much conviction.

GOSPEL

Matthew 22:15-21

The Pharisees went off and plotted how they might entrap Jesus in speech. They sent their disciples to him, with the Herodians, saying, "Teacher, we know that you are a truthful man and that you teach the way of God in accordance with the truth. And you are not concerned with anyone's opinion, for you do not regard a person's status. Tell us, then, what is your opinion: Is it lawful to pay the census tax to Caesar or not?" Knowing their malice, Jesus said, "Why are you testing me, you hypocrites? Show me the coin that pays the census tax." Then they handed him the Roman coin. He said to them, "Whose image is this and whose inscription?" They replied, "Caesar's." At that he said to them, "Then repay to Caesar what belongs to Caesar and to God what belongs to God."

TWENTY-NINTH SUNDAY IN ORDINARY TIME / B   1083

READING I

Isaiah 53:10-11 / 146

The LORD was pleased
  to crush him in infirmity.

If he gives his life as an offering for sin,
  he shall see his descendants in a
  long life,
    and the will of the LORD shall be
    accomplished through him.

Because of his affliction
  he shall see the light in fullness
  of days;
through his suffering, my servant shall
  justify many,
    and their guilt he shall bear.

RESPONSORIAL PSALM   *Psalm 33:4-5, 18-19, 20, 22*

℟. **Lord, let your mercy be on us, as we place our trust in you.**

Upright is the word of the LORD,
  and all his works are trustworthy.
He loves justice and right;
  of the kindness of the LORD the
  earth is full. ℟.

See, the eyes of the LORD are upon those
  who fear him,
  upon those who hope for his

kindness,
to deliver them from death
  and preserve them in spite of
  famine. ℟.

Our soul waits for the LORD,
  who is our help and our shield.
May your kindness, O LORD, be upon us
  who have put our hope in you. ℟.

READING II   *Hebrews 4:14-16*

Brothers and sisters: Since we have a great high priest who has passed through the heavens, Jesus, the Son of God, let us hold fast to our confession. For we do not have a high priest who is unable to sympathize with our weaknesses, but one who has similarly been tested in every way, yet without sin. So let us confidently approach the throne of grace to receive mercy and to find grace for timely help.

GOSPEL   *Mark 10:35-45 or 10:42-45*
For short form read only the part in brackets.

James and John, the sons of Zebedee, came to Jesus and said to him, "Teacher, we want you to do for us whatever we ask of you." He replied, "What do you wish me to do for you?" They answered him, "Grant that in your glory we may sit one at your right and the other at your left." Jesus said to them, "You do not know what you are asking. Can you drink the cup that I drink or be baptized with the baptism with which I am baptized?" They said to him, "We can." Jesus said to them, "The cup that I drink, you will drink, and with the baptism with which I am baptized, you will be baptized; but to sit at my right or at my left is not mine to give but is for those for whom it has been prepared." When the ten heard this, they became indignant at James and John. [Jesus summoned them and said to them, "You know that those who are recognized as rulers over the Gentiles lord it over them, and their great ones make their authority over them felt. But it shall not be so among you. Rather, whoever wishes to be great among you will be your servant; whoever wishes to be first among you will be the slave of all. For the Son of Man did not come to be served but to serve and to give his life as a ransom for many."]

1084 # TWENTY-NINTH SUNDAY IN ORDINARY TIME / C

READING I   *Exodus 17:8-13 / 147*

In those days, Amalek came and waged war against Israel. Moses, therefore, said to Joshua, "Pick out certain men, and tomorrow go out and engage Amalek in battle. I will be standing on top of the hill with the staff of God in my hand." So Joshua did as Moses told him: he engaged Amalek in battle after Moses had climbed to the top of the hill with Aaron and Hur. As long as Moses kept his hands raised up, Israel had the better of the fight, but when he let his hands rest, Amalek had the better of the fight. Moses' hands, however, grew tired; so they put a rock in place for him to sit on. Meanwhile Aaron and Hur supported his hands, one on one side and one on the other, so that his hands remained steady till sunset. And Joshua mowed down Amalek and his people with the edge of the sword.

RESPONSORIAL PSALM   *Psalm 121:1-2, 3-4, 5-6, 7-8*
℞. Our help is from the Lord, who made heaven and earth.

I lift up my eyes toward the mountains;
    whence shall help come to me?
My help is from the LORD,
    who made heaven and earth. ℞.

May he not suffer your foot to slip;
    may he slumber not who guards you:
indeed he neither slumbers nor sleeps,
    the guardian of Israel. ℞.

The LORD is your guardian; the LORD is
    your shade;
he is beside you at your right hand.
The sun shall not harm you by day,
    nor the moon by night. ℞.

The LORD will guard you from all evil;
    he will guard your life.
The LORD will guard your coming and
    your going,
both now and forever. ℞.

READING II   *2 Timothy 3:14—4:2*
Beloved: Remain faithful to what you have learned and believed, because you know from whom you learned it, and that from infancy you have known the sacred Scriptures, which are capable of giving you wisdom for salvation through faith in Christ Jesus. All Scripture is inspired by God and is useful for teaching, for refutation, for correction, and for training in righteousness, so that one who belongs to God may be competent, equipped for every good work.
    I charge you in the presence of God and of Christ Jesus, who will judge the living and the dead, and by his appearing and his kingly power: proclaim the word; be persistent whether it is convenient or inconvenient; convince, reprimand, encourage through all patience and teaching.

GOSPEL   *Luke 18:1-8*
Jesus told his disciples a parable about the necessity for them to pray always without becoming weary. He said, "There was a judge in a certain town who neither feared God nor respected any human being. And a widow in that town used to come to him and say, 'Render a just decision for me against my adversary.' For a long time the judge was unwilling, but eventually he thought, 'While it is true that I neither fear God nor respect any human being, because this widow keeps bothering me I shall deliver a just decision for her lest she finally come and strike me.'" The Lord said, "Pay attention to what the dishonest judge says. Will not God then secure the rights of his chosen ones who call out to him day and night? Will he be slow to answer them? I tell you, he will see to it that justice is done for them speedily. But when the Son of Man comes, will he find faith on earth?'"

THIRTIETH SUNDAY IN ORDINARY TIME / A   1085

READING I   *Exodus 22:20-26 / 148*
Thus says the Lord: "You shall not molest or oppress an alien, for you were once aliens yourselves in the land of Egypt. You shall not wrong any widow or orphan. If ever you wrong them and they cry out to me, I will surely hear their cry. My wrath will flare up, and I will kill you with the sword; then your own wives will be widows, and your children orphans.
    "If you lend money to one of your poor neighbors among my people, you shall not act like an extortioner toward him by demanding interest from him. If you take your neighbor's cloak as a pledge, you shall return it to him before sunset; for this cloak of his is the only covering he has for his body. What else has he to sleep in? If he cries out to me, I will hear him; for I am compassionate."

RESPONSORIAL PSALM   *Psalm 18:2-3, 3-4, 47, 51*

℟. **I love you, Lord, my strength.**

I love you, O LORD, my strength,
    O LORD, my rock, my fortress, my
        deliverer. ℟.

My God, my rock of refuge,
    my shield, the horn of my salvation,
        my stronghold!
Praised be the LORD, I exclaim,

and I am safe from my enemies. ℟.

The LORD lives and blessed be my rock!
    Extolled be God my savior.
You who gave great victories to your
        king
    and showed kindness to your
        anointed. ℟.

READING II   *1 Thessalonians 1:5c-10*

Brothers and sisters: You know what sort of people we were among you for your sake. And you became imitators of us and of the Lord, receiving the word in great affliction, with joy from the Holy Spirit, so that you became a model for all the believers in Macedonia and in Achaia. For from you the word of the Lord has sounded forth not only in Macedonia and in Achaia, but in every place your faith in God has gone forth, so that we have no need to say anything. For they themselves openly declare about us what sort of reception we had among you, and how you turned to God from idols to serve the living and true God and to await his Son from heaven, whom he raised from the dead, Jesus, who delivers us from the coming wrath.

GOSPEL   *Matthew 22:34-40*

When the Pharisees heard that Jesus had silenced the Sadducees, they gathered together, and one of them, a scholar of the law, tested him by asking, "Teacher, which commandment in the law is the greatest?" He said to him, "You shall love the Lord, your God, with all your heart, with all your soul, and with all your mind. This is the greatest and the first commandment. The second is like it: You shall love your neighbor as yourself. The whole law and the prophets depend on these two commandments."

1086   THIRTIETH SUNDAY IN ORDINARY TIME / B

READING I   *Jeremiah 31:7-9 / 149*

Thus says the LORD:
Shout with joy for Jacob,
    exult at the head of the nations;
    proclaim your praise and say:
The LORD has delivered his people,
    the remnant of Israel.
Behold, I will bring them back
    from the land of the north;
I will gather them from the ends of the
        world,
    with the blind and the lame in their
        midst,

the mothers and those with child;
    they shall return as an immense
        throng.
They departed in tears,
    but I will console them and guide
        them;
I will lead them to brooks of water,
    on a level road, so that none shall
        stumble.
For I am a father to Israel,
    Ephraim is my first-born.

RESPONSORIAL PSALM   *Psalm 126:1-2, 2-3, 4-5, 6*

℟. **The Lord has done great things for us; we are filled with joy.**

When the LORD brought back the
        captives of Zion,
    we were like men dreaming.
Then our mouth was filled with laughter,
    and our tongue with rejoicing. ℟.

Then they said among the nations,
    "The LORD has done great things for
        them."
The LORD has done great things for us;
    we are glad indeed. ℟.

Restore our fortunes, O LORD,
like the torrents in the southern
desert.
Those that sow in tears
shall reap rejoicing. ℟.

Although they go forth weeping,
carrying the seed to be sown,
they shall come back rejoicing,
carrying their sheaves. ℟.

READING II
Hebrews 5:1-6

Brothers and sisters: Every high priest is taken from among men and made their representative before God, to offer gifts and sacrifices for sins. He is able to deal patiently with the ignorant and erring, for he himself is beset by weakness and so, for this reason, must make sin offerings for himself as well as for the people. No one takes this honor upon himself but only when called by God, just as Aaron was. In the same way, it was not Christ who glorified himself in becoming high priest, but rather the one who said to him:
"You are my son:
this day I have begotten you";
just as he says in another place:
"You are a priest forever
according to the order of Melchizedek."

GOSPEL
Mark 10:46-52

As Jesus was leaving Jericho with his disciples and a sizable crowd, Bartimaeus, a blind man, the son of Timaeus, sat by the roadside begging. On hearing that it was Jesus of Nazareth, he began to cry out and say, "Jesus, son of David, have pity on me." And many rebuked him, telling him to be silent. But he kept calling out all the more, "Son of David, have pity on me." Jesus stopped and said, "Call him." So they called the blind man, saying to him, "Take courage; get up, Jesus is calling you." He threw aside his cloak, sprang up, and came to Jesus. Jesus said to him in reply, "What do you want me to do for you?" The blind man replied to him, "Master, I want to see." Jesus told him, "Go your way; your faith has saved you." Immediately he received his sight and followed him on the way.

THIRTIETH SUNDAY IN ORDINARY TIME / C
1087

READING I
Sirach 35:12-14, 16-18 / 150

The LORD is a God of justice,
who knows no favorites.
Though not unduly partial toward the
weak,
yet he hears the cry of the oppressed.
The Lord is not deaf to the wail of the
orphan,
nor to the widow when she pours out
her complaint.
The one who serves God willingly is
heard;
his petition reaches the heavens.
The prayer of the lowly pierces the
clouds;
it does not rest till it reaches its goal,
nor will it withdraw till the Most High
responds,
judges justly and affirms the right,
and the Lord will not delay.

RESPONSORIAL PSALM
Psalm 34:2-3, 17-18, 19, 23

℟. **The Lord hears the cry of the poor.**

I will bless the LORD at all times;
his praise shall be ever in my mouth.
Let my soul glory in the Lord;
the lowly will hear me and be glad. ℟.

The LORD confronts the evildoers,
to destroy remembrance of them
from the earth.
When the just cry out, the Lord hears
them,

and from all their distress he rescues
them. ℟.

The Lord is close to the brokenhearted;
and those who are crushed in spirit

he saves.
The Lord redeems the lives of his
servants;
no one incurs guilt who takes refuge
in him. ℟.

READING II
2 Timothy 4:6-8, 16-18

Beloved: I am already being poured out like a libation, and the time of my departure is at hand. I have competed well; I have finished the race; I have kept the faith. From now on the crown of righteousness awaits me, which the Lord, the just judge, will award to me on that day, and not only to me, but to all who have longed for his appearance.

At my first defense no one appeared on my behalf, but everyone deserted me. May it not be held against them! But the Lord stood by me and gave me strength, so that through me the proclamation might be completed and all the Gentiles might hear it. And I was rescued from the lion's mouth. The Lord will rescue me from every evil threat and will bring me safe to his heavenly kingdom. To him be glory forever and ever. Amen.

GOSPEL
Luke 18:9-14

Jesus addressed this parable to those who were convinced of their own righteousness and despised everyone else. "Two people went up to the temple area to pray; one was a Pharisee and the other was a tax collector. The Pharisee took up his position and spoke this prayer to himself, 'O God, I thank you that I am not like the rest of humanity— greedy, dishonest, adulterous—or even like this tax collector. I fast twice a week, and I pay tithes on my whole income.' But the tax collector stood off at a distance and would not even raise his eyes to heaven but beat his breast and prayed, 'O God, be merciful to me a sinner.' I tell you, the latter went home justified, not the former; for whoever exalts himself will be humbled, and the one who humbles himself will be exalted."

1088 THIRTY-FIRST SUNDAY IN ORDINARY TIME / A

READING I
Malachi 1:14b-2:2b, 8-10 / 151

A great King am I, says the Lord of
hosts,
and my name will be feared among
the nations.
And now, O priests, this commandment
is for you:
If you do not listen,
if you do not lay it to heart,
to give glory to my name, says the
Lord of hosts,
I will send a curse upon you
and of your blessing I will make a
curse.
You have turned aside from the way,

and have caused many to falter by
your instruction;
you have made void the covenant of
Levi,
says the Lord of hosts.
I, therefore, have made you contemptible
and base before all the people,
since you do not keep my ways,
but show partiality in your decisions.
Have we not all the one father?
Has not the one God created us?
Why then do we break faith with one
another,
violating the covenant of our fathers?

RESPONSORIAL PSALM
Psalm 131:1, 2, 3

℟. In you, Lord, I have found my peace.

O Lord, my heart is not proud,
nor are my eyes haughty;
I busy not myself with great things,
nor with things too sublime for me. ℟.

Nay rather, I have stilled and quieted

my soul like a weaned child.
Like a weaned child on its mother's lap,
so is my soul within me. ℟.

O Israel, hope in the Lord,
both now and forever. ℟.

READING II   *1 Thessalonians 2:7b-9, 13*

Brothers and sisters: We were gentle among you, as a nursing mother cares for her children. With such affection for you, we were determined to share with you not only the gospel of God, but our very selves as well, so dearly beloved had you become to us. You recall, brothers and sisters, our toil and drudgery. Working night and day in order not to burden any of you, we proclaimed to you the gospel of God.

And for this reason we too give thanks to God unceasingly, that, in receiving the word of God from hearing us, you received not a human word but, as it truly is, the word of God, which is now at work in you who believe.

GOSPEL   *Matthew 23:1-12*

Jesus spoke to the crowds and to his disciples, saying, "The scribes and the Pharisees have taken their seat on the chair of Moses. Therefore, do and observe all things whatsoever they tell you, but do not follow their example. For they preach but they do not practice. They tie up heavy burdens hard to carry and lay them on people's shoulders, but they will not lift a finger to move them. All their works are performed to be seen. They widen their phylacteries and lengthen their tassels. They love places of honor at banquets, seats of honor in synagogues, greetings in marketplaces, and the salutation 'Rabbi.' As for you, do not be called 'Rabbi.' You have but one teacher, and you are all brothers. Call no one on earth your father; you have but one Father in heaven. Do not be called 'Master'; you have but one master, the Christ. The greatest among you must be your servant. Whoever exalts himself will be humbled; but whoever humbles himself will be exalted."

THIRTY-FIRST SUNDAY IN ORDINARY TIME / B   1089

READING I   *Deuteronomy 6:2-6 / 152*

Moses spoke to the people, saying: "Fear the LORD, your God, and keep, throughout the days of your lives, all his statutes and commandments which I enjoin on you, and thus have long life. Hear then, Israel, and be careful to observe them, that you may grow and prosper the more, in keeping with the promise of the LORD, the God of your fathers, to give you a land flowing with milk and honey.

"Hear, O Israel! The LORD is our God, the LORD alone! Therefore, you shall love the LORD, your God, with all your heart, and with all your soul, and with all your strength. Take to heart these words which I enjoin on you today."

RESPONSORIAL PSALM   *Psalm 18:2-3, 3-4, 47, 51*

℟. **I love you, Lord, my strength.**

I love you, O LORD, my strength,
    O LORD, my rock, my fortress, my
      deliverer. ℟.

My God, my rock of refuge,
    my shield, the horn of my salvation,
      my stronghold!
Praised be the LORD, I exclaim,
    and I am safe from my enemies. ℟.

The LORD lives! And blessed be my
    rock!
Extolled be God my savior,
you who gave great victories to your
    king
    and showed kindness to your
      anointed. ℟.

READING II   *Hebrews 7:23-28*

Brothers and sisters: The levitical priests were many because they were prevented by death from remaining in office, but Jesus, because he remains forever, has a priesthood that does not pass away. Therefore, he is always able to save those who approach God through him, since he lives forever to make intercession for them.

It was fitting that we should have such a high priest: holy, innocent, undefiled, separated from sinners, higher than the heavens. He has no need, as did the high priests, to offer sacrifice day after day, first for his own sins and then for those of the people; he did that once for all when he offered himself. For the law appoints men subject to weakness to be high priests, but the word of the oath, which was taken after the law, appoints a son, who has been made perfect forever.

GOSPEL *Mark 12:28b-34*

One of the scribes came to Jesus and asked him, "Which is the first of all the commandments?" Jesus replied, "The first is this: 'Hear, O Israel! The Lord our God is Lord alone! You shall love the Lord your God with all your heart, with all your soul, with all your mind, and with all your strength.' The second is this: 'You shall love your neighbor as yourself.' There is no other commandment greater than these." The scribe said to him, "Well said, teacher. You are right in saying, 'He is One and there is no other than he.' And 'to love him with all your heart, with all your understanding, with all your strength, and to love your neighbor as yourself' is worth more than all burnt offerings and sacrifices." And when Jesus saw that he answered with understanding, he said to him, "You are not far from the kingdom of God." And no one dared to ask him any more questions.

1090 THIRTY-FIRST SUNDAY IN ORDINARY TIME / C

READING I *Wisdom 11:22—12:2 / 153*

Before the LORD the whole universe is as a grain
    from a balance
    or a drop of morning dew come down upon the earth.
But you have mercy on all, because you can do all things;
    and you overlook people's sins that they may repent.
For you love all things that are
    and loathe nothing that you have made;
    for what you hated, you would not have fashioned.
And how could a thing remain, unless you willed it;
    or be preserved, had it not been called forth by you?
But you spare all things, because they are yours,
    O LORD and lover of souls,
    for your imperishable spirit is in all things!
Therefore you rebuke offenders little by little,
    warn them and remind them of the sins
        they are committing,
    that they may abandon their wickedness
        and believe in you, O LORD!

RESPONSORIAL PSALM *Psalm 145:1-2, 8-9, 10-11, 13, 14*

℟. **I will praise your name for ever, my king and my God.**

I will extol you, O my God and King,
    and I will bless your name forever
    and ever.
Every day will I bless you,
    and I will praise your name forever
    and ever. ℟.

The LORD is gracious and merciful,
    slow to anger and of great kindness.

The LORD is good to all
    and compassionate toward all his
    works. ℟.

Let all your works give you thanks, O
    LORD,
    and let your faithful ones bless you.
Let them discourse of the glory of your
    kingdom
    and speak of your might. ℟.

The LORD is faithful in all his words
and holy in all his works.

The LORD lifts up all who are falling
and raises up all who are bowed
down. ℟.

READING II
2 Thessalonians 1:11—2:2

Brothers and sisters: We always pray for you, that our God may make you worthy of his calling and powerfully bring to fulfillment every good purpose and every effort of faith, that the name of our Lord Jesus may be glorified in you, and you in him, in accord with the grace of our God and Lord Jesus Christ.

We ask you, brothers and sisters, with regard to the coming of our Lord Jesus Christ and our assembling with him, not to be shaken out of your minds suddenly, or to be alarmed either by a "spirit," or by an oral statement, or by a letter allegedly from us to the effect that the day of the Lord is at hand.

GOSPEL
Luke 19:1-10

At that time, Jesus came to Jericho and intended to pass through the town. Now a man there named Zacchaeus, who was a chief tax collector and also a wealthy man, was seeking to see who Jesus was; but he could not see him because of the crowd, for he was short in stature. So he ran ahead and climbed a sycamore tree in order to see Jesus, who was about to pass that way. When he reached the place, Jesus looked up and said, "Zacchaeus, come down quickly, for today I must stay at your house." And he came down quickly and received him with joy. When they all saw this, they began to grumble, saying, "He has gone to stay at the house of a sinner." But Zacchaeus stood there and said to the Lord, "Behold, half of my possessions, Lord, I shall give to the poor, and if I have extorted anything from anyone I shall repay it four times over." And Jesus said to him, "Today salvation has come to this house because this man too is a descendant of Abraham. For the Son of Man has come to seek and to save what was lost."

THIRTY-SECOND SUNDAY IN ORDINARY TIME / A   1091

READING I
Wisdom 6:12-16 / 154

Resplendent and unfading is wisdom,
    and she is readily perceived by those
        who love her,
    and found by those who seek her.
She hastens to make herself known in
        anticipation of their desire;
    whoever watches for her at dawn
        shall not be disappointed,
    for he shall find her sitting by his
        gate.

For taking thought of wisdom is the
        perfection of prudence,
    and whoever for her sake keeps vigil
        shall quickly be free from care;
    because she makes her own rounds,
        seeking those worthy of her,
    and graciously appears to them in
        the ways,
    and meets them with all solicitude.

RESPONSORIAL PSALM
Psalm 63:2, 3-4, 5-6, 7-8

℟. **My soul is thirsting for you, O Lord my God.**

O God, you are my God whom I seek;
    for you my flesh pines and my soul
        thirsts
    like the earth, parched, lifeless and
        without water. ℟.

Thus have I gazed toward you in the
    sanctuary

to see your power and your glory,
for your kindness is a greater good than
        life;
    my lips shall glorify you. ℟.

Thus will I bless you while I live;
    lifting up my hands, I will call upon
        your name.

As with the riches of a banquet shall my
soul be satisfied,
and with exultant lips my mouth
shall praise you. ℟.

I will remember you upon my couch,

and through the night-watches I will
meditate on you:
you are my help,
and in the shadow of your wings I
shout for joy. ℟.

READING II   *1 Thessalonians 4:13-18 or 4:13-14*
For short form read only the part in brackets.

[We do not want you to be unaware, brothers and sisters, about those who have fallen asleep, so that you may not grieve like the rest, who have no hope. For if we believe that Jesus died and rose, so too will God, through Jesus, bring with him those who have fallen asleep.] Indeed, we tell you this, on the word of the Lord, that we who are alive, who are left until the coming of the Lord, will surely not precede those who have fallen asleep. For the Lord himself, with a word of command, with the voice of an archangel and with the trumpet of God, will come down from heaven, and the dead in Christ will rise first. Then we who are alive, who are left, will be caught up together with them in the clouds to meet the Lord in the air. Thus we shall always be with the Lord. Therefore, console one another with these words.

GOSPEL   *Matthew 25:1-13*
Jesus told his disciples this parable: "The kingdom of heaven will be like ten virgins who took their lamps and went out to meet the bridegroom. Five of them were foolish and five were wise. The foolish ones, when taking their lamps, brought no oil with them, but the wise brought flasks of oil with their lamps. Since the bridegroom was long delayed, they all became drowsy and fell asleep. At midnight, there was a cry, 'Behold, the bridegroom! Come out to meet him!' Then all those virgins got up and trimmed their lamps. The foolish ones said to the wise, 'Give us some of your oil, for our lamps are going out.' But the wise ones replied, 'No, for there may not be enough for us and you. Go instead to the merchants and buy some for yourselves.' While they went off to buy it, the bridegroom came and those who were ready went into the wedding feast with him. Then the door was locked. Afterwards the other virgins came and said, 'Lord, Lord, open the door for us!' But he said in reply, 'Amen, I say to you, I do not know you.' Therefore, stay awake, for you know neither the day nor the hour."

1092 **THIRTY-SECOND SUNDAY IN ORDINARY TIME / B**

READING I   *1 Kings 17:10-16 / 155*
In those days, Elijah the prophet went to Zarephath. As he arrived at the entrance of the city, a widow was gathering sticks there; he called out to her, "Please bring me a small cupful of water to drink." She left to get it, and he called out after her, "Please bring along a bit of bread." She answered, "As the LORD, your God, lives, I have nothing baked; there is only a handful of flour in my jar and a little oil in my jug. Just now I was collecting a couple of sticks, to go in and prepare something for myself and my son; when we have eaten it, we shall die." Elijah said to her, "Do not be afraid. Go and do as you propose. But first make me a little cake and bring it to me. Then you can prepare something for yourself and your son. For the LORD, the God of Israel, says, 'The jar of flour shall not go empty, nor the jug of oil run dry, until the day when the LORD sends rain upon the earth.'" She left and did as Elijah had said. She was able to eat for a year, and he and her son as well; the jar of flour did not go empty, nor the jug of oil run dry, as the LORD had foretold through Elijah.

RESPONSORIAL PSALM *Psalm 146:7, 8-9, 9-10*
℟. **Praise the Lord, my soul!**
or:
Alleluia.

The LORD keeps faith forever,
  secures justice for the oppressed,
  gives food to the hungry.
The LORD sets captives free. ℟.

The LORD gives sight to the blind;
  the LORD raises up those who were
  bowed down.

The LORD loves the just;
  the LORD protects strangers. ℟.

The fatherless and the widow he sustains,
  but the way of the wicked he thwarts.
The LORD shall reign forever;
  your God, O Zion, through all
  generations. Alleluia. ℟.

READING II *Hebrews 9:24-28*
Christ did not enter into a sanctuary made by hands, a copy of the true one, but heaven itself, that he might now appear before God on our behalf. Not that he might offer himself repeatedly, as the high priest enters each year into the sanctuary with blood that is not his own; if that were so, he would have had to suffer repeatedly from the foundation of the world. But now once for all he has appeared at the end of the ages to take away sin by his sacrifice. Just as it is appointed that human beings die once, and after this the judgment, so also Christ, offered once to take away the sins of many, will appear a second time, not to take away sin but to bring salvation to those who eagerly await him.

GOSPEL *Mark 12:38-44 or 12:41-44*
For short form read only the part in brackets.

In the course of his teaching Jesus said to the crowds, "Beware of the scribes, who like to go around in long robes and accept greetings in the marketplaces, seats of honor in synagogues, and places of honor at banquets. They devour the houses of widows and, as a pretext recite lengthy prayers. They will receive a very severe condemnation."

[He sat down opposite the treasury and observed how the crowd put money into the treasury. Many rich people put in large sums. A poor widow also came and put in two small coins worth a few cents. Calling his disciples to himself, he said to them, "Amen, I say to you, this poor widow put in more than all the other contributors to the treasury. For they have all contributed from their surplus wealth, but she, from her poverty, has contributed all she had, her whole livelihood."]

THIRTY-SECOND SUNDAY IN ORDINARY TIME / C 1093

READING I *2 Maccabees 7:1-2, 9-14 / 156*
It happened that seven brothers with their mother were arrested and tortured with whips and scourges by the king, to force them to eat pork in violation of God's law. One of the brothers, speaking for the others, said: "What do you expect to achieve by questioning us? We are ready to die rather than transgress the laws of our ancestors."

At the point of death he said: "You accursed fiend, you are depriving us of this present life, but the King of the world will raise us up to live again forever. It is for his laws that we are dying."

After him the third suffered their cruel sport. He put out his tongue at once when told to do so, and bravely held out his hands, as he spoke these noble words: "It was from Heaven that I received these; for the sake of his laws I disdain them; from him I hope to receive them again." Even the king and his attendants marveled at the young man's courage, because he regarded his sufferings as nothing.

After he had died, they tortured and maltreated the fourth brother in the same way. When he was near death, he said, "It is my choice to die at the hands of men with the hope God gives of being raised up by him; but for you, there will be no resurrection to life."

RESPONSORIAL PSALM   *Psalm 17:1, 5-6, 8, 15*
℟. **Lord, when your glory appears, my joy will be full.**

Hear, O LORD, a just suit;
   attend to my outcry;
   hearken to my prayer from lips
     without deceit. ℟.

My steps have been steadfast in your
   paths,
   my feet have not faltered.
I call upon you, for you will answer

me, O God;
   incline your ear to me; hear my
   word. ℟.

Keep me as the apple of your eye,
   hide me in the shadow of your wings.
But I in justice shall behold your face;
   on waking I shall be content in your
   presence. ℟.

READING II   *2 Thessalonians 2:16—3:5*
Brothers and sisters: May our Lord Jesus Christ himself and God our Father, who has loved us and given us everlasting encouragement and good hope through his grace, encourage your hearts and strengthen them in every good deed and word.

Finally, brothers and sisters, pray for us, so that the word of the Lord may speed forward and be glorified, as it did among you, and that we may be delivered from perverse and wicked people, for not all have faith. But the Lord is faithful; he will strengthen you and guard you from the evil one. We are confident of you in the Lord that what we instruct you, you are doing and will continue to do. May the Lord direct your hearts to the love of God and to the endurance of Christ.

GOSPEL   *Luke 20:27-38 or 20:27, 34-38*
For short form read only the parts in brackets.

[Some Sadducees, those who deny that there is a resurrection, came forward] and put this question to Jesus, saying, "Teacher, Moses wrote for us, 'If someone's brother dies leaving a wife but no child, his brother must take the wife and raise up descendants for his brother.' Now there were seven brothers; the first married a woman but died childless. Then the second and the third married her, and likewise all the seven died childless. Finally the woman also died. Now at the resurrection whose wife will that woman be? For all seven had been married to her." [Jesus said to them, "The children of this age marry and remarry; but those who are deemed worthy to attain to the coming age and to the resurrection of the dead neither marry nor are given in marriage. They can no longer die, for they are like angels; and they are the children of God because they are the ones who will rise. That the dead will rise even Moses made known in the passage about the bush, when he called out 'Lord,' the God of Abraham, the God of Isaac, and the God of Jacob; and he is not God of the dead, but of the living, for to him all are alive."]

1094 **THIRTY-THIRD SUNDAY IN ORDINARY TIME / A**

READING I   *Proverbs 31:10-13, 19-20, 30-31 / 157*
When one finds a worthy wife,
   her value is far beyond pearls.
Her husband, entrusting his heart to her,
   has an unfailing prize.
She brings him good, and not evil,
   all the days of her life.

She obtains wool and flax
   and works with loving hands.
She puts her hands to the distaff,
   and her fingers ply the spindle.
She reaches out her hands to the poor,
   and extends her arms to the needy.

Charm is deceptive and beauty fleeting;
the woman who fears the LORD is to
be praised.

Give her a reward for her labors,
and let her works praise her at the
city gates.

RESPONSORIAL PSALM
Psalm 128:1-2, 3, 4-5

℞. **Blessed are those who fear the Lord.**

Blessed are you who fear the LORD,
who walk in his ways!
For you shall eat the fruit of your
handiwork;
blessed shall you be, and favored. ℞.

Your wife shall be like a fruitful vine
in the recesses of your home;
your children like olive plants

around your table. ℞.

Behold, thus is the man blessed
who fears the LORD.
The LORD bless you from Zion:
may you see the prosperity of
Jerusalem
all the days of your life. ℞.

READING II
1 Thessalonians 5:1-6

Concerning times and seasons, brothers and sisters, you have no need for anything to be written to you. For you yourselves know very well that the day of the Lord will come like a thief at night. When people are saying, "Peace and security," then sudden disaster comes upon them, like labor pains upon a pregnant woman, and they will not escape.

But you, brothers and sisters, are not in darkness, for that day to overtake you like a thief. For all of you are children of the light and children of the day. We are not of the night or of darkness. Therefore, let us not sleep as the rest do, but let us stay alert and sober.

GOSPEL
Matthew 25:14-30 or 25:14-15, 19-21

For short form read only the parts in brackets.

[Jesus told his disciples this parable: "A man going on a journey called in his servants and entrusted his possessions to them. To one he gave five talents; to another, two; to a third, one—to each according to his ability. Then he went away.] Immediately the one who received five talents went and traded with them, and made another five. Likewise, the one who received two made another two. But the man who received one went off and dug a hole in the ground and buried his master's money.

[After a long time the master of those servants came back and settled accounts with them. The one who had received five talents came forward bringing the additional five. He said, 'Master, you gave me five talents. See, I have made five more.' His master said to him, 'Well done, my good and faithful servant. Since you were faithful in small matters, I will give you great responsibilities. Come, share your master's joy.'] Then the one who had received two talents also came forward and said, 'Master, you gave me two talents. See, I have made two more.' His master said to him, 'Well done, my good and faithful servant. Since you were faithful in small matters, I will give you great responsibilities. Come, share your master's joy.' Then the one who had received the one talent came forward and said, 'Master, I knew you were a demanding person, harvesting where you did not plant and gathering where you did not scatter; so out of fear I went off and buried your talent in the ground. Here it is back.' His master said to him in reply, 'You wicked, lazy servant! So you knew that I harvest where I did not plant and gather where I did not scatter? Should you not then have put my money in the bank so that I could have got it back with interest on my return? Now then! Take the talent from him and give it to the one with ten. For to everyone who has, more will be given and he will grow rich; but from the one who has not, even what he has will be taken away. And throw this useless servant into the darkness outside, where there will be wailing and grinding of teeth.'"

1095 THIRTY-THIRD SUNDAY IN ORDINARY TIME / B

READING I
Daniel 12:1-3 / 158

In those days, I Daniel,
    heard this word of the Lord:
"At that time there shall arise
    Michael, the great prince,
    guardian of your people;
it shall be a time unsurpassed in distress
    since nations began until that time.
At that time your people shall escape,
    everyone who is found written in the
    book.

Many of those who sleep in the dust of
    the earth shall awake;
some shall live forever,
others shall be an everlasting horror
    and disgrace.

But the wise shall shine brightly
    like the splendor of the firmament,
and those who lead the many to justice
    shall be like the stars forever."

RESPONSORIAL PSALM
Psalm 16:5, 8, 9-10, 11

℟. You are my inheritance, O Lord!

O LORD, my allotted portion and my cup,
    you it is who hold fast my lot.
I set the LORD ever before me;
    with him at my right hand I shall not
    be disturbed. ℟.

Therefore my heart is glad and my soul
    rejoices,
    my body, too, abides in confidence;

because you will not abandon my soul to
    the netherworld,
nor will you suffer your faithful one
    to undergo corruption. ℟.

You will show me the path to life,
    fullness of joys in your presence,
    the delights at your right hand
    forever. ℟.

READING II
Hebrews 10:11-14, 18

Brothers and sisters: Every priest stands daily at his ministry, offering frequently those same sacrifices that can never take away sins. But this one offered one sacrifice for sins, and took his seat forever at the right hand of God; now he waits until his enemies are made his footstool. For by one offering he has made perfect forever those who are being consecrated.
    Where there is forgiveness of these, there is no longer offering for sin.

GOSPEL
Mark 13:24-32

Jesus said to his disciples: "In those days after that tribulation
    the sun will be darkened,
        and the moon will not give its light,
    and the stars will be falling from the sky,
        and the powers in the heavens will be shaken.
"And then they will see 'the Son of Man coming in the clouds' with great power and glory, and then he will send out the angels and gather his elect from the four winds, from the end of the earth to the end of the sky.
    "Learn a lesson from the fig tree. When its branch becomes tender and sprouts leaves, you know that summer is near. In the same way, when you see these things happening, know that he is near, at the gates. Amen, I say to you, this generation will not pass away until all these things have taken place. Heaven and earth will pass away, but my words will not pass away.
    "But of that day or hour, no one knows, neither the angels in heaven, nor the Son, but only the Father."

THIRTY-THIRD SUNDAY IN ORDINARY TIME / C

READING I
Malachi 3:19-20a / 159

Lo, the day is coming, blazing like an oven,
when all the proud and all evildoers will be stubble,
and the day that is coming will set them on fire,
leaving them neither root nor branch, says the LORD of hosts.
But for you who fear my name, there will arise
the sun of justice with its healing rays.

RESPONSORIAL PSALM
Psalm 98:5-6, 7-8, 9

℟. The Lord comes to rule the earth with justice.

Sing praise to the LORD with the harp,
with the harp and melodious song.
With trumpets and the sound of the horn
sing joyfully before the King, the LORD. ℟.

Let the sea and what fills it resound,
the world and those who dwell in it;

let the rivers clap their hands,
the mountains shout with them for joy. ℟.

Before the LORD, for he comes,
for he comes to rule the earth;
he will rule the world with justice
and the peoples with equity. ℟.

READING II
2 Thessalonians 3:7-12

Brothers and sisters: You know how one must imitate us. For we did not act in a disorderly way among you, nor did we eat food received free from anyone. On the contrary, in toil and drudgery, night and day we worked, so as not to burden any of you. Not that we do not have the right. Rather, we wanted to present ourselves as a model for you, so that you might imitate us. In fact, when we were with you, we instructed you that if anyone was unwilling to work, neither should that one eat. We hear that some are conducting themselves among you in a disorderly way, by not keeping busy but minding the business of others. Such people we instruct and urge in the Lord Jesus Christ to work quietly and to eat their own food.

GOSPEL
Luke 21:5-19

While some people were speaking about how the temple was adorned with costly stones and votive offerings, Jesus said, "All that you see here—the days will come when there will not be left a stone upon another stone that will not be thrown down."

Then they asked him, "Teacher, when will this happen? And what sign will there be when all these things are about to happen?" He answered, "See that you not be deceived, for many will come in my name, saying, 'I am he,' and 'The time has come.' Do not follow them! When you hear of wars and insurrections, do not be terrified; for such things must happen first, but it will not immediately be the end." Then he said to them, "Nation will rise against nation, and kingdom against kingdom. There will be powerful earthquakes, famines, and plagues from place to place; and awesome sights and mighty signs will come from the sky.

"Before all this happens, however, they will seize and persecute you, they will hand you over to the synagogues and to prisons, and they will have you led before kings and governors because of my name. It will lead to your giving testimony. Remember, you are not to prepare your defense beforehand, for I myself shall give you a wisdom in speaking that all your adversaries will be powerless to resist or refute. You will even be handed over by parents, brothers, relatives, and friends, and they will put some of you to death. You will be hated by all because of my name, but not a hair on your head will be destroyed. By your perseverance you will secure your lives."

1097 LAST SUNDAY IN ORDINARY TIME
CHRIST THE KING / A

READING I   *Ezekiel 34:11-12, 15-17 / 160*

Thus says the Lord GOD: I myself will look after and tend my sheep. As a shepherd tends his flock when he finds himself among his scattered sheep, so will I tend my sheep. I will rescue them from every place where they were scattered when it was cloudy and dark. I myself will pasture my sheep; I myself will give them rest, says the Lord GOD. The lost I will seek out, the strayed I will bring back, the injured I will bind up, the sick I will heal, but the sleek and the strong I will destroy, shepherding them rightly.

As for you, my sheep, says the Lord GOD, I will judge between one sheep and another, between rams and goats.

RESPONSORIAL PSALM   *Psalm 23:1-2, 2-3, 5-6*

℟. The Lord is my shepherd; there is nothing I shall want.

The LORD is my shepherd; I shall not
    want.
In verdant pastures he gives me
    repose. ℟.

Beside restful waters he leads me;
    he refreshes my soul.
He guides me in right paths
    for his name's sake. ℟.

You spread the table before me
    in the sight of my foes;
you anoint my head with oil;
    my cup overflows. ℟.

Only goodness and kindness follow me
    all the days of my life;
and I shall dwell in the house of the
    LORD
    for years to come. ℟.

READING II   *1 Corinthians 15:20-26, 28*

Brothers and sisters: Christ has been raised from the dead, the firstfruits of those who have fallen asleep. For since death came through man, the resurrection of the dead came also through man. For just as in Adam all die, so too in Christ shall all be brought to life, but each one in proper order: Christ the firstfruits; then, at his coming, those who belong to Christ; then comes the end, when he hands over the kingdom to his God and Father, when he has destroyed every sovereignty and every authority and power. For he must reign until he has put all his enemies under his feet. The last enemy to be destroyed is death. When everything is subjected to him, then the Son himself will also be subjected to the one who subjected everything to him, so that God may be all in all.

GOSPEL   *Matthew 25:31-46*

Jesus said to his disciples: "When the Son of Man comes in his glory, and all the angels with him, he will sit upon his glorious throne, and all the nations will be assembled before him. And he will separate them one from another, as a shepherd separates the sheep from the goats. He will place the sheep on his right and the goats on his left. Then the king will say to those on his right, 'Come, you who are blessed by my Father. Inherit the kingdom prepared for you from the foundation of the world. For I was hungry and you gave me food, I was thirsty and you gave me drink, a stranger and you welcomed me, naked and you clothed me, ill and you cared for me, in prison and you visited me.' Then the righteous will answer him and say, 'Lord, when did we see you hungry and feed you, or thirsty and give you drink? When did we see you a stranger and welcome you, or naked and clothe you? When did we see you ill or in prison, and visit you?' And the king will say to them in reply, 'Amen, I say to you, whatever you did for one of the least brothers of mine, you did for me.' Then he will say to those on his left, 'Depart from me, you accursed, into the eternal fire prepared for the devil and his angels. For I was hungry and you gave me no food, I was thirsty and you gave me no drink, a stranger and you gave me no welcome, naked and you gave me no clothing, ill and in prison, and you did not care for me.' Then they will answer and say, 'Lord, when did we see you hungry or thirsty or a stranger or naked or ill or in prison, and not minister to your needs?' He will answer them, 'Amen, I say to you, what you did not do for one of these least ones, you did not do for me.' And these will go off to eternal punishment, but the righteous to eternal life."

LAST SUNDAY IN ORDINARY TIME
CHRIST THE KING / B

1098

READING I
Daniel 7:13-14 / 161

As the visions during the night continued,
    I saw
one like a Son of man coming,
    on the clouds of heaven;
when he reached the Ancient One
    and was presented before him,
the one like a Son of man received
    dominion, glory, and kingship;

all peoples, nations, and
    languages serve him.
His dominion is an everlasting
    dominion
that shall not be taken away,
    his kingship shall not be
    destroyed.

RESPONSORIAL PSALM
Psalm 93:1, 1-2, 5

℟. The Lord is king; he is robed in majesty.

The LORD is king, in splendor robed;
    robed is the LORD and girt about
    with strength. ℟.

And he has made the world firm,
    not to be moved.

Your throne stands firm from of old;
    from everlasting you are, O Lord. ℟.

Your decrees are worthy of trust indeed;
    holiness befits your house,
    O Lord, for length of days. ℟.

READING II
Revelation 1:5-8

Jesus Christ is the faithful witness, the firstborn of the dead and ruler of the kings of the earth. To him who loves us and has freed us from our sins by his blood, who has made us into a kingdom, priests for his God and Father, to him be glory and power forever and ever. Amen.
    Behold, he is coming amid the clouds,
        and every eye will see him,
        even those who pierced him.
    All the peoples of the earth will lament him.
        Yes. Amen.
"I am the Alpha and the Omega," says the Lord God, "the one who is and who was and who is to come, the almighty."

GOSPEL
John 18:33b-37

Pilate said to Jesus, "Are you the King of the Jews?" Jesus answered, "Do you say this on your own or have others told you about me?" Pilate answered, "I am not a Jew, am I? Your own nation and the chief priests handed you over to me. What have you done?" Jesus answered, "My kingdom does not belong to this world. If my kingdom did belong to this world, my attendants would be fighting to keep me from being handed over to the Jews. But as it is, my kingdom is not here." So Pilate said to him, "Then you are a king?" Jesus answered, "You say I am a king. For this I was born and for this I came into the world, to testify to the truth. Everyone who belongs to the truth listens to my voice."

1099 LAST SUNDAY IN ORDINARY TIME
CHRIST THE KING / C

READING I   *2 Samuel 5:1-3 / 162*

In those days, all the tribes of Israel came to David in Hebron and said: "Here we are, your bone and your flesh. In days past, when Saul was our king, it was you who led the Israelites out and brought them back. And the LORD said to you, 'You shall shepherd my people Israel and shall be commander of Israel.'" When all the elders of Israel came to David in Hebron, King David made an agreement with them there before the LORD, and they anointed him king of Israel.

RESPONSORIAL PSALM   *Psalm 122:1-2, 3-4, 4-5*

℞. Let us go rejoicing to the house of the Lord.

I rejoiced because they said to me,
  "We will go up to the house of the
    LORD."
And now we have set foot
  within your gates, O Jerusalem. ℞.

Jerusalem, built as a city
  with compact unity.

To it the tribes go up,
  the tribes of the LORD. ℞.

According to the decree for Israel,
  to give thanks to the name of the
    LORD.
In it are set up judgment seats,
  seats for the house of David. ℞.

READING II   *Colossians 1:12-20*

Brothers and sisters: Let us give thanks to the Father, who has made you fit to share in the inheritance of the holy ones in light. He delivered us from the power of darkness and transferred us to the kingdom of his beloved Son, in whom we have redemption, the forgiveness of sins.
    He is the image of the invisible God,
      the firstborn of all creation.
    For in him were created all things in heaven and on earth,
      the visible and the invisible,
      whether thrones or dominions or principalities or powers;
      all things were created through him and for him.
    He is before all things,
      and in him all things hold together.
    He is the head of the body, the church.
    He is the beginning, the firstborn from the dead,
      that in all things he himself might be preeminent.
    For in him all the fullness was pleased to dwell,
      and through him to reconcile all things for him,
      making peace by the blood of his cross
      through him, whether those on earth or those in heaven.

GOSPEL   *Luke 23:35-43*

The rulers sneered at Jesus and said, "He saved others, let him save himself if he is the chosen one, the Christ of God." Even the soldiers jeered at him. As they approached to offer him wine they called out, "If you are King of the Jews, save yourself." Above him there was an inscription that read, "This is the King of the Jews."
    Now one of the criminals hanging there reviled Jesus, saying, "Are you not the Christ? Save yourself and us." The other, however, rebuking him, said in reply, "Have you no fear of God, for you are subject to the same condemnation? And indeed, we have been condemned justly, for the sentence we received corresponds to our crimes, but this man has done nothing criminal." Then he said, "Jesus, remember me when you come into your kingdom." He replied to him, "Amen, I say to you, today you will be with me in Paradise."

Seasons:
Weekday Psalm Responses

FIRST WEEK OF ADVENT 1100

Monday / *175*
I rejoiced when I heard them say:
let us go to the house of the Lord.

Tuesday / *176*
Justice shall flourish in his time,
and fullness of peace for ever.

Wednesday / *177*
I shall live in the house of the Lord
all the days of my life.

Thursday / *178*
Blessed is he who comes in the
name of the Lord.
Or: Alleluia.

Friday / *179*
The Lord is my light and my
salvation.
Or: Alleluia.

Saturday / *180*
Happy are all who long for the
coming of the Lord.
Or: Alleluia.

SECOND WEEK OF ADVENT 1101

Monday / *181*
Our God will come to save us!

Tuesday / *182*
The Lord our God comes in
strength.

Wednesday / *183*
O bless the Lord, my soul.

Thursday / *184*
The Lord is kind and merciful;
slow to anger, and rich in
compassion.

Friday / *185*
Those who follow you, Lord, will
   have the light of life.

Saturday / *186*
Lord, make us turn to you,
let us see your face and we shall be
   saved.

1102 THIRD WEEK OF ADVENT

Monday / *187*
Teach me your ways, O Lord.

Tuesday / *188*
The Lord hears the cry of the poor.

Wednesday / *189*
Let the clouds rain down the Just
   One,
and the earth bring forth a savior.

Thursday / *190*
I will praise you, Lord,
for you have rescued me.

Friday / *191*
O God, let all the nations praise
you!

1103 LAST DAYS OF ADVENT

December 17 / *193*
Justice shall flourish in his time,
and fullness of peace for ever.

December 18 / *194*
Justice shall flourish in his time,
and fullness of peace for ever.

December 19 / *195*
Fill me with your praise
and I will sing your glory!

December 20 / *196*
Let the Lord enter;
he is king of glory.

December 21 / *197*
Cry out with joy in the Lord, you
   holy ones;
sing a new song to him.

December 22 / *198*
My heart rejoices in the Lord, my
   Savior.

December 23 / *199*
Lift up your heads and see;
your redemption is near at hand.

December 24 / *200*
Mass in the Morning
For ever I will sing the goodness of
   the Lord.

1104 SEASON OF CHRISTMAS

December 29 / *202*
Let heaven and earth exult in joy!

December 30 / *203*
Let heaven and earth exult in joy!

December 31 / *204*
Let heaven and earth exult in joy!

January 2 / *205*
All the ends of the earth have seen
   the saving power of God.

January 3 / *206*
All the ends of the earth have seen
   the saving power of God.

January 4 / *207*
All the ends of the earth have seen
the saving power of God.

January 5 / *208*
Let all the earth cry out to God
with joy.

January 6 / *209*
Praise the Lord, Jerusalem.
Or: Alleluia.

January 7 / *210*
The Lord takes delight in his
people.
Or: Alleluia.

AFTER EPIPHANY   1105

Monday / *212*
I will give you all the nations for
your heritage.

Tuesday / *213*
Lord, every nation on earth will
adore you.

Wednesday / *214*
Lord, every nation on earth will
adore you.

Thursday / *215*
Lord, every nation on earth will
adore you.

Friday / *216*
Praise the Lord, Jerusalem.
Or: Alleluia.

Saturday / *217*
The Lord takes delight in his
people.
Or: Alleluia.

ASH WEDNESDAY   1106

READING I   *Joel 2:12-18 / 219*

Even now, says the Lord,
    return to me with your whole heart,
    with fasting, and weeping, and
        mourning;
Rend your hearts, not your garments,
    and return to the Lord, your God.
For gracious and merciful is he,
    slow to anger, rich in kindness,
    and relenting in punishment.
Perhaps he will again relent
    and leave behind him a blessing,
Offerings and libations,
    for the Lord, your God.
Blow the trumpet in Zion!
    Proclaim a fast,
    call an assembly;
Gather the people,
    notify the congregation;

Assemble the elders,
    gather the children
    and the infants at the breast;
Let the bridegroom quit his room,
    and the bride her chamber.
Between the porch and the altar
    let the priests, the ministers of the
        Lord, weep,
And say, "Spare, O Lord, your people,
    and make not your heritage a
        reproach,
    with the nations ruling over them!
Why should they say among the
        peoples,
    'Where is their God?'"
Then the Lord was stirred to
        concern for his
    land and took pity on his people.

RESPONSORIAL PSALM *Psalm 51:3-4, 5-6, 12-13, 14, 17*
℟. Be merciful, O Lord, for we have sinned.

Have mercy on me, O God, in your
  goodness
in the greatness of your compassion
  wipe out my offense.
Thoroughly wash me from my guilt
  and of my sin cleanse me. ℟.

For I acknowledge my offense,
  and my sin is before me always:
"Against you only have I sinned,
  and done what is evil in your
  sight." ℟.

A clean heart create for me, O God,
  and a steadfast spirit renew within
  me.
Cast me not out from your presence,
  and your Holy spirit take not from
  me. ℟.

Give me back the joy of your salvation,
  and a willing spirit sustain in me.
O Lord, open my lips,
  and my mouth shall proclaim your
  praise. ℟.

READING II *2 Corinthians 5:20—6:2*
We are ambassadors for Christ, God as it were appealing through us. We implore you, in Christ's name: be reconciled to God! For our sakes God made him who did not know sin to be sin, so that in him we might become the very holiness of God.

As your fellow workers we beg you not to receive the grace of God in vain. For he says, "In an acceptable time I have heard you; on a day of salvation I have helped you." Now is the acceptable time! Now is the day of salvation!

GOSPEL *Matthew 6:1-6, 16-18*
Jesus said to his disciples: "Take care not to perform righteous deeds in order that people may see them; otherwise, you will have no recompense from your heavenly Father. When you give alms, do not blow a trumpet before you, as the hypocrites do in the synagogues and in the streets to win the praise of others. Amen, I say to you, they have received their reward. But when you give alms, do not let your left hand know what your right is doing, so that your almsgiving may be secret. And your Father who sees in secret will repay you.

"When you pray, do not be like the hypocrites, who love to stand and pray in the synagogues and on street corners so that others may see them. Amen, I say to you, they have received their reward. But when you pray, go to your inner room, close the door, and pray to your Father in secret. And your Father who sees in secret will repay you.

"When you fast, do not look gloomy like the hypocrites. They neglect their appearance, so that they may appear to others to be fasting. Amen, I say to you, they have received their reward. But when you fast, anoint your head and wash your face, so that you may not appear to be fasting, except to your Father who is hidden. And your Father who sees what is hidden will repay you."

1107 AFTER ASH WEDNESDAY

Thursday / 220
Happy are they who hope in the
  Lord.

Friday / 221
A broken, humbled heart, O God,
  you will not scorn.

Saturday / 222
Teach me your way, O Lord, that I
  may be faithful in your sight.

FIRST WEEK OF LENT

Monday / *224*
Your words, Lord, are spirit and life.

Tuesday / *225*
From all their afflictions God will deliver the just.

Wednesday / *226*
A broken, humbled heart, O God, you will not scorn.

Thursday / *227*
Lord, on the day I called for help, you answered me.

Friday / *228*
If you, O Lord, laid bare our guilt who could endure it?

Saturday / *229*
Happy are they who follow the law of the Lord.

SECOND WEEK OF LENT

Monday / *230*
Lord, do not deal with us as our sins deserve.

Tuesday / *231*
To the upright I will show the saving power of God.

Wednesday / *232*
Save me, O Lord, in your steadfast love.

Thursday / *233*
Happy are they who hope in the Lord.

Friday / *234*
Remember the marvels the Lord has done.

Saturday / *235*
The Lord is kind and merciful.

THIRD WEEK OF LENT

Monday / *237*
My soul is thirsting for the living God:
when shall I see him face to face?

Tuesday / *238*
Remember your mercies, O Lord.

Wednesday / *239*
Praise the Lord, Jerusalem.

Thursday / *240*
If today you hear his voice, harden not your hearts.

Friday / *241*
I am the Lord, your God: hear my voice.

Saturday / *242*
It is steadfast love, not sacrifice, that God desires.

FOURTH WEEK OF LENT

Monday / *244*
I will praise you, Lord, for you have rescued me.

Tuesday / *245*
The mighty Lord is with us;
The God of Jacob is our refuge.

Wednesday / *246*
The Lord is kind and merciful.

Thursday / *247*
Lord, remember us,
for the love you bear your people.

Friday / *248*
The Lord is near to broken hearts.

Saturday / *249*
Lord, my God, I take shelter in you.

1112 FIFTH WEEK OF LENT

Monday / *251*
Though I walk in the valley of
   darkness,
I fear no evil, for you are with me.

Tuesday / *252*
O Lord, hear my prayer,
and let my cry come to you.

Wednesday / *253*
Glory and praise for ever!

Thursday / *254*
The Lord remembers his covenant
   for ever.

Friday / *255*
In my distress I called upon the
   Lord,
and he heard my voice.

Saturday / *256*
The Lord will guard us,
like a shepherd guarding his flock.

1113 HOLY WEEK

Monday / *257*
The Lord is my light and my
   salvation.

Tuesday / *258*
I will sing of your salvation.

Wednesday / *259*
Lord, in your great love, answer
   me.

1114 OCTAVE OF EASTER

Monday / *261*
Keep me safe, O God;
you are my hope.
Or: Alleluia.

Tuesday / *262*
The earth is full of the goodness of
   the Lord.
Or: Alleluia.

Wednesday / *263*
The earth is full of the goodness of
   the Lord.
Or: Alleluia.

Thursday / *264*
O Lord, our God,
how wonderful your name in all the
   earth!
Or: Alleluia.

Friday / *265*
The stone rejected by the builders
   has become the cornerstone.
Or: Alleluia.

Saturday / *266*
I praise you, Lord,
for you have answered me.
Or: Alleluia.

SECOND WEEK OF EASTER

Monday / *267*
Happy are all who put their trust in
    the Lord.
Or: Alleluia.

Tuesday / *268*
The Lord is king;
he is robed in majesty.
Or: Alleluia.

Wednesday / *269*
The Lord hears the cry of the poor.
Or: Alleluia.

Thursday / *270*
The Lord hears the cry of the poor.
Or: Alleluia.

Friday / *271*
One thing I seek: to dwell in the
    house of the Lord.
Or: Alleluia.

Saturday / *272*
Lord, let your mercy be on us,
as we place our trust in you.
Or: Alleluia.

THIRD WEEK OF EASTER

Monday / *273*
Happy are those of blameless life.
Or: Alleluia.

Tuesday / *274*
Into your hands, O Lord,
I entrust my spirit.
Or: Alleluia.

Wednesday / *275*
Let all the earth cry out to God
    with joy.
Or: Alleluia.

Thursday / *276*
Let all the earth cry out to God
    with joy.
Or: Alleluia.

Friday / *277*
Go out to all the world,
and tell the Good News.
Or: Alleluia.

Saturday / *278*
What return can I make to the Lord
for all that he gives to me?
Or: Alleluia.

FOURTH WEEK OF EASTER

Monday / *279*
My soul is thirsting for the living
    God.
Or: Alleluia.

Tuesday / *280*
All you nations, praise the Lord.
Or: Alleluia.

Wednesday / *281*
O God, let all the nations praise
    you!
Or: Alleluia.

Thursday / *282*
For ever I will sing the goodness of
    the Lord.
Or: Alleluia.

Friday / *283*
You are my Son;
this day have I begotten you.
Or: Alleluia.

Saturday / *284*
All the ends of the earth have seen
   the saving power of God.
Or: Alleluia.

1118 FIFTH WEEK OF EASTER

Monday / *285*
Not to us, O Lord,
but to your name give the glory.
Or: Alleluia.

Thursday / *288*
Proclaim his marvelous deeds
to all the nations.
Or: Alleluia.

Tuesday / *286*
Your friends tell the glory of your
   kingship, Lord.
Or: Alleluia.

Friday / *289*
I will praise you among the nations,
   O Lord.
Or: Alleluia.

Wednesday / *287*
I rejoiced when I heard them say:
let us go to the house of the Lord.
Or: Alleluia.

Saturday / *290*
Let all the earth cry out to God
   with joy.
Or: Alleluia.

1119 SIXTH WEEK OF EASTER

Monday / *291*
The Lord takes delight in his people.
Or: Alleluia.

Thursday / *294*
The Lord has revealed to the nations
   his saving power.
Or: Alleluia.

Tuesday / *292*
Your right hand has saved me, O
   Lord.
Or: Alleluia.

Friday / *295*
God is king of all the earth.
Or: Alleluia.

Wednesday / *293*
Heaven and earth are filled with
   your glory.
Or: Alleluia.

Saturday / *296*
God is king of all the earth.
Or: Alleluia.

1120 SEVENTH WEEK OF EASTER

Monday / *297*
Sing to God, O kingdoms of the
   earth.
Or: Alleluia.

Tuesday / *298*
Sing to God, O kingdoms of the
   earth.
Or: Alleluia.

Wednesday / *299*
Sing to God, O kingdoms of the
earth.
Or: Alleluia.

Thursday / *300*
Keep me safe, O God;
you are my hope.
Or: Alleluia.

Friday / *301*
The Lord has set his throne in
heaven.
Or: Alleluia.

Saturday / *302*
The just will gaze on your face, O
Lord.
Or: Alleluia.

Ordinary Time: Psalm Responses

1121 FIRST WEEK IN ORDINARY TIME

Monday / *305*

I Let all his angels worship him.

II To you, Lord, I will offer a sacrifice of praise.

Or: Alleluia.

Tuesday / *306*

I You gave your Son authority over all creation.

II My heart rejoices in the Lord, my Savior.

Wednesday / *307*

I The Lord remembers his covenant for ever.

Or: Alleluia.

II Here am I, Lord; I come to do your will.

Thursday / *308*

I If today you hear his voice, harden not your hearts.

II Save us, Lord, in your mercy.

Friday / *309*

I Do not forget the works of the Lord!

II For ever I will sing the goodness of the Lord.

Saturday / *310*

I Your words, Lord, are spirit and life.

II Lord, your strength gives joy to the king.

1122 SECOND WEEK IN ORDINARY TIME

Monday / *311*

I You are a priest for ever, in the line of Melchizedek.

II To the upright I will show the saving power of God.

Tuesday / *312*

I The Lord will remember his covenant for ever.

Or: Alleluia.

II I have found David, my servant.

Wednesday / *313*
I   You are a priest for ever,
    in the line of Melchizedek.
II Blessed be the Lord, my Rock!

Thursday / *314*
I   Here am I, Lord;
    I come to do your will.
II In God I trust;
    I shall not fear.

Friday / *315*
I   Kindness and truth shall meet.
II Have mercy on me, God, have
    mercy.

Saturday / *316*
I   God mounts his throne to
    shouts of joy;
    a blare of trumpets for the Lord.
II Let us see your face, Lord,
    and we shall be saved.

THIRD WEEK IN ORDINARY TIME   1123

Monday / *317*
I   Sing to the Lord a new song,
    for he has done marvelous
    deeds.
II My faithfulness and love shall
    be with him.

Tuesday / *318*
I   Here am I, Lord;
    I come to do your will.
II Who is the king of glory?
    It is the Lord!

Wednesday / *319*
I   You are a priest for ever,
    in the line of Melchizedek.
II For ever I will keep my love for
    him.

Thursday / *320*
I   Lord, this is the people that
    longs to see your face.
II God will give him the throne of
    David, his father.

Friday / *321*
I   The salvation of the just comes
    from the Lord.
II Be merciful, O Lord, for we
    have sinned.

Saturday / *322*
I   Blessed be the Lord God of
    Israel,
    for he has visited his people.
II Create a clean heart in me, O
    God.

FOURTH WEEK IN ORDINARY TIME   1124

Monday / *323*
I   Let your hearts take comfort,
    all who hope in the Lord.
II Lord, rise up and save me.

Tuesday / *324*
I   They will praise you, Lord,
    who long for you.
II Listen, Lord, and answer me.

Wednesday / *325*
I   The Lord's kindness is
    everlasting to those who
    fear him.
II Lord, forgive the wrong I
    have done.

Thursday / *326*
I   God, in your temple, we ponder
    your love.
II Lord, you are exalted over all.

Friday / *327*

I   The Lord is my light and my
    salvation.

II Blessed be God my salvation!

Saturday / *328*

I   The Lord is my shepherd;
    there is nothing I shall want.

II Lord, teach me your decrees.

1125   FIFTH WEEK IN ORDINARY TIME

Monday / *329*

I   May the Lord be glad in his
    works.

II Lord, go up to the place of
    your rest!

Tuesday / *330*

I   O Lord, our God,
    how wonderful your name in all
    the earth!

II How lovely is your dwelling
    place,
    Lord, mighty God!

Wednesday / *331*

I   Oh, bless the Lord, my soul!

II The mouth of the just man
    murmurs wisdom.

Thursday / *332*

I   Happy are those who fear the
    Lord.

II Lord, remember us,
    for the love you bear your
    people.

Friday / *333*

I   Happy are those whose sins are
    forgiven.

II I am the Lord, your God:
    hear my voice.

Saturday / *334*

I   In every age, O Lord, you
    have been our refuge.

II Lord, remember us,
    for the love you bear your
    people.

1126   SIXTH WEEK IN ORDINARY TIME

Monday / *335*

I   Offer to God a sacrifice of
    praise.

II Be kind to me, Lord, and I
    shall live.

Tuesday / *336*

I   The Lord will bless his people
    with peace.

II Happy the man you teach,
    O Lord.

Wednesday / *337*

I   To you, Lord, I will offer a
    sacrifice of praise.

    Or: Alleluia.

II He who does justice shall live
    on the Lord's holy mountain.

Thursday / *338*

I   From heaven the Lord looks
    down on the earth.

II The Lord hears the cry of the
    poor.

Friday / *339*

I   Happy the people the Lord has
    chosen to be his own.

II Happy are those who do what
    the Lord commands.

Saturday / *340*

I   I will praise your name for
    ever, Lord.

II You will protect us, Lord.

SEVENTH WEEK IN ORDINARY TIME 1127

Monday / *341*

I   The Lord is king; he is robed in majesty.

II The precepts of the Lord give joy to the heart.

Tuesday / *342*

I   Commit your life to the Lord, and he will help you.

II Throw your cares on the Lord, and he will support you.

Wednesday / *343*

I   O Lord, great peace have they who love the law.

II Happy the poor in spirit; the kingdom of heaven is theirs!

Thursday / *344*

I   Happy are they who hope in the Lord.

II Happy the poor in spirit; the kingdom of heaven is theirs!

Friday / *345*

I   Guide me, Lord, in the way of your commands.

II The Lord is kind and merciful.

Saturday / *346*

I   The Lord's kindness is everlasting to those who fear him.

II Let my prayer come like incense before you.

EIGHTH WEEK IN ORDINARY TIME 1128

Monday / *347*

I   Let the just exult and rejoice in the Lord.

II The Lord will remember his covenant for ever.

Or: Alleluia.

Tuesday / *348*

I   To the upright I will show the saving power of God.

II The Lord has made known his salvation.

Wednesday / *349*

I   Show us, O Lord, the light of your kindness.

II Praise the Lord, Jerusalem.

Or: Alleluia.

Thursday / *350*

I   By the word of the Lord the heavens were made.

II Come with joy into the presence of the Lord.

Friday / *351*

I   The Lord takes delight in his people.

II The Lord comes to judge the earth.

Saturday / *352*

I   The precepts of the Lord give joy to the heart.

II My soul is thirsting for you, O Lord my God.

1129   NINTH WEEK IN ORDINARY TIME

Monday / *353*

I   Happy the man who fears the Lord.

Or: Alleluia.

II   In you, my God, I place my trust.

Tuesday / *354*

I   The heart of the just man is secure, trusting in the Lord.

Or: Alleluia.

II   In every age, O Lord, you have been our refuge.

Wednesday / *355*

I   To you, O Lord, I lift my soul.

II   To you, O Lord, I lift up my eyes.

Thursday / *356*

I   Happy are those who fear the Lord.

II   Teach me your ways, O Lord.

Friday / *357*

I   Praise the Lord, my soul!

Or: Alleluia.

II   O Lord, great peace have they who love your law.

Saturday / *358*

I   Blessed be God, who lives for ever.

II   I will sing of your salvation.

1130   TENTH WEEK IN ORDINARY TIME

Monday / *359*

I   Taste and see the goodness of the Lord.

II   Our help is from the Lord who made heaven and earth.

Tuesday / *360*

I   Lord, let your face shine on me.

II   Lord, let your face shine on us.

Wednesday / *361*

I   Holy is the Lord our God.

II   Keep me safe, O God; you are my hope.

Thursday / *362*

I   The glory of the Lord will dwell in our land.

II   It is right to praise you in Zion, O God.

Friday / *363*

I   To you, Lord, I will offer a sacrifice of praise.

Or: Alleluia.

II   I long to see your face, O Lord.

Saturday / *364*

I   The Lord is kind and merciful.

II   You are my inheritance, O Lord.

1131   ELEVENTH WEEK IN ORDINARY TIME

Monday / *365*

I   The Lord has made known his salvation.

II   Lord, listen to my groaning.

Tuesday / *366*

I   Praise the Lord, my soul!

Or: Alleluia.

II   Be merciful, O Lord, for we have sinned.

Wednesday / *367*

I Happy the man who fears the Lord.

Or: Alleluia.

II Let your hearts take comfort, all who hope in the Lord.

Thursday / *368*

I Your works, O Lord, are justice and truth.

Or: Alleluia.

II Let good men rejoice in the Lord.

Friday / *369*

I From all their afflictions God will deliver the just.

II The Lord has chosen Zion for his dwelling.

Saturday / *370*

I Taste and see the goodness of the Lord.

II For ever I will keep my love for him.

TWELFTH WEEK IN ORDINARY TIME 1132

Monday / *371*

I Happy the people the Lord has chosen to be his own.

II Help us with your right hand, O Lord, and answer us.

Tuesday / *372*

I He who does justice will live in the presence of the Lord.

II God upholds his city for ever.

Wednesday / *373*

I The Lord remembers his covenant for ever.

Or: Alleluia.

II Teach me the way of your decrees, O Lord.

Thursday / *374*

I Give thanks to the Lord for he is good.

Or: Alleluia.

II For the glory of your name, O Lord, deliver us.

Friday / *375*

I See how the Lord blesses those who fear him.

II Let my tongue be silenced, if I ever forget you!

Saturday / *376*

I The Lord has remembered his mercy.

II Lord, forget not the life of your poor ones.

THIRTEENTH WEEK IN ORDINARY TIME 1133

Monday / *377*

I The Lord is kind and merciful.

II Remember this, you who never think of God.

Tuesday / *378*

I O Lord, your kindness is before my eyes.

II Lead me in your justice, Lord.

Wednesday / *379*
I   The Lord hears the cry of the poor.
II To the upright I will show the saving power of God.

Thursday / *380*
I   I will walk in the presence of the Lord,
    in the land of the living.
    Or: Alleluia.
II The judgments of the Lord are true,
    and all of them just.

Friday / *381*
I   Give thanks to the Lord for he is good.
    Or: Alleluia.
II Man does not live on bread alone,
    but on every word that comes from the mouth of God.

Saturday / *382*
I   Praise the Lord for he is good!
    Or: Alleluia.
II The Lord speaks of peace to his people.

1134   FOURTEENTH WEEK IN ORDINARY TIME

Monday / *383*
I   In you, my God, I place my trust.
II The Lord is kind and merciful.

Tuesday / *384*
I   In my justice, I shall see your face, O Lord.
II The house of Israel trusts in the Lord.
    Or: Alleluia.

Wednesday / *385*
I   Lord, let your mercy be on us, as we place our trust in you.
II Seek always the face of the Lord.
    Or: Alleluia.

Thursday / *386*
I   Remember the marvels the Lord has done.
    Or: Alleluia.
II Let us see your face, Lord, and we shall be saved.

Friday / *387*
I   The salvation of the just comes from the Lord.
II My mouth will declare your praise.

Saturday / *388*
I   Turn to the Lord in your need, and you will live.
II The Lord is king;
    he is robed in majesty.

1135   FIFTEENTH WEEK IN ORDINARY TIME

Monday / *389*
I   Our help is in the name of the Lord.
II To the upright I will show the saving power of God.

Tuesday / *390*
I   Turn to the Lord in your need, and you will live.
II God upholds his city for ever.

Wednesday / *391*

I   The Lord is kind and merciful.

II The Lord will not abandon his people.

Thursday / *392*

I   The Lord remembers his covenant for ever.

Or: Alleluia.

II From heaven the Lord looks down on the earth.

Friday / *393*

I   I will take the cup of salvation, and call on the name of the Lord.

Or: Alleluia.

II You saved my life, O Lord; I shall not die.

Saturday / *394*

I   His love is everlasting.

Or: Alleluia.

II Do not forget the poor, O Lord!

SIXTEENTH WEEK IN ORDINARY TIME   1136

Monday / *395*

I   Let us sing to the Lord; he has covered himself in glory.

II To the upright I will show the saving power of God.

Tuesday / *396*

I   Let us sing to the Lord; he has covered himself in glory.

II Lord, let us see your kindness.

Wednesday / *397*

I   The Lord gave them bread from heaven.

II I will sing of your salvation.

Thursday / *398*

I   Glory and praise for ever!

II You are the source of life, O Lord.

Friday / *399*

I   Lord, you have the words of everlasting life.

II The Lord will guard us, like a shepherd guarding his flock.

Saturday / *400*

I   Offer to God a sacrifice of praise.

II How lovely is your dwelling place, Lord, mighty God!

SEVENTEENTH WEEK IN ORDINARY TIME   1137

Monday / *401*

I   Give thanks to the Lord for he is good.

Or: Alleluia.

II You have forgotten God who gave you birth.

Tuesday / *402*

I   The Lord is kind and merciful.

II For the glory of your name, O Lord, deliver us.

Wednesday / *403*

I   Holy is the Lord our God.

II God is my refuge on the day of distress.

Thursday / *404*

I   How lovely is your dwelling place,
Lord, mighty God!

II Blest are they whose help is the God of Jacob.

Or: Alleluia.

Friday / *405*

I   Sing with joy to God our help.

II Lord, in your great love, answer me.

Saturday / *406*

I   O God, let all the nations praise you!

II Lord, in your great love, answer me.

1138   EIGHTEENTH WEEK IN ORDINARY TIME

Monday / *407*

I   Sing with joy to God our help.

II Teach me your laws, O Lord.

Tuesday / *408*

I   Be merciful, O Lord, for we have sinned.

II The Lord will build up Zion again,
and appear in all his glory.

Wednesday / *409*

I   Lord, remember us,
for the love you bear your people.

Or: Alleluia.

II The Lord will guard us,
like a shepherd guarding his flock.

Thursday / *410*

I   If today you hear his voice, harden not your hearts.

II Create a clean heart in me, O God.

Friday / *411*

I   I remember the deeds of the Lord.

II It is I who deal death and give life.

Saturday / *412*

I   I love you, Lord, my strength.

II You will never abandon those who seek you, Lord.

1139   NINETEENTH WEEK IN ORDINARY TIME

Monday / *413*

I   Praise the Lord, Jerusalem.

Or: Alleluia.

II Heaven and earth are filled with your glory.

Or: Alleluia.

Tuesday / *414*

I   The portion of the Lord is his people.

II How sweet to my taste is your promise!

Wednesday / *415*

I   Blessed be God who filled my
     soul with life!

II The glory of the Lord is higher
     than the skies.

     Or: Alleluia.

Thursday / *416*

I   Alleluia.

II Do not forget the works of the
     Lord!

Friday / *417*

I   His love is everlasting.

     Or: Alleluia.

II You have turned from your
     anger to comfort me.

Saturday / *418*

I   You are my inheritance, O
     Lord.

II Create a clean heart in me, O
     God.

TWENTIETH WEEK IN ORDINARY TIME   1140

Monday / *419*

I   Lord, remember us,
     for the love you bear your
     people.

II You have forgotten God who
     gave you birth.

Tuesday / *420*

I   The Lord speaks of peace to his
     people.

II It is I who deal death and give
     life.

Wednesday / *421*

I   Lord, your strength gives joy to
     the king.

II The Lord is my shepherd;
     there is nothing I shall want.

Thursday / *422*

I   Here am I, Lord;
     I come to do your will.

II I will pour clean water on you
     and wash away all your sins.

Friday / *423*

I   Praise the Lord, my soul!

     Or: Alleluia.

II Give thanks to the Lord,
     his love is everlasting.

     Or: Alleluia.

Saturday / *424*

I   See how the Lord blesses those
     who fear him.

II The glory of the Lord will
     dwell in our land.

TWENTY-FIRST WEEK IN ORDINARY TIME   1141

Monday / *425*

I   The Lord takes delight in his
     people.

     Or: Alleluia.

II Proclaim his marvelous deeds to
     all the nations.

Tuesday / *426*

I   You have searched me
     and you know me, Lord.

II The Lord comes to judge the
     earth.

Wednesday / *427*
I   You have searched me and you know me, Lord.
II   Happy are those who fear the Lord.

Thursday / *428*
I   Fill us with your love, O Lord, and we will sing for joy!
II   I will praise your name for ever, Lord.

Friday / *429*
I   Let good men rejoice in the Lord.
II   The earth is full of the goodness of the Lord.

Saturday / *430*
I   The Lord comes to rule the earth with justice.
II   Happy the people the Lord has chosen to be his own.

1142   TWENTY-SECOND WEEK IN ORDINARY TIME

Monday / *431*
I   The Lord comes to judge the earth.
II   Lord, I love your commands.

Tuesday / *432*
I   I believe that I shall see the good things of the Lord in the land of the living.
II   The Lord is just in all his ways.

Wednesday / *433*
I   I trust in the kindness of God for ever.
II   Happy the people the Lord has chosen to be his own.

Thursday / *434*
I   The Lord has made known his salvation.
II   To the Lord belongs the earth and all that fills it.

Friday / *435*
I   Come with joy into the presence of the Lord.
II   The salvation of the just comes from the Lord.

Saturday / *436*
I   God himself is my help.
II   The Lord is near to all who call him.

1143   TWENTY-THIRD WEEK IN ORDINARY TIME

Monday / *437*
I   In God is my safety and my glory.
II   Lead me in your justice, Lord.

Tuesday / *438*
I   The Lord is compassionate to all his creatures.
II   The Lord takes delight in his people.
Or: Alleluia.

Wednesday / *439*
I   The Lord is compassionate to all his creatures.
II   Listen to me, daughter; see and bend your ear.

Thursday/ *440*
I   Let everything that breathes praise the Lord!
Or: Alleluia.
II   Guide me, Lord, along the everlasting way.

Friday / *441*

I   You are my inheritance, O
     Lord.

II   How lovely is your dwelling
     place,
     Lord, mighty God!

Saturday / *442*

I   Blessed be the name of the
     Lord for ever.

Or: Alleluia.

II   To you, Lord, I will offer a
     sacrifice of praise.

TWENTY-FOURTH WEEK IN ORDINARY TIME   1144

Monday / *443*

I   Blest be the Lord for he has
     heard my prayer.

II   Proclaim the death of the Lord
     until he comes again.

Tuesday / *444*

I   I will walk with blameless
     heart.

II   We are his people:
     the sheep of his flock.

Wednesday / *445*

I   How great are the works of the
     Lord!

Or: Alleluia.

II   Happy the people the Lord has
     chosen to be his own.

Thursday / *446*

I   How great are the works of the
     Lord!

Or: Alleluia.

II   Give thanks to the Lord, for he
     is good.

Or: Alleluia.

Friday / *447*

I   Happy the poor in spirit;
     the kingdom of heaven is theirs!

II   Lord, when your glory appears,
     my joy will be full.

Saturday / *448*

I   Come with joy into the
     presence of the Lord.

II   I will walk in the presence of
     God,
     with the light of the living.

TWENTY-FIFTH WEEK IN ORDINARY TIME   1145

Monday / *449*

I   The Lord has done marvels for
     us.

II   He who does justice shall live
     on the Lord's holy
     mountain.

Tuesday / *450*

I   I rejoiced when I heard them
     say:
     let us go to the house of the
     Lord.

II   Guide me, Lord, in the way of
     your commands.

Wednesday / *451*

I   Blessed be God, who lives for
     ever.

II   Your word, O Lord, is a lamp
     for my feet.

Thursday / *452*

I   The Lord takes delight in his
     people.

II   In every age, O Lord, you have
     been our refuge.

Friday / *453*

I Hope in God; I will praise him, my savior and my God.

II Blessed be the Lord, my Rock!

Saturday / *454*

I The Lord will guard us, like a shepherd guarding his flock.

II In every age, O Lord, you have been our refuge.

1146 TWENTY-SIXTH WEEK IN ORDINARY TIME

Monday / *455*

I The Lord will build up Zion again,
and appear in all his glory.

II Lord, bend your ear and hear my prayer.

Tuesday / *456*

I God is with us.

II Let my prayer come before you, Lord.

Wednesday / *457*

I Let my tongue be silenced, if I ever forget you!

II Let my prayer come before you, Lord.

Thursday / *458*

I The precepts of the Lord give joy to the heart.

II I believe that I shall see the good things of the Lord in the land of the living.

Friday / *459*

I For the glory of your name, O Lord, deliver us.

II Guide me, Lord, along the everlasting way.

Saturday / *460*

I The Lord listens to the poor.

II Lord, let your face shine on me.

1147 TWENTY-SEVENTH WEEK IN ORDINARY TIME

Monday / *461*

I You will rescue my life from the pit, O Lord.

II The Lord will remember his covenant for ever.
Or: Alleluia.

Tuesday / *462*

I If you, O Lord, laid bare our guilt,
who could endure it?

II Guide me, Lord, along the everlasting way.

Wednesday / *463*

I Lord, you are tender and full of love.

II Go out to all the world, and tell the Good News.
Or: Alleluia.

Thursday / *464*

I Happy are they who hope in the Lord.

II Blessed be the Lord God of Israel,
for he has visited his people.

Friday / *465*

I The Lord will judge the world with justice.

II The Lord will remember his covenant for ever.

Or: Alleluia.

Saturday / *466*

I Let good men rejoice in the Lord.

II The Lord remembers his covenant for ever.

Or: Alleluia.

TWENTY-EIGHTH WEEK IN ORDINARY TIME 1148

Monday / *467*

I The Lord has made known his salvation.

II Blessed be the name of the Lord for ever.

Or: Alleluia.

Tuesday / *468*

I The heavens proclaim the glory of God.

II Let your loving kindness come to me, O Lord.

Wednesday / *469*

I Lord, you give back to every man,
according to his works.

II Those who follow you, Lord, will have the light of life.

Thursday / *470*

I With the Lord there is mercy, and fullness of redemption.

II The Lord has made known his salvation.

Friday / *471*

I I turn to you, Lord, in time of trouble,
and you fill me with the joy of salvation.

II Happy the people the Lord has chosen to be his own.

Saturday / *472*

I The Lord remembers his covenant for ever.

Or: Alleluia.

II You gave your Son authority over all your creation.

TWENTY-NINTH WEEK IN ORDINARY TIME 1149

Monday / *473*

I Blessed be the Lord God of Israel,
for he has visited his people.

II The Lord made us, we belong to him.

Tuesday / *474*

I Here am I, Lord;
I come to do your will.

II The Lord speaks of peace to his people.

Wednesday / *475*

I Our help is in the name of the Lord.

II You will draw water joyfully from the springs of salvation.

Thursday / *476*

I Happy are they who hope in the Lord.

II The earth is full of the goodness of the Lord.

Friday / *477*

I   Teach me your laws, O Lord.

II Lord, this is the people that
    longs to see your face.

Saturday / *478*

I   Lord, this is the people that
    longs to see your face.

II I rejoiced when I heard them
    say:
    let us go to the house of the Lord.

1150   THIRTIETH WEEK IN ORDINARY TIME

Monday / *479*

I   Our God is the God of
    salvation.

II Behave like God as his very
    dear children.

Tuesday / *480*

I   The Lord has done marvels for
    us.

II Happy are those who fear the
    Lord.

Wednesday / *481*

I   All my hope, O Lord,
    is in your loving kindness.

II The Lord is faithful in all his
    words.

Thursday / *482*

I   Save me, O Lord,
    in your kindness.

II Blessed be the Lord, my Rock!

Friday / *483*

I   Praise the Lord, Jerusalem.

II How great are the works of the
    Lord!

    Or: Alleluia.

Saturday / *484*

I   The Lord will not abandon his
    people.

II My soul is thirsting for the
    living God.

1151   THIRTY-FIRST WEEK IN ORDINARY TIME

Monday / *485*

I   Lord, in your great love,
    answer me.

II In you, Lord, I have found my
    peace.

Tuesday / *486*

I   In you, Lord, I have found my
    peace.

II I will praise you, Lord, in the
    assembly of your people.

Wednesday / *487*

I   Happy the man who is merciful
    and lends to those in need.

    Or: Alleluia.

II The Lord is my light and my
    salvation.

Thursday / *488*

I   I believe that I shall see the
    good things of the Lord in
    the land of the living.

II Let hearts rejoice who search
    for the Lord.

    Or: Alleluia.

Friday / *489*

I The Lord has revealed to the nations his saving power.

II I rejoiced when I heard them say:
Let us go to the house of the Lord.

Saturday / *490*

I I will praise your name for ever, Lord.

II Happy the man who fears the Lord.

Or: Alleluia.

THIRTY-SECOND WEEK IN ORDINARY TIME   1152

Monday / *491*

I Guide me, Lord, along the everlasting way.

II Lord, this is the people that longs to see your face.

Tuesday / *492*

I I will bless the Lord at all times.

II The salvation of the just comes from the Lord.

Wednesday / *493*

I Rise up, O God, bring judgment to the earth.

II The Lord is my shepherd; there is nothing I shall want.

Thursday / *494*

I Your word is for ever, O Lord.

II Blest are they whose help is the God of Jacob.

Or: Alleluia.

Friday / 495

I The heavens proclaim the glory of God.

II Happy are they who follow the law of the Lord!

Saturday / *496*

I Remember the marvels the Lord has done.

Or: Alleluia.

II Happy the man who fears the Lord.

Or: Alleluia.

THIRTY-THIRD WEEK IN ORDINARY TIME   1153

Monday / *497*

I Give me life, O Lord, and I will do your commands.

II Those who are victorious I will feed from the tree of life.

Tuesday / *498*

I The Lord upholds me.

II Him who is victorious I will sit beside me on my throne.

Wednesday / *499*

I Lord, when your glory appears, my joy will be full.

II Holy, holy, holy Lord, mighty God!

Thursday / *500*

I To the upright I will show the saving power of God.

II The Lamb has made us a kingdom of priests to serve our God.

Or: Alleluia.

Friday / 501

I We praise your glorious name,
O mighty God.

II How sweet to my taste is your
promise!

Saturday / 502

I I will rejoice in your salvation,
O Lord.

II Blessed be the Lord, my Rock!

1154 THIRTY-FOURTH WEEK IN ORDINARY TIME

Monday / 503

I Glory and praise for ever!

II Lord, this is the people that
longs to see your face.

Tuesday / 504

I Give glory and eternal praise to
him.

II The Lord comes to judge the
earth.

Wednesday / 505

I Give glory and eternal praise to
him.

II Great and wonderful are all
your works,
Lord, mighty God!

Thursday / 506

I Give glory and eternal praise to
him.

II Blessed are they who are called
to the wedding feast of the
Lamb.

Friday / 507

I Give glory and eternal praise to
him.

II Here God lives among his
people.

Saturday / 508

I Give glory and eternal praise to
him.

II Maranatha! Come, Lord Jesus!

Saints:
Weekday Psalm Responses

January 2 / *510*
**BASIL THE GREAT
AND GREGORY NAZIANZEN**
cf. 1198 or 1199

January 4
ELIZABETH ANN SETON
cf. 1201

January 5
JOHN NEUMANN
Proclaim his marvelous deeds
to all the nations.

January 6
ANDRE BESSETTE
cf. 1201

January 7 / *511*
RAYMOND OF PENYAFORT
cf. 1198

January 13 / *512*
HILARY
cf. 1198 or 1199

January 17 / *513*
ANTHONY
cf. 1201

January 20 / *514*
FABIAN
cf. 1197 or 1198

SEBASTIAN / *515*
cf. 1197

January 21 / *516*
AGNES
cf. 1197 or 1200

January 22 / *517*
VINCENT
cf. 1197

January 24 / *518*
FRANCIS DE SALES
cf. 1198 or 1199

January 25 / *519*
CONVERSION OF PAUL
Go out to all the world,
and tell the Good News.

Or: Alleluia.

January 26 / 520
TIMOTHY AND TITUS
cf. 1198

January 27 / 521
ANGELA MERICI
cf. 1200 or 1201

January 28 / 522
THOMAS AQUINAS
cf. 1198 or 1199

January 31 / 523
JOHN BOSCO
cf. 1198 or 1201

1156 FEBRUARY 2: PRESENTATION OF THE LORD

Forty days after the celebration of Christmas, this feast tells of how Mary and Joseph brought the child to the Temple. There the aged Simeon took the baby in his arms and proclaimed that Jesus would be "a light to the Gentiles, the glory of Israel." These words have been sung for centuries on February 2 as Christians have blessed and carried lighted candles in procession.

BLESSING OF CANDLES AND PROCESSION

As the candles are lighted, this antiphon (with optional verses) may be sung:

Antiphon

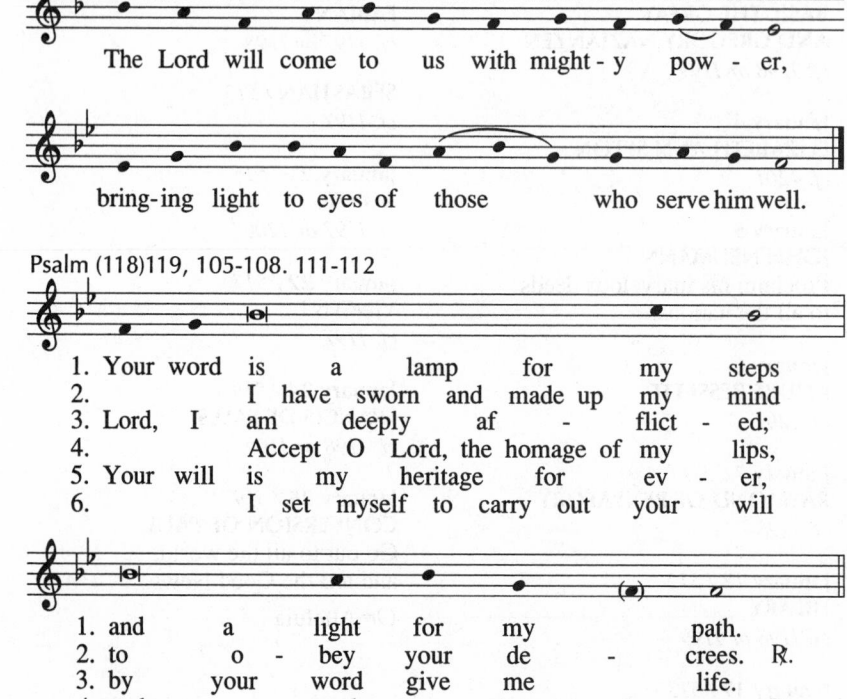

The Lord will come to us with might-y pow-er,
bring-ing light to eyes of those who serve him well.

Psalm (118)119, 105-108. 111-112

1. Your word is a lamp for my steps
2. I have sworn and made up my mind
3. Lord, I am deeply af - flict - ed;
4. Accept O Lord, the homage of my lips,
5. Your will is my heritage for ev - er,
6. I set myself to carry out your will

1. and a light for my path.
2. to o - bey your de - crees. ℟.
3. by your word give me life.
4. and teach me your de - crees. ℟.
5. the joy of my heart.
6. in full - ness for ev - er. ℟.

Music: Chant Mode VIII; setting by Richard Proulx, © 1985, GIA Publications, Inc.

When the candles have been blessed, the presider invites all: "Let us go forth **1157**
in peace to meet the Lord." During the procession, the following may be sung:

Antiphon

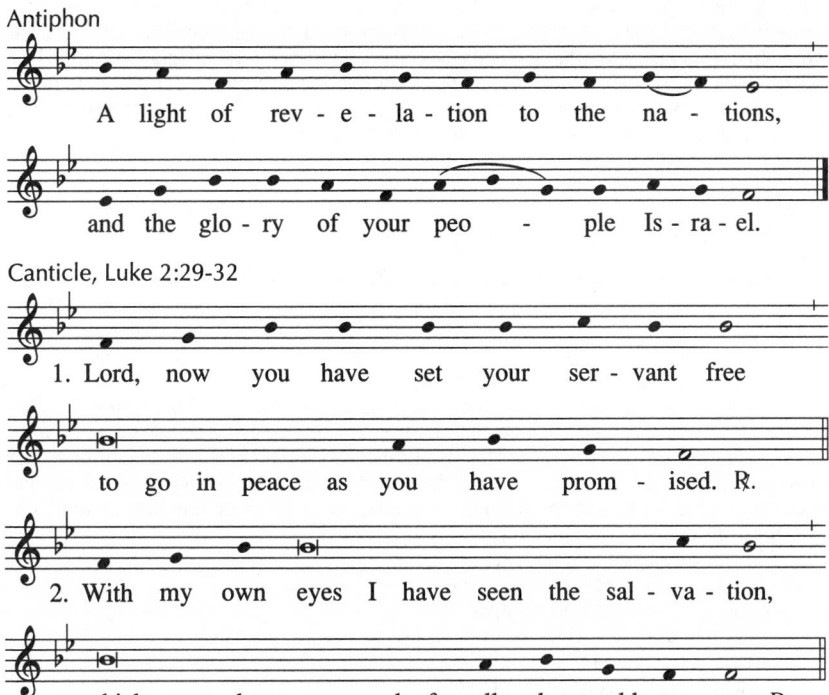

A light of rev - e - la - tion to the na - tions,

and the glo - ry of your peo - ple Is - ra - el.

Canticle, Luke 2:29-32

1. Lord, now you have set your ser - vant free

to go in peace as you have prom - ised. ℟.

2. With my own eyes I have seen the sal - va - tion,

which you have prepared for all the world to see. ℟.

Music: Chant Mode VIII; setting by Richard Proulx, © 1985, GIA Publications, Inc.

READING I
Malachi 3:1-4 / 524

Thus says the Lord God:
Lo, I am sending my messenger
to prepare the way before me;
and suddenly there will come to the
temple
the Lord whom you seek,
and the messenger of the covenant whom
you desire.
Yes, he is coming, says the LORD of
hosts.
But who will endure the day of his
coming?

And who can stand when he appears?
For he is like the refiner's fire,
or like the fuller's lye.
He will sit refining and purifying silver,
and he will purify the sons of Levi,
refining them like gold or like silver
that they may offer due sacrifice to
the LORD.
Then the sacrifice of Judah and Jerusalem
will please the LORD,
as in the days of old, as in years
gone by.

RESPONSORIAL PSALM
Psalm 24:7, 8, 9, 10

℟. Who is this king of glory? It is the Lord!

Lift up, O gates, your lintels;
reach up, you ancient portals,
that the king of glory may come in! ℟.

Who is this king of glory?
The LORD, strong and mighty,
the LORD, mighty in battle. ℟.

Lift up, O gates, your lintels;
reach up, you ancient portals,
that the king of glory may come in! ℟.

Who is this king of glory?
The LORD of hosts; he is the king of
glory. ℟.

READING II *Hebrews 2:14-18*

Since the children share in blood and flesh, Jesus likewise shared in them, that through death he might destroy the one who has the power of death, that is, the devil, and free those who through fear of death had been subject to slavery all their life. Surely he did not help angels but rather the descendants of Abraham; therefore, he had to become like his brothers and sisters in every way, that he might be a merciful and faithful high priest before God to expiate the sins of the people. Because he himself was tested through what he suffered, he is able to help those who are being tested.

GOSPEL *Luke 2:22-40 or 2:22-32*
For short form, read only the part in brackets.

[When the days were completed for their purification according to the law of Moses, Mary and Joseph took Jesus up to Jerusalem to present him to the Lord, just as it is written in the law of the Lord, "Every male that opens the womb shall be consecrated to the Lord," and to offer the sacrifice of "a pair of turtledoves or two young pigeons," in accordance with the dictate in the law of the Lord.

Now there was a man in Jerusalem whose name was Simeon. This man was righteous and devout, awaiting the consolation of Israel, and the Holy Spirit was upon him. It had been revealed to him by the Holy Spirit that he should not see death before he had seen the Christ of the Lord. He came in the Spirit into the temple; and when the parents brought in the child Jesus to perform the custom of the law in regard to him, he took him into his arms and blessed God, saying:

"Now, Master, you may let your servant go
    in peace, according to your word,
for my eyes have seen your salvation,
    which you prepared in sight of all the peoples,
a light for revelation to the Gentiles,
    and glory for your people Israel."]

The child's father and mother were amazed at what was said about him; and Simeon blessed them and said to Mary his mother, "Behold, this child is destined for the fall and rise of many in Israel, and to be a sign that will be contradicted (and you yourself a sword will pierce) so that the thoughts of many hearts may be revealed." There was also a prophetess, Anna, the daughter of Phanuel, of the tribe of Asher. She was advanced in years, having lived seven years with her husband after her marriage, and then as a widow until she was eighty-four. She never left the temple, but worshipped night and day with fasting and prayer. And coming forward at that very time, she gave thanks to God and spoke about the child to all who were awaiting the redemption of Jerusalem.

When they had fulfilled all the prescriptions of the law of the Lord, they returned to Galilee, to their own town of Nazareth. The child grew and became strong, filled with wisdom; and the favor of God was upon him.

1158

February 3 / 525
BLASE
cf. 1197 or 1198

ANSGAR / 526
cf. 1198

February 5 / 527
AGATHA
cf. 1197 or 1200

February 6 / 528
PAUL MIKI AND COMPANIONS
cf. 1197

February 8 / 529
JEROME EMILIANI
cf. 1201

February 10 / 530
SCHOLASTICA
cf. 1200 or 1201

February 11 / *531*
OUR LADY OF LOURDES
cf. 1196

February 14 / *532*
CYRIL AND METHODIUS
cf. 1198 or 1201

February 17 / *533*
**SEVEN FOUNDERS OF THE
ORDER OF SERVITES**
cf. 1201

February 21 / *534*
PETER DAMIAN
cf. 1198 or 1199 or 1201

February 22 / *535*
CHAIR OF PETER
The Lord is my shepherd;
there is nothing I shall want.

February 23 / *536*
POLYCARP
cf. 1197 or 1198

MARCH 1159

March 3
KATHARINE DREXEL
cf. 1200

March 4 / *537*
CASIMIR
cf. 1201

March 7 / *538*
PERPETUA AND FELICITY
cf. 1197

March 8 / *539*
JOHN OF GOD
cf. 1201

March 9 / *540*
FRANCES OF ROME
cf. 1201

March 17 / *541*
PATRICK
cf. 1198

March 18 / *542*
CYRIL OF JERUSALEM
cf. 1198 or 1199

MARCH 19: JOSEPH, HUSBAND OF MARY 1160

READING I *2 Samuel 7:4-5a, 12-14a, 16 / *543**
The Lord spoke to Nathan and said: "Go, tell my servant David, 'When your time comes and you rest with your ancestors, I will raise up your heir after you, sprung from your loins, and I will make his kingdom firm. It is he who shall build a house for my name. And I will make his royal throne firm forever. I will be a father to him, and he shall be a son to me. Your house and your kingdom shall endure forever before me; your throne shall stand firm forever.'"

RESPONSORIAL PSALM *Psalm 89:2-3, 4-5, 27, 29*
℟. **The son of David will live for ever.**

The promises of the LORD I will sing
   forever,
  through all generations my mouth
    will proclaim your faithfulness,
for you have said, "My kindness is
   established for ever;"
  In heaven you have confirmed your
   faithfulness. ℟.

"I have made a covenant with my
   chosen one;
  I have sworn to David my servant:
forever will I confirm your posterity
  and establish your throne for all
   generations." ℟.

"He shall say of me, 'You are my father,
my God, the Rock my savior!'
Forever I will maintain my kindness
toward him,
my covenant with him stands
firm." ℟.

READING II
Romans 4:13, 16-18, 22

Brothers and sisters: It was not through the law that the promise was made to Abraham and his descendants that he would inherit the world, but through the righteousness that comes from faith. For this reason, it depends on faith, so that it may be a gift, and the promise may be guaranteed to all his descendants, not to those who only adhere to the law but to those who follow the faith of Abraham, who is the father of all of us, as it is written, 'I have made you father of many nations.' He is our father in the sight of God, in whom he believed, who gives life to the dead and calls into being what does not exist. He believed, hoping against hope, that he would become "the father of many nations," according to what was said, "Thus shall your descendants be." That is why "it was credited to him as righteousness."

GOSPEL
Matthew 1:16, 18-21, 24a

Jacob was the father of Joseph, the husband of Mary. Of her was born Jesus who is called the Christ.

Now this is how the birth of Jesus Christ came about. When his mother Mary was betrothed to Joseph, but before they lived together, she was found with child through the Holy Spirit. Joseph her husband, since he was a righteous man, yet unwilling to expose her to shame, decided to divorce her quietly. Such was his intention when, behold, the angel of the Lord appeared to him in a dream and said, "Joseph, son of David, do not be afraid to take Mary your wife into your home. For it is through the Holy Spirit that this child has been conceived in her. She will bear a son and you are to name him Jesus, because he will save his people from their sins." When Joseph awoke, he did as the angel of the Lord had commanded him and took his wife into his home.

Or:

GOSPEL
Luke 2:41-51a

Each year Jesus' parents went to Jerusalem for the feast of Passover, and when he was twelve years old, they went up according to festival custom. After they had completed its days, as they were returning, the boy Jesus remained behind in Jerusalem, but his parents did not know it. Thinking that he was in the caravan, they journeyed for a day and looked for him among their relatives and acquaintances, but not finding him, they returned to Jerusalem to look for him. After three days they found him in the temple, sitting in the midst of the teachers, listening to them and asking them questions, and all who heard him were astounded at his understanding and his answers. When his parents saw him, they were astonished, and his mother said to him, "Son, why have you done this to us? Your father and I have been looking for you with great anxiety." And he said to them, "Why were you looking for me? Did you not know that I must be in my Father's house?" But they did not understand what he said to them. He went down with them and came to Nazareth, and was obedient to them.

1161   **March 23 / 544**
TURIBUS DE MOGROVEJO
cf. 1198

MARCH 25: ANNUNCIATION OF OUR LORD 1162

READING I *Isaiah 7:10-14; 8:10 / 545*

The LORD spoke to Ahaz, saying: Ask for a sign from the LORD, your God; let it be deep as the nether world, or high as the sky! But Ahaz answered, "I will not ask! I will not tempt the LORD!" Then Isaiah said: Listen, O house of David! Is it not enough for you to weary people, must you also weary my God? Therefore the Lord himself will give you this sign: the virgin shall conceive, and bear a son, and shall name him Emmanuel, which means "God is with us!"

RESPONSORIAL PSALM *Psalm 40:7-8, 8-9, 10, 11*

℟. **Here am I, Lord; I come to do your will.**

Sacrifice or offering you wished not,
  but ears open to obedience you gave
    me.
Holocausts and sin-offerings you sought
    not;
  then said I, "Behold, I come." ℟.

"In the written scroll it is prescribed for
    me.
To do your will, O God, is my delight,
  and your law is within my heart!" ℟.

I announced your justice in the vast
    assembly;
  I did not restrain my lips, as you, O
    LORD, know. ℟.

Your justice I kept not hid within my
    heart;
  your faithfulness and your salvation
    I have spoken of;
I have made no secret of your kindness
    and your truth
  in the vast assembly. ℟.

READING II *Hebrews 10:4-10*

Brothers and sisters: It is impossible that the blood of bulls and goats takes away sins. For this reason, when Christ came into the world, he said:
"Sacrifice and offering you did not desire,
  but a body you prepared for me;
in holocausts and sin offerings you took no delight.
Then I said, 'As is written of me in the scroll,
  behold, I come to do your will, O God.'"
First Christ says, "Sacrifices and offerings, holocausts and sin offerings, you neither desired nor delighted in." These are offered according to the law. Then he says, "Behold, I come to do your will." He takes away the first to establish the second. By this "will," we have been consecrated through the offering of the body of Jesus Christ once for all.

GOSPEL *Luke 1:26-38*

The angel Gabriel was sent from God to a town of Galilee called Nazareth, to a virgin betrothed to a man named Joseph, of the house of David, and the virgin's name was Mary. And coming to her, he said, "Hail, full of grace! The Lord is with you." But she was greatly troubled at what was said and pondered what sort of greeting this might be. Then the angel said to her, "Do not be afraid, Mary, for you have found favor with God. Behold, you will conceive in your womb and bear a son, and you shall name him Jesus. He will be great and will be called Son of the Most High, and the Lord God will give him the throne of David his father, and he will rule over the house of Jacob forever, and of his kingdom there will be no end." But Mary said to the angel, "How can this be, since I have no relations with a man?" And the angel said to her in reply, "The Holy Spirit will come upon you, and the power of the Most High will overshadow you. Therefore the child to be born will be called holy, the Son of God. And behold, Elizabeth, your relative, has also conceived a son in her old age, and this is the sixth month for her who was called barren; for nothing will be impossible for God." Mary said, "Behold, I am the handmaid of the Lord. May it be done to me according to your word." Then the angel departed from her.

1163 APRIL

April 2 / 546
FRANCIS OF PAOLA
cf. 1201

April 4 / 547
ISIDORE
cf. 1198 or 1199

April 5 / 548
VINCENT FERRER
cf. 1198

April 7 / 549
JOHN BAPTIST DE LA SALLE
cf. 1198 or 1201

April 11 / 550
STANISLAUS
cf. 1197 or 1198

April 13 / 551
MARTIN I
cf. 1197 or 1198

April 21 / 552
ANSELM
cf. 1198 or 1199

April 23 / 553
GEORGE
cf. 1197

ADALBERT
cf. 1199

April 24 / 554
FIDELIS OF SIGMARINGEN
cf. 1197 or 1198

April 25 / 555
MARK
For ever I will sing the
goodness of the Lord.

Or: Alleluia.

April 28 / 556
PETER CHANEL
cf. 1197 or 1198

LOUIS DE MONTFORT
cf. 1201

April 29 / 557
CATHERINE OF SIENA
cf. 1200

April 30 / 558
PIUS V
cf. 1198

1164 MAY

May 1 / 559
JOSEPH THE WORKER
Lord, give success to the work of
our hands.

Or: Alleluia.

May 2 / 560
ATHANASIUS
cf. 1198 or 1199

May 3 / 561
PHILIP AND JAMES
Their message goes out through
all the earth.

Or: Alleluia.

May 12 / 562
NEREUS AND ACHILLEUS
cf. 1197

PANCRAS / 563
cf. 1197

May 14 / 564
MATTHIAS
The Lord will give him a seat with
the leaders of his people.

Or: Alleluia.

May 15
ISIDORE
cf. 1201

May 18 / *565*
JOHN I
cf. 1197 or 1198

May 20 / *566*
BERNARDINE OF SIENA
cf. 1198

May 25 / *567*
VENERABLE BEDE
cf. 1198 or 1199

GREGORY VII / *568*
cf. 1198

MARY MAGDALENE DE PAZZI / *569*
cf. 1200 or 1201

May 26 / *570*
PHILIP NERI
cf. 1198 or 1201

May 27 / *571*
AUGUSTINE OF CANTERBURY
cf. 1198

May 31 / *572*
VISITATION
Among you is the great and Holy
    One of Israel.

Saturday following the Second
Sunday after Pentecost / *573*
IMMACULATE HEART OF MARY
cf. 1196

JUNE 1165

June 1 / *574*
JUSTIN
cf. 1197

June 2 / *575*
MARCELLINUS AND PETER
cf. 1197

June 3 / *576*
CHARLES LWANGA AND
COMPANIONS
cf. 1197

June 5 / *577*
BONIFACE
cf. 1197 or 1198

June 6 / *578*
NORBERT
cf. 1198 or 1201

June 9 / *579*
EPHREM
cf. 1199

June 11 / *580*
BARNABAS
The Lord has revealed to the
    nations his saving power.

June 13 / *581*
ANTHONY OF PADUA
cf. 1198 or 1199 or 1201

June 19 / *582*
ROMUALD
cf. 1201

June 21 / *583*
ALOYSIUS GONZAGA
cf. 1201

June 22 / *584*
PAULINUS OF NOLA
cf. 1198

JOHN FISHER / *585*
AND THOMAS MORE
cf. 1197

JUNE 24: BIRTH OF JOHN THE BAPTIST / VIGIL 1166

READING I *Jeremiah 1:4-10 / 586*

In the days of King Josiah, the word of
the LORD came to me, saying:
    Before I formed you in the womb I
        knew you,
before you were born I
    dedicated you,
a prophet to the nations I
    appointed you.

"Ah, Lord GOD!" I said,
"I know not how to speak; I am
too young."
But the LORD answered me,
Say not, "I am too young."
To whomever I send you, you
shall go;
whatever I command you, you
shall speak.
Have no fear before them,
because I am with you to
deliver you, says the Lord.

Then the LORD extended his hand and
touched my mouth, saying,
See, I place my words in your
mouth!
This day I set you
over nations and over kingdoms,
to root up and to tear down,
to destroy and to demolish,
to build and to plant.

RESPONSORIAL PSALM
Psalm 71:1-2, 3-4, 5-6, 15, 17

℟. **Since my mother's womb, you have been my strength.**

In you, O LORD, I take refuge;
let me never be put to shame.
In your justice rescue me, and deliver me;
incline your ear to me, and save
me. ℟.

Be my rock of refuge,
a stronghold to give me safety,
for you are my rock and my fortress.
O my God, rescue me from the hand of
the wicked. ℟.

For you are my hope, O Lord;
my trust, O Lord, from my youth.
On you I depend from birth;
from my mother's womb you are my
strength. ℟.

My mouth shall declare your justice,
day by day your salvation.
O God, you have taught me from my
youth,
and till the present I proclaim your
wondrous deeds. ℟.

READING II
1 Peter 1:8-12

Beloved: Although you have not seen Jesus Christ you love him; even though you do not see him now yet believe in him, you rejoice with an indescribable and glorious joy, as you attain the goal of your faith, the salvation of your souls.

Concerning this salvation, prophets who prophesied about the grace that was to be yours searched and investigated it, investigating the time and circumstances that the Spirit of Christ within them indicated when he testified in advance to the sufferings destined for Christ and the glories to follow them. It was revealed to them that they were serving not themselves but you with regard to the things that have now been announced to you by those who preached the good news to you through the Holy Spirit sent from heaven, things into which angels longed to look.

GOSPEL
Luke 1:5-17

In the days of Herod, King of Judea, there was a priest named Zechariah of the priestly division of Abijah; his wife was from the daughters of Aaron, and her name was Elizabeth. Both were righteous in the eyes of God, observing all the commandments and ordinances of the Lord blamelessly. But they had no child, because Elizabeth was barren and both were advanced in years. Once when he was serving as priest in his division's turn before God, according to the practice of the priestly service, he was chosen by lot to enter the sanctuary of the Lord to burn incense. Then, when the whole assembly of the people was praying outside at the hour of the incense offering, the angel of the Lord appeared to him, standing at the right of the altar of incense. Zechariah was troubled by what he saw, and fear came upon him. But the angel said to him, "Do not be afraid, Zechariah, because your prayer has been heard. Your wife Elizabeth will bear you a son, and you shall name him John. And you will have joy and gladness, and many will rejoice at his birth, for he will be great in the sight of the Lord. John will drink neither wine nor strong drink. He will be filled with the Holy Spirit even from his mother's womb, and he will turn many of the children of Israel to the Lord their God. He will go before him in the spirit and power of Elijah to turn their hearts toward their children and the disobedient to the understanding of the righteous, to prepare a people fit for the Lord."

JUNE 24: BIRTH OF JOHN THE BAPTIST / DURING THE DAY 1167

READING I
Isaiah 49:1-6 / 587

Hear me, O coastlands
   listen, O distant peoples.
The LORD called me from birth,
   from my mother's womb he gave me
     my name.
He made of me a sharp-edged sword
   and concealed me in the shadow of
     his arm.
He made me a polished arrow,
   in his quiver he hid me.
You are my servant, he said to me,
   Israel, through whom I show my
     glory.

Though I thought I had toiled in vain,
   and for nothing, uselessly, spent my
     strength,

yet my reward is with the LORD,
   my recompense is with my God.
For now the LORD has spoken
   who formed me as his servant from
     the womb,
that Jacob may be brought back to him
   and Israel gathered to him;
and I am made glorious in the sight of
     the Lord,
   and my God is now my strength!
It is too little, he says, for you to be my
     servant,
   to raise up the tribes of Jacob,
   and restore the survivors of Israel;
I will make you a light to the nations,
   that my salvation may reach to the
     ends of the earth.

RESPONSORIAL PSALM
Psalm 139:1-3, 13-14, 14-15

℟. **I praise you for I am wonderfully made.**

O LORD you have probed me and you
   know me;
   you know when I sit and when I
     stand;
   you understand my thoughts from
     afar.
My journeys and my rest you scrutinize,
   with all my ways you are familiar. ℟.

Truly you have formed my inmost being;

   you knit me in my mother's womb.
I give you thanks that I am fearfully,
   wonderfully made;
   wonderful are your works. ℟.

My soul also you knew full well;
   nor was my frame unknown to you
when I was made in secret,
   when I was fashioned in the depths
     of the earth. ℟.

READING II
Acts 13:22-26

In those days, Paul said: "God raised up David as their king; of him he testified, 'I have found David, son of Jesse, a man after my own heart; he will carry out my every wish.' From this man's descendants God, according to his promise, has brought to Israel a savior, Jesus. John heralded his coming by proclaiming a baptism of repentance to all the people of Israel; and as John was completing his course, he would say, 'What do you suppose that I am? I am not he. Behold, one is coming after me; I am not worthy to unfasten the sandals of his feet.'

"My brothers, children of the family of Abraham, and those others among you who are God-fearing, to us this word of salvation has been sent."

GOSPEL *Luke 1:57-66, 80*

When the time arrived for Elizabeth to have her child she gave birth to a son. Her neighbors and relatives heard that the Lord had shown his great mercy toward her, and they rejoiced with her. When they came on the eighth day to circumcise the child, they were going to call him Zechariah after his father, but his mother said in reply, "No. He will be called John." But they answered her, "There is no one among your relatives who has this name." So they made signs, asking his father what he wished him to be called. He asked for a tablet and wrote, "John is his name," and all were amazed. Immediately his mouth was opened, his tongue freed, and he spoke blessing God. Then fear came upon all their neighbors, and all these matters were discussed throughout the hill country of Judea. All who heard these things took them to heart, saying, "What, then, will this child be?" For surely the hand of the Lord was with him.

The child grew and became strong in spirit, and he was in the desert until the day of his manifestation to Israel.

1168

June 27 / *588*	**June 28** / *589*
CYRIL OF ALEXANDRIA	**IRENAEUS**
cf. 1198 or 1199	*cf. 1197 or 1199*

1169 JUNE 29: PETER AND PAUL / VIGIL

READING I *Acts 3:1-10 / 590*

Peter and John were going up to the temple area for the three o'clock hour of prayer. And a man crippled from birth was carried and placed at the gate of the temple called "the Beautiful Gate" every day to beg for alms from the people who entered the temple. When he saw Peter and John about to go into the temple, he asked for alms. But Peter looked intently at him, as did John, and said, "Look at us." He paid attention to them, expecting to receive something from them. Peter said, "I have neither silver nor gold, but what I do have I give you: in the name of Jesus Christ the Nazarene, rise and walk." Then Peter took him by the right hand and raised him up, and immediately his feet and ankles grew strong. He leaped up, stood, and walked around, and went into the temple with them, walking and jumping and praising God. When all the people saw the man walking and praising God, they recognized him as the one who used to sit begging at the Beautiful Gate of the temple, and they were filled with amazement and astonishment at what had happened to him.

RESPONSORIAL PSALM *Psalm 19:2-3, 4-5*
℞. **Their message goes out through all the earth.**

The heavens declare the glory of God,
  and the firmament proclaims his
    handiwork.
Day pours out the word to day,
  and night to night imparts
    knowledge. ℞.

Not a word nor a discourse
  whose voice is not heard;
through all the earth their voice
    resounds,
  and to the ends of the world, their
    message. ℞.

READING II *Galatians 1:11-20*

I want you to know, brothers and sisters, that the gospel preached by me is not of human origin. For I did not receive it from a human being, nor was I taught it, but it came through a revelation of Jesus Christ.

For you heard of my former way of life in Judaism, how I persecuted the church of God beyond measure and tried to destroy it, and progressed in Judaism beyond many of my contemporaries among my race, since I was even more a zealot for my ancestral traditions. But when God, who from my mother's womb had set me apart and called me through his grace, was pleased to reveal his Son to me, so that I might proclaim him to the Gentiles, I did not immediately consult flesh and blood, nor did I go up to Jerusalem to those who were apostles before me; rather, I went into Arabia and then returned to Damascus.

Then after three years I went up to Jerusalem to confer with Cephas and remained with him for fifteen days. But I did not see any other of the apostles, only James the brother of the Lord. (As to what I am writing to you, behold, before God, I am not lying.)

GOSPEL   *John 21:15-19*

Jesus revealed himself to his disciples and, when they had finished breakfast, said to Simon Peter, "Simon, son of John, do you love me more than these?" He answered him, "Yes, Lord, you know that I love you." Jesus said to him, "Feed my lambs."

He then said to him a second time, "Simon, son of John, do you love me?" He answered him, "Yes, Lord, you know that I love you." He said to him, "Tend my sheep."

He said to him the third time, "Simon, son of John, do you love me?" Peter was distressed that Jesus had said to him a third time, "Do you love me?" and he said to him, "Lord, you know everything; you know that I love you." Jesus said to him, "Feed my sheep. Amen, amen, I say to you, when you were younger, you used to dress yourself and go where you wanted; but when you grow old, you will stretch out your hands, and someone else will dress you and lead you where you do not want to go." He said this signifying by what kind of death he would glorify God. And when he had said this, he said to him, "Follow me."

JUNE 29: PETER AND PAUL / MASS DURING THE DAY   1170

READING I   *Acts 12:1-11 / 591*

In those days, King Herod laid hands upon some members of the church to harm them. He had James, the brother of John, killed by the sword, and when he saw that this was pleasing to the Jews he proceeded to arrest Peter also. (It was [the] feast of Unleavened Bread.) He had him taken into custody and put in prison under the guard of four squads of four soldiers each. He intended to bring him before the people after Passover. Peter thus was being kept in prison, but prayer by the church was fervently being made to God on his behalf.

On the very night before Herod was to bring him to trial, Peter, secured by double chains, was sleeping between two soldiers, while outside the door guards kept watch on the prison. Suddenly the angel of the Lord stood by him and a light shone in the cell. He tapped Peter on the side and awakened him, saying, "Get up quickly." The chains fell from his wrists. The angel said to him, "Put on your belt and your sandals." He did so. Then he said to him, "Put on your cloak and follow me." So he followed him out, not realizing that what was happening through the angel was real; he thought he was seeing a vision. They passed the first guard, then the second, and came to the iron gate leading out to the city, which opened for them by itself. They emerged and made their way down an alley, and suddenly the angel left him.

RESPONSORIAL PSALM   *Psalm 34:2-3, 4-5, 6-7, 8-9*

℟. The angel of the Lord will rescue those who fear him.

I will bless the LORD at all times;
  his praise shall be ever in my mouth.
Let my soul glory in the LORD;
  the lowly will hear me and be
    glad. ℟.

Glorify the LORD with me,
  let us together extol his name.
I sought the LORD, and he answered me
  and delivered me from all my
    fears. ℟.

Look to him that you may be radiant
  with joy,
and your faces may not blush with
  shame.
When the poor one called out, the LORD
  heard,
and from all his distress he saved
  him. ℟.

The angel of the LORD encamps
  around those who fear him, and
  delivers them.
Taste and see how good the LORD is;
  blessed the man who takes refuge in
  him. ℟.

READING II   *2 Timothy 4:6-8, 17-18*

I, Paul, am already being poured out like a libation, and the time of my departure is at hand. I have competed well; I have finished the race; I have kept the faith. From now on the crown of righteousness awaits me, which the Lord, the just judge, will award to me on that day, and not only to me, but to all who have longed for his appearance.

The Lord stood by me and gave me strength, so that through me the proclamation might be completed and all the Gentiles might hear it. And I was rescued from the lion's mouth. The Lord will rescue me from every evil threat and will bring me safe to his heavenly kingdom. To him be glory forever and ever. Amen.

GOSPEL   *Matthew 16:13-19*

When Jesus went into the region of Caesarea Philippi he asked his disciples, "Who do people say that the Son of Man is?" They replied, "Some say John the Baptist, others Elijah, still others Jeremiah or one of the prophets." He said to them, "But who do you say that I am?" Simon Peter said in reply, "You are the Christ, the Son of the living God." Jesus said to him in reply, "Blessed are you, Simon son of Jonah. For flesh and blood has not revealed this to you, but my heavenly Father. And so I say to you, you are Peter, and upon this rock I will build my church, and the gates of the nether world shall not prevail against it. I will give you the keys to the kingdom of heaven. Whatever you bind on earth shall be bound in heaven; and whatever you loose on earth shall be loosed in heaven."

1171   **June 30 / 592**
        FIRST MARTYRS OF THE CHURCH OF ROME
        cf. 1197

1172   **JULY**

        July 1
        JUNÍPERO SERRA
        cf. 1198

        July 3 / 593
        THOMAS
        Go out to all the world,
        and tell the Good News.

        July 4 / 594
        ELIZABETH OF PORTUGAL
        cf. 1201

JULY 4: INDEPENDENCE DAY   1173

RESPONSORIAL PSALM   *Psalm 85:9-10, 11-12, 13-14*
℟. **The Lord speaks of peace to his people.**

I will hear what the Lord God has to say,
    a voice that speaks of peace,
peace for his people and his friends
    and those who turn to him in their
    hearts.
His help is near for those who fear him
    and his glory will dwell in our
    land. ℟.

Mercy and faithfulness have met;

justice and peace have embraced.
Faithfulness shall spring from the earth
    and justice look down from
    heaven. ℟.

The Lord will make us prosper
    and our earth shall yield its fruit.
Justice shall march before him
    and peace shall follow his steps. ℟.

July 5 / 595
ANTHONY ZACCARIA
cf. 1198 or 1201

July 6 / 596
MARIA GORETTI
cf. 1197 or 1200

July 11 / 597
BENEDICT
cf. 1201

July 13 / 598
HENRY
cf. 1201

July 14 / 599
KATERI TEKAKWITHA
cf. 1200

CAMILLUS DE LELLIS
cf. 1201

July 15 / 600
BONAVENTURE
cf. 1198 or 1199

July 16 / 601
OUR LADY OF MOUNT CARMEL
cf. 1196

July 21 / 602   1174
LAWRENCE OF BRINDISI
cf. 1198 or 1199

July 22 / 603
MARY MAGDALENE
My soul is thirsting for you, O
    Lord, my God.

July 23 / 604
BRIDGET
cf. 1201

July 25 / 605
JAMES
Those who sow in tears, shall reap
    with shouts of joy.

July 26 / 606
JOACHIM AND ANN
God will give him the throne of
    David, his father.

July 29 / 607
MARTHA
cf. 1201

July 30 / 608
PETER CHRYSOLOGUS
cf. 1198 or 1199

July 31 / 609
IGNATIUS OF LOYOLA
cf. 1198 or 1201

1175 AUGUST

August 1 / 610
ALPHONSUS LIGUORI
cf. 1198 or 1199

August 2 / 611
EUSEBIUS OF VERCELLI
cf. 1198

PETER JULIAN EYMARD
cf. 1198

August 4 / 612
JOHN VIANNEY
cf. 1198

August 5 / 613
DEDICATION OF SAINT MARY MAJOR
cf. 1195

1176 AUGUST 6: TRANSFIGURATION

READING I   *Daniel 7:9-10, 13-14 / 614*

As I watched:
    Thrones were set up
        and the Ancient One took his throne.
    His clothing was snow bright,
        and the hair on his head as white as wool;
    his throne was flames of fire,
        with wheels of burning fire.
    A surging stream of fire
        flowed out from where he sat;
    thousands upon thousands were ministering to him,
        and myriads upon myriads attended him.
The court was convened and the books were opened. As the visions during the night continued, I saw
    One like a Son of man coming,
        on the clouds of heaven;
    When he reached the Ancient One
        and was presented before him,
    The one like a Son of man received dominion, glory, and kingship;
        all peoples, nations, and languages serve him.
    His dominion is an everlasting dominion
        that shall not be taken away,
        his kingship shall not be destroyed.

RESPONSORIAL PSALM   *Psalm 97:1-2, 5-6, 9*
℞. The Lord is king, the most high over all the earth.

The LORD is king; let the earth rejoice;
    let the many islands be glad.
Clouds and darkness are round about him;
    justice and judgment are the foundation of his throne. ℞.

The mountains melt like wax before the LORD,
    before the LORD of all the earth.
The heavens proclaim his justice;
    all peoples see his glory. ℞.

Because you, O LORD, are the Most High over all the earth,
    exalted far above all gods. ℞.

READING II   *2 Peter 1:16-19*

Beloved: We did not follow cleverly devised myths when we made known to you the power and coming of our Lord Jesus Christ, but we had been eyewitnesses of his majesty. For he received honor and glory from God the Father when that unique declaration came to him from the majestic glory, "This is my Son, my beloved, with whom I am well pleased." We ourselves heard this voice come from heaven while we were with him on the holy mountain. Moreover, we possess the prophetic message that is altogether reliable. You will do well to be attentive to it, as to a lamp shining in a dark place, until day dawns and the morning star rises in your hearts.

GOSPEL / A   *Matthew 17:1-9*

Jesus took Peter, James, and his brother, John, and led them up a high mountain by themselves. And he was transfigured before them; his face shone like the sun and his clothes became white as light. And behold, Moses and Elijah appeared to them, conversing with him. Then Peter said to Jesus in reply, "Lord, it is good that we are here. If you wish, I will make three tents here, one for you, one for Moses, and one for Elijah." While he was still speaking, behold, a bright cloud cast a shadow over them, then from the cloud came a voice that said, "This is my beloved Son, with whom I am well pleased; listen to him." When the disciples heard this, they fell prostrate and were very much afraid. But Jesus came and touched them, saying, "Rise, and do not be afraid." And when the disciples raised their eyes, they saw no one else but Jesus alone.

As they were coming down from the mountain, Jesus charged them, "Do not tell the vision to anyone until the Son of Man has been raised from the dead."

GOSPEL / B   *Mark 9:2-10*

Jesus took Peter, James, and John and led them up a high mountain apart by themselves. And he was transfigured before them, and his clothes became dazzling white, such as no fuller on earth could bleach them. Then Elijah appeared to them along with Moses, and they were conversing with Jesus. Then Peter said to Jesus in reply, "Rabbi, it is good that we are here! Let us make three tents: one for you, one for Moses, and one for Elijah." He hardly knew what to say, they were so terrified. Then a cloud came, casting a shadow over them; from the cloud came a voice, "This is my beloved Son. Listen to him." Suddenly, looking around, they no longer saw anyone but Jesus alone with them.

As they were coming down from the mountain, he charged them not to relate what they had seen to anyone, except when the Son of Man had risen from the dead. So they kept the matter to themselves, questioning what rising from the dead meant.

GOSPEL / C   *Luke 9:28b-36*

Jesus took Peter, John, and James and went up a mountain to pray. While he was praying his face changed in appearance and his clothing became dazzling white. And behold, two men were conversing with him, Moses and Elijah, who appeared in glory and spoke of his exodus that he was going to accomplish in Jerusalem. Peter and his companions had been overcome by sleep, but becoming fully awake, they saw his glory and the two men standing with him. As they were about to part from him, Peter said to Jesus, "Master, it is good that we are here; let us make three tents, one for you, one for Moses, and one for Elijah." But he did not know what he was saying. While he was still speaking, a cloud came and cast a shadow over them, and they became frightened when they entered the cloud. Then from the cloud came a voice that said, "This is my chosen Son; listen to him." After the voice had spoken, Jesus was found alone. They fell silent and did not at that time tell anyone what they had seen.

August 7 / *616*   **CAJETAN**   1177
SIXTUS II   *cf. 1198 or 1201*
cf. 1197

August 8 / *617*
DOMINIC
cf. 1198 or 1201

August 13 / *620*
PONTIAN AND HIPPOLYTUS
cf. 1197 or 1198

August 10 / *618*
LAWRENCE
Happy the man who is merciful
and lends to those in need.

August 14
MAXIMILIAN MARY KOLBE
Precious in the eyes of the Lord
is the death of his faithful ones.

August 11 / *619*
CLARE
cf. 1201

1178 AUGUST 15: ASSUMPTION / VIGIL

READING I *1 Chronicles 15:3-4, 15-16; 16:1-2 / 621*
David assembled all Israel in Jerusalem to bring the ark of the LORD to the place that he had prepared for it. David also called together the sons of Aaron and the Levites.

The Levites bore the ark of God on their shoulders with poles, as Moses had ordained according to the word of the LORD.

David commanded the chiefs of the Levites to appoint their kinsmen as chanters, to play on musical instruments, harps, lyres, and cymbals, to make a loud sound of rejoicing.

They brought in the ark of God and set it within the tent which David had pitched for it. Then they offered up burnt offerings and peace offerings to God. When David had finished offering up the burnt offerings and peace offerings, he blessed the people in the name of the LORD.

RESPONSORIAL PSALM *Psalm 132:6-7, 9-10, 13-14*
℟. **Lord, go up to the place of your rest, you and the ark of your holiness.**

Behold, we heard of it in Ephrathah;
    we found it in the fields of Jaar.
Let us enter into his dwelling,
    let us worship at his footstool. ℟.

May your priests be clothed with justice;
    let your faithful ones shout merrily
        for joy.
For the sake of David your servant,

reject not the plea of your
    anointed. ℟.

For the LORD has chosen Zion;
    he prefers her for his dwelling.
"Zion is my resting place forever;
    in her will I dwell, for I prefer
        her." ℟.

READING II *1 Corinthians 15:54b-57*
Brothers and sisters: When that which is mortal clothes itself with immortality, then the word that is written shall come about:
    "Death is swallowed up in victory.
    Where, O death, is your victory?
    Where, O death, is your sting?"
The sting of death is sin, and the power of sin is the law. But thanks be to God who gives us the victory through our Lord Jesus Christ.

GOSPEL *Luke 11:27-28*

While Jesus was speaking, a woman from the crowd called out and said to him, "Blessed is the womb that carried you and the breasts at which you nursed." He replied, "Rather, blessed are those who hear the word of God and observe it."

AUGUST 15: ASSUMPTION / MASS DURING THE DAY   1179

READING I *Revelation 11:19a; 12:1-6a, 10ab / 622*

God's temple in heaven was opened, and the ark of his covenant could be seen in the temple.

A great sign appeared in the sky, a woman clothed with the sun, with the moon beneath her feet, and on her head a crown of twelve stars. She was with child and wailed aloud in pain as she labored to give birth. Then another sign appeared in the sky; it was a huge red dragon, with seven heads and ten horns, and on its heads were seven diadems. Its tail swept away a third of the stars in the sky and hurled them down to the earth. Then the dragon stood before the woman about to give birth, to devour her child when she gave birth. She gave birth to a son, a male child, destined to rule all the nations with an iron rod. Her child was caught up to God and his throne. The woman herself fled into the desert where she had a place prepared by God.

Then I heard a loud voice in heaven say:
"Now have salvation and power come,
   and the kingdom of our God
   and the authority of his Anointed One."

RESPONSORIAL PSALM *Psalm 45:10, 11, 12, 16*

℟. **The queen stands at your right hand, arrayed in gold.**

The queen takes her place at your right
   hand in gold of Ophir. ℟.

So shall the king desire your beauty;
   for he is your lord. ℟.

Hear, O daughter, and see; turn your ear,
   forget your people and your father's
   house. ℟.

They are borne in with gladness and joy;
   they enter the palace of the king. ℟.

READING II *1 Corinthians 15:20-27*

Brothers and sisters: Christ has been raised from the dead, the first fruits of those who have fallen asleep. For since death came through man, the resurrection of the dead came also through man. For just as in Adam all die, so too in Christ shall all be brought to life, but each one in proper order: Christ the first fruits; then, at his coming, those who belong to Christ; then comes the end, when he hands over the kingdom to his God and Father, when he has destroyed every sovereignty and every authority and power. For he must reign until he has put all his enemies under his feet. The last enemy to be destroyed is death, for "he subjected everything under his feet."

GOSPEL *Luke 1:39-56*

Mary set out and traveled to the hill country in haste to a town of Judah, where she entered the house of Zechariah and greeted Elizabeth. When Elizabeth heard Mary's greeting, the infant leaped in her womb, and Elizabeth, filled with the Holy Spirit, cried out in a loud voice and said, "Blessed are you among women, and blessed is the fruit of your womb. And how does this happen to me, that the mother of my Lord should come to me? For at the moment the sound of your greeting reached my ears, the infant in my womb leaped for joy. Blessed are you who believed that what was spoken to you by the Lord would be fulfilled."

And Mary said:
"My soul proclaims the greatness of the Lord;
my spirit rejoices in God my Savior
for he has looked upon his lowly servant.
From this day all generations will call me blessed:
the Almighty has done great things for me,
and holy is his Name.
He has mercy on those who fear him
in every generation.
He has shown the strength of his arm,
and has scattered the proud in their conceit.
He has cast down the mighty from their thrones,
and has lifted up the lowly.
He has filled the hungry with good things,
and the rich he has sent away empty.
He has come to the help of his servant Israel
for he has remembered his promise of mercy,
the promise he made to our fathers,
to Abraham and his children for ever."

Mary remained with her about three months and then returned to her home.

1180

August 16 / 623
STEPHEN OF HUNGARY
cf. 1201

August 18
JANE FRANCES DE CHANTAL
cf. 1200

August 19 / 624
JOHN EUDES
cf. 1198 or 1201

August 20 / 625
BERNARD
cf. 1199 or 1201

August 21 / 626
PIUS X
cf. 1198

August 22 / 627
QUEENSHIP OF MARY
cf. 1196

August 23 / 628
ROSE OF LIMA
cf. 1200 or 1201

August 24 / 629
BARTHOLOMEW
Your friends tell the glory of your kingship, Lord.

August 25 / 630
LOUIS
cf. 1201

JOSEPH CALASANZ / 631
cf. 1198 or 1201

August 27 / 632
MONICA
cf. 1201

August 28 / 633
AUGUSTINE
cf. 1198 or 1199

August 29 / 634
BEHEADING OF JOHN THE BAPTIST
I will sing of your salvation.

FIRST MONDAY IN SEPTEMBER: LABOR DAY 1181

RESPONSORIAL PSALM *Psalm 90:2, 3-4, 12-13, 14, 16*

℟. **Lord, give success to the work of our hands.**

Before the mountains were born,
the earth and the world brought
forth,
from eternity to eternity you are God. ℟.

You turn man back to dust,
saying, "Return, O children of men."
For a thousand years in your sight
are as yesterday, now that it is past,
or as a watch of the night. ℟.

Teach us to number our days aright,
that we may gain wisdom of heart.
Return, O Lord! How long?
Have pity on your servants! ℟.

Fill us at daybreak with your kindness,
that we may shout for joy and
gladness all our days.
Show your deeds to your servants,
your glory to their children. ℟.

SEPTEMBER 1182

September 3 / *635*
GREGORY THE GREAT
cf. 1198 or 1199

September 9
PETER CLAVER
cf. 1198

September 8 / *636*
BIRTH OF MARY
With delight I rejoice in the Lord.

September 13 / *637*
JOHN CHRYSOSTOM
cf. 1198 or 1199

SEPTEMBER 14: EXALTATION OF THE HOLY CROSS 1183

READING I *Numbers 21:4b-9 / 638*

With their patience worn out by the journey, the people complained against God and Moses, "Why have you brought us up from Egypt to die in this desert, where there is no food or water? We are disgusted with this wretched food!"

In punishment the LORD sent among the people saraph serpents, which bit the people so that many of them died. Then the people came to Moses and said, "We have sinned in complaining against the LORD and you. Pray the LORD to take the serpents from us." So Moses prayed for the people, and the LORD said to Moses, "Make a saraph and mount it on a pole, and if any who have been bitten look at it, they will live." Moses accordingly made a bronze serpent and mounted it on a pole, and whenever anyone who had been bitten by a serpent looked at the bronze serpent, he lived.

RESPONSORIAL PSALM *Psalm 78:1-2, 34-35, 36-37, 38*

℟. **Do not forget the works of the Lord!**

Hearken, my people, to my teaching;
incline your ears to the words of my
mouth.
I will open my mouth in a parable,
I will utter mysteries from of old. ℟.

While he slew them they sought him
and inquired after God again,
remembering that God was their rock
and the Most High God, their
redeemer. ℟.

But they flattered him with their mouths
and lied to him with their tongues,
though their hearts were not steadfast
toward him,
nor were they faithful to his
covenant. ℟.

READING II
Philippians 2:6-11

Brothers and sisters:
Christ Jesus, though he was in the
form of God,
did not regard equality with God
something to be grasped.
Rather, he emptied himself,
taking the form of a slave,
coming in human likeness;
and found human in appearance,
he humbled himself,
becoming obedient to the point
of death,

even death on a cross.
Because of this, God greatly exalted
him
and bestowed on him the name
which is above every name,
that at the name of Jesus
every knee should bend,
of those in heaven and on earth
and under the earth,
and every tongue confess that
Jesus Christ is Lord,
to the glory of God the Father.

Yet he, being merciful, forgave their sin
and destroyed them not;
often he turned back his anger
and let none of his wrath be
roused. ℟.

GOSPEL
John 3:13-17

Jesus said to Nicodemus: "No one has gone up to heaven except the one who has come down from heaven, the Son of Man. And just as Moses lifted up the serpent in the desert, so must the Son of Man be lifted up, so that everyone who believes in him may have eternal life."

For God so loved the world that he gave his only Son, so that he who believes in him might not perish but might have eternal life. For God did not send his Son into the world to condemn the world, but that the world might be saved through him.

1184

September 15 / *639*
OUR LADY OF SORROWS
Save me, O Lord, in your steadfast
love.

September 16 / *640*
CORNELIUS AND CYPRIAN
cf. 1197 or 1198

September 17 / *641*
ROBERT BELLARMINE
cf. 1198 or 1199

September 19 / *642*
JANUARIUS
cf. 1197 or 1198

September 20
ANDREW KIM TAEGŎN,
PAUL CHŎNG HASANG,
AND COMPANIONS
Those who sow in tears shall sing
for joy when they reap.

September 21 / *643*
MATTHEW
Their message goes out through all
the earth.

September 26 / *644*
COSMAS AND DAMIAN
cf. 1197

September 27 / *645*
VINCENT DE PAUL
cf. 1198 or 1201

September 28 / *646*
WENCESLAUS
cf. 1197

September 29 / *647*
MICHAEL, GABRIEL, AND RAPHAEL
In the sight of the angels
I will sing your praise, Lord.

September 30 / *648*
JEROME
cf. 1198 or 1199

OCTOBER

October 1 / *649*
THERESA OF THE CHILD JESUS
cf. 1200 or 1201

October 2 / *650*
GUARDIAN ANGELS
He has put his angels in charge of
    you,
to guard you in all your ways.

October 4 / *651*
FRANCIS OF ASSISI
cf. 1201

October 6 / *652*
BRUNO
cf. 1198 or 1201

MARIE ROSE DUROCHER
cf. 1200

October 7 / *653*
OUR LADY OF THE ROSARY
cf. 1196

October 9 / *654*
DENIS AND COMPANIONS
cf. 1197

JOHN LEONARDI / *655*
cf. 1198 or 1201

October 14 / *656*
CALLISTUS I
cf. 1197 or 1198

October 15 / *657*
TERESA OF JESUS
cf. 1200 or 1201

October 16 / *658*
HEDWIG
cf. 1201

MARGARET MARY ALACOQUE / *659*
cf. 1200 or 1201

October 17 / *660*
IGNATIUS OF ANTIOCH
cf. 1197 or 1198

October 18 / *661*
LUKE
Your friends tell the glory of your
    kingship, Lord.

October 19 / *662*
**ISAAC JOGUES,
JOHN DE BRÉBEUF AND
COMPANIONS**
cf. 1197 or 1198

October 20 / *663*
PAUL OF THE CROSS
cf. 1198 or 1201

October 23 / *664*
JOHN OF CAPISTRANO
cf. 1198

October 24 / *665*
ANTHONY CLARET
cf. 1198

October 28 / *666*
SIMON AND JUDE
Their message goes out through all
    the earth.

NOVEMBER 1: ALL SAINTS

READING I   *Revelation 7:2-4, 9-14* / *667*
I, John, saw another angel come up from the East, holding the seal of the living God. He cried out in a loud voice to the four angels who were given power to damage the land and the sea, "Do not damage the land or the sea or the trees until we put the seal on the foreheads of the servants of our God." I heard the number of those who had been marked with the seal, one hundred and forty-four thousand marked from every tribe of the Israelites.

After this I had a vision of a great multitude, which no one could count, from every nation, race, people, and tongue. They stood before the throne and before the Lamb, wearing white robes and holding palm branches in their hands. They cried out in a loud voice:
"Salvation comes from our God,
    who is seated on the throne,
and from the Lamb."
All the angels stood around the throne and around the elders and the four living creatures. They prostrated themselves before the throne, worshipped God, and exclaimed:
"Amen. Blessing and glory, wisdom and thanksgiving,
    honor, power, and might
    be to our God forever and ever. Amen."
Then one of the elders spoke up and said to me, "Who are these wearing white robes, and where did they come from?" I said to him, "My lord, you are the one who knows." He said to me, "These are the ones who have survived the time of great distress; they have washed their robes and made them white in the blood of the Lamb."

RESPONSORIAL PSALM   *Psalm 24:1-2, 3-4, 5-6*
℟. **Lord, this is the people that longs to see your face.**

The LORD's are the earth and its fullness;
    the world and those who dwell in it.
For he founded it upon the seas
    and established it upon the rivers. ℟.

Who can ascend the mountain of the
        LORD?
    or who may stand in his holy place?
One whose hands are sinless, whose
heart is clean,
who desires not what is vain. ℟.

He shall receive a blessing from the
        LORD,
    a reward from God his savior.
Such is the race that seeks for him,
    that seeks the face of the God of
        Jacob. ℟.

READING II   *1 John 3:1-3*
Beloved: See what love the Father has bestowed on us that we may be called the children of God. Yet so we are. The reason the world does not know us is that it did not know him. Beloved, we are God's children now; what we shall be has not yet been revealed. We do know that when it is revealed we shall be like him, for we shall see him as he is. Everyone who has this hope based on him makes himself pure, as he is pure.

GOSPEL   *Matthew 5:1-12a*
When Jesus saw the crowds, he went up the mountain, and after he had sat down, his disciples came to him. He began to teach them, saying:
"Blessed are the poor in spirit,
    for theirs is the kingdom of heaven.
Blessed are they who mourn,
    for they will be comforted.
Blessed are the meek,
    for they will inherit the land.
Blessed are they who hunger and
        thirst for righteousness,
    for they will be satisfied.
Blessed are the merciful,
    for they will be shown mercy.
Blessed are the clean of heart,
    for they will see God.
Blessed are the peacemakers,
    for they will be called children of God.
Blessed are they who are persecuted for the sake of righteousness,

for theirs is the kingdom of heaven.

Blessed are you when they insult you and persecute you and utter every kind of evil against you falsely because of me. Rejoice and be glad, for your reward will be great in heaven."

NOVEMBER 2: ALL SOULS　　　　　　　　　　　　　　1187

RESPONSORIAL PSALM　　　　　　　　*Psalm 23:1-3a, 3b-4, 5, 6 / 668*
℟. **The Lord is my shepherd; there is nothing I shall want.**
　　or:
Though I walk in the valley of darkness, I fear no evil, for you are with me.

The LORD is my shepherd; I shall not
　　want.
　In verdant pastures he gives me
　　repose;
beside restful waters he leads me;
　he refreshes my soul. ℟.

He guides me in right paths
　for his name's sake.
Even though I walk in the dark valley
　I fear no evil; for you are at my side

with your rod and your staff
　that give me courage. ℟.

You spread the table before me
　in the sight of my foes;
you anoint my head with oil;
　my cup overflows. ℟.

Only goodness and kindness follow me
　all the days of my life;
and I shall dwell in the house of the Lord
　for years to come. ℟.

Or:

RESPONSORIAL PSALM　　　　　　　　*Psalm 25:6 and 7b, 17-18, 20-21*
℟. **To you, O Lord, I lift my soul.**
　　or:
No one who waits for you, O Lord, will ever be put to shame.

Remember that your compassion, O
　LORD;
　and your love are from of old.
In your kindness remember me,
　because of your goodness, O LORD. ℟.

Relieve the troubles of my heart,
　and bring me out of my distress.
Put an end to my affliction and my

suffering;
　and take away all my sins. ℟.

Preserve my life, and rescue me;
　let me not be put to shame, for I take
　　refuge in you,
Let integrity and uprightness preserve
　me,
　because I wait for you, O LORD. ℟.

Or:

RESPONSORIAL PSALM　　　　　　　　*Psalm 27:1, 4, 7 and 8b and 9a, 13-14*
℟. **The Lord is my light and my salvation.**
　　or:
I believe that I shall see the good things of the Lord in the land of the living.

The LORD is my light and my salvation;
　whom should I fear?
The LORD is my life's refuge;
　of whom should I be afraid? ℟.

One thing I ask of the LORD;
　this I seek:
to dwell in the house of the LORD
　all the days of my life,
that I may gaze on the loveliness of the
　LORD

and contemplate his temple. ℟.

Hear, O LORD, the sound of my call;
have pity on me and answer me.
Your presence, O LORD, I seek!
Hide not your face from me. ℟.

I believe that I shall see the bounty of
the LORD
in the land of the living.
Wait for the LORD with courage;
be stouthearted and wait for the
LORD! ℟.

1188 **November 3 / 669**
MARTIN DE PORRES
cf. 1201

November 4 / 670
CHARLES BORROMEO
cf. 1198

1189 # NOVEMBER 9: DEDICATION OF SAINT JOHN LATERAN

READING I *Ezekiel 47:1-2, 8-9, 12 / 671*

The angel brought me back to the entrance of the temple, and I saw water flowing out from beneath the threshold of the temple toward the east, for the facade of the temple was toward the east; the water flowed down from the southern side of the temple, south of the altar. He led me outside by the north gate, and around to the outer gate facing the east, where I saw water trickling from the southern side. He said to me, "This water flows into the eastern district down upon the Arabah, and empties into the sea, the salt waters, which it makes fresh. Wherever the river flows, every sort of living creature that can multiply shall live, and there shall be abundant fish, for wherever this water comes the sea shall be made fresh. Along both banks of the river, fruit trees of every kind shall grow; their leaves shall not fade, nor their fruit fail. Every month they shall bear fresh fruit, for they shall be watered by the flow from the sanctuary. Their fruit shall serve for food, and their leaves for medicine."

RESPONSORIAL PSALM *Psalm 46:2-3, 5-6, 8-9*

℟. The waters of the river gladden the city of God,
the holy dwelling of the Most High.

God is our refuge and our strength,
an ever-present help in distress.
Therefore we fear not, though the earth
be shaken
and mountains plunge into the depths
of the sea. ℟.

There is a stream whose runlets gladden
the city of God,
the holy dwelling of the Most High.

God is in its midst; it shall not be
disturbed;
God will help it at the break of
dawn. ℟.

The Lord of hosts is with us;
our stronghold is the God of Jacob.
Come! behold the deeds of the Lord,
the astounding things he has wrought
on earth. ℟.

READING II *1 Corinthians 3:9c-11, 16-17*

Brothers and sisters: You are God's building. According to the grace of God given to me, like a wise master builder I laid a foundation, and another is building upon it. But each one must be careful how he builds upon it, for no one can lay a foundation other than the one that is there, namely, Jesus Christ.

Do you not know that you are the temple of God, and that the Spirit of God dwells in you? If anyone destroys God's temple, God will destroy that person; for the temple of God, which you are, is holy.

GOSPEL *John 2:13-22*

Since the Passover of the Jews was near, Jesus went up to Jerusalem. He found in the temple area those who sold oxen, sheep, and doves, as well as the money changers seated there. He made a whip out of cords and drove them all out of the temple area, with the sheep and oxen, and spilled the coins of the money changers and overturned their tables, and to those who sold doves he said, "Take these out of here, and stop making my Father's house a marketplace." His disciples recalled the words of Scripture, 'Zeal for your house will consume me.' At this the Jews answered and said to him, "What sign can you show us for doing this?" Jesus answered and said to them, "Destroy this temple and in three days I will raise it up." The Jews said, "This temple has been under construction for forty-six years, and you will raise it up in three days?" But he was speaking about the temple of his body. Therefore, when he was raised from the dead, his disciples remembered that he had said this, and they came to believe the Scripture and the word Jesus had spoken.

November 10 / *672*
LEO THE GREAT
cf. 1198 or 1199

November 11 / *673*
MARTIN OF TOURS
cf. 1201

November 12 / *674*
JOSAPHAT
cf. 1197 or 1198

November 13
FRANCES XAVIER CABRINI
cf. 1200

November 15 / *675*
ALBERT THE GREAT
cf. 1198 or 1199

November 16 / *676*
MARGARET OF SCOTLAND
cf. 1201

GERTRUDE / *677*
cf. 1200 or 1201

November 17 / *678*
ELIZABETH OF HUNGARY
cf. 1201

November 18 / *679*
DEDICATION OF THE CHURCHES OF PETER AND PAUL
The Lord has revealed to the
     nations his saving power.

ROSE PHILIPPINE DUCHESNE
cf. 1200

November 21 / *680*
PRESENTATION OF MARY
cf. 1196

November 22 / *681*
CECILIA
cf. 1197 or 1200

November 23 / *682*
CLEMENT I
cf. 1197 or 1198

COLUMBAN / *683*
cf. 1198 or 1201

MIGUEL AGUSTIN PRO
cf. 1197

November 30 / *684*
ANDREW
Their message goes out through all
     the earth.

THANKSGIVING DAY

RESPONSORIAL PSALM I   *Psalm 67:2-3, 5, 7-8*
℟. **The earth has yielded its fruits; God, our God, has blessed us.**

May God have pity on us and bless us;
     may he let his face shine upon us.
So may your way be known upon earth;
     among all nations, your salvation. ℟.

May the nations be glad and exult
     because you rule the peoples in
     equity;
the nations on the earth you
     guide. ℟.

The earth has yielded its fruits;
God, our God, has blessed us.

May God bless us,
and may all the ends of the earth
fear him! ℟.

Or:

RESPONSORIAL PSALM II *Psalm 138:1-2, 2-3, 4-5*
℟. **I will give thanks to your name, because of your kindness and your truth.**

I will give thanks to you, O Lord, with
all my heart,
[for you have heard the words of my
mouth;]
in the presence of the angels I will
sing your praise;
I will worship at your holy temple. ℟.

I will give thanks to your name,
because of your kindness and your
truth;

For you have made great above all things
your name and your promise.
When I called, you answered me;
you built up strength within me. ℟.

All the kings of the earth shall give
thanks to you, O Lord,
when they hear the words of your
mouth;
And they shall sing of the ways of the
Lord:
"Great is the glory of the Lord." ℟.

1192 **DECEMBER**

December 3 / *685*
FRANCIS XAVIER
cf. 1198

December 4 / *686*
JOHN DAMASCENE
cf. 1198 or 1199

December 6 / *687*
NICHOLAS
cf. 1198

December 7 / *688*
AMBROSE
cf. 1198 or 1199

1193 **DECEMBER 8: IMMACULATE CONCEPTION**

READING I *Genesis 3:9-15, 20* / *689*
After the man, Adam, had eaten of the tree, the LORD God called to the man and asked him, "Where are you?" He answered, "I heard you in the garden; but I was afraid, because I was naked, so I hid myself." Then he asked, "Who told you that you were naked? You have eaten, then, from the tree of which I had forbidden you to eat!" The man replied, "The woman whom you put here with me—she gave me fruit from the tree, and so I ate it." The LORD God then asked the woman, "Why did you do such a thing?" The woman answered, "The serpent tricked me into it, so I ate it."

Then the LORD God said to the serpent:
"Because you have done this, you shall be banned
from all the animals
and from all the wild creatures;
on your belly shall you crawl,
and dirt shall you eat
all the days of your life.
I will put enmity between you and the woman,
and between your offspring and hers;
he will strike at your head,
while you strike at his heel."
The man called his wife Eve, because she became the mother of all the living.

RESPONSORIAL PSALM
Psalm 98:1, 2-3, 3-4

℟. **Sing to the Lord a new song, for he has done marvelous deeds.**

Sing to the LORD a new song,
for he has done wondrous deeds;
his right hand has won victory for him,
his holy arm. ℟.

The LORD has made his salvation known:
in the sight of the nations he has
revealed his justice.

He has remembered his kindness and his
faithfulness
toward the house of Israel. ℟.

All the ends of the earth have seen
the salvation by our God.
Sing joyfully to the LORD, all you lands;
break into song; sing praise. ℟.

READING II
Ephesians 1:3-6, 11-12

Brothers and sisters: Blessed be the God and Father of our Lord Jesus Christ, who has blessed us in Christ with every spiritual blessing in the heavens, as he chose us in him, before the foundation of the world, to be holy and without blemish before him. In love he destined us for adoption to himself through Jesus Christ, in accord with the favor of his will, for the praise of the glory of his grace that he granted us in the beloved.

In him we were also chosen, destined in accord with the purpose of the One who accomplishes all things according to the intention of his will, so that we might exist for the praise of his glory, we who first hoped in Christ.

GOSPEL
Luke 1:26-38

The angel Gabriel was sent from God to a town of Galilee called Nazareth, to a virgin betrothed to a man named Joseph, of the house of David, and the virgin's name was Mary. And coming to her, he said, "Hail, full of grace! The Lord is with you." But she was greatly troubled at what was said and pondered what sort of greeting this might be. Then the angel said to her, "Do not be afraid, Mary, for you have found favor with God. Behold, you will conceive in your womb and bear a son, and you shall name him Jesus. He will be great and will be called Son of the Most High, and the Lord God will give him the throne of David his father, and he will rule over the house of Jacob forever, and of his kingdom there will be no end." But Mary said to the angel, "How can this be, since I have no relations with a man?" And the angel said to her in reply, "The Holy Spirit will come upon you, and the power of the Most High will overshadow you. Therefore the child to be born will be called holy, the Son of God. And behold, Elizabeth, your relative, has also conceived a son in her old age, and this is the sixth month for her who was called barren; for nothing will be impossible for God." Mary said, "Behold, I am the handmaid of the Lord. May it be done to me according to your word." Then the angel departed from her.

December 23 / 695
JOHN OF KANTY
cf. 1198

December 26 / 696
STEPHEN
Into your hands, O Lord,
I entrust my spirit.

December 27 / 697
JOHN
Let good men rejoice in the Lord.

December 28 / 698
HOLY INNOCENTS
Our soul has escaped like a bird
from the hunter's net.

December 29 / 699
THOMAS BECKET
cf. 1197 or 1198

December 31 / 700
SYLVESTER I
cf. 1198

Commons: Psalm Responses

DEDICATION OF A CHURCH / *703*   1195
1   We praise your glorious name, O mighty God.
2   How lovely is your dwelling place, Lord, mighty God!
    Or: Here God lives among his people.
3   Let us come before the Lord and praise him.
4   I rejoiced when I heard them say: let us go to the house of the Lord.
    Or: Let us go rejoicing to the house of the Lord.

COMMON OF THE BLESSED VIRGIN MARY / *709*   1196
1   My heart rejoices in the Lord, my Savior.
2   You are the highest honor of our race.
3   Listen to me, daughter; see and bend your ear.
4   Blessed be the name of the Lord for ever.
    Or: Alleluia.
5   The Almighty has done great things for me and holy is his name.
    Or: O Blessed Virgin Mary, you carried the Son of the eternal Father.

COMMON OF MARTYRS / *715*   1197
1   Into your hands, O Lord, I entrust my spirit.
2   The Lord set me free from all my fears.
3   Our soul has escaped like a bird from the hunter's net.
4   Those who sow in tears, shall reap with shouts of joy.

COMMON OF PASTORS / *721*   1198
1   You are my inheritance, O Lord.
2   The Lord is my shepherd; there is nothing I shall want.

3   For ever I will sing the goodness of the Lord.

4   Proclaim his marvelous deeds to all the nations.

5   You are a priest for ever, in the line of Melchizedek.

6   Go out to all the world, and tell the Good News.
    Or: Alleluia.

1199   **COMMON OF DOCTORS OF THE CHURCH** / *727*

1   The judgments of the Lord are true, and all of them just.
    Or: Your words, Lord, are spirit and life.

2   The mouth of the just man murmurs wisdom.

3   Lord, teach me your decrees.

1200   **COMMON OF VIRGINS** / *733*

1   Listen to me, daughter; see and bend your ear.
    Or: The bridegroom is here; let us go out to meet Christ the Lord.

2   Alleluia.

1201   **COMMON OF SAINTS** / *739*

1   Happy are they who hope in the Lord.
    Or: The just man will flourish like a palm tree in the garden of the Lord.

2   He who does justice shall live on the Lord's holy mountain.

3   You are my inheritance, O Lord.

4   I will bless the Lord at all times.
    Or: Taste and see the goodness of the Lord.

5   Oh, bless the Lord, my soul.

6   Happy the man who fears the Lord.
    Or: Alleluia.

7   Happy are those who fear the Lord.

8   In you, Lord, I have found my peace.

Seasonal Psalms

The psalm as a rule is drawn from the lectionary because the individual psalm texts are directly connected with the individual readings: the choice of psalm depends therefore on the readings.

Nevertheless, in order that the people may be able to join in the responsorial psalm more readily, some texts of responses and psalms have been chosen for optional use whenever the psalm is sung. These texts, chosen according to the different seasons of the year, may be used in place of the text corresponding to the reading.

These responsorial psalms are either printed below, or a reference is given to where they may be found elsewhere in the hymnal.

ADVENT SEASON
Psalm 25:4-5, 8-9, 10, 14 / 174
Use no. 899.

Or:

RESPONSORIAL PSALM   *Psalm 85:9-10, 11-12, 13-14*   1202
℟. **Lord, show us your mercy and love.**

I will hear what God proclaims;
   the LORD—for he proclaims peace.
Near indeed is his salvation to those who
   fear him,
   glory dwelling in our land. ℟.

Kindness and truth shall meet;
   justice and peace shall kiss.

Truth shall spring out of the earth,
   and justice shall look down from
   heaven. ℟.

The LORD himself will give his benefits;
   our land shall yield its increase.
Justice shall walk before him,
   and prepare the way of his steps. ℟.

CHRISTMAS SEASON
Psalm 98:1, 2-3ab, 3cd-4, 5-6
Use no. 912

EPIPHANY
Psalm 72:1-2, 7-8, 10-11, 12-13
Use no. 917.

LENTEN SEASON
Psalm 51:3-4, 5-6, 12-13, 14 & 17
Use no. 922.

Or:

Psalm 91:1-2, 10-11, 12-13, 14, 16
Use no. 924.

Or:

Psalm 130:1-2, 3-4, 5-6, 7-8
Use no. 934.

HOLY WEEK
Psalm 22:8-9, 17-18, 19-20, 23-24
Use no. 941.

EASTER VIGIL

1203 **RESPONSORIAL PSALM**

Psalm 136:1-3, 4-6, 7-9, 24-26
or 1, 3, 16, 21-23, 24-26

℟. **God's love is everlasting.**

Give thanks to the LORD, for he is good,
    for his mercy endures forever;
give thanks to the God of gods,
    for his mercy endures forever;
give thanks to the LORD of lords,
    for his mercy endures forever. ℟.

Who alone does great wonders,
    for his mercy endures forever;
who made the heavens in wisdom,
    for his mercy endures forever;
who spread out the earth upon the waters,
    for his mercy endures forever. ℟.

Or:

Give thanks to the LORD, for he is good,
    for his mercy endures forever;
give thanks to the LORD of lords,
    for his mercy endures forever;
who led his people through the
    wilderness,
    for his mercy endures forever. ℟.

Who made the great lights,
    for his mercy endures forever;
the sun to rule over the day,
    for his mercy endures forever;
the moon and the stars to rule over the
    night,
    for his mercy endures forever. ℟.

Who freed us from our foes,
    for his mercy endures forever;
who gives food to all flesh,
    for his mercy endures forever;
give thanks to the God of heaven,
    for his mercy endures forever. ℟.

Who made their land a heritage,
    for his mercy endures forever;
the heritage of Israel, his servant,
    for his mercy endures forever;
who remembered us in our abjection,
    for his mercy endures forever. ℟.

Who freed us from our foes,
for his mercy endures forever;
who gives food to all flesh,

for his mercy endures forever;
give thanks to the God of heaven,
for his mercy endures forever. ℟.

EASTER SEASON

Psalm 118:1-2, 16-17, 22-23
Use no. 971.

Or:

Psalm 66:1-3, 4-5, 6-7, 16, 20
Use no. 982.

ASCENSION   1204
RESPONSORIAL PSALM   *Psalm 47:2-3, 6-7, 8-9*
℟. **God mounts his throne to shouts of joy.**

All you peoples, clap your hands,
shout to God with cries of gladness,
for the LORD, the Most High, the
awesome,
is the great king over all the earth. ℟.

God mounts his throne amid shouts of
joy;
the LORD, amid trumpet blasts.

Sing praise to God, sing praise;
sing praise to our king, sing praise. ℟.

For king of all the earth is God;
sing hymns of praise.
God reigns over the nations,
God sits upon his holy throne. ℟.

PENTECOST

Psalm 104:1, 24, 29-30, 31, 34
Use no. 990.

ORDINARY TIME

Psalm 19:8, 9, 10, 11
Use no. 929.

Or:

Psalm 27:1, 4, 13-14
Use no. 1004.

Or:

RESPONSORIAL PSALM   *Psalm 34:2-3, 4-5, 6-7* 1205
℟. **I will bless the Lord at all times.**
    or:
Taste and see the goodness of the Lord.

I will bless the LORD at all times;
his praise shall be ever in my mouth.
Let my soul glory in the LORD;
the lowly will hear me and be glad. ℟.

Glorify the LORD with me;
let us extol his name.
I sought the LORD, and he answered me,
and delivered me from all my
fears. ℟.

Look to him that you may be radiant
    with joy,
and your faces may not blush with
    shame.
When the poor one called out, the LORD
    heard
    and from all his distress he saved
    him. ℟.

The angel of the LORD encamps
    around those who fear him, and
    delivers them.
Taste and see how good the LORD is;
    blessed the man who takes refuge in
    him. ℟.

Or:

Psalm 63:2, 3-4, 5-6, 8-9
Use no. 1033.

Or:

Psalm 95:1-2, 6-7, 8-9
Use no. 928.

Or:

Psalm 100:1-2, 3, 5
Use no. 978.

Or:

Psalm 103:1-2, 3-4, 8, 10, 12-13
Use no. 1016.

Or:

Psalm 145:1-2, 8-9, 10-11, 13-14
Use no. 1037.

LAST WEEKS

Psalm 122:1-2, 3-4, 4-5, 6-7, 8-9
Use no. 897.

1206 Acknowledgements

SERVICE MUSIC

Acknowledgements/*continued*

Acknowledgements/*continued*

233 Through 240: Deutsche Mass, adapt. © 1985, 1989, GIA Publications, Inc.

241 © 1988, GIA Publications, Inc

242 Refrain trans. © 1973, ICEL. Verse text and tune © 1994, GIA Publications, Inc.

243 Refrain trans. © 1973, ICEL. Verse text and tune © 1994, GIA Publications, Inc.

244 Music: © 1983, GIA Publications, Inc.

245 Tune: © 1977, ICEL.

246 Tune: © 1993, GIA Publications, Inc.

247 Tune: © 1981, GIA Publications, Inc.

248 Tune: © 1979, GIA Publications, Inc.

249 Music: © John B. Foley, SJ, and New Dawn Music, P.O. Box 13248, Portland, OR 97213-0248. All rights reserved. Used with permission.

250 Music: © 1979, 1988, Les Presses de Taizé, GIA Publications, Inc., agent.

251 Music: © 1992, GIA Publications, Inc.

252 Music: © 1987, GIA Publications, Inc.

253 Music: © 1972, 1973, GIA Publications, Inc.

254 Music: © 1970, GIA Publications, Inc.

255 Acc.: © 1986, GIA Publications, Inc.

256 Music: © 1966, 1973, 1986, GIA Publications, Inc.

257 Music: © 1984, Les Presses de Taizé, GIA Publications, Inc., agent.

258 © 1985, Fintan O'Carroll and Christopher Walker. Published by OCP Publications. All rights reserved.

259 Arrangement: © 1990, Iona Community, GIA Publications, Inc., agent.

260 © 1992, GIA Publications, Inc.

261 Music: © 1958, The Grail, GIA Publications, agent.

262 Music: © 1973, 1979, GIA Publications, Inc.

263 Music: © 1973, 1982, GIA Publications, Inc.

264 Music: © 1980, ICEL

265 Music: © 1971, Manna Music, arr. © 1971, 1975, Celebration

266 © 1983, GIA Publications, Inc.

267 Music: © 1975, GIA Publications, Inc.

268 © 1987, GIA Publications, Inc.

269 Text and Music: © 1984 by Bob Hurd. Accompaniment: © 1984, OCP Publications. Published by OCP Publications. All rights reserved.

270 Music: © 1983, GIA Publications, Inc.

271 Music: © 1980, Les Presses de Taizé, GIA Publications, Inc., agent.

272 Arrangement: © 1990, Iona Community, GIA Publications, Inc., agent.

273 Tune: © 1987, Dinah Reindorf. Arrangement: © 1990, Iona Community, GIA Publications, Inc., agent.

274 Music: © 1977, GIA Publications, Inc.

275 through 281: Music © 1993, GIA Publications, Inc.

282 Music: © 1984, GIA Publications, Inc.

283 Music: © 1989, GIA Publications, Inc.

284 Music: © 1984, GIA Publications, Inc.

285 through 287: Music © 1989, GIA Publications, Inc.

288 Music: © 1984, GIA Publications, Inc.

289 through 296: Music © 1990, GIA Publications, Inc.

297 Music: © 1973, Robert J. Dufford, SJ and Daniel L. Schutte. Administered by New Dawn Music, P.O. Box 13248, Portland, OR 97213-0248. All rights reserved. Used with permission.

298 Music: © 1977, 1979, Robert J. Dufford, SJ and Daniel L. Schutte. Administered by New Dawn Music, P.O. Box 13248, Portland, OR 97213-0248. All rights reserved. Used with permission.

299 Music: © 1973, Robert J. Dufford, SJ and Daniel L. Schutte. Administered by New Dawn Music, P.O. Box 13248, Portland, OR 97213-0248. All rights reserved. Used with permission.

300 through 302: Adaptation: © 1980, Church Pension Fund.

303 Adaptation: © 1975, GIA Publications, Inc.

304 Adaptation: © 1980, GIA Publications, Inc.

305 Acc. © 1986, GIA Publications, Inc.

306 Music: © 1971, 1972, GIA Publications, Inc.

307 Music: © 1975, GIA Publications, Inc.

308 Music: © 1993, GIA Publications, Inc.

309 Music: © Text: ICEL, Addl. Text © 1990, GIA Publications, Inc. Music © 1990, GIA Publications, Inc.

310 Music: © 1993, Tony Way. Published and distributed in North America by GIA Publications, Inc.

311 Music: © 1975, GIA Publications, Inc.

312 Acc. © 1993, GIA Publications, Inc.

313 Music: © 1983, GIA Publications, Inc.

314 Music: © 1979, GIA Publications, Inc.

315 © 1993, GIA Publications, Inc.

316 © 1993, GIA Publications, Inc.

317 Harm: © 1975, GIA Publications, Inc.

318 Text: © David Higham Assoc. Ltd.

319 © 1990, GIA Publications, Inc.

320 Arr. © 1994, GIA Publications, Inc.

322 © 1974, 1975 CELEBRATION. (Administered by THE COPYRIGHT COMPANY, NASHVILLE, TN) All Rights Reserved. International Copyright Secured. Used By Permission.

323 Harm: © National Christian Education Council

324 © 1993, GIA Publications, Inc.

325 Text and Music: © 1976, Robert J. Dufford, SJ, and New Dawn Music, P.O. Box 13248, Portland, OR 97213-0248. All rights reserved. Used with permission.

327 Text: © 1982, Hope Publishing Co., Carol Stream, IL 60188

328 © 1982, GIA Publications, Inc.

329 © 1994, GIA Publications, Inc.

330 © 1993, GIA Publications, Inc.

331 © 1988, GIA Publications, Inc.

332 © 1984, Les Presses de Taizé, GIA Publications, Inc., agent.

333 Harm: © 1958, Basilian Fathers, assigned to Ralph Jusko Publications, Inc.

335 Text: © 1982, Hope Publishing Co., Carol Stream, IL 60188

336 © 1984, Les Presses de Taizé, GIA Publications, Inc., agent.

337 Text © 1985, The Church Pension Fund. Harm: © 1986, GIA Publications, Inc.

338 Text and Music: © 1982, Bernadette Farrell. Administered in England by the St. Thomas More Group. Published by OCP Publications. All rights reserved.

339 Text and Tune: © 1971, The United Church Press. Reprinted from *A New Song 3*. Accompaniment: © 1987, GIA Publications, Inc.

340 © 1983, GIA Publications, Inc.

341 Descant with accompaniment: From *Carols for Choirs,* © 1961, Oxford University Press.

342 © 1984, GIA Publications, Inc.

344 © 1994, GIA Publications, Inc.

345 © Text and Tune: © 1945, Boosey and Co., Ltd.; Copyright Renewed. Reprinted by permission of Boosey & Hawkes, Inc. Accompaniment: © 1993, GIA Publications, Inc.

346 © 1983, GIA Publications, Inc.

348 Descant with accompaniment: From *Carols for Choirs,* © 1961, Oxford University Press

349 © 1992, GIA Publications, Inc.

350 © 1987, Iona Community, GIA Publications, Inc., agent.

351 Harm © 1985, GIA Publications, Inc.

353 Harm © Oxford University Press

354 Harm: © Rosalind Rushbridge, 44 Archfield Rd., Bristol, BS6 6BQ, England

355 © 1992, GIA Publications, Inc.

356 © Text: "A Christmas Hymn" from *Advice to a Prophet and Other Poems* ©1961, Richard Wilbur. Reprinted by permission of Harcourt Brace and Company. Music: © 1992, GIA Publications, Inc.

357 © 1991, GIA Publications, Inc.

359 Text: By permission of Mrs. John W. Work III. Harm: © 1971, Walton Music Corp.

Acknowledgements/*continued*

361 Text: English Text by J. E. Middleton: © The Frederick Harris Music Co., Limited, Oakville, Ontario, Canada. All rights reserved. Arrangement: © 1992, GIA Publications, Inc.

364 Text: © 1980 by Hope Publishing Co., Carol Stream, IL 60188. All rights reserved. Used by permission. Music: © 1985, GIA Publications, Inc.

365 © 1992, GIA Publications, Inc

369 © 1987, GIA Publications, Inc.

370 Arrangement: © 1990, Iona Community, GIA Publications, Inc., agent.

371 © 1987, Iona Community, GIA Publications, Inc., agent.

372 Harm: © 1957, Novello and Co. Ltd.

375 © 1978, Damean Music. Distributed by GIA Publications, Inc.

377 Harm: © Oxford University Press

379 Harmonization: © 1987, GIA Publications, Inc.

381 Text: © 1989 by Hope Publishing Co., Carol Stream, IL 60188. All rights reserved. Used by permission. Music: © 1991, GIA Publications, Inc.

382 Text © Peter J Scagnelli

383 Psalm Text: © 1963, The Grail. Harm: © 1986, GIA Publications, Inc.

385 Text: © 1982, Thomas H. Cain. Music: © 1988, GIA Publications, Inc.

386 © 1972, 1980, The Benedictine Foundation of the State of Vermont, Inc., Weston Priory, Weston, Vermont.

387 Text: © 1980, International Committee on English in the Liturgy, Inc. All rights reserved.
Harm: © 1975, GIA Publications, Inc.

389 © 1990, 1991, GIA Publications, Inc.

390 © 1990, GIA Publications, Inc.

391 © 1990, Bernadette Farrell. Administered in England by the St. Thomas More Group. Published by OCP Publications. All rights reserved.

393 Harm: © 1975, GIA Publications

394 Copyright © 1984, North American Liturgy Resources, 11036 N. 23rd Ave., Phoenix, AZ 85029. All rights reserved.

395 Harm: © 1986, GIA Publications

396 Music: © 1984, GIA Publications, Inc.

397 © 1984, GIA Publications, Inc.

398 © 1993, GIA Publications, Inc.

399 © 1987, GIA Publications, Inc.

400 © 1990, GIA Publications, Inc.

401 Text: © 1971, Faber Music Ltd., London. Reprinted from *New Catholic Hymnal* by permission of the publishers. Harm: © 1986, GIA Publications, Inc.

403 © 1988, GIA Publications, Inc.

404 © 1981, Les Presses de Taizé, GIA Publications, Inc., agent.

405 Text: Verses 3-9 © 1991, GIA Publications, Inc. Harmonization: © 1987, GIA Publications, Inc.

406 Text: (except first verse for Holy Thursday and Good Friday, and final two verses for Easter Vigil) © 1987, GIA Publications, Inc. Accompaniment: © 1987, GIA Publications, Inc.

407 Text: © 1969, James Quinn, SJ. By permission of Geoffrey Chapman, a division of Cassell Ltd.

408 © 1979, Les Presses de Taizé, GIA Publications, Inc., agent.

409 © 1982 by Hope Publishing Co., Carol Stream, IL 60188. All rights reserved. Used by permission.

410 © 1992, GIA Publications, Inc.

411 © 1984, Les Presses de Taizé, GIA Publications, Inc., agent.

412 © 1988, GIA Publications, Inc.

413 Copyright © 1986, North American Liturgy Resources, 11036 N. 23rd Ave., Phoenix, AZ 85029. All rights reserved.

414 © 1986, GIA Publications, Inc.

416 Harmonization: © 1987, GIA Publications, Inc.

417 © 1991, Les Presses de Taizé, GIA Publications, Inc., agent.

418 Text and Music: © 1981, Robert F. O'Connor, SJ, and New Dawn Music, P.O. Box 13248, Portland, OR 97213-0248. All rights reserved. Used with permission.

420 Text and Music: © 1976, Daniel L. Schutte and New Dawn Music, P.O. Box 13248, Portland, OR 97213-0248. All rights reserved. Used with permission.

421 © 1984, Les Presses de Taizé, GIA Publications, Inc., agent.

423 Harm: © 1975, GIA Publications, Inc.

424 © 1986, GIA Publications, Inc.

425 Harm: © 1975, Romda Ltd.

427 © 1993, GIA Publications, Inc.

428 © 1978, Les Presses de Taizé, GIA Publications, Inc.

429 Melody: © 1975, Richard Hillert from Setting One of Holy Communion in the *Lutheran Book of Worship* © 1978. Permission to use the melody in additional arrangements must be obtained from the copyright holder.

431 Text: © 1986, by Hope Publishing Co., Carol Stream, IL 60188. All rights reserved. Used by permission. Music: © 1991, GIA Publications, Inc.

432 Text and Tune: © 1972, Francisco Gómez Argüello y Ediciones Musical PAX. All rights reserved. Sole U.S. Agent: OCP Publications. English text: © 1988, OCP Publications. All rights reserved. Accompaniment: © 1993, GIA Publications, Inc.

434 Harm: From *Lutheran Worship* © 1969, Concordia Publishing House.

435 Text and Music: © 1975, Robert J. Dufford, SJ, and New Dawn Music, P.O. Box 13248, Portland, OR 97213-0248. All rights reserved. Used with permission.

436 © 1984, Les Presses de Taizé, GIA Publications, Inc., agent.

438 Text trans. © 1983, Peter J. Scagnelli. Music © 1975, GIA Publications, Inc.

439 © 1969 by Hope Publishing Co., Carol Stream, IL 60188. All rights reserved. Used by permission.

440 Harmonization: © 1984, Jack W. Burnam

443 Text and Tune: © 1973, The Word of God. All rights reserved. P.O. Box 8617, Ann Arbor, MI 48107, U.S.A. Descant harmonization: © 1979 CELEBRATION (Administered by MARANATHA! MUSIC c/o THE COPYRIGHT COMPANY, NASHVILLE, TN) All Rights Reserved. International Copyright Secured. Used By Permission.

444 Text: From *Oxford Book of Carols,* © Oxford University Press. Accompaniment: © 1987, GIA Publications, Inc.

447 Harm: © 1986, GIA Publications, Inc.

448 © 1988, Iona Community, GIA Publications, Inc., agent.

449 © 1980, GIA Publications, Inc.

450 Text: © Oxford University Press. Music: From *English Hymnal* © Oxford University Press

451 © 1988, Iona Community, GIA Publications, Inc. agent.

452 Copyright © 1987, North American Liturgy Resources, 11036 N. 23rd Ave., Phoenix, AZ 85029. All rights reserved.

453 Harm: From the *English Hymnal* © Oxford University Press

454 © 1981 by Word Music (a div. of WORD, INC.). All Rights Reserved. Used by Permission.

455 © 1983, GIA Publications, Inc.

456 Text: © 1978, Jeffrey W Rowthorn. Music © 1942, Renewal 1970, Hope Publishing Co., Carol Stream, IL 60188

458 © 1970, 1973, World Library Publications, Inc.

459 Text and music: © 1988, Bob Hurd. Accompaniment and arrangement: © 1988, OCP Publications. Published by OCP Publications. All rights reserved.

460 Harm: © 1975, GIA Publications, Inc.

461 Text © 1971, John Webster Grant. Harm © 1975, GIA Publications, Inc.

462 © 1987, GIA Publications, Inc.

463 © 1979, Les Presses de Taizé, GIA Publications, Inc., agent.

464 Text: © 1983, Peter J. Scagnelli. Music: © Interkerkelijke Stichting voor het Kerklied.

465 Music: From the *English Hymnal* © Oxford University Press

466 © 1989, GIA Publications, Inc.

467 © 1969 and this arrangement © 1987 by Hope Publishing Co., Carol Stream, IL 60188. All rights reserved. Used by permission.

Acknowledgements/*continued*

556 © 1990, GIA Publications, Inc.

557 © 1979, Les Presses de Taizé, GIA Publications, Inc., agent.

558 Text and Tune: © 1981, Robert F. O'Connor, SJ, and New Dawn Music, P.O. Box 13248, Portland, OR 97213-0248. All rights reserved. Used with permission. Accompaniment: ©1994, GIA Publications, Inc.

559 Text: Stanzas 1-4 © 1982 by Hope Publishing Co., Carol Stream, IL 60188. All rights reserved. Used by permission. Stanzas 5-6 © 1993, GIA Publications, Inc. Harmonization: © 1992, GIA Publications, Inc.

560 Text: © 1972, Hope Publishing Co., Carol Stream, IL 60188

561 Text: © 1972 by Hope Publishing Co., Carol Stream, IL 60188. All rights reserved. Used by permission. Music: © 1989, GIA Publications, Inc.

562 © 1984, Utryck, Walton Music Corporation, agent.

563 © 1993, 1994, GIA Publications, Inc.

564 Harm: © 1986, GIA Publications, Inc.

566 © 1986, 1991, Les presses de Taizé, GIA Publications, Inc., agent.

567 Text: © 1939 E.C. Schirmer Music Co. Harm: Executors of S. H. Knight

568 Text: © 1940, The Church Pension Fund

569 © 1990, GIA Publications, Inc.

570 © 1982, 1991, Les Presses de Taizé, GIA Publications, Inc., agent.

573 © 1985, Damean Music. Distributed by GIA Publications, Inc.

574 © 1953, Doris Akers. All rights administered by Unichappell Music, Inc. International Copyright Secured. All Rights Reserved.

575 © 1989, Iona Community, GIA Publications, Inc., agent.

576 Text: © 1979, Stainer and Bell, Ltd., London, England. Music: © 1987, GIA Publications, Inc.

577 Music: © 1911, Stainer and Bell, Ltd. Used by permission of Galaxy Music Corp., New York, NY, sole US agent

578 Text: From *Enlarged Songs of Praise* © Oxford University Press. Harm: © 1985, Hope Publishing Co., Carol Stream, IL 60188

580 Text: © 1979 by The Hymn Society, Texas Christian University, Fort Worth, TX 76129. All rights reserved. Used by permission. Music: © 1989, GIA Publications, Inc.

581 Music: © 1991, Iona Community, GIA Publications, Inc., agent.

582 Text: © 1983, The Pastoral Press. Music: © 1991, GIA Publications, Inc.

583 © 1989, Iona Community, GIA Publications, Inc., agent.

584 Text and Tune: © Copyright 1964 (Renewed) by Appleseed Music, Inc., 200 West 57th St., New York, NY 10019. Arrangement: ©1982, GIA Publications, Inc.

585 © 1987, GIA Publications, Inc.

586 © 1982, Les Presses de Taizé, GIA Publications, Inc., agent.

588 © 1993, GIA Publications, Inc.

589 Tune: Adapt. © 1983 by Abingdon Press. Used from *Hymns from the Four Winds*. Accompaniment: © 1993, GIA Publications, Inc.

590 Music: © 1984, GIA Publications, Inc.

591 Text: © 1986 by Hope Publishing Co., Carol Stream, IL 60188. All rights reserved. Used by permission. Music: © 1990, GIA Publications, Inc.

592 Music: © 1990, Iona Community, GIA Publications, Inc., agent.

593 © 1980, GIA Publications, Inc.

594 © 1976, John B. Foley, SJ, and New Dawn Music, P.O. Box 13248, Portland, OR 97213-0248. All rights reserved. Used with permission.

595 © 1988, GIA Publications, Inc.

596 Copyright © 1986, North American Liturgy Resources, 10636 N. 23rd Ave., Phoenix, AZ 85029. All rights reserved.

597 © 1989, GIA Publications, Inc.

598 Music and refrain text: © 1985, Paul Inwood. Administered in England by the St. Thomas More Group. Published by OCP Publications. All rights reserved. Verse text: © 1963, 1993, The Grail, GIA Publications, Inc., agent.

599 © 1967, Gooi en Sticht, bv., Baarn, The Netherlands. All rights reserved. Exclusive English-language agent: OCP Publications.

601 © 1969, 1979, Damean Music. Distributed by GIA Publications, Inc.

602 © 1975, Daniel L. Schutte and New Dawn Music, P.O. Box 13248, Portland, OR 97213-0248. All rights reserved. Used with permission.

603 Text: © 1957, 1964, Sanga Music, Inc., 250 W. 57th St., Ste. 710, New York, NY 10107. Harmonization: © 1987, GIA Publications, Inc.

604 © 1971, Daniel L. Schutte. Administered by New Dawn Music, P.O. Box 13248, Portland, OR 97213-0248. All rights reserved. Used with permission.

605 © 1980, Savgos Music, Inc.

606 Harm: © 1975, GIA Publications, Inc.

607 Text: © 1982, Hope Publishing Co., Carol Stream, IL 60188

608 © 1975, Robert J. Dufford, SJ, and New Dawn Music, P.O. Box 13248, Portland, OR 07213-0248. All rights reserved. Used with permission.

609 © 1978, Damean Music. Distributed by GIA Publications, Inc.

610 © 1982, Dennis Vessels.

611 © 1979, New Dawn Music, P.O. Box 13248, Portland, OR 07213-0248. All rights reserved. Used with permission.

612 Accompaniment: © 1993, GIA Publications, Inc.

613 Text and Tune: © 1989, M. D. Ridge. Accompaniment: © 1990, OCP Publications. Published by OCP Publications. All rights reserved.

615 ©1972, Maranatha! Music

616 © 1970, John B. Foley, SJ. Administered by New Dawn Music, P.O. Box 13248, Portland, OR 07213-0248. All rights reserved. Used with permission

617 © 1976, 1979, Daniel L. Schutte and New Dawn Music, P.O. Box 13248, Portland, OR 07213-0248. All rights reserved. Used with permission.

618 © 1989, Iona Community, GIA Publications, Inc., agent

619 © 1979, New Dawn Music, P.O. Box 13248, Portland, OR 07213-0248. All rights reserved. Used with permission.

620 Text and Tune: © 1981, New Dawn Music, P.O. Box 13248, Portland, OR 07213-0248. All rights reserved. Used with permission. Accompaniment: © 1994, GIA Publications, Inc.

621 © 1976, John B. Foley, SJ, and New Dawn Music, P.O. Box 13248, Portland, OR 07213-0248. All rights reserved. Used with permission.

623 Text: © 1985 by Hope Publishing Co., Carol Stream, IL 60188. All rights reserved. Used by permission. Music: © 1988, GIA Publications, Inc.

624 © 1992, GIA Publications, Inc.

625 © 1961, 1962, World Library Publications, Inc.

627 Harm: From *Cantate Domino* © 1980, Oxford University Press

628 © 1988, GIA Publications, Inc.

629 © 1987, GIA Publications, Inc.

630 © 1983, GIA Publications, Inc.

631 Trans: © 1975, 1986, GIA Publications, Inc. Harm: © 1986, GIA Publications, Inc.

632 Text and tune: © 1973, Damean Music. Distributed by GIA Publications, Inc. Accompaniment: © 1993, GIA Publications, Inc.

633 Text and Music: © 1987, 1989, Daniel L. Schutte. Published by OCP Publications. All rights reserved.

634 Text and harm: © 1969, Concordia Publishing House

635 Harm: © A. Gregory Murray, Downside Abbey, Stratton on the Fosse, Bath BA3 4RH

636 Text and Tune: © 1984, Bob Hurd. Accompaniment: © 1984, OCP Publications. Published by OCP Publications. All rights reserved.

637 Text: © 1991, GIA Publications, Inc. Music: © 1993, GIA Publications, Inc.

638 © 1982, GIA Publications, Inc.

Acknowledgements/*continued*

727 Text: © 1992, GIA Publications, Inc. Harmonization: © 989 The United Methodist Publishing House. Used from *The United Methodist Hymnal*.

728 Accompaniment: © 1993, GIA Publications, Inc.

729 © 1987, GIA Publications, Inc.

730 Accompaniment: © 1994, GIA Publications, Inc.

731 Text and Tune: © 1955, 1983, Jan-Lee Music. Used with permission. Accompaniment: © 1993, GIA Publications, Inc.

732 Verse text and Tune: © 1985, GIA Publications, Inc.

733 © 1980, 1986 GIA Publications, Inc.

734 © 1993, GIA Publications, Inc.

735 © 1966, F.E.L. Publications, assigned to The Lorenz Corp., 1991. All rights reserved. Reproduced by permission of The Lorenz Corp., Dayton, OH.

736 Text translation: © Verbum Forlong AB, Sweden. Tune: © Olle Widestrand, Sweden. Accompaniment: © 1987, GIA Publications, Inc.

737 Text and Accompaniment: © 1993, Iona Community, GIA Publications, Inc., agent.

739 Text: © 1992, GIA Publications, Inc.

740 © 1982, GIA Publications, Inc.

741 Text: © 1979, and music: © 1942. Renewal 1970, Hope Publishing Co., Carol Stream, IL 60188

742 © 1992, GIA Publications, Inc.

743 Copyright © 1986 by North American Liturgy Resources (NALR), 11036 N. 23rd Ave., Phoenix, AZ 85029. All rights reserved.

744 © 1982, GIA Publications, Inc.

745 © 1988, GIA Publications, Inc.

746 Text: © 1968, Hope Publishing Co., Carol Stream, IL 60188. Music: From the *Clarendon Hymnbook* © Oxford University Press

748 Text: © 1967, Gooi en Sticht, bv., Baarn, The Netherlands. All rights reserved. Exclusive agent for English-language countries: OCP Publications. Accompaniment: © 1987, GIA Publications, Inc.

749 © Copyright 1972, Dawn Treader Music (a division of Star Song Communications). Administered by Gaither Copyright Management. All rights reserved. Used by permission.

750 Text: © 1991, GIA Publications, Inc. Music: © 1993, GIA Publications, Inc.

751 Text and Accompaniment: © 1989, Iona Community, GIA Publications, Inc., agent.

752 © 1989, OCP Publications. All rights reserved.

753 © 1994, GIA Publications, Inc.

754 © 1969, Hope Publishing Co., Carol Stream, IL 60188

755 © 1989, Iona Community, GIA Publications, Inc., agent.

756 Text: From "The Children's Bells," published by Oxford University Press. © David Higham Assoc., Ltd. Accompaniment: © 1987, GIA Publications, Inc.

757 Text: © 1969, James Quinn, SJ. Used by permission of Selah Publishing Co., Kingston, NY. Music: © 1993, GIA Publications, Inc.

758 Text: © 1969, James Quinn, SJ. By permission of Geoffrey Chapman, a division of Cassel Ltd.

759 Text: © 1974 by Hope Publishing Co., Carol Stream, IL 60188. All rights reserved. Used by permission. Music: © 1985, GIA Publications, Inc.

760 Text: © 1989 by Hope Publishing Co., Carol Stream, IL 60188. All rights reserved. Used by permission. Music: © 1993, GIA Publications, Inc.

761 Text: © 1985, 1994, GIA Publications, Inc. Harmonization: © 1985, GIA Publications, Inc.

762 © 1987, 1990, GIA Publications, Inc.

763 © 1991, Les Presses de Taizé, GIA Publications, Inc., agent.

764 Text: © Oxford University Press. Harm: © A. Gregory Murray, Downside Abbey, stratton on the Fosse, Bath BA3 4RH

765 Text: © 1967, Hope Publishing Co., Carol Stream, IL 60188. All rights reserved. Used by permission. Music: © 1993, GIA Publications, Inc.

767 Text: © Harper and Row. Harm: © 1940, The Church Pension Fund

768 Text and Tune: © 1973, Gooi en sticht, bv., Baarn, The Netherlands. All rights reserved. Exclusive agent for English-language countries: OCP Publications.

769 © 1991, GIA Publications, Inc.

770 © 1976, Bud John Songs, Inc./Crouch Music.

771 Harm: © 1975, GIA Publications, Inc.

772 © 1987, GIA Publications, Inc.

775 Text: © 1992, GIA Publications, Inc. Harmonization: © 1987, GIA Publications, Inc.

776 Text: © 1992, GIA Publications, Inc. Accompaniment: © 1986, GIA Publications, Inc.

778 Text: © Esme. D. E. Bird

779 Trans: © 1954 and harm: © 1986, GIA Publications, Inc.

781 Text and Harmonization: © 1987, GIA Publications, Inc.

782 Copyright © 1975 by North American Liturgy Resources, 11036 N. 23rd Ave., Phoenix, AZ 85029. All rights reserved.

783 Harm: © 1986, GIA Publications, Inc.

784 Harm: © Willis Music Company

785 © 1993, GIA Publications, Inc.

786 Text: From *English Praise* © 1975, Oxford University Press

787 Harmonization: © 1987, GIA Publications, Inc.

788 © 1990, GIA Publications, Inc.

789 Harm: © 1986, GIA Publications, Inc.

790 Text: © 1971, Faber Music Ltd., London. reprinted from *New Catholic Hymnal* by permission of the publishers

791 © Hymns Ancient and Modern, Ltd.

792 Text: © 1985 by Hope Publishing Co., Carol Stream, IL 60188. All rights reserved. Used by permission. Music: © 1987, GIA Publications, Inc.

793 Music: From the *English Hymnal* © Oxford University Press

794 Text and Harm: From the *English Hymnal* © Oxford University Press

796 © 1987, John D. Becker, published by OCP Publications. All rights reserved.

797 © 1993, GIA Publications, Inc.

798 Text: © 1982 by Hope Publishing Co., Carol Stream, IL 60188. All rights reserved. Used by permission. Accompaniment: © 1987, GIA Publications, Inc.

799 © 1991, GIA Publications, Inc.

800 Harm: © A. Gregory Murray, Downside Abbey, Stratton on the Fosse, Bath BA3 4RH

801 © 1993, GIA Publications, Inc.

802 © 1987, GIA Publications, Inc.

803 © 1993, GIA Publications, Inc.

805 © 1979, Kevin Yancy

806 Text: © 1971, Hope Publishing Co., Carol Stream, IL 60188. Harm: © 1938, J. Fisher and Bro.

807 Text: © 1971, Faber Music Ltd., London. reprinted from *New Catholic Hymnal* by permission of the publishers.

808 © 1991, GIA Publications, Inc.

809 © 1984, Les Presses de Taizé, GIA Publications,Inc., agent.

810 © 1988, GIA Publications, Inc.

811 © 1988, GIA Publications, Inc.

812 Harmonization: © 1994, GIA Publications, Inc.

813 Copyright © 1986 by North American Liturgy Resources, 11036 N. 23rd Ave., Phoenix, AZ 85029. All rights reserved.

814 © 1983, GIA Publications, Inc.

815 © 1977 Archdiocese of Philadelphia

816 © 1990, GIA Publications, Inc.

817 © 1985, GIA Publications, Inc.

818 Copyright © 1987 by North American Liturgy Resources, 11036 N. 23rd Ave., Phoenix, AZ 95029. All rights reserved.

819 © 1979, New Dawn Music, P.O. Box 13248, Portland, OR 97213-0248. All rights reserved. Used with permission.

820 Text: © 1991, GIA Publications, Inc. Music: © 1993, GIA Publications, Inc.

821 © 1982, 1987, Bernadette Farrell. Administered in England by the St. Thomas More Group. Published by OCP Publications. All rights reserved.

Acknowledgements/*continued*

822 © 1987, GIA Publications, Inc.

823 Text and Music: © 1984, OCP Publications. All rights reserved.

824 Copyright © 1987 by North American Liturgy Resources, 11036 N. 23rd Ave., Phoenix, AZ 95029. All rights reserved.

825 © 1990, GIA Publications, Inc.

826 © 1992, GIA Publications, Inc.

827 © 1990, Bernadette Farrell. Administered in England by the St. Thomas More Group. Published by OCP Publications. All rights reserved.

828 © 1966, 1970, 1986, 1993, GIA Publications, Inc.

829 © 1988, GIA Publications, Inc.

830 Text and Music: © 1978, John B. Foley, SJ, and New Dawn Music, P.O. Box 13248, Portland, OR 97213-0248. All rights reserved. Used with permission.

831 Verse text: © 1969, James Quinn, SJ. Used by permission of Selah Publishing Co., Inc., Kingston, N.Y. Refrain text and Tune: © 1989, GIA Publications, Inc.

832 Harm: © 1983, GIA Publications, Inc.

833 © 1986, GIA Publications, Inc.

834 © 1987, EKKLESIA Music, Inc., P.O. Box 22967, Denver, CO 80222.

835 © 1993, GIA Publications, Inc.

836 © 1992, GIA Publications, Inc.

837 © 1992, GIA Publications, Inc.

838 © 1984, Les Presses de Taizé, GIA Publications, Inc., agent.

839 © 1992, GIA Publications, Inc.

840 Harm: © 1986, GIA Publications, Inc.

841 English text and Tune: © 1984, Bob Hurd. Revised English Text: © 1987, Bob Hurd and Michael Downey. Spanish text: © 1989, OCP Publications. Accompaniment: © 1984, OCP Publications. All rights reserved. Published and distributed by OCP Publications.

842 © 1992, GIA Publications, Inc.

843 © 1969, 1979, Damean Music. Distributed by GIA Publications, Inc.

844 © 1993, GIA Publications, Inc.

845 Text: © 1988, Iona Community, GIA Publications, Inc., agent. Accompaniment: © 1993, Iona Community, GIA Publications, Inc., agent.

846 © 1993, GIA Publications, Inc.

847 © 1989, GIA Publications, Inc.

848 Text and Tune: © 1988, Bob Hurd. Accompaniment and arrangement: © 1988, OCP Publications. All rights reserved. Published by OCP Publications.

849 © 1991, GIA Publications, Inc.

850 © 1994, GIA Publications, Inc.

851 Harm: © 1986, GIA Publications, Inc.

854 © 1990, GIA Publications, Inc.

855 Text: © 1991, Jean Janzen. Music: © 1993, GIA Publications, Inc.

856 © 1993, GIA Publications, Inc.

857 © 1970, 1977 ICEL

858 Text: © 1970, ICEL. Music: © 1977, ICEL.

859 Refrain and verse 1 text and Music: © 1994, GIA Publications, Inc. Verse 2 text from *In paradisum; Rite of Funerals*, © 1970, International Commission on English in the Liturgy.

860 Copyright © 1983 by North American Liturgy Resources, 11036 N. 23rd Ave., Phoenix, AZ 95029. All rights reserved.

861 © 1980, GIA Publications, Inc.

862 Text: *Order of Christian Funerals*, © 1985, International Commission on English in the Liturgy. Music: © 1990, GIA Publications, Inc.

864 Refrain text: © 1973, International Commission on English in the Liturgy. Verse text and Music: © 1988, GIA Publications, Inc.

865 © 1983 by Hope Publishing Co., Carol Stream, IL 60188. All rights reserved. Used by permission.

866 Text: © 1981, Concordia Publishing House. Music: © 1993, GIA Publications, Inc.

867 © 1993, GIA Publications, Inc.

868 Text: © 1989, Iona Community, GIA Publications, Inc. agent. Harmonization: © 1975 by Hope Publishing Co., Carol Stream, IL 60188. All rights reserved. Used by permission.

869 © 1993, GIA Publications, Inc.

870 © 1989, GIA Publications, Inc.

871 Text: © 1989, Iona Community, GIA Publications, Inc. agent.

872 © 1972, 1980, The Benedictine Foundation of the State of Vermont, Inc., Weston Priory, Weston, Vermont.

873 © 1993, GIA Publications, Inc.

874 Text and Tune: © 1938 by Unichappell Music, Inc. Copyright Renewed. International Copyright Secured. All Rights Reserved. Arrangement: © 1994, GIA Publications, Inc.

875 © 1988, GIA Publications, Inc.

876 Text: © 1982 by Hope Publishing Co., Carol Stream, IL 60188. All rights reserved. Used by permission. Music: © 1988, GIA Publications, Inc.

877 Text: © 1992, GIA Publications, Inc. Music: © 1994, GIA Publications, Inc.

878 Text: © 1965, GIA Publications, Inc. Harm: © 1986, GIA Publications, Inc.

879 Text: © Oxford University Press. Harm: Executors of G. H. Knight.

880 © 1993, GIA Publications, Inc.

881 © 1978, Damean Music. Distributed by GIA Publications, Inc.

882 © 1987, GIA Publications, Inc.

883 © 1978, New Dawn Music, P.O. Box 13248, Portland, OR 97213-0248. All rights reserved. Used with permission.

884 © 1989, GIA Publications, Inc.

885 Verse text: © 1963, 1993, The Grail, GIA Publications, Inc. agent. Refrain text and Music: © 1987, Paul Inwood. Published by OCP Publications. All rights reserved.

888 Trans: © 1969, James Quinn SJ. By permission of Geoffrey Chapman, a division of Cassell Ltd.

892 Text: © 1989 by Hope Publishing Co., Carol Stream, IL 60188. All rights reserved. Used by permission. Music: © 1994, GIA Publications, Inc.

893 Text: © 1989 by Hope Publishing Co., Carol Stream, IL 60188. All rights reserved. Used by permission. Music: © 1994, GIA Publications, Inc.

894 Text and Arrangement: © 1989, Iona Community, GIA Publications, Inc., agent.

895 Text: © 1969, Concordia Publishing House. Music: © 1989, Selah Publishing Co., Inc., Kingston, NY.

938 Acc. © 1985, GIA Publications, Inc.

961 Text © 1998, Confraternity of Christian Doctrine

1156 Acc. © 1985, GIA Publications, Inc.

1157 Acc. © 1985, GIA Publications, Inc.

GENESIS

1:	Joyful Is the Dark	760
1:	Many and Great	498
1:	Song over the Waters	585
1:	The Earth Is the Lord's	495
1:	This Day God Gives Me	757
1:	This Is the Day When Light Was First Created	746
1:2-3	Psalm 107 Give Thanks to the Lord	102
1:3-5	Morning Has Broken	756
1:14-19	All Things New	427
1:26-27	God, beyond All Names	491
1:26-28	Psalm 112 A Light Rises in the Darkness	104
1:27-30	God of Adam, God of Joseph	893
2:15	God of Adam, God of Joseph	893
2:18-23	Blessing the Marriage	871
2:18-23	God, in the Planning	868
8:22	Now Join We to Praise the Creator	720
12:1	The God of Abraham Praise	544
12:1-4	God It Was	701
12:1-5	God of Abraham	391
14:18	The God of Abraham Praise	544
18:	This Is the Day	449
18:9-15	God It Was	701
18:9-15	God of Abraham	391
22:16-17	The God of Abraham Praise	544
28:10-15	We Are Climbing Jacob's Ladder	693
28:12-13	Calvary	419

EXODUS

3:	Go Down, Moses	715
3:6-14	The God of Abraham Praise	544
3:9-10	God It Was	701
3:13-15	I Am for You	704
4:1-17	God of Abraham	391
12:1-14	As We Remember	818
13:3-16	Bless the Feast	752
13:21	Eternal Lord of Love	385
14:	All Things New	427
14:	Go Down, Moses	715
14:29	Come, Ye Faithful, Raise the Strain	441
15:	At the Lamb's High Feast We Sing	433
15:	Come, Ye Faithful, Raise the Strain	441
15:	Go Down, Moses	715
15:1-6	Song at the Sea: Exodus 15	143
15:17-18	Song at the Sea: Exodus 15	143
15:20-21	God It Was	701
16:	Shepherd of Our Hearts	829
16:	Shepherd of Souls	840
16:4	All Things New	427
16:13-15	Change Our Hearts	394
16:21	Psalm 78 The Lord Gave them Bread	73
17:	Shepherd of Our Hearts	829
17:	Shepherd of Souls	840
17:5-7	Change Our Hearts	394
19:4	The God of Abraham Praise	544
20:	O Come, O Come, Emmanuel	317
33:18-23	Holy, Holy, Holy! Lord God Almighty	474
34:	I Will Not Die	657

LEVITICUS

19:9	The Harvest of Justice	711
23:22	The Harvest of Justice	711
25:8-12	Sign Me Up	805
25:42	Psalm 81 Sing with Joy to God	76

NUMBERS

6:22-27	Bwana Awabariki / May God Grant You a Blessing	587
6:24	A Nuptial Blessing	870
6:24-26	May the Lord, Mighty God	589
14:33	May We Be One	316
24:17	What Star Is This	378

DEUTERONOMY

8:3	Not by Bread Alone	517
8:3	Shepherd of Our Hearts	829
8:3	Shepherd of Souls	840
24:19	The Harvest of Justice	711
32:3	Sing Praise to God Who Reigns Above	539

JOSHUA

24:14-24	We Will Serve the Lord	665
24:15	We Will Serve the Lord	869

RUTH

1:	God of Abraham	391
1:16	Covenant Hymn	797
1:16	Wherever You Go	867
1:16	Wherever You Go	872

1 SAMUEL

2:1-10	Canticle of the Turning	556
2:1-10	Psalm 113 Praise the Lord	106
2:1-11	Holy Is Your Name / Luke 1:46-55	
2:1-11	Magnificat / Luke 1:46-55	146
3:1-10	God of Abraham	391

2 SAMUEL

22:	The Lord Is My Hope	613

1 KINGS

19:8	May We Be One	247

2 KINGS

18:32	Psalm 137 Let My Tongue Be Silent	132

1 CHRONICLES

16:	When in Our Music God Is Glorified	560
16:	When in Our Music God Is Glorified	561

JOB

3:17-18	Jesus Shall Reign	482
19:25	I Know That My Redeemer Lives	430
19:25	I Know That My Redeemer Lives	857
19:25-27	I Know That My Redeemer Lives	854
19:25-27	I Shall See My God	856
31:16-23	Psalm 112 A Light Rises in the Darkness	104
42:1-6	I Say "Yes," Lord / Digo "Sí," Señor	597

Scripture Passages Related to Hymns/*continued*

PSALMS

1:1-4	Psalm 1 Happy Are They 18
1:6	Psalm 1 Happy Are They 18
3:5	With a Shepherd's Care 654
4:2	Psalm 4 Let Your Face Shine upon Us 19
4:2	Standin' in the Need of Prayer 579
4:8-9	Psalm 4 Let Your Face Shine upon Us 19
8:	The Works of the Lord Are Created in Wisdom 493
8:	Psalm 8 How Glorious Is Your Name 20
8:1-10	Psalm 8 How Great Is Your Name 21
8:4	O God of Matchless Glory 546
9:3	Amen Siakudumisa 536
9:9	You Are Mine 649
15:2-5	Psalm 15 They Who Do Justice 22
16:	Center of My Life 598
16:	For You Are My God 616
16:	Shelter Me, O God 636
16:	Show Us the Path of Life 645
16:1	Psalm 16 You Will Show Me the Path of Life 24
16:5-8	Psalm 16 You Will Show Me the Path of Life 24
16:7-11	Psalm 16 Keep Me Safe, O God 23
16:11	Psalm 16 You Will Show Me the Path of Life 24
17:1-2	Psalm 17 Lord, When Your Glory Appears 25
17:5-6	Psalm 17 Lord, When Your Glory Appears 25
17:6-9	Shelter Me, O God 636
17:8-9	Psalm 17 Lord, When Your Glory Appears 25
17:15	Psalm 17 Lord, When Your Glory Appears 25
18:2-4	Psalm 18 I Love You Lord, My Strength 26
18:47	Psalm 18 I Love You Lord, My Strength 26
18:50-51	Psalm 18 I Love You Lord, My Strength 26
19:	Cantemos al Señor / Let's Sing unto the Lord 553
19:	O Taste and See 835
19:	Psalm 19 Lord, You Have the Words 27
19:	The Stars Declare His Glory 489
19:2	Canticle of the Sun 496
19:4-6	Jesus Shall Reign 482
19:9-11	Not by Bread Alone 517
22:	Psalm 22 My God, My God 29
22:23-24	Psalm 22 I Will Praise You, Lord 28
22:28-32	Psalm 22 I Will Praise You, Lord 28
23:	Jesus, Shepherd of Our Souls 725
23:	Psalm 23 Shepherd Me, O God 31
23:	Shepherd of My Heart 641
23:	The King of Love My Shepherd Is 635
23:	The Lord Is My Shepherd 643
23:	We Shall Rise Again 772
23:	With a Shepherd's Care 654
23:1-2	Without Seeing You 844

23:1-6	Psalm 23 My Shepherd Is the Lord 30
23:1-6	Psalm 23 The Lord Is My Shepherd 32
23:1-6	Psalm 23 Nada Me Falta 33
23:5	The Carpenter 483
24:	Hail the Day That Sees Him Rise 457
24:	The King of Glory 486
24:1-6	Psalm 24 We Long to See Your Face 34
24:3	I Have Loved You 504
24:7-10	All Glory, Laud, and Honor 402
25:	Hold Me in Life 423
25:	Psalm 25 To You, O Lord 36
25:	Servant Song 683
25:1-7	Psalm 25 Levanto Mi Alma 37
25:4-9	Psalm 25 Remember Your Mercies 35
25:4-9	Remember Your Mercy, Lord 885
25:5	My Soul in Stillness Waits 328
25:15-16	Psalm 25 Levanto Mi Alma 37
27:	I Need You to Listen 582
27:	May the Angels Lead You into Paradise 858
27:	Psalm 27 The Lord Is My Light 39
27:	The Lord Is My Light 605
27:	The Lord Is Near 619
27:1	Psalm 27 In the Land of the Living 38
27:1-8	Remember Your Love 881
27:4	Psalm 27 In the Land of the Living 38
27:7-8	Psalm 27 In the Land of the Living 38
27:11	Lead Me, Guide Me 574
27:13	Psalm 27 In the Land of the Living 38
27:14	Wait for the Lord 332
28:7	With a Shepherd's Care 654
29:	All Glory, Laud, and Honor 402
29:1-4	Psalm 29 The Lord Will Bless His People 40
29:9-10	Psalm 29 The Lord Will Bless His People 40
30:	Psalm 30 I Will Praise You, Lord 41
30:	The Lord Is My Hope 613
31:	My Refuge 610
31:2-6	Psalm 31 I Put My Life in Your Hands 42
31:2-6	Psalm 31 I Put My Life in Your Hands 43
31:4	Lead Me, Guide Me 574
31:5	The Hand of God Shall Hold You 859
31:6	You Are All We Have 505
31:12-17	Psalm 31 I Put My Life in Your Hands 42
31:12-17	Psalm 31 I Put My Life in Your Hands 43
31:15	The Hand of God Shall Hold You 859
32:1-5	Psalm 32 I Turn to You 44
32:11	Psalm 32 I Turn to You 44
33:	Psalm 33 Let Your Mercy Be on Us 45
33:	Song of the Chosen 813
33:	There's a Wideness in God's Mercy 626

85:8-13	Psalm 85 Come, O Lord, and Set Us Free 80	
85:9-14	Ps. 80/85/Lk. 1 Lord, Make Us Turn to You 75	
85:11-12	The Day Is Near 768	
86:5-6	Psalm 86 Lord, You Are Good and Forgiving 81	
86:9-10	Psalm 86 Lord, You Are Good and Forgiving 81	
86:15-16	Psalm 86 Lord, You Are Good and Forgiving 81	
89:	Psalm 89 For Ever I Will Sing 82	
89:1-16	Let Heaven Your Wonders Proclaim 538	
90:	The Lord Is My Hope 613	
90:1-5	O God, Our Help in Ages Past 614	
90:2	Remember Your Love 881	
90:3-6	Psalm 90 In Ev'ry Age 83	
90:12-14	Psalm 90 In Ev'ry Age 83	
90:12-17	Psalm 90 Fill Us with Your Love, O Lord 84	
90:17	Psalm 90 In Ev'ry Age 83	
91:	Blest Be the Lord 617	
91:	On Eagle's Wings 611	
91:	Psalm 91 Be with Me 85	
91:11-12	Saints of God 862	
92:2-3	Psalm 92 Lord, It Is Good 86	
92:13-16	Psalm 92 Lord, It Is Good 86	
93:1-5	Psalm 93 The Lord Is King for Evermore 88	
93:1-2	Psalm 93 The Lord Is King 87	
93:5	Psalm 93 The Lord Is King 87	
95:	My Soul in Stillness Waits 328	
95:	Psalm 95 If Today You Hear God's Voice 89	
95:	Rejoice, the Lord Is King 487	
95:	This Is the Day 449	
95:	To God with Gladness Sing 535	
96:	Sing a New Song to the Lord 521	
96:	Sing a New Song 537	
96:	This Is the Day 449	
96:1	A New Song 530	
96:1	Sing Our God Together 523	
96:1-3	Psalm 96 Proclaim to All the Nations 93	
96:1-3	Psalm 96 Today Is Born Our Savior 90	
96:1-13	Psalm 96 Great Is the Lord 92	
96:7-10	Psalm 96 Today Is Born Our Savior 91	
96:7-10	Psalm 96 Proclaim to All the Nations 93	
96:11-13	Psalm 96 Today Is Born Our Savior 90	
97:1	Lord, Today 375	
97:1-2	Psalm 97 The Lord Is King 94	
97:6-7	Psalm 97 The Lord Is King 94	
97:9	Psalm 97 The Lord Is King 94	
98:	All the Ends of the earth 520	
98:	Cantai ao Senhor 526	
98:	Psalm 98 All the Ends of the Earth 95	
98:	Sing a New Song to the Lord 521	
98:	Sing a New Song 537	
98:49	Joy to the World 343	
100:	All People That on Earth Do Dwell 747	
100:	All the Earth, Proclaim God's Glory 552	
100:	Joyfully Singing 548	

100:	Jubilate Deo / In the Lord Rejoicing 555	
100:	Jubilate Servite 557	
100:	Lift Up Your Hearts 558	
100:	Praise to the Lord, the Almighty 527	
100:	Sing of the Lord's Goodness 547	
100:	To God with Gladness Sing 535	
100:	Psalm 100 We Are God's People 97	
100:1-5	Psalm 100 Arise, Come to Your God 96	
100:3	Be Still, and Know That I Am God 618	
102:2	O Lord, Hear My Prayer 586	
102:2	Standin' in the Need of Prayer 579	
103:	Blessed Be God 477	
103:	Deep Down in My Soul 880	
103:	Jesus, Heal Us 875	
103:	Our God Is Rich in Love 652	
103:	Praise the Lord, My Soul 554	
103:	Praise to the Lord, the Almighty 527	
103:	Praise, My Soul, the King of Heaven 551	
103:	Psalm 103 The Lord Is Kind and Merciful 100	
103:1-2	Psalm 103 The Lord Is Kind and Merciful 99	
103:1-22	Psalm 103 My Soul, Give Thanks to the Lord 98	
103:3-6	Psalm 146 Happy the Poor in Spirit 139	
103:6	Psalm 103 The Lord Is Kind and Merciful 99	
103:8	Psalm 103 The Lord Is Kind and Merciful 99	
103:17-18	Psalm 103 The Lord Is Kind and Merciful 99	
104:	Blessed Be God 477	
104:	God of All Creation 497	
104:	Joyful, Joyful, We Adore You 528	
104:	Praise and Thanksgiving 764	
104:	Psalm 104 Lord, Send Out Your Spirit 101	
104:	Spirit Blowing through Creation 462	
104:	The Works of the Lord Are Created in Wisdom 493	
104:	This Day God Gives Me 757	
104:	World without End 532	
104:	You Are the Voice 549	
104:24	We Praise You 541	
104:30	Envía Tu Espíritu / Send Out Your Spirit 459	
104:30	Send Down the Fire 466	
104:30	Send Us Your Spirit 470	
104:30	Wa Wa Wa Emimimo 471	
104:33	A New Song 530	
104:33	My Lord Will Come Again 769	
105:	All Creatures of Our God and King 533	
105:	For the Beauty of the Earth 572	
107:23-24	Psalm 107 Give Thanks to the Lord 102	
107:25-26	Psalm 107 Give Thanks to the Lord 102	
107:28-29	Psalm 107 Give Thanks to the Lord 102	
109:	The Works of the Lord Are Created in Wisdom 493	
110:1-4	Psalm 110 You Are a Priest for Ever 103	

6:9-10	Thy Kingdom Come 656
6:9-13	Mayenziwe / Your Will Be Done 592
6:9-15	Forgive Our Sins 879
6:16-18	Again We Keep This Solemn Fast 382
6:25-34	Lord of All Hopefulness 578
6:25-34	Praise and Thanksgiving 764
6:25-34	Today I Awake 755
6:28-34	Come to Me 650
6:33	Seek Ye First the Kingdom of God 615
7:7	Seek Ye First the Kingdom of God 615
7:7-8	Come to Me 650
9:11-13	The Master Came to Bring Good News 878
9:21-22	I Danced in the Morning 708
10:28	Now Go Forward 691
10:42	There's a Spirit in the Air 550
11:2-6	Hold Me in Life 599
11:25-30	I Heard the Voice of Jesus Say 646
11:28	Come to Us 743
11:28	Like a Shepherd 325
11:28-30	Come to Me 647
11:28-30	Come to Me, O Weary Traveler 637
11:28-30	Come to the Water 502
11:29-30	O God of Matchless Glory 546
11:29-30	We Shall Rise Again 772
13:4-30	Anthem 690
13:4-23	Bring Forth the Kingdom 658
13:21-43	Come, Ye Thankful People, Come 564
14:14	Love Divine, All Loves Excelling 622
14:22-33	How Firm a Foundation 606
16:21-27	Take Up Your Cross 698
17:1-9	'Tis Good, Lord, to Be Here 778
17:1-9	The Glory of These Forty Days 388
18:10-14	The King of Love My Shepherd Is 635
18:20	The God of All Eternity 894
18:20	You Are Our Living Bread 819
21:1-17	All Glory, Laud, and Honor 402
21:9	Hosanna 403
21:33-43	Christ Is Made the Sure Foundation 662
22:1-10	The Kingdom of God 655
25:1-13	Wake, O Wake, and Sleep No Longer 335
25:3-12	Whatsoever You Do 670
25:13	Sign Me Up 805
25:31-46	Bread for the World 827
25:31-46	One Is the Body 846
25:31-46	There's a Spirit in the Air 550
25:35-44	A Nuptial Blessing 870
25:39-40	God of Day and God of Darkness 761
25:40	A Touching Place 640
26:26	Take and Eat 831
26:26	Take and Eat this Bread 842
26:30	When in Our Music God Is Glorified 560
26:30	When, in Our Music, God Is Glorified 561
26:36-46	Stay Here and Keep Watch 411
26:38	Nada Te Turbe / Nothing Can Trouble 639
27:35	Were You There 416
27:45	A Stable Lamp Is Lighted 356

27:50	Calvary 419
28:1-10	Christ Has Risen 451
28:5-6	Now the Green Blade Rises 444
28:5-6	Surrexit Christus 436
28:5-6	Surrexit Dominus Vere II 428
28:6-9	Christ the Lord Is Risen Today 437
28:6-9	Jesus Christ Is Risen Today 422
28:16-20	Go 454
28:16-20	Hail the Day That Sees Him Rise 457
28:18	Alleluia! Sing to Jesus 853
28:18	I Will Be with You 455
28:18	Lord, You Give the Great Commission 456
28:18-20	Halleluya! We Sing Your Praises 562
28:18-20	Now Go Forward 691
28:19-20	Go Make of All Disciples 687
28:19-20	I Am for You 704
28:20	We Gather in Worship 750
28:46	All You Who Pass This Way 421

MARK

1:1-4	The Glory of These Forty Days 388
1:1-8	Comfort, Comfort, O My People 326
1:3	On Jordan's Bank 321
1:3	On Jordan's Bank 322
1:12-15	Lord, Who throughout These Forty Days 392
1:14-20	Anthem 690
1:14-20	I Danced in the Morning 708
1:14-20	Two Fishermen 688
1:16-20	Lord, When You Came / Pescador de Hombres 696
1:16-20	Sing Hey for the Carpenter 692
1:32-34	The Carpenter 483
2:1-12	I Danced in the Morning 708
2:1-12	Now in This Banquet 833
2:1-12	Songs of Thankfulness and Praise 376
2:21	You Are Mine 649
3:1-6	I Danced in the Morning 708
4:3-6	Seed, Scattered and Sown 834
4:26-34	The Kingdom of God 655
4:35-41	How Firm a Foundation 606
4:35-41	Psalm 107 Give Thanks to the Lord 102
4:39	Be Still, And Know That I Am God 618
6:30-34	I Heard the Voice of Jesus Say 646
6:30-34	There's a Wideness in God's Mercy 626
6:41-44	The Word of Life 514
6:45-52	I Am for You 704
8:34-38	Gifts That Last 583
8:34	Take Up Your Cross 698
9:2-10	'Tis Good, Lord, to Be Here 778
9:2-10	The Glory of These Forty Days 388
9:2-8	Tree of Life 397
9:49	Shake Up the Morning 529
10:31	Walk in the Reign 319
10:32	Jesus, Lead the Way 642
10:38-39	We Will Drink the Cup 709
11:1-11	All Glory, Laud, and Honor 402
11:9	Ride On, Jesus, Ride 405
11:9-10	Alleluia! Alleluia! Let the Holy Anthem Rise 425
11:9-10	Hosanna 403
13:5-13	Go Make of All Disciples 687

11:43	I Want to Call You	884
11:43-44	Up from the Earth	452
12:	Behold the Wood	420
12:12-13	Hosanna	403
12:13	Ride On, Jesus, Ride	405
12:20-33	Now the Green Blade Rises	444
12:23-24	Table Song	849
12:24-26	Never the Blade Shall Rise	706
12:24-26	Unless a Grain of Wheat	697
12:46	I Want to Walk as a Child of the Light 507	
13:1-5	Pan de Vida	848
13:1-15	Jesus Took a Towel	414
13:1-17	Jesu, Jesu	409
13:1-17	No Greater Love	628
13:1-17	Triduum Hymn: Wondrous Love 406	
13:3-5	Stand Up, Friends	478
13:14	Serving You	410
13:34-35	Faithful Family	413
13:35	They'll Know We Are Christians 735	
14:1-8	Triduum Hymn: Wondrous Love 406	
14:1-12	I Know That My Redeemer Lives 430	
14:3	Bread of Life, Hope of the World 821	
14:6	Come, My Way, My Truth, My Life 577	
14:6	I Received the Living God	851
14:6	Jesus Christ, Yesterday, Today and Forever 745	
14:15-21	Come Down, O Love Divine	465
14:16	Spirit Friend	467
14:23-27	Unless a Grain of Wheat	697
14:24-26	Come, Holy Ghost	469
14:24-26	Veni Creator Spiritus	460
14:27	Dona Nobis Pacem	730
14:27	Let There Be Peace on Earth	731
14:27	Make Me a Channel of Your Peace 726	
14:27	Take and Eat	831
14:27	World Peace Prayer	732
14:27	You Are Mine	649
14:34	Serving You	410
14:34-35	Triduum Hymn: Wondrous Love 406	
15:	Lord of All Nations, Grant Me Grace 634	
15:1-10	I Am the Vine	672
15:4	I Danced in the Morning	444
15:4	Now We Remain	694
15:4-5	Unless a Grain of Wheat	697
15:4-5	We Have Been Told	699
15:5	Many Are the Light Beams	736
15:5	Serving You	410
15:7-8	Unless a Grain of Wheat	697
15:9	Let Us Be Bread	816
15:9-14	No Greater Love	628
15:9-17	Faithful Family	413
15:9-17	The Master Came to Bring Good News 878	
15:11-27	Serving You	410
15:14	Let Us Be Bread	816
15:14-15	Christ Is Risen! Shout Hosanna!	431
15:15	Stand Up, Friends	478
16:13	Come, Now Almighty King	475
16:22	Bread of Life, Hope of the World 821	

17:	At That First Eucharist	852
17:1-8	Your Love, O God, Has All the World Created 713	
17:21	Bread of Life, Hope of the World 821	
17:21-23	The Broken Body	737
19:	O Sacred Head Surrounded	415
19:	What Wondrous Love Is This	627
19:25	At the Cross Her Station Keeping 401	
19:25	Calvary	419
19:25	Immaculate Mary	790
19:25	Sing We of the Blessed Mother	786
19:28	All You Who Pass This Way	421
19:34	Come and Let Us Drink of That New River 807	
19:34	O Food of Exiles Lowly	886
19:35-37	A Stable Lamp Is Lighted	356
19:36-42	I Danced in the Morning	708
20:	O Sons and Daughters	423
20:	That Easter Day with Joy Was Bright 445	
20:1	Were You There	416
20:1-9	This Is the Day When Light Was First Created 746	
20:11-18	Christ the Lord Is Risen Today	437
20:14-16	The Word of Life	514
20:19-23	Christ Has Risen	451
20:27-29	We Walk by Faith	590
21:15-17	Go	454

ACTS

1:1-11	A Hymn of Glory Let Us Sing	453
1:8	Come Down, O Love Divine	465
1:8	Come, Holy Ghost	469
1:8	O Holy Spirit, by Whose Breath	461
1:8	Veni Creator Spiritus	460
1:9-11	Hail the Day That Sees Him Rise 457	
2:1-2	Song over the Waters	585
2:1-11	Diverse in Culture, Nation, Race 739	
2:1-11	Spirit of God within Me	468
2:1-11	This Is the Day When Light Was First Created 746	
2:1-11	Veni Sancte Spiritus	463
3:6	The Love of the Lord	702
10:37	On Jordan's Bank	321
10:37	On Jordan's Bank	322

ROMANS

5:2-17	Amazing Grace	612
6:1-4	Baptized in Water	798
6:3-11	I Know That My Redeemer Lives 430	
6:3-11	Triduum Hymn: Wondrous Love 406	
8:	Alive in Christ Jesus	799
8:14-17	In Christ There Is No East or West 738	
8:15	All Things New	427
8:18-23	On Holy Ground	712
8:18-39	There's a Wideness in God's Mercy 626	
8:20-22	Song at the Center	490
10:8	The Word Is in Your Heart	518
11:33-35	There's a Wideness in God's Mercy 626	
12:15	The Servant Song	669

12:15	The Servant Song 683
14:7-8	Resucitó 432
14:8	Pues Si Vivimos / If We Are Living 666
14:17	The Kingdom of God 655

1 CORINTHIANS

1:18	Lift High the Cross 791
1:25	Darkness Is Gone 448
1:27	Do Not Fear to Hope 596
2:9	We Live a Mystery 595
2:9-10	Eye Has Not Seen 638
3:13-15	Come, Ye Thankful People, Come 564
5:6-8	Steal Away to Jesus 773
10:16-17	One Bread, One Body 830
10:16-17	Seed, Scattered and Sown 834
10:16-17	You Satisfy the Hungry Heart 815
10:17	Song of Gathering 740
10:17	We Know and Believe 836
11:23-26	I Come with Joy to Meet My Lord 806
11:23-29	Let Us Break Bread Together 832
11:23-26	Life-Giving Bread, Saving Cup 822
11:23-26	Now We Remain 694
11:23-26	Song of the Lord's Supper 412
11:24	Take and Eat this Bread 842
11:24-26	The Song of the Supper 845
11:26	May We Be One 316
11:26	The Living Bread of God 826
12:	Glorious in Majesty 671
12:	In Christ There Is No East or West 738
12:	Many Are the Light Beams 736
12:	There Is One Lord 809
12:	We Are Many Parts 733
12:	When Love Is Found 865
12:4	One Bread, One Body 830
12:4-11	Come, Holy Ghost 469
12:4-11	Veni Creator Spiritus 460
12:27-33	God Is Here! As We His People 741
13:	In Love We Choose to Live 873
13:	Not for Tongues of Heaven's Angels 623
13:	We Are Many Parts 733
13:2-8	Ubi Caritas 408
13:2-8	Where True Love and Charity Are Found / Ubi Caritas 631
13:13	Faith, Hope and Love 624
15:14-19	This Joyful Eastertide 434
15:20	Sing with All the Saints in Glory 442
15:20-28	Come, Ye Faithful, Raise the Strain 441
15:22-23	Spirit of God within Me 468
15:51-54	The Strife Is O'er 446
15:54-56	Resucitó 432
15:55	Christ the Lord Is Risen Today 437

2 CORINTHIANS

4:5	God Is Here! As We His People 741
5:7	We Walk by Faith 590
5:17	Come Away to the Skies 440
5:17	Love Divine, All Loves Excelling 622
6:2	Return to God 389
9:10-14	Come, Ye Thankful People, Come 564
9:10-14	Now Join We to Praise the Creator 720

9:14	Amazing Grace 612
12:9	Amazing Grace 612

GALATIANS

2:19	Alleluia, Alleluia, Give Thanks 443
2:20	God, beyond All Names 491
2:20	I Heard the Voice of Jesus Say 646
3:28	God Is Love 629
3:28	In Christ There Is No East or West 738
3:28	One Bread, One Body 830
3:28-29	Pan de Vida 848
3:28-30	Song of Gathering 740
4:4	Hark! The Herald Angels Sing 348
6:14	Crucem Tuam / O Lord, Your Cross 417
7:	All Who Claim the Faith of Jesus 787

EPHESIANS

1:2	Dwelling Place 594
1:4	You Are God's Work of Art 810
1:19-23	Holy God, We Praise Thy Name 524
2:1	We Are God's Work of Art/Somos la Creación de Dios 808
2:4-7	We Are God's Work of Art/Somos la Creación de Dios 808
2:7-10	Lover of Us All 633
2:10	We Are God's Work of Art/Somos la Creación de Dios 808
2:10	You Are God's Work of Art 810
2:12-22	We Are God's Work of Art/Somos la Creación de Dios 808
2:19	We Are God's Work of Art/Somos la Creación de Dios 808
2:19-20	No Longer Strangers 734
3:14-17	Dwelling Place 594
3:14	You Are Called to Tell the Story 680
3:16-19	The Word Is in Your Heart 518
4:	There Is One Lord 809
4:1-6	In Christ There Is No East or West 738
4:4-6	Let Us Be Bread 816
4:4-6	The Broken Body 737
5:8	Morning Hymn 2
5:8	We Are Marching 512
5:8	You Are God's Work of Art 810
5:8-9	Church of God 664
5:8-9	Out of Darkness 689
5:8-10	I Want to Walk as a Child of the Light 507
5:14	Awake, O Sleeper 803
5:14	I Am the Light of the World 510
5:14	Light of Christ/Exsultet 511
5:14	Wake, O Wake, and Sleep No Longer 335
5:19-20	Lover of Us All 633
5:27	Love Divine, All Loves Excelling 622

PHILIPPIANS

1:11	The Harvest of Justice 711
2:1-18	Lord of All Nations, Grant Me Grace 634
2:5-7	Stand Up, Friends 478
2:8	Hark! The Herald Angels Sing 348
2:9-10	All Hail the Power of Jesus' Name 484

Scripture Passages Related to Hymns/*continued*

Scripture Passages Related to Hymns/*continued*

ADVENT
Seasonal Psalms
Psalm 25: To You, O Lord 36
Psalm 25: Levanto Mi Alma 37
Psalm 85: Lord, Let Us See Your Kindness 79
Psalm 85: Come, O Lord, and Set Us Free 80

ADVENT I
A - Psalm 122: Let Us Go Rejoicing 120
Psalm 122: I Was Glad 121
B - Psalm 80/85/Luke 1: Lord, Make Us Turn to You 75
C - Psalm 25: To You, O Lord 36
Psalm 25: Levanto Mi Alma 37

ADVENT II
A - Psalm 72: Every Nation on Earth 72
B - Psalm 85: Lord, Let Us See Your Kindness 79
Psalm 85: Come, O Lord, and Set Us Free 80
C - Psalm126: God Has Done Great Things for Us 124
Psalm126: The Lord Has Done Great Things 123

ADVENT III
A - Psalm 146: Happy the Poor in Spirit 139
Psalm 146: Lord, Come and Save Us 140
B - Canticle of Mary / Luke 1:46-55 145
Magnificat / Luke 1:46-55 146
Holy Is Your Name / Luke 1:46-55 147
C - Isaiah 12:2-3, 4, 6 148

ADVENT IV
A - Psalm 24: We Long to See Your Face 34
B - Psalm 89: For Ever I Will Sing 82
C - Psalm 80/85/Luke 1: Lord, Make Us Turn to You 75

CHRISTMAS
Seasonal Psalm
Psalm 98: All the Ends of the Earth 95

CHRISTMAS/VIGIL
Psalm 89: For Ever I Will Sing 82

CHRISTMAS/MASS AT MIDNIGHT
Psalm 96: Today Is Born Our Savior 90
Psalm 96: Today Is Born Our Savior 91

CHRISTMAS/MASS AT DAWN
Psalm 97: The Lord Is King 94

CHRISTMAS/MASS DURING THE DAY
Psalm 98: All the Ends of the Earth 95

HOLY FAMILY
Psalm128: Blest Are Those Who Love You 125

MARY, MOTHER OF GOD
Psalm 67: May God Bless Us in His Mercy 66

EPIPHANY
Psalm 72: Every Nation on Earth 72

BAPTISM OF THE LORD
Psalm 29: The Lord Will Bless His People 40

LENT
Seasonal Psalms
Psalm 51: Be Merciful, O Lord 56
Psalm 51: Have Mercy, Lord 55
Psalm 91: Be with Me 85
Psalm 130: With the Lord There Is Mercy 127

ASH WEDNESDAY
Psalm 51: Be Merciful, O Lord 56
Psalm 51: Have Mercy, Lord 55

LENT I
A - Psalm 51: Be Merciful, O Lord 56
Psalm 51: Have Mercy, Lord 55
B - Psalm 25: Remember Your Mercies 35
C - Psalm 91: Be with Me 85

LENT II
A - Psalm 33: Let Your Mercy Be on Us 45
B - Psalm 116: I Will Walk in the Presence 108
Psalm 116: I Will Walk in the Presence of God 109
C - Psalm 27: The Lord Is My Light 39

LENT III
A - Psalm 95: If Today You Hear God's Voice 89
B - Psalm19: Lord, You Have the Words 27
C - Psalm 103: The Lord Is Kind and Merciful 99
Psalm 103: The Lord Is Kind and Merciful 100

LENT IV
A - Psalm 23: My Shepherd Is the Lord 30
Psalm 23: Shepherd Me, O God 31
Psalm 23: The Lord Is My Shepherd 32
Psalm 23: Nada Me Falta 33
B - Psalm 137: Let My Tongue Be Silent 132
C - Psalm 34: Taste and See 47

LENT V
A - Psalm 130: With the Lord, There Is Mercy 127
B - Psalm 51: Create in Me 57
C - Psalm 126: God Has Done Great Things for Us 124
Psalm126: The Lord Has Done Great Things 123

HOLY WEEK
Seasonal Psalm
Psalm 22: My God, My God 29

PASSION SUNDAY
Psalm 22: My God, My God 29

HOLY THURSDAY
Psalm 116: Our Blessing Cup 107
Psalm 116: The Name of God 110

GOOD FRIDAY
Psalm 31: I Put My Life in Your Hands / Pongo Mi Vida 42
Psalm 31: I Put My Life in Your Hands 43

EASTER VIGIL
Seasonal Psalm
Psalm 136: Love Is Never Ending 131

EASTER VIGIL
1 - Psalm 104: Lord, Send Out Your Spirit 101
Psalm 33: Let Your Mercy Be on Us 45
2 - Psalm 16: Keep Me Safe, O God 23
Psalm 16: You Will Show Me the Path of Life 24
3 - Song at the Sea / Exodus 15 143
4 - Psalm 30: I Will Praise You, Lord 41
5 - Isaiah 12:2-3,4,6 148
6 - Psalm 19: Lord, You Have the Words 27
7 - Psalm 41-42: Song of Longing 51
Psalm 51: Create in Me 57

Suggested Psalms for the Church Year/*continued*

EASTER
Seasonal Psalms
Psalm 118: Alleluia, Alleluia 113
Psalm 118: Let Us Rejoice 114
Psalm 118: This Is the Day 115
Psalm 66: Let All the Earth 65

EASTER SUNDAY
Psalm 118: Alleluia, Alleluia 113
Psalm 118: Let Us Rejoice 114
Psalm 118: This Is the Day 115

EASTER II
Psalm 118: Alleluia, Alleluia 113
Psalm 118: Let Us Rejoice 114
Psalm 118: This Is the Day 115

EASTER III
A - Psalm 16: You Will Show Me the Path of Life 24
B - Psalm 4: Lord, Let Your Face Shine upon Us 19
C - Psalm 30: I Will Praise You, Lord 41

EASTER IV
A - Psalm 23: My Shepherd Is the Lord 30
    Psalm 23: Shepherd Me, O God 31
    Psalm 23: The Lord Is My Shepherd 32
    Psalm 23: Nada Me Falta 33
B - Psalm 118: Alleluia, Alleluia 113
    Psalm 118: Let Us Rejoice 114
    Psalm 118: This Is the Day 115
C - Psalm 100: Arise, Come to Your God 96
    Psalm 100: We Are God's People 97

EASTER V
A - Psalm 33: Let Your Mercy Be on Us 45
B - Psalm 22: I Will Praise You, Lord 28
C - Psalm 145: I Will Praise Your Name 137

EASTER VI
A - Psalm 66: Let All the Earth 65
B - Psalm 98: All the Ends of the Earth 95
C - Psalm 67: May God Bless Us in His Mercy 66

ASCENSION
Psalm 47: God Mounts His Throne 53

EASTER VII
A - Psalm 27: In the Land of the Living 38
B - Psalm 103: The Lord Is Kind and Merciful 99
    Psalm 103: The Lord Is Kind and Merciful 100
C - Psalm 97: The Lord Is King 94

PENTECOST
Psalm 104: Lord, Send Out Your Spirit 101

TRINITY SUNDAY
A - Song of the Three Children / Daniel 3:52-56 150
    Song of the Three Children / Daniel 3:52-57 151
B - Psalm 33: Let Your Mercy Be on Us 45
C - Psalm 8: How Glorious Your Name 20
    Psalm 8: How Great Is Your Name 21

BODY AND BLOOD OF CHRIST
A - Psalm 147: Bless the Lord, My Soul 141
B - Psalm 116: The Name of God 110
C - Psalm 110: You Are a Priest for Ever 103

SACRED HEART
A - Psalm 103: The Lord Is Kind and Merciful 99
    Psalm 103: The Lord Is Kind and Merciful 100

B - Isaiah 12:2-3,4,6 148
C - Psalm 23: My Shepherd Is the Lord 30
    Psalm 23: Shepherd Me, O God 31
    Psalm 23: The Lord Is My Shepherd 32
    Psalm 23: Nada Me Falta 33

ORDINARY TIME
Seasonal Psalms
Psalm 19: Lord, You Have the Words 27
Psalm 27: The Lord Is My Light and My Salvation 39
Psalm 34: I Will Bless the Lord 46
Psalm 34: Taste and See 47
Psalm 63: My Soul Is Thirsting 60
Psalm 63: My Soul Is Thirsting 61
Psalm 63: Your Love Is Finer Than Life 62
Psalm 95: If Today You Hear God's Voice 89
Psalm 100: Arise, Come to Your God 96
Psalm 100: We Are God's People 87
Psalm 103: The Lord Is Kind and Merciful 99
Psalm 103: The Lord Is Kind and Merciful 100
Psalm 145: I Will Praise Your Name 137

LAST WEEKS IN ORDINARY TIME
Seasonal Psalms
Psalm 122: Let Us Go Rejoicing 120
Psalm 122: I Was Glad 121

ORDINARY TIME
SECOND SUNDAY
A - Psalm 40: Here I Am, O God 49
B - Psalm 40: Here I Am, O God 49
C - Psalm 96: Great Is the Lord 92
    Psalm 96: Proclaim to All the Nations 93

THIRD SUNDAY
A - Psalm 27: The Lord Is My Light 39
B - Psalm 25: Remember Your Mercies 35
C - Psalm 19: Lord, You Have the Words 27

FOURTH SUNDAY
A - Psalm 146: Happy the Poor in Spirit 139
B - Psalm 95: If Today You Hear God's Voice 89
C - Psalm 71: I Will Sing 71

FIFTH SUNDAY
A - Psalm 112: A Light Rises in the Darkness 104
B - Psalm 147: Bless the Lord, My Soul 141
C - Psalm 138: The Fragrance of Christ 134

SIXTH SUNDAY
A - Psalm 119: Happy Are Those Who Follow 116
B - Psalm 32: I Turn to You 44
C - Psalm 1: Happy Are They 18

SEVENTH SUNDAY
A - Psalm 103: The Lord Is Kind and Merciful 99
    Psalm 103: The Lord Is Kind and Merciful 100
B - Psalm 41: Lord, Heal My Soul 50
C - Psalm 103: The Lord Is Kind and Merciful 99
    Psalm 103: The Lord Is Kind and Merciful 100

EIGHTH SUNDAY
A - Psalm 62: In God Alone 59
B - Psalm 103: The Lord Is Kind and Merciful 99
    Psalm 103: The Lord Is Kind and Merciful 100
C - Psalm 92: Lord, It Is Good to Give Thanks to You 86

Suggested Psalms for the Church Year/*continued*

NINTH SUNDAY
A - Psalm 31: I Put My Life in Your Hands / Pongo Mi
    Vida 42
    Psalm 31: I Put My Life in Your Hands 43
B - Psalm 81: Sing with Joy to God 76
C - Psalm 117: Go out to All the World 112

TENTH SUNDAY
A - Psalm 50: To the Upright 54
B - Psalm 130: With the Lord There Is Mercy 127
C - Psalm 30: I Will Praise You, Lord 41

ELEVENTH SUNDAY
A - Psalm 100: Arise, Come to Your God 96
    Psalm 100: We Are God's People 87
B - Psalm 92: Lord, It Is Good 86
C - Psalm 32: I Turn to You 44

TWELFTH SUNDAY
A - Psalm 69: Lord, in Your Great Love 68
B - Psalm 107: Give Thanks to the Lord 102
C - Psalm 63: My Soul Is Thirsting 60
    Psalm 63: My Soul Is Thirsting 61
    Psalm 63: Your Love Is Finer Than Life 62

THIRTEENTH SUNDAY
A - Psalm 89: For Ever I Will Sing 82
B - Psalm 30: I Will Praise You, Lord 41
C - Psalm 16: You Will Show Me the Path of Life 24

FOURTEENTH SUNDAY
A - Psalm 145: I Will Praise Your Name 137
B - Psalm 123: Our Eyes Are Fixed on the Lord 122
C - Psalm 66: Let All the Earth 65

FIFTEENTH SUNDAY
A - Psalm 65: The Seed That Falls on Good Ground 64
B - Psalm 85: Let Us See Your Kindness 79
    Psalm 85: Come, O Lord, and Set Us Free 80
C - Psalm 69: Turn to the Lord in Your Need 69
    Psalm 69: Turn to the Lord in Your Need 70

SIXTEENTH SUNDAY
A - Psalm 86: Lord, You Are Good and Forgiving 81
B - Psalm 23: My Shepherd Is the Lord 30
    Psalm 23: Shepherd Me, O God 31
    Psalm 23: The Lord Is My Shepherd 32
    Psalm 23: Nada Me Falta 33
C - Psalm 15: They Who Do Justice 22

SEVENTEENTH SUNDAY
A - Psalm 119: Lord, I Love Your Commands 117
B - Psalm 145: I Will Praise Your Name 137
    Psalm 145: Our God Is Compassion 138
C - Psalm 138: The Fragrance of Christ 134

EIGHTEENTH SUNDAY
A - Psalm 145: I Will Praise Your Name 137
    Psalm 145: Our God Is Compassion 138
B - Psalm 78: The Lord Gave Them Bread 73
C - Psalm 95: If Today You Hear God's Voice 89

NINETEENTH SUNDAY
A - Psalm 85: Lord, Let Us See Your Kindness 79
    Psalm 85: Come, O Lord, and Set Us Free 80
B - Psalm 34: Taste and See 47
    Psalm 34: I Will Bless the Lord 46
C - Psalm 33: Let Your Mercy Be on Us 45

TWENTIETH SUNDAY
A - Psalm 67: May God Bless Us in His Mercy 66
B - Psalm 34: Taste and See 47
    Psalm 34: I Will Bless the Lord 46
C - Psalm 40: Here I Am 49

TWENTY-FIRST SUNDAY
A - Psalm 138: Lord, Your Love Is Eternal 133
B - Psalm 34: Taste and See 47
    Psalm 34: I Will Bless the Lord 46
C - Psalm 117: Go out to All the World 112

TWENTY-SECOND SUNDAY
A - Psalm 63: My Soul Is Thirsting 60
    Psalm 63: My Soul Is Thirsting 61
    Psalm 63: Your Love Is Finer Than Life 62
B - Psalm 15: They Who Do Justice 22
C - Psalm 68: You Have Made a Home for the Poor 67

TWENTY-THIRD SUNDAY
A - Psalm 95: If Today You Hear God's Voice 89
B - Psalm 146: Happy the Poor in Spirit 139
C - Psalm 90: In Every Age 83

TWENTY-FOURTH SUNDAY
A - Psalm 103: The Lord Is Kind and Merciful 99
    Psalm 103: The Lord Is Kind and Merciful 100
B - Psalm 116: I Will Walk in the Presence 108
    Psalm 116: I Will Walk in the Presence of God 109
C - Psalm 51: Create in Me a Clean Heart, O God 57

TWENTY-FIFTH SUNDAY
A - Psalm 145: I Will Praise Your Name 137
B - Psalm 54: The Lord Upholds My Life 58
C - Psalm 113: Praise God's Name 105
    Psalm 113: Praise the Lord 106

TWENTY-SIXTH SUNDAY
A - Psalm 25: Remember Your Mercies 35
B - Psalm 19: Lord, You Have the Words 27
C - Psalm 146: Happy the Poor in Spirit 139
    Psalm 146: Lord, Come and Save Us 140

TWENTY-SEVENTH SUNDAY
A - Psalm 80: The Vineyard of the Lord 74
B - Psalm 128: Blest Are Those Who Love You 125
C - Psalm 95: If Today You Hear God's Voice 89

TWENTY-EIGHTH SUNDAY
A - Psalm 23: My Shepherd Is the Lord 30
    Psalm 23: Shepherd Me, O God 31
    Psalm 23: The Lord Is My Shepherd 32
    Psalm 23: Nada Me Falta 33
B - Psalm 90: Fill Us with Your Love, O Lord 84
C - Psalm 98: All the Ends of the Earth 95

TWENTY-NINTH SUNDAY
A - Psalm 96: Great Is the Lord 92
    Psalm 96: Proclaim to All the Nations 93
B - Psalm 33: Let Your Mercy Be on Us 45
C - Psalm 121: Our Help Comes From the Lord 119

THIRTIETH SUNDAY
A - Psalm 18: I Love You Lord, My Strength 26
B - Psalm 126: God Has Done Great Things for Us 124
C - Psalm 34: The Lord Hears the Cry of the Poor 48

Suggested Psalms for the Church Year/*continued*

THIRTY-FIRST SUNDAY
A - Psalm 131: My Soul Is Still 129
B - Psalm 18: I Love You Lord, My Strength 26
C - Psalm 145: I Will Praise Your Name 137

THIRTY-SECOND SUNDAY
A - Psalm 63: My Soul Is Thirsting 60
Psalm 63: My Soul Is Thirsting 61
Psalm 63: Your Love Is Finer Than Life 62
B - Psalm 146: Happy the Poor in Spirit 139
Psalm 146: Lord, Come and Save Us 140
C - Psalm 17: Lord, When Your Glory Appears 25

THIRTY-THIRD SUNDAY
A - Psalm 128: Blest Are Those Who Love You 125
B - Psalm 16: Keep Me Safe, O God 23
Psalm 16: You Will Show Me the Path of Life 24
C - Psalm 98: All the Ends of the Earth 95

CHRIST THE KING
A - Psalm 23: My Shepherd Is the Lord 30
Psalm 23: Shepherd Me, O God 31
Psalm 23: The Lord Is My Shepherd 32
Psalm 23: Nada Me Falta 33
B - Psalm 93: The Lord Is King 87
C - Psalm 122: Let Us Go Rejoicing 120
Psalm 122: I Was Glad 121

ASSUMPTION
Psalm 45: The Queen Stands at Your Right Hand 52

ALL SAINTS
Psalm 24: We Long to See Your Face 34

IMMACULATE CONCEPTION
Psalm 98: All the Ends of the Earth 95

Liturgical Index/*continued*

Liturgical Index/*continued*

Liturgical Index/*continued*

1210 Topical Index

Topical Index/*continued*

Topical Index/*continued*

Topical Index/*continued*

Topical Index/*continued*

Topical Index/*continued*

Topical Index/*continued*

Topical Index/*continued*

513 This Little Light of Mine
602 Though the Mountains May Fall
778 'Tis Good, Lord, to Be Here
488 To Jesus Christ, Our Sovereign King
721 Voices that Challenge
512 We Are Marching
724 We Shall Overcome
709 We Will Drink the Cup
561 When, in Our Music, God Is
　　Glorified
532 World without End

GOSPEL *(see Word of God)*

GRACE
820 All Who Hunger
492 All You Works of God
612 Amazing Grace
752 Bless the Feast
431 Christ Is Risen! Shout Hosanna!
465 Come Down, O Love Divine
469 Come, Holy Ghost
337 Creator of the Stars of Night
739 Diverse in Culture, Nation, Race
596 Do Not Fear to Hope
730 Dona Nobis Pacem
594 Dwelling Place
572 For the Beauty of the Earth
583 Gifts That Last
741 God Is Here! As We His People
895 Greet Now the Swiftly Changing
　　Year
782 Hail Mary: Gentle Woman
506 Immortal, Invisible, God Only Wise
734 No Longer Strangers
565 Now Thank We All Our God
886 O Food of Exiles Lowly
767 O Holy City, Seen of John
321 On Jordan's Bank
551 Praise, My Soul, the King of Heaven
138 Psalm 145 - Our God Is Compassion
389 Return to God
737 The Broken Body
388 The Glory of These Forty Days
544 The God of Abraham Praise
894 The God of All Eternity
655 The Kingdom of God
626 There's a Wideness in God's Mercy
808 We Are God's Work of Art / Somos
　　la Creación de Dios
575 We Cannot Measure How You Heal
750 We Gather in Worship
378 What Star Is This

GRIEVING
640 A Touching Place
647 Come to Me
637 Come to Me, O Weary Traveler
503 Come to the Feast
339 Each Winter As the Year Grows
　　Older
877 Out of the Depths
874 Precious Lord, Take My Hand
110 Psalm 116 - The Name of God
132 Psalm 137 - Let My Tongue Be
　　Silent
666 Pues Si Vivimos / If We Are Living
770 Soon and Very Soon
483 The Carpenter
859 The Hand of God Shall Hold You
613 The Lord Is My Hope
644 Within Our Darkest Night

GROWTH
883 Ashes
707 Guide My Feet
727 How Good It Is
516 Sow the Word
700 The Summons
532 World without End

GUIDANCE
453 A Hymn of Glory Let Us Sing
870 A Nuptial Blessing
577 Come, My Way, My Truth, My Life
391 God of Abraham
497 God of All Creation
707 Guide My Feet
606 How Firm a Foundation
855 How Lovely Is Your Dwelling
646 I Heard the Voice of Jesus Say
582 I Need You to Listen
860 I, the Lord
642 Jesus, Lead the Way
725 Jesus, Shepherd of Our Souls
574 Lead Me, Guide Me
567 Let All Things Now Living
633 Lover of Us All
519 May We Praise You
610 My Refuge
639 Nada Te Turbe / Nothing Can
　　Trouble
517 Not by Bread Alone
565 Now Thank We All Our God
614 O God, Our Help in Ages Past
660 Onward to the Kingdom
874 Precious Lord, Take My Hand
23 Psalm 16 - Keep Me Safe, O God
30 Psalm 23 - My Shepherd Is the Lord
36 Psalm 25 - Levanto Mi Alma
35 Psalm 25 - Remember Your Mercies
36 Psalm 25 - To You, O Lord
66 Psalm 67 - May God Bless Us in
　　His Mercy
72 Psalm 72 - Every Nation on Earth
885 Remember Your Mercy, Lord
464 Sequence for Pentecost
641 Shepherd of My Heart
829 Shepherd of Our Hearts
737 The Broken Body
894 The God of All Eternity
859 The Hand of God Shall Hold You
635 The King of Love My Shepherd Is
489 The Stars Declare His Glory
757 This Day God Gives Me
571 We Gather Together
378 What Star Is This
654 With a Shepherd's Care
732 World Peace Prayer
505 You Are All We Have
604 You Are Near

HARVEST
564 Come, Ye Thankful People, Come
691 Now Go Forward
720 Now Join We to Praise the Creator
764 Praise and Thanksgiving
64 Psalm 65 - The Seed that Falls on
　　Good Ground
66 Psalm 67 - May God Bless Us in
　　His Mercy
80 Psalm 85 - Come, O Lord and Set
　　Us Free
711 The Harvest of Justice

HEALING
552 All the Earth, Proclaim God's Glory
387 Attende Domine / Hear Us,
　　Almighty Lord
509 Be Light For Our Eyes
503 Come to the Feast
739 Diverse in Culture, Nation, Race
459 Envía Tú Espíritu / Send Our Your
　　Spirit
391 God of Abraham
679 Good News
876 He Healed the Darkness of My
　　Mind
882 Healer of Our Every Ill
584 Healing River
398 Hold Us in Your Mercy

704 I Am for You
390 Jerusalem, My Destiny
875 Jesus, Heal Us
817 Jesus, Wine of Peace
321 On Jordan's Bank
322 On Jordan's Bank
621 Only in God
877 Out of the Depths
728 Peace Is Flowing Like a River
31 Psalm 23 - Shepherd Me, O God
140 Psalm 146 - Lord, Come and Save
　　Us
141 Psalm 147 - Bless the Lord, My
　　Soul
389 Return to God
539 Sing Praise to God Who Reigns
　　Above
847 Song of the Body of Christ
376 Songs of Thankfulness and Praise
462 Spirit Blowing through Creation
411 Stay Here and Keep Watch
673 Take This Moment
349 The Age of Expectation
483 The Carpenter
486 The King of Glory
648 There Is a Balm in Gilead
626 There's a Wideness in God's Mercy
755 Today I Awake
452 Up from the Earth
319 Walk in the Reign
400 Wash Me, Cleanse Me
575 We Cannot Measure How You Heal
593 We Remember
867 Wherever You Go
872 Wherever You Go
644 Within Our Darkest Night
532 World without End
649 You Are Mine

HEAVEN
374 As with Gladness Men of Old
401 At the Cross Her Station Keeping
437 Christ the Lord Is Risen Today
564 Come, Ye Thankful People, Come
758 Day Is Done
793 For All the Saints
828 I Am the Bread of Life
507 I Want to Walk as a Child of the
　　Light
771 Jerusalem, My Happy Home
642 Jesus, Lead the Way
528 Joyful, Joyful, We Adore You
392 Lord, Who throughout These Forty
　　Days
622 Love Divine, All Loves Excelling
769 My Lord Will Come Again
639 Nada Te Turbe / Nothing Can
　　Trouble
565 Now Thank We All Our God
767 O Holy City, Seen of John
887 O Saving Victim / O Salutaris
372 Once in Royal David's City
660 Onward to the Kingdom
110 Psalm 116 - The Name of God
487 Rejoice, the Lord Is King
149 Revelation 19:1-7
774 Shall We Gather at the River
641 Shepherd of My Heart
805 Sign Me Up
786 Sing We of the Blessed Mother
442 Sing with All the Saints in Glory
773 Steal Away to Jesus
544 The God of Abraham Praise
653 The People of God
335 Wake, O Wake, and Sleep No
　　Longer
670 Whatsoever You Do
649 You Are Mine

Topical Index/*continued*

JESUS CHRIST

Topical Index/*continued*

Topical Index/*continued*

Topical Index/*continued*

Topical Index/*continued*

Topical Index/*continued*

Topical Index/*continued*

Topical Index/*continued*

Topical Index/*continued*

Topical Index/*continued*

Topical Index/*continued*

Topical Index/*continued*

Topical Index/*continued*

Topical Index/*continued*

SHARING
825 As the Grains of Wheat
759 At Evening
752 Bless the Feast
588 Blest Are You
827 Bread for the World
624 Faith, Hope and Love
719 For the Healing of the Nations
839 Here in This Place
727 How Good It Is
824 I, Myself, Am the Bread of Life
409 Jesu, Jesu
725 Jesus, Shepherd of Our Souls
731 Let There Be Peace on Earth
816 Let Us Be Bread
720 Now Join We to Praise the Creator
764 Praise and Thanksgiving
22 Psalm 15 - They Who Do Justice
666 Pues Si Vivimos / If We Are Living
692 Sing Hey for the Carpenter
412 Song of the Lord's Supper
711 The Harvest of Justice
733 We Are Many Parts
850 We Come to Your Feast
724 We Shall Overcome
665 We Will Serve the Lord
680 You Are Called to Tell the Story

SHEPHERD
747 All People That on Earth Do Dwell
424 Easter Alleluia
725 Jesus, Shepherd of Our Souls
817 Jesus, Wine of Peace
325 Like a Shepherd
415 O Sacred Head Surrounded
30 Psalm 23 - My Shepherd Is the Lord
33 Psalm 23 - Nada Me Falta
31 Psalm 23 - Shepherd Me, O God
32 Psalm 23 - The Lord Is My Shepherd
360 Rise Up, Shepherd, and Follow
641 Shepherd of My Heart
829 Shepherd of Our Hearts
840 Shepherd of Souls
675 The God Who Sends Us Forth
635 The King of Love My Shepherd Is
613 The Lord Is My Hope
643 The Lord Is My Shepherd
535 To God with Gladness Sing
654 With a Shepherd's Care
844 Without Seeing You
815 You Satisfy the Hungry Heart

SICKNESS (see Comfort, Healing, Suffering; Liturgical Index: Pastoral Care of the Sick)

SIN
823 Behold the Lamb
477 Blessed Be God
439 Christ the Lord Is Risen!
879 Forgive Our Sins
876 He Healed the Darkness of My Mind
884 I Want to Call You
519 May We Praise You
5 Now Bless the God of Israel
830 One Bread, One Body
383 Parce Domine
44 Psalm 32 - I Turn to You
56 Psalm 51 - Be Merciful, O Lord
57 Psalm 51 - Create in Me
55 Psalm 51 - Have Mercy, Lord
62 Psalm 63 - Your Love Is Finer Than Life
100 Psalm 103 - The Lord Is Kind and Merciful
101 Psalm 104 - Lord, Send Out Your Spirit
105 Psalm 113 - Praise God's Name

125 Psalm 128 - Blest Are Those Who Love You
126 Psalm 130 - If You, O God, Laid Bare Our Guilt
703 Song of St. Patrick
737 The Broken Body
878 The Master Came to Bring Good News
626 There's a Wideness in God's Mercy
656 Thy Kingdom Come
535 To God with Gladness Sing
397 Tree of Life

SOCIAL CONCERN
870 A Nuptial Blessing
640 A Touching Place
820 All Who Hunger
501 All You Who Are Thirsty
690 Anthem
663 As a Fire Is Meant for Burning
759 At Evening
827 Bread for the World
556 Canticle of the Turning
369 Carol at the Manger
678 City of God
503 Come to the Feast
502 Come to the Water
580 Creating God
730 Dona Nobis Pacem
381 Dust and Ashes
339 Each Winter As the Year Grows Older
838 Eat This Bread
719 For the Healing of the Nations
801 For the Life of the World
717 Free at Last
723 Freedom Is Coming
583 Gifts That Last
671 Glorious in Majesty
715 Go Down, Moses
682 God Has Chosen Me
761 God of Day and God of Darkness
350 God's Surprise
714 God, Whose Purpose Is to Kindle
679 Good News
684 Great Is the Lord
782 Hail Mary: Gentle Woman
584 Healing River
686 Here I Am, Lord
603 How Can I Keep from Singing
727 How Good It Is
668 I Bind My Heart
597 I Say "Yes," Lord / Digo "Sí," Señor
500 I Will Lift Up My Eyes
657 I Will Not Die
722 If You Believe and I Believe
738 In Christ There Is No East or West
409 Jesu, Jesu
725 Jesus, Shepherd of Our Souls
548 Joyfully Singing
762 Joyous Light of Heavenly Glory
581 Kyrie Guarany
716 Let Justice Roll Like a River
731 Let There Be Peace on Earth
634 Lord of All Nations, Grant Me Grace
696 Lord, When You Came / Pescador de Hombres
456 Lord, You Give the Great Commission
788 Magnificat
766 Mine Eyes Have Seen the Glory
720 Now Join We to Praise the Creator
767 O Holy City, Seen of John
712 On Holy Ground
846 One Is the Body
764 Praise and Thanksgiving
22 Psalm 15 - They Who Do Justice

67 Psalm 68 - You Have Made a Home for the Poor
104 Psalm 112 - A Light Rises in the Darkness
132 Psalm 137 - Let My Tongue Be Silent
139 Psalm 146 - Happy the Poor in Spirit
666 Pues Si Vivimos / If We Are Living
389 Return to God
466 Send Down the Fire
529 Shake Up the Morning
559 Shout for Joy
805 Sign Me Up
499 Sing Out Earth and Skies
847 Song of the Body of Christ
813 Song of the Chosen
585 Song Over the Waters
837 Taste and See
569 Thanks Be to You
483 The Carpenter
768 The Day Is Near
675 The God Who Sends Us Forth
711 The Harvest of Justice
878 The Master Came to Bring Good News
700 The Summons
809 There Is One Lord
550 There's a Spirit in the Air
408 Ubi Caritas
721 Voices that Challenge
319 Walk in the Reign
718 We Are Called
508 We Are the Light of the World
724 We Shall Overcome
665 We Will Serve the Lord
625 Where Charity and Love Prevail
631 Where True Love and Charity Are Found / Ubi Caritas
532 World without End
620 You Will Draw Water
713 Your Love, O God, Has All the World Created

SONG
453 A Hymn of Glory Let Us Sing
542 Alabaré
533 All Creatures of Our God and King
484 All Hail the Power of Jesus' Name
747 All People That on Earth Do Dwell
552 All the Earth, Proclaim God's Glory
520 All the Ends of the Earth
427 All Things New
492 All You Works of God
853 Alleluia! Sing to Jesus
433 At the Lamb's High Feast We Sing
526 Cantai ao Senhor
553 Cantemos al Señor / Let's Sing unto the Lord
496 Canticle of the Sun
481 Christ Is the King
664 Church of God
440 Come Away to the Skies
485 Crown Him with Many Crowns
448 Darkness Is Gone
793 For All the Saints
715 Go Down, Moses
391 God of Abraham
784 Hail, Holy Queen Enthroned Above
524 Holy God, We Praise Thy Name
474 Holy, Holy, Holy! Lord God Almighty
603 How Can I Keep from Singing
591 How Shall I Sing to God?
884 I Want to Call You
531 I Want to Praise Your Name
543 I Will Sing, I Will Sing
749 In Christ There Is a Table Set for All
148 Isaiah 12:2-3, 4, 6

Topical Index/*continued*

Topical Index/*continued*

Topical Index/*continued*

Index of Service Music/*continued*

Index of Composers, Authors and Sources   1212

Index of Composers, Authors and Sources/*continued*

Index of Composers, Authors and Sources/*continued*

Index of Composers, Authors and Sources/*continued*

CM (COMMON METER - 86 86)

	343	ANTIOCH
	625	CHRISTIAN LOVE
	879	DETROIT
	484	DIADEM
	727	DOVE OF PEACE
771	806	LAND OF REST
	738	MC KEE
	320	MORNING SONG
	612	NEW BRITAIN
	840	ST. AGNES
	614	ST. ANNE
635 751	800	ST. COLUMBA
	392	ST. FLAVIAN
	590	SHANTI

CMD (COMMON METER DOUBLE)

	367	CAROL
	775	FOREST GREEN
646	685	KINGSFOLD
	890	MATERNA
	5	MELBOURNE

LM (LONG METER - 88 88)

	876	ARLINGTON
	634	BEATUS VIR
337	776	CONDITOR ALME SIDERUM
	887	DUGUET
430 4	82	DUKE STREET
	469	LAMBILLOTTE
382 388	747	OLD HUNDREDTH
698 865	894	O WALY WALY
	580	PRESENCE
	472	PROSPECT
378	445	PUER NOBIS
	10	RADIANT LIGHT
	322	ST. JOHN THE BAPTIST
	480	SWEET SACRAMENT
	739	TALLIS' CANON
	460	VENI CREATOR SPIRITUS
		(Chant)
	461	VENI CREATOR SPIRITUS
		(Rhythmic)
	321	WINCHESTER NEW

LMD (LONG METER DOUBLE)

	14	MAGNIFICAT
	575	YE BANKS AND BRAES

LM WITH REFRAIN

453 533	794	LASST UNS ERFREUEN
	600	ST. CATHERINE
	317	VENI, VENI EMMANUEL

5 5 5 4 D

	757	ANDREA
756 764	798	BUNESSAN
	759	EVENING HYMN
	866	SHADE

66 4 666 4

	889	AMERICA
	475	ITALIAN HYMN

6 6 6 6 4 44 4

	535	CYMBALA
	487	DARWALL'S 148TH

6 69 D

	440	MIDDLEBURY
	874	PRECIOUS LORD

7 6 7 6 D

	349	ASHWOOD
	661	AURELIA
	687	ELLACOMBE
327	441	GAUDEAMUS PARITER
	415	PASSION CHORALE
	402	ST. THEODULPH

7 6 7 6 WITH REFRAIN

	359	GO TELL IT ON THE MOUNTAIN
	479	GOTT VATER SEI GEPRIESSEN

77 77

	384	HEINLEIN
	550	LAUDS
	334	NUN KOM DER HEIDEN HEILAND
	577	THE CALL

7 7 7 7 WITH REFRAIN

	422	EASTER HYMN
	347	GLORIA
	851	LIVING GOD
437	457	LLANFAIR
	499	SING OUT

77 77 D

	564	ST. GEORGE'S WINDSOR
376	433	SALZBURG

8 7 8 7

	737	BARBARA ALLEN
	637	DUNSTAN
	323	STUTTGART

8 7 8 7 WITH REFRAIN

	623	COMFORT
892 893		FARRELL
	380	GREENSLEEVES
	603	HOW CAN I KEEP FROM SINGING
488	878	ICH GLAUB AN GOTT
	710	LA GRANGE

8 7 8 7 D

456	741	ABBOT'S LEIGH
663	761	BEACH SPRING
	425	HOLY ANTHEM
	431	HOSANNA
622	853	HYFRYDOL
442 528	714	HYMN TO JOY
626	681	IN BABILONE
369	762	JOYOUS LIGHT
	786	OMNE DIE
	783	PLEADING SAVIOR
	451	TRANSFORMATION

8 7 8 7 8 7

	680	GHENT
	551	LAUDA ANIMA
	407	PANGE LINGUA
	540	PICARDY
	358	REGENT SQUARE
662 719	888	ST. THOMAS
	787	TILLFLYKT

Metrical Index of Tunes/*continued*

Index of First Lines and Common Titles/*continued*

Index of First Lines and Common Titles/*continued*

Index of First Lines and Common Titles/*continued*

Index of First Lines and Common Titles/*continued*

Index of First Lines and Common Titles/*continued*

Index of First Lines and Common Titles/*continued*

Index of First Lines and Common Titles/*continued*